ILLINOIS

W9-AQS-610

A12901 690092

WITHDRAWN

PREBIND   MANY FACES OF SNOOPY

9780005266854

CM

SCHULZ

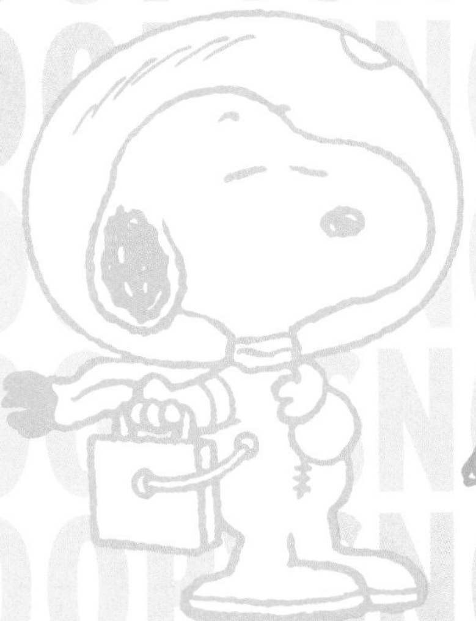

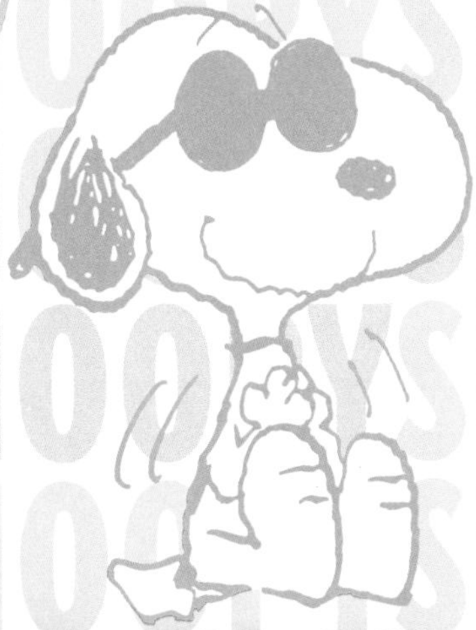

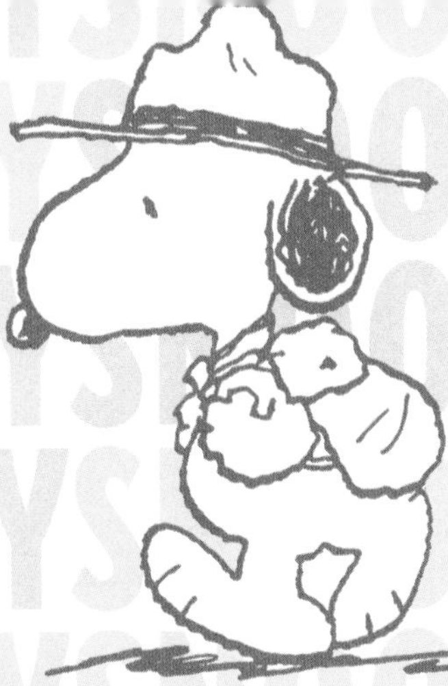

THE MANY FACES OF SNOOPY

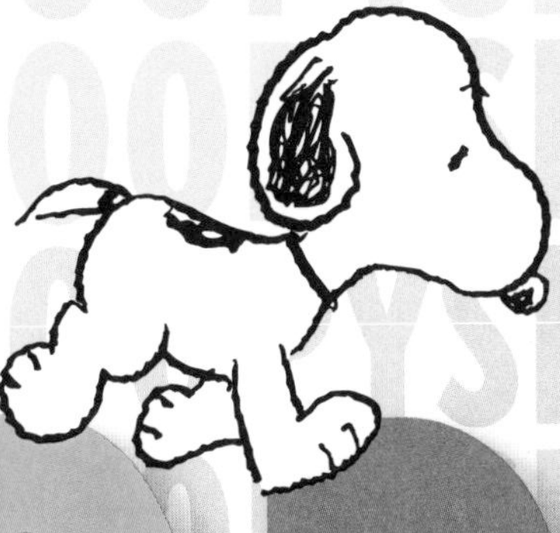

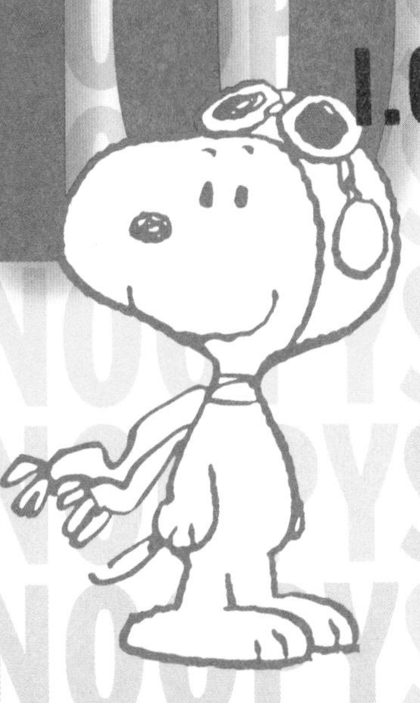

CHARLES M. SCHULZ

Balantine Books · New York

PN
6728
.P4
S32475
2006

A Ballantine Books Trade Paperback Original

Copyright © 2006 United Feature Syndicate, Inc.

All rights reserved.

Published in the United States by Ballantine Books, an imprint of The Random House Publishing Group, a division of Random House, Inc., New York.

BALLANTINE and colophon are registered trademarks of Random House, Inc.

The comic strips in this book were originally published in newspapers worldwide.

ISBN 0-345-47983-1

Printed in the United States of America

www.ballantinebooks.com

9 8 7 6 5 4 3 2 1

Designed by Diane Hobbing of Snap-Haus Graphics

SNOOPY

Joe Cool

JOE
COOL

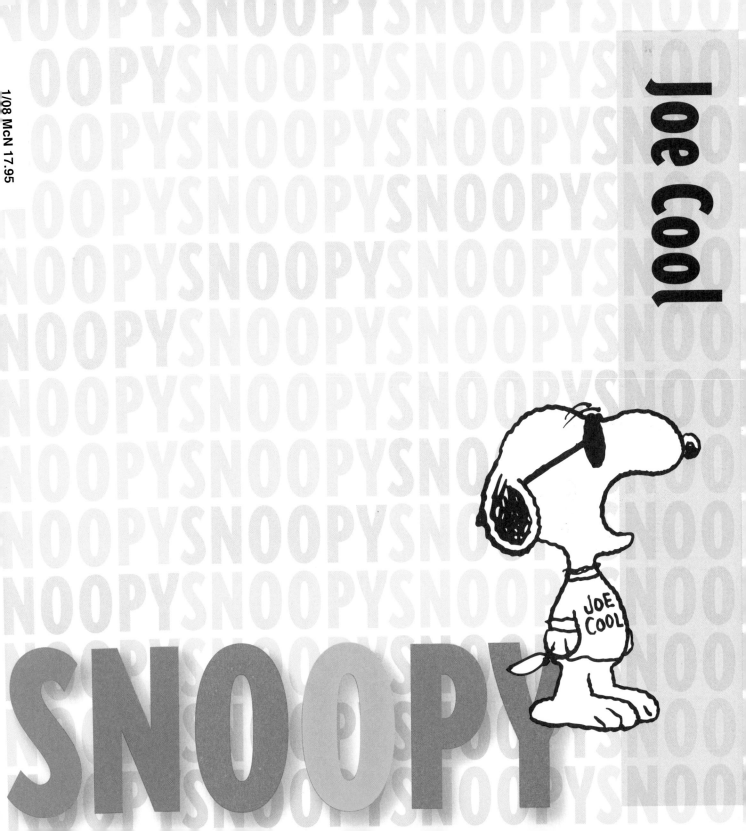

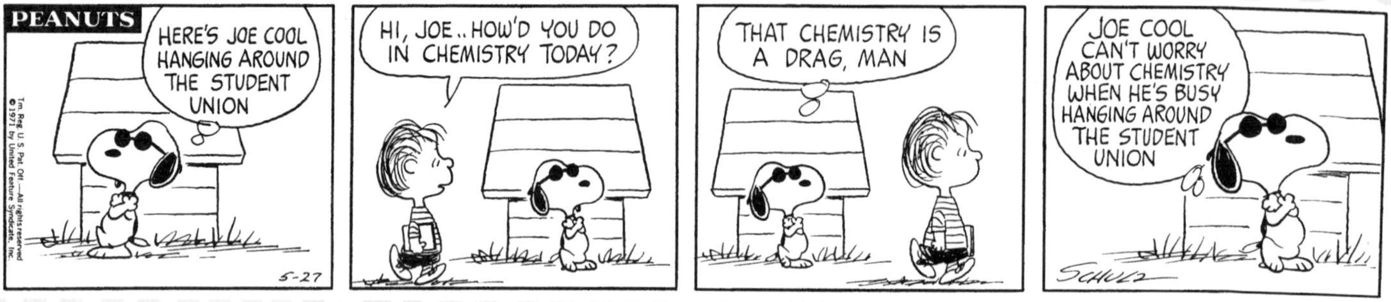
PEANUTS
Tm. Reg. U.S. Pat. Off.—All rights reserved © 1971 by United Feature Syndicate, Inc.
HERE'S JOE COOL HANGING AROUND THE STUDENT UNION
5-27
HI, JOE.. HOW'D YOU DO IN CHEMISTRY TODAY?
THAT CHEMISTRY IS A DRAG, MAN
JOE COOL CAN'T WORRY ABOUT CHEMISTRY WHEN HE'S BUSY HANGING AROUND THE STUDENT UNION
SCHULZ

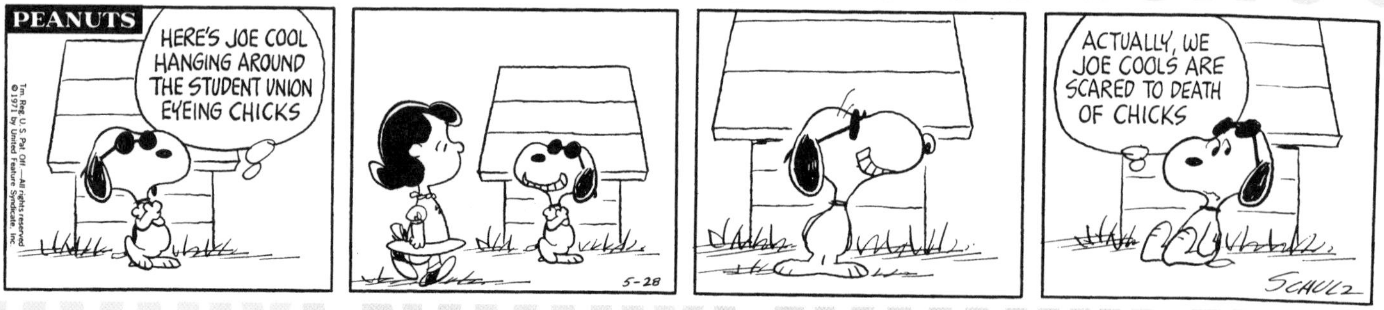
PEANUTS
Tm. Reg. U.S. Pat. Off.—All rights reserved © 1971 by United Feature Syndicate, Inc.
HERE'S JOE COOL HANGING AROUND THE STUDENT UNION EYEING CHICKS
5-28
ACTUALLY, WE JOE COOLS ARE SCARED TO DEATH OF CHICKS
SCHULZ

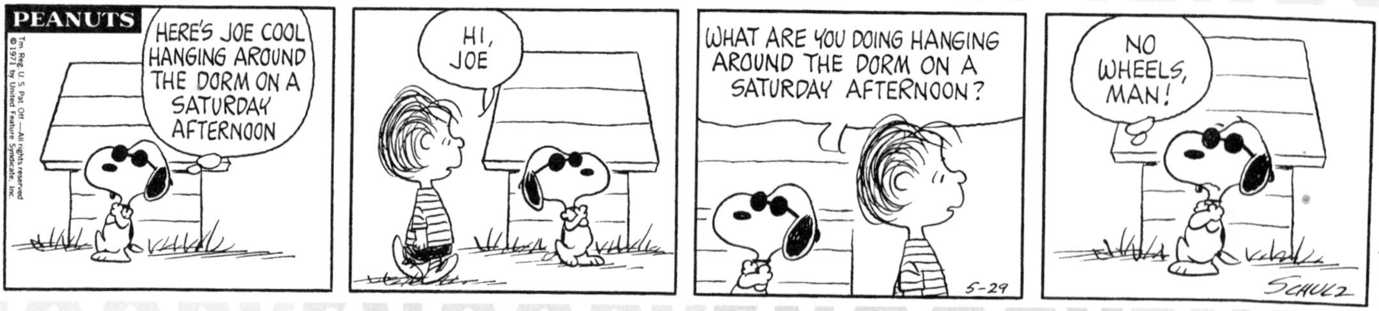
PEANUTS
Tm. Reg. U.S. Pat. Off.—All rights reserved © 1971 by United Feature Syndicate, Inc.
HERE'S JOE COOL HANGING AROUND THE DORM ON A SATURDAY AFTERNOON
HI, JOE
WHAT ARE YOU DOING HANGING AROUND THE DORM ON A SATURDAY AFTERNOON?
5-29
NO WHEELS, MAN!
SCHULZ

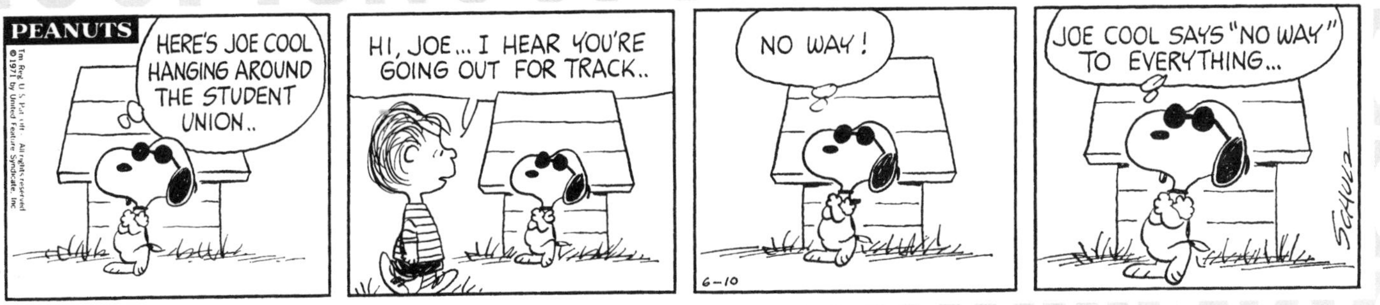
PEANUTS
HERE'S JOE COOL HANGING AROUND THE STUDENT UNION..
HI, JOE... I HEAR YOU'RE GOING OUT FOR TRACK..
NO WAY!
JOE COOL SAYS "NO WAY" TO EVERYTHING...
6-10
SCHULZ

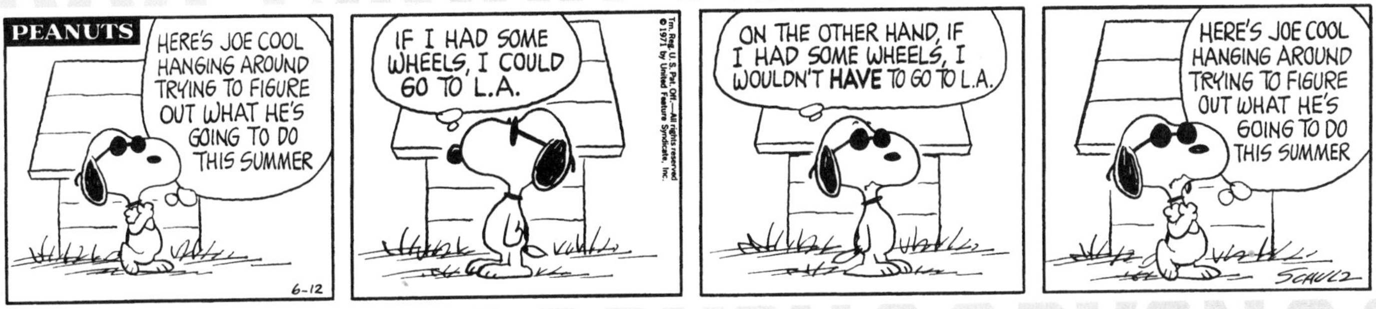
PEANUTS
HERE'S JOE COOL HANGING AROUND TRYING TO FIGURE OUT WHAT HE'S GOING TO DO THIS SUMMER
6-12
IF I HAD SOME WHEELS, I COULD GO TO L.A.
Tm. Reg. U.S. Pat. Off.—All rights reserved © 1971 by United Feature Syndicate, Inc.
ON THE OTHER HAND, IF I HAD SOME WHEELS, I WOULDN'T HAVE TO GO TO L.A.
HERE'S JOE COOL HANGING AROUND TRYING TO FIGURE OUT WHAT HE'S GOING TO DO THIS SUMMER
SCHULZ

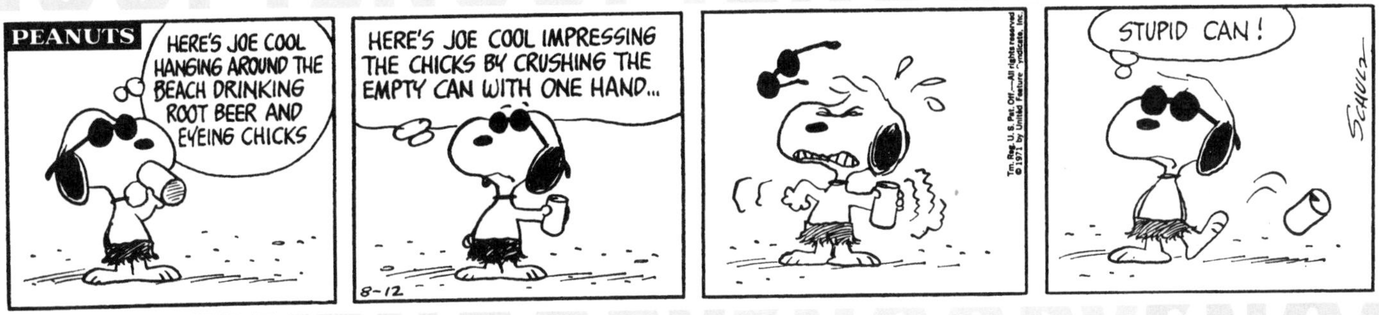
PEANUTS
HERE'S JOE COOL HANGING AROUND THE BEACH DRINKING ROOT BEER AND EYEING CHICKS
HERE'S JOE COOL IMPRESSING THE CHICKS BY CRUSHING THE EMPTY CAN WITH ONE HAND...
8-12
Tm. Reg. U.S. Pat. Off.—All rights reserved
STUPID CAN!
SCHULZ

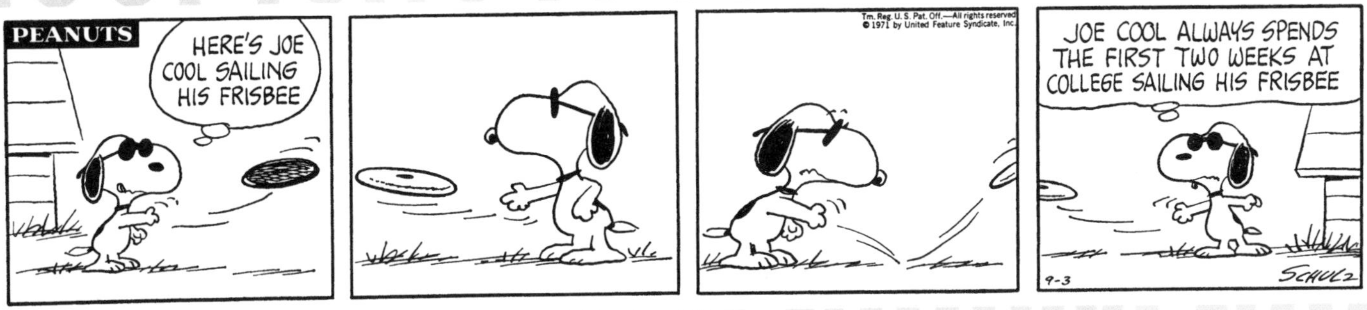
PEANUTS
HERE'S JOE COOL SAILING HIS FRISBEE
Tm. Reg. U.S. Pat. Off.—All rights reserved © 1971 by United Feature Syndicate, Inc.
JOE COOL ALWAYS SPENDS THE FIRST TWO WEEKS AT COLLEGE SAILING HIS FRISBEE
9-3
SCHULZ

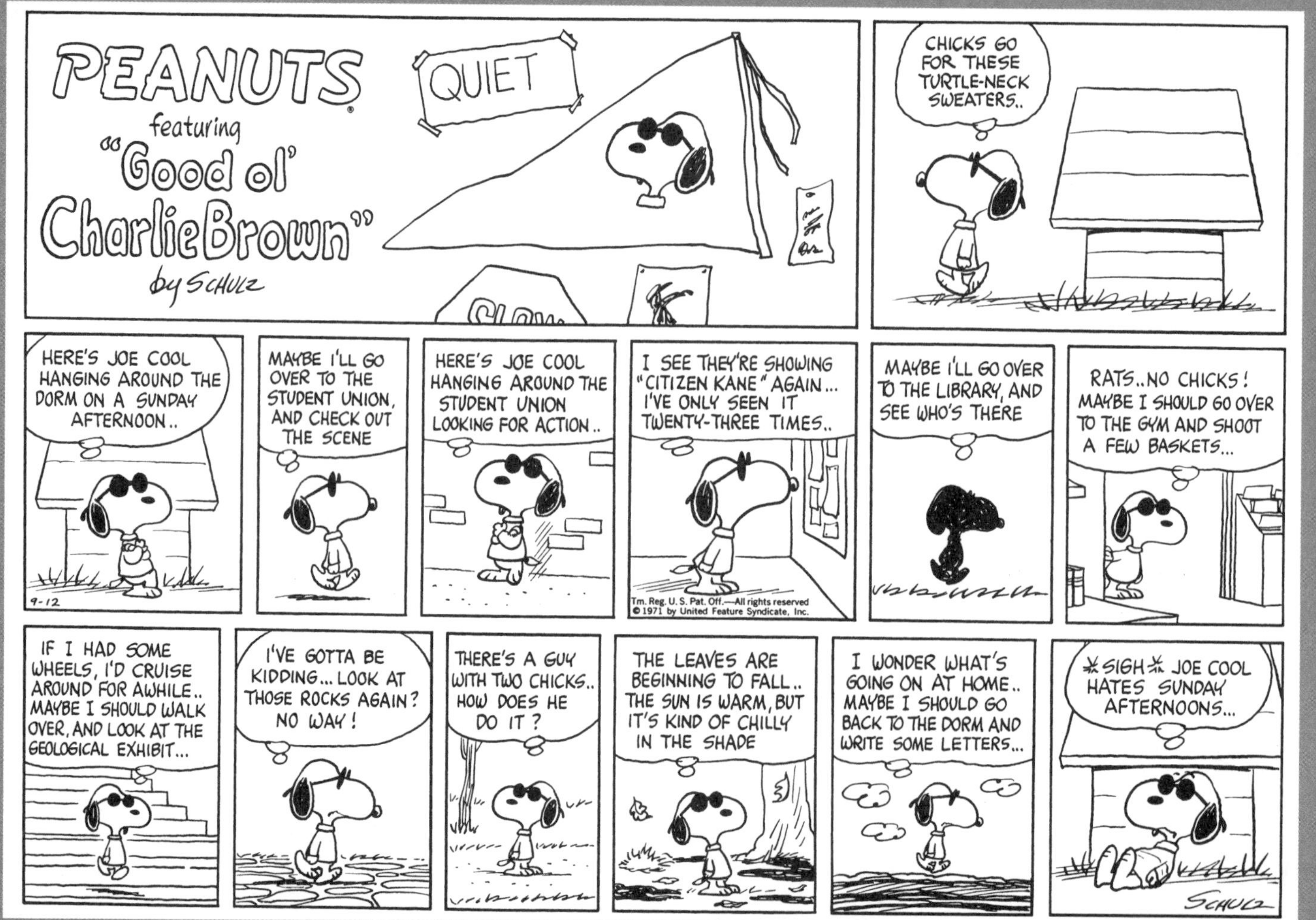
PEANUTS
featuring
"Good ol' CharlieBrown"
by SCHULZ
QUIET
CHICKS GO FOR THESE TURTLE-NECK SWEATERS..
HERE'S JOE COOL HANGING AROUND THE DORM ON A SUNDAY AFTERNOON..
9-12
MAYBE I'LL GO OVER TO THE STUDENT UNION, AND CHECK OUT THE SCENE
HERE'S JOE COOL HANGING AROUND THE STUDENT UNION LOOKING FOR ACTION..
I SEE THEY'RE SHOWING "CITIZEN KANE" AGAIN... I'VE ONLY SEEN IT TWENTY-THREE TIMES..
Tm. Reg. U. S. Pat. Off.—All rights reserved © 1971 by United Feature Syndicate, Inc.
MAYBE I'LL GO OVER TO THE LIBRARY, AND SEE WHO'S THERE
RATS..NO CHICKS! MAYBE I SHOULD GO OVER TO THE GYM AND SHOOT A FEW BASKETS...
IF I HAD SOME WHEELS, I'D CRUISE AROUND FOR AWHILE.. MAYBE I SHOULD WALK OVER, AND LOOK AT THE GEOLOGICAL EXHIBIT...
I'VE GOTTA BE KIDDING... LOOK AT THOSE ROCKS AGAIN? NO WAY!
THERE'S A GUY WITH TWO CHICKS.. HOW DOES HE DO IT?
THE LEAVES ARE BEGINNING TO FALL.. THE SUN IS WARM, BUT IT'S KIND OF CHILLY IN THE SHADE
I WONDER WHAT'S GOING ON AT HOME.. MAYBE I SHOULD GO BACK TO THE DORM AND WRITE SOME LETTERS...
SIGH JOE COOL HATES SUNDAY AFTERNOONS...
SCHULZ

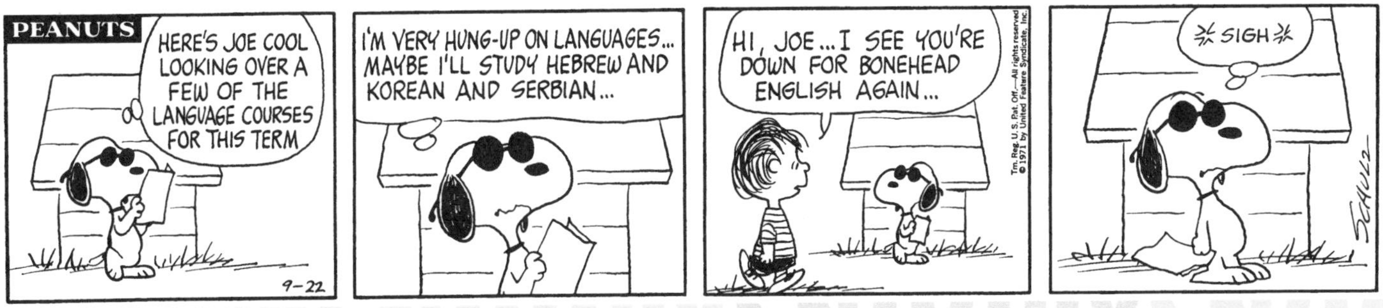
PEANUTS
HERE'S JOE COOL LOOKING OVER A FEW OF THE LANGUAGE COURSES FOR THIS TERM
9-22
I'M VERY HUNG-UP ON LANGUAGES... MAYBE I'LL STUDY HEBREW AND KOREAN AND SERBIAN...
HI, JOE... I SEE YOU'RE DOWN FOR BONEHEAD ENGLISH AGAIN...
Tm. Reg. U. S. Pat. Off.—All rights reserved © 1971 by United Feature Syndicate, Inc.
SIGH
SCHULZ

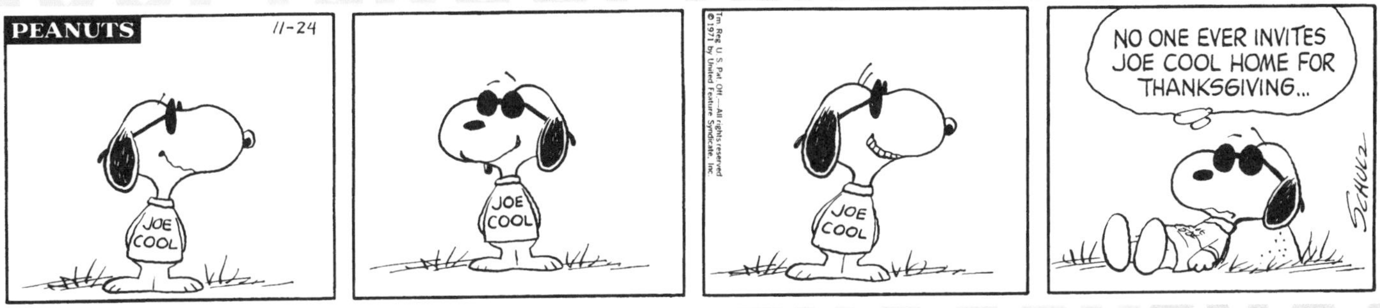
PEANUTS
11-24
JOE COOL
JOE COOL
Tm. Reg. U. S. Pat. Off.—All rights reserved © 1971 by United Feature Syndicate, Inc.
JOE COOL
NO ONE EVER INVITES JOE COOL HOME FOR THANKSGIVING...
SCHULZ

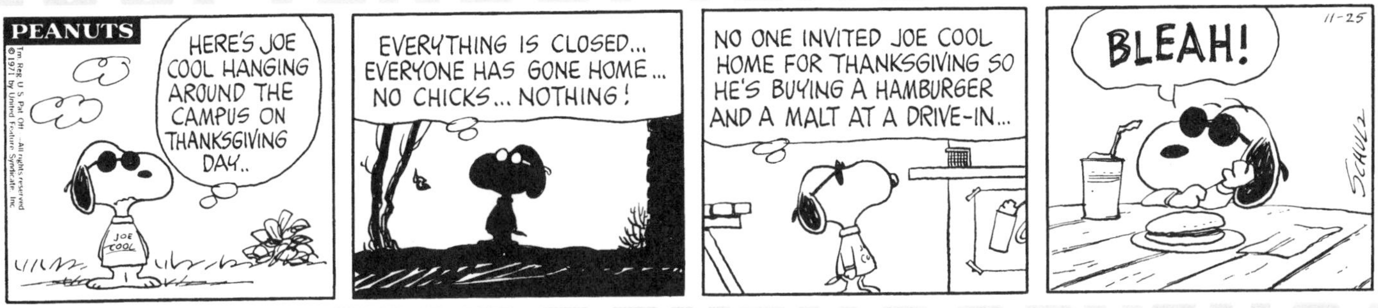
PEANUTS
Tm. Reg. U. S. Pat. Off.—All rights reserved © 1971 by United Feature Syndicate, Inc.
HERE'S JOE COOL HANGING AROUND THE CAMPUS ON THANKSGIVING DAY..
JOE COOL
EVERYTHING IS CLOSED... EVERYONE HAS GONE HOME... NO CHICKS... NOTHING!
NO ONE INVITED JOE COOL HOME FOR THANKSGIVING SO HE'S BUYING A HAMBURGER AND A MALT AT A DRIVE-IN...
11-25
BLEAH!
SCHULZ

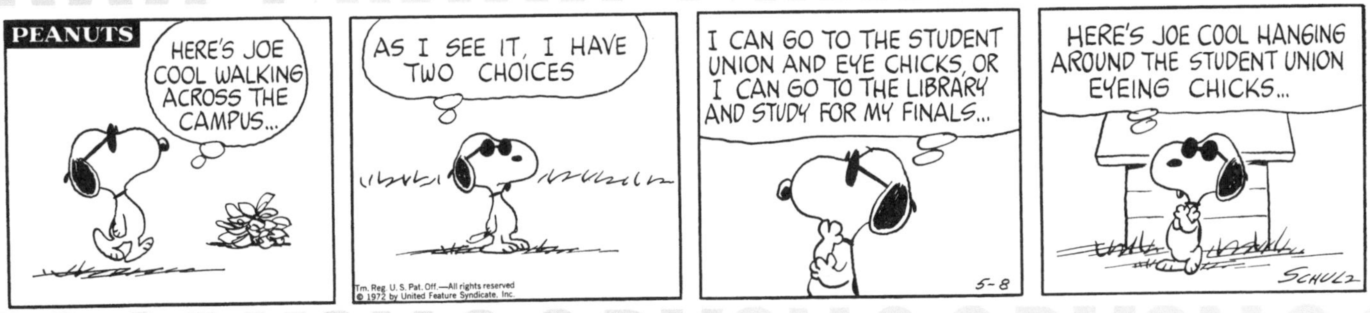
PEANUTS
HERE'S JOE COOL WALKING ACROSS THE CAMPUS...
AS I SEE IT, I HAVE TWO CHOICES
Tm. Reg. U. S. Pat. Off.—All rights reserved © 1972 by United Feature Syndicate, Inc.
I CAN GO TO THE STUDENT UNION AND EYE CHICKS, OR I CAN GO TO THE LIBRARY AND STUDY FOR MY FINALS...
5-8
HERE'S JOE COOL HANGING AROUND THE STUDENT UNION EYEING CHICKS...
SCHULZ

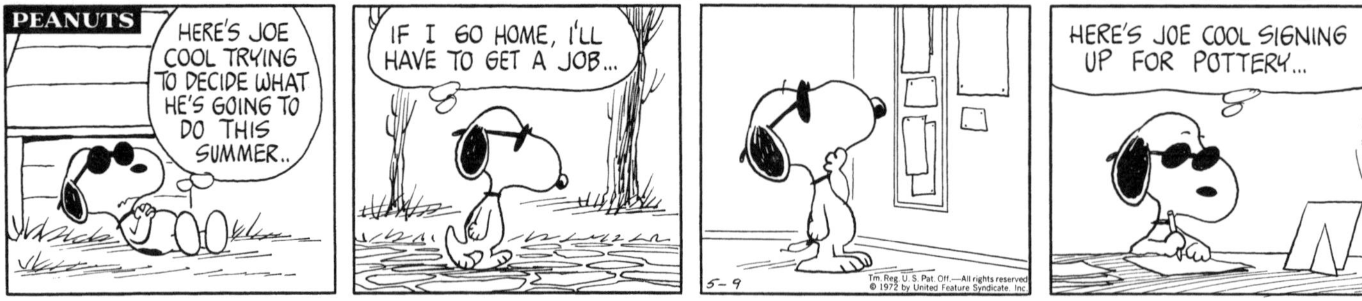
PEANUTS
HERE'S JOE COOL TRYING TO DECIDE WHAT HE'S GOING TO DO THIS SUMMER..
IF I GO HOME, I'LL HAVE TO GET A JOB...
5-9
Tm. Reg. U.S. Pat. Off.—All rights reserved © 1972 by United Feature Syndicate, Inc.
HERE'S JOE COOL SIGNING UP FOR POTTERY...
SCHULZ

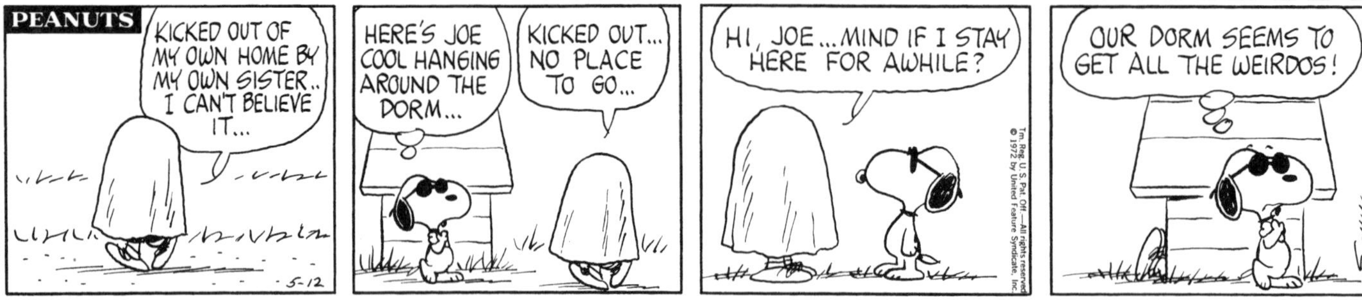
PEANUTS
KICKED OUT OF MY OWN HOME BY MY OWN SISTER.. I CAN'T BELIEVE IT...
5-12
HERE'S JOE COOL HANGING AROUND THE DORM...
KICKED OUT... NO PLACE TO GO...
HI, JOE... MIND IF I STAY HERE FOR AWHILE?
Tm. Reg. U.S. Pat. Off.—All rights reserved © 1972 by United Feature Syndicate, Inc.
OUR DORM SEEMS TO GET ALL THE WEIRDOS!
SCHULZ

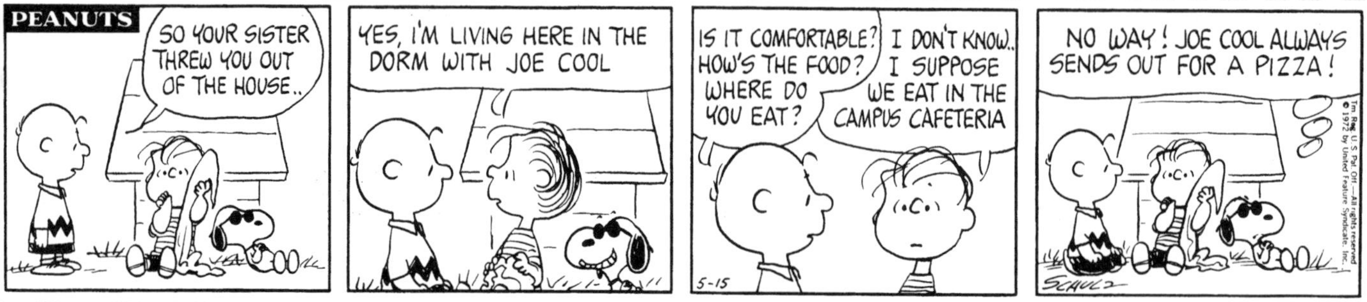
PEANUTS
SO YOUR SISTER THREW YOU OUT OF THE HOUSE..
YES, I'M LIVING HERE IN THE DORM WITH JOE COOL
IS IT COMFORTABLE? HOW'S THE FOOD? WHERE DO YOU EAT?
I DON'T KNOW.. I SUPPOSE WE EAT IN THE CAMPUS CAFETERIA
5-15
NO WAY! JOE COOL ALWAYS SENDS OUT FOR A PIZZA!
Tm. Reg. U.S. Pat. Off.—All rights reserved © 1972 by United Feature Syndicate, Inc.
SCHULZ

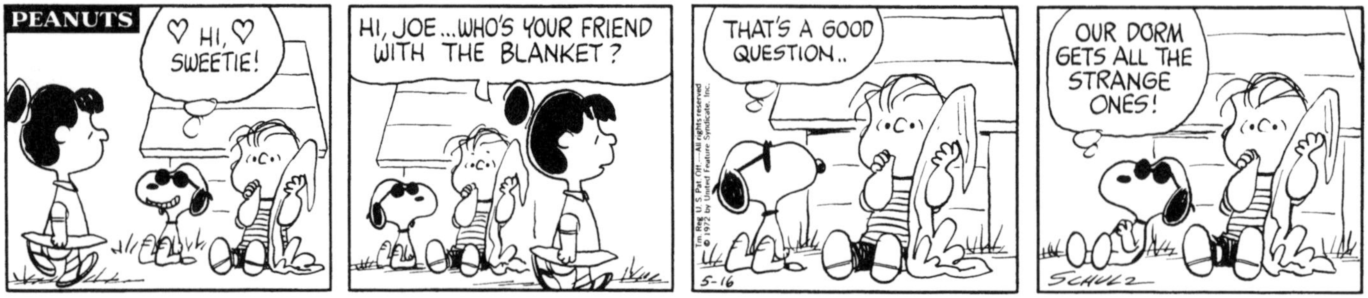
PEANUTS
♡ HI, ♡ SWEETIE!
HI, JOE... WHO'S YOUR FRIEND WITH THE BLANKET?
Tm. Reg. U.S. Pat. Off.—All rights reserved © 1972 by United Feature Syndicate, Inc.
THAT'S A GOOD QUESTION..
5-16
OUR DORM GETS ALL THE STRANGE ONES!
SCHULZ

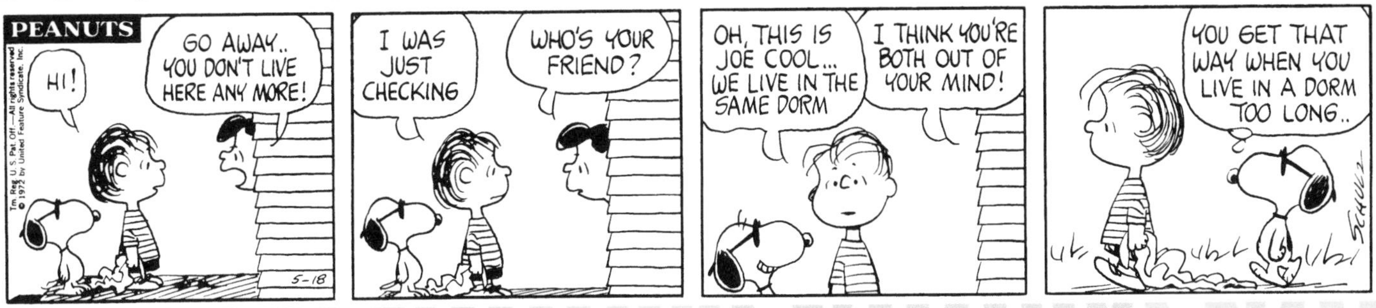
PEANUTS
Tm. Reg. U.S. Pat. Off.—All rights reserved © 1972 by United Feature Syndicate, Inc.
HI!
GO AWAY.. YOU DON'T LIVE HERE ANY MORE!
I WAS JUST CHECKING
WHO'S YOUR FRIEND?
OH, THIS IS JOE COOL... WE LIVE IN THE SAME DORM
I THINK YOU'RE BOTH OUT OF YOUR MIND!
YOU GET THAT WAY WHEN YOU LIVE IN A DORM TOO LONG..

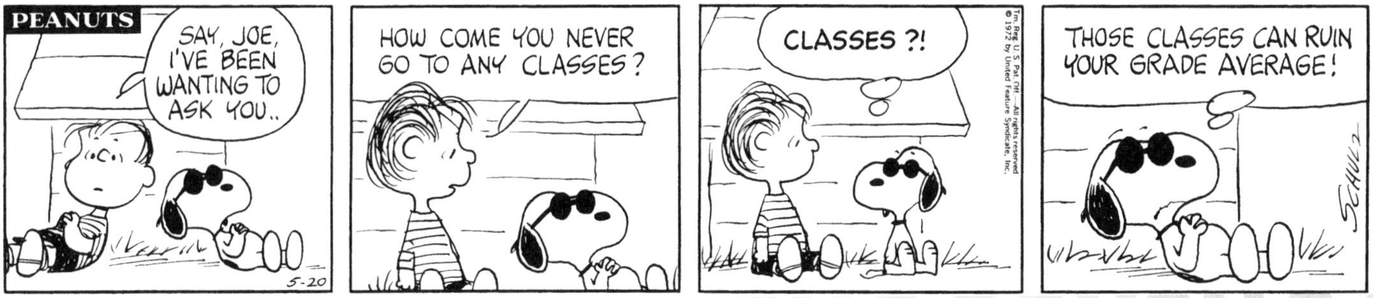
PEANUTS
SAY, JOE, I'VE BEEN WANTING TO ASK YOU..
HOW COME YOU NEVER GO TO ANY CLASSES?
CLASSES?!
Tm. Reg. U.S. Pat. Off.—All rights reserved © 1972 by United Feature Syndicate, Inc.
THOSE CLASSES CAN RUIN YOUR GRADE AVERAGE!

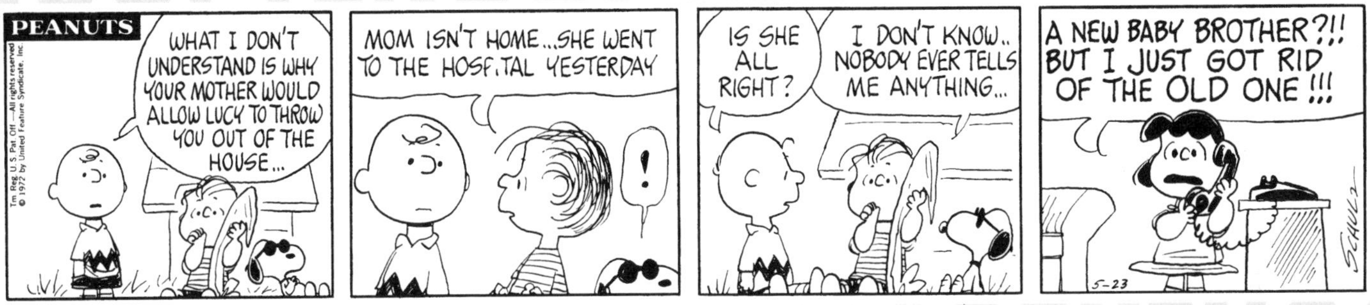
PEANUTS
Tm. Reg. U.S. Pat. Off.—All rights reserved © 1972 by United Feature Syndicate, Inc.
WHAT I DON'T UNDERSTAND IS WHY YOUR MOTHER WOULD ALLOW LUCY TO THROW YOU OUT OF THE HOUSE...
MOM ISN'T HOME...SHE WENT TO THE HOSPITAL YESTERDAY
!
IS SHE ALL RIGHT?
I DON'T KNOW.. NOBODY EVER TELLS ME ANYTHING...
A NEW BABY BROTHER?!! BUT I JUST GOT RID OF THE OLD ONE!!!

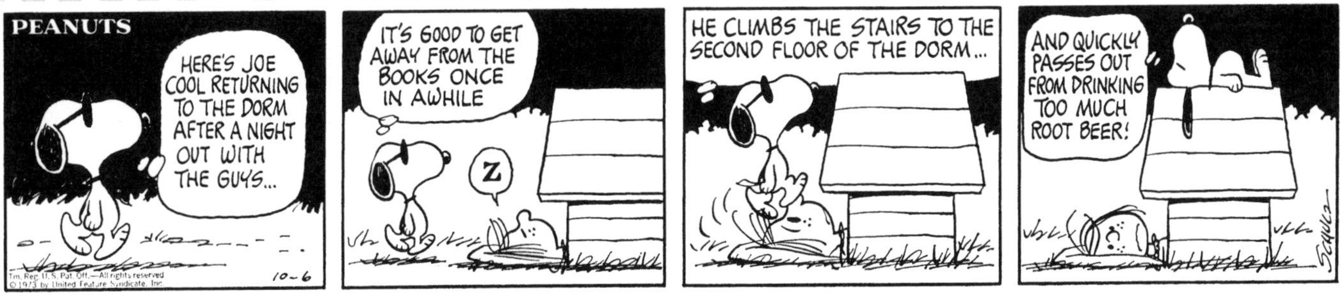
PEANUTS
HERE'S JOE COOL RETURNING TO THE DORM AFTER A NIGHT OUT WITH THE GUYS...
Tm. Reg. U.S. Pat. Off.—All rights reserved © 1973 by United Feature Syndicate, Inc.
IT'S GOOD TO GET AWAY FROM THE BOOKS ONCE IN AWHILE
Z
HE CLIMBS THE STAIRS TO THE SECOND FLOOR OF THE DORM...
AND QUICKLY PASSES OUT FROM DRINKING TOO MUCH ROOT BEER!

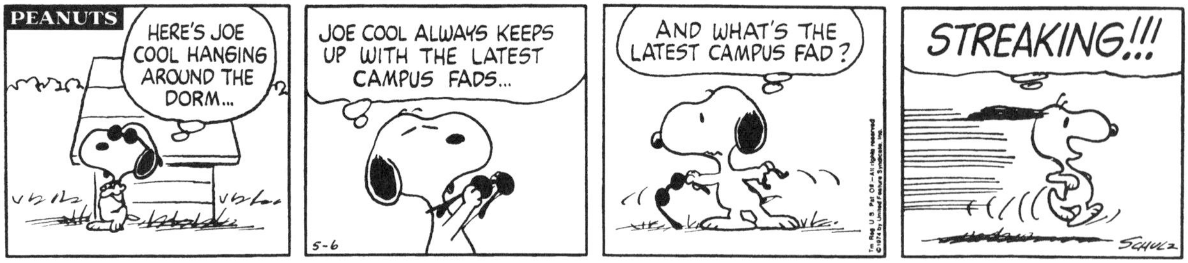
PEANUTS
HERE'S JOE COOL HANGING AROUND THE DORM...
JOE COOL ALWAYS KEEPS UP WITH THE LATEST CAMPUS FADS...
5-6
AND WHAT'S THE LATEST CAMPUS FAD?
STREAKING!!!
SCHULZ

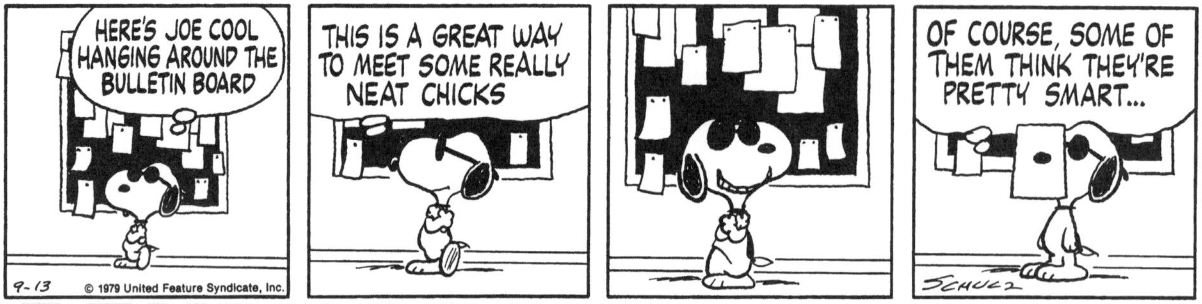
HERE'S JOE COOL HANGING AROUND THE BULLETIN BOARD
9-13
© 1979 United Feature Syndicate, Inc.
THIS IS A GREAT WAY TO MEET SOME REALLY NEAT CHICKS
OF COURSE, SOME OF THEM THINK THEY'RE PRETTY SMART...
SCHULZ

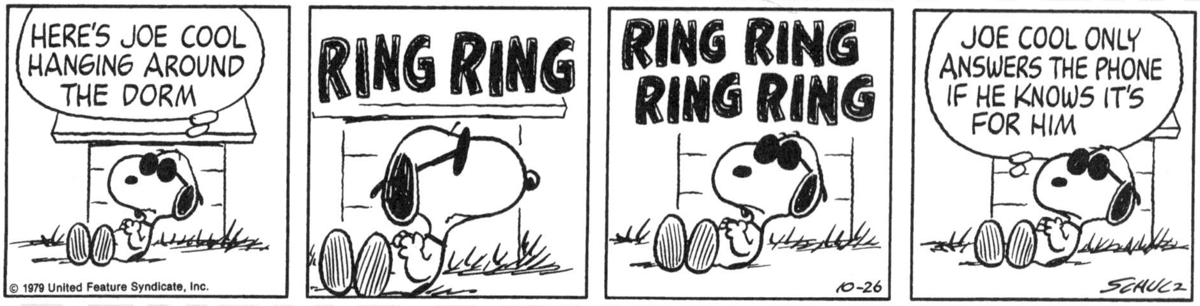
HERE'S JOE COOL HANGING AROUND THE DORM
© 1979 United Feature Syndicate, Inc.
RING RING
RING RING RING RING
10-26
JOE COOL ONLY ANSWERS THE PHONE IF HE KNOWS IT'S FOR HIM
SCHULZ

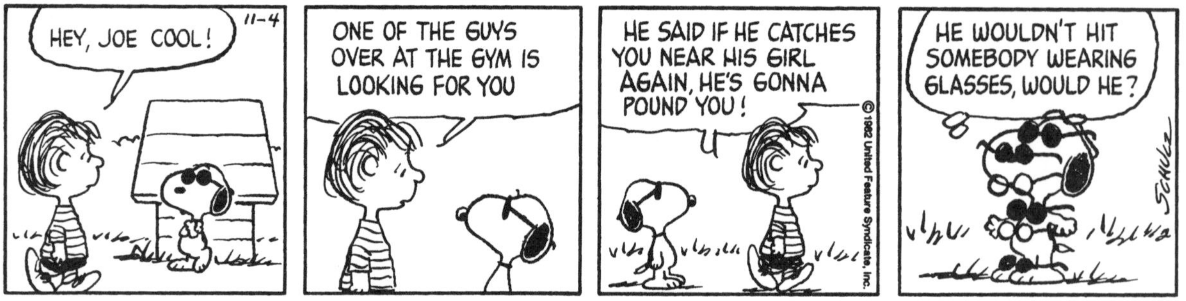
HEY, JOE COOL!
11-4
ONE OF THE GUYS OVER AT THE GYM IS LOOKING FOR YOU
HE SAID IF HE CATCHES YOU NEAR HIS GIRL AGAIN, HE'S GONNA POUND YOU!
© 1982 United Feature Syndicate, Inc.
HE WOULDN'T HIT SOMEBODY WEARING GLASSES, WOULD HE?
SCHULZ

HERE'S JOE COOL ON HIS WAY TO REGISTER FOR THE FALL SEMESTER...
© 1991 United Feature Syndicate, Inc.
RATS!
IF BROOMBALL IS FILLED, I'M GOING TO BE VERY DISAPPOINTED
SCHULZ
8-21

HERE'S JOE COOL SIGNING UP FOR A CLASS IN FIGURE DRAWING...
© 1991 United Feature Syndicate, Inc.
"ALL STUDENTS SHOULD BE PREPARED TO SHOW A SAMPLE OF THEIR WORK"
8-22
SCHULZ

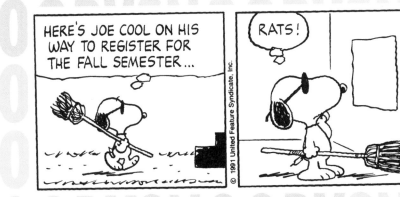

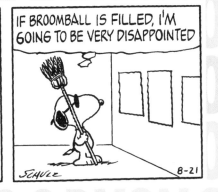

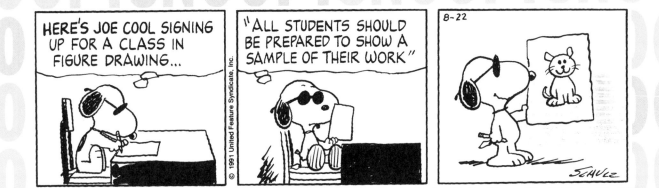

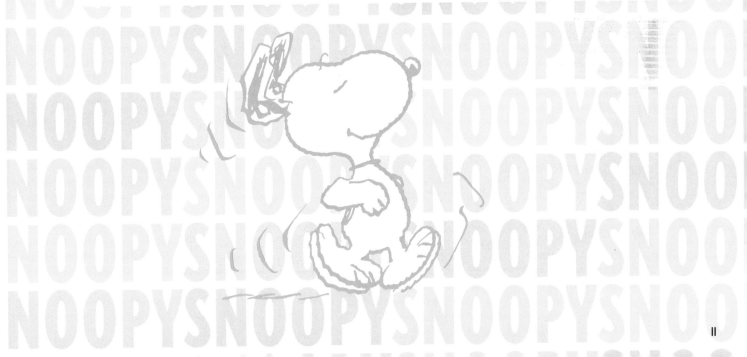

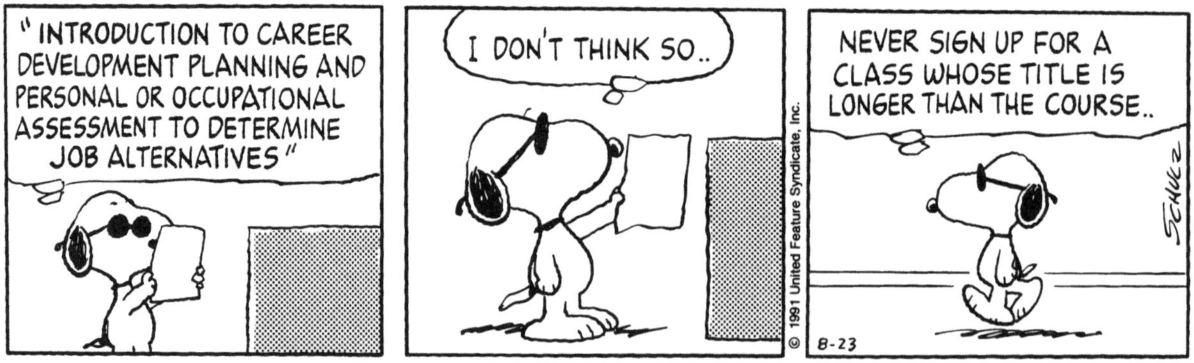
"INTRODUCTION TO CAREER DEVELOPMENT PLANNING AND PERSONAL OR OCCUPATIONAL ASSESSMENT TO DETERMINE JOB ALTERNATIVES"
I DON'T THINK SO..
NEVER SIGN UP FOR A CLASS WHOSE TITLE IS LONGER THAN THE COURSE..
© 1991 United Feature Syndicate, Inc.
SCHULZ
8-23

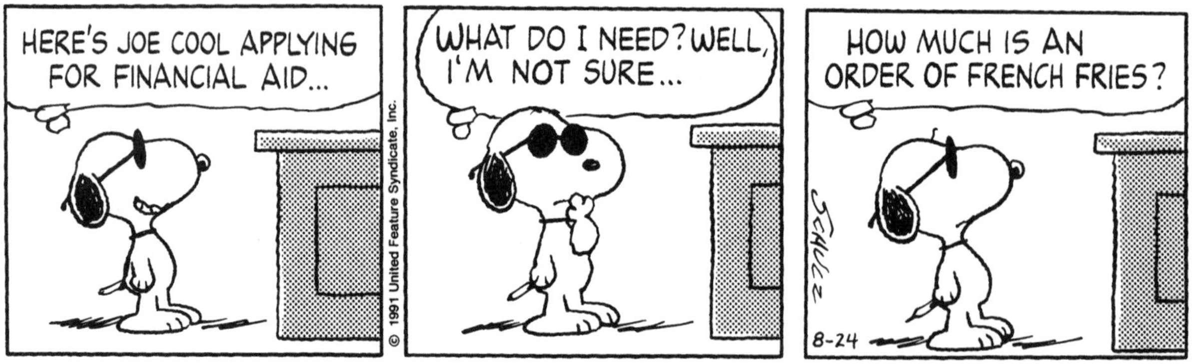
HERE'S JOE COOL APPLYING FOR FINANCIAL AID...
WHAT DO I NEED? WELL, I'M NOT SURE...
HOW MUCH IS AN ORDER OF FRENCH FRIES?
© 1991 United Feature Syndicate, Inc.
SCHULZ
8-24

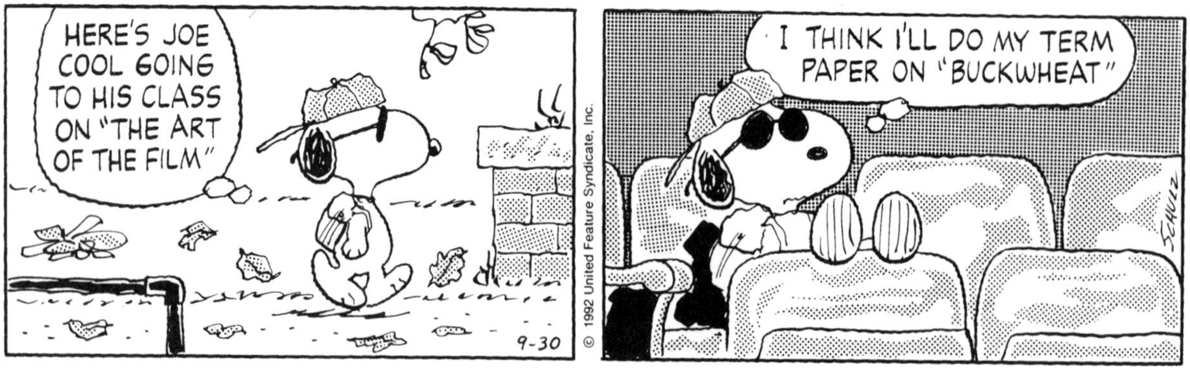
HERE'S JOE COOL GOING TO HIS CLASS ON "THE ART OF THE FILM"
I THINK I'LL DO MY TERM PAPER ON "BUCKWHEAT"
© 1992 United Feature Syndicate, Inc.
SCHULZ
9-30

Legal Beagle

SNOOPY

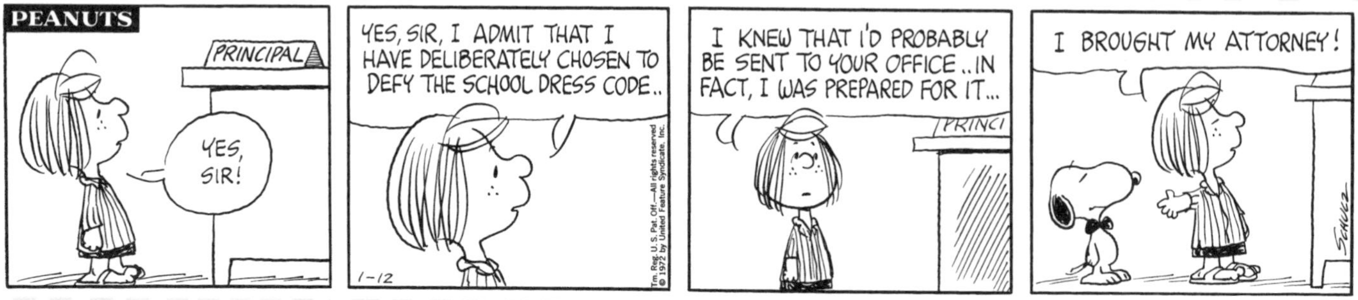
PEANUTS
PRINCIPAL
YES, SIR!
YES, SIR, I ADMIT THAT I HAVE DELIBERATELY CHOSEN TO DEFY THE SCHOOL DRESS CODE..
1-12
Tm. Reg. U.S. Pat. Off.—All rights reserved © 1972 by United Feature Syndicate, Inc.
I KNEW THAT I'D PROBABLY BE SENT TO YOUR OFFICE..IN FACT, I WAS PREPARED FOR IT...
PRINCI
I BROUGHT MY ATTORNEY!
SCHULZ

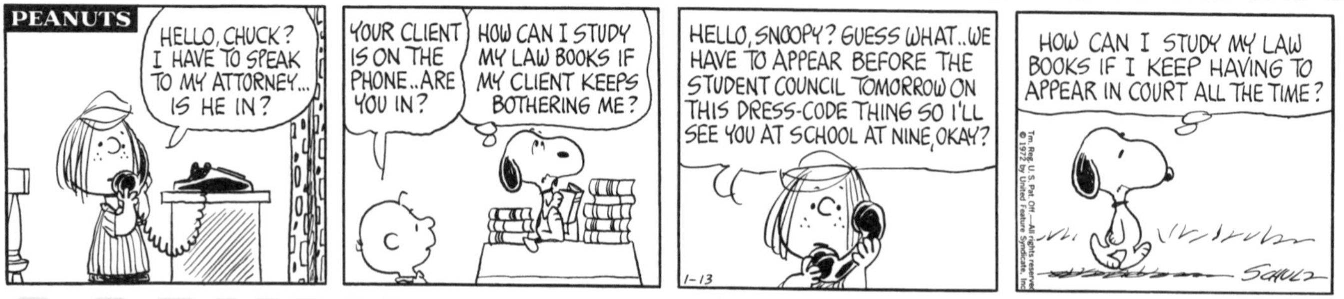
PEANUTS
HELLO, CHUCK? I HAVE TO SPEAK TO MY ATTORNEY... IS HE IN?
YOUR CLIENT IS ON THE PHONE..ARE YOU IN?
HOW CAN I STUDY MY LAW BOOKS IF MY CLIENT KEEPS BOTHERING ME?
HELLO, SNOOPY? GUESS WHAT..WE HAVE TO APPEAR BEFORE THE STUDENT COUNCIL TOMORROW ON THIS DRESS-CODE THING SO I'LL SEE YOU AT SCHOOL AT NINE, OKAY?
1-13
Tm. Reg. U.S. Pat. Off.—All rights reserved © 1972 by United Feature Syndicate, Inc.
HOW CAN I STUDY MY LAW BOOKS IF I KEEP HAVING TO APPEAR IN COURT ALL THE TIME?
SCHULZ

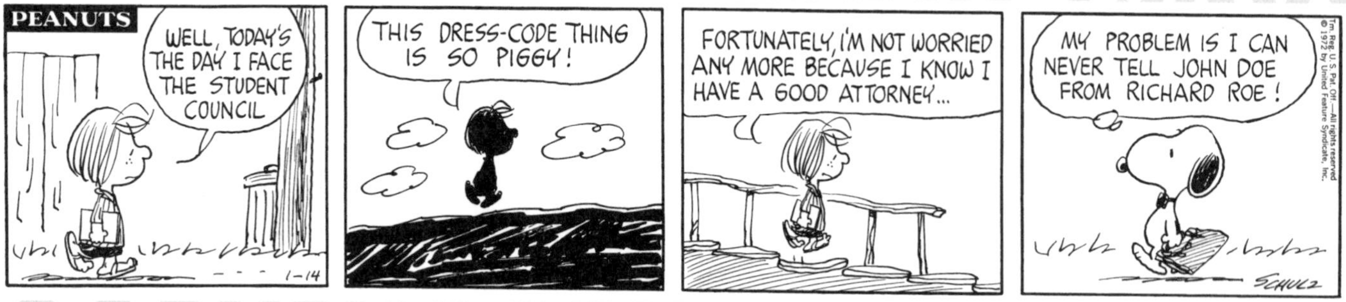
PEANUTS
WELL, TODAY'S THE DAY I FACE THE STUDENT COUNCIL
1-14
THIS DRESS-CODE THING IS SO PIGGY!
FORTUNATELY, I'M NOT WORRIED ANY MORE BECAUSE I KNOW I HAVE A GOOD ATTORNEY...
MY PROBLEM IS I CAN NEVER TELL JOHN DOE FROM RICHARD ROE!
Tm. Reg. U.S. Pat. Off.—All rights reserved © 1972 by United Feature Syndicate, Inc.
SCHULZ

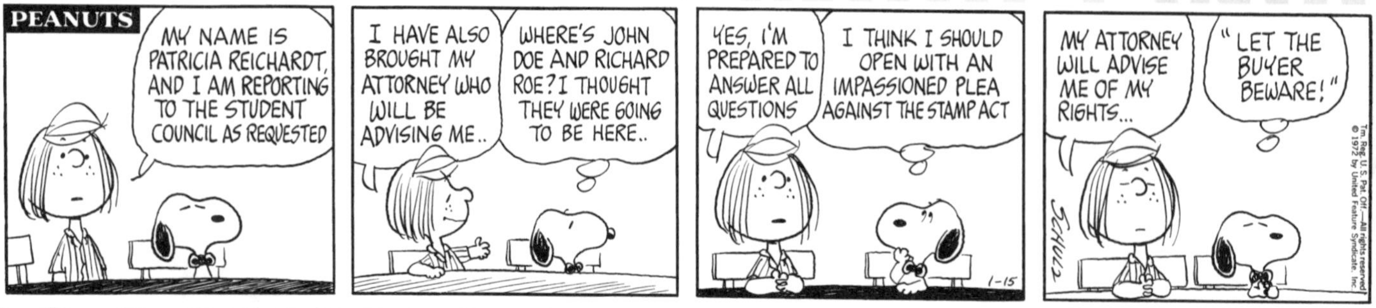
PEANUTS
MY NAME IS PATRICIA REICHARDT, AND I AM REPORTING TO THE STUDENT COUNCIL AS REQUESTED
I HAVE ALSO BROUGHT MY ATTORNEY WHO WILL BE ADVISING ME..
WHERE'S JOHN DOE AND RICHARD ROE? I THOUGHT THEY WERE GOING TO BE HERE..
YES, I'M PREPARED TO ANSWER ALL QUESTIONS
I THINK I SHOULD OPEN WITH AN IMPASSIONED PLEA AGAINST THE STAMP ACT
1-15
MY ATTORNEY WILL ADVISE ME OF MY RIGHTS...
"LET THE BUYER BEWARE!"
SCHULZ
Tm. Reg. U.S. Pat. Off.—All rights reserved © 1972 by United Feature Syndicate, Inc.

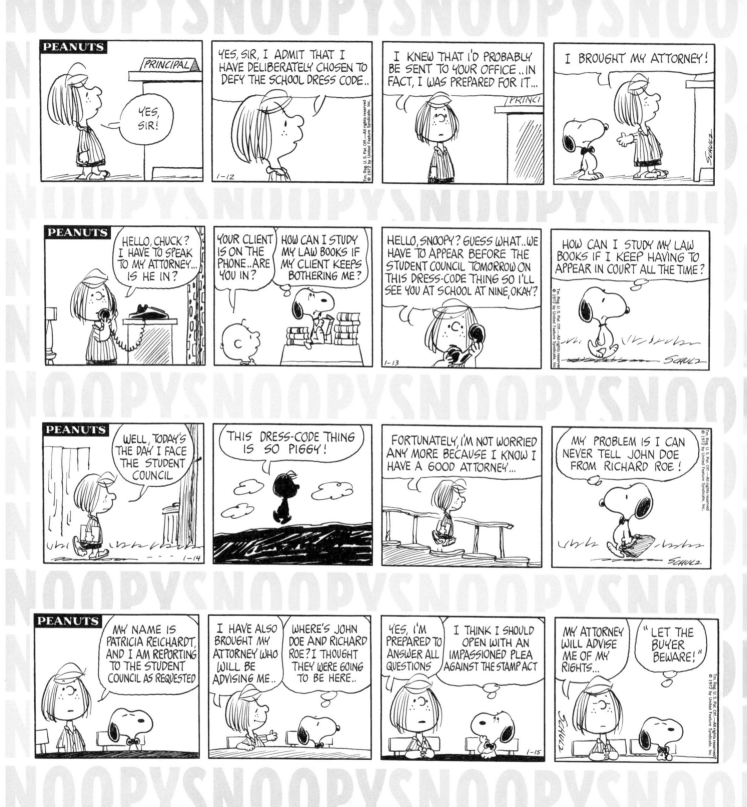

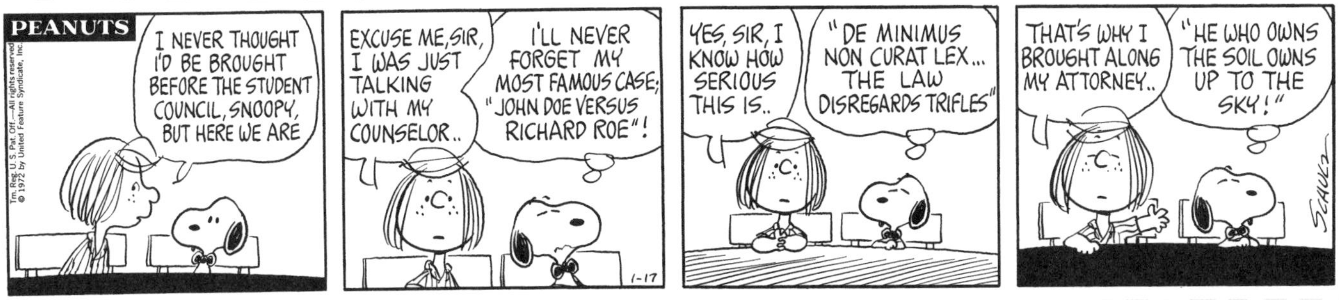
PEANUTS
Tm. Reg. U.S. Pat. Off.—All rights reserved © 1972 by United Feature Syndicate, Inc.
I NEVER THOUGHT I'D BE BROUGHT BEFORE THE STUDENT COUNCIL, SNOOPY, BUT HERE WE ARE
EXCUSE ME, SIR, I WAS JUST TALKING WITH MY COUNSELOR..
I'LL NEVER FORGET MY MOST FAMOUS CASE; "JOHN DOE VERSUS RICHARD ROE"!
1-17
YES, SIR, I KNOW HOW SERIOUS THIS IS..
"DE MINIMUS NON CURAT LEX... THE LAW DISREGARDS TRIFLES"
THAT'S WHY I BROUGHT ALONG MY ATTORNEY..
"HE WHO OWNS THE SOIL OWNS UP TO THE SKY!"
SCHULZ

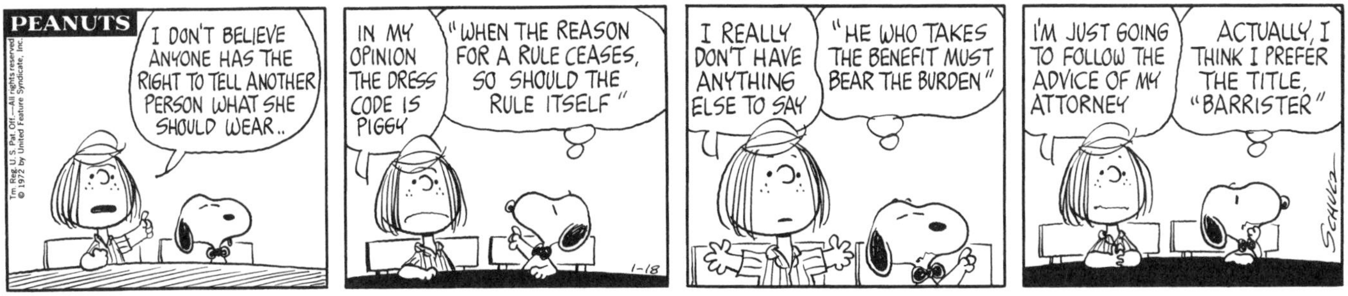
PEANUTS
Tm. Reg. U.S. Pat. Off.—All rights reserved © 1972 by United Feature Syndicate, Inc.
I DON'T BELIEVE ANYONE HAS THE RIGHT TO TELL ANOTHER PERSON WHAT SHE SHOULD WEAR..
IN MY OPINION THE DRESS CODE IS PIGGY
"WHEN THE REASON FOR A RULE CEASES, SO SHOULD THE RULE ITSELF"
1-18
I REALLY DON'T HAVE ANYTHING ELSE TO SAY
"HE WHO TAKES THE BENEFIT MUST BEAR THE BURDEN"
I'M JUST GOING TO FOLLOW THE ADVICE OF MY ATTORNEY
ACTUALLY, I THINK I PREFER THE TITLE, "BARRISTER"
SCHULZ

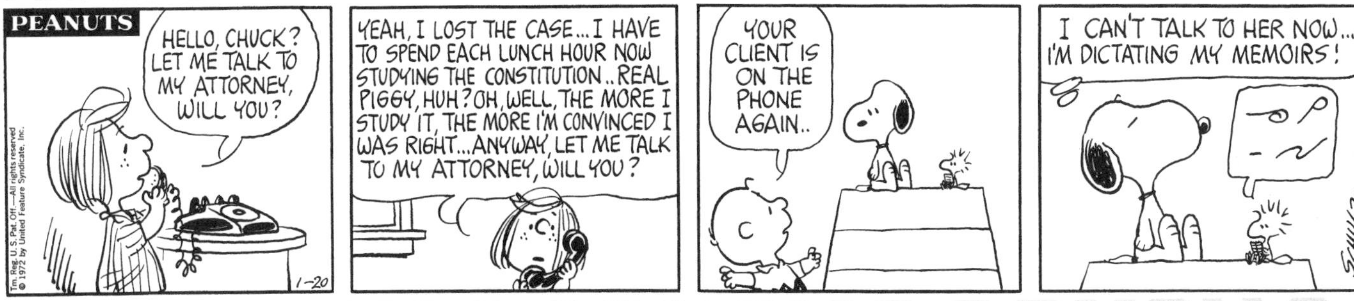
PEANUTS
Tm. Reg. U.S. Pat. Off.—All rights reserved © 1972 by United Feature Syndicate, Inc.
HELLO, CHUCK? LET ME TALK TO MY ATTORNEY, WILL YOU?
1-20
YEAH, I LOST THE CASE... I HAVE TO SPEND EACH LUNCH HOUR NOW STUDYING THE CONSTITUTION.. REAL PIGGY, HUH? OH, WELL, THE MORE I STUDY IT, THE MORE I'M CONVINCED I WAS RIGHT... ANYWAY, LET ME TALK TO MY ATTORNEY, WILL YOU?
YOUR CLIENT IS ON THE PHONE AGAIN..
I CAN'T TALK TO HER NOW... I'M DICTATING MY MEMOIRS!
SCHULZ

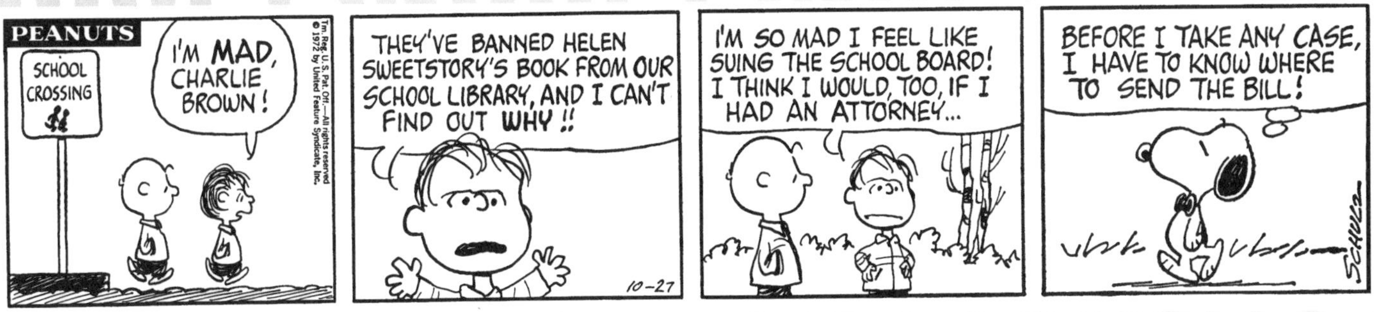
PEANUTS
SCHOOL CROSSING
I'M MAD, CHARLIE BROWN!
Tm. Reg. U.S. Pat. Off.—All rights reserved © 1972 by United Feature Syndicate, Inc.
THEY'VE BANNED HELEN SWEETSTORY'S BOOK FROM OUR SCHOOL LIBRARY, AND I CAN'T FIND OUT WHY!!
10-27
I'M SO MAD I FEEL LIKE SUING THE SCHOOL BOARD! I THINK I WOULD, TOO, IF I HAD AN ATTORNEY...
BEFORE I TAKE ANY CASE, I HAVE TO KNOW WHERE TO SEND THE BILL!
SCHULZ

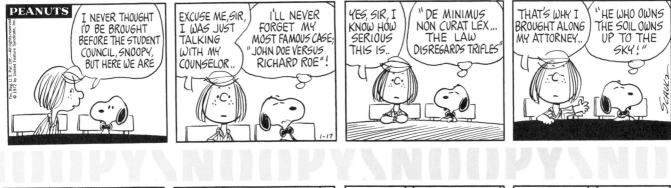

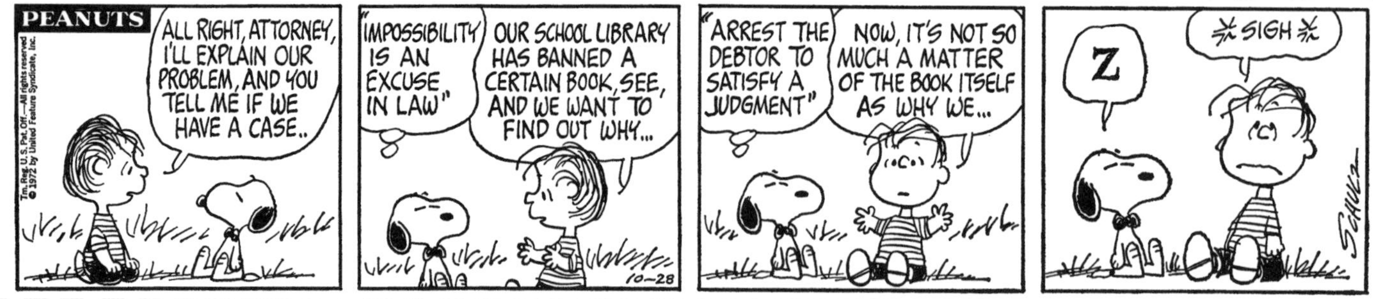
PEANUTS
Tm. Reg. U.S. Pat. Off.—All rights reserved © 1972 by United Feature Syndicate, Inc.
ALL RIGHT, ATTORNEY, I'LL EXPLAIN OUR PROBLEM, AND YOU TELL ME IF WE HAVE A CASE..
"IMPOSSIBILITY IS AN EXCUSE IN LAW"
OUR SCHOOL LIBRARY HAS BANNED A CERTAIN BOOK, SEE, AND WE WANT TO FIND OUT WHY...
10-28
"ARREST THE DEBTOR TO SATISFY A JUDGMENT"
NOW, IT'S NOT SO MUCH A MATTER OF THE BOOK ITSELF AS WHY WE...
Z
SIGH
SCHULZ

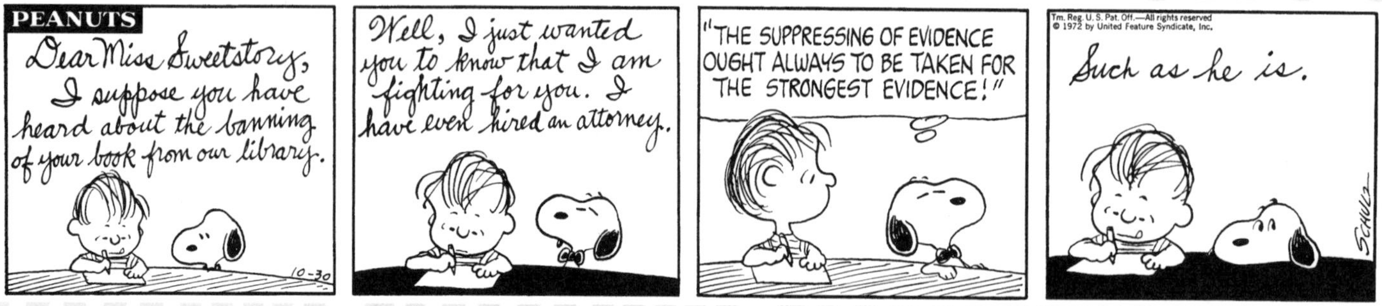
PEANUTS
Dear Miss Sweetstory, I suppose you have heard about the banning of your book from our library.
10-30
Well, I just wanted you to know that I am fighting for you. I have even hired an attorney.
"THE SUPPRESSING OF EVIDENCE OUGHT ALWAYS TO BE TAKEN FOR THE STRONGEST EVIDENCE!"
Tm. Reg. U. S. Pat. Off.—All rights reserved © 1972 by United Feature Syndicate, Inc.
Such as he is.
SCHULZ

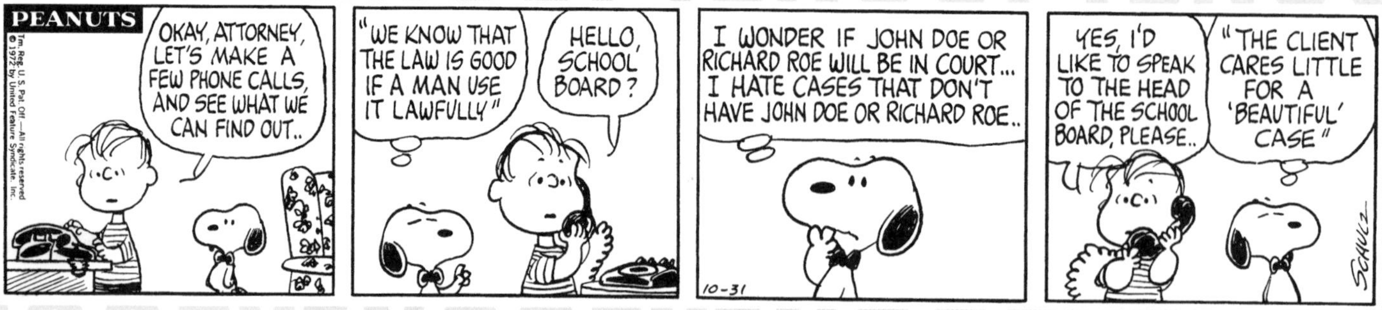
PEANUTS
Tm. Reg. U.S. Pat. Off.—All rights reserved © 1972 by United Feature Syndicate, Inc.
OKAY, ATTORNEY, LET'S MAKE A FEW PHONE CALLS, AND SEE WHAT WE CAN FIND OUT..
"WE KNOW THAT THE LAW IS GOOD IF A MAN USE IT LAWFULLY"
HELLO, SCHOOL BOARD?
I WONDER IF JOHN DOE OR RICHARD ROE WILL BE IN COURT... I HATE CASES THAT DON'T HAVE JOHN DOE OR RICHARD ROE..
10-31
YES, I'D LIKE TO SPEAK TO THE HEAD OF THE SCHOOL BOARD, PLEASE..
"THE CLIENT CARES LITTLE FOR A 'BEAUTIFUL' CASE"
SCHULZ

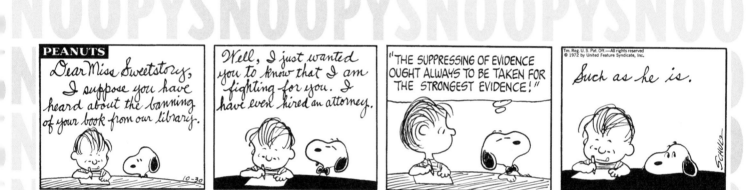

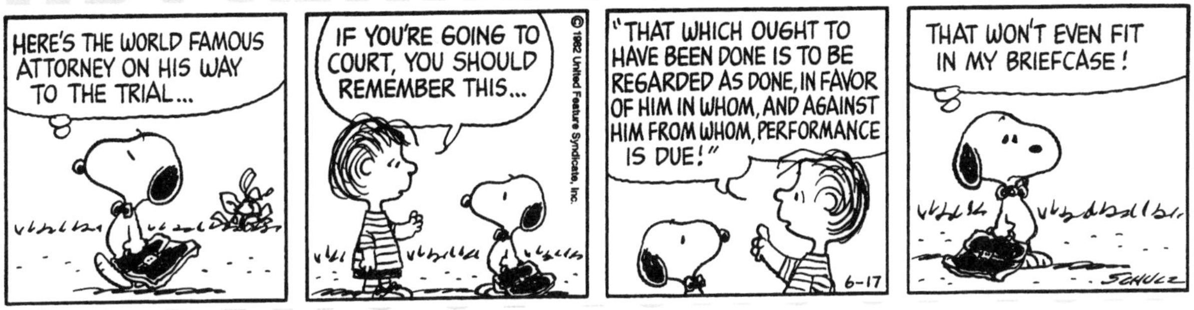
HERE'S THE WORLD FAMOUS ATTORNEY ON HIS WAY TO THE TRIAL...
IF YOU'RE GOING TO COURT, YOU SHOULD REMEMBER THIS...
© 1982 United Feature Syndicate, Inc.
"THAT WHICH OUGHT TO HAVE BEEN DONE IS TO BE REGARDED AS DONE, IN FAVOR OF HIM IN WHOM, AND AGAINST HIM FROM WHOM, PERFORMANCE IS DUE!"
6-17
THAT WON'T EVEN FIT IN MY BRIEFCASE!
SCHULZ

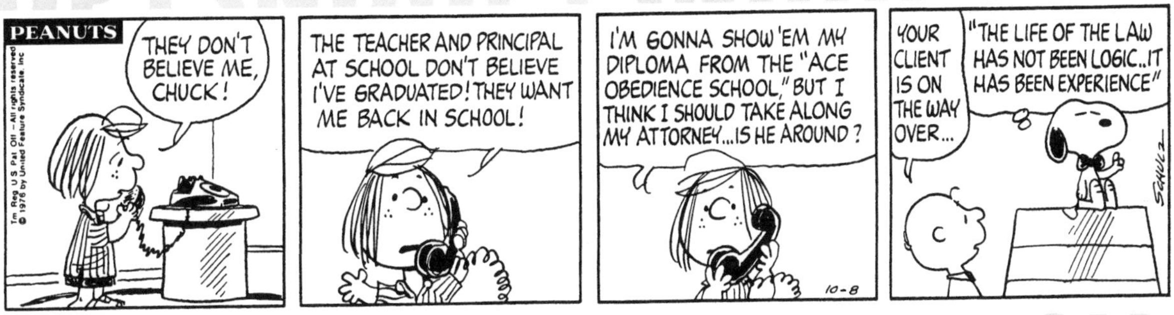
PEANUTS
Tm Reg U S Pat Off – All rights reserved © 1976 by United Feature Syndicate, Inc
THEY DON'T BELIEVE ME, CHUCK!
THE TEACHER AND PRINCIPAL AT SCHOOL DON'T BELIEVE I'VE GRADUATED! THEY WANT ME BACK IN SCHOOL!
I'M GONNA SHOW 'EM MY DIPLOMA FROM THE "ACE OBEDIENCE SCHOOL," BUT I THINK I SHOULD TAKE ALONG MY ATTORNEY...IS HE AROUND?
10-8
YOUR CLIENT IS ON THE WAY OVER...
"THE LIFE OF THE LAW HAS NOT BEEN LOGIC..IT HAS BEEN EXPERIENCE"
SCHULZ

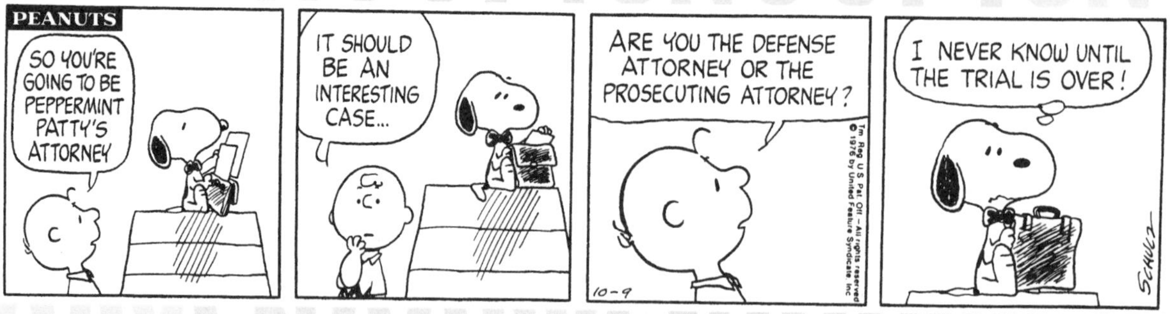
PEANUTS
SO YOU'RE GOING TO BE PEPPERMINT PATTY'S ATTORNEY
IT SHOULD BE AN INTERESTING CASE...
ARE YOU THE DEFENSE ATTORNEY OR THE PROSECUTING ATTORNEY?
Tm Reg U S Pat Off — All rights reserved © 1976 by United Feature Syndicate, Inc
10-9
I NEVER KNOW UNTIL THE TRIAL IS OVER!
SCHULZ

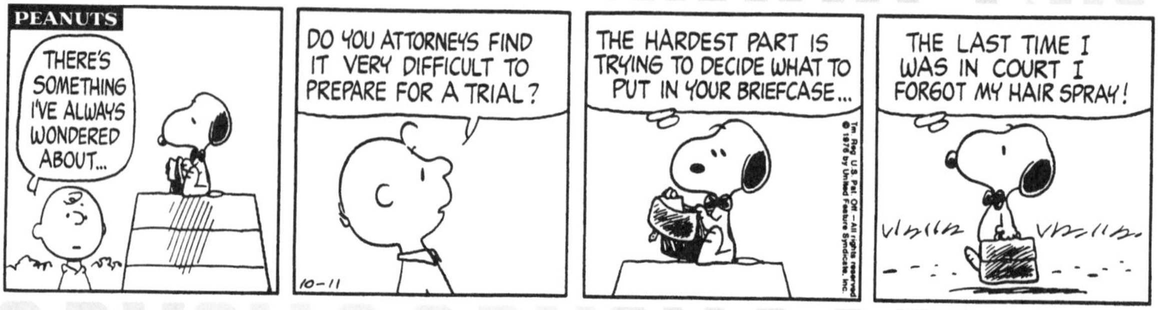
PEANUTS
THERE'S SOMETHING I'VE ALWAYS WONDERED ABOUT...
DO YOU ATTORNEYS FIND IT VERY DIFFICULT TO PREPARE FOR A TRIAL?
10-11
THE HARDEST PART IS TRYING TO DECIDE WHAT TO PUT IN YOUR BRIEFCASE...
Tm Reg U S Pat Off — All rights reserved © 1976 by United Feature Syndicate, Inc
THE LAST TIME I WAS IN COURT I FORGOT MY HAIR SPRAY!

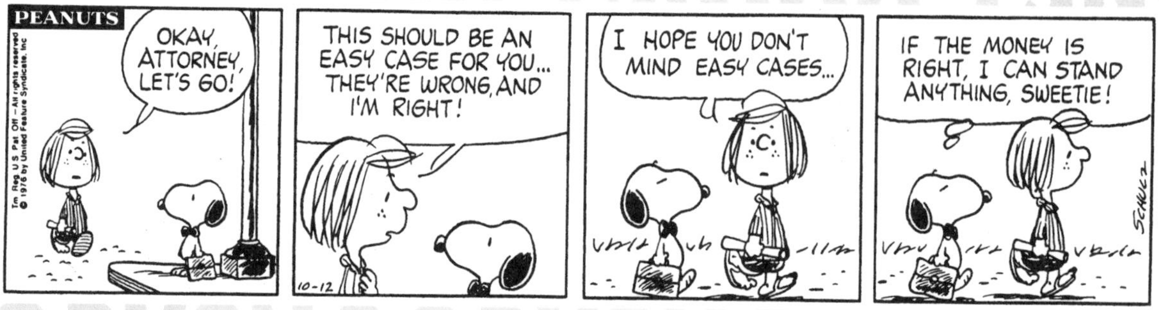
PEANUTS
Tm Reg U S Pat Off — All rights reserved © 1976 by United Feature Syndicate, Inc
OKAY, ATTORNEY, LET'S GO!
THIS SHOULD BE AN EASY CASE FOR YOU... THEY'RE WRONG, AND I'M RIGHT!
10-12
I HOPE YOU DON'T MIND EASY CASES...
IF THE MONEY IS RIGHT, I CAN STAND ANYTHING, SWEETIE!
SCHULZ

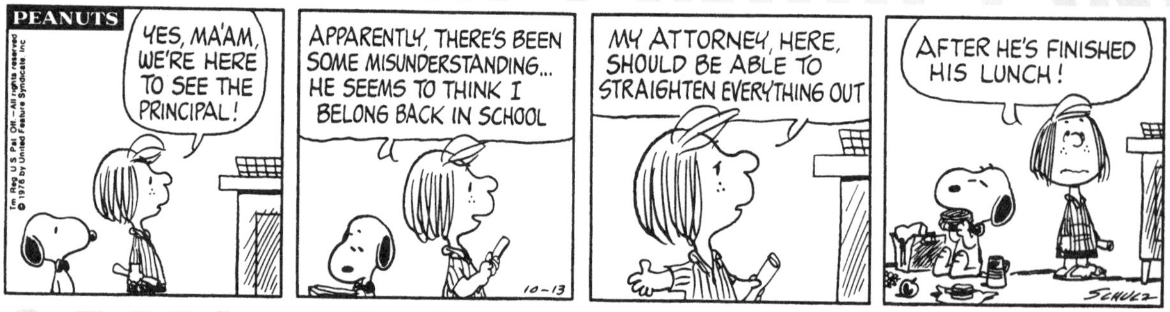
PEANUTS
Tm Reg U S Pat Off — All rights reserved © 1976 by United Feature Syndicate, Inc
YES, MA'AM, WE'RE HERE TO SEE THE PRINCIPAL!
APPARENTLY, THERE'S BEEN SOME MISUNDERSTANDING... HE SEEMS TO THINK I BELONG BACK IN SCHOOL
10-13
MY ATTORNEY, HERE, SHOULD BE ABLE TO STRAIGHTEN EVERYTHING OUT
AFTER HE'S FINISHED HIS LUNCH!
SCHULZ

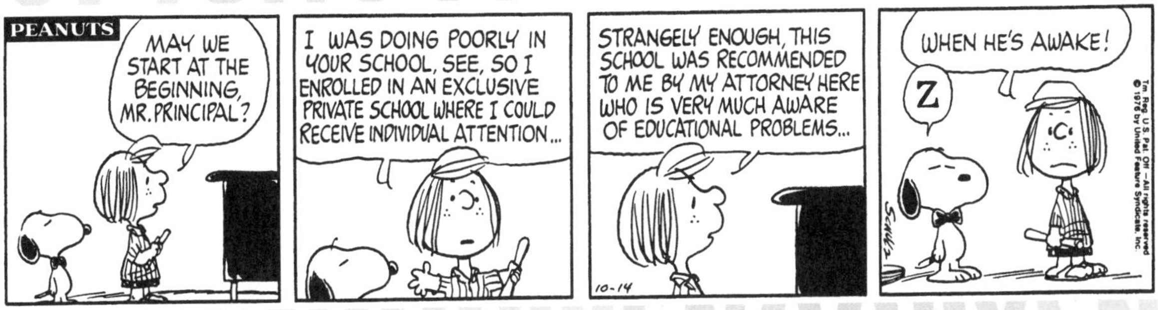
PEANUTS
MAY WE START AT THE BEGINNING, MR. PRINCIPAL?
I WAS DOING POORLY IN YOUR SCHOOL, SEE, SO I ENROLLED IN AN EXCLUSIVE PRIVATE SCHOOL WHERE I COULD RECEIVE INDIVIDUAL ATTENTION...
STRANGELY ENOUGH, THIS SCHOOL WAS RECOMMENDED TO ME BY MY ATTORNEY HERE WHO IS VERY MUCH AWARE OF EDUCATIONAL PROBLEMS...
10-14
Z
WHEN HE'S AWAKE!
Tm Reg U.S. Pat Off—All rights reserved © 1976 by United Feature Syndicate, Inc.
SCHULZ

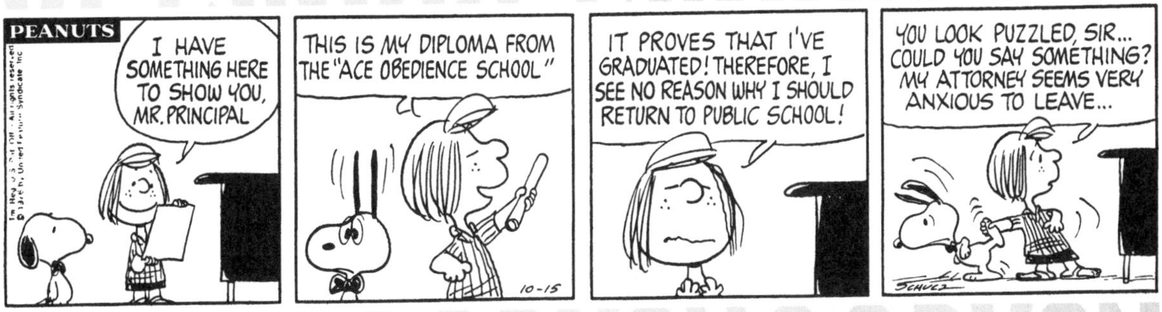
PEANUTS
I HAVE SOMETHING HERE TO SHOW YOU, MR. PRINCIPAL
THIS IS MY DIPLOMA FROM THE "ACE OBEDIENCE SCHOOL"
10-15
IT PROVES THAT I'VE GRADUATED! THEREFORE, I SEE NO REASON WHY I SHOULD RETURN TO PUBLIC SCHOOL!
YOU LOOK PUZZLED, SIR... COULD YOU SAY SOMETHING? MY ATTORNEY SEEMS VERY ANXIOUS TO LEAVE...
SCHULZ

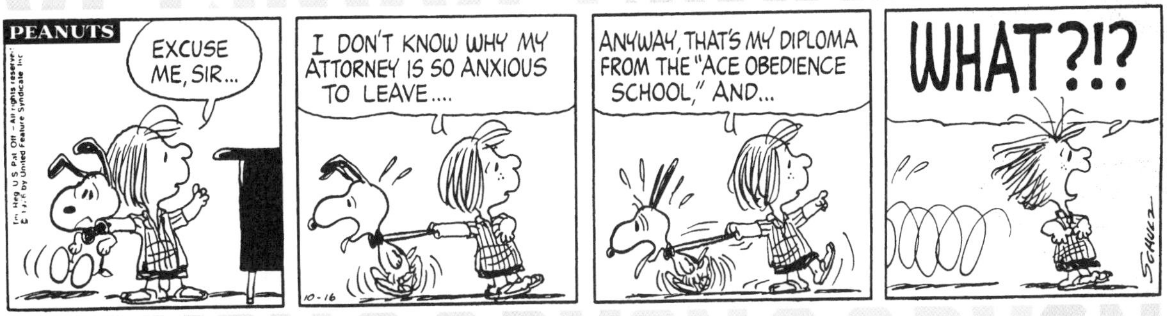
PEANUTS
EXCUSE ME, SIR...
Tm Reg U.S. Pat Off—All rights reserved © 1976 by United Feature Syndicate Inc
I DON'T KNOW WHY MY ATTORNEY IS SO ANXIOUS TO LEAVE....
10-16
ANYWAY, THAT'S MY DIPLOMA FROM THE "ACE OBEDIENCE SCHOOL," AND...
WHAT?!?
SCHULZ

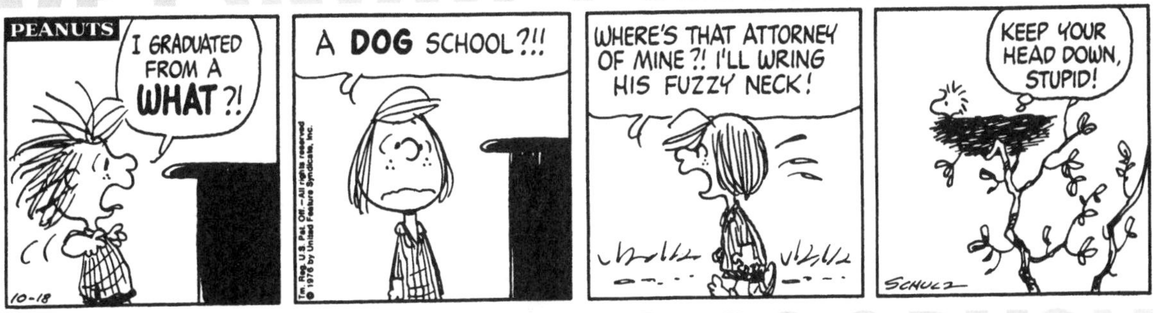
PEANUTS
I GRADUATED FROM A WHAT?!
10-18
A DOG SCHOOL?!!
Tm Reg U.S. Pat Off—All rights reserved © 1976 by United Feature Syndicate, Inc.
WHERE'S THAT ATTORNEY OF MINE?! I'LL WRING HIS FUZZY NECK!
SCHULZ
KEEP YOUR HEAD DOWN, STUPID!

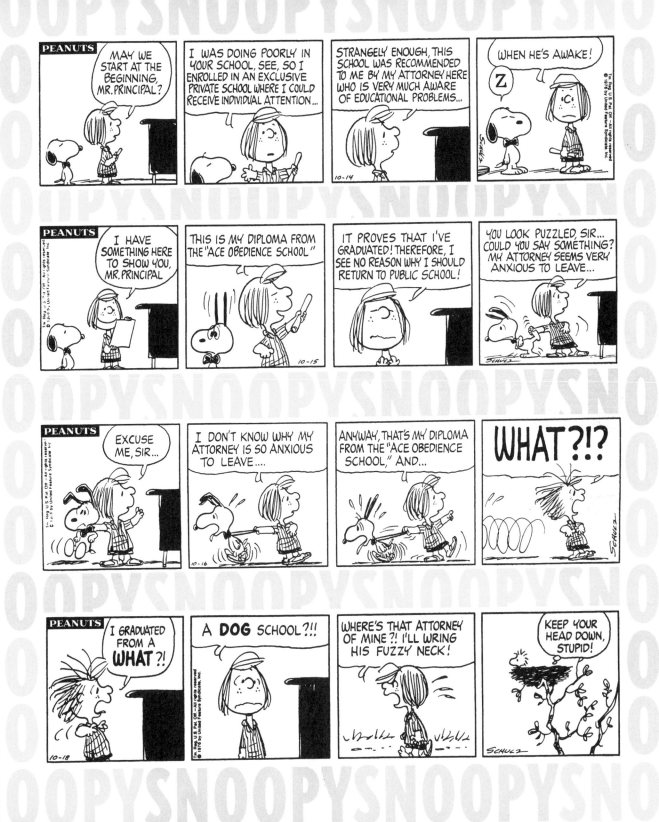

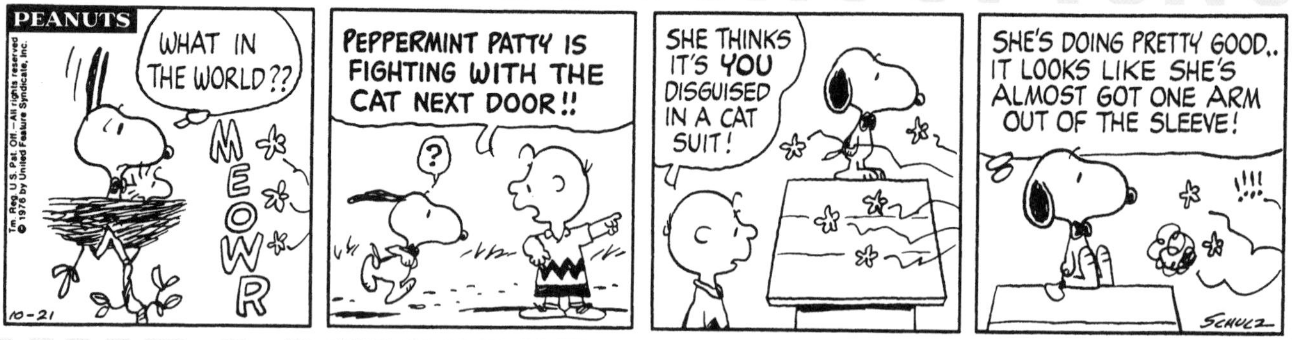
PEANUTS
Tm. Reg. U.S. Pat. Off.—All rights reserved © 1976 by United Feature Syndicate, Inc.
WHAT IN THE WORLD??
MEOWR
10-21
PEPPERMINT PATTY IS FIGHTING WITH THE CAT NEXT DOOR!!
?
SHE THINKS IT'S YOU DISGUISED IN A CAT SUIT!
SHE'S DOING PRETTY GOOD.. IT LOOKS LIKE SHE'S ALMOST GOT ONE ARM OUT OF THE SLEEVE!
!!!
SCHULZ

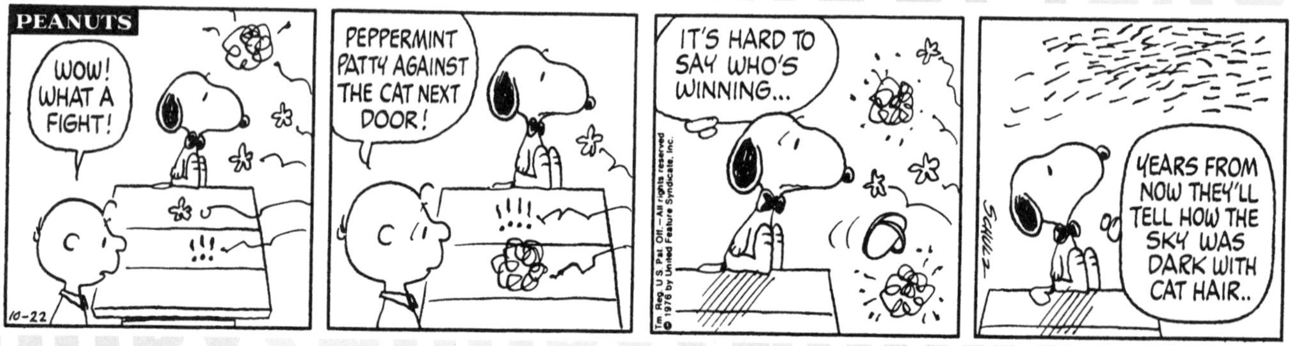
PEANUTS
WOW! WHAT A FIGHT!
!!!
10-22
PEPPERMINT PATTY AGAINST THE CAT NEXT DOOR!
!!!
IT'S HARD TO SAY WHO'S WINNING...
Tm. Reg. U.S. Pat. Off.—All rights reserved © 1976 by United Feature Syndicate, Inc.
YEARS FROM NOW THEY'LL TELL HOW THE SKY WAS DARK WITH CAT HAIR..
SCHULZ

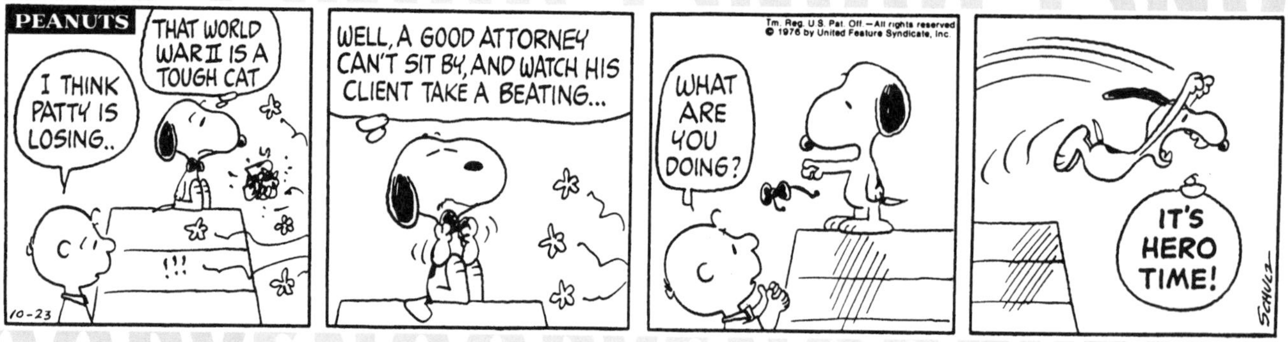
PEANUTS
I THINK PATTY IS LOSING..
THAT WORLD WAR II IS A TOUGH CAT
!!!
10-23
WELL, A GOOD ATTORNEY CAN'T SIT BY, AND WATCH HIS CLIENT TAKE A BEATING...
Tm. Reg. U.S. Pat. Off.—All rights reserved © 1976 by United Feature Syndicate, Inc.
WHAT ARE YOU DOING?
IT'S HERO TIME!
SCHULZ

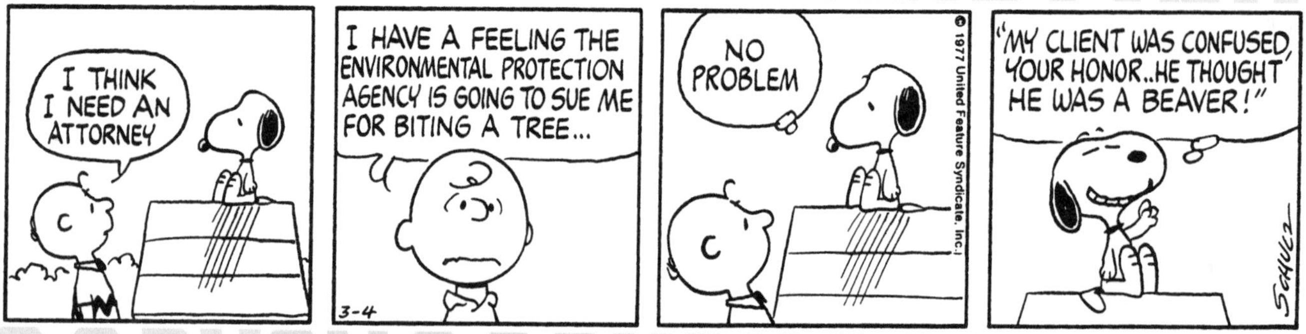
I THINK I NEED AN ATTORNEY
I HAVE A FEELING THE ENVIRONMENTAL PROTECTION AGENCY IS GOING TO SUE ME FOR BITING A TREE...
3-4
NO PROBLEM
© 1977 United Feature Syndicate, Inc.
"MY CLIENT WAS CONFUSED, YOUR HONOR..HE THOUGHT HE WAS A BEAVER!"
SCHULZ

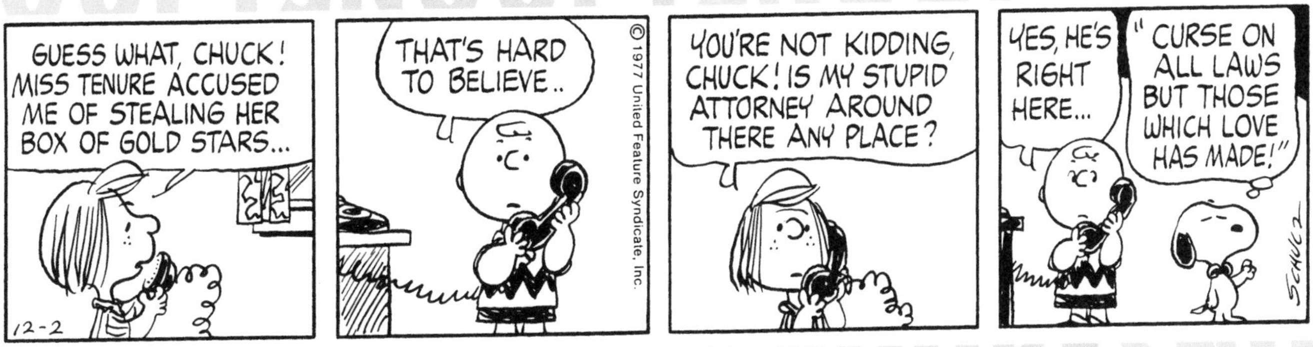
GUESS WHAT, CHUCK! MISS TENURE ACCUSED ME OF STEALING HER BOX OF GOLD STARS...
12-2
THAT'S HARD TO BELIEVE..
© 1977 United Feature Syndicate, Inc.
YOU'RE NOT KIDDING, CHUCK! IS MY STUPID ATTORNEY AROUND THERE ANY PLACE?
YES, HE'S RIGHT HERE...
"CURSE ON ALL LAWS BUT THOSE WHICH LOVE HAS MADE!"
SCHULZ

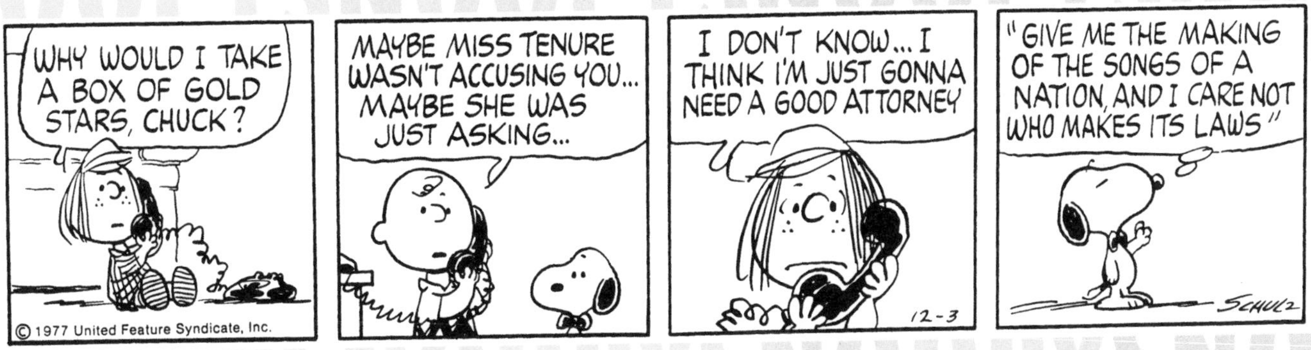
WHY WOULD I TAKE A BOX OF GOLD STARS, CHUCK?
© 1977 United Feature Syndicate, Inc.
MAYBE MISS TENURE WASN'T ACCUSING YOU... MAYBE SHE WAS JUST ASKING...
I DON'T KNOW... I THINK I'M JUST GONNA NEED A GOOD ATTORNEY
12-3
"GIVE ME THE MAKING OF THE SONGS OF A NATION, AND I CARE NOT WHO MAKES ITS LAWS"
SCHULZ

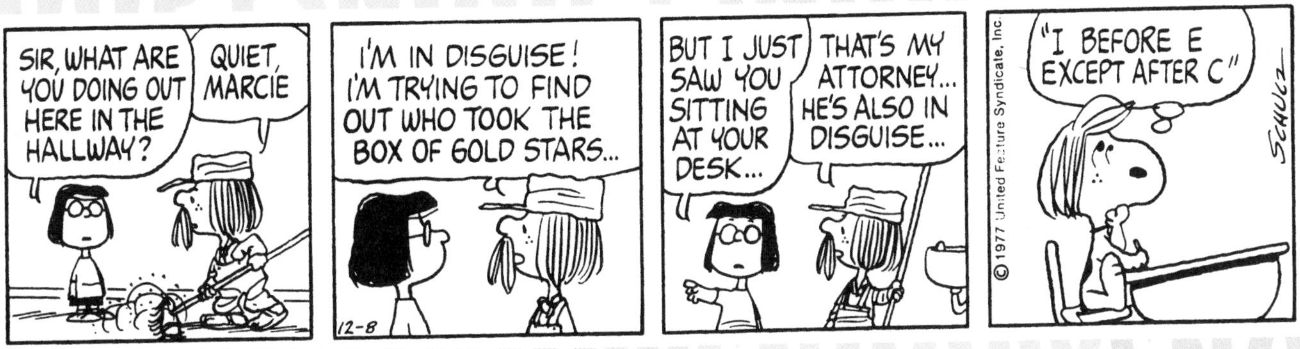
SIR, WHAT ARE YOU DOING OUT HERE IN THE HALLWAY?
QUIET, MARCIE
I'M IN DISGUISE! I'M TRYING TO FIND OUT WHO TOOK THE BOX OF GOLD STARS...
12-8
BUT I JUST SAW YOU SITTING AT YOUR DESK...
THAT'S MY ATTORNEY... HE'S ALSO IN DISGUISE...
© 1977 United Feature Syndicate, Inc.
"I BEFORE E EXCEPT AFTER C"
SCHULZ

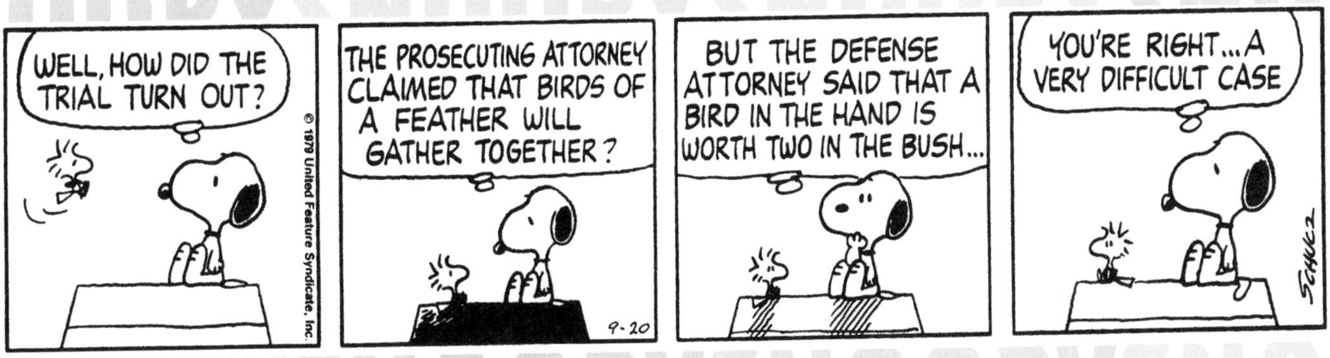
WELL, HOW DID THE TRIAL TURN OUT?
© 1979 United Feature Syndicate, Inc.
THE PROSECUTING ATTORNEY CLAIMED THAT BIRDS OF A FEATHER WILL GATHER TOGETHER?
9-20
BUT THE DEFENSE ATTORNEY SAID THAT A BIRD IN THE HAND IS WORTH TWO IN THE BUSH...
YOU'RE RIGHT... A VERY DIFFICULT CASE
SCHULZ

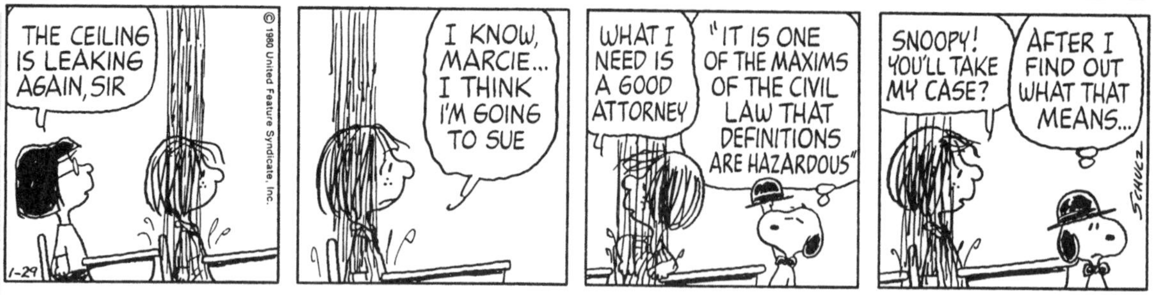
THE CEILING IS LEAKING AGAIN, SIR
© 1980 United Feature Syndicate, Inc.
1-29
I KNOW, MARCIE... I THINK I'M GOING TO SUE
WHAT I NEED IS A GOOD ATTORNEY
"IT IS ONE OF THE MAXIMS OF THE CIVIL LAW THAT DEFINITIONS ARE HAZARDOUS"
SNOOPY! YOU'LL TAKE MY CASE?
AFTER I FIND OUT WHAT THAT MEANS...
SCHULZ

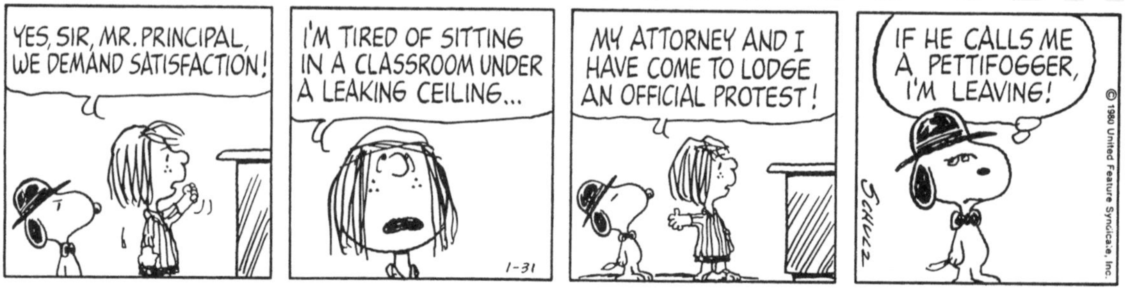
YES, SIR, MR. PRINCIPAL, WE DEMAND SATISFACTION!
I'M TIRED OF SITTING IN A CLASSROOM UNDER A LEAKING CEILING...
1-31
MY ATTORNEY AND I HAVE COME TO LODGE AN OFFICIAL PROTEST!
IF HE CALLS ME A PETTIFOGGER, I'M LEAVING!
SCHULZ
© 1980 United Feature Syndicate, Inc.

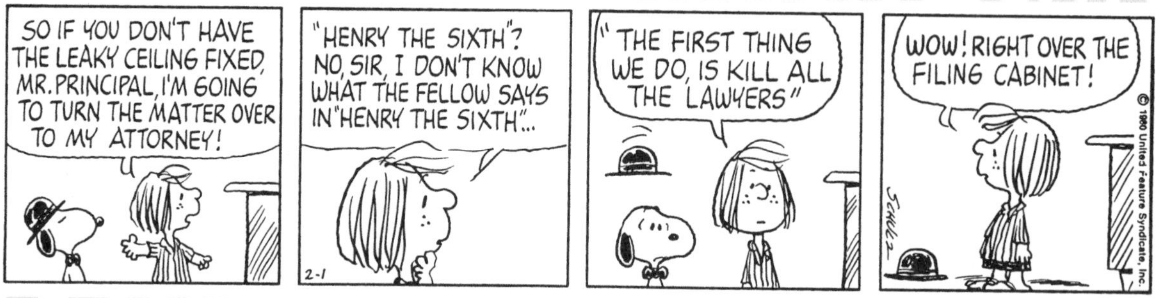
SO IF YOU DON'T HAVE THE LEAKY CEILING FIXED, MR. PRINCIPAL, I'M GOING TO TURN THE MATTER OVER TO MY ATTORNEY!
"HENRY THE SIXTH"? NO, SIR, I DON'T KNOW WHAT THE FELLOW SAYS IN "HENRY THE SIXTH"...
2-1
"THE FIRST THING WE DO, IS KILL ALL THE LAWYERS"
WOW! RIGHT OVER THE FILING CABINET!
SCHULZ
© 1980 United Feature Syndicate, Inc.

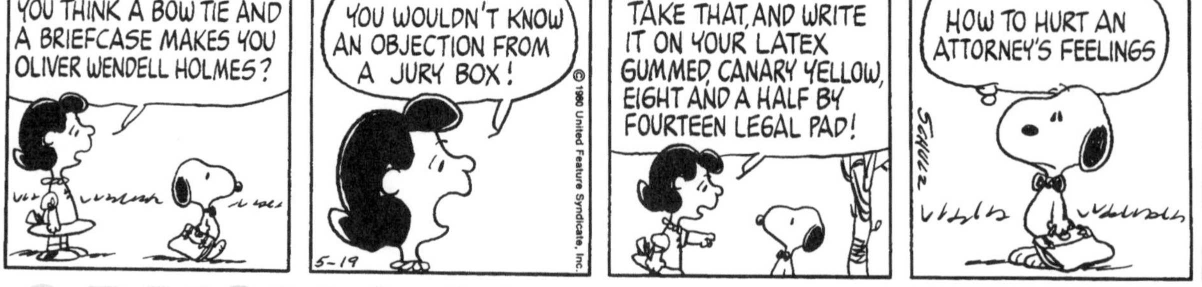
YOU THINK A BOW TIE AND A BRIEFCASE MAKES YOU OLIVER WENDELL HOLMES?
YOU WOULDN'T KNOW AN OBJECTION FROM A JURY BOX!
5-19
© 1980 United Feature Syndicate, Inc.
TAKE THAT, AND WRITE IT ON YOUR LATEX GUMMED, CANARY YELLOW, EIGHT AND A HALF BY FOURTEEN LEGAL PAD!
HOW TO HURT AN ATTORNEY'S FEELINGS
SCHULZ

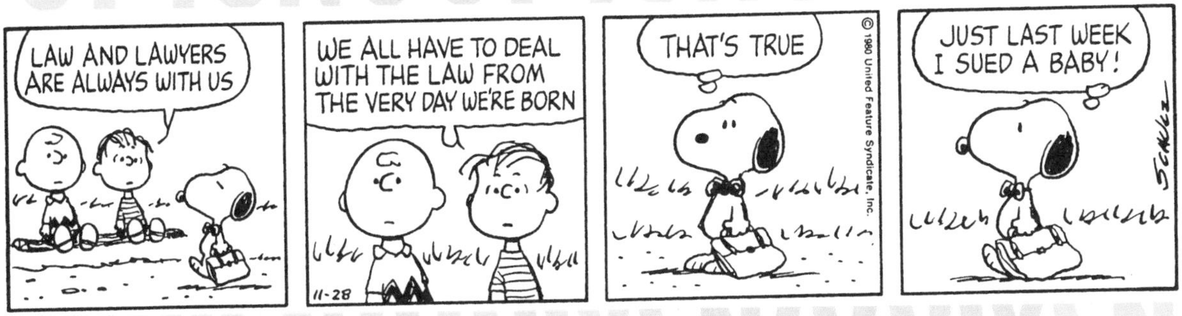
LAW AND LAWYERS ARE ALWAYS WITH US
WE ALL HAVE TO DEAL WITH THE LAW FROM THE VERY DAY WE'RE BORN
11-28
THAT'S TRUE
© 1980 United Feature Syndicate, Inc.
JUST LAST WEEK I SUED A BABY!
SCHULZ

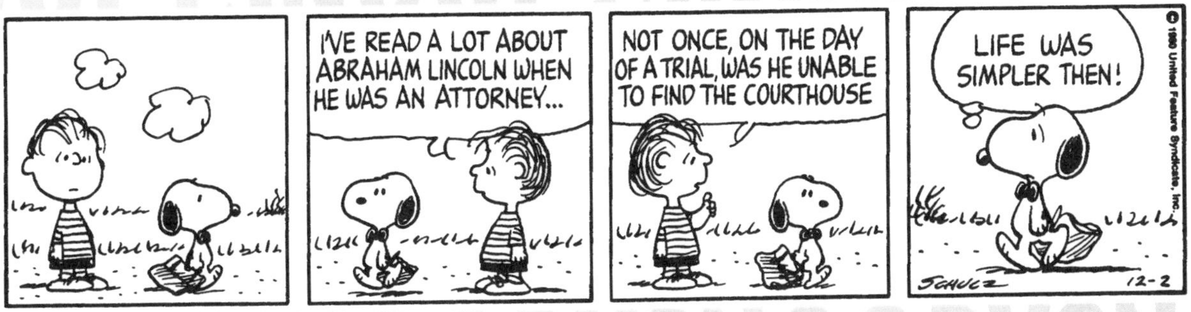
I'VE READ A LOT ABOUT ABRAHAM LINCOLN WHEN HE WAS AN ATTORNEY...
NOT ONCE, ON THE DAY OF A TRIAL, WAS HE UNABLE TO FIND THE COURTHOUSE
LIFE WAS SIMPLER THEN!
© 1980 United Feature Syndicate, Inc.
SCHULZ
12-2

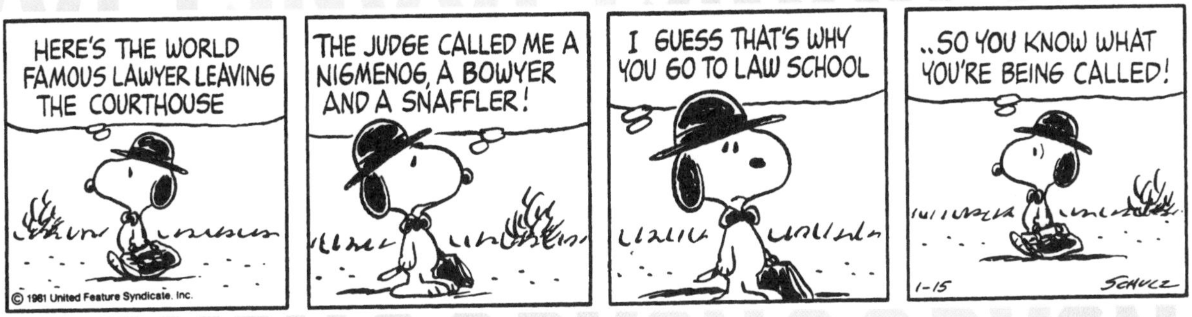
HERE'S THE WORLD FAMOUS LAWYER LEAVING THE COURTHOUSE
© 1981 United Feature Syndicate, Inc.
THE JUDGE CALLED ME A NIGMENOG, A BOWYER AND A SNAFFLER!
I GUESS THAT'S WHY YOU GO TO LAW SCHOOL
..SO YOU KNOW WHAT YOU'RE BEING CALLED!
1-15
SCHULZ

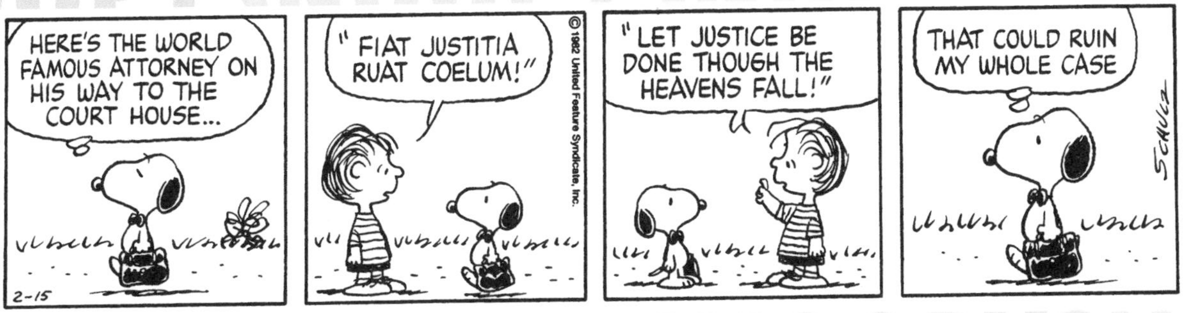
HERE'S THE WORLD FAMOUS ATTORNEY ON HIS WAY TO THE COURT HOUSE...
2-15
"FIAT JUSTITIA RUAT COELUM!"
© 1982 United Feature Syndicate, Inc.
"LET JUSTICE BE DONE THOUGH THE HEAVENS FALL!"
THAT COULD RUIN MY WHOLE CASE
SCHULZ

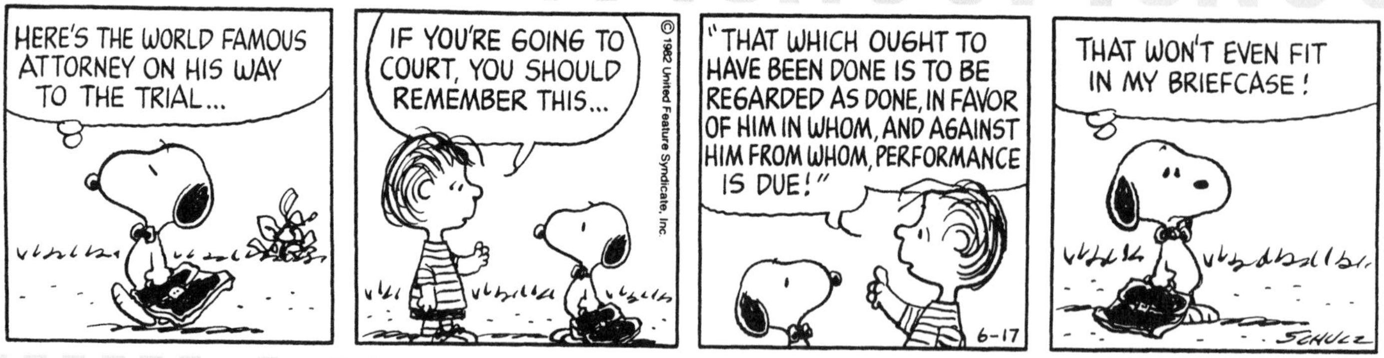
HERE'S THE WORLD FAMOUS ATTORNEY ON HIS WAY TO THE TRIAL...
IF YOU'RE GOING TO COURT, YOU SHOULD REMEMBER THIS...
© 1982 United Feature Syndicate, Inc.
"THAT WHICH OUGHT TO HAVE BEEN DONE IS TO BE REGARDED AS DONE, IN FAVOR OF HIM IN WHOM, AND AGAINST HIM FROM WHOM, PERFORMANCE IS DUE!"
6-17
THAT WON'T EVEN FIT IN MY BRIEFCASE!
SCHULZ

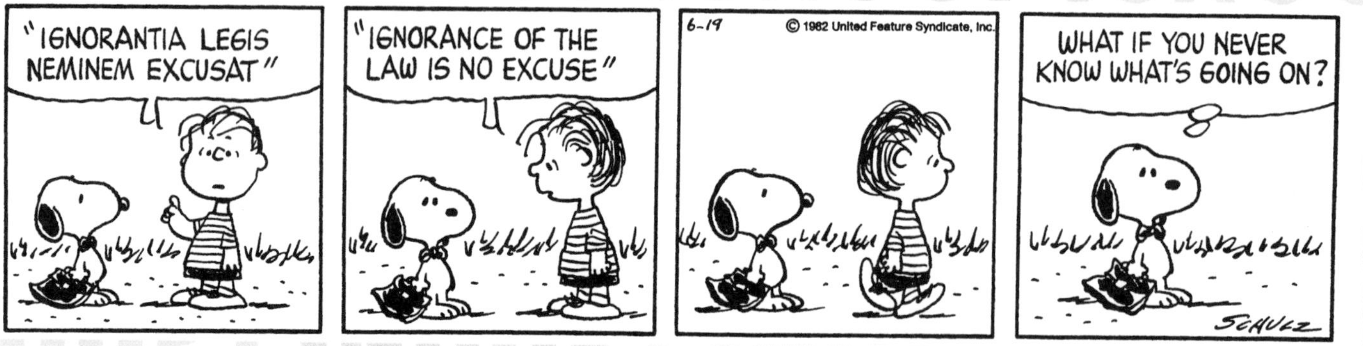
"IGNORANTIA LEGIS NEMINEM EXCUSAT"
"IGNORANCE OF THE LAW IS NO EXCUSE"
6-19
© 1982 United Feature Syndicate, Inc.
WHAT IF YOU NEVER KNOW WHAT'S GOING ON?
SCHULZ

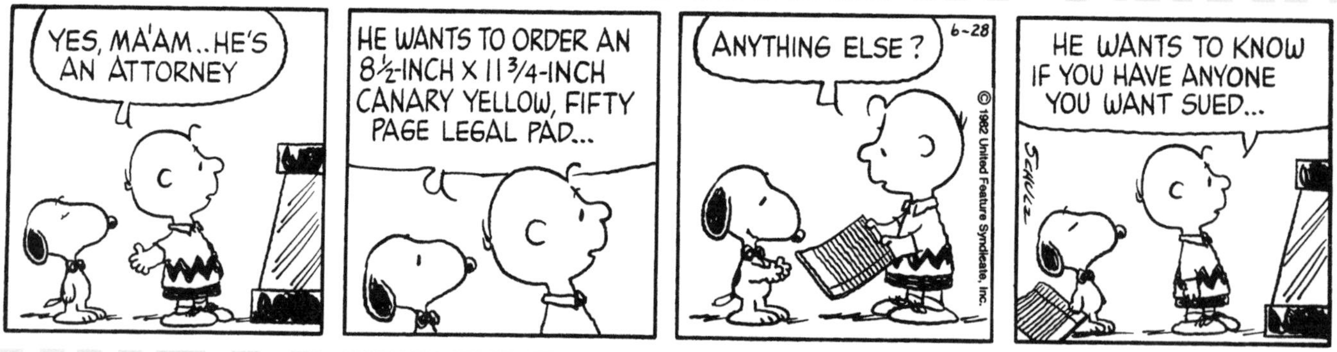
YES, MA'AM.. HE'S AN ATTORNEY
HE WANTS TO ORDER AN 8½-INCH X 11¾-INCH CANARY YELLOW, FIFTY PAGE LEGAL PAD...
ANYTHING ELSE?
6-28
© 1982 United Feature Syndicate, Inc.
SCHULZ
HE WANTS TO KNOW IF YOU HAVE ANYONE YOU WANT SUED...

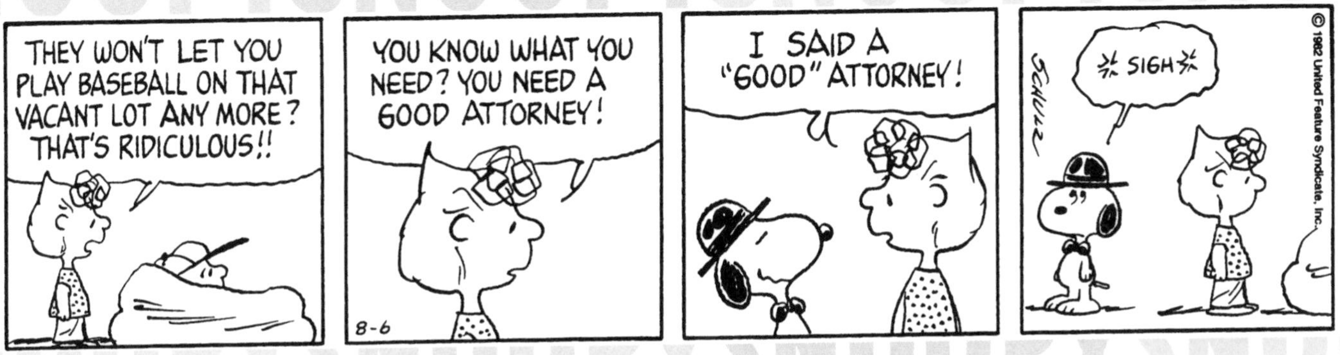
THEY WON'T LET YOU PLAY BASEBALL ON THAT VACANT LOT ANY MORE? THAT'S RIDICULOUS!!
YOU KNOW WHAT YOU NEED? YOU NEED A GOOD ATTORNEY!
8-6
I SAID A "GOOD" ATTORNEY!
SIGH
SCHULZ
© 1982 United Feature Syndicate, Inc.

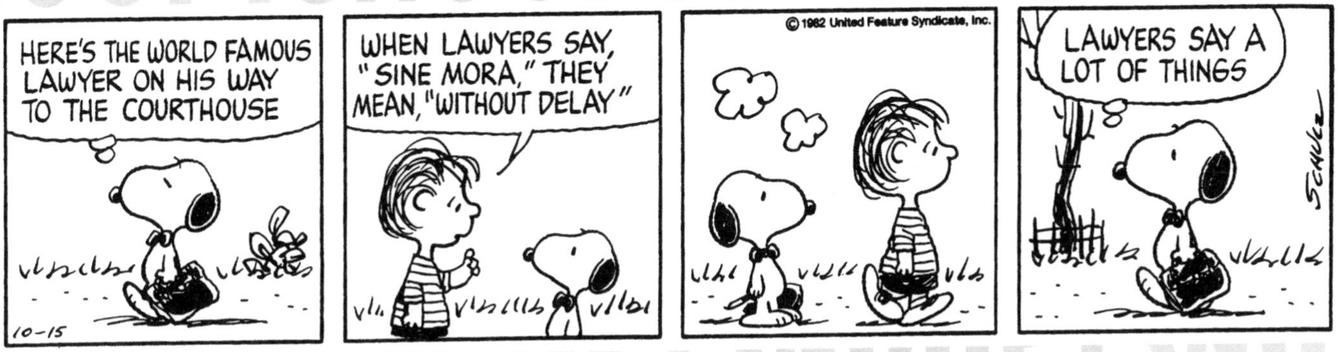
HERE'S THE WORLD FAMOUS LAWYER ON HIS WAY TO THE COURTHOUSE
10-15
WHEN LAWYERS SAY, "SINE MORA," THEY MEAN, "WITHOUT DELAY"
© 1982 United Feature Syndicate, Inc.
LAWYERS SAY A LOT OF THINGS
SCHULZ

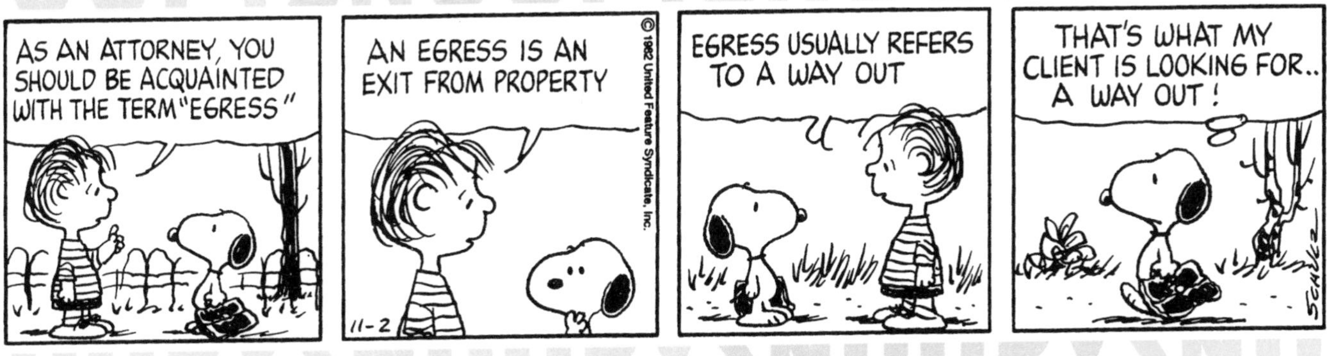
AS AN ATTORNEY, YOU SHOULD BE ACQUAINTED WITH THE TERM "EGRESS"
AN EGRESS IS AN EXIT FROM PROPERTY
11-2
© 1982 United Feature Syndicate, Inc.
EGRESS USUALLY REFERS TO A WAY OUT
THAT'S WHAT MY CLIENT IS LOOKING FOR.. A WAY OUT!
SCHULZ

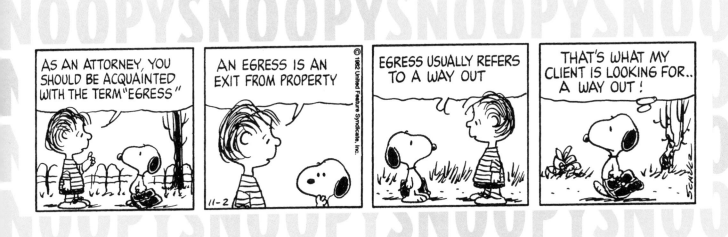

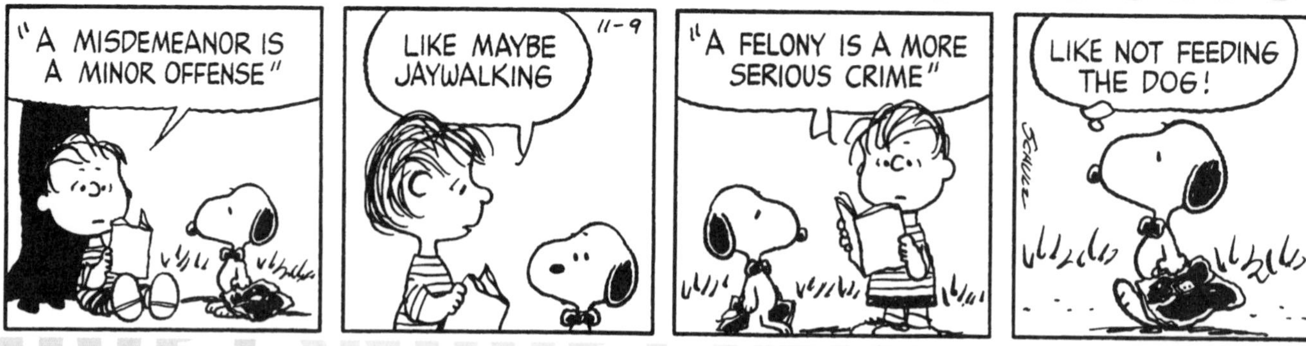
"A MISDEMEANOR IS A MINOR OFFENSE"
LIKE MAYBE JAYWALKING
11-9
"A FELONY IS A MORE SERIOUS CRIME"
LIKE NOT FEEDING THE DOG!
© 1982 United Feature Syndicate, Inc.
SCHULZ

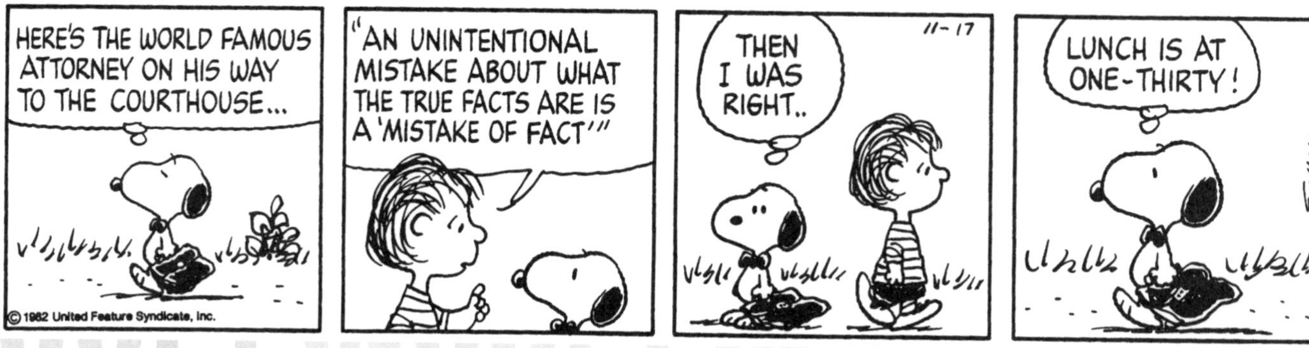
HERE'S THE WORLD FAMOUS ATTORNEY ON HIS WAY TO THE COURTHOUSE...
© 1982 United Feature Syndicate, Inc.
"AN UNINTENTIONAL MISTAKE ABOUT WHAT THE TRUE FACTS ARE IS A 'MISTAKE OF FACT'"
11-17
THEN I WAS RIGHT..
LUNCH IS AT ONE-THIRTY!
SCHULZ

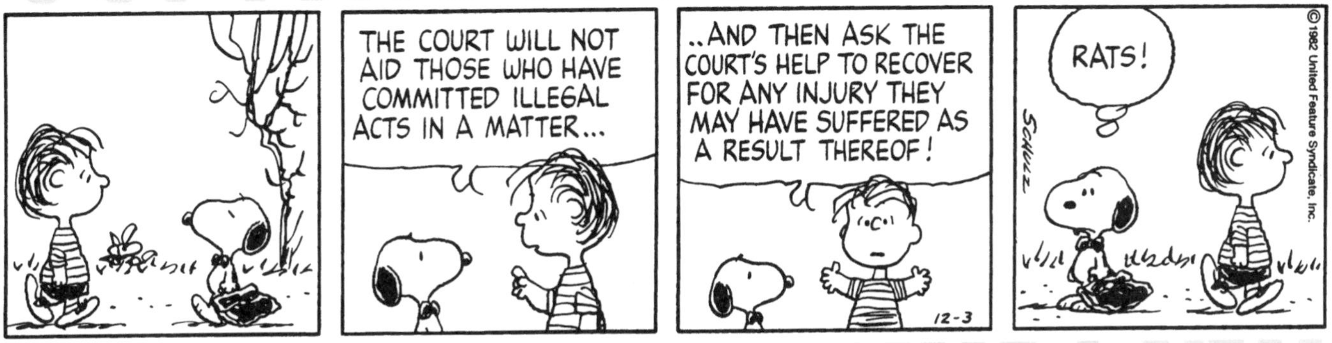
THE COURT WILL NOT AID THOSE WHO HAVE COMMITTED ILLEGAL ACTS IN A MATTER...
..AND THEN ASK THE COURT'S HELP TO RECOVER FOR ANY INJURY THEY MAY HAVE SUFFERED AS A RESULT THEREOF!
12-3
RATS!
SCHULZ
© 1982 United Feature Syndicate, Inc.

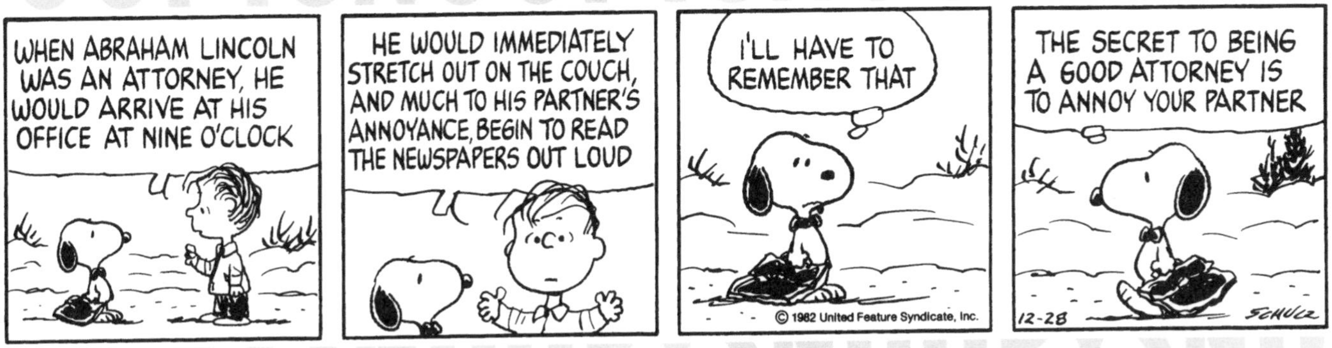
WHEN ABRAHAM LINCOLN WAS AN ATTORNEY, HE WOULD ARRIVE AT HIS OFFICE AT NINE O'CLOCK
HE WOULD IMMEDIATELY STRETCH OUT ON THE COUCH, AND MUCH TO HIS PARTNER'S ANNOYANCE, BEGIN TO READ THE NEWSPAPERS OUT LOUD
I'LL HAVE TO REMEMBER THAT
© 1982 United Feature Syndicate, Inc.
THE SECRET TO BEING A GOOD ATTORNEY IS TO ANNOY YOUR PARTNER
12-28
SCHULZ

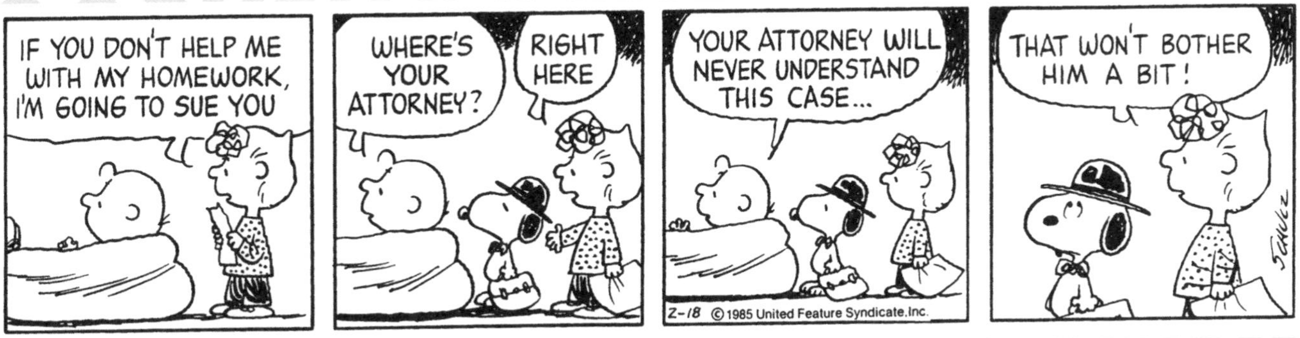
IF YOU DON'T HELP ME WITH MY HOMEWORK, I'M GOING TO SUE YOU
WHERE'S YOUR ATTORNEY?
RIGHT HERE
YOUR ATTORNEY WILL NEVER UNDERSTAND THIS CASE...
2-18 © 1985 United Feature Syndicate, Inc.
THAT WON'T BOTHER HIM A BIT!
SCHULZ

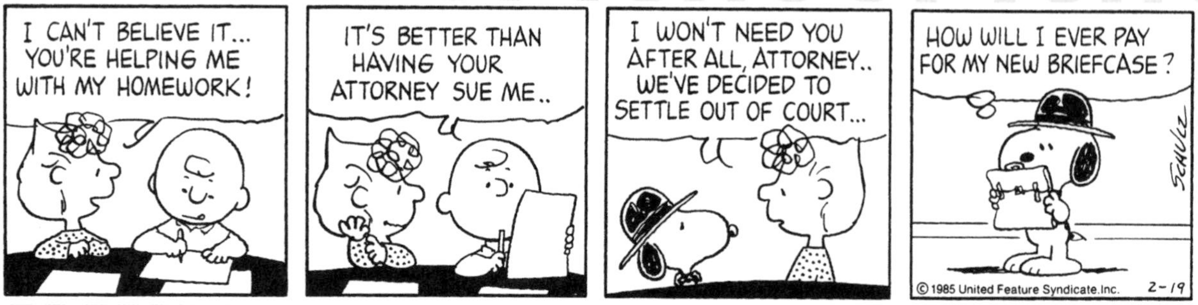
I CAN'T BELIEVE IT... YOU'RE HELPING ME WITH MY HOMEWORK!
IT'S BETTER THAN HAVING YOUR ATTORNEY SUE ME..
I WON'T NEED YOU AFTER ALL, ATTORNEY.. WE'VE DECIDED TO SETTLE OUT OF COURT...
HOW WILL I EVER PAY FOR MY NEW BRIEFCASE?
SCHULZ
© 1985 United Feature Syndicate, Inc.
2-19

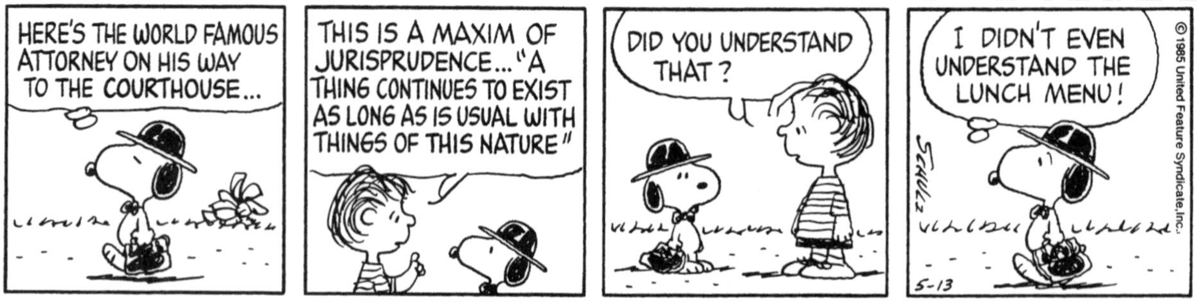
HERE'S THE WORLD FAMOUS ATTORNEY ON HIS WAY TO THE COURTHOUSE...
THIS IS A MAXIM OF JURISPRUDENCE..."A THING CONTINUES TO EXIST AS LONG AS IS USUAL WITH THINGS OF THIS NATURE"
DID YOU UNDERSTAND THAT?
I DIDN'T EVEN UNDERSTAND THE LUNCH MENU!
SCHULZ
© 1985 United Feature Syndicate, Inc.
5-13

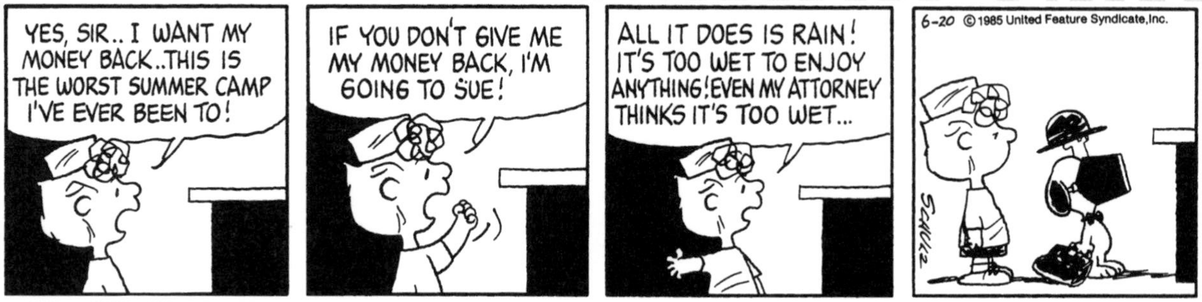
YES, SIR.. I WANT MY MONEY BACK..THIS IS THE WORST SUMMER CAMP I'VE EVER BEEN TO!
IF YOU DON'T GIVE ME MY MONEY BACK, I'M GOING TO SUE!
ALL IT DOES IS RAIN! IT'S TOO WET TO ENJOY ANYTHING! EVEN MY ATTORNEY THINKS IT'S TOO WET...
6-20 © 1985 United Feature Syndicate, Inc.
SCHULZ

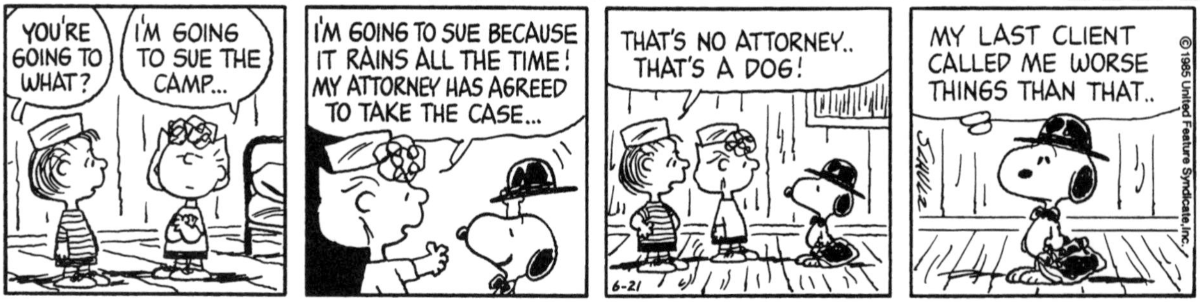
YOU'RE GOING TO WHAT?
I'M GOING TO SUE THE CAMP...
I'M GOING TO SUE BECAUSE IT RAINS ALL THE TIME! MY ATTORNEY HAS AGREED TO TAKE THE CASE...
THAT'S NO ATTORNEY.. THAT'S A DOG!
6-21
MY LAST CLIENT CALLED ME WORSE THINGS THAN THAT..
SCHULZ
© 1985 United Feature Syndicate, Inc.

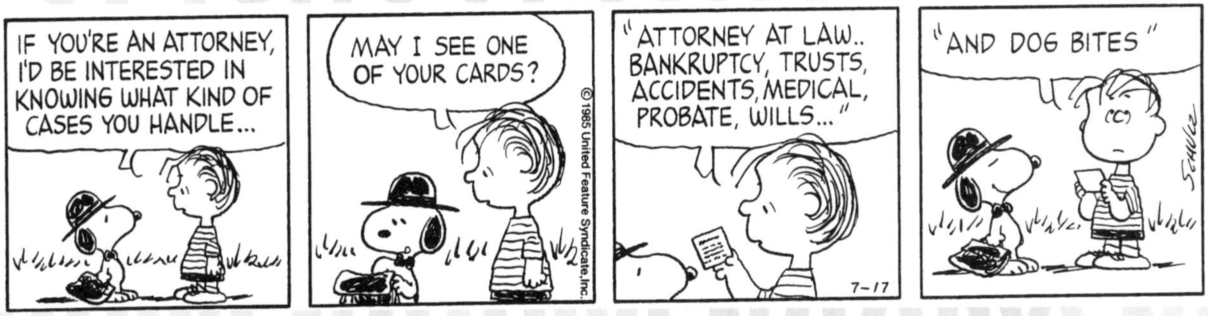
IF YOU'RE AN ATTORNEY, I'D BE INTERESTED IN KNOWING WHAT KIND OF CASES YOU HANDLE...
MAY I SEE ONE OF YOUR CARDS?
© 1985 United Feature Syndicate, Inc.
"ATTORNEY AT LAW.. BANKRUPTCY, TRUSTS, ACCIDENTS, MEDICAL, PROBATE, WILLS..."
7-17
"AND DOG BITES"
SCHULZ

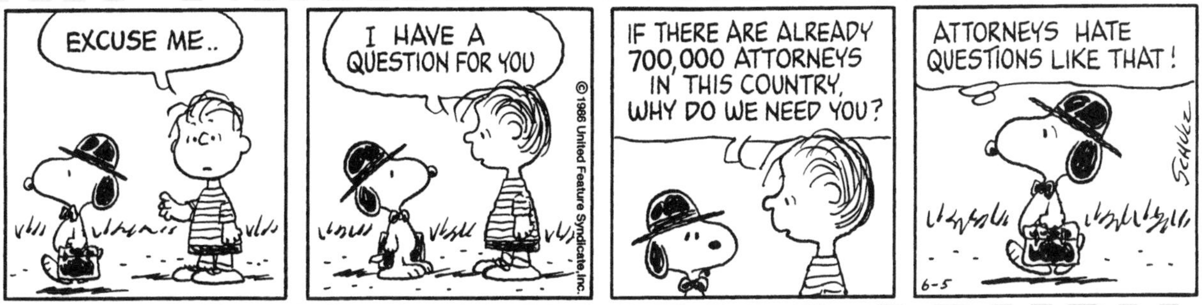
EXCUSE ME..
I HAVE A QUESTION FOR YOU
© 1986 United Feature Syndicate, Inc.
IF THERE ARE ALREADY 700,000 ATTORNEYS IN THIS COUNTRY, WHY DO WE NEED YOU?
ATTORNEYS HATE QUESTIONS LIKE THAT!
SCHULZ
6-5

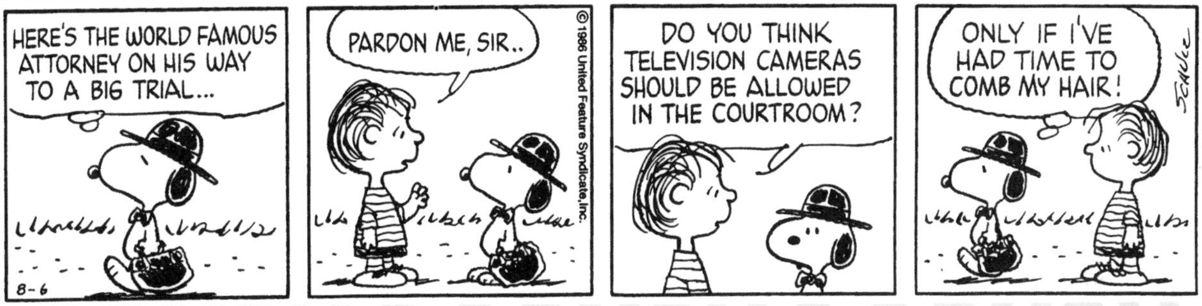
HERE'S THE WORLD FAMOUS ATTORNEY ON HIS WAY TO A BIG TRIAL...
8-6
PARDON ME, SIR..
© 1986 United Feature Syndicate, Inc.
DO YOU THINK TELEVISION CAMERAS SHOULD BE ALLOWED IN THE COURTROOM?
ONLY IF I'VE HAD TIME TO COMB MY HAIR!
SCHULZ

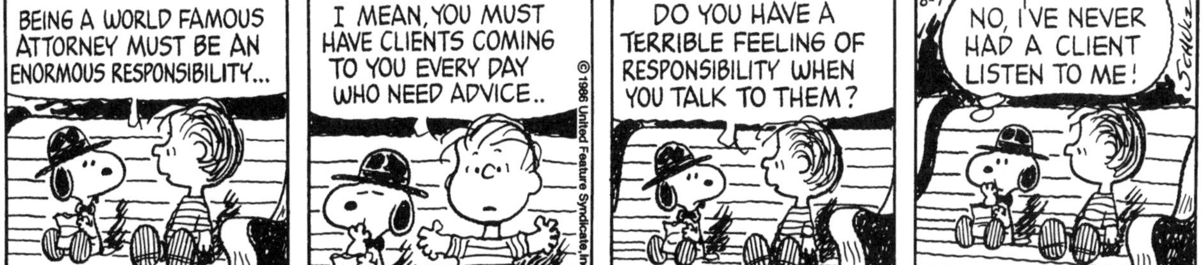
BEING A WORLD FAMOUS ATTORNEY MUST BE AN ENORMOUS RESPONSIBILITY...
I MEAN, YOU MUST HAVE CLIENTS COMING TO YOU EVERY DAY WHO NEED ADVICE..
© 1986 United Feature Syndicate, Inc.
DO YOU HAVE A TERRIBLE FEELING OF RESPONSIBILITY WHEN YOU TALK TO THEM?
8-7
NO, I'VE NEVER HAD A CLIENT LISTEN TO ME!
SCHULZ

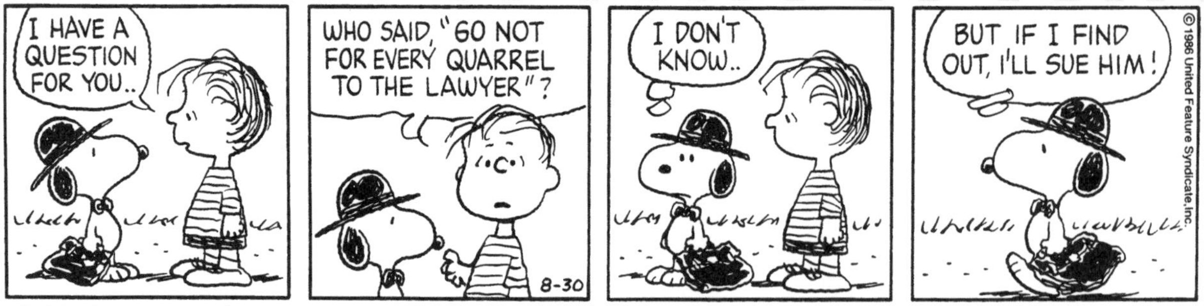
I HAVE A QUESTION FOR YOU..
WHO SAID, "GO NOT FOR EVERY QUARREL TO THE LAWYER"?
8-30
I DON'T KNOW..
BUT IF I FIND OUT, I'LL SUE HIM!
© 1986 United Feature Syndicate, Inc.

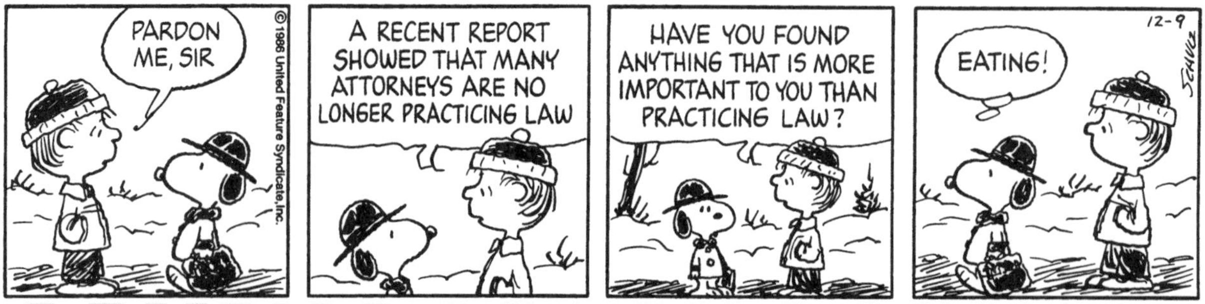
PARDON ME, SIR
© 1986 United Feature Syndicate, Inc.
A RECENT REPORT SHOWED THAT MANY ATTORNEYS ARE NO LONGER PRACTICING LAW
HAVE YOU FOUND ANYTHING THAT IS MORE IMPORTANT TO YOU THAN PRACTICING LAW?
12-9
EATING!
SCHULZ

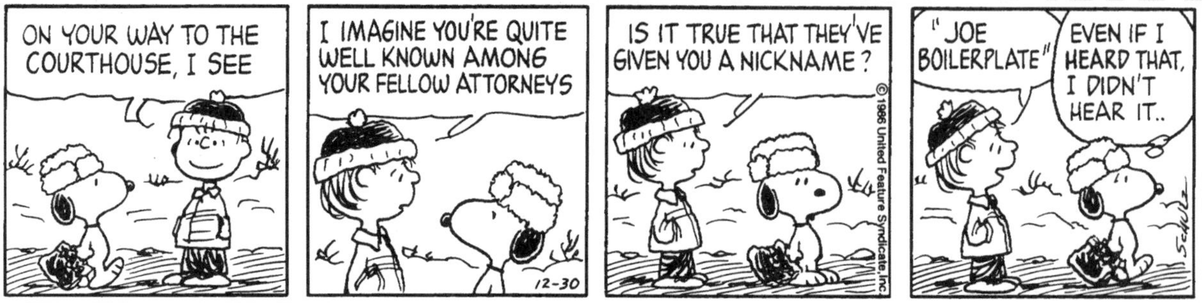
ON YOUR WAY TO THE COURTHOUSE, I SEE
I IMAGINE YOU'RE QUITE WELL KNOWN AMONG YOUR FELLOW ATTORNEYS
12-30
IS IT TRUE THAT THEY'VE GIVEN YOU A NICKNAME?
© 1986 United Feature Syndicate, Inc.
"JOE BOILERPLATE"
EVEN IF I HEARD THAT, I DIDN'T HEAR IT..
SCHULZ

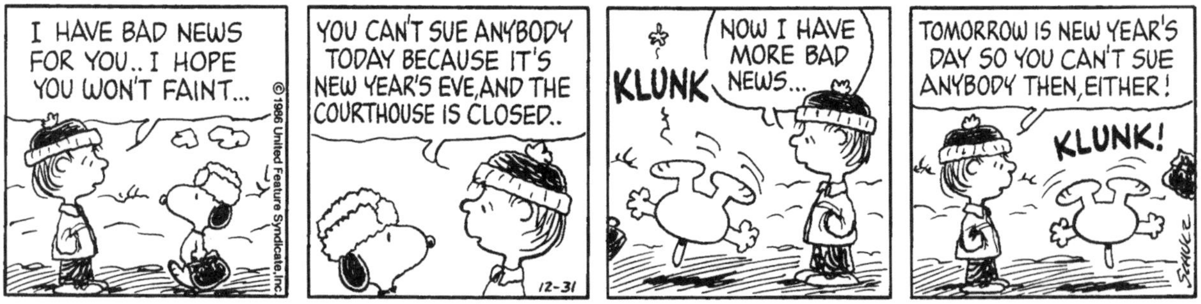
I HAVE BAD NEWS FOR YOU.. I HOPE YOU WON'T FAINT...
© 1986 United Feature Syndicate, Inc.
YOU CAN'T SUE ANYBODY TODAY BECAUSE IT'S NEW YEAR'S EVE, AND THE COURTHOUSE IS CLOSED..
12-31
KLUNK
NOW I HAVE MORE BAD NEWS...
TOMORROW IS NEW YEAR'S DAY SO YOU CAN'T SUE ANYBODY THEN, EITHER!
KLUNK!
SCHULZ

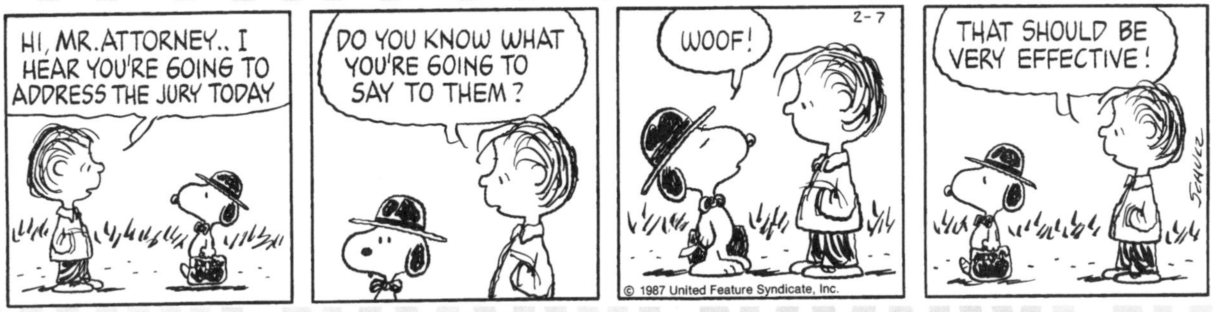
HI, MR. ATTORNEY.. I HEAR YOU'RE GOING TO ADDRESS THE JURY TODAY
DO YOU KNOW WHAT YOU'RE GOING TO SAY TO THEM?
WOOF!
2-7
THAT SHOULD BE VERY EFFECTIVE!
© 1987 United Feature Syndicate, Inc.
SCHULZ

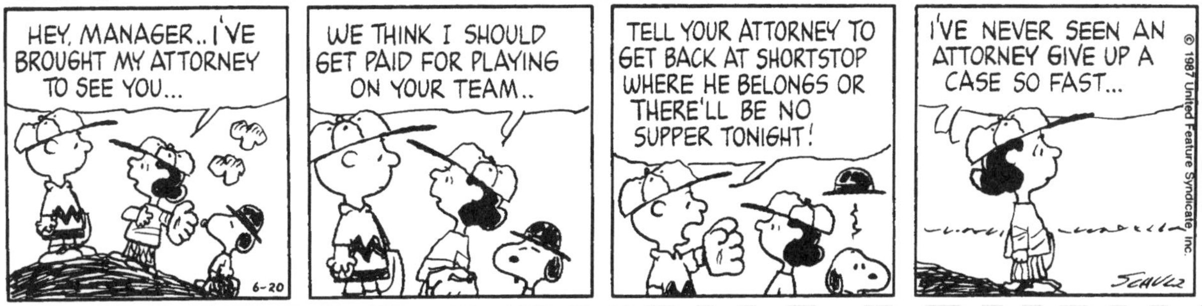
HEY, MANAGER.. I'VE BROUGHT MY ATTORNEY TO SEE YOU...
6-20
WE THINK I SHOULD GET PAID FOR PLAYING ON YOUR TEAM..
TELL YOUR ATTORNEY TO GET BACK AT SHORTSTOP WHERE HE BELONGS OR THERE'LL BE NO SUPPER TONIGHT!
I'VE NEVER SEEN AN ATTORNEY GIVE UP A CASE SO FAST...
© 1987 United Feature Syndicate, Inc.
SCHULZ

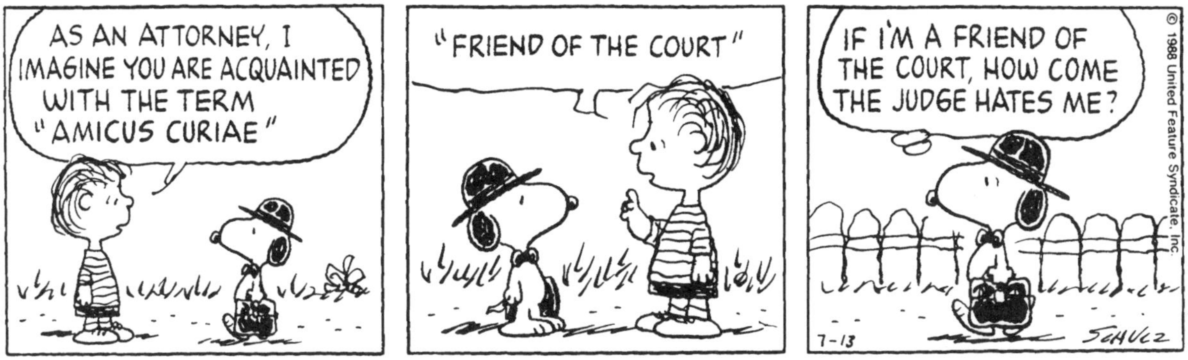
AS AN ATTORNEY, I IMAGINE YOU ARE ACQUAINTED WITH THE TERM "AMICUS CURIAE"
"FRIEND OF THE COURT"
IF I'M A FRIEND OF THE COURT, HOW COME THE JUDGE HATES ME?
© 1988 United Feature Syndicate, Inc.
7-13
SCHULZ

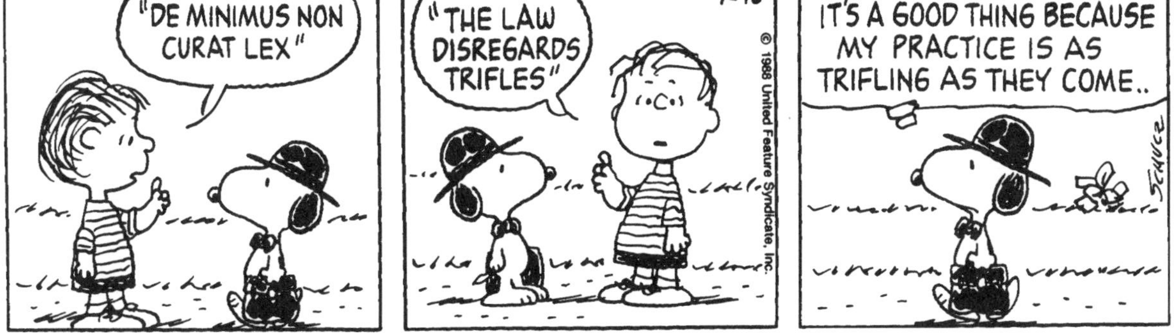
"DE MINIMUS NON CURAT LEX"
7-18
"THE LAW DISREGARDS TRIFLES"
© 1988 United Feature Syndicate, Inc.
IT'S A GOOD THING BECAUSE MY PRACTICE IS AS TRIFLING AS THEY COME..
SCHULZ

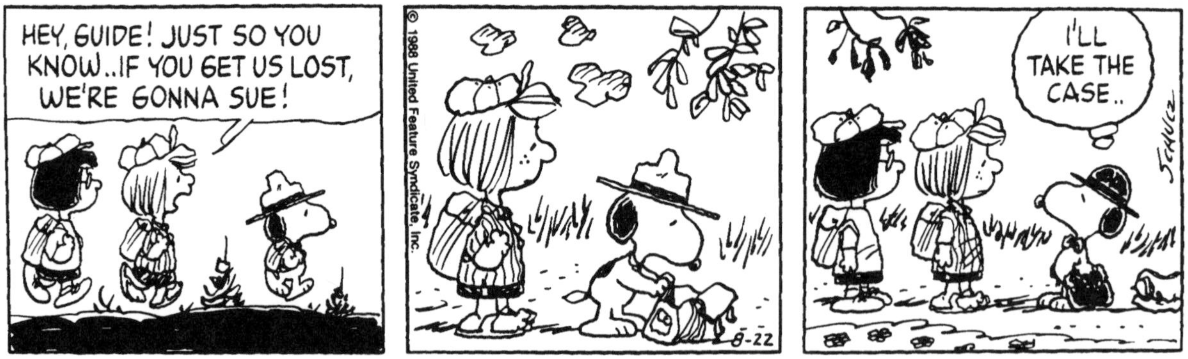
HEY, GUIDE! JUST SO YOU KNOW..IF YOU GET US LOST, WE'RE GONNA SUE!
© 1988 United Feature Syndicate, Inc.
8-22
I'LL TAKE THE CASE..
SCHULZ

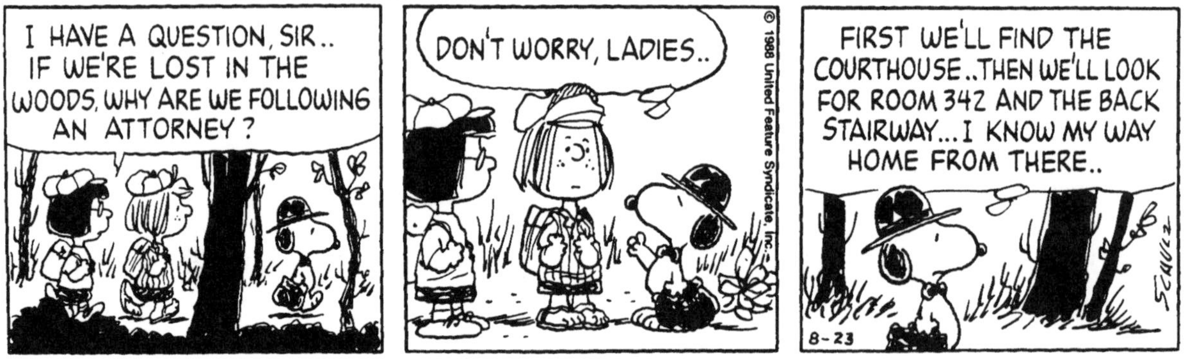
I HAVE A QUESTION, SIR.. IF WE'RE LOST IN THE WOODS, WHY ARE WE FOLLOWING AN ATTORNEY?
DON'T WORRY, LADIES..
© 1988 United Feature Syndicate, Inc.
FIRST WE'LL FIND THE COURTHOUSE..THEN WE'LL LOOK FOR ROOM 342 AND THE BACK STAIRWAY...I KNOW MY WAY HOME FROM THERE..
SCHULZ
8-23

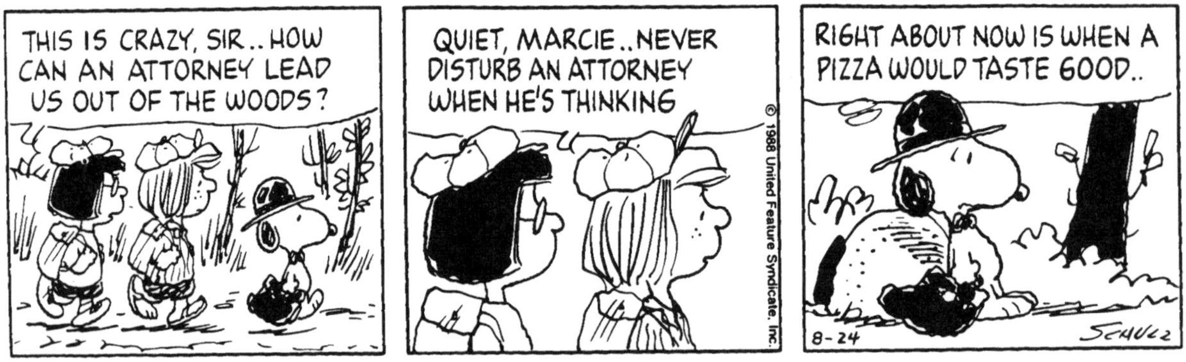
THIS IS CRAZY, SIR..HOW CAN AN ATTORNEY LEAD US OUT OF THE WOODS?
QUIET, MARCIE..NEVER DISTURB AN ATTORNEY WHEN HE'S THINKING
© 1988 United Feature Syndicate, Inc.
RIGHT ABOUT NOW IS WHEN A PIZZA WOULD TASTE GOOD..
8-24
SCHULZ

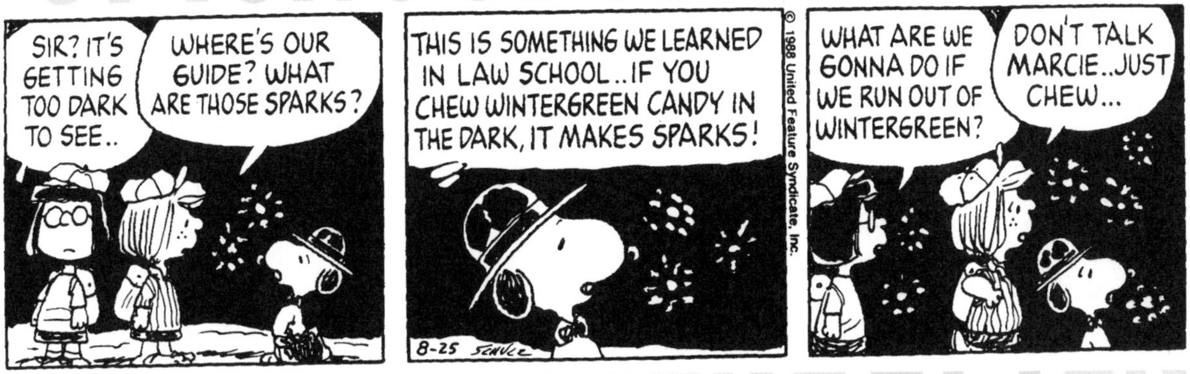
SIR? IT'S GETTING TOO DARK TO SEE..
WHERE'S OUR GUIDE? WHAT ARE THOSE SPARKS?
THIS IS SOMETHING WE LEARNED IN LAW SCHOOL..IF YOU CHEW WINTERGREEN CANDY IN THE DARK, IT MAKES SPARKS!
© 1988 United Feature Syndicate, Inc.
8-25 SCHULZ
WHAT ARE WE GONNA DO IF WE RUN OUT OF WINTERGREEN?
DON'T TALK MARCIE..JUST CHEW...

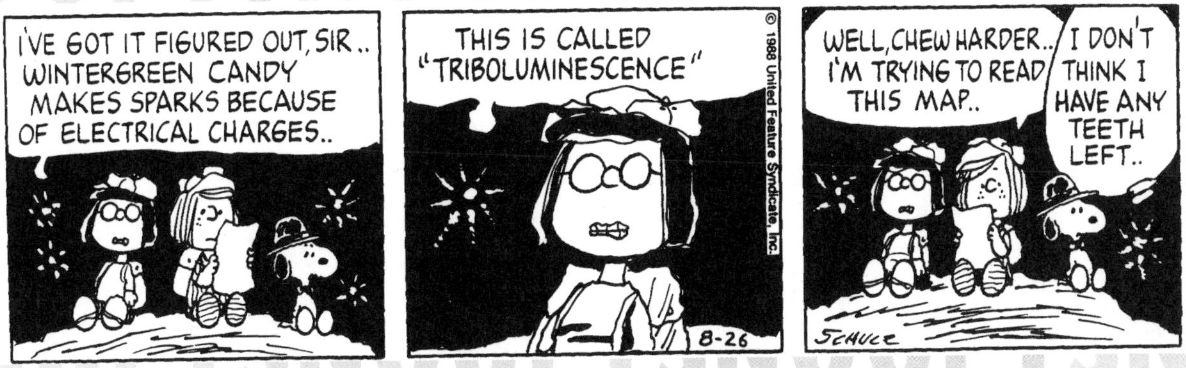
I'VE GOT IT FIGURED OUT, SIR.. WINTERGREEN CANDY MAKES SPARKS BECAUSE OF ELECTRICAL CHARGES..
THIS IS CALLED "TRIBOLUMINESCENCE"
© 1988 United Feature Syndicate, Inc.
8-26
WELL, CHEW HARDER.. I'M TRYING TO READ THIS MAP..
I DON'T THINK I HAVE ANY TEETH LEFT..
SCHULZ

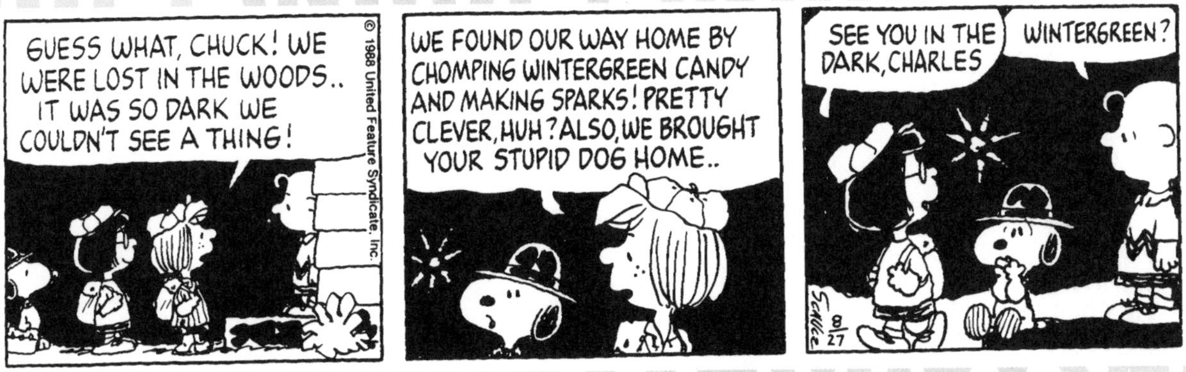
GUESS WHAT, CHUCK! WE WERE LOST IN THE WOODS.. IT WAS SO DARK WE COULDN'T SEE A THING!
© 1988 United Feature Syndicate, Inc.
WE FOUND OUR WAY HOME BY CHOMPING WINTERGREEN CANDY AND MAKING SPARKS! PRETTY CLEVER, HUH? ALSO, WE BROUGHT YOUR STUPID DOG HOME..
SEE YOU IN THE DARK, CHARLES
WINTERGREEN?
SCHULZ 8/27

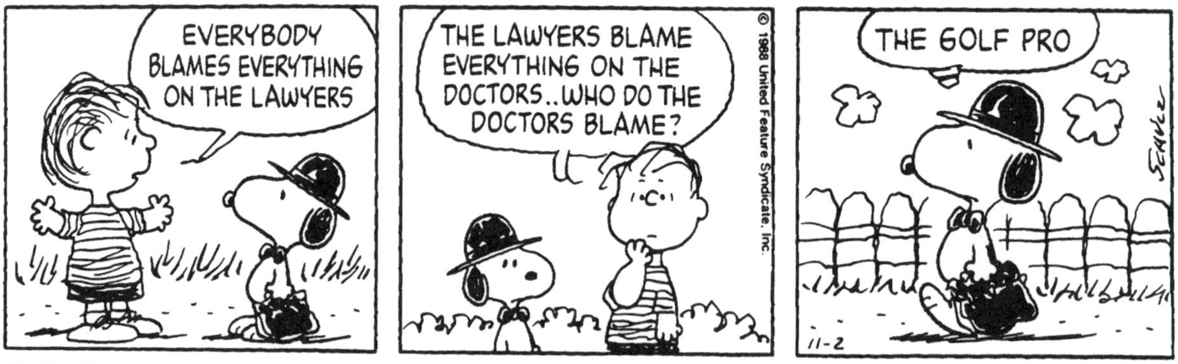
EVERYBODY BLAMES EVERYTHING ON THE LAWYERS
THE LAWYERS BLAME EVERYTHING ON THE DOCTORS..WHO DO THE DOCTORS BLAME?
© 1988 United Feature Syndicate, Inc.
THE GOLF PRO
SCHULZ
11-2

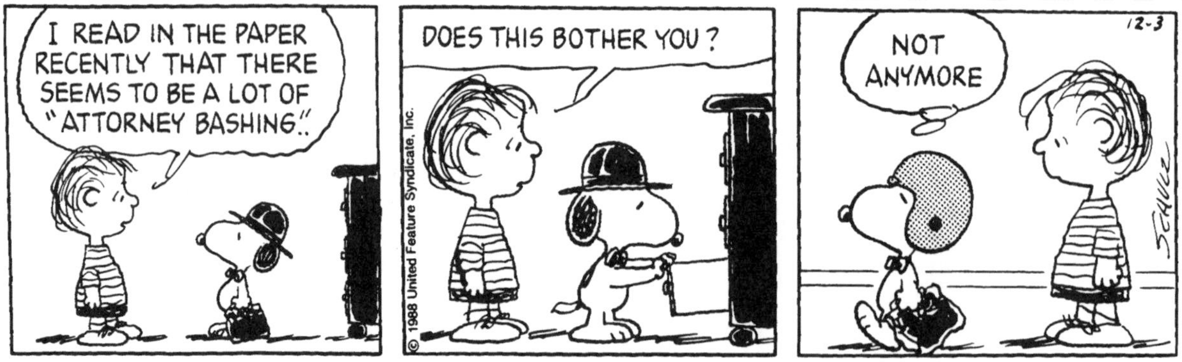
I READ IN THE PAPER RECENTLY THAT THERE SEEMS TO BE A LOT OF "ATTORNEY BASHING."
DOES THIS BOTHER YOU?
© 1988 United Feature Syndicate, Inc.
12-3
NOT ANYMORE
SCHULZ

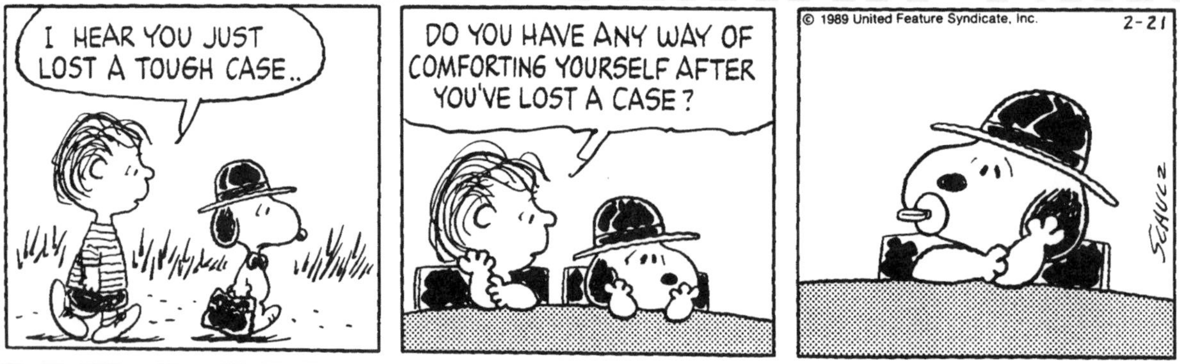
I HEAR YOU JUST LOST A TOUGH CASE..
DO YOU HAVE ANY WAY OF COMFORTING YOURSELF AFTER YOU'VE LOST A CASE?
© 1989 United Feature Syndicate, Inc.
2-21
SCHULZ

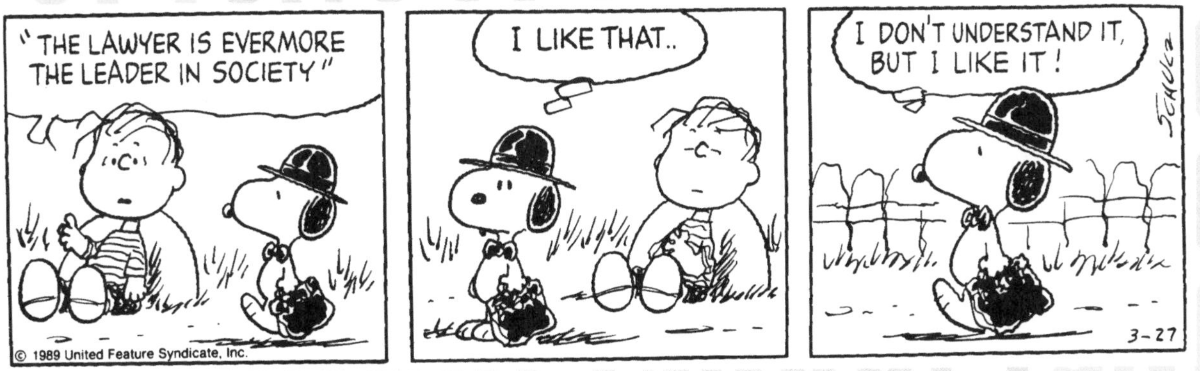
"THE LAWYER IS EVERMORE THE LEADER IN SOCIETY"
I LIKE THAT..
I DON'T UNDERSTAND IT, BUT I LIKE IT!
© 1989 United Feature Syndicate, Inc.
3-27

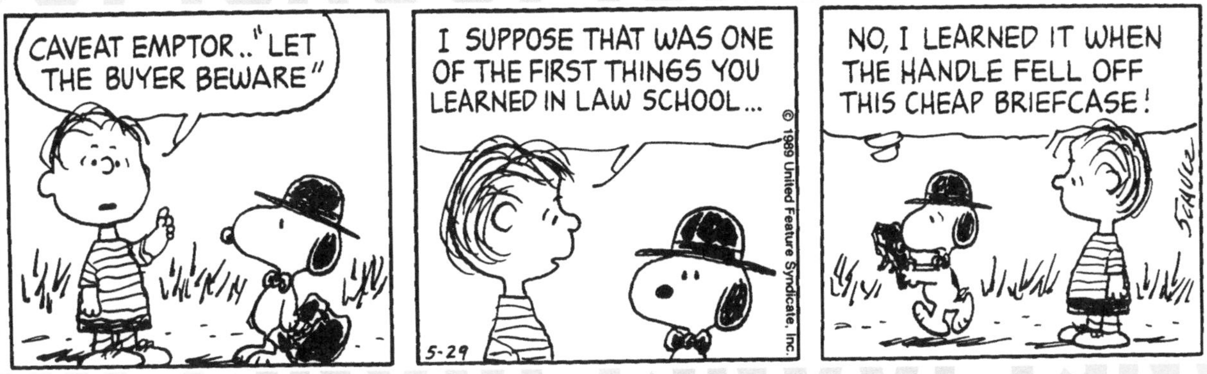
CAVEAT EMPTOR.."LET THE BUYER BEWARE"
I SUPPOSE THAT WAS ONE OF THE FIRST THINGS YOU LEARNED IN LAW SCHOOL...
NO, I LEARNED IT WHEN THE HANDLE FELL OFF THIS CHEAP BRIEFCASE!
© 1989 United Feature Syndicate, Inc.
5-29

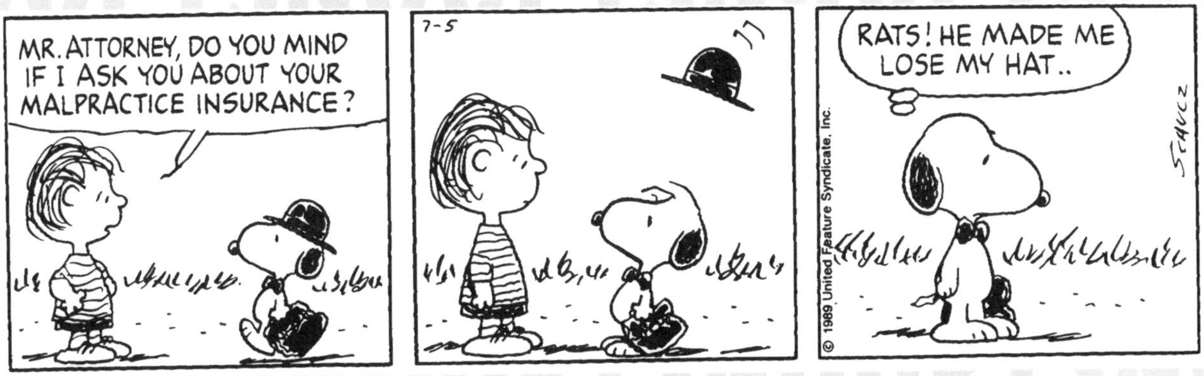
MR. ATTORNEY, DO YOU MIND IF I ASK YOU ABOUT YOUR MALPRACTICE INSURANCE?
7-5
RATS! HE MADE ME LOSE MY HAT..
© 1989 United Feature Syndicate, Inc.

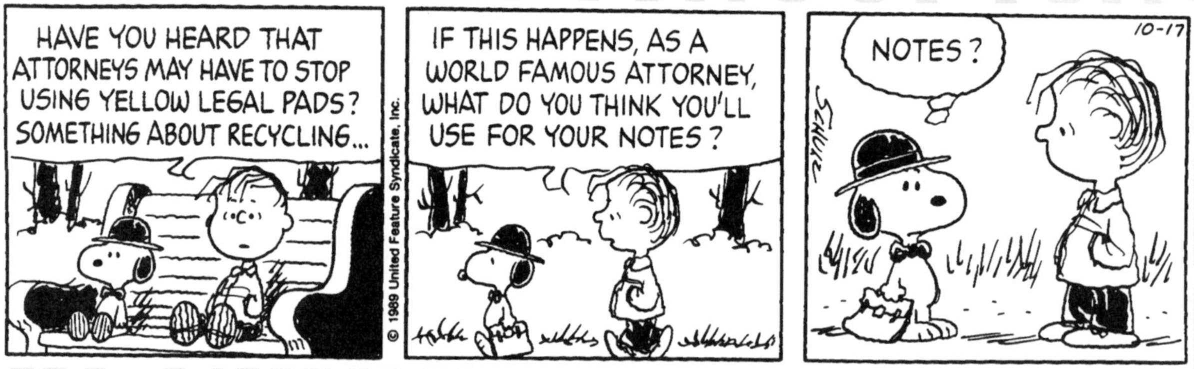
HAVE YOU HEARD THAT ATTORNEYS MAY HAVE TO STOP USING YELLOW LEGAL PADS? SOMETHING ABOUT RECYCLING...
© 1989 United Feature Syndicate, Inc.
IF THIS HAPPENS, AS A WORLD FAMOUS ATTORNEY, WHAT DO YOU THINK YOU'LL USE FOR YOUR NOTES?
10-17
NOTES?
SCHULZ

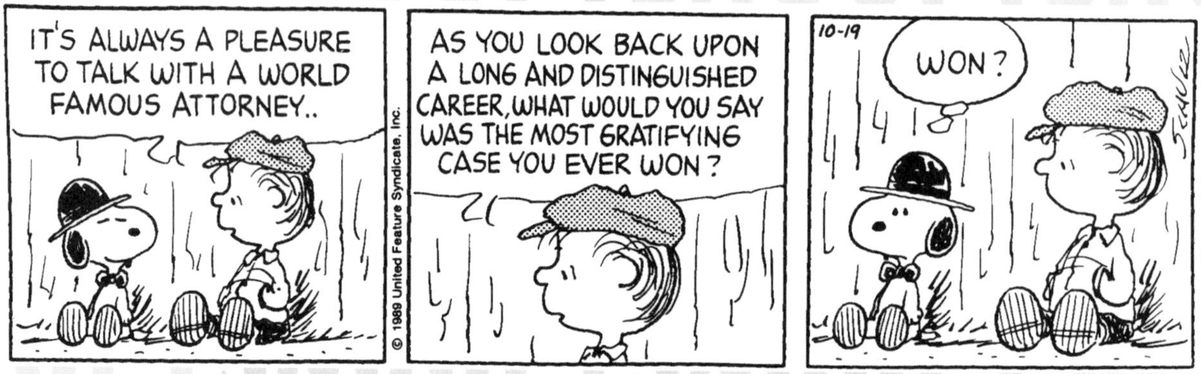
IT'S ALWAYS A PLEASURE TO TALK WITH A WORLD FAMOUS ATTORNEY..
© 1989 United Feature Syndicate, Inc.
AS YOU LOOK BACK UPON A LONG AND DISTINGUISHED CAREER, WHAT WOULD YOU SAY WAS THE MOST GRATIFYING CASE YOU EVER WON?
10-19
WON?
SCHULZ

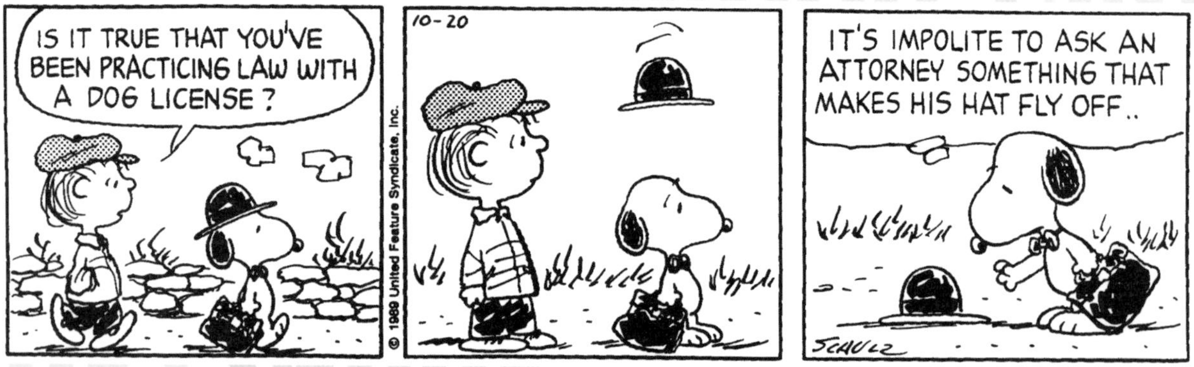
IS IT TRUE THAT YOU'VE BEEN PRACTICING LAW WITH A DOG LICENSE?
© 1989 United Feature Syndicate, Inc.
10-20
IT'S IMPOLITE TO ASK AN ATTORNEY SOMETHING THAT MAKES HIS HAT FLY OFF..
SCHULZ

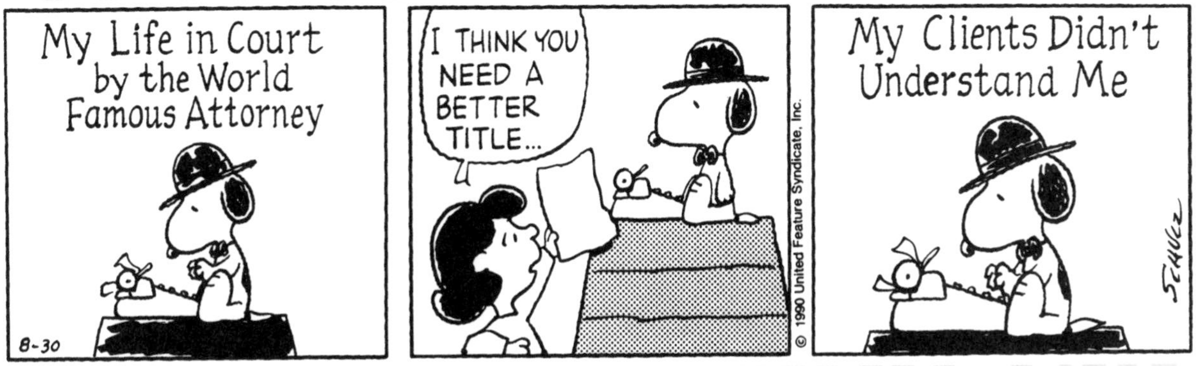
My Life in Court by the World Famous Attorney
8-30
I THINK YOU NEED A BETTER TITLE...
© 1990 United Feature Syndicate, Inc.
My Clients Didn't Understand Me
SCHULZ

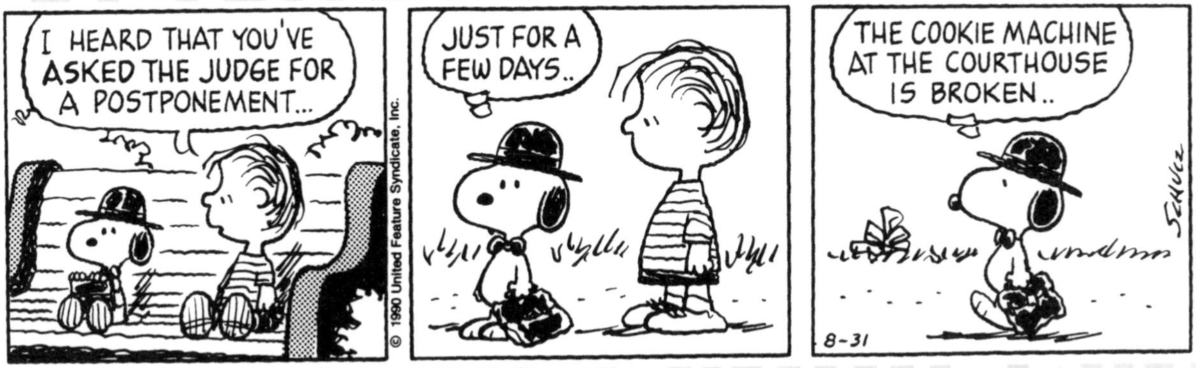
I HEARD THAT YOU'VE ASKED THE JUDGE FOR A POSTPONEMENT...
© 1990 United Feature Syndicate, Inc.
JUST FOR A FEW DAYS..
THE COOKIE MACHINE AT THE COURTHOUSE IS BROKEN..
SCHULZ
8-31

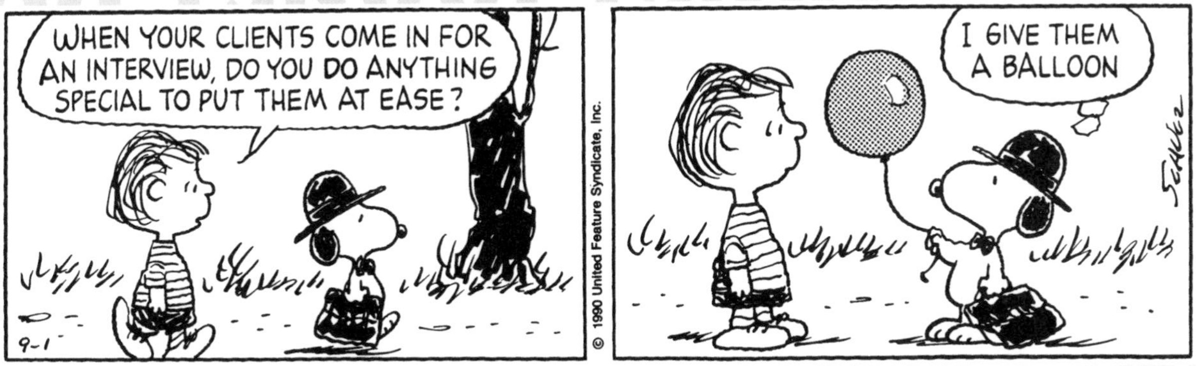
WHEN YOUR CLIENTS COME IN FOR AN INTERVIEW, DO YOU DO ANYTHING SPECIAL TO PUT THEM AT EASE?
9-1
© 1990 United Feature Syndicate, Inc.
I GIVE THEM A BALLOON
SCHULZ

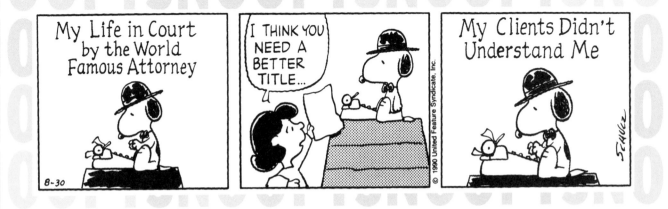

IS IT TRUE THAT ATTORNEYS ARE MORE LIKELY TO SUFFER DEPRESSION THAN OTHER PEOPLE?
© 1991 United Feature Syndicate, Inc.
I DOUBT IT...
1-25
AFTER A TRIAL, MY CLIENTS ARE ALWAYS MORE DEPRESSED THAN I AM..
SCHULZ

..AND THEN YOUR STUPID SISTER HIT ME WITH HER LUNCH BOX...SANDWICHES FLEW ALL OVER..AND THEN MY ATTORNEY SHOWED UP..
© 1991 United Feature Syndicate, Inc.
2-15
DID HE TAKE THE CASE?
NO, HE ATE ALL THE SANDWICHES!
SCHULZ

MY ATTORNEY AND I ARE HERE TO SUE YOU FOR HITTING ME WITH YOUR LUNCH BOX..
THAT'S WHAT YOU THINK!
2-16
I'VE GOT HIS SUPPER DISH, SEE? IF YOU SUE ME, I'LL THROW IT OVER THE FENCE!
© 1991 United Feature Syndicate, Inc.
AFTER CAREFUL CONSIDERATION, I'VE DECIDED WE DON'T HAVE A CASE..
SCHULZ

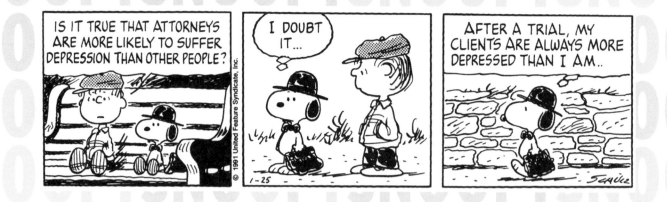

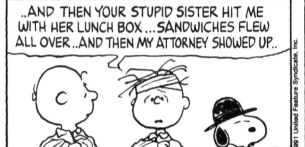

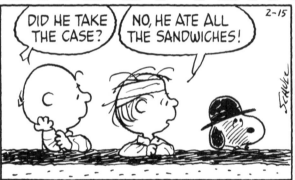

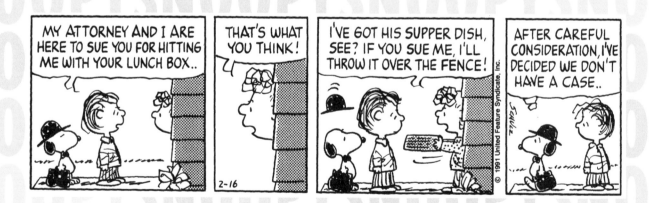

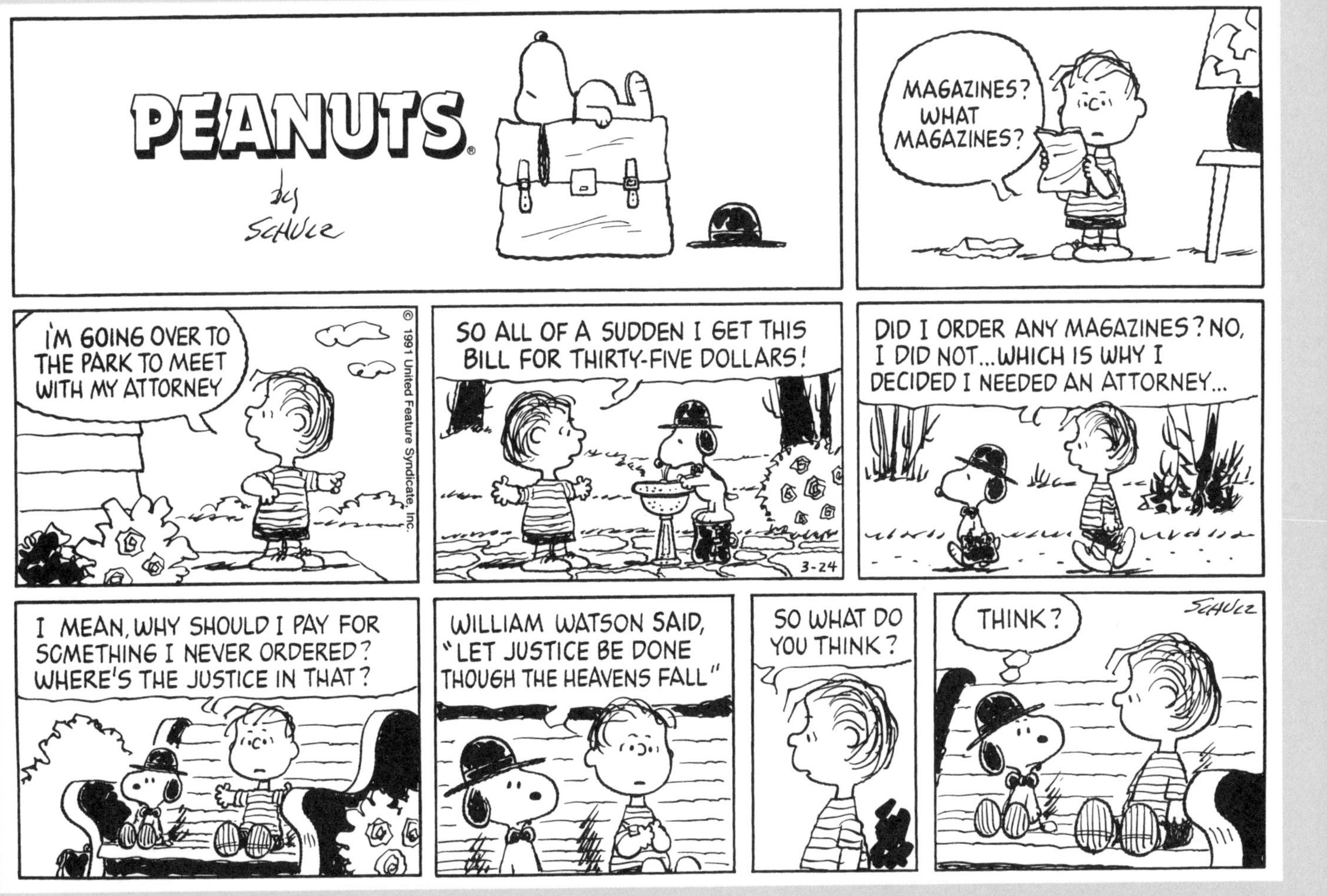
PEANUTS
by SCHULZ
MAGAZINES? WHAT MAGAZINES?
I'M GOING OVER TO THE PARK TO MEET WITH MY ATTORNEY
© 1991 United Feature Syndicate, Inc.
SO ALL OF A SUDDEN I GET THIS BILL FOR THIRTY-FIVE DOLLARS!
3-24
DID I ORDER ANY MAGAZINES? NO, I DID NOT...WHICH IS WHY I DECIDED I NEEDED AN ATTORNEY...
I MEAN, WHY SHOULD I PAY FOR SOMETHING I NEVER ORDERED? WHERE'S THE JUSTICE IN THAT?
WILLIAM WATSON SAID, "LET JUSTICE BE DONE THOUGH THE HEAVENS FALL"
SO WHAT DO YOU THINK?
THINK?
SCHULZ

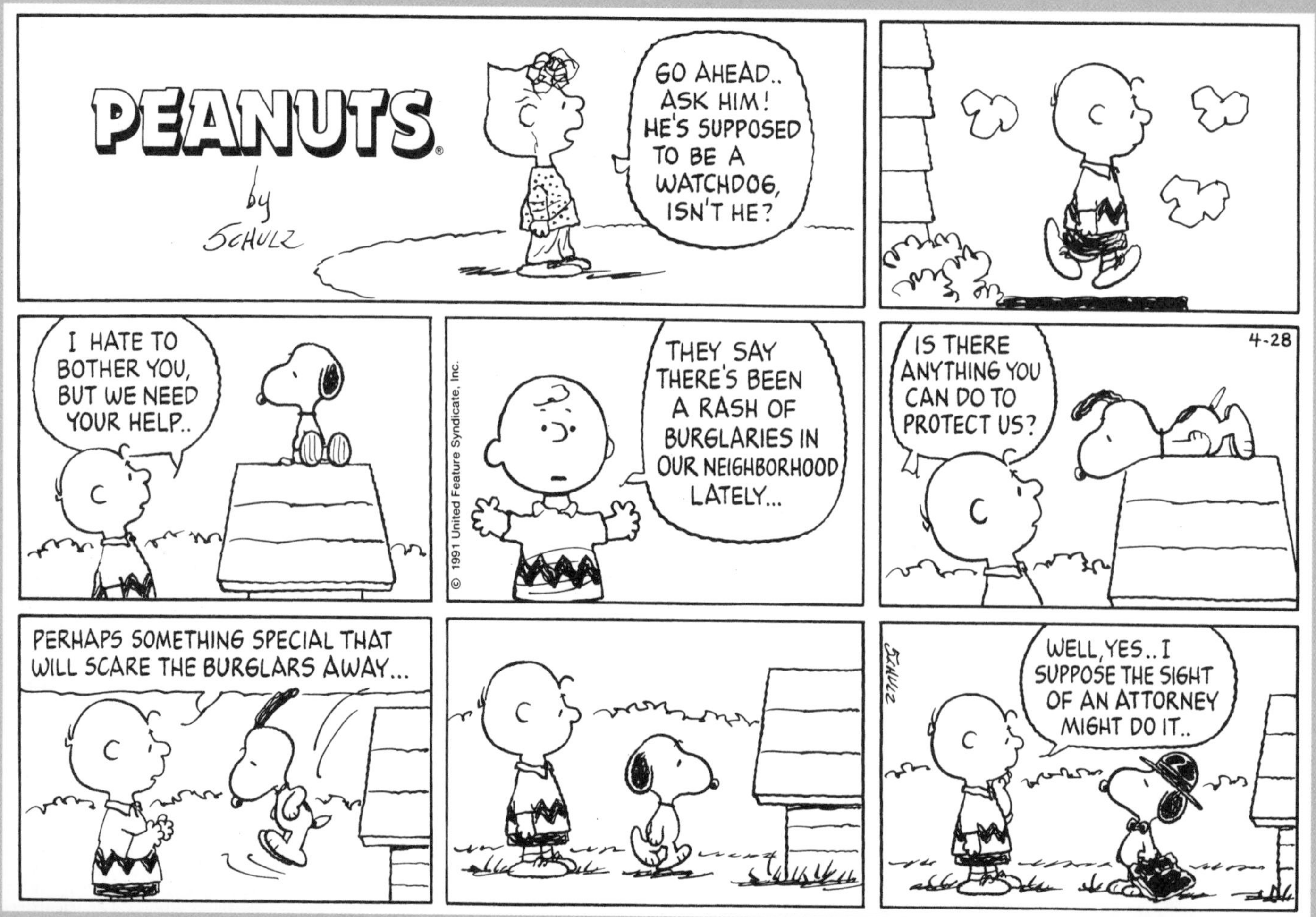
PEANUTS
by SCHULZ
GO AHEAD.. ASK HIM! HE'S SUPPOSED TO BE A WATCHDOG, ISN'T HE?
I HATE TO BOTHER YOU, BUT WE NEED YOUR HELP..
© 1991 United Feature Syndicate, Inc.
THEY SAY THERE'S BEEN A RASH OF BURGLARIES IN OUR NEIGHBORHOOD LATELY...
4-28
IS THERE ANYTHING YOU CAN DO TO PROTECT US?
PERHAPS SOMETHING SPECIAL THAT WILL SCARE THE BURGLARS AWAY...
SCHULZ
WELL, YES.. I SUPPOSE THE SIGHT OF AN ATTORNEY MIGHT DO IT..

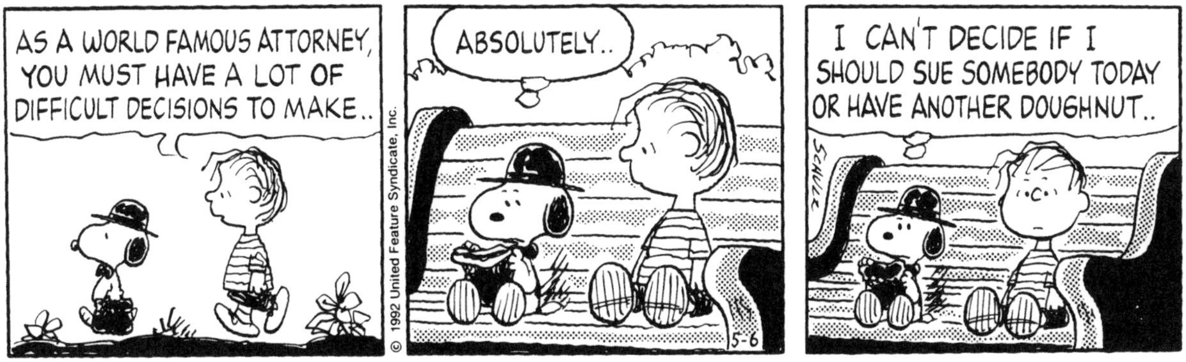
AS A WORLD FAMOUS ATTORNEY, YOU MUST HAVE A LOT OF DIFFICULT DECISIONS TO MAKE..
ABSOLUTELY..
I CAN'T DECIDE IF I SHOULD SUE SOMEBODY TODAY OR HAVE ANOTHER DOUGHNUT..
© 1992 United Feature Syndicate, Inc.
5-6
SCHULZ

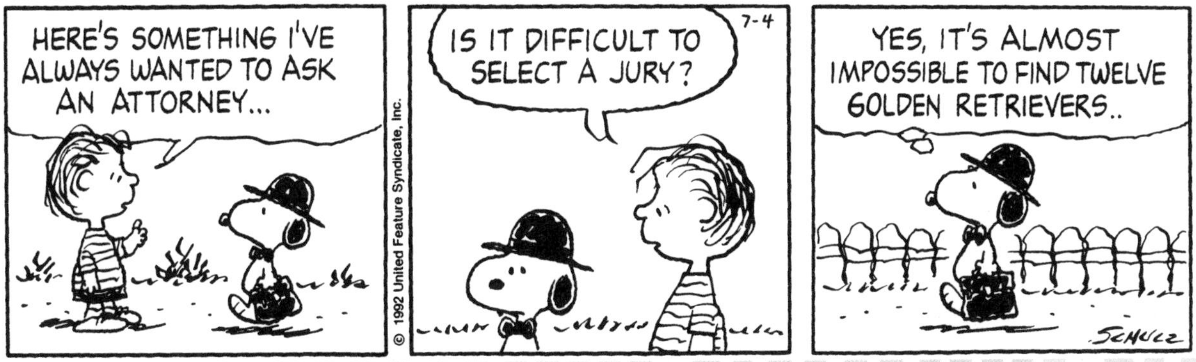
HERE'S SOMETHING I'VE ALWAYS WANTED TO ASK AN ATTORNEY...
IS IT DIFFICULT TO SELECT A JURY?
YES, IT'S ALMOST IMPOSSIBLE TO FIND TWELVE GOLDEN RETRIEVERS..
© 1992 United Feature Syndicate, Inc.
7-4
SCHULZ

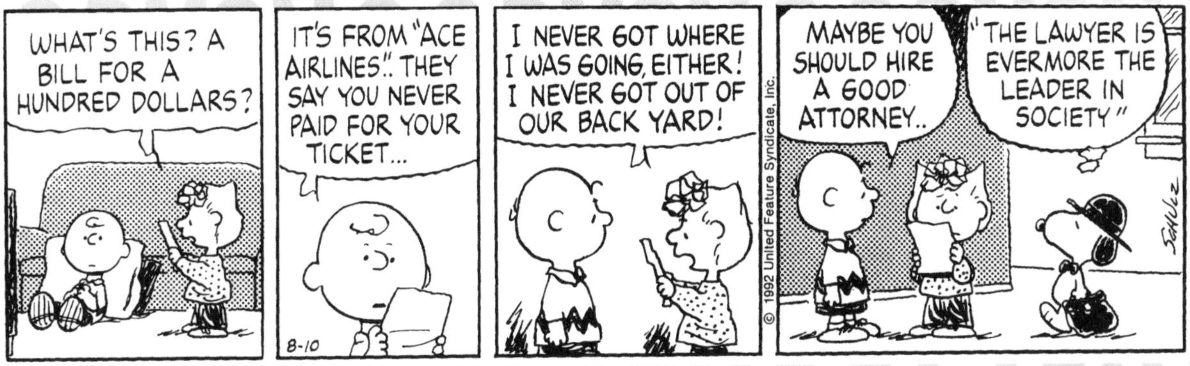
WHAT'S THIS? A BILL FOR A HUNDRED DOLLARS?
IT'S FROM "ACE AIRLINES". THEY SAY YOU NEVER PAID FOR YOUR TICKET...
I NEVER GOT WHERE I WAS GOING, EITHER! I NEVER GOT OUT OF OUR BACK YARD!
MAYBE YOU SHOULD HIRE A GOOD ATTORNEY..
"THE LAWYER IS EVERMORE THE LEADER IN SOCIETY"
© 1992 United Feature Syndicate, Inc.
8-10
SCHULZ

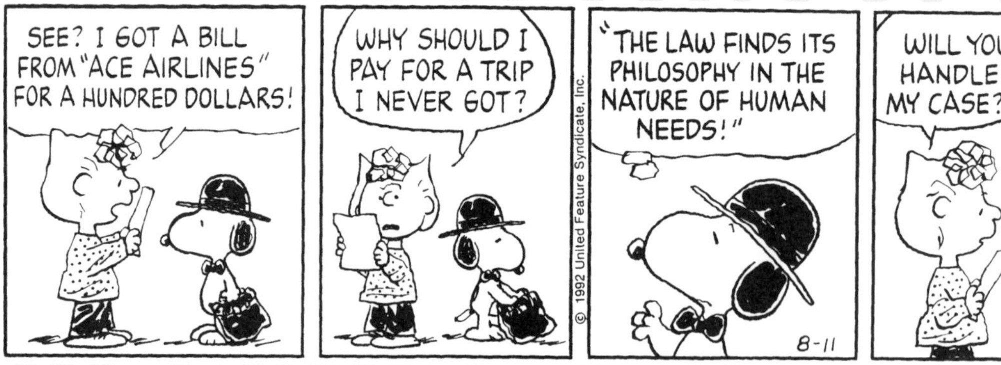
SEE? I GOT A BILL FROM "ACE AIRLINES" FOR A HUNDRED DOLLARS!
WHY SHOULD I PAY FOR A TRIP I NEVER GOT?
© 1992 United Feature Syndicate, Inc.
"THE LAW FINDS ITS PHILOSOPHY IN THE NATURE OF HUMAN NEEDS!"
8-11
WILL YOU HANDLE MY CASE?
AFTER I FINISH THIS DOUGHNUT..
SCHULZ

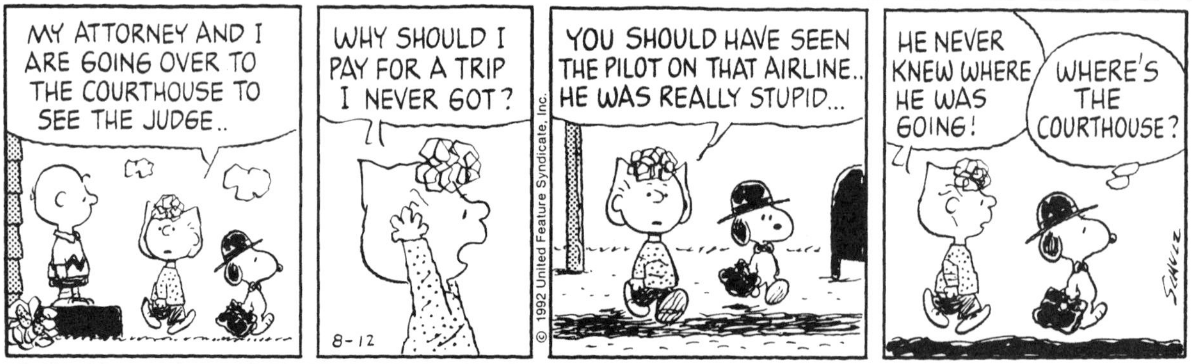
MY ATTORNEY AND I ARE GOING OVER TO THE COURTHOUSE TO SEE THE JUDGE..
WHY SHOULD I PAY FOR A TRIP I NEVER GOT?
8-12
© 1992 United Feature Syndicate, Inc.
YOU SHOULD HAVE SEEN THE PILOT ON THAT AIRLINE.. HE WAS REALLY STUPID...
HE NEVER KNEW WHERE HE WAS GOING!
WHERE'S THE COURTHOUSE?
SCHULZ

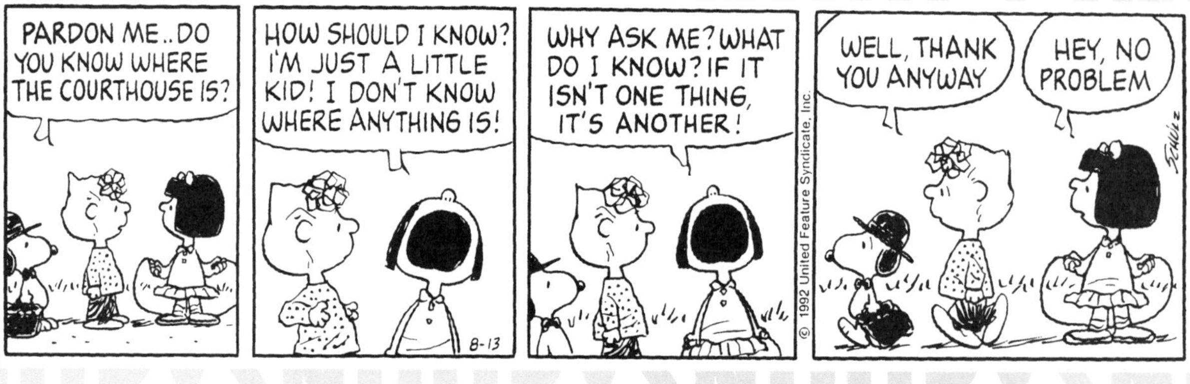
PARDON ME..DO YOU KNOW WHERE THE COURTHOUSE IS?
HOW SHOULD I KNOW? I'M JUST A LITTLE KID! I DON'T KNOW WHERE ANYTHING IS!
8-13
WHY ASK ME? WHAT DO I KNOW? IF IT ISN'T ONE THING, IT'S ANOTHER!
© 1992 United Feature Syndicate, Inc.
WELL, THANK YOU ANYWAY
HEY, NO PROBLEM
SCHULZ

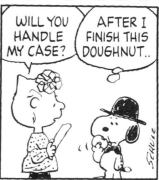

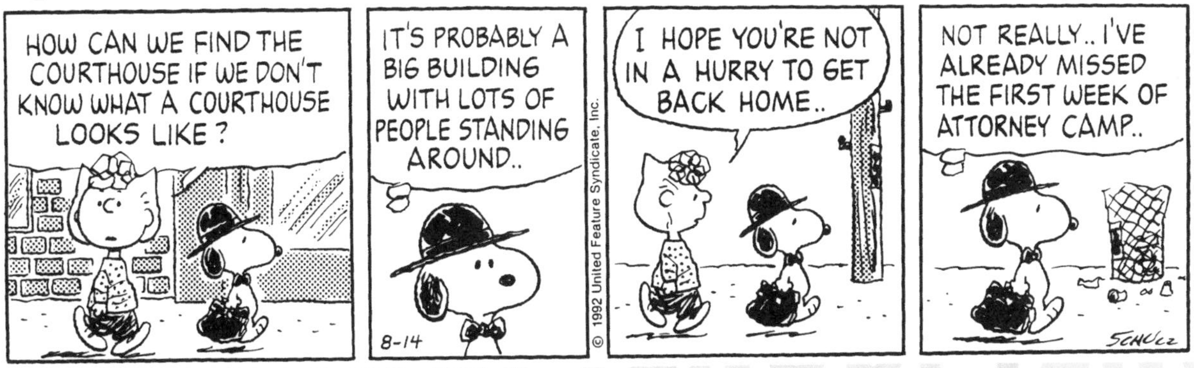
HOW CAN WE FIND THE COURTHOUSE IF WE DON'T KNOW WHAT A COURTHOUSE LOOKS LIKE?
IT'S PROBABLY A BIG BUILDING WITH LOTS OF PEOPLE STANDING AROUND..
8-14
© 1992 United Feature Syndicate, Inc.
I HOPE YOU'RE NOT IN A HURRY TO GET BACK HOME..
NOT REALLY.. I'VE ALREADY MISSED THE FIRST WEEK OF ATTORNEY CAMP..
SCHULZ

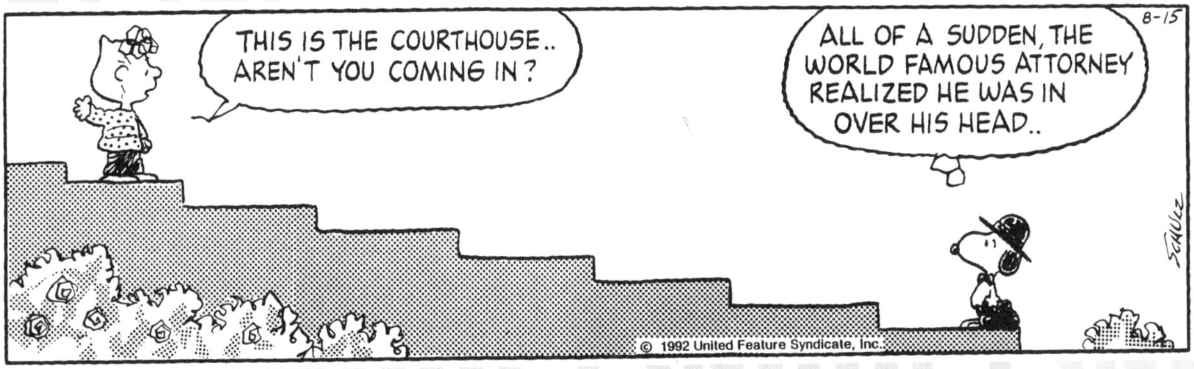
THIS IS THE COURTHOUSE.. AREN'T YOU COMING IN?
8-15
ALL OF A SUDDEN, THE WORLD FAMOUS ATTORNEY REALIZED HE WAS IN OVER HIS HEAD..
SCHULZ
© 1992 United Feature Syndicate, Inc.

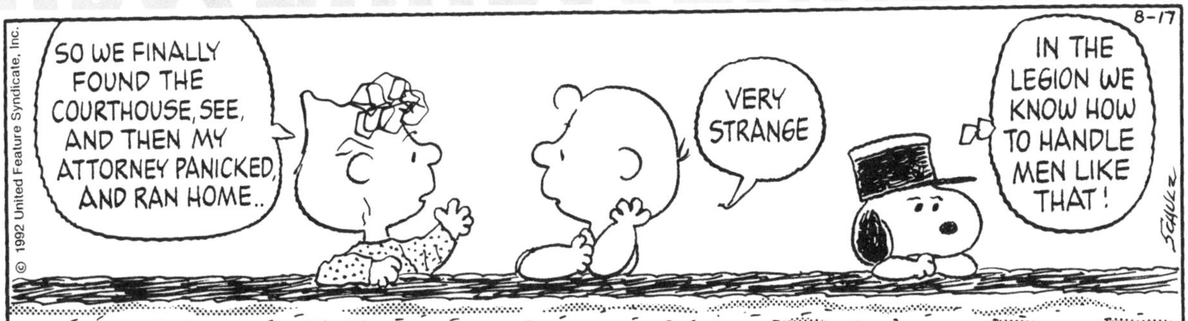
© 1992 United Feature Syndicate, Inc.
SO WE FINALLY FOUND THE COURTHOUSE, SEE, AND THEN MY ATTORNEY PANICKED, AND RAN HOME..
VERY STRANGE
8-17
IN THE LEGION WE KNOW HOW TO HANDLE MEN LIKE THAT!
SCHULZ

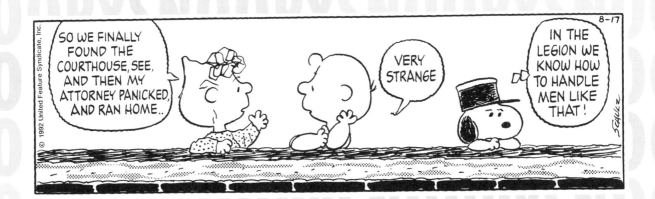

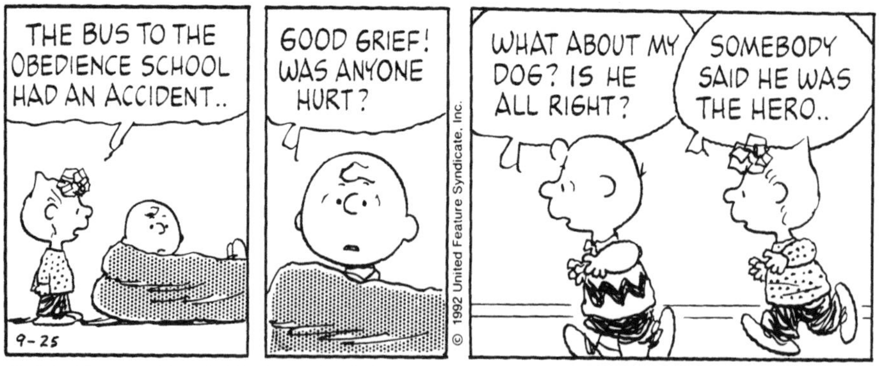
THE BUS TO THE OBEDIENCE SCHOOL HAD AN ACCIDENT..
GOOD GRIEF! WAS ANYONE HURT?
WHAT ABOUT MY DOG? IS HE ALL RIGHT?
SOMEBODY SAID HE WAS THE HERO..
I'M HANDLING ALL THE LAWSUITS..
9-25
© 1992 United Feature Syndicate, Inc.
SCHULZ

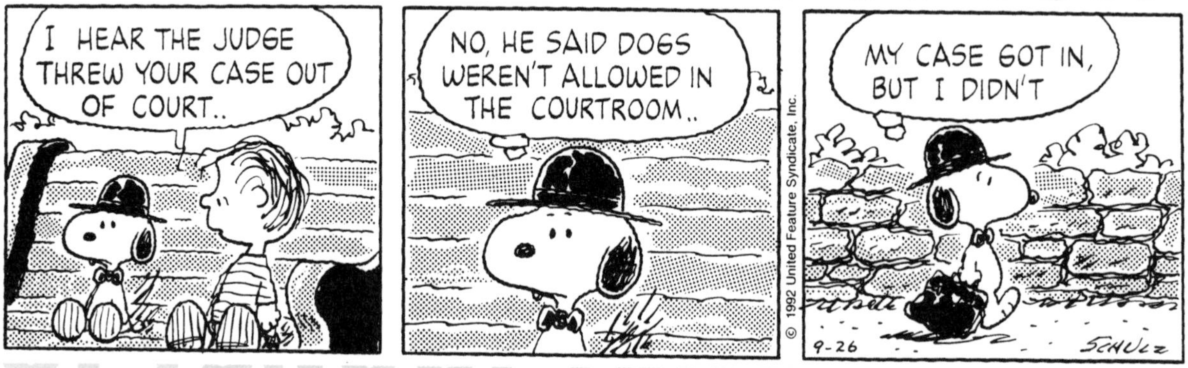
I HEAR THE JUDGE THREW YOUR CASE OUT OF COURT..
NO, HE SAID DOGS WEREN'T ALLOWED IN THE COURTROOM..
MY CASE GOT IN, BUT I DIDN'T
9-26
© 1992 United Feature Syndicate, Inc.
SCHULZ

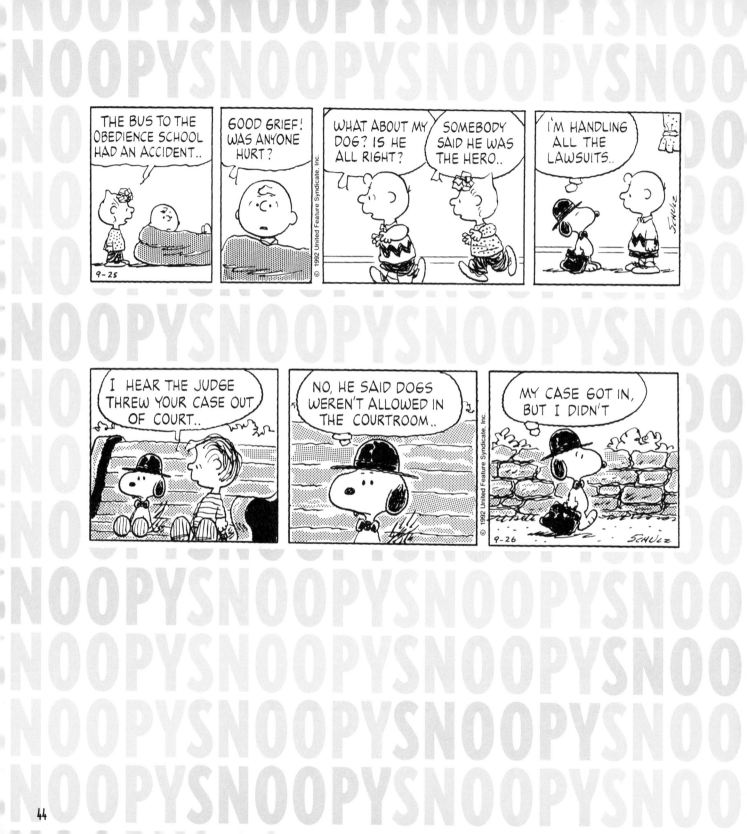

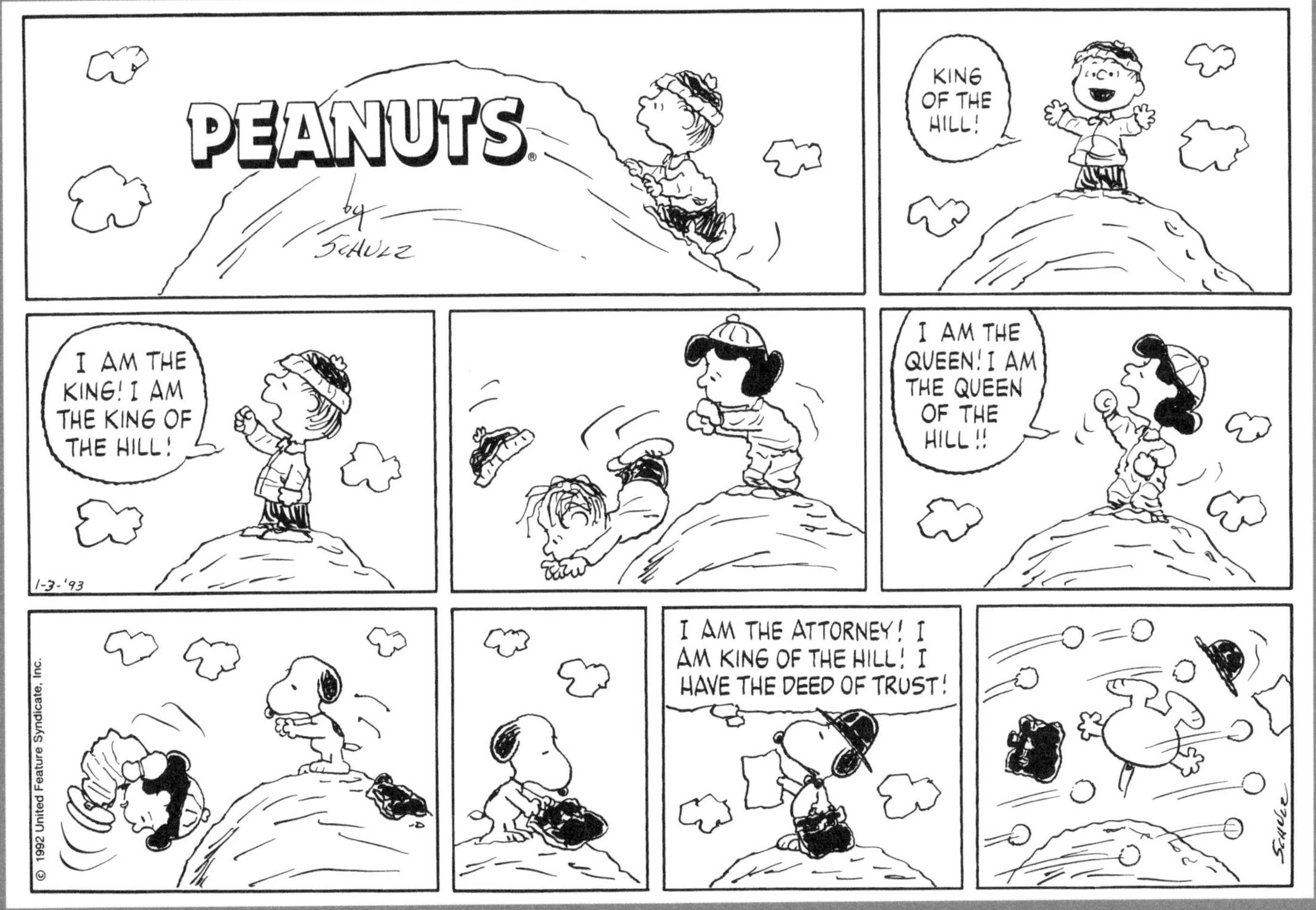
PEANUTS
by SCHULZ
KING OF THE HILL!
I AM THE KING! I AM THE KING OF THE HILL!
1-3-'93
I AM THE QUEEN! I AM THE QUEEN OF THE HILL!!
© 1992 United Feature Syndicate, Inc.
I AM THE ATTORNEY! I AM KING OF THE HILL! I HAVE THE DEED OF TRUST!
SCHULZ

5-19
AS A WORLD FAMOUS ATTORNEY, WOULD YOU EVER BE INTERESTED IN BECOMING A MEMBER OF THE SUPREME COURT?
WHY NOT?
© 1993 United Feature Syndicate, Inc.
OF COURSE, YOU'D HAVE TO MOVE TO WASHINGTON..
WHERE'S THAT?
SCHULZ

Dear Mr. President,
Apparently there is soon to be an opening on the Supreme Court.
© 1993 United Feature Syndicate, Inc.
I would like to recommend a friend of mine who is a world famous attorney.
WHERE SHOULD I TELL HIM YOU WENT TO LAW SCHOOL?
YOU'D BETTER SKIP THAT PART..
SCHULZ
5-20

5-21
© 1993 United Feature Syndicate, Inc.
I CAN SEE YOU NOW SITTING ON THE BENCH OF THE SUPREME COURT..THEY'D PROBABLY PUT YOU RIGHT NEXT TO JUDGE SANDRA DAY O'CONNOR..
IS SHE CUTE?
SCHULZ

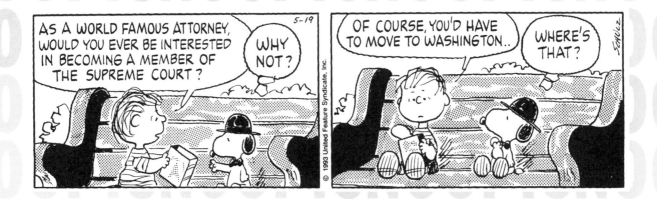

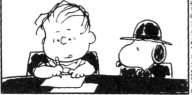

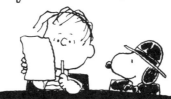

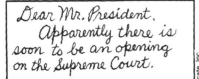

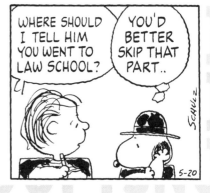

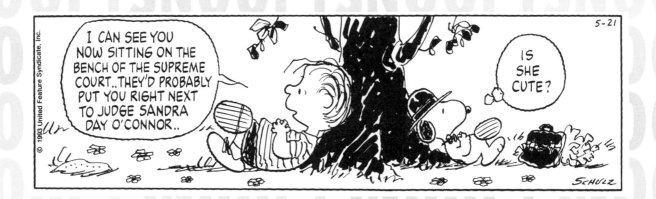

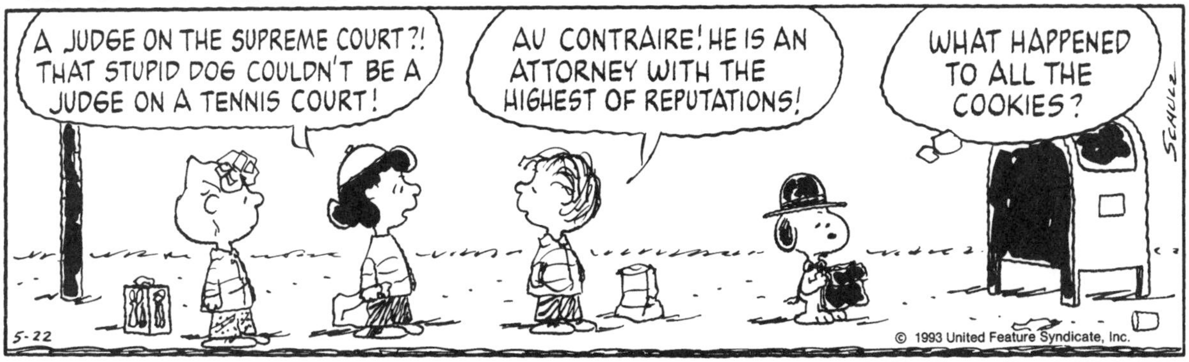
A JUDGE ON THE SUPREME COURT?! THAT STUPID DOG COULDN'T BE A JUDGE ON A TENNIS COURT!
AU CONTRAIRE! HE IS AN ATTORNEY WITH THE HIGHEST OF REPUTATIONS!
WHAT HAPPENED TO ALL THE COOKIES?
5-22
© 1993 United Feature Syndicate, Inc.

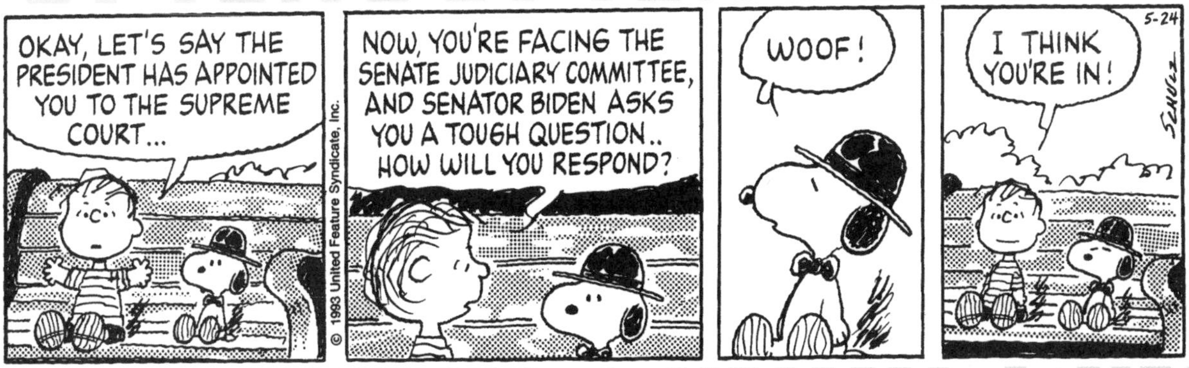
OKAY, LET'S SAY THE PRESIDENT HAS APPOINTED YOU TO THE SUPREME COURT...
© 1993 United Feature Syndicate, Inc.
NOW, YOU'RE FACING THE SENATE JUDICIARY COMMITTEE, AND SENATOR BIDEN ASKS YOU A TOUGH QUESTION.. HOW WILL YOU RESPOND?
WOOF!
I THINK YOU'RE IN!
5-24

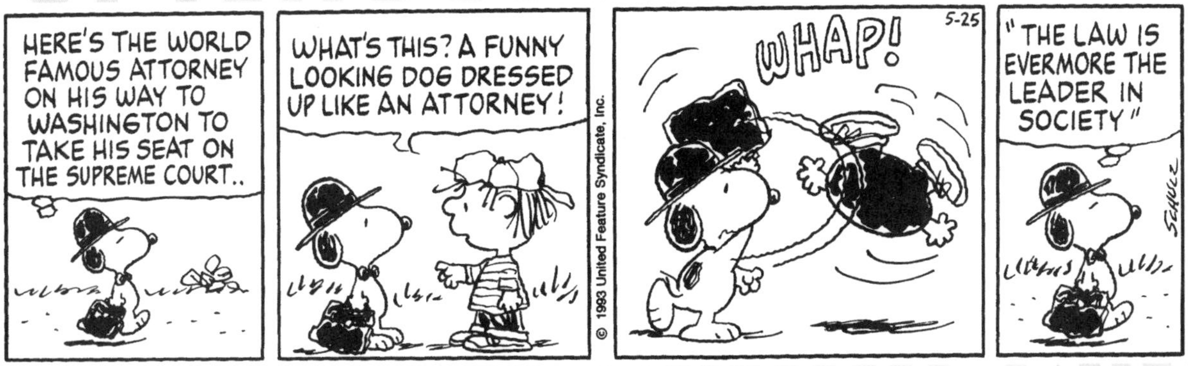
HERE'S THE WORLD FAMOUS ATTORNEY ON HIS WAY TO WASHINGTON TO TAKE HIS SEAT ON THE SUPREME COURT..
WHAT'S THIS? A FUNNY LOOKING DOG DRESSED UP LIKE AN ATTORNEY!
© 1993 United Feature Syndicate, Inc.
WHAP!
5-25
"THE LAW IS EVERMORE THE LEADER IN SOCIETY"

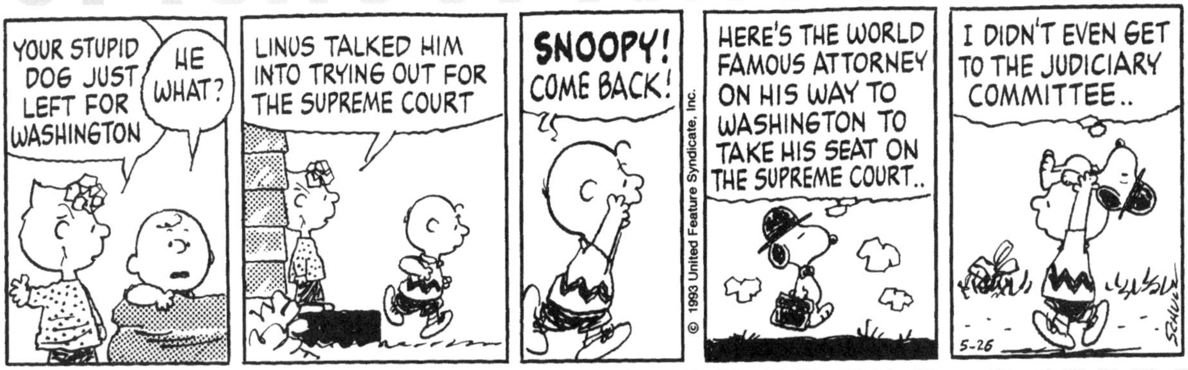
YOUR STUPID DOG JUST LEFT FOR WASHINGTON
HE WHAT?
LINUS TALKED HIM INTO TRYING OUT FOR THE SUPREME COURT
SNOOPY! COME BACK!
© 1993 United Feature Syndicate, Inc.
HERE'S THE WORLD FAMOUS ATTORNEY ON HIS WAY TO WASHINGTON TO TAKE HIS SEAT ON THE SUPREME COURT..
I DIDN'T EVEN GET TO THE JUDICIARY COMMITTEE..
5-26

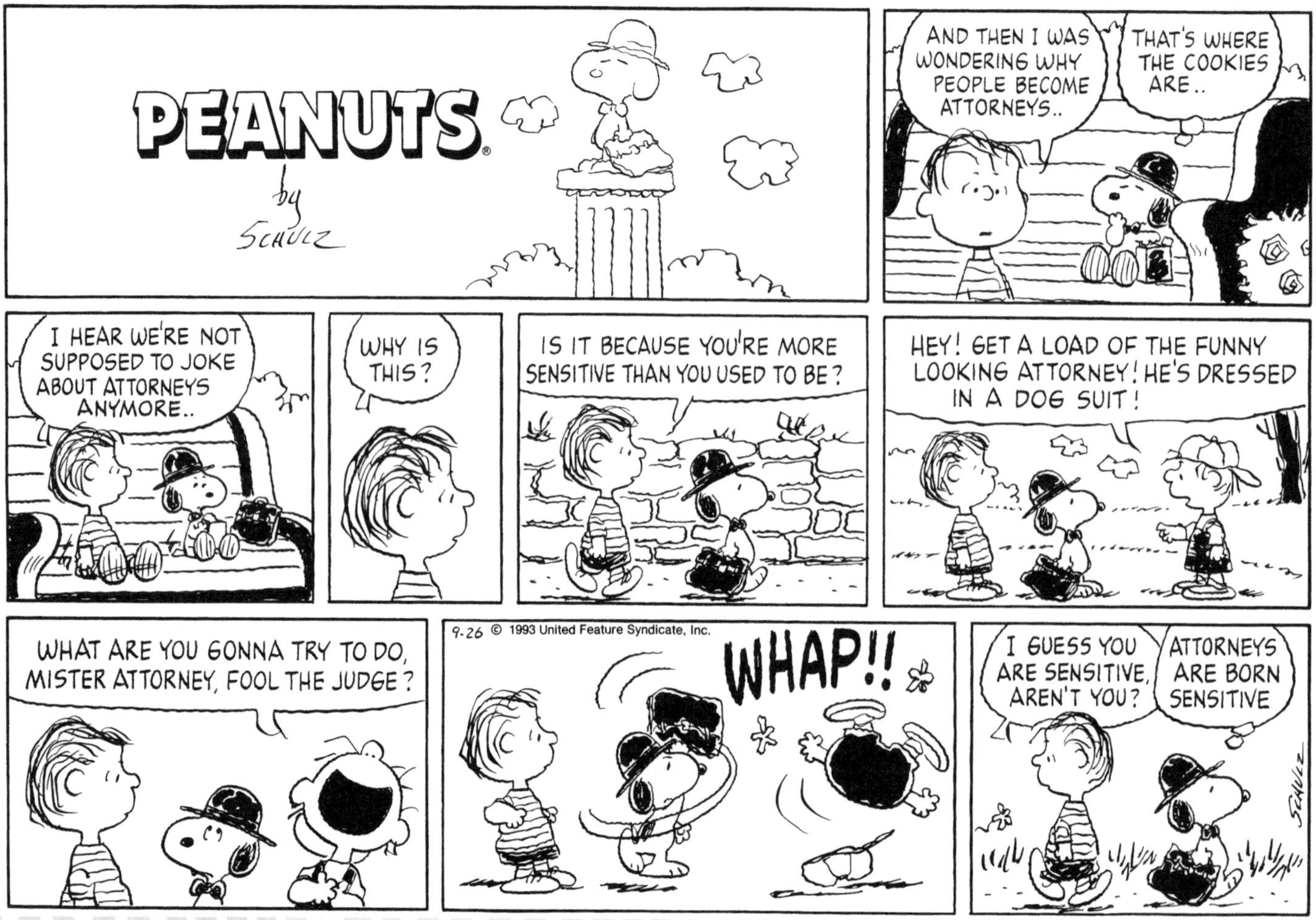
PEANUTS
by SCHULZ
AND THEN I WAS WONDERING WHY PEOPLE BECOME ATTORNEYS..
THAT'S WHERE THE COOKIES ARE..
I HEAR WE'RE NOT SUPPOSED TO JOKE ABOUT ATTORNEYS ANYMORE..
WHY IS THIS?
IS IT BECAUSE YOU'RE MORE SENSITIVE THAN YOU USED TO BE?
HEY! GET A LOAD OF THE FUNNY LOOKING ATTORNEY! HE'S DRESSED IN A DOG SUIT!
WHAT ARE YOU GONNA TRY TO DO, MISTER ATTORNEY, FOOL THE JUDGE?
9-26 © 1993 United Feature Syndicate, Inc.
WHAP!!
I GUESS YOU ARE SENSITIVE, AREN'T YOU?
ATTORNEYS ARE BORN SENSITIVE
SCHULZ

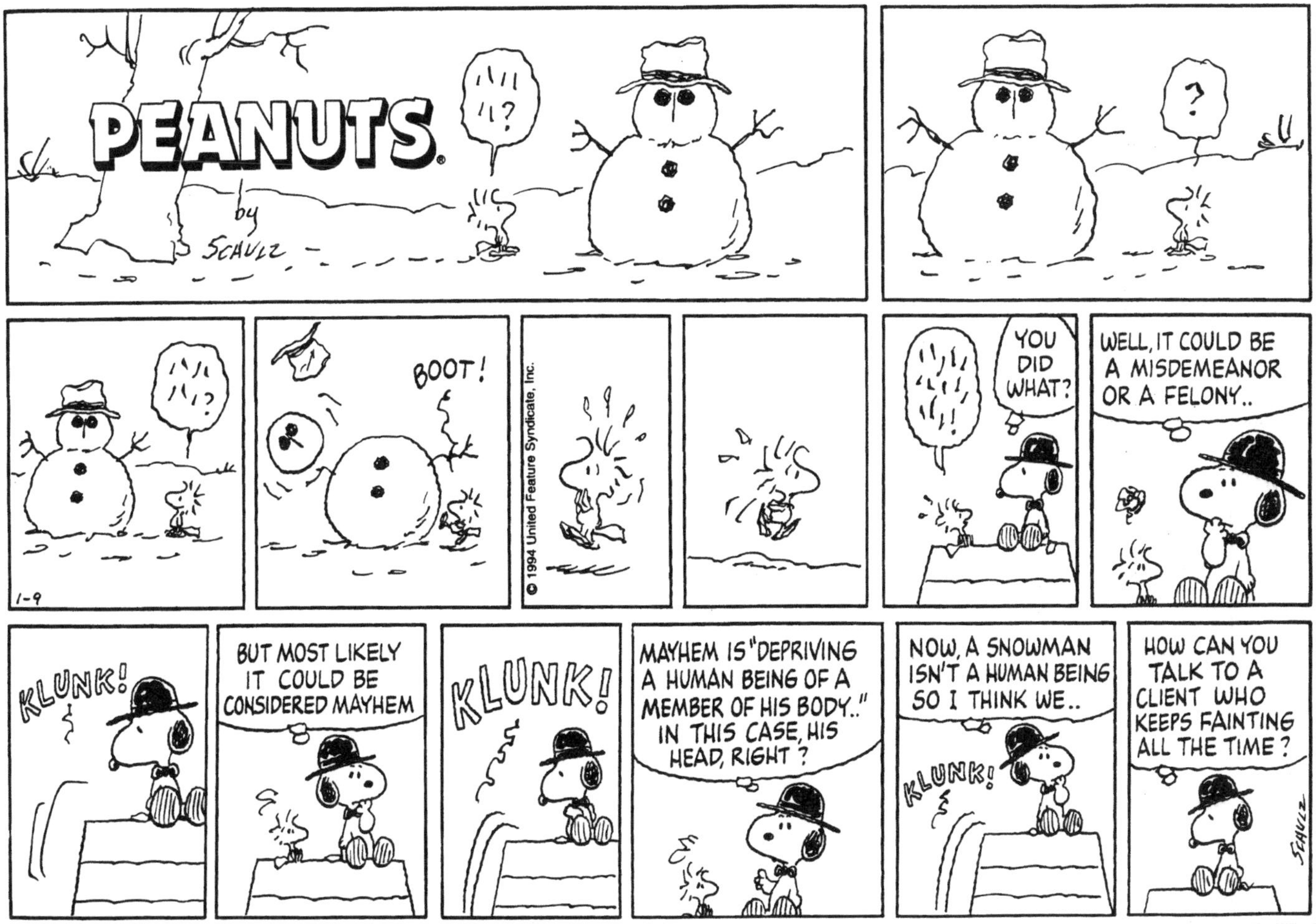
PEANUTS
by SCHULZ
?
BOOT!
© 1994 United Feature Syndicate, Inc.
1-9
YOU DID WHAT?
WELL, IT COULD BE A MISDEMEANOR OR A FELONY..
KLUNK!
BUT MOST LIKELY IT COULD BE CONSIDERED MAYHEM
KLUNK!
MAYHEM IS "DEPRIVING A HUMAN BEING OF A MEMBER OF HIS BODY.." IN THIS CASE, HIS HEAD, RIGHT ?
NOW, A SNOWMAN ISN'T A HUMAN BEING SO I THINK WE..
KLUNK!
HOW CAN YOU TALK TO A CLIENT WHO KEEPS FAINTING ALL THE TIME ?
SCHULZ

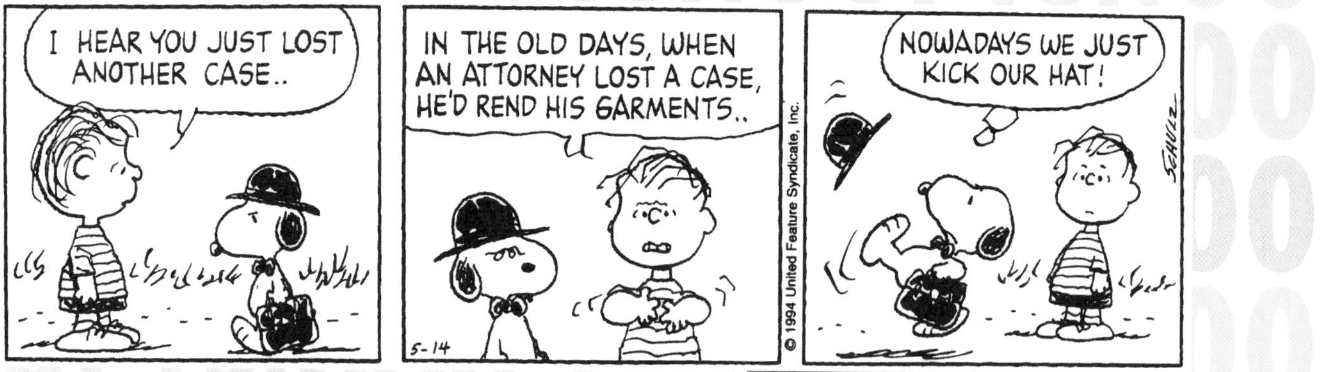

I HEAR YOU JUST LOST ANOTHER CASE..
IN THE OLD DAYS, WHEN AN ATTORNEY LOST A CASE, HE'D REND HIS GARMENTS..
5-14
© 1994 United Feature Syndicate, Inc.
NOWADAYS WE JUST KICK OUR HAT!
SCHULZ

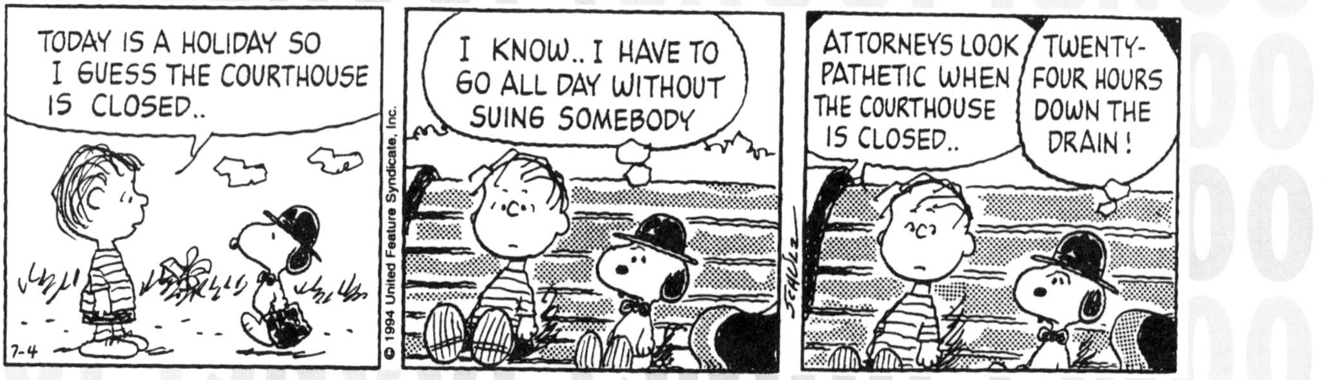

TODAY IS A HOLIDAY SO I GUESS THE COURTHOUSE IS CLOSED..
7-4
© 1994 United Feature Syndicate, Inc.
I KNOW.. I HAVE TO GO ALL DAY WITHOUT SUING SOMEBODY
SCHULZ
ATTORNEYS LOOK PATHETIC WHEN THE COURTHOUSE IS CLOSED..
TWENTY-FOUR HOURS DOWN THE DRAIN!

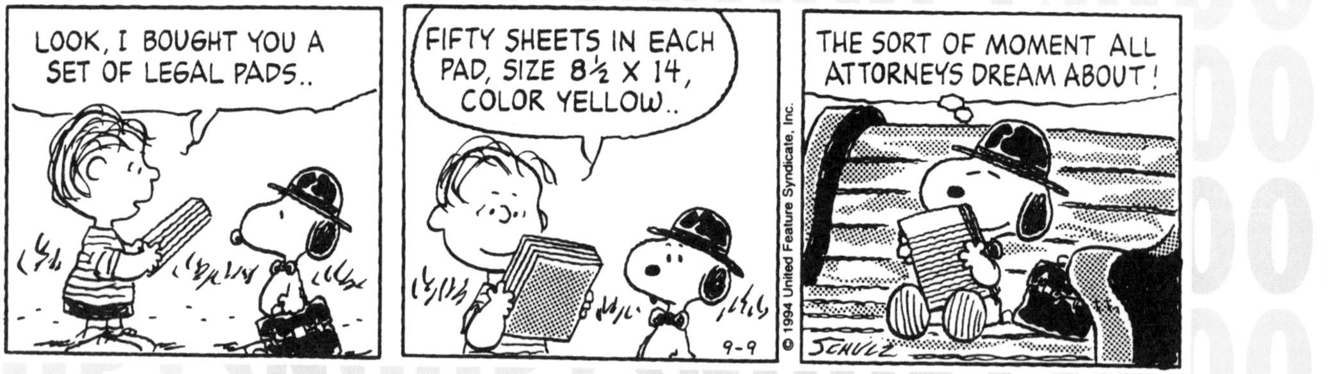

LOOK, I BOUGHT YOU A SET OF LEGAL PADS..
FIFTY SHEETS IN EACH PAD, SIZE 8½ X 14, COLOR YELLOW..
9-9
© 1994 United Feature Syndicate, Inc.
THE SORT OF MOMENT ALL ATTORNEYS DREAM ABOUT!
SCHULZ

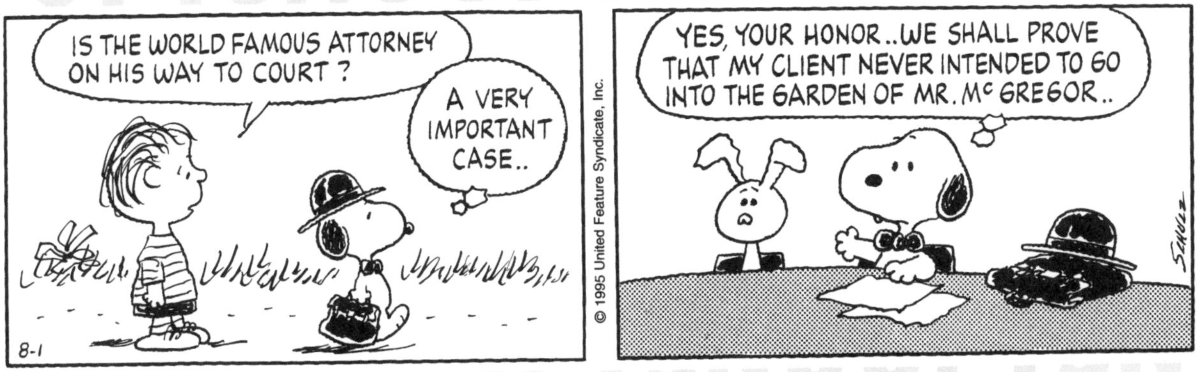

IS THE WORLD FAMOUS ATTORNEY ON HIS WAY TO COURT ?
A VERY IMPORTANT CASE..
8-1
© 1995 United Feature Syndicate, Inc.
YES, YOUR HONOR..WE SHALL PROVE THAT MY CLIENT NEVER INTENDED TO GO INTO THE GARDEN OF MR. MC GREGOR..
SCHULZ

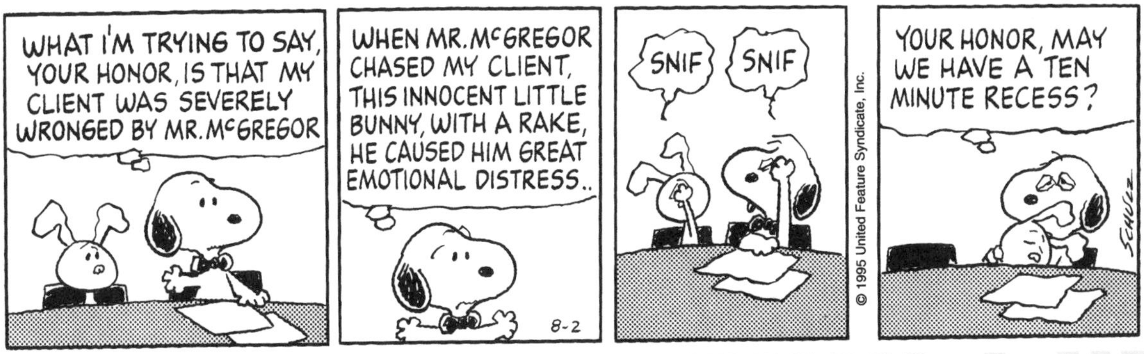

WHAT I'M TRYING TO SAY, YOUR HONOR, IS THAT MY CLIENT WAS SEVERELY WRONGED BY MR. MCGREGOR
WHEN MR. MCGREGOR CHASED MY CLIENT, THIS INNOCENT LITTLE BUNNY, WITH A RAKE, HE CAUSED HIM GREAT EMOTIONAL DISTRESS..
8-2
SNIF
SNIF
© 1995 United Feature Syndicate, Inc.
YOUR HONOR, MAY WE HAVE A TEN MINUTE RECESS ?
SCHULZ

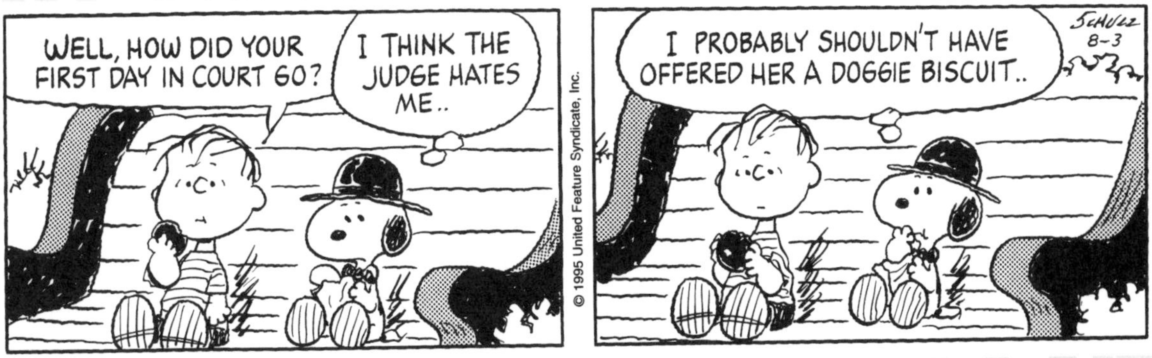

WELL, HOW DID YOUR FIRST DAY IN COURT GO?
I THINK THE JUDGE HATES ME..
© 1995 United Feature Syndicate, Inc.
I PROBABLY SHOULDN'T HAVE OFFERED HER A DOGGIE BISCUIT..
SCHULZ 8-3

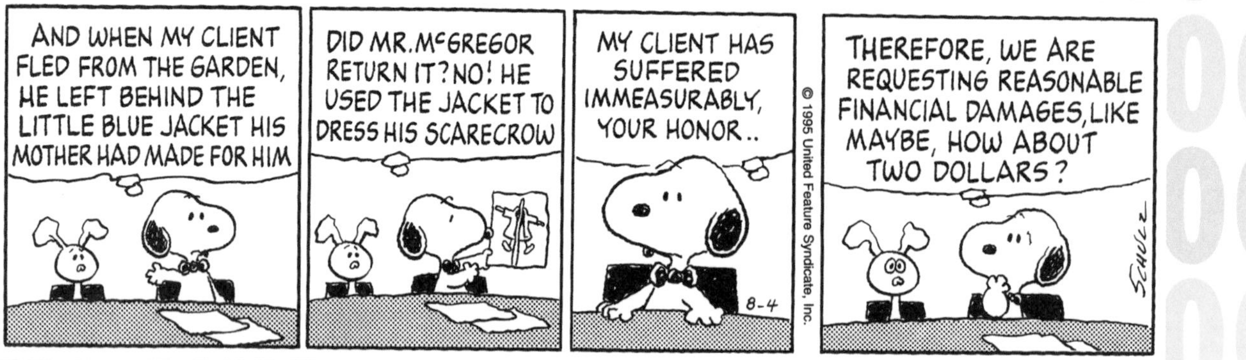
AND WHEN MY CLIENT FLED FROM THE GARDEN, HE LEFT BEHIND THE LITTLE BLUE JACKET HIS MOTHER HAD MADE FOR HIM
DID MR. McGREGOR RETURN IT? NO! HE USED THE JACKET TO DRESS HIS SCARECROW
MY CLIENT HAS SUFFERED IMMEASURABLY, YOUR HONOR..
8-4
© 1995 United Feature Syndicate, Inc.
THEREFORE, WE ARE REQUESTING REASONABLE FINANCIAL DAMAGES, LIKE MAYBE, HOW ABOUT TWO DOLLARS?
SCHULZ

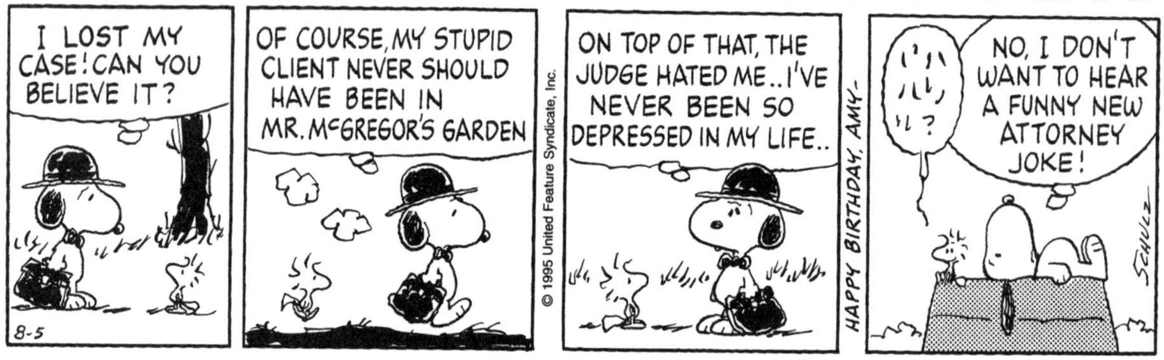
I LOST MY CASE! CAN YOU BELIEVE IT?
8-5
OF COURSE, MY STUPID CLIENT NEVER SHOULD HAVE BEEN IN MR. McGREGOR'S GARDEN
© 1995 United Feature Syndicate, Inc.
ON TOP OF THAT, THE JUDGE HATED ME.. I'VE NEVER BEEN SO DEPRESSED IN MY LIFE..
HAPPY BIRTHDAY, AMY-
NO, I DON'T WANT TO HEAR A FUNNY NEW ATTORNEY JOKE!
SCHULZ

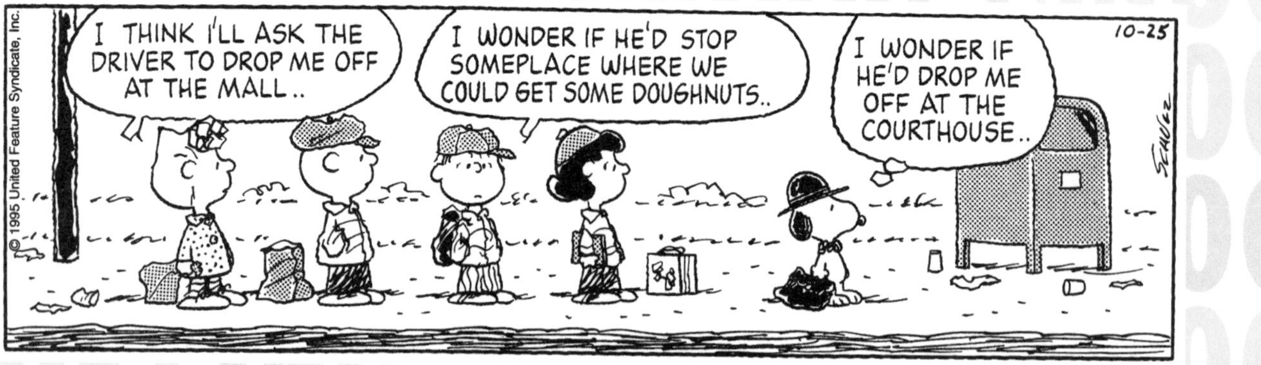
© 1995 United Feature Syndicate, Inc.
I THINK I'LL ASK THE DRIVER TO DROP ME OFF AT THE MALL..
I WONDER IF HE'D STOP SOMEPLACE WHERE WE COULD GET SOME DOUGHNUTS..
I WONDER IF HE'D DROP ME OFF AT THE COURTHOUSE..
10-25
SCHULZ

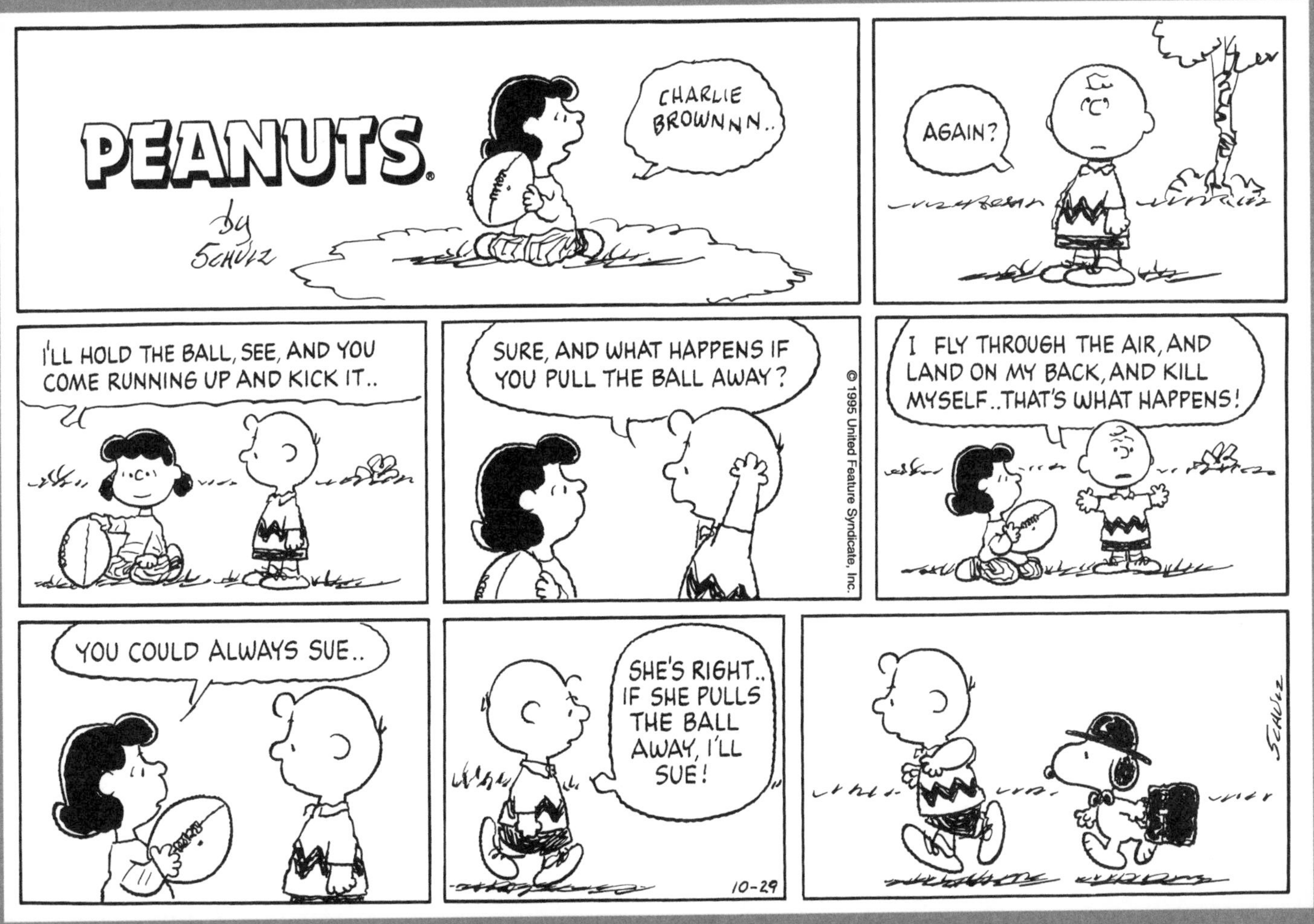
PEANUTS
by SCHULZ
CHARLIE BROWNNN..
AGAIN?
I'LL HOLD THE BALL, SEE, AND YOU COME RUNNING UP AND KICK IT..
SURE, AND WHAT HAPPENS IF YOU PULL THE BALL AWAY?
© 1995 United Feature Syndicate, Inc.
I FLY THROUGH THE AIR, AND LAND ON MY BACK, AND KILL MYSELF..THAT'S WHAT HAPPENS!
YOU COULD ALWAYS SUE..
SHE'S RIGHT.. IF SHE PULLS THE BALL AWAY, I'LL SUE!
10-29
SCHULZ

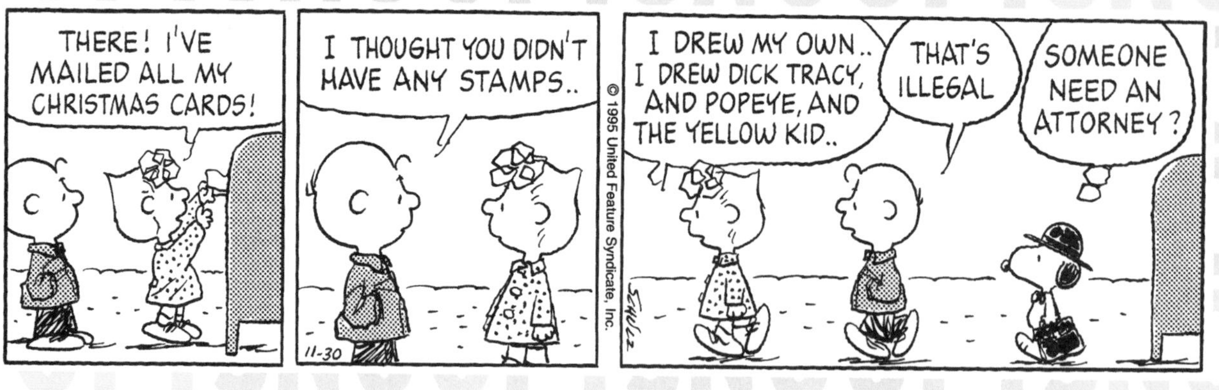
THERE! I'VE MAILED ALL MY CHRISTMAS CARDS!
I THOUGHT YOU DIDN'T HAVE ANY STAMPS..
I DREW MY OWN.. I DREW DICK TRACY, AND POPEYE, AND THE YELLOW KID..
THAT'S ILLEGAL
SOMEONE NEED AN ATTORNEY?
11-30
© 1995 United Feature Syndicate, Inc.
SCHULZ

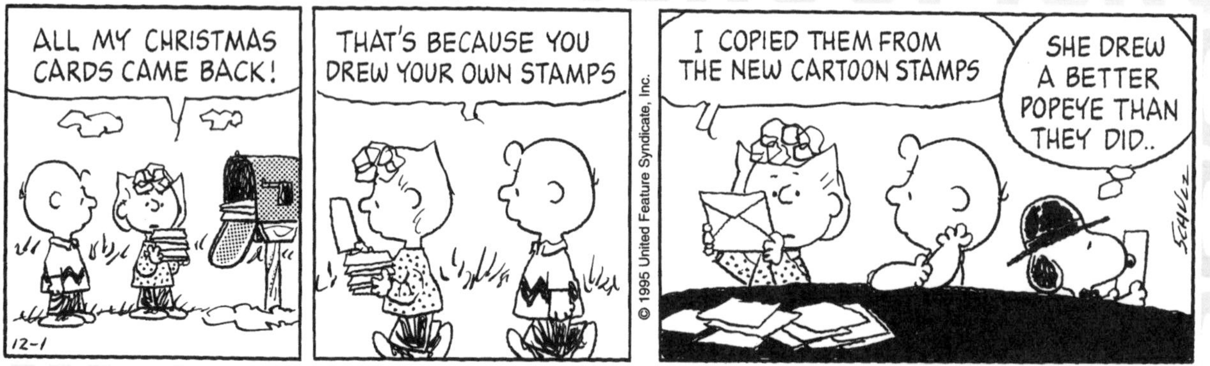
ALL MY CHRISTMAS CARDS CAME BACK!
THAT'S BECAUSE YOU DREW YOUR OWN STAMPS
I COPIED THEM FROM THE NEW CARTOON STAMPS
SHE DREW A BETTER POPEYE THAN THEY DID..
12-1
© 1995 United Feature Syndicate, Inc.
SCHULZ

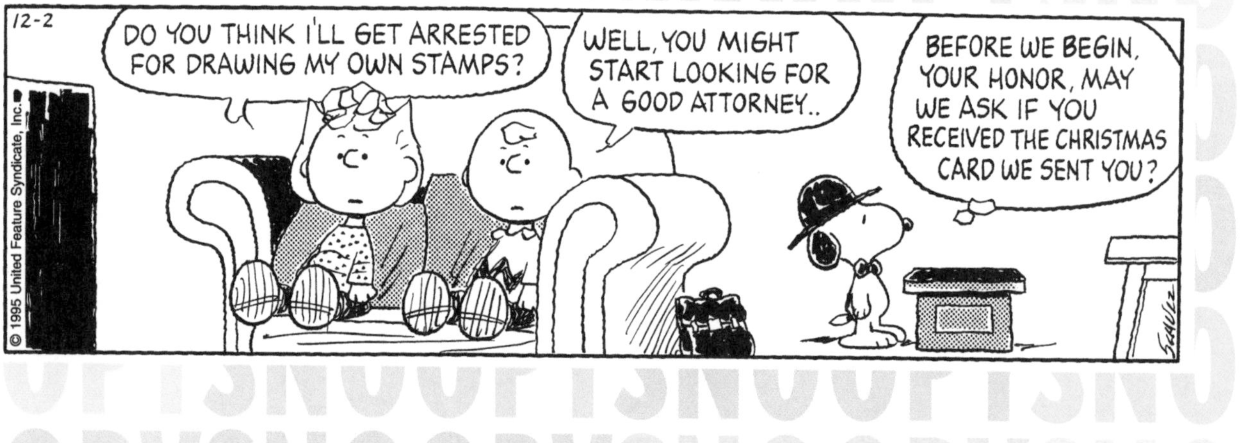
12-2
DO YOU THINK I'LL GET ARRESTED FOR DRAWING MY OWN STAMPS?
WELL, YOU MIGHT START LOOKING FOR A GOOD ATTORNEY..
BEFORE WE BEGIN, YOUR HONOR, MAY WE ASK IF YOU RECEIVED THE CHRISTMAS CARD WE SENT YOU?
© 1995 United Feature Syndicate, Inc.
SCHULZ

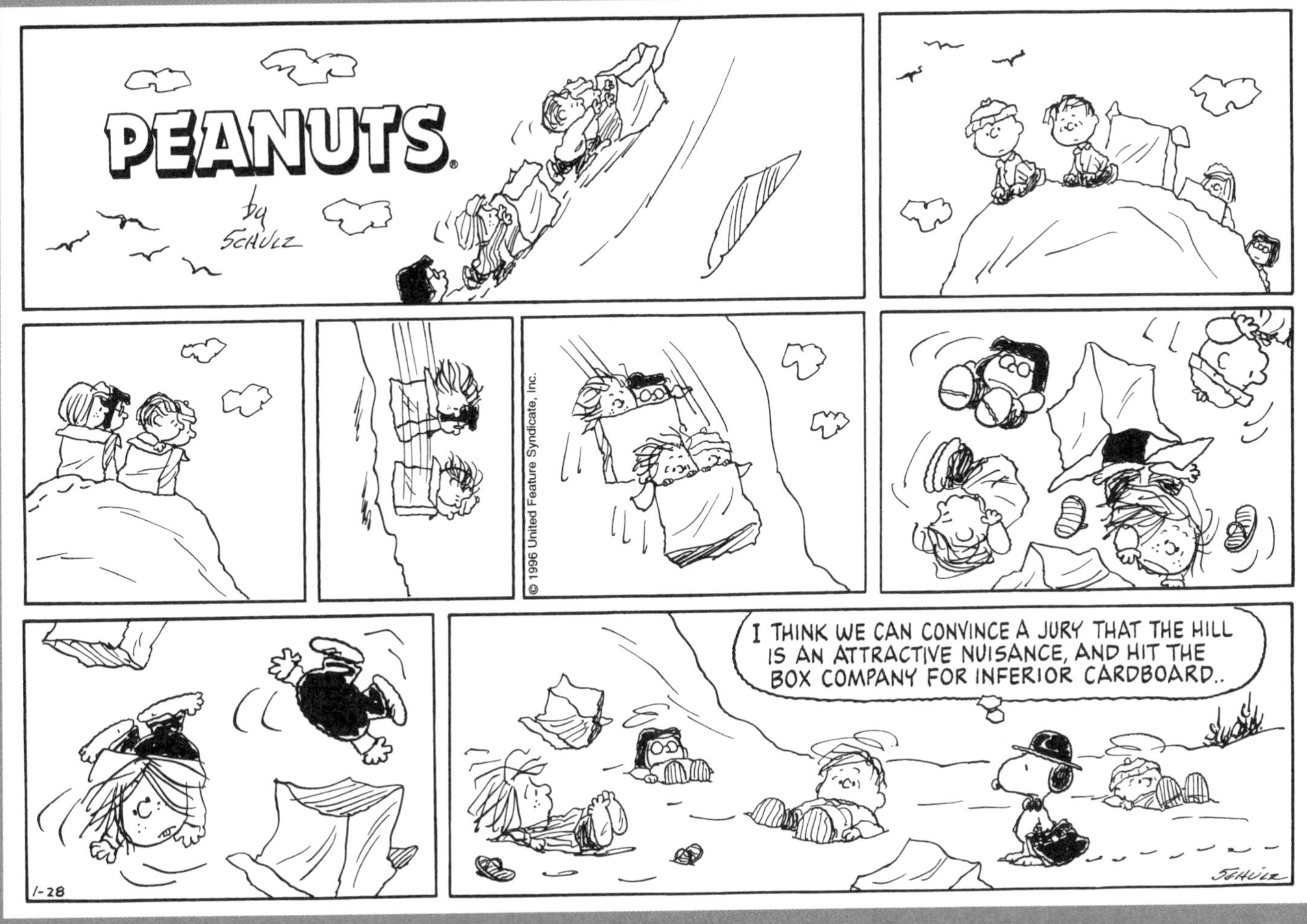
PEANUTS®
by SCHULZ
© 1996 United Feature Syndicate, Inc.
I THINK WE CAN CONVINCE A JURY THAT THE HILL IS AN ATTRACTIVE NUISANCE, AND HIT THE BOX COMPANY FOR INFERIOR CARDBOARD..
1-28
SCHULZ

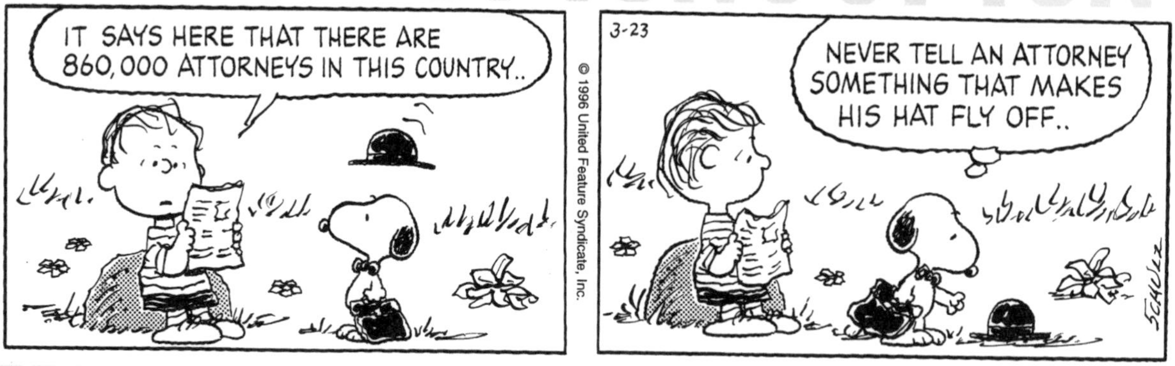
IT SAYS HERE THAT THERE ARE 860,000 ATTORNEYS IN THIS COUNTRY..
© 1996 United Feature Syndicate, Inc.
3-23
NEVER TELL AN ATTORNEY SOMETHING THAT MAKES HIS HAT FLY OFF..
SCHULZ

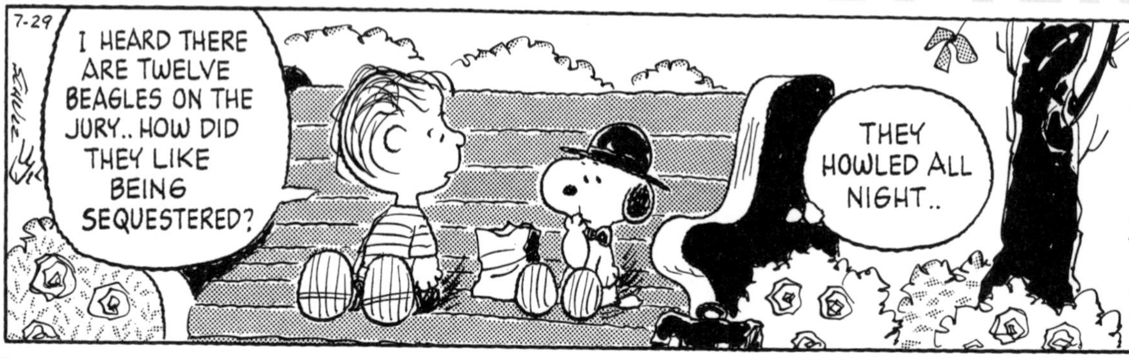
7-29
I HEARD THERE ARE TWELVE BEAGLES ON THE JURY.. HOW DID THEY LIKE BEING SEQUESTERED?
THEY HOWLED ALL NIGHT..
© 1996 United Feature Syndicate, Inc.

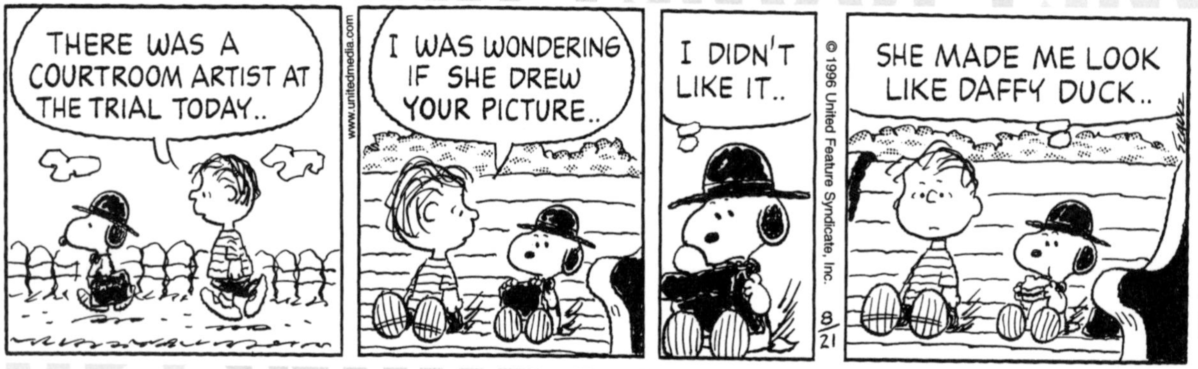
THERE WAS A COURTROOM ARTIST AT THE TRIAL TODAY..
www.unitedmedia.com
I WAS WONDERING IF SHE DREW YOUR PICTURE..
I DIDN'T LIKE IT..
© 1996 United Feature Syndicate, Inc.
8/21
SHE MADE ME LOOK LIKE DAFFY DUCK..

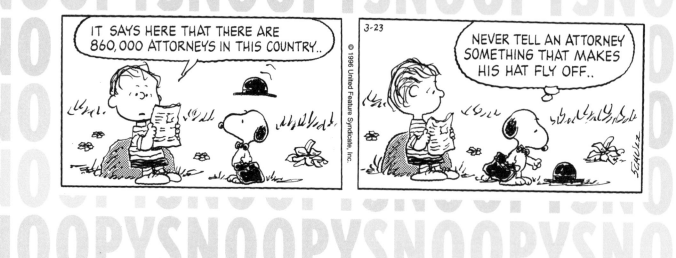

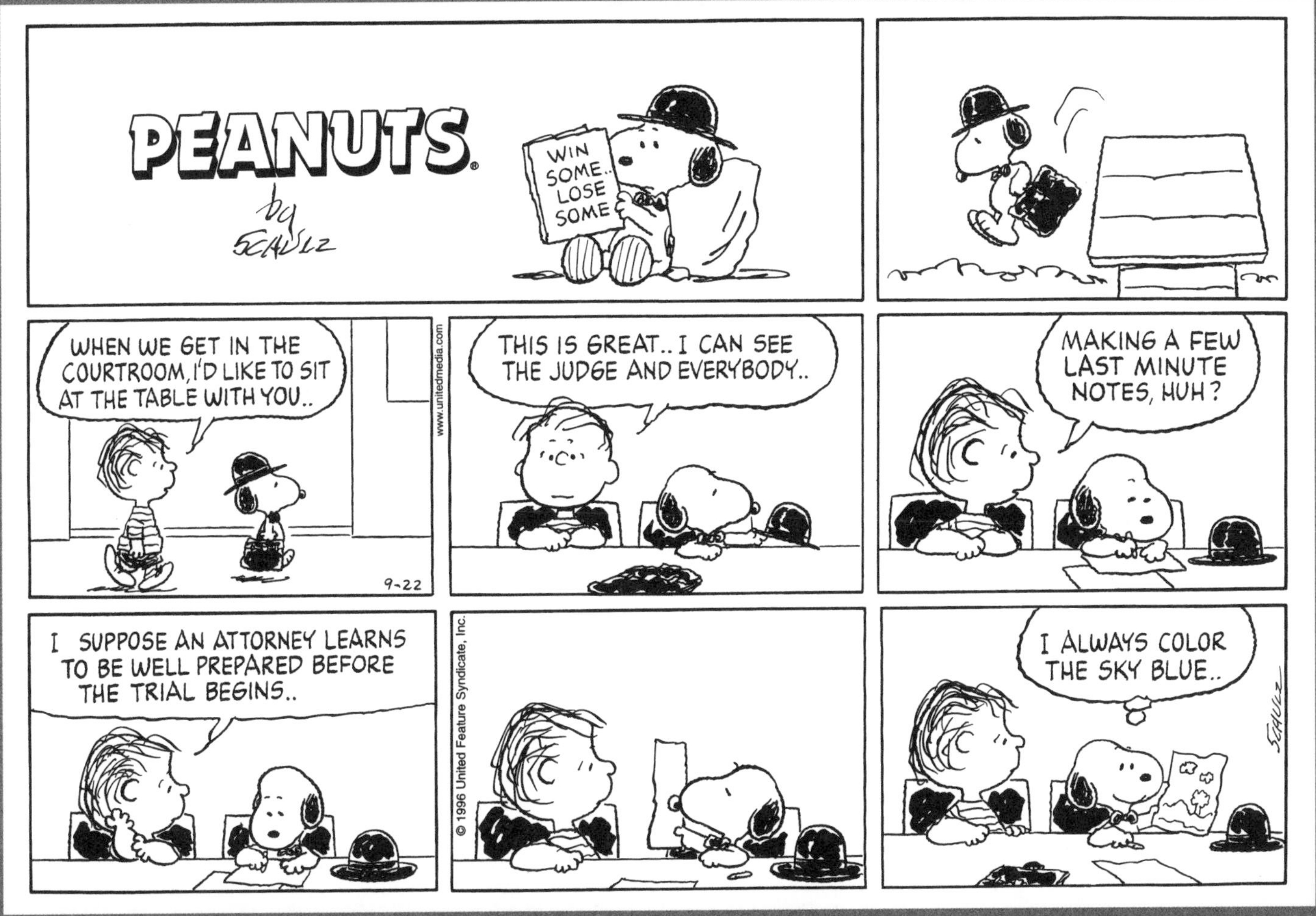
PEANUTS
by SCHULZ
WIN SOME.. LOSE SOME
WHEN WE GET IN THE COURTROOM, I'D LIKE TO SIT AT THE TABLE WITH YOU..
www.unitedmedia.com
9-22
THIS IS GREAT.. I CAN SEE THE JUDGE AND EVERYBODY..
MAKING A FEW LAST MINUTE NOTES, HUH?
I SUPPOSE AN ATTORNEY LEARNS TO BE WELL PREPARED BEFORE THE TRIAL BEGINS..
© 1996 United Feature Syndicate, Inc.
I ALWAYS COLOR THE SKY BLUE..
SCHULZ

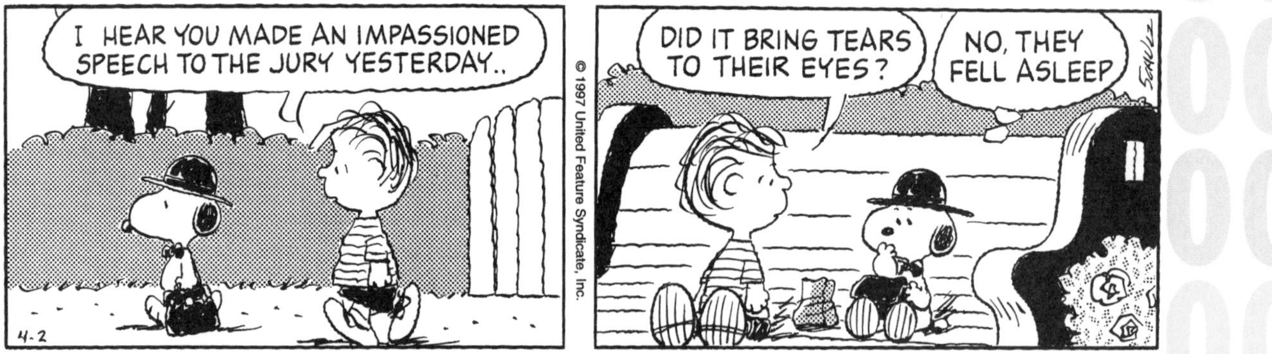
I HEAR YOU MADE AN IMPASSIONED SPEECH TO THE JURY YESTERDAY..
DID IT BRING TEARS TO THEIR EYES?
NO, THEY FELL ASLEEP
© 1997 United Feature Syndicate, Inc.
SCHULZ
4-2

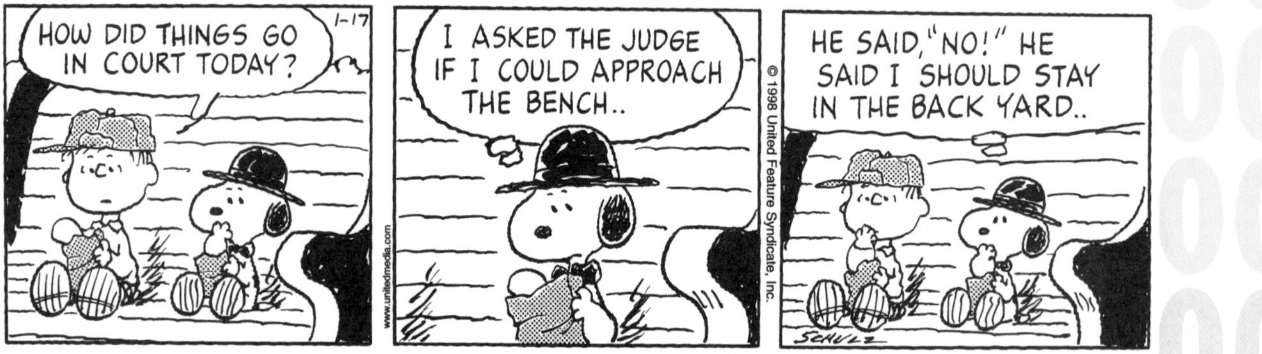
1-17
HOW DID THINGS GO IN COURT TODAY?
I ASKED THE JUDGE IF I COULD APPROACH THE BENCH..
HE SAID, "NO!" HE SAID I SHOULD STAY IN THE BACK YARD..
© 1998 United Feature Syndicate, Inc.
www.unitedmedia.com
SCHULZ

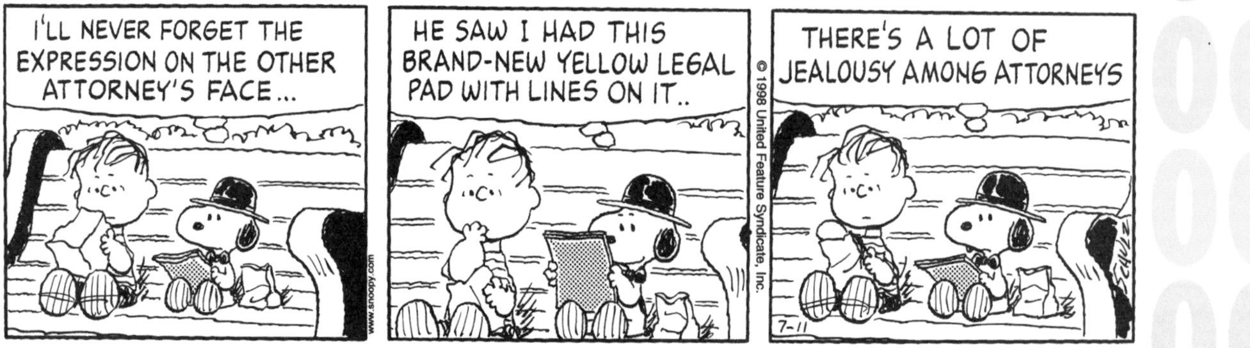
I'LL NEVER FORGET THE EXPRESSION ON THE OTHER ATTORNEY'S FACE...
HE SAW I HAD THIS BRAND-NEW YELLOW LEGAL PAD WITH LINES ON IT..
THERE'S A LOT OF JEALOUSY AMONG ATTORNEYS
© 1998 United Feature Syndicate, Inc.
www.snoopy.com
SCHULZ
7-11

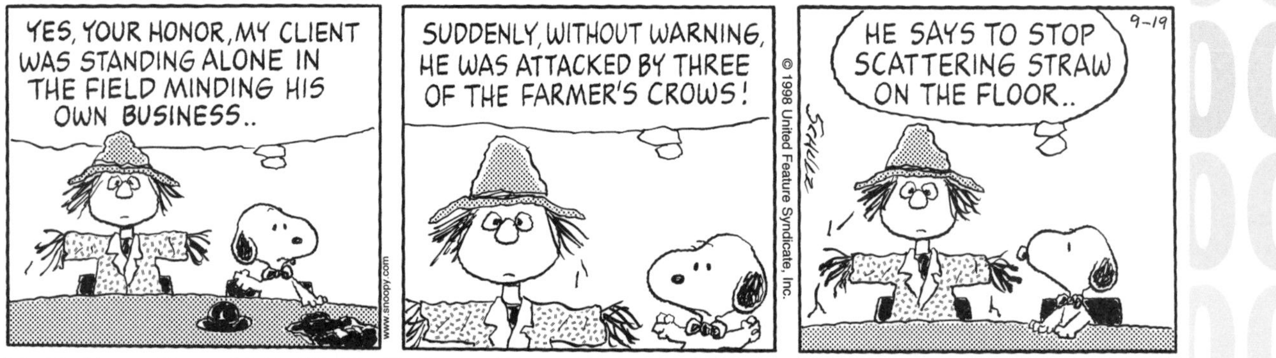
YES, YOUR HONOR, MY CLIENT WAS STANDING ALONE IN THE FIELD MINDING HIS OWN BUSINESS..
SUDDENLY, WITHOUT WARNING, HE WAS ATTACKED BY THREE OF THE FARMER'S CROWS!
HE SAYS TO STOP SCATTERING STRAW ON THE FLOOR..
9-19
© 1998 United Feature Syndicate, Inc.
www.snoopy.com
SCHULZ

Flying Ace

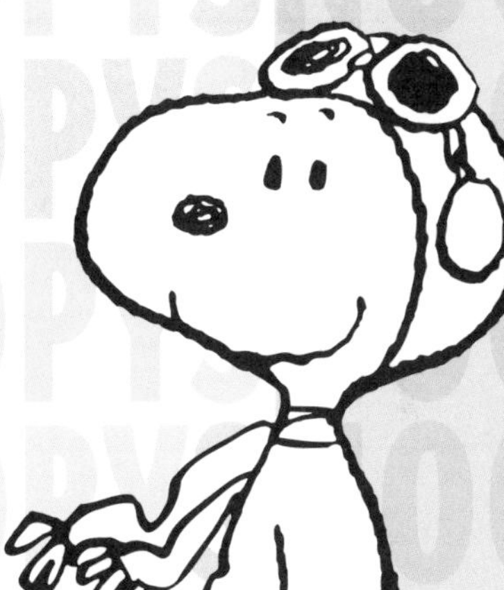

SNOOPY

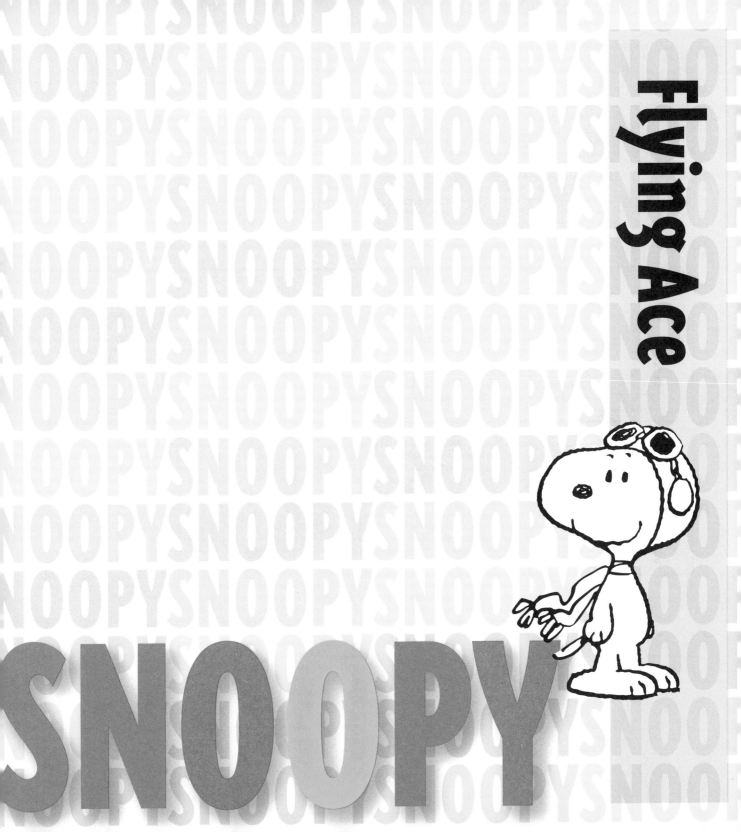

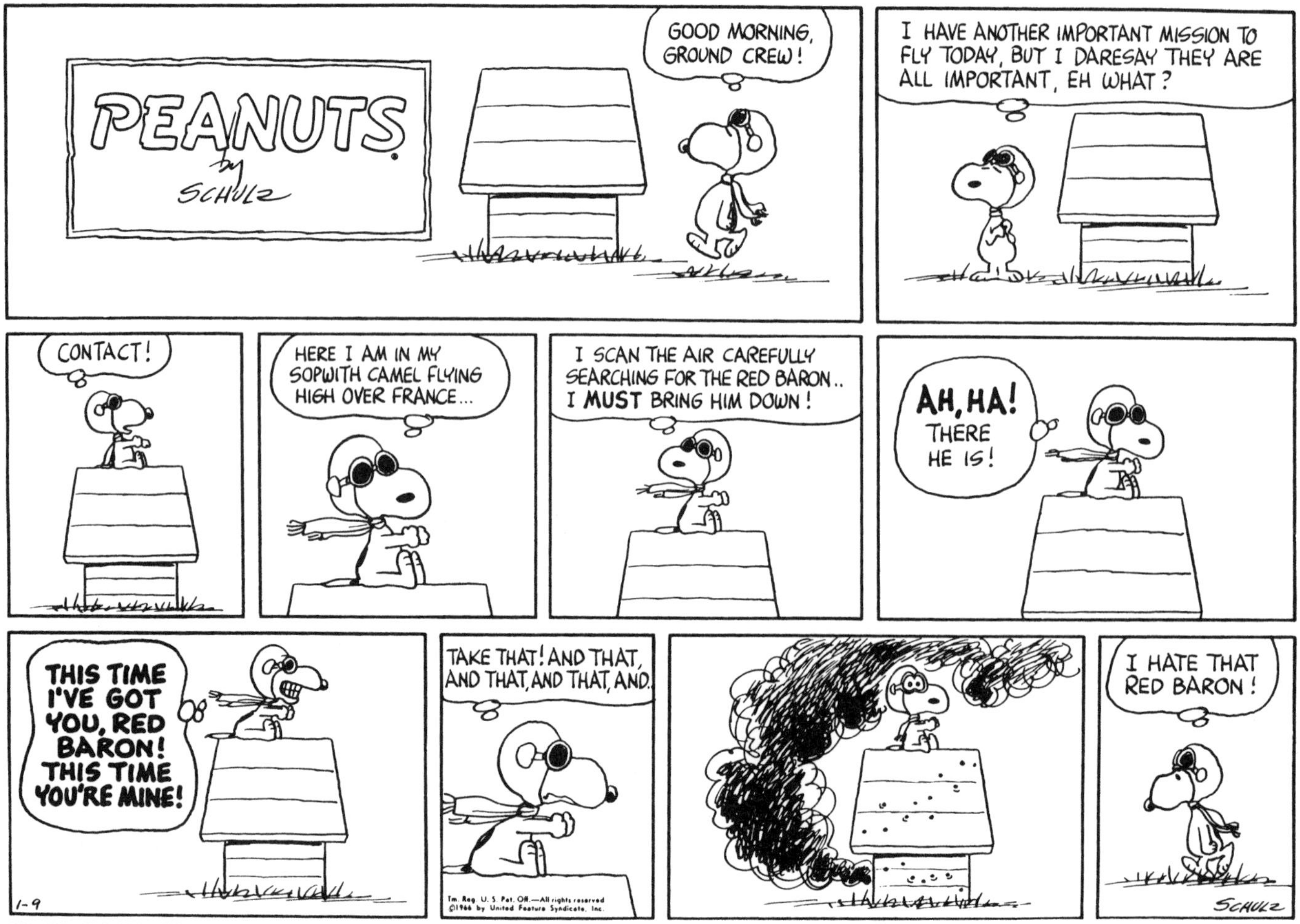
PEANUTS
by SCHULZ
GOOD MORNING, GROUND CREW!
I HAVE ANOTHER IMPORTANT MISSION TO FLY TODAY, BUT I DARESAY THEY ARE ALL IMPORTANT, EH WHAT?
CONTACT!
HERE I AM IN MY SOPWITH CAMEL FLYING HIGH OVER FRANCE...
I SCAN THE AIR CAREFULLY SEARCHING FOR THE RED BARON.. I MUST BRING HIM DOWN!
AH, HA! THERE HE IS!
THIS TIME I'VE GOT YOU, RED BARON! THIS TIME YOU'RE MINE!
1-9
TAKE THAT! AND THAT, AND THAT, AND THAT, AND.
Tm. Reg. U. S. Pat. Off.—All rights reserved ©1966 by United Feature Syndicate, Inc.
I HATE THAT RED BARON!
SCHULZ

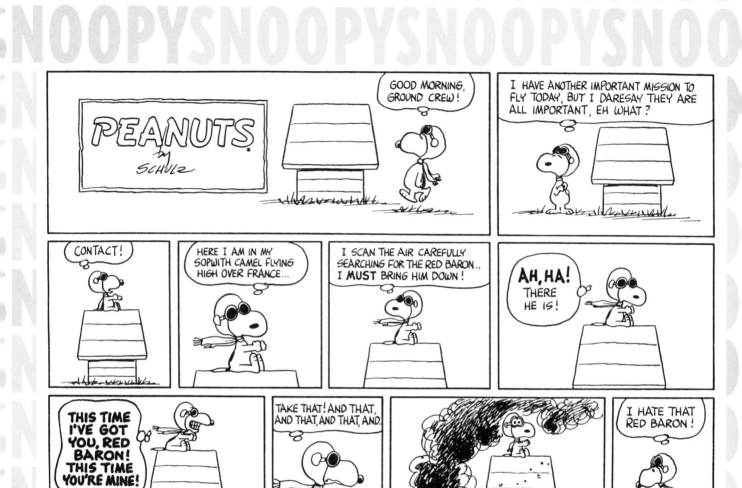

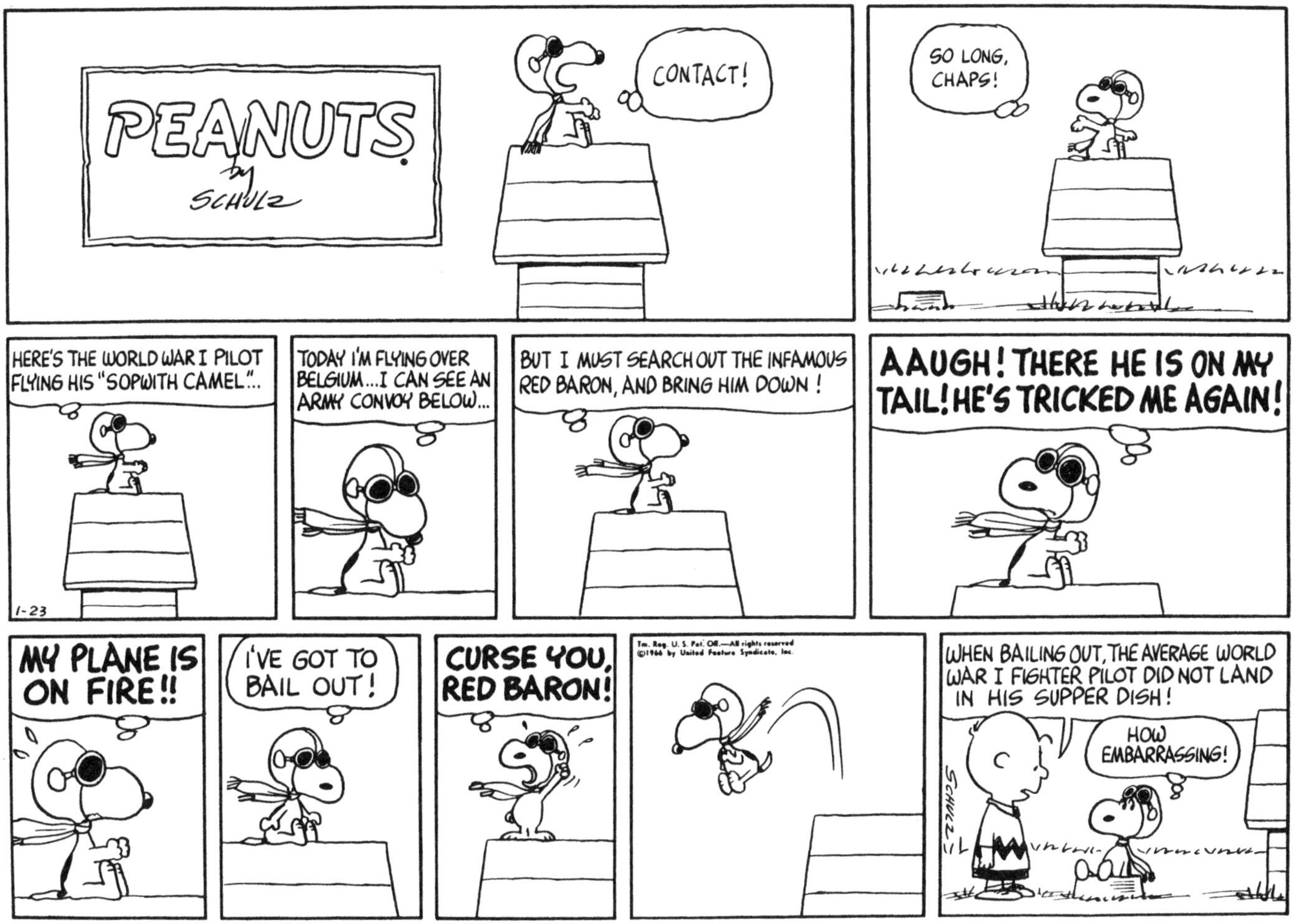

PEANUTS
by SCHULZ
CONTACT!
SO LONG, CHAPS!
HERE'S THE WORLD WAR I PILOT FLYING HIS "SOPWITH CAMEL"...
1-23
TODAY I'M FLYING OVER BELGIUM...I CAN SEE AN ARMY CONVOY BELOW...
BUT I MUST SEARCH OUT THE INFAMOUS RED BARON, AND BRING HIM DOWN!
AAUGH! THERE HE IS ON MY TAIL! HE'S TRICKED ME AGAIN!
MY PLANE IS ON FIRE!!
I'VE GOT TO BAIL OUT!
CURSE YOU, RED BARON!
Tm. Reg. U. S. Pat. Off.—All rights reserved ©1966 by United Feature Syndicate, Inc.
WHEN BAILING OUT, THE AVERAGE WORLD WAR I FIGHTER PILOT DID NOT LAND IN HIS SUPPER DISH!
HOW EMBARRASSING!
SCHULZ

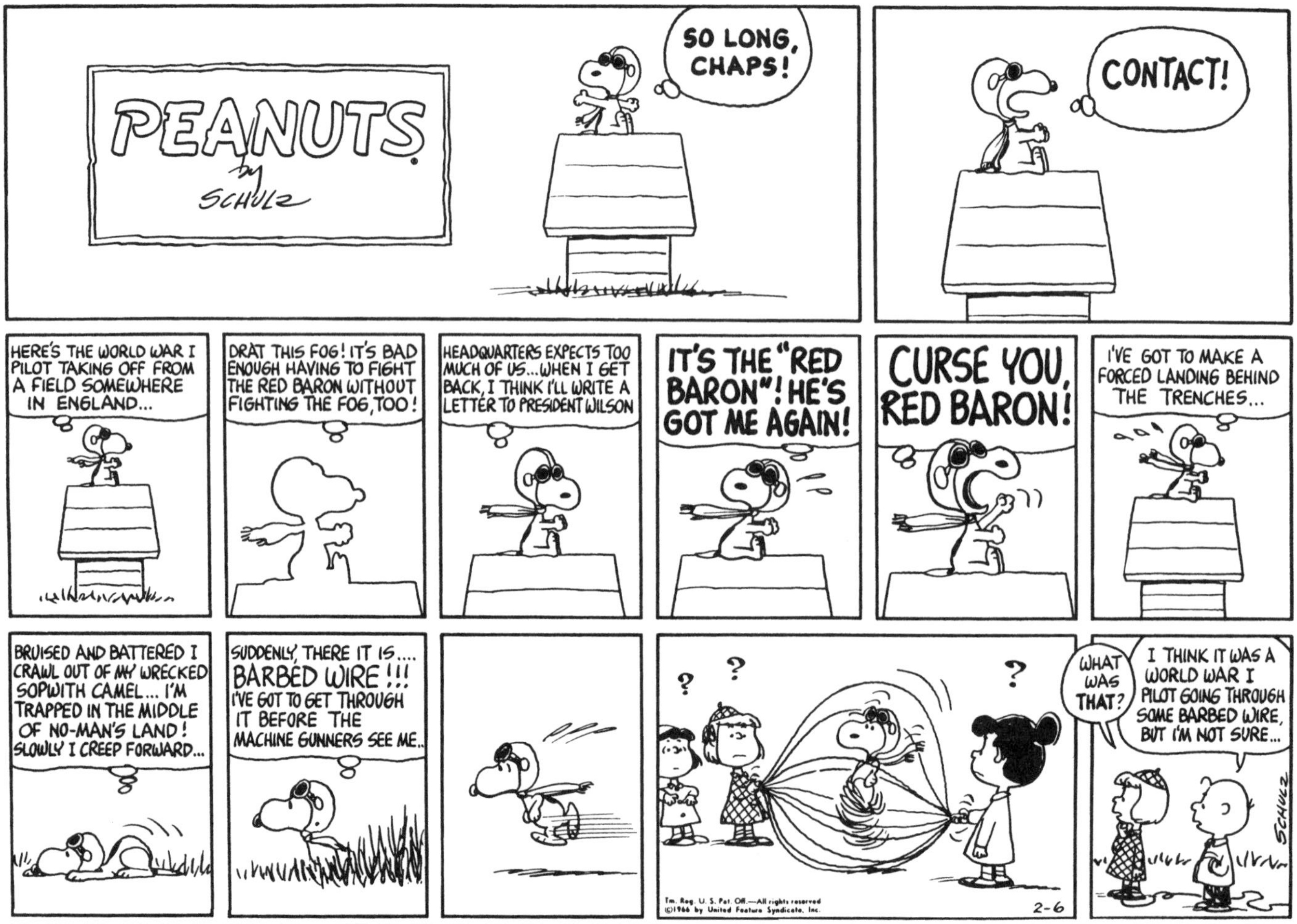
PEANUTS
by SCHULZ
SO LONG, CHAPS!
CONTACT!
HERE'S THE WORLD WAR I PILOT TAKING OFF FROM A FIELD SOMEWHERE IN ENGLAND...
DRAT THIS FOG! IT'S BAD ENOUGH HAVING TO FIGHT THE RED BARON WITHOUT FIGHTING THE FOG, TOO!
HEADQUARTERS EXPECTS TOO MUCH OF US...WHEN I GET BACK, I THINK I'LL WRITE A LETTER TO PRESIDENT WILSON
IT'S THE "RED BARON"! HE'S GOT ME AGAIN!
CURSE YOU, RED BARON!
I'VE GOT TO MAKE A FORCED LANDING BEHIND THE TRENCHES...
BRUISED AND BATTERED I CRAWL OUT OF MY WRECKED SOPWITH CAMEL... I'M TRAPPED IN THE MIDDLE OF NO-MAN'S LAND! SLOWLY I CREEP FORWARD...
SUDDENLY, THERE IT IS.... BARBED WIRE!!! I'VE GOT TO GET THROUGH IT BEFORE THE MACHINE GUNNERS SEE ME..
?
?
?
Tm. Reg. U. S. Pat. Off.—All rights reserved ©1966 by United Feature Syndicate, Inc.
2-6
WHAT WAS THAT?
I THINK IT WAS A WORLD WAR I PILOT GOING THROUGH SOME BARBED WIRE, BUT I'M NOT SURE...
SCHULZ

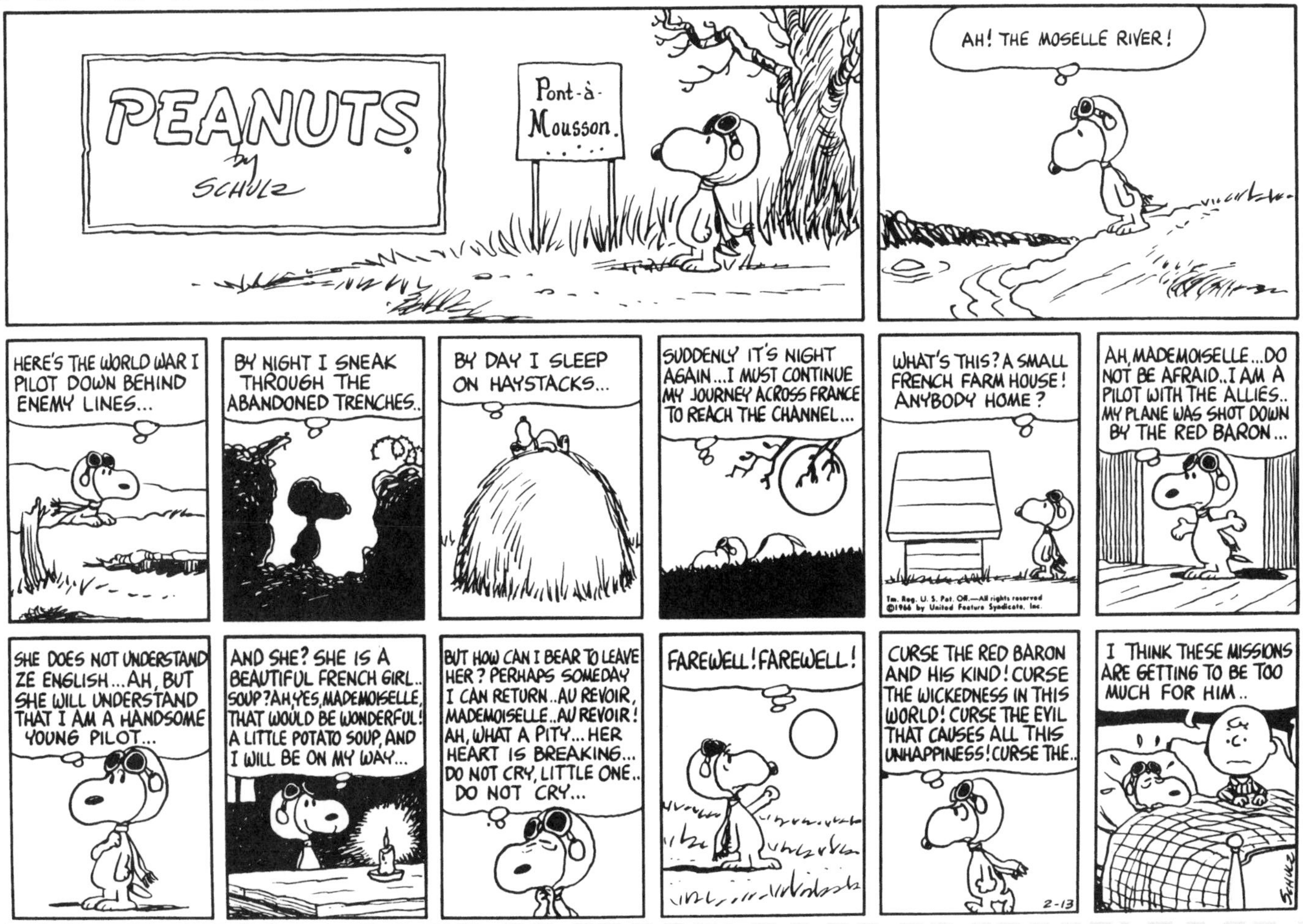
PEANUTS
by SCHULZ
Pont-à-Mousson
AH! THE MOSELLE RIVER!
HERE'S THE WORLD WAR I PILOT DOWN BEHIND ENEMY LINES...
BY NIGHT I SNEAK THROUGH THE ABANDONED TRENCHES..
BY DAY I SLEEP ON HAYSTACKS...
SUDDENLY IT'S NIGHT AGAIN...I MUST CONTINUE MY JOURNEY ACROSS FRANCE TO REACH THE CHANNEL...
WHAT'S THIS? A SMALL FRENCH FARM HOUSE! ANYBODY HOME?
Tm. Reg. U. S. Pat. Off.—All rights reserved ©1966 by United Feature Syndicate, Inc.
AH, MADEMOISELLE...DO NOT BE AFRAID..I AM A PILOT WITH THE ALLIES.. MY PLANE WAS SHOT DOWN BY THE RED BARON...
SHE DOES NOT UNDERSTAND ZE ENGLISH...AH, BUT SHE WILL UNDERSTAND THAT I AM A HANDSOME YOUNG PILOT...
AND SHE? SHE IS A BEAUTIFUL FRENCH GIRL.. SOUP? AH, YES, MADEMOISELLE, THAT WOULD BE WONDERFUL! A LITTLE POTATO SOUP, AND I WILL BE ON MY WAY...
BUT HOW CAN I BEAR TO LEAVE HER? PERHAPS SOMEDAY I CAN RETURN..AU REVOIR, MADEMOISELLE..AU REVOIR! AH, WHAT A PITY...HER HEART IS BREAKING... DO NOT CRY, LITTLE ONE.. DO NOT CRY...
FAREWELL! FAREWELL!
CURSE THE RED BARON AND HIS KIND! CURSE THE WICKEDNESS IN THIS WORLD! CURSE THE EVIL THAT CAUSES ALL THIS UNHAPPINESS! CURSE THE..
2-13
I THINK THESE MISSIONS ARE GETTING TO BE TOO MUCH FOR HIM..
SCHULZ

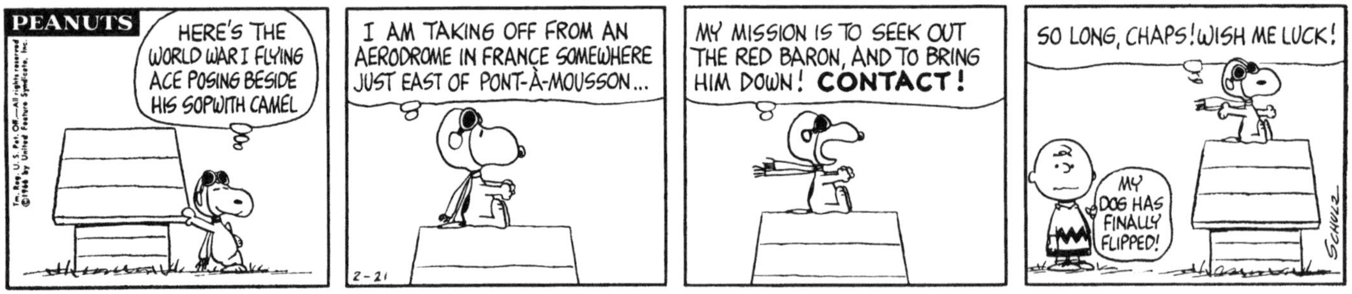
PEANUTS
Tm. Reg. U.S. Pat. Off.—All rights reserved ©1966 by United Feature Syndicate, Inc.
HERE'S THE WORLD WAR I FLYING ACE POSING BESIDE HIS SOPWITH CAMEL
I AM TAKING OFF FROM AN AERODROME IN FRANCE SOMEWHERE JUST EAST OF PONT-À-MOUSSON...
2-21
MY MISSION IS TO SEEK OUT THE RED BARON, AND TO BRING HIM DOWN! CONTACT!
SO LONG, CHAPS! WISH ME LUCK!
MY DOG HAS FINALLY FLIPPED!
SCHULZ

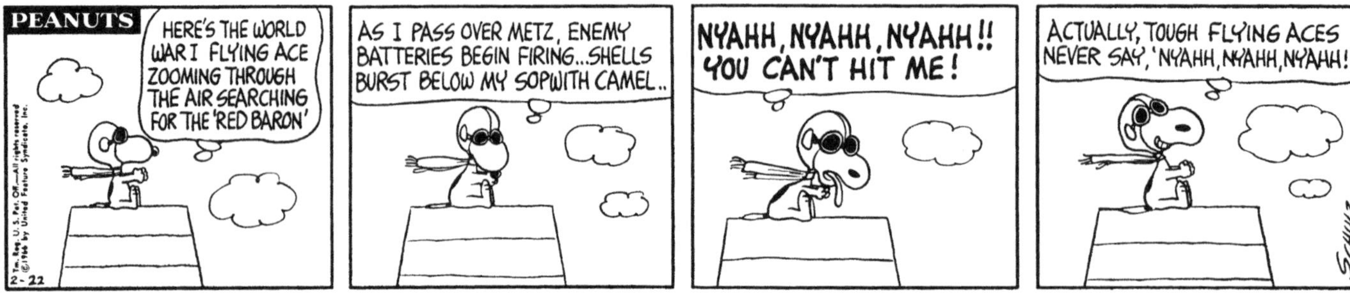
PEANUTS
Tm. Reg. U.S. Pat. Off.—All rights reserved ©1966 by United Feature Syndicate, Inc.
2-22
HERE'S THE WORLD WAR I FLYING ACE ZOOMING THROUGH THE AIR SEARCHING FOR THE 'RED BARON'
AS I PASS OVER METZ, ENEMY BATTERIES BEGIN FIRING...SHELLS BURST BELOW MY SOPWITH CAMEL..
NYAHH, NYAHH, NYAHH!! YOU CAN'T HIT ME!
ACTUALLY, TOUGH FLYING ACES NEVER SAY, 'NYAHH, NYAHH, NYAHH!'
SCHULZ

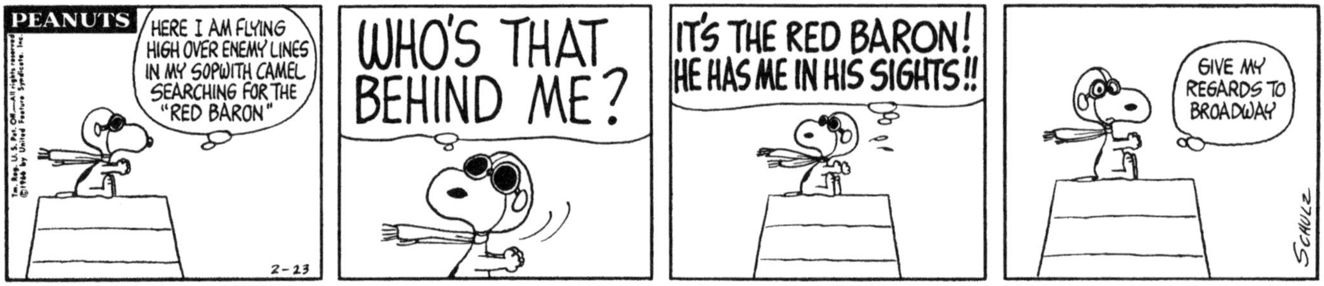
PEANUTS
Tm. Reg. U.S. Pat. Off.—All rights reserved ©1966 by United Feature Syndicate, Inc.
HERE I AM FLYING HIGH OVER ENEMY LINES IN MY SOPWITH CAMEL SEARCHING FOR THE "RED BARON"
2-23
WHO'S THAT BEHIND ME?
IT'S THE RED BARON! HE HAS ME IN HIS SIGHTS!!
GIVE MY REGARDS TO BROADWAY
SCHULZ

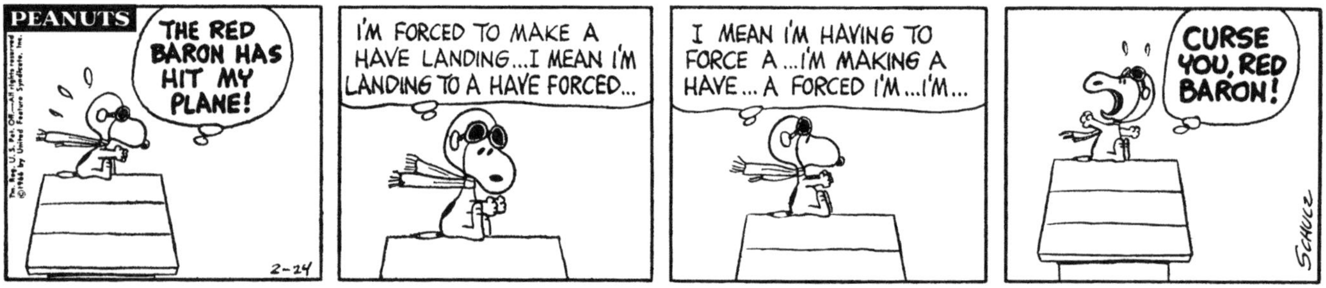
PEANUTS
Tm. Reg. U.S. Pat. Off.—All rights reserved ©1966 by United Feature Syndicate, Inc.
THE RED BARON HAS HIT MY PLANE!
2-24
I'M FORCED TO MAKE A HAVE LANDING...I MEAN I'M LANDING TO A HAVE FORCED...
I MEAN I'M HAVING TO FORCE A ...I'M MAKING A HAVE... A FORCED I'M...I'M...
CURSE YOU, RED BARON!
SCHULZ

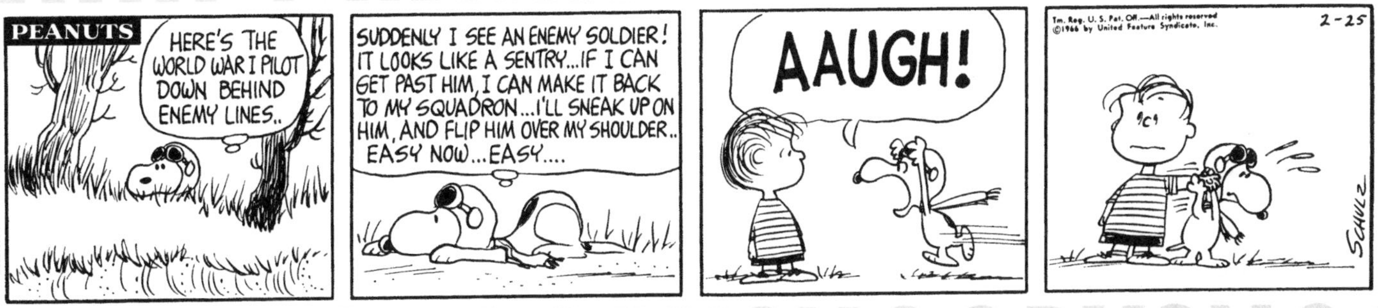
PEANUTS
HERE'S THE WORLD WAR I PILOT DOWN BEHIND ENEMY LINES..
SUDDENLY I SEE AN ENEMY SOLDIER! IT LOOKS LIKE A SENTRY...IF I CAN GET PAST HIM, I CAN MAKE IT BACK TO MY SQUADRON...I'LL SNEAK UP ON HIM, AND FLIP HIM OVER MY SHOULDER.. EASY NOW...EASY....
AAUGH!
Tm. Reg. U. S. Pat. Off.—All rights reserved ©1966 by United Feature Syndicate, Inc.
2-25
SCHULZ

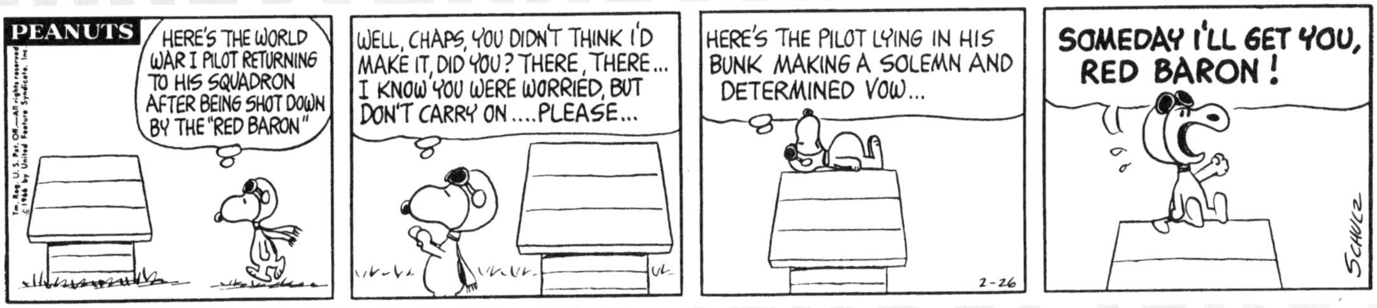
PEANUTS
HERE'S THE WORLD WAR I PILOT RETURNING TO HIS SQUADRON AFTER BEING SHOT DOWN BY THE "RED BARON"
Tm. Reg. U. S. Pat. Off.—All rights reserved ©1966 by United Feature Syndicate, Inc.
WELL, CHAPS, YOU DIDN'T THINK I'D MAKE IT, DID YOU? THERE, THERE... I KNOW YOU WERE WORRIED, BUT DON'T CARRY ON....PLEASE...
HERE'S THE PILOT LYING IN HIS BUNK MAKING A SOLEMN AND DETERMINED VOW...
2-26
SOMEDAY I'LL GET YOU, RED BARON!
SCHULZ

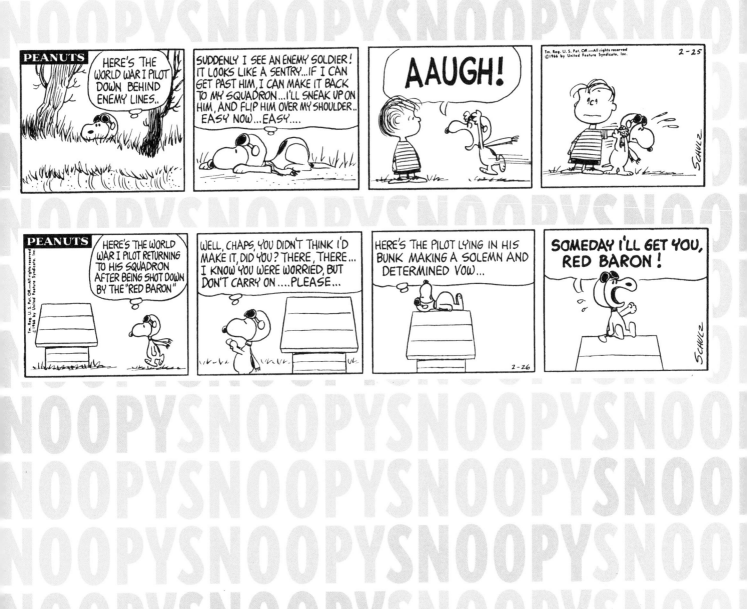

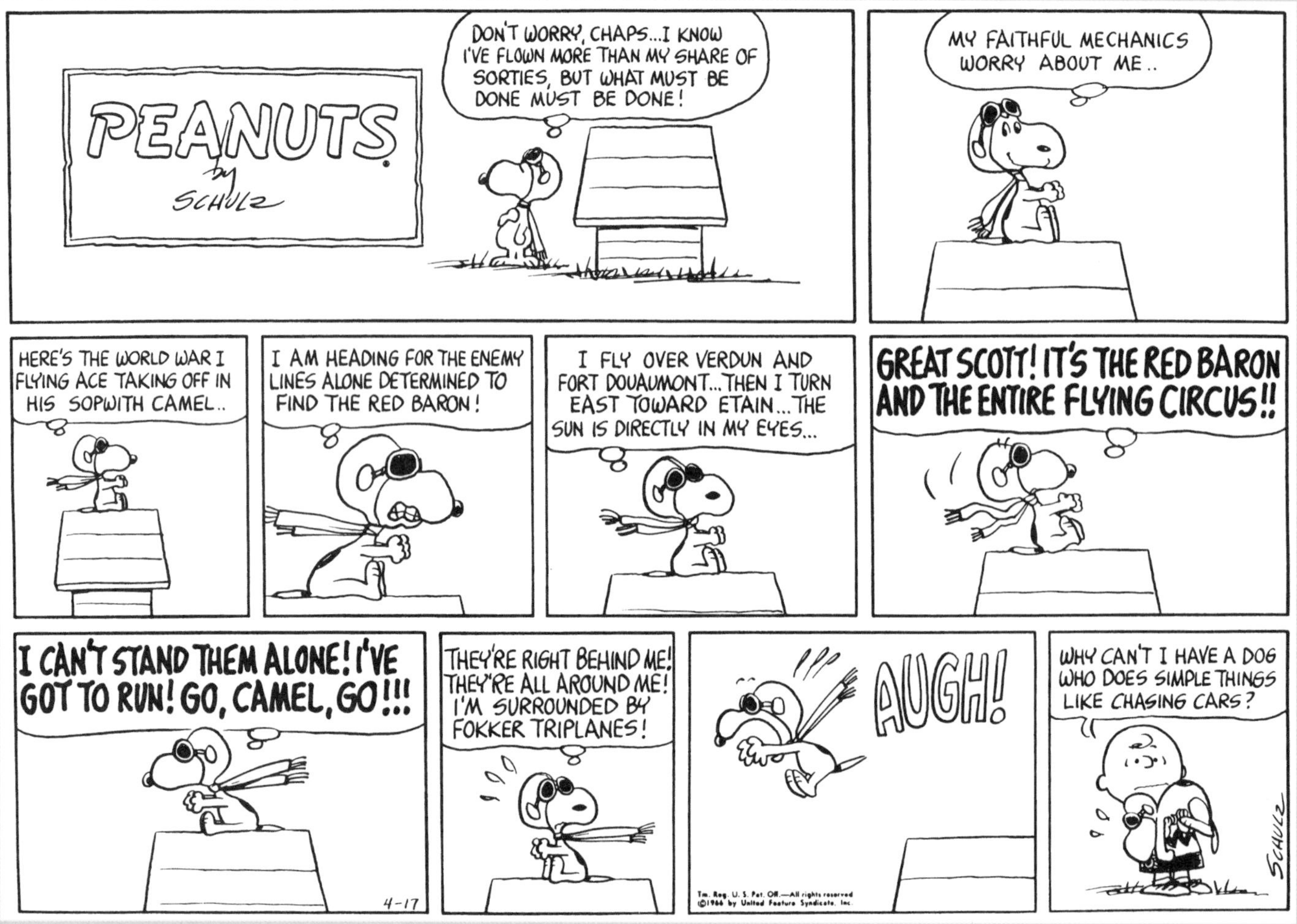
PEANUTS
by
SCHULZ
DON'T WORRY, CHAPS...I KNOW I'VE FLOWN MORE THAN MY SHARE OF SORTIES, BUT WHAT MUST BE DONE MUST BE DONE!
MY FAITHFUL MECHANICS WORRY ABOUT ME..
HERE'S THE WORLD WAR I FLYING ACE TAKING OFF IN HIS SOPWITH CAMEL..
I AM HEADING FOR THE ENEMY LINES ALONE DETERMINED TO FIND THE RED BARON!
I FLY OVER VERDUN AND FORT DOUAUMONT...THEN I TURN EAST TOWARD ETAIN...THE SUN IS DIRECTLY IN MY EYES...
GREAT SCOTT! IT'S THE RED BARON AND THE ENTIRE FLYING CIRCUS!!
I CAN'T STAND THEM ALONE! I'VE GOT TO RUN! GO, CAMEL, GO!!!
4-17
THEY'RE RIGHT BEHIND ME! THEY'RE ALL AROUND ME! I'M SURROUNDED BY FOKKER TRIPLANES!
AUGH!
Tm. Reg. U. S. Pat. Off.—All rights reserved
©1966 by United Feature Syndicate, Inc.
WHY CAN'T I HAVE A DOG WHO DOES SIMPLE THINGS LIKE CHASING CARS?
SCHULZ

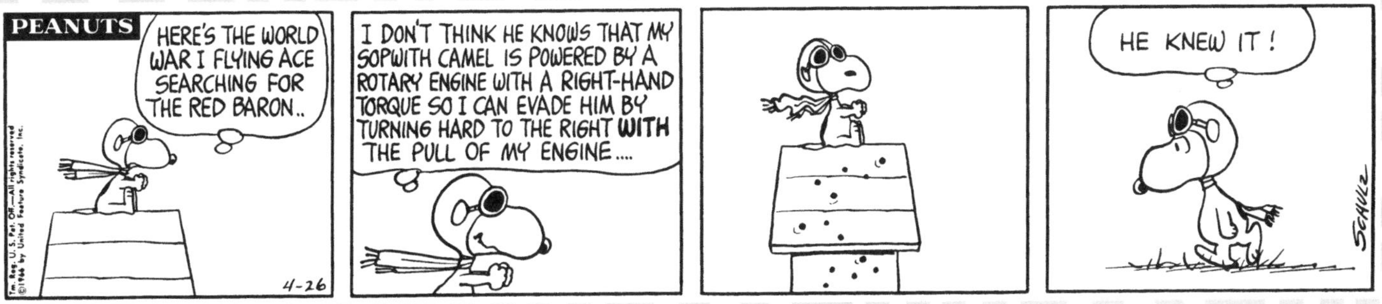
PEANUTS
HERE'S THE WORLD WAR I FLYING ACE SEARCHING FOR THE RED BARON..
I DON'T THINK HE KNOWS THAT MY SOPWITH CAMEL IS POWERED BY A ROTARY ENGINE WITH A RIGHT-HAND TORQUE SO I CAN EVADE HIM BY TURNING HARD TO THE RIGHT WITH THE PULL OF MY ENGINE....
HE KNEW IT!
4-26
SCHULZ

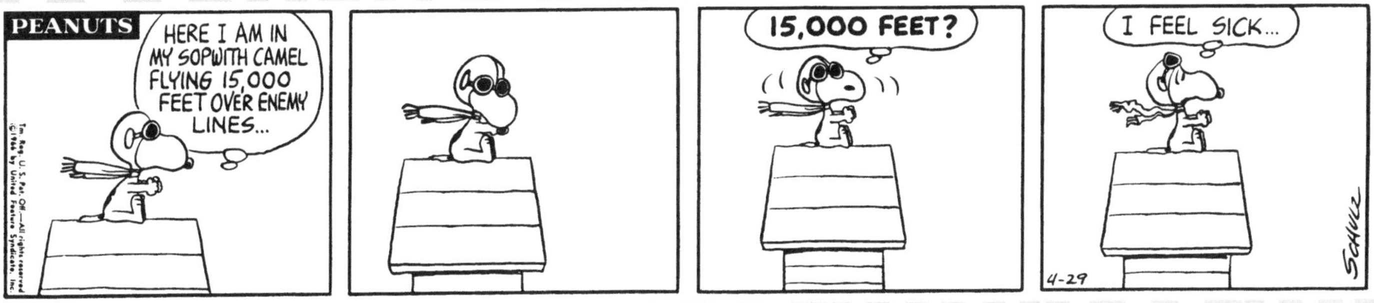
PEANUTS
HERE I AM IN MY SOPWITH CAMEL FLYING 15,000 FEET OVER ENEMY LINES...
15,000 FEET?
I FEEL SICK...
4-29
SCHULZ

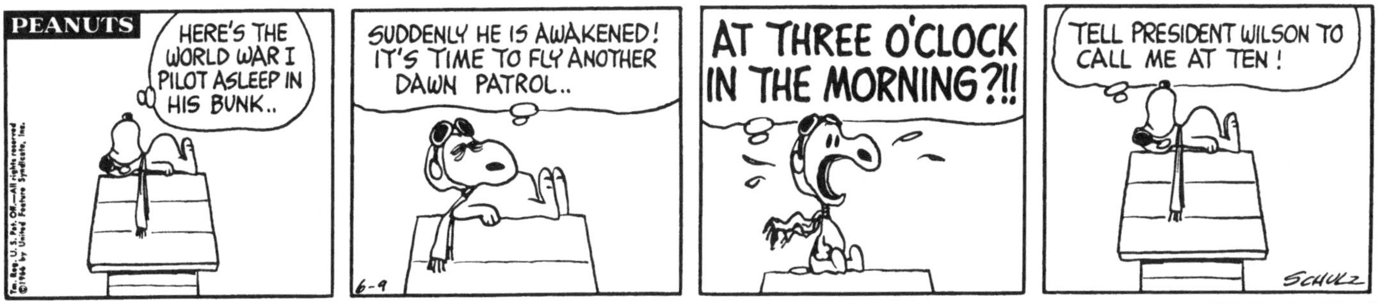
PEANUTS
HERE'S THE WORLD WAR I PILOT ASLEEP IN HIS BUNK..
SUDDENLY HE IS AWAKENED! IT'S TIME TO FLY ANOTHER DAWN PATROL..
AT THREE O'CLOCK IN THE MORNING?!!
TELL PRESIDENT WILSON TO CALL ME AT TEN!
6-9
SCHULZ

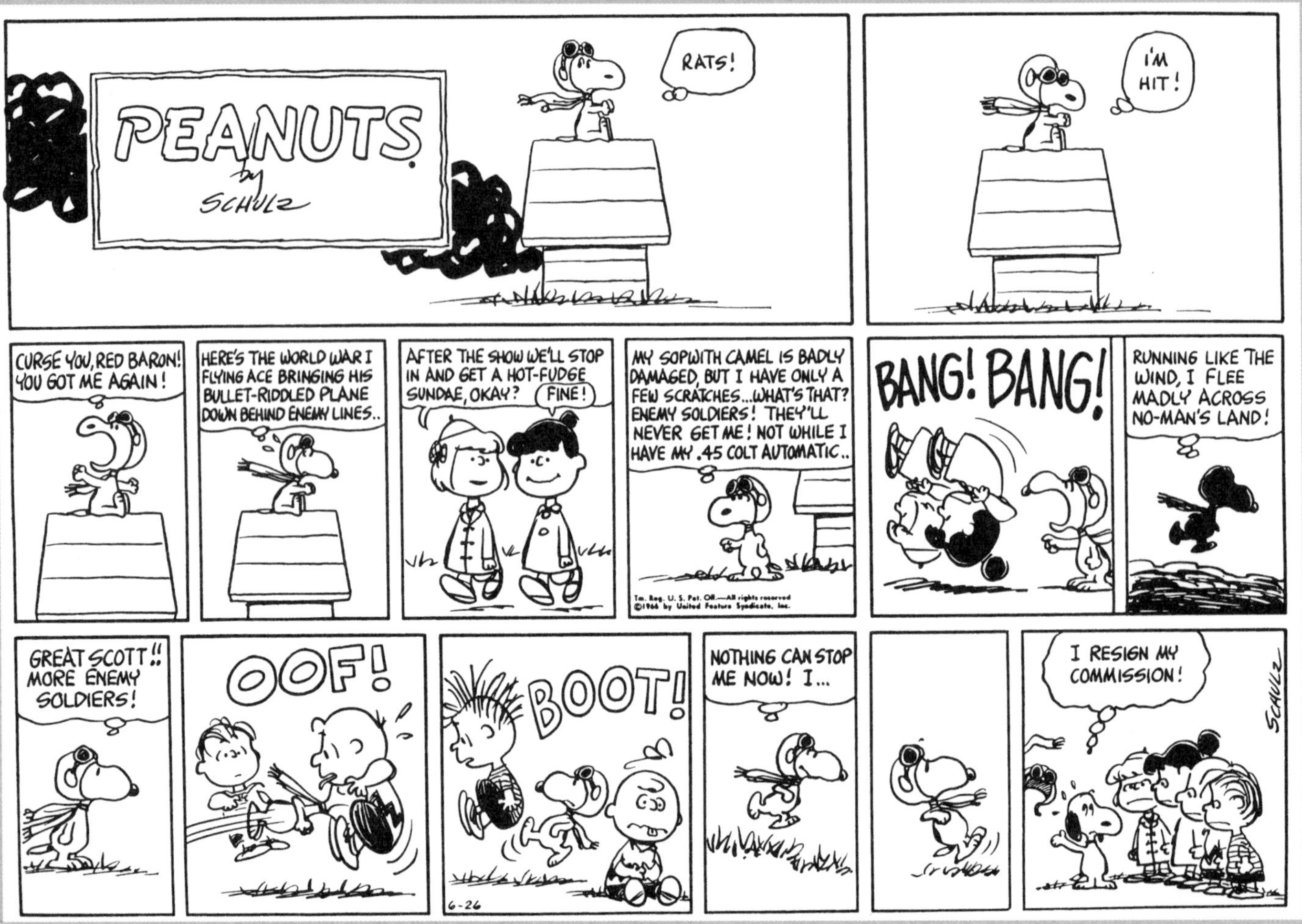
PEANUTS
by
SCHULZ
RATS!
I'M HIT!
CURSE YOU, RED BARON! YOU GOT ME AGAIN!
HERE'S THE WORLD WAR I FLYING ACE BRINGING HIS BULLET-RIDDLED PLANE DOWN BEHIND ENEMY LINES..
AFTER THE SHOW WE'LL STOP IN AND GET A HOT-FUDGE SUNDAE, OKAY?
FINE!
MY SOPWITH CAMEL IS BADLY DAMAGED, BUT I HAVE ONLY A FEW SCRATCHES...WHAT'S THAT? ENEMY SOLDIERS! THEY'LL NEVER GET ME! NOT WHILE I HAVE MY .45 COLT AUTOMATIC..
Tm. Reg. U. S. Pat. Off.—All rights reserved ©1966 by United Feature Syndicate, Inc.
BANG! BANG!
RUNNING LIKE THE WIND, I FLEE MADLY ACROSS NO-MAN'S LAND!
GREAT SCOTT!! MORE ENEMY SOLDIERS!
OOF!
BOOT!
6-26
NOTHING CAN STOP ME NOW! I...
I RESIGN MY COMMISSION!
SCHULZ

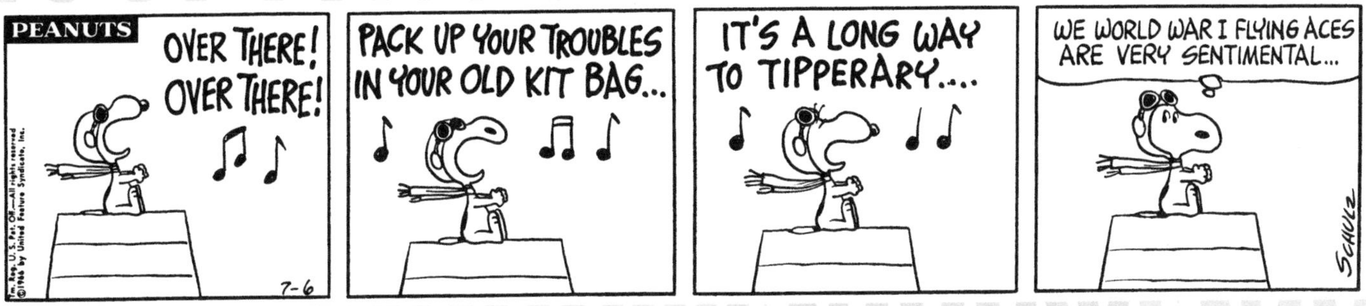
PEANUTS
OVER THERE! OVER THERE!
Tm. Reg. U. S. Pat. Off.—All rights reserved ©1966 by United Feature Syndicate, Inc.
7-6
PACK UP YOUR TROUBLES IN YOUR OLD KIT BAG...
IT'S A LONG WAY TO TIPPERARY....
WE WORLD WAR I FLYING ACES ARE VERY SENTIMENTAL...
SCHULZ

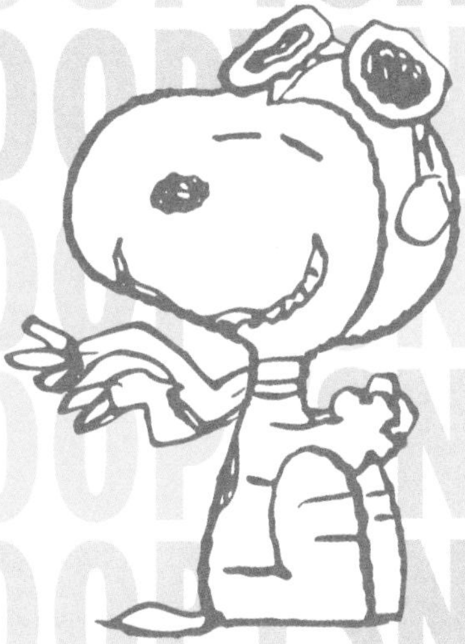

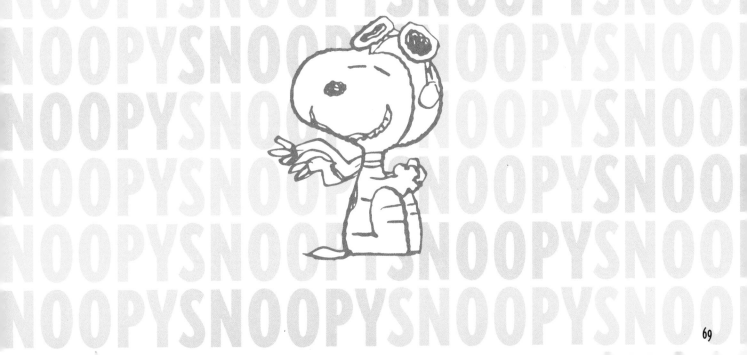

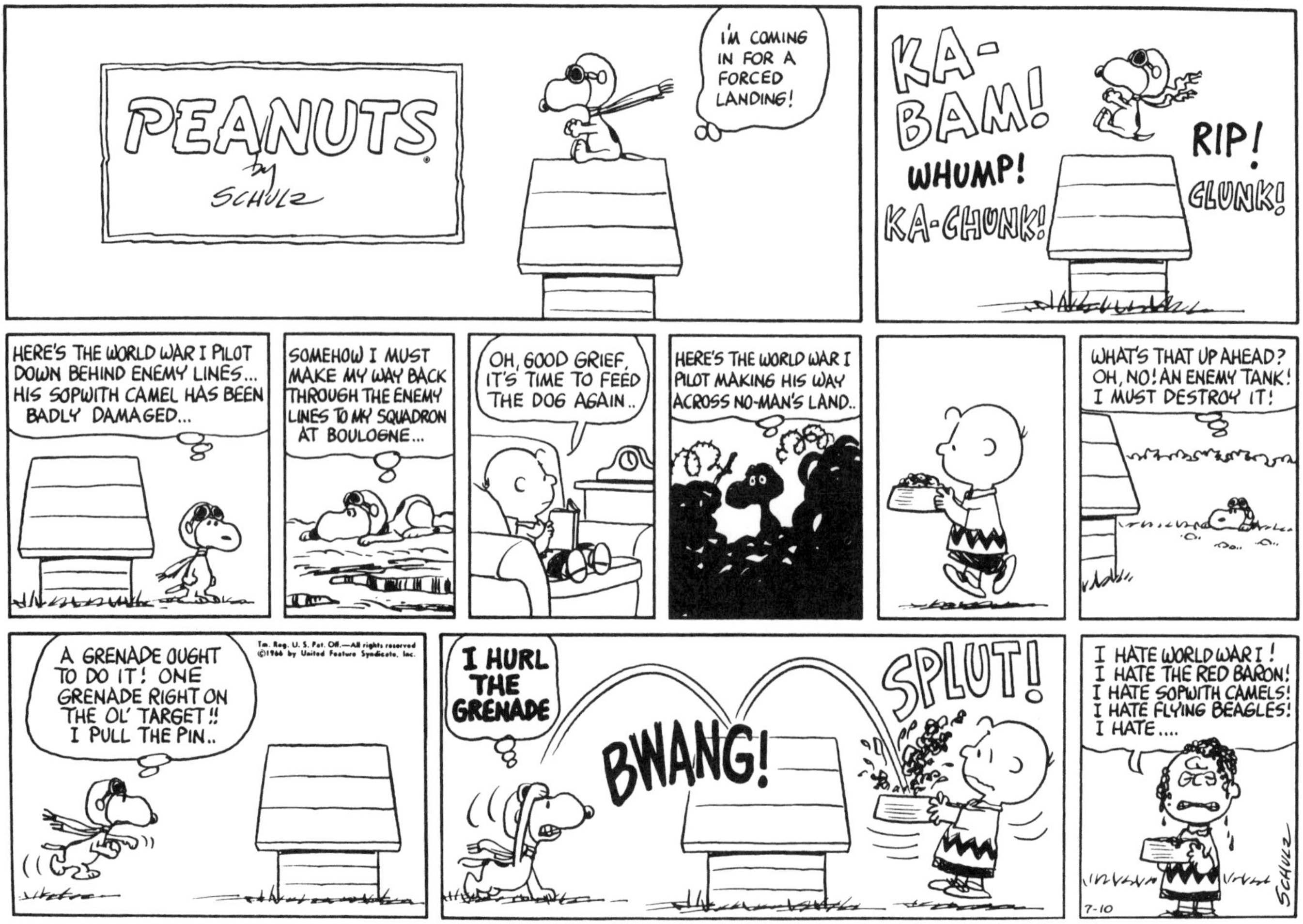
PEANUTS
by SCHULZ
I'M COMING IN FOR A FORCED LANDING!
KA-BAM!
RIP!
WHUMP!
KA-CHUNK!
GLUNK!
HERE'S THE WORLD WAR I PILOT DOWN BEHIND ENEMY LINES... HIS SOPWITH CAMEL HAS BEEN BADLY DAMAGED...
SOMEHOW I MUST MAKE MY WAY BACK THROUGH THE ENEMY LINES TO MY SQUADRON AT BOULOGNE...
OH, GOOD GRIEF, IT'S TIME TO FEED THE DOG AGAIN..
HERE'S THE WORLD WAR I PILOT MAKING HIS WAY ACROSS NO-MAN'S LAND..
WHAT'S THAT UP AHEAD? OH, NO! AN ENEMY TANK! I MUST DESTROY IT!
A GRENADE OUGHT TO DO IT! ONE GRENADE RIGHT ON THE OL' TARGET!! I PULL THE PIN..
Tm. Reg. U. S. Pat. Off.—All rights reserved ©1966 by United Feature Syndicate, Inc.
I HURL THE GRENADE
SPLUT!
BWANG!
I HATE WORLD WAR I! I HATE THE RED BARON! I HATE SOPWITH CAMELS! I HATE FLYING BEAGLES! I HATE....
7-10
SCHULZ

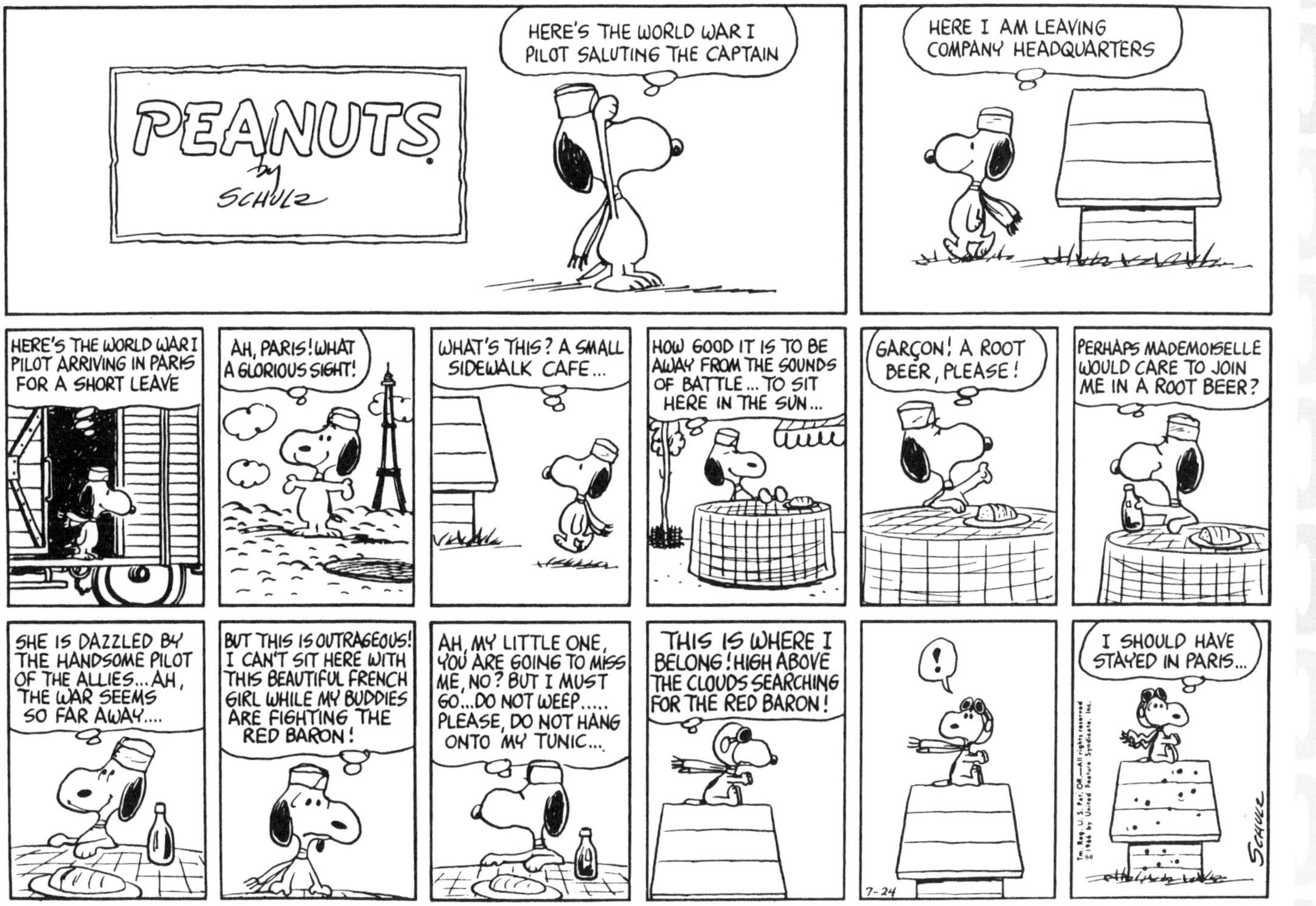
PEANUTS
by SCHULZ
HERE'S THE WORLD WAR I PILOT SALUTING THE CAPTAIN
HERE I AM LEAVING COMPANY HEADQUARTERS
HERE'S THE WORLD WAR I PILOT ARRIVING IN PARIS FOR A SHORT LEAVE
AH, PARIS! WHAT A GLORIOUS SIGHT!
WHAT'S THIS? A SMALL SIDEWALK CAFE...
HOW GOOD IT IS TO BE AWAY FROM THE SOUNDS OF BATTLE... TO SIT HERE IN THE SUN...
GARÇON! A ROOT BEER, PLEASE!
PERHAPS MADEMOISELLE WOULD CARE TO JOIN ME IN A ROOT BEER?
SHE IS DAZZLED BY THE HANDSOME PILOT OF THE ALLIES...AH, THE WAR SEEMS SO FAR AWAY....
BUT THIS IS OUTRAGEOUS! I CAN'T SIT HERE WITH THIS BEAUTIFUL FRENCH GIRL WHILE MY BUDDIES ARE FIGHTING THE RED BARON!
AH, MY LITTLE ONE, YOU ARE GOING TO MISS ME, NO? BUT I MUST GO...DO NOT WEEP..... PLEASE, DO NOT HANG ONTO MY TUNIC....
THIS IS WHERE I BELONG! HIGH ABOVE THE CLOUDS SEARCHING FOR THE RED BARON!
!
7-24
I SHOULD HAVE STAYED IN PARIS...
Tm. Reg. U. S. Pat. Off.—All rights reserved © 1966 by United Feature Syndicate, Inc.
SCHULZ

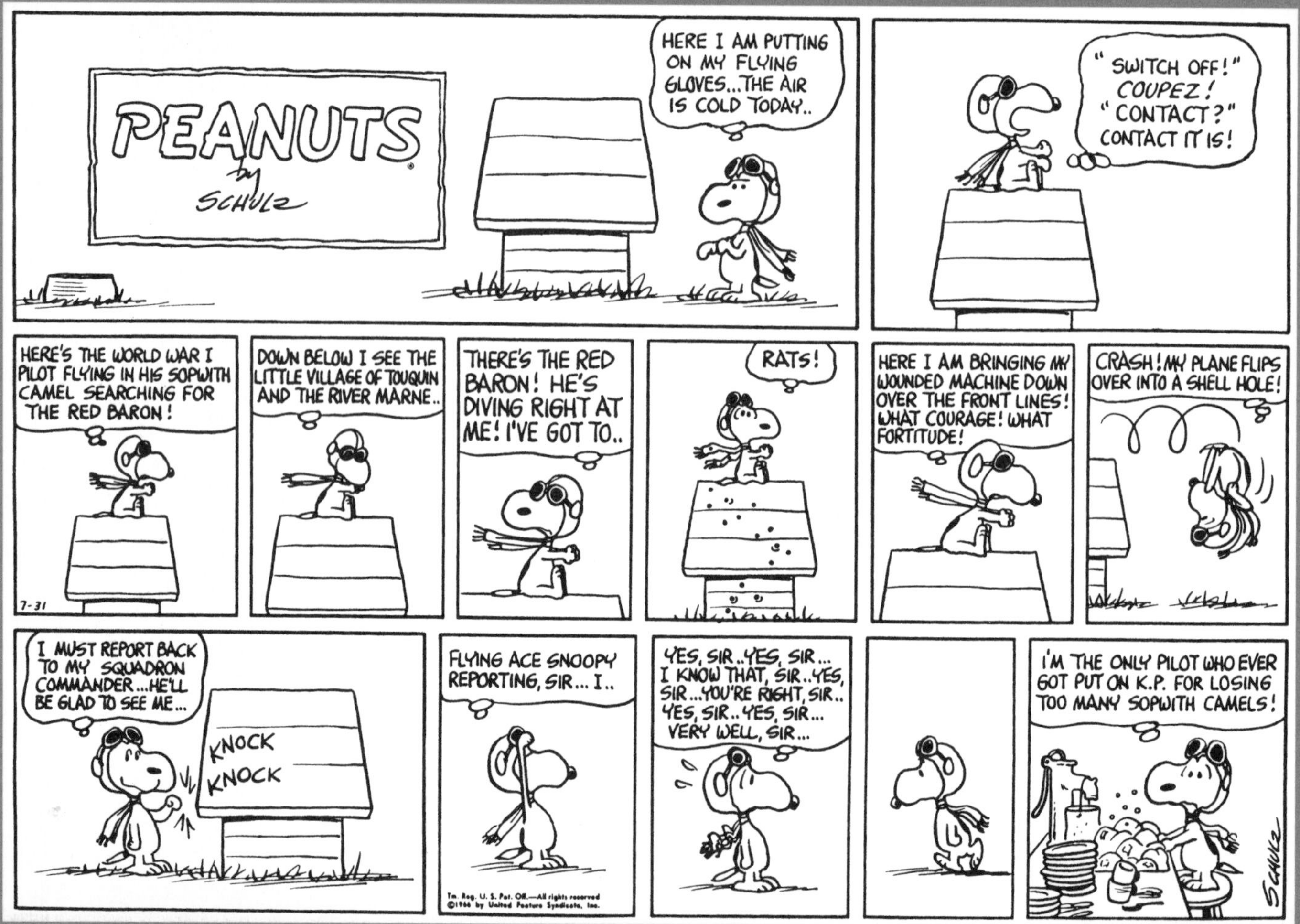
PEANUTS
by SCHULZ
HERE I AM PUTTING ON MY FLYING GLOVES...THE AIR IS COLD TODAY..
"SWITCH OFF!" COUPEZ! "CONTACT?" CONTACT IT IS!
HERE'S THE WORLD WAR I PILOT FLYING IN HIS SOPWITH CAMEL SEARCHING FOR THE RED BARON!
7-31
DOWN BELOW I SEE THE LITTLE VILLAGE OF TOUQUIN AND THE RIVER MARNE..
THERE'S THE RED BARON! HE'S DIVING RIGHT AT ME! I'VE GOT TO..
RATS!
HERE I AM BRINGING MY WOUNDED MACHINE DOWN OVER THE FRONT LINES! WHAT COURAGE! WHAT FORTITUDE!
CRASH! MY PLANE FLIPS OVER INTO A SHELL HOLE!
I MUST REPORT BACK TO MY SQUADRON COMMANDER...HE'LL BE GLAD TO SEE ME...
KNOCK KNOCK
FLYING ACE SNOOPY REPORTING, SIR... I..
Tm. Reg. U. S. Pat. Off.—All rights reserved ©1966 by United Feature Syndicate, Inc.
YES, SIR..YES, SIR... I KNOW THAT, SIR..YES, SIR...YOU'RE RIGHT, SIR.. YES, SIR..YES, SIR... VERY WELL, SIR...
I'M THE ONLY PILOT WHO EVER GOT PUT ON K.P. FOR LOSING TOO MANY SOPWITH CAMELS!
SCHULZ

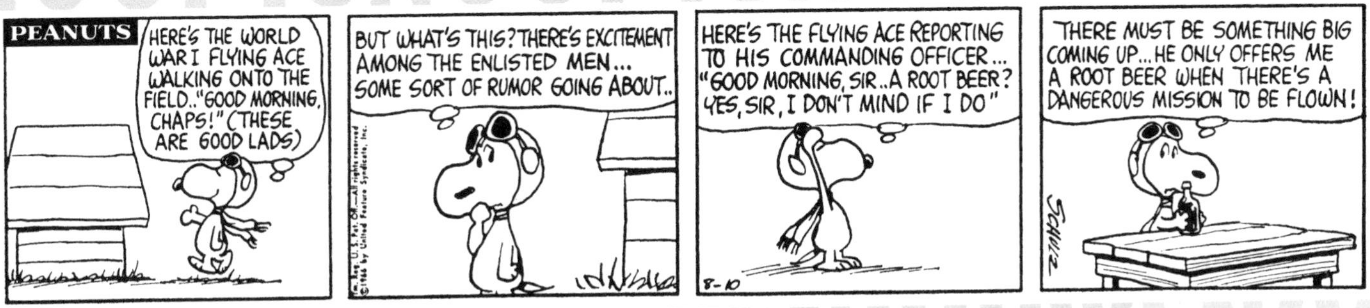
PEANUTS
HERE'S THE WORLD WAR I FLYING ACE WALKING ONTO THE FIELD.."GOOD MORNING, CHAPS!" (THESE ARE GOOD LADS)
BUT WHAT'S THIS? THERE'S EXCITEMENT AMONG THE ENLISTED MEN... SOME SORT OF RUMOR GOING ABOUT..
Tm. Reg. U.S. Pat. Off.—All rights reserved ©1966 by United Feature Syndicate, Inc.
HERE'S THE FLYING ACE REPORTING TO HIS COMMANDING OFFICER... "GOOD MORNING, SIR..A ROOT BEER? YES, SIR, I DON'T MIND IF I DO"
8-10
THERE MUST BE SOMETHING BIG COMING UP... HE ONLY OFFERS ME A ROOT BEER WHEN THERE'S A DANGEROUS MISSION TO BE FLOWN!
SCHULZ

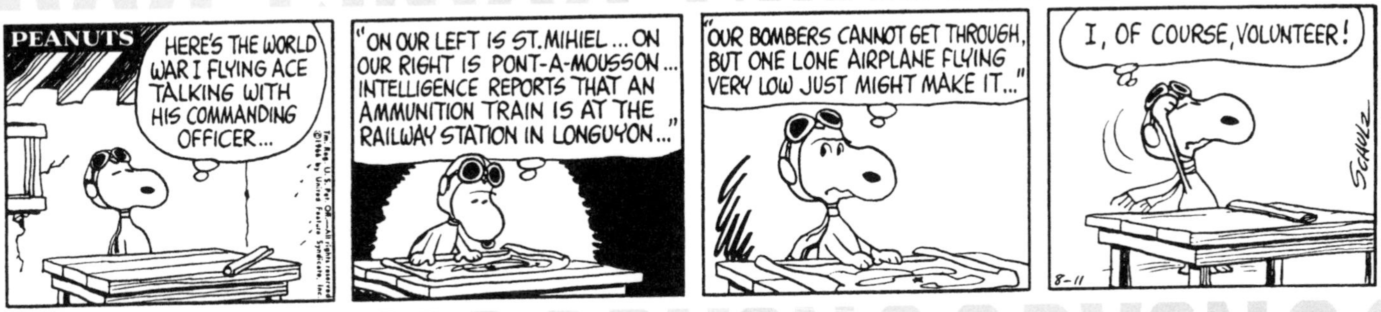
PEANUTS
HERE'S THE WORLD WAR I FLYING ACE TALKING WITH HIS COMMANDING OFFICER...
Tm. Reg. U.S. Pat. Off.—All rights reserved ©1966 by United Feature Syndicate, Inc.
"ON OUR LEFT IS ST. MIHIEL... ON OUR RIGHT IS PONT-A-MOUSSON... INTELLIGENCE REPORTS THAT AN AMMUNITION TRAIN IS AT THE RAILWAY STATION IN LONGUYON..."
"OUR BOMBERS CANNOT GET THROUGH, BUT ONE LONE AIRPLANE FLYING VERY LOW JUST MIGHT MAKE IT..."
I, OF COURSE, VOLUNTEER!
SCHULZ
8-11

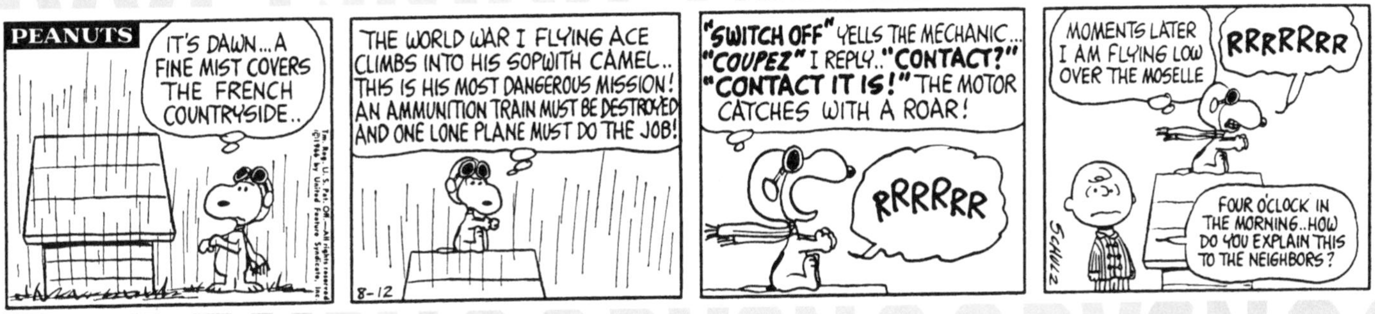
PEANUTS
IT'S DAWN... A FINE MIST COVERS THE FRENCH COUNTRYSIDE..
Tm. Reg. U.S. Pat. Off.—All rights reserved ©1966 by United Feature Syndicate, Inc.
THE WORLD WAR I FLYING ACE CLIMBS INTO HIS SOPWITH CAMEL.. THIS IS HIS MOST DANGEROUS MISSION! AN AMMUNITION TRAIN MUST BE DESTROYED AND ONE LONE PLANE MUST DO THE JOB!
8-12
"SWITCH OFF" YELLS THE MECHANIC... "COUPEZ" I REPLY.."CONTACT?" "CONTACT IT IS!" THE MOTOR CATCHES WITH A ROAR!
RRRRRR
MOMENTS LATER I AM FLYING LOW OVER THE MOSELLE
RRRRRRR
FOUR O'CLOCK IN THE MORNING..HOW DO YOU EXPLAIN THIS TO THE NEIGHBORS?
SCHULZ

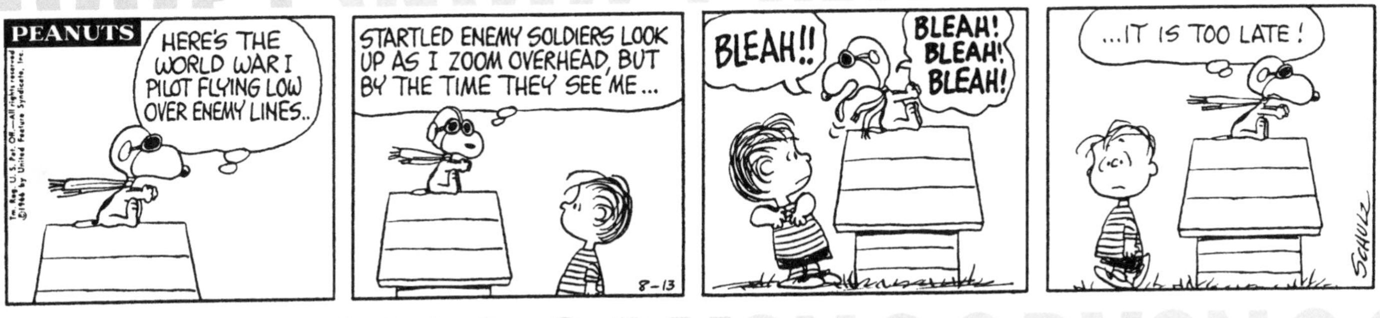
PEANUTS
Tm. Reg. U.S. Pat. Off.—All rights reserved ©1966 by United Feature Syndicate, Inc.
HERE'S THE WORLD WAR I PILOT FLYING LOW OVER ENEMY LINES..
STARTLED ENEMY SOLDIERS LOOK UP AS I ZOOM OVERHEAD, BUT BY THE TIME THEY SEE ME...
8-13
BLEAH!!
BLEAH! BLEAH! BLEAH!
...IT IS TOO LATE!
SCHULZ

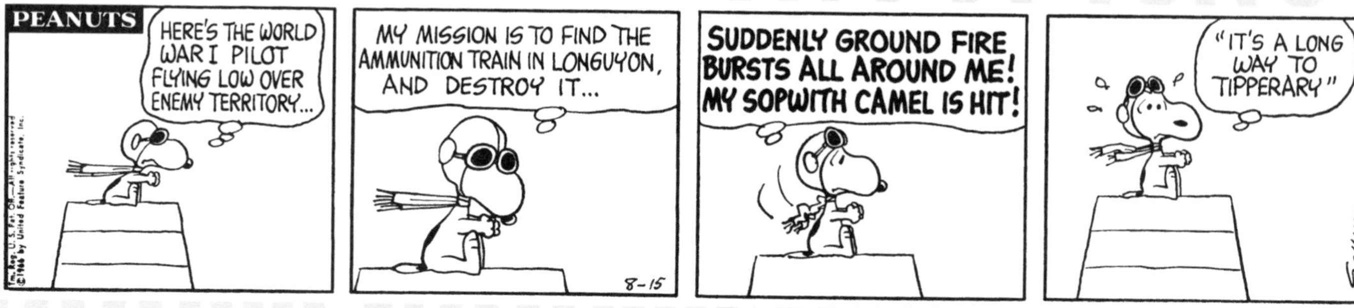
PEANUTS
HERE'S THE WORLD WAR I PILOT FLYING LOW OVER ENEMY TERRITORY...
Tm. Reg. U. S. Pat. Off.—All rights reserved ©1966 by United Feature Syndicate, Inc.
MY MISSION IS TO FIND THE AMMUNITION TRAIN IN LONGUYON, AND DESTROY IT...
8-15
SUDDENLY GROUND FIRE BURSTS ALL AROUND ME! MY SOPWITH CAMEL IS HIT!
"IT'S A LONG WAY TO TIPPERARY"
SCHULZ

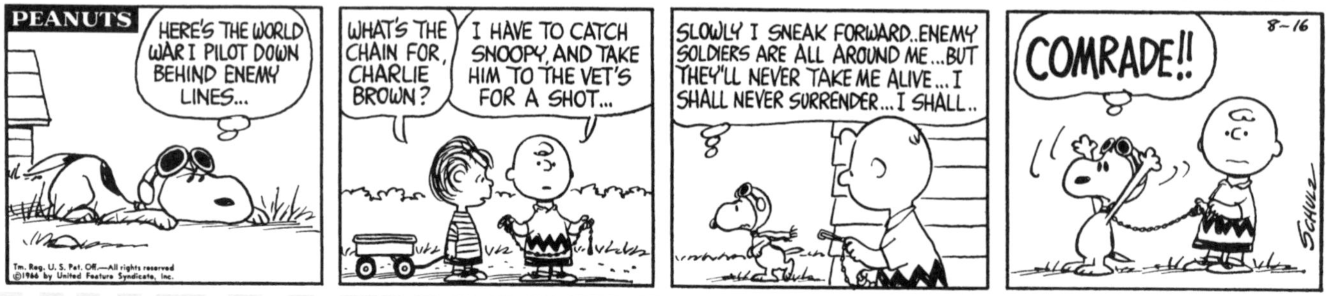
PEANUTS
HERE'S THE WORLD WAR I PILOT DOWN BEHIND ENEMY LINES...
Tm. Reg. U. S. Pat. Off.—All rights reserved ©1966 by United Feature Syndicate, Inc.
WHAT'S THE CHAIN FOR, CHARLIE BROWN?
I HAVE TO CATCH SNOOPY, AND TAKE HIM TO THE VET'S FOR A SHOT...
SLOWLY I SNEAK FORWARD..ENEMY SOLDIERS ARE ALL AROUND ME...BUT THEY'LL NEVER TAKE ME ALIVE...I SHALL NEVER SURRENDER...I SHALL..
8-16
COMRADE!!
SCHULZ

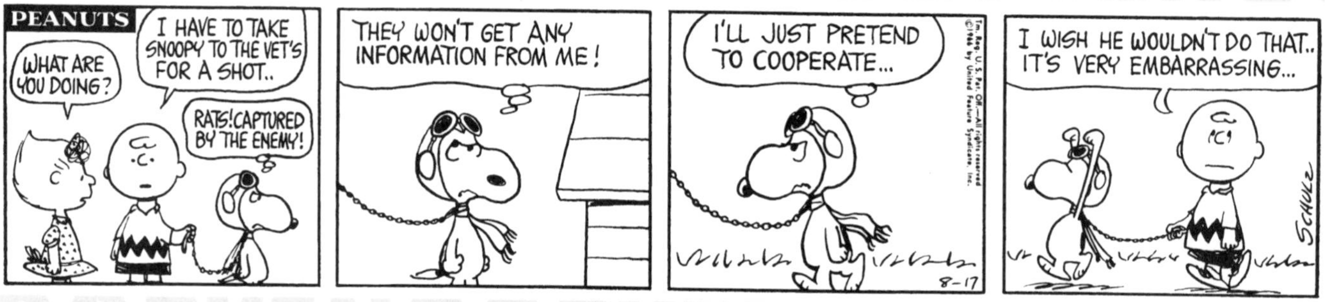
PEANUTS
WHAT ARE YOU DOING?
I HAVE TO TAKE SNOOPY TO THE VET'S FOR A SHOT..
RATS! CAPTURED BY THE ENEMY!
THEY WON'T GET ANY INFORMATION FROM ME!
I'LL JUST PRETEND TO COOPERATE...
Tm. Reg. U. S. Pat. Off.—All rights reserved ©1966 by United Feature Syndicate, Inc.
8-17
I WISH HE WOULDN'T DO THAT.. IT'S VERY EMBARRASSING...
SCHULZ

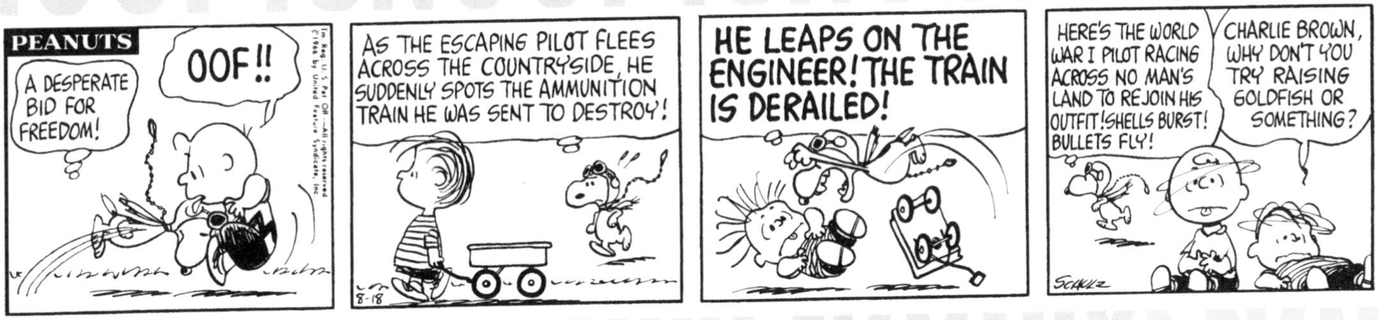
PEANUTS
A DESPERATE BID FOR FREEDOM!
OOF!!
AS THE ESCAPING PILOT FLEES ACROSS THE COUNTRYSIDE, HE SUDDENLY SPOTS THE AMMUNITION TRAIN HE WAS SENT TO DESTROY!
8-18
HE LEAPS ON THE ENGINEER! THE TRAIN IS DERAILED!
HERE'S THE WORLD WAR I PILOT RACING ACROSS NO MAN'S LAND TO REJOIN HIS OUTFIT! SHELLS BURST! BULLETS FLY!
CHARLIE BROWN, WHY DON'T YOU TRY RAISING GOLDFISH OR SOMETHING?
SCHULZ

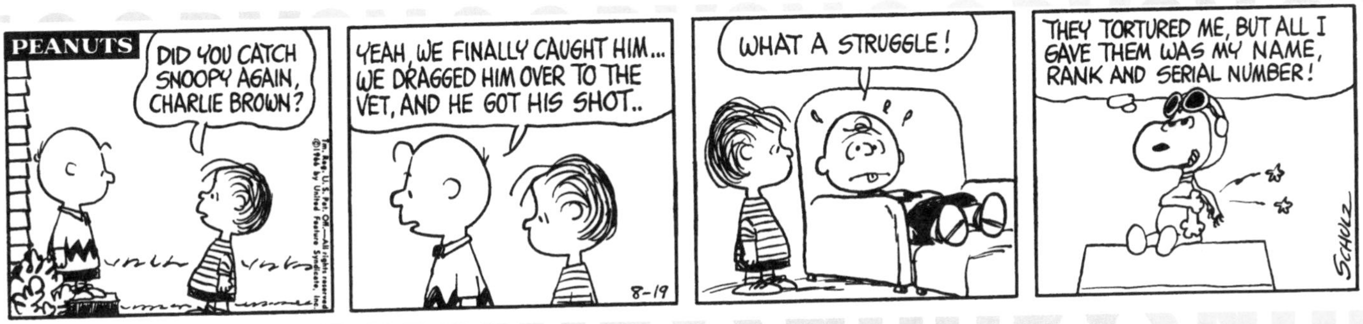
PEANUTS
DID YOU CATCH SNOOPY AGAIN, CHARLIE BROWN?
YEAH, WE FINALLY CAUGHT HIM... WE DRAGGED HIM OVER TO THE VET, AND HE GOT HIS SHOT..
8-19
WHAT A STRUGGLE!
THEY TORTURED ME, BUT ALL I GAVE THEM WAS MY NAME, RANK AND SERIAL NUMBER!
SCHULZ

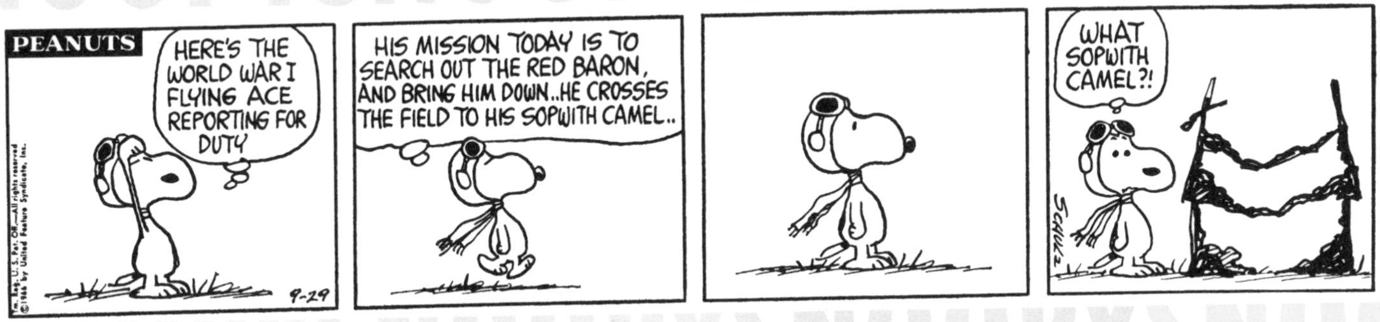
PEANUTS
HERE'S THE WORLD WAR I FLYING ACE REPORTING FOR DUTY
Tm. Reg. U.S. Pat. Off.—All rights reserved ©1966 by United Feature Syndicate, Inc.
9-29
HIS MISSION TODAY IS TO SEARCH OUT THE RED BARON, AND BRING HIM DOWN..HE CROSSES THE FIELD TO HIS SOPWITH CAMEL..
WHAT SOPWITH CAMEL?!
SCHULZ

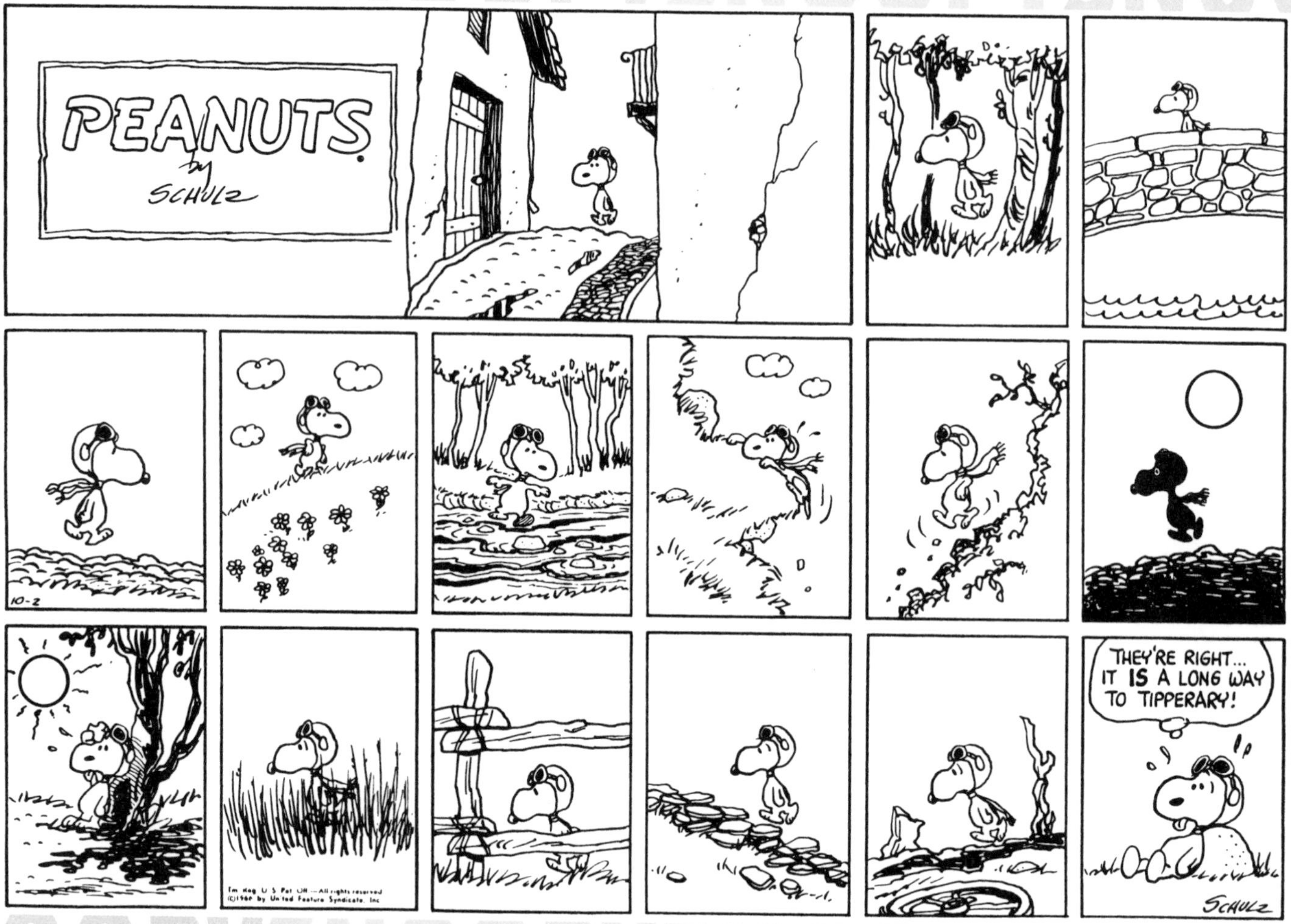
PEANUTS
by
SCHULZ
10-2
Tm Reg U S Pat Off —All rights reserved
(C)1966 by United Feature Syndicate, Inc
THEY'RE RIGHT... IT IS A LONG WAY TO TIPPERARY!
SCHULZ

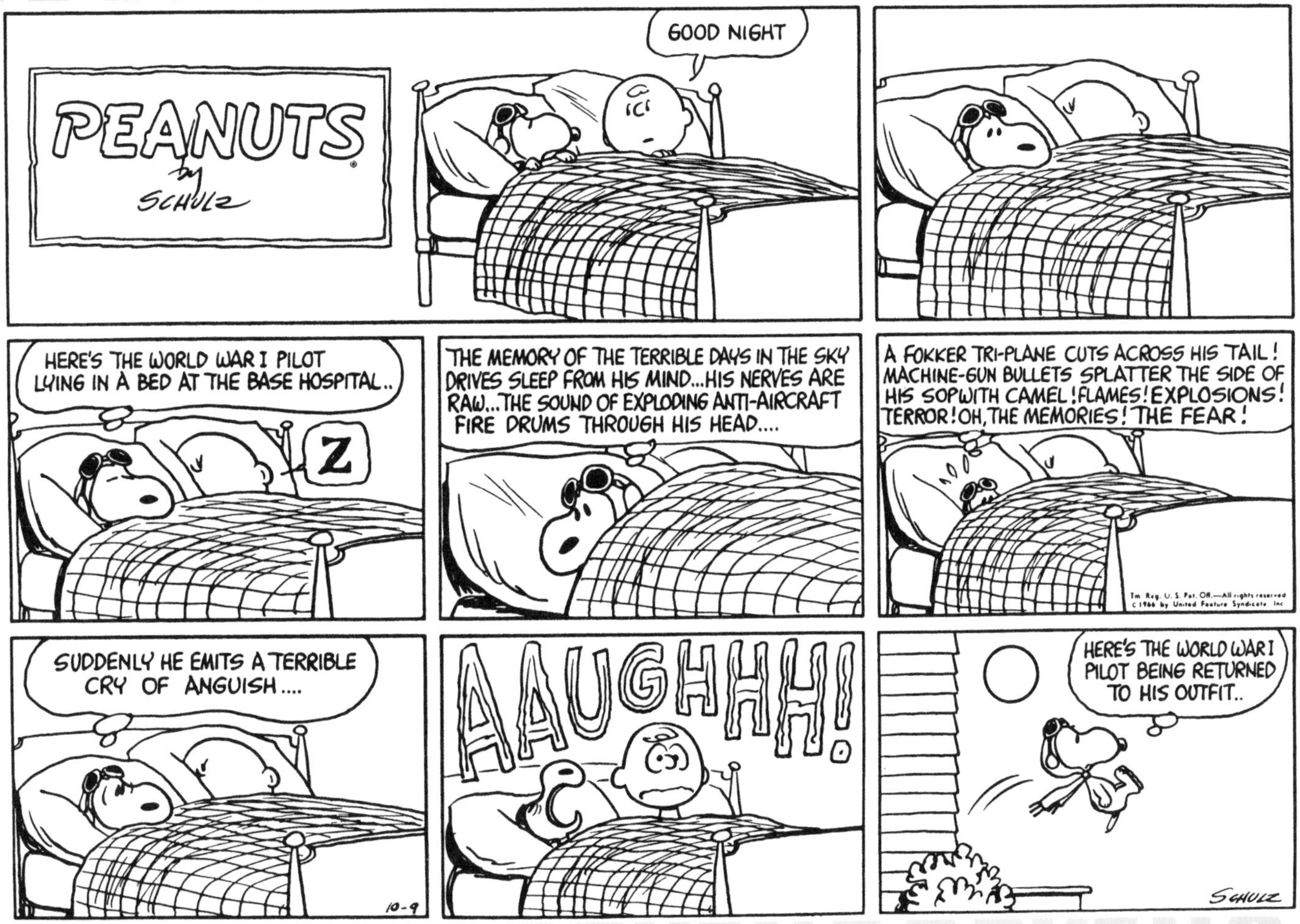
PEANUTS
by SCHULZ
GOOD NIGHT
HERE'S THE WORLD WAR I PILOT LYING IN A BED AT THE BASE HOSPITAL..
Z
THE MEMORY OF THE TERRIBLE DAYS IN THE SKY DRIVES SLEEP FROM HIS MIND...HIS NERVES ARE RAW...THE SOUND OF EXPLODING ANTI-AIRCRAFT FIRE DRUMS THROUGH HIS HEAD....
A FOKKER TRI-PLANE CUTS ACROSS HIS TAIL! MACHINE-GUN BULLETS SPLATTER THE SIDE OF HIS SOPWITH CAMEL! FLAMES! EXPLOSIONS! TERROR! OH, THE MEMORIES! THE FEAR!
Tm Reg. U. S. Pat. Off.—All rights reserved
©1966 by United Feature Syndicate, Inc
SUDDENLY HE EMITS A TERRIBLE CRY OF ANGUISH....
10-9
AAUGHHH!
HERE'S THE WORLD WAR I PILOT BEING RETURNED TO HIS OUTFIT..
SCHULZ

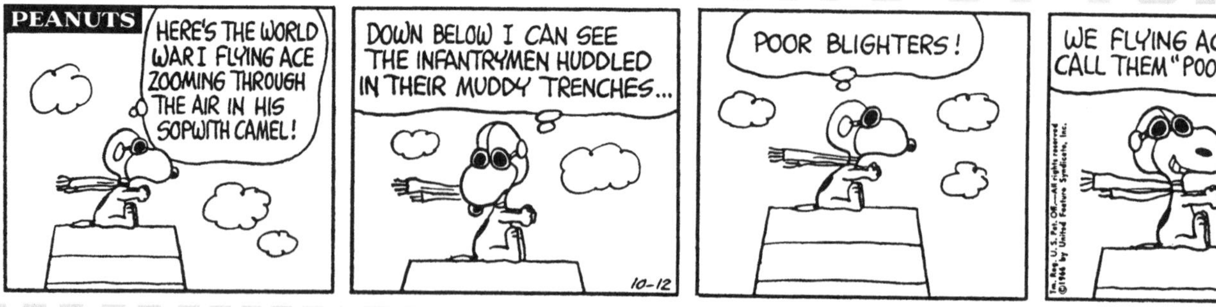
PEANUTS
HERE'S THE WORLD WAR I FLYING ACE ZOOMING THROUGH THE AIR IN HIS SOPWITH CAMEL!
DOWN BELOW I CAN SEE THE INFANTRYMEN HUDDLED IN THEIR MUDDY TRENCHES...
10-12
POOR BLIGHTERS!
WE FLYING ACES ALWAYS CALL THEM "POOR BLIGHTERS"
Tm. Reg. U. S. Pat. Off.—All rights reserved ©1966 by United Feature Syndicate, Inc.
SCHULZ

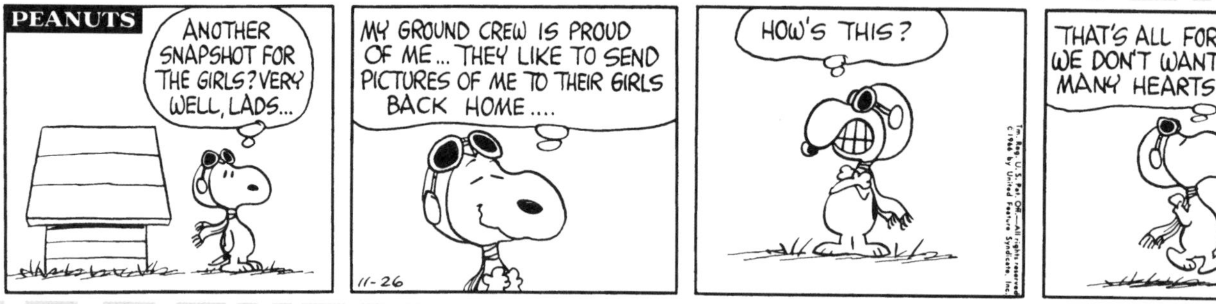
PEANUTS
ANOTHER SNAPSHOT FOR THE GIRLS? VERY WELL, LADS...
MY GROUND CREW IS PROUD OF ME... THEY LIKE TO SEND PICTURES OF ME TO THEIR GIRLS BACK HOME....
11-26
HOW'S THIS?
Tm. Reg. U. S. Pat. Off.—All rights reserved ©1966 by United Feature Syndicate, Inc.
THAT'S ALL FOR NOW, LADS... WE DON'T WANT TO SET TOO MANY HEARTS FLUTTERING!
SCHULZ

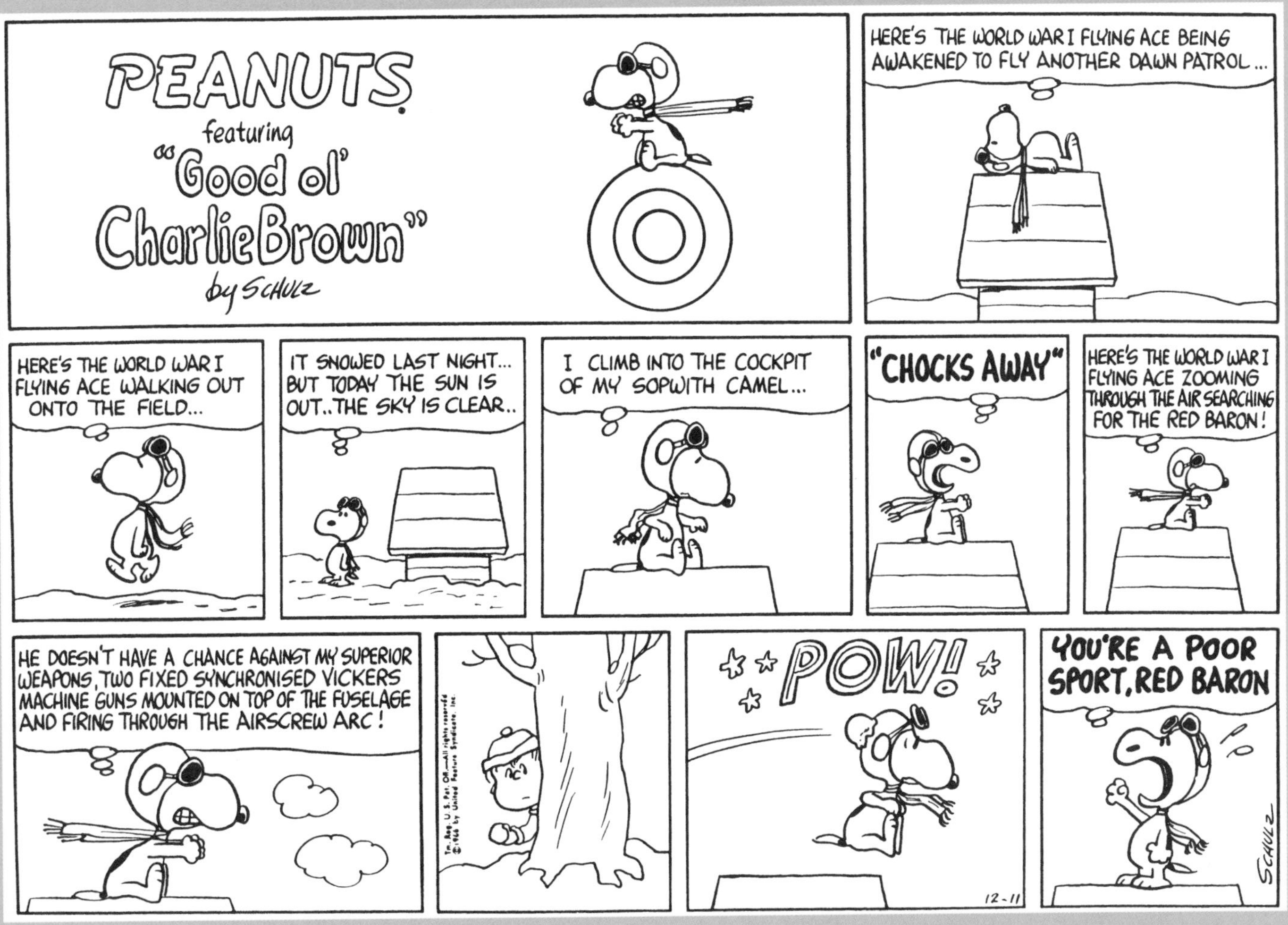
PEANUTS
featuring
"Good ol' CharlieBrown"
by SCHULZ
HERE'S THE WORLD WAR I FLYING ACE BEING AWAKENED TO FLY ANOTHER DAWN PATROL...
HERE'S THE WORLD WAR I FLYING ACE WALKING OUT ONTO THE FIELD...
IT SNOWED LAST NIGHT... BUT TODAY THE SUN IS OUT..THE SKY IS CLEAR..
I CLIMB INTO THE COCKPIT OF MY SOPWITH CAMEL...
"CHOCKS AWAY"
HERE'S THE WORLD WAR I FLYING ACE ZOOMING THROUGH THE AIR SEARCHING FOR THE RED BARON!
HE DOESN'T HAVE A CHANCE AGAINST MY SUPERIOR WEAPONS, TWO FIXED SYNCHRONISED VICKERS MACHINE GUNS MOUNTED ON TOP OF THE FUSELAGE AND FIRING THROUGH THE AIRSCREW ARC!
Tm. Reg. U. S. Pat. Off.—All rights reserved © 1966 by United Feature Syndicate, Inc.
POW!
12-11
YOU'RE A POOR SPORT, RED BARON
SCHULZ

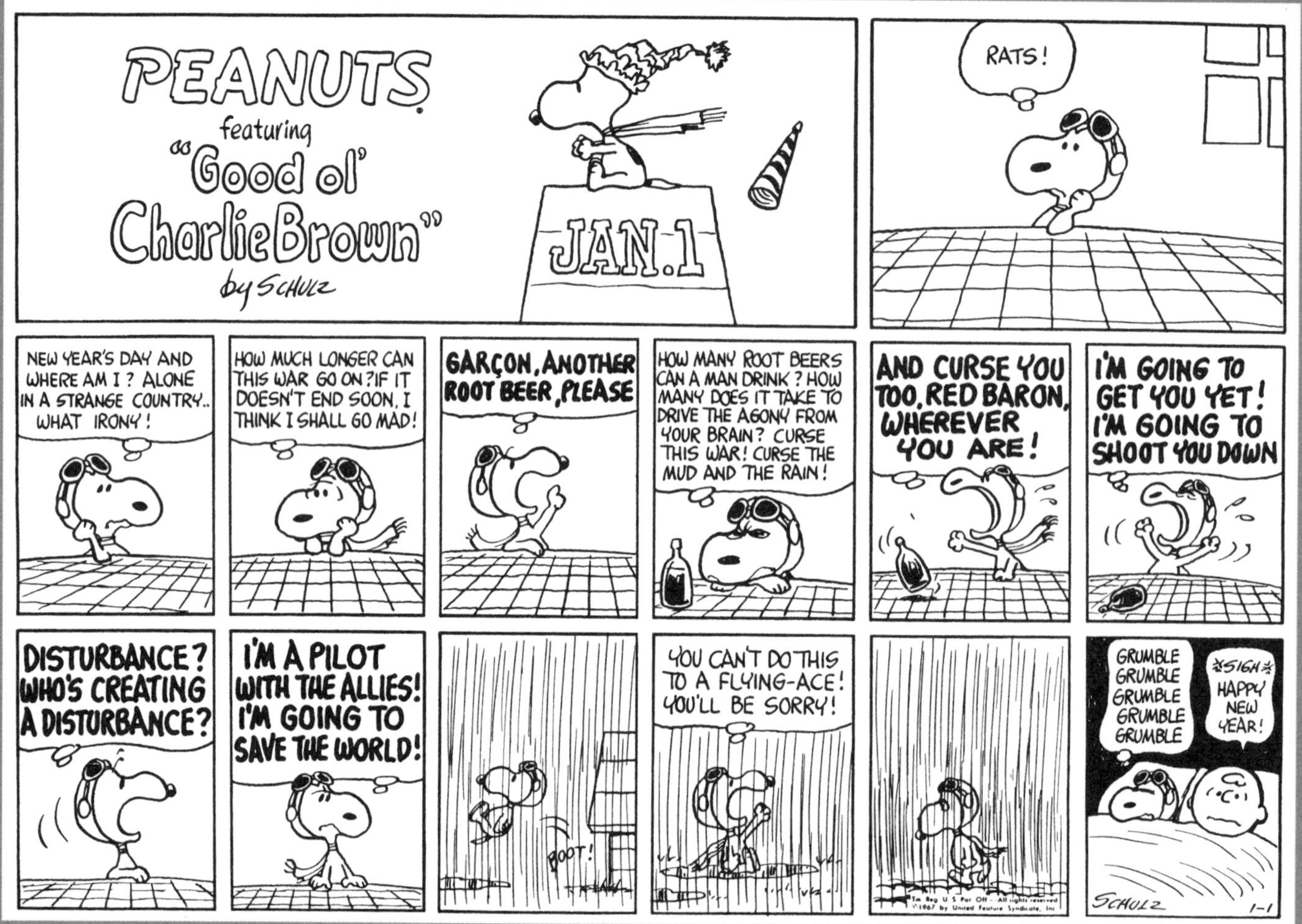
PEANUTS
featuring
"Good ol' Charlie Brown"
by SCHULZ
JAN. 1
RATS!
NEW YEAR'S DAY AND WHERE AM I? ALONE IN A STRANGE COUNTRY.. WHAT IRONY!
HOW MUCH LONGER CAN THIS WAR GO ON? IF IT DOESN'T END SOON, I THINK I SHALL GO MAD!
GARÇON, ANOTHER ROOT BEER, PLEASE
HOW MANY ROOT BEERS CAN A MAN DRINK? HOW MANY DOES IT TAKE TO DRIVE THE AGONY FROM YOUR BRAIN? CURSE THIS WAR! CURSE THE MUD AND THE RAIN!
AND CURSE YOU TOO, RED BARON, WHEREVER YOU ARE!
I'M GOING TO GET YOU YET! I'M GOING TO SHOOT YOU DOWN
DISTURBANCE? WHO'S CREATING A DISTURBANCE?
I'M A PILOT WITH THE ALLIES! I'M GOING TO SAVE THE WORLD!
BOOT!
YOU CAN'T DO THIS TO A FLYING-ACE! YOU'LL BE SORRY!
Tm Reg U S Pat Off - All rights reserved ©1967 by United Feature Syndicate, Inc
GRUMBLE GRUMBLE GRUMBLE GRUMBLE GRUMBLE
SIGH HAPPY NEW YEAR!
SCHULZ
1-1

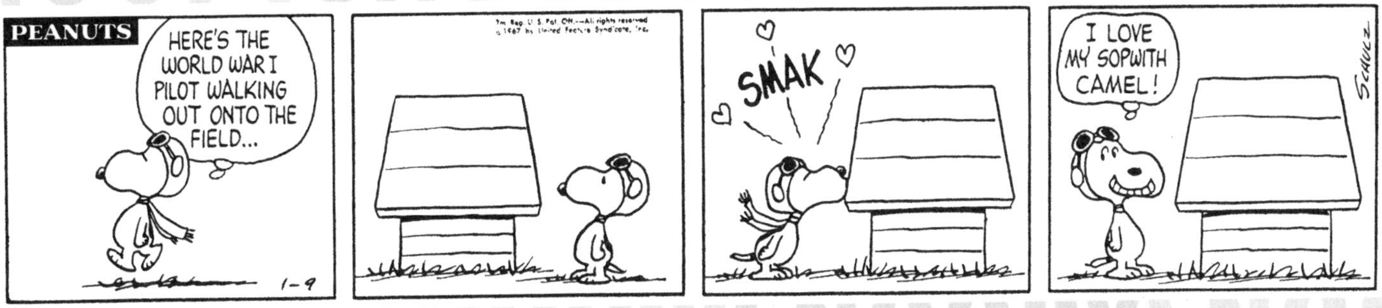
PEANUTS
HERE'S THE WORLD WAR I PILOT WALKING OUT ONTO THE FIELD...
1-9
Tm. Reg. U.S. Pat. Off.—All rights reserved ©1967 by United Feature Syndicate, Inc.
SMAK
I LOVE MY SOPWITH CAMEL!
SCHULZ

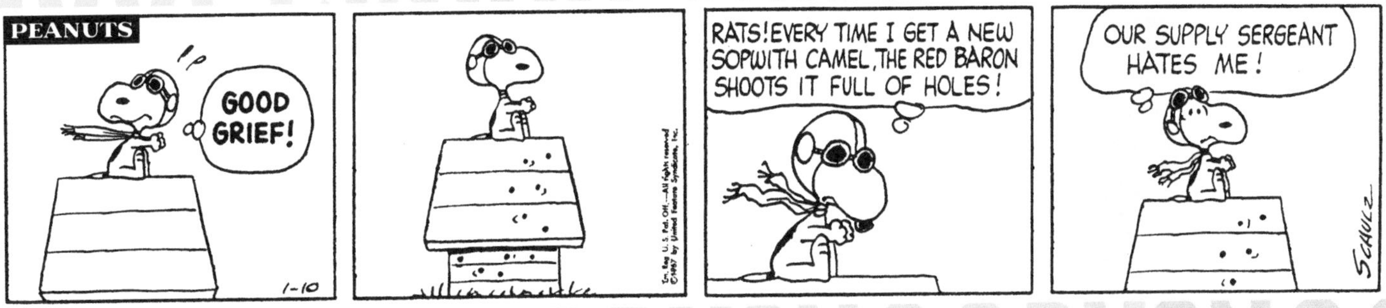
PEANUTS
GOOD GRIEF!
1-10
Tm. Reg. U.S. Pat. Off.—All rights reserved ©1967 by United Feature Syndicate, Inc.
RATS! EVERY TIME I GET A NEW SOPWITH CAMEL, THE RED BARON SHOOTS IT FULL OF HOLES!
OUR SUPPLY SERGEANT HATES ME!
SCHULZ

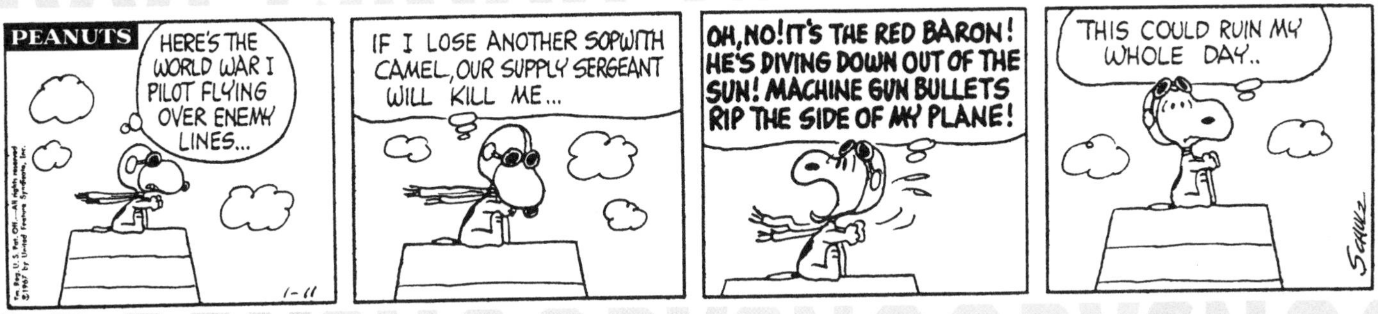
PEANUTS
HERE'S THE WORLD WAR I PILOT FLYING OVER ENEMY LINES...
Tm. Reg. U.S. Pat. Off.—All rights reserved ©1967 by United Feature Syndicate, Inc.
1-11
IF I LOSE ANOTHER SOPWITH CAMEL, OUR SUPPLY SERGEANT WILL KILL ME...
OH, NO! IT'S THE RED BARON! HE'S DIVING DOWN OUT OF THE SUN! MACHINE GUN BULLETS RIP THE SIDE OF MY PLANE!
THIS COULD RUIN MY WHOLE DAY..
SCHULZ

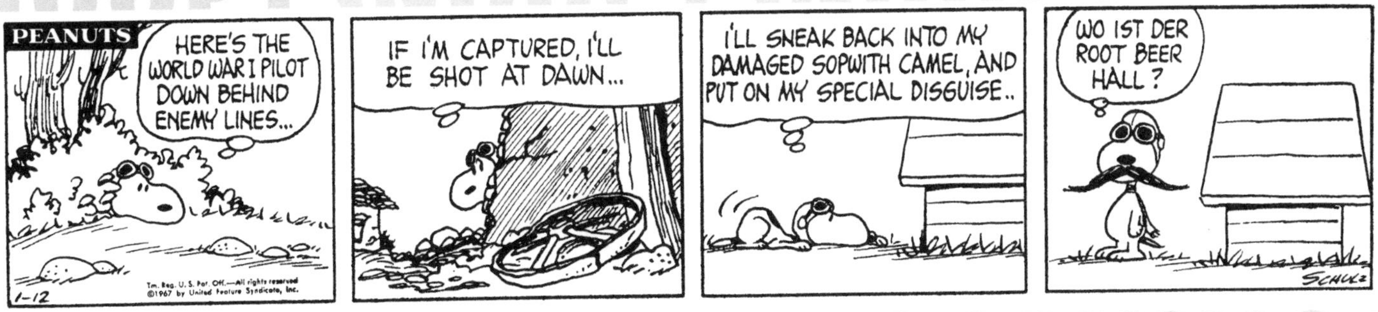
PEANUTS
HERE'S THE WORLD WAR I PILOT DOWN BEHIND ENEMY LINES...
1-12
Tm. Reg. U.S. Pat. Off.—All rights reserved ©1967 by United Feature Syndicate, Inc.
IF I'M CAPTURED, I'LL BE SHOT AT DAWN...
I'LL SNEAK BACK INTO MY DAMAGED SOPWITH CAMEL, AND PUT ON MY SPECIAL DISGUISE..
WO IST DER ROOT BEER HALL?
SCHULZ

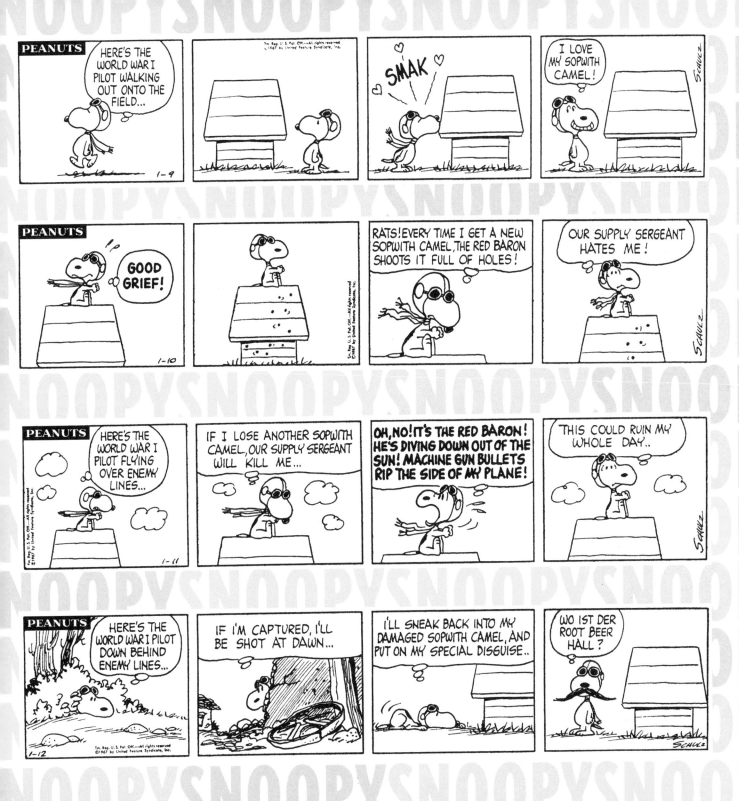

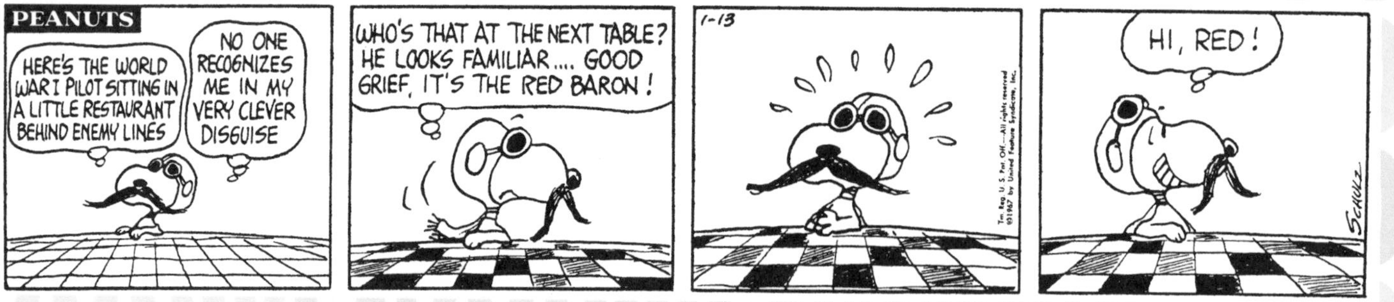
PEANUTS
HERE'S THE WORLD WAR I PILOT SITTING IN A LITTLE RESTAURANT BEHIND ENEMY LINES
NO ONE RECOGNIZES ME IN MY VERY CLEVER DISGUISE
WHO'S THAT AT THE NEXT TABLE? HE LOOKS FAMILIAR.... GOOD GRIEF, IT'S THE RED BARON!
1-13
HI, RED!
SCHULZ

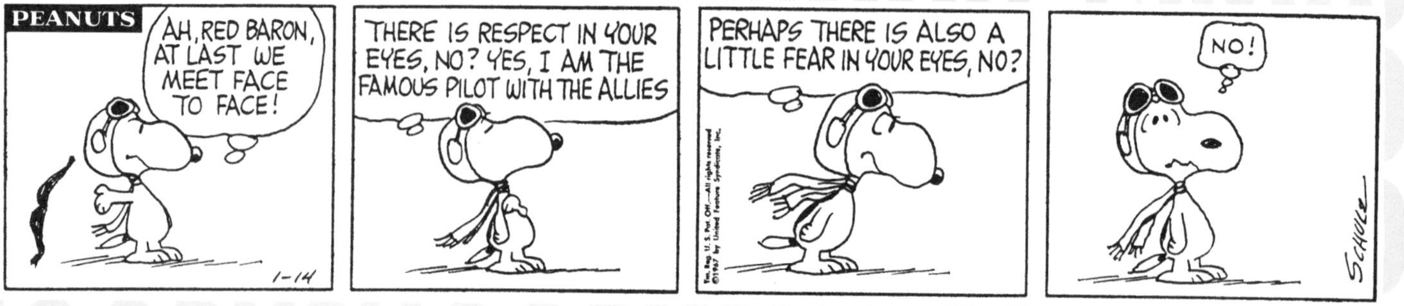
PEANUTS
AH, RED BARON, AT LAST WE MEET FACE TO FACE!
1-14
THERE IS RESPECT IN YOUR EYES, NO? YES, I AM THE FAMOUS PILOT WITH THE ALLIES
PERHAPS THERE IS ALSO A LITTLE FEAR IN YOUR EYES, NO?
NO!
SCHULZ

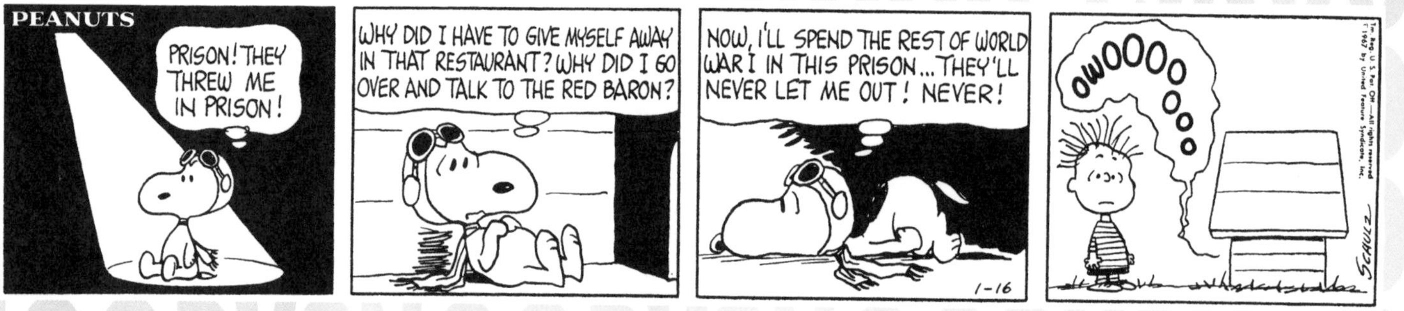
PEANUTS
PRISON! THEY THREW ME IN PRISON!
WHY DID I HAVE TO GIVE MYSELF AWAY IN THAT RESTAURANT? WHY DID I GO OVER AND TALK TO THE RED BARON?
NOW, I'LL SPEND THE REST OF WORLD WAR I IN THIS PRISON... THEY'LL NEVER LET ME OUT! NEVER!
1-16
OWOOOOOOOO
SCHULZ

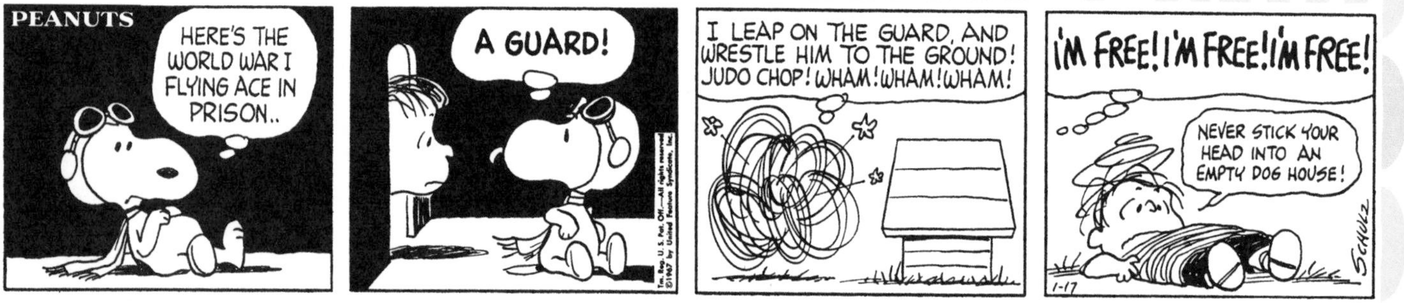
PEANUTS
HERE'S THE WORLD WAR I FLYING ACE IN PRISON..
A GUARD!
I LEAP ON THE GUARD, AND WRESTLE HIM TO THE GROUND! JUDO CHOP! WHAM! WHAM! WHAM!
I'M FREE! I'M FREE! I'M FREE!
NEVER STICK YOUR HEAD INTO AN EMPTY DOG HOUSE!
1-17
SCHULZ

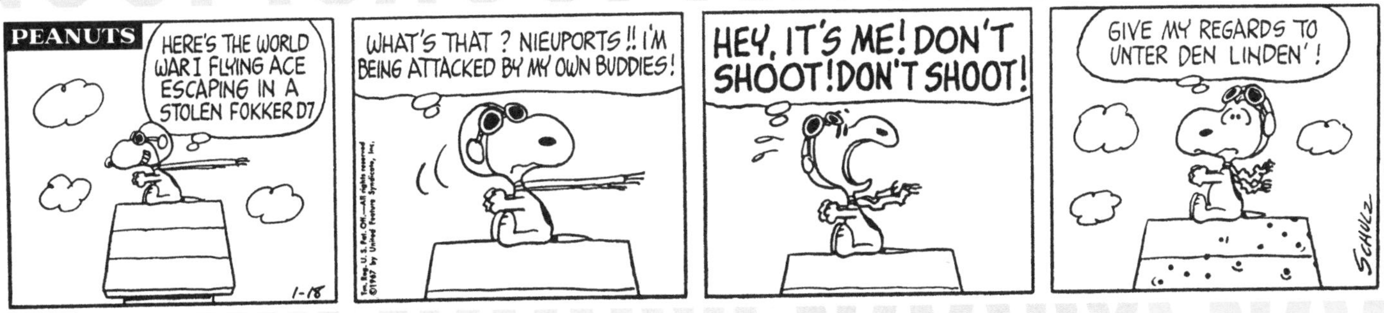
PEANUTS
HERE'S THE WORLD WAR I FLYING ACE ESCAPING IN A STOLEN FOKKER D7
1-18
Tm. Reg. U. S. Pat. Off.—All rights reserved ©1967 by United Feature Syndicate, Inc.
WHAT'S THAT ? NIEUPORTS !! I'M BEING ATTACKED BY MY OWN BUDDIES!
HEY, IT'S ME! DON'T SHOOT! DON'T SHOOT!
GIVE MY REGARDS TO UNTER DEN LINDEN' !
SCHULZ

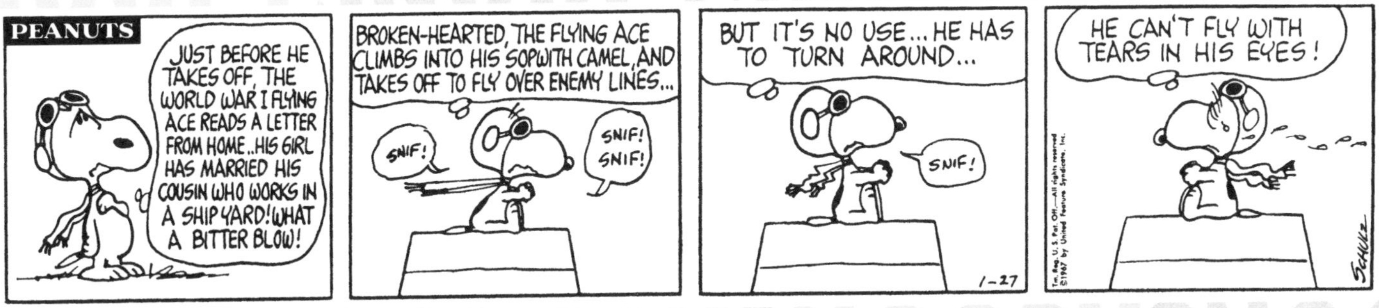
PEANUTS
JUST BEFORE HE TAKES OFF, THE WORLD WAR I FLYING ACE READS A LETTER FROM HOME..HIS GIRL HAS MARRIED HIS COUSIN WHO WORKS IN A SHIP YARD! WHAT A BITTER BLOW!
BROKEN-HEARTED, THE FLYING ACE CLIMBS INTO HIS SOPWITH CAMEL, AND TAKES OFF TO FLY OVER ENEMY LINES...
SNIF!
SNIF! SNIF!
BUT IT'S NO USE... HE HAS TO TURN AROUND...
SNIF!
1-27
HE CAN'T FLY WITH TEARS IN HIS EYES!
Tm. Reg. U. S. Pat. Off.—All rights reserved ©1967 by United Feature Syndicate, Inc.
SCHULZ

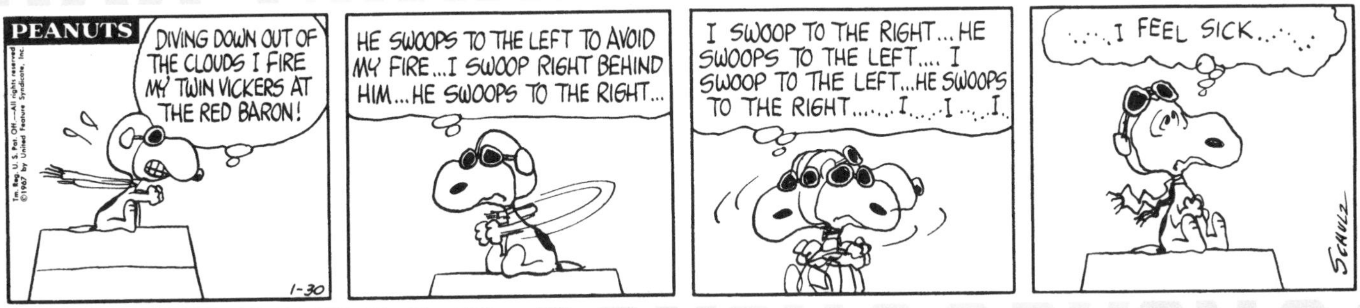
PEANUTS
Tm. Reg. U. S. Pat. Off.—All rights reserved ©1967 by United Feature Syndicate, Inc.
DIVING DOWN OUT OF THE CLOUDS I FIRE MY TWIN VICKERS AT THE RED BARON!
1-30
HE SWOOPS TO THE LEFT TO AVOID MY FIRE...I SWOOP RIGHT BEHIND HIM... HE SWOOPS TO THE RIGHT...
I SWOOP TO THE RIGHT... HE SWOOPS TO THE LEFT.... I SWOOP TO THE LEFT...HE SWOOPS TO THE RIGHT.......I.....I.....I.
.......I FEEL SICK.........
SCHULZ

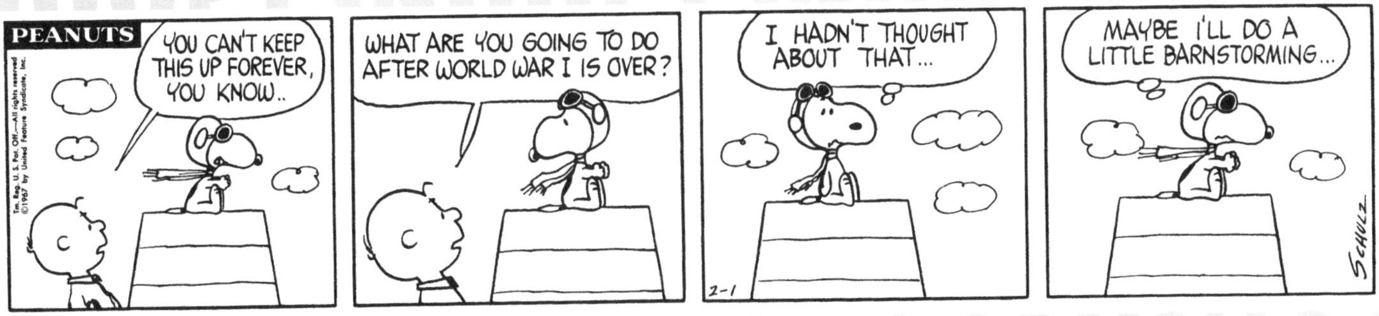
PEANUTS
Tm. Reg. U. S. Pat. Off.—All rights reserved ©1967 by United Feature Syndicate, Inc.
YOU CAN'T KEEP THIS UP FOREVER, YOU KNOW..
WHAT ARE YOU GOING TO DO AFTER WORLD WAR I IS OVER?
I HADN'T THOUGHT ABOUT THAT...
2-1
MAYBE I'LL DO A LITTLE BARNSTORMING...
SCHULZ

PEANUTS
HERE'S THE WORLD WAR I PILOT WALKING OUT TO HIS SOPWITH CAMEL
WHERE'S MY MECHANIC ? HOW CAN I FLY THIS PLANE WITHOUT MY MECHANIC ?!
Tm. Reg. U. S. Pat. Off.—All rights reserved
© 1967 by United Feature Syndicate, Inc.
4-7
THEY DON'T CARE WHO THEY DRAFT THESE DAYS !
SCHULZ

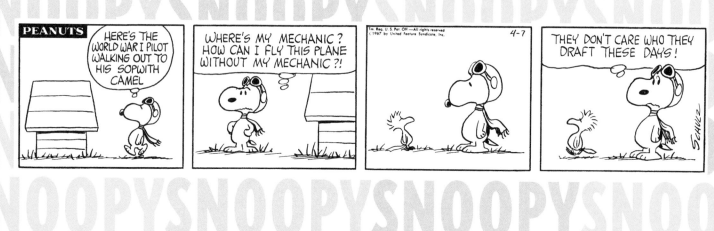

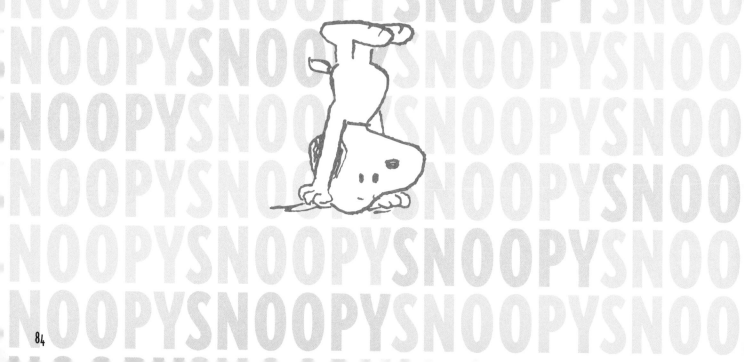

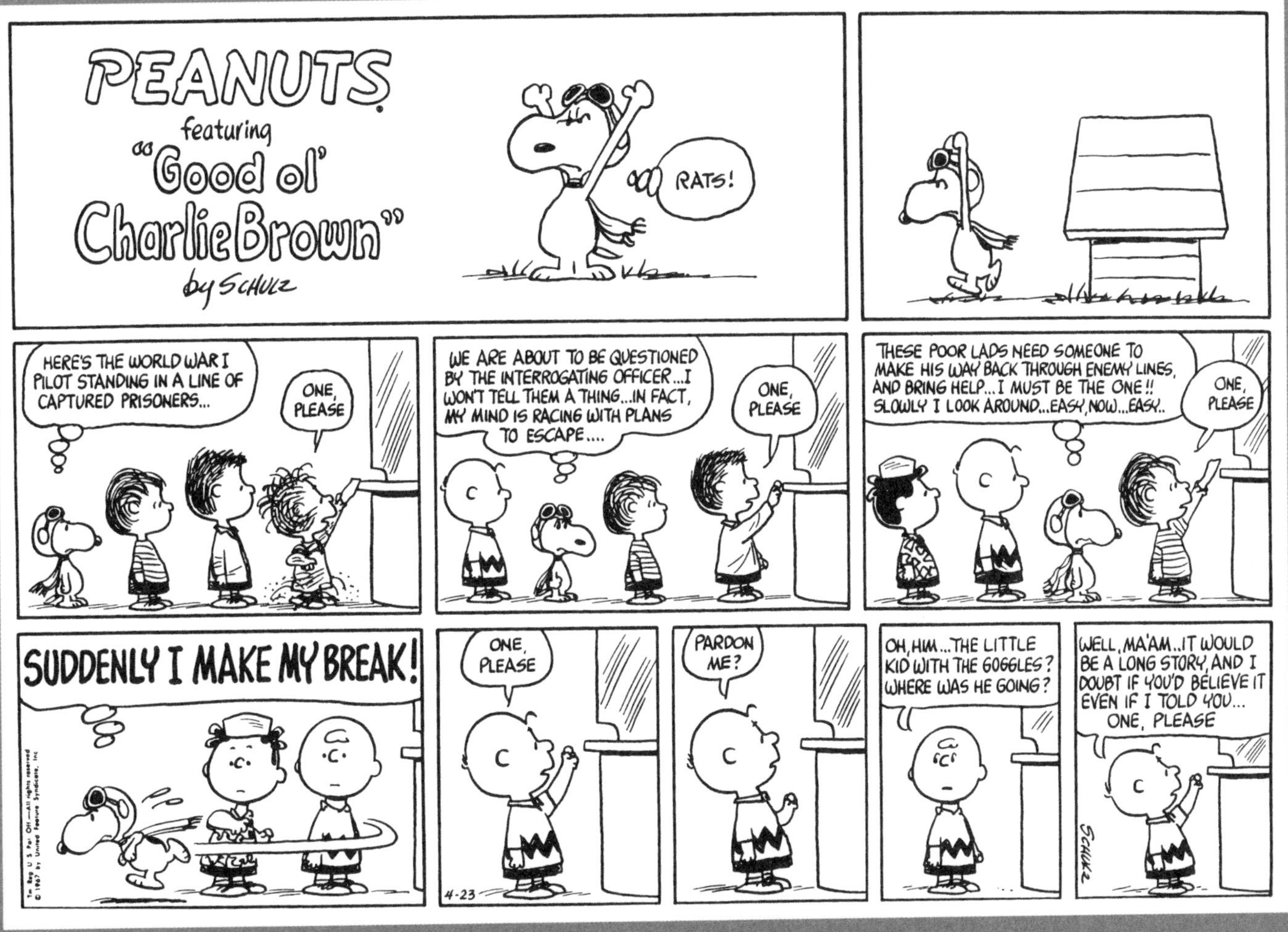
PEANUTS
featuring
"Good ol' CharlieBrown"
by SCHULZ
RATS!
HERE'S THE WORLD WAR I PILOT STANDING IN A LINE OF CAPTURED PRISONERS...
ONE, PLEASE
WE ARE ABOUT TO BE QUESTIONED BY THE INTERROGATING OFFICER...I WON'T TELL THEM A THING...IN FACT, MY MIND IS RACING WITH PLANS TO ESCAPE....
ONE, PLEASE
THESE POOR LADS NEED SOMEONE TO MAKE HIS WAY BACK THROUGH ENEMY LINES, AND BRING HELP...I MUST BE THE ONE!! SLOWLY I LOOK AROUND...EASY, NOW...EASY..
ONE, PLEASE
SUDDENLY I MAKE MY BREAK!
Tm Reg U S Pat Off—All rights reserved © 1967 by United Feature Syndicate, Inc
ONE, PLEASE
4-23
PARDON ME?
OH, HIM...THE LITTLE KID WITH THE GOGGLES? WHERE WAS HE GOING?
WELL, MA'AM..IT WOULD BE A LONG STORY, AND I DOUBT IF YOU'D BELIEVE IT EVEN IF I TOLD YOU... ONE, PLEASE
SCHULZ

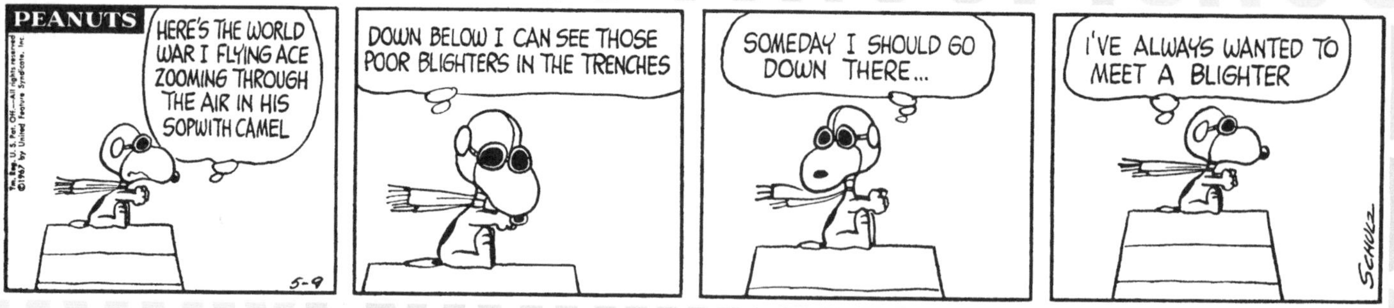
PEANUTS
Tm. Reg. U.S. Pat. Off.—All rights reserved ©1967 by United Feature Syndicate, Inc.
HERE'S THE WORLD WAR I FLYING ACE ZOOMING THROUGH THE AIR IN HIS SOPWITH CAMEL
5-9
DOWN BELOW I CAN SEE THOSE POOR BLIGHTERS IN THE TRENCHES
SOMEDAY I SHOULD GO DOWN THERE...
I'VE ALWAYS WANTED TO MEET A BLIGHTER
SCHULZ

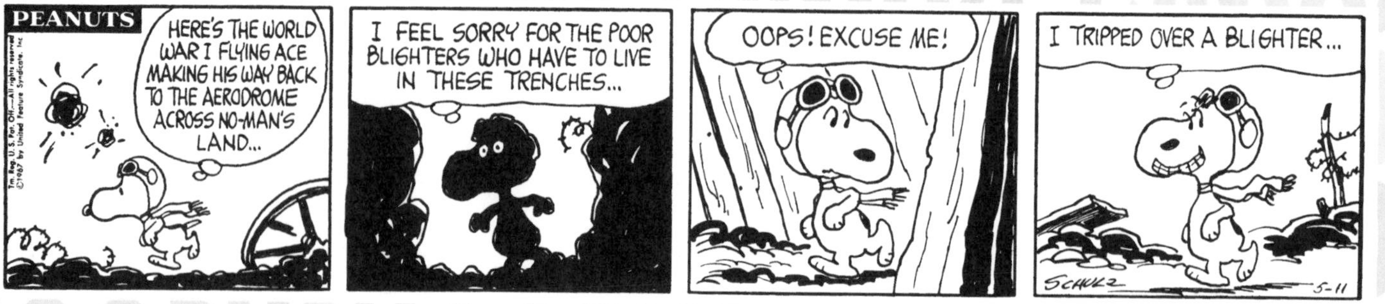
PEANUTS
Tm. Reg. U.S. Pat. Off.—All rights reserved ©1967 by United Feature Syndicate, Inc.
HERE'S THE WORLD WAR I FLYING ACE MAKING HIS WAY BACK TO THE AERODROME ACROSS NO-MAN'S LAND...
I FEEL SORRY FOR THE POOR BLIGHTERS WHO HAVE TO LIVE IN THESE TRENCHES...
OOPS! EXCUSE ME!
I TRIPPED OVER A BLIGHTER...
SCHULZ
5-11

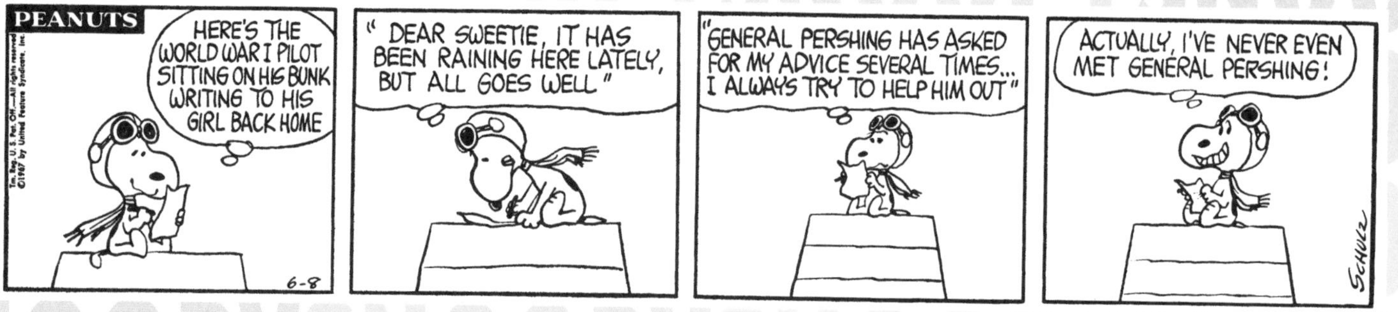
PEANUTS
Tm. Reg. U.S. Pat. Off.—All rights reserved ©1967 by United Feature Syndicate, Inc.
HERE'S THE WORLD WAR I PILOT SITTING ON HIS BUNK WRITING TO HIS GIRL BACK HOME
6-8
"DEAR SWEETIE, IT HAS BEEN RAINING HERE LATELY, BUT ALL GOES WELL"
"GENERAL PERSHING HAS ASKED FOR MY ADVICE SEVERAL TIMES... I ALWAYS TRY TO HELP HIM OUT"
ACTUALLY, I'VE NEVER EVEN MET GENERAL PERSHING!
SCHULZ

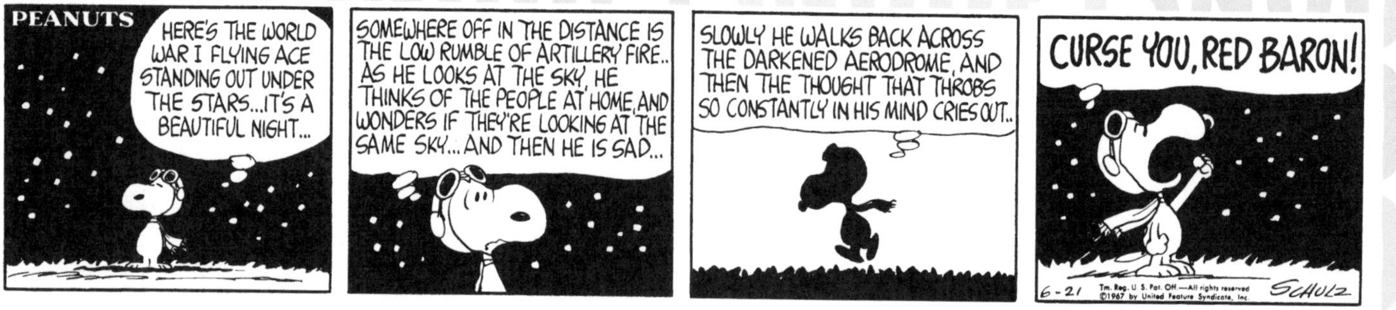
PEANUTS
HERE'S THE WORLD WAR I FLYING ACE STANDING OUT UNDER THE STARS...IT'S A BEAUTIFUL NIGHT...
SOMEWHERE OFF IN THE DISTANCE IS THE LOW RUMBLE OF ARTILLERY FIRE.. AS HE LOOKS AT THE SKY, HE THINKS OF THE PEOPLE AT HOME, AND WONDERS IF THEY'RE LOOKING AT THE SAME SKY... AND THEN HE IS SAD...
SLOWLY HE WALKS BACK ACROSS THE DARKENED AERODROME, AND THEN THE THOUGHT THAT THROBS SO CONSTANTLY IN HIS MIND CRIES OUT..
CURSE YOU, RED BARON!
6-21
Tm. Reg. U.S. Pat. Off.—All rights reserved ©1967 by United Feature Syndicate, Inc.
SCHULZ

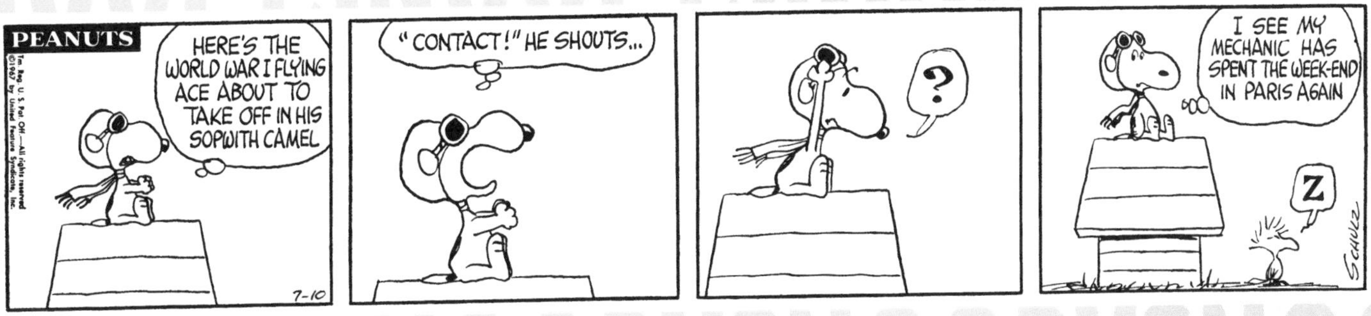
PEANUTS
Tm. Reg. U. S. Pat. Off.—All rights reserved ©1967 by United Feature Syndicate, Inc.
HERE'S THE WORLD WAR I FLYING ACE ABOUT TO TAKE OFF IN HIS SOPWITH CAMEL
7-10
"CONTACT!" HE SHOUTS...
?
I SEE MY MECHANIC HAS SPENT THE WEEK-END IN PARIS AGAIN
Z
SCHULZ

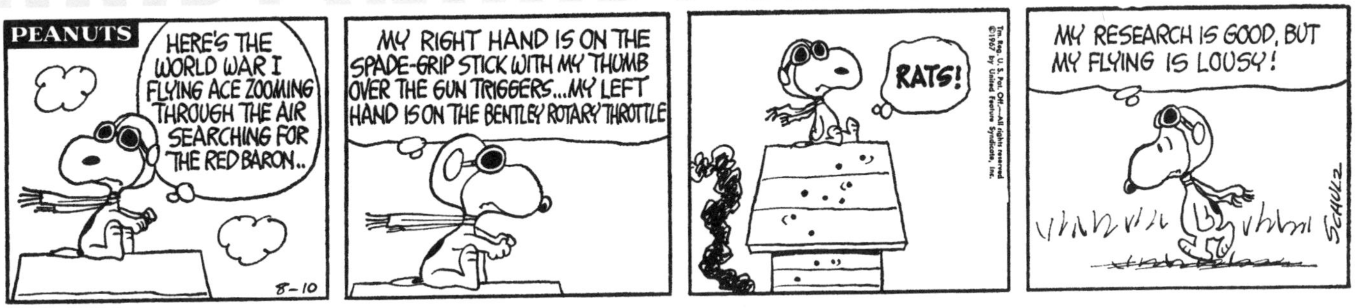
PEANUTS
HERE'S THE WORLD WAR I FLYING ACE ZOOMING THROUGH THE AIR SEARCHING FOR THE RED BARON..
8-10
MY RIGHT HAND IS ON THE SPADE-GRIP STICK WITH MY THUMB OVER THE GUN TRIGGERS...MY LEFT HAND IS ON THE BENTLEY ROTARY THROTTLE
RATS!
Tm. Reg. U. S. Pat. Off.—All rights reserved ©1967 by United Feature Syndicate, Inc.
MY RESEARCH IS GOOD, BUT MY FLYING IS LOUSY!
SCHULZ

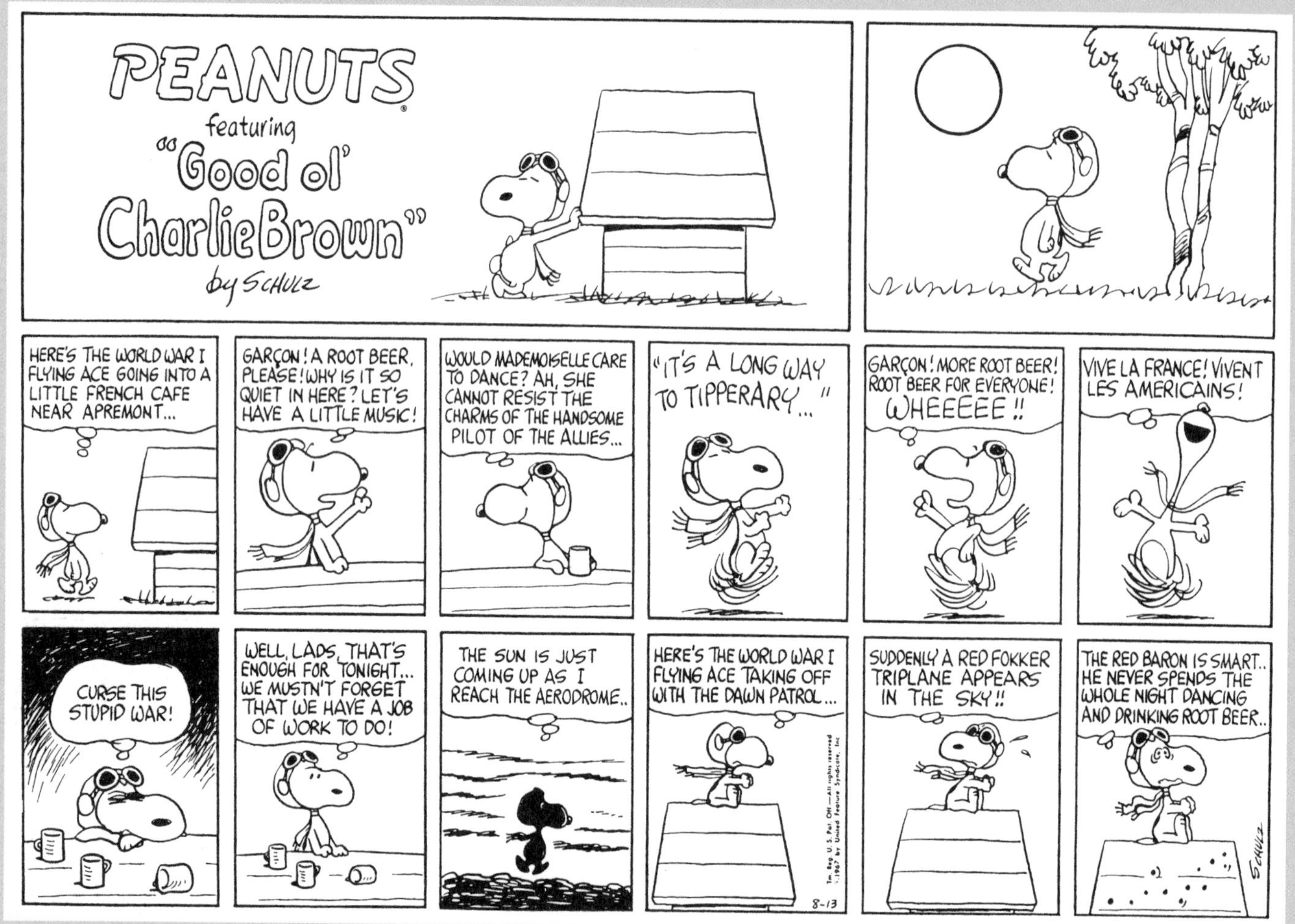
PEANUTS®
featuring
"Good ol' Charlie Brown"
by SCHULZ
HERE'S THE WORLD WAR I FLYING ACE GOING INTO A LITTLE FRENCH CAFE NEAR APREMONT...
GARÇON! A ROOT BEER, PLEASE! WHY IS IT SO QUIET IN HERE? LET'S HAVE A LITTLE MUSIC!
WOULD MADEMOISELLE CARE TO DANCE? AH, SHE CANNOT RESIST THE CHARMS OF THE HANDSOME PILOT OF THE ALLIES...
"IT'S A LONG WAY TO TIPPERARY..."
GARÇON! MORE ROOT BEER! ROOT BEER FOR EVERYONE! WHEEEEE!!
VIVE LA FRANCE! VIVENT LES AMERICAINS!
CURSE THIS STUPID WAR!
WELL, LADS, THAT'S ENOUGH FOR TONIGHT... WE MUSTN'T FORGET THAT WE HAVE A JOB OF WORK TO DO!
THE SUN IS JUST COMING UP AS I REACH THE AERODROME..
HERE'S THE WORLD WAR I FLYING ACE TAKING OFF WITH THE DAWN PATROL...
Tm. Reg. U. S. Pat. Off.—All rights reserved
©1967 by United Feature Syndicate, Inc
8-13
SUDDENLY A RED FOKKER TRIPLANE APPEARS IN THE SKY!!
THE RED BARON IS SMART.. HE NEVER SPENDS THE WHOLE NIGHT DANCING AND DRINKING ROOT BEER..
SCHULZ

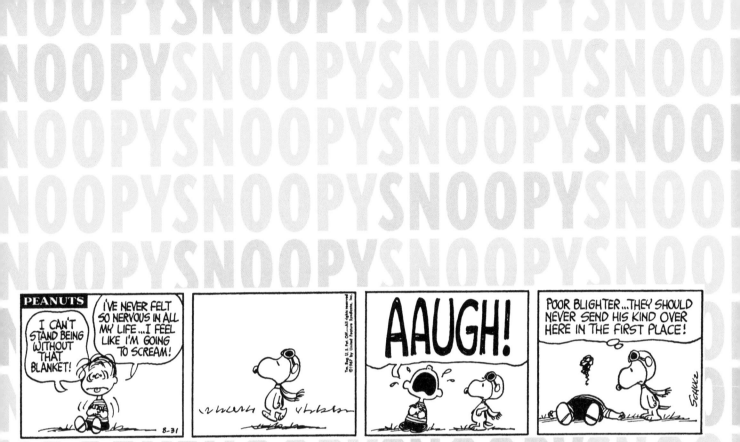

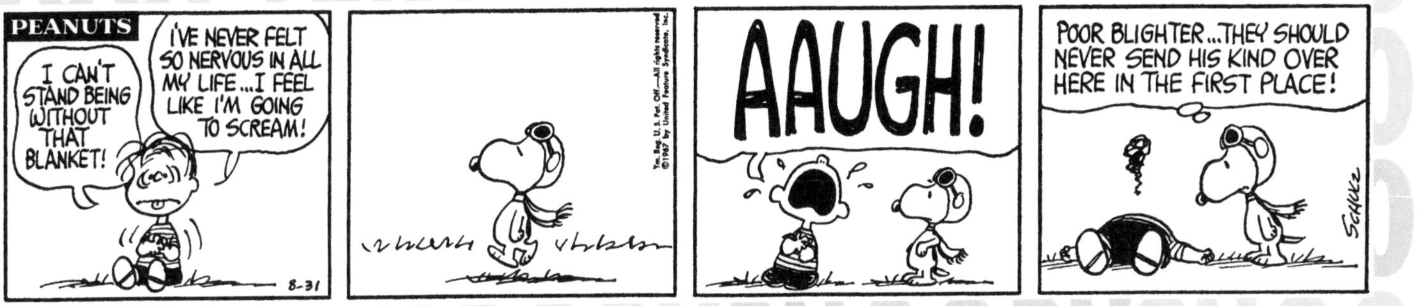
PEANUTS
I CAN'T STAND BEING WITHOUT THAT BLANKET!
I'VE NEVER FELT SO NERVOUS IN ALL MY LIFE...I FEEL LIKE I'M GOING TO SCREAM!
8-31
Tm. Reg. U.S. Pat. Off.—All rights reserved
©1987 by United Feature Syndicate, Inc.
AAUGH!
POOR BLIGHTER...THEY SHOULD NEVER SEND HIS KIND OVER HERE IN THE FIRST PLACE!
SCHULZ

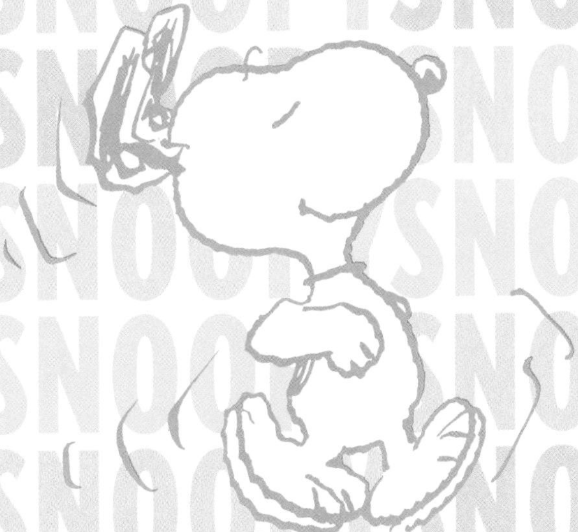

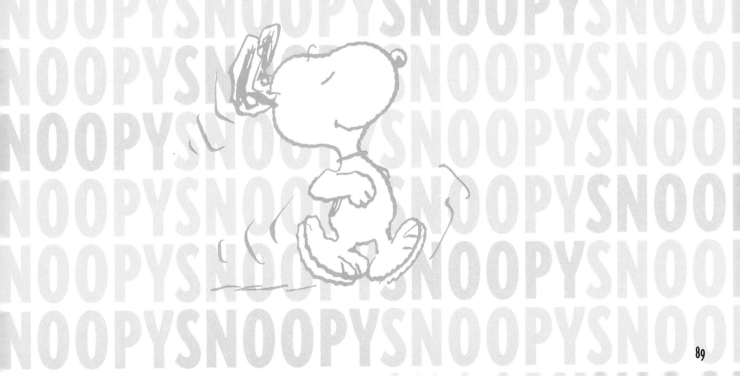

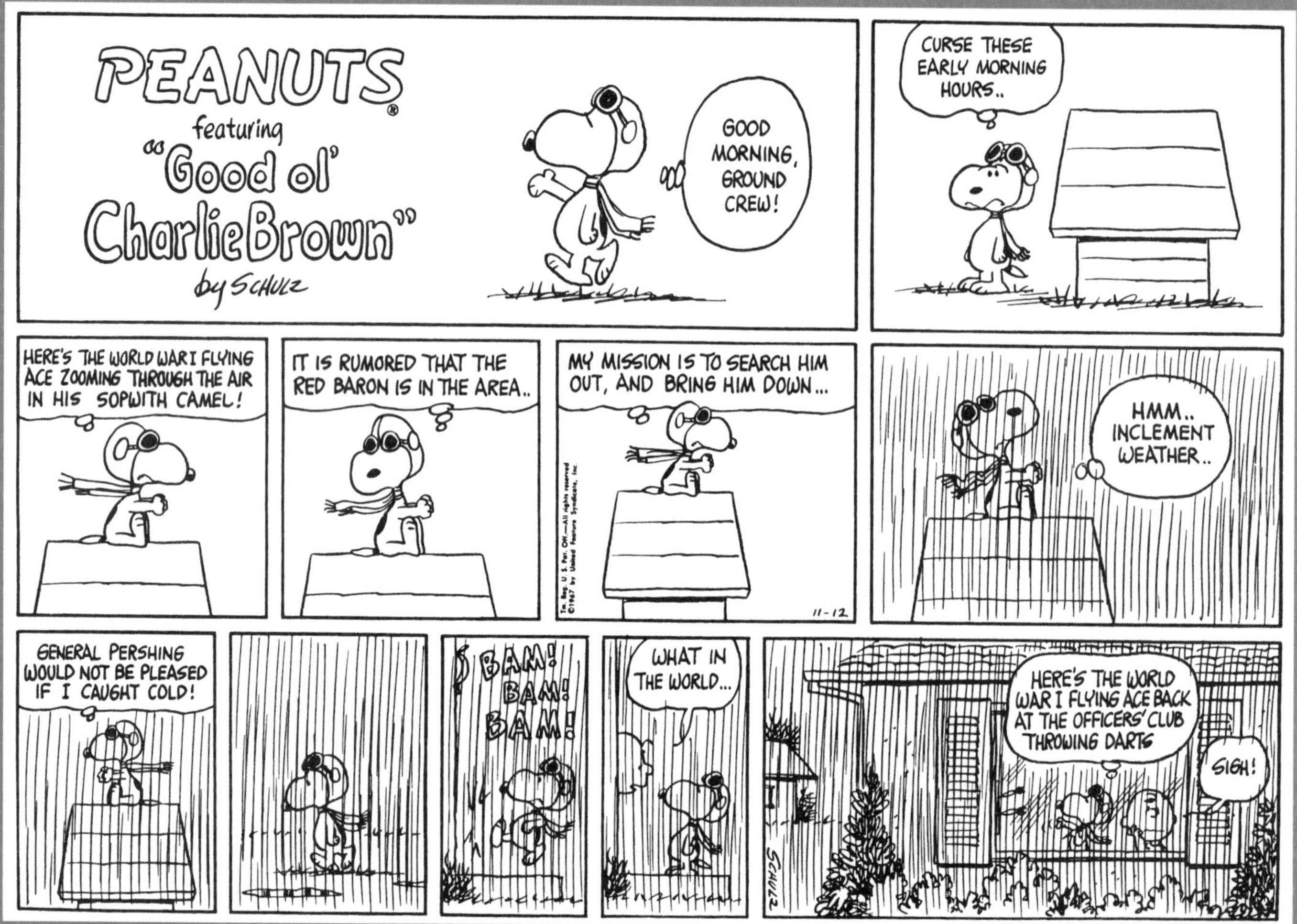
PEANUTS
featuring
"Good ol' CharlieBrown"
by SCHULZ
GOOD MORNING, GROUND CREW!
CURSE THESE EARLY MORNING HOURS..
HERE'S THE WORLD WAR I FLYING ACE ZOOMING THROUGH THE AIR IN HIS SOPWITH CAMEL!
IT IS RUMORED THAT THE RED BARON IS IN THE AREA..
MY MISSION IS TO SEARCH HIM OUT, AND BRING HIM DOWN...
11-12
HMM.. INCLEMENT WEATHER..
GENERAL PERSHING WOULD NOT BE PLEASED IF I CAUGHT COLD!
BAM! BAM! BAM!
WHAT IN THE WORLD...
SCHULZ
HERE'S THE WORLD WAR I FLYING ACE BACK AT THE OFFICERS' CLUB THROWING DARTS
SIGH!

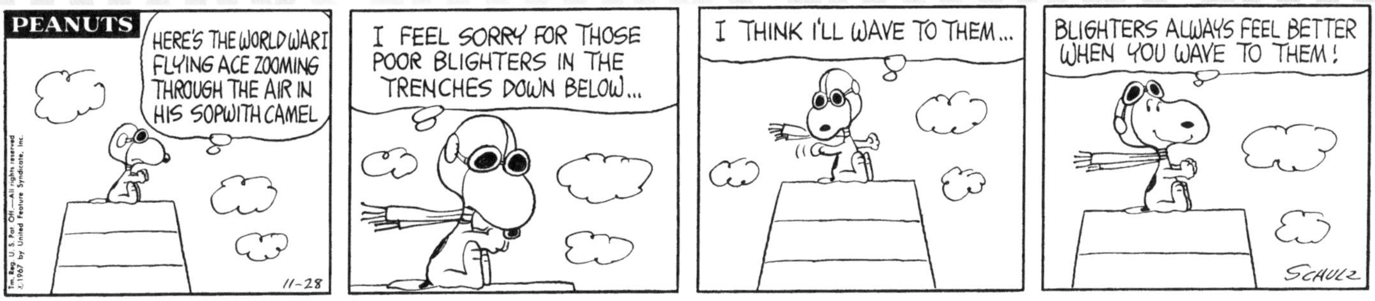
PEANUTS
HERE'S THE WORLD WAR I FLYING ACE ZOOMING THROUGH THE AIR IN HIS SOPWITH CAMEL
Tm. Reg. U.S. Pat. Off.—All rights reserved © 1967 by United Feature Syndicate, Inc.
11-28
I FEEL SORRY FOR THOSE POOR BLIGHTERS IN THE TRENCHES DOWN BELOW...
I THINK I'LL WAVE TO THEM...
BLIGHTERS ALWAYS FEEL BETTER WHEN YOU WAVE TO THEM!
SCHULZ

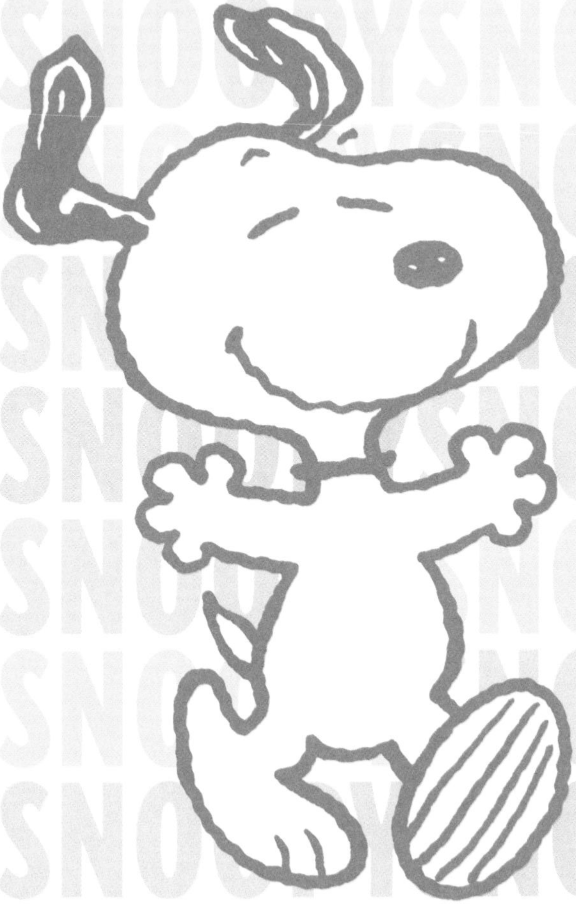

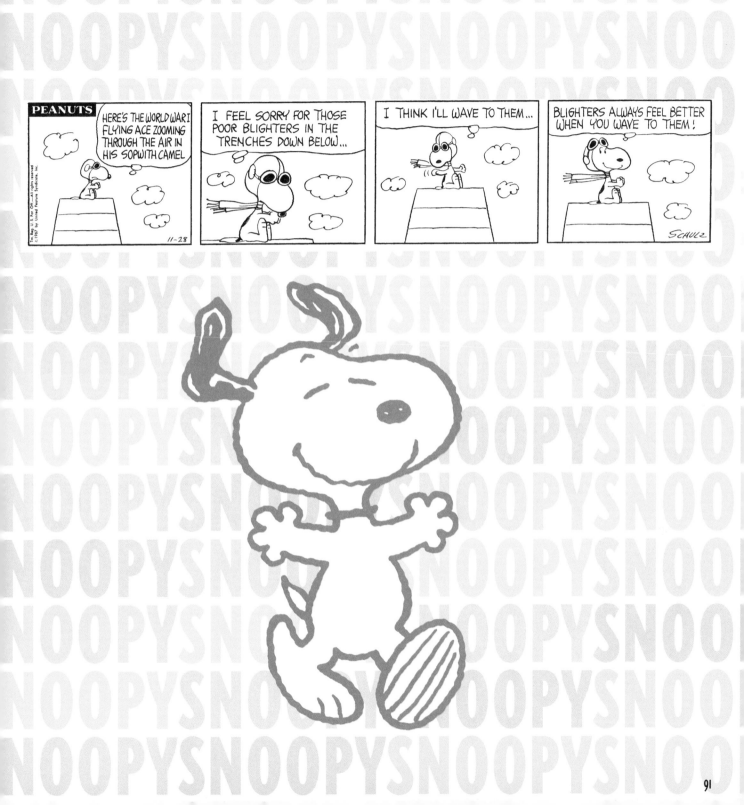

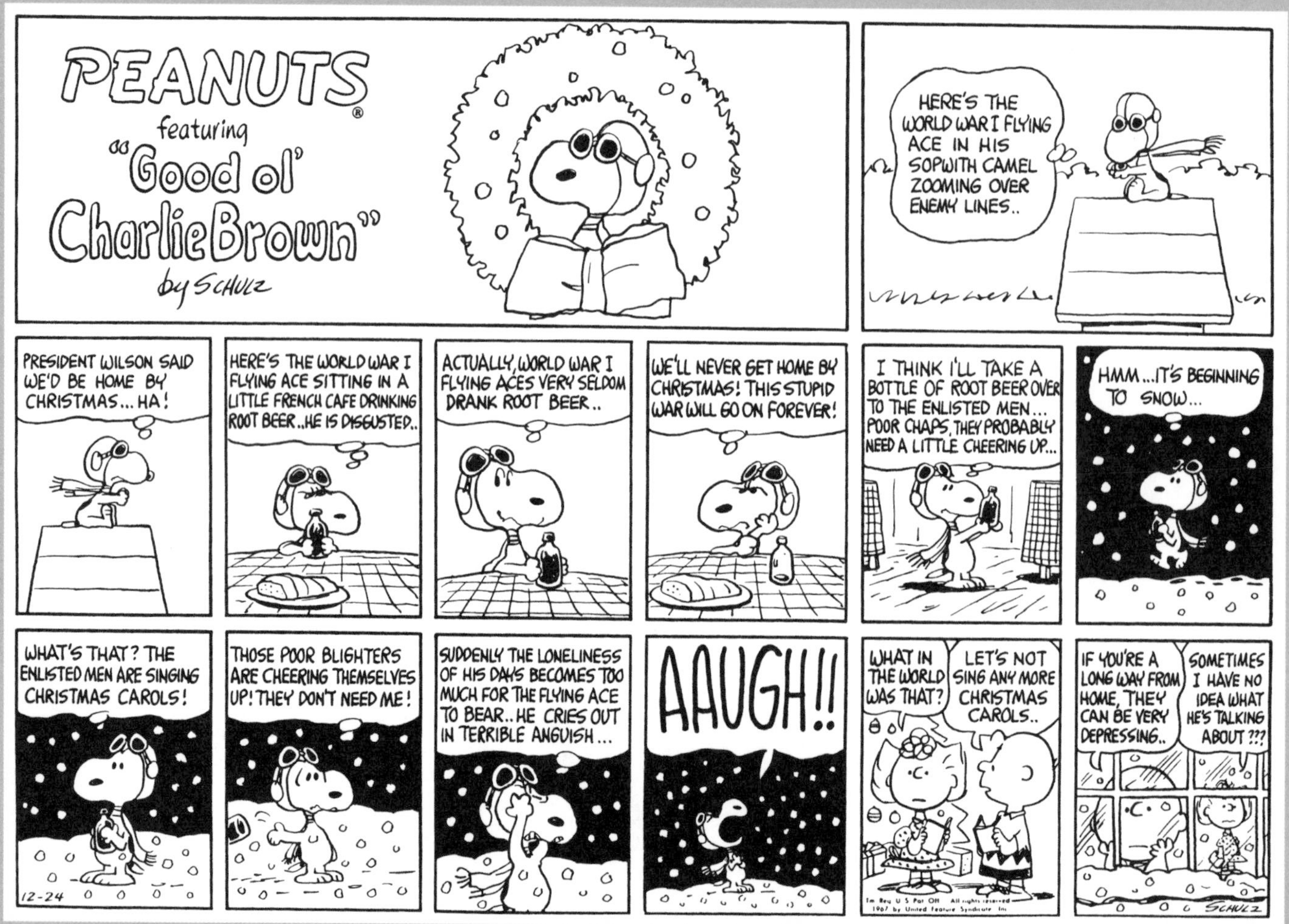
PEANUTS®
featuring
"Good ol' Charlie Brown"
by SCHULZ
HERE'S THE WORLD WAR I FLYING ACE IN HIS SOPWITH CAMEL ZOOMING OVER ENEMY LINES..
PRESIDENT WILSON SAID WE'D BE HOME BY CHRISTMAS... HA!
HERE'S THE WORLD WAR I FLYING ACE SITTING IN A LITTLE FRENCH CAFE DRINKING ROOT BEER..HE IS DISGUSTED..
ACTUALLY, WORLD WAR I FLYING ACES VERY SELDOM DRANK ROOT BEER..
WE'LL NEVER GET HOME BY CHRISTMAS! THIS STUPID WAR WILL GO ON FOREVER!
I THINK I'LL TAKE A BOTTLE OF ROOT BEER OVER TO THE ENLISTED MEN... POOR CHAPS, THEY PROBABLY NEED A LITTLE CHEERING UP...
HMM...IT'S BEGINNING TO SNOW...
WHAT'S THAT? THE ENLISTED MEN ARE SINGING CHRISTMAS CAROLS!
12-24
THOSE POOR BLIGHTERS ARE CHEERING THEMSELVES UP! THEY DON'T NEED ME!
SUDDENLY THE LONELINESS OF HIS DAYS BECOMES TOO MUCH FOR THE FLYING ACE TO BEAR.. HE CRIES OUT IN TERRIBLE ANGUISH...
AAUGH!!
WHAT IN THE WORLD WAS THAT?
LET'S NOT SING ANY MORE CHRISTMAS CAROLS..
Tm Reg U S Pat Off All rights reserved
1967 by United Feature Syndicate Inc
IF YOU'RE A LONG WAY FROM HOME, THEY CAN BE VERY DEPRESSING..
SOMETIMES I HAVE NO IDEA WHAT HE'S TALKING ABOUT???
SCHULZ

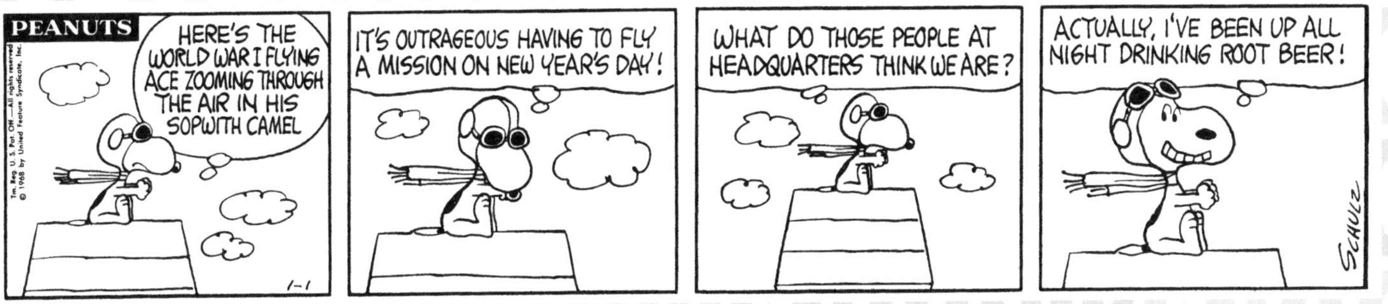
PEANUTS
HERE'S THE WORLD WAR I FLYING ACE ZOOMING THROUGH THE AIR IN HIS SOPWITH CAMEL
Tm. Reg. U. S. Pat. Off.—All rights reserved © 1968 by United Feature Syndicate, Inc.
1-1
IT'S OUTRAGEOUS HAVING TO FLY A MISSION ON NEW YEAR'S DAY!
WHAT DO THOSE PEOPLE AT HEADQUARTERS THINK WE ARE?
ACTUALLY, I'VE BEEN UP ALL NIGHT DRINKING ROOT BEER!
SCHULZ

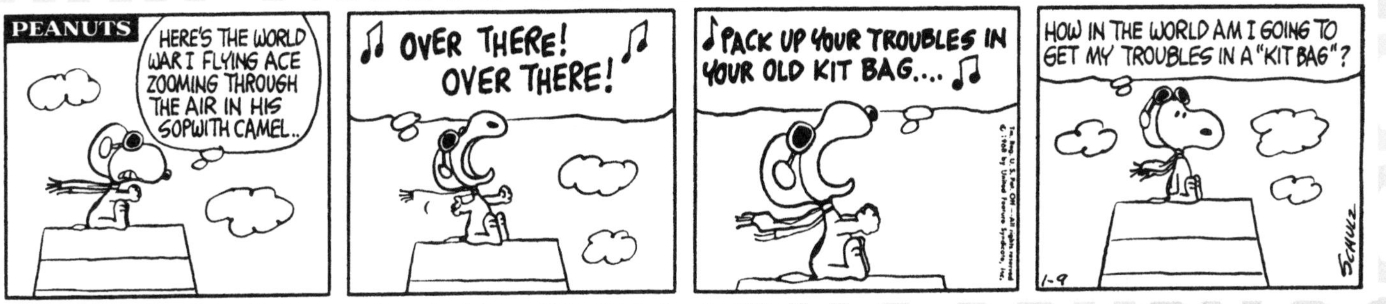
PEANUTS
HERE'S THE WORLD WAR I FLYING ACE ZOOMING THROUGH THE AIR IN HIS SOPWITH CAMEL..
♫ OVER THERE! OVER THERE! ♫
♪ PACK UP YOUR TROUBLES IN YOUR OLD KIT BAG.... ♫
Tm. Reg. U. S. Pat. Off.—All rights reserved © 1968 by United Feature Syndicate, Inc.
1-9
HOW IN THE WORLD AM I GOING TO GET MY TROUBLES IN A "KIT BAG"?
SCHULZ

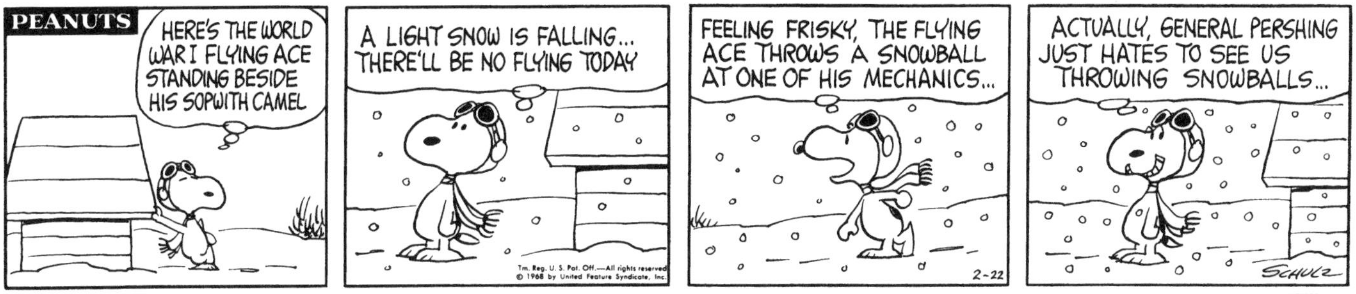
PEANUTS
HERE'S THE WORLD WAR I FLYING ACE STANDING BESIDE HIS SOPWITH CAMEL
A LIGHT SNOW IS FALLING... THERE'LL BE NO FLYING TODAY
Tm. Reg. U. S. Pat. Off.—All rights reserved © 1968 by United Feature Syndicate, Inc.
FEELING FRISKY, THE FLYING ACE THROWS A SNOWBALL AT ONE OF HIS MECHANICS...
2-22
ACTUALLY, GENERAL PERSHING JUST HATES TO SEE US THROWING SNOWBALLS...
SCHULZ

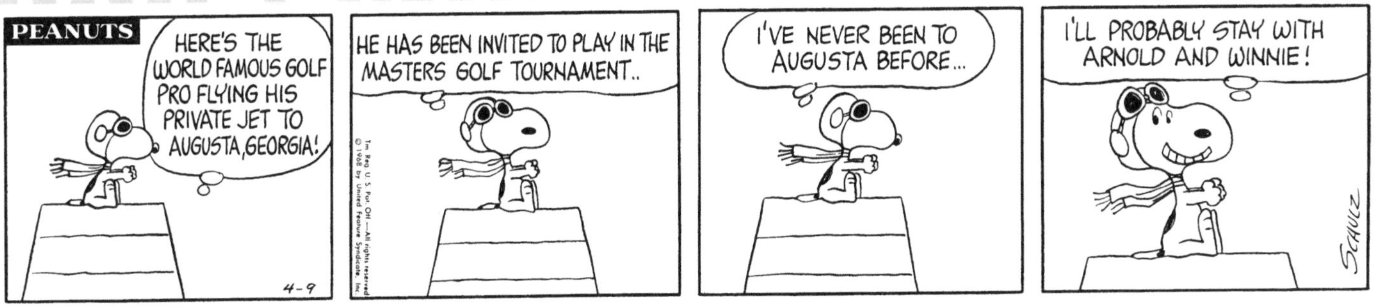
PEANUTS
HERE'S THE WORLD FAMOUS GOLF PRO FLYING HIS PRIVATE JET TO AUGUSTA, GEORGIA!
4-9
HE HAS BEEN INVITED TO PLAY IN THE MASTERS GOLF TOURNAMENT..
Tm. Reg. U. S. Pat. Off.—All rights reserved © 1968 by United Feature Syndicate, Inc.
I'VE NEVER BEEN TO AUGUSTA BEFORE...
I'LL PROBABLY STAY WITH ARNOLD AND WINNIE!
SCHULZ

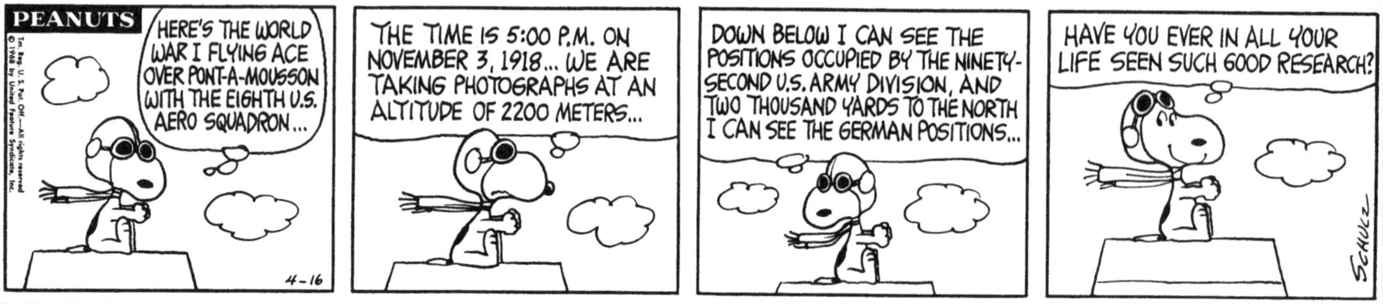
PEANUTS
Tm. Reg. U. S. Pat. Off.—All rights reserved © 1968 by United Feature Syndicate, Inc.
HERE'S THE WORLD WAR I FLYING ACE OVER PONT-A-MOUSSON WITH THE EIGHTH U.S. AERO SQUADRON...
4-16
THE TIME IS 5:00 P.M. ON NOVEMBER 3, 1918... WE ARE TAKING PHOTOGRAPHS AT AN ALTITUDE OF 2200 METERS...
DOWN BELOW I CAN SEE THE POSITIONS OCCUPIED BY THE NINETY-SECOND U.S. ARMY DIVISION, AND TWO THOUSAND YARDS TO THE NORTH I CAN SEE THE GERMAN POSITIONS...
HAVE YOU EVER IN ALL YOUR LIFE SEEN SUCH GOOD RESEARCH?
SCHULZ

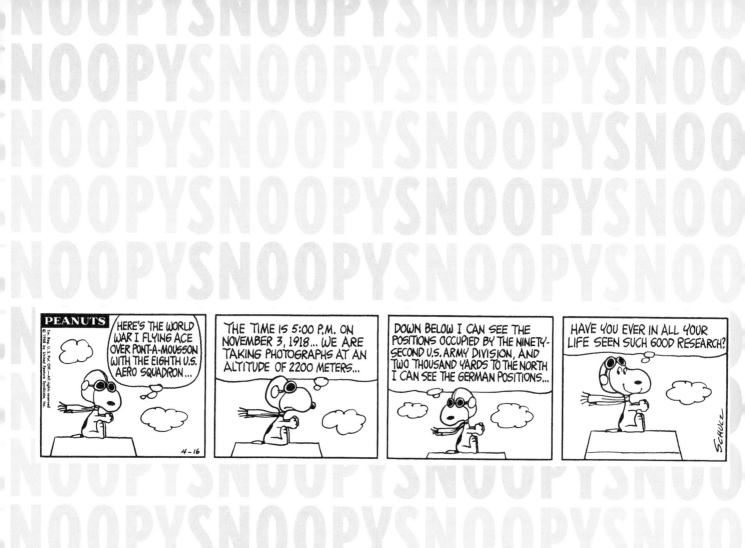

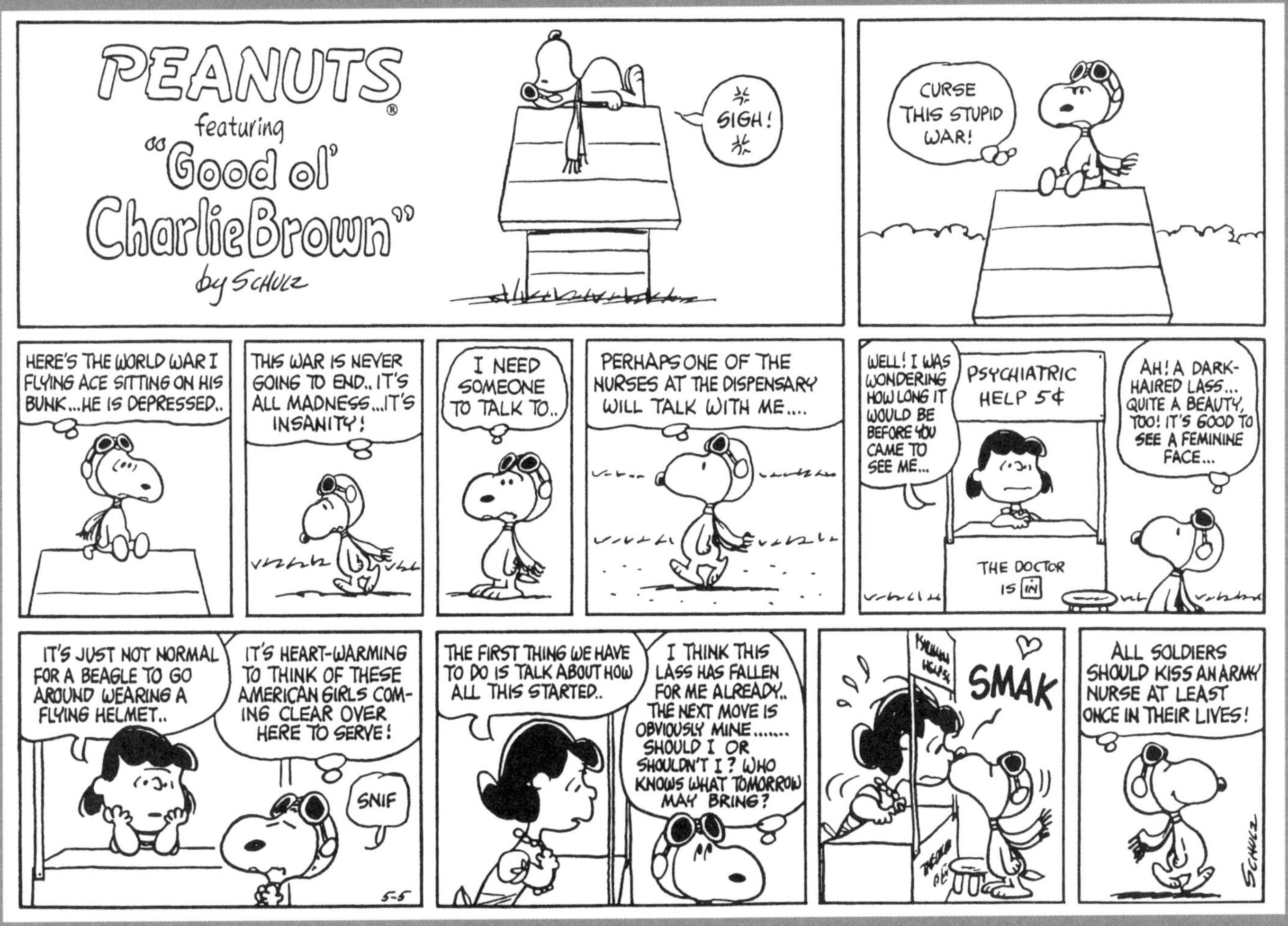
PEANUTS®
featuring "Good ol' CharlieBrown"
by SCHULZ
SIGH!
CURSE THIS STUPID WAR!
HERE'S THE WORLD WAR I FLYING ACE SITTING ON HIS BUNK...HE IS DEPRESSED..
THIS WAR IS NEVER GOING TO END.. IT'S ALL MADNESS...IT'S INSANITY!
I NEED SOMEONE TO TALK TO..
PERHAPS ONE OF THE NURSES AT THE DISPENSARY WILL TALK WITH ME....
WELL! I WAS WONDERING HOW LONG IT WOULD BE BEFORE YOU CAME TO SEE ME...
PSYCHIATRIC HELP 5¢
AH! A DARK-HAIRED LASS... QUITE A BEAUTY, TOO! IT'S GOOD TO SEE A FEMININE FACE...
THE DOCTOR IS IN
IT'S JUST NOT NORMAL FOR A BEAGLE TO GO AROUND WEARING A FLYING HELMET..
IT'S HEART-WARMING TO THINK OF THESE AMERICAN GIRLS COMING CLEAR OVER HERE TO SERVE!
SNIF
5-5
THE FIRST THING WE HAVE TO DO IS TALK ABOUT HOW ALL THIS STARTED..
I THINK THIS LASS HAS FALLEN FOR ME ALREADY.. THE NEXT MOVE IS OBVIOUSLY MINE....... SHOULD I OR SHOULDN'T I? WHO KNOWS WHAT TOMORROW MAY BRING?
SMAK
ALL SOLDIERS SHOULD KISS AN ARMY NURSE AT LEAST ONCE IN THEIR LIVES!
SCHULZ

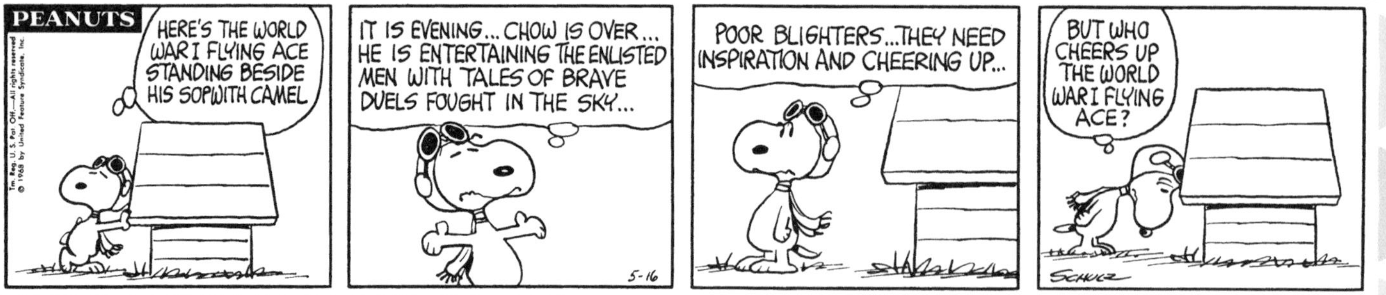
PEANUTS
Tm. Reg. U.S. Pat. Off.—All rights reserved © 1968 by United Feature Syndicate, Inc.
HERE'S THE WORLD WAR I FLYING ACE STANDING BESIDE HIS SOPWITH CAMEL
IT IS EVENING... CHOW IS OVER... HE IS ENTERTAINING THE ENLISTED MEN WITH TALES OF BRAVE DUELS FOUGHT IN THE SKY...
5-16
POOR BLIGHTERS...THEY NEED INSPIRATION AND CHEERING UP...
BUT WHO CHEERS UP THE WORLD WAR I FLYING ACE?
SCHULZ

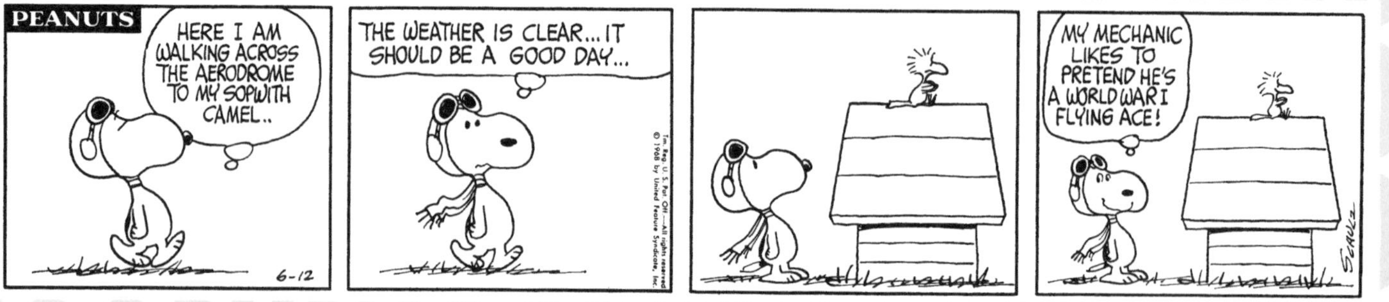
PEANUTS
HERE I AM WALKING ACROSS THE AERODROME TO MY SOPWITH CAMEL..
6-12
THE WEATHER IS CLEAR... IT SHOULD BE A GOOD DAY...
Tm. Reg. U.S. Pat. Off.—All rights reserved © 1968 by United Feature Syndicate, Inc.
MY MECHANIC LIKES TO PRETEND HE'S A WORLD WAR I FLYING ACE!
SCHULZ

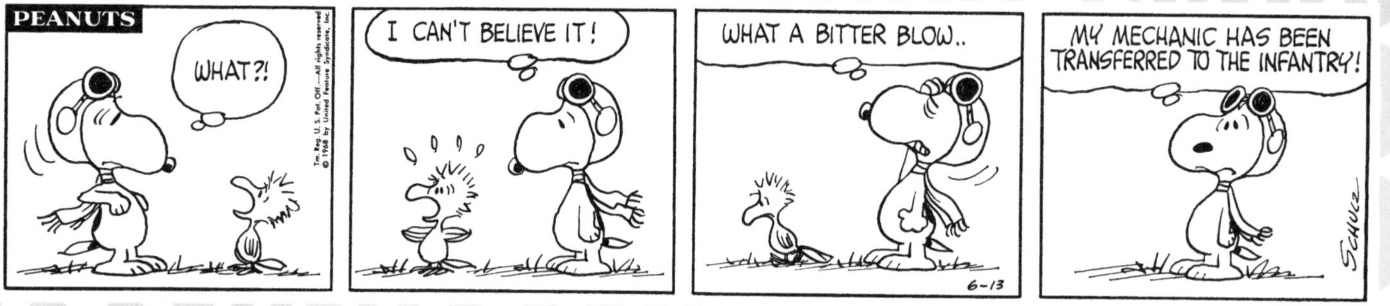
PEANUTS
WHAT?!
Tm. Reg. U.S. Pat. Off.—All rights reserved © 1968 by United Feature Syndicate, Inc.
I CAN'T BELIEVE IT!
WHAT A BITTER BLOW..
6-13
MY MECHANIC HAS BEEN TRANSFERRED TO THE INFANTRY!
SCHULZ

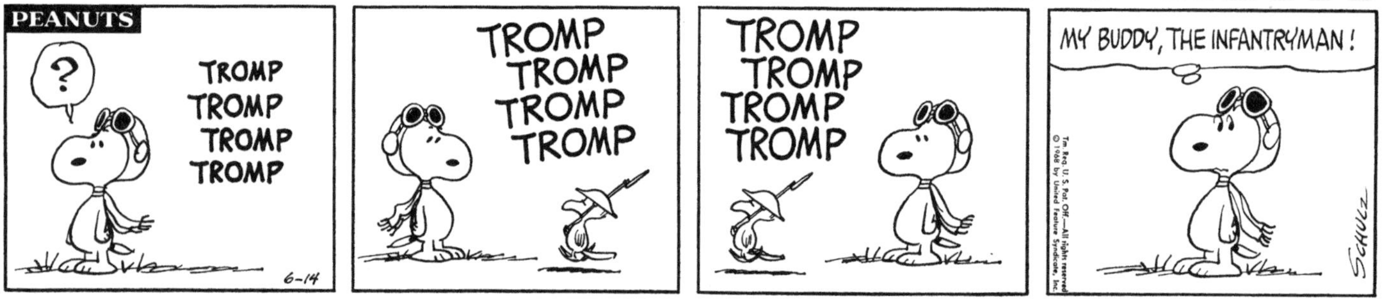
PEANUTS
?
TROMP TROMP TROMP TROMP
6-14
TROMP TROMP TROMP TROMP
TROMP TROMP TROMP TROMP
MY BUDDY, THE INFANTRYMAN!
Tm. Reg. U.S. Pat. Off.—All rights reserved © 1968 by United Feature Syndicate, Inc.
SCHULZ

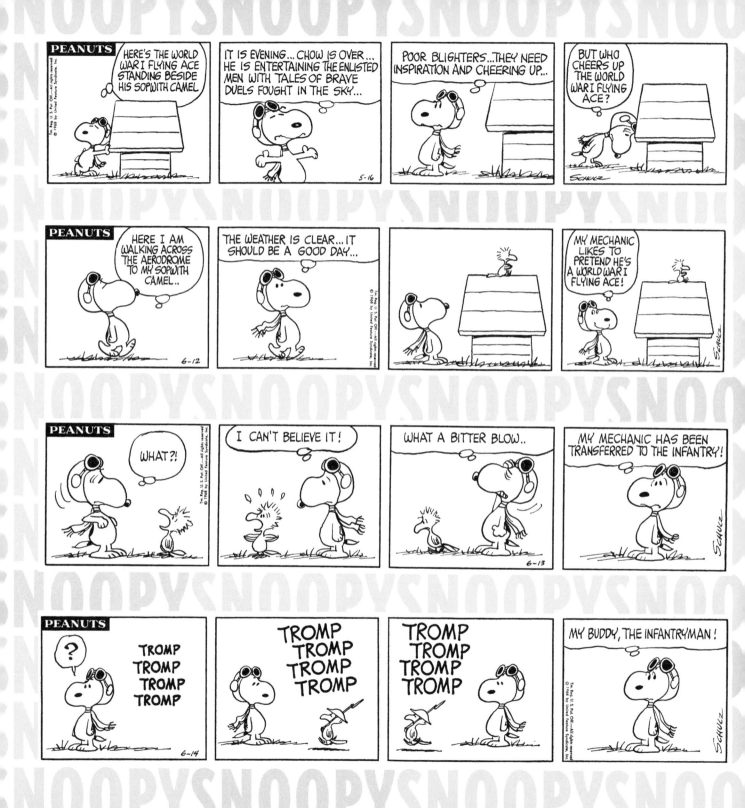

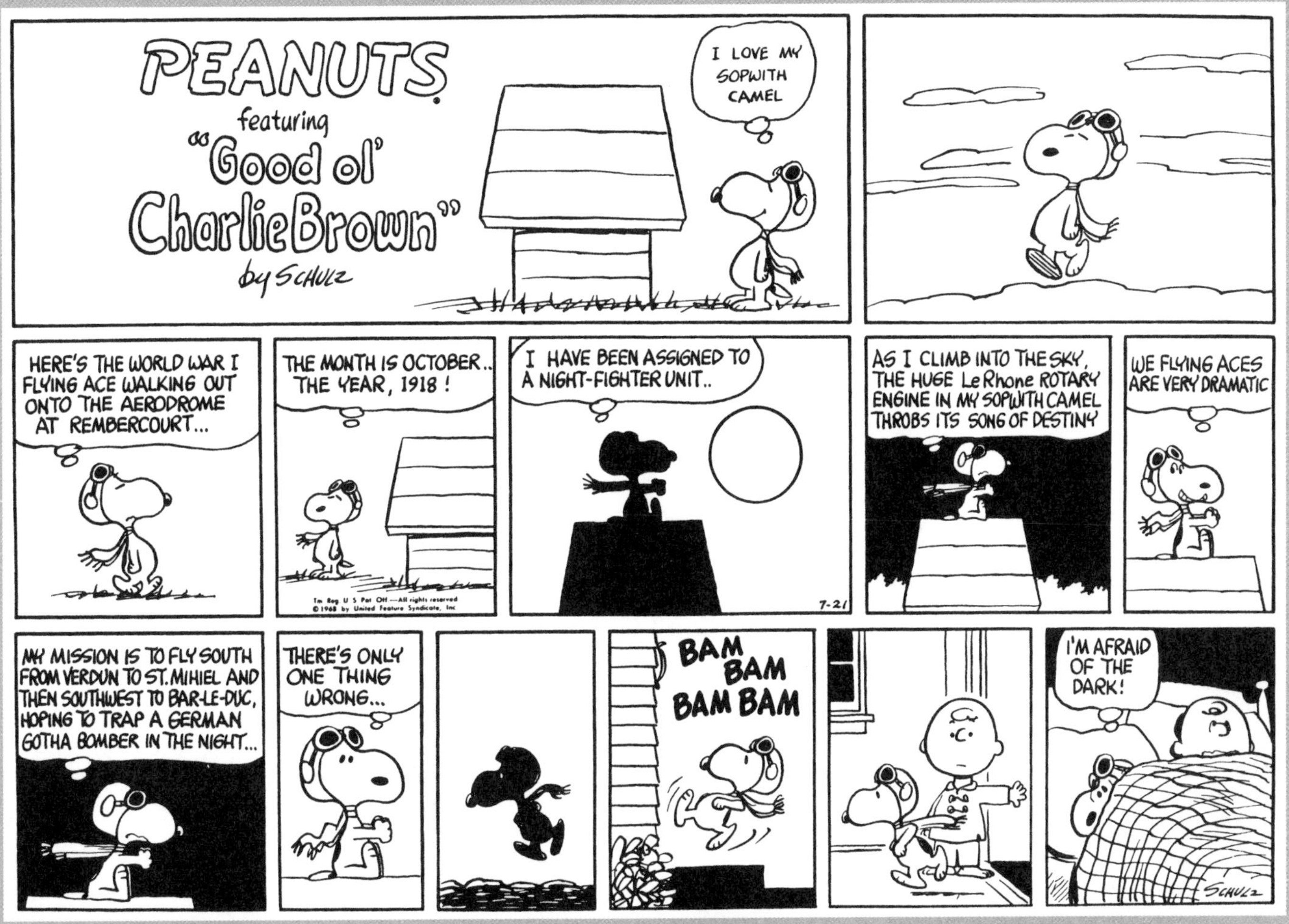
PEANUTS
featuring
"Good ol' CharlieBrown"
by SCHULZ
I LOVE MY SOPWITH CAMEL
HERE'S THE WORLD WAR I FLYING ACE WALKING OUT ONTO THE AERODROME AT REMBERCOURT...
THE MONTH IS OCTOBER.. THE YEAR, 1918 !
Tm Reg U S Pat Off —All rights reserved
© 1968 by United Feature Syndicate, Inc
I HAVE BEEN ASSIGNED TO A NIGHT-FIGHTER UNIT..
7-21
AS I CLIMB INTO THE SKY, THE HUGE Le Rhone ROTARY ENGINE IN MY SOPWITH CAMEL THROBS ITS SONG OF DESTINY
WE FLYING ACES ARE VERY DRAMATIC
MY MISSION IS TO FLY SOUTH FROM VERDUN TO ST. MIHIEL AND THEN SOUTHWEST TO BAR-LE-DUC, HOPING TO TRAP A GERMAN GOTHA BOMBER IN THE NIGHT...
THERE'S ONLY ONE THING WRONG...
BAM BAM BAM BAM
I'M AFRAID OF THE DARK!
SCHULZ

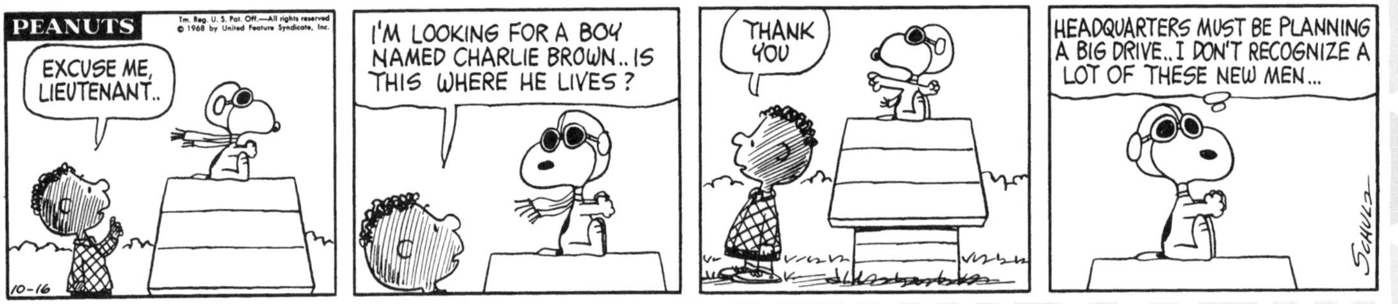
PEANUTS
Tm. Reg. U. S. Pat. Off.—All rights reserved © 1968 by United Feature Syndicate, Inc.
EXCUSE ME, LIEUTENANT..
10-16
I'M LOOKING FOR A BOY NAMED CHARLIE BROWN.. IS THIS WHERE HE LIVES?
THANK YOU
HEADQUARTERS MUST BE PLANNING A BIG DRIVE.. I DON'T RECOGNIZE A LOT OF THESE NEW MEN...
SCHULZ

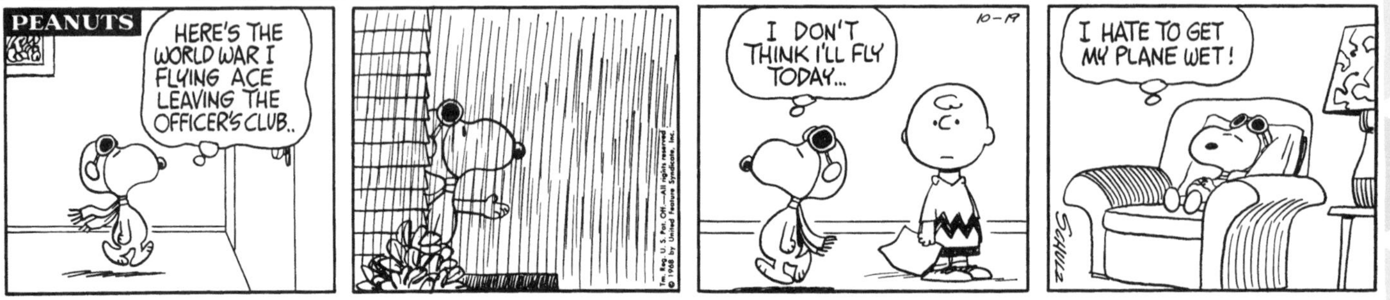
PEANUTS
HERE'S THE WORLD WAR I FLYING ACE LEAVING THE OFFICER'S CLUB..
Tm. Reg. U. S. Pat. Off.—All rights reserved © 1968 by United Feature Syndicate, Inc.
I DON'T THINK I'LL FLY TODAY...
10-19
SCHULZ
I HATE TO GET MY PLANE WET!

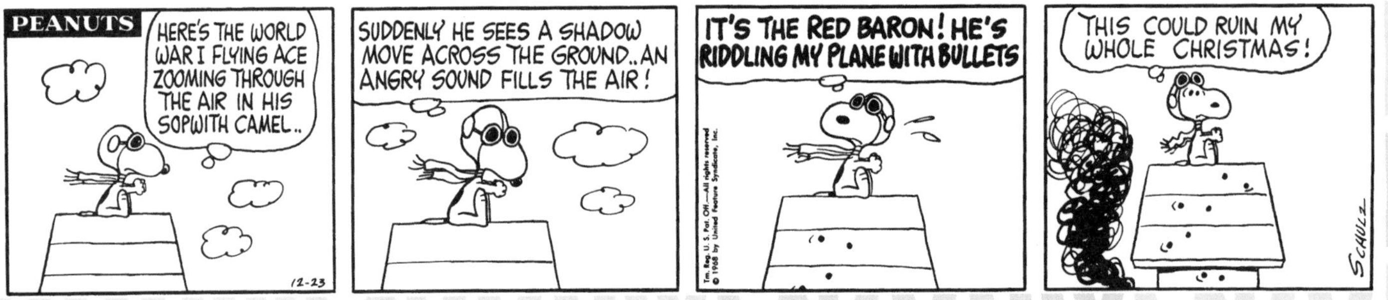
PEANUTS
HERE'S THE WORLD WAR I FLYING ACE ZOOMING THROUGH THE AIR IN HIS SOPWITH CAMEL..
12-23
SUDDENLY HE SEES A SHADOW MOVE ACROSS THE GROUND.. AN ANGRY SOUND FILLS THE AIR!
IT'S THE RED BARON! HE'S RIDDLING MY PLANE WITH BULLETS
Tm. Reg. U. S. Pat. Off.—All rights reserved © 1968 by United Feature Syndicate, Inc.
THIS COULD RUIN MY WHOLE CHRISTMAS!
SCHULZ

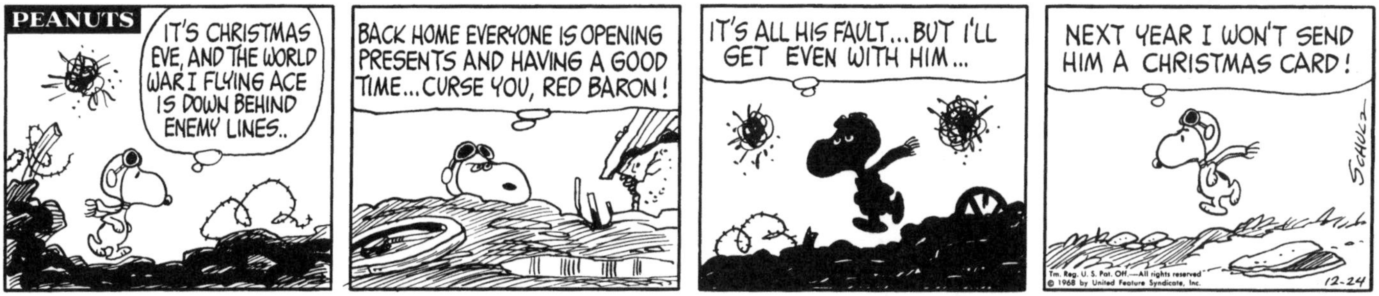
PEANUTS
IT'S CHRISTMAS EVE, AND THE WORLD WAR I FLYING ACE IS DOWN BEHIND ENEMY LINES..
BACK HOME EVERYONE IS OPENING PRESENTS AND HAVING A GOOD TIME...CURSE YOU, RED BARON!
IT'S ALL HIS FAULT...BUT I'LL GET EVEN WITH HIM...
NEXT YEAR I WON'T SEND HIM A CHRISTMAS CARD!
SCHULZ
Tm. Reg. U. S. Pat. Off.—All rights reserved © 1968 by United Feature Syndicate, Inc.
12-24

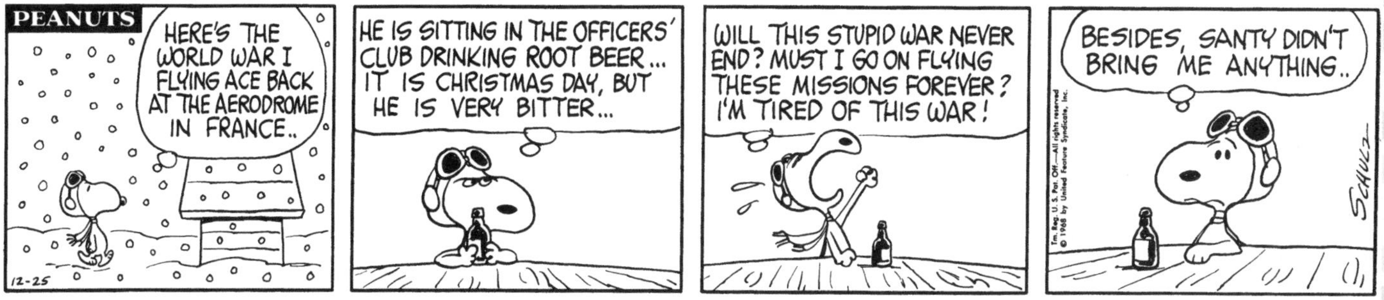
PEANUTS
HERE'S THE WORLD WAR I FLYING ACE BACK AT THE AERODROME IN FRANCE..
12-25
HE IS SITTING IN THE OFFICERS' CLUB DRINKING ROOT BEER... IT IS CHRISTMAS DAY, BUT HE IS VERY BITTER...
WILL THIS STUPID WAR NEVER END? MUST I GO ON FLYING THESE MISSIONS FOREVER? I'M TIRED OF THIS WAR!
Tm. Reg. U. S. Pat. Off.—All rights reserved © 1968 by United Feature Syndicate, Inc.
BESIDES, SANTY DIDN'T BRING ME ANYTHING..
SCHULZ

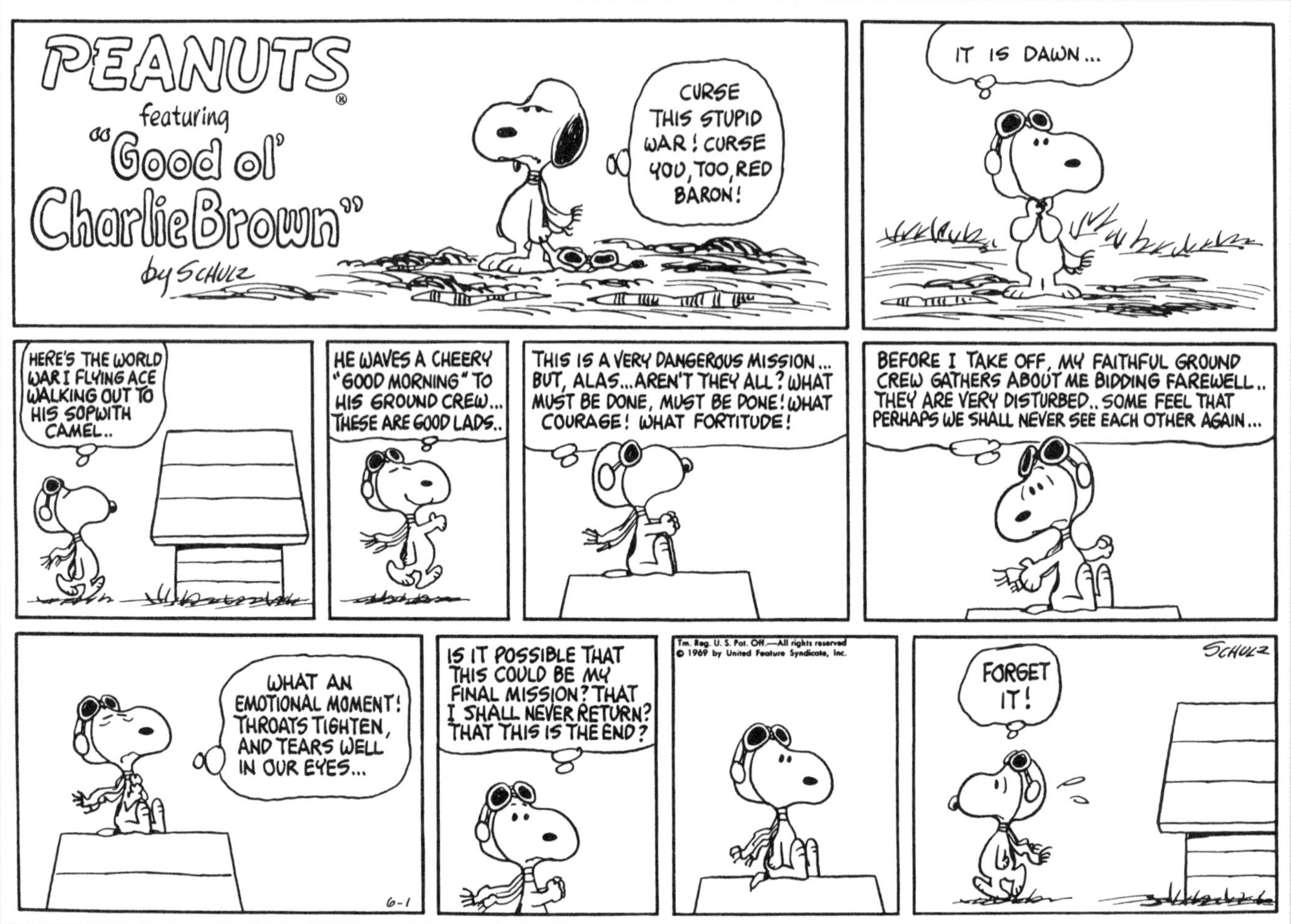
PEANUTS® featuring "Good ol' CharlieBrown" by SCHULZ
CURSE THIS STUPID WAR! CURSE YOU, TOO, RED BARON!
IT IS DAWN...
HERE'S THE WORLD WAR I FLYING ACE WALKING OUT TO HIS SOPWITH CAMEL..
HE WAVES A CHEERY "GOOD MORNING" TO HIS GROUND CREW... THESE ARE GOOD LADS..
THIS IS A VERY DANGEROUS MISSION... BUT, ALAS...AREN'T THEY ALL? WHAT MUST BE DONE, MUST BE DONE! WHAT COURAGE! WHAT FORTITUDE!
BEFORE I TAKE OFF, MY FAITHFUL GROUND CREW GATHERS ABOUT ME BIDDING FAREWELL.. THEY ARE VERY DISTURBED.. SOME FEEL THAT PERHAPS WE SHALL NEVER SEE EACH OTHER AGAIN...
WHAT AN EMOTIONAL MOMENT! THROATS TIGHTEN, AND TEARS WELL IN OUR EYES...
6-1
IS IT POSSIBLE THAT THIS COULD BE MY FINAL MISSION? THAT I SHALL NEVER RETURN? THAT THIS IS THE END?
Tm. Reg. U. S. Pat. Off.—All rights reserved © 1969 by United Feature Syndicate, Inc.
FORGET IT!
SCHULZ

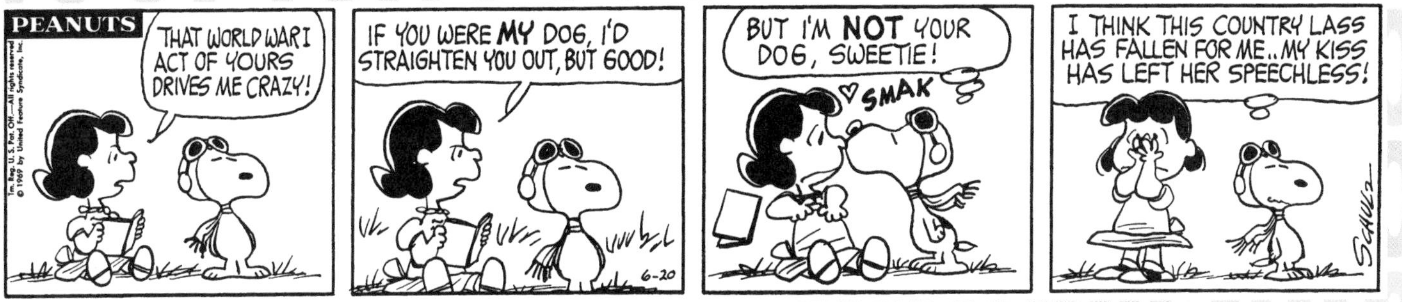
PEANUTS
Tm. Reg. U.S. Pat. Off.—All rights reserved © 1969 by United Feature Syndicate, Inc.
THAT WORLD WAR I ACT OF YOURS DRIVES ME CRAZY!
IF YOU WERE MY DOG, I'D STRAIGHTEN YOU OUT, BUT GOOD!
6-20
BUT I'M NOT YOUR DOG, SWEETIE!
SMAK
I THINK THIS COUNTRY LASS HAS FALLEN FOR ME.. MY KISS HAS LEFT HER SPEECHLESS!
SCHULZ

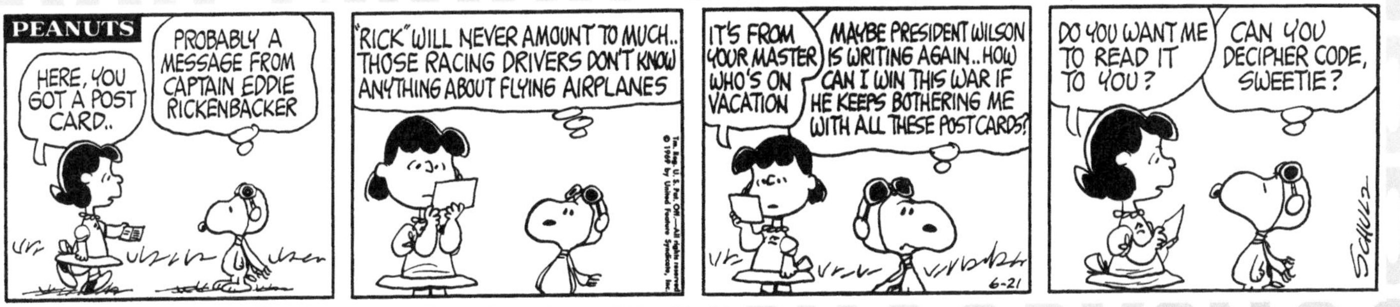
PEANUTS
HERE, YOU GOT A POST CARD..
PROBABLY A MESSAGE FROM CAPTAIN EDDIE RICKENBACKER
"RICK" WILL NEVER AMOUNT TO MUCH.. THOSE RACING DRIVERS DON'T KNOW ANYTHING ABOUT FLYING AIRPLANES
Tm. Reg. U.S. Pat. Off.—All rights reserved © 1969 by United Feature Syndicate, Inc.
IT'S FROM YOUR MASTER WHO'S ON VACATION
MAYBE PRESIDENT WILSON IS WRITING AGAIN.. HOW CAN I WIN THIS WAR IF HE KEEPS BOTHERING ME WITH ALL THESE POSTCARDS?
6-21
DO YOU WANT ME TO READ IT TO YOU?
CAN YOU DECIPHER CODE, SWEETIE?
SCHULZ

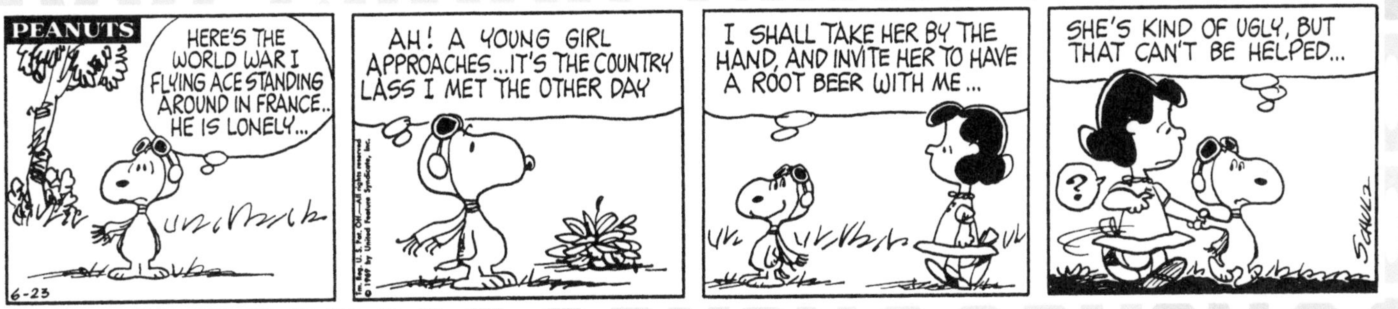
PEANUTS
HERE'S THE WORLD WAR I FLYING ACE STANDING AROUND IN FRANCE.. HE IS LONELY...
6-23
AH! A YOUNG GIRL APPROACHES...IT'S THE COUNTRY LASS I MET THE OTHER DAY
Tm. Reg. U.S. Pat. Off.—All rights reserved © 1969 by United Feature Syndicate, Inc.
I SHALL TAKE HER BY THE HAND, AND INVITE HER TO HAVE A ROOT BEER WITH ME...
SHE'S KIND OF UGLY, BUT THAT CAN'T BE HELPED...
?
SCHULZ

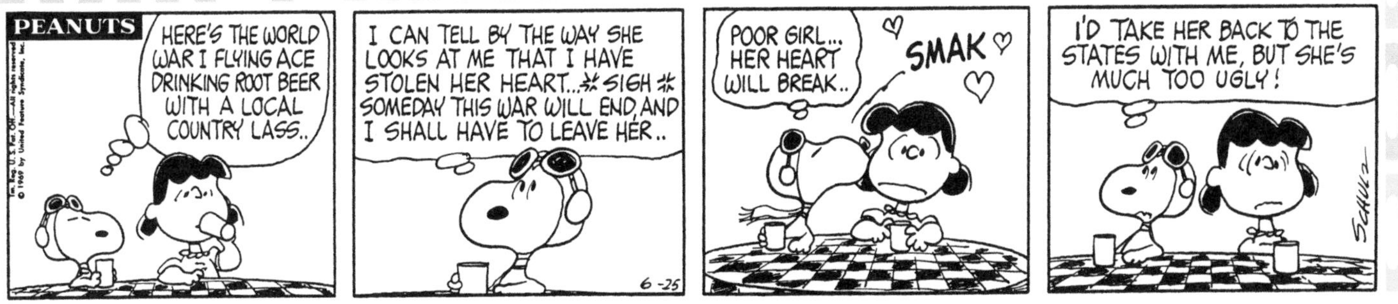
PEANUTS
Tm. Reg. U.S. Pat. Off.—All rights reserved © 1969 by United Feature Syndicate, Inc.
HERE'S THE WORLD WAR I FLYING ACE DRINKING ROOT BEER WITH A LOCAL COUNTRY LASS..
I CAN TELL BY THE WAY SHE LOOKS AT ME THAT I HAVE STOLEN HER HEART... *SIGH* SOMEDAY THIS WAR WILL END, AND I SHALL HAVE TO LEAVE HER..
6-25
POOR GIRL... HER HEART WILL BREAK..
SMAK
I'D TAKE HER BACK TO THE STATES WITH ME, BUT SHE'S MUCH TOO UGLY!
SCHULZ

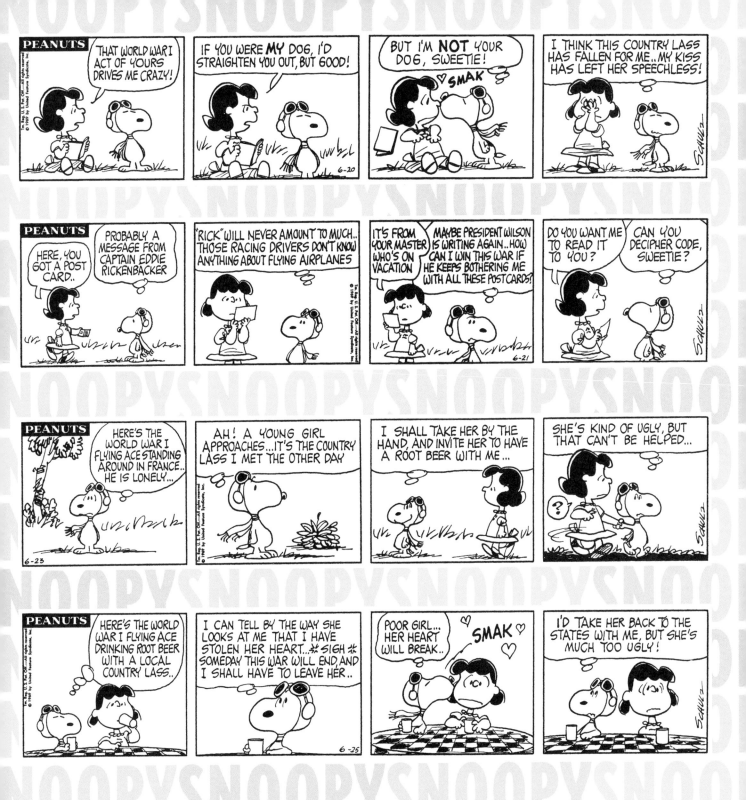

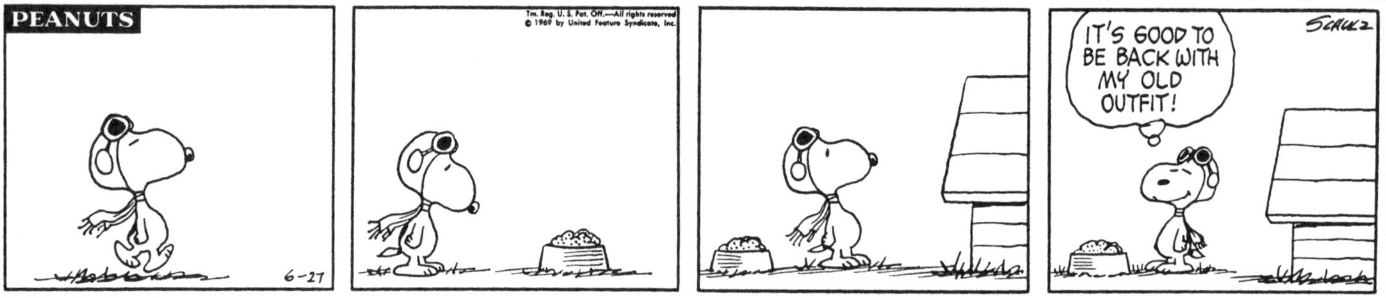
PEANUTS
Tm. Reg. U. S. Pat. Off.—All rights reserved © 1969 by United Feature Syndicate, Inc.
6-27
IT'S GOOD TO BE BACK WITH MY OLD OUTFIT!
SCHULZ

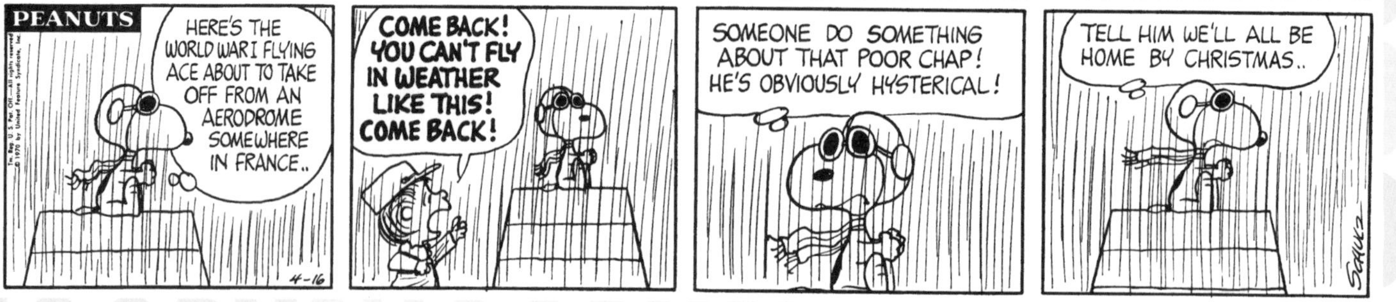
PEANUTS
HERE'S THE WORLD WAR I FLYING ACE ABOUT TO TAKE OFF FROM AN AERODROME SOMEWHERE IN FRANCE..
4-16
COME BACK! YOU CAN'T FLY IN WEATHER LIKE THIS! COME BACK!
SOMEONE DO SOMETHING ABOUT THAT POOR CHAP! HE'S OBVIOUSLY HYSTERICAL!
TELL HIM WE'LL ALL BE HOME BY CHRISTMAS..
SCHULZ

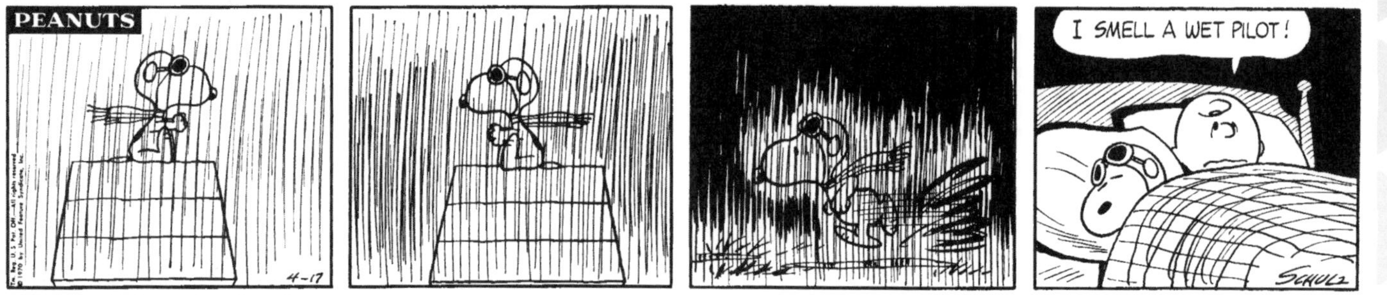
PEANUTS
4-17
I SMELL A WET PILOT!
SCHULZ

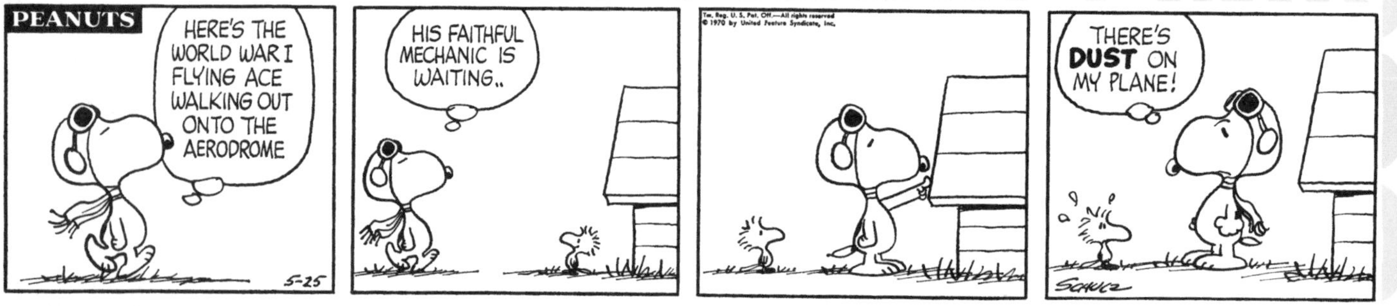
PEANUTS
HERE'S THE WORLD WAR I FLYING ACE WALKING OUT ONTO THE AERODROME
5-25
HIS FAITHFUL MECHANIC IS WAITING..
Tm. Reg. U. S. Pat. Off.—All rights reserved © 1970 by United Feature Syndicate, Inc.
THERE'S **DUST** ON MY PLANE!
SCHULZ

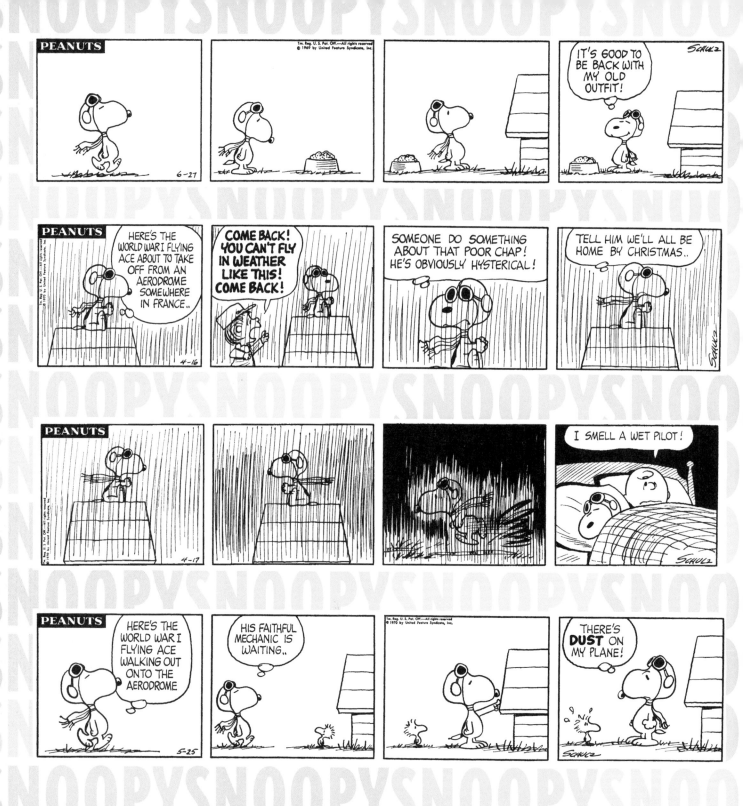

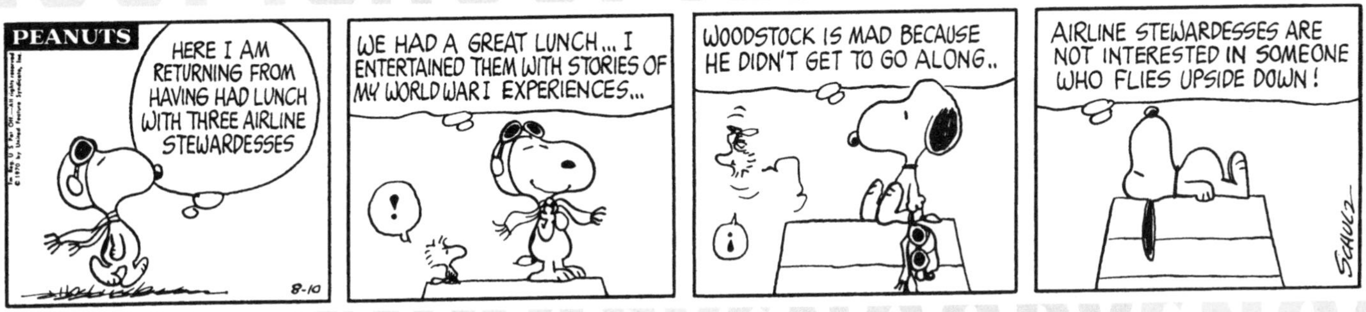
PEANUTS
HERE I AM RETURNING FROM HAVING HAD LUNCH WITH THREE AIRLINE STEWARDESSES
8-10
WE HAD A GREAT LUNCH... I ENTERTAINED THEM WITH STORIES OF MY WORLD WAR I EXPERIENCES...
!
WOODSTOCK IS MAD BECAUSE HE DIDN'T GET TO GO ALONG..
AIRLINE STEWARDESSES ARE NOT INTERESTED IN SOMEONE WHO FLIES UPSIDE DOWN!
SCHULZ

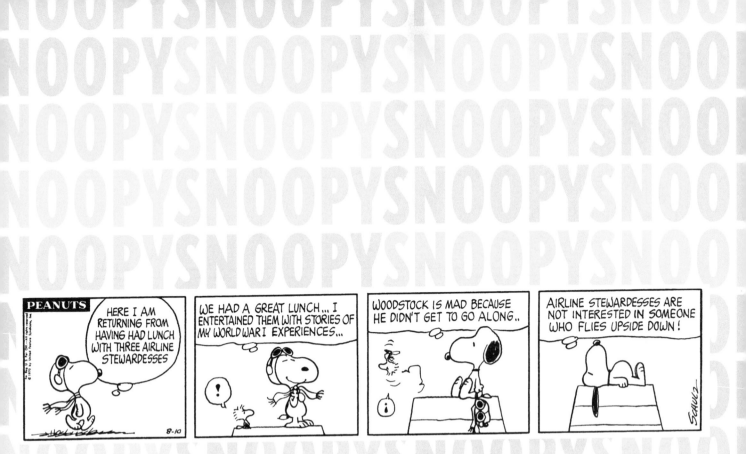

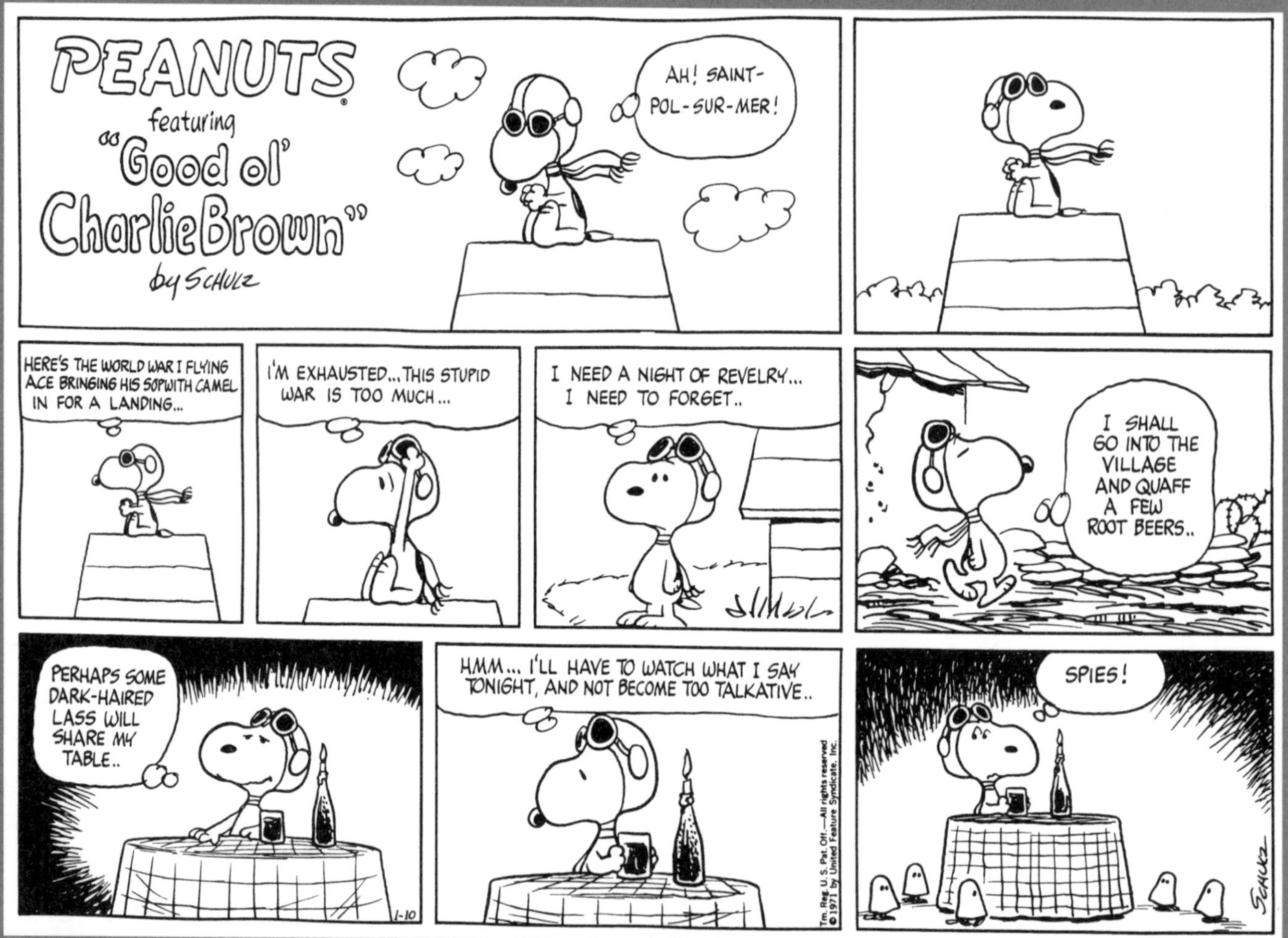
PEANUTS
featuring
"Good ol' CharlieBrown"
by SCHULZ
AH! SAINT-POL-SUR-MER!
HERE'S THE WORLD WAR I FLYING ACE BRINGING HIS SOPWITH CAMEL IN FOR A LANDING...
I'M EXHAUSTED... THIS STUPID WAR IS TOO MUCH...
I NEED A NIGHT OF REVELRY... I NEED TO FORGET..
I SHALL GO INTO THE VILLAGE AND QUAFF A FEW ROOT BEERS..
PERHAPS SOME DARK-HAIRED LASS WILL SHARE MY TABLE..
1-10
HMM... I'LL HAVE TO WATCH WHAT I SAY TONIGHT, AND NOT BECOME TOO TALKATIVE..
Tm. Reg. U. S. Pat. Off.—All rights reserved
© 1971 by United Feature Syndicate, Inc.
SPIES!
SCHULZ

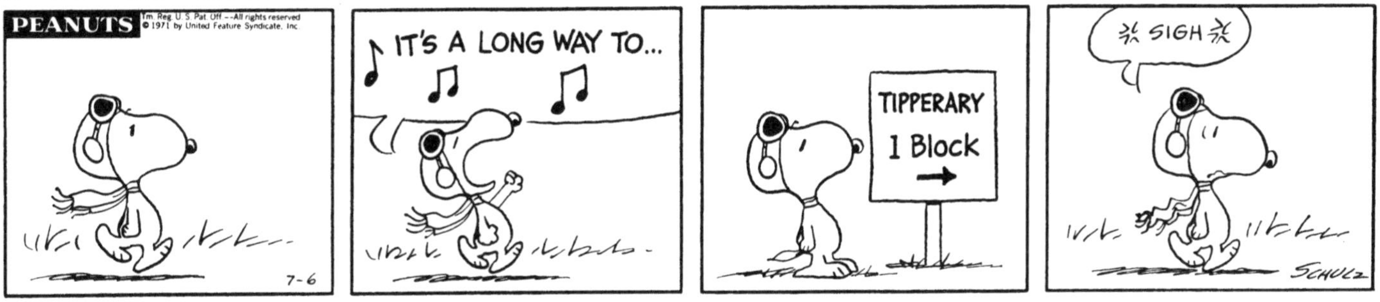
PEANUTS
Tm. Reg. U.S. Pat. Off.—All rights reserved © 1971 by United Feature Syndicate, Inc.
7-6
IT'S A LONG WAY TO...
TIPPERARY
1 Block
SIGH
SCHULZ

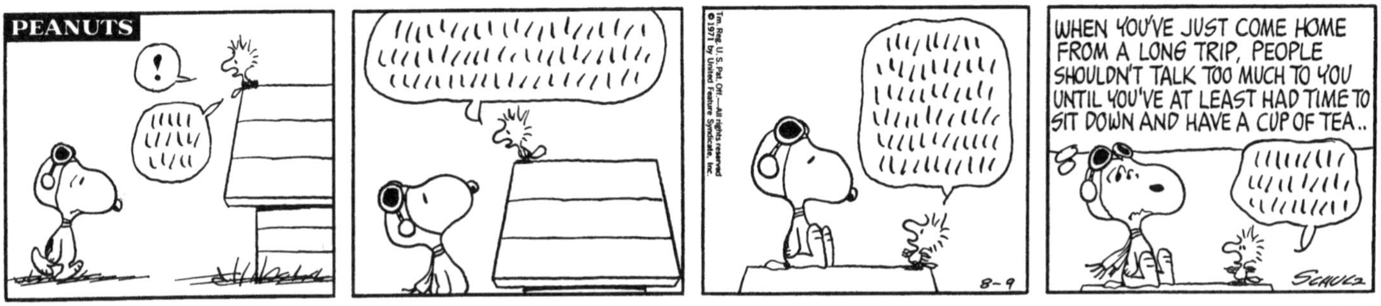
PEANUTS
!
Tm. Reg. U.S. Pat. Off.—All rights reserved © 1971 by United Feature Syndicate, Inc.
8-9
WHEN YOU'VE JUST COME HOME FROM A LONG TRIP, PEOPLE SHOULDN'T TALK TOO MUCH TO YOU UNTIL YOU'VE AT LEAST HAD TIME TO SIT DOWN AND HAVE A CUP OF TEA..
SCHULZ

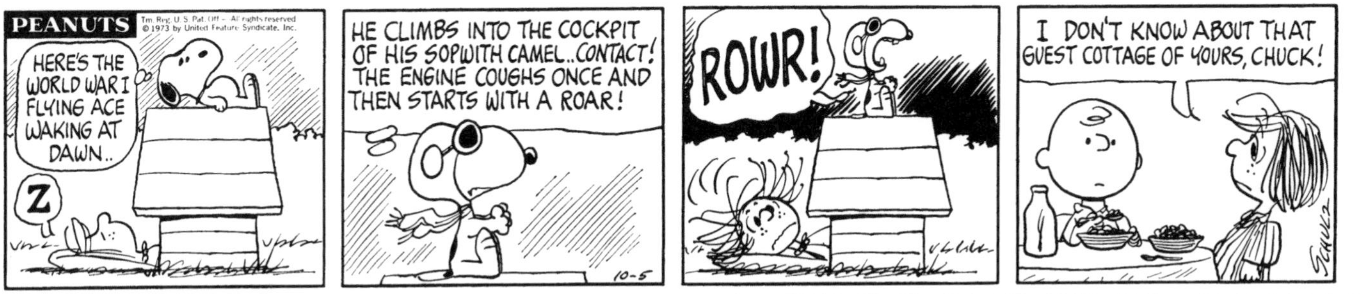
PEANUTS
Tm. Reg. U.S. Pat. Off.—All rights reserved © 1973 by United Feature Syndicate, Inc.
HERE'S THE WORLD WAR I FLYING ACE WAKING AT DAWN..
Z
HE CLIMBS INTO THE COCKPIT OF HIS SOPWITH CAMEL..CONTACT! THE ENGINE COUGHS ONCE AND THEN STARTS WITH A ROAR!
10-5
ROWR!
I DON'T KNOW ABOUT THAT GUEST COTTAGE OF YOURS, CHUCK!
SCHULZ

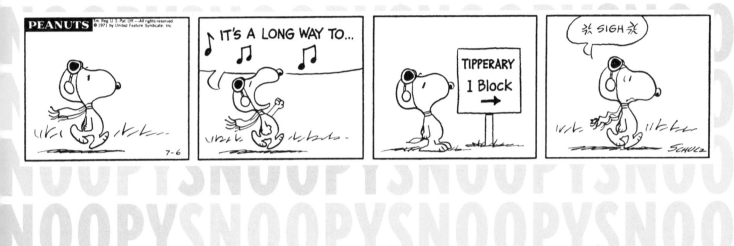

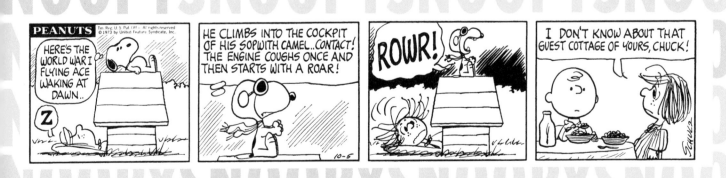

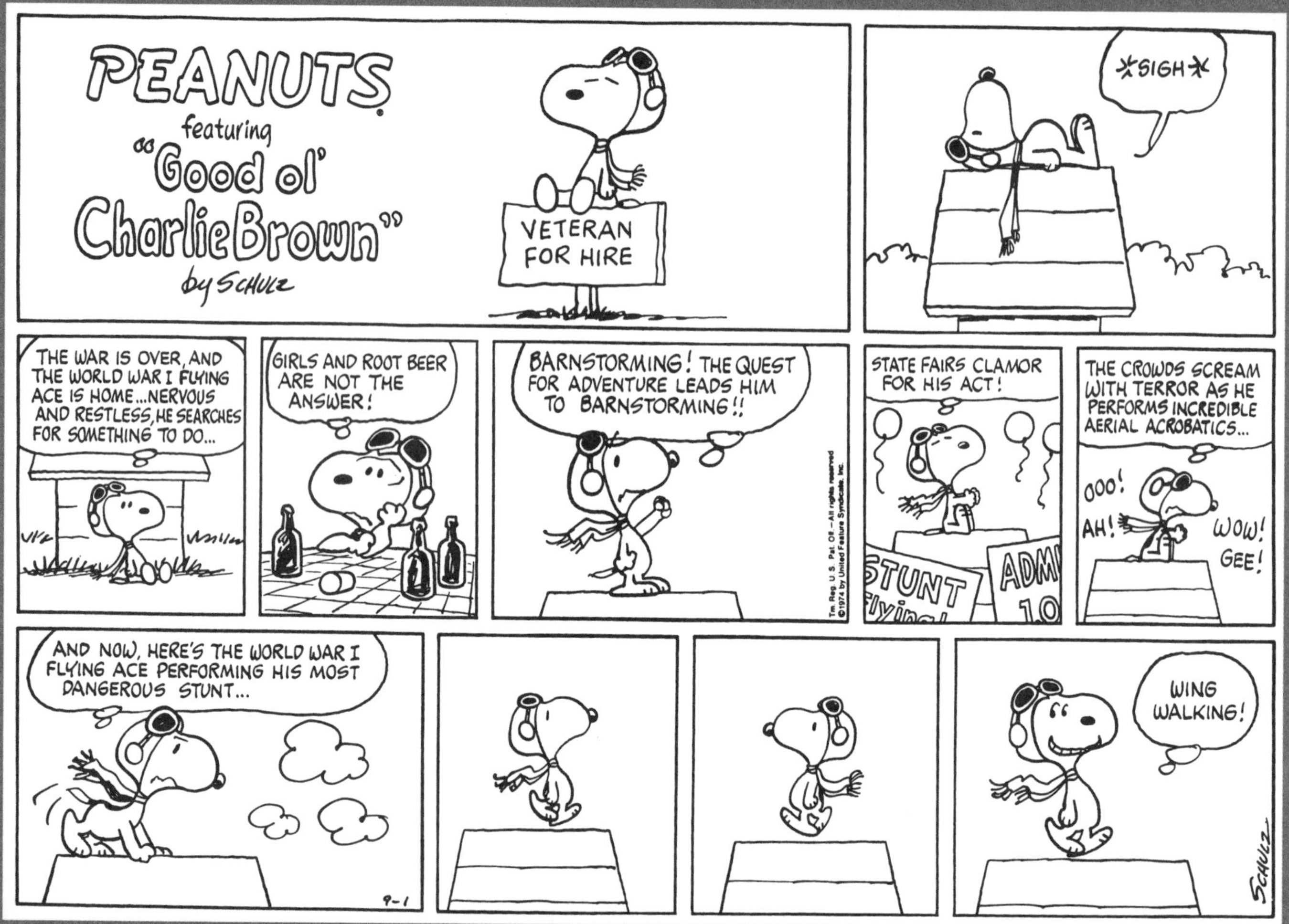
PEANUTS
featuring
"Good ol' Charlie Brown"
by SCHULZ
VETERAN FOR HIRE
SIGH
THE WAR IS OVER, AND THE WORLD WAR I FLYING ACE IS HOME...NERVOUS AND RESTLESS, HE SEARCHES FOR SOMETHING TO DO...
GIRLS AND ROOT BEER ARE NOT THE ANSWER!
BARNSTORMING! THE QUEST FOR ADVENTURE LEADS HIM TO BARNSTORMING!!
Tm. Reg. U.S. Pat. Off.—All rights reserved
©1974 by United Feature Syndicate, Inc.
STATE FAIRS CLAMOR FOR HIS ACT!
STUNT
ADM
10
THE CROWDS SCREAM WITH TERROR AS HE PERFORMS INCREDIBLE AERIAL ACROBATICS...
OOO!
AH!
WOW!
GEE!
AND NOW, HERE'S THE WORLD WAR I FLYING ACE PERFORMING HIS MOST DANGEROUS STUNT...
9-1
WING WALKING!
SCHULZ

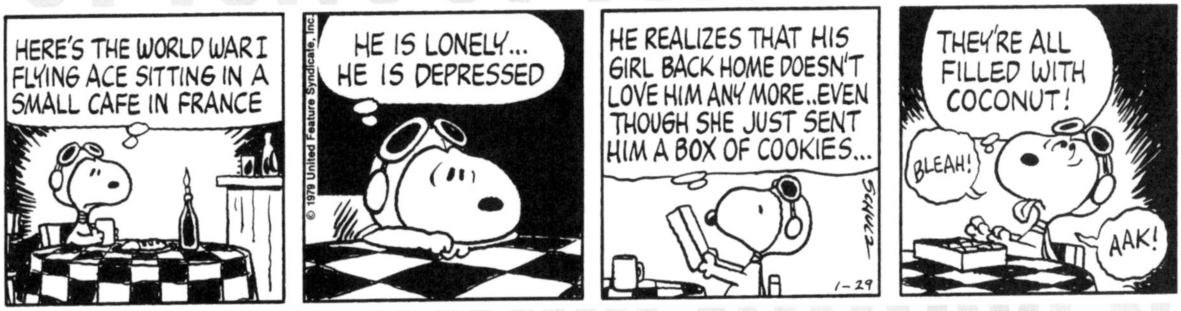
HERE'S THE WORLD WAR I FLYING ACE SITTING IN A SMALL CAFE IN FRANCE
HE IS LONELY... HE IS DEPRESSED
© 1979 United Feature Syndicate, Inc.
HE REALIZES THAT HIS GIRL BACK HOME DOESN'T LOVE HIM ANY MORE..EVEN THOUGH SHE JUST SENT HIM A BOX OF COOKIES...
SCHULZ
1-29
THEY'RE ALL FILLED WITH COCONUT!
BLEAH!
AAK!

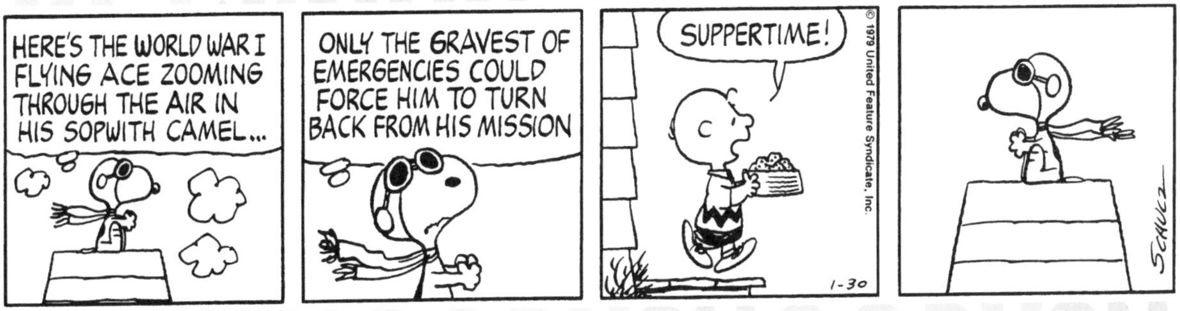
HERE'S THE WORLD WAR I FLYING ACE ZOOMING THROUGH THE AIR IN HIS SOPWITH CAMEL...
ONLY THE GRAVEST OF EMERGENCIES COULD FORCE HIM TO TURN BACK FROM HIS MISSION
SUPPERTIME!
© 1979 United Feature Syndicate, Inc.
1-30
SCHULZ

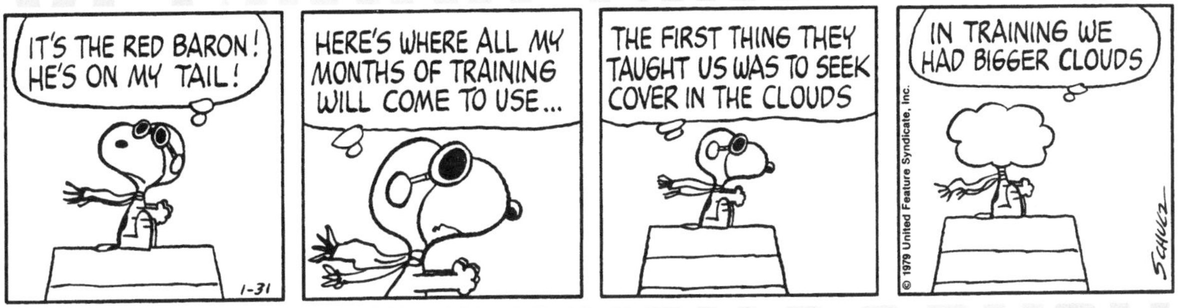
IT'S THE RED BARON! HE'S ON MY TAIL!
1-31
HERE'S WHERE ALL MY MONTHS OF TRAINING WILL COME TO USE...
THE FIRST THING THEY TAUGHT US WAS TO SEEK COVER IN THE CLOUDS
© 1979 United Feature Syndicate, Inc.
IN TRAINING WE HAD BIGGER CLOUDS
SCHULZ

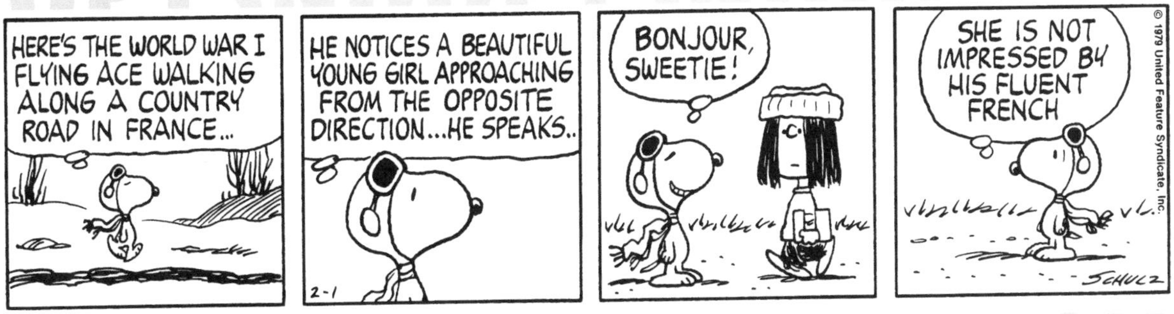
HERE'S THE WORLD WAR I FLYING ACE WALKING ALONG A COUNTRY ROAD IN FRANCE...
HE NOTICES A BEAUTIFUL YOUNG GIRL APPROACHING FROM THE OPPOSITE DIRECTION...HE SPEAKS..
2-1
BONJOUR, SWEETIE!
SHE IS NOT IMPRESSED BY HIS FLUENT FRENCH
© 1979 United Feature Syndicate, Inc.
SCHULZ

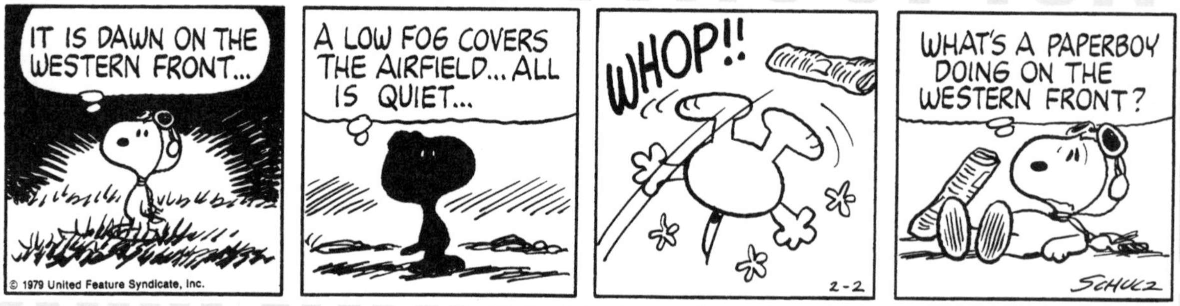
IT IS DAWN ON THE WESTERN FRONT...
A LOW FOG COVERS THE AIRFIELD... ALL IS QUIET...
WHOP!!
WHAT'S A PAPERBOY DOING ON THE WESTERN FRONT?
© 1979 United Feature Syndicate, Inc.
2-2
SCHULZ

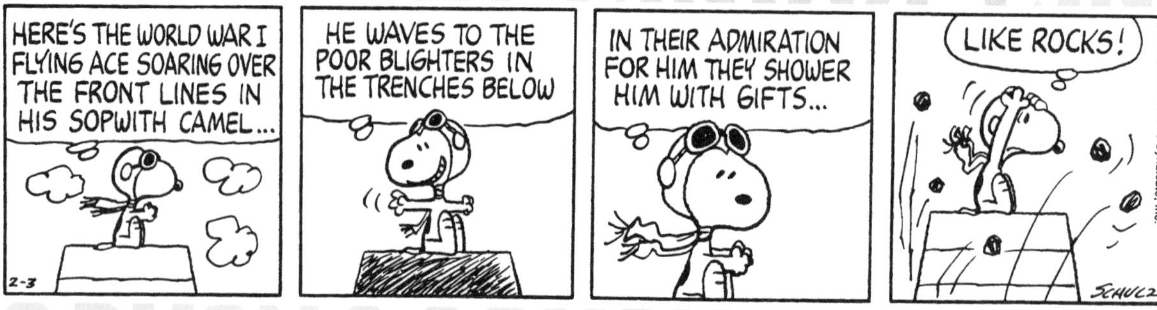
HERE'S THE WORLD WAR I FLYING ACE SOARING OVER THE FRONT LINES IN HIS SOPWITH CAMEL...
HE WAVES TO THE POOR BLIGHTERS IN THE TRENCHES BELOW
IN THEIR ADMIRATION FOR HIM THEY SHOWER HIM WITH GIFTS...
LIKE ROCKS!
2-3
© 1979 United Feature Syndicate, Inc.
SCHULZ

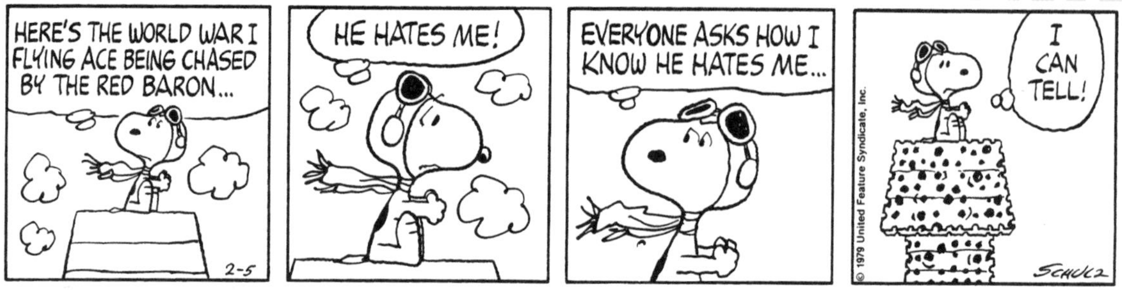
HERE'S THE WORLD WAR I FLYING ACE BEING CHASED BY THE RED BARON...
HE HATES ME!
EVERYONE ASKS HOW I KNOW HE HATES ME...
I CAN TELL!
2-5
© 1979 United Feature Syndicate, Inc.
SCHULZ

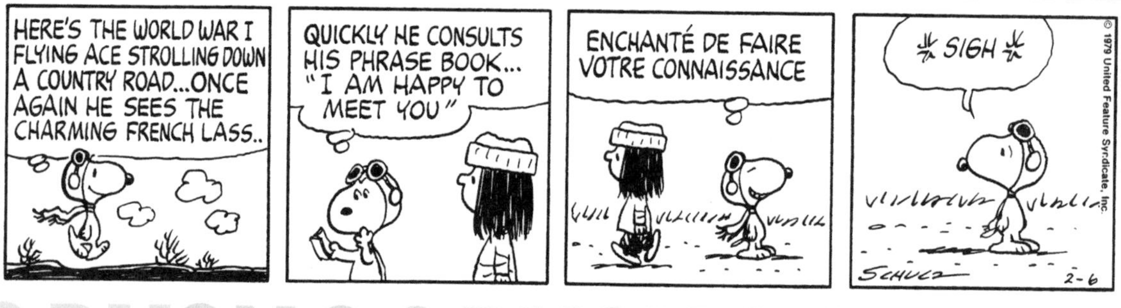
HERE'S THE WORLD WAR I FLYING ACE STROLLING DOWN A COUNTRY ROAD...ONCE AGAIN HE SEES THE CHARMING FRENCH LASS..
QUICKLY HE CONSULTS HIS PHRASE BOOK... "I AM HAPPY TO MEET YOU"
ENCHANTÉ DE FAIRE VOTRE CONNAISSANCE
SIGH
© 1979 United Feature Syndicate, Inc.
SCHULZ
2-6

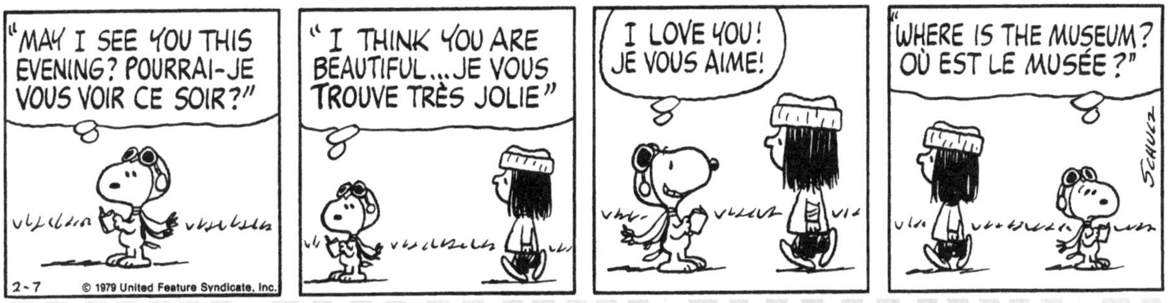
"MAY I SEE YOU THIS EVENING? POURRAI-JE VOUS VOIR CE SOIR?"
2-7
© 1979 United Feature Syndicate, Inc.
"I THINK YOU ARE BEAUTIFUL...JE VOUS TROUVE TRÈS JOLIE"
I LOVE YOU! JE VOUS AIME!
"WHERE IS THE MUSEUM? OÙ EST LE MUSÉE?"
SCHULZ

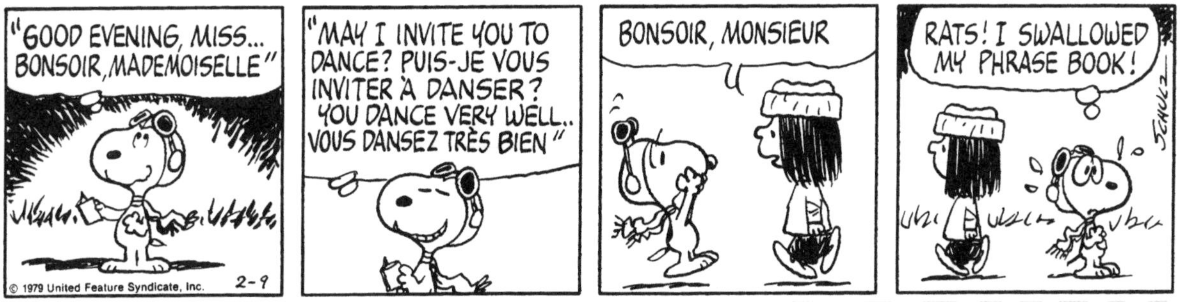
"GOOD EVENING, MISS... BONSOIR, MADEMOISELLE"
© 1979 United Feature Syndicate, Inc.
2-9
"MAY I INVITE YOU TO DANCE? PUIS-JE VOUS INVITER À DANSER? YOU DANCE VERY WELL.. VOUS DANSEZ TRÈS BIEN"
BONSOIR, MONSIEUR
RATS! I SWALLOWED MY PHRASE BOOK!
SCHULZ

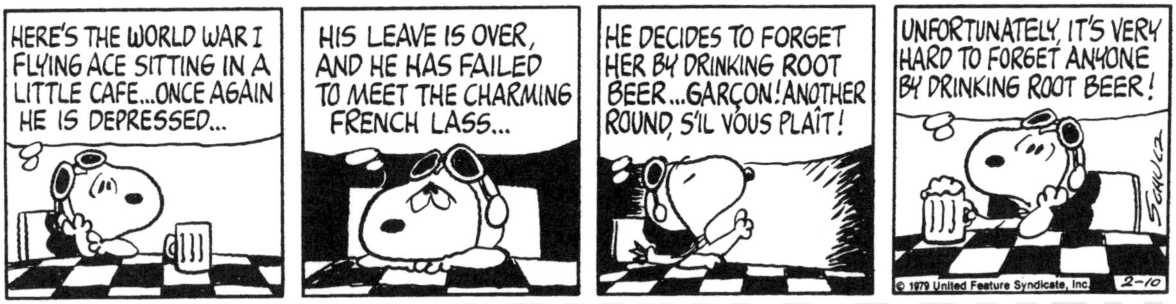
HERE'S THE WORLD WAR I FLYING ACE SITTING IN A LITTLE CAFE...ONCE AGAIN HE IS DEPRESSED...
HIS LEAVE IS OVER, AND HE HAS FAILED TO MEET THE CHARMING FRENCH LASS...
HE DECIDES TO FORGET HER BY DRINKING ROOT BEER...GARÇON! ANOTHER ROUND, S'IL VOUS PLAÎT!
UNFORTUNATELY, IT'S VERY HARD TO FORGET ANYONE BY DRINKING ROOT BEER!
SCHULZ
© 1979 United Feature Syndicate, Inc.
2-10

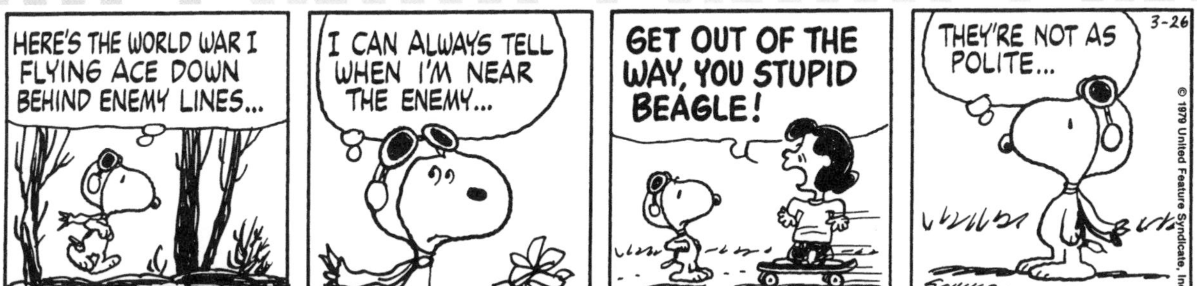
HERE'S THE WORLD WAR I FLYING ACE DOWN BEHIND ENEMY LINES...
I CAN ALWAYS TELL WHEN I'M NEAR THE ENEMY...
GET OUT OF THE WAY, YOU STUPID BEAGLE!
THEY'RE NOT AS POLITE...
3-26
© 1979 United Feature Syndicate, Inc.
SCHULZ

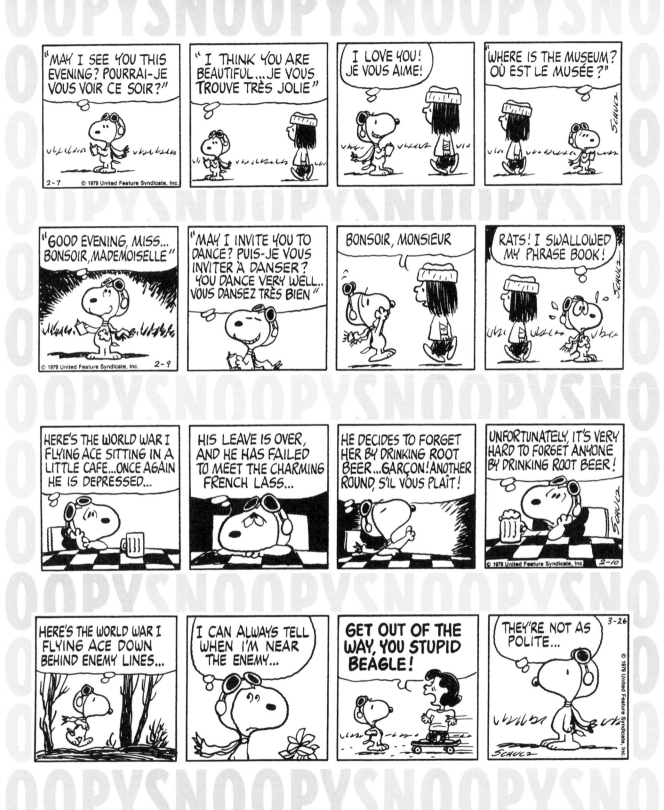

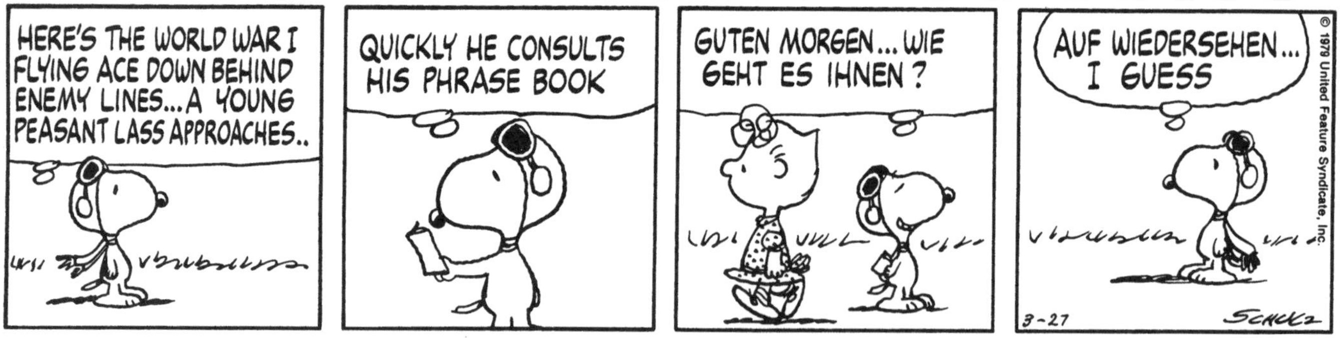
HERE'S THE WORLD WAR I FLYING ACE DOWN BEHIND ENEMY LINES...A YOUNG PEASANT LASS APPROACHES..
QUICKLY HE CONSULTS HIS PHRASE BOOK
GUTEN MORGEN... WIE GEHT ES IHNEN?
AUF WIEDERSEHEN... I GUESS
© 1979 United Feature Syndicate, Inc.
3-27
SCHULZ

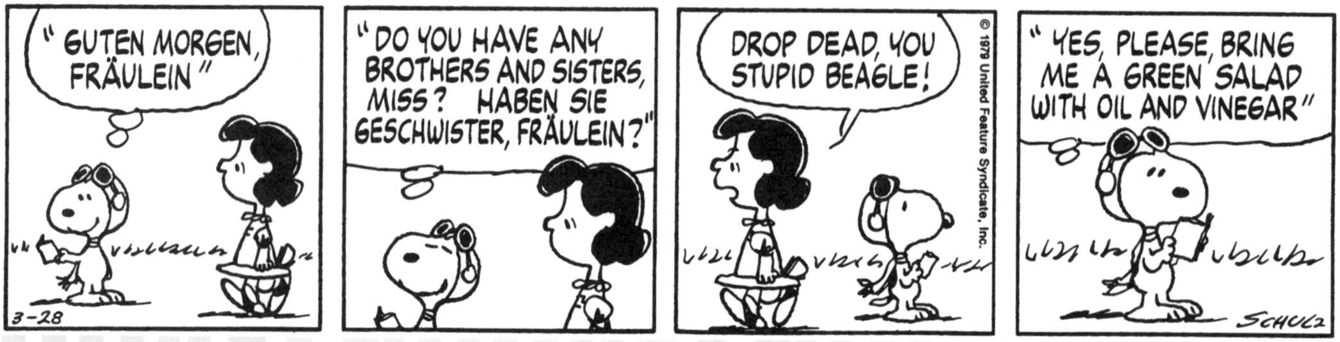
"GUTEN MORGEN, FRÄULEIN"
3-28
"DO YOU HAVE ANY BROTHERS AND SISTERS, MISS? HABEN SIE GESCHWISTER, FRÄULEIN?"
DROP DEAD, YOU STUPID BEAGLE!
© 1979 United Feature Syndicate, Inc.
"YES, PLEASE, BRING ME A GREEN SALAD WITH OIL AND VINEGAR"
SCHULZ

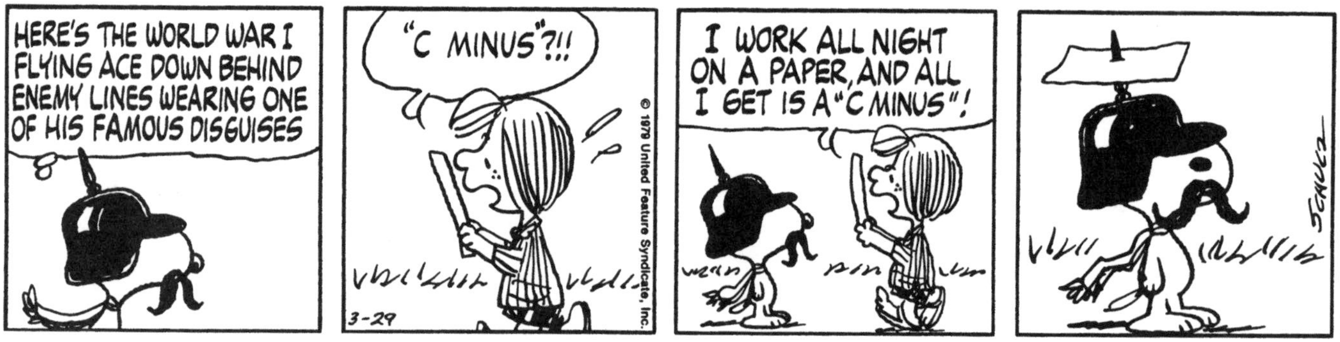
HERE'S THE WORLD WAR I FLYING ACE DOWN BEHIND ENEMY LINES WEARING ONE OF HIS FAMOUS DISGUISES
"C MINUS"?!!
3-29
© 1979 United Feature Syndicate, Inc.
I WORK ALL NIGHT ON A PAPER, AND ALL I GET IS A "C MINUS"!
SCHULZ

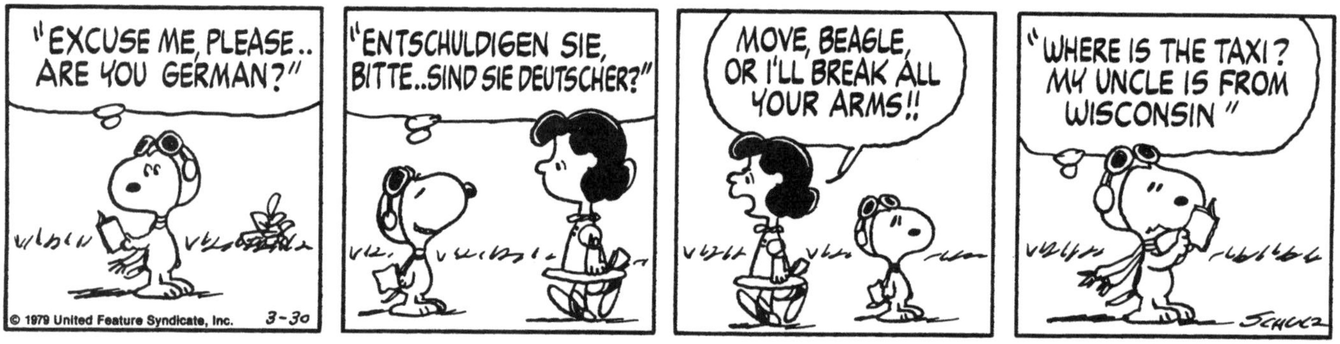
"EXCUSE ME, PLEASE.. ARE YOU GERMAN?"
© 1979 United Feature Syndicate, Inc.
3-30
"ENTSCHULDIGEN SIE, BITTE..SIND SIE DEUTSCHER?"
MOVE, BEAGLE, OR I'LL BREAK ALL YOUR ARMS!!
"WHERE IS THE TAXI? MY UNCLE IS FROM WISCONSIN"
SCHULZ

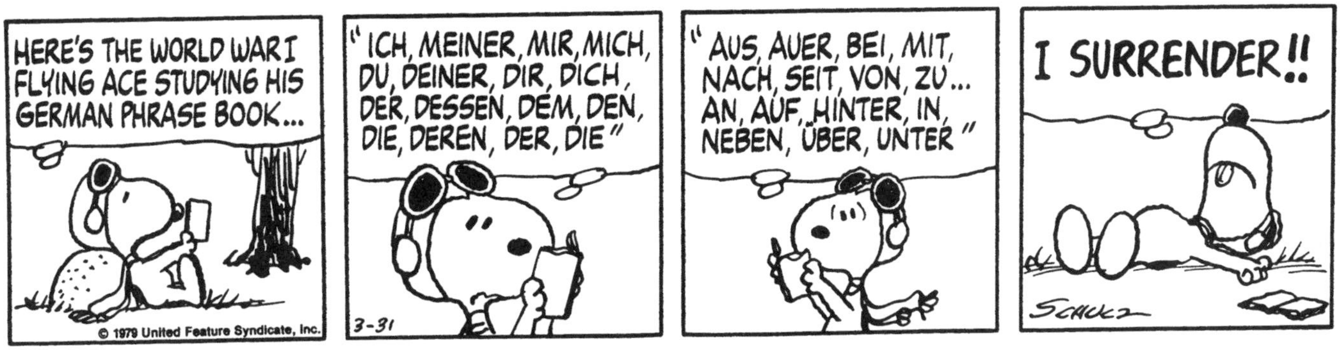
HERE'S THE WORLD WAR I FLYING ACE STUDYING HIS GERMAN PHRASE BOOK...
© 1979 United Feature Syndicate, Inc.
"ICH, MEINER, MIR, MICH, DU, DEINER, DIR, DICH, DER, DESSEN, DEM, DEN, DIE, DEREN, DER, DIE"
3-31
"AUS, AUER, BEI, MIT, NACH, SEIT, VON, ZU... AN, AUF, HINTER, IN, NEBEN, ÜBER, UNTER"
I SURRENDER!!
SCHULZ

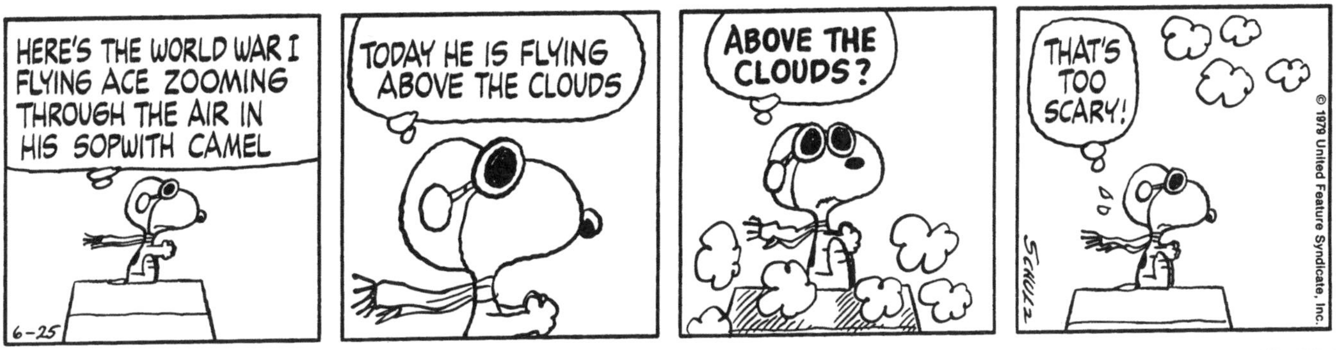
HERE'S THE WORLD WAR I FLYING ACE ZOOMING THROUGH THE AIR IN HIS SOPWITH CAMEL
6-25
TODAY HE IS FLYING ABOVE THE CLOUDS
ABOVE THE CLOUDS?
THAT'S TOO SCARY!
SCHULZ
© 1979 United Feature Syndicate, Inc.

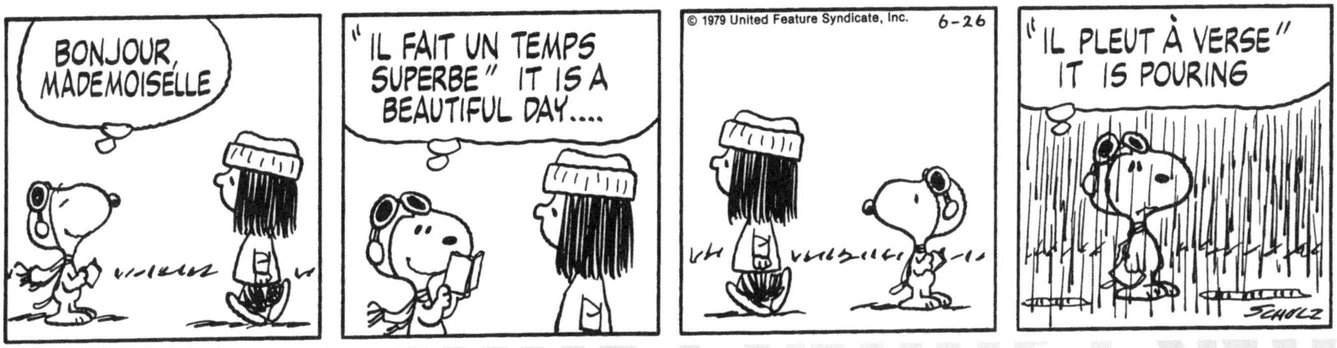
BONJOUR, MADEMOISELLE
"IL FAIT UN TEMPS SUPERBE" IT IS A BEAUTIFUL DAY....
© 1979 United Feature Syndicate, Inc.
6-26
"IL PLEUT À VERSE" IT IS POURING
SCHULZ

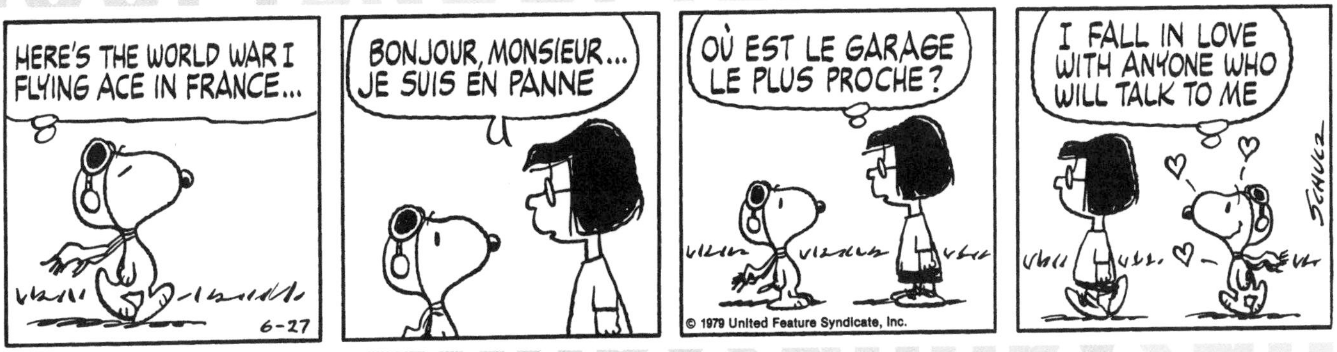
HERE'S THE WORLD WAR I FLYING ACE IN FRANCE...
6-27
BONJOUR, MONSIEUR... JE SUIS EN PANNE
OÙ EST LE GARAGE LE PLUS PROCHE?
© 1979 United Feature Syndicate, Inc.
I FALL IN LOVE WITH ANYONE WHO WILL TALK TO ME
SCHULZ

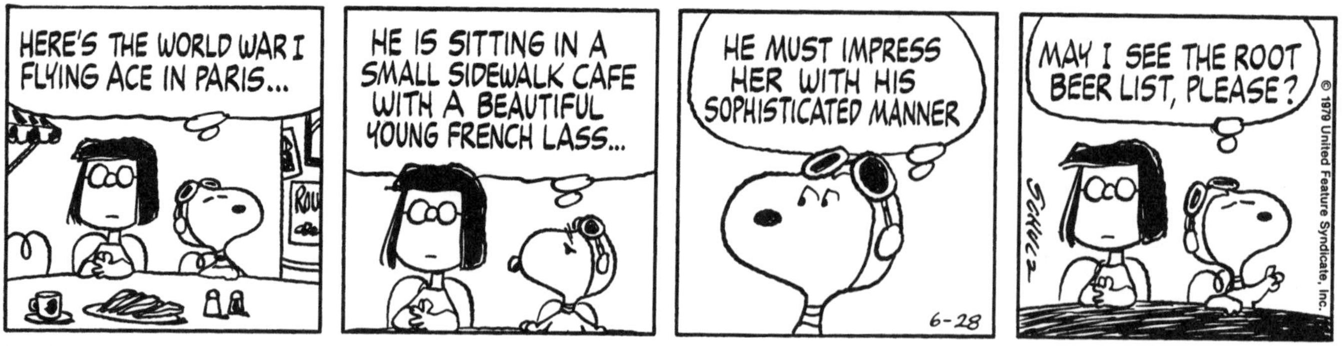
HERE'S THE WORLD WAR I FLYING ACE IN PARIS...
HE IS SITTING IN A SMALL SIDEWALK CAFE WITH A BEAUTIFUL YOUNG FRENCH LASS...
HE MUST IMPRESS HER WITH HIS SOPHISTICATED MANNER
6-28
MAY I SEE THE ROOT BEER LIST, PLEASE?
SCHULZ
© 1979 United Feature Syndicate, Inc.

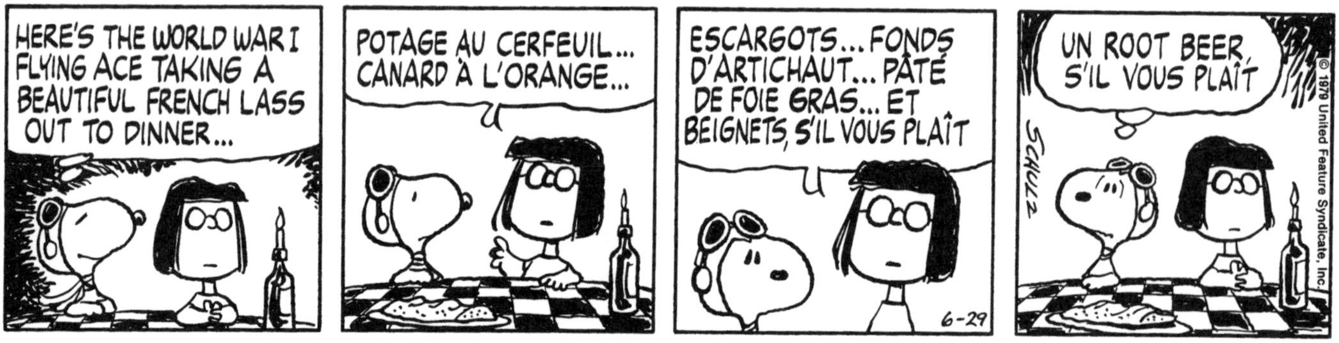
HERE'S THE WORLD WAR I FLYING ACE TAKING A BEAUTIFUL FRENCH LASS OUT TO DINNER...
POTAGE AU CERFEUIL... CANARD À L'ORANGE...
ESCARGOTS... FONDS D'ARTICHAUT... PÂTÉ DE FOIE GRAS... ET BEIGNETS, S'IL VOUS PLAÎT
6-29
UN ROOT BEER, S'IL VOUS PLAÎT
SCHULZ
© 1979 United Feature Syndicate, Inc.

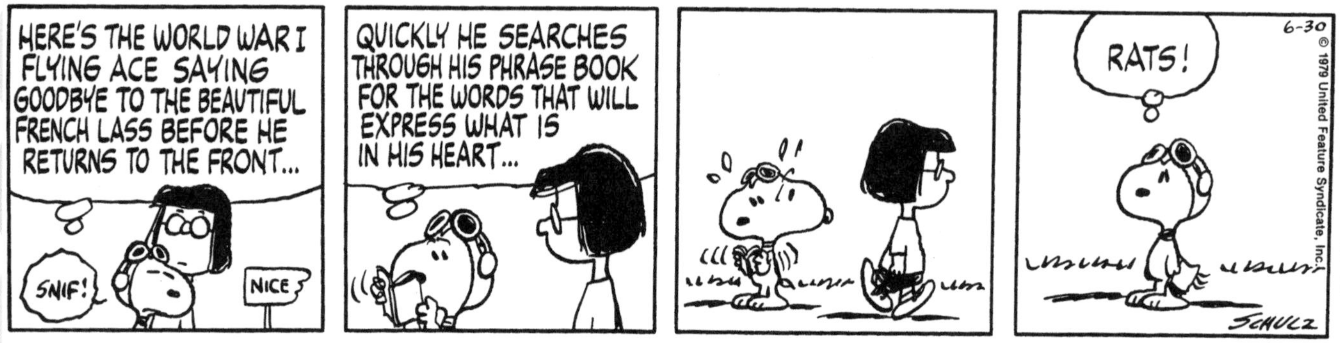
HERE'S THE WORLD WAR I FLYING ACE SAYING GOODBYE TO THE BEAUTIFUL FRENCH LASS BEFORE HE RETURNS TO THE FRONT...
SNIF!
NICE
QUICKLY HE SEARCHES THROUGH HIS PHRASE BOOK FOR THE WORDS THAT WILL EXPRESS WHAT IS IN HIS HEART...
6-30
RATS!
SCHULZ
© 1979 United Feature Syndicate, Inc.

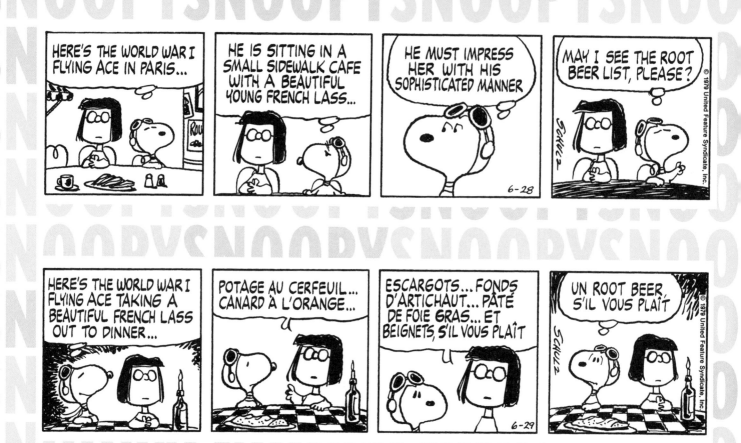

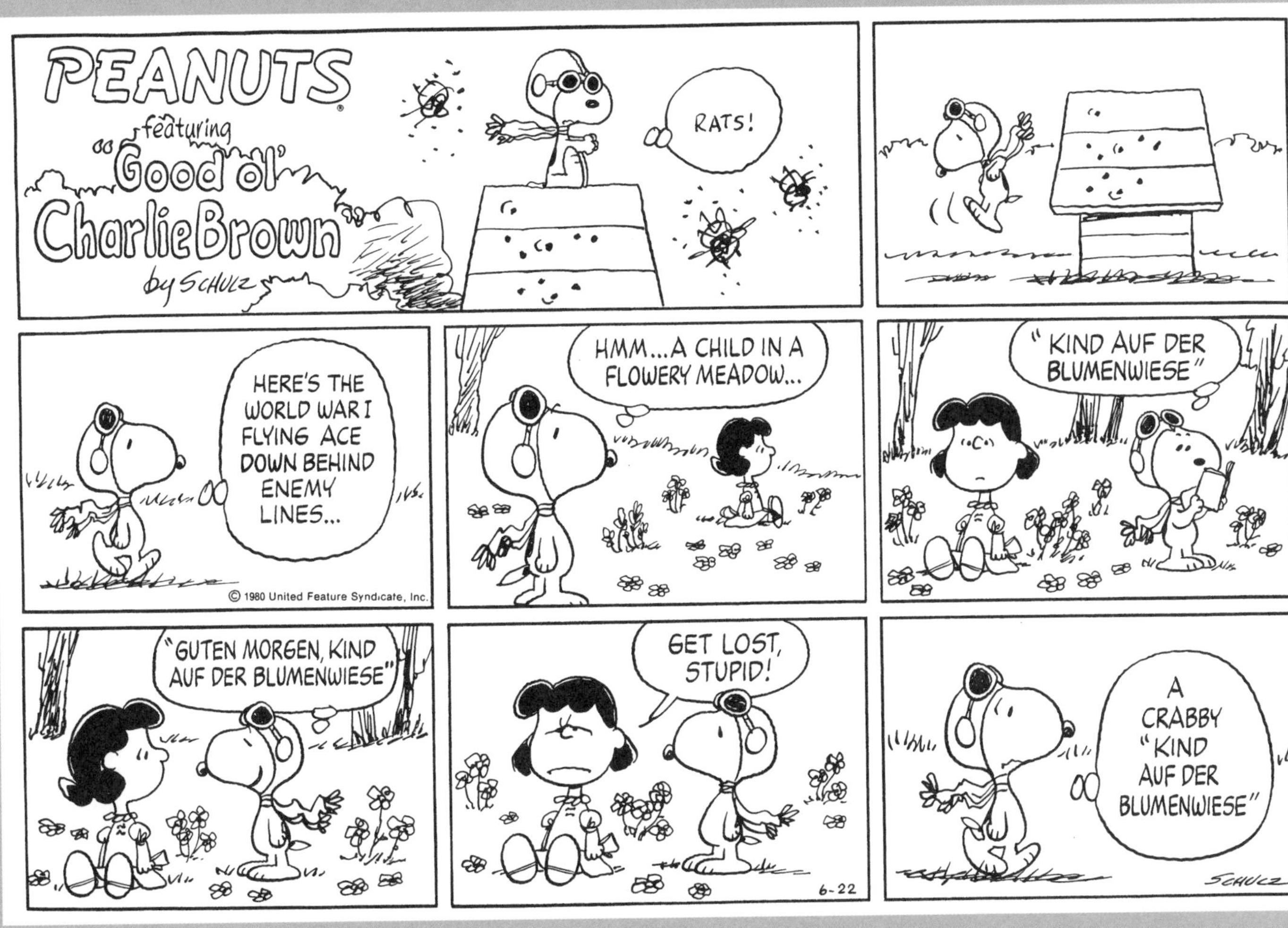
PEANUTS
featuring "Good ol' Charlie Brown"
by SCHULZ
RATS!
HERE'S THE WORLD WAR I FLYING ACE DOWN BEHIND ENEMY LINES...
© 1980 United Feature Syndicate, Inc.
HMM...A CHILD IN A FLOWERY MEADOW...
"KIND AUF DER BLUMENWIESE"
"GUTEN MORGEN, KIND AUF DER BLUMENWIESE"
GET LOST, STUPID!
6-22
A CRABBY "KIND AUF DER BLUMENWIESE"
SCHULZ

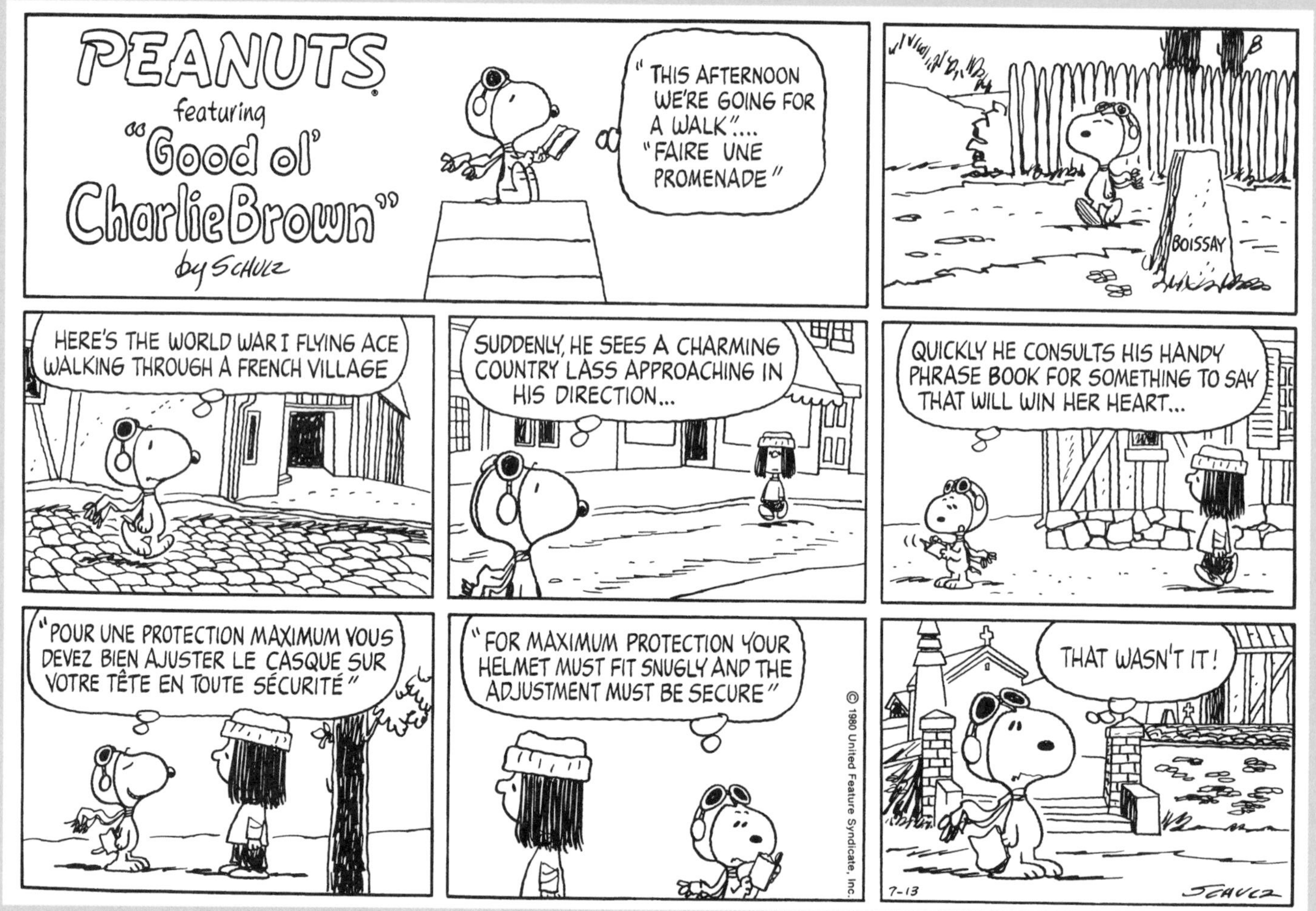
PEANUTS
featuring "Good ol' CharlieBrown"
by SCHULZ
" THIS AFTERNOON WE'RE GOING FOR A WALK"....
"FAIRE UNE PROMENADE"
BOISSAY
HERE'S THE WORLD WAR I FLYING ACE WALKING THROUGH A FRENCH VILLAGE
SUDDENLY, HE SEES A CHARMING COUNTRY LASS APPROACHING IN HIS DIRECTION...
QUICKLY HE CONSULTS HIS HANDY PHRASE BOOK FOR SOMETHING TO SAY THAT WILL WIN HER HEART...
"POUR UNE PROTECTION MAXIMUM VOUS DEVEZ BIEN AJUSTER LE CASQUE SUR VOTRE TÊTE EN TOUTE SÉCURITÉ"
"FOR MAXIMUM PROTECTION YOUR HELMET MUST FIT SNUGLY AND THE ADJUSTMENT MUST BE SECURE"
© 1980 United Feature Syndicate, Inc.
THAT WASN'T IT!
7-13
SCHULZ

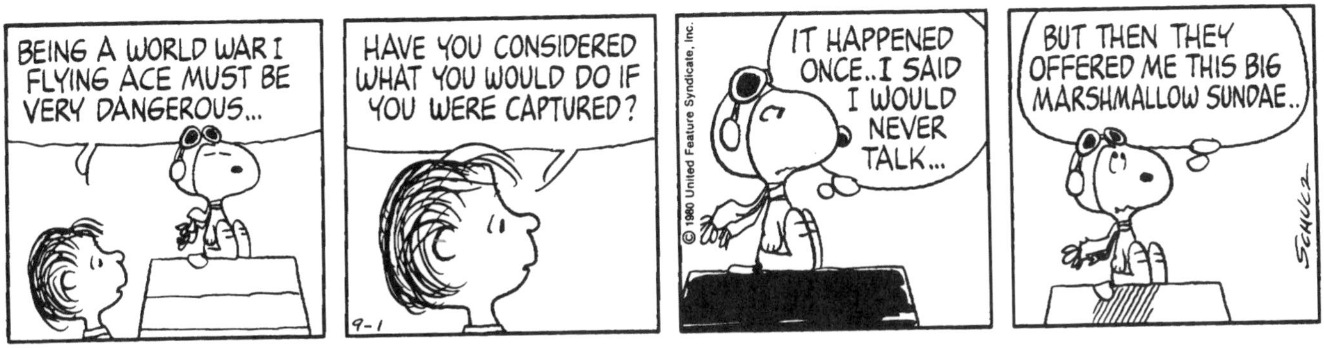
BEING A WORLD WAR I FLYING ACE MUST BE VERY DANGEROUS...
HAVE YOU CONSIDERED WHAT YOU WOULD DO IF YOU WERE CAPTURED?
9-1
© 1980 United Feature Syndicate, Inc.
IT HAPPENED ONCE..I SAID I WOULD NEVER TALK...
BUT THEN THEY OFFERED ME THIS BIG MARSHMALLOW SUNDAE..
SCHULZ

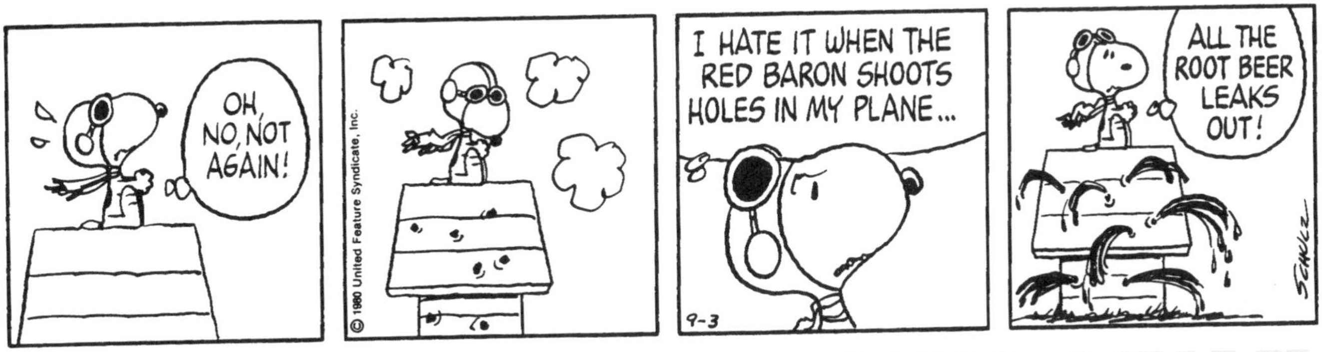
OH, NO, NOT AGAIN!
© 1980 United Feature Syndicate, Inc.
I HATE IT WHEN THE RED BARON SHOOTS HOLES IN MY PLANE...
9-3
ALL THE ROOT BEER LEAKS OUT!
SCHULZ

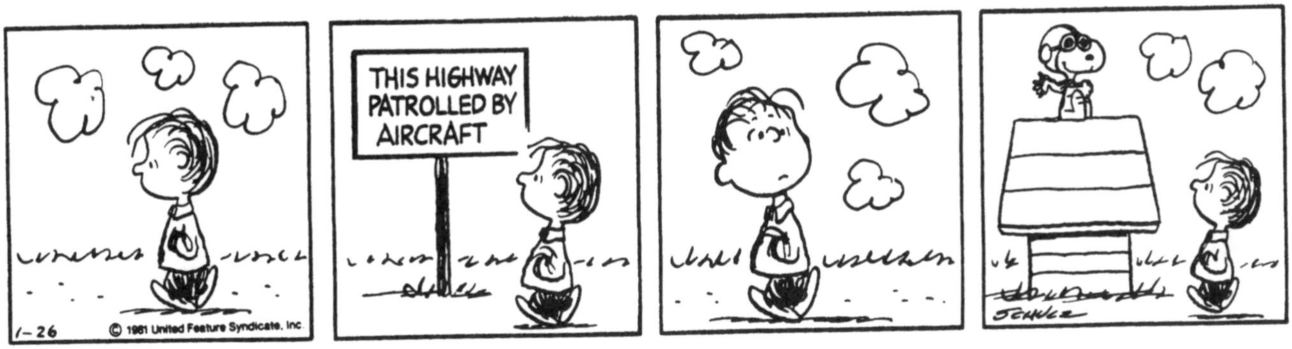
1-26
© 1981 United Feature Syndicate, Inc.
THIS HIGHWAY PATROLLED BY AIRCRAFT
SCHULZ

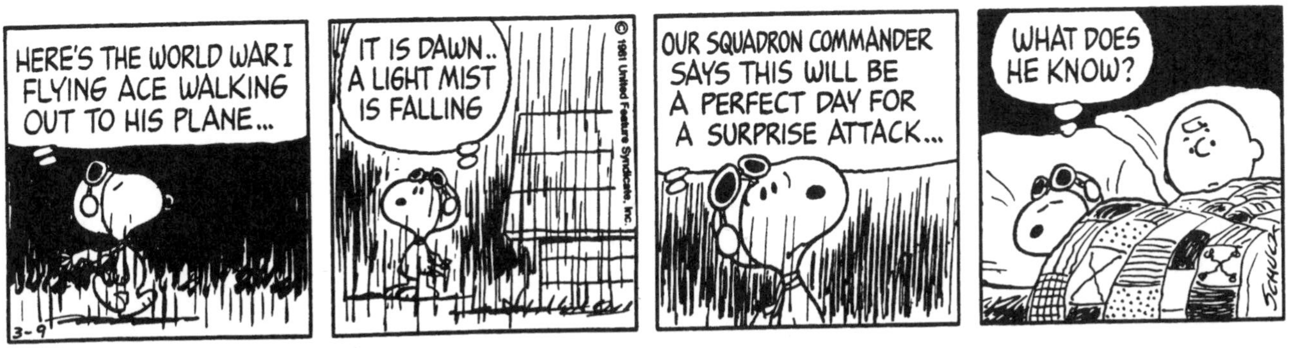
HERE'S THE WORLD WAR I FLYING ACE WALKING OUT TO HIS PLANE...
3-9
IT IS DAWN.. A LIGHT MIST IS FALLING
© 1981 United Feature Syndicate, Inc.
OUR SQUADRON COMMANDER SAYS THIS WILL BE A PERFECT DAY FOR A SURPRISE ATTACK...
WHAT DOES HE KNOW?
SCHULZ

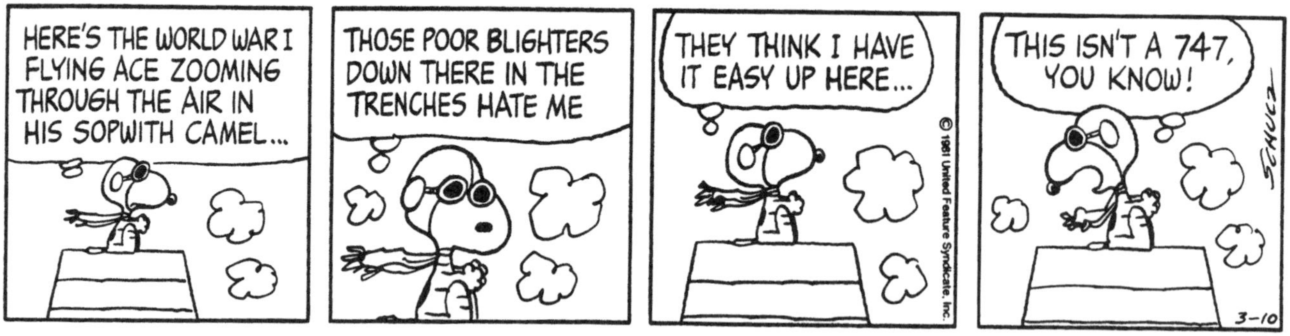
HERE'S THE WORLD WAR I FLYING ACE ZOOMING THROUGH THE AIR IN HIS SOPWITH CAMEL...
THOSE POOR BLIGHTERS DOWN THERE IN THE TRENCHES HATE ME
THEY THINK I HAVE IT EASY UP HERE...
THIS ISN'T A 747, YOU KNOW!
© 1981 United Feature Syndicate, Inc.
SCHULZ
3-10

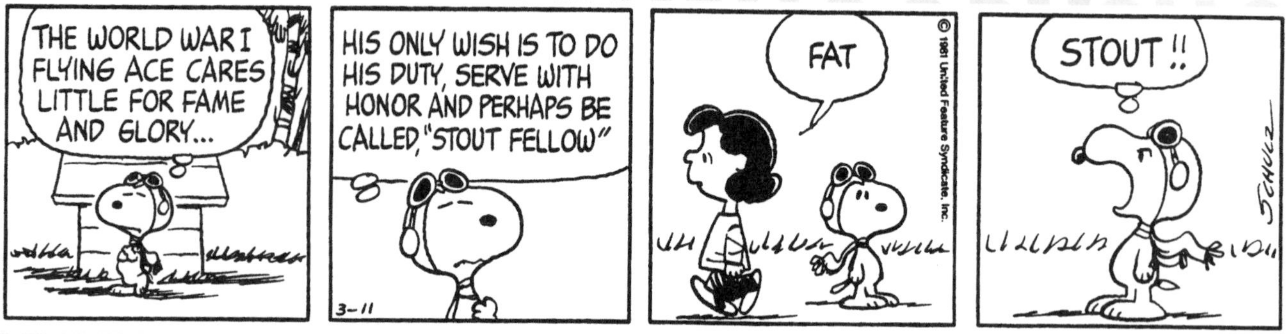
THE WORLD WAR I FLYING ACE CARES LITTLE FOR FAME AND GLORY...
HIS ONLY WISH IS TO DO HIS DUTY, SERVE WITH HONOR AND PERHAPS BE CALLED, "STOUT FELLOW"
3-11
FAT
© 1981 United Feature Syndicate, Inc.
STOUT!!
SCHULZ

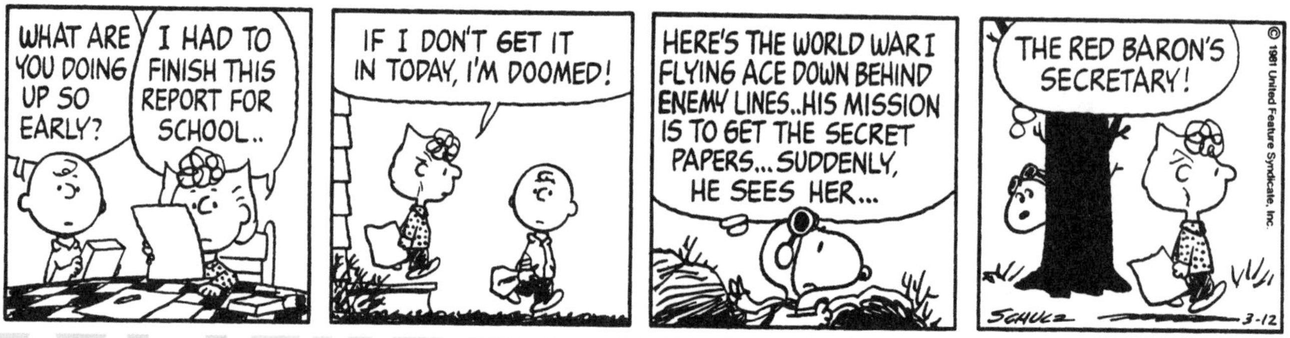
WHAT ARE YOU DOING UP SO EARLY?
I HAD TO FINISH THIS REPORT FOR SCHOOL..
IF I DON'T GET IT IN TODAY, I'M DOOMED!
HERE'S THE WORLD WAR I FLYING ACE DOWN BEHIND ENEMY LINES..HIS MISSION IS TO GET THE SECRET PAPERS...SUDDENLY, HE SEES HER...
SCHULZ
THE RED BARON'S SECRETARY!
© 1981 United Feature Syndicate, Inc.
3-12

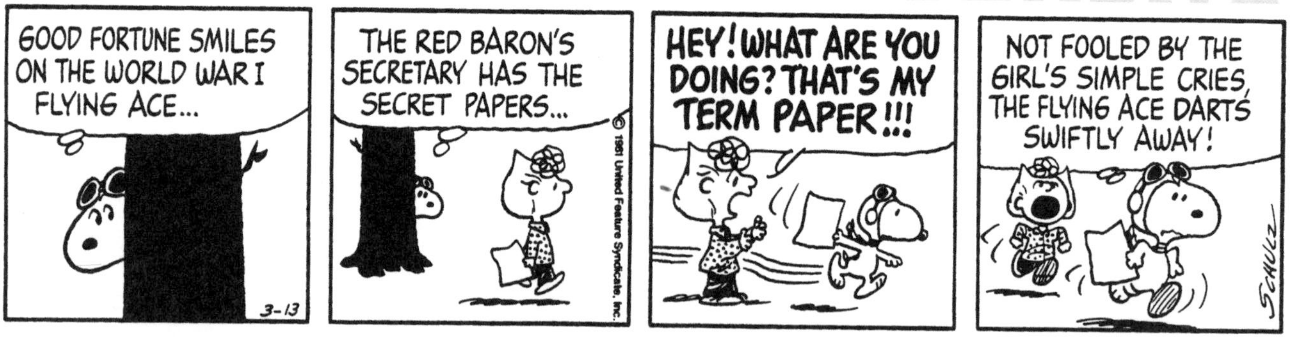
GOOD FORTUNE SMILES ON THE WORLD WAR I FLYING ACE...
3-13
THE RED BARON'S SECRETARY HAS THE SECRET PAPERS...
© 1981 United Feature Syndicate, Inc.
HEY! WHAT ARE YOU DOING? THAT'S MY TERM PAPER!!!
NOT FOOLED BY THE GIRL'S SIMPLE CRIES, THE FLYING ACE DARTS SWIFTLY AWAY!
SCHULZ

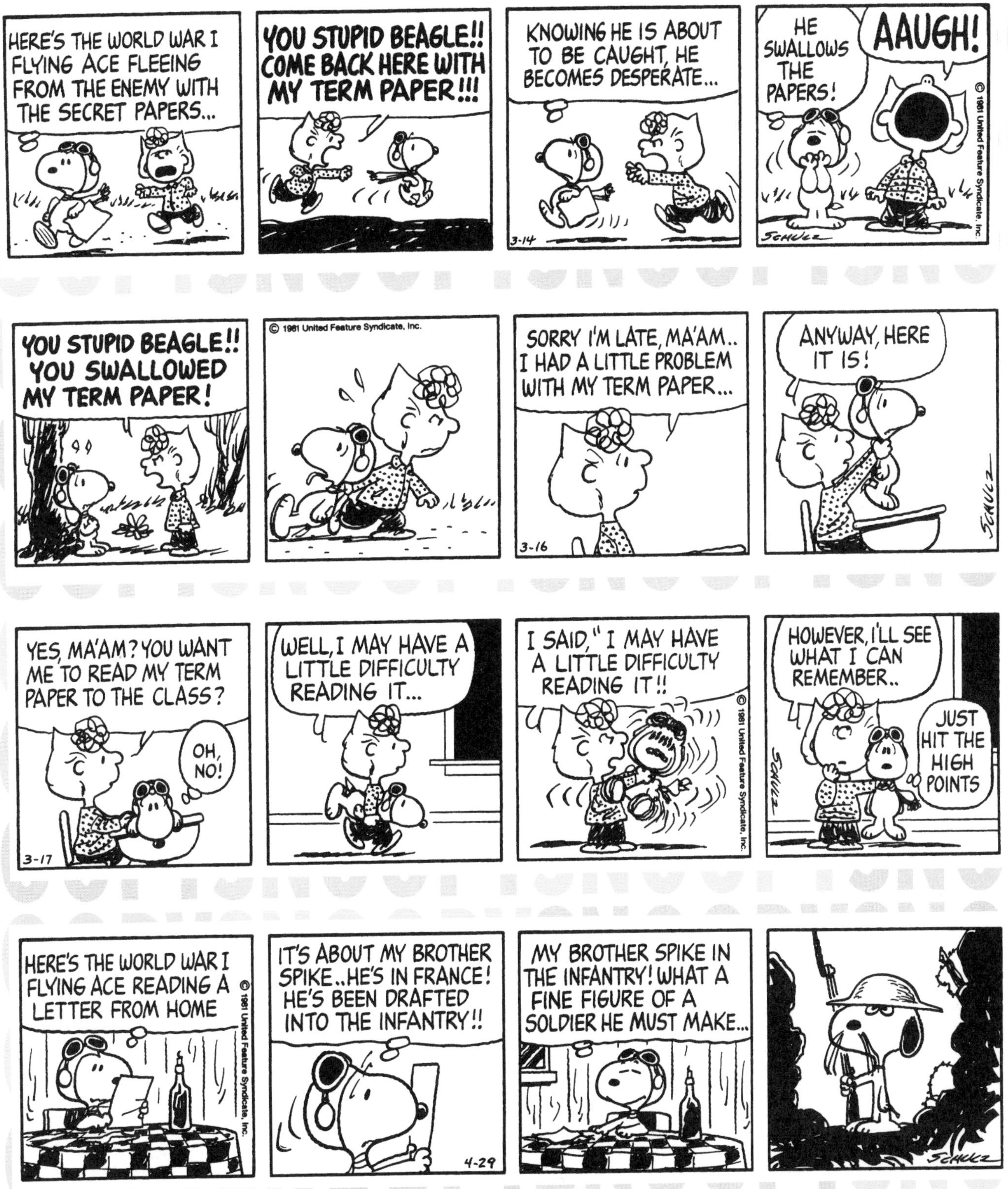
HERE'S THE WORLD WAR I FLYING ACE FLEEING FROM THE ENEMY WITH THE SECRET PAPERS...
YOU STUPID BEAGLE!! COME BACK HERE WITH MY TERM PAPER!!!
KNOWING HE IS ABOUT TO BE CAUGHT, HE BECOMES DESPERATE...
3-14
HE SWALLOWS THE PAPERS!
AAUGH!
© 1981 United Feature Syndicate, Inc.
SCHULZ
YOU STUPID BEAGLE!! YOU SWALLOWED MY TERM PAPER!
© 1981 United Feature Syndicate, Inc.
SORRY I'M LATE, MA'AM.. I HAD A LITTLE PROBLEM WITH MY TERM PAPER...
3-16
ANYWAY, HERE IT IS!
SCHULZ
YES, MA'AM? YOU WANT ME TO READ MY TERM PAPER TO THE CLASS?
OH, NO!
3-17
WELL, I MAY HAVE A LITTLE DIFFICULTY READING IT...
I SAID, "I MAY HAVE A LITTLE DIFFICULTY READING IT!!
© 1981 United Feature Syndicate, Inc.
SCHULZ
HOWEVER, I'LL SEE WHAT I CAN REMEMBER..
JUST HIT THE HIGH POINTS
HERE'S THE WORLD WAR I FLYING ACE READING A LETTER FROM HOME
© 1981 United Feature Syndicate, Inc.
IT'S ABOUT MY BROTHER SPIKE..HE'S IN FRANCE! HE'S BEEN DRAFTED INTO THE INFANTRY!!
4-29
MY BROTHER SPIKE IN THE INFANTRY! WHAT A FINE FIGURE OF A SOLDIER HE MUST MAKE...
SCHULZ

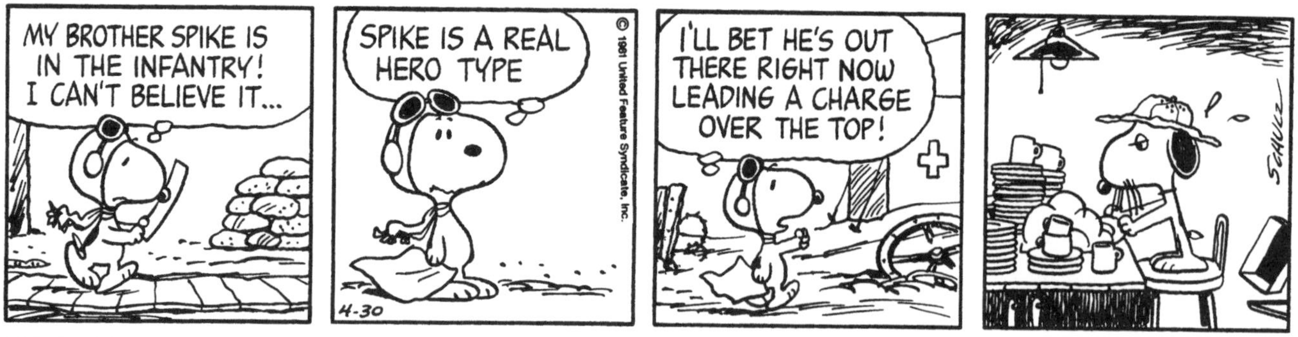
MY BROTHER SPIKE IS IN THE INFANTRY! I CAN'T BELIEVE IT...
SPIKE IS A REAL HERO TYPE
© 1981 United Feature Syndicate, Inc.
4-30
I'LL BET HE'S OUT THERE RIGHT NOW LEADING A CHARGE OVER THE TOP!
!
SCHULZ

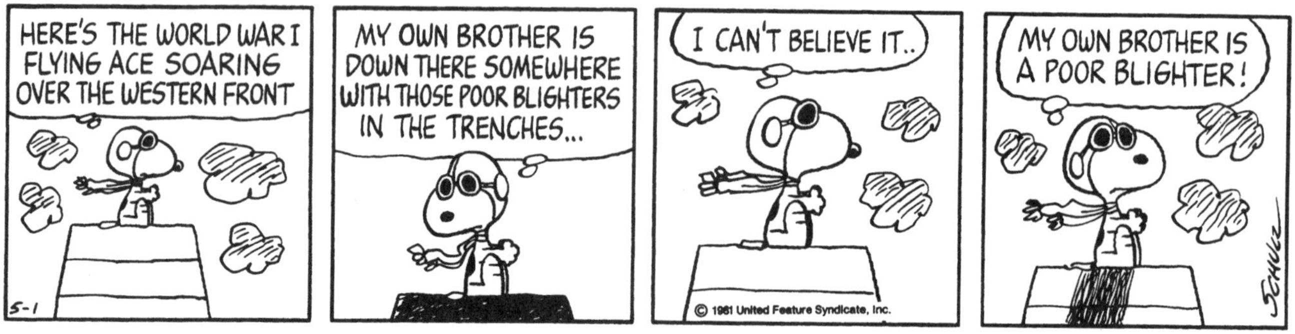
HERE'S THE WORLD WAR I FLYING ACE SOARING OVER THE WESTERN FRONT
5-1
MY OWN BROTHER IS DOWN THERE SOMEWHERE WITH THOSE POOR BLIGHTERS IN THE TRENCHES...
I CAN'T BELIEVE IT..
© 1981 United Feature Syndicate, Inc.
MY OWN BROTHER IS A POOR BLIGHTER!
SCHULZ

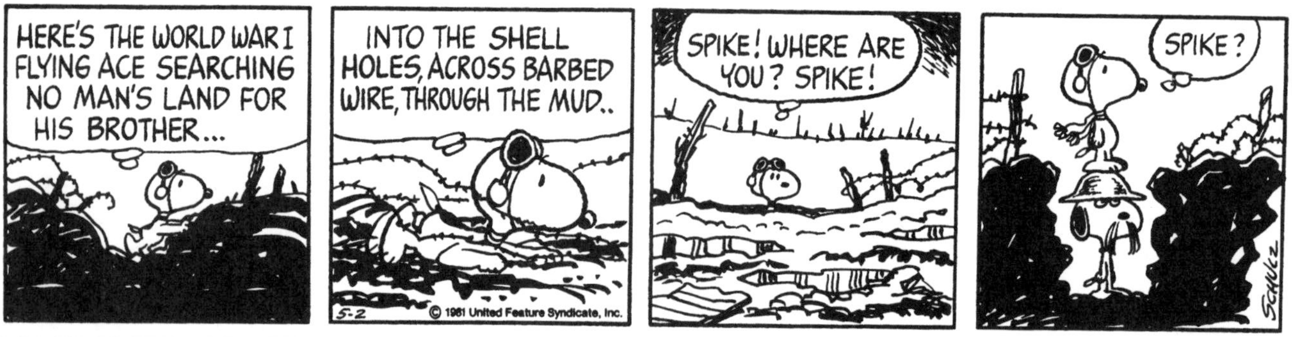
HERE'S THE WORLD WAR I FLYING ACE SEARCHING NO MAN'S LAND FOR HIS BROTHER...
INTO THE SHELL HOLES, ACROSS BARBED WIRE, THROUGH THE MUD..
5-2
© 1981 United Feature Syndicate, Inc.
SPIKE! WHERE ARE YOU? SPIKE!
SPIKE?
SCHULZ

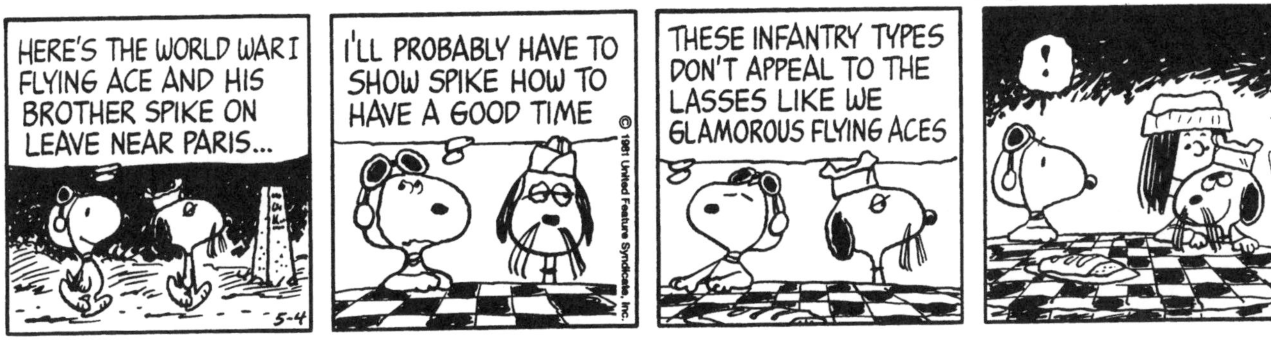
HERE'S THE WORLD WAR I FLYING ACE AND HIS BROTHER SPIKE ON LEAVE NEAR PARIS...
5-4
I'LL PROBABLY HAVE TO SHOW SPIKE HOW TO HAVE A GOOD TIME
© 1981 United Feature Syndicate, Inc.
THESE INFANTRY TYPES DON'T APPEAL TO THE LASSES LIKE WE GLAMOROUS FLYING ACES
!
SCHULZ

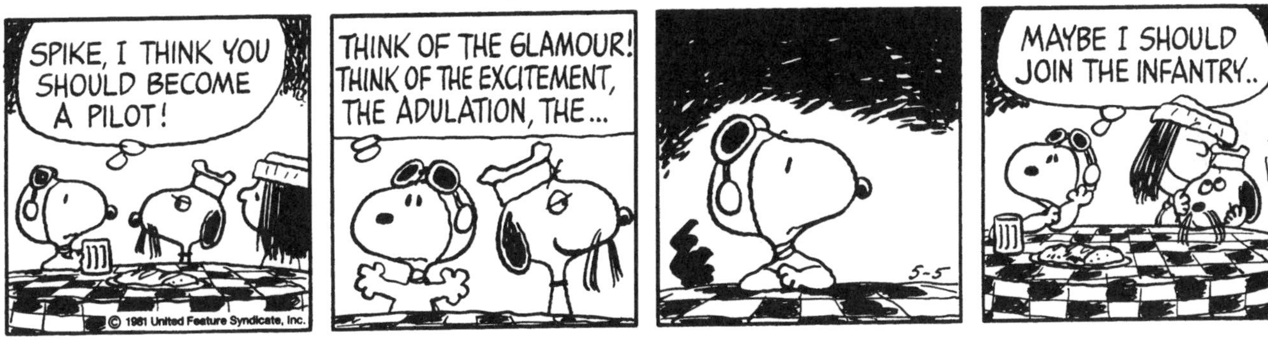
SPIKE, I THINK YOU SHOULD BECOME A PILOT!
© 1981 United Feature Syndicate, Inc.
THINK OF THE GLAMOUR! THINK OF THE EXCITEMENT, THE ADULATION, THE...
5-5
MAYBE I SHOULD JOIN THE INFANTRY..
SCHULZ

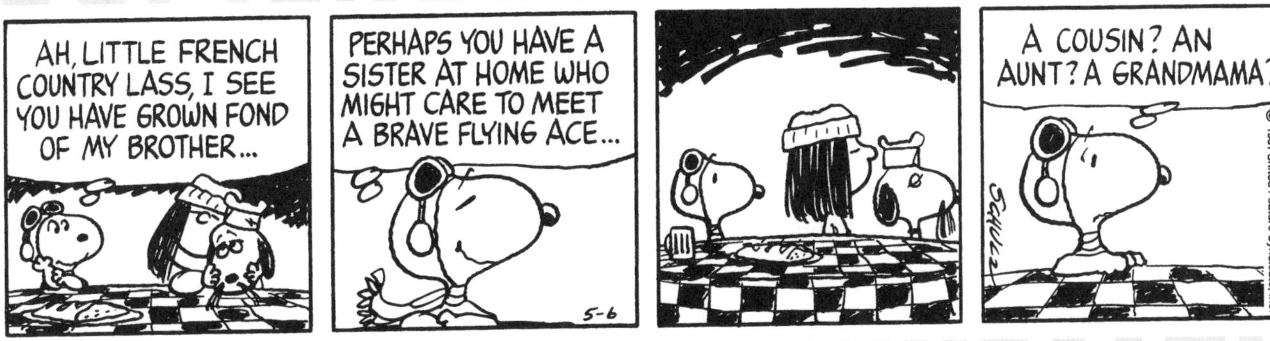
AH, LITTLE FRENCH COUNTRY LASS, I SEE YOU HAVE GROWN FOND OF MY BROTHER...
PERHAPS YOU HAVE A SISTER AT HOME WHO MIGHT CARE TO MEET A BRAVE FLYING ACE...
5-6
SCHULZ
A COUSIN? AN AUNT? A GRANDMAMA?
© 1981 United Feature Syndicate, Inc.

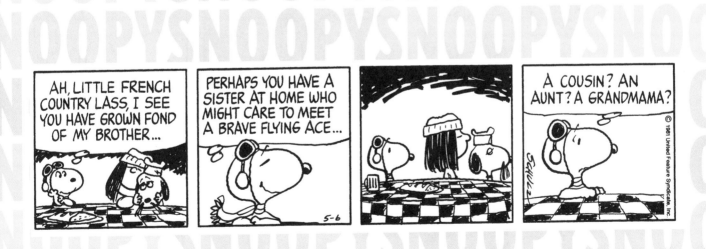

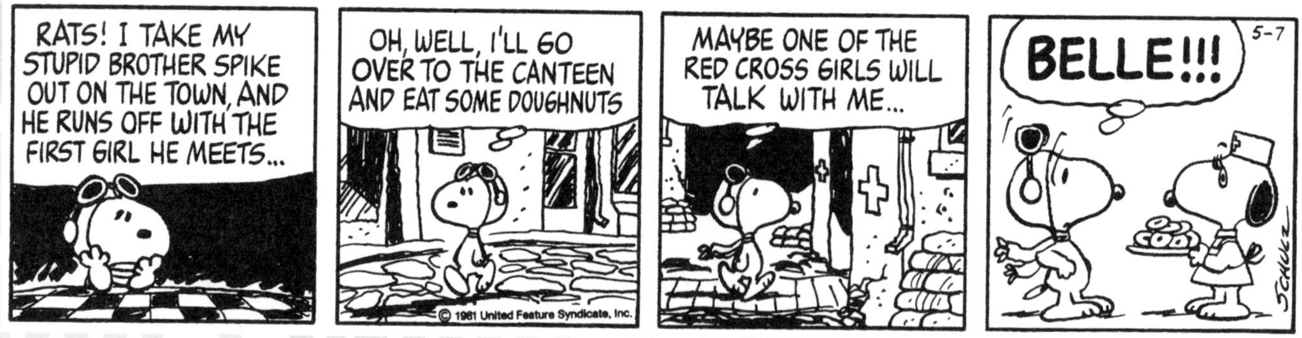
RATS! I TAKE MY STUPID BROTHER SPIKE OUT ON THE TOWN, AND HE RUNS OFF WITH THE FIRST GIRL HE MEETS...
OH, WELL, I'LL GO OVER TO THE CANTEEN AND EAT SOME DOUGHNUTS
© 1981 United Feature Syndicate, Inc.
MAYBE ONE OF THE RED CROSS GIRLS WILL TALK WITH ME...
BELLE!!!
5-7
SCHULZ

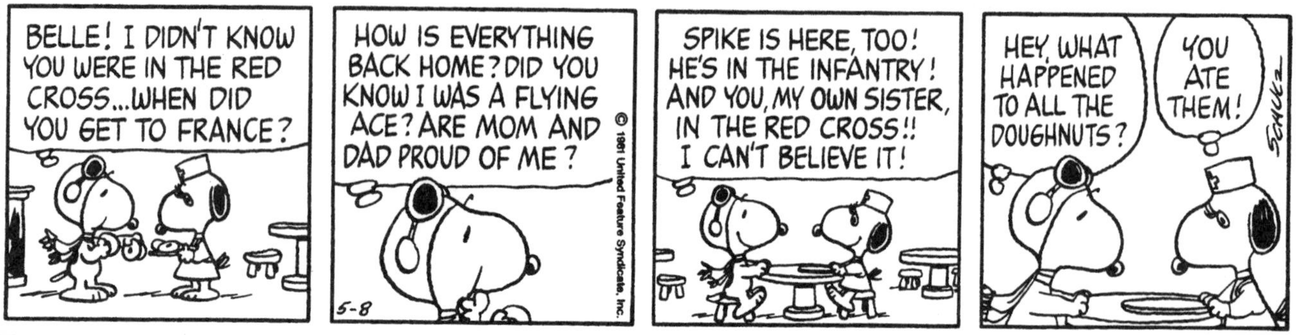
BELLE! I DIDN'T KNOW YOU WERE IN THE RED CROSS...WHEN DID YOU GET TO FRANCE?
HOW IS EVERYTHING BACK HOME? DID YOU KNOW I WAS A FLYING ACE? ARE MOM AND DAD PROUD OF ME?
5-8
© 1981 United Feature Syndicate, Inc.
SPIKE IS HERE, TOO! HE'S IN THE INFANTRY! AND YOU, MY OWN SISTER, IN THE RED CROSS!! I CAN'T BELIEVE IT!
HEY, WHAT HAPPENED TO ALL THE DOUGHNUTS?
YOU ATE THEM!
SCHULZ

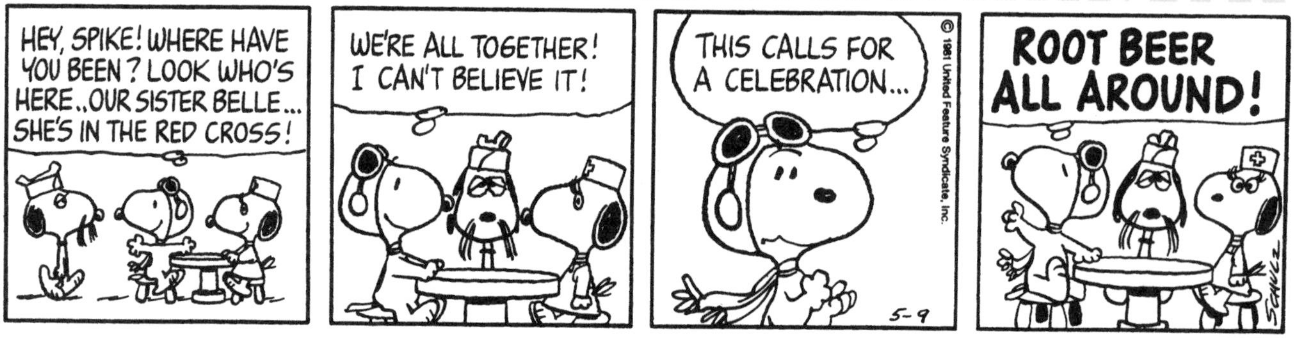
HEY, SPIKE! WHERE HAVE YOU BEEN? LOOK WHO'S HERE..OUR SISTER BELLE... SHE'S IN THE RED CROSS!
WE'RE ALL TOGETHER! I CAN'T BELIEVE IT!
THIS CALLS FOR A CELEBRATION...
5-9
© 1981 United Feature Syndicate, Inc.
ROOT BEER ALL AROUND!
SCHULZ

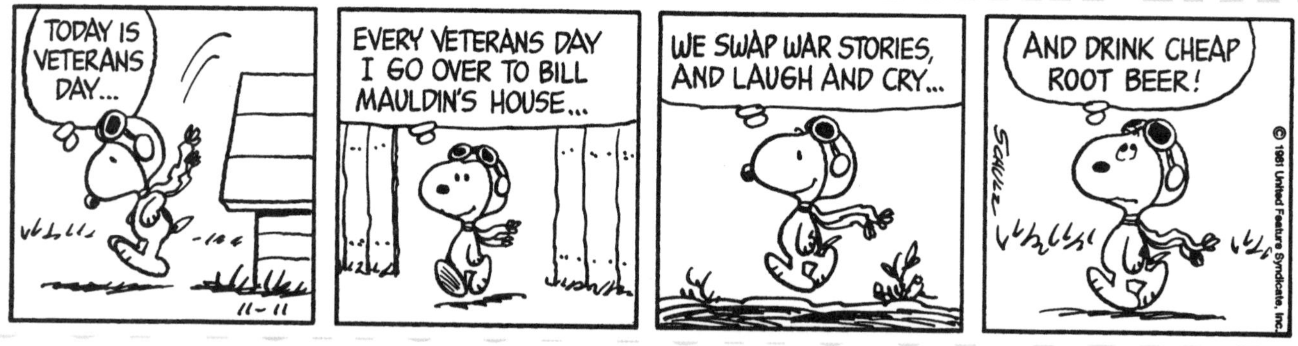
TODAY IS VETERANS DAY...
11-11
EVERY VETERANS DAY I GO OVER TO BILL MAULDIN'S HOUSE...
WE SWAP WAR STORIES, AND LAUGH AND CRY...
SCHULZ
AND DRINK CHEAP ROOT BEER!
© 1981 United Feature Syndicate, Inc.

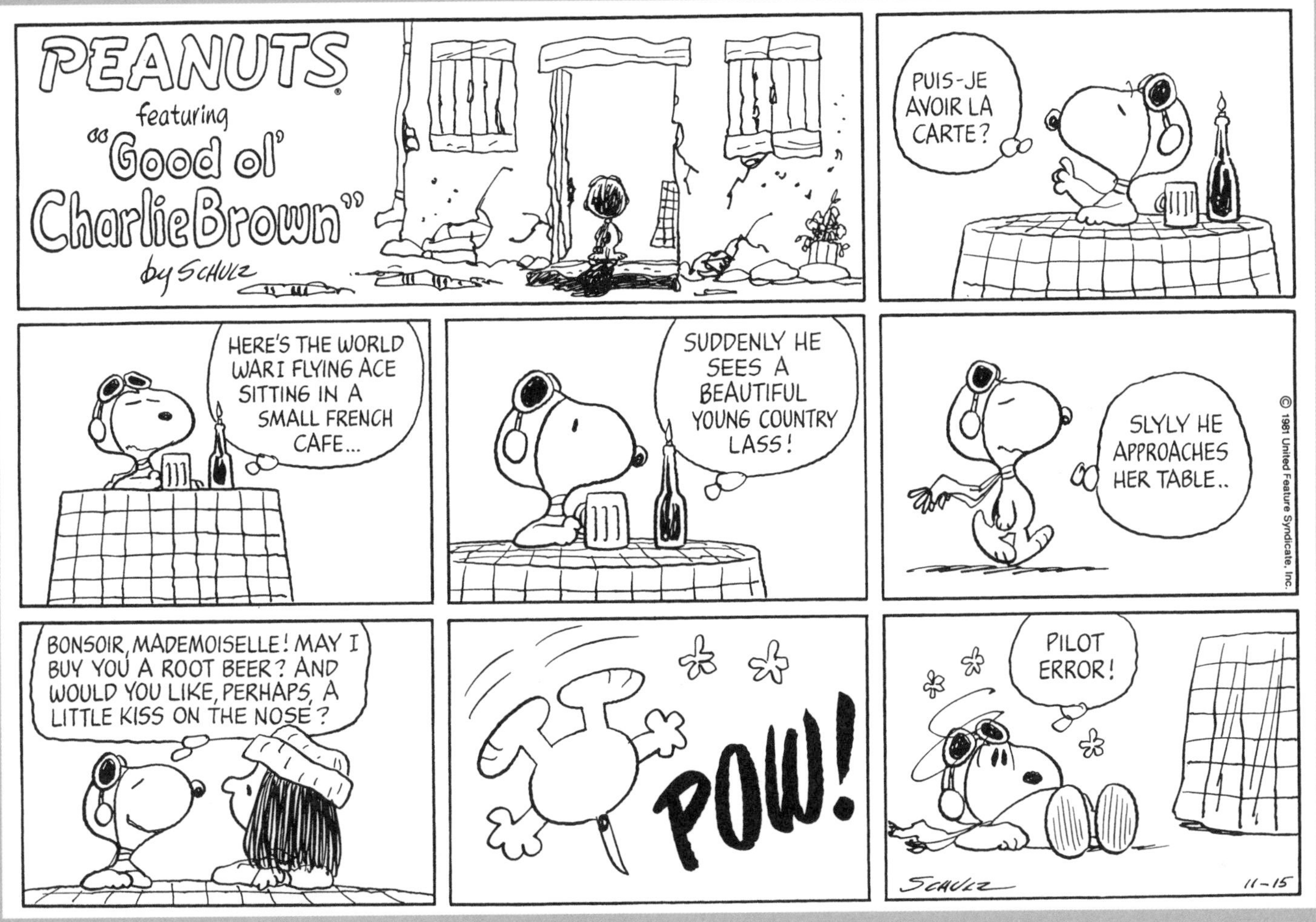
PEANUTS
featuring
"Good ol' Charlie Brown"
by SCHULZ
PUIS-JE AVOIR LA CARTE?
HERE'S THE WORLD WAR I FLYING ACE SITTING IN A SMALL FRENCH CAFE...
SUDDENLY HE SEES A BEAUTIFUL YOUNG COUNTRY LASS!
SLYLY HE APPROACHES HER TABLE..
© 1981 United Feature Syndicate, Inc.
BONSOIR, MADEMOISELLE! MAY I BUY YOU A ROOT BEER? AND WOULD YOU LIKE, PERHAPS, A LITTLE KISS ON THE NOSE?
POW!
PILOT ERROR!
SCHULZ
11-15

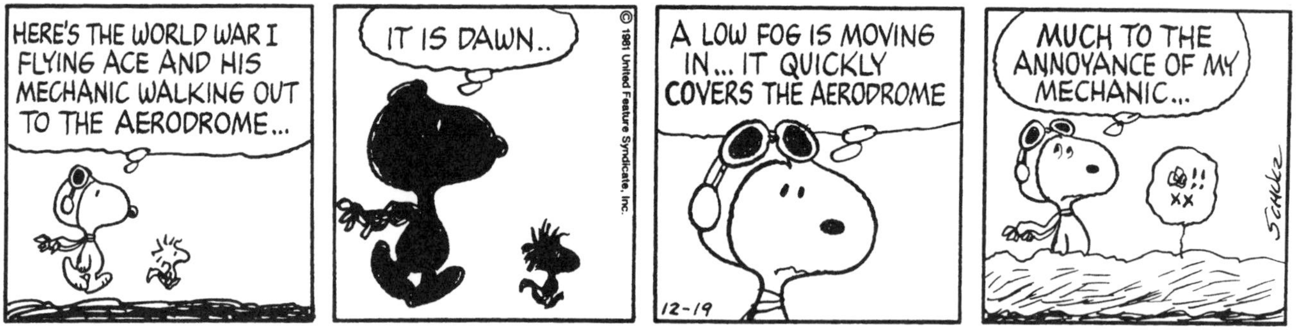
HERE'S THE WORLD WAR I FLYING ACE AND HIS MECHANIC WALKING OUT TO THE AERODROME...
IT IS DAWN..
© 1981 United Feature Syndicate, Inc.
A LOW FOG IS MOVING IN... IT QUICKLY COVERS THE AERODROME
12-19
MUCH TO THE ANNOYANCE OF MY MECHANIC...
SCHULZ

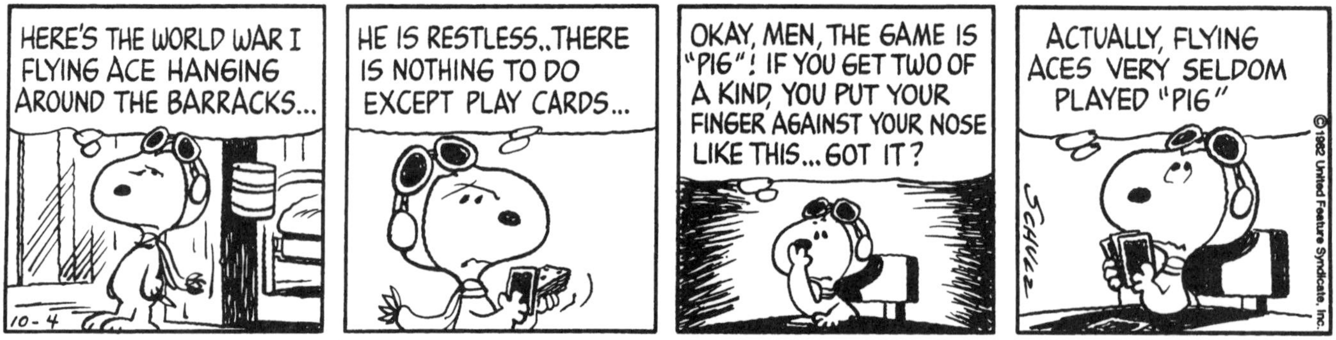
HERE'S THE WORLD WAR I FLYING ACE HANGING AROUND THE BARRACKS...
10-4
HE IS RESTLESS..THERE IS NOTHING TO DO EXCEPT PLAY CARDS...
OKAY, MEN, THE GAME IS "PIG"! IF YOU GET TWO OF A KIND, YOU PUT YOUR FINGER AGAINST YOUR NOSE LIKE THIS...GOT IT?
SCHULZ
ACTUALLY, FLYING ACES VERY SELDOM PLAYED "PIG"
© 1982 United Feature Syndicate, Inc.

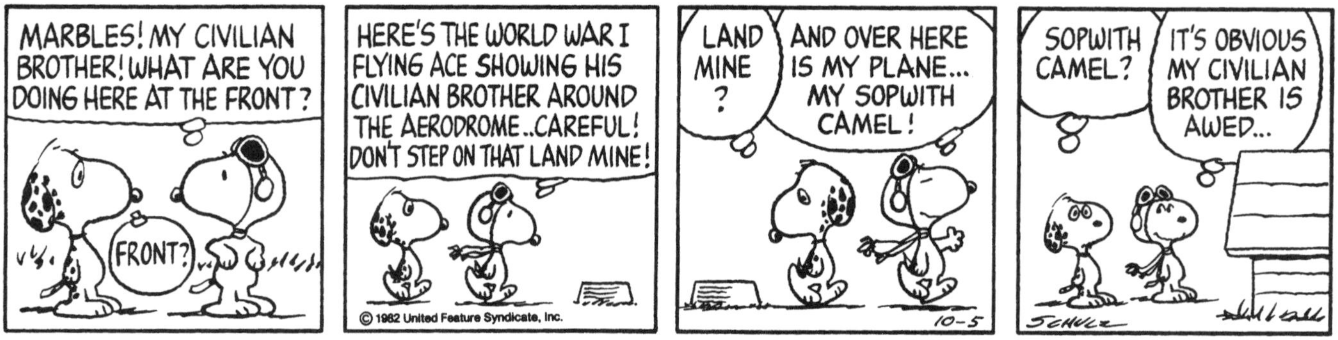
MARBLES! MY CIVILIAN BROTHER! WHAT ARE YOU DOING HERE AT THE FRONT?
FRONT?
HERE'S THE WORLD WAR I FLYING ACE SHOWING HIS CIVILIAN BROTHER AROUND THE AERODROME..CAREFUL! DON'T STEP ON THAT LAND MINE!
© 1982 United Feature Syndicate, Inc.
LAND MINE?
AND OVER HERE IS MY PLANE... MY SOPWITH CAMEL!
10-5
SOPWITH CAMEL?
IT'S OBVIOUS MY CIVILIAN BROTHER IS AWED...
SCHULZ

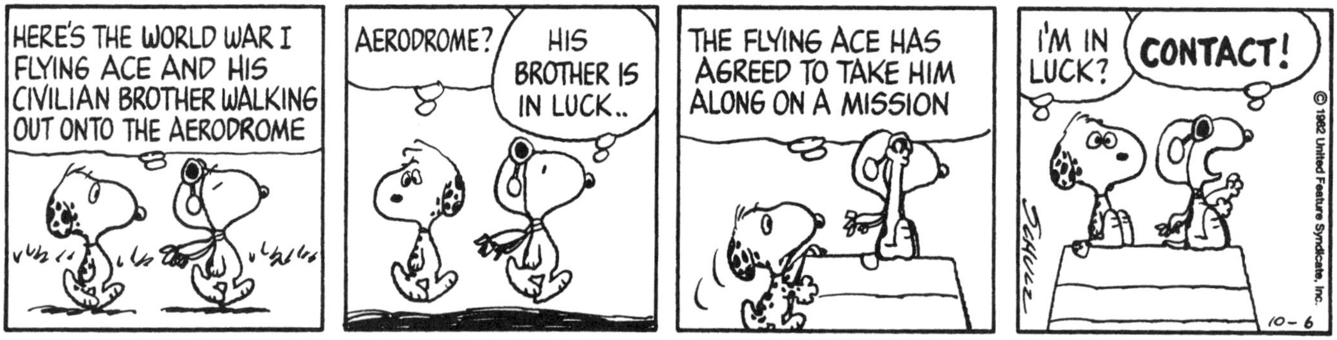
HERE'S THE WORLD WAR I FLYING ACE AND HIS CIVILIAN BROTHER WALKING OUT ONTO THE AERODROME
AERODROME?
HIS BROTHER IS IN LUCK..
THE FLYING ACE HAS AGREED TO TAKE HIM ALONG ON A MISSION
I'M IN LUCK?
CONTACT!
SCHULZ
© 1982 United Feature Syndicate, Inc.
10-6

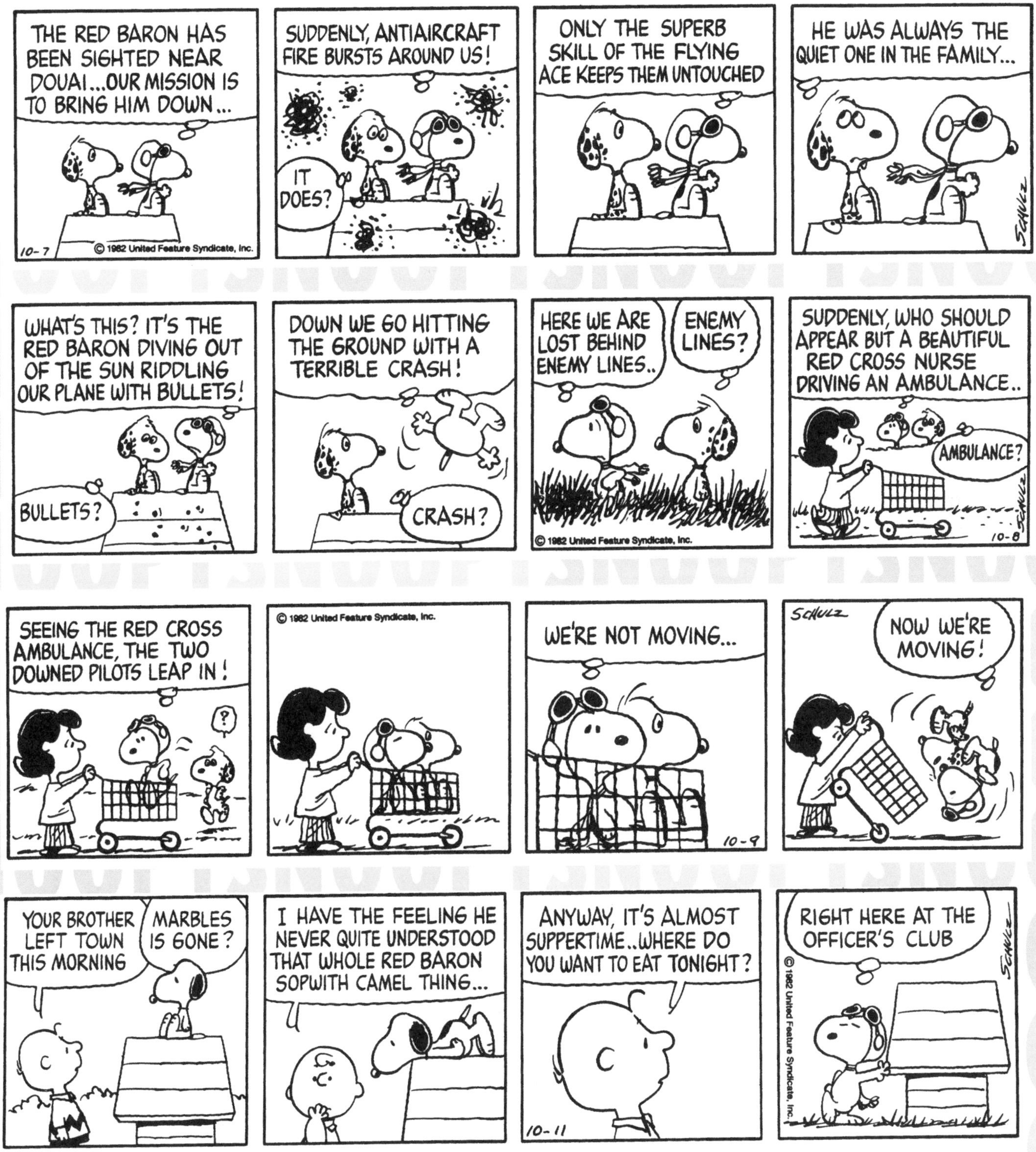
THE RED BARON HAS BEEN SIGHTED NEAR DOUAI...OUR MISSION IS TO BRING HIM DOWN...
10-7
© 1982 United Feature Syndicate, Inc.
SUDDENLY, ANTIAIRCRAFT FIRE BURSTS AROUND US!
IT DOES?
ONLY THE SUPERB SKILL OF THE FLYING ACE KEEPS THEM UNTOUCHED
HE WAS ALWAYS THE QUIET ONE IN THE FAMILY...
SCHULZ
WHAT'S THIS? IT'S THE RED BARON DIVING OUT OF THE SUN RIDDLING OUR PLANE WITH BULLETS!
BULLETS?
DOWN WE GO HITTING THE GROUND WITH A TERRIBLE CRASH!
CRASH?
HERE WE ARE LOST BEHIND ENEMY LINES..
ENEMY LINES?
© 1982 United Feature Syndicate, Inc.
SUDDENLY, WHO SHOULD APPEAR BUT A BEAUTIFUL RED CROSS NURSE DRIVING AN AMBULANCE..
AMBULANCE?
SCHULZ
10-8
SEEING THE RED CROSS AMBULANCE, THE TWO DOWNED PILOTS LEAP IN!
?
© 1982 United Feature Syndicate, Inc.
WE'RE NOT MOVING...
10-9
SCHULZ
NOW WE'RE MOVING!
YOUR BROTHER LEFT TOWN THIS MORNING
MARBLES IS GONE?
I HAVE THE FEELING HE NEVER QUITE UNDERSTOOD THAT WHOLE RED BARON SOPWITH CAMEL THING...
ANYWAY, IT'S ALMOST SUPPERTIME..WHERE DO YOU WANT TO EAT TONIGHT?
10-11
© 1982 United Feature Syndicate, Inc.
RIGHT HERE AT THE OFFICER'S CLUB
SCHULZ

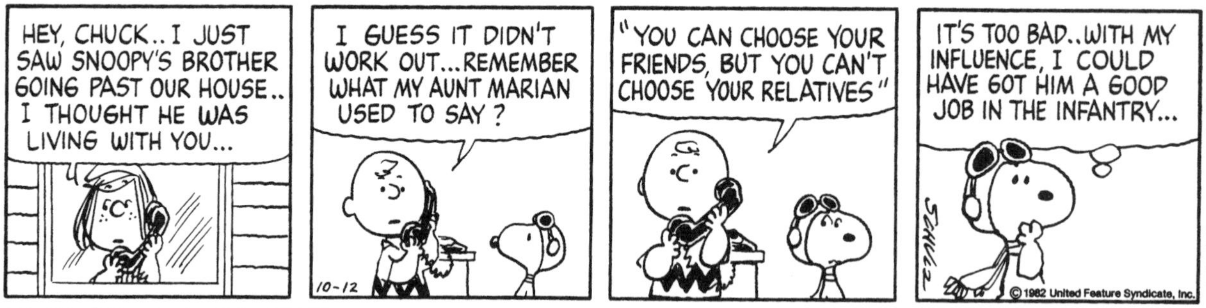
HEY, CHUCK.. I JUST SAW SNOOPY'S BROTHER GOING PAST OUR HOUSE.. I THOUGHT HE WAS LIVING WITH YOU...
I GUESS IT DIDN'T WORK OUT... REMEMBER WHAT MY AUNT MARIAN USED TO SAY?
"YOU CAN CHOOSE YOUR FRIENDS, BUT YOU CAN'T CHOOSE YOUR RELATIVES"
IT'S TOO BAD.. WITH MY INFLUENCE, I COULD HAVE GOT HIM A GOOD JOB IN THE INFANTRY...
10-12
SCHULZ
© 1982 United Feature Syndicate, Inc.

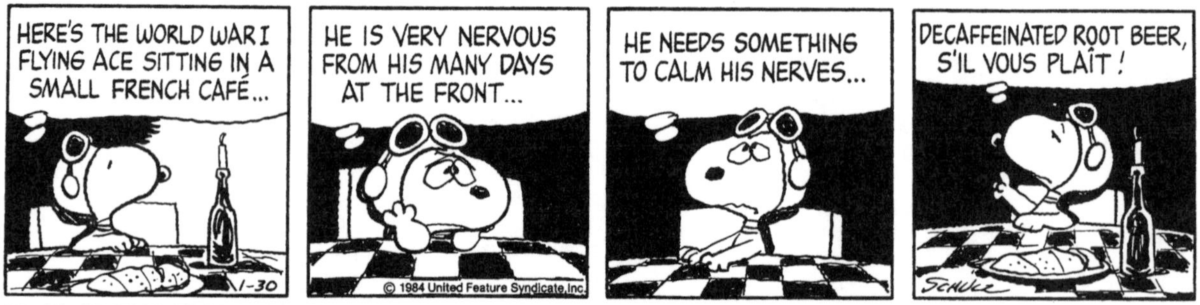
HERE'S THE WORLD WAR I FLYING ACE SITTING IN A SMALL FRENCH CAFÉ...
HE IS VERY NERVOUS FROM HIS MANY DAYS AT THE FRONT...
HE NEEDS SOMETHING TO CALM HIS NERVES...
DECAFFEINATED ROOT BEER, S'IL VOUS PLAÎT!
1-30
© 1984 United Feature Syndicate, Inc.
SCHULZ

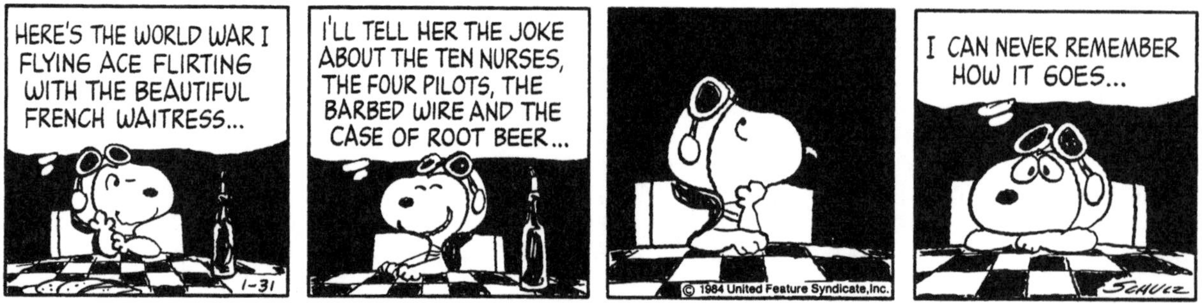
HERE'S THE WORLD WAR I FLYING ACE FLIRTING WITH THE BEAUTIFUL FRENCH WAITRESS...
I'LL TELL HER THE JOKE ABOUT THE TEN NURSES, THE FOUR PILOTS, THE BARBED WIRE AND THE CASE OF ROOT BEER...
I CAN NEVER REMEMBER HOW IT GOES...
1-31
© 1984 United Feature Syndicate, Inc.
SCHULZ

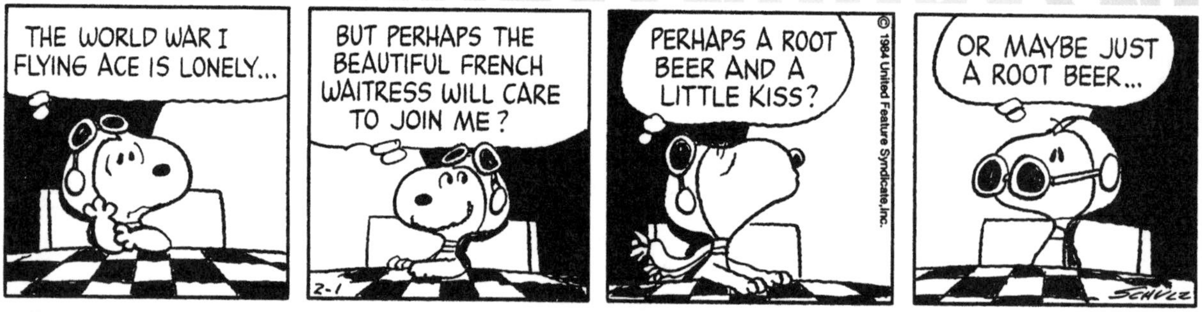
THE WORLD WAR I FLYING ACE IS LONELY...
BUT PERHAPS THE BEAUTIFUL FRENCH WAITRESS WILL CARE TO JOIN ME?
PERHAPS A ROOT BEER AND A LITTLE KISS?
OR MAYBE JUST A ROOT BEER...
2-1
© 1984 United Feature Syndicate, Inc.
SCHULZ

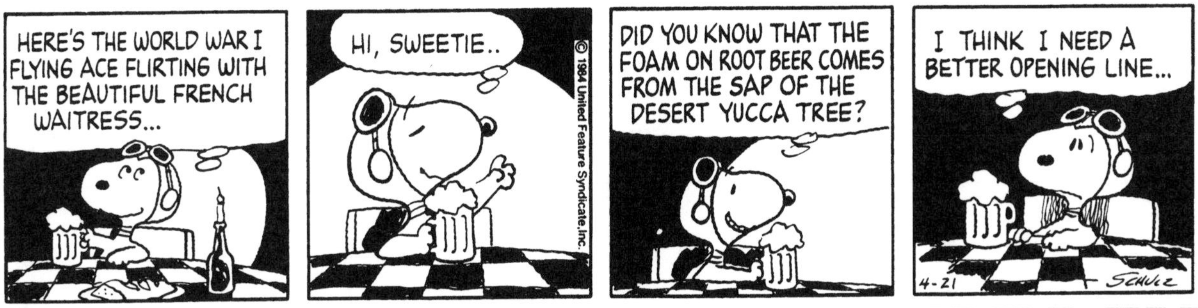
HERE'S THE WORLD WAR I FLYING ACE FLIRTING WITH THE BEAUTIFUL FRENCH WAITRESS...
HI, SWEETIE..
© 1984 United Feature Syndicate, Inc.
DID YOU KNOW THAT THE FOAM ON ROOT BEER COMES FROM THE SAP OF THE DESERT YUCCA TREE?
I THINK I NEED A BETTER OPENING LINE...
4-21
SCHULZ

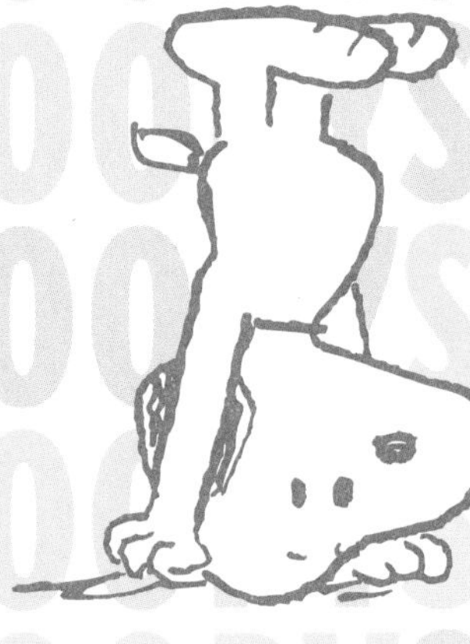

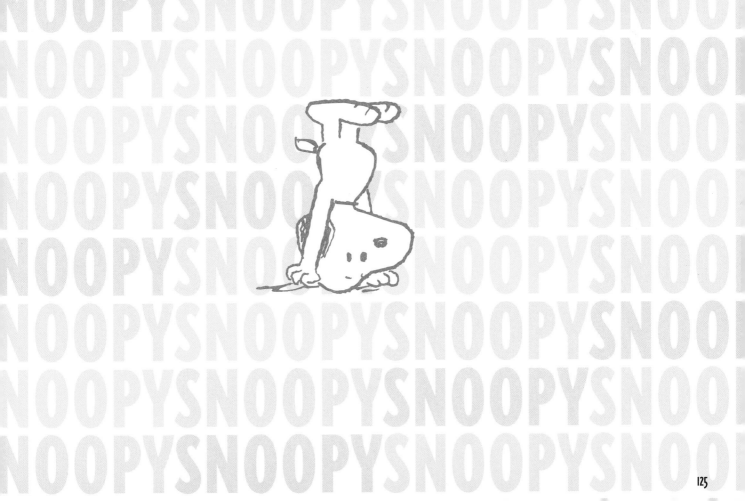

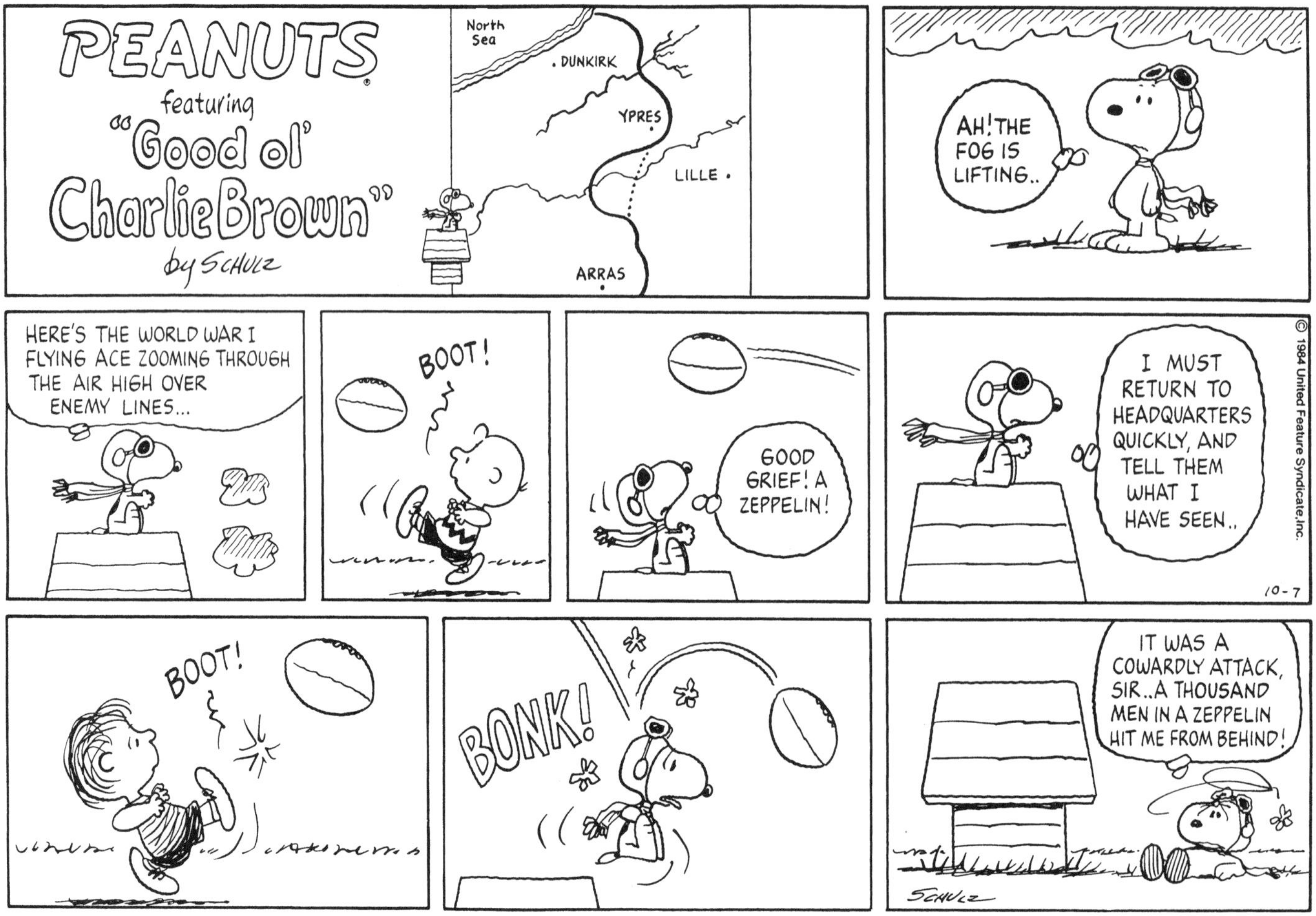
PEANUTS
featuring
"Good ol' CharlieBrown"
by SCHULZ
North Sea
DUNKIRK
YPRES
LILLE
ARRAS
AH! THE FOG IS LIFTING..
HERE'S THE WORLD WAR I FLYING ACE ZOOMING THROUGH THE AIR HIGH OVER ENEMY LINES...
BOOT!
GOOD GRIEF! A ZEPPELIN!
I MUST RETURN TO HEADQUARTERS QUICKLY, AND TELL THEM WHAT I HAVE SEEN..
© 1984 United Feature Syndicate, Inc.
10-7
BOOT!
BONK!
IT WAS A COWARDLY ATTACK, SIR..A THOUSAND MEN IN A ZEPPELIN HIT ME FROM BEHIND!
SCHULZ

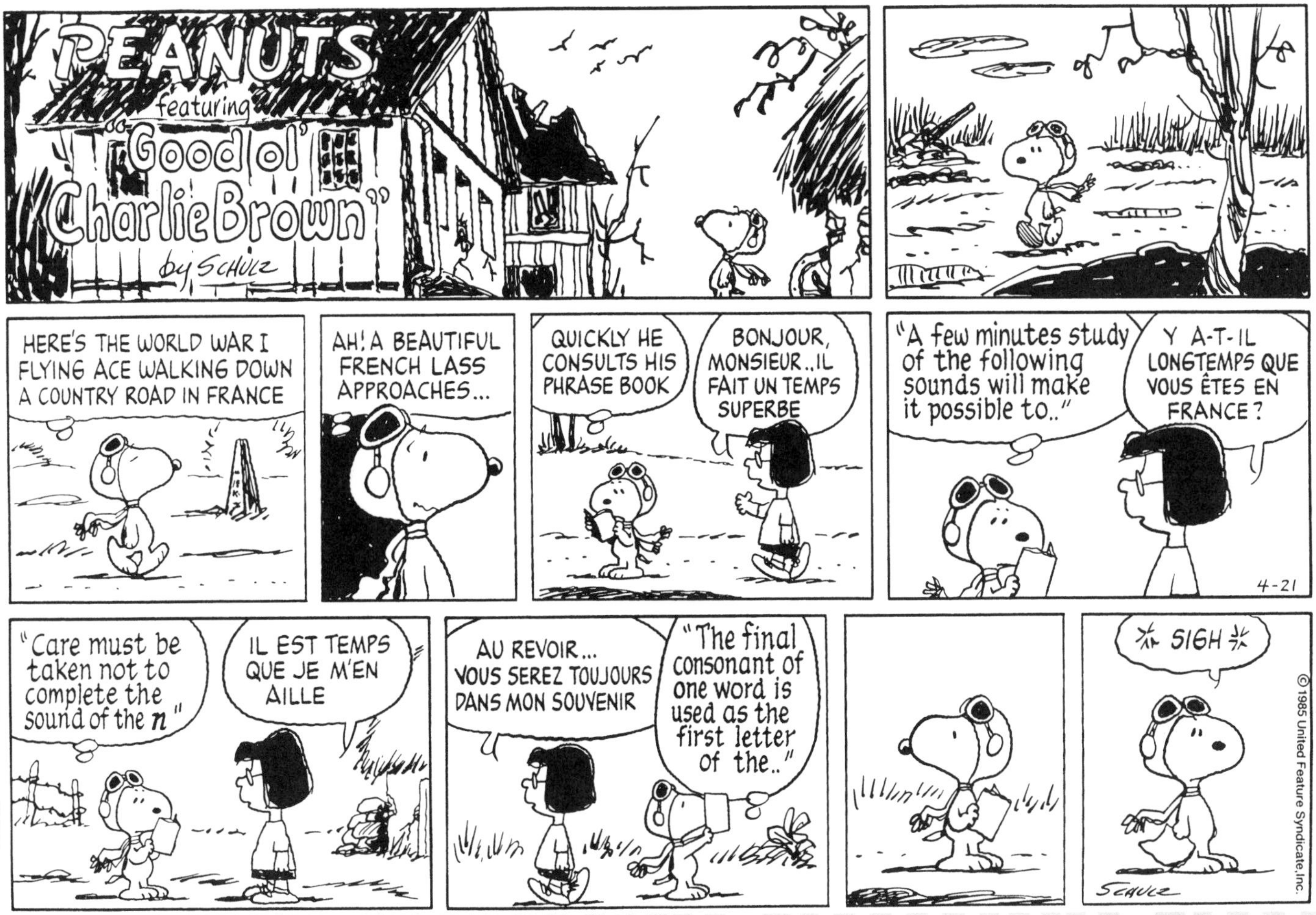
PEANUTS
featuring "Good ol' Charlie Brown"
by SCHULZ
HERE'S THE WORLD WAR I FLYING ACE WALKING DOWN A COUNTRY ROAD IN FRANCE
AH! A BEAUTIFUL FRENCH LASS APPROACHES...
QUICKLY HE CONSULTS HIS PHRASE BOOK
BONJOUR, MONSIEUR..IL FAIT UN TEMPS SUPERBE
"A few minutes study of the following sounds will make it possible to.."
Y A-T-IL LONGTEMPS QUE VOUS ÊTES EN FRANCE?
4-21
"Care must be taken not to complete the sound of the n"
IL EST TEMPS QUE JE M'EN AILLE
AU REVOIR... VOUS SEREZ TOUJOURS DANS MON SOUVENIR
"The final consonant of one word is used as the first letter of the.."
SIGH
SCHULZ
© 1985 United Feature Syndicate, Inc.

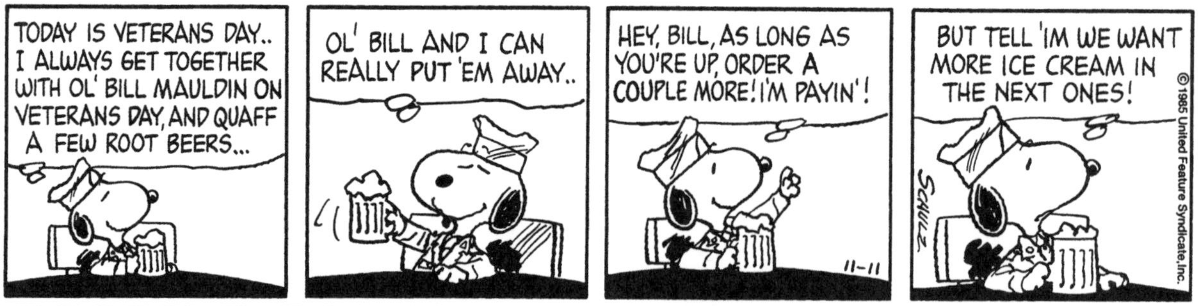
TODAY IS VETERANS DAY.. I ALWAYS GET TOGETHER WITH OL' BILL MAULDIN ON VETERANS DAY, AND QUAFF A FEW ROOT BEERS...
OL' BILL AND I CAN REALLY PUT 'EM AWAY..
HEY, BILL, AS LONG AS YOU'RE UP, ORDER A COUPLE MORE! I'M PAYIN'!
11-11
BUT TELL 'IM WE WANT MORE ICE CREAM IN THE NEXT ONES!
SCHULZ
© 1985 United Feature Syndicate, Inc.

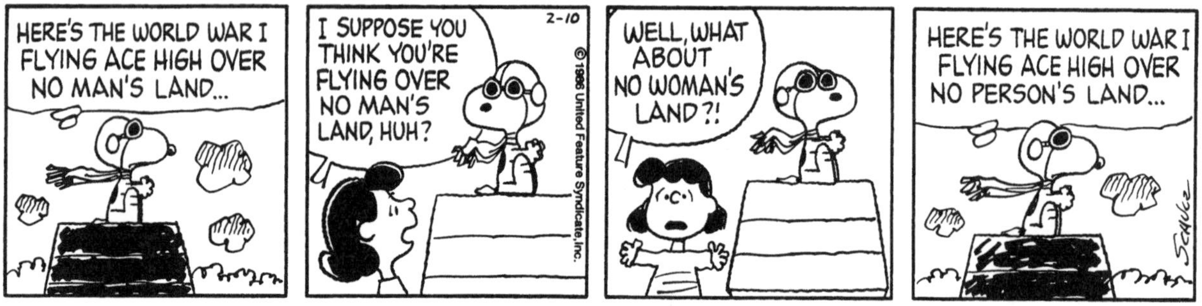
HERE'S THE WORLD WAR I FLYING ACE HIGH OVER NO MAN'S LAND...
I SUPPOSE YOU THINK YOU'RE FLYING OVER NO MAN'S LAND, HUH?
2-10
© 1986 United Feature Syndicate, Inc.
WELL, WHAT ABOUT NO WOMAN'S LAND?!
HERE'S THE WORLD WAR I FLYING ACE HIGH OVER NO PERSON'S LAND...
SCHULZ

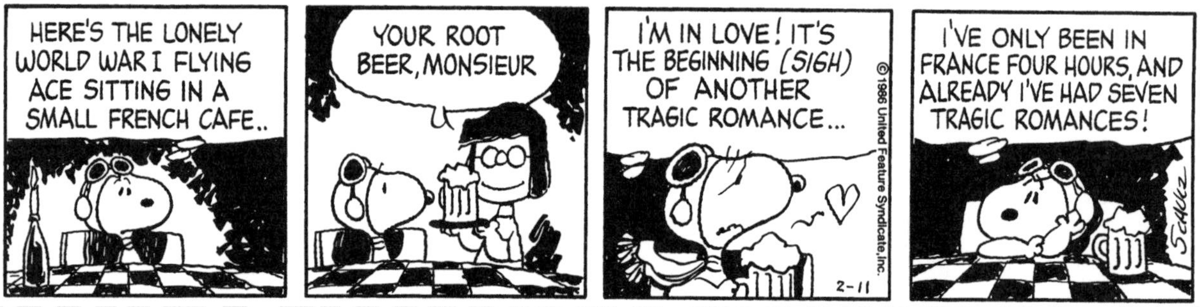
HERE'S THE LONELY WORLD WAR I FLYING ACE SITTING IN A SMALL FRENCH CAFE..
YOUR ROOT BEER, MONSIEUR
I'M IN LOVE! IT'S THE BEGINNING (SIGH) OF ANOTHER TRAGIC ROMANCE...
2-11
© 1986 United Feature Syndicate, Inc.
I'VE ONLY BEEN IN FRANCE FOUR HOURS, AND ALREADY I'VE HAD SEVEN TRAGIC ROMANCES!
SCHULZ

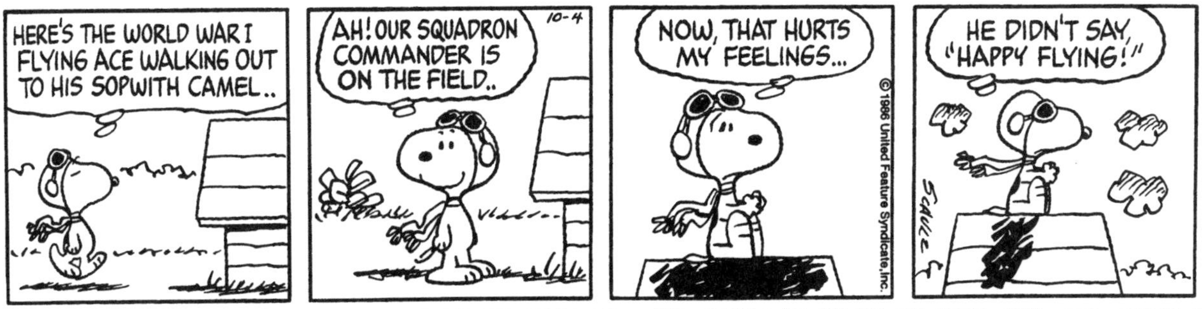
HERE'S THE WORLD WAR I FLYING ACE WALKING OUT TO HIS SOPWITH CAMEL..
AH! OUR SQUADRON COMMANDER IS ON THE FIELD..
10-4
NOW, THAT HURTS MY FEELINGS...
© 1986 United Feature Syndicate, Inc.
HE DIDN'T SAY, "HAPPY FLYING!"
SCHULZ

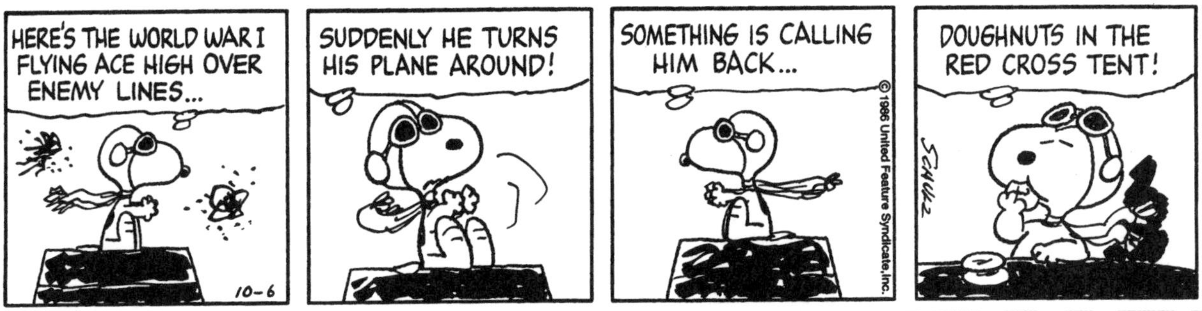
HERE'S THE WORLD WAR I FLYING ACE HIGH OVER ENEMY LINES...
10-6
SUDDENLY HE TURNS HIS PLANE AROUND!
SOMETHING IS CALLING HIM BACK...
© 1986 United Feature Syndicate, Inc.
DOUGHNUTS IN THE RED CROSS TENT!
SCHULZ

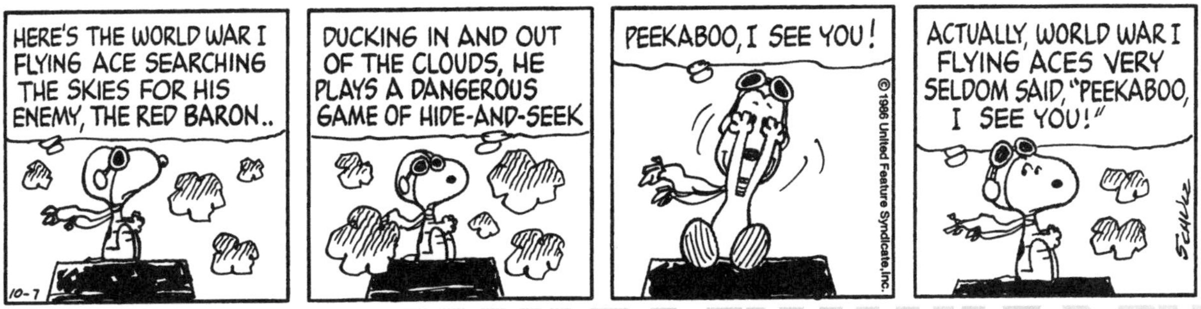
HERE'S THE WORLD WAR I FLYING ACE SEARCHING THE SKIES FOR HIS ENEMY, THE RED BARON..
10-7
DUCKING IN AND OUT OF THE CLOUDS, HE PLAYS A DANGEROUS GAME OF HIDE-AND-SEEK
PEEKABOO, I SEE YOU!
© 1986 United Feature Syndicate, Inc.
ACTUALLY, WORLD WAR I FLYING ACES VERY SELDOM SAID, "PEEKABOO, I SEE YOU!"
SCHULZ

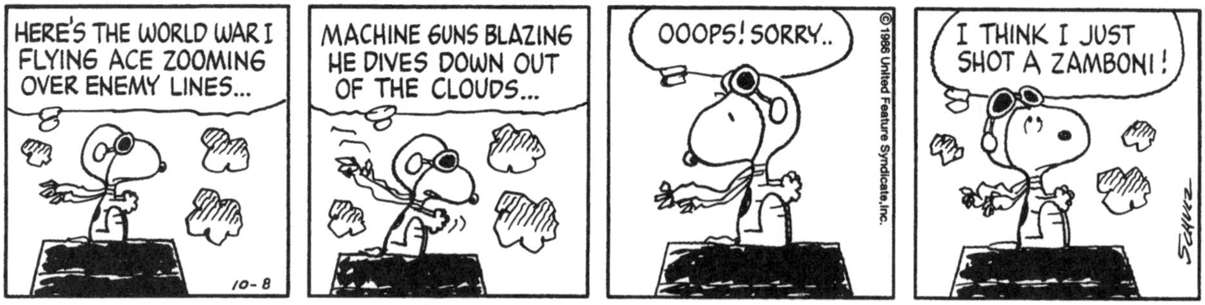
HERE'S THE WORLD WAR I FLYING ACE ZOOMING OVER ENEMY LINES...
MACHINE GUNS BLAZING HE DIVES DOWN OUT OF THE CLOUDS...
OOOPS! SORRY..
I THINK I JUST SHOT A ZAMBONI!
10-8
© 1986 United Feature Syndicate, Inc.
SCHULZ

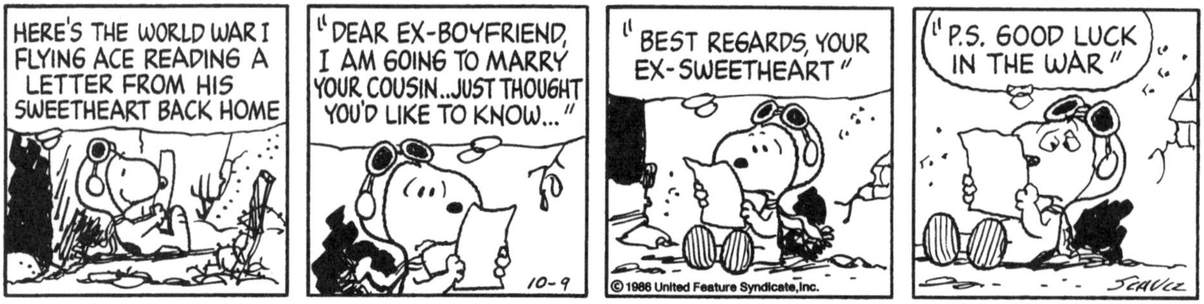
HERE'S THE WORLD WAR I FLYING ACE READING A LETTER FROM HIS SWEETHEART BACK HOME
"DEAR EX-BOYFRIEND, I AM GOING TO MARRY YOUR COUSIN...JUST THOUGHT YOU'D LIKE TO KNOW..."
"BEST REGARDS, YOUR EX-SWEETHEART"
"P.S. GOOD LUCK IN THE WAR"
10-9
© 1986 United Feature Syndicate, Inc.
SCHULZ

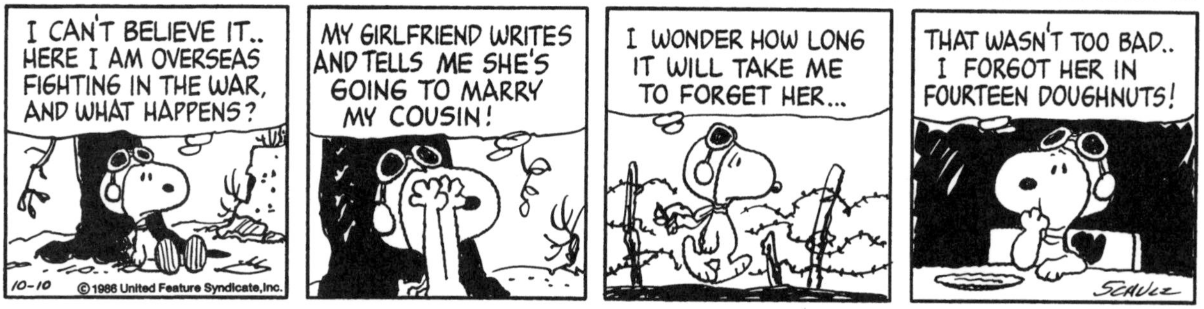
I CAN'T BELIEVE IT.. HERE I AM OVERSEAS FIGHTING IN THE WAR, AND WHAT HAPPENS?
MY GIRLFRIEND WRITES AND TELLS ME SHE'S GOING TO MARRY MY COUSIN!
I WONDER HOW LONG IT WILL TAKE ME TO FORGET HER...
THAT WASN'T TOO BAD.. I FORGOT HER IN FOURTEEN DOUGHNUTS!
10-10
© 1986 United Feature Syndicate, Inc.
SCHULZ

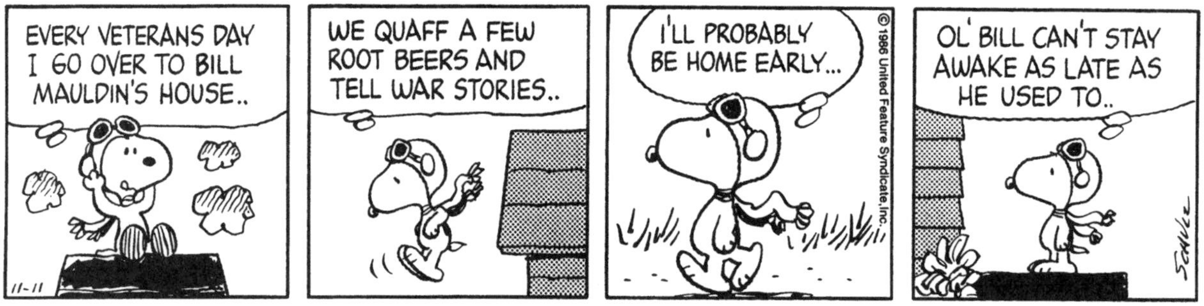
EVERY VETERANS DAY I GO OVER TO BILL MAULDIN'S HOUSE..
WE QUAFF A FEW ROOT BEERS AND TELL WAR STORIES..
I'LL PROBABLY BE HOME EARLY...
OL' BILL CAN'T STAY AWAKE AS LATE AS HE USED TO..
11-11
© 1986 United Feature Syndicate, Inc.
SCHULZ

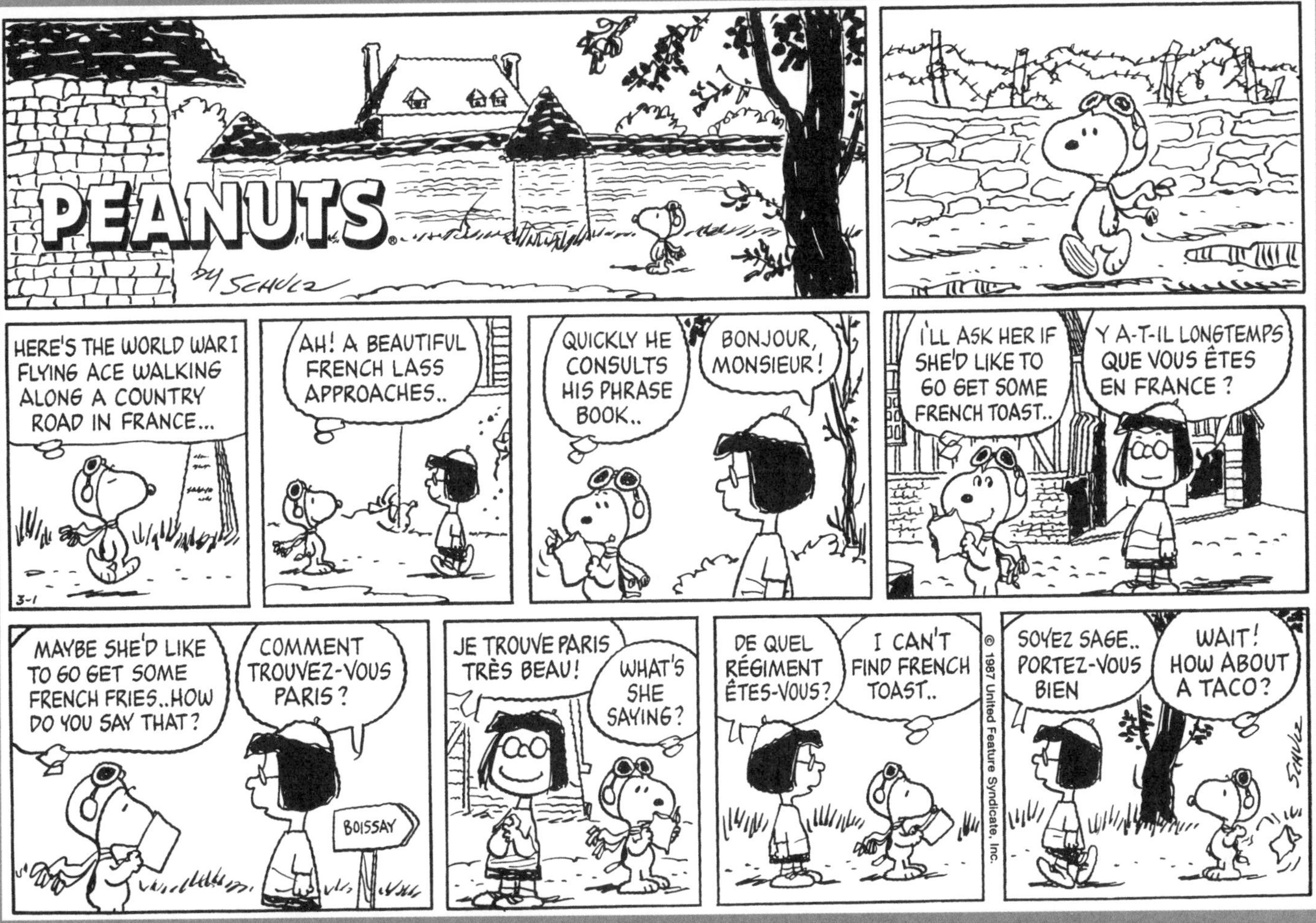
PEANUTS
BY SCHULZ
HERE'S THE WORLD WAR I FLYING ACE WALKING ALONG A COUNTRY ROAD IN FRANCE...
3-1
AH! A BEAUTIFUL FRENCH LASS APPROACHES..
QUICKLY HE CONSULTS HIS PHRASE BOOK..
BONJOUR, MONSIEUR!
I'LL ASK HER IF SHE'D LIKE TO GO GET SOME FRENCH TOAST..
Y A-T-IL LONGTEMPS QUE VOUS ÊTES EN FRANCE ?
MAYBE SHE'D LIKE TO GO GET SOME FRENCH FRIES..HOW DO YOU SAY THAT?
COMMENT TROUVEZ-VOUS PARIS ?
BOISSAY
JE TROUVE PARIS TRÈS BEAU!
WHAT'S SHE SAYING?
DE QUEL RÉGIMENT ÊTES-VOUS?
I CAN'T FIND FRENCH TOAST..
© 1987 United Feature Syndicate, Inc.
SOYEZ SAGE.. PORTEZ-VOUS BIEN
WAIT! HOW ABOUT A TACO?
SCHULZ

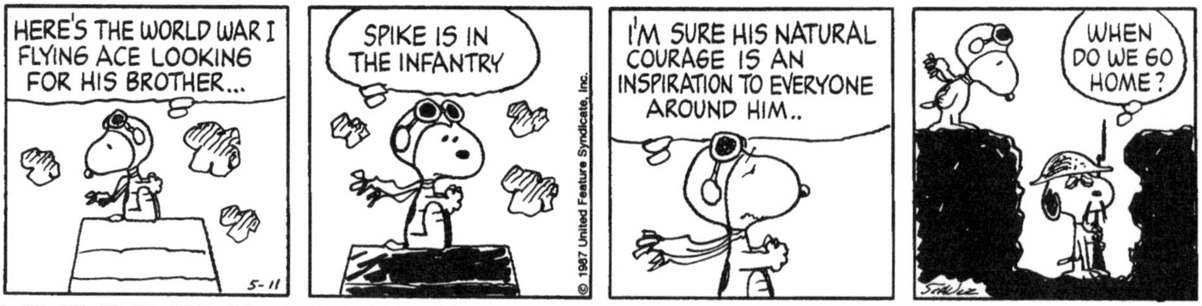
HERE'S THE WORLD WAR I FLYING ACE LOOKING FOR HIS BROTHER...
SPIKE IS IN THE INFANTRY
I'M SURE HIS NATURAL COURAGE IS AN INSPIRATION TO EVERYONE AROUND HIM..
WHEN DO WE GO HOME?
5-11
© 1987 United Feature Syndicate, Inc.
SCHULZ

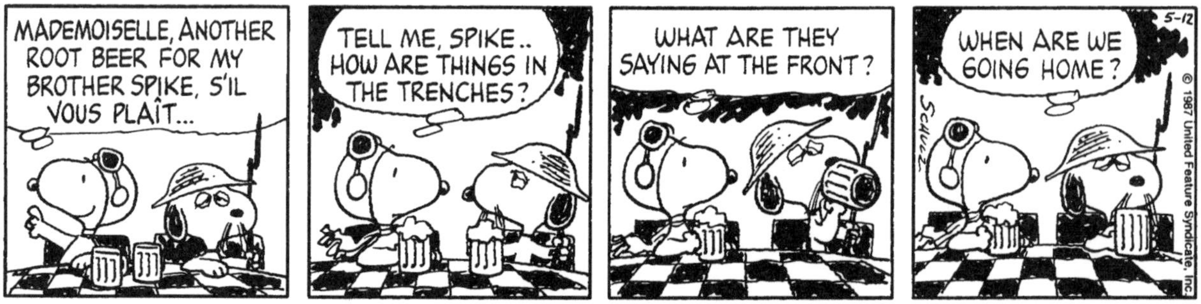
MADEMOISELLE, ANOTHER ROOT BEER FOR MY BROTHER SPIKE, S'IL VOUS PLAÎT...
TELL ME, SPIKE.. HOW ARE THINGS IN THE TRENCHES?
WHAT ARE THEY SAYING AT THE FRONT?
WHEN ARE WE GOING HOME?
5-12
© 1987 United Feature Syndicate, Inc.
SCHULZ

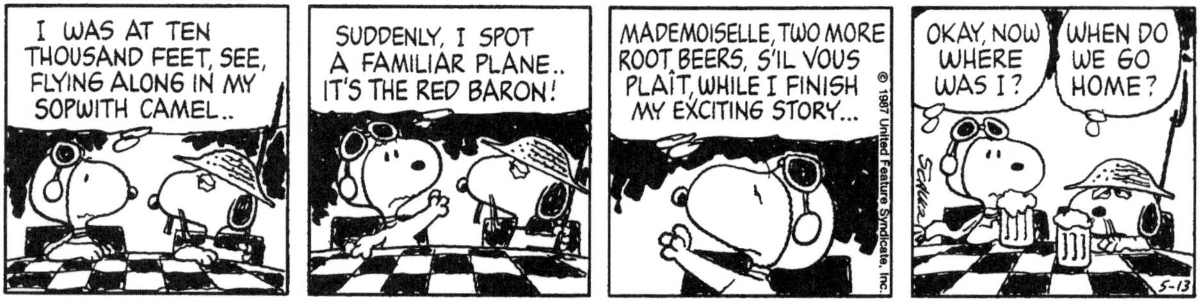
I WAS AT TEN THOUSAND FEET, SEE, FLYING ALONG IN MY SOPWITH CAMEL..
SUDDENLY, I SPOT A FAMILIAR PLANE.. IT'S THE RED BARON!
MADEMOISELLE, TWO MORE ROOT BEERS, S'IL VOUS PLAÎT, WHILE I FINISH MY EXCITING STORY...
OKAY, NOW WHERE WAS I?
WHEN DO WE GO HOME?
5-13
© 1987 United Feature Syndicate, Inc.
SCHULZ

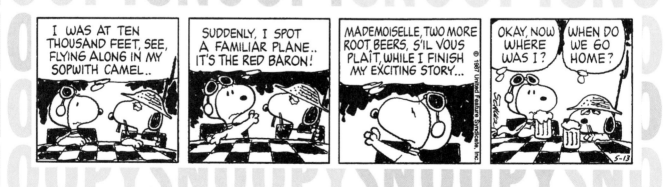

SO LONG, SPIKE..I HOPE WE'LL SEE EACH OTHER AGAIN...
© 1987 United Feature Syndicate, Inc.
FIGHTING IN THE AIR IS SO IMPERSONAL.. SOMETIMES, I ALMOST ENVY SPIKE...
5-14
AT LEAST IN THE INFANTRY HE CAN SEE THE ENEMY FACE TO FACE..
WHEN DO WE GO HOME?
SCHULZ

Dear Mom and Dad, I am writing from an aerodrome somewhere in France.
© 1987 United Feature Syndicate, Inc.
5-15
I saw Spike yesterday. He is fine. I expect he will be an officer someday.
He has obvious leadership qualities, and would make a good general.
WHEN DO WE GO HOME?
SCHULZ

HEY, SPIKE! THE WAR IS OVER!
5-16
© 1987 United Feature Syndicate, Inc.
WE WON!
WE DID?
I FORGOT WHICH SIDE I WAS ON..
SCHULZ

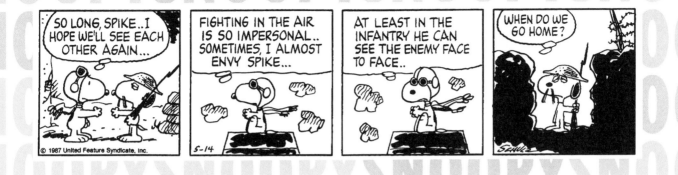

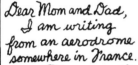

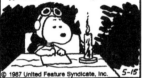

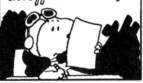

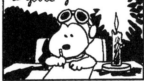

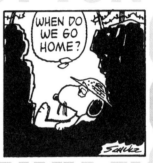

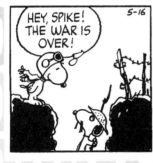

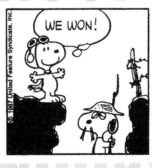

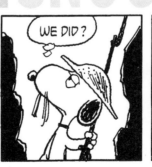

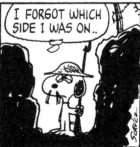

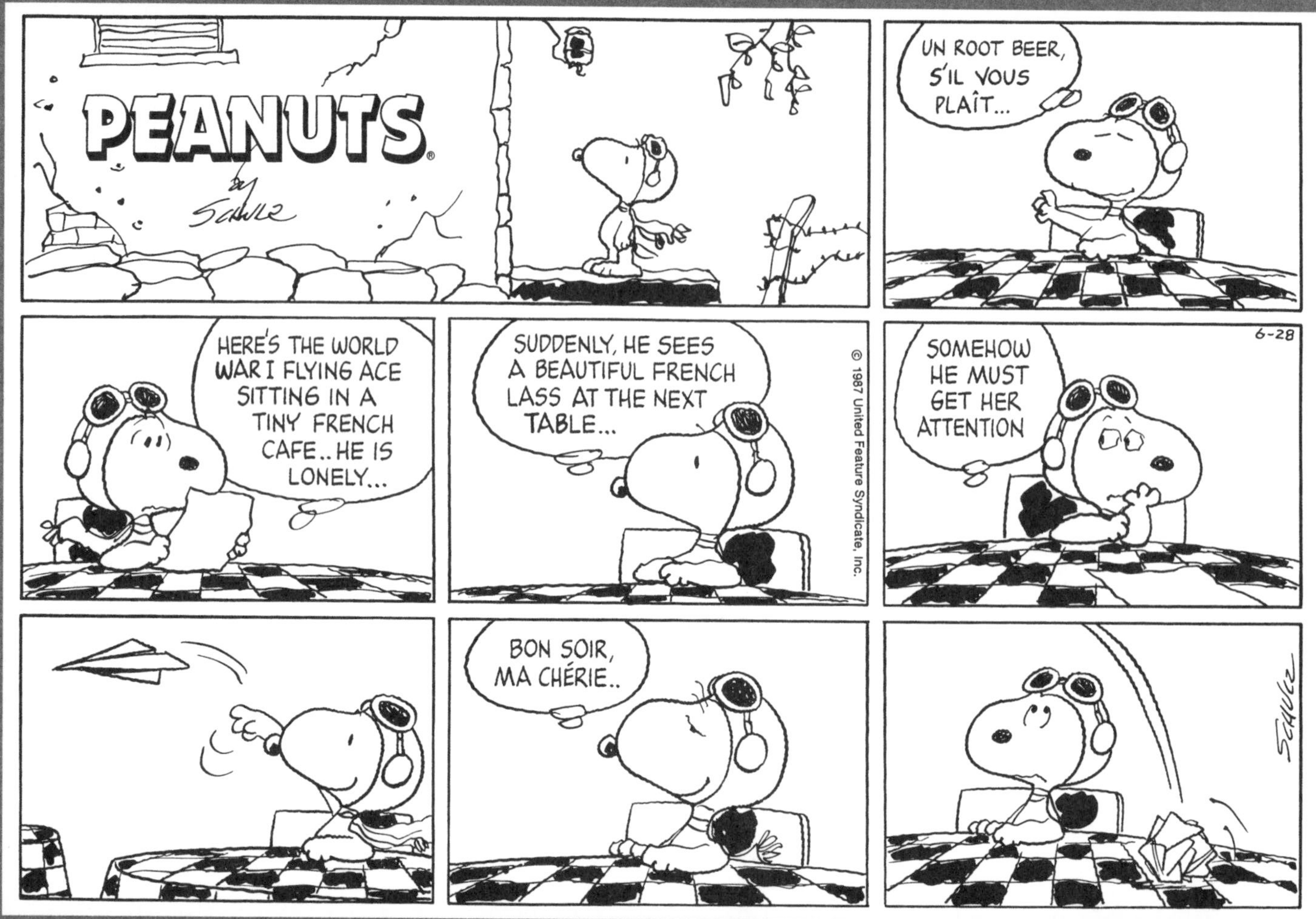
PEANUTS
by SCHULZ
UN ROOT BEER, S'IL VOUS PLAÎT...
HERE'S THE WORLD WAR I FLYING ACE SITTING IN A TINY FRENCH CAFE.. HE IS LONELY...
SUDDENLY, HE SEES A BEAUTIFUL FRENCH LASS AT THE NEXT TABLE...
© 1987 United Feature Syndicate, Inc.
6-28
SOMEHOW HE MUST GET HER ATTENTION
BON SOIR, MA CHÉRIE..
SCHULZ

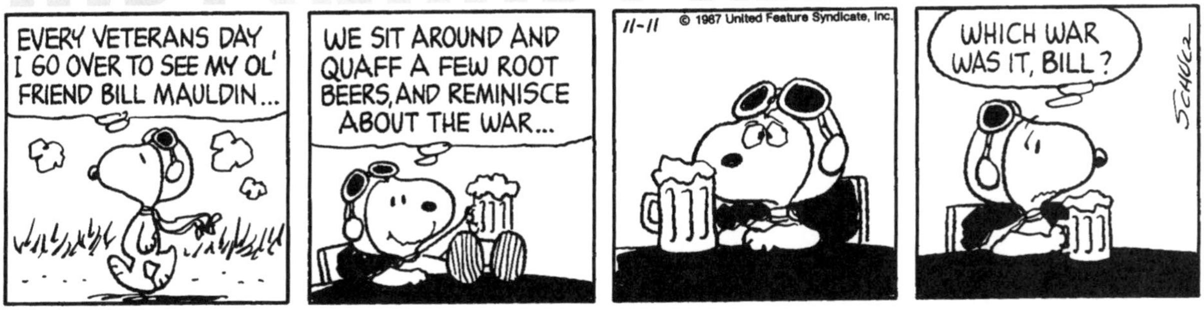
EVERY VETERANS DAY I GO OVER TO SEE MY OL' FRIEND BILL MAULDIN...
WE SIT AROUND AND QUAFF A FEW ROOT BEERS, AND REMINISCE ABOUT THE WAR...
11-11
© 1987 United Feature Syndicate, Inc.
WHICH WAR WAS IT, BILL?
SCHULZ

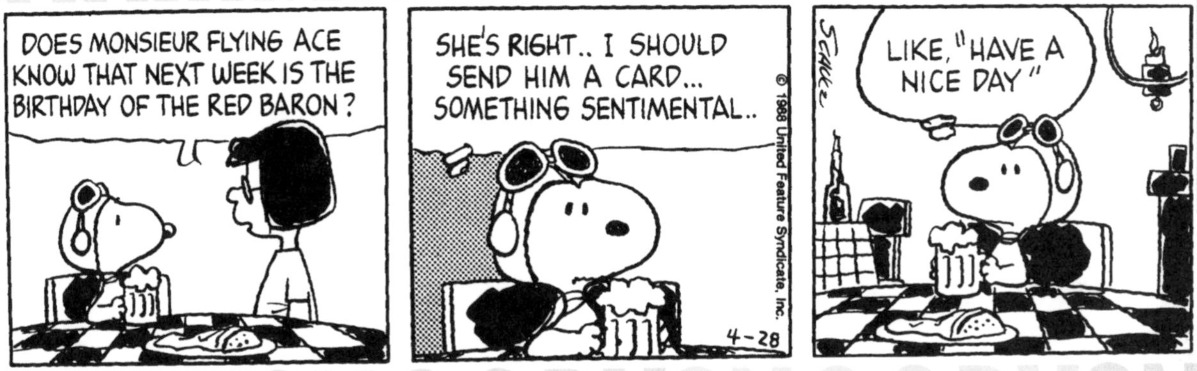
DOES MONSIEUR FLYING ACE KNOW THAT NEXT WEEK IS THE BIRTHDAY OF THE RED BARON?
SHE'S RIGHT.. I SHOULD SEND HIM A CARD... SOMETHING SENTIMENTAL..
© 1988 United Feature Syndicate, Inc.
4-28
SCHULZ
LIKE, "HAVE A NICE DAY"

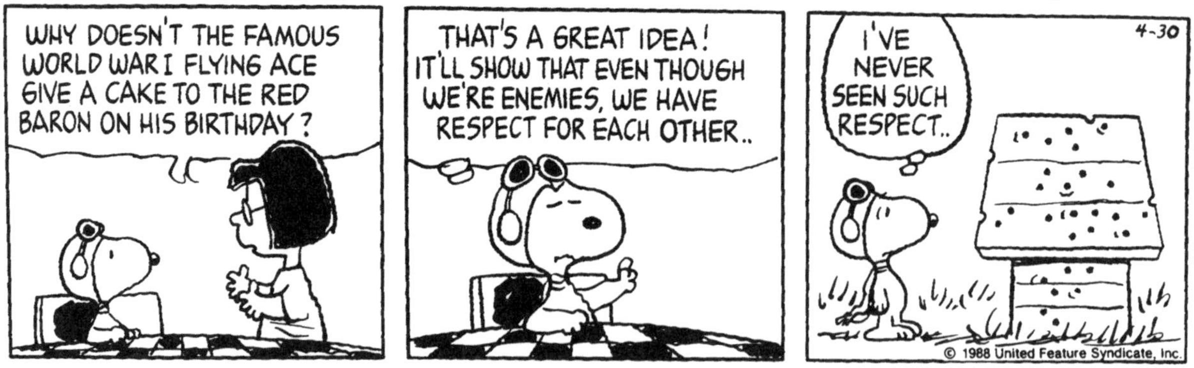
WHY DOESN'T THE FAMOUS WORLD WAR I FLYING ACE GIVE A CAKE TO THE RED BARON ON HIS BIRTHDAY ?
THAT'S A GREAT IDEA! IT'LL SHOW THAT EVEN THOUGH WE'RE ENEMIES, WE HAVE RESPECT FOR EACH OTHER..
4-30
I'VE NEVER SEEN SUCH RESPECT..
© 1988 United Feature Syndicate, Inc.

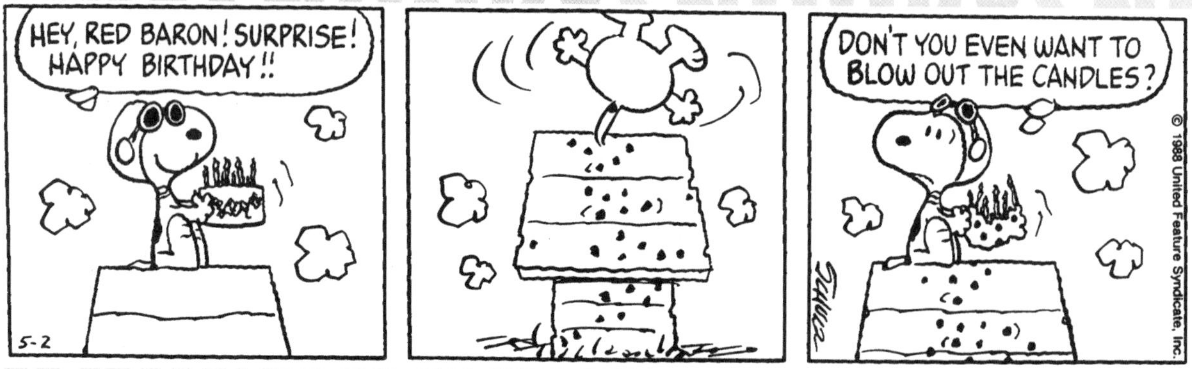
HEY, RED BARON! SURPRISE! HAPPY BIRTHDAY!!
5-2
DON'T YOU EVEN WANT TO BLOW OUT THE CANDLES?
© 1988 United Feature Syndicate, Inc.

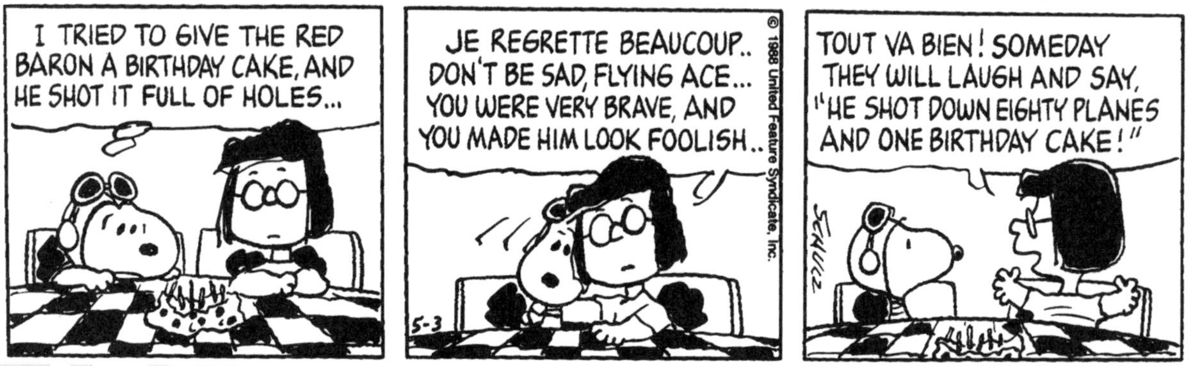
I TRIED TO GIVE THE RED BARON A BIRTHDAY CAKE, AND HE SHOT IT FULL OF HOLES...
JE REGRETTE BEAUCOUP.. DON'T BE SAD, FLYING ACE... YOU WERE VERY BRAVE, AND YOU MADE HIM LOOK FOOLISH..
5-3
© 1988 United Feature Syndicate, Inc.
TOUT VA BIEN! SOMEDAY THEY WILL LAUGH AND SAY, "HE SHOT DOWN EIGHTY PLANES AND ONE BIRTHDAY CAKE!"

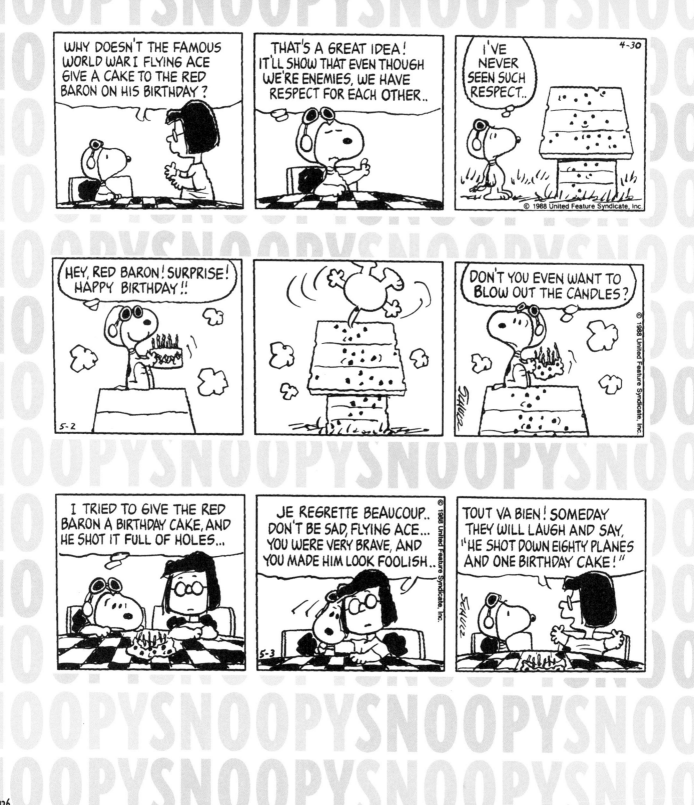

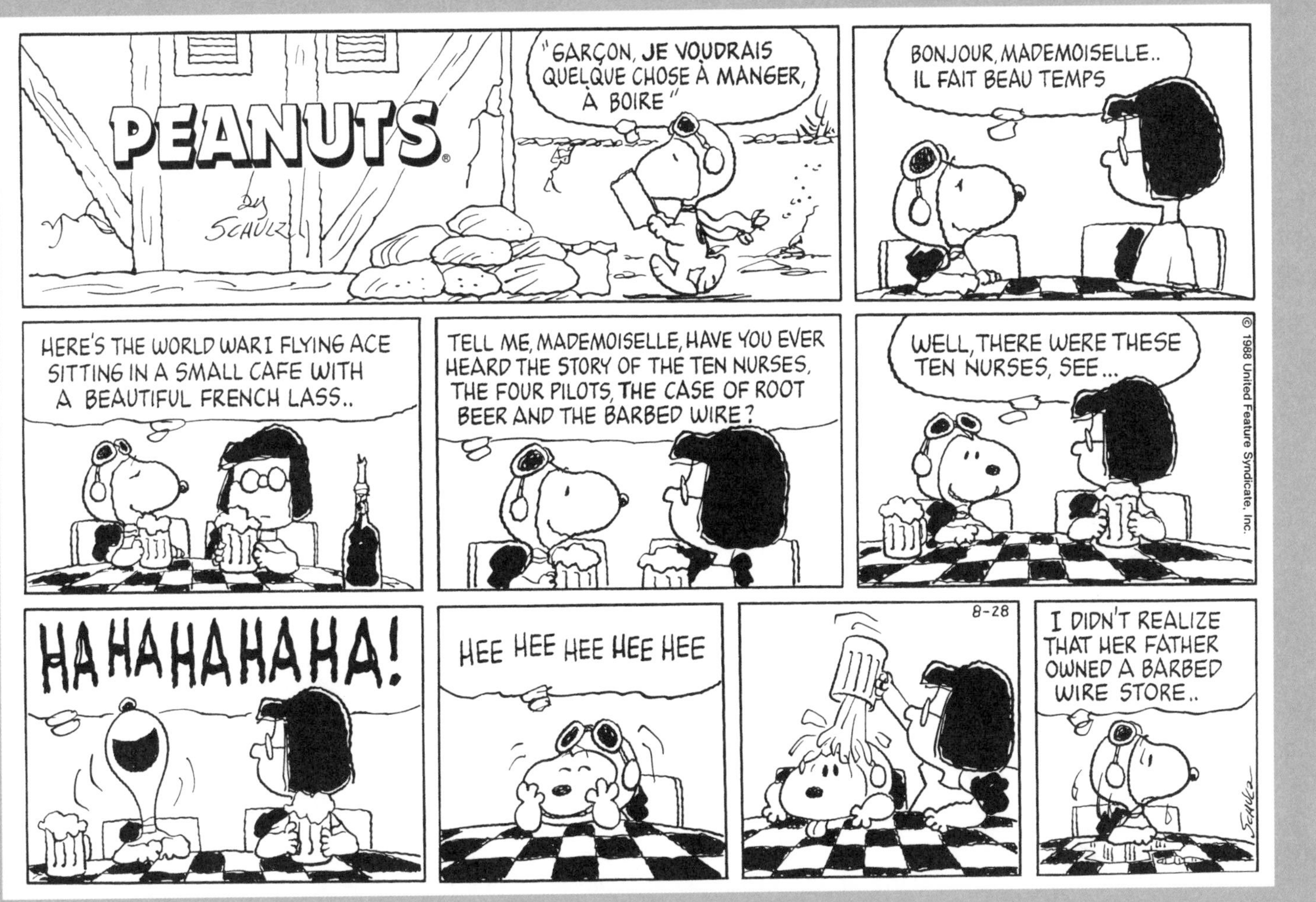
PEANUTS
by SCHULZ
"GARÇON, JE VOUDRAIS QUELQUE CHOSE À MANGER, À BOIRE"
BONJOUR, MADEMOISELLE.. IL FAIT BEAU TEMPS
HERE'S THE WORLD WAR I FLYING ACE SITTING IN A SMALL CAFE WITH A BEAUTIFUL FRENCH LASS..
TELL ME, MADEMOISELLE, HAVE YOU EVER HEARD THE STORY OF THE TEN NURSES, THE FOUR PILOTS, THE CASE OF ROOT BEER AND THE BARBED WIRE?
WELL, THERE WERE THESE TEN NURSES, SEE...
© 1988 United Feature Syndicate, Inc.
HAHAHAHAHA!
HEE HEE HEE HEE HEE
8-28
I DIDN'T REALIZE THAT HER FATHER OWNED A BARBED WIRE STORE..

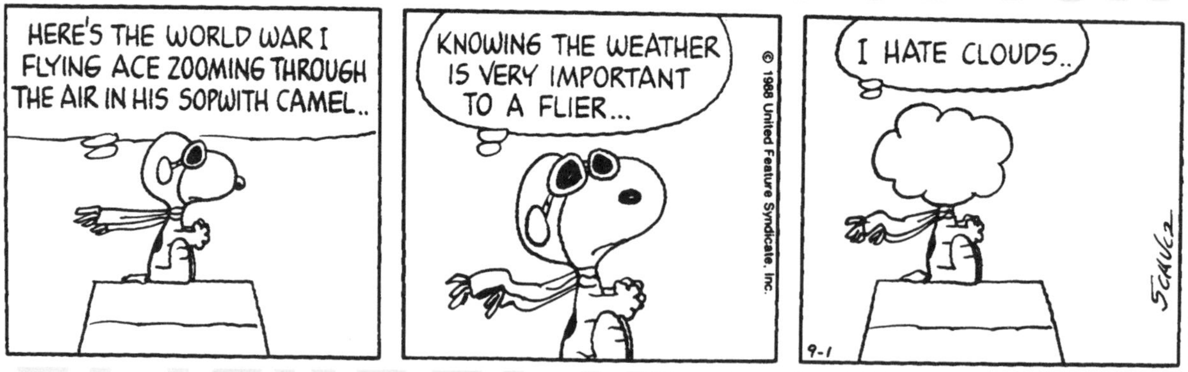
HERE'S THE WORLD WAR I FLYING ACE ZOOMING THROUGH THE AIR IN HIS SOPWITH CAMEL..
KNOWING THE WEATHER IS VERY IMPORTANT TO A FLIER...
© 1988 United Feature Syndicate, Inc.
I HATE CLOUDS..
SCHULZ
9-1

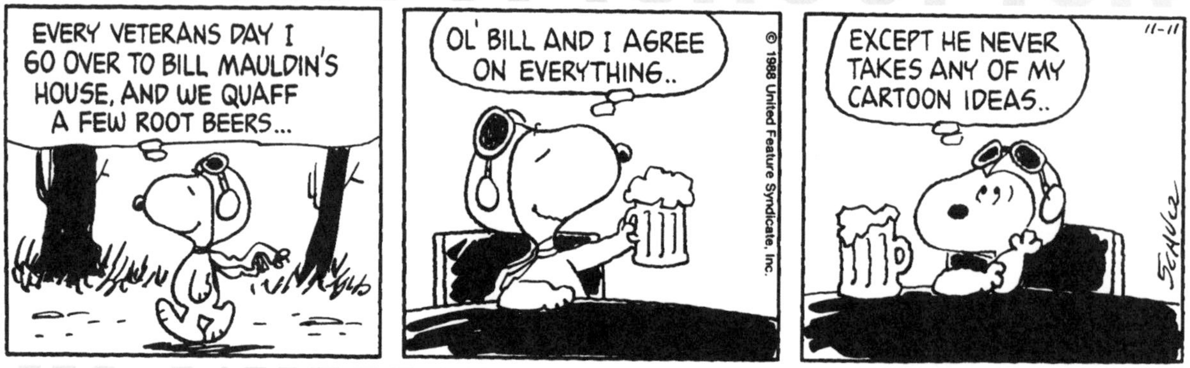
EVERY VETERANS DAY I GO OVER TO BILL MAULDIN'S HOUSE, AND WE QUAFF A FEW ROOT BEERS...
OL' BILL AND I AGREE ON EVERYTHING..
© 1988 United Feature Syndicate, Inc.
11-11
EXCEPT HE NEVER TAKES ANY OF MY CARTOON IDEAS..
SCHULZ

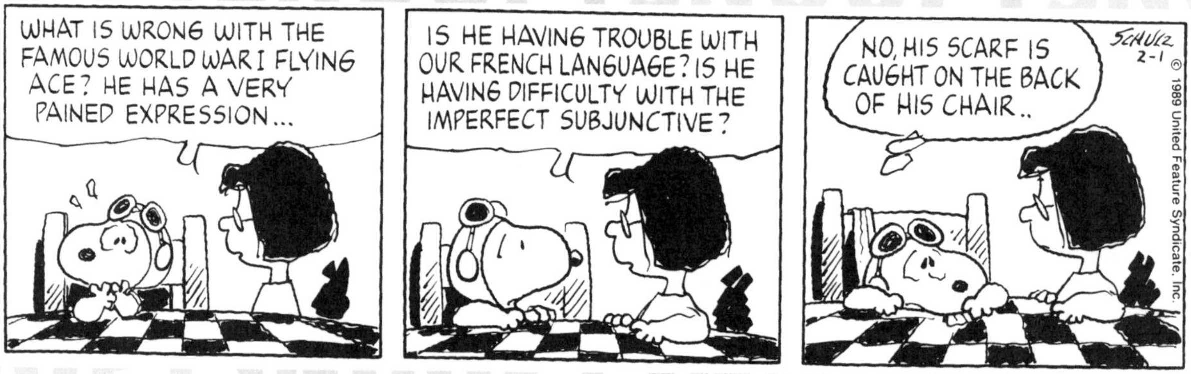
WHAT IS WRONG WITH THE FAMOUS WORLD WAR I FLYING ACE? HE HAS A VERY PAINED EXPRESSION...
IS HE HAVING TROUBLE WITH OUR FRENCH LANGUAGE? IS HE HAVING DIFFICULTY WITH THE IMPERFECT SUBJUNCTIVE?
SCHULZ
2-1
© 1989 United Feature Syndicate, Inc.
NO, HIS SCARF IS CAUGHT ON THE BACK OF HIS CHAIR..

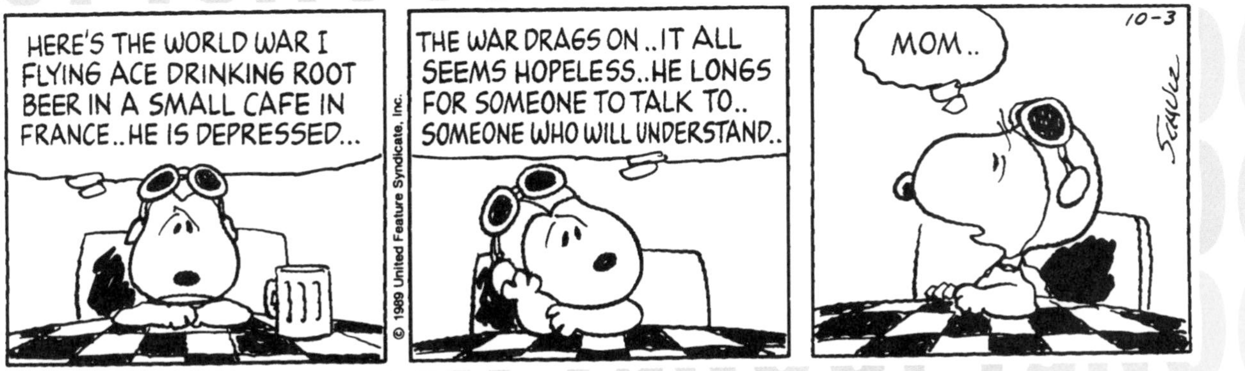
HERE'S THE WORLD WAR I FLYING ACE DRINKING ROOT BEER IN A SMALL CAFE IN FRANCE..HE IS DEPRESSED...
THE WAR DRAGS ON..IT ALL SEEMS HOPELESS..HE LONGS FOR SOMEONE TO TALK TO.. SOMEONE WHO WILL UNDERSTAND..
© 1989 United Feature Syndicate, Inc.
10-3
MOM..
SCHULZ

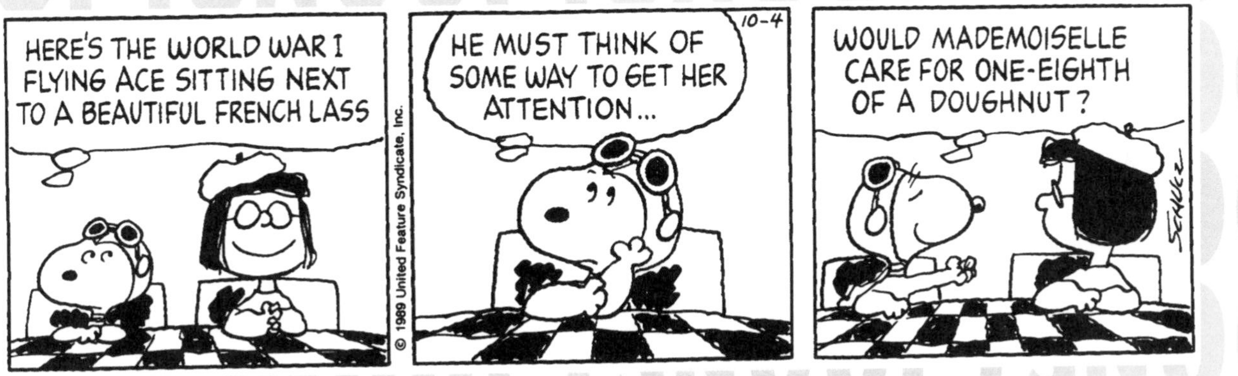
HERE'S THE WORLD WAR I FLYING ACE SITTING NEXT TO A BEAUTIFUL FRENCH LASS
© 1989 United Feature Syndicate, Inc.
10-4
HE MUST THINK OF SOME WAY TO GET HER ATTENTION...
WOULD MADEMOISELLE CARE FOR ONE-EIGHTH OF A DOUGHNUT?
SCHULZ

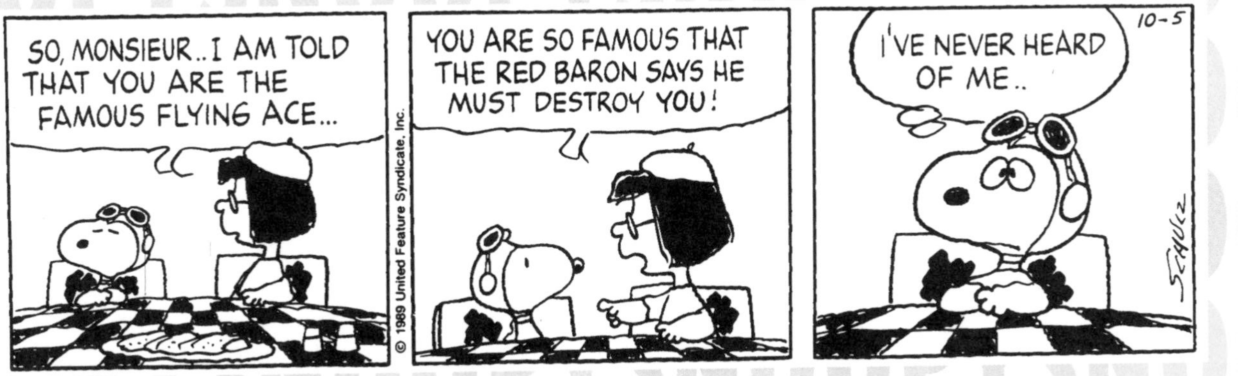
SO, MONSIEUR..I AM TOLD THAT YOU ARE THE FAMOUS FLYING ACE...
© 1989 United Feature Syndicate, Inc.
YOU ARE SO FAMOUS THAT THE RED BARON SAYS HE MUST DESTROY YOU!
10-5
I'VE NEVER HEARD OF ME..
SCHULZ

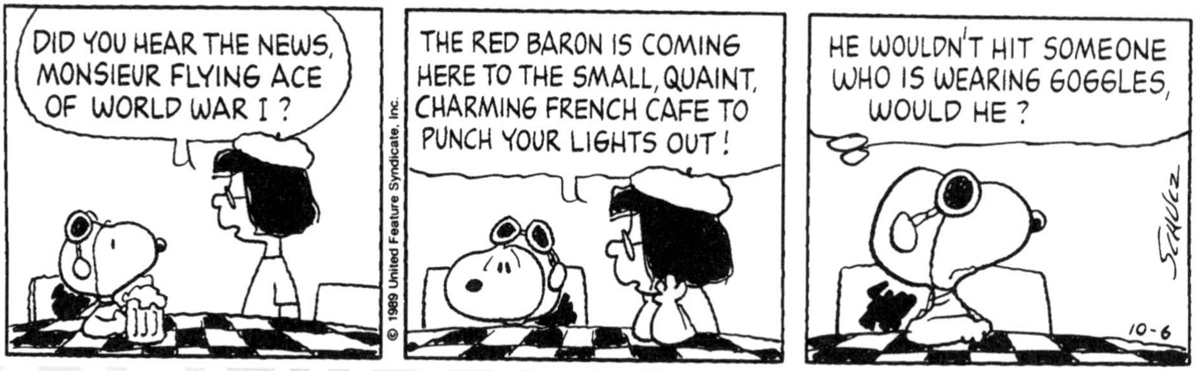
DID YOU HEAR THE NEWS, MONSIEUR FLYING ACE OF WORLD WAR I ?
© 1989 United Feature Syndicate, Inc.
THE RED BARON IS COMING HERE TO THE SMALL, QUAINT, CHARMING FRENCH CAFE TO PUNCH YOUR LIGHTS OUT !
HE WOULDN'T HIT SOMEONE WHO IS WEARING GOGGLES, WOULD HE ?
10-6

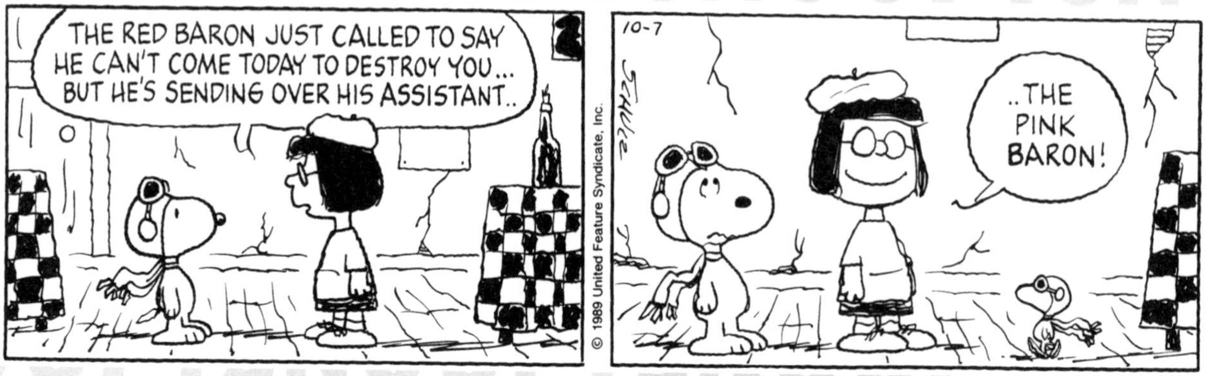
THE RED BARON JUST CALLED TO SAY HE CAN'T COME TODAY TO DESTROY YOU... BUT HE'S SENDING OVER HIS ASSISTANT..
© 1989 United Feature Syndicate, Inc.
10-7
..THE PINK BARON !

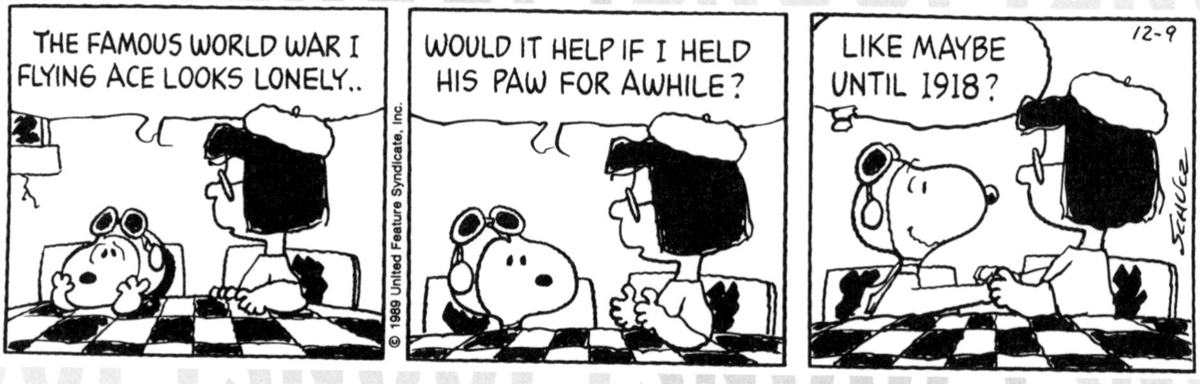
THE FAMOUS WORLD WAR I FLYING ACE LOOKS LONELY..
© 1989 United Feature Syndicate, Inc.
WOULD IT HELP IF I HELD HIS PAW FOR AWHILE ?
12-9
LIKE MAYBE UNTIL 1918 ?

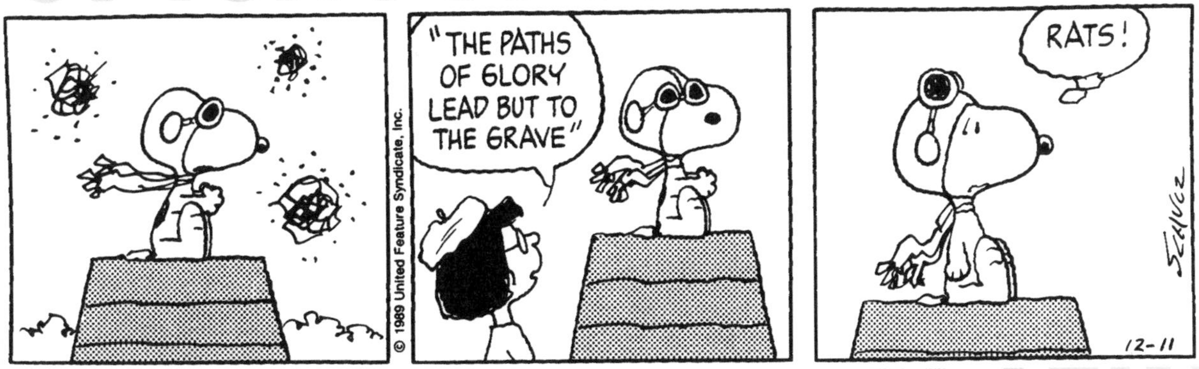
"THE PATHS OF GLORY LEAD BUT TO THE GRAVE"
RATS!
12-11

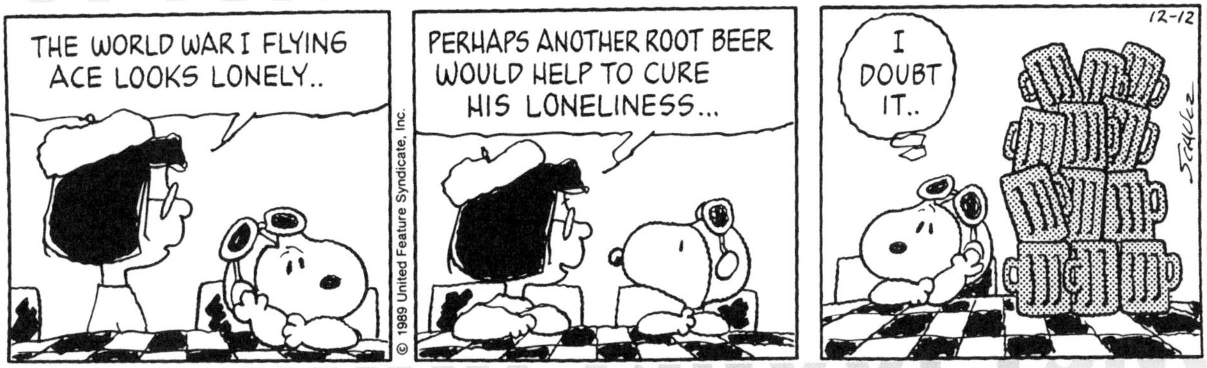
THE WORLD WAR I FLYING ACE LOOKS LONELY..
PERHAPS ANOTHER ROOT BEER WOULD HELP TO CURE HIS LONELINESS...
I DOUBT IT..
12-12

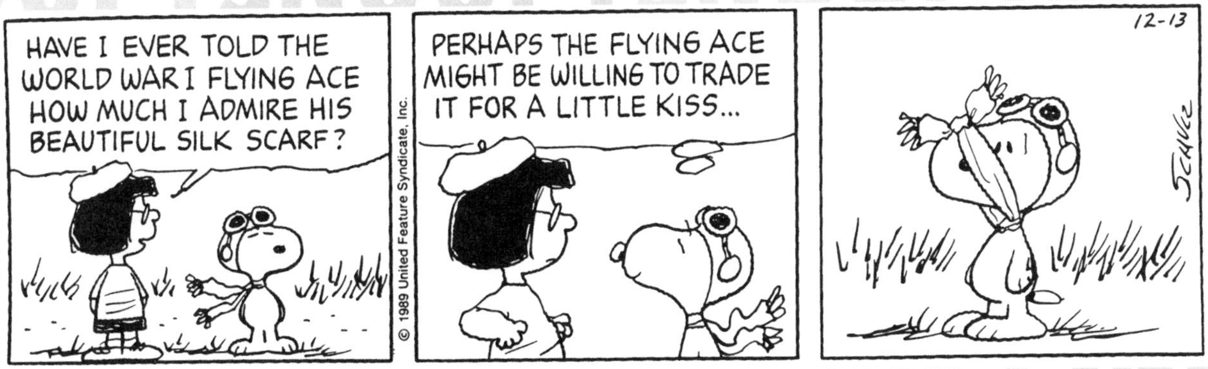
HAVE I EVER TOLD THE WORLD WAR I FLYING ACE HOW MUCH I ADMIRE HIS BEAUTIFUL SILK SCARF?
PERHAPS THE FLYING ACE MIGHT BE WILLING TO TRADE IT FOR A LITTLE KISS...
12-13

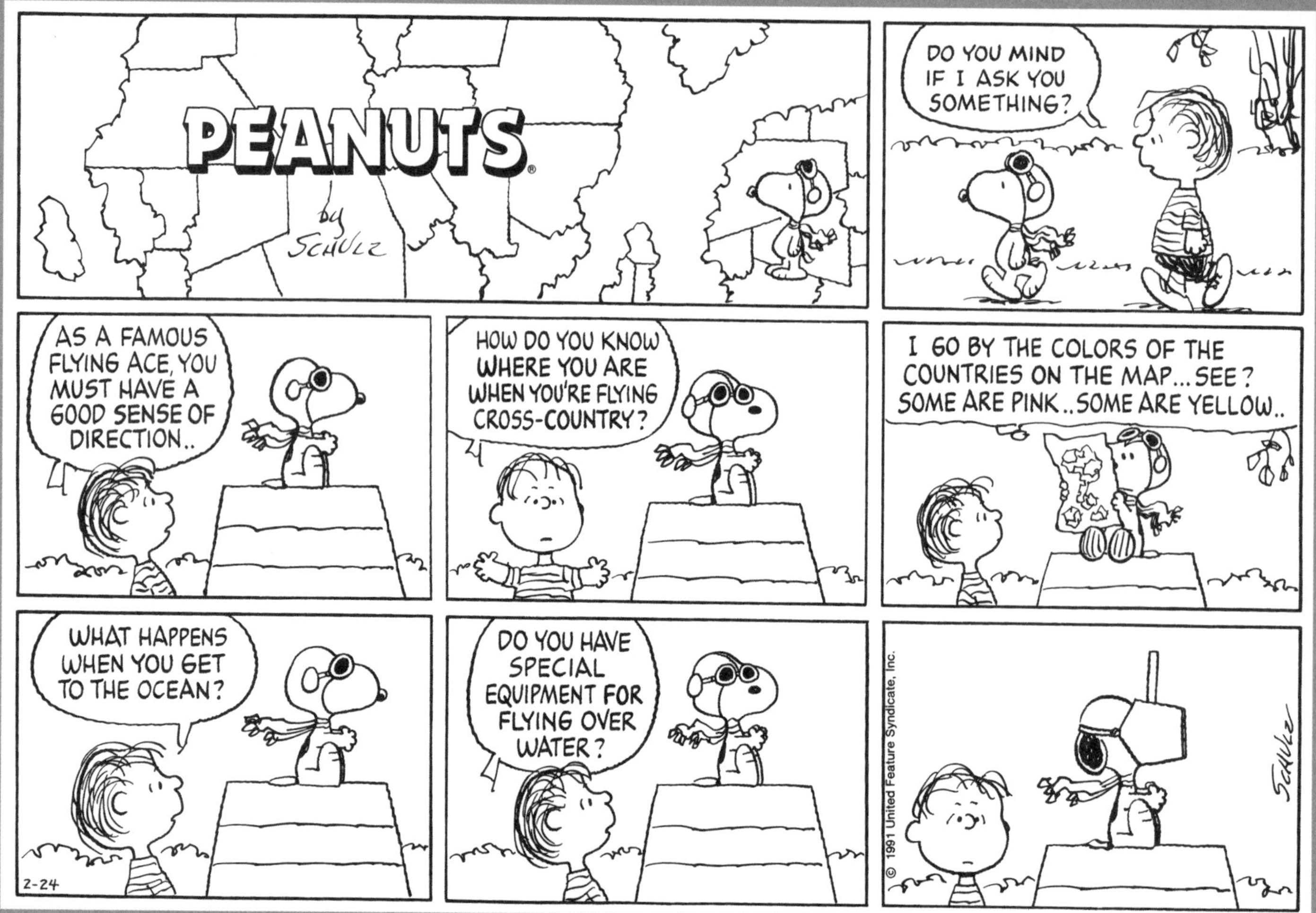
PEANUTS
by SCHULZ
DO YOU MIND IF I ASK YOU SOMETHING?
AS A FAMOUS FLYING ACE, YOU MUST HAVE A GOOD SENSE OF DIRECTION..
HOW DO YOU KNOW WHERE YOU ARE WHEN YOU'RE FLYING CROSS-COUNTRY?
I GO BY THE COLORS OF THE COUNTRIES ON THE MAP... SEE? SOME ARE PINK..SOME ARE YELLOW..
WHAT HAPPENS WHEN YOU GET TO THE OCEAN?
DO YOU HAVE SPECIAL EQUIPMENT FOR FLYING OVER WATER?
2-24
© 1991 United Feature Syndicate, Inc.
SCHULZ

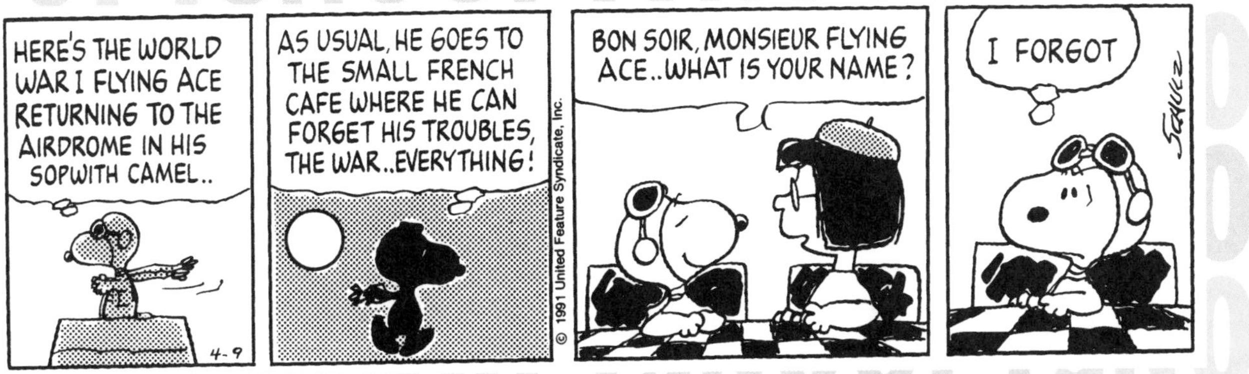
HERE'S THE WORLD WAR I FLYING ACE RETURNING TO THE AIRDROME IN HIS SOPWITH CAMEL..
4-9
AS USUAL, HE GOES TO THE SMALL FRENCH CAFE WHERE HE CAN FORGET HIS TROUBLES, THE WAR..EVERYTHING!
© 1991 United Feature Syndicate, Inc.
BON SOIR, MONSIEUR FLYING ACE..WHAT IS YOUR NAME?
I FORGOT
SCHULZ

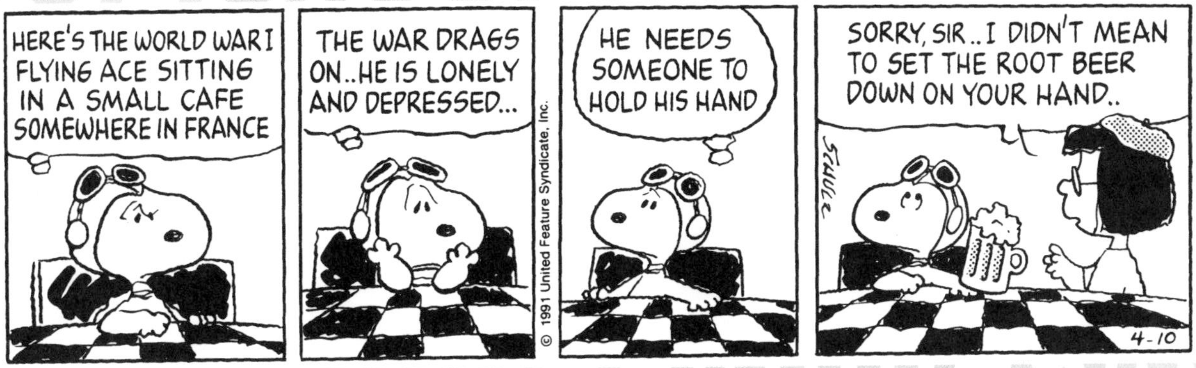
HERE'S THE WORLD WAR I FLYING ACE SITTING IN A SMALL CAFE SOMEWHERE IN FRANCE
THE WAR DRAGS ON..HE IS LONELY AND DEPRESSED...
© 1991 United Feature Syndicate, Inc.
HE NEEDS SOMEONE TO HOLD HIS HAND
SORRY, SIR..I DIDN'T MEAN TO SET THE ROOT BEER DOWN ON YOUR HAND..
SCHULZ
4-10

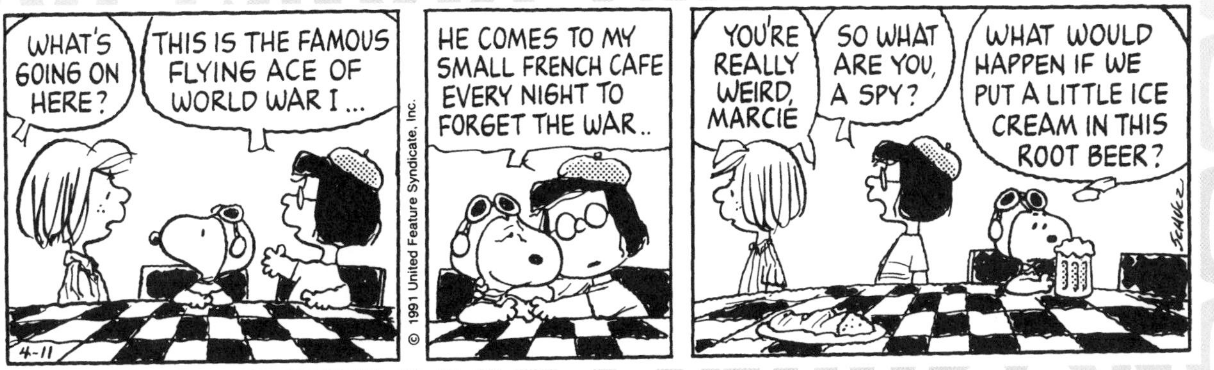
WHAT'S GOING ON HERE?
THIS IS THE FAMOUS FLYING ACE OF WORLD WAR I ...
4-11
© 1991 United Feature Syndicate, Inc.
HE COMES TO MY SMALL FRENCH CAFE EVERY NIGHT TO FORGET THE WAR..
YOU'RE REALLY WEIRD, MARCIE
SO WHAT ARE YOU, A SPY?
WHAT WOULD HAPPEN IF WE PUT A LITTLE ICE CREAM IN THIS ROOT BEER?
SCHULZ

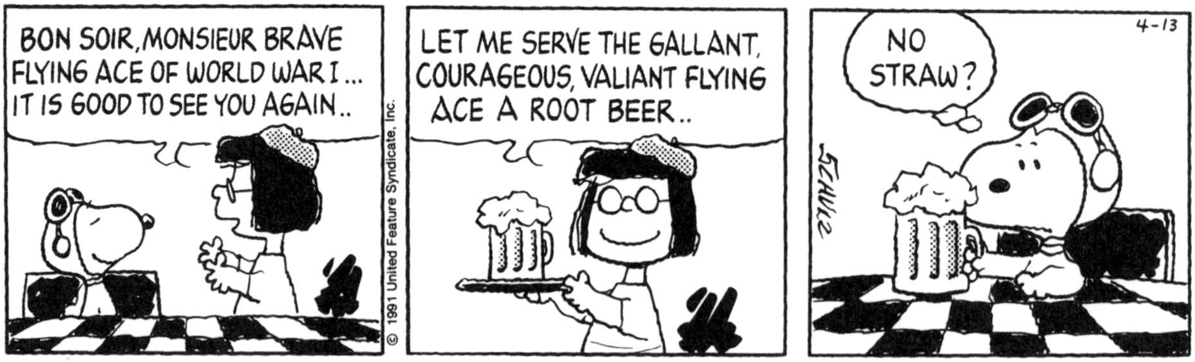
BON SOIR, MONSIEUR BRAVE FLYING ACE OF WORLD WAR I... IT IS GOOD TO SEE YOU AGAIN..
© 1991 United Feature Syndicate, Inc.
LET ME SERVE THE GALLANT, COURAGEOUS, VALIANT FLYING ACE A ROOT BEER..
NO STRAW?
4-13
SCHULZ

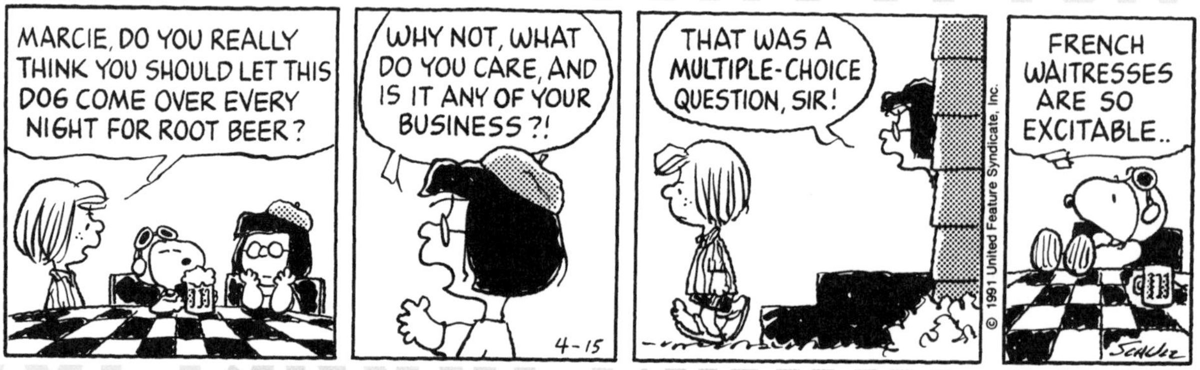
MARCIE, DO YOU REALLY THINK YOU SHOULD LET THIS DOG COME OVER EVERY NIGHT FOR ROOT BEER?
WHY NOT, WHAT DO YOU CARE, AND IS IT ANY OF YOUR BUSINESS?!
4-15
THAT WAS A MULTIPLE-CHOICE QUESTION, SIR!
© 1991 United Feature Syndicate, Inc.
FRENCH WAITRESSES ARE SO EXCITABLE..
SCHULZ

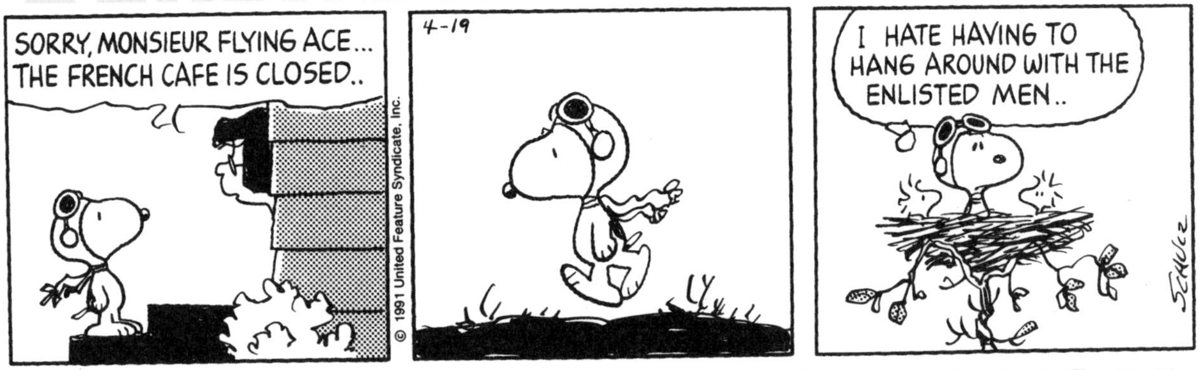
SORRY, MONSIEUR FLYING ACE... THE FRENCH CAFE IS CLOSED..
© 1991 United Feature Syndicate, Inc.
4-19
I HATE HAVING TO HANG AROUND WITH THE ENLISTED MEN..
SCHULZ

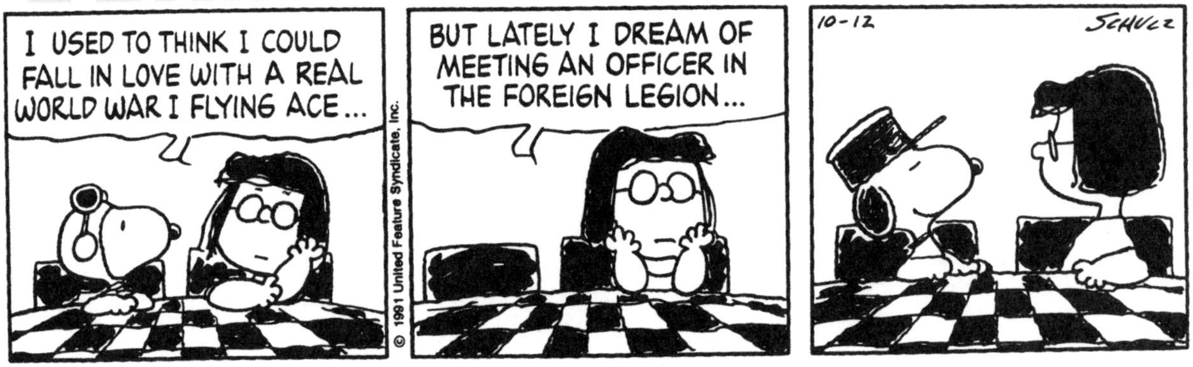
I USED TO THINK I COULD FALL IN LOVE WITH A REAL WORLD WAR I FLYING ACE...
© 1991 United Feature Syndicate, Inc.
BUT LATELY I DREAM OF MEETING AN OFFICER IN THE FOREIGN LEGION...
10-12
SCHULZ

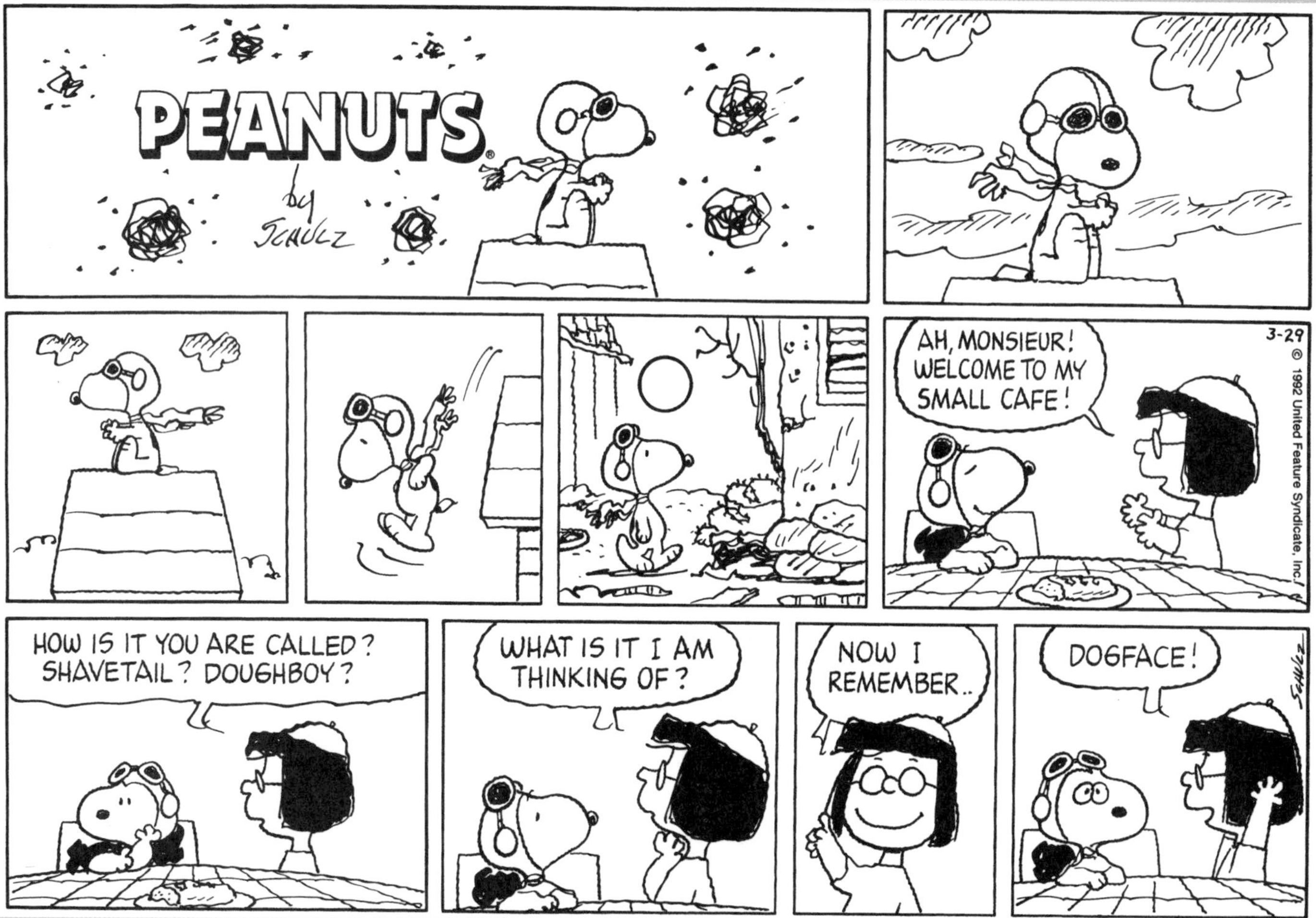
PEANUTS
by SCHULZ
AH, MONSIEUR! WELCOME TO MY SMALL CAFE!
3-29
© 1992 United Feature Syndicate, Inc.
HOW IS IT YOU ARE CALLED? SHAVETAIL? DOUGHBOY?
WHAT IS IT I AM THINKING OF?
NOW I REMEMBER..
DOGFACE!
SCHULZ

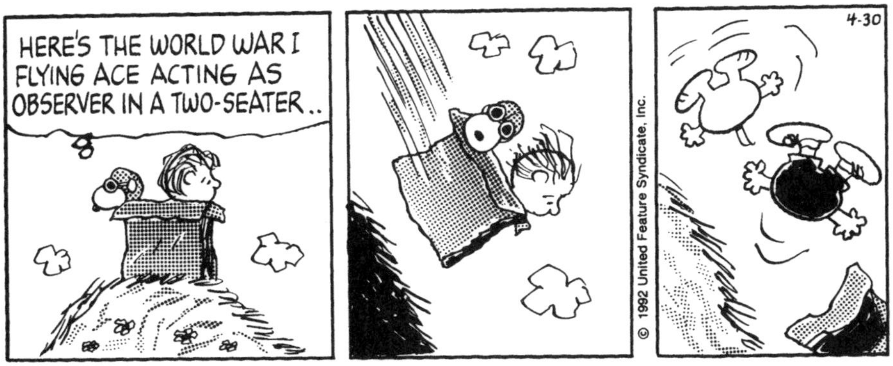
HERE'S THE WORLD WAR I FLYING ACE ACTING AS OBSERVER IN A TWO-SEATER..
© 1992 United Feature Syndicate, Inc.
4-30
I HAVE OBSERVED THAT I DON'T THINK I WANT TO DO THAT AGAIN..

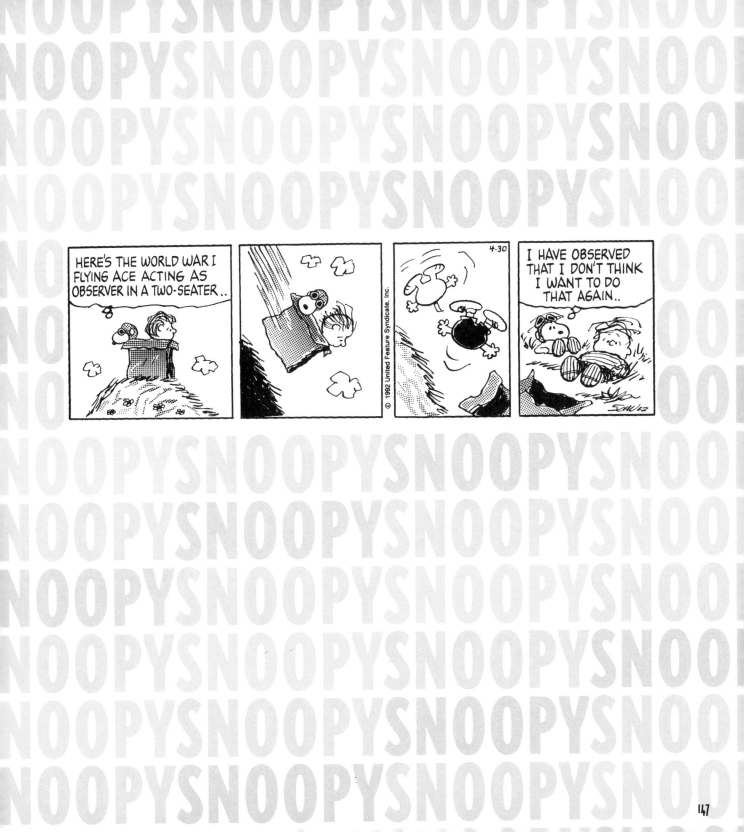

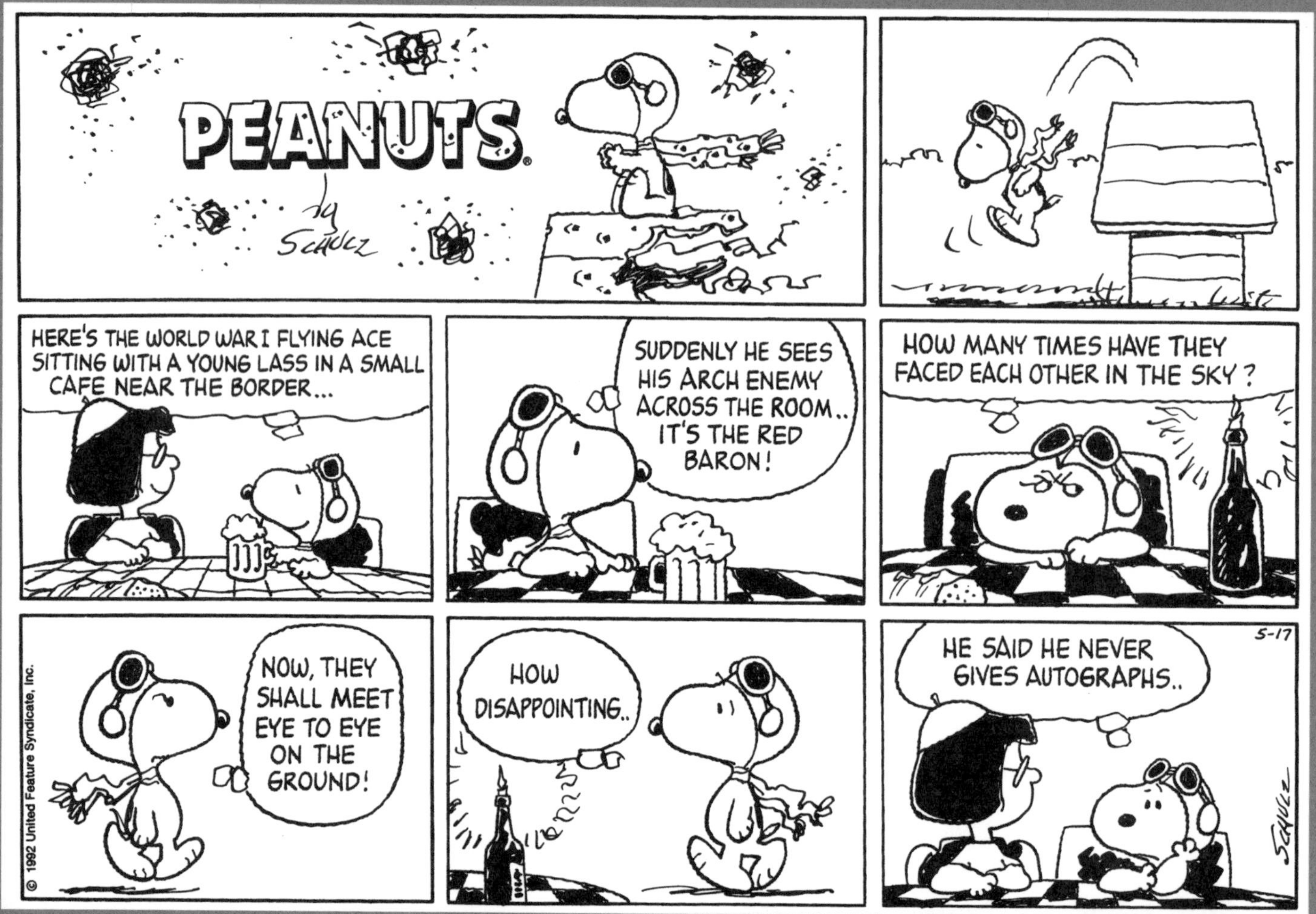
PEANUTS
SCHULZ
HERE'S THE WORLD WAR I FLYING ACE SITTING WITH A YOUNG LASS IN A SMALL CAFE NEAR THE BORDER...
SUDDENLY HE SEES HIS ARCH ENEMY ACROSS THE ROOM.. IT'S THE RED BARON!
HOW MANY TIMES HAVE THEY FACED EACH OTHER IN THE SKY?
© 1992 United Feature Syndicate, Inc.
NOW, THEY SHALL MEET EYE TO EYE ON THE GROUND!
HOW DISAPPOINTING..
5-17
HE SAID HE NEVER GIVES AUTOGRAPHS..
SCHULZ

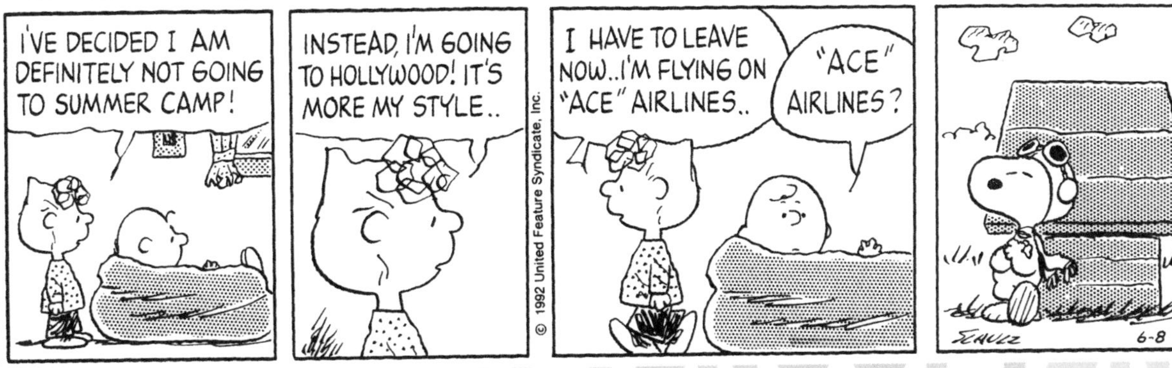
I'VE DECIDED I AM DEFINITELY NOT GOING TO SUMMER CAMP!
INSTEAD, I'M GOING TO HOLLYWOOD! IT'S MORE MY STYLE..
© 1992 United Feature Syndicate, Inc.
I HAVE TO LEAVE NOW..I'M FLYING ON "ACE" AIRLINES..
"ACE" AIRLINES?
SCHULZ
6-8

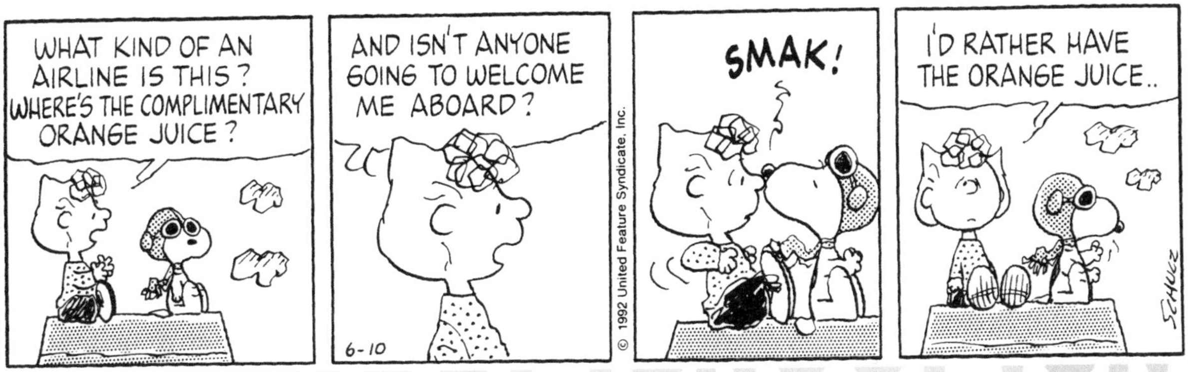
WHAT KIND OF AN AIRLINE IS THIS? WHERE'S THE COMPLIMENTARY ORANGE JUICE?
AND ISN'T ANYONE GOING TO WELCOME ME ABOARD?
6-10
© 1992 United Feature Syndicate, Inc.
SMAK!
I'D RATHER HAVE THE ORANGE JUICE..
SCHULZ

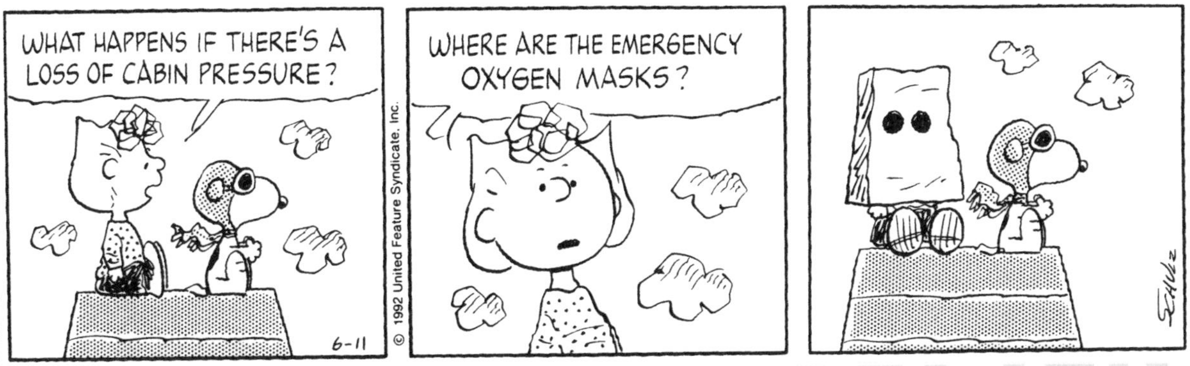
WHAT HAPPENS IF THERE'S A LOSS OF CABIN PRESSURE?
6-11
© 1992 United Feature Syndicate, Inc.
WHERE ARE THE EMERGENCY OXYGEN MASKS?
SCHULZ

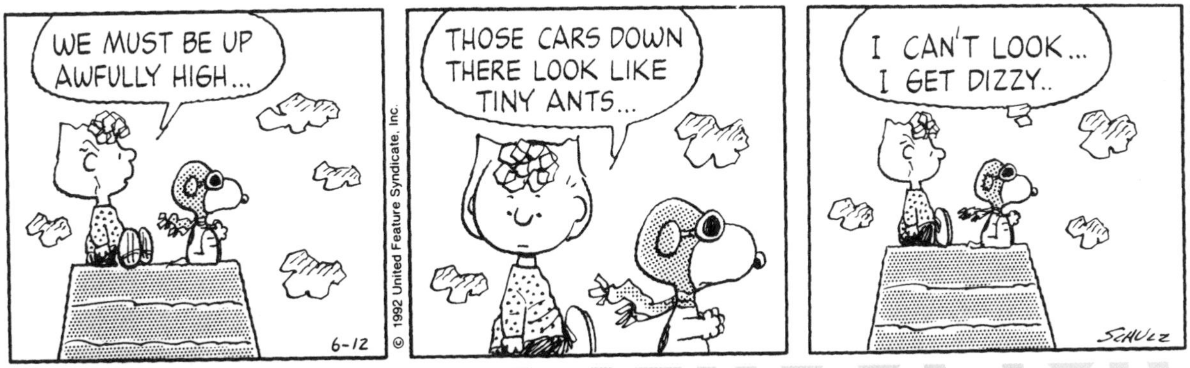
WE MUST BE UP AWFULLY HIGH...
6-12
© 1992 United Feature Syndicate, Inc.
THOSE CARS DOWN THERE LOOK LIKE TINY ANTS...
I CAN'T LOOK... I GET DIZZY..
SCHULZ

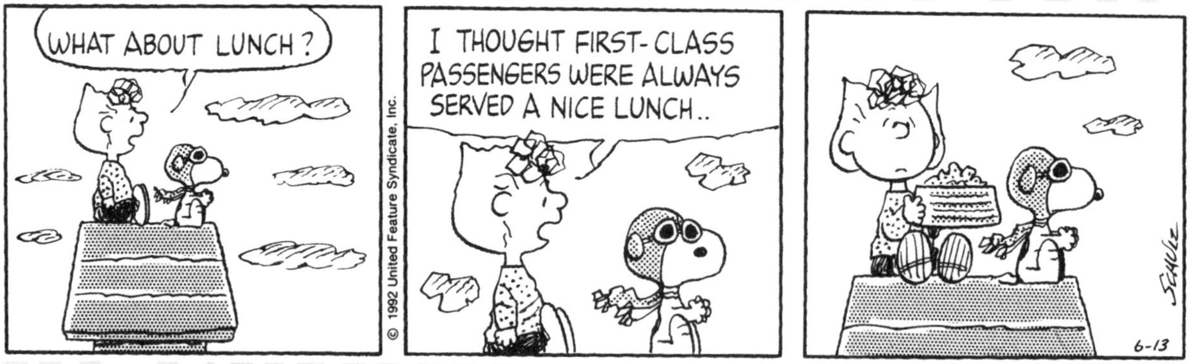
WHAT ABOUT LUNCH?
I THOUGHT FIRST-CLASS PASSENGERS WERE ALWAYS SERVED A NICE LUNCH..
© 1992 United Feature Syndicate, Inc.
SCHULZ
6-13

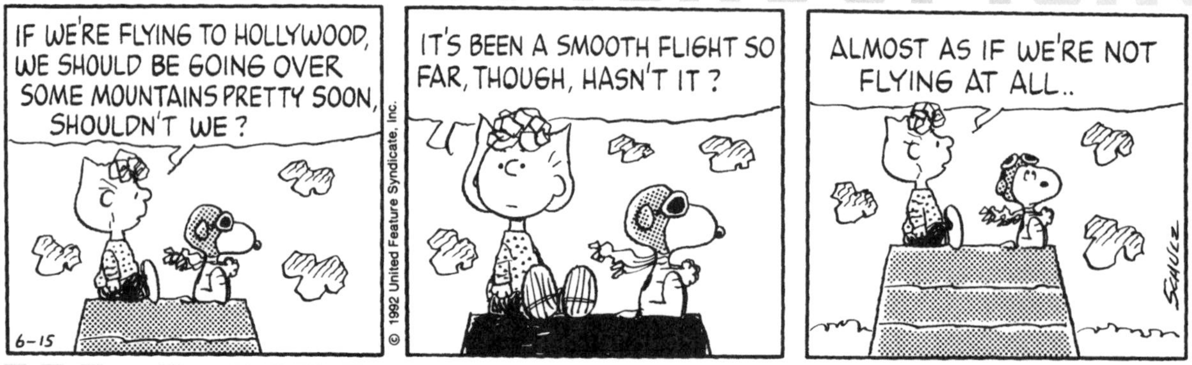
IF WE'RE FLYING TO HOLLYWOOD, WE SHOULD BE GOING OVER SOME MOUNTAINS PRETTY SOON, SHOULDN'T WE?
6-15
IT'S BEEN A SMOOTH FLIGHT SO FAR, THOUGH, HASN'T IT?
© 1992 United Feature Syndicate, Inc.
ALMOST AS IF WE'RE NOT FLYING AT ALL..
SCHULZ

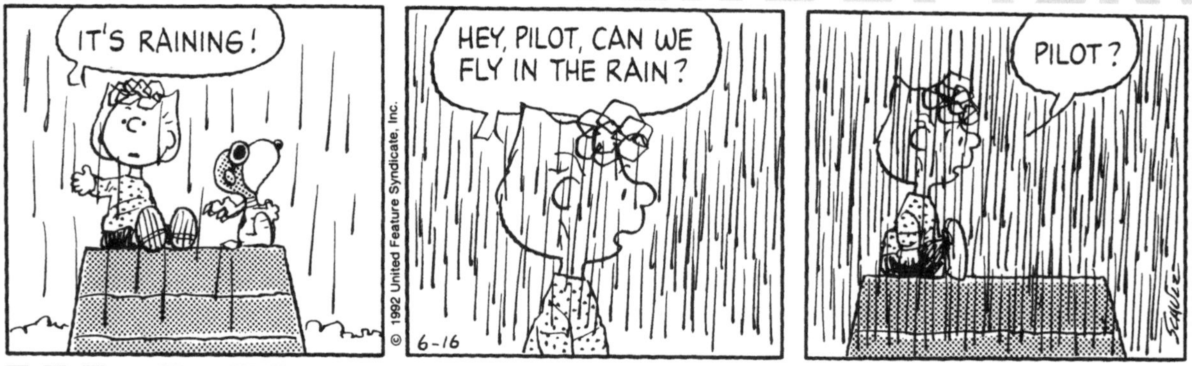
IT'S RAINING!
© 1992 United Feature Syndicate, Inc.
HEY, PILOT, CAN WE FLY IN THE RAIN?
6-16
PILOT?
SCHULZ

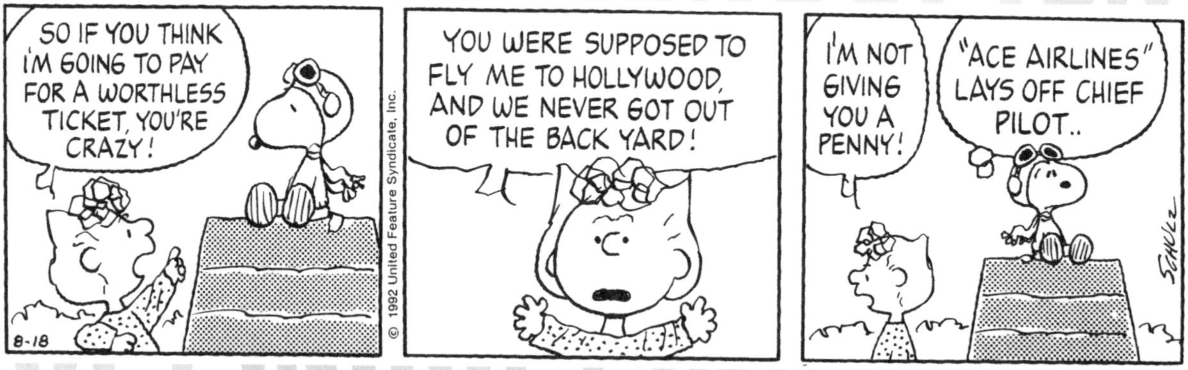
SO IF YOU THINK I'M GOING TO PAY FOR A WORTHLESS TICKET, YOU'RE CRAZY!
8-18
© 1992 United Feature Syndicate, Inc.
YOU WERE SUPPOSED TO FLY ME TO HOLLYWOOD, AND WE NEVER GOT OUT OF THE BACK YARD!
I'M NOT GIVING YOU A PENNY!
"ACE AIRLINES" LAYS OFF CHIEF PILOT..
SCHULZ

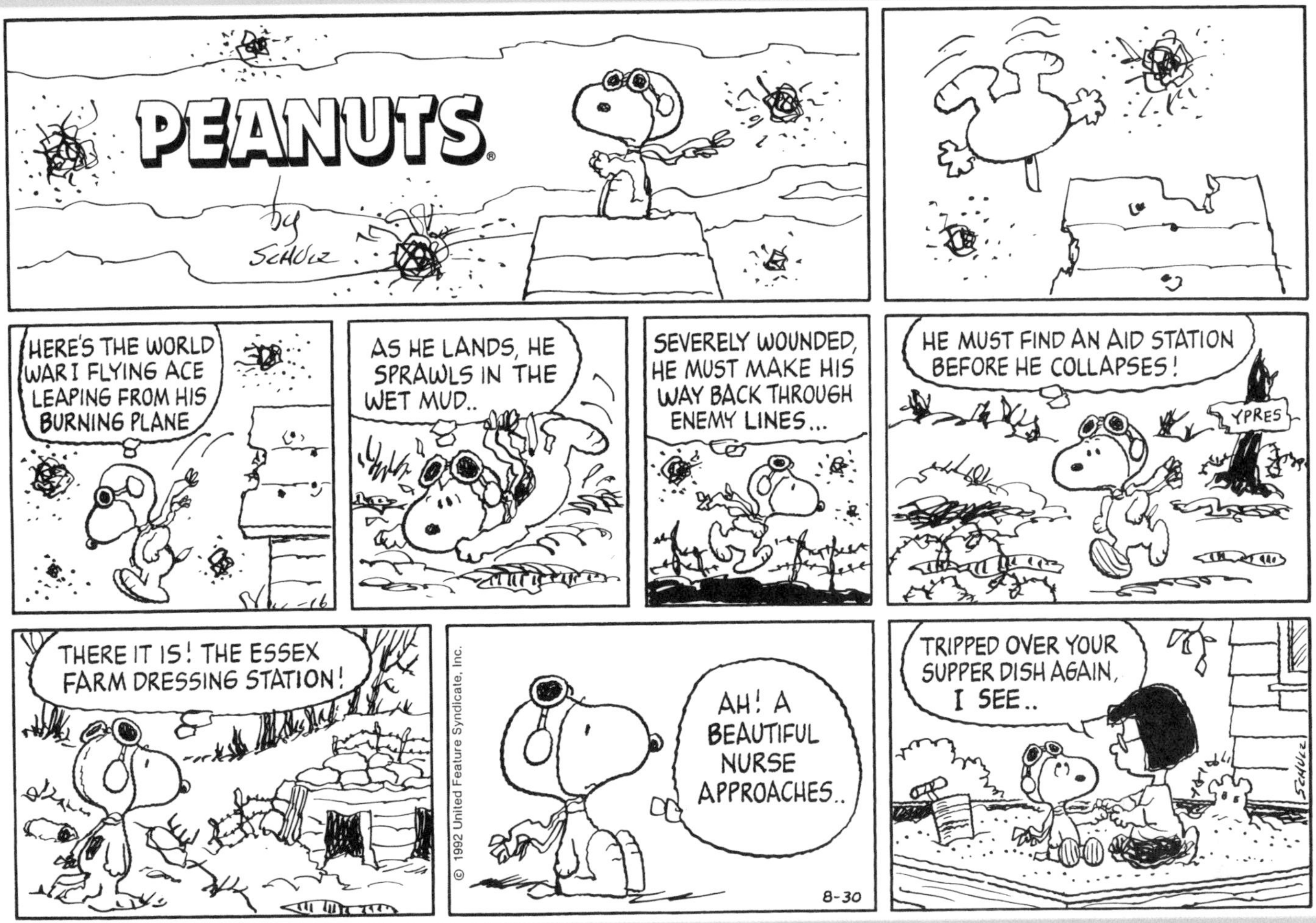
PEANUTS
by SCHULZ
HERE'S THE WORLD WAR I FLYING ACE LEAPING FROM HIS BURNING PLANE
AS HE LANDS, HE SPRAWLS IN THE WET MUD..
SEVERELY WOUNDED, HE MUST MAKE HIS WAY BACK THROUGH ENEMY LINES...
HE MUST FIND AN AID STATION BEFORE HE COLLAPSES!
YPRES
THERE IT IS! THE ESSEX FARM DRESSING STATION!
© 1992 United Feature Syndicate, Inc.
AH! A BEAUTIFUL NURSE APPROACHES..
8-30
TRIPPED OVER YOUR SUPPER DISH AGAIN, I SEE..
SCHULZ

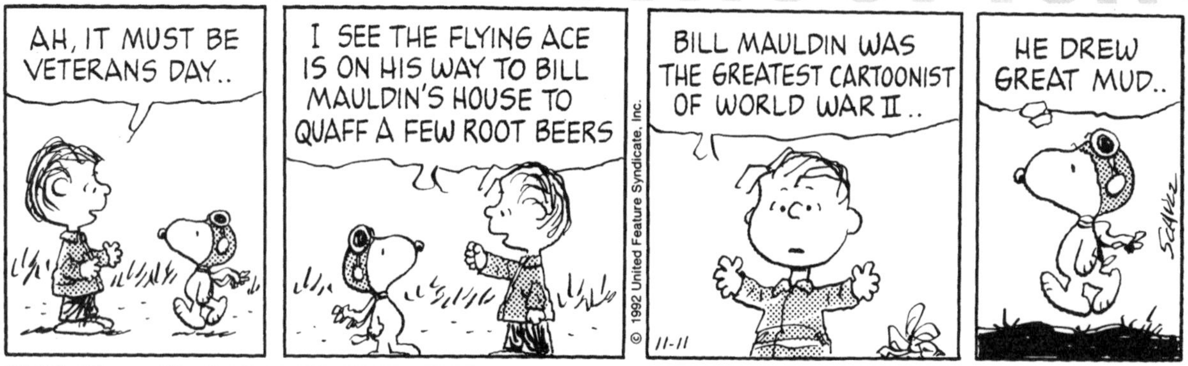
AH, IT MUST BE VETERANS DAY..
I SEE THE FLYING ACE IS ON HIS WAY TO BILL MAULDIN'S HOUSE TO QUAFF A FEW ROOT BEERS
© 1992 United Feature Syndicate, Inc.
BILL MAULDIN WAS THE GREATEST CARTOONIST OF WORLD WAR II..
11-11
HE DREW GREAT MUD..
SCHULZ

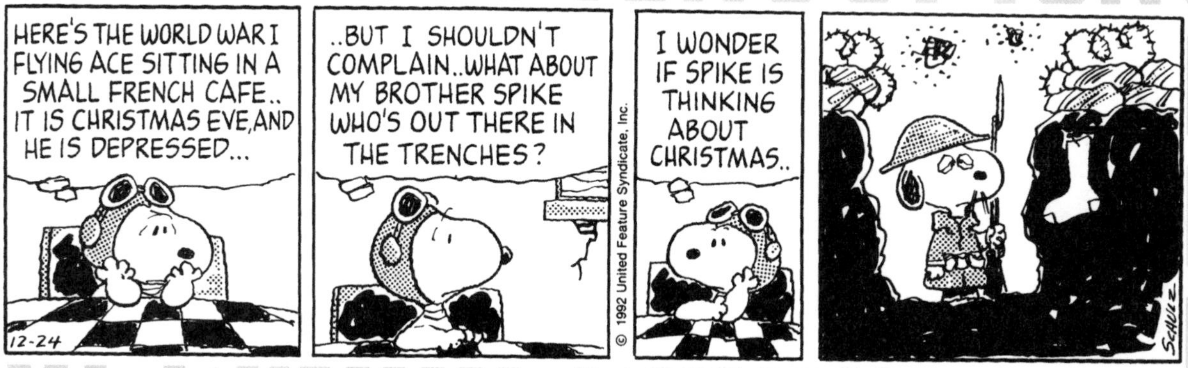
HERE'S THE WORLD WAR I FLYING ACE SITTING IN A SMALL FRENCH CAFE.. IT IS CHRISTMAS EVE, AND HE IS DEPRESSED...
12-24
..BUT I SHOULDN'T COMPLAIN..WHAT ABOUT MY BROTHER SPIKE WHO'S OUT THERE IN THE TRENCHES?
© 1992 United Feature Syndicate, Inc.
I WONDER IF SPIKE IS THINKING ABOUT CHRISTMAS..
SCHULZ

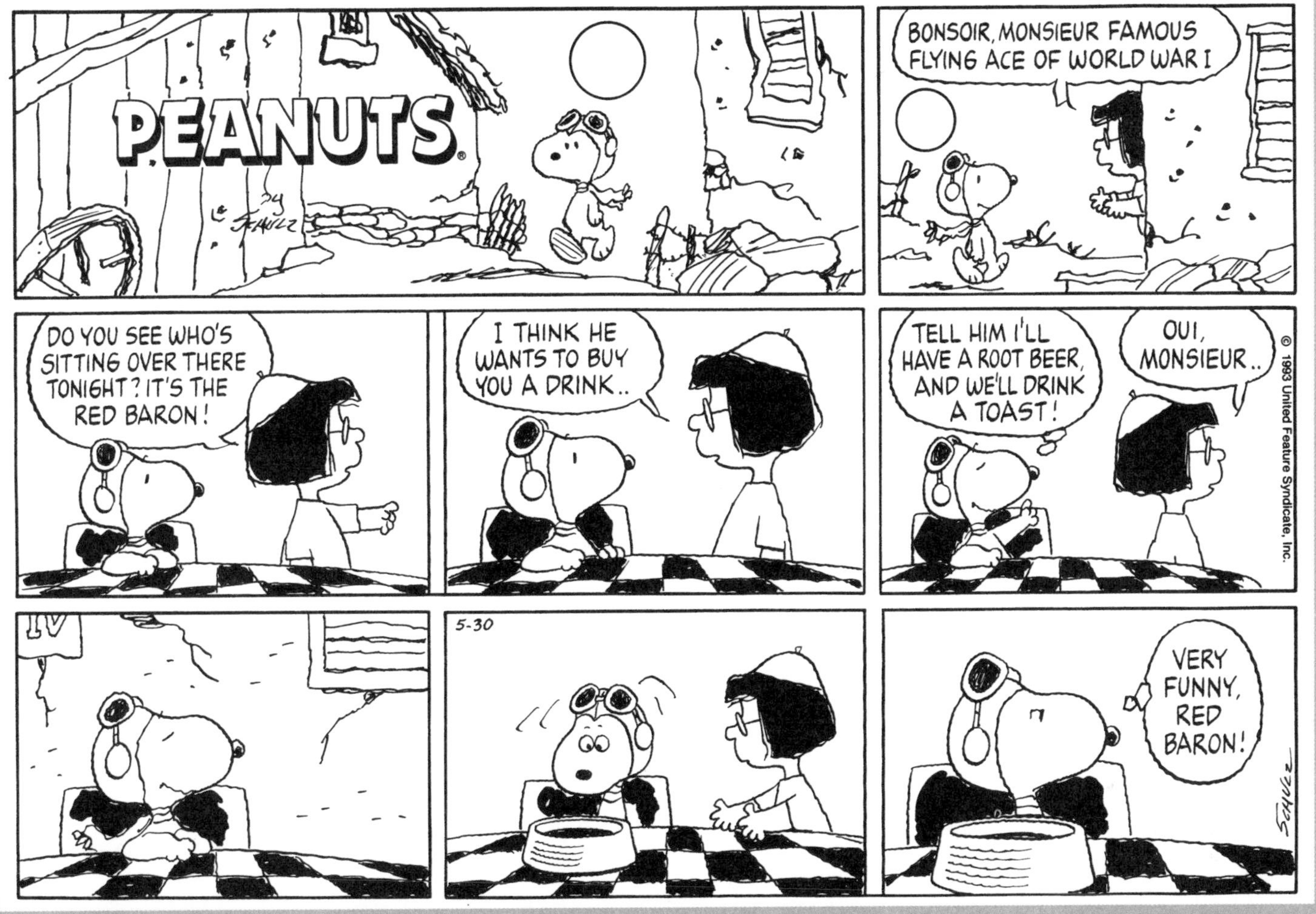
PEANUTS
by SCHULZ
BONSOIR, MONSIEUR FAMOUS FLYING ACE OF WORLD WAR I
DO YOU SEE WHO'S SITTING OVER THERE TONIGHT? IT'S THE RED BARON!
I THINK HE WANTS TO BUY YOU A DRINK..
TELL HIM I'LL HAVE A ROOT BEER, AND WE'LL DRINK A TOAST!
OUI, MONSIEUR..
© 1993 United Feature Syndicate, Inc.
5-30
VERY FUNNY, RED BARON!
SCHULZ

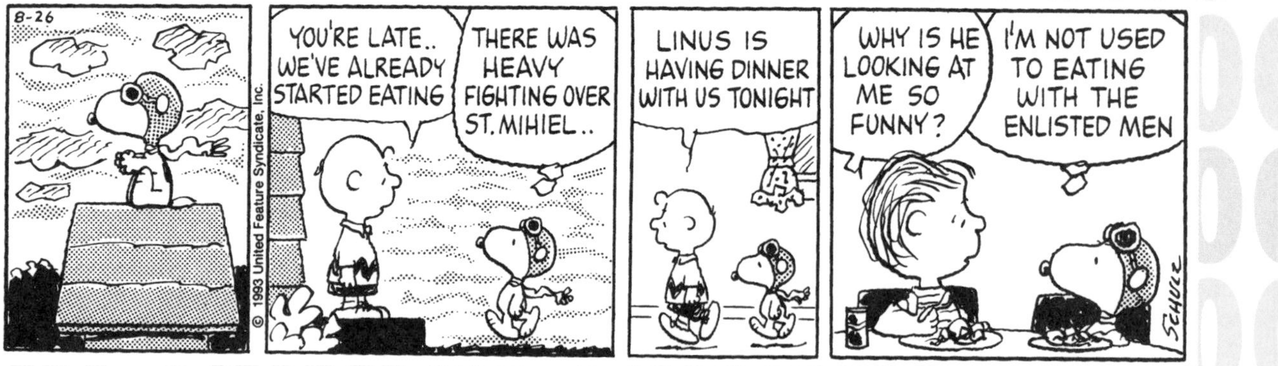
8-26
© 1993 United Feature Syndicate, Inc.
YOU'RE LATE.. WE'VE ALREADY STARTED EATING
THERE WAS HEAVY FIGHTING OVER ST. MIHIEL..
LINUS IS HAVING DINNER WITH US TONIGHT
WHY IS HE LOOKING AT ME SO FUNNY?
I'M NOT USED TO EATING WITH THE ENLISTED MEN
SCHULZ

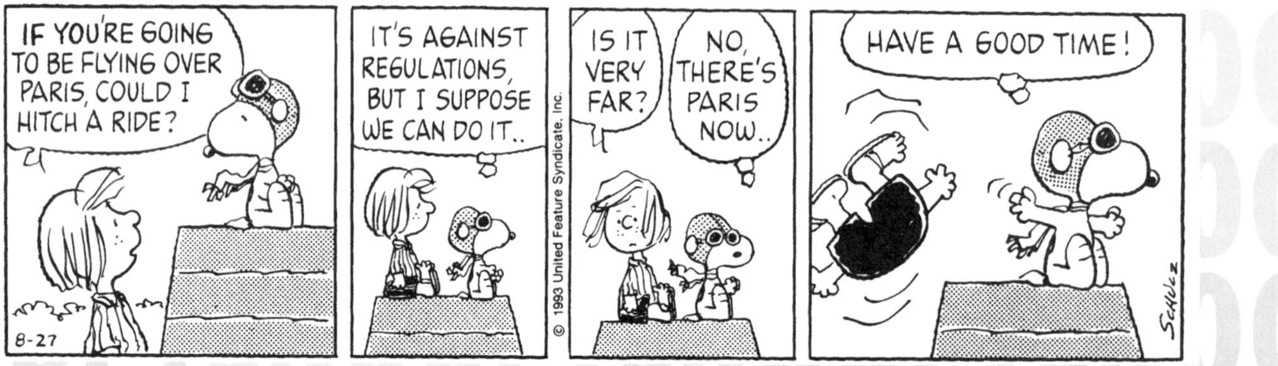
IF YOU'RE GOING TO BE FLYING OVER PARIS, COULD I HITCH A RIDE?
8-27
IT'S AGAINST REGULATIONS, BUT I SUPPOSE WE CAN DO IT..
© 1993 United Feature Syndicate, Inc.
IS IT VERY FAR?
NO, THERE'S PARIS NOW..
HAVE A GOOD TIME!
SCHULZ

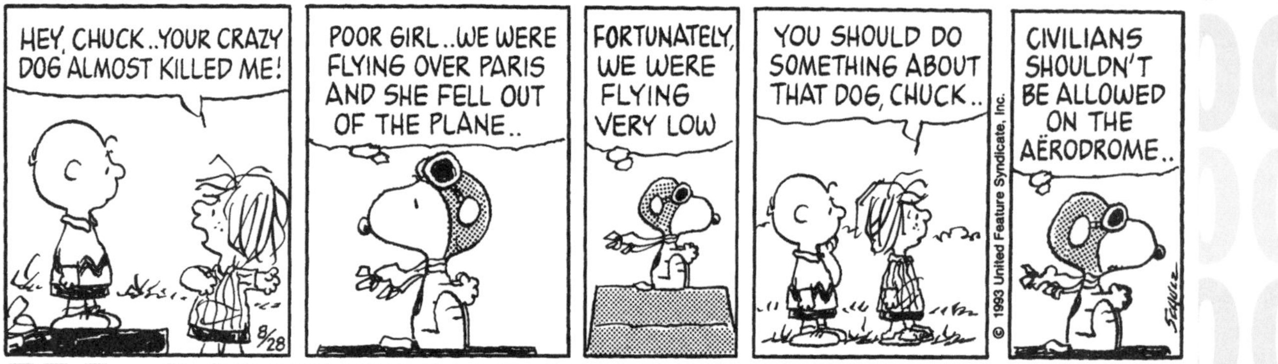
HEY, CHUCK..YOUR CRAZY DOG ALMOST KILLED ME!
8/28
POOR GIRL..WE WERE FLYING OVER PARIS AND SHE FELL OUT OF THE PLANE..
FORTUNATELY, WE WERE FLYING VERY LOW
YOU SHOULD DO SOMETHING ABOUT THAT DOG, CHUCK..
© 1993 United Feature Syndicate, Inc.
CIVILIANS SHOULDN'T BE ALLOWED ON THE AËRODROME..
SCHULZ

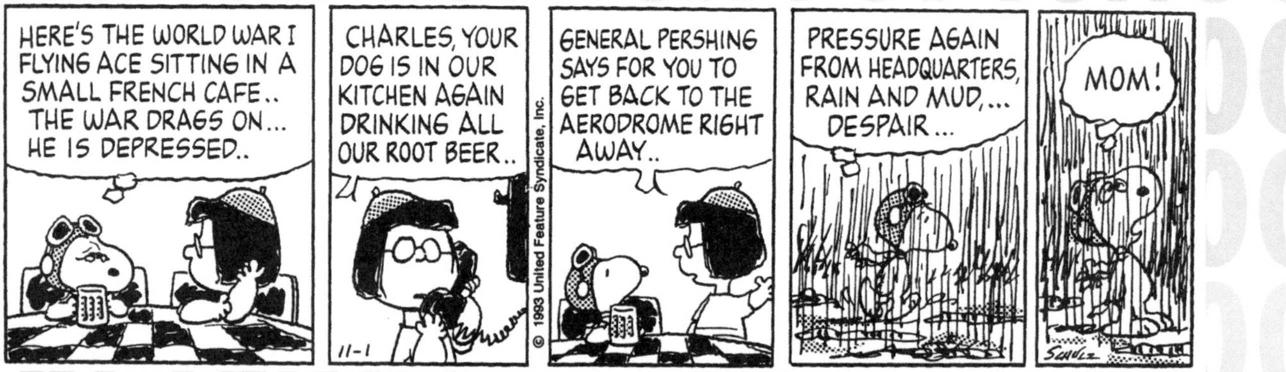
HERE'S THE WORLD WAR I FLYING ACE SITTING IN A SMALL FRENCH CAFE.. THE WAR DRAGS ON... HE IS DEPRESSED..
CHARLES, YOUR DOG IS IN OUR KITCHEN AGAIN DRINKING ALL OUR ROOT BEER..
11-1
© 1993 United Feature Syndicate, Inc.
GENERAL PERSHING SAYS FOR YOU TO GET BACK TO THE AERODROME RIGHT AWAY..
PRESSURE AGAIN FROM HEADQUARTERS, RAIN AND MUD,... DESPAIR...
MOM!
SCHULZ

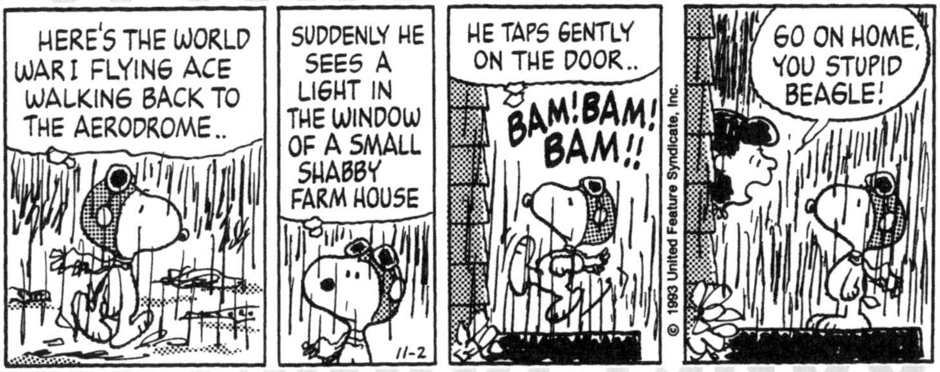
HERE'S THE WORLD WAR I FLYING ACE WALKING BACK TO THE AERODROME..
SUDDENLY HE SEES A LIGHT IN THE WINDOW OF A SMALL SHABBY FARM HOUSE
11-2
HE TAPS GENTLY ON THE DOOR..
BAM! BAM! BAM!!
© 1993 United Feature Syndicate, Inc.
GO ON HOME, YOU STUPID BEAGLE!
SOMETIMES THE UNIFORM FRIGHTENS THEM..
SCHULZ

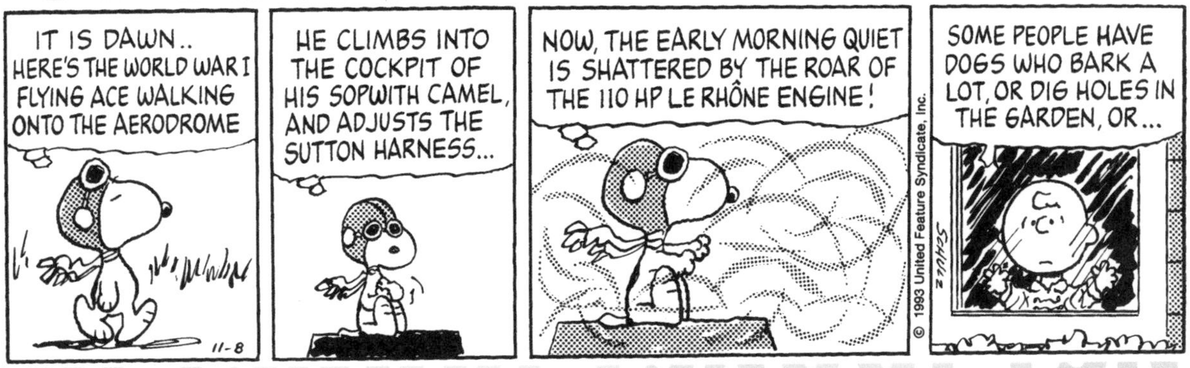
IT IS DAWN.. HERE'S THE WORLD WAR I FLYING ACE WALKING ONTO THE AERODROME
11-8
HE CLIMBS INTO THE COCKPIT OF HIS SOPWITH CAMEL, AND ADJUSTS THE SUTTON HARNESS...
NOW, THE EARLY MORNING QUIET IS SHATTERED BY THE ROAR OF THE 110 HP LE RHÔNE ENGINE!
© 1993 United Feature Syndicate, Inc.
SOME PEOPLE HAVE DOGS WHO BARK A LOT, OR DIG HOLES IN THE GARDEN, OR...
SCHULZ

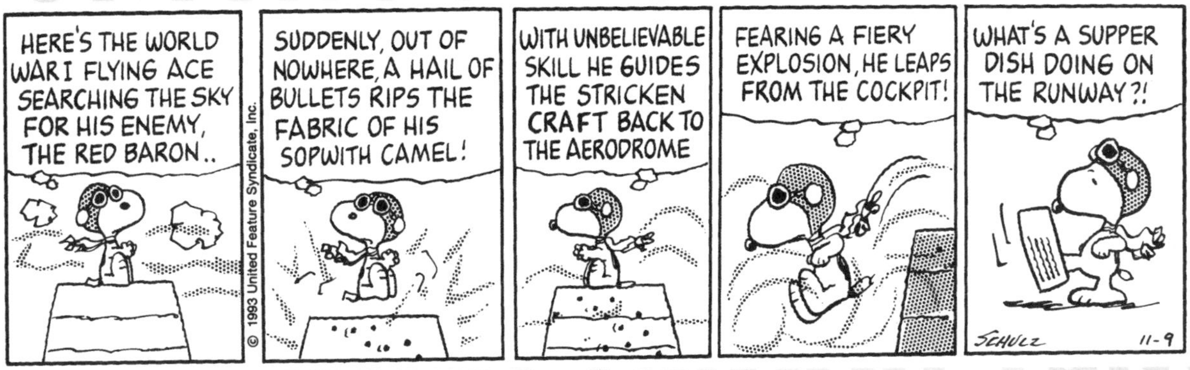
HERE'S THE WORLD WAR I FLYING ACE SEARCHING THE SKY FOR HIS ENEMY, THE RED BARON..
© 1993 United Feature Syndicate, Inc.
SUDDENLY, OUT OF NOWHERE, A HAIL OF BULLETS RIPS THE FABRIC OF HIS SOPWITH CAMEL!
WITH UNBELIEVABLE SKILL HE GUIDES THE STRICKEN CRAFT BACK TO THE AERODROME
FEARING A FIERY EXPLOSION, HE LEAPS FROM THE COCKPIT!
WHAT'S A SUPPER DISH DOING ON THE RUNWAY?!
SCHULZ
11-9

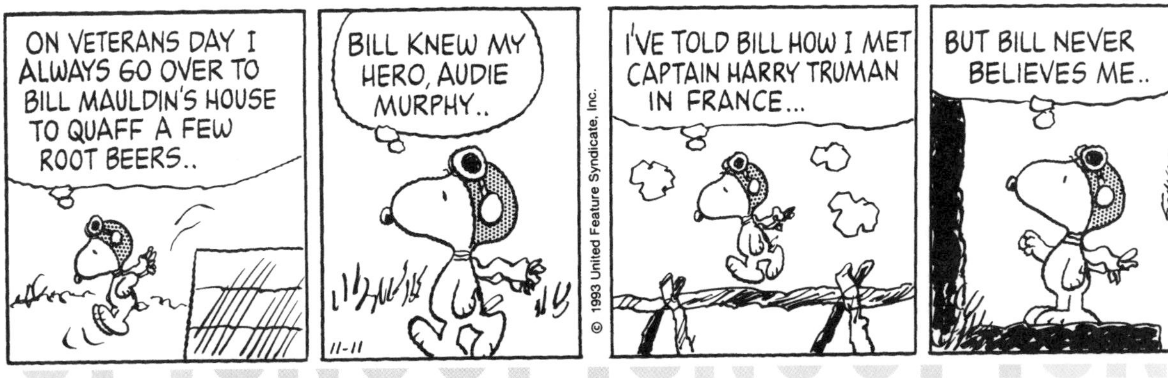
ON VETERANS DAY I ALWAYS GO OVER TO BILL MAULDIN'S HOUSE TO QUAFF A FEW ROOT BEERS..
BILL KNEW MY HERO, AUDIE MURPHY..
11-11
© 1993 United Feature Syndicate, Inc.
I'VE TOLD BILL HOW I MET CAPTAIN HARRY TRUMAN IN FRANCE...
BUT BILL NEVER BELIEVES ME..
SCHULZ

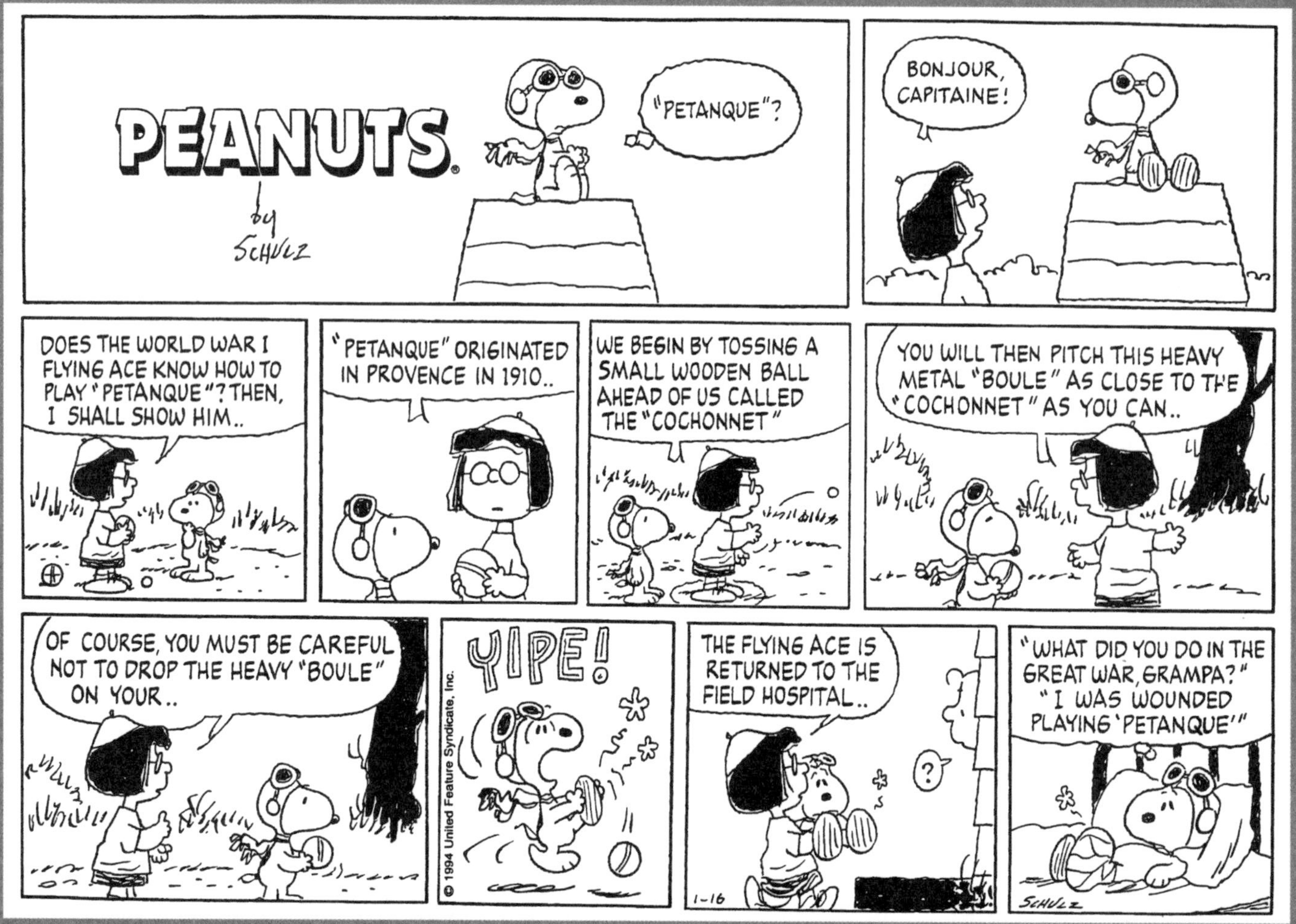
PEANUTS
by SCHULZ
"PETANQUE"?
BONJOUR, CAPITAINE!
DOES THE WORLD WAR I FLYING ACE KNOW HOW TO PLAY "PETANQUE"? THEN, I SHALL SHOW HIM..
"PETANQUE" ORIGINATED IN PROVENCE IN 1910..
WE BEGIN BY TOSSING A SMALL WOODEN BALL AHEAD OF US CALLED THE "COCHONNET"
YOU WILL THEN PITCH THIS HEAVY METAL "BOULE" AS CLOSE TO THE "COCHONNET" AS YOU CAN..
OF COURSE, YOU MUST BE CAREFUL NOT TO DROP THE HEAVY "BOULE" ON YOUR..
YIPE!
© 1994 United Feature Syndicate, Inc.
THE FLYING ACE IS RETURNED TO THE FIELD HOSPITAL..
?
1-16
"WHAT DID YOU DO IN THE GREAT WAR, GRAMPA?" "I WAS WOUNDED PLAYING 'PETANQUE'"
SCHULZ

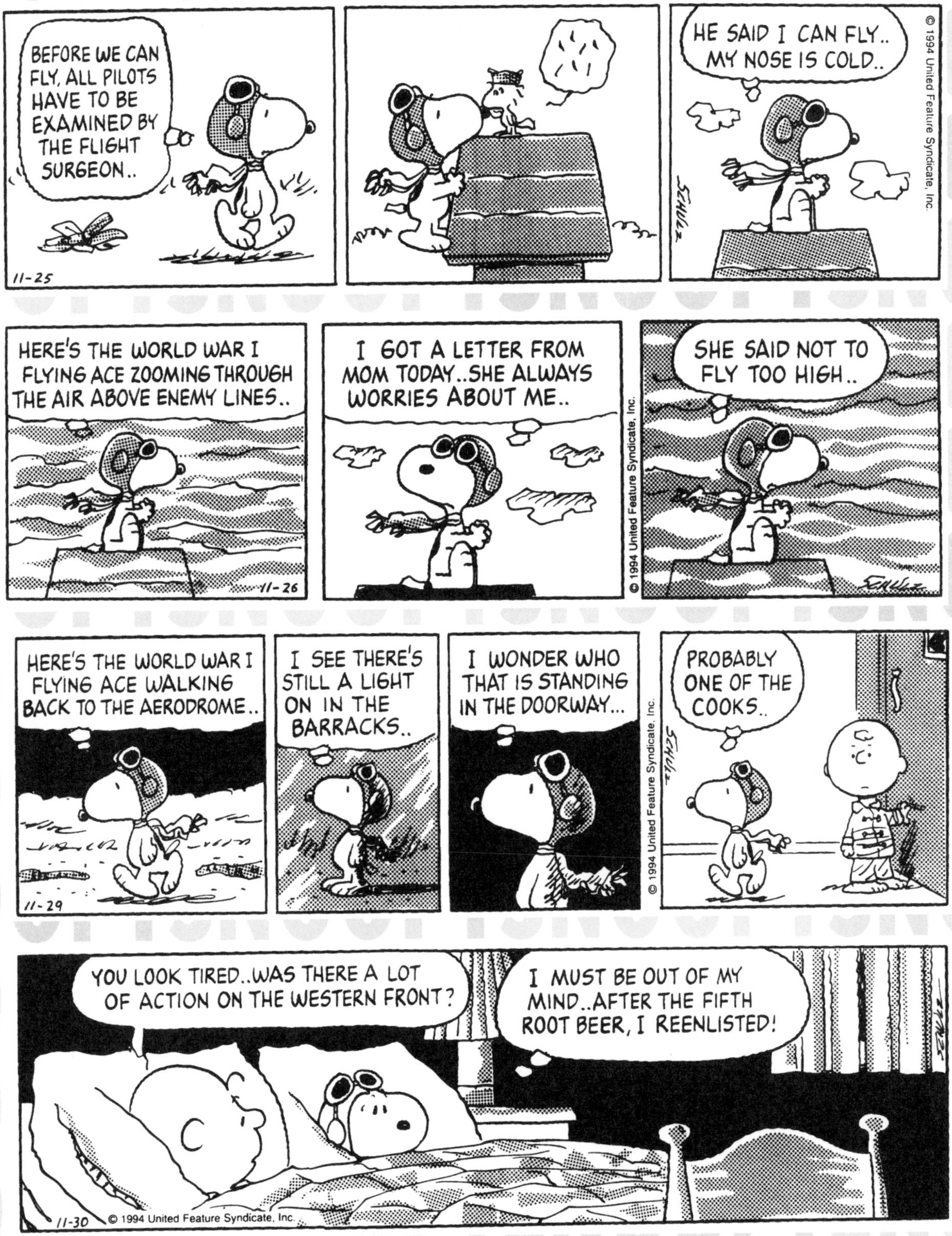

BEFORE WE CAN FLY, ALL PILOTS HAVE TO BE EXAMINED BY THE FLIGHT SURGEON..
HE SAID I CAN FLY.. MY NOSE IS COLD..
© 1994 United Feature Syndicate, Inc.
11-25
HERE'S THE WORLD WAR I FLYING ACE ZOOMING THROUGH THE AIR ABOVE ENEMY LINES..
I GOT A LETTER FROM MOM TODAY..SHE ALWAYS WORRIES ABOUT ME..
SHE SAID NOT TO FLY TOO HIGH..
11-26
© 1994 United Feature Syndicate, Inc.
HERE'S THE WORLD WAR I FLYING ACE WALKING BACK TO THE AERODROME..
I SEE THERE'S STILL A LIGHT ON IN THE BARRACKS..
I WONDER WHO THAT IS STANDING IN THE DOORWAY...
PROBABLY ONE OF THE COOKS..
11-29
© 1994 United Feature Syndicate, Inc.
YOU LOOK TIRED..WAS THERE A LOT OF ACTION ON THE WESTERN FRONT?
I MUST BE OUT OF MY MIND..AFTER THE FIFTH ROOT BEER, I REENLISTED!
11-30
© 1994 United Feature Syndicate, Inc.

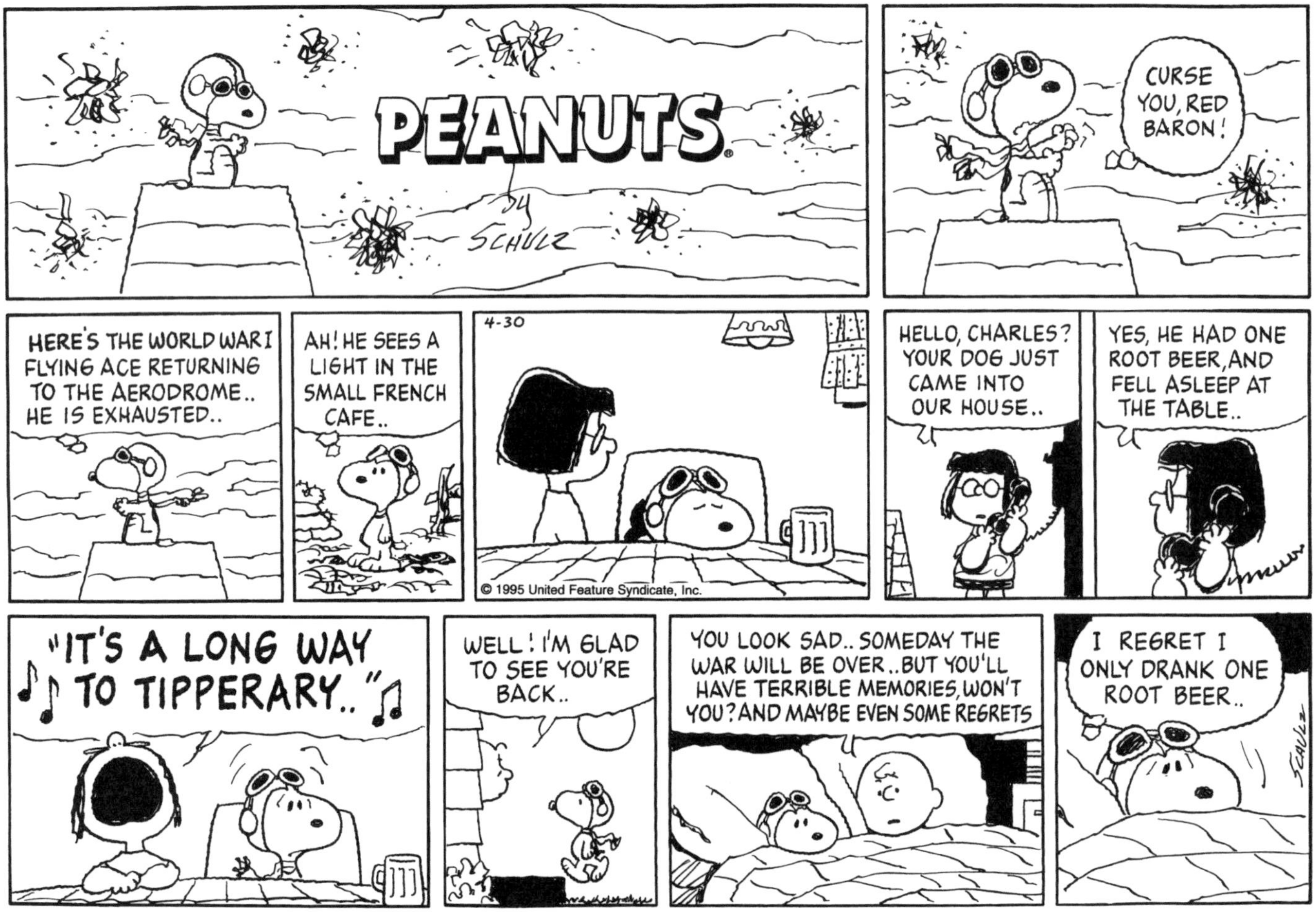
PEANUTS
SCHULZ
CURSE YOU, RED BARON!
HERE'S THE WORLD WAR I FLYING ACE RETURNING TO THE AERODROME.. HE IS EXHAUSTED..
AH! HE SEES A LIGHT IN THE SMALL FRENCH CAFE..
4-30
© 1995 United Feature Syndicate, Inc.
HELLO, CHARLES? YOUR DOG JUST CAME INTO OUR HOUSE..
YES, HE HAD ONE ROOT BEER, AND FELL ASLEEP AT THE TABLE..
"IT'S A LONG WAY TO TIPPERARY.."
WELL! I'M GLAD TO SEE YOU'RE BACK..
YOU LOOK SAD.. SOMEDAY THE WAR WILL BE OVER..BUT YOU'LL HAVE TERRIBLE MEMORIES, WON'T YOU? AND MAYBE EVEN SOME REGRETS
I REGRET I ONLY DRANK ONE ROOT BEER..
SCHULZ

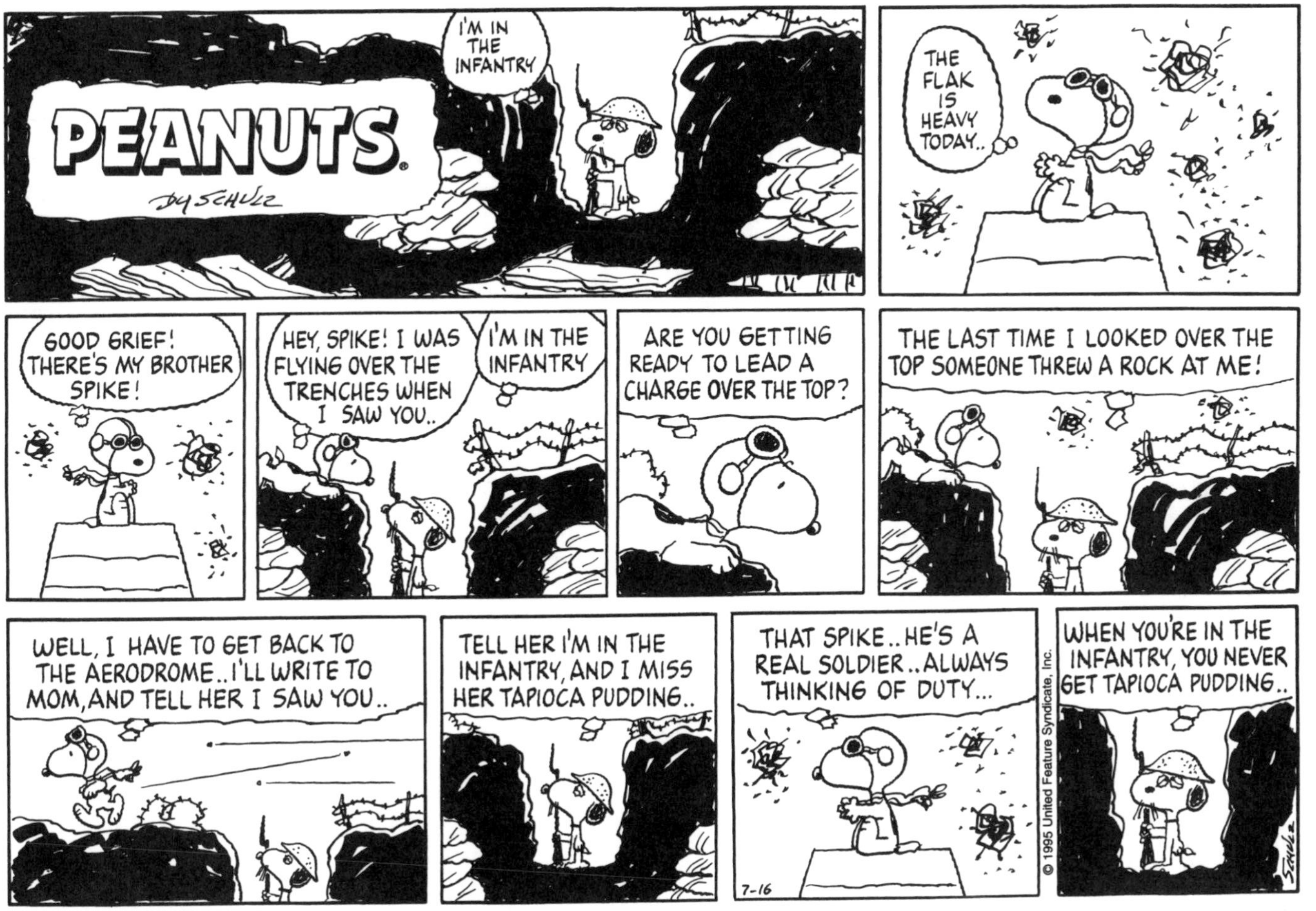
PEANUTS
I'M IN THE INFANTRY
THE FLAK IS HEAVY TODAY..
GOOD GRIEF! THERE'S MY BROTHER SPIKE!
HEY, SPIKE! I WAS FLYING OVER THE TRENCHES WHEN I SAW YOU..
I'M IN THE INFANTRY
ARE YOU GETTING READY TO LEAD A CHARGE OVER THE TOP?
THE LAST TIME I LOOKED OVER THE TOP SOMEONE THREW A ROCK AT ME!
WELL, I HAVE TO GET BACK TO THE AERODROME..I'LL WRITE TO MOM, AND TELL HER I SAW YOU..
TELL HER I'M IN THE INFANTRY, AND I MISS HER TAPIOCA PUDDING..
THAT SPIKE..HE'S A REAL SOLDIER..ALWAYS THINKING OF DUTY...
7-16
© 1995 United Feature Syndicate, Inc.
WHEN YOU'RE IN THE INFANTRY, YOU NEVER GET TAPIOCA PUDDING..

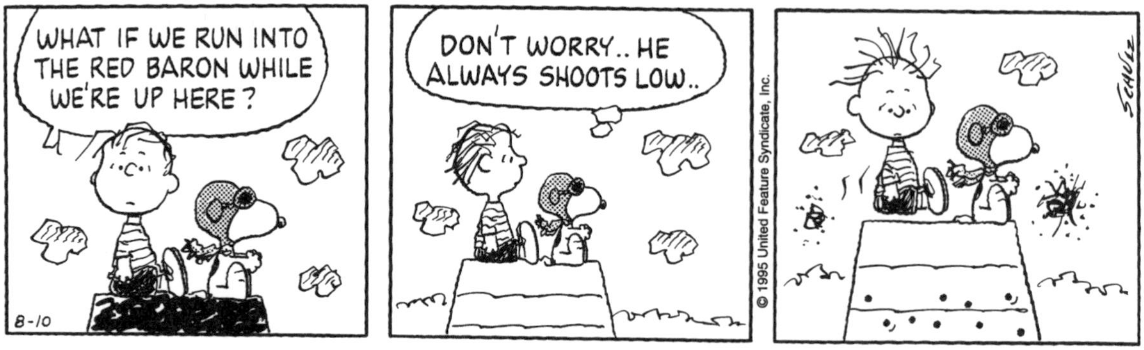
WHAT IF WE RUN INTO THE RED BARON WHILE WE'RE UP HERE ?
8-10
DON'T WORRY.. HE ALWAYS SHOOTS LOW..
© 1995 United Feature Syndicate, Inc.
SCHULZ

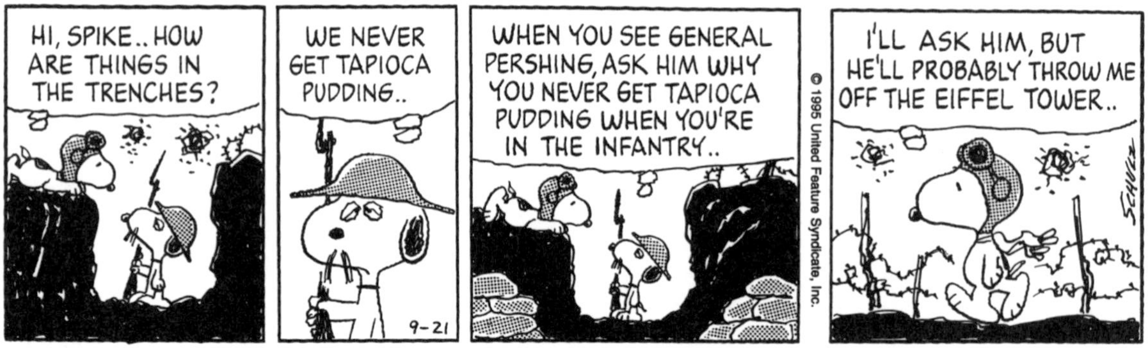
HI, SPIKE.. HOW ARE THINGS IN THE TRENCHES?
WE NEVER GET TAPIOCA PUDDING..
9-21
WHEN YOU SEE GENERAL PERSHING, ASK HIM WHY YOU NEVER GET TAPIOCA PUDDING WHEN YOU'RE IN THE INFANTRY..
© 1995 United Feature Syndicate, Inc.
I'LL ASK HIM, BUT HE'LL PROBABLY THROW ME OFF THE EIFFEL TOWER..
SCHULZ

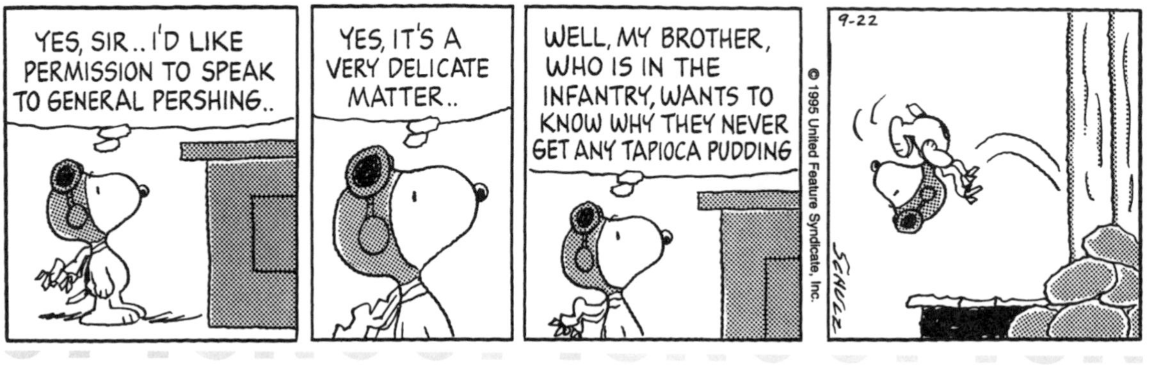
YES, SIR.. I'D LIKE PERMISSION TO SPEAK TO GENERAL PERSHING..
YES, IT'S A VERY DELICATE MATTER..
WELL, MY BROTHER, WHO IS IN THE INFANTRY, WANTS TO KNOW WHY THEY NEVER GET ANY TAPIOCA PUDDING
© 1995 United Feature Syndicate, Inc.
SCHULZ
9-22

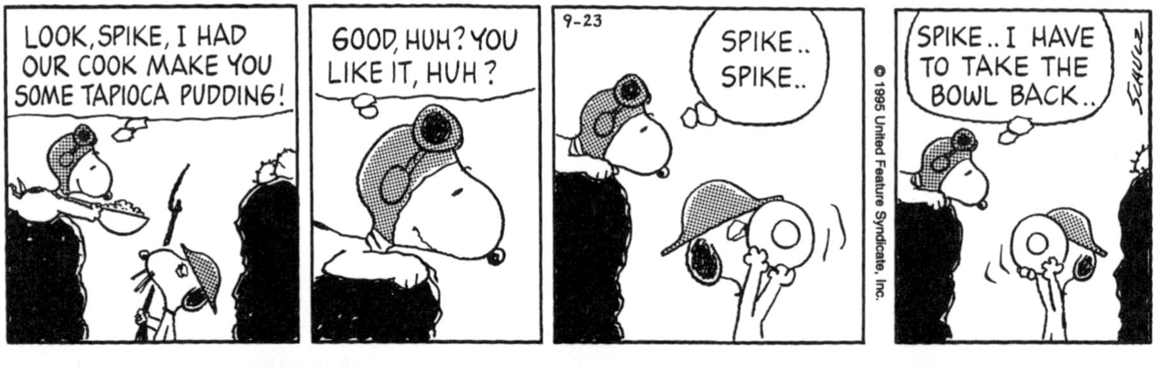
LOOK, SPIKE, I HAD OUR COOK MAKE YOU SOME TAPIOCA PUDDING!
GOOD, HUH? YOU LIKE IT, HUH ?
9-23
SPIKE.. SPIKE..
© 1995 United Feature Syndicate, Inc.
SPIKE.. I HAVE TO TAKE THE BOWL BACK..
SCHULZ

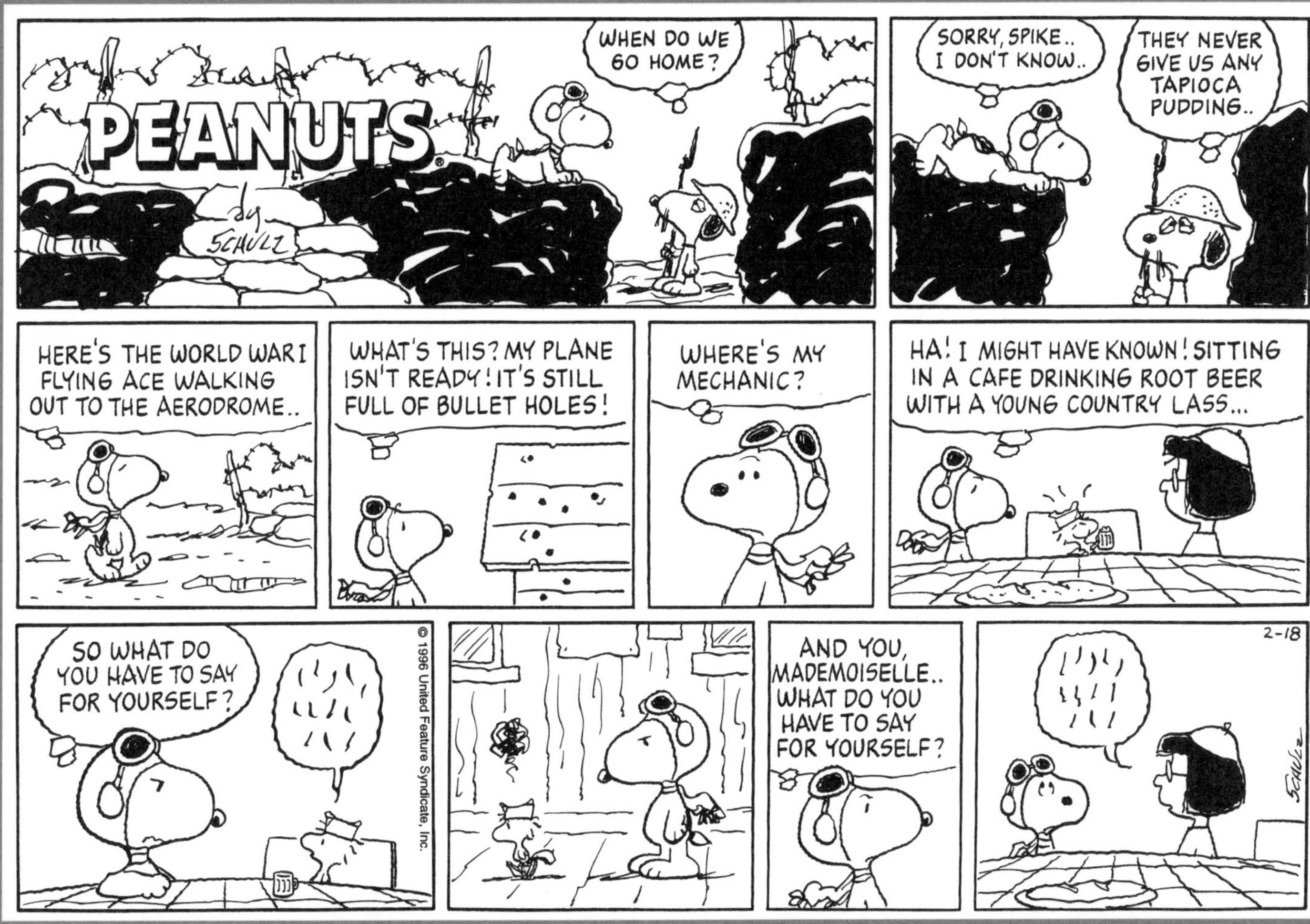
PEANUTS
by SCHULZ
WHEN DO WE GO HOME?
SORRY, SPIKE.. I DON'T KNOW..
THEY NEVER GIVE US ANY TAPIOCA PUDDING..
HERE'S THE WORLD WAR I FLYING ACE WALKING OUT TO THE AERODROME..
WHAT'S THIS? MY PLANE ISN'T READY! IT'S STILL FULL OF BULLET HOLES!
WHERE'S MY MECHANIC?
HA! I MIGHT HAVE KNOWN! SITTING IN A CAFE DRINKING ROOT BEER WITH A YOUNG COUNTRY LASS...
SO WHAT DO YOU HAVE TO SAY FOR YOURSELF?
© 1996 United Feature Syndicate, Inc.
AND YOU, MADEMOISELLE.. WHAT DO YOU HAVE TO SAY FOR YOURSELF?
2-18
SCHULZ

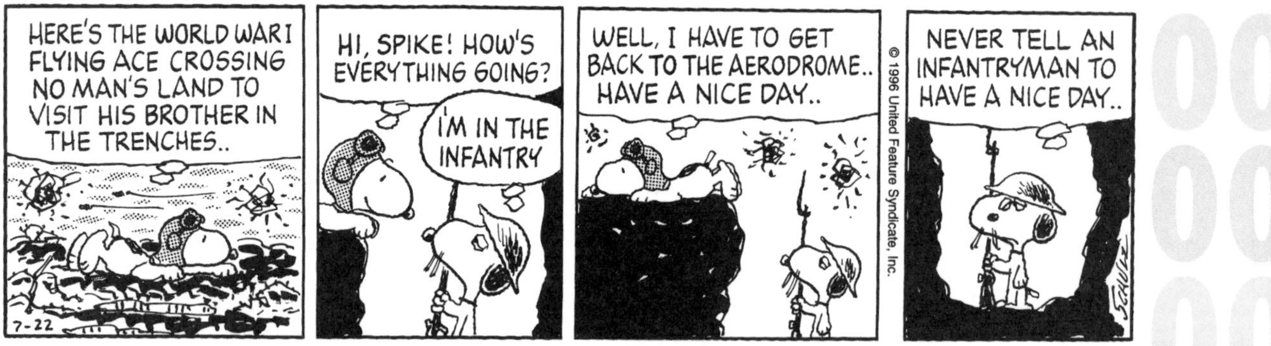
HERE'S THE WORLD WAR I FLYING ACE CROSSING NO MAN'S LAND TO VISIT HIS BROTHER IN THE TRENCHES..
7-22
HI, SPIKE! HOW'S EVERYTHING GOING?
I'M IN THE INFANTRY
WELL, I HAVE TO GET BACK TO THE AERODROME.. HAVE A NICE DAY..
© 1996 United Feature Syndicate, Inc.
NEVER TELL AN INFANTRYMAN TO HAVE A NICE DAY..
SCHULZ

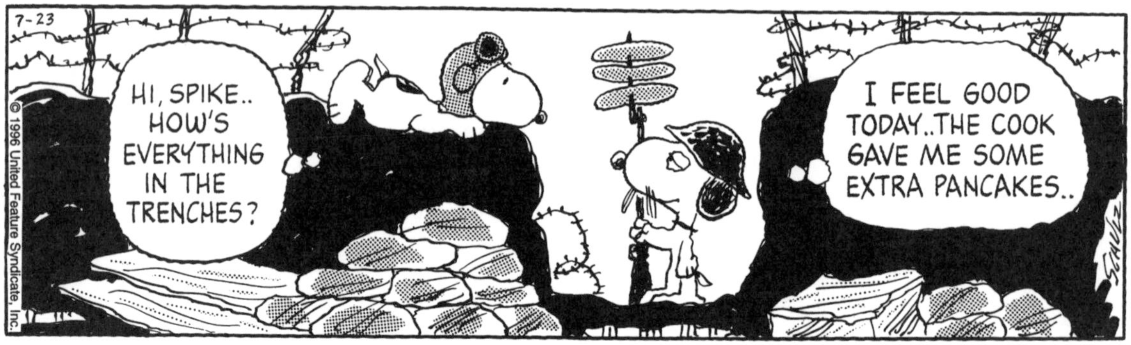
7-23
© 1996 United Feature Syndicate, Inc.
HI, SPIKE.. HOW'S EVERYTHING IN THE TRENCHES?
I FEEL GOOD TODAY..THE COOK GAVE ME SOME EXTRA PANCAKES..
SCHULZ

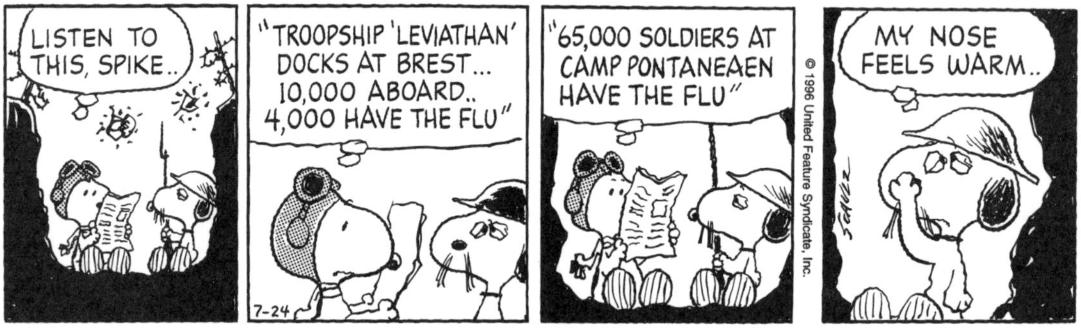
LISTEN TO THIS, SPIKE..
"TROOPSHIP 'LEVIATHAN' DOCKS AT BREST... 10,000 ABOARD.. 4,000 HAVE THE FLU"
7-24
"65,000 SOLDIERS AT CAMP PONTANEAEN HAVE THE FLU"
© 1996 United Feature Syndicate, Inc.
SCHULZ
MY NOSE FEELS WARM..

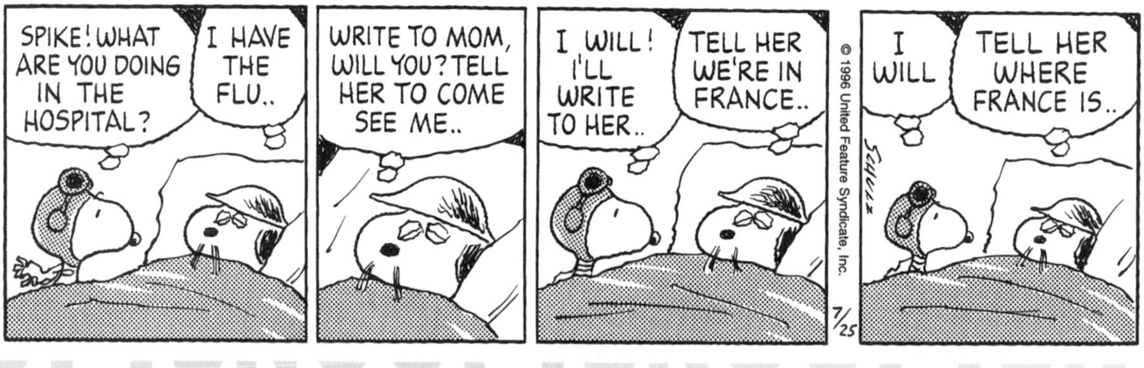
SPIKE! WHAT ARE YOU DOING IN THE HOSPITAL?
I HAVE THE FLU..
WRITE TO MOM, WILL YOU? TELL HER TO COME SEE ME..
I WILL! I'LL WRITE TO HER..
TELL HER WE'RE IN FRANCE..
© 1996 United Feature Syndicate, Inc.
SCHULZ
7/25
I WILL
TELL HER WHERE FRANCE IS..

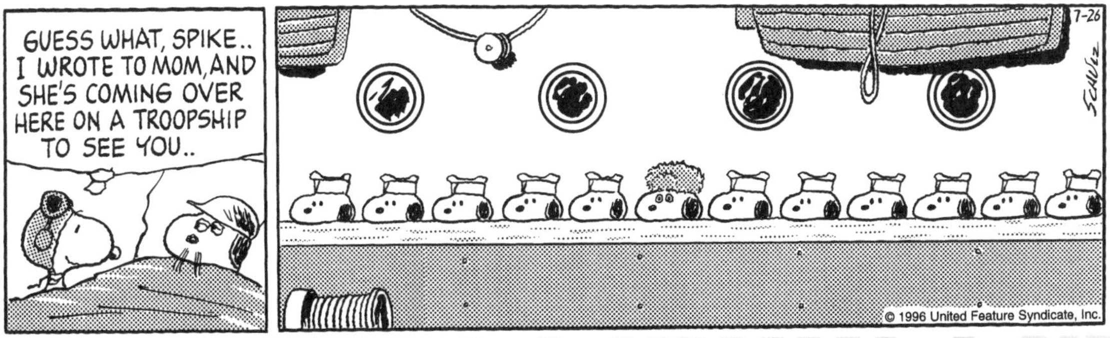
GUESS WHAT, SPIKE.. I WROTE TO MOM, AND SHE'S COMING OVER HERE ON A TROOPSHIP TO SEE YOU..
7-26
SCHULZ
© 1996 United Feature Syndicate, Inc.

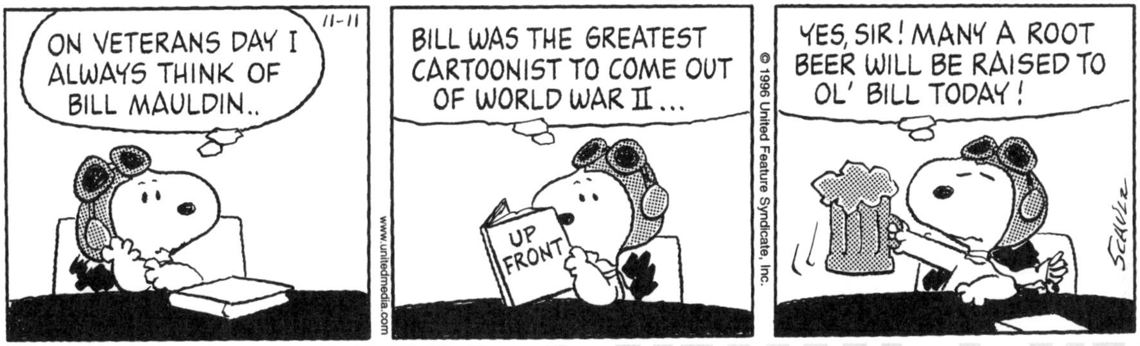
11-11
ON VETERANS DAY I ALWAYS THINK OF BILL MAULDIN..
www.unitedmedia.com
BILL WAS THE GREATEST CARTOONIST TO COME OUT OF WORLD WAR II...
UP FRONT
© 1996 United Feature Syndicate, Inc.
YES, SIR! MANY A ROOT BEER WILL BE RAISED TO OL' BILL TODAY!
SCHULZ

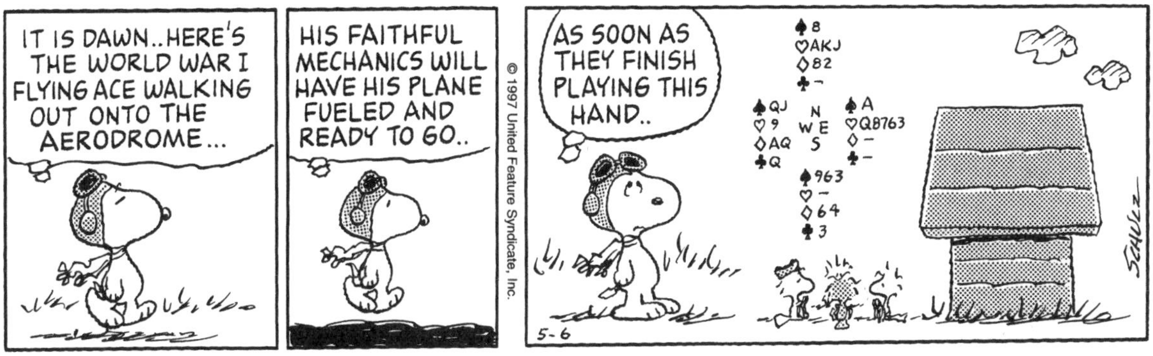
IT IS DAWN..HERE'S THE WORLD WAR I FLYING ACE WALKING OUT ONTO THE AERODROME...
HIS FAITHFUL MECHANICS WILL HAVE HIS PLANE FUELED AND READY TO GO..
© 1997 United Feature Syndicate, Inc.
AS SOON AS THEY FINISH PLAYING THIS HAND..
♠8
♡AKJ
◇82
♣–
♠QJ
♡9
◇AQ
♣Q
N
W E
S
♠A
♡Q8763
◇–
♣–
♠963
♡–
◇64
♣3
SCHULZ
5-6

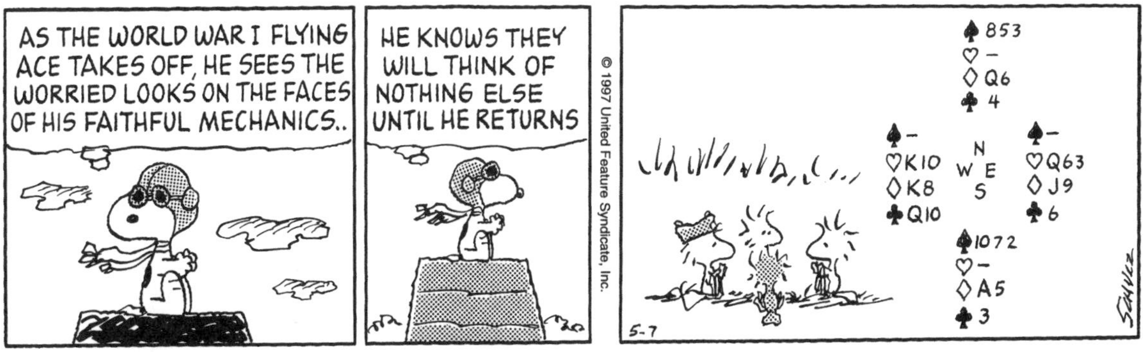
AS THE WORLD WAR I FLYING ACE TAKES OFF, HE SEES THE WORRIED LOOKS ON THE FACES OF HIS FAITHFUL MECHANICS..
HE KNOWS THEY WILL THINK OF NOTHING ELSE UNTIL HE RETURNS
© 1997 United Feature Syndicate, Inc.
♠853
♡–
◇Q6
♣4
♠–
♡K10
◇K8
♣Q10
N
W E
S
♠–
♡Q63
◇J9
♣6
♠1072
♡–
◇A5
♣3
SCHULZ
5-7

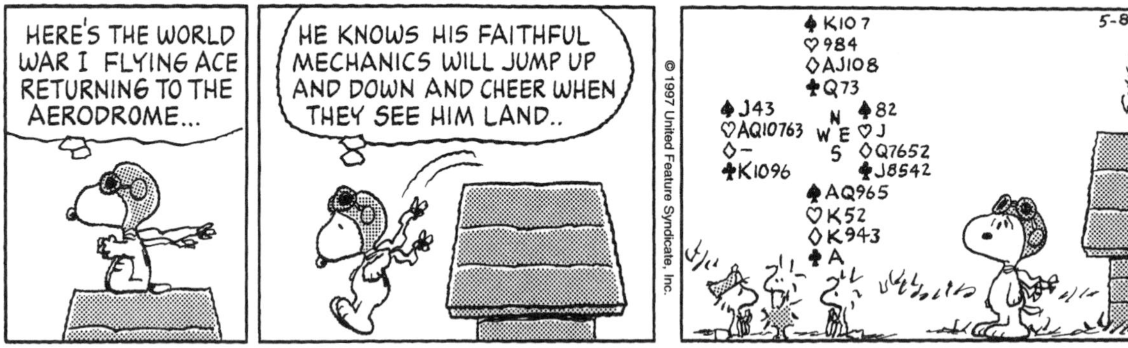
HERE'S THE WORLD WAR I FLYING ACE RETURNING TO THE AERODROME...
HE KNOWS HIS FAITHFUL MECHANICS WILL JUMP UP AND DOWN AND CHEER WHEN THEY SEE HIM LAND..
© 1997 United Feature Syndicate, Inc.
♠K10 7
♡984
◇AJ108
♣Q73
♠J43
♡AQ10763
◇–
♣K1096
N
W E
S
♠82
♡J
◇Q7652
♣J8542
♠AQ965
♡K52
◇K943
♣A
5-8
SCHULZ

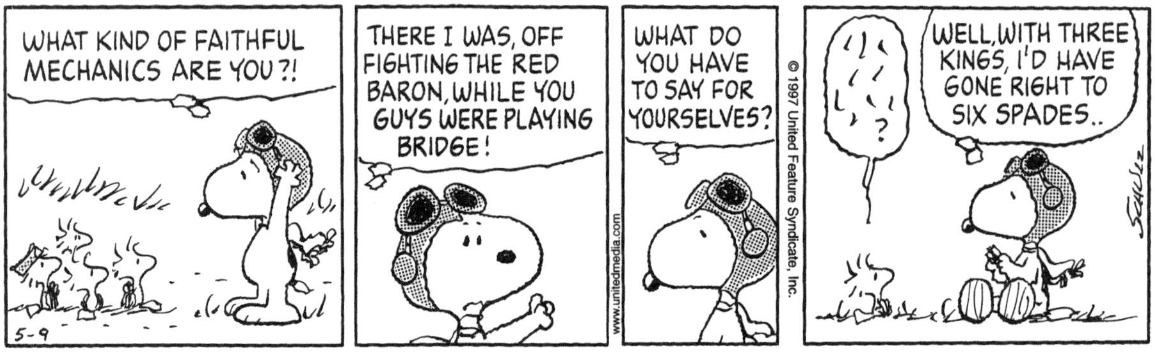
WHAT KIND OF FAITHFUL MECHANICS ARE YOU?!
5-9
THERE I WAS, OFF FIGHTING THE RED BARON, WHILE YOU GUYS WERE PLAYING BRIDGE!
www.unitedmedia.com
WHAT DO YOU HAVE TO SAY FOR YOURSELVES?
© 1997 United Feature Syndicate, Inc.
?
WELL, WITH THREE KINGS, I'D HAVE GONE RIGHT TO SIX SPADES..
SCHULZ

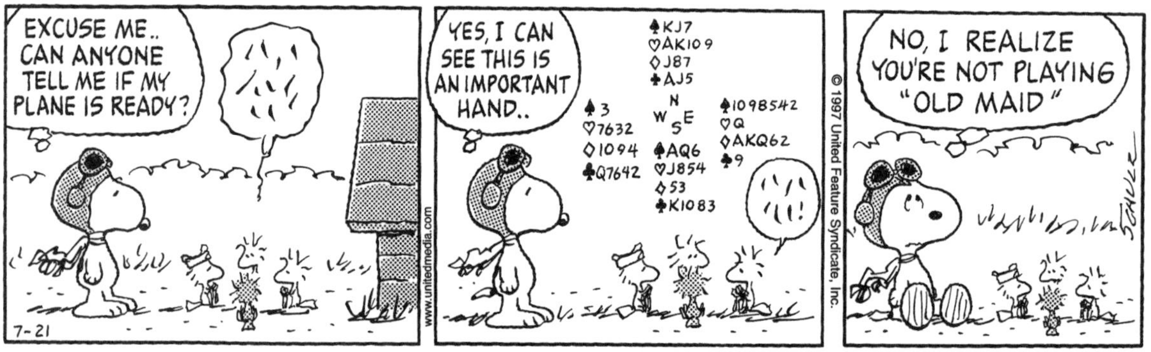
EXCUSE ME.. CAN ANYONE TELL ME IF MY PLANE IS READY?
7-21
www.unitedmedia.com
YES, I CAN SEE THIS IS AN IMPORTANT HAND..
♠KJ7
♡AK109
◇J87
♣AJ5
♠3
♡7632
◇1094
♣Q7642
N
W E
S
♠1098542
♡Q
◇AKQ62
♣9
♠AQ6
♡J854
◇53
♣K1083
!
© 1997 United Feature Syndicate, Inc.
NO, I REALIZE YOU'RE NOT PLAYING "OLD MAID"
SCHULZ

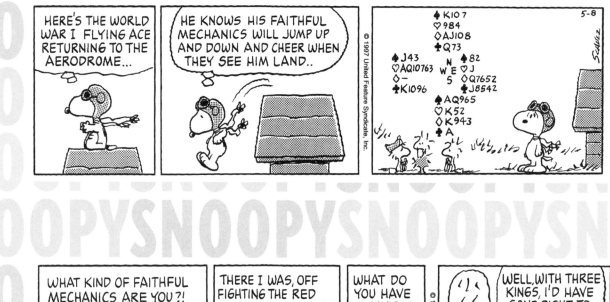

Beagle Scout

SNOOPY

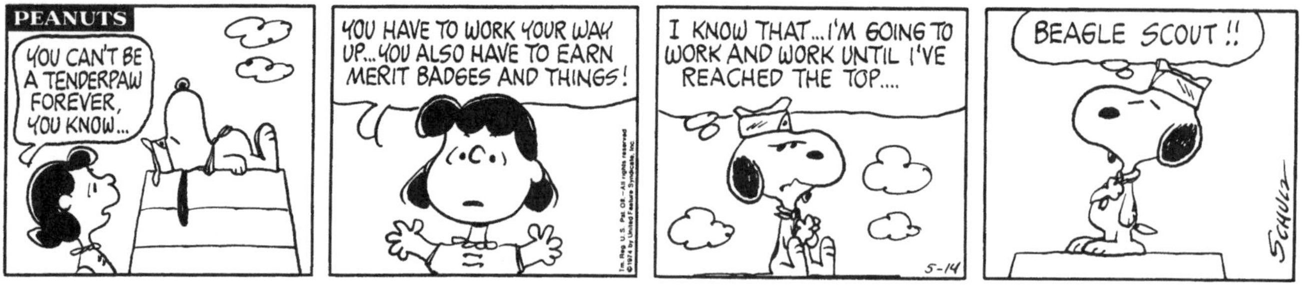
PEANUTS
YOU CAN'T BE A TENDERPAW FOREVER, YOU KNOW...
YOU HAVE TO WORK YOUR WAY UP...YOU ALSO HAVE TO EARN MERIT BADGES AND THINGS!
I KNOW THAT...I'M GOING TO WORK AND WORK UNTIL I'VE REACHED THE TOP....
5-14
BEAGLE SCOUT!!
SCHULZ

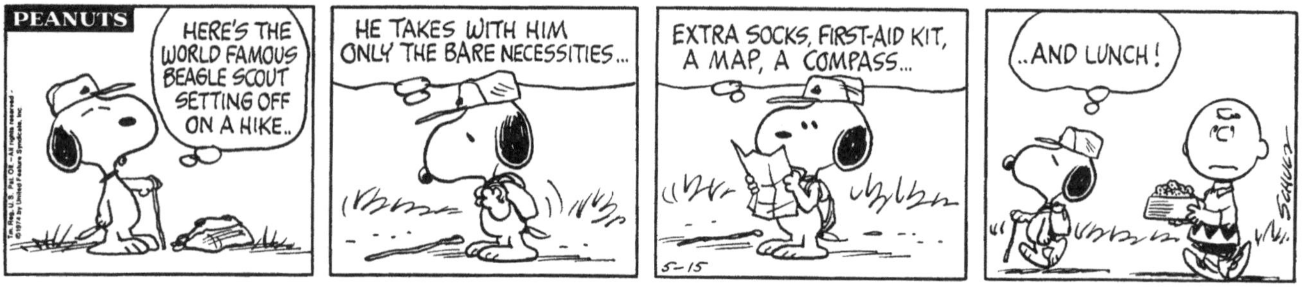
PEANUTS
HERE'S THE WORLD FAMOUS BEAGLE SCOUT SETTING OFF ON A HIKE..
HE TAKES WITH HIM ONLY THE BARE NECESSITIES...
EXTRA SOCKS, FIRST-AID KIT, A MAP, A COMPASS...
5-15
..AND LUNCH!
SCHULZ

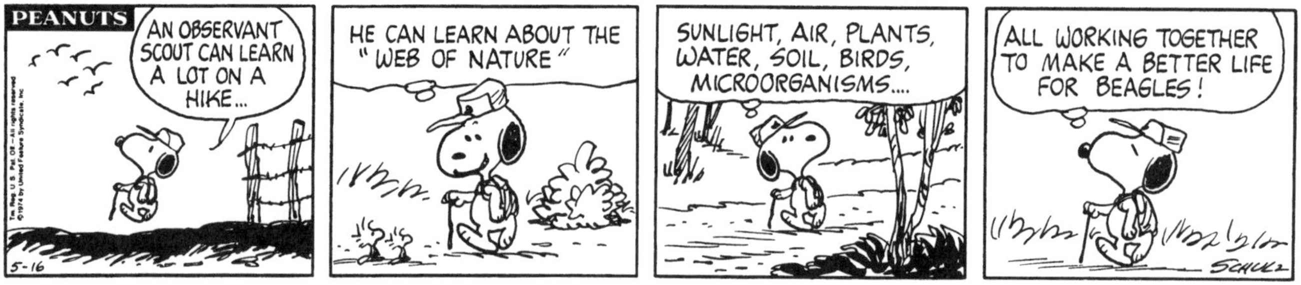
PEANUTS
AN OBSERVANT SCOUT CAN LEARN A LOT ON A HIKE...
5-16
HE CAN LEARN ABOUT THE "WEB OF NATURE"
SUNLIGHT, AIR, PLANTS, WATER, SOIL, BIRDS, MICROORGANISMS....
ALL WORKING TOGETHER TO MAKE A BETTER LIFE FOR BEAGLES!
SCHULZ

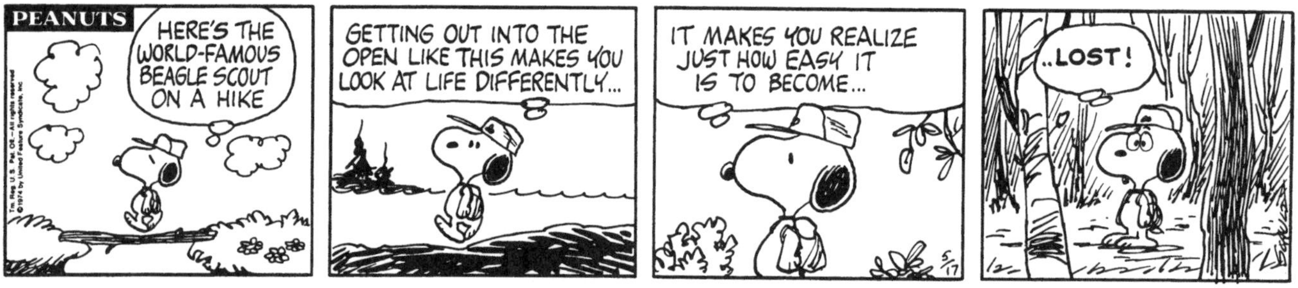
PEANUTS
HERE'S THE WORLD-FAMOUS BEAGLE SCOUT ON A HIKE
GETTING OUT INTO THE OPEN LIKE THIS MAKES YOU LOOK AT LIFE DIFFERENTLY...
IT MAKES YOU REALIZE JUST HOW EASY IT IS TO BECOME...
5/17
..LOST!
SCHULZ

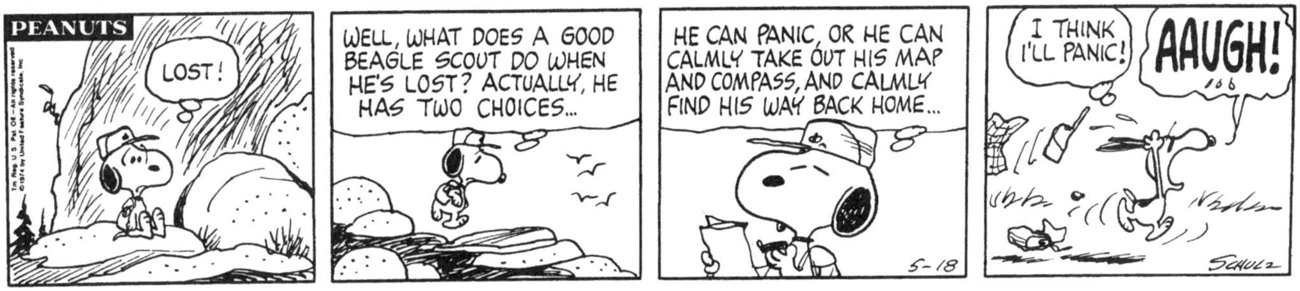
PEANUTS
Tm Reg. U.S. Pat. Off.—All rights reserved ©1974 by United Feature Syndicate, Inc.
LOST!
WELL, WHAT DOES A GOOD BEAGLE SCOUT DO WHEN HE'S LOST? ACTUALLY, HE HAS TWO CHOICES...
HE CAN PANIC, OR HE CAN CALMLY TAKE OUT HIS MAP AND COMPASS, AND CALMLY FIND HIS WAY BACK HOME...
5-18
I THINK I'LL PANIC!
AAUGH!
SCHULZ

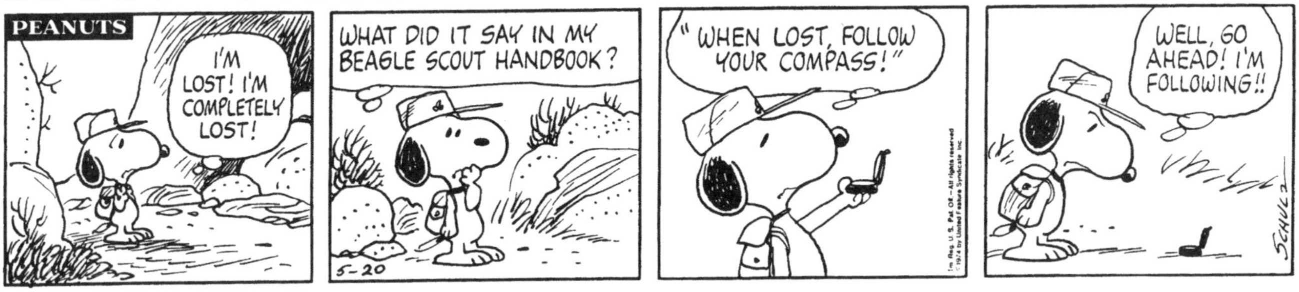
PEANUTS
I'M LOST! I'M COMPLETELY LOST!
WHAT DID IT SAY IN MY BEAGLE SCOUT HANDBOOK?
5-20
"WHEN LOST, FOLLOW YOUR COMPASS!"
Tm Reg. U.S. Pat. Off.—All rights reserved ©1974 by United Feature Syndicate, Inc.
WELL, GO AHEAD! I'M FOLLOWING!!
SCHULZ

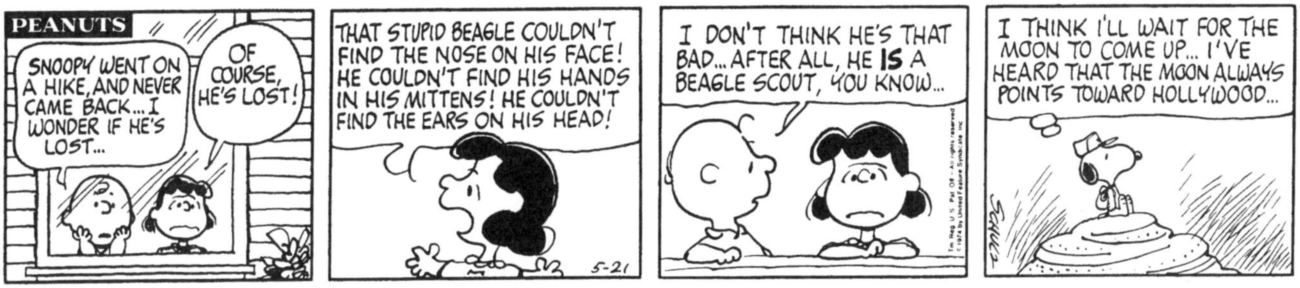
PEANUTS
SNOOPY WENT ON A HIKE, AND NEVER CAME BACK... I WONDER IF HE'S LOST...
OF COURSE, HE'S LOST!
THAT STUPID BEAGLE COULDN'T FIND THE NOSE ON HIS FACE! HE COULDN'T FIND HIS HANDS IN HIS MITTENS! HE COULDN'T FIND THE EARS ON HIS HEAD!
5-21
I DON'T THINK HE'S THAT BAD... AFTER ALL, HE **IS** A BEAGLE SCOUT, YOU KNOW...
Tm Reg. U.S. Pat. Off.—All rights reserved ©1974 by United Feature Syndicate, Inc.
I THINK I'LL WAIT FOR THE MOON TO COME UP... I'VE HEARD THAT THE MOON ALWAYS POINTS TOWARD HOLLYWOOD...
SCHULZ

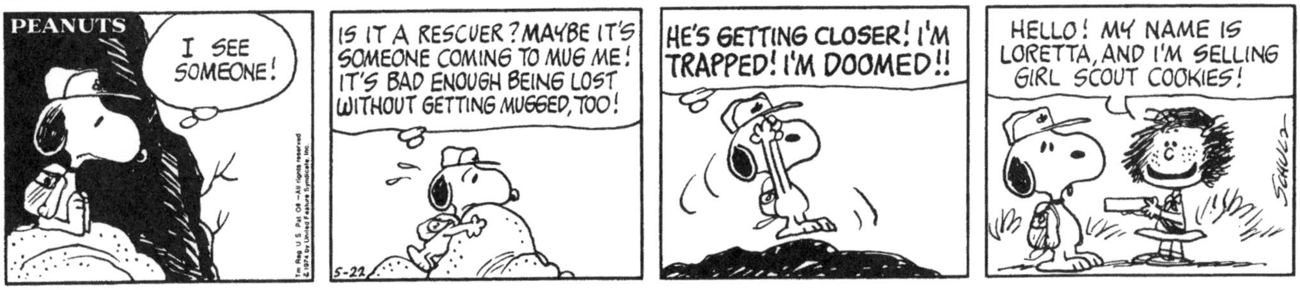
PEANUTS
I SEE SOMEONE!
Tm Reg. U.S. Pat. Off.—All rights reserved ©1974 by United Feature Syndicate, Inc.
IS IT A RESCUER? MAYBE IT'S SOMEONE COMING TO MUG ME! IT'S BAD ENOUGH BEING LOST WITHOUT GETTING MUGGED, TOO!
5-22
HE'S GETTING CLOSER! I'M TRAPPED! I'M DOOMED!!
HELLO! MY NAME IS LORETTA, AND I'M SELLING GIRL SCOUT COOKIES!
SCHULZ

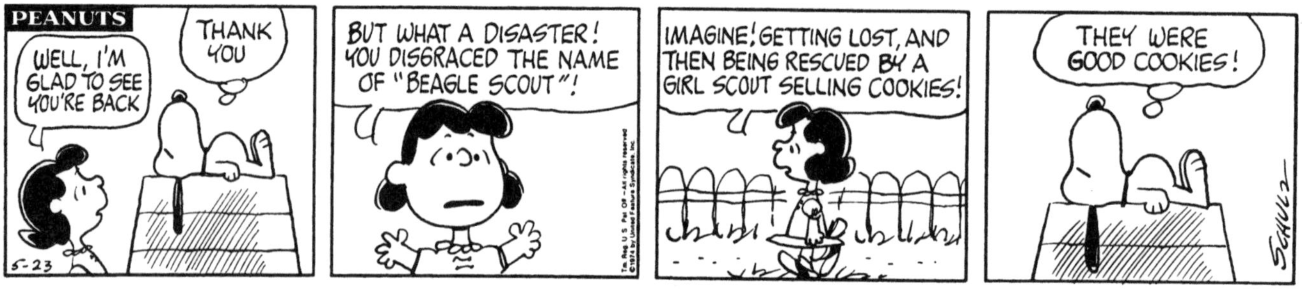
PEANUTS
WELL, I'M GLAD TO SEE YOU'RE BACK
THANK YOU
BUT WHAT A DISASTER! YOU DISGRACED THE NAME OF "BEAGLE SCOUT"!
IMAGINE! GETTING LOST, AND THEN BEING RESCUED BY A GIRL SCOUT SELLING COOKIES!
THEY WERE GOOD COOKIES!
5-23
SCHULZ

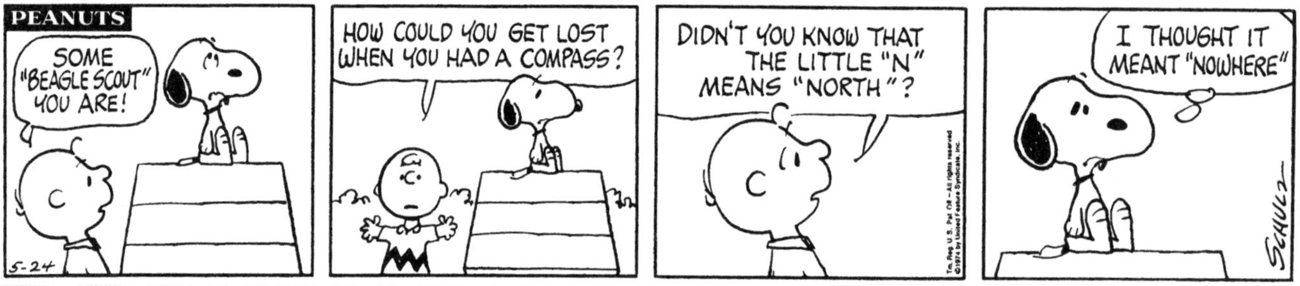
PEANUTS
SOME "BEAGLE SCOUT" YOU ARE!
HOW COULD YOU GET LOST WHEN YOU HAD A COMPASS?
DIDN'T YOU KNOW THAT THE LITTLE "N" MEANS "NORTH"?
I THOUGHT IT MEANT "NOWHERE"
5-24
SCHULZ

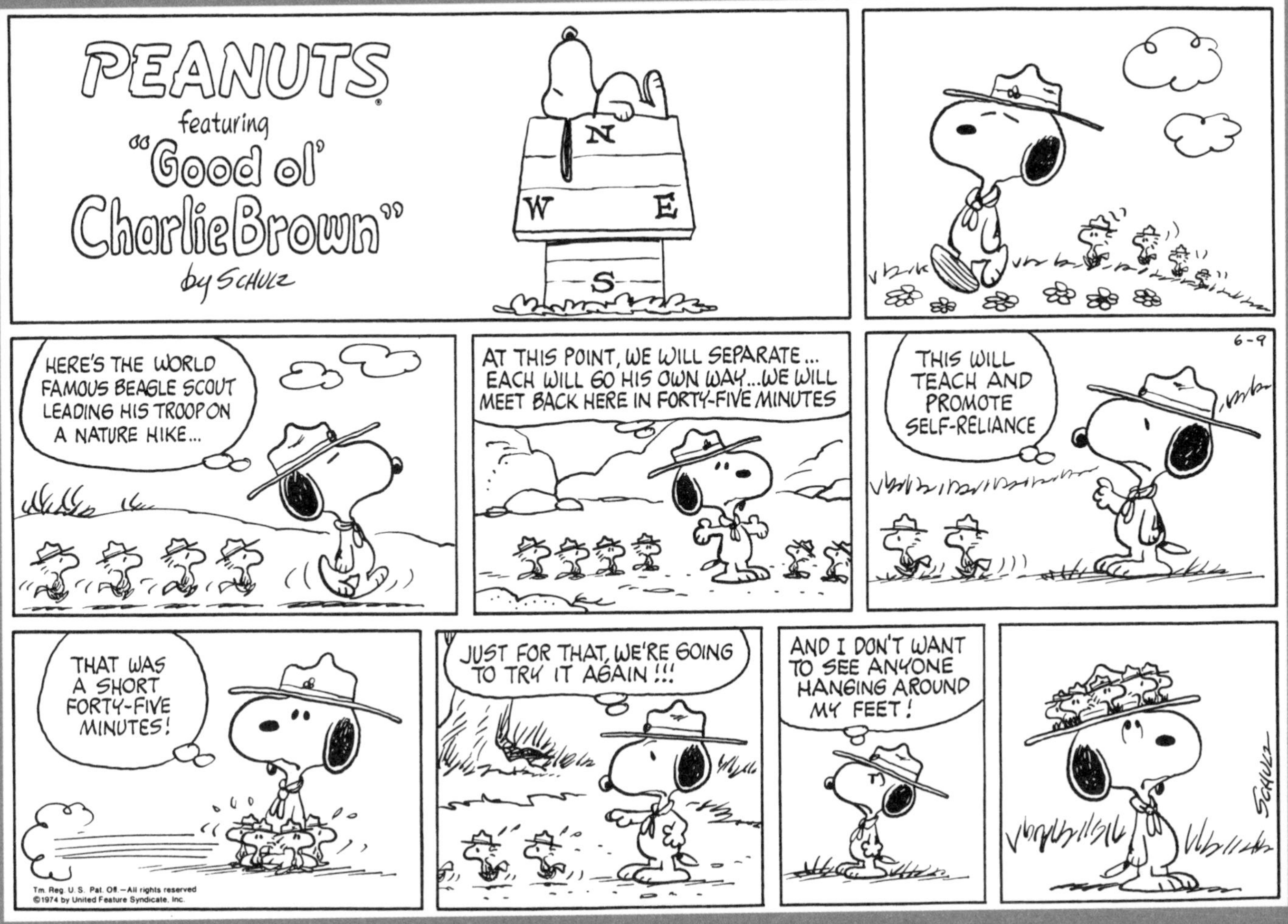

PEANUTS
featuring "Good ol' Charlie Brown"
by SCHULZ
N
W
E
S
HERE'S THE WORLD FAMOUS BEAGLE SCOUT LEADING HIS TROOP ON A NATURE HIKE...
AT THIS POINT, WE WILL SEPARATE... EACH WILL GO HIS OWN WAY...WE WILL MEET BACK HERE IN FORTY-FIVE MINUTES
6-9
THIS WILL TEACH AND PROMOTE SELF-RELIANCE
THAT WAS A SHORT FORTY-FIVE MINUTES!
JUST FOR THAT, WE'RE GOING TO TRY IT AGAIN!!!
AND I DON'T WANT TO SEE ANYONE HANGING AROUND MY FEET!
SCHULZ

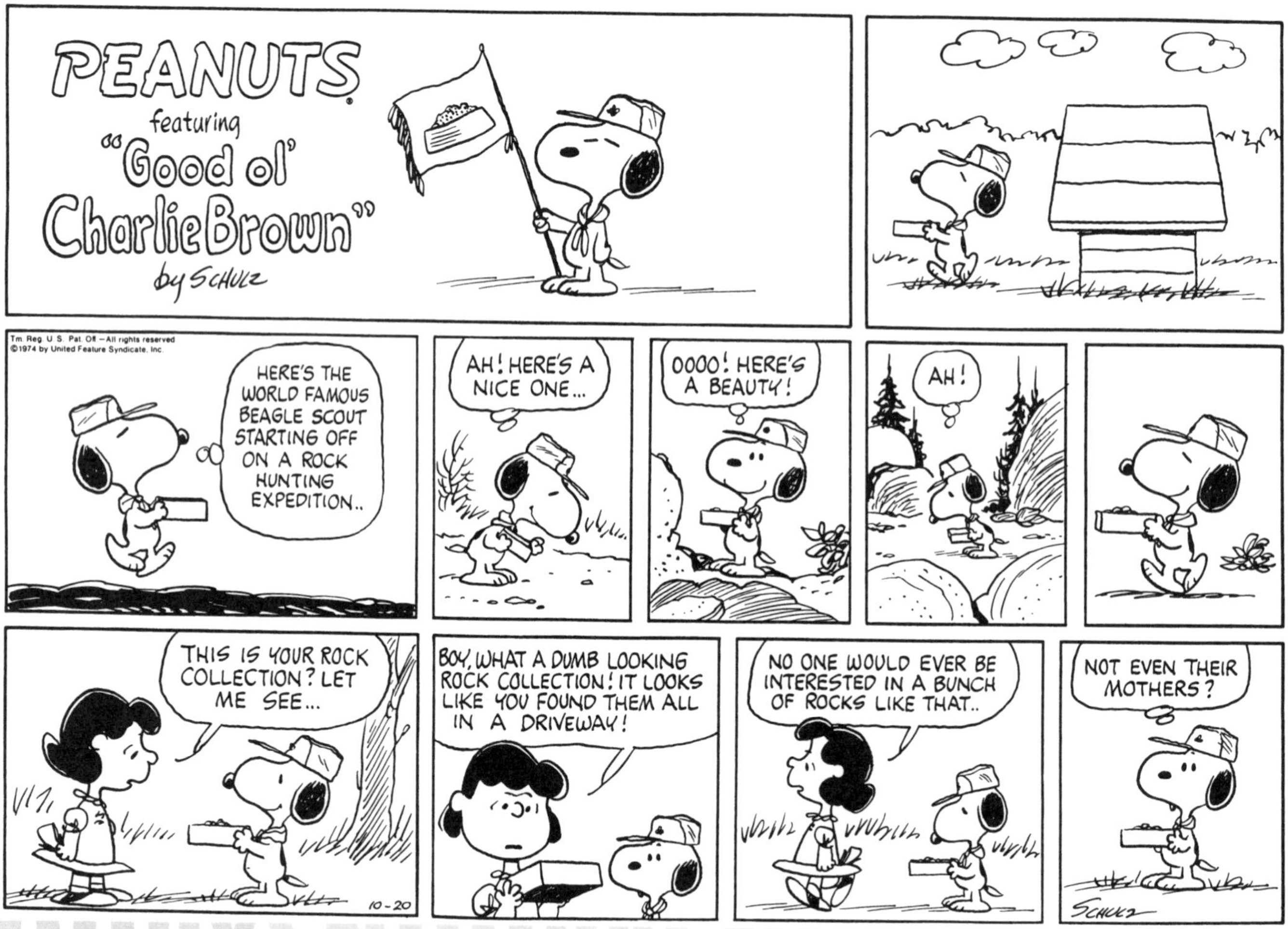
PEANUTS
featuring "Good ol' Charlie Brown"
by SCHULZ
Tm. Reg. U.S. Pat. Off.—All rights reserved
©1974 by United Feature Syndicate, Inc.
HERE'S THE WORLD FAMOUS BEAGLE SCOUT STARTING OFF ON A ROCK HUNTING EXPEDITION..
AH! HERE'S A NICE ONE...
OOOO! HERE'S A BEAUTY!
AH!
THIS IS YOUR ROCK COLLECTION? LET ME SEE...
10-20
BOY, WHAT A DUMB LOOKING ROCK COLLECTION! IT LOOKS LIKE YOU FOUND THEM ALL IN A DRIVEWAY!
NO ONE WOULD EVER BE INTERESTED IN A BUNCH OF ROCKS LIKE THAT..
NOT EVEN THEIR MOTHERS?
SCHULZ

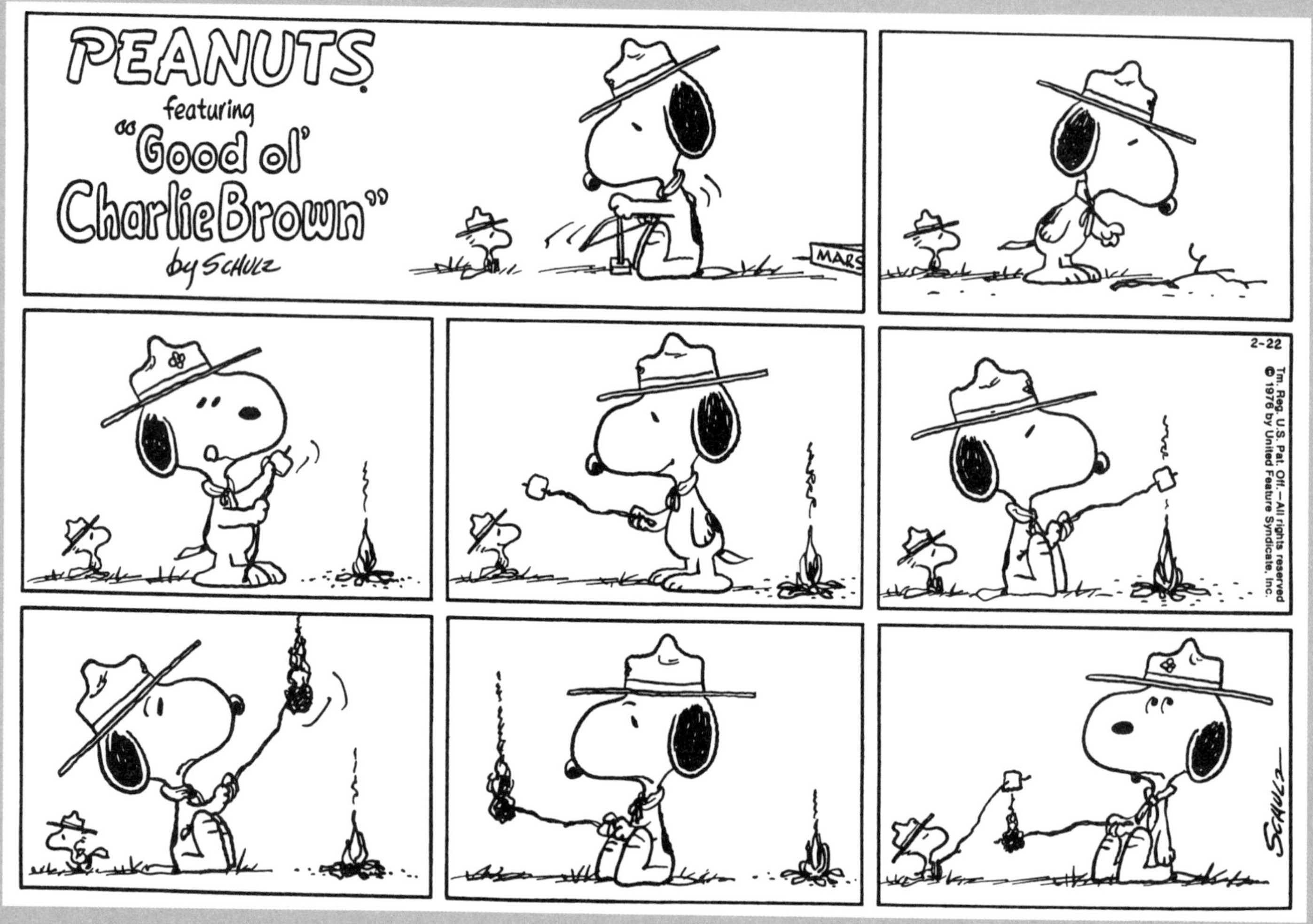
PEANUTS
featuring
"Good ol' CharlieBrown"
by SCHULZ
MARS
2-22
Tm. Reg. U.S. Pat. Off.—All rights reserved
© 1976 by United Feature Syndicate, Inc.
SCHULZ

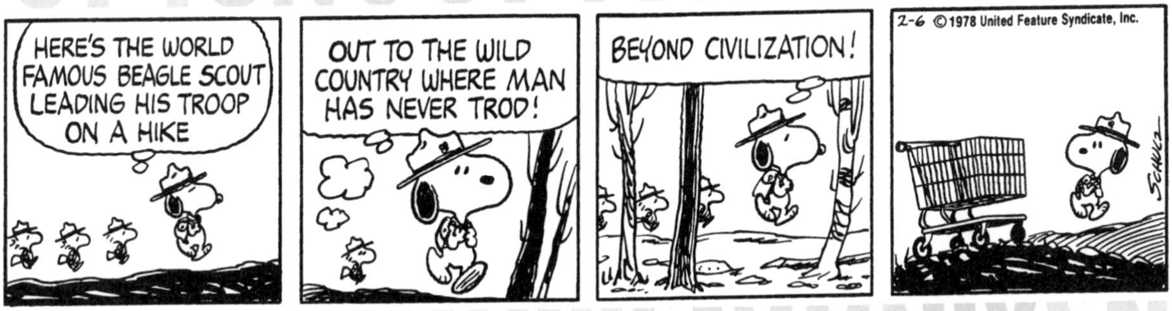
HERE'S THE WORLD FAMOUS BEAGLE SCOUT LEADING HIS TROOP ON A HIKE
OUT TO THE WILD COUNTRY WHERE MAN HAS NEVER TROD!
BEYOND CIVILIZATION!
2-6 © 1978 United Feature Syndicate, Inc.
SCHULZ

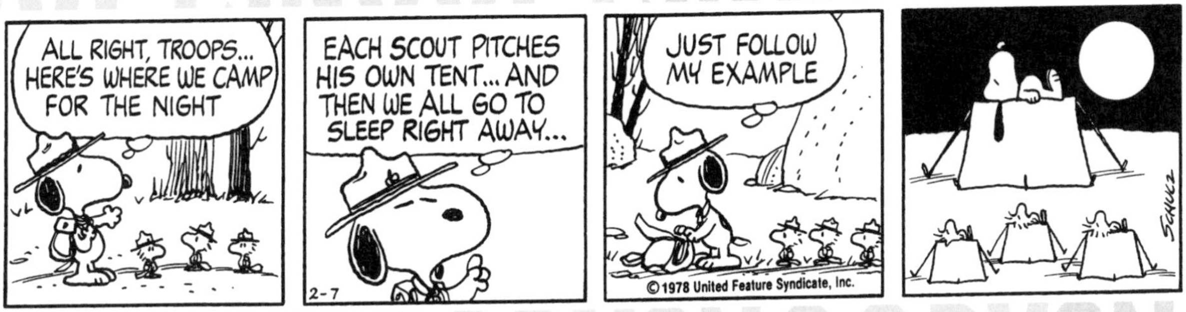
ALL RIGHT, TROOPS... HERE'S WHERE WE CAMP FOR THE NIGHT
EACH SCOUT PITCHES HIS OWN TENT... AND THEN WE ALL GO TO SLEEP RIGHT AWAY...
2-7
JUST FOLLOW MY EXAMPLE
© 1978 United Feature Syndicate, Inc.
SCHULZ

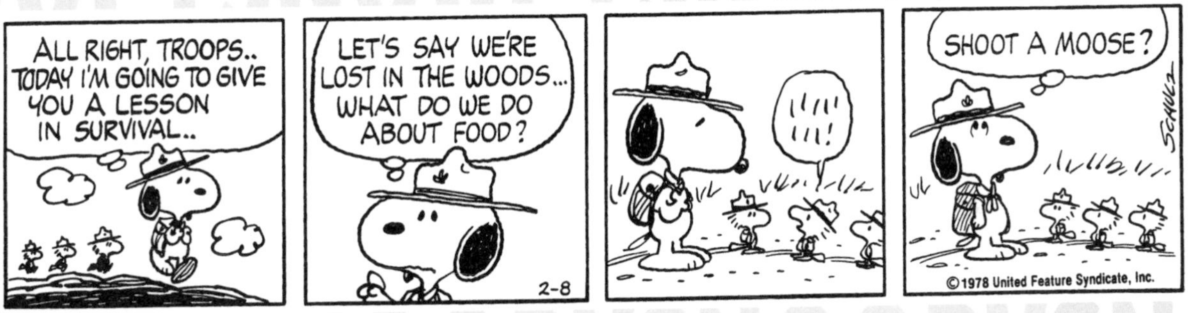
ALL RIGHT, TROOPS.. TODAY I'M GOING TO GIVE YOU A LESSON IN SURVIVAL..
LET'S SAY WE'RE LOST IN THE WOODS... WHAT DO WE DO ABOUT FOOD?
2-8
SHOOT A MOOSE?
SCHULZ
© 1978 United Feature Syndicate, Inc.

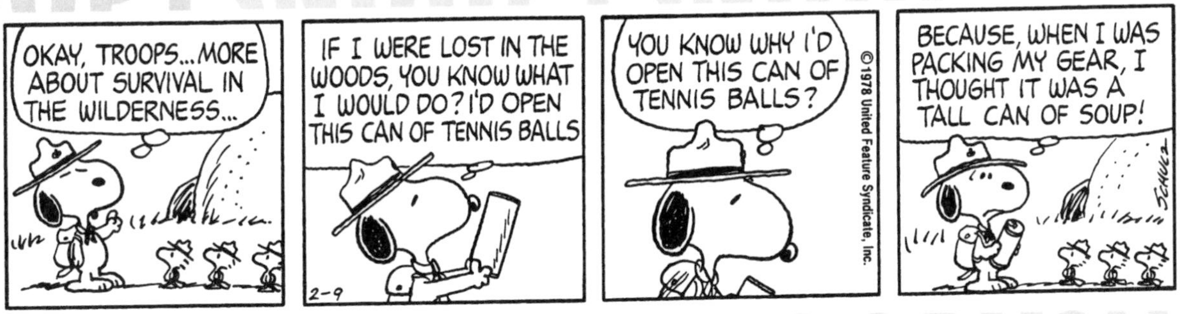
OKAY, TROOPS... MORE ABOUT SURVIVAL IN THE WILDERNESS...
IF I WERE LOST IN THE WOODS, YOU KNOW WHAT I WOULD DO? I'D OPEN THIS CAN OF TENNIS BALLS
2-9
YOU KNOW WHY I'D OPEN THIS CAN OF TENNIS BALLS?
© 1978 United Feature Syndicate, Inc.
BECAUSE, WHEN I WAS PACKING MY GEAR, I THOUGHT IT WAS A TALL CAN OF SOUP!
SCHULZ

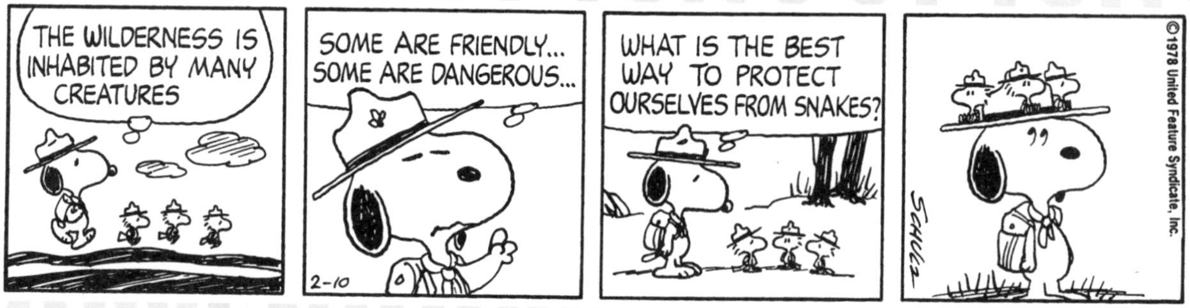
THE WILDERNESS IS INHABITED BY MANY CREATURES
SOME ARE FRIENDLY... SOME ARE DANGEROUS...
2-10
WHAT IS THE BEST WAY TO PROTECT OURSELVES FROM SNAKES?
SCHULZ
© 1978 United Feature Syndicate, Inc.

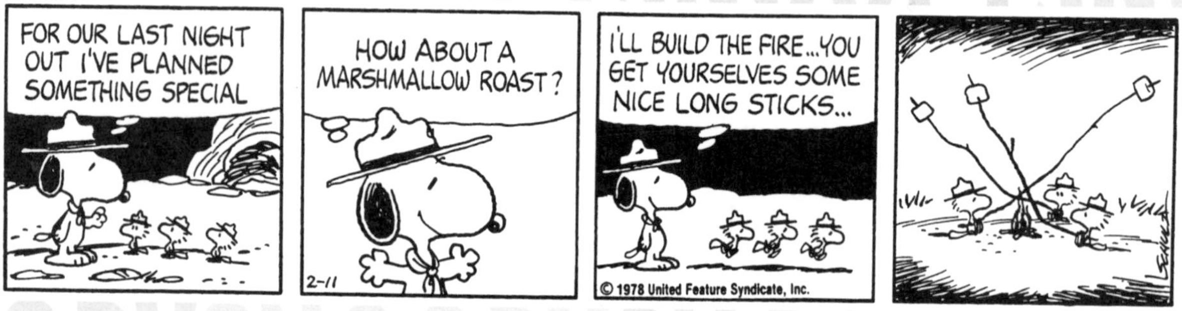
FOR OUR LAST NIGHT OUT I'VE PLANNED SOMETHING SPECIAL
HOW ABOUT A MARSHMALLOW ROAST?
2-11
I'LL BUILD THE FIRE...YOU GET YOURSELVES SOME NICE LONG STICKS...
© 1978 United Feature Syndicate, Inc.
SCHULZ

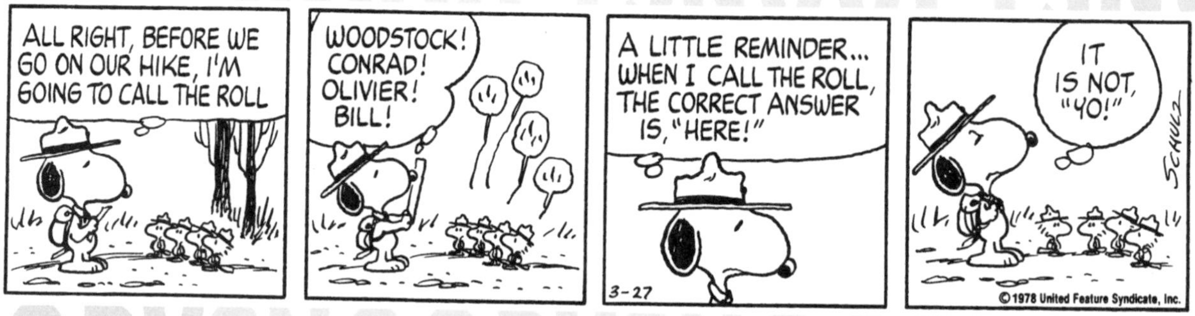
ALL RIGHT, BEFORE WE GO ON OUR HIKE, I'M GOING TO CALL THE ROLL
WOODSTOCK! CONRAD! OLIVIER! BILL!
A LITTLE REMINDER... WHEN I CALL THE ROLL, THE CORRECT ANSWER IS, "HERE!"
3-27
IT IS NOT, "YO!"
SCHULZ
© 1978 United Feature Syndicate, Inc.

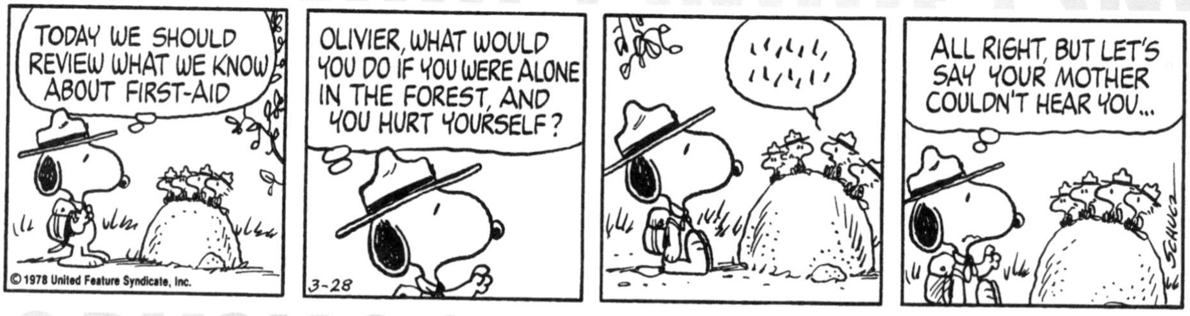
TODAY WE SHOULD REVIEW WHAT WE KNOW ABOUT FIRST-AID
© 1978 United Feature Syndicate, Inc.
OLIVIER, WHAT WOULD YOU DO IF YOU WERE ALONE IN THE FOREST, AND YOU HURT YOURSELF?
3-28
ALL RIGHT, BUT LET'S SAY YOUR MOTHER COULDN'T HEAR YOU...
SCHULZ

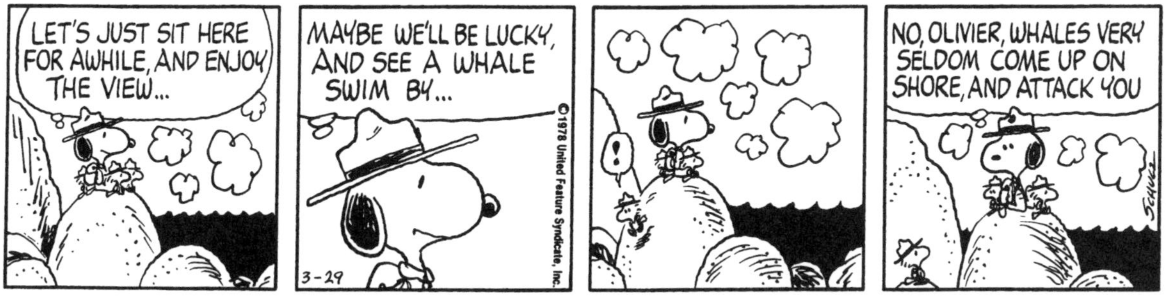
LET'S JUST SIT HERE FOR AWHILE, AND ENJOY THE VIEW...
MAYBE WE'LL BE LUCKY, AND SEE A WHALE SWIM BY...
© 1978 United Feature Syndicate, Inc.
3-29
!
NO, OLIVIER, WHALES VERY SELDOM COME UP ON SHORE, AND ATTACK YOU
SCHULZ

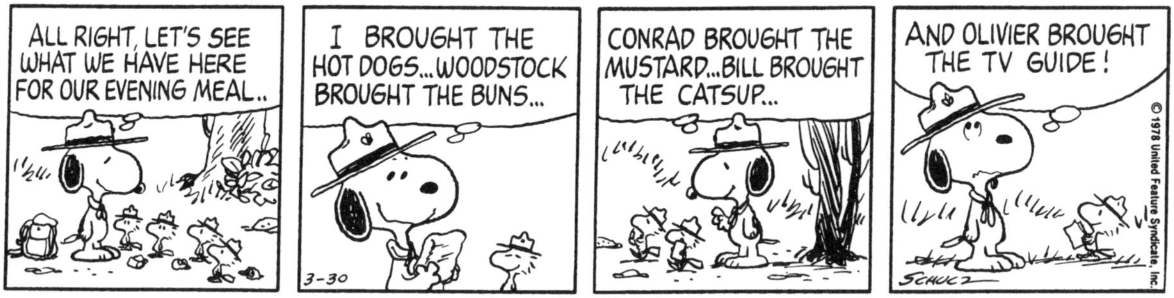
ALL RIGHT, LET'S SEE WHAT WE HAVE HERE FOR OUR EVENING MEAL..
I BROUGHT THE HOT DOGS...WOODSTOCK BROUGHT THE BUNS...
3-30
CONRAD BROUGHT THE MUSTARD...BILL BROUGHT THE CATSUP...
AND OLIVIER BROUGHT THE TV GUIDE!
© 1978 United Feature Syndicate, Inc.
SCHULZ

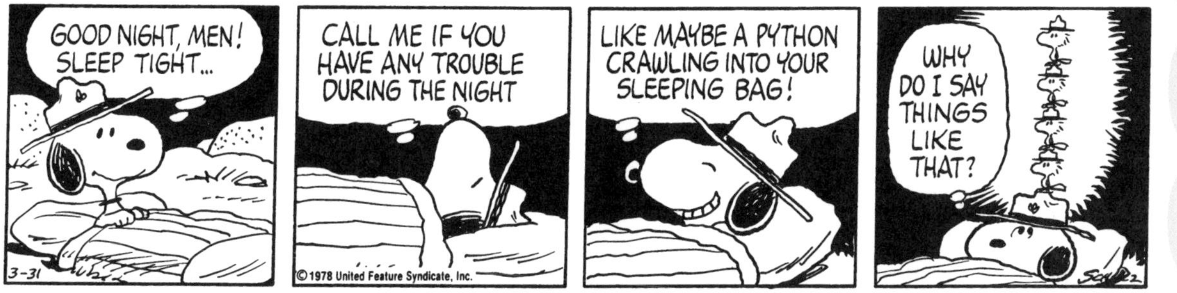
GOOD NIGHT, MEN! SLEEP TIGHT...
3-31
CALL ME IF YOU HAVE ANY TROUBLE DURING THE NIGHT
© 1978 United Feature Syndicate, Inc.
LIKE MAYBE A PYTHON CRAWLING INTO YOUR SLEEPING BAG!
WHY DO I SAY THINGS LIKE THAT?
SCHULZ

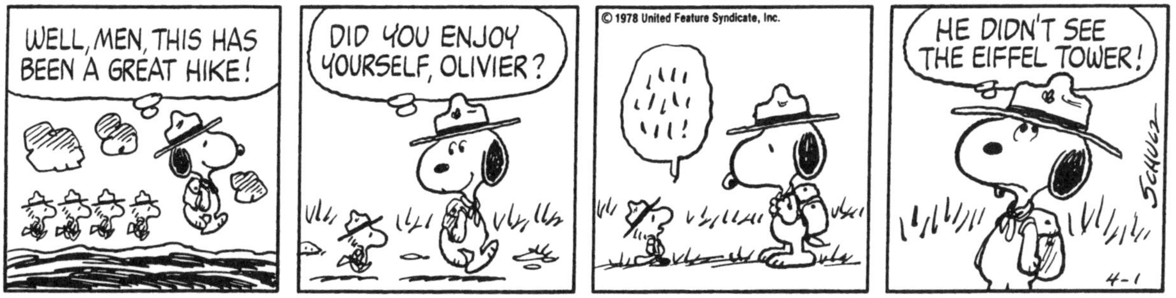
WELL, MEN, THIS HAS BEEN A GREAT HIKE!
DID YOU ENJOY YOURSELF, OLIVIER?
© 1978 United Feature Syndicate, Inc.
HE DIDN'T SEE THE EIFFEL TOWER!
SCHULZ
4-1

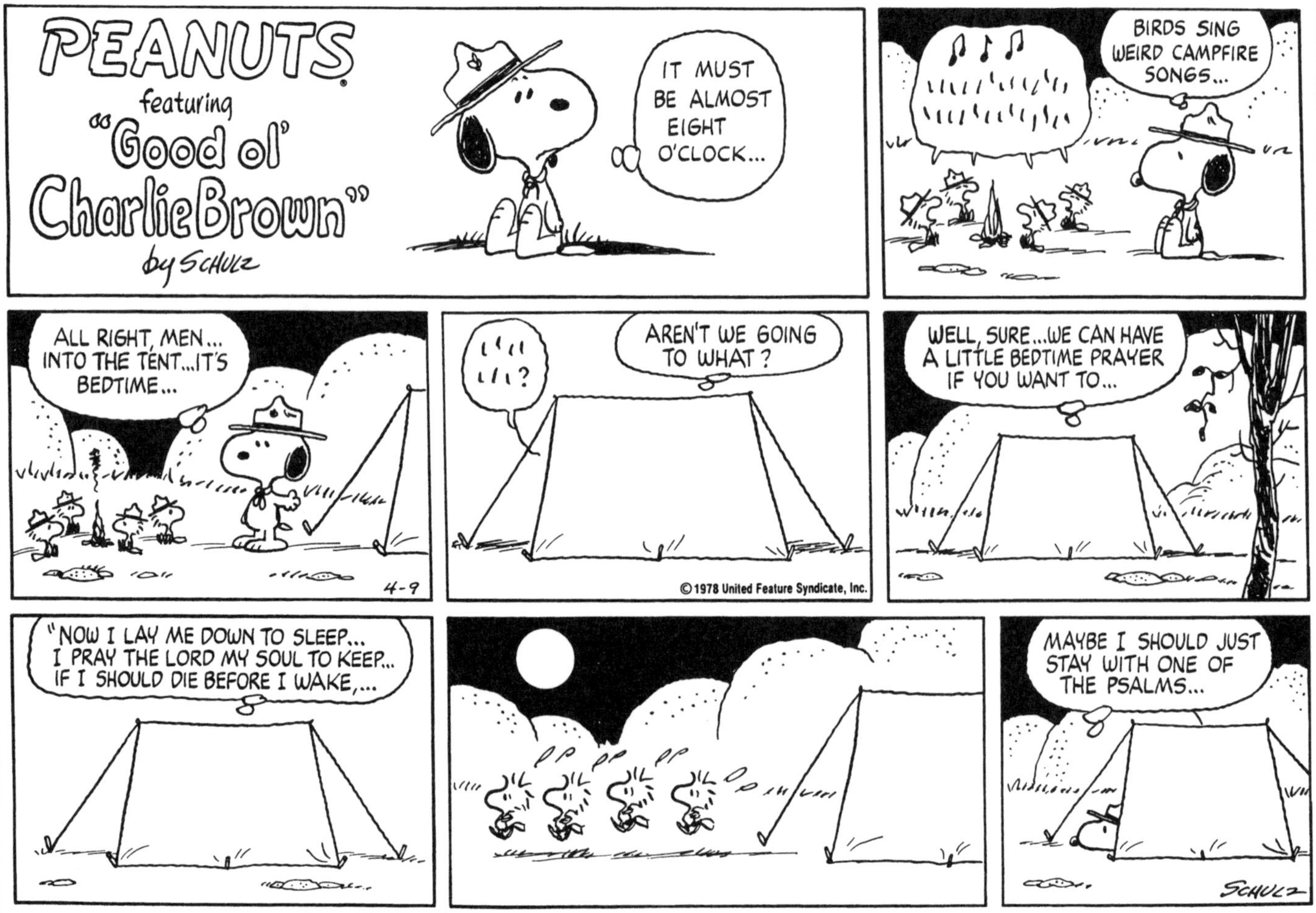
PEANUTS
featuring "Good ol' Charlie Brown"
by SCHULZ
IT MUST BE ALMOST EIGHT O'CLOCK...
BIRDS SING WEIRD CAMPFIRE SONGS...
ALL RIGHT, MEN... INTO THE TENT...IT'S BEDTIME...
4-9
?
AREN'T WE GOING TO WHAT ?
© 1978 United Feature Syndicate, Inc.
WELL, SURE...WE CAN HAVE A LITTLE BEDTIME PRAYER IF YOU WANT TO...
"NOW I LAY ME DOWN TO SLEEP... I PRAY THE LORD MY SOUL TO KEEP... IF I SHOULD DIE BEFORE I WAKE,...
MAYBE I SHOULD JUST STAY WITH ONE OF THE PSALMS...
SCHULZ

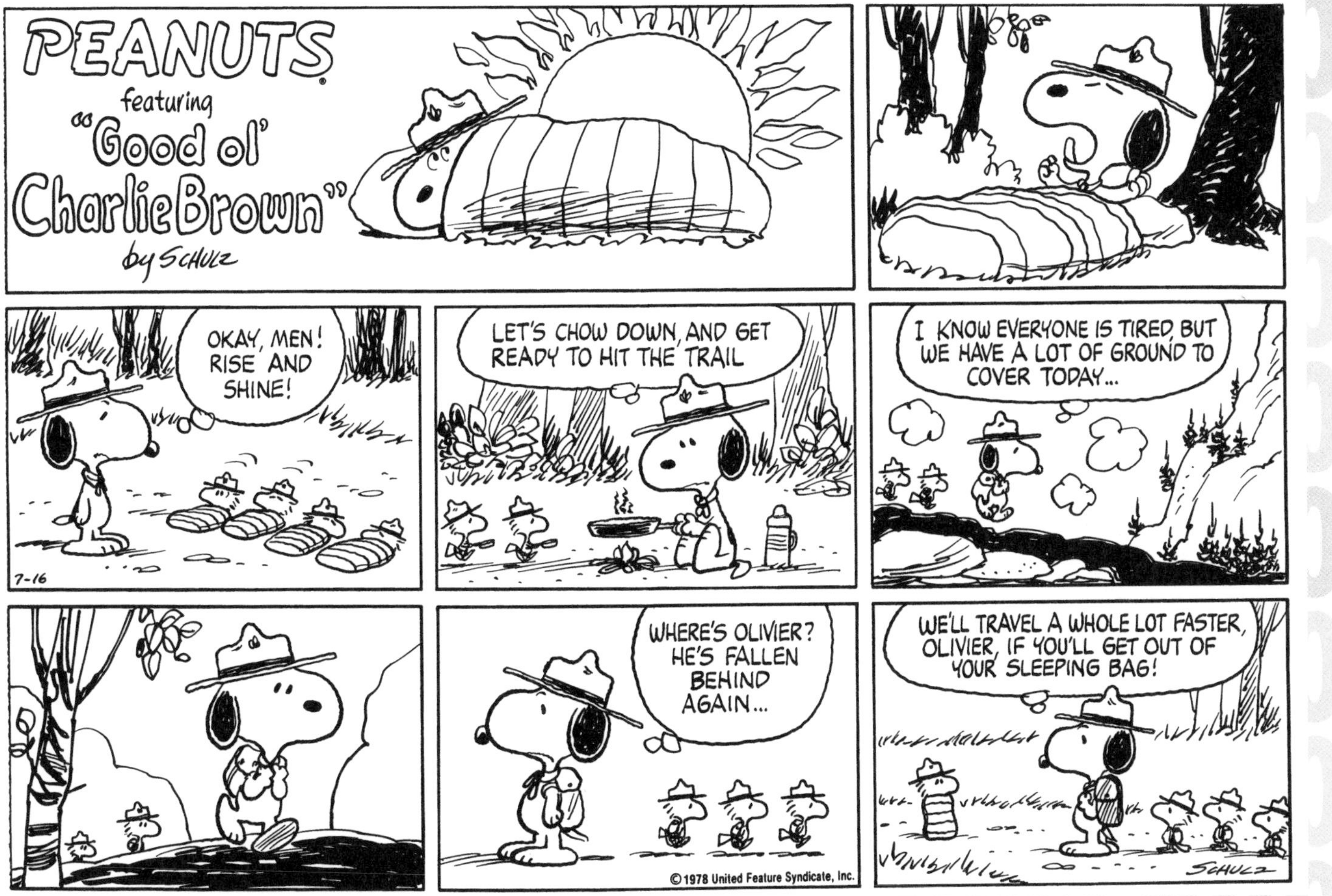
PEANUTS
featuring
"Good ol' CharlieBrown"
by SCHULZ
OKAY, MEN! RISE AND SHINE!
7-16
LET'S CHOW DOWN, AND GET READY TO HIT THE TRAIL
I KNOW EVERYONE IS TIRED, BUT WE HAVE A LOT OF GROUND TO COVER TODAY...
WHERE'S OLIVIER? HE'S FALLEN BEHIND AGAIN...
©1978 United Feature Syndicate, Inc.
WE'LL TRAVEL A WHOLE LOT FASTER, OLIVIER, IF YOU'LL GET OUT OF YOUR SLEEPING BAG!
SCHULZ

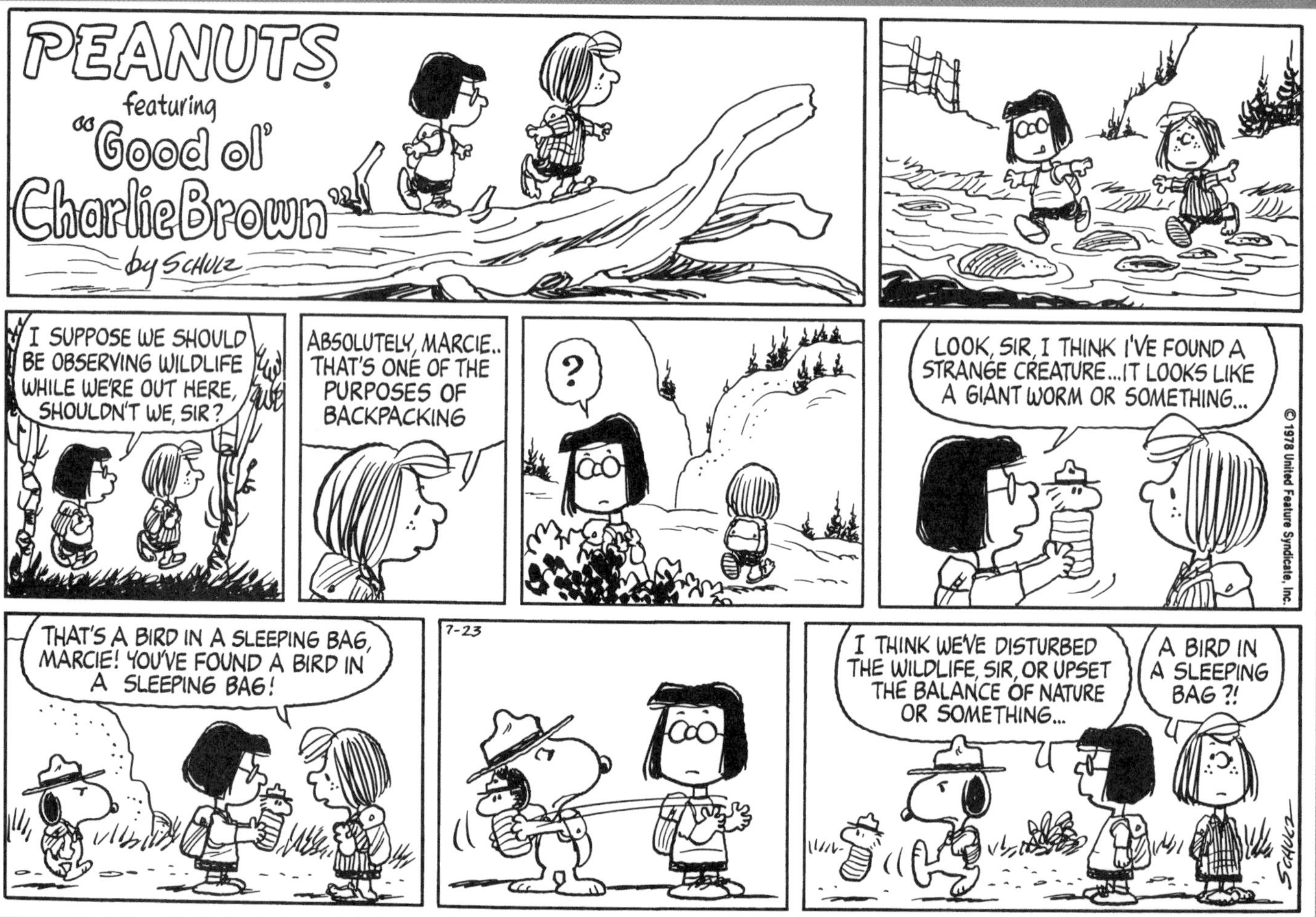
PEANUTS
featuring "Good ol' Charlie Brown"
by SCHULZ
I SUPPOSE WE SHOULD BE OBSERVING WILDLIFE WHILE WE'RE OUT HERE, SHOULDN'T WE, SIR?
ABSOLUTELY, MARCIE.. THAT'S ONE OF THE PURPOSES OF BACKPACKING
?
LOOK, SIR, I THINK I'VE FOUND A STRANGE CREATURE...IT LOOKS LIKE A GIANT WORM OR SOMETHING...
© 1978 United Feature Syndicate, Inc.
THAT'S A BIRD IN A SLEEPING BAG, MARCIE! YOU'VE FOUND A BIRD IN A SLEEPING BAG!
7-23
I THINK WE'VE DISTURBED THE WILDLIFE, SIR, OR UPSET THE BALANCE OF NATURE OR SOMETHING...
A BIRD IN A SLEEPING BAG ?!
SCHULZ

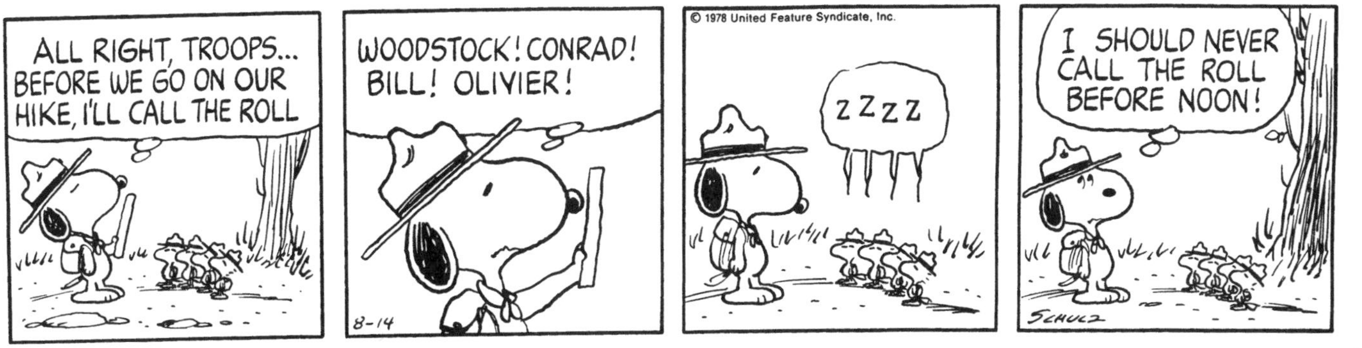
ALL RIGHT, TROOPS... BEFORE WE GO ON OUR HIKE, I'LL CALL THE ROLL
WOODSTOCK! CONRAD! BILL! OLIVIER!
8-14
© 1978 United Feature Syndicate, Inc.
ZZZZ
I SHOULD NEVER CALL THE ROLL BEFORE NOON!
SCHULZ

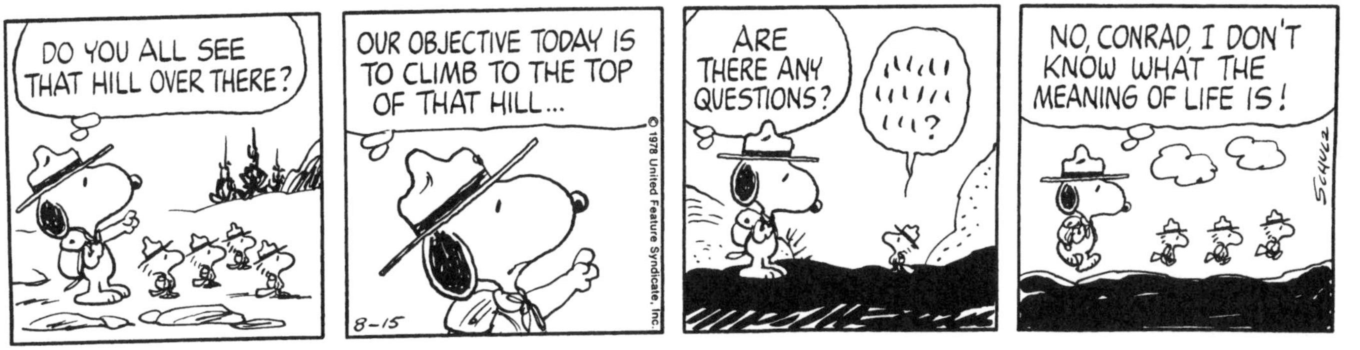
DO YOU ALL SEE THAT HILL OVER THERE?
OUR OBJECTIVE TODAY IS TO CLIMB TO THE TOP OF THAT HILL...
8-15
© 1978 United Feature Syndicate, Inc.
ARE THERE ANY QUESTIONS?
NO, CONRAD, I DON'T KNOW WHAT THE MEANING OF LIFE IS!
SCHULZ

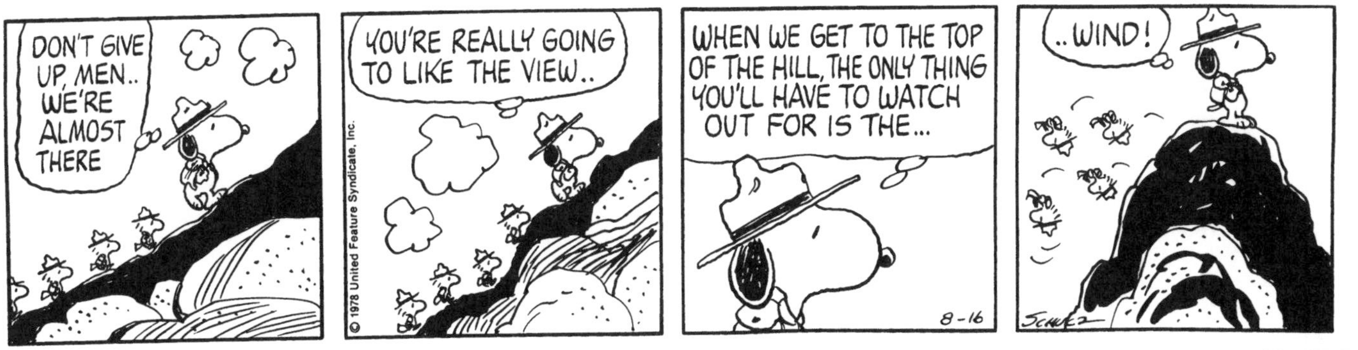
DON'T GIVE UP, MEN.. WE'RE ALMOST THERE
© 1978 United Feature Syndicate, Inc.
YOU'RE REALLY GOING TO LIKE THE VIEW..
WHEN WE GET TO THE TOP OF THE HILL, THE ONLY THING YOU'LL HAVE TO WATCH OUT FOR IS THE...
8-16
..WIND!
SCHULZ

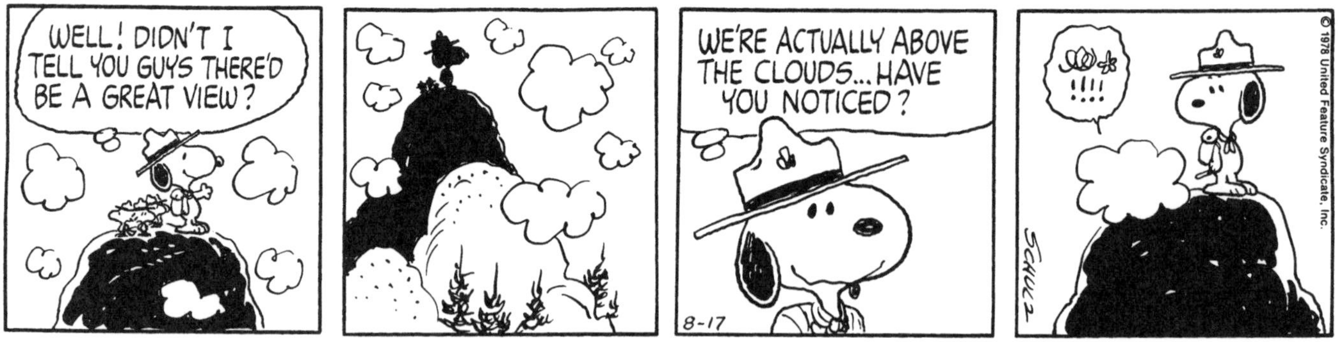
WELL! DIDN'T I TELL YOU GUYS THERE'D BE A GREAT VIEW?
WE'RE ACTUALLY ABOVE THE CLOUDS...HAVE YOU NOTICED?
8-17
SCHULZ
!!!!
© 1978 United Feature Syndicate, Inc.

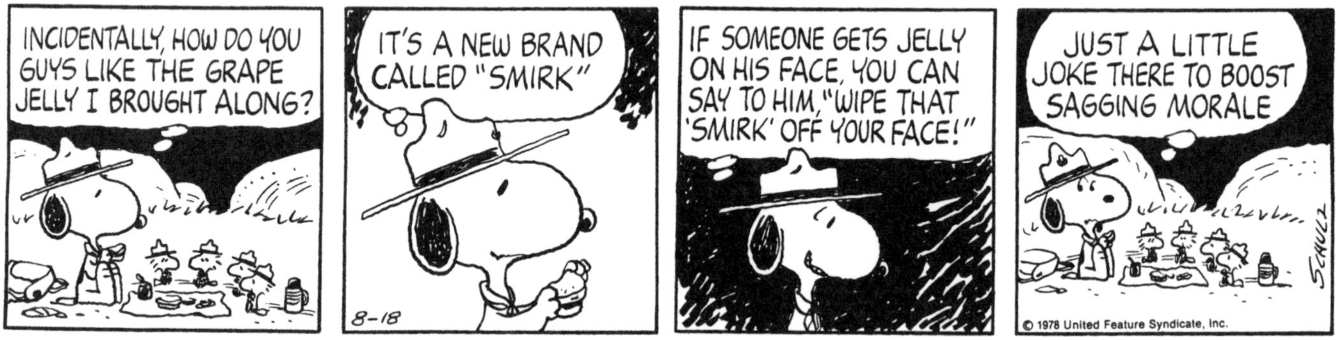
INCIDENTALLY, HOW DO YOU GUYS LIKE THE GRAPE JELLY I BROUGHT ALONG?
IT'S A NEW BRAND CALLED "SMIRK"
8-18
IF SOMEONE GETS JELLY ON HIS FACE, YOU CAN SAY TO HIM, "WIPE THAT 'SMIRK' OFF YOUR FACE!"
JUST A LITTLE JOKE THERE TO BOOST SAGGING MORALE
SCHULZ
© 1978 United Feature Syndicate, Inc.

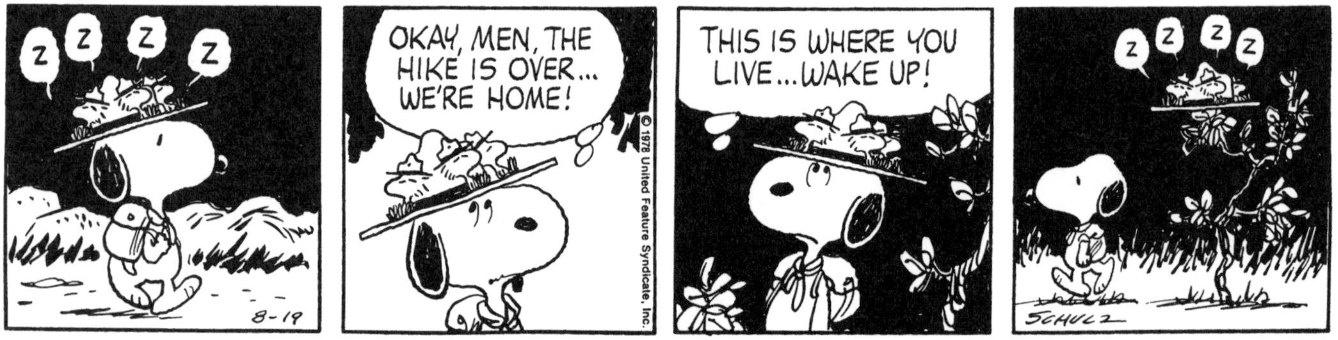
Z Z Z Z
8-19
OKAY, MEN, THE HIKE IS OVER... WE'RE HOME!
© 1978 United Feature Syndicate, Inc.
THIS IS WHERE YOU LIVE...WAKE UP!
Z Z Z Z
SCHULZ

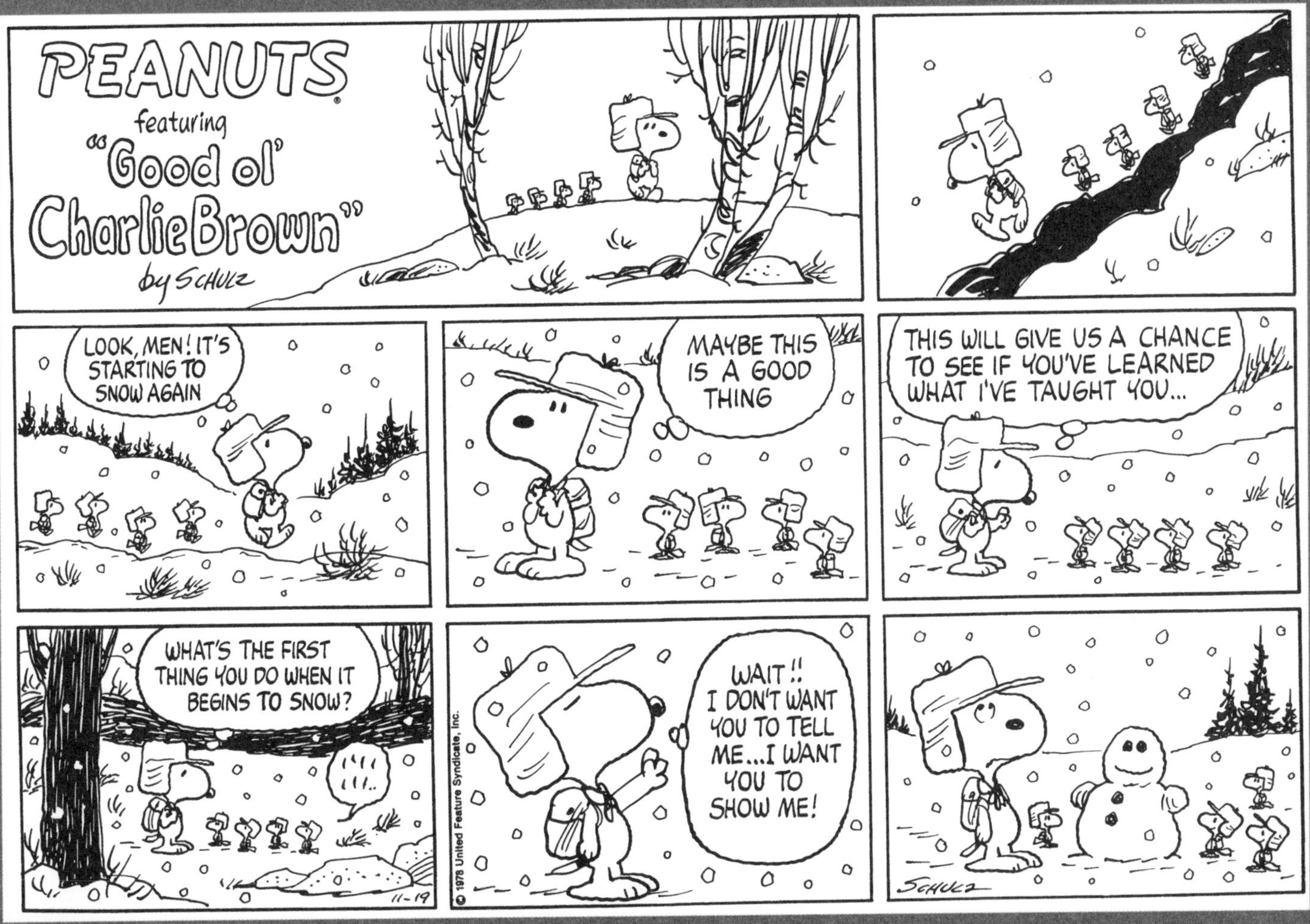
PEANUTS
featuring
"Good ol' CharlieBrown"
by SCHULZ
LOOK, MEN! IT'S STARTING TO SNOW AGAIN
MAYBE THIS IS A GOOD THING
THIS WILL GIVE US A CHANCE TO SEE IF YOU'VE LEARNED WHAT I'VE TAUGHT YOU...
WHAT'S THE FIRST THING YOU DO WHEN IT BEGINS TO SNOW?
11-19
© 1978 United Feature Syndicate, Inc.
WAIT!! I DON'T WANT YOU TO TELL ME...I WANT YOU TO SHOW ME!
SCHULZ

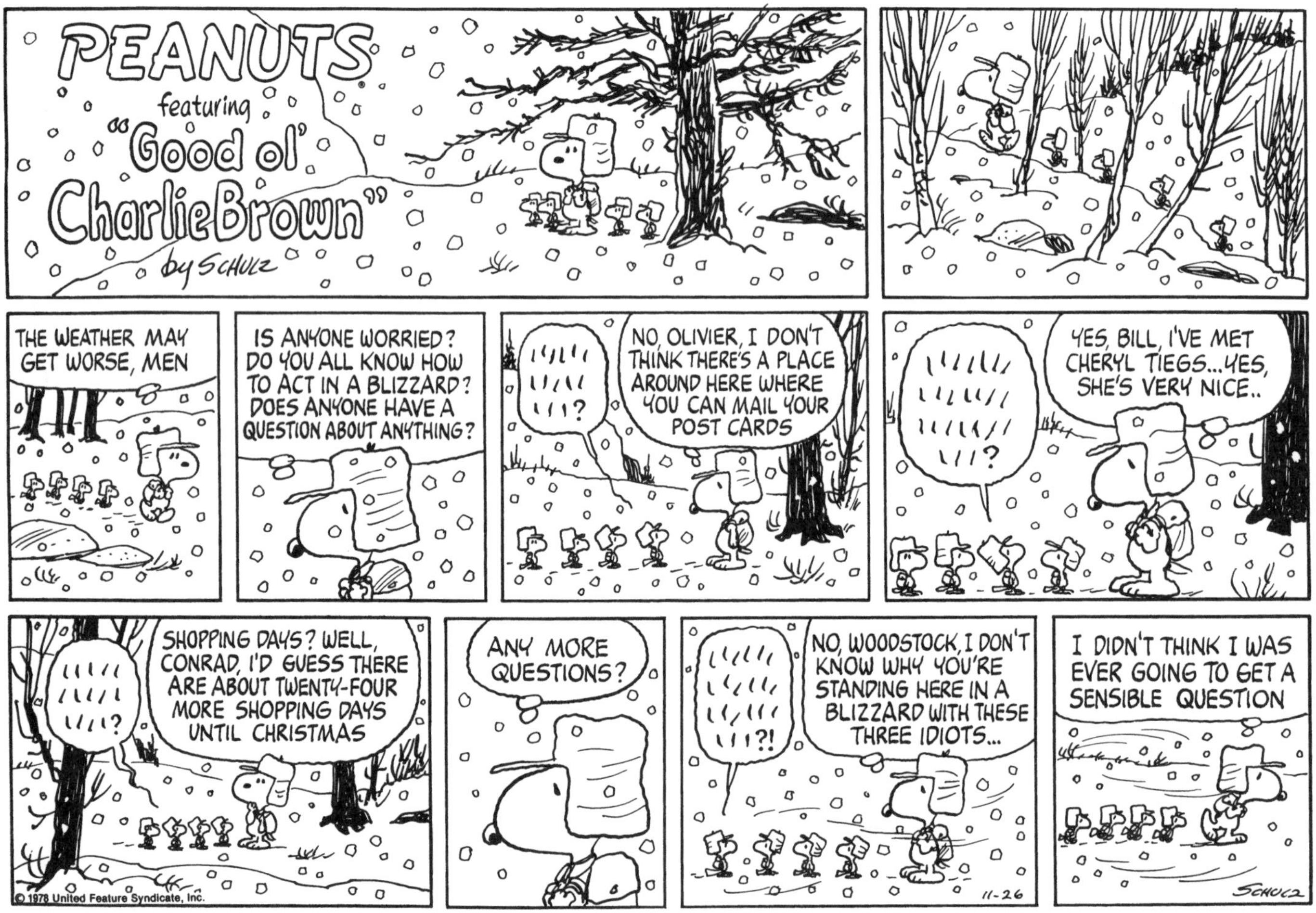
PEANUTS featuring "Good ol' Charlie Brown" by SCHULZ
THE WEATHER MAY GET WORSE, MEN
IS ANYONE WORRIED? DO YOU ALL KNOW HOW TO ACT IN A BLIZZARD? DOES ANYONE HAVE A QUESTION ABOUT ANYTHING?
NO, OLIVIER, I DON'T THINK THERE'S A PLACE AROUND HERE WHERE YOU CAN MAIL YOUR POST CARDS
YES, BILL, I'VE MET CHERYL TIEGS...YES, SHE'S VERY NICE..
SHOPPING DAYS? WELL, CONRAD, I'D GUESS THERE ARE ABOUT TWENTY-FOUR MORE SHOPPING DAYS UNTIL CHRISTMAS
ANY MORE QUESTIONS?
NO, WOODSTOCK, I DON'T KNOW WHY YOU'RE STANDING HERE IN A BLIZZARD WITH THESE THREE IDIOTS...
I DIDN'T THINK I WAS EVER GOING TO GET A SENSIBLE QUESTION
© 1978 United Feature Syndicate, Inc.
11-26
SCHULZ

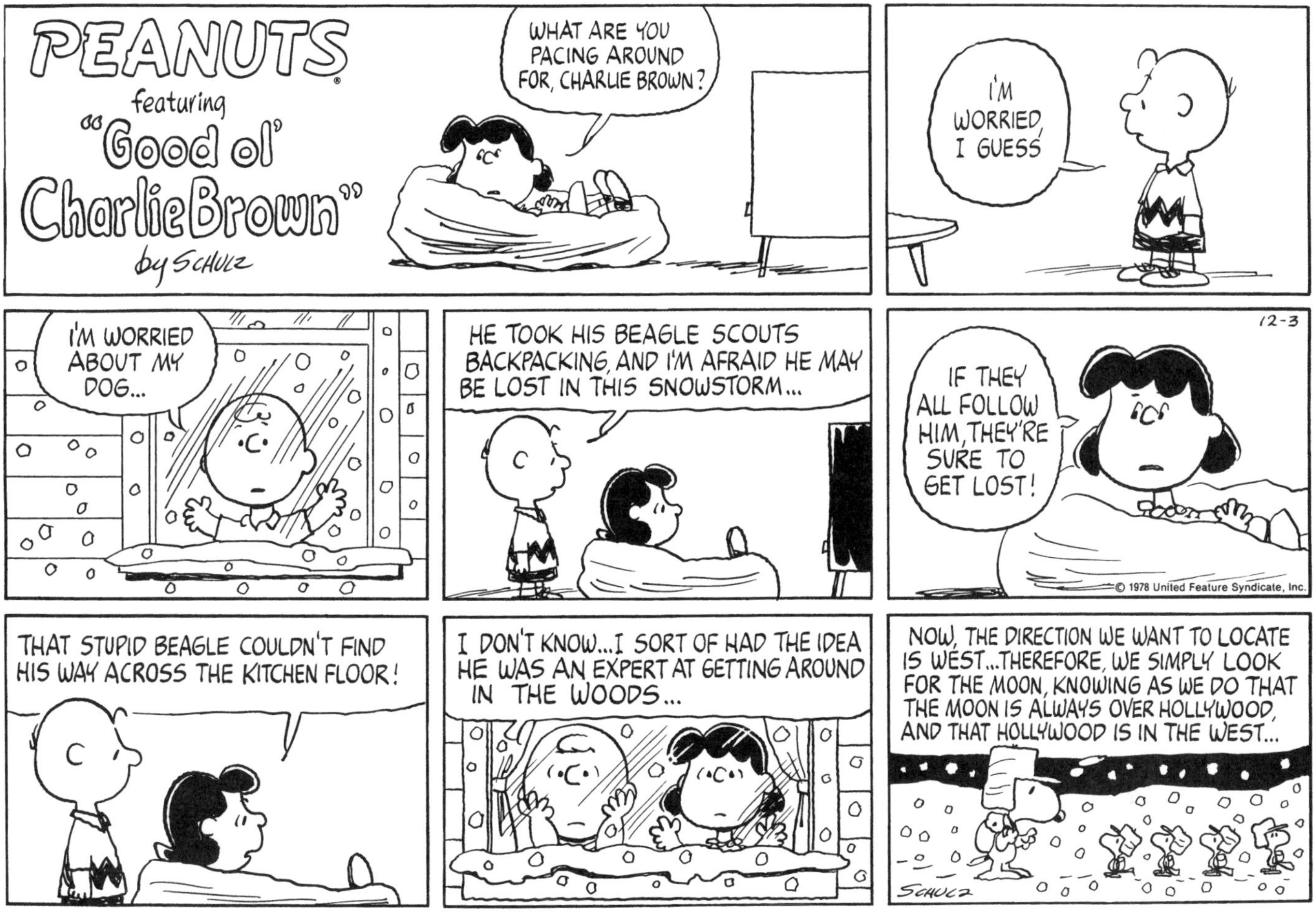
PEANUTS
featuring
"Good ol' Charlie Brown"
by SCHULZ
WHAT ARE YOU PACING AROUND FOR, CHARLIE BROWN?
I'M WORRIED, I GUESS
I'M WORRIED ABOUT MY DOG...
HE TOOK HIS BEAGLE SCOUTS BACKPACKING, AND I'M AFRAID HE MAY BE LOST IN THIS SNOWSTORM...
12-3
IF THEY ALL FOLLOW HIM, THEY'RE SURE TO GET LOST!
© 1978 United Feature Syndicate, Inc.
THAT STUPID BEAGLE COULDN'T FIND HIS WAY ACROSS THE KITCHEN FLOOR!
I DON'T KNOW...I SORT OF HAD THE IDEA HE WAS AN EXPERT AT GETTING AROUND IN THE WOODS...
NOW, THE DIRECTION WE WANT TO LOCATE IS WEST...THEREFORE, WE SIMPLY LOOK FOR THE MOON, KNOWING AS WE DO THAT THE MOON IS ALWAYS OVER HOLLYWOOD, AND THAT HOLLYWOOD IS IN THE WEST...
SCHULZ

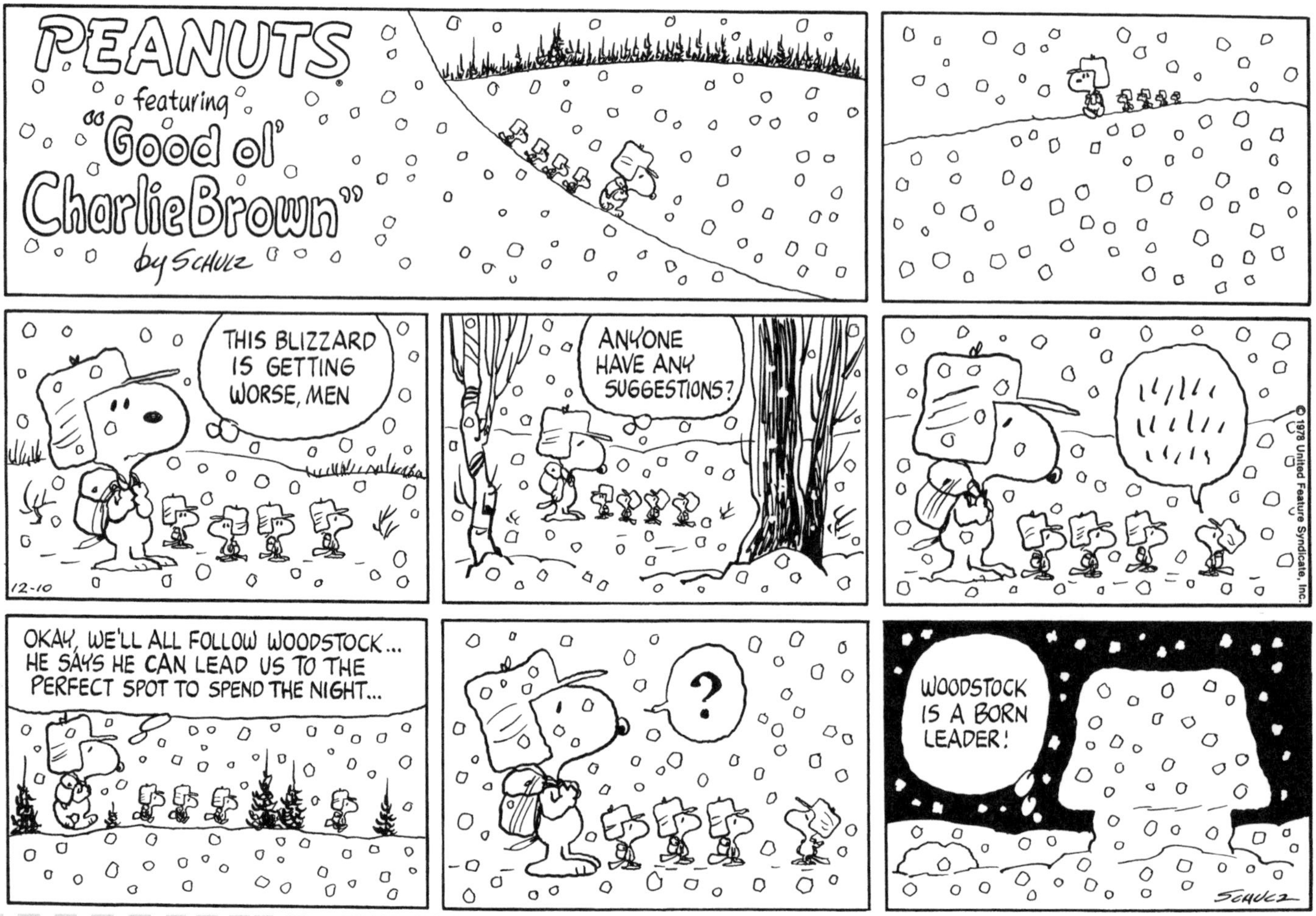
PEANUTS
featuring
"Good ol' Charlie Brown"
by SCHULZ
THIS BLIZZARD IS GETTING WORSE, MEN
12-10
ANYONE HAVE ANY SUGGESTIONS?
© 1978 United Feature Syndicate, Inc.
OKAY, WE'LL ALL FOLLOW WOODSTOCK... HE SAYS HE CAN LEAD US TO THE PERFECT SPOT TO SPEND THE NIGHT...
?
WOODSTOCK IS A BORN LEADER!
SCHULZ

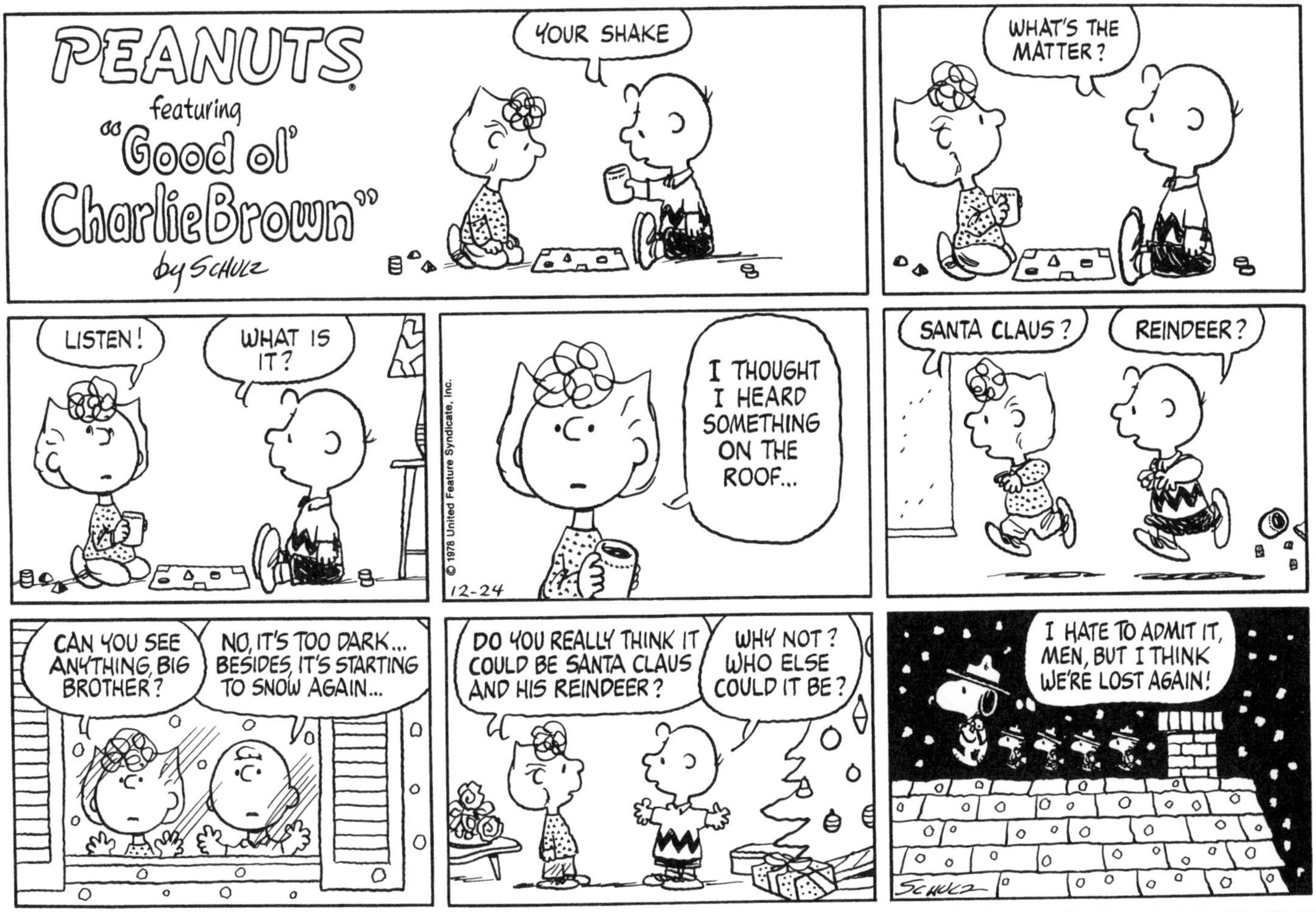
PEANUTS
featuring "Good ol' CharlieBrown"
by SCHULZ
YOUR SHAKE
WHAT'S THE MATTER?
LISTEN!
WHAT IS IT?
© 1978 United Feature Syndicate, Inc.
12-24
I THOUGHT I HEARD SOMETHING ON THE ROOF...
SANTA CLAUS?
REINDEER?
CAN YOU SEE ANYTHING, BIG BROTHER?
NO, IT'S TOO DARK... BESIDES, IT'S STARTING TO SNOW AGAIN...
DO YOU REALLY THINK IT COULD BE SANTA CLAUS AND HIS REINDEER?
WHY NOT? WHO ELSE COULD IT BE?
I HATE TO ADMIT IT, MEN, BUT I THINK WE'RE LOST AGAIN!
SCHULZ

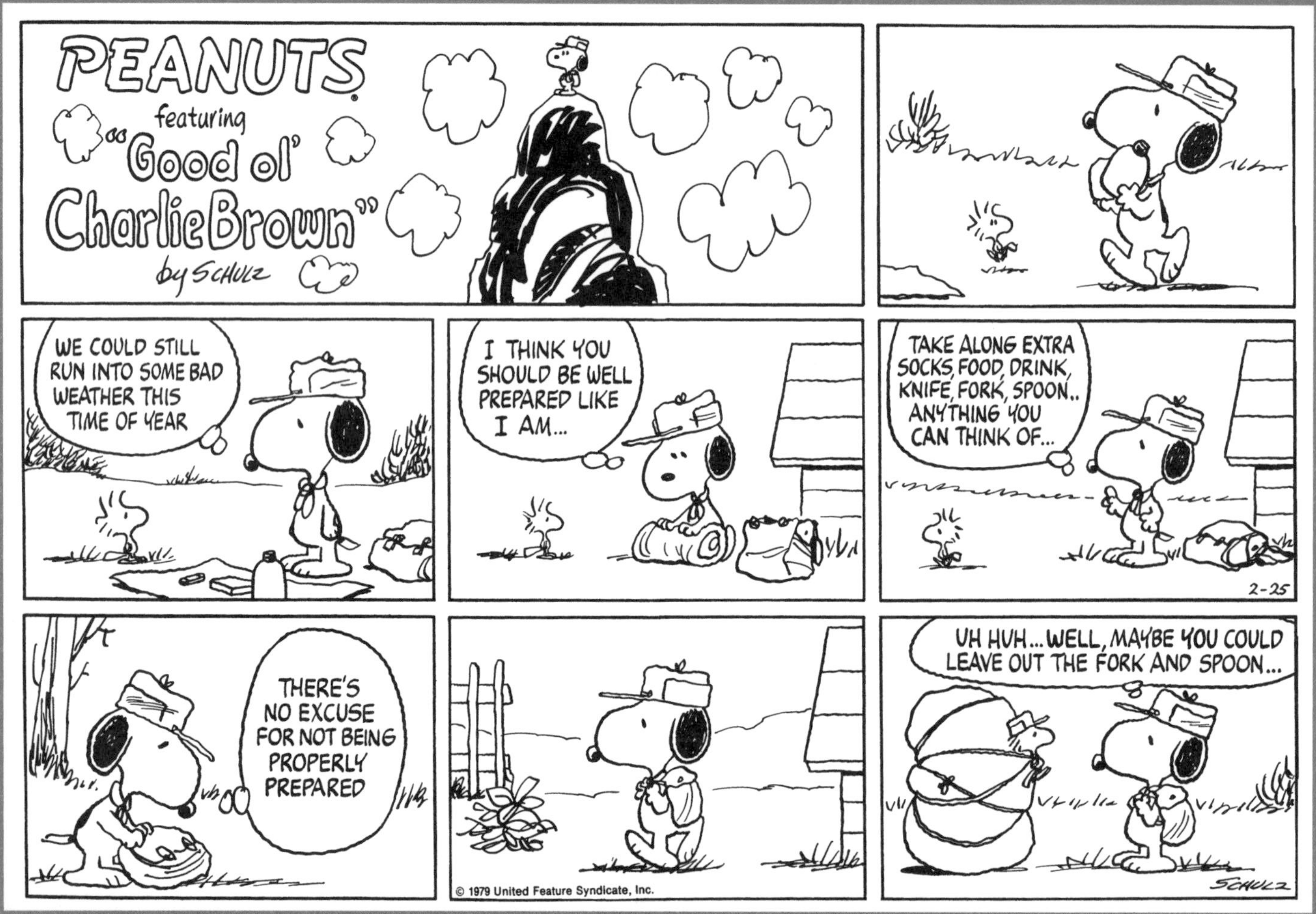
PEANUTS
featuring "Good ol' Charlie Brown"
by SCHULZ
WE COULD STILL RUN INTO SOME BAD WEATHER THIS TIME OF YEAR
I THINK YOU SHOULD BE WELL PREPARED LIKE I AM...
TAKE ALONG EXTRA SOCKS, FOOD, DRINK, KNIFE, FORK, SPOON.. ANYTHING YOU CAN THINK OF...
2-25
THERE'S NO EXCUSE FOR NOT BEING PROPERLY PREPARED
© 1979 United Feature Syndicate, Inc.
UH HUH... WELL, MAYBE YOU COULD LEAVE OUT THE FORK AND SPOON...
SCHULZ

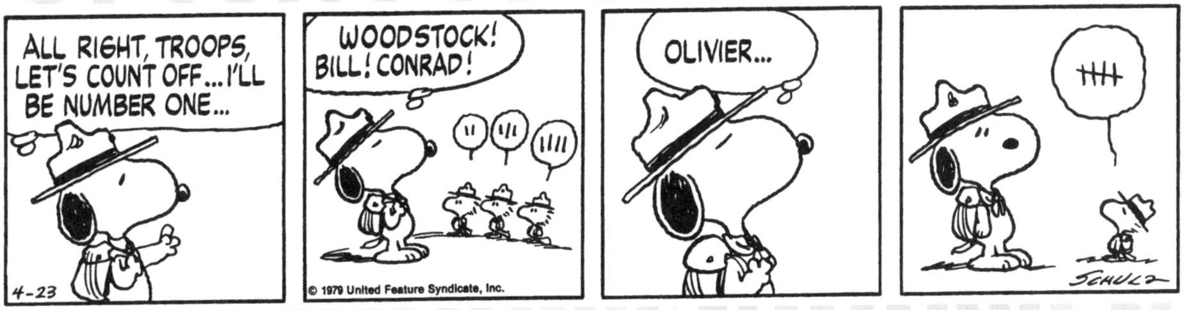
ALL RIGHT, TROOPS, LET'S COUNT OFF...I'LL BE NUMBER ONE...
4-23
WOODSTOCK! BILL! CONRAD!
© 1979 United Feature Syndicate, Inc.
OLIVIER...
SCHULZ

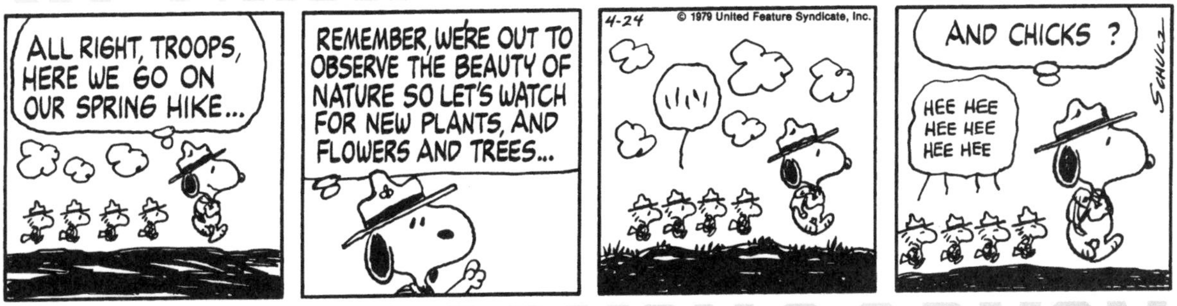
ALL RIGHT, TROOPS, HERE WE GO ON OUR SPRING HIKE...
REMEMBER, WE'RE OUT TO OBSERVE THE BEAUTY OF NATURE SO LET'S WATCH FOR NEW PLANTS, AND FLOWERS AND TREES...
4-24
© 1979 United Feature Syndicate, Inc.
AND CHICKS ?
HEE HEE HEE HEE HEE HEE
SCHULZ

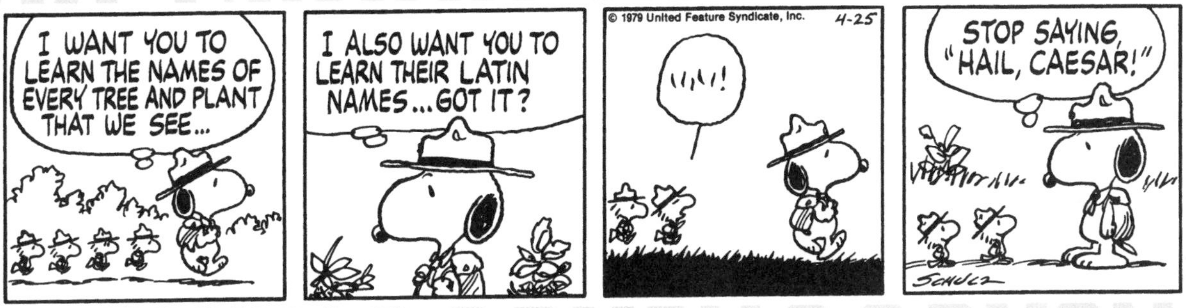
I WANT YOU TO LEARN THE NAMES OF EVERY TREE AND PLANT THAT WE SEE...
I ALSO WANT YOU TO LEARN THEIR LATIN NAMES...GOT IT?
© 1979 United Feature Syndicate, Inc.
4-25
STOP SAYING, "HAIL, CAESAR!"
SCHULZ

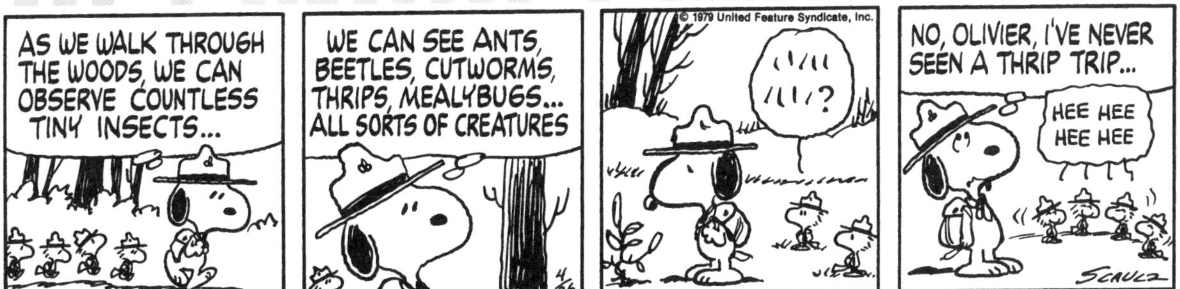
AS WE WALK THROUGH THE WOODS, WE CAN OBSERVE COUNTLESS TINY INSECTS...
WE CAN SEE ANTS, BEETLES, CUTWORMS, THRIPS, MEALYBUGS... ALL SORTS OF CREATURES
4/26
© 1979 United Feature Syndicate, Inc.
NO, OLIVIER, I'VE NEVER SEEN A THRIP TRIP...
HEE HEE HEE HEE
SCHULZ

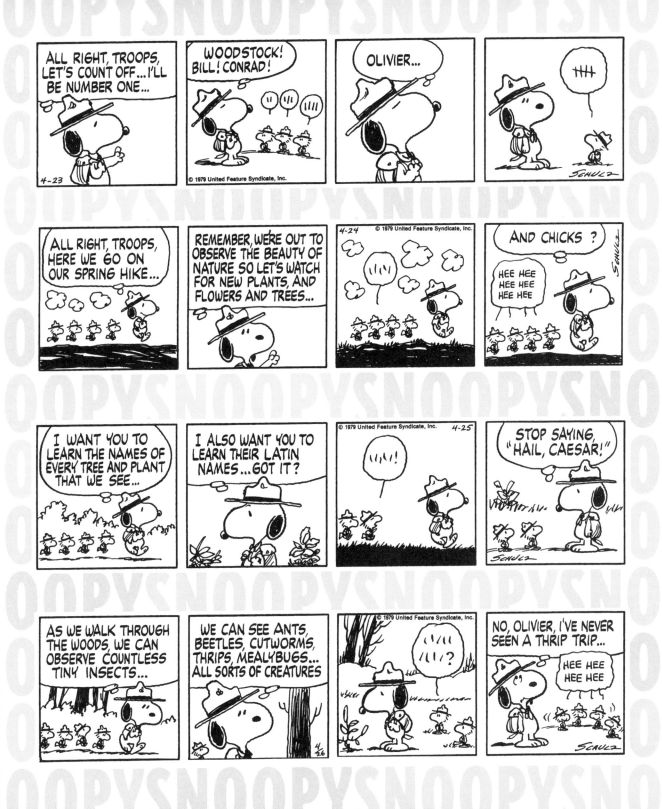

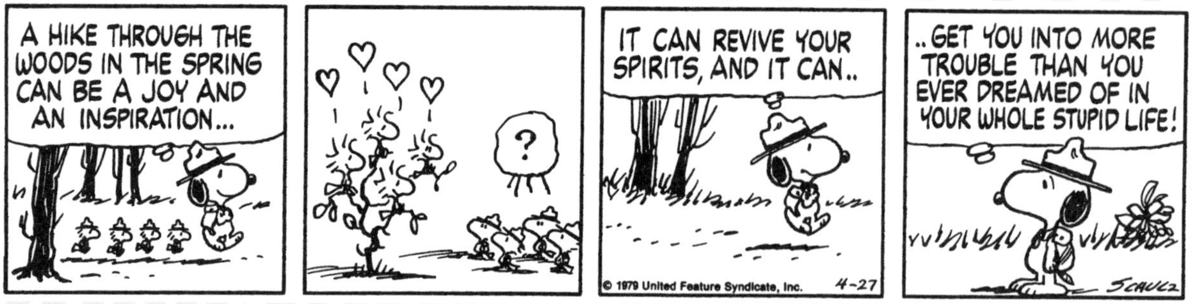
A HIKE THROUGH THE WOODS IN THE SPRING CAN BE A JOY AND AN INSPIRATION...
?
IT CAN REVIVE YOUR SPIRITS, AND IT CAN..
..GET YOU INTO MORE TROUBLE THAN YOU EVER DREAMED OF IN YOUR WHOLE STUPID LIFE!
© 1979 United Feature Syndicate, Inc.
4-27
SCHULZ

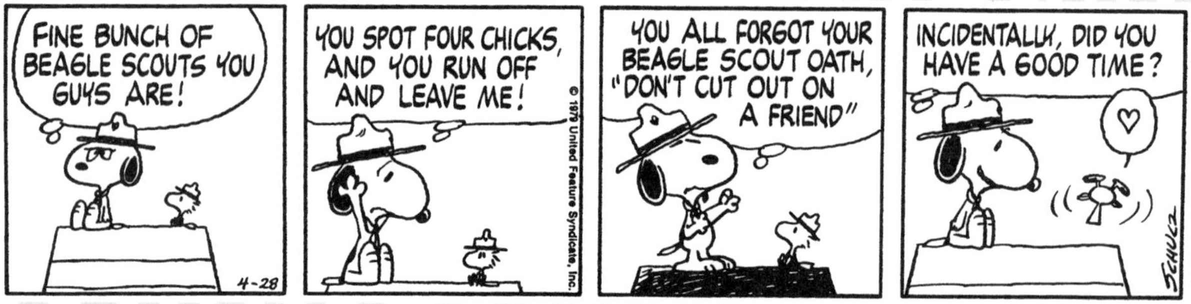
FINE BUNCH OF BEAGLE SCOUTS YOU GUYS ARE!
YOU SPOT FOUR CHICKS, AND YOU RUN OFF AND LEAVE ME!
YOU ALL FORGOT YOUR BEAGLE SCOUT OATH, "DON'T CUT OUT ON A FRIEND"
INCIDENTALLY, DID YOU HAVE A GOOD TIME?
4-28
© 1979 United Feature Syndicate, Inc.
SCHULZ

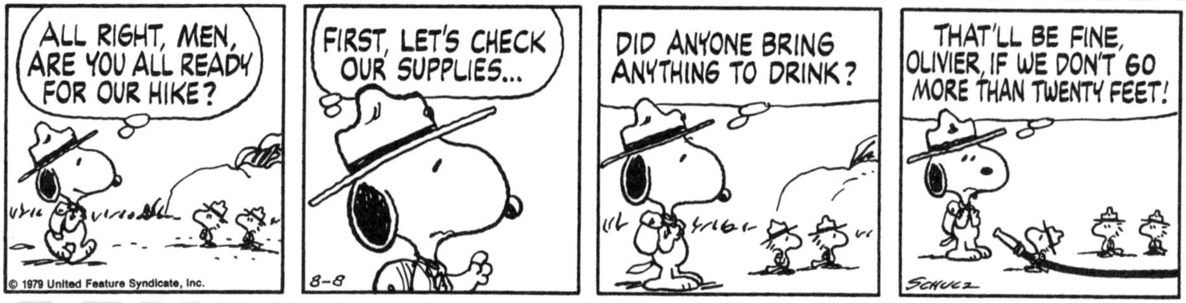
ALL RIGHT, MEN, ARE YOU ALL READY FOR OUR HIKE?
FIRST, LET'S CHECK OUR SUPPLIES...
DID ANYONE BRING ANYTHING TO DRINK?
THAT'LL BE FINE, OLIVIER, IF WE DON'T GO MORE THAN TWENTY FEET!
© 1979 United Feature Syndicate, Inc.
8-8
SCHULZ

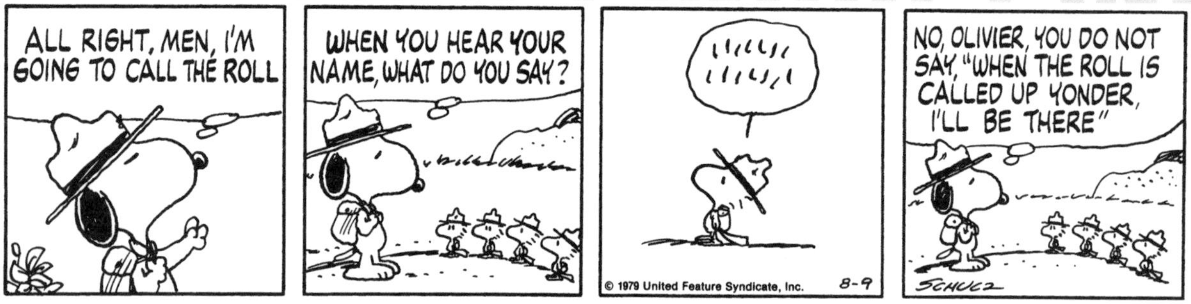
ALL RIGHT, MEN, I'M GOING TO CALL THE ROLL
WHEN YOU HEAR YOUR NAME, WHAT DO YOU SAY?
NO, OLIVIER, YOU DO NOT SAY, "WHEN THE ROLL IS CALLED UP YONDER, I'LL BE THERE"
© 1979 United Feature Syndicate, Inc.
8-9
SCHULZ

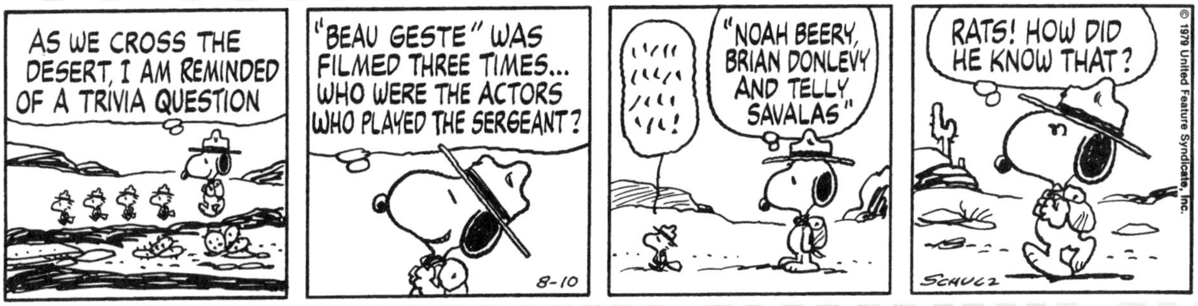
AS WE CROSS THE DESERT, I AM REMINDED OF A TRIVIA QUESTION
"BEAU GESTE" WAS FILMED THREE TIMES... WHO WERE THE ACTORS WHO PLAYED THE SERGEANT?
8-10
"NOAH BEERY, BRIAN DONLEVY AND TELLY SAVALAS"
RATS! HOW DID HE KNOW THAT?
SCHULZ
© 1979 United Feature Syndicate, Inc.

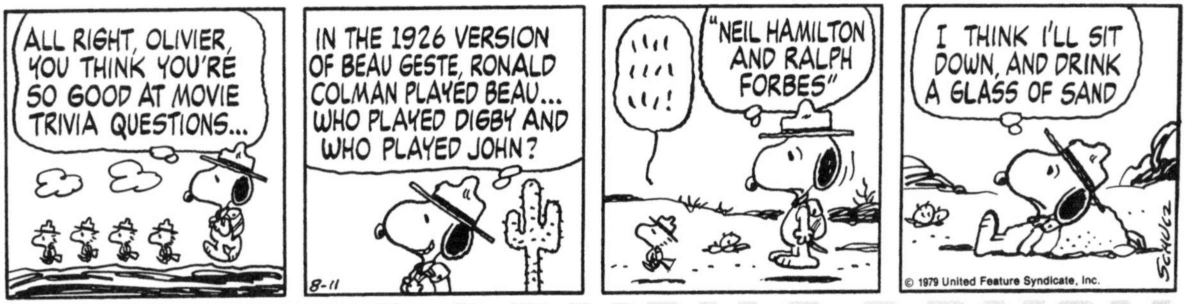
ALL RIGHT, OLIVIER, YOU THINK YOU'RE SO GOOD AT MOVIE TRIVIA QUESTIONS...
IN THE 1926 VERSION OF BEAU GESTE, RONALD COLMAN PLAYED BEAU... WHO PLAYED DIGBY AND WHO PLAYED JOHN?
8-11
"NEIL HAMILTON AND RALPH FORBES"
I THINK I'LL SIT DOWN, AND DRINK A GLASS OF SAND
SCHULZ
© 1979 United Feature Syndicate, Inc.

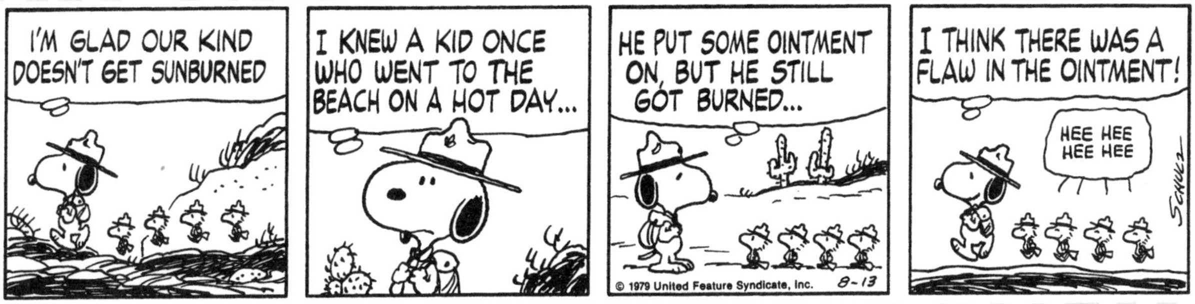
I'M GLAD OUR KIND DOESN'T GET SUNBURNED
I KNEW A KID ONCE WHO WENT TO THE BEACH ON A HOT DAY...
HE PUT SOME OINTMENT ON, BUT HE STILL GOT BURNED...
© 1979 United Feature Syndicate, Inc.
8-13
I THINK THERE WAS A FLAW IN THE OINTMENT!
HEE HEE HEE HEE
SCHULZ

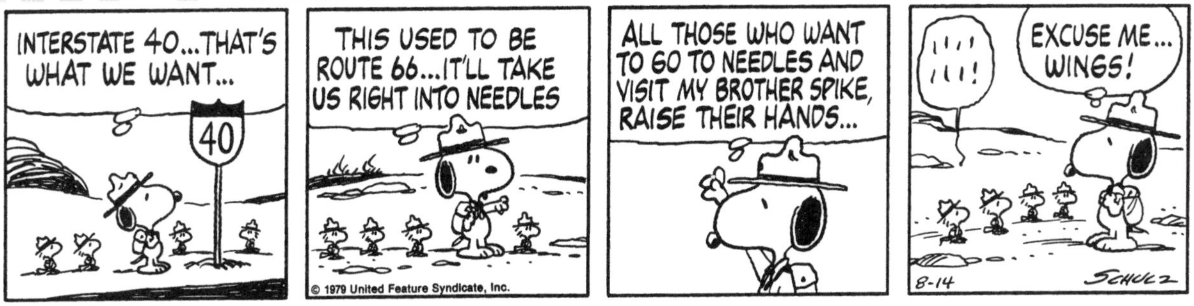
INTERSTATE 40...THAT'S WHAT WE WANT...
40
THIS USED TO BE ROUTE 66...IT'LL TAKE US RIGHT INTO NEEDLES
© 1979 United Feature Syndicate, Inc.
ALL THOSE WHO WANT TO GO TO NEEDLES AND VISIT MY BROTHER SPIKE, RAISE THEIR HANDS...
EXCUSE ME... WINGS!
8-14
SCHULZ

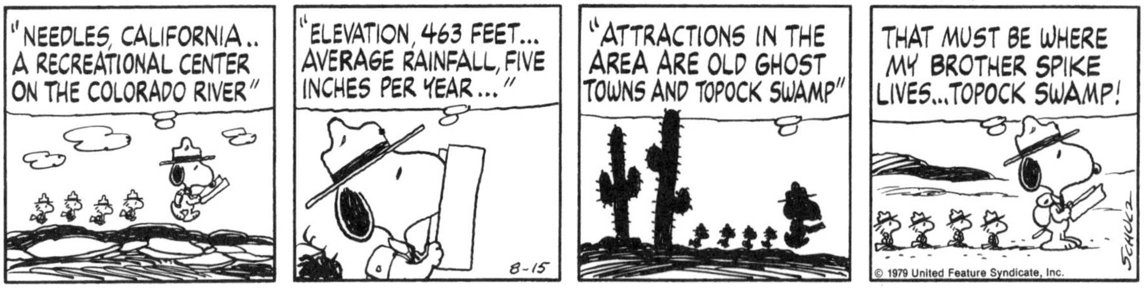
"NEEDLES, CALIFORNIA.. A RECREATIONAL CENTER ON THE COLORADO RIVER"
"ELEVATION, 463 FEET... AVERAGE RAINFALL, FIVE INCHES PER YEAR..."
8-15
"ATTRACTIONS IN THE AREA ARE OLD GHOST TOWNS AND TOPOCK SWAMP"
THAT MUST BE WHERE MY BROTHER SPIKE LIVES...TOPOCK SWAMP!
SCHULZ
© 1979 United Feature Syndicate, Inc.

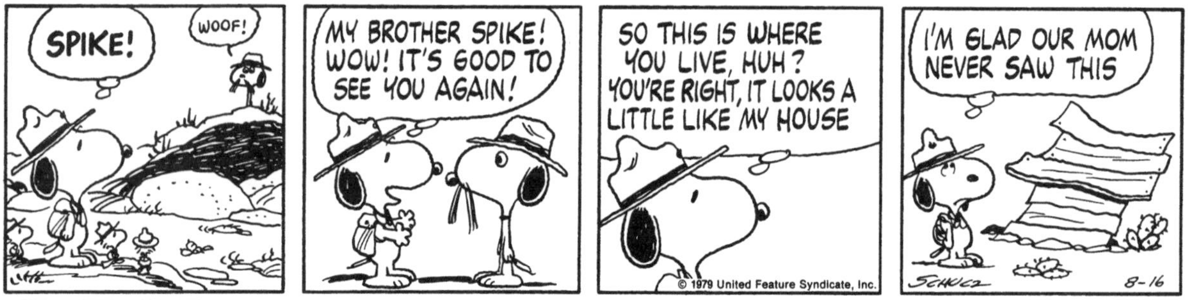
SPIKE!
WOOF!
MY BROTHER SPIKE! WOW! IT'S GOOD TO SEE YOU AGAIN!
SO THIS IS WHERE YOU LIVE, HUH? YOU'RE RIGHT, IT LOOKS A LITTLE LIKE MY HOUSE
© 1979 United Feature Syndicate, Inc.
I'M GLAD OUR MOM NEVER SAW THIS
SCHULZ
8-16

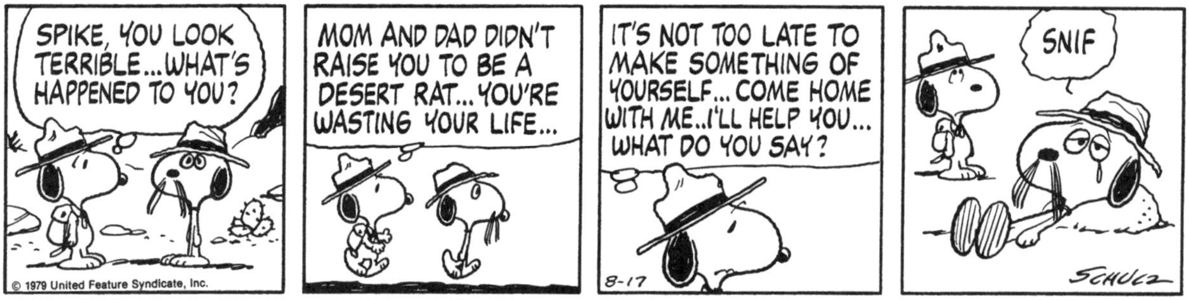
SPIKE, YOU LOOK TERRIBLE...WHAT'S HAPPENED TO YOU?
© 1979 United Feature Syndicate, Inc.
MOM AND DAD DIDN'T RAISE YOU TO BE A DESERT RAT...YOU'RE WASTING YOUR LIFE...
IT'S NOT TOO LATE TO MAKE SOMETHING OF YOURSELF...COME HOME WITH ME..I'LL HELP YOU... WHAT DO YOU SAY?
8-17
SNIF
SCHULZ

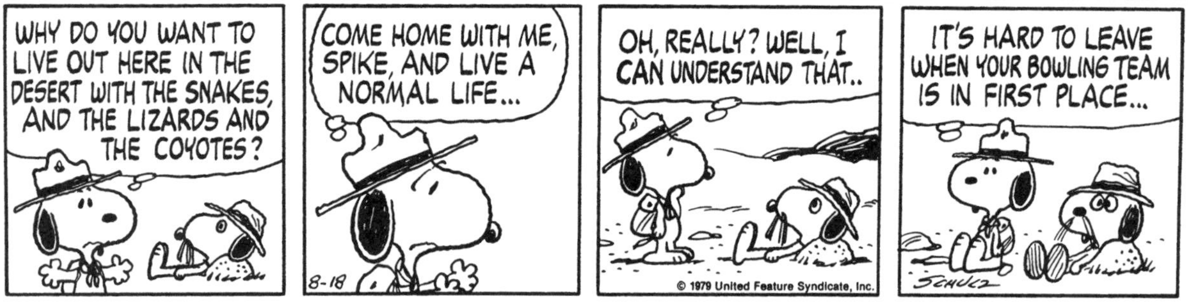
WHY DO YOU WANT TO LIVE OUT HERE IN THE DESERT WITH THE SNAKES, AND THE LIZARDS AND THE COYOTES?
COME HOME WITH ME, SPIKE, AND LIVE A NORMAL LIFE...
8-18
OH, REALLY? WELL, I CAN UNDERSTAND THAT..
© 1979 United Feature Syndicate, Inc.
IT'S HARD TO LEAVE WHEN YOUR BOWLING TEAM IS IN FIRST PLACE...
SCHULZ

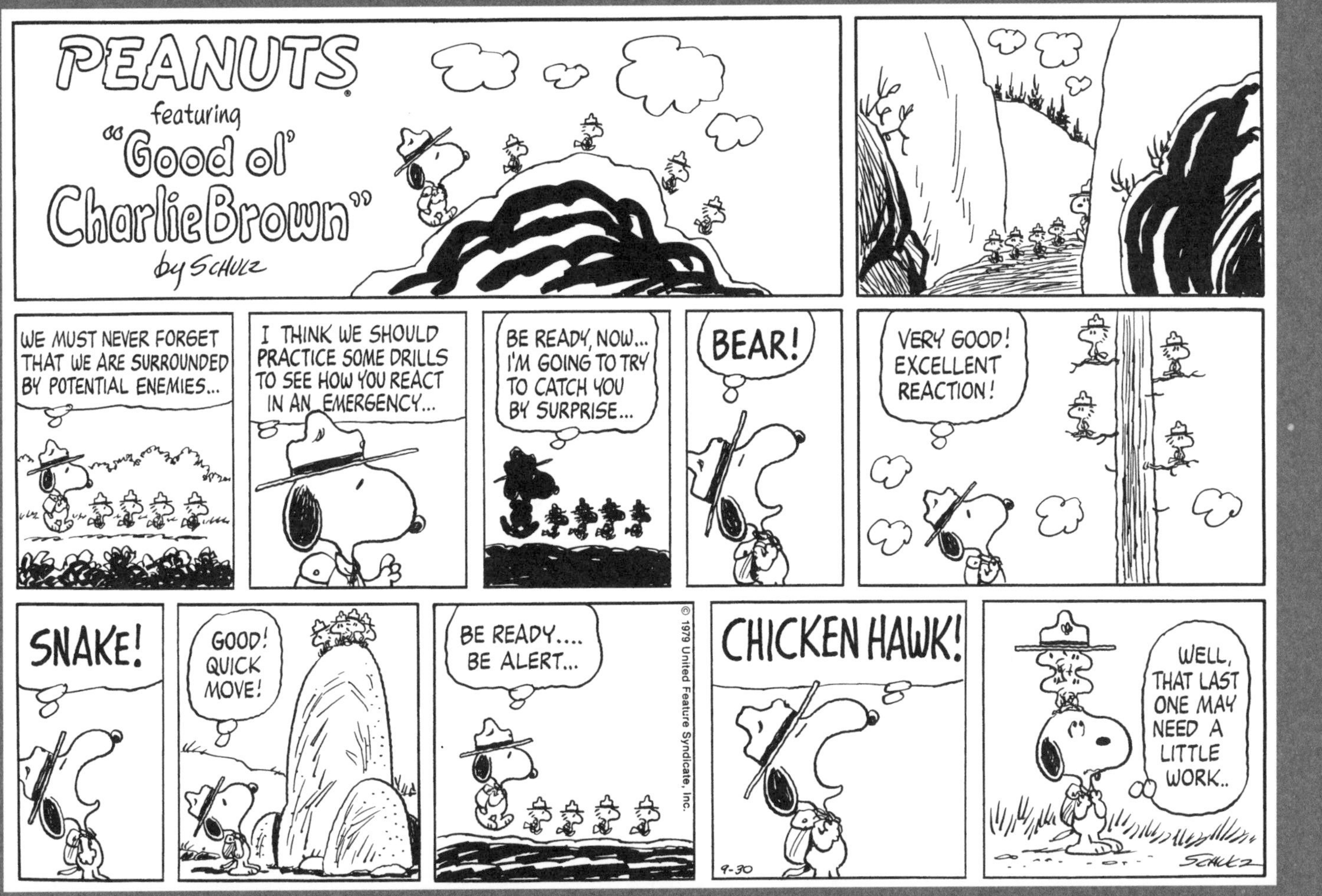
PEANUTS
featuring "Good ol' CharlieBrown"
by SCHULZ
WE MUST NEVER FORGET THAT WE ARE SURROUNDED BY POTENTIAL ENEMIES...
I THINK WE SHOULD PRACTICE SOME DRILLS TO SEE HOW YOU REACT IN AN EMERGENCY...
BE READY, NOW... I'M GOING TO TRY TO CATCH YOU BY SURPRISE...
BEAR!
VERY GOOD! EXCELLENT REACTION!
SNAKE!
GOOD! QUICK MOVE!
BE READY.... BE ALERT...
© 1979 United Feature Syndicate, Inc.
CHICKEN HAWK!
9-30
WELL, THAT LAST ONE MAY NEED A LITTLE WORK..
SCHULZ

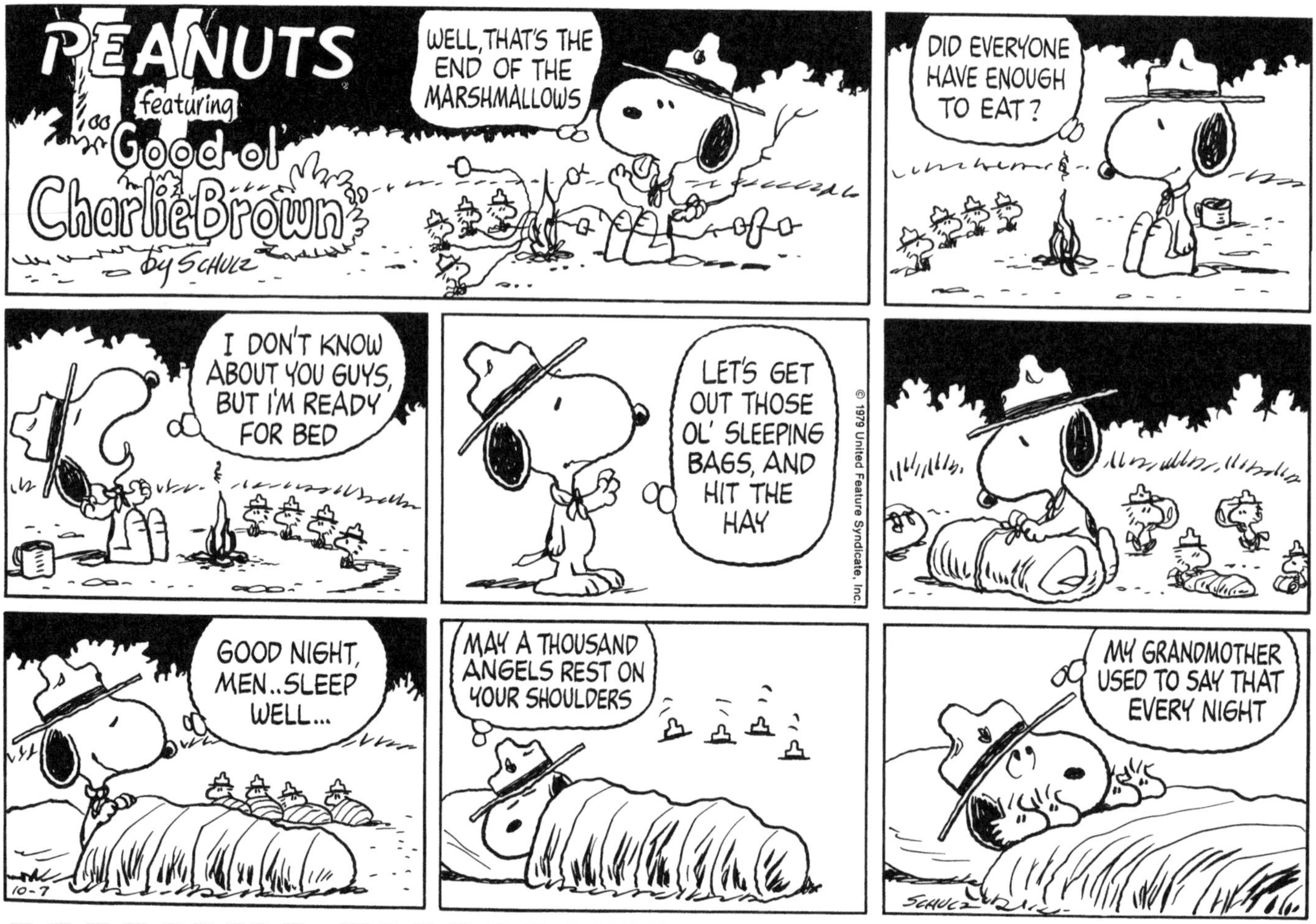
PEANUTS
featuring
Good ol' Charlie Brown
by SCHULZ
WELL, THAT'S THE END OF THE MARSHMALLOWS
DID EVERYONE HAVE ENOUGH TO EAT?
I DON'T KNOW ABOUT YOU GUYS, BUT I'M READY FOR BED
LET'S GET OUT THOSE OL' SLEEPING BAGS, AND HIT THE HAY
© 1979 United Feature Syndicate, Inc.
GOOD NIGHT, MEN..SLEEP WELL...
10-7
MAY A THOUSAND ANGELS REST ON YOUR SHOULDERS
MY GRANDMOTHER USED TO SAY THAT EVERY NIGHT
SCHULZ

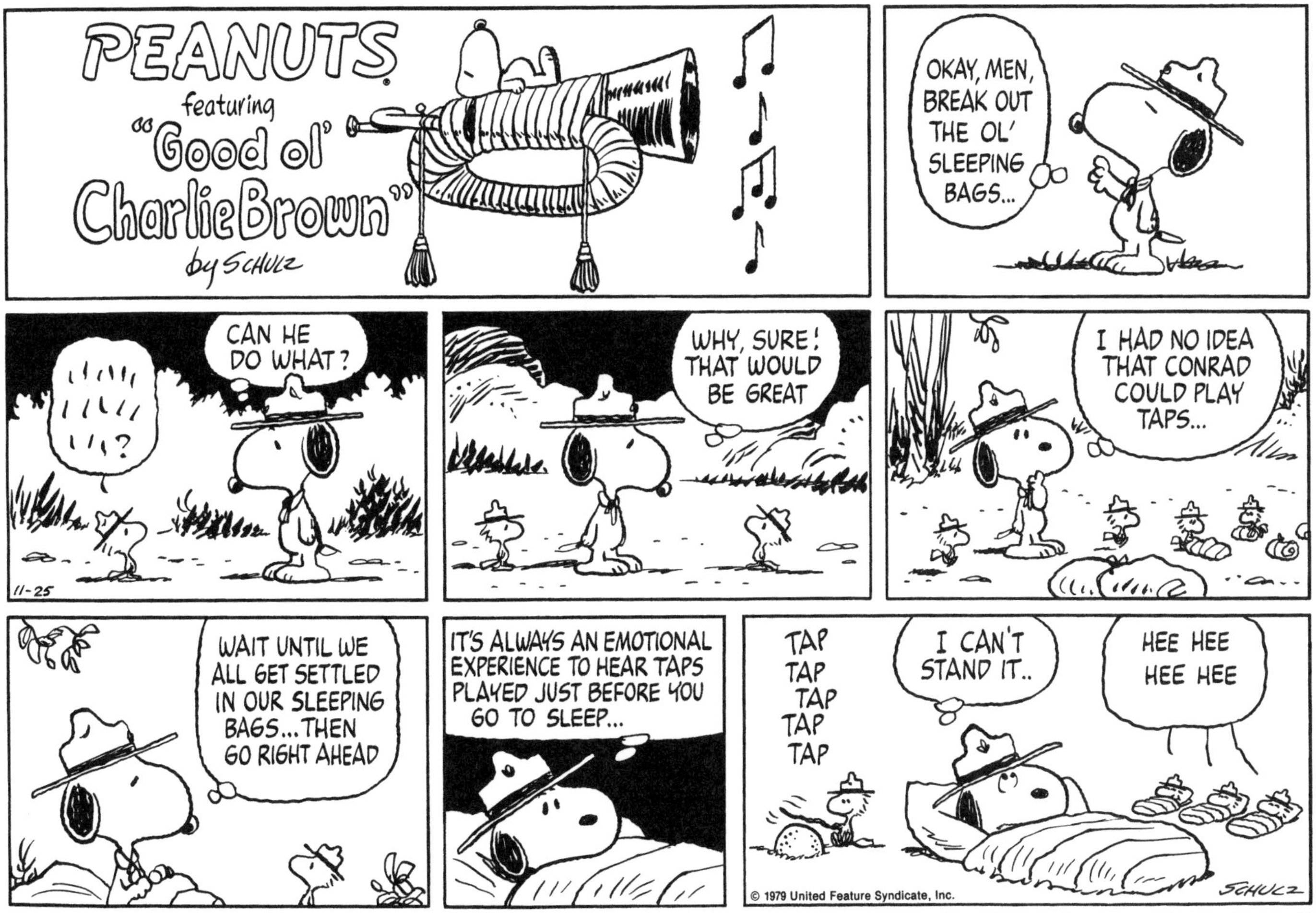
PEANUTS
featuring
"Good ol' Charlie Brown"
by SCHULZ
OKAY, MEN, BREAK OUT THE OL' SLEEPING BAGS...
11-25
CAN HE DO WHAT?
WHY, SURE! THAT WOULD BE GREAT
I HAD NO IDEA THAT CONRAD COULD PLAY TAPS...
WAIT UNTIL WE ALL GET SETTLED IN OUR SLEEPING BAGS...THEN GO RIGHT AHEAD
IT'S ALWAYS AN EMOTIONAL EXPERIENCE TO HEAR TAPS PLAYED JUST BEFORE YOU GO TO SLEEP...
TAP
TAP
TAP
TAP
TAP
I CAN'T STAND IT..
HEE HEE HEE HEE
© 1979 United Feature Syndicate, Inc.
SCHULZ

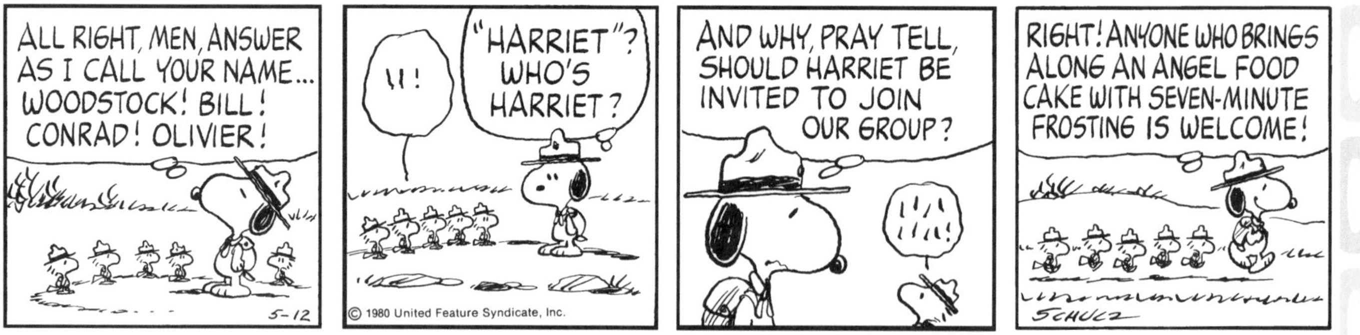
ALL RIGHT, MEN, ANSWER AS I CALL YOUR NAME... WOODSTOCK! BILL! CONRAD! OLIVIER!
5-12
"HARRIET"? WHO'S HARRIET?
© 1980 United Feature Syndicate, Inc.
AND WHY, PRAY TELL, SHOULD HARRIET BE INVITED TO JOIN OUR GROUP?
RIGHT! ANYONE WHO BRINGS ALONG AN ANGEL FOOD CAKE WITH SEVEN-MINUTE FROSTING IS WELCOME!
SCHULZ

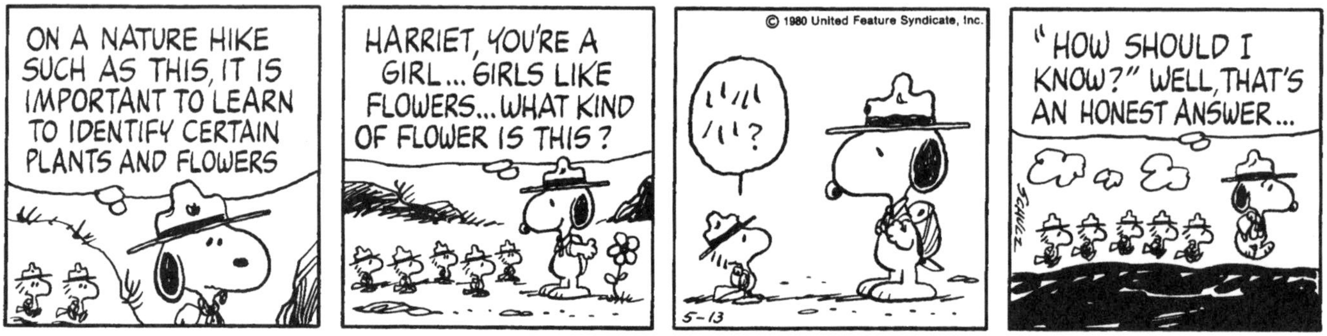
ON A NATURE HIKE SUCH AS THIS, IT IS IMPORTANT TO LEARN TO IDENTIFY CERTAIN PLANTS AND FLOWERS
HARRIET, YOU'RE A GIRL... GIRLS LIKE FLOWERS... WHAT KIND OF FLOWER IS THIS?
© 1980 United Feature Syndicate, Inc.
5-13
"HOW SHOULD I KNOW?" WELL, THAT'S AN HONEST ANSWER...
SCHULZ

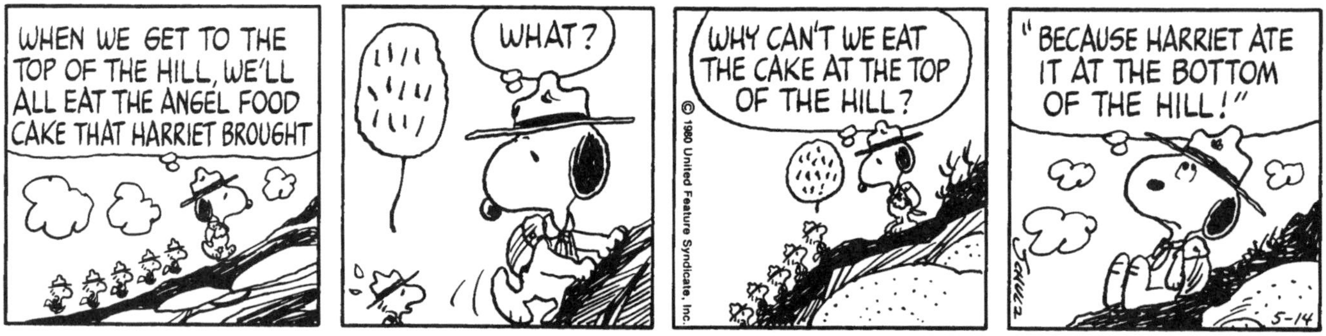
WHEN WE GET TO THE TOP OF THE HILL, WE'LL ALL EAT THE ANGEL FOOD CAKE THAT HARRIET BROUGHT
WHAT?
© 1980 United Feature Syndicate, Inc.
WHY CAN'T WE EAT THE CAKE AT THE TOP OF THE HILL?
"BECAUSE HARRIET ATE IT AT THE BOTTOM OF THE HILL!"
SCHULZ
5-14

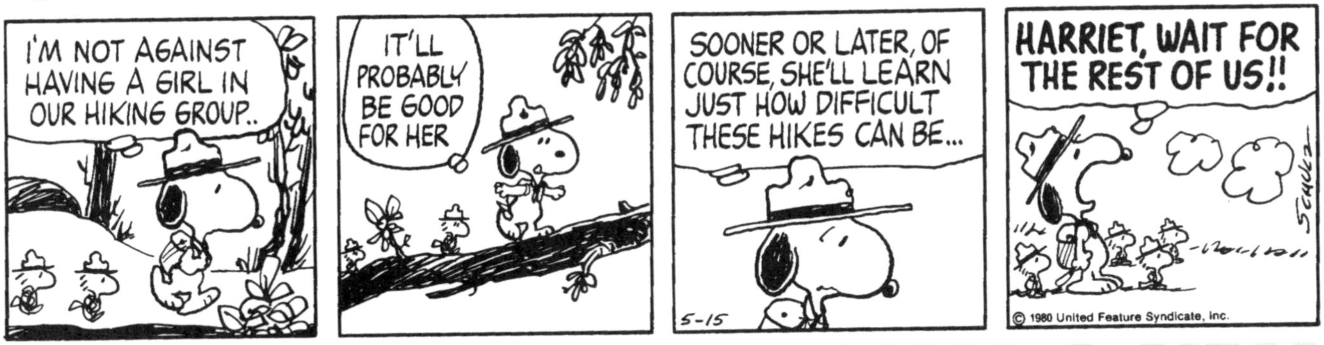
I'M NOT AGAINST HAVING A GIRL IN OUR HIKING GROUP..
IT'LL PROBABLY BE GOOD FOR HER
SOONER OR LATER, OF COURSE, SHE'LL LEARN JUST HOW DIFFICULT THESE HIKES CAN BE...
5-15
HARRIET, WAIT FOR THE REST OF US!!
SCHULZ
© 1980 United Feature Syndicate, Inc.

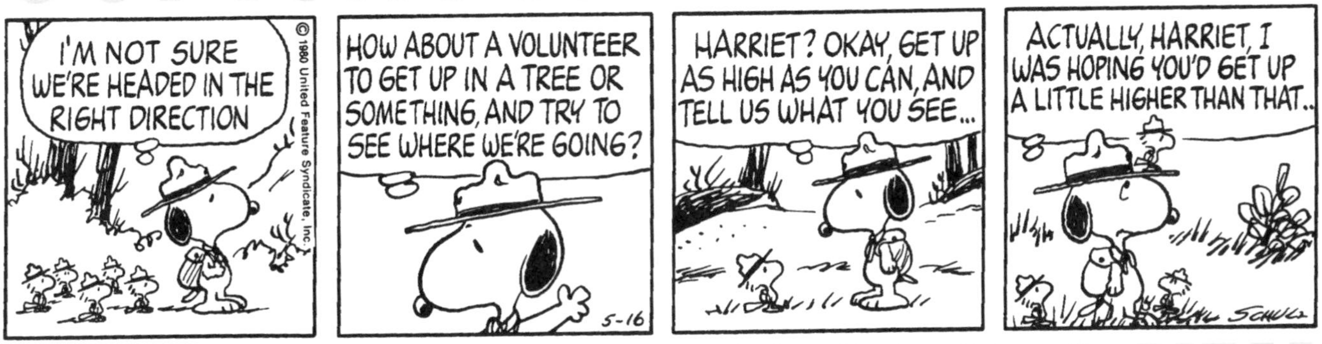
I'M NOT SURE WE'RE HEADED IN THE RIGHT DIRECTION
© 1980 United Feature Syndicate, Inc.
HOW ABOUT A VOLUNTEER TO GET UP IN A TREE OR SOMETHING, AND TRY TO SEE WHERE WE'RE GOING?
5-16
HARRIET? OKAY, GET UP AS HIGH AS YOU CAN, AND TELL US WHAT YOU SEE...
ACTUALLY, HARRIET, I WAS HOPING YOU'D GET UP A LITTLE HIGHER THAN THAT..
SCHULZ

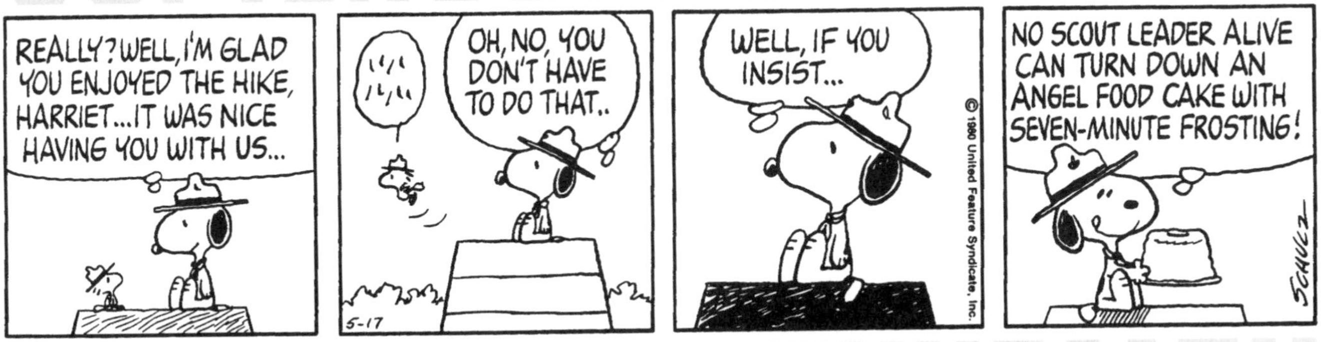
REALLY? WELL, I'M GLAD YOU ENJOYED THE HIKE, HARRIET...IT WAS NICE HAVING YOU WITH US...
OH, NO, YOU DON'T HAVE TO DO THAT..
5-17
WELL, IF YOU INSIST...
© 1980 United Feature Syndicate, Inc.
NO SCOUT LEADER ALIVE CAN TURN DOWN AN ANGEL FOOD CAKE WITH SEVEN-MINUTE FROSTING!
SCHULZ

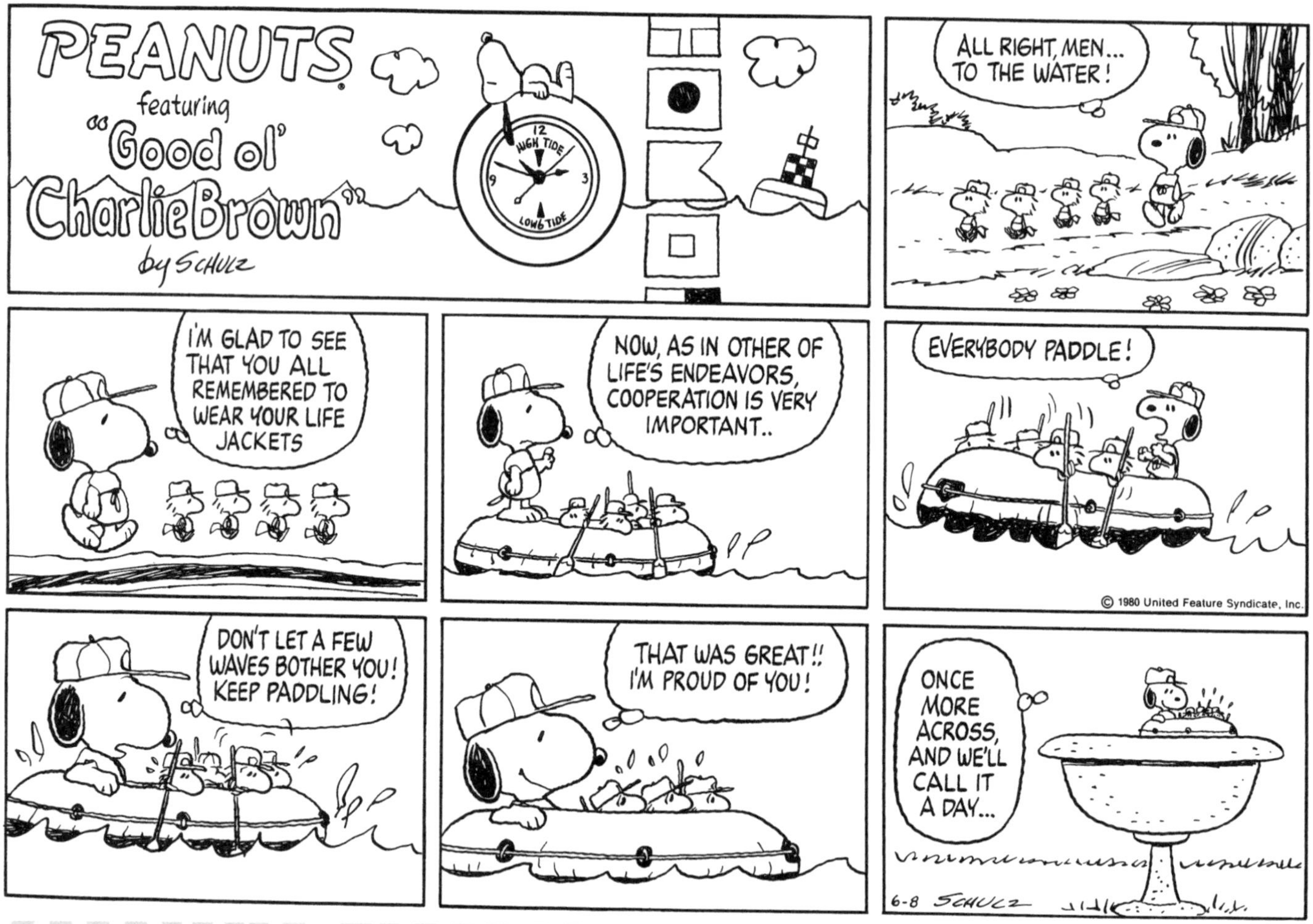
PEANUTS
featuring
"Good ol' Charlie Brown"
by SCHULZ
12
HIGH TIDE
9
3
LOW 6 TIDE
ALL RIGHT, MEN... TO THE WATER!
I'M GLAD TO SEE THAT YOU ALL REMEMBERED TO WEAR YOUR LIFE JACKETS
NOW, AS IN OTHER OF LIFE'S ENDEAVORS, COOPERATION IS VERY IMPORTANT..
EVERYBODY PADDLE!
© 1980 United Feature Syndicate, Inc.
DON'T LET A FEW WAVES BOTHER YOU! KEEP PADDLING!
THAT WAS GREAT!! I'M PROUD OF YOU!
ONCE MORE ACROSS, AND WE'LL CALL IT A DAY...
6-8 SCHULZ

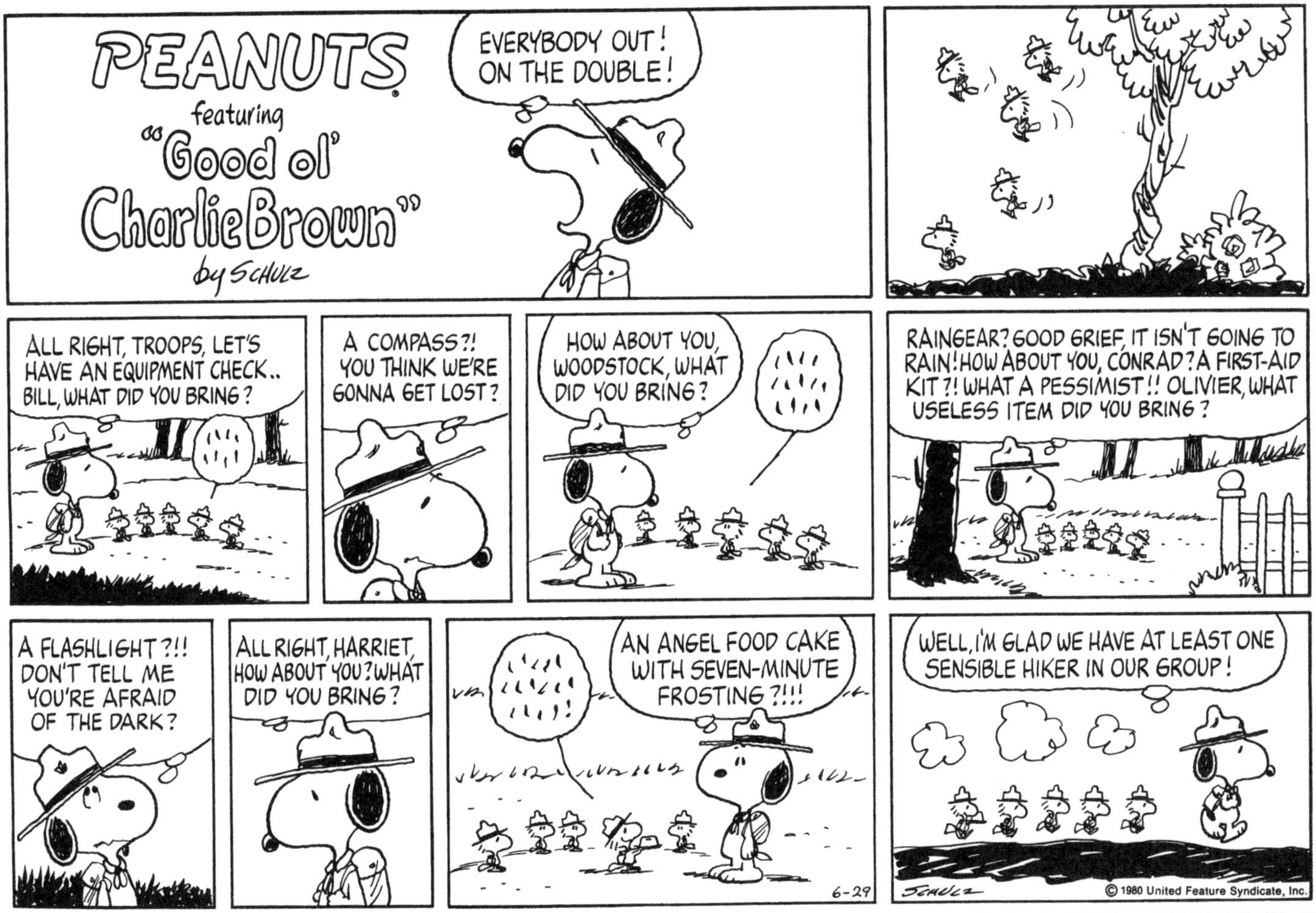
PEANUTS
featuring "Good ol' Charlie Brown"
by SCHULZ
EVERYBODY OUT! ON THE DOUBLE!
ALL RIGHT, TROOPS, LET'S HAVE AN EQUIPMENT CHECK.. BILL, WHAT DID YOU BRING?
A COMPASS?! YOU THINK WE'RE GONNA GET LOST?
HOW ABOUT YOU, WOODSTOCK, WHAT DID YOU BRING?
RAINGEAR? GOOD GRIEF, IT ISN'T GOING TO RAIN! HOW ABOUT YOU, CONRAD? A FIRST-AID KIT?! WHAT A PESSIMIST!! OLIVIER, WHAT USELESS ITEM DID YOU BRING?
A FLASHLIGHT?!! DON'T TELL ME YOU'RE AFRAID OF THE DARK?
ALL RIGHT, HARRIET, HOW ABOUT YOU? WHAT DID YOU BRING?
AN ANGEL FOOD CAKE WITH SEVEN-MINUTE FROSTING?!!!
6-29
WELL, I'M GLAD WE HAVE AT LEAST ONE SENSIBLE HIKER IN OUR GROUP!
SCHULZ
© 1980 United Feature Syndicate, Inc.

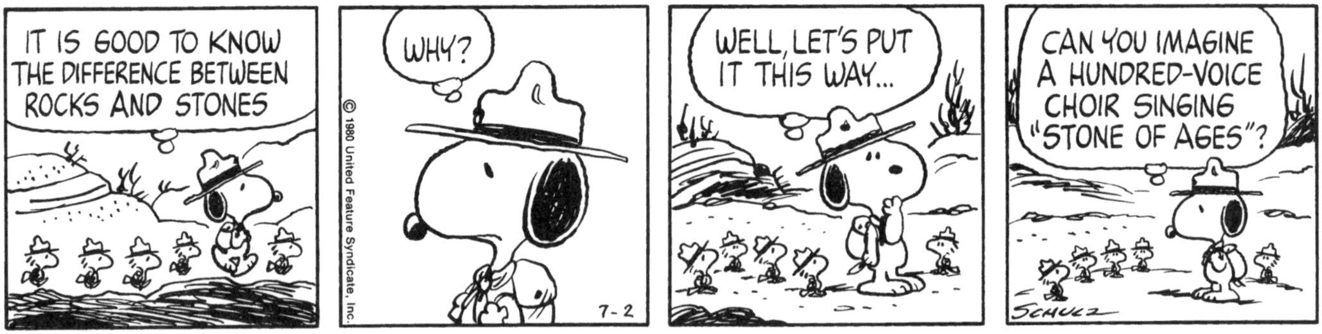
IT IS GOOD TO KNOW THE DIFFERENCE BETWEEN ROCKS AND STONES
WHY?
© 1980 United Feature Syndicate, Inc.
7-2
WELL, LET'S PUT IT THIS WAY...
CAN YOU IMAGINE A HUNDRED-VOICE CHOIR SINGING "STONE OF AGES"?
SCHULZ

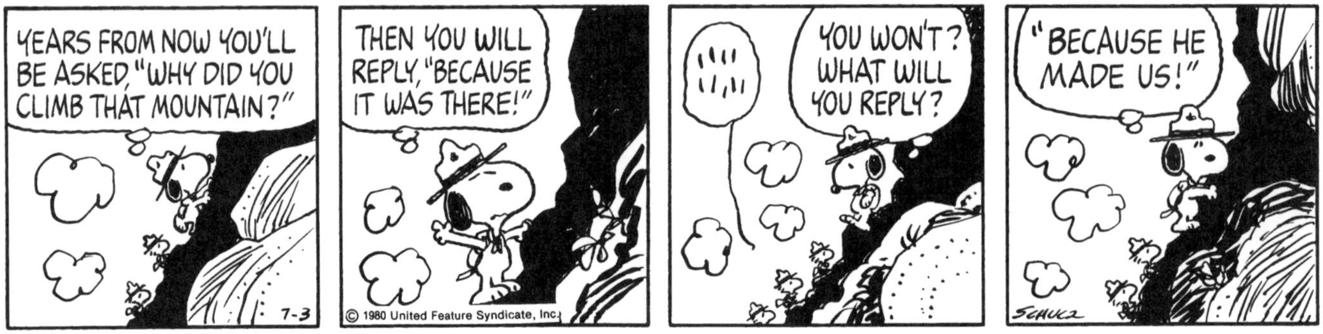
YEARS FROM NOW YOU'LL BE ASKED, "WHY DID YOU CLIMB THAT MOUNTAIN?"
7-3
THEN YOU WILL REPLY, "BECAUSE IT WAS THERE!"
© 1980 United Feature Syndicate, Inc.
YOU WON'T? WHAT WILL YOU REPLY?
"BECAUSE HE MADE US!"
SCHULZ

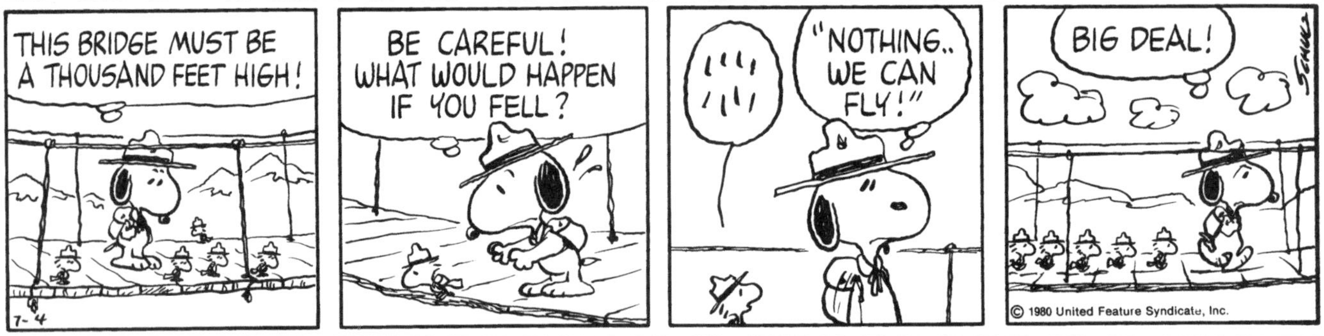
THIS BRIDGE MUST BE A THOUSAND FEET HIGH!
7-4
BE CAREFUL! WHAT WOULD HAPPEN IF YOU FELL?
"NOTHING.. WE CAN FLY!"
BIG DEAL!
SCHULZ
© 1980 United Feature Syndicate, Inc.

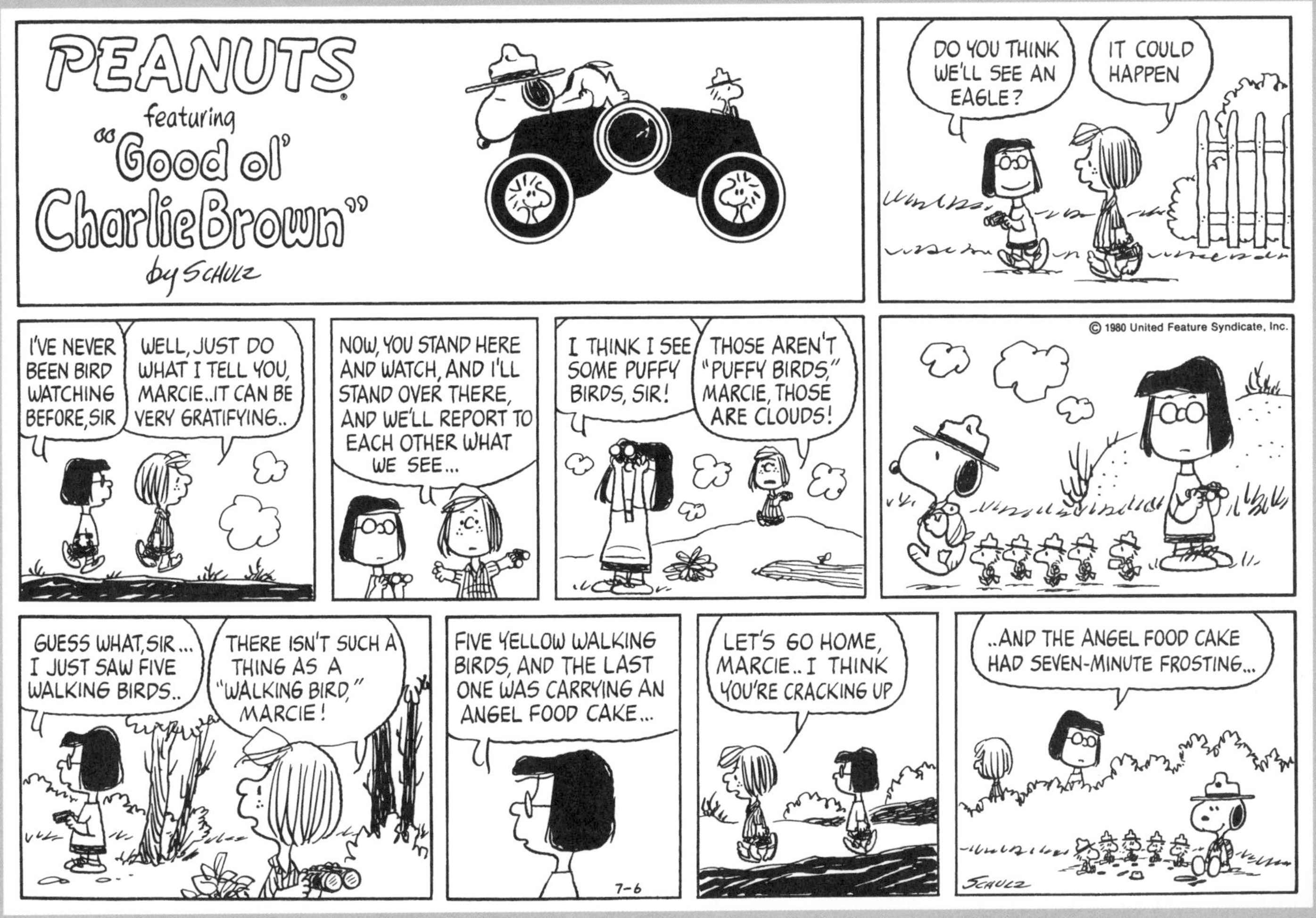
PEANUTS
featuring "Good ol' CharlieBrown"
by SCHULZ
DO YOU THINK WE'LL SEE AN EAGLE?
IT COULD HAPPEN
I'VE NEVER BEEN BIRD WATCHING BEFORE, SIR
WELL, JUST DO WHAT I TELL YOU, MARCIE..IT CAN BE VERY GRATIFYING..
NOW, YOU STAND HERE AND WATCH, AND I'LL STAND OVER THERE, AND WE'LL REPORT TO EACH OTHER WHAT WE SEE...
I THINK I SEE SOME PUFFY BIRDS, SIR!
THOSE AREN'T "PUFFY BIRDS," MARCIE, THOSE ARE CLOUDS!
© 1980 United Feature Syndicate, Inc.
GUESS WHAT, SIR... I JUST SAW FIVE WALKING BIRDS..
THERE ISN'T SUCH A THING AS A "WALKING BIRD," MARCIE!
FIVE YELLOW WALKING BIRDS, AND THE LAST ONE WAS CARRYING AN ANGEL FOOD CAKE...
7-6
LET'S GO HOME, MARCIE.. I THINK YOU'RE CRACKING UP
..AND THE ANGEL FOOD CAKE HAD SEVEN-MINUTE FROSTING...
SCHULZ

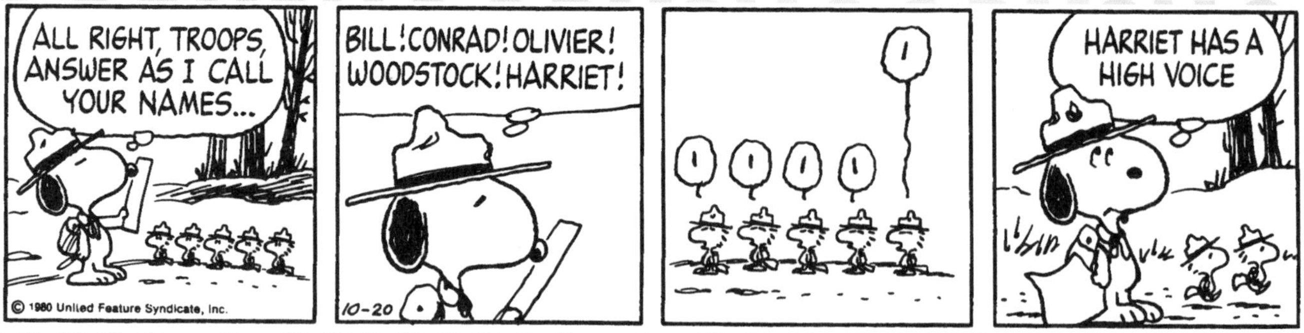
ALL RIGHT, TROOPS, ANSWER AS I CALL YOUR NAMES...
© 1980 United Feature Syndicate, Inc.
BILL! CONRAD! OLIVIER! WOODSTOCK! HARRIET!
10-20
HARRIET HAS A HIGH VOICE

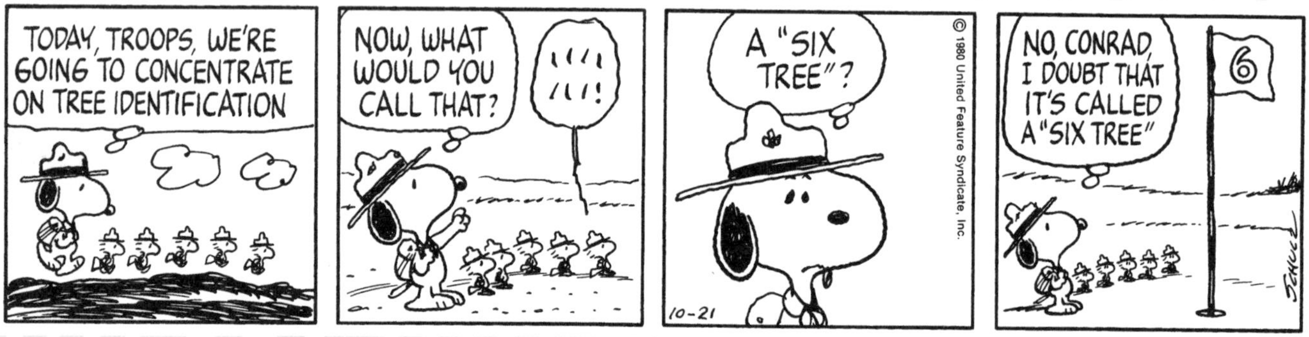
TODAY, TROOPS, WE'RE GOING TO CONCENTRATE ON TREE IDENTIFICATION
NOW, WHAT WOULD YOU CALL THAT?
A "SIX TREE"?
© 1980 United Feature Syndicate, Inc.
10-21
NO, CONRAD, I DOUBT THAT IT'S CALLED A "SIX TREE"
6
SCHULZ

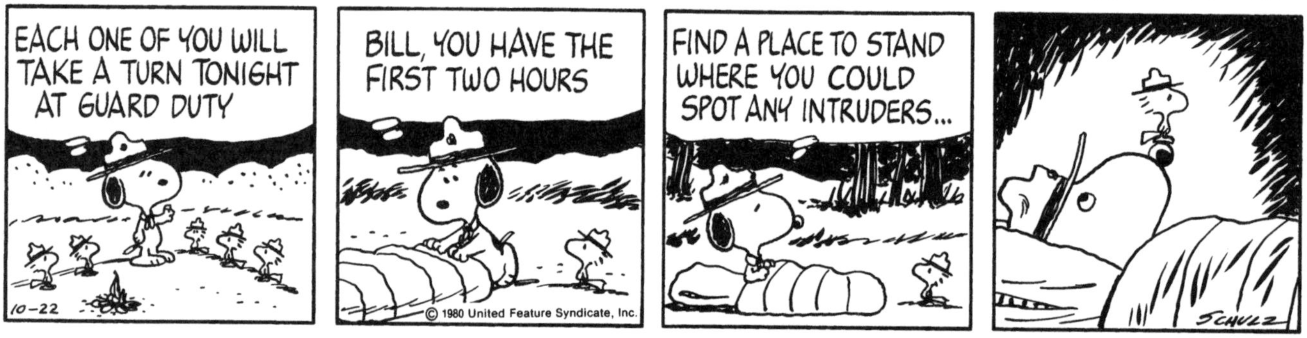
EACH ONE OF YOU WILL TAKE A TURN TONIGHT AT GUARD DUTY
10-22
BILL, YOU HAVE THE FIRST TWO HOURS
© 1980 United Feature Syndicate, Inc.
FIND A PLACE TO STAND WHERE YOU COULD SPOT ANY INTRUDERS...
SCHULZ

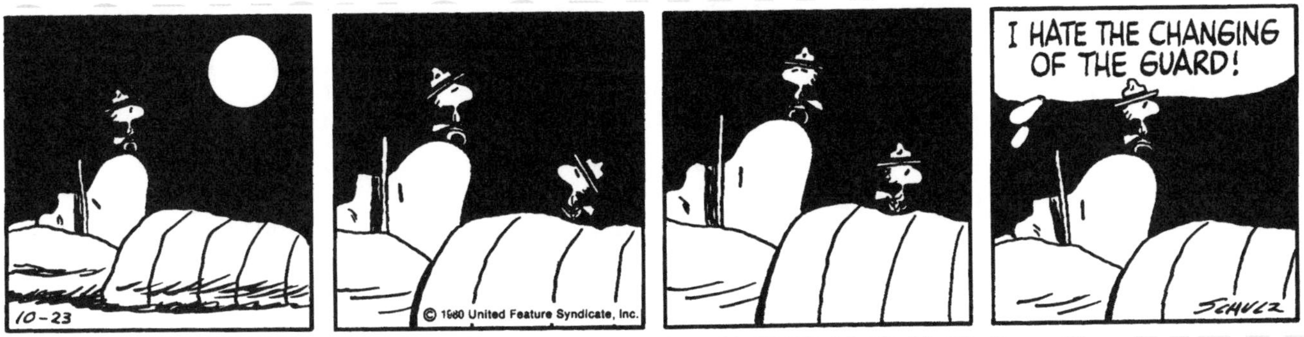
10-23
© 1980 United Feature Syndicate, Inc.
I HATE THE CHANGING OF THE GUARD!
SCHULZ

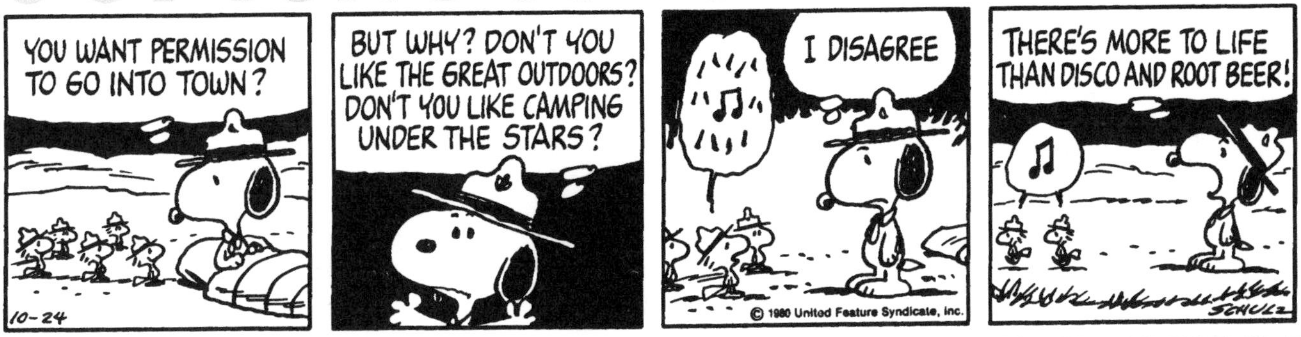
YOU WANT PERMISSION TO GO INTO TOWN?
10-24
BUT WHY? DON'T YOU LIKE THE GREAT OUTDOORS? DON'T YOU LIKE CAMPING UNDER THE STARS?
I DISAGREE
© 1980 United Feature Syndicate, Inc.
THERE'S MORE TO LIFE THAN DISCO AND ROOT BEER!
SCHULZ

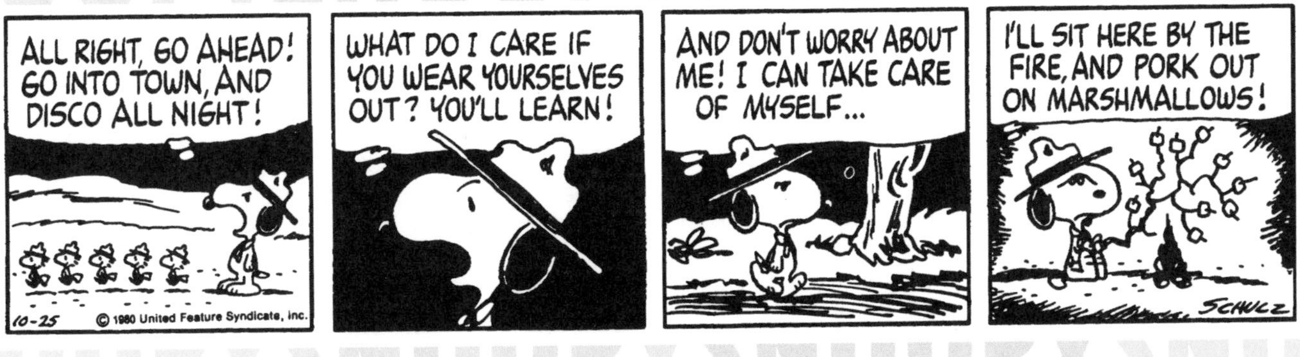
ALL RIGHT, GO AHEAD! GO INTO TOWN, AND DISCO ALL NIGHT!
10-25
© 1980 United Feature Syndicate, Inc.
WHAT DO I CARE IF YOU WEAR YOURSELVES OUT? YOU'LL LEARN!
AND DON'T WORRY ABOUT ME! I CAN TAKE CARE OF MYSELF...
I'LL SIT HERE BY THE FIRE, AND PORK OUT ON MARSHMALLOWS!
SCHULZ

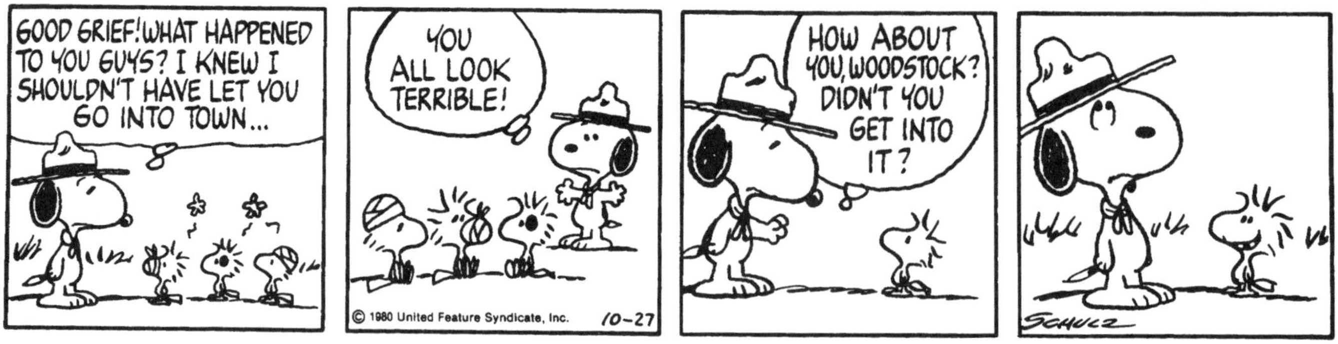
GOOD GRIEF! WHAT HAPPENED TO YOU GUYS? I KNEW I SHOULDN'T HAVE LET YOU GO INTO TOWN...
YOU ALL LOOK TERRIBLE!
© 1980 United Feature Syndicate, Inc.
10-27
HOW ABOUT YOU, WOODSTOCK? DIDN'T YOU GET INTO IT?
SCHULZ

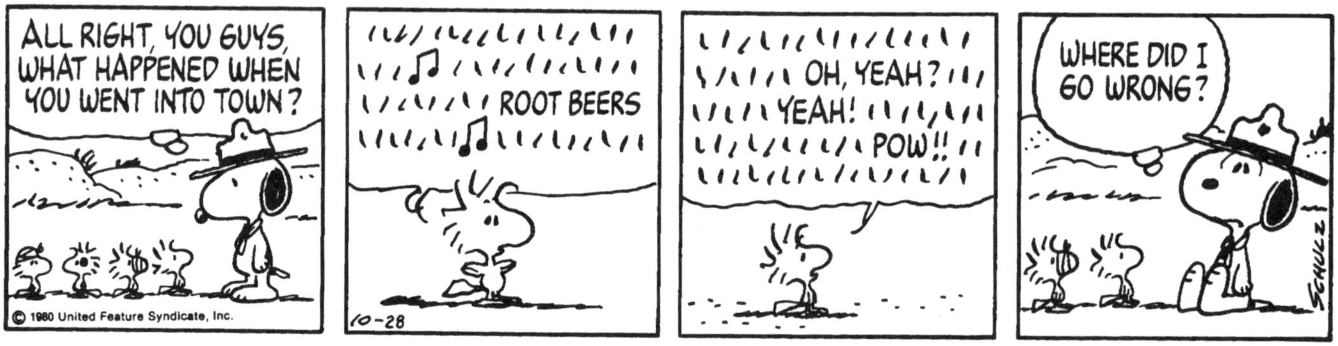
ALL RIGHT, YOU GUYS, WHAT HAPPENED WHEN YOU WENT INTO TOWN?
© 1980 United Feature Syndicate, Inc.
ROOT BEERS
10-28
OH, YEAH? YEAH! POW!!
WHERE DID I GO WRONG?
SCHULZ

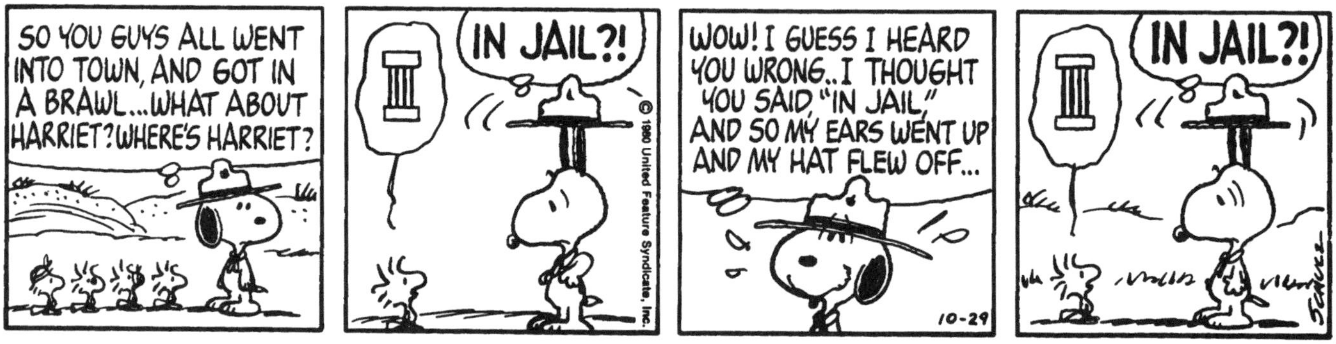
SO YOU GUYS ALL WENT INTO TOWN, AND GOT IN A BRAWL...WHAT ABOUT HARRIET? WHERE'S HARRIET?
IN JAIL?!
© 1980 United Feature Syndicate, Inc.
WOW! I GUESS I HEARD YOU WRONG..I THOUGHT YOU SAID, "IN JAIL," AND SO MY EARS WENT UP AND MY HAT FLEW OFF...
10-29
IN JAIL?!
SCHULZ

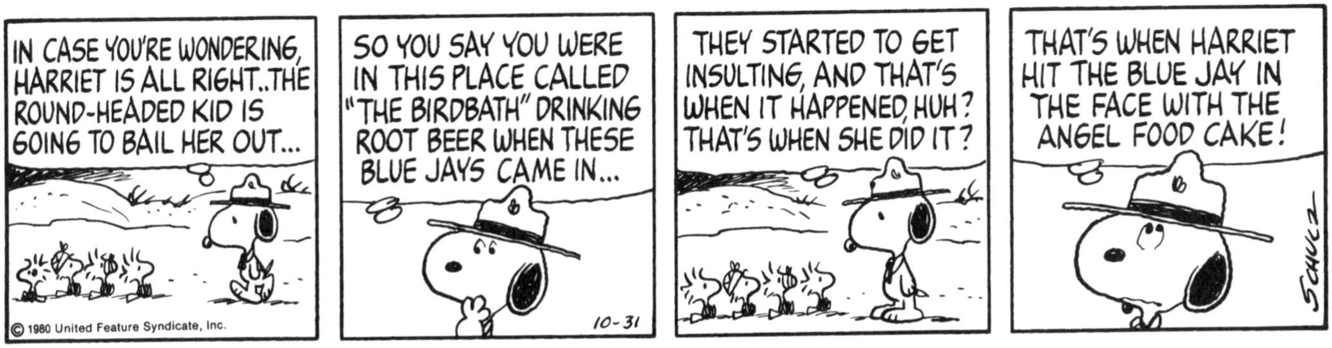
IN CASE YOU'RE WONDERING, HARRIET IS ALL RIGHT..THE ROUND-HEADED KID IS GOING TO BAIL HER OUT...
© 1980 United Feature Syndicate, Inc.
SO YOU SAY YOU WERE IN THIS PLACE CALLED "THE BIRDBATH" DRINKING ROOT BEER WHEN THESE BLUE JAYS CAME IN...
10-31
THEY STARTED TO GET INSULTING, AND THAT'S WHEN IT HAPPENED, HUH? THAT'S WHEN SHE DID IT?
THAT'S WHEN HARRIET HIT THE BLUE JAY IN THE FACE WITH THE ANGEL FOOD CAKE!
SCHULZ

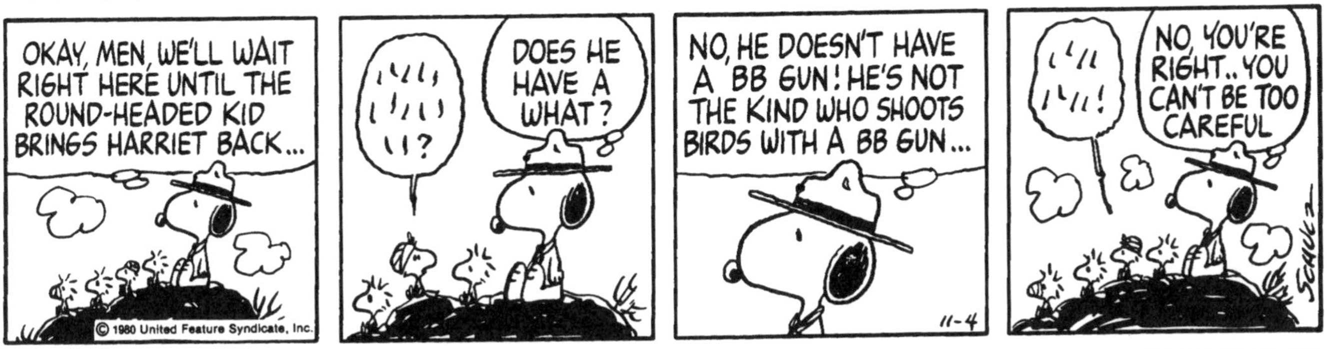
OKAY, MEN, WE'LL WAIT RIGHT HERE UNTIL THE ROUND-HEADED KID BRINGS HARRIET BACK...
© 1980 United Feature Syndicate, Inc.
DOES HE HAVE A WHAT?
NO, HE DOESN'T HAVE A BB GUN! HE'S NOT THE KIND WHO SHOOTS BIRDS WITH A BB GUN...
11-4
NO, YOU'RE RIGHT.. YOU CAN'T BE TOO CAREFUL
SCHULZ

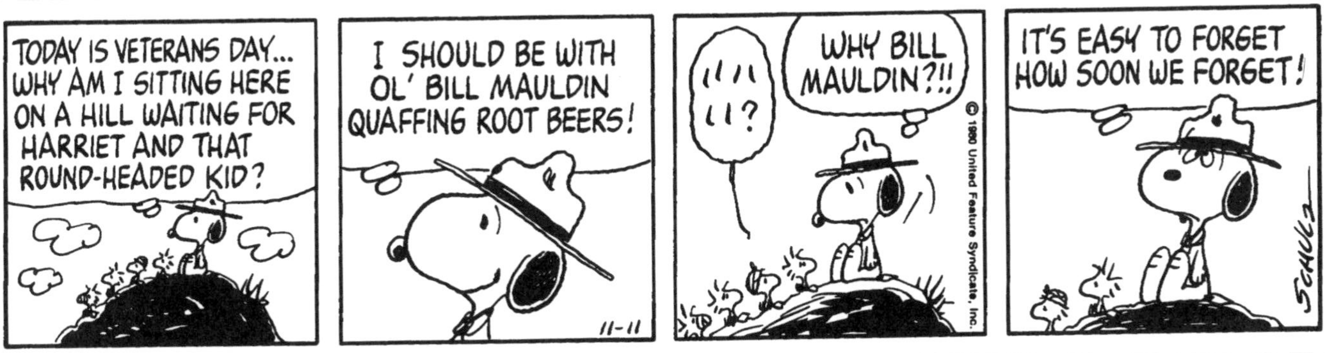
TODAY IS VETERANS DAY... WHY AM I SITTING HERE ON A HILL WAITING FOR HARRIET AND THAT ROUND-HEADED KID?
I SHOULD BE WITH OL' BILL MAULDIN QUAFFING ROOT BEERS!
11-11
WHY BILL MAULDIN?!!
© 1980 United Feature Syndicate, Inc.
IT'S EASY TO FORGET HOW SOON WE FORGET!
SCHULZ

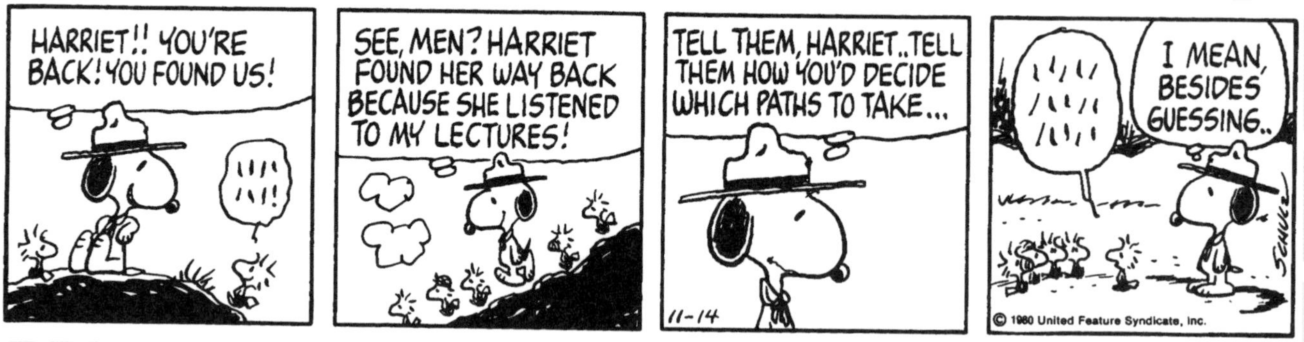
HARRIET!! YOU'RE BACK! YOU FOUND US!
SEE, MEN? HARRIET FOUND HER WAY BACK BECAUSE SHE LISTENED TO MY LECTURES!
TELL THEM, HARRIET..TELL THEM HOW YOU'D DECIDE WHICH PATHS TO TAKE...
11-14
I MEAN, BESIDES GUESSING..
SCHULZ
© 1980 United Feature Syndicate, Inc.

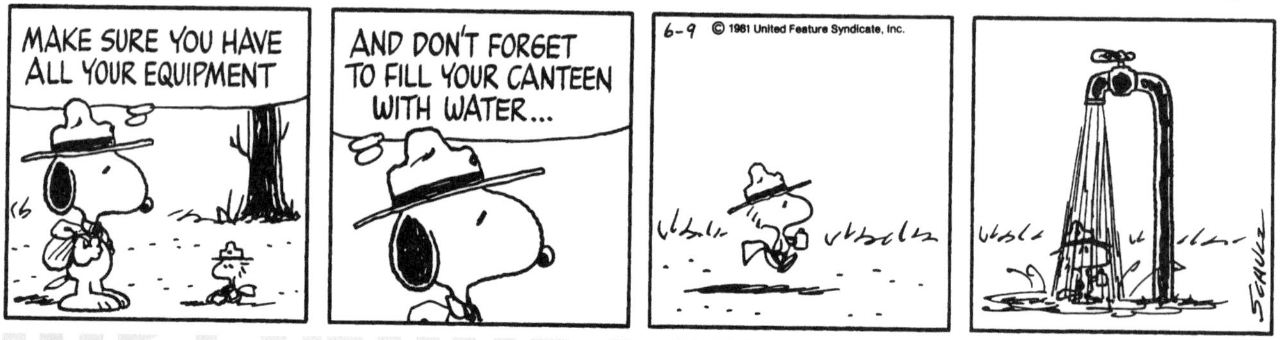
MAKE SURE YOU HAVE ALL YOUR EQUIPMENT
AND DON'T FORGET TO FILL YOUR CANTEEN WITH WATER...
6-9
© 1981 United Feature Syndicate, Inc.
SCHULZ

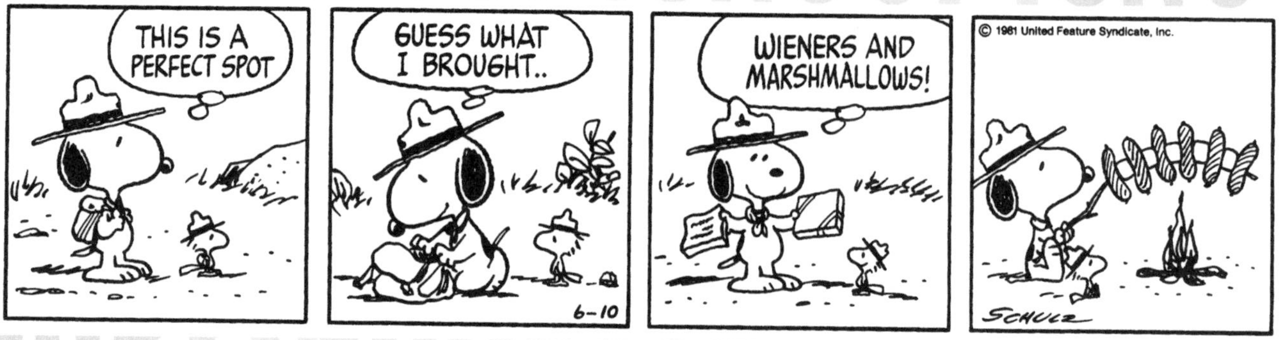
THIS IS A PERFECT SPOT
GUESS WHAT I BROUGHT..
6-10
WIENERS AND MARSHMALLOWS!
© 1981 United Feature Syndicate, Inc.
SCHULZ

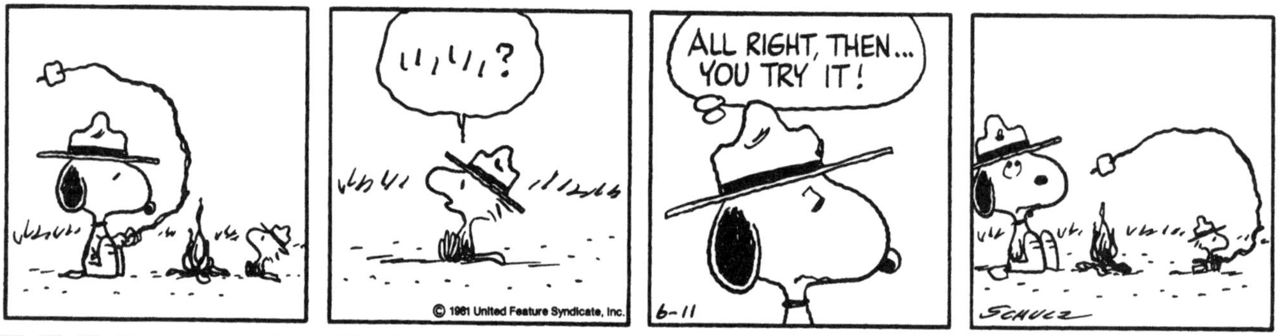
© 1981 United Feature Syndicate, Inc.
ALL RIGHT, THEN... YOU TRY IT!
6-11
SCHULZ

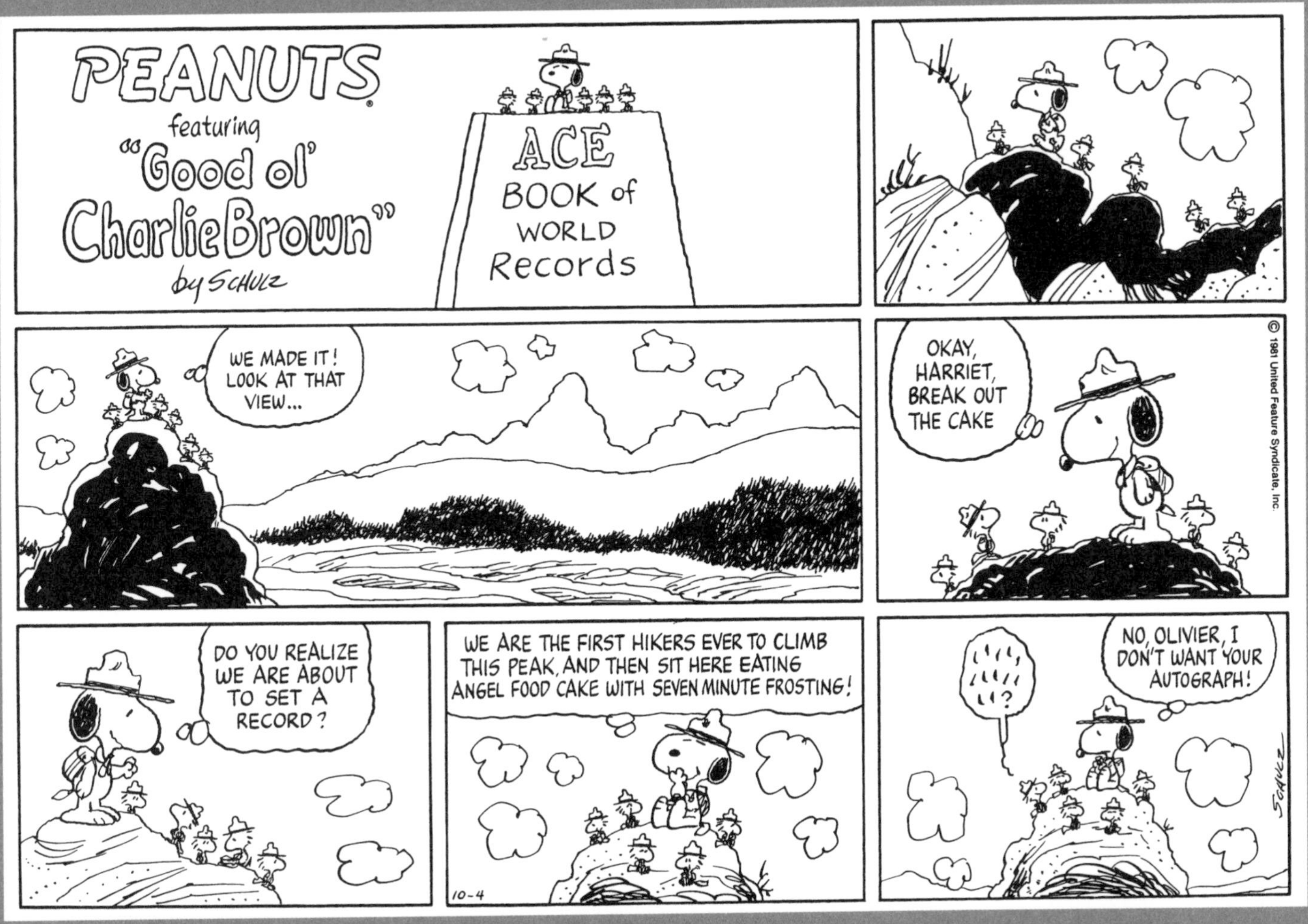
PEANUTS
featuring "Good ol' Charlie Brown"
by SCHULZ
ACE BOOK of WORLD Records
WE MADE IT! LOOK AT THAT VIEW...
OKAY, HARRIET, BREAK OUT THE CAKE
© 1981 United Feature Syndicate, Inc.
DO YOU REALIZE WE ARE ABOUT TO SET A RECORD?
WE ARE THE FIRST HIKERS EVER TO CLIMB THIS PEAK, AND THEN SIT HERE EATING ANGEL FOOD CAKE WITH SEVEN MINUTE FROSTING!
10-4
?
NO, OLIVIER, I DON'T WANT YOUR AUTOGRAPH!
SCHULZ

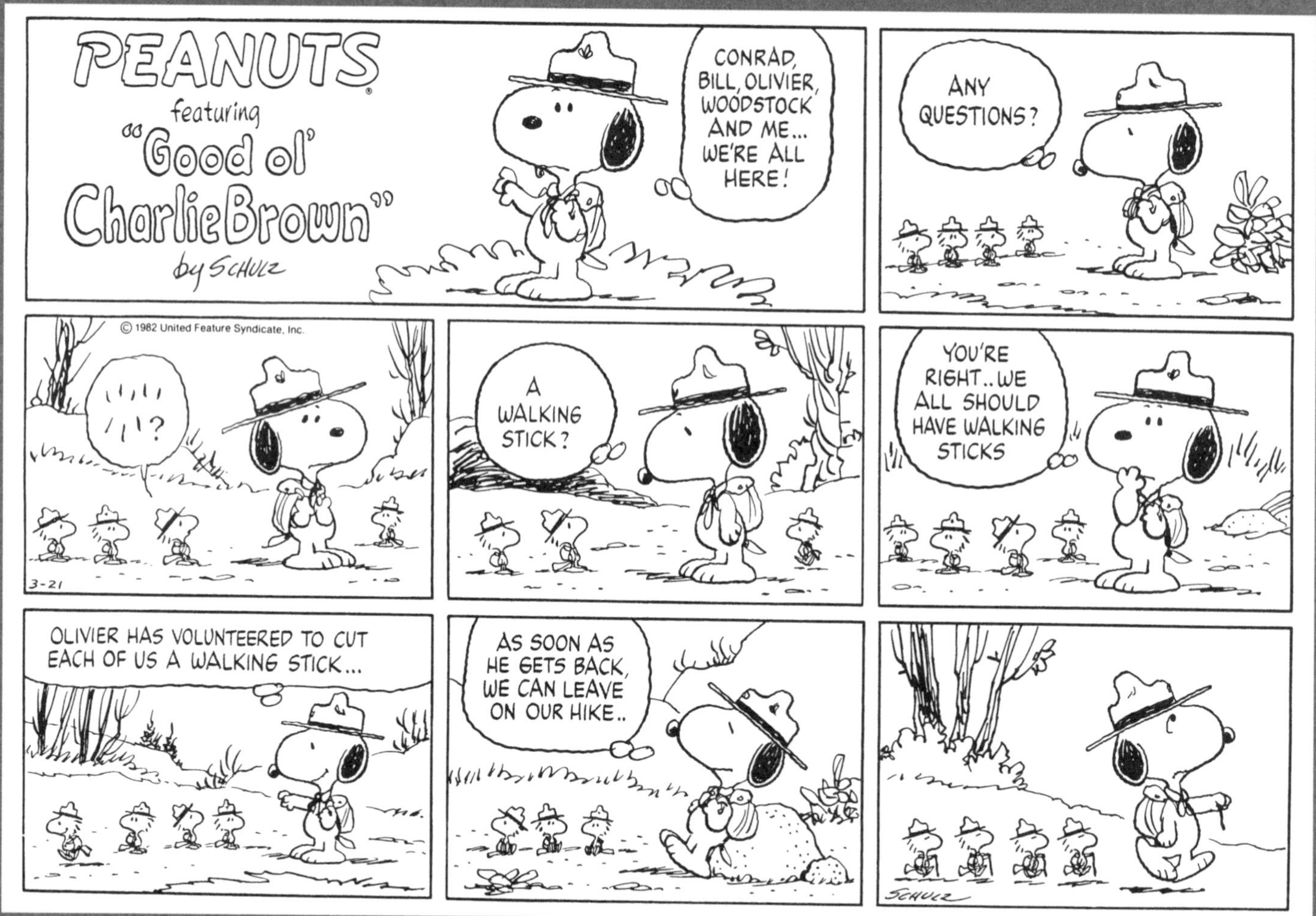
PEANUTS
featuring "Good ol' Charlie Brown"
by SCHULZ
CONRAD, BILL, OLIVIER, WOODSTOCK AND ME... WE'RE ALL HERE!
ANY QUESTIONS?
© 1982 United Feature Syndicate, Inc.
3-21
A WALKING STICK?
YOU'RE RIGHT.. WE ALL SHOULD HAVE WALKING STICKS
OLIVIER HAS VOLUNTEERED TO CUT EACH OF US A WALKING STICK...
AS SOON AS HE GETS BACK, WE CAN LEAVE ON OUR HIKE..
SCHULZ

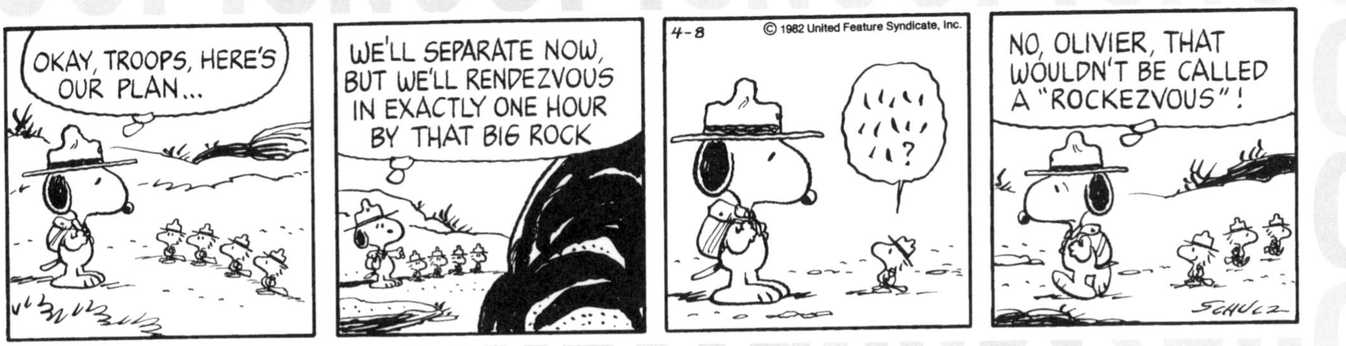
OKAY, TROOPS, HERE'S OUR PLAN...
WE'LL SEPARATE NOW, BUT WE'LL RENDEZVOUS IN EXACTLY ONE HOUR BY THAT BIG ROCK
4-8
© 1982 United Feature Syndicate, Inc.
?
NO, OLIVIER, THAT WOULDN'T BE CALLED A "ROCKEZVOUS"!
SCHULZ

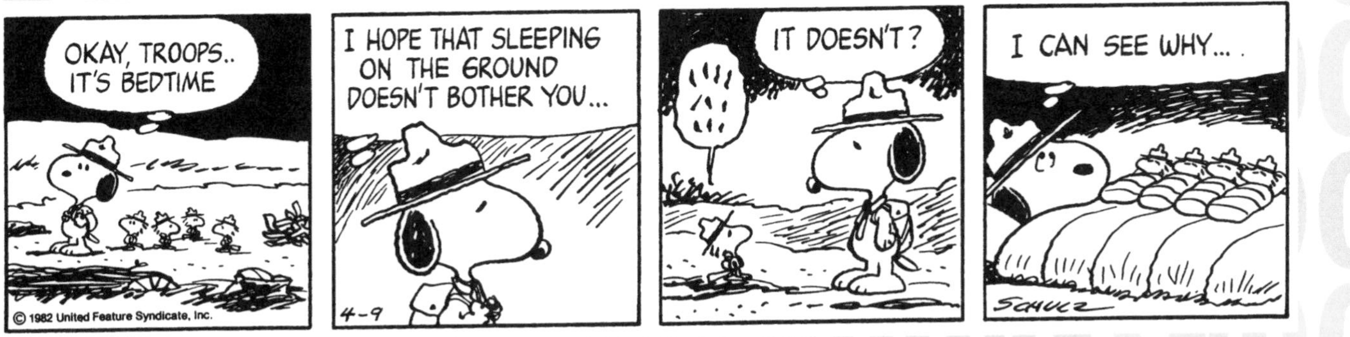
OKAY, TROOPS.. IT'S BEDTIME
© 1982 United Feature Syndicate, Inc.
I HOPE THAT SLEEPING ON THE GROUND DOESN'T BOTHER YOU...
4-9
IT DOESN'T?
I CAN SEE WHY... .
SCHULZ

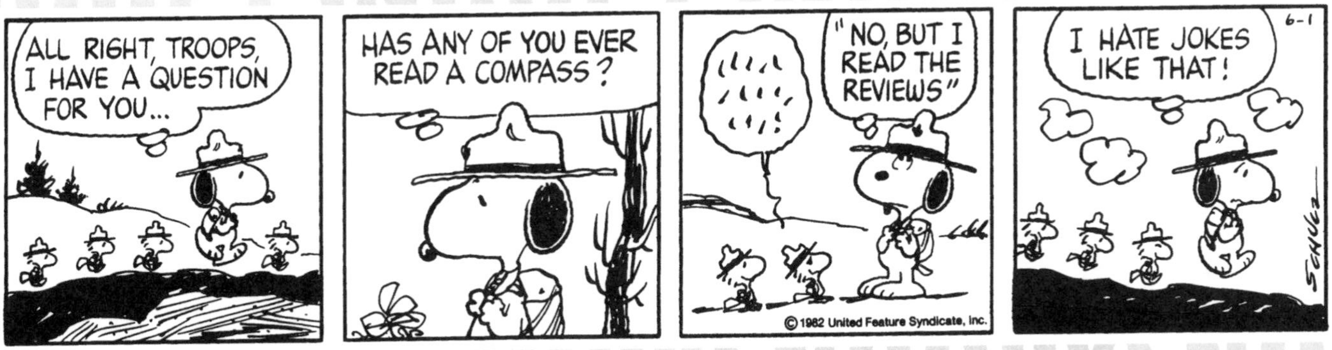
ALL RIGHT, TROOPS, I HAVE A QUESTION FOR YOU...
HAS ANY OF YOU EVER READ A COMPASS?
"NO, BUT I READ THE REVIEWS"
© 1982 United Feature Syndicate, Inc.
6-1
I HATE JOKES LIKE THAT!
SCHULZ

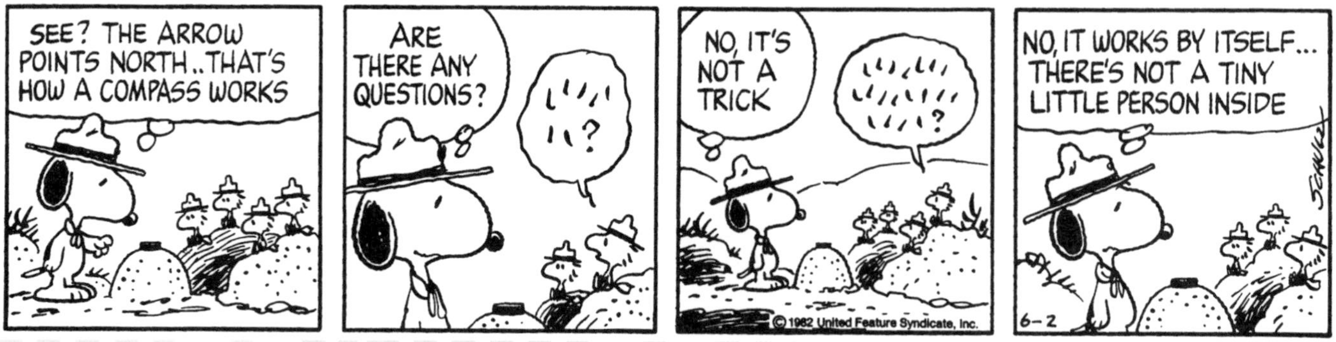
SEE? THE ARROW POINTS NORTH..THAT'S HOW A COMPASS WORKS
ARE THERE ANY QUESTIONS?
NO, IT'S NOT A TRICK
NO, IT WORKS BY ITSELF... THERE'S NOT A TINY LITTLE PERSON INSIDE
© 1982 United Feature Syndicate, Inc.
6-2
SCHULZ

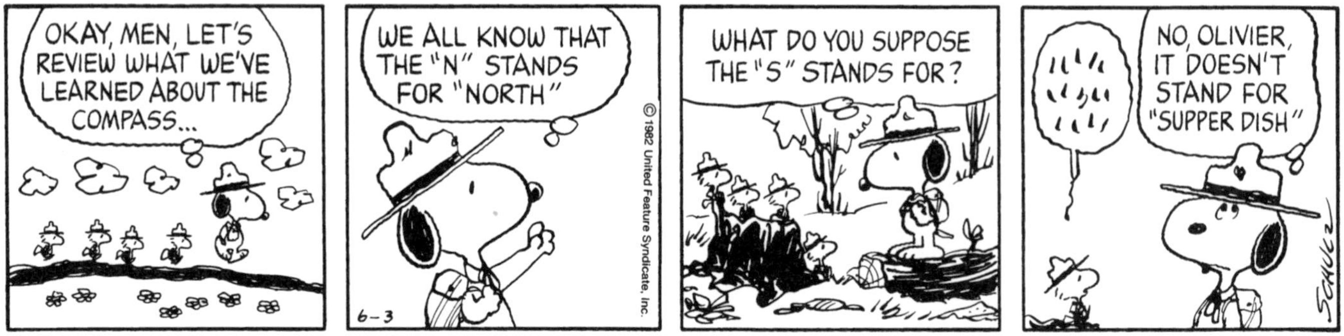
OKAY, MEN, LET'S REVIEW WHAT WE'VE LEARNED ABOUT THE COMPASS...
WE ALL KNOW THAT THE "N" STANDS FOR "NORTH"
© 1982 United Feature Syndicate, Inc.
6-3
WHAT DO YOU SUPPOSE THE "S" STANDS FOR?
NO, OLIVIER, IT DOESN'T STAND FOR "SUPPER DISH"
SCHULZ

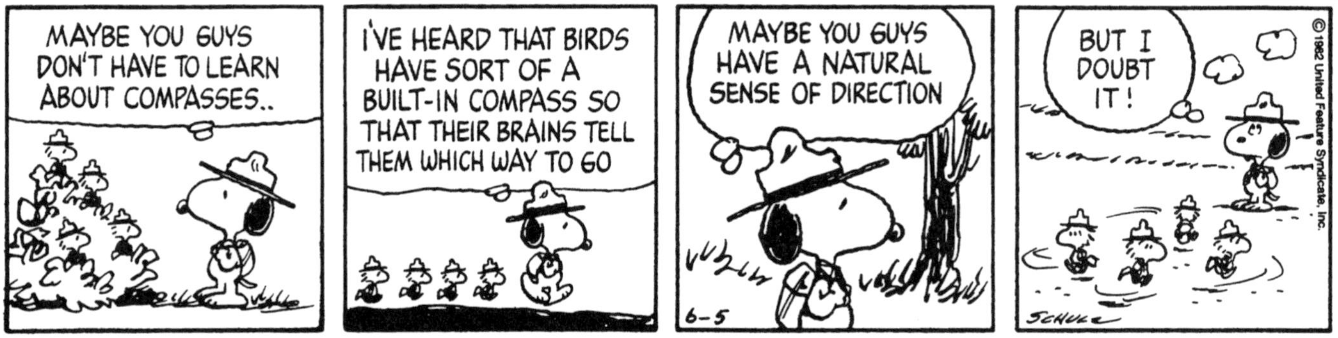
MAYBE YOU GUYS DON'T HAVE TO LEARN ABOUT COMPASSES..
I'VE HEARD THAT BIRDS HAVE SORT OF A BUILT-IN COMPASS SO THAT THEIR BRAINS TELL THEM WHICH WAY TO GO
MAYBE YOU GUYS HAVE A NATURAL SENSE OF DIRECTION
6-5
BUT I DOUBT IT!
© 1982 United Feature Syndicate, Inc.
SCHULZ

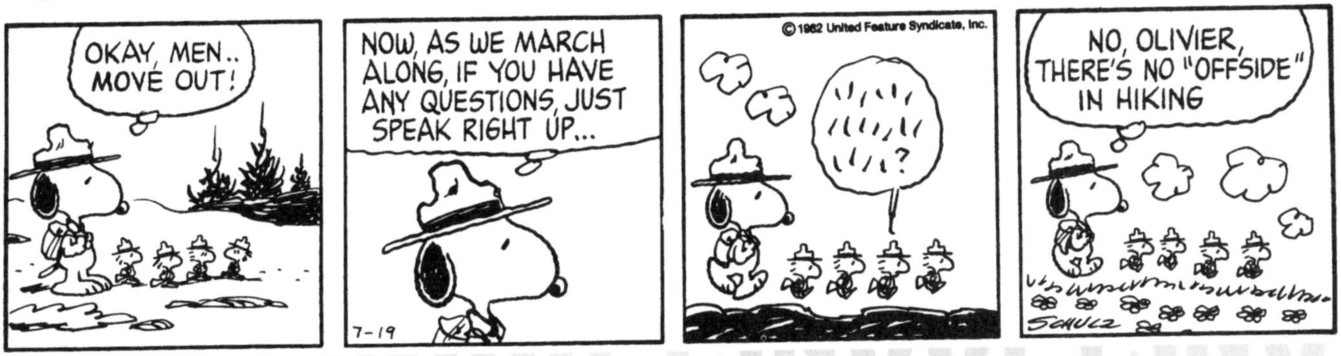
OKAY, MEN.. MOVE OUT!
NOW, AS WE MARCH ALONG, IF YOU HAVE ANY QUESTIONS, JUST SPEAK RIGHT UP...
7-19
© 1982 United Feature Syndicate, Inc.
?
NO, OLIVIER, THERE'S NO "OFFSIDE" IN HIKING
SCHULZ

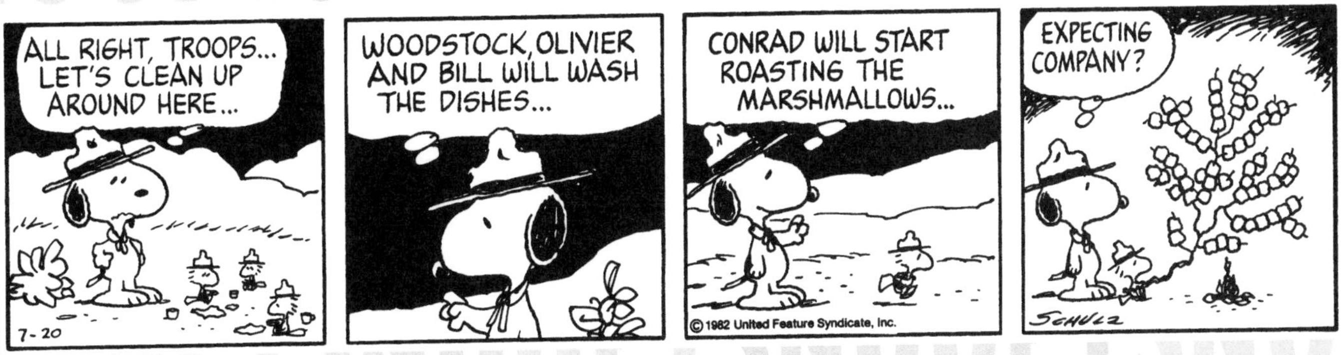
ALL RIGHT, TROOPS... LET'S CLEAN UP AROUND HERE...
7-20
WOODSTOCK, OLIVIER AND BILL WILL WASH THE DISHES...
CONRAD WILL START ROASTING THE MARSHMALLOWS...
© 1982 United Feature Syndicate, Inc.
EXPECTING COMPANY?
SCHULZ

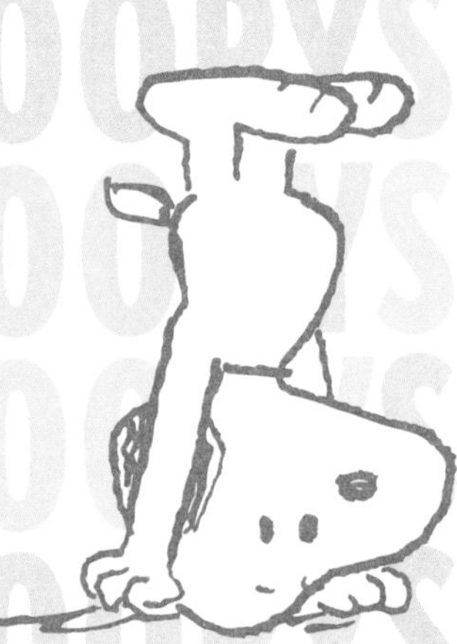

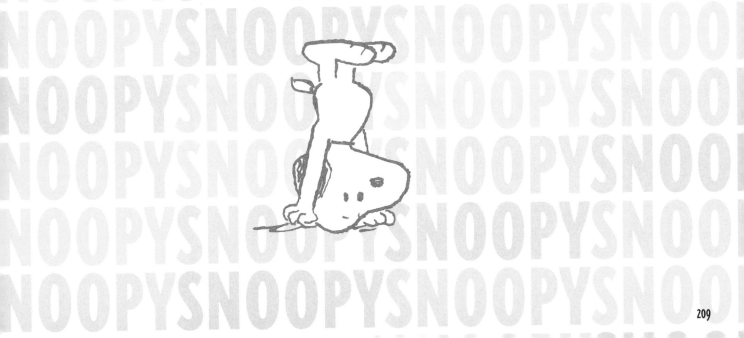

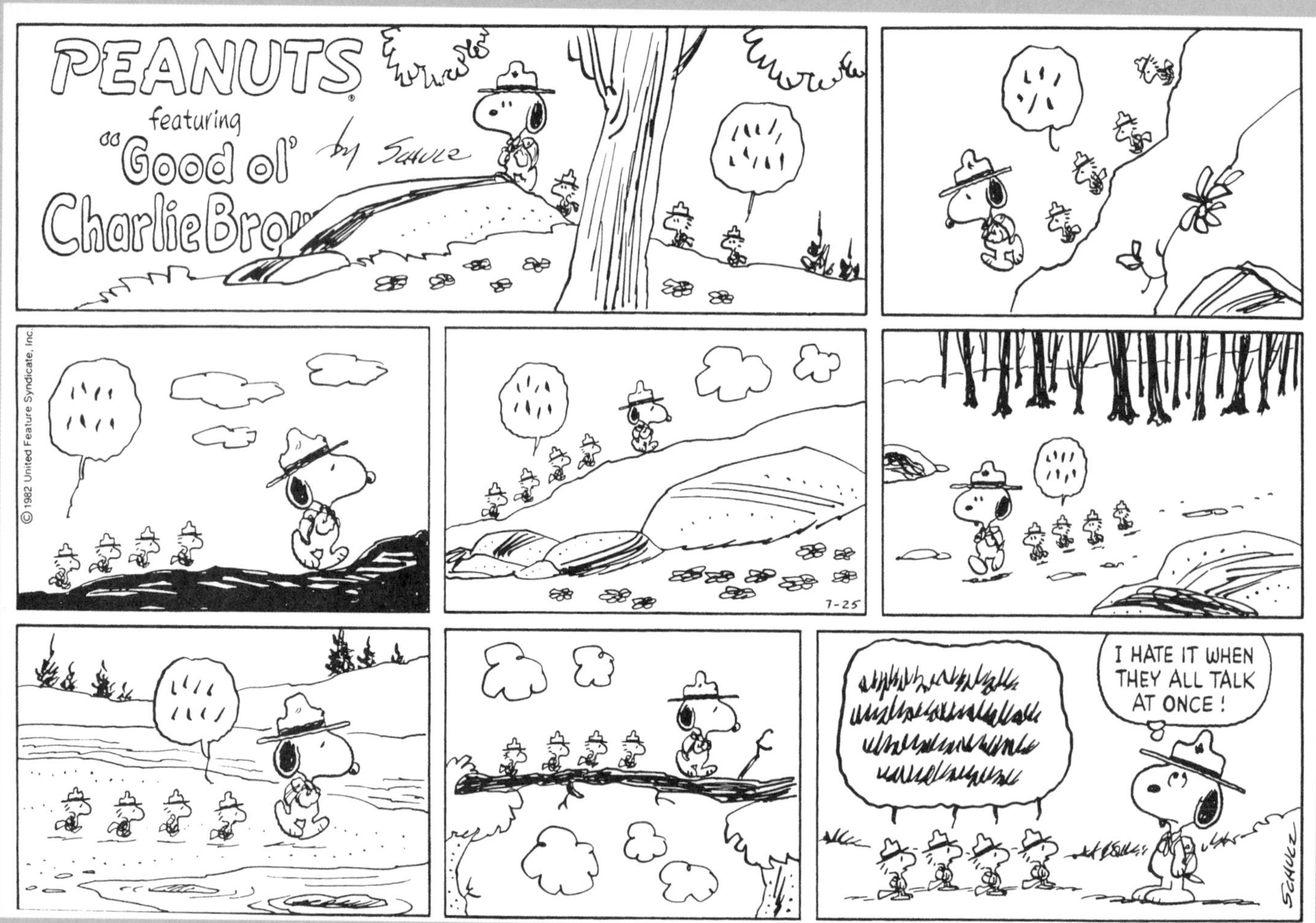
PEANUTS
featuring
"Good ol' CharlieBrown"
by Schulz
© 1982 United Feature Syndicate, Inc.
7-25
I HATE IT WHEN THEY ALL TALK AT ONCE!
SCHULZ

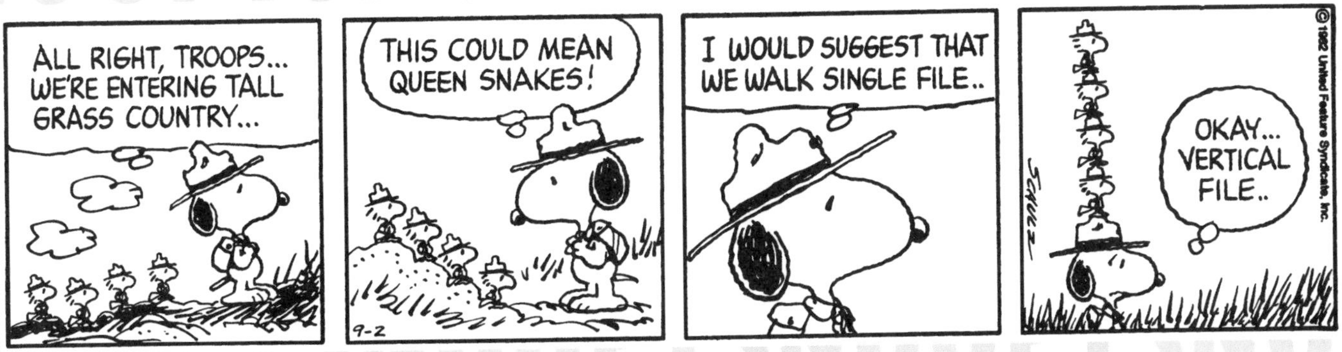
ALL RIGHT, TROOPS... WE'RE ENTERING TALL GRASS COUNTRY...
THIS COULD MEAN QUEEN SNAKES!
9-2
I WOULD SUGGEST THAT WE WALK SINGLE FILE..
OKAY... VERTICAL FILE..
SCHULZ
© 1982 United Feature Syndicate, Inc.

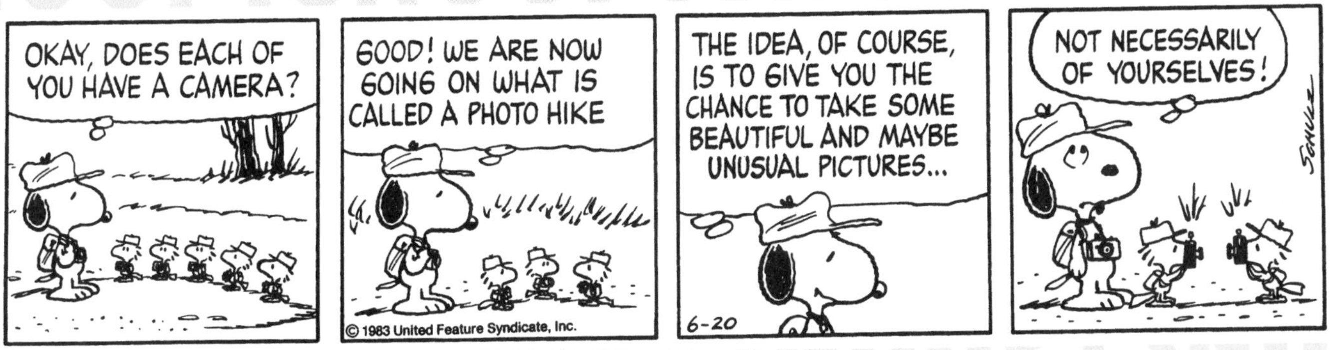
OKAY, DOES EACH OF YOU HAVE A CAMERA?
GOOD! WE ARE NOW GOING ON WHAT IS CALLED A PHOTO HIKE
© 1983 United Feature Syndicate, Inc.
THE IDEA, OF COURSE, IS TO GIVE YOU THE CHANCE TO TAKE SOME BEAUTIFUL AND MAYBE UNUSUAL PICTURES...
6-20
NOT NECESSARILY OF YOURSELVES!
SCHULZ

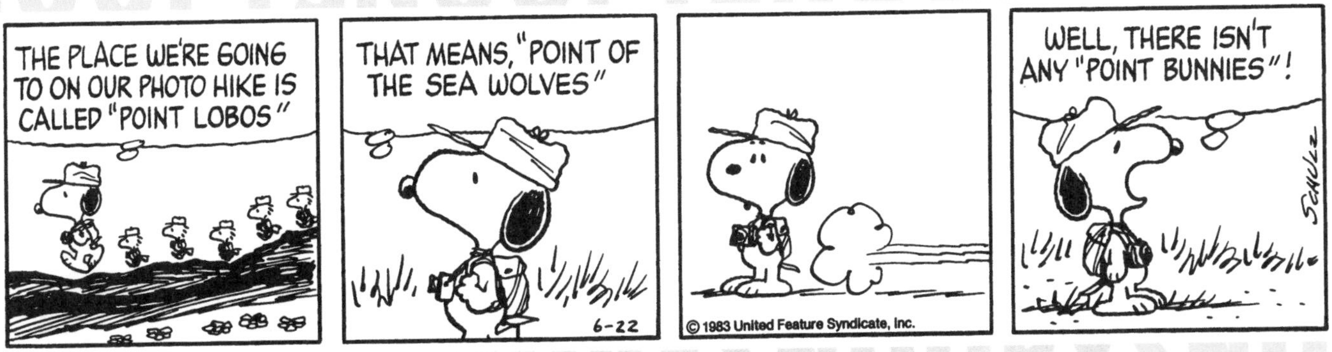
THE PLACE WE'RE GOING TO ON OUR PHOTO HIKE IS CALLED "POINT LOBOS"
THAT MEANS, "POINT OF THE SEA WOLVES"
6-22
© 1983 United Feature Syndicate, Inc.
WELL, THERE ISN'T ANY "POINT BUNNIES"!
SCHULZ

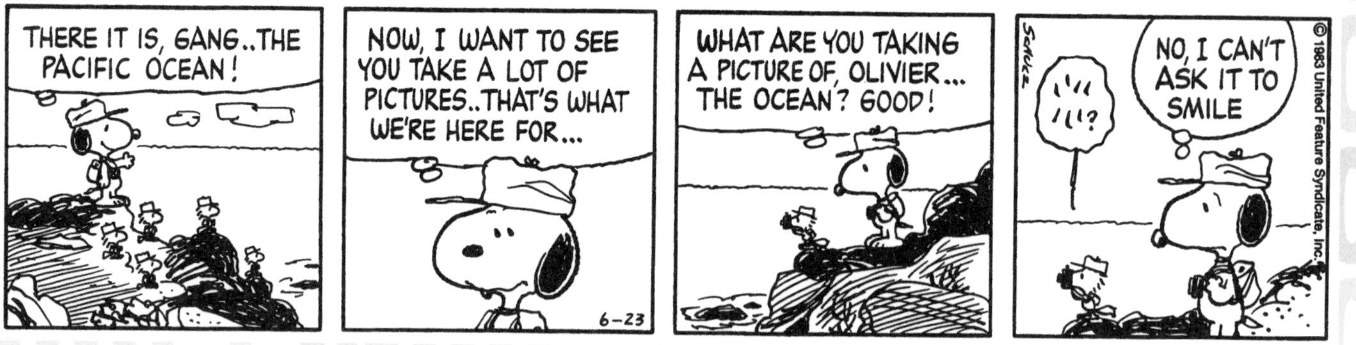
THERE IT IS, GANG..THE PACIFIC OCEAN!
NOW, I WANT TO SEE YOU TAKE A LOT OF PICTURES..THAT'S WHAT WE'RE HERE FOR...
6-23
WHAT ARE YOU TAKING A PICTURE OF, OLIVIER... THE OCEAN? GOOD!
NO, I CAN'T ASK IT TO SMILE
© 1983 United Feature Syndicate, Inc.

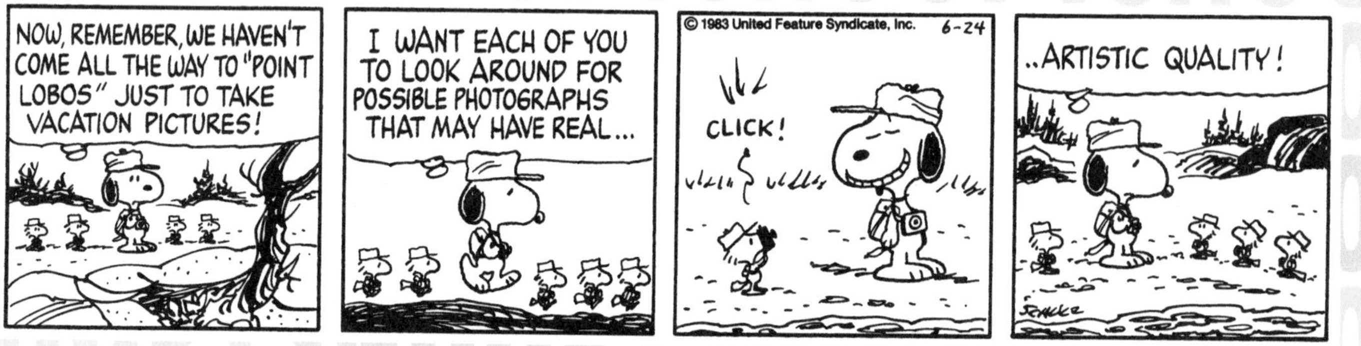
NOW, REMEMBER, WE HAVEN'T COME ALL THE WAY TO "POINT LOBOS" JUST TO TAKE VACATION PICTURES!
I WANT EACH OF YOU TO LOOK AROUND FOR POSSIBLE PHOTOGRAPHS THAT MAY HAVE REAL...
© 1983 United Feature Syndicate, Inc.
6-24
CLICK!
..ARTISTIC QUALITY!

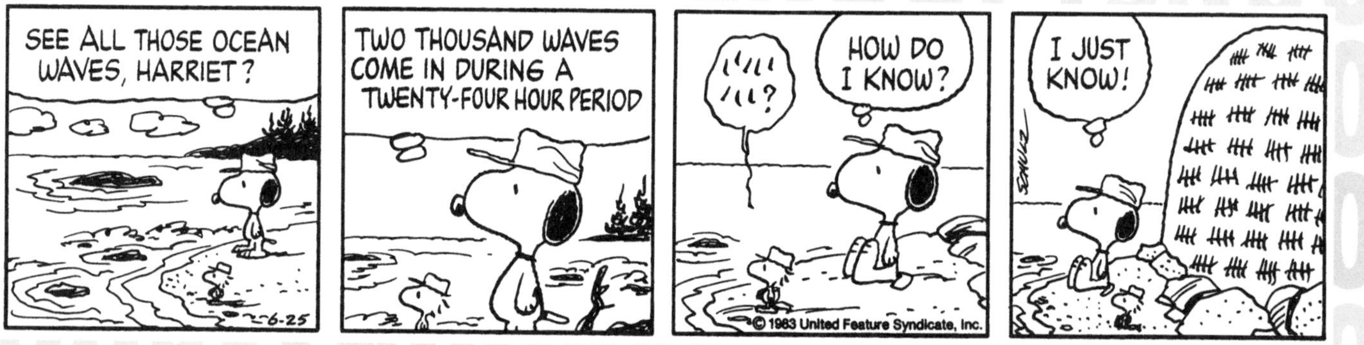
SEE ALL THOSE OCEAN WAVES, HARRIET?
6-25
TWO THOUSAND WAVES COME IN DURING A TWENTY-FOUR HOUR PERIOD
HOW DO I KNOW?
© 1983 United Feature Syndicate, Inc.
I JUST KNOW!

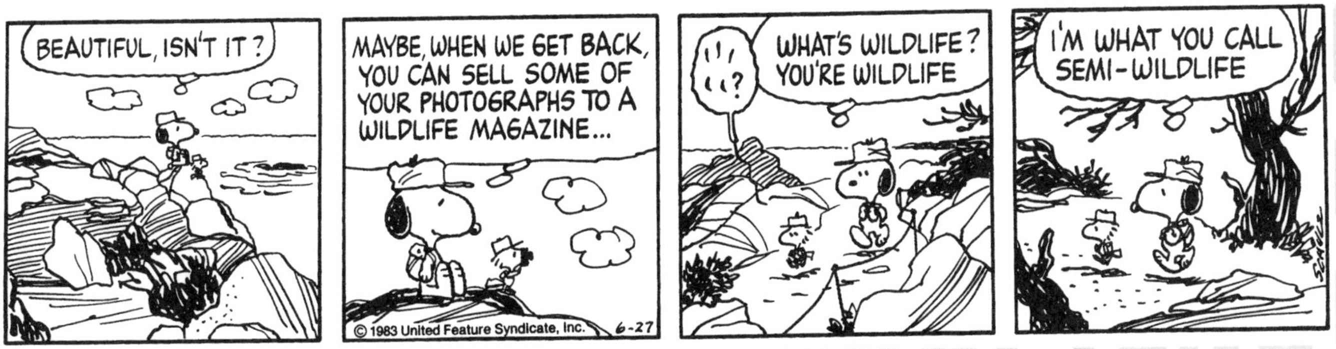
BEAUTIFUL, ISN'T IT?
MAYBE, WHEN WE GET BACK, YOU CAN SELL SOME OF YOUR PHOTOGRAPHS TO A WILDLIFE MAGAZINE...
© 1983 United Feature Syndicate, Inc.
6-27
??
WHAT'S WILDLIFE? YOU'RE WILDLIFE
I'M WHAT YOU CALL SEMI-WILDLIFE
SCHULZ

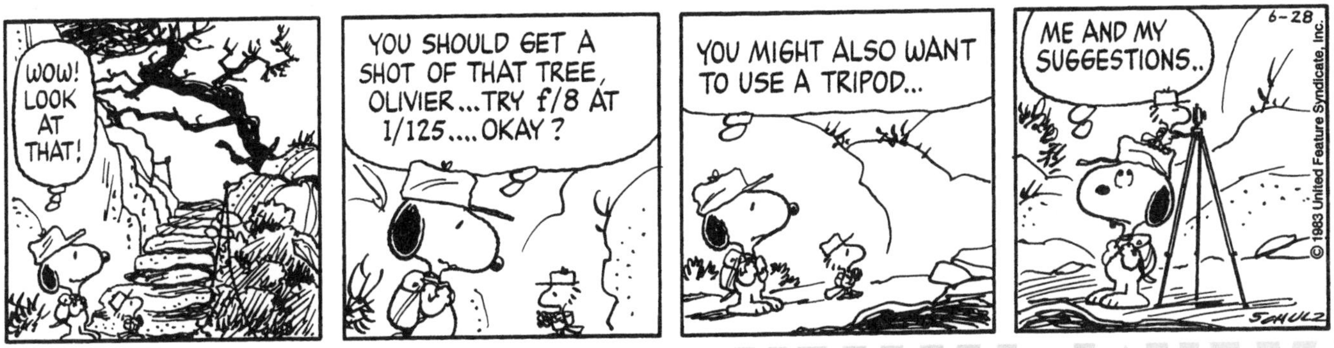
WOW! LOOK AT THAT!
YOU SHOULD GET A SHOT OF THAT TREE, OLIVIER...TRY f/8 AT 1/125....OKAY?
YOU MIGHT ALSO WANT TO USE A TRIPOD...
ME AND MY SUGGESTIONS..
6-28
© 1983 United Feature Syndicate, Inc.
SCHULZ

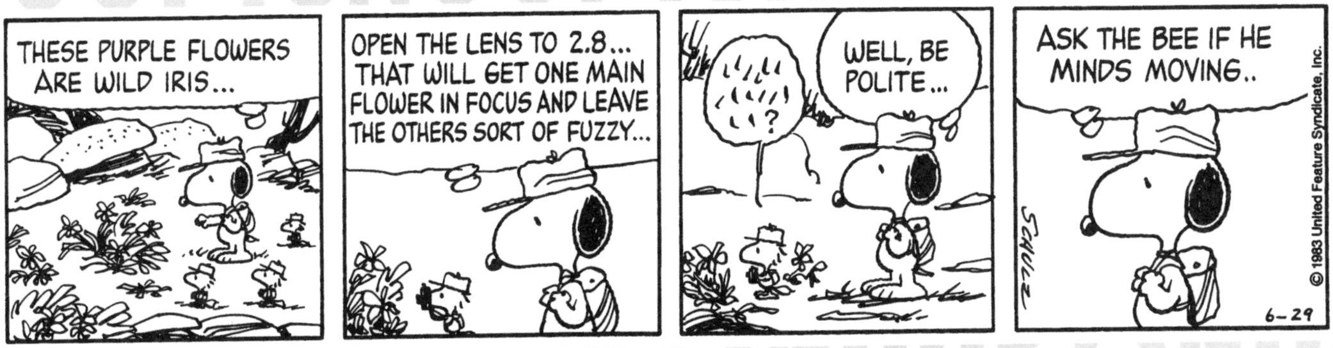
THESE PURPLE FLOWERS ARE WILD IRIS...
OPEN THE LENS TO 2.8... THAT WILL GET ONE MAIN FLOWER IN FOCUS AND LEAVE THE OTHERS SORT OF FUZZY...
?
WELL, BE POLITE...
SCHULZ
ASK THE BEE IF HE MINDS MOVING..
© 1983 United Feature Syndicate, Inc.
6-29

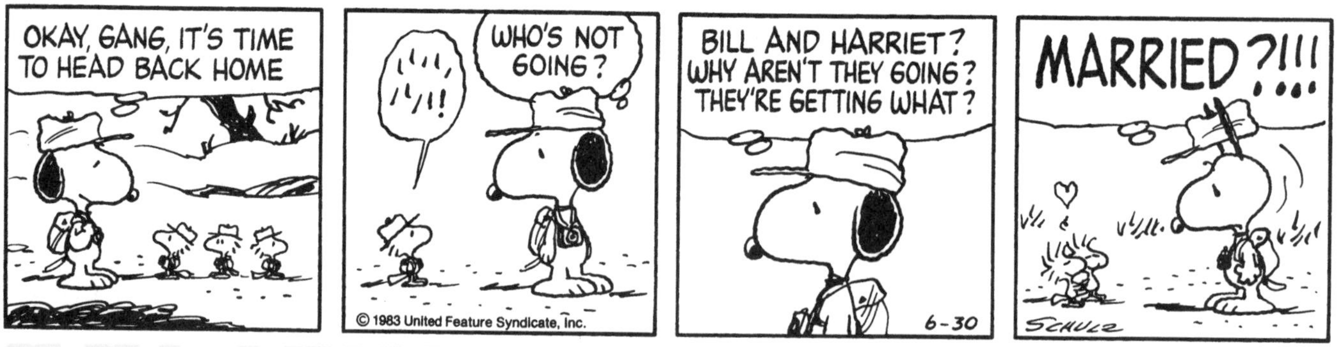
OKAY, GANG, IT'S TIME TO HEAD BACK HOME
WHO'S NOT GOING?
© 1983 United Feature Syndicate, Inc.
BILL AND HARRIET? WHY AREN'T THEY GOING? THEY'RE GETTING WHAT?
6-30
MARRIED?!!!
SCHULZ

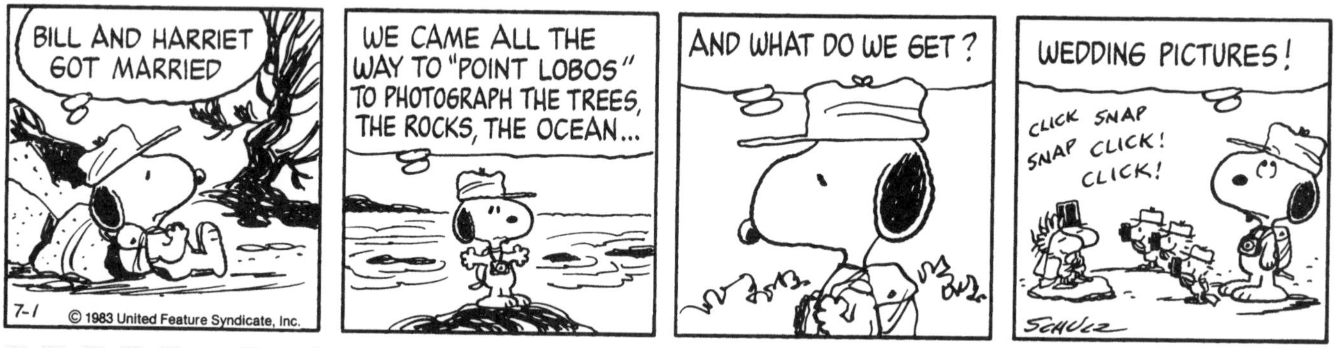
BILL AND HARRIET GOT MARRIED
7-1
© 1983 United Feature Syndicate, Inc.
WE CAME ALL THE WAY TO "POINT LOBOS" TO PHOTOGRAPH THE TREES, THE ROCKS, THE OCEAN...
AND WHAT DO WE GET?
WEDDING PICTURES!
CLICK SNAP
SNAP CLICK!
CLICK!
SCHULZ

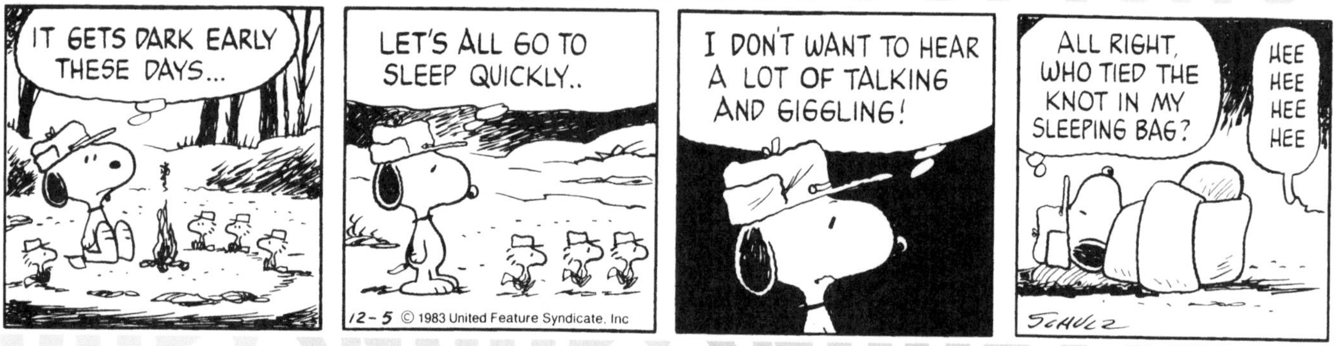
IT GETS DARK EARLY THESE DAYS...
LET'S ALL GO TO SLEEP QUICKLY..
12-5
© 1983 United Feature Syndicate, Inc
I DON'T WANT TO HEAR A LOT OF TALKING AND GIGGLING!
ALL RIGHT, WHO TIED THE KNOT IN MY SLEEPING BAG?
HEE HEE HEE HEE
SCHULZ

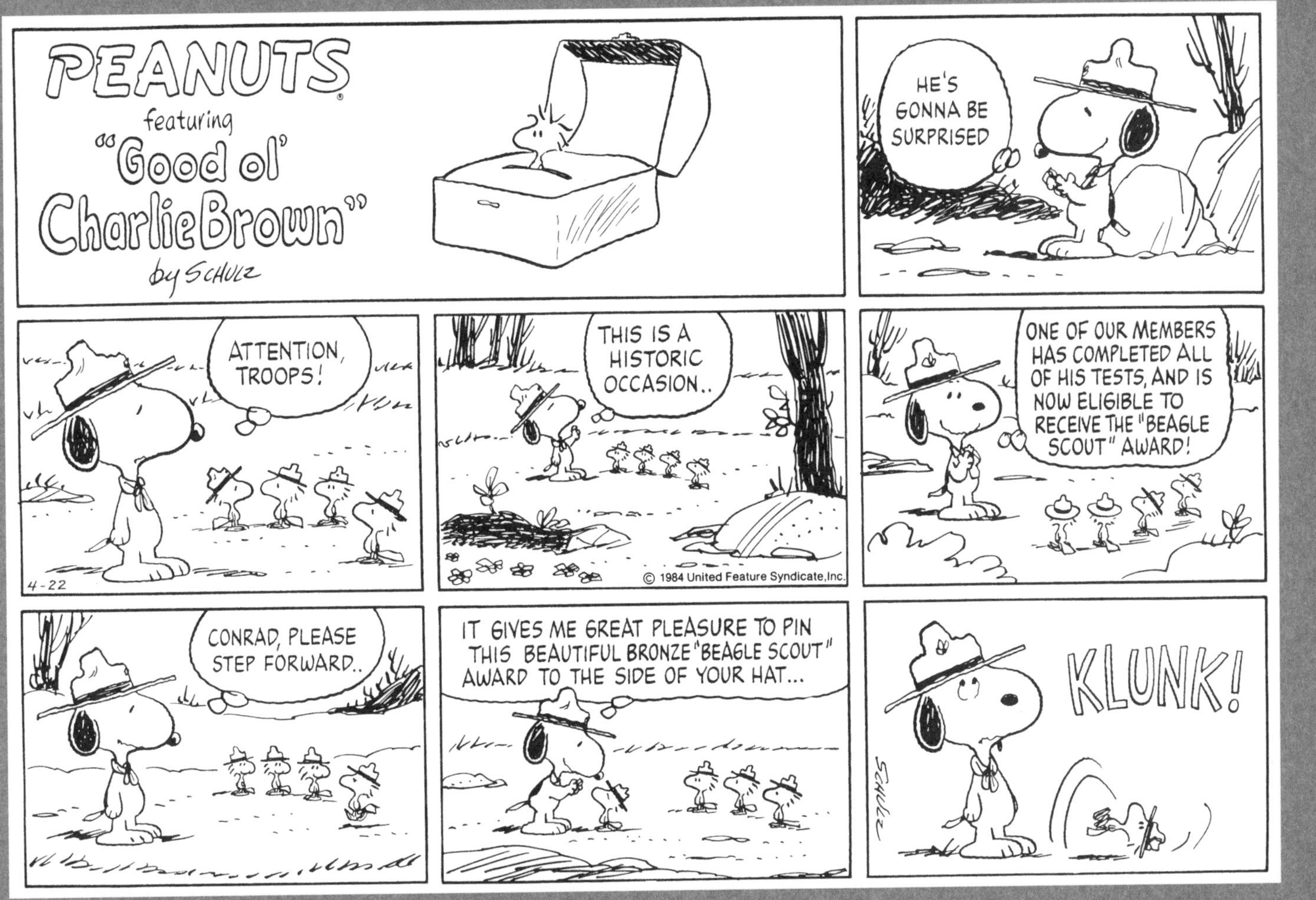
PEANUTS
featuring
"Good ol' Charlie Brown"
by SCHULZ
HE'S GONNA BE SURPRISED
ATTENTION, TROOPS!
4-22
THIS IS A HISTORIC OCCASION..
© 1984 United Feature Syndicate, Inc.
ONE OF OUR MEMBERS HAS COMPLETED ALL OF HIS TESTS, AND IS NOW ELIGIBLE TO RECEIVE THE "BEAGLE SCOUT" AWARD!
CONRAD, PLEASE STEP FORWARD..
IT GIVES ME GREAT PLEASURE TO PIN THIS BEAUTIFUL BRONZE "BEAGLE SCOUT" AWARD TO THE SIDE OF YOUR HAT...
SCHULZ
KLUNK!

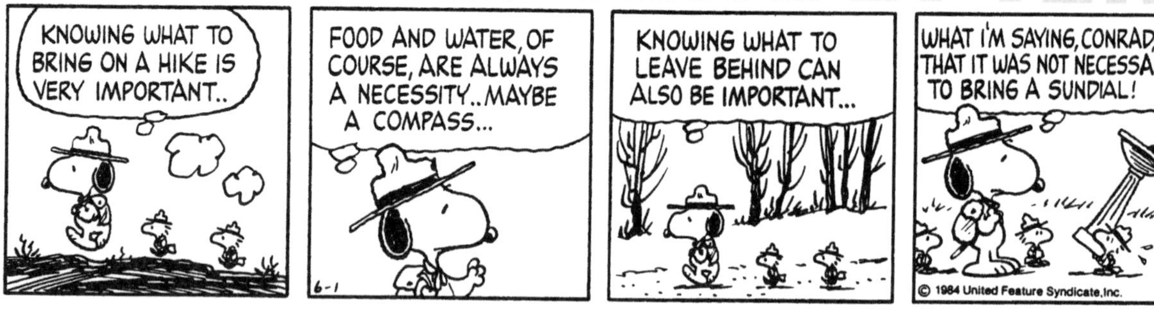
KNOWING WHAT TO BRING ON A HIKE IS VERY IMPORTANT..
FOOD AND WATER, OF COURSE, ARE ALWAYS A NECESSITY..MAYBE A COMPASS...
6-1
KNOWING WHAT TO LEAVE BEHIND CAN ALSO BE IMPORTANT...
WHAT I'M SAYING, CONRAD, IS THAT IT WAS NOT NECESSARY TO BRING A SUNDIAL!
SCHULZ
© 1984 United Feature Syndicate, Inc.

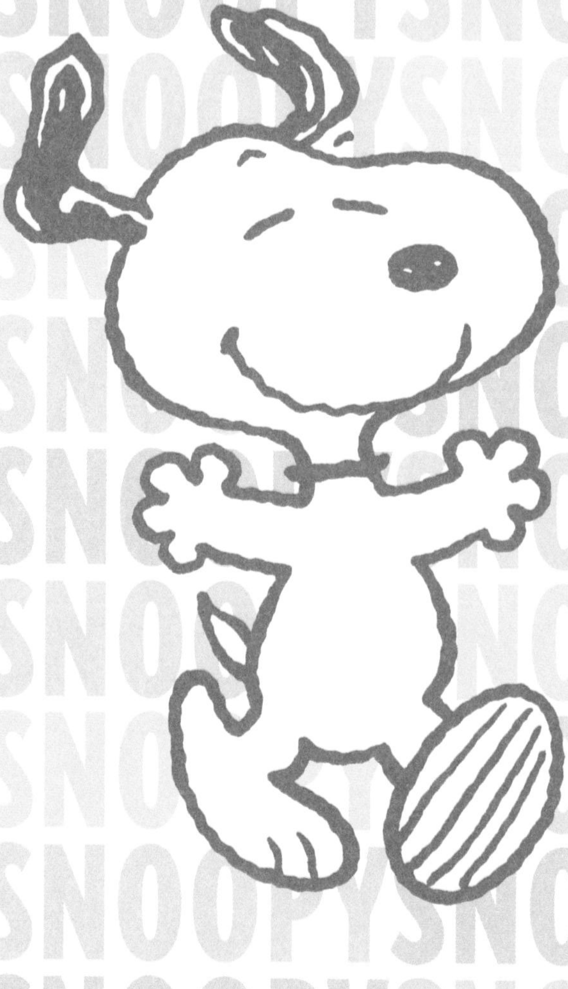

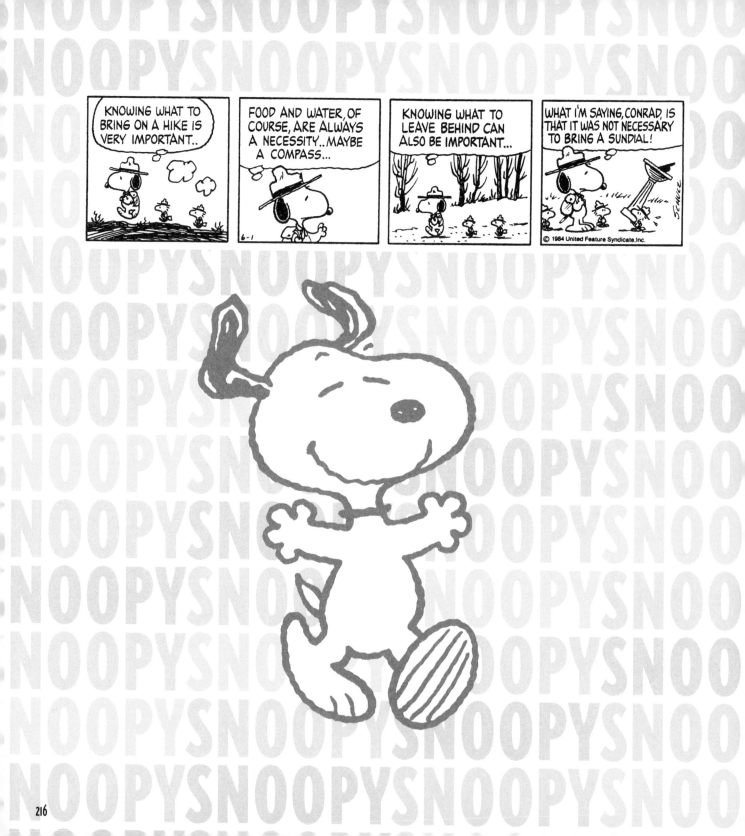

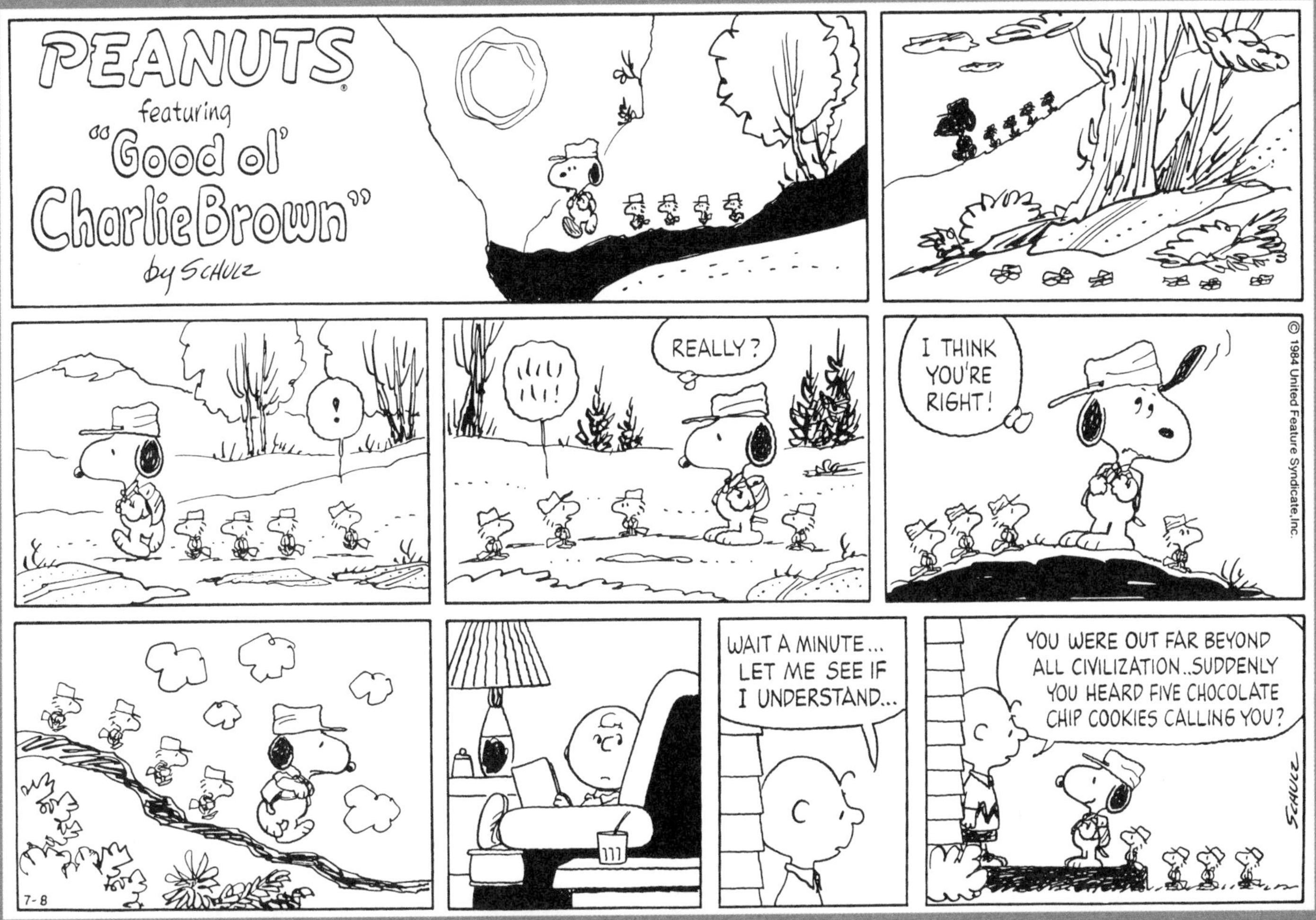
PEANUTS
featuring "Good ol' Charlie Brown"
by SCHULZ
!
REALLY?
I THINK YOU'RE RIGHT!
© 1984 United Feature Syndicate, Inc.
7-8
WAIT A MINUTE... LET ME SEE IF I UNDERSTAND...
YOU WERE OUT FAR BEYOND ALL CIVILIZATION..SUDDENLY YOU HEARD FIVE CHOCOLATE CHIP COOKIES CALLING YOU?
SCHULZ

THIS IS MY FAVORITE TIME OF DAY...

ONE OF THE GREAT JOYS OF LIFE IS SHARING A MEAL AROUND A CAMPFIRE...

8-4

© 1984 United Feature Syndicate, Inc.

NO, CONRAD, I DON'T KNOW HOW YOU KEEP THE BUTTER FROM FALLING OFF THE BREAD STICKS...

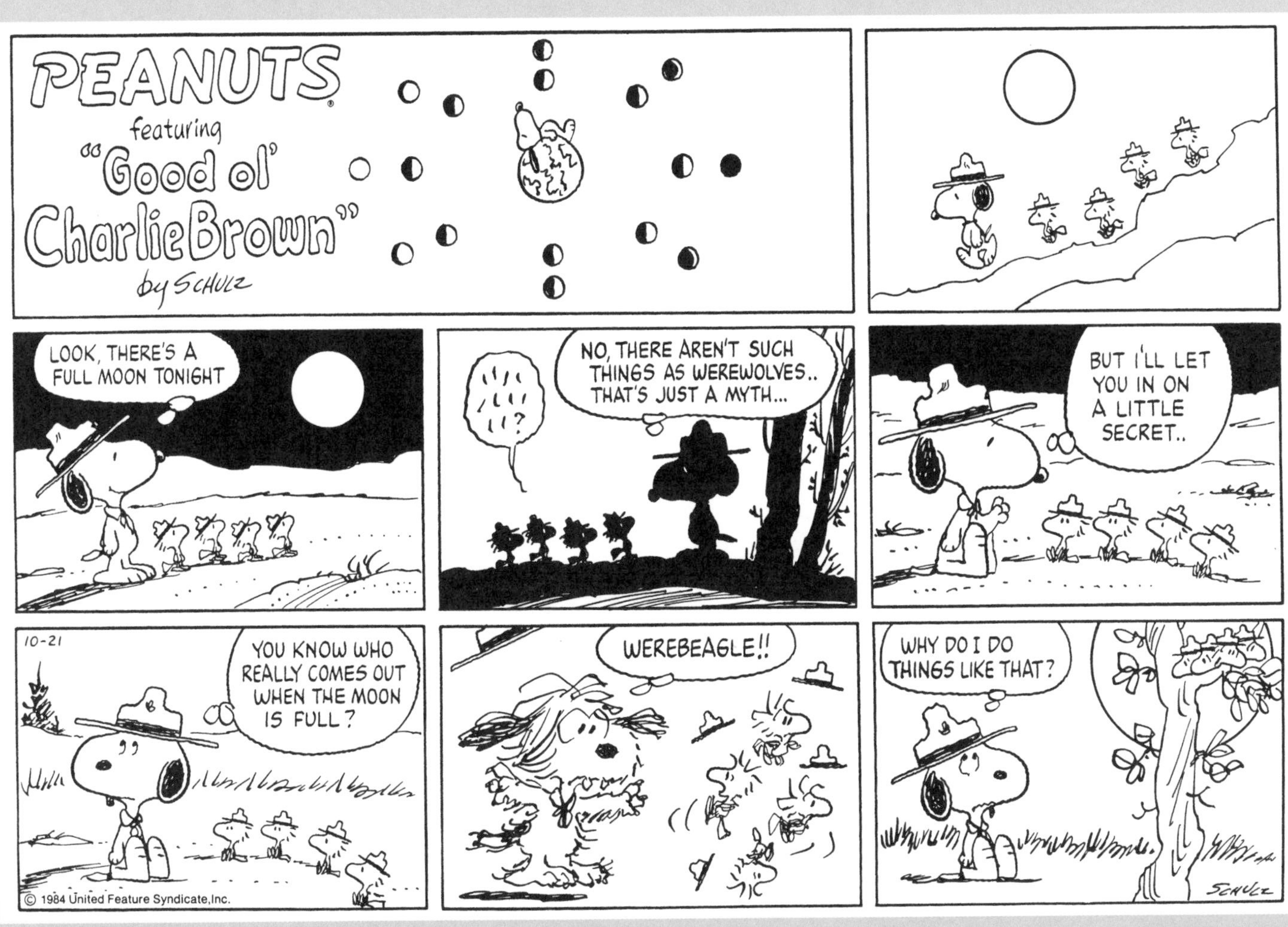

PEANUTS
featuring
"Good ol' Charlie Brown"
by SCHULZ
LOOK, THERE'S A FULL MOON TONIGHT
NO, THERE AREN'T SUCH THINGS AS WEREWOLVES.. THAT'S JUST A MYTH...
?
BUT I'LL LET YOU IN ON A LITTLE SECRET..
10-21
YOU KNOW WHO REALLY COMES OUT WHEN THE MOON IS FULL?
© 1984 United Feature Syndicate, Inc.
WEREBEAGLE!!
WHY DO I DO THINGS LIKE THAT?
SCHULZ

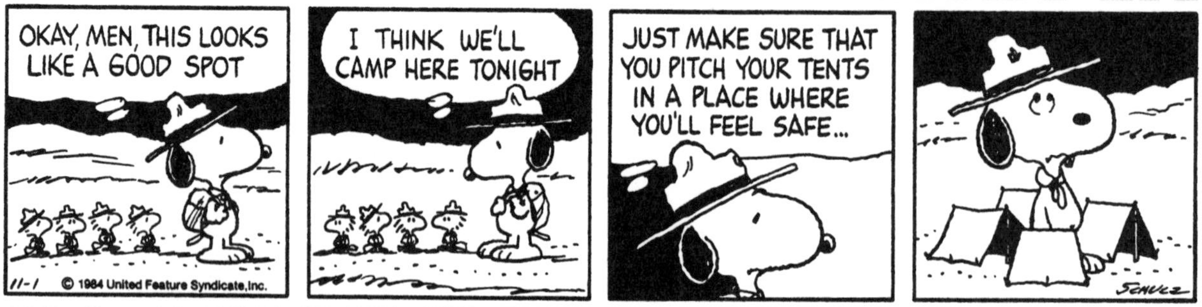
OKAY, MEN, THIS LOOKS LIKE A GOOD SPOT
11-1 © 1984 United Feature Syndicate, Inc.
I THINK WE'LL CAMP HERE TONIGHT
JUST MAKE SURE THAT YOU PITCH YOUR TENTS IN A PLACE WHERE YOU'LL FEEL SAFE...
SCHULZ

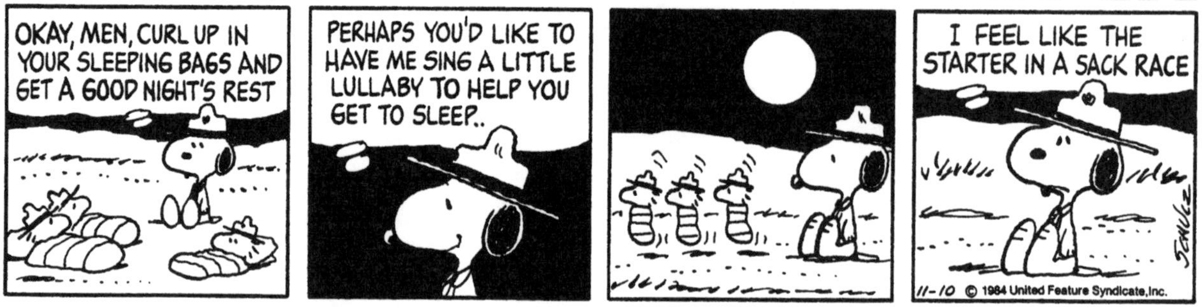
OKAY, MEN, CURL UP IN YOUR SLEEPING BAGS AND GET A GOOD NIGHT'S REST
PERHAPS YOU'D LIKE TO HAVE ME SING A LITTLE LULLABY TO HELP YOU GET TO SLEEP..
I FEEL LIKE THE STARTER IN A SACK RACE
SCHULZ
11-10 © 1984 United Feature Syndicate, Inc.

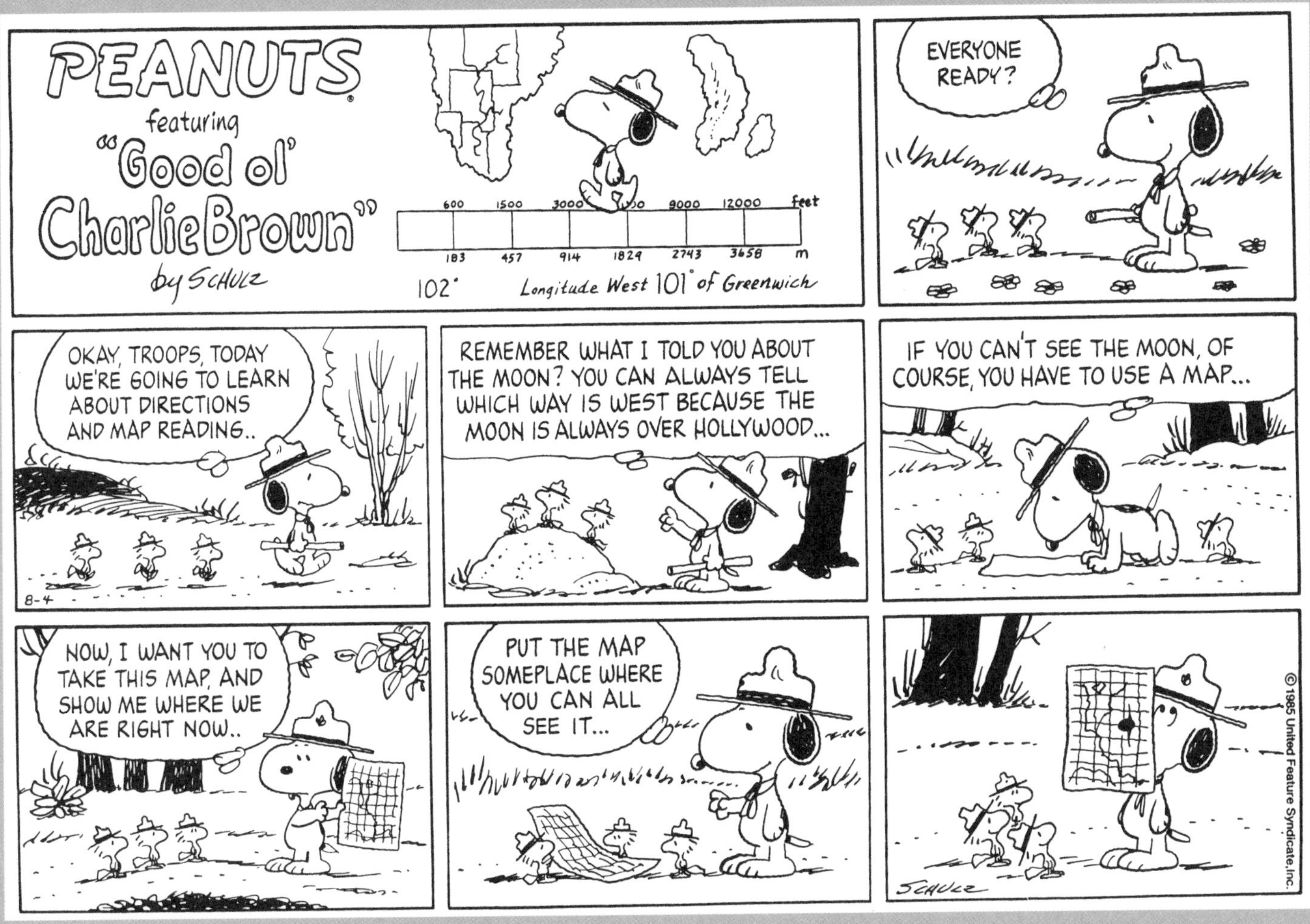
PEANUTS
featuring
"Good ol' CharlieBrown"
by SCHULZ
600 1500 3000 9000 12000 feet
183 457 914 1829 2743 3658 m
102°
Longitude West 101° of Greenwich
EVERYONE READY?
OKAY, TROOPS, TODAY WE'RE GOING TO LEARN ABOUT DIRECTIONS AND MAP READING..
8-4
REMEMBER WHAT I TOLD YOU ABOUT THE MOON? YOU CAN ALWAYS TELL WHICH WAY IS WEST BECAUSE THE MOON IS ALWAYS OVER HOLLYWOOD...
IF YOU CAN'T SEE THE MOON, OF COURSE, YOU HAVE TO USE A MAP...
NOW, I WANT YOU TO TAKE THIS MAP, AND SHOW ME WHERE WE ARE RIGHT NOW..
PUT THE MAP SOMEPLACE WHERE YOU CAN ALL SEE IT...
SCHULZ
©1985 United Feature Syndicate, Inc.

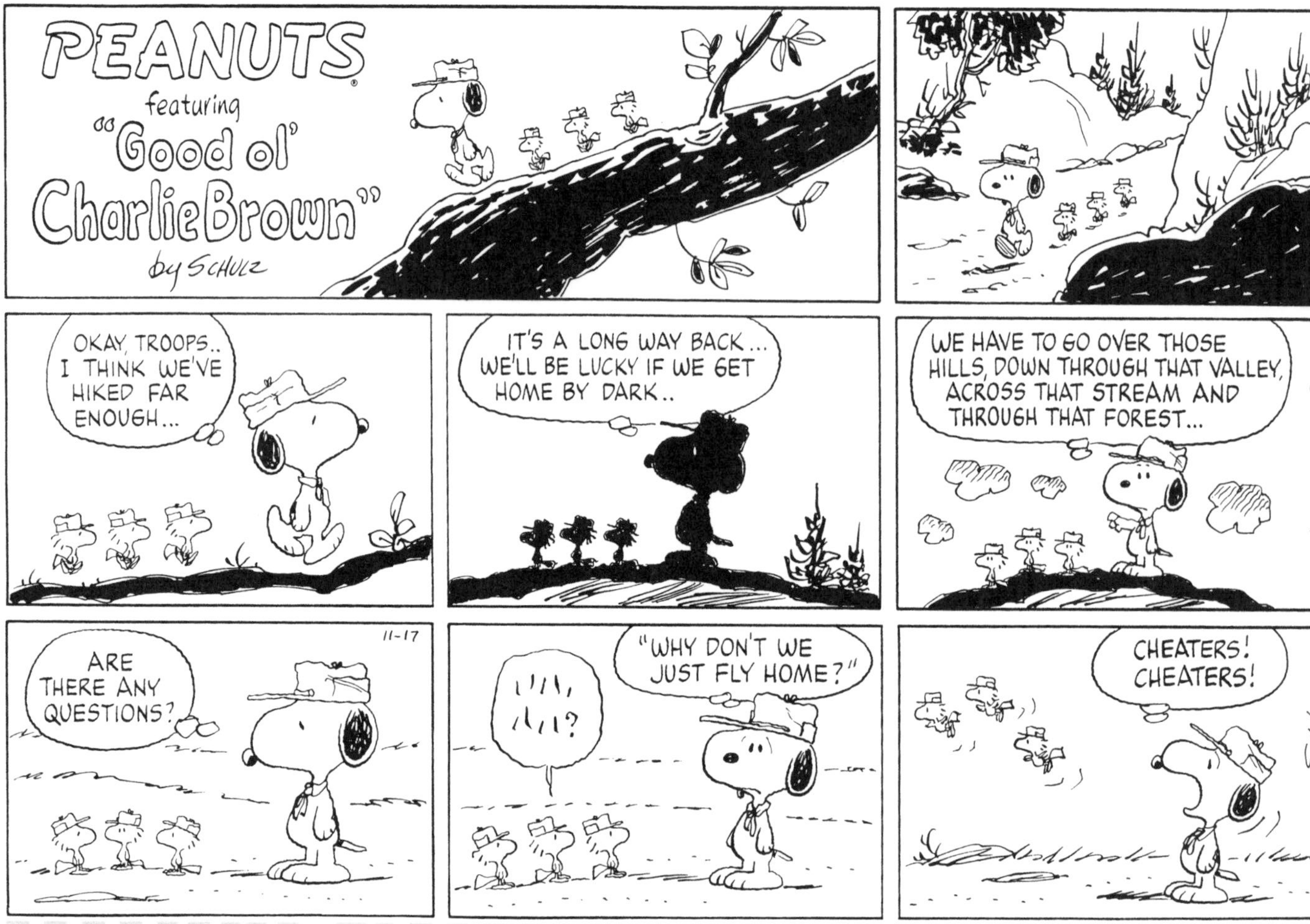
PEANUTS
featuring "Good ol' CharlieBrown"
by SCHULZ
OKAY, TROOPS.. I THINK WE'VE HIKED FAR ENOUGH...
IT'S A LONG WAY BACK... WE'LL BE LUCKY IF WE GET HOME BY DARK..
WE HAVE TO GO OVER THOSE HILLS, DOWN THROUGH THAT VALLEY, ACROSS THAT STREAM AND THROUGH THAT FOREST...
© 1985 United Feature Syndicate, Inc.
11-17
ARE THERE ANY QUESTIONS?
"WHY DON'T WE JUST FLY HOME?"
CHEATERS! CHEATERS!
SCHULZ

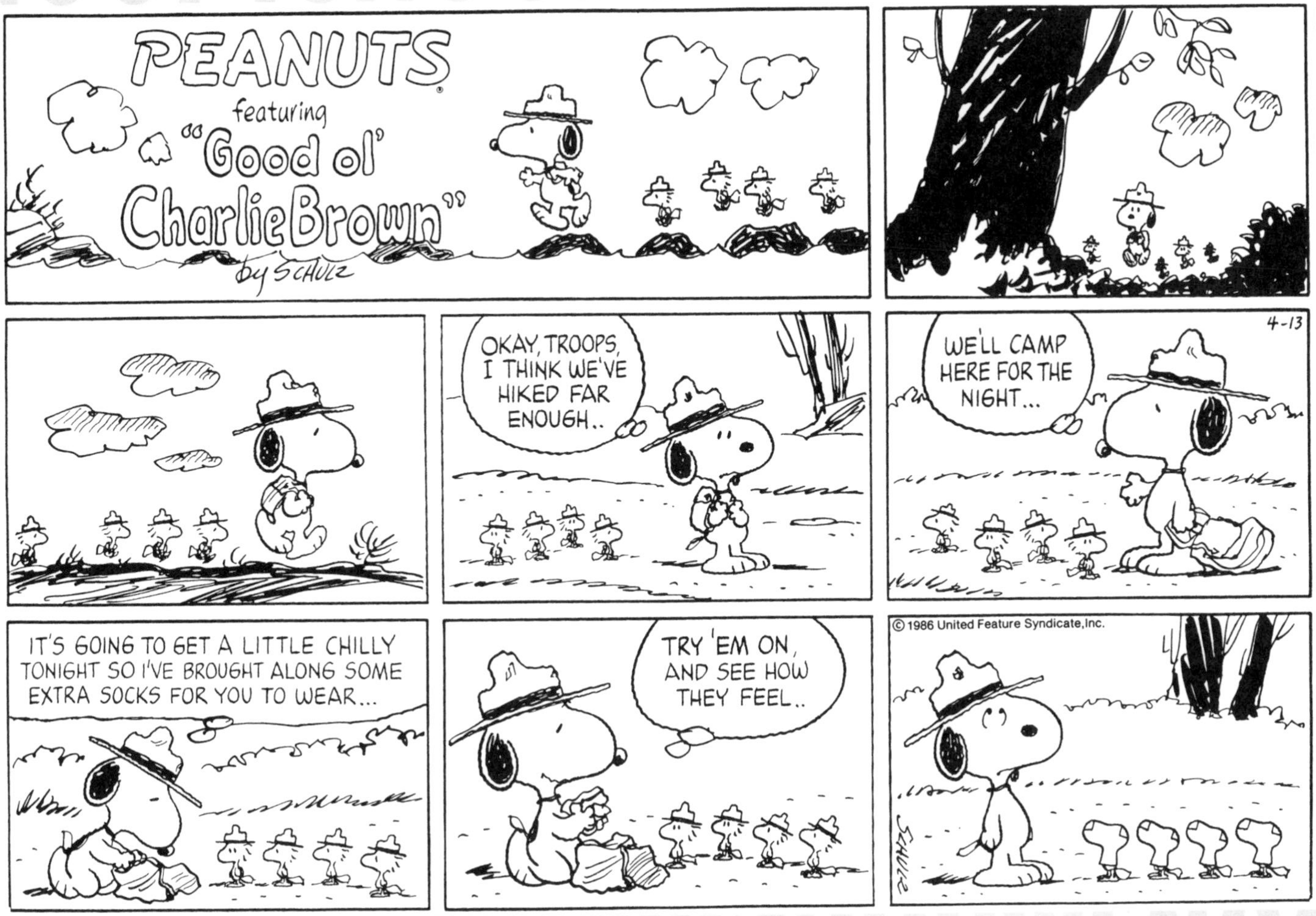
PEANUTS
featuring
"Good ol' Charlie Brown"
by SCHULZ
OKAY, TROOPS, I THINK WE'VE HIKED FAR ENOUGH..
4-13
WE'LL CAMP HERE FOR THE NIGHT...
IT'S GOING TO GET A LITTLE CHILLY TONIGHT SO I'VE BROUGHT ALONG SOME EXTRA SOCKS FOR YOU TO WEAR...
TRY 'EM ON, AND SEE HOW THEY FEEL..
© 1986 United Feature Syndicate, Inc.
SCHULZ

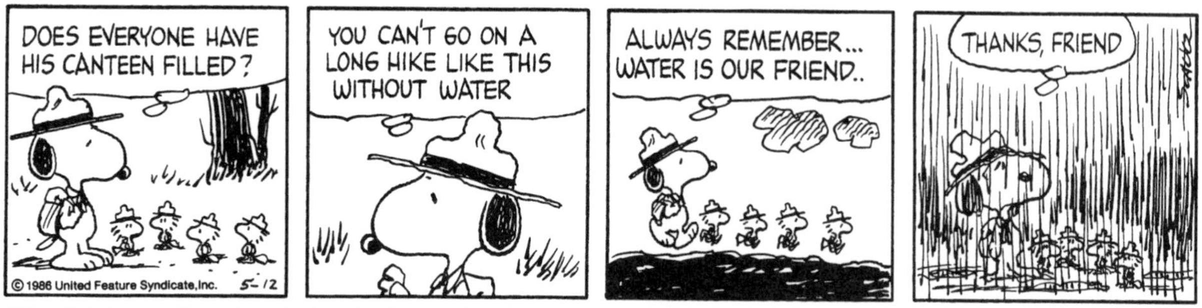
DOES EVERYONE HAVE HIS CANTEEN FILLED?
© 1986 United Feature Syndicate,Inc.
5-12
YOU CAN'T GO ON A LONG HIKE LIKE THIS WITHOUT WATER
ALWAYS REMEMBER... WATER IS OUR FRIEND..
THANKS, FRIEND
SCHULZ

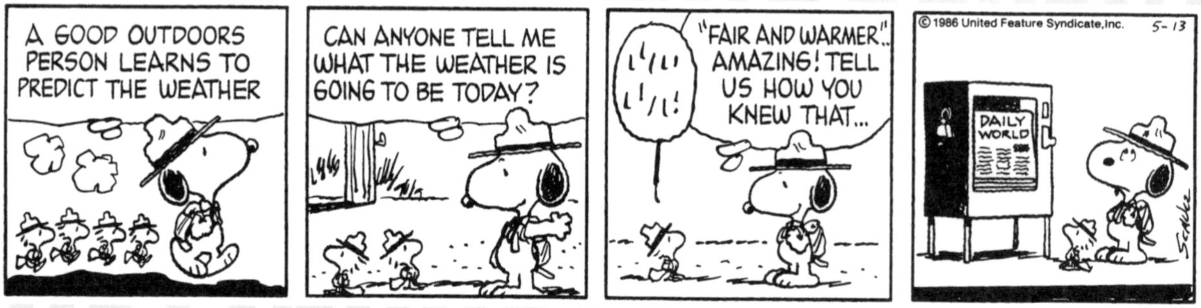
A GOOD OUTDOORS PERSON LEARNS TO PREDICT THE WEATHER
CAN ANYONE TELL ME WHAT THE WEATHER IS GOING TO BE TODAY?
"FAIR AND WARMER".. AMAZING! TELL US HOW YOU KNEW THAT...
© 1986 United Feature Syndicate,Inc.
5-13
DAILY WORLD
SCHULZ

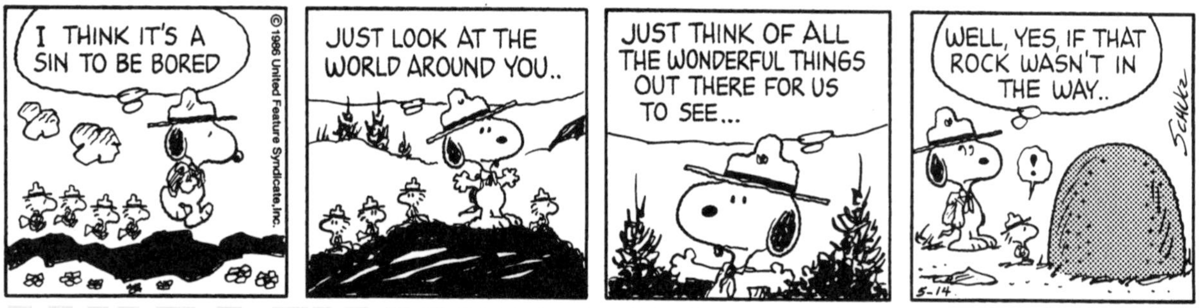
I THINK IT'S A SIN TO BE BORED
© 1986 United Feature Syndicate,Inc.
JUST LOOK AT THE WORLD AROUND YOU..
JUST THINK OF ALL THE WONDERFUL THINGS OUT THERE FOR US TO SEE...
WELL, YES, IF THAT ROCK WASN'T IN THE WAY..
!
SCHULZ
5-14

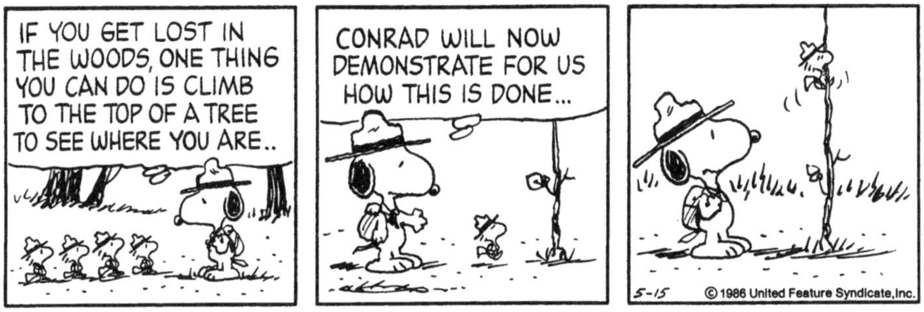
IF YOU GET LOST IN THE WOODS, ONE THING YOU CAN DO IS CLIMB TO THE TOP OF A TREE TO SEE WHERE YOU ARE..
CONRAD WILL NOW DEMONSTRATE FOR US HOW THIS IS DONE...
5-15
© 1986 United Feature Syndicate, Inc.
SCHULZ

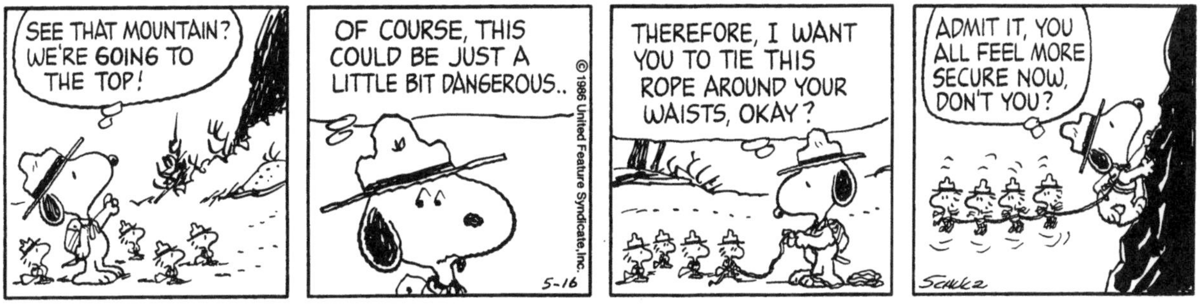
SEE THAT MOUNTAIN? WE'RE GOING TO THE TOP!
OF COURSE, THIS COULD BE JUST A LITTLE BIT DANGEROUS..
© 1986 United Feature Syndicate, Inc.
5-16
THEREFORE, I WANT YOU TO TIE THIS ROPE AROUND YOUR WAISTS, OKAY?
ADMIT IT, YOU ALL FEEL MORE SECURE NOW, DON'T YOU?
SCHULZ

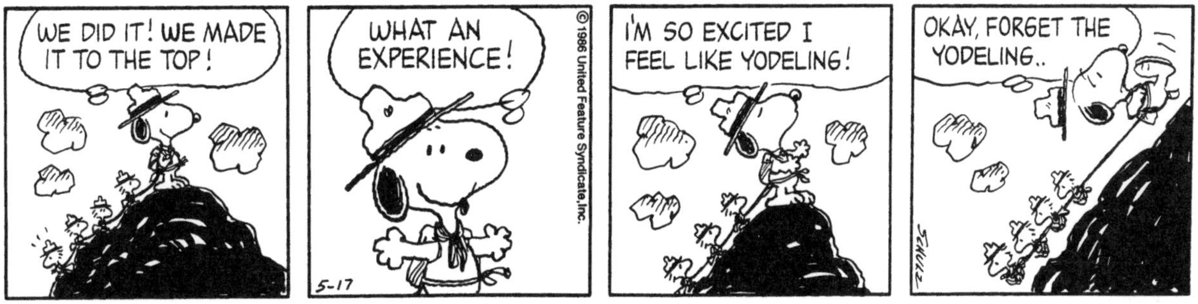
WE DID IT! WE MADE IT TO THE TOP!
WHAT AN EXPERIENCE!
5-17
© 1986 United Feature Syndicate, Inc.
I'M SO EXCITED I FEEL LIKE YODELING!
OKAY, FORGET THE YODELING..
SCHULZ

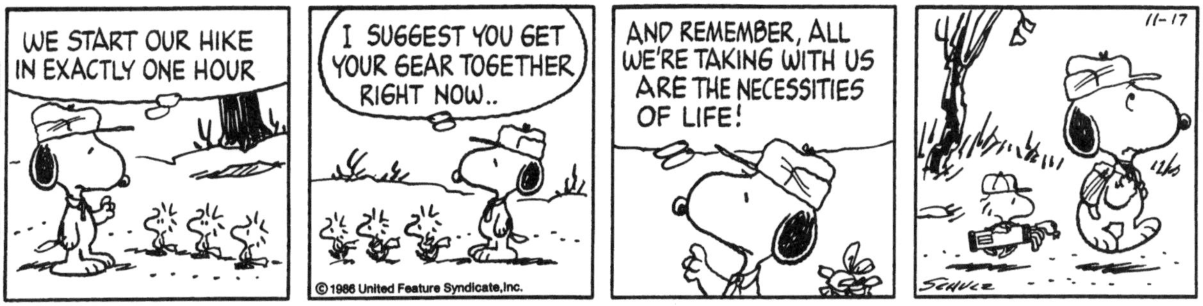
WE START OUR HIKE IN EXACTLY ONE HOUR
I SUGGEST YOU GET YOUR GEAR TOGETHER RIGHT NOW..
© 1986 United Feature Syndicate, Inc.
AND REMEMBER, ALL WE'RE TAKING WITH US ARE THE NECESSITIES OF LIFE!
11-17
SCHULZ

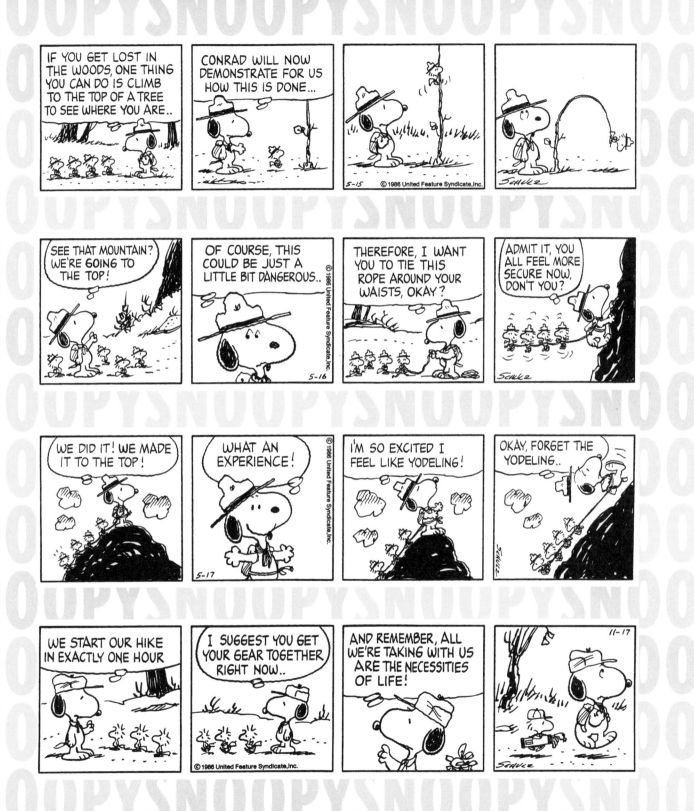

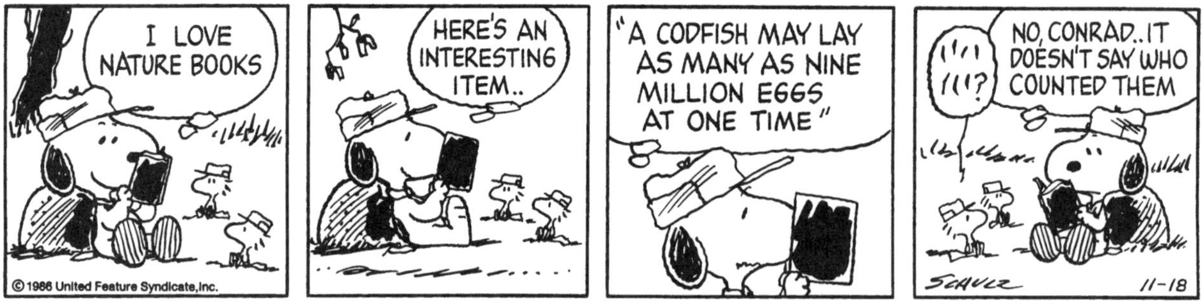
I LOVE NATURE BOOKS
©1986 United Feature Syndicate,Inc.
HERE'S AN INTERESTING ITEM..
"A CODFISH MAY LAY AS MANY AS NINE MILLION EGGS AT ONE TIME"
NO, CONRAD..IT DOESN'T SAY WHO COUNTED THEM
11-18

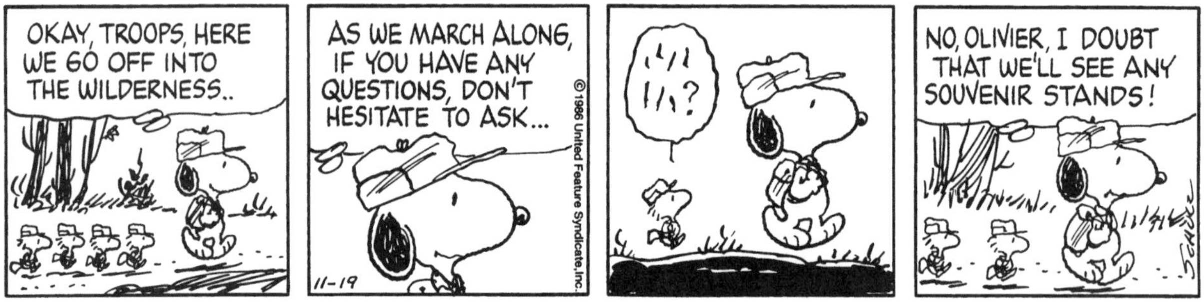
OKAY, TROOPS, HERE WE GO OFF INTO THE WILDERNESS..
AS WE MARCH ALONG, IF YOU HAVE ANY QUESTIONS, DON'T HESITATE TO ASK...
© 1986 United Feature Syndicate,Inc.
11-19
NO, OLIVIER, I DOUBT THAT WE'LL SEE ANY SOUVENIR STANDS!

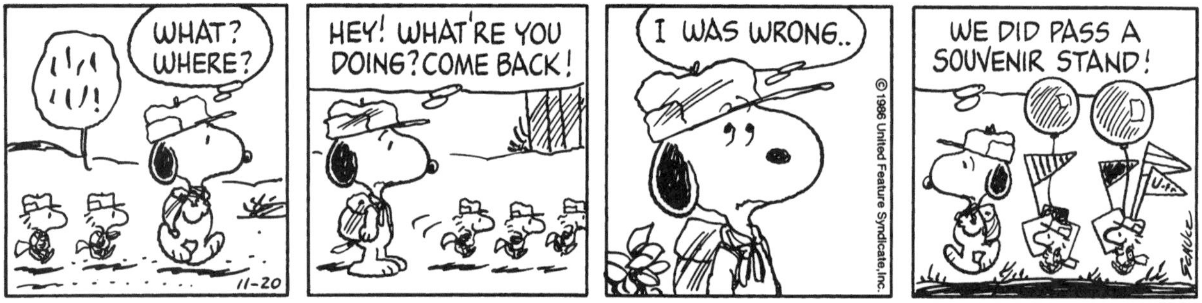
WHAT? WHERE?
11-20
HEY! WHAT'RE YOU DOING? COME BACK!
I WAS WRONG..
© 1986 United Feature Syndicate,Inc.
WE DID PASS A SOUVENIR STAND!

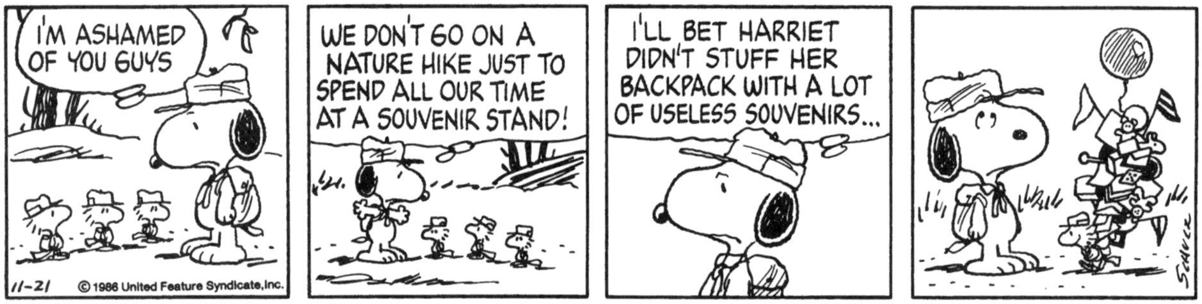
I'M ASHAMED OF YOU GUYS
11-21
© 1986 United Feature Syndicate,Inc.
WE DON'T GO ON A NATURE HIKE JUST TO SPEND ALL OUR TIME AT A SOUVENIR STAND!
I'LL BET HARRIET DIDN'T STUFF HER BACKPACK WITH A LOT OF USELESS SOUVENIRS...

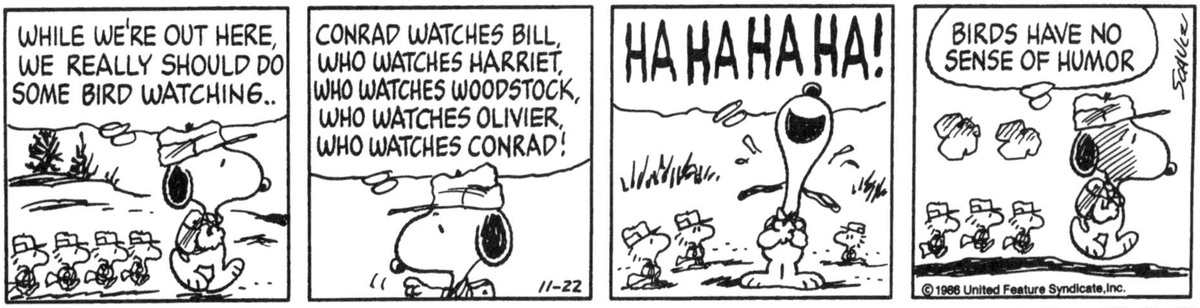
WHILE WE'RE OUT HERE, WE REALLY SHOULD DO SOME BIRD WATCHING..
CONRAD WATCHES BILL, WHO WATCHES HARRIET, WHO WATCHES WOODSTOCK, WHO WATCHES OLIVIER, WHO WATCHES CONRAD!
11-22
HA HA HA HA!
BIRDS HAVE NO SENSE OF HUMOR
SCHULZ
© 1986 United Feature Syndicate, Inc.

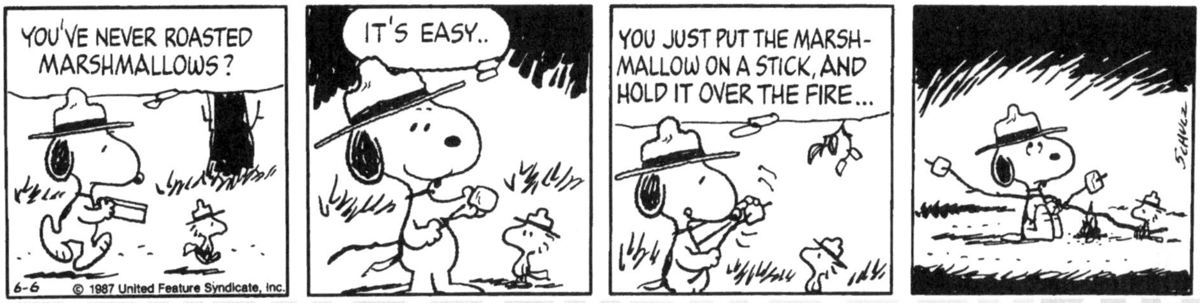
YOU'VE NEVER ROASTED MARSHMALLOWS?
6-6
© 1987 United Feature Syndicate, Inc.
IT'S EASY..
YOU JUST PUT THE MARSH-MALLOW ON A STICK, AND HOLD IT OVER THE FIRE...
SCHULZ

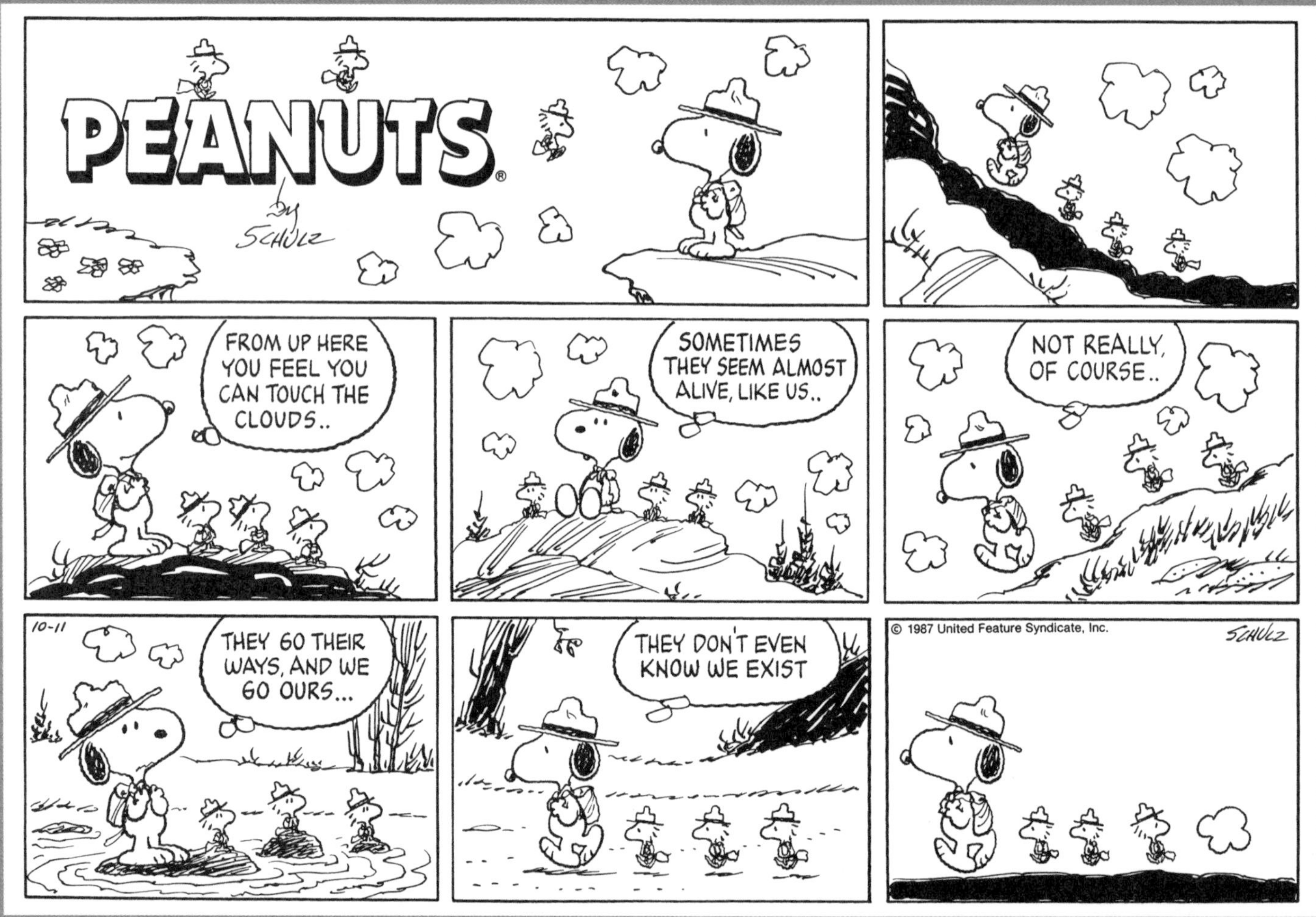
PEANUTS
by SCHULZ
FROM UP HERE YOU FEEL YOU CAN TOUCH THE CLOUDS..
SOMETIMES THEY SEEM ALMOST ALIVE, LIKE US..
NOT REALLY, OF COURSE..
10-11
THEY GO THEIR WAYS, AND WE GO OURS...
THEY DON'T EVEN KNOW WE EXIST
© 1987 United Feature Syndicate, Inc.
SCHULZ

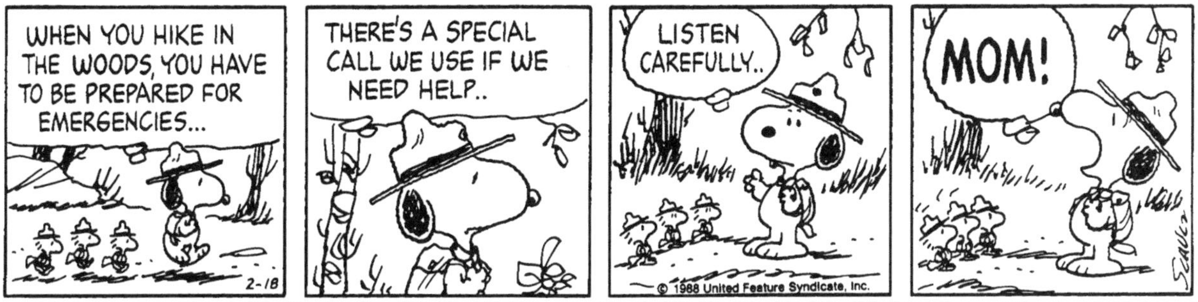
WHEN YOU HIKE IN THE WOODS, YOU HAVE TO BE PREPARED FOR EMERGENCIES...
2-18
THERE'S A SPECIAL CALL WE USE IF WE NEED HELP..
LISTEN CAREFULLY..
© 1988 United Feature Syndicate, Inc.
MOM!

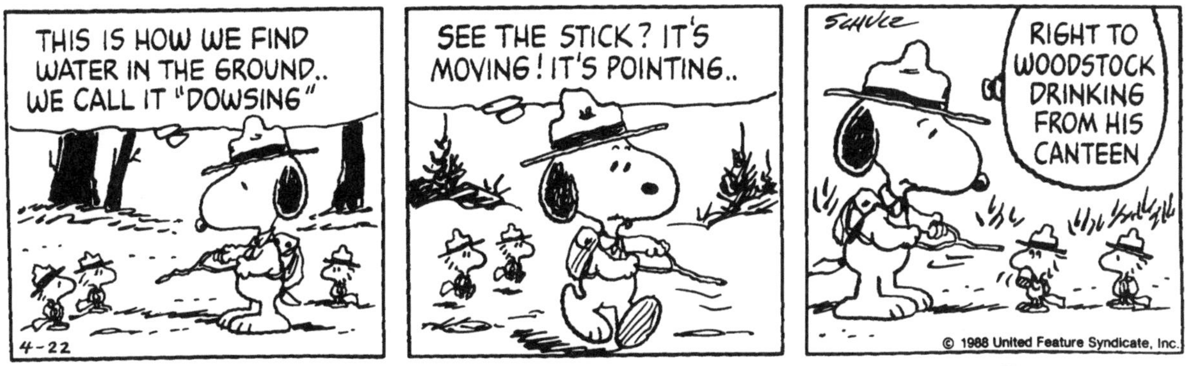
THIS IS HOW WE FIND WATER IN THE GROUND.. WE CALL IT "DOWSING"
4-22
SEE THE STICK? IT'S MOVING! IT'S POINTING..
RIGHT TO WOODSTOCK DRINKING FROM HIS CANTEEN
© 1988 United Feature Syndicate, Inc.

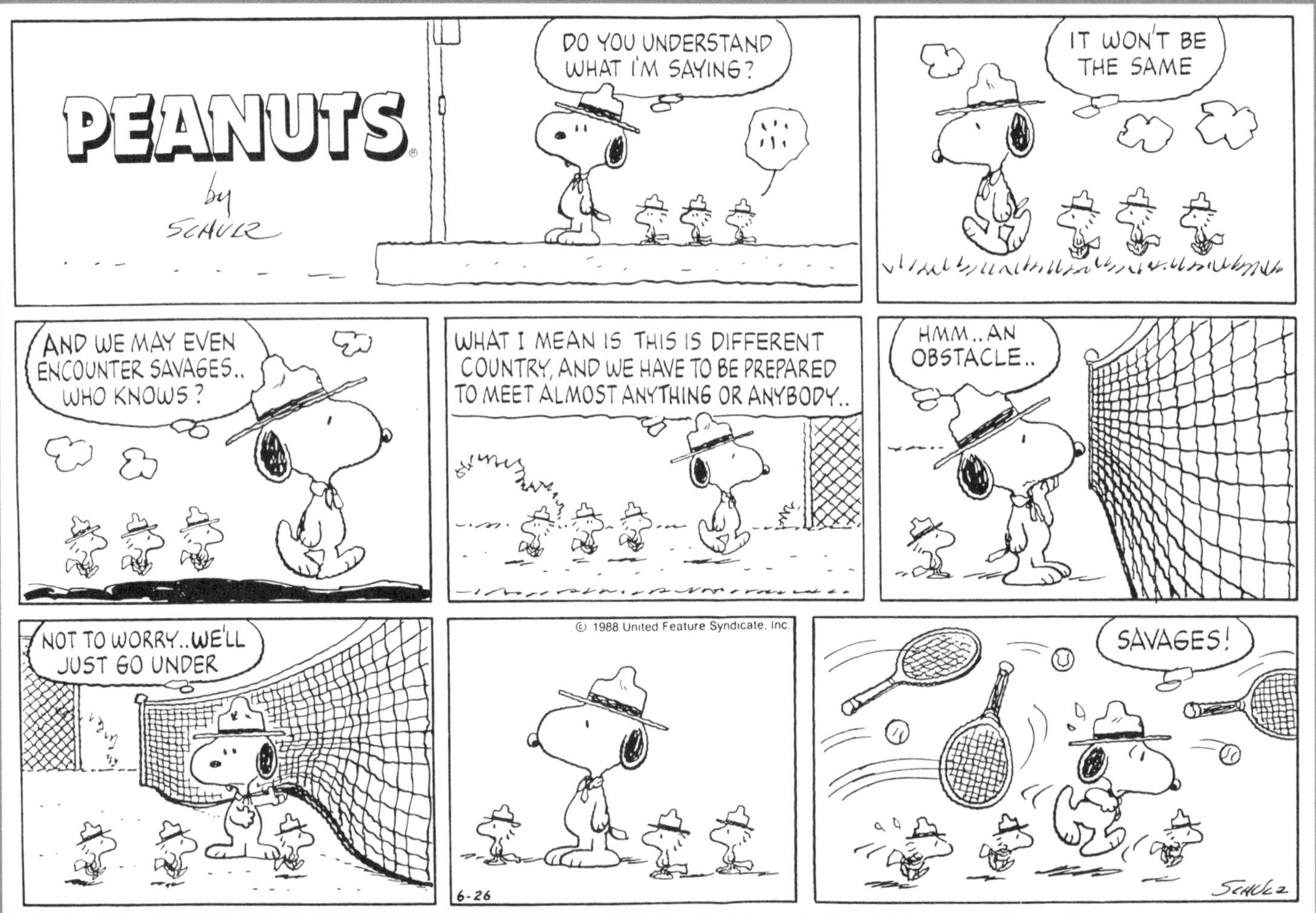
PEANUTS
by SCHULZ
DO YOU UNDERSTAND WHAT I'M SAYING?
IT WON'T BE THE SAME
AND WE MAY EVEN ENCOUNTER SAVAGES.. WHO KNOWS?
WHAT I MEAN IS THIS IS DIFFERENT COUNTRY, AND WE HAVE TO BE PREPARED TO MEET ALMOST ANYTHING OR ANYBODY..
HMM..AN OBSTACLE..
NOT TO WORRY..WE'LL JUST GO UNDER
© 1988 United Feature Syndicate, Inc.
6-26
SAVAGES!
SCHULZ

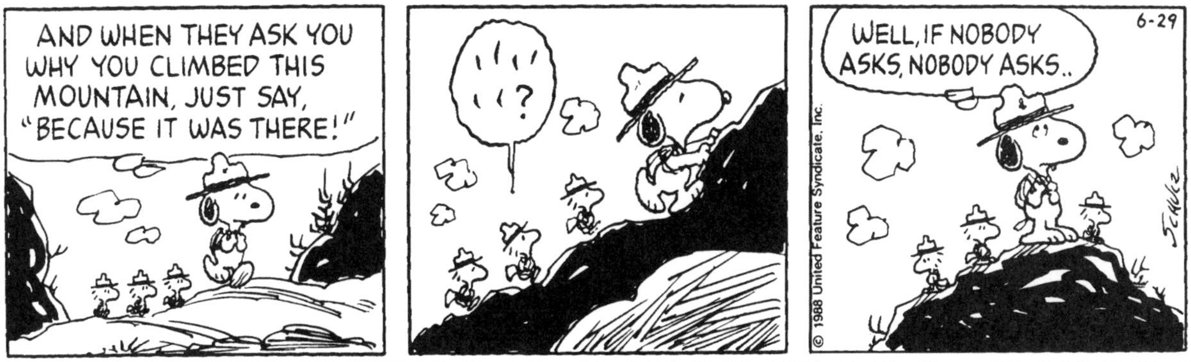
AND WHEN THEY ASK YOU WHY YOU CLIMBED THIS MOUNTAIN, JUST SAY, "BECAUSE IT WAS THERE!"
WELL, IF NOBODY ASKS, NOBODY ASKS..
6-29
© 1988 United Feature Syndicate, Inc.
SCHULZ

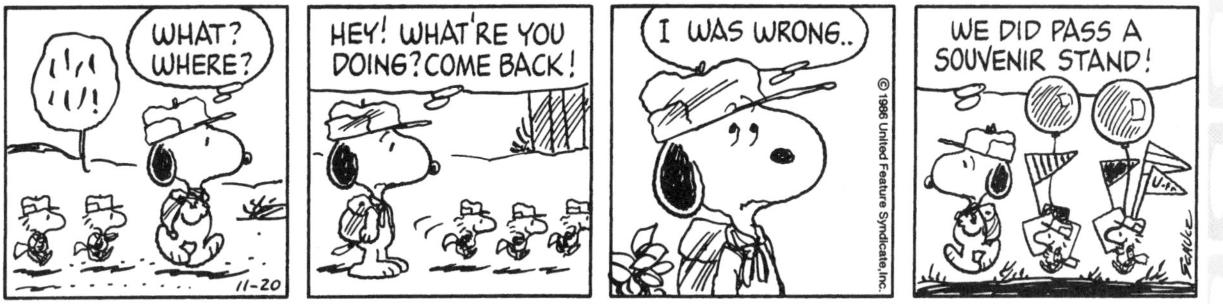
WHAT? WHERE?
11-20
HEY! WHAT'RE YOU DOING? COME BACK!
I WAS WRONG..
© 1986 United Feature Syndicate, Inc.
WE DID PASS A SOUVENIR STAND!
SCHULZ

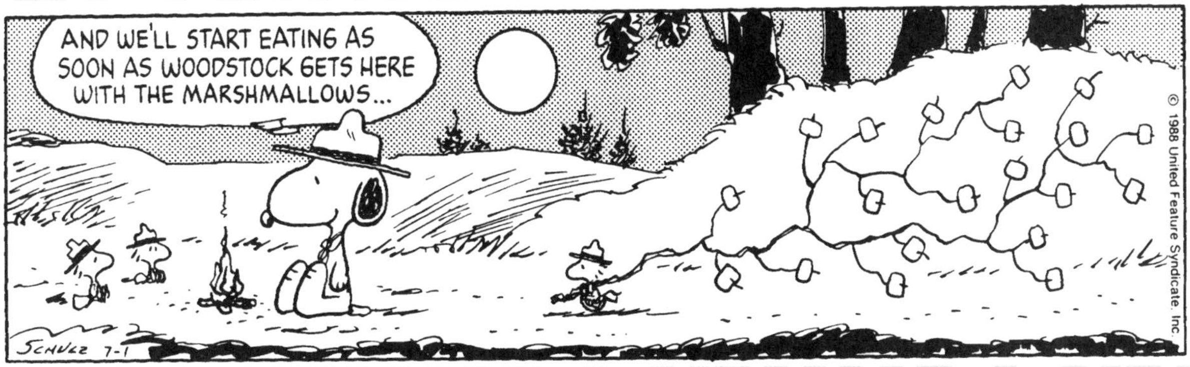
AND WE'LL START EATING AS SOON AS WOODSTOCK GETS HERE WITH THE MARSHMALLOWS...
© 1988 United Feature Syndicate, Inc.
SCHULZ 7-1

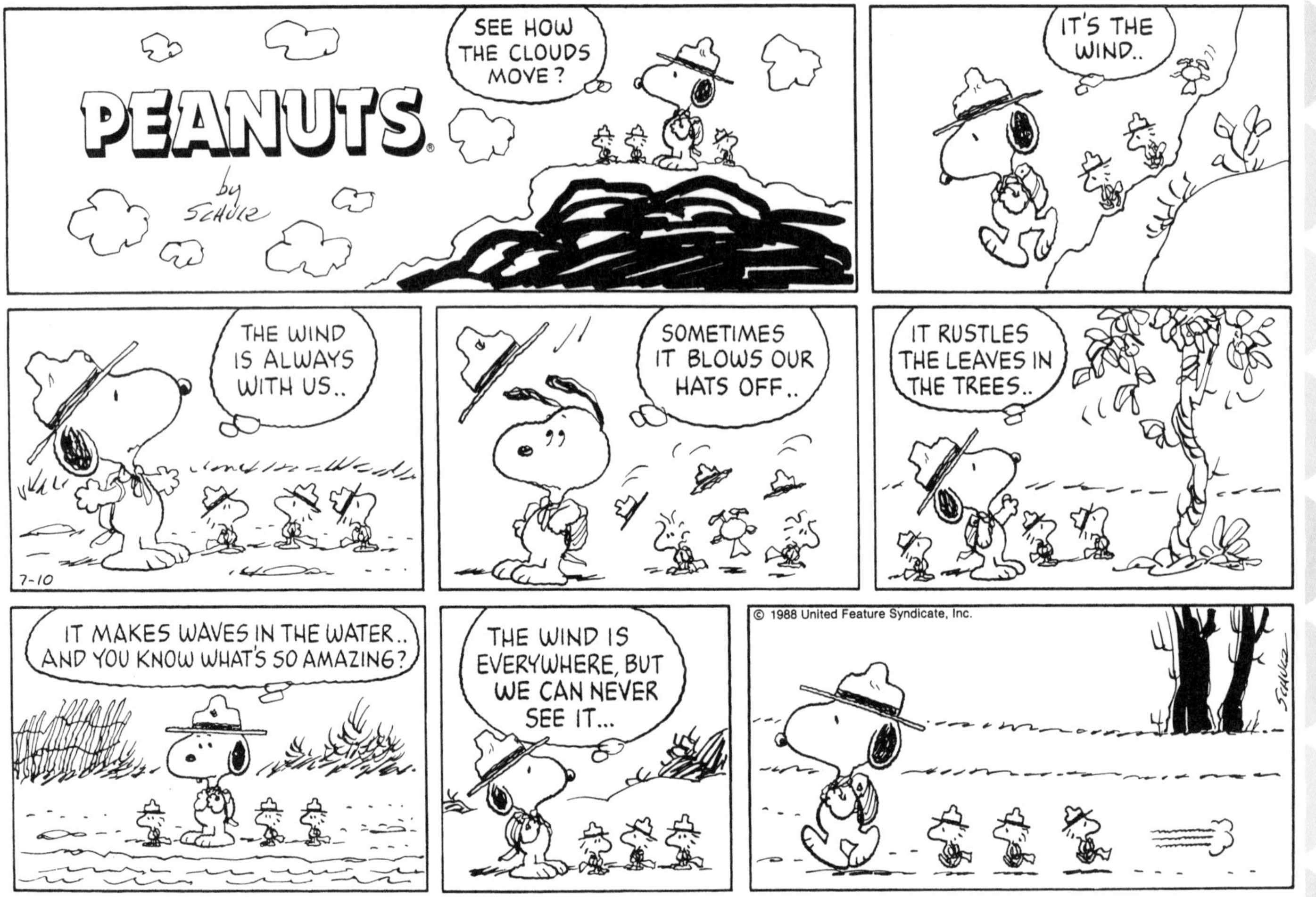
PEANUTS
by SCHULZ
SEE HOW THE CLOUDS MOVE?
IT'S THE WIND..
THE WIND IS ALWAYS WITH US..
7-10
SOMETIMES IT BLOWS OUR HATS OFF..
IT RUSTLES THE LEAVES IN THE TREES..
IT MAKES WAVES IN THE WATER.. AND YOU KNOW WHAT'S SO AMAZING?
THE WIND IS EVERYWHERE, BUT WE CAN NEVER SEE IT...
© 1988 United Feature Syndicate, Inc.
SCHULZ

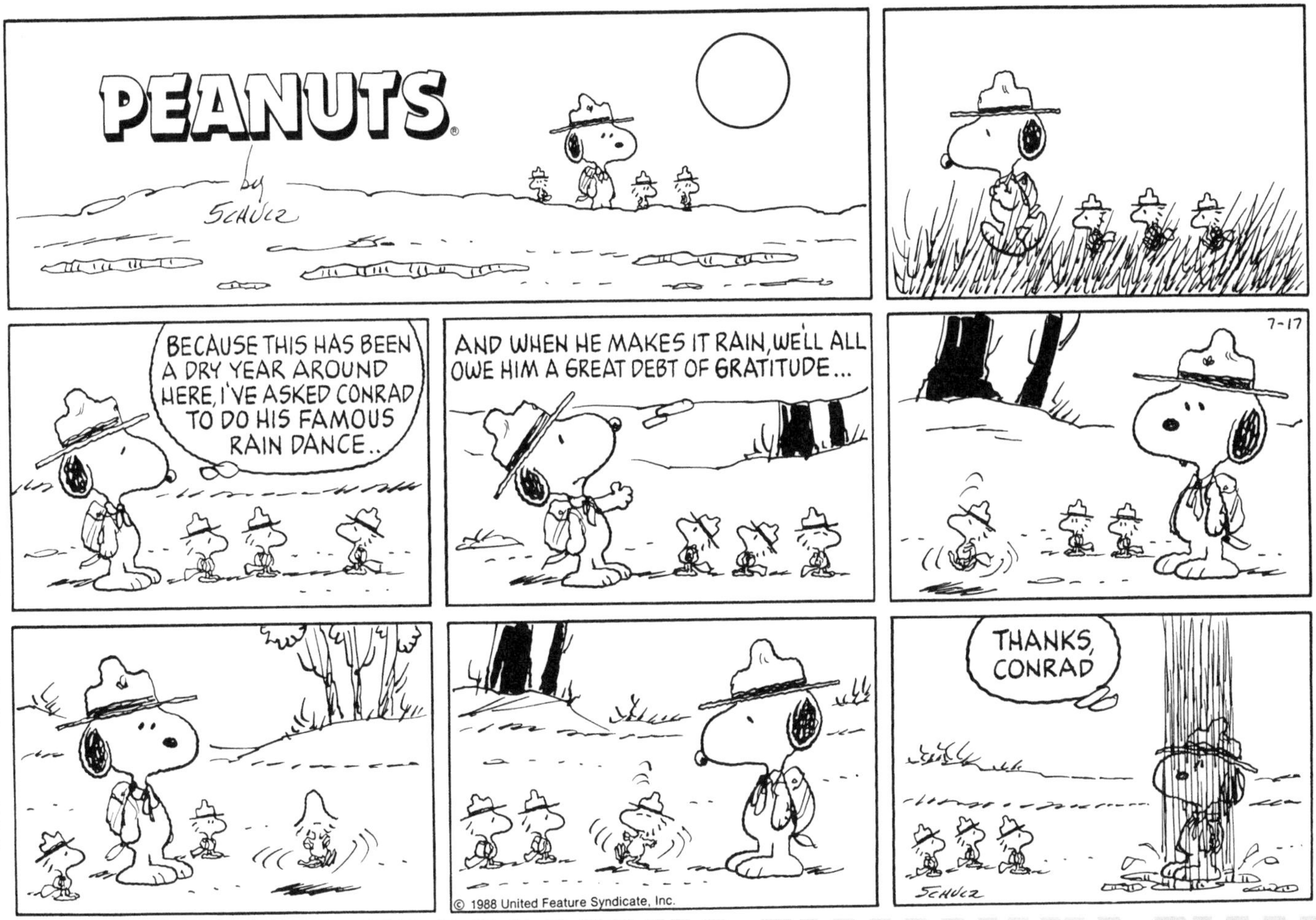
PEANUTS
by SCHULZ
BECAUSE THIS HAS BEEN A DRY YEAR AROUND HERE, I'VE ASKED CONRAD TO DO HIS FAMOUS RAIN DANCE..
AND WHEN HE MAKES IT RAIN, WE'LL ALL OWE HIM A GREAT DEBT OF GRATITUDE...
7-17
THANKS, CONRAD
SCHULZ

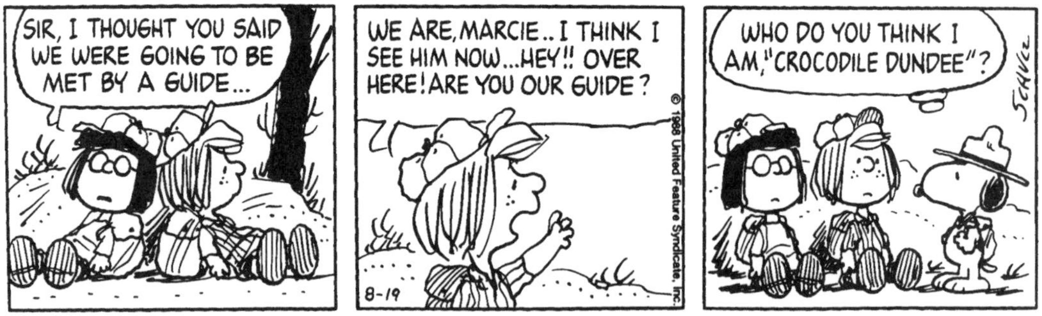
SIR, I THOUGHT YOU SAID WE WERE GOING TO BE MET BY A GUIDE...
WE ARE, MARCIE.. I THINK I SEE HIM NOW...HEY!! OVER HERE! ARE YOU OUR GUIDE?
© 1988 United Feature Syndicate, Inc.
8-19
WHO DO YOU THINK I AM, "CROCODILE DUNDEE"?
SCHULZ

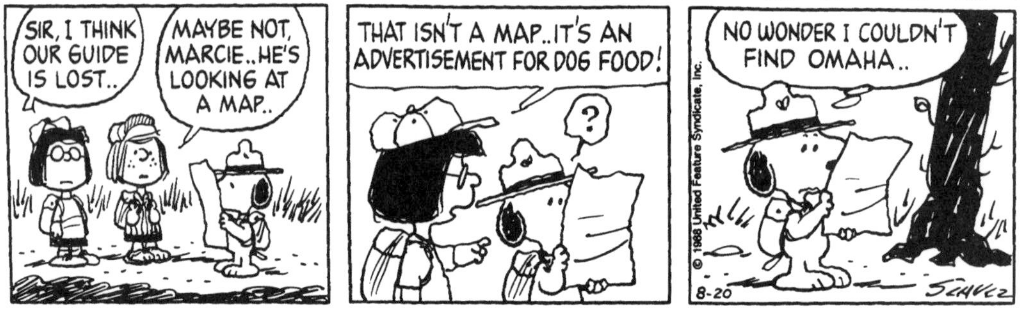
SIR, I THINK OUR GUIDE IS LOST..
MAYBE NOT, MARCIE..HE'S LOOKING AT A MAP..
THAT ISN'T A MAP..IT'S AN ADVERTISEMENT FOR DOG FOOD!
?
NO WONDER I COULDN'T FIND OMAHA..
© 1988 United Feature Syndicate, Inc.
8-20
SCHULZ

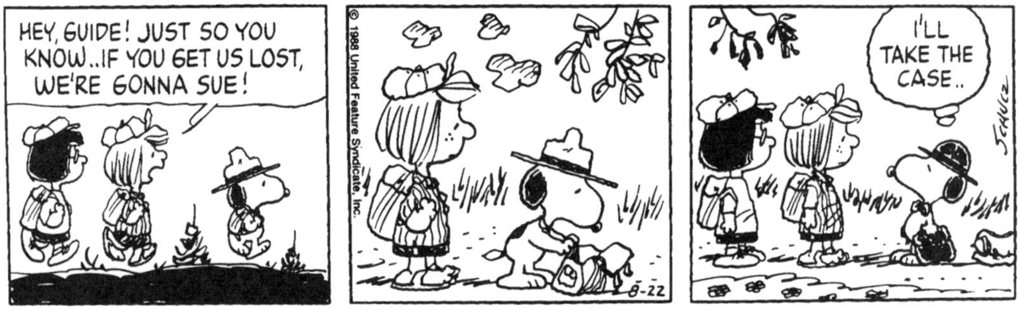
HEY, GUIDE! JUST SO YOU KNOW..IF YOU GET US LOST, WE'RE GONNA SUE!
© 1988 United Feature Syndicate, Inc.
8-22
I'LL TAKE THE CASE..
SCHULZ

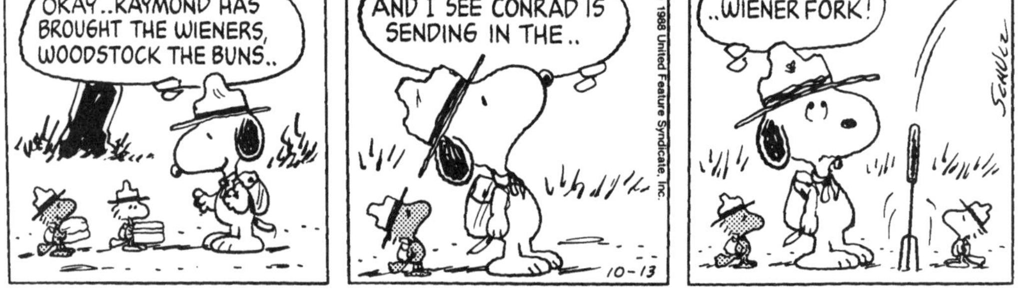
OKAY..RAYMOND HAS BROUGHT THE WIENERS, WOODSTOCK THE BUNS..
AND I SEE CONRAD IS SENDING IN THE..
© 1988 United Feature Syndicate, Inc.
10-13
..WIENER FORK!
SCHULZ

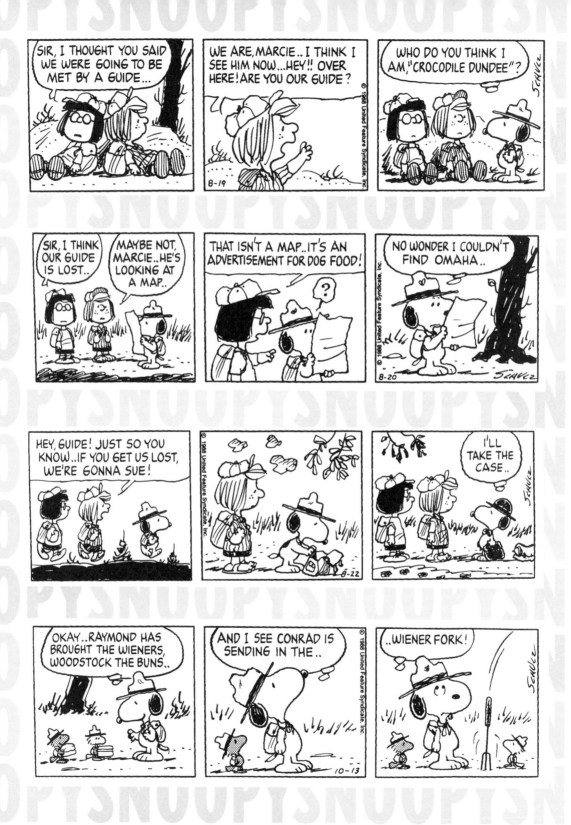

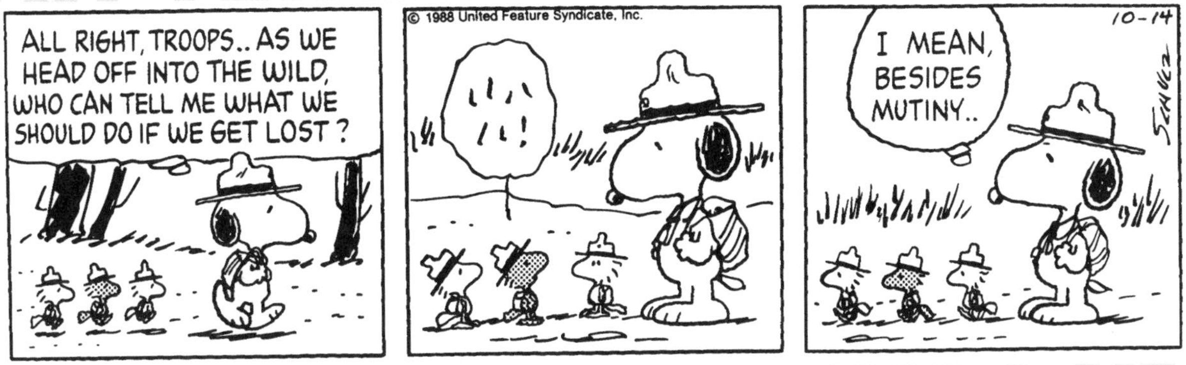
ALL RIGHT, TROOPS.. AS WE HEAD OFF INTO THE WILD, WHO CAN TELL ME WHAT WE SHOULD DO IF WE GET LOST ?
© 1988 United Feature Syndicate, Inc.
I MEAN, BESIDES MUTINY..
10-14
SCHULZ

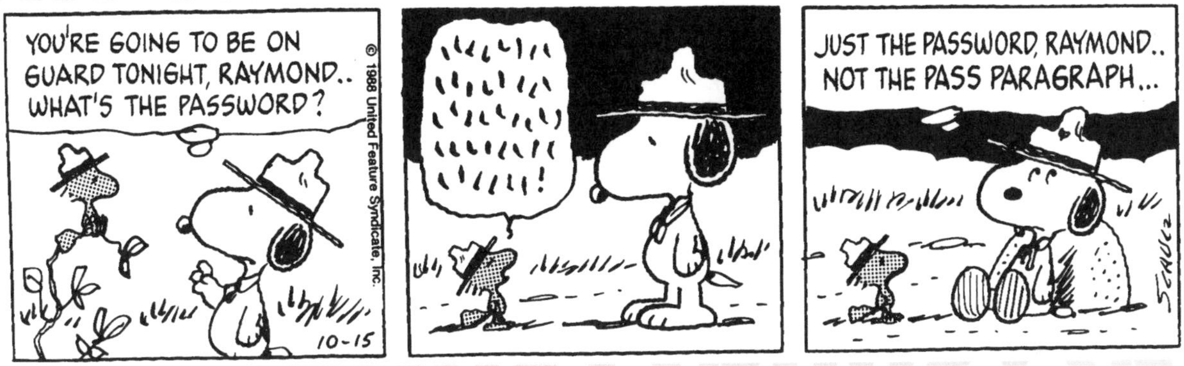
YOU'RE GOING TO BE ON GUARD TONIGHT, RAYMOND.. WHAT'S THE PASSWORD ?
© 1988 United Feature Syndicate, Inc.
10-15
JUST THE PASSWORD, RAYMOND.. NOT THE PASS PARAGRAPH...
SCHULZ

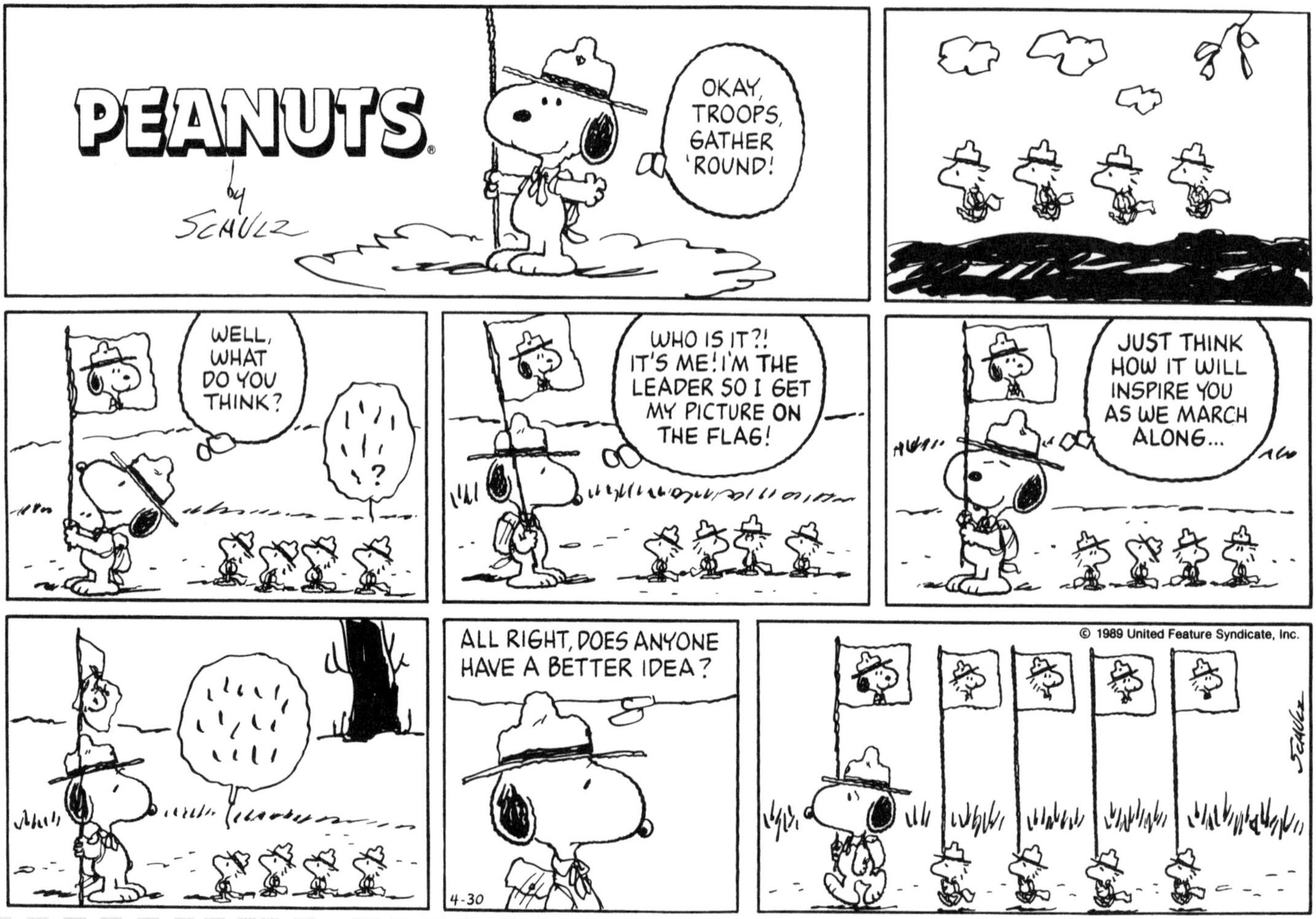
PEANUTS
by SCHULZ
OKAY, TROOPS, GATHER 'ROUND!
WELL, WHAT DO YOU THINK?
?
WHO IS IT?! IT'S ME! I'M THE LEADER SO I GET MY PICTURE ON THE FLAG!
JUST THINK HOW IT WILL INSPIRE YOU AS WE MARCH ALONG...
ALL RIGHT, DOES ANYONE HAVE A BETTER IDEA?
4-30
© 1989 United Feature Syndicate, Inc.
SCHULZ

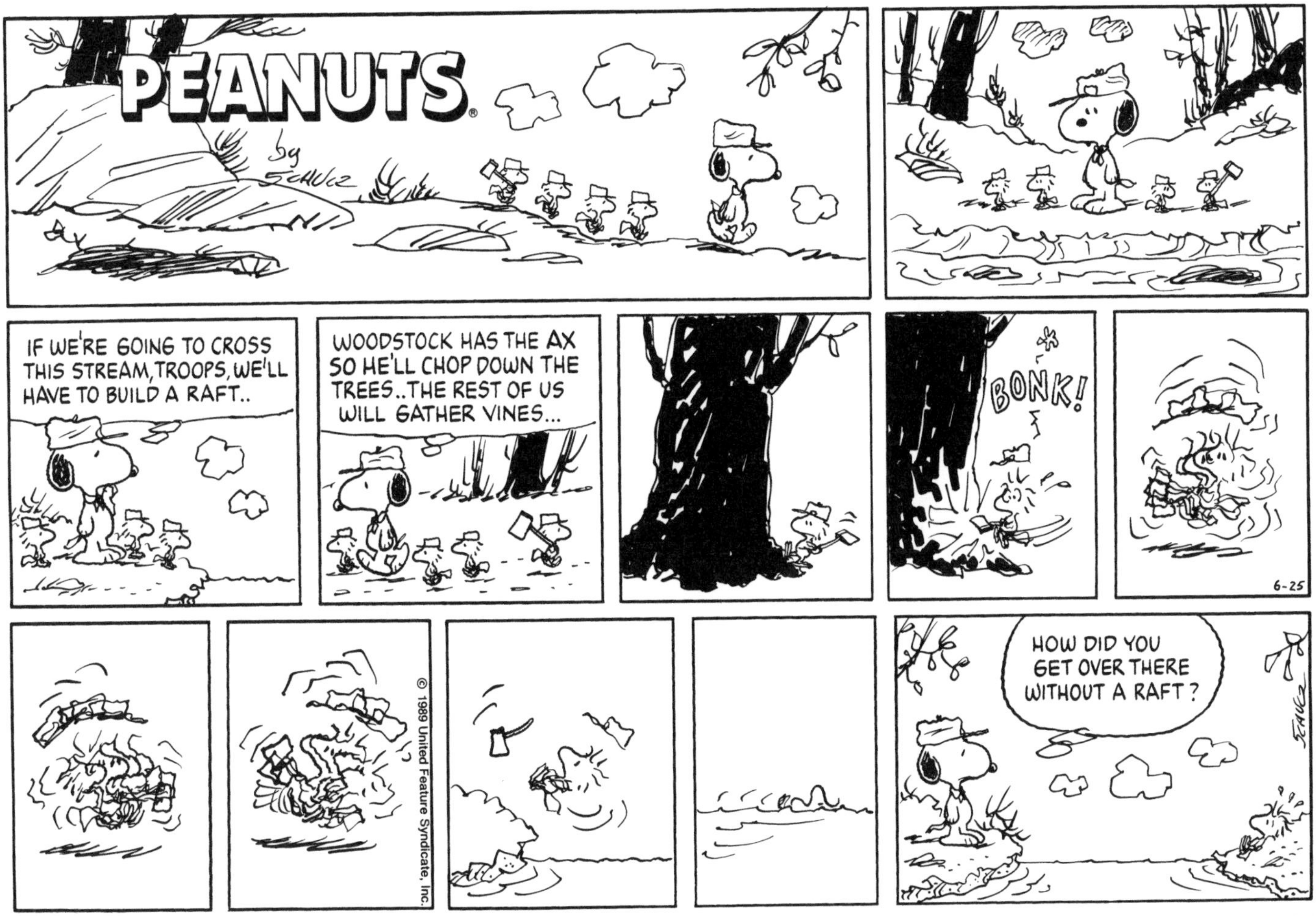
PEANUTS
by SCHULZ
IF WE'RE GOING TO CROSS THIS STREAM, TROOPS, WE'LL HAVE TO BUILD A RAFT..
WOODSTOCK HAS THE AX SO HE'LL CHOP DOWN THE TREES..THE REST OF US WILL GATHER VINES...
BONK!
6-25
© 1989 United Feature Syndicate, Inc.
HOW DID YOU GET OVER THERE WITHOUT A RAFT?
SCHULZ

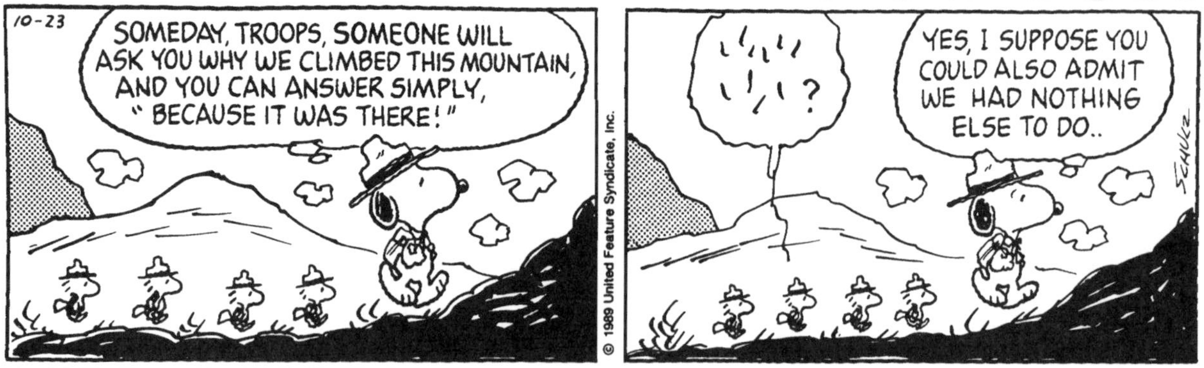
10-23
SOMEDAY, TROOPS, SOMEONE WILL ASK YOU WHY WE CLIMBED THIS MOUNTAIN, AND YOU CAN ANSWER SIMPLY, "BECAUSE IT WAS THERE!"
YES, I SUPPOSE YOU COULD ALSO ADMIT WE HAD NOTHING ELSE TO DO..
?
SCHULZ
© 1989 United Feature Syndicate, Inc.

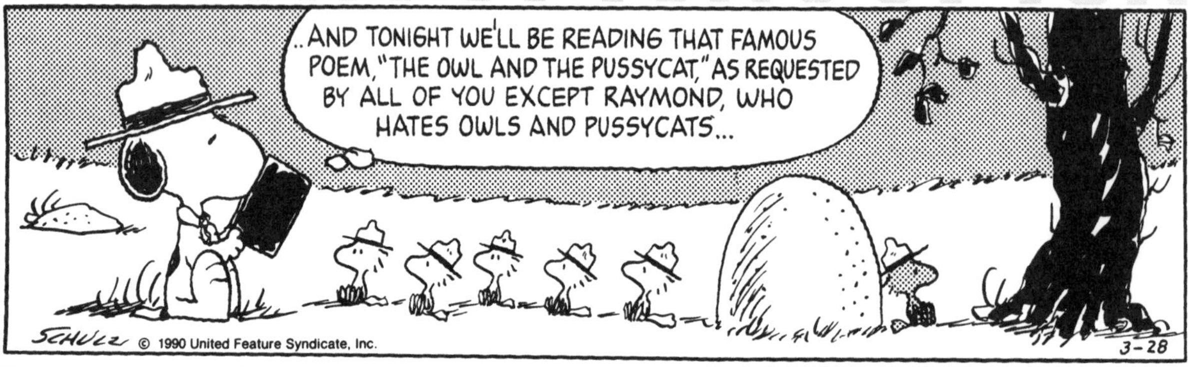
..AND TONIGHT WE'LL BE READING THAT FAMOUS POEM, "THE OWL AND THE PUSSYCAT," AS REQUESTED BY ALL OF YOU EXCEPT RAYMOND, WHO HATES OWLS AND PUSSYCATS...
SCHULZ © 1990 United Feature Syndicate, Inc.
3-28

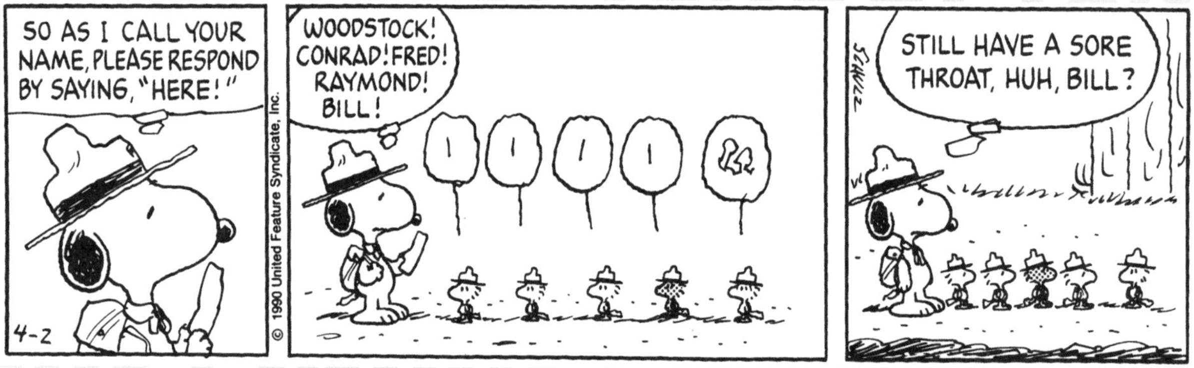
SO AS I CALL YOUR NAME, PLEASE RESPOND BY SAYING, "HERE!"
4-2
© 1990 United Feature Syndicate, Inc.
WOODSTOCK! CONRAD! FRED! RAYMOND! BILL!
STILL HAVE A SORE THROAT, HUH, BILL?
SCHULZ

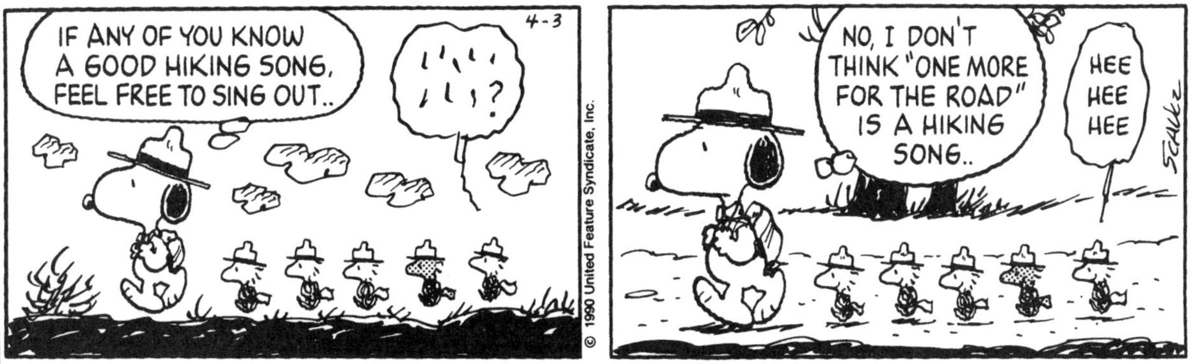
4-3
IF ANY OF YOU KNOW A GOOD HIKING SONG, FEEL FREE TO SING OUT..
?
NO, I DON'T THINK "ONE MORE FOR THE ROAD" IS A HIKING SONG..
HEE HEE HEE
SCHULZ
© 1990 United Feature Syndicate, Inc.

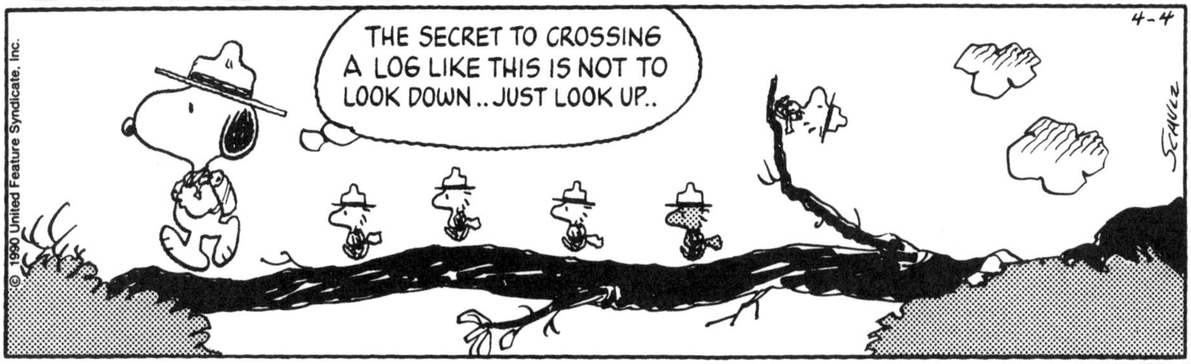
4-4
THE SECRET TO CROSSING A LOG LIKE THIS IS NOT TO LOOK DOWN.. JUST LOOK UP..
SCHULZ
© 1990 United Feature Syndicate, Inc.

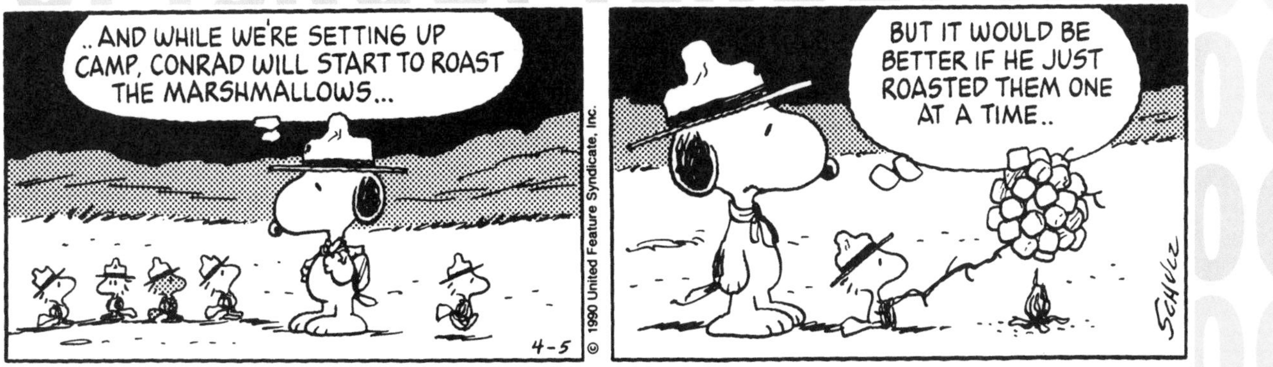
.. AND WHILE WE'RE SETTING UP CAMP, CONRAD WILL START TO ROAST THE MARSHMALLOWS...
4-5
BUT IT WOULD BE BETTER IF HE JUST ROASTED THEM ONE AT A TIME..
SCHULZ
© 1990 United Feature Syndicate, Inc.

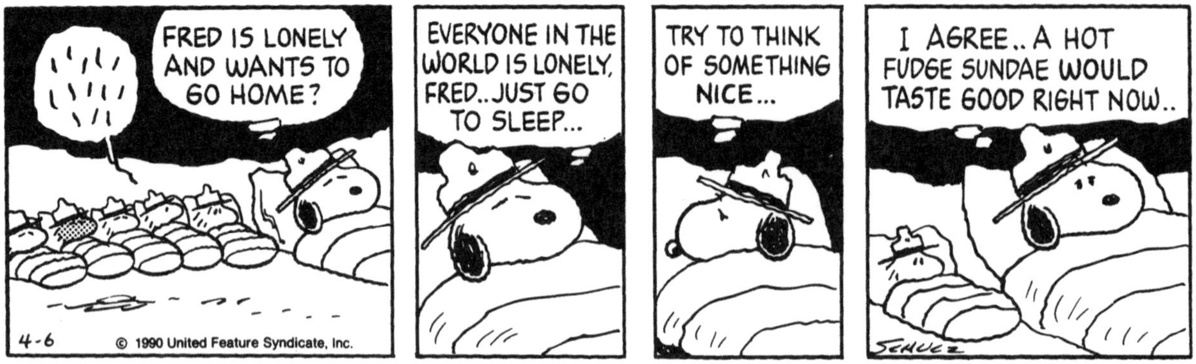
FRED IS LONELY AND WANTS TO GO HOME?
EVERYONE IN THE WORLD IS LONELY, FRED..JUST GO TO SLEEP...
TRY TO THINK OF SOMETHING NICE...
I AGREE.. A HOT FUDGE SUNDAE WOULD TASTE GOOD RIGHT NOW..
4-6
© 1990 United Feature Syndicate, Inc.

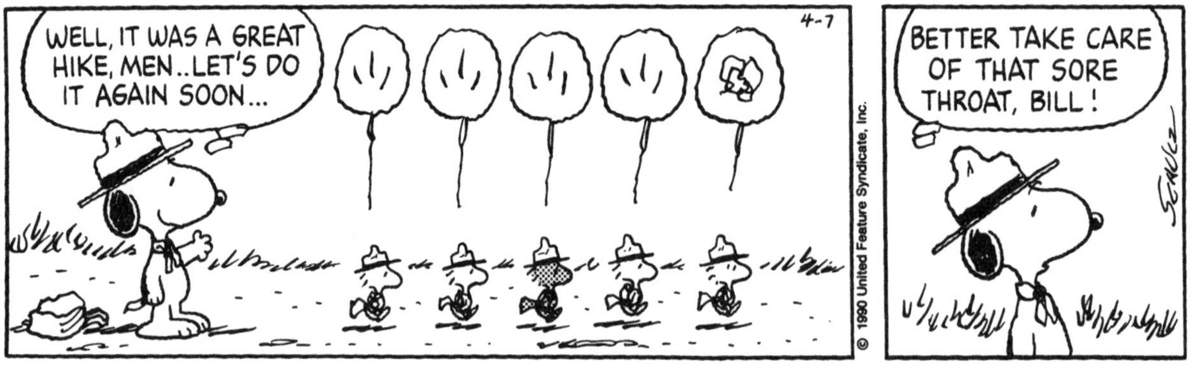
4-7
WELL, IT WAS A GREAT HIKE, MEN..LET'S DO IT AGAIN SOON...
BETTER TAKE CARE OF THAT SORE THROAT, BILL!
© 1990 United Feature Syndicate, Inc.

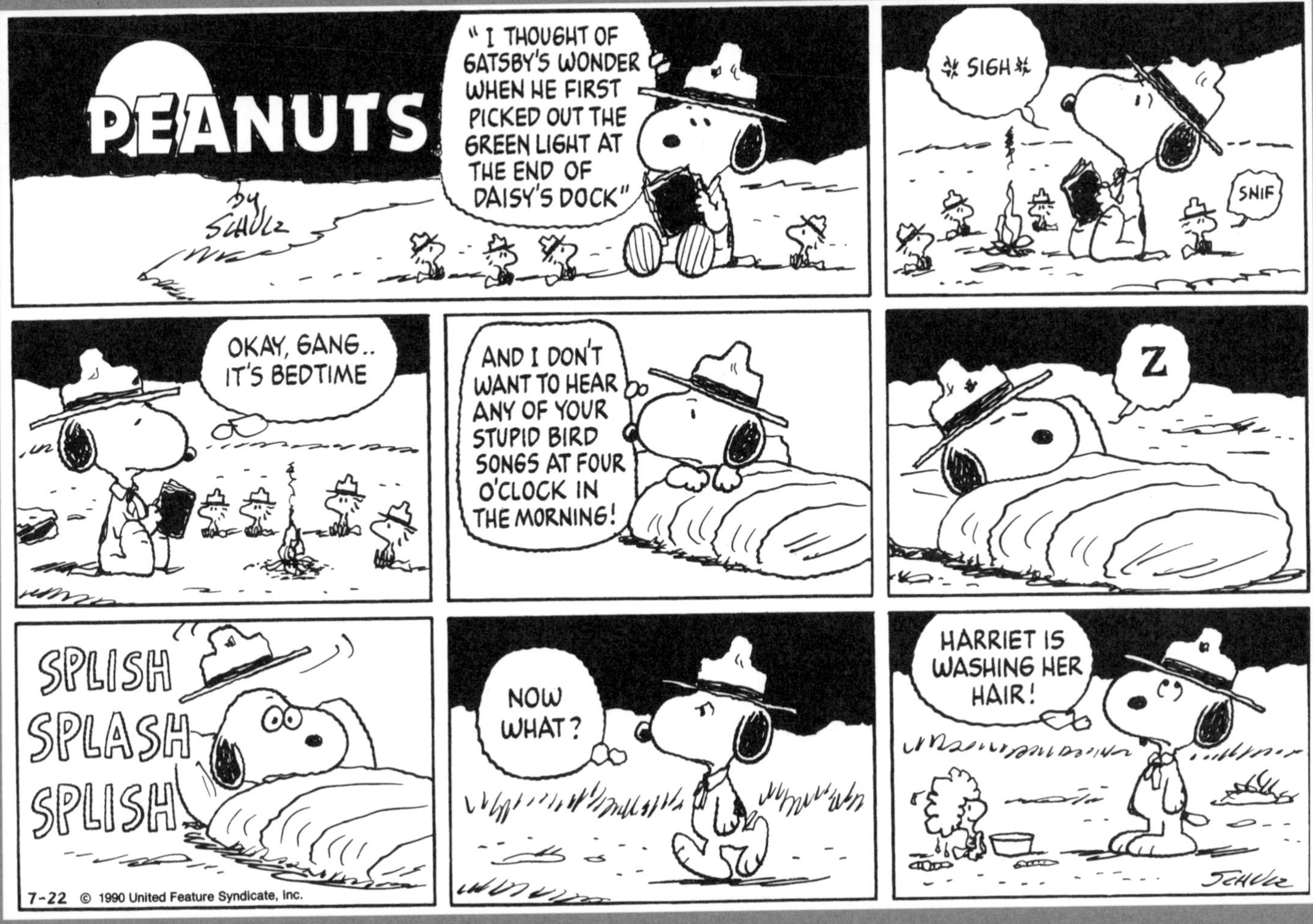
PEANUTS
by SCHULZ
" I THOUGHT OF GATSBY'S WONDER WHEN HE FIRST PICKED OUT THE GREEN LIGHT AT THE END OF DAISY'S DOCK"
SIGH
SNIF
OKAY, GANG.. IT'S BEDTIME
AND I DON'T WANT TO HEAR ANY OF YOUR STUPID BIRD SONGS AT FOUR O'CLOCK IN THE MORNING!
Z
SPLISH
SPLASH
SPLISH
NOW WHAT?
HARRIET IS WASHING HER HAIR!
SCHULZ
7-22 © 1990 United Feature Syndicate, Inc.

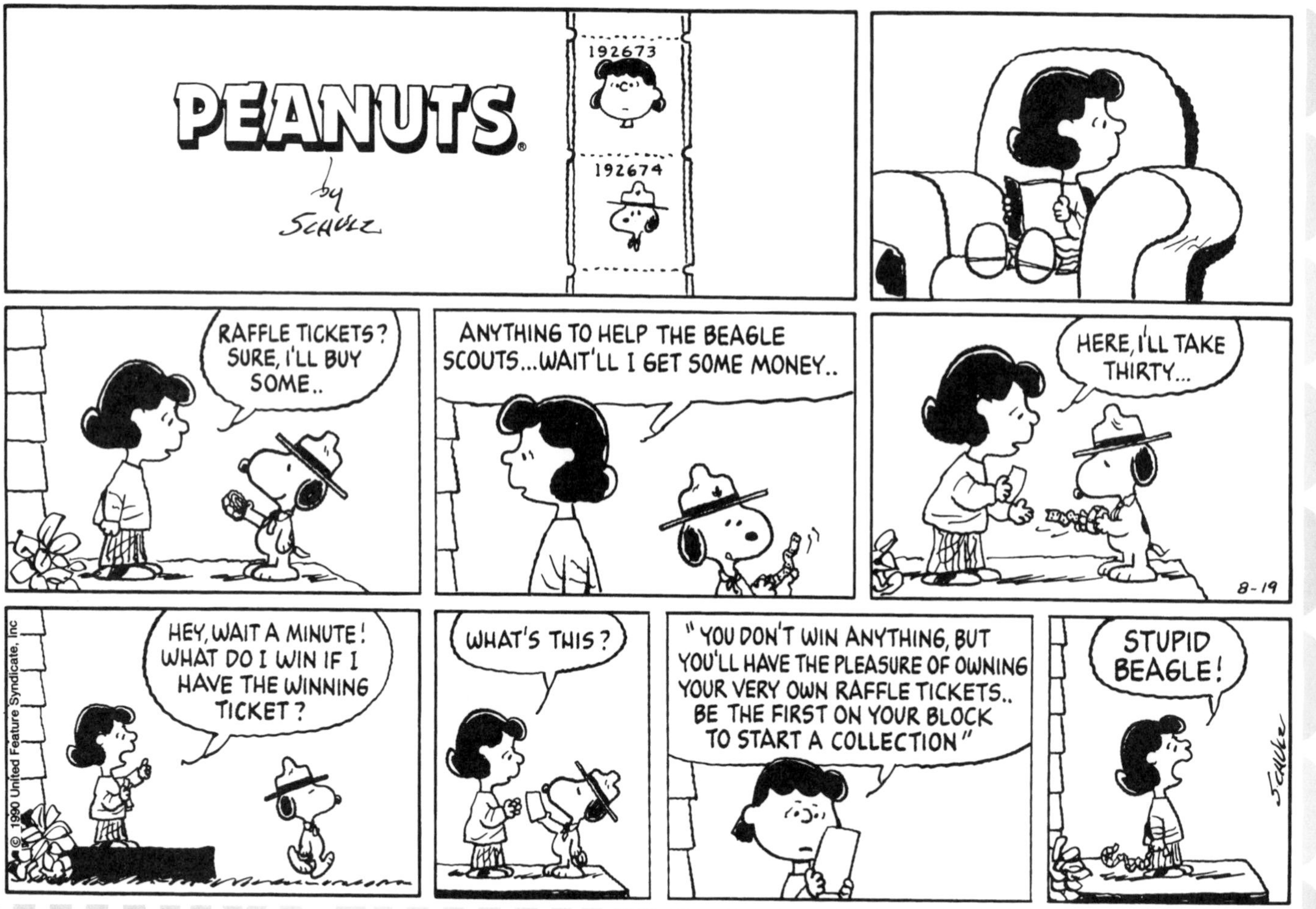
192673
PEANUTS
by SCHULZ
192674
RAFFLE TICKETS? SURE, I'LL BUY SOME..
ANYTHING TO HELP THE BEAGLE SCOUTS...WAIT'LL I GET SOME MONEY..
HERE, I'LL TAKE THIRTY...
8-19
HEY, WAIT A MINUTE! WHAT DO I WIN IF I HAVE THE WINNING TICKET?
© 1990 United Feature Syndicate, Inc
WHAT'S THIS?
"YOU DON'T WIN ANYTHING, BUT YOU'LL HAVE THE PLEASURE OF OWNING YOUR VERY OWN RAFFLE TICKETS.. BE THE FIRST ON YOUR BLOCK TO START A COLLECTION"
STUPID BEAGLE!
SCHULZ

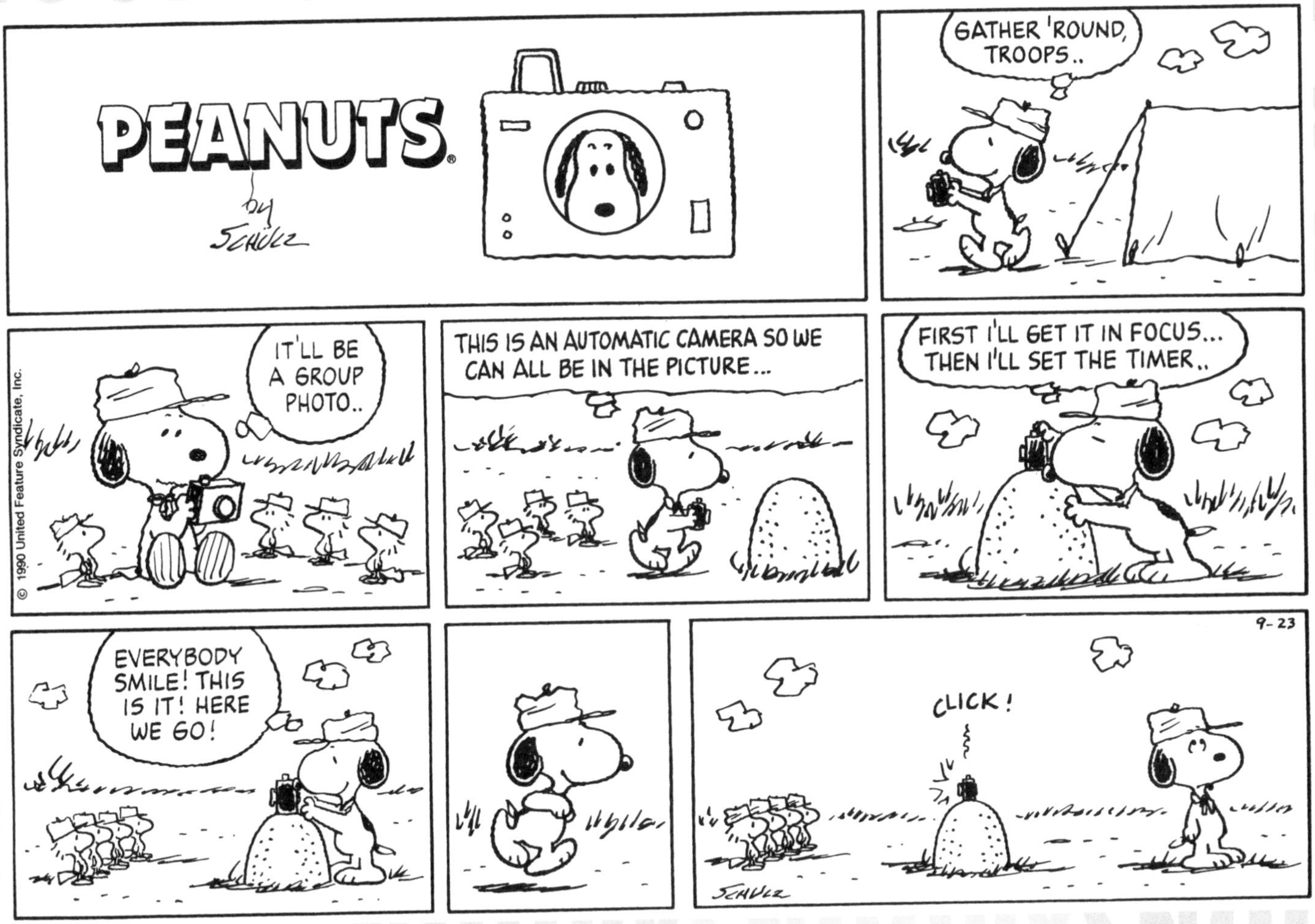
PEANUTS
by SCHULZ
GATHER 'ROUND, TROOPS..
IT'LL BE A GROUP PHOTO..
THIS IS AN AUTOMATIC CAMERA SO WE CAN ALL BE IN THE PICTURE...
FIRST I'LL GET IT IN FOCUS... THEN I'LL SET THE TIMER..
EVERYBODY SMILE! THIS IS IT! HERE WE GO!
9-23
CLICK!
SCHULZ
© 1990 United Feature Syndicate, Inc.

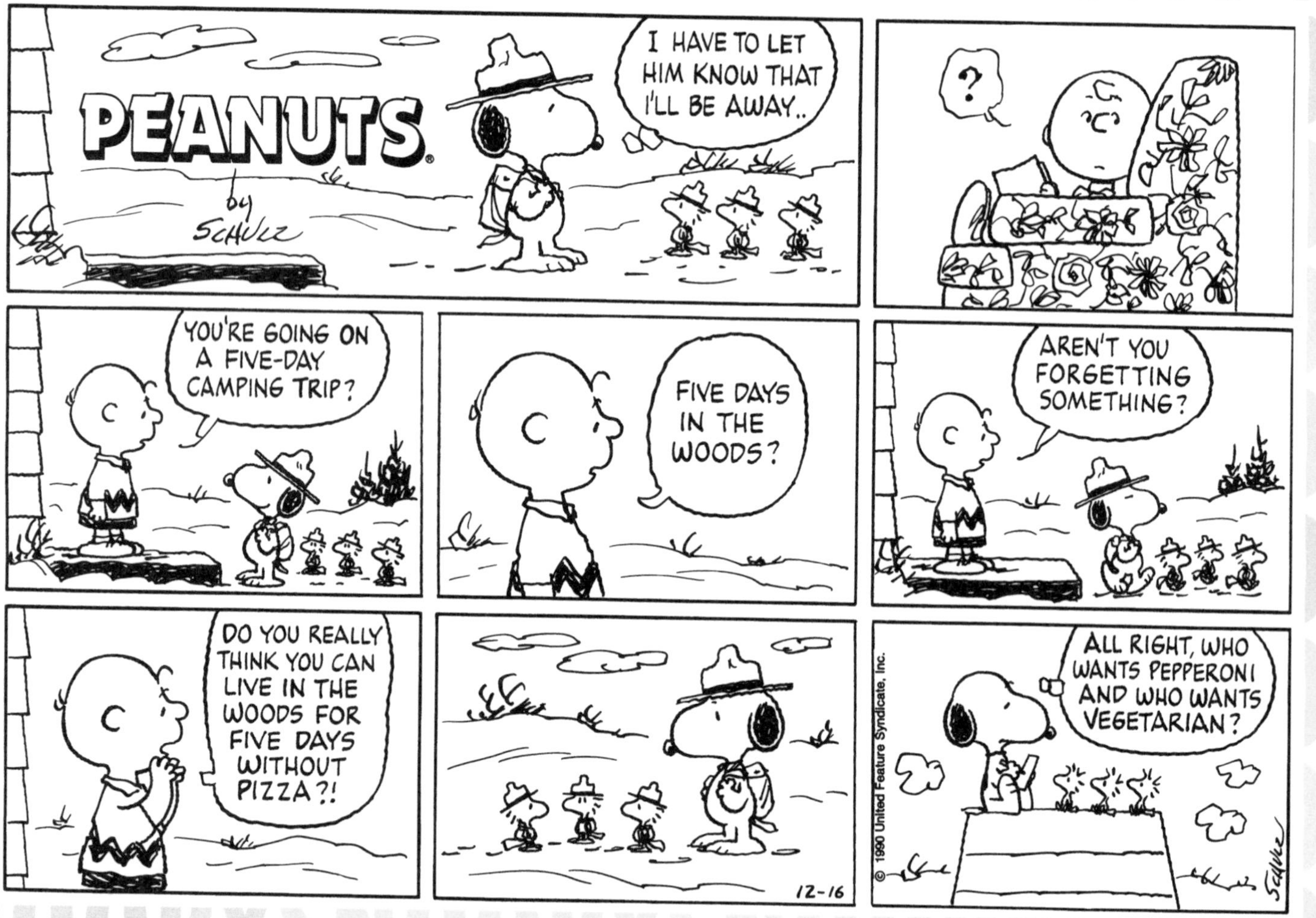
PEANUTS
by SCHULZ
I HAVE TO LET HIM KNOW THAT I'LL BE AWAY..
?
YOU'RE GOING ON A FIVE-DAY CAMPING TRIP?
FIVE DAYS IN THE WOODS?
AREN'T YOU FORGETTING SOMETHING?
DO YOU REALLY THINK YOU CAN LIVE IN THE WOODS FOR FIVE DAYS WITHOUT PIZZA?!
12-16
© 1990 United Feature Syndicate, Inc.
ALL RIGHT, WHO WANTS PEPPERONI AND WHO WANTS VEGETARIAN?
SCHULZ

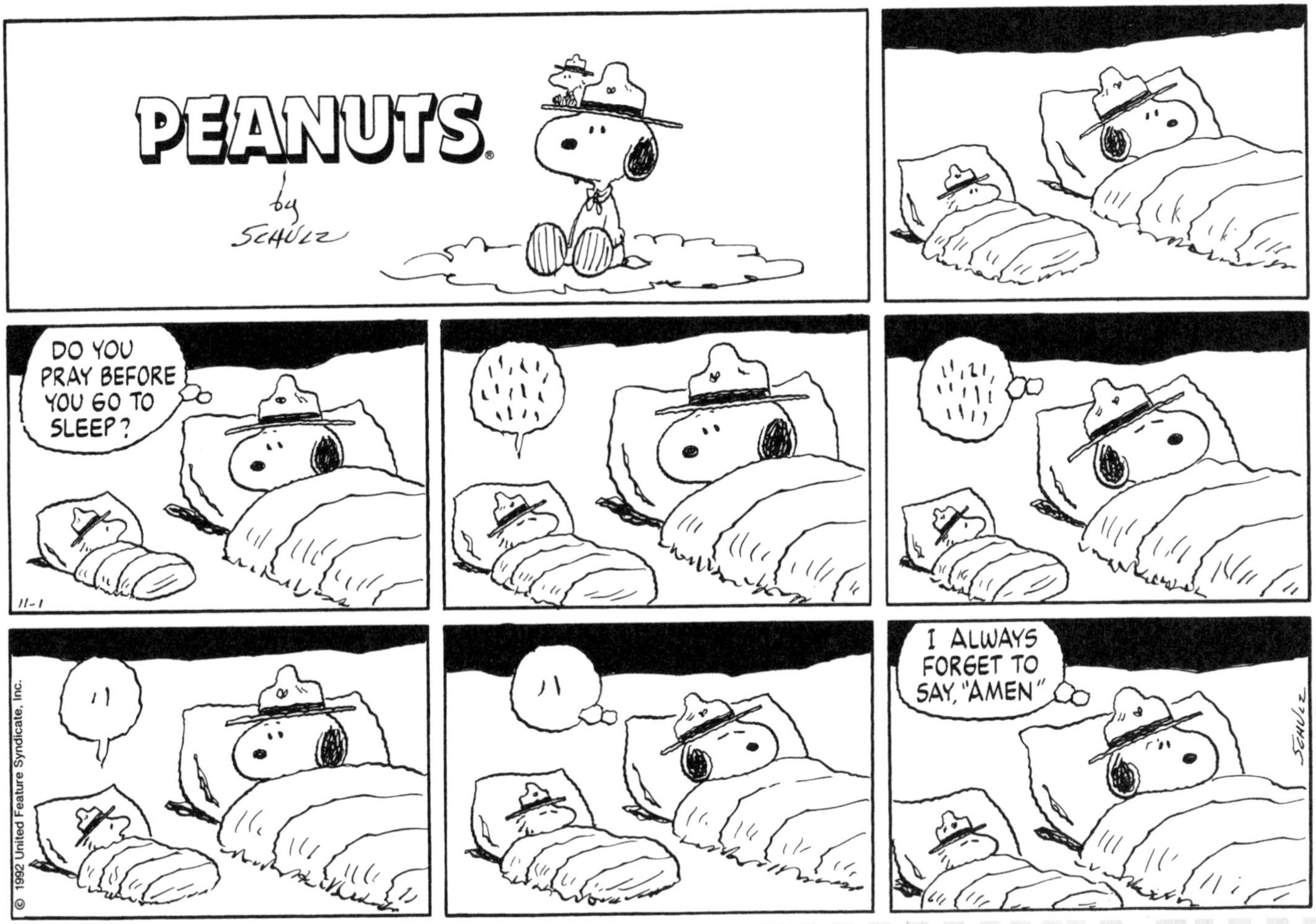
PEANUTS
by SCHULZ
DO YOU PRAY BEFORE YOU GO TO SLEEP?
11-1
© 1992 United Feature Syndicate, Inc.
I ALWAYS FORGET TO SAY, "AMEN"
SCHULZ

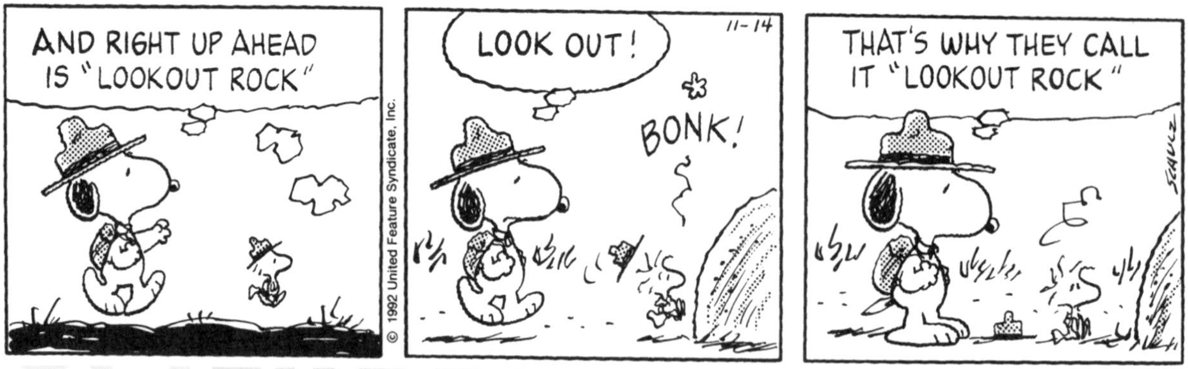
AND RIGHT UP AHEAD IS "LOOKOUT ROCK"
© 1992 United Feature Syndicate, Inc.
LOOK OUT!
11-14
BONK!
THAT'S WHY THEY CALL IT "LOOKOUT ROCK"
SCHULZ

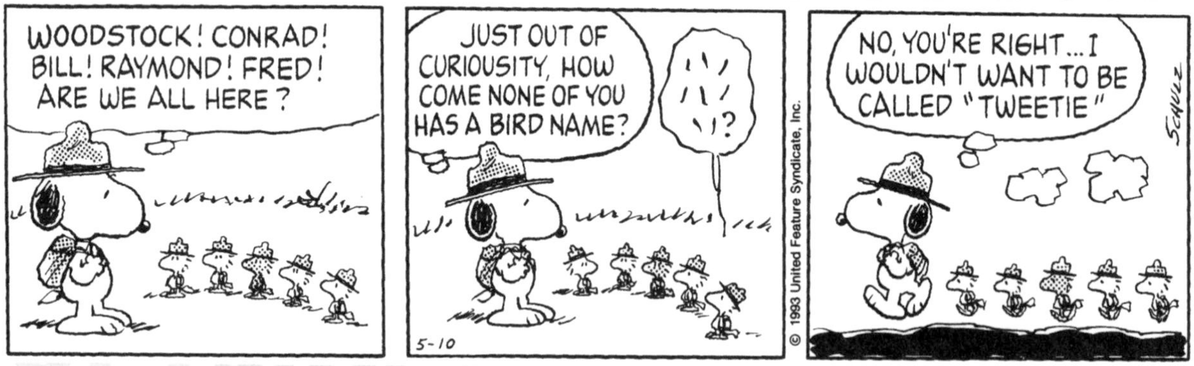
WOODSTOCK! CONRAD! BILL! RAYMOND! FRED! ARE WE ALL HERE?
JUST OUT OF CURIOUSITY, HOW COME NONE OF YOU HAS A BIRD NAME?
5-10
© 1993 United Feature Syndicate, Inc.
NO, YOU'RE RIGHT... I WOULDN'T WANT TO BE CALLED "TWEETIE"
SCHULZ

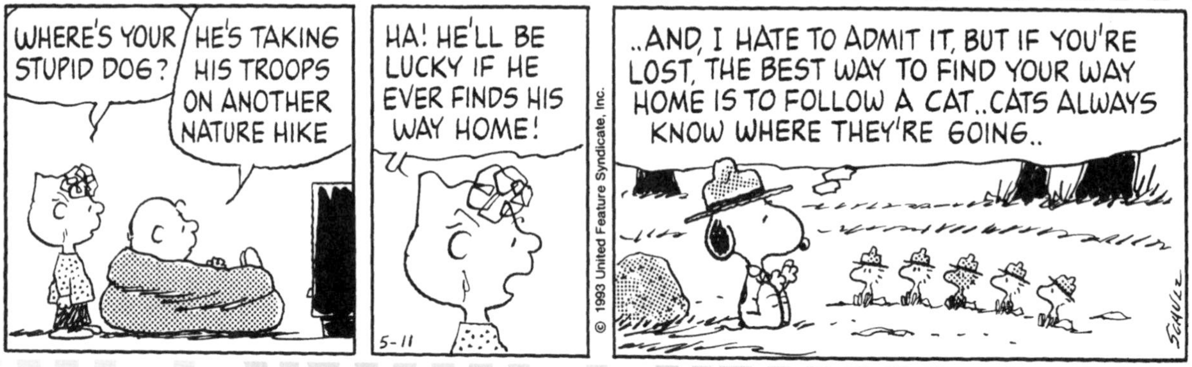
WHERE'S YOUR STUPID DOG?
HE'S TAKING HIS TROOPS ON ANOTHER NATURE HIKE
HA! HE'LL BE LUCKY IF HE EVER FINDS HIS WAY HOME!
5-11
© 1993 United Feature Syndicate, Inc.
..AND, I HATE TO ADMIT IT, BUT IF YOU'RE LOST, THE BEST WAY TO FIND YOUR WAY HOME IS TO FOLLOW A CAT..CATS ALWAYS KNOW WHERE THEY'RE GOING..
SCHULZ

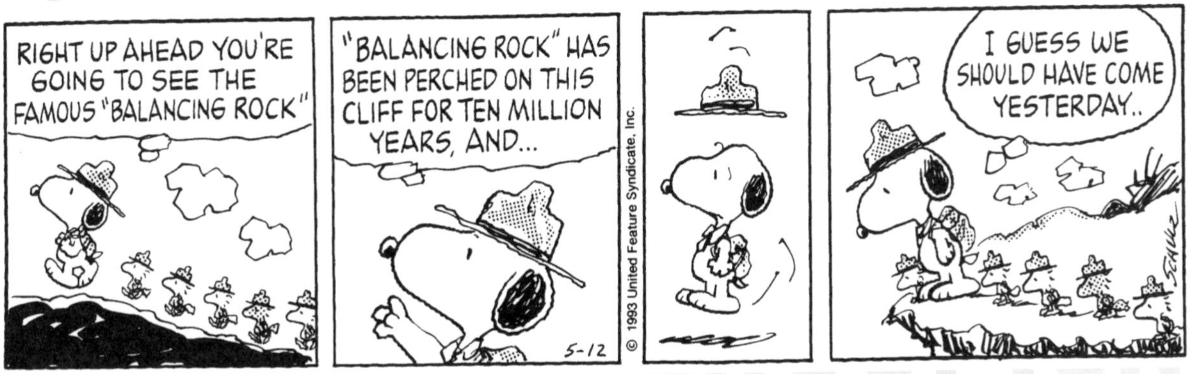
RIGHT UP AHEAD YOU'RE GOING TO SEE THE FAMOUS "BALANCING ROCK"
"BALANCING ROCK" HAS BEEN PERCHED ON THIS CLIFF FOR TEN MILLION YEARS, AND...
5-12
© 1993 United Feature Syndicate, Inc.
I GUESS WE SHOULD HAVE COME YESTERDAY..
SCHULZ

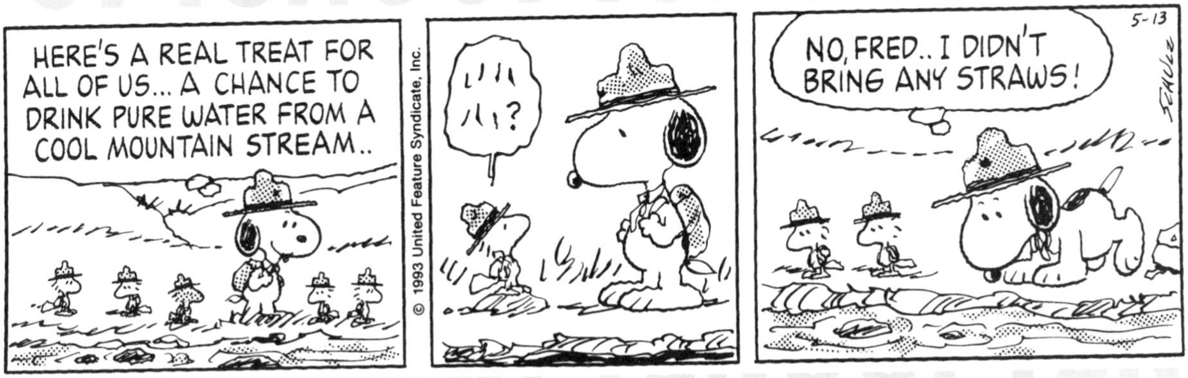
HERE'S A REAL TREAT FOR ALL OF US... A CHANCE TO DRINK PURE WATER FROM A COOL MOUNTAIN STREAM..
© 1993 United Feature Syndicate, Inc.
?
5-13
NO, FRED.. I DIDN'T BRING ANY STRAWS!
SCHULZ

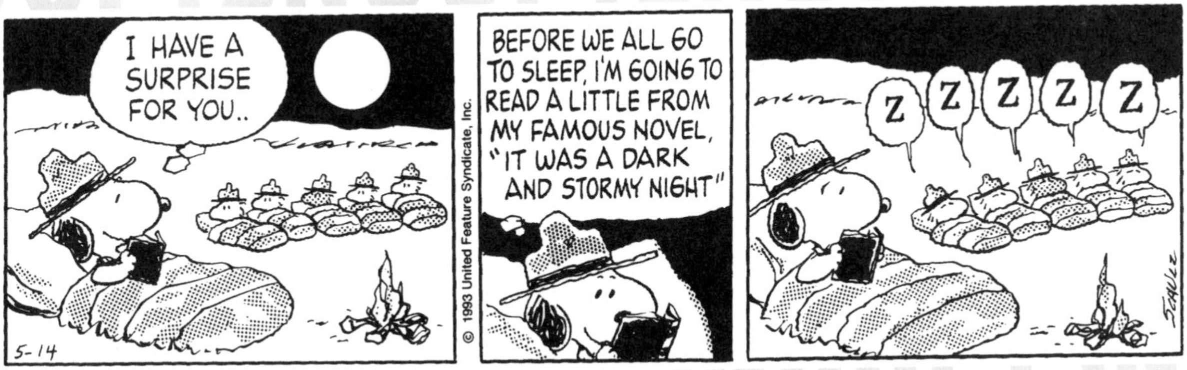
I HAVE A SURPRISE FOR YOU..
5-14
© 1993 United Feature Syndicate, Inc.
BEFORE WE ALL GO TO SLEEP, I'M GOING TO READ A LITTLE FROM MY FAMOUS NOVEL, "IT WAS A DARK AND STORMY NIGHT"
Z Z Z Z Z
SCHULZ

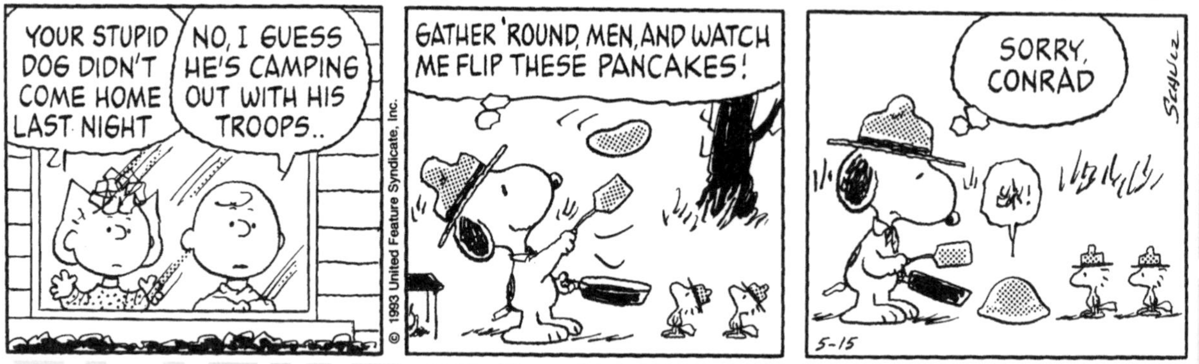
YOUR STUPID DOG DIDN'T COME HOME LAST NIGHT
NO, I GUESS HE'S CAMPING OUT WITH HIS TROOPS..
© 1993 United Feature Syndicate, Inc.
GATHER 'ROUND, MEN, AND WATCH ME FLIP THESE PANCAKES!
SORRY, CONRAD
SCHULZ
5-15

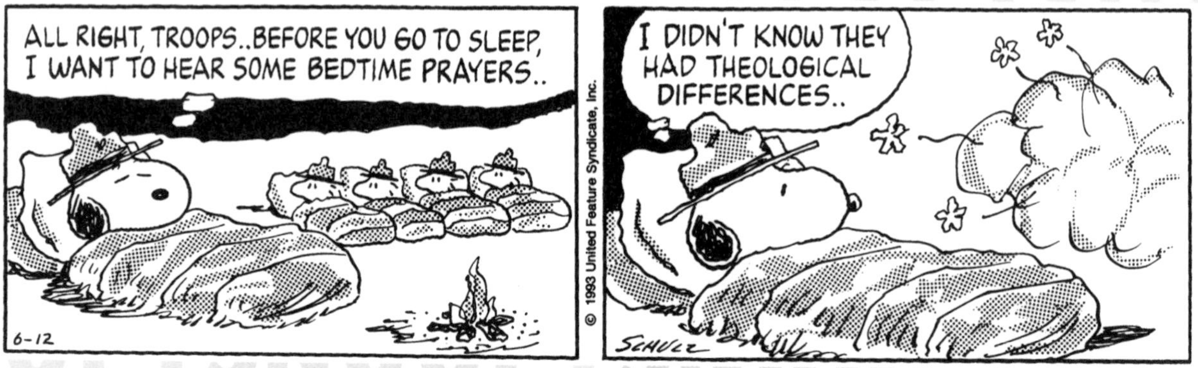
ALL RIGHT, TROOPS..BEFORE YOU GO TO SLEEP, I WANT TO HEAR SOME BEDTIME PRAYERS..
6-12
© 1993 United Feature Syndicate, Inc.
I DIDN'T KNOW THEY HAD THEOLOGICAL DIFFERENCES..
SCHULZ

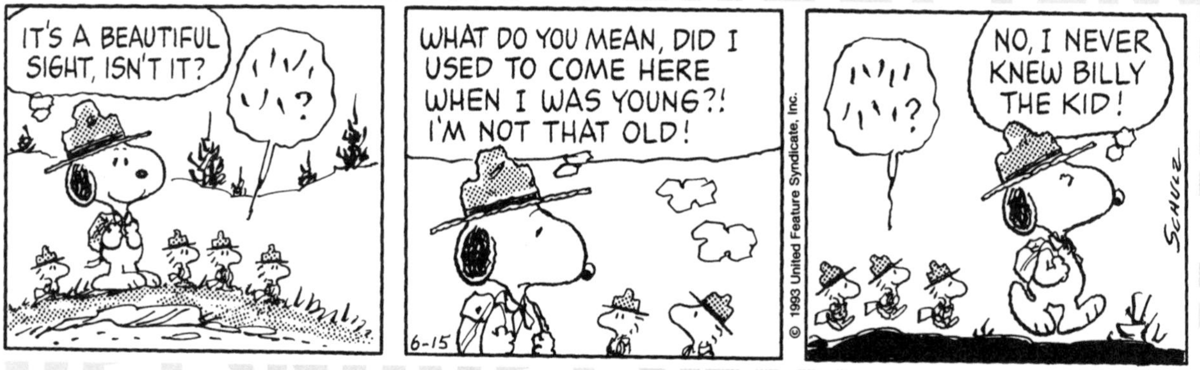
IT'S A BEAUTIFUL SIGHT, ISN'T IT?
WHAT DO YOU MEAN, DID I USED TO COME HERE WHEN I WAS YOUNG?! I'M NOT THAT OLD!
6-15
© 1993 United Feature Syndicate, Inc.
NO, I NEVER KNEW BILLY THE KID!
SCHULZ

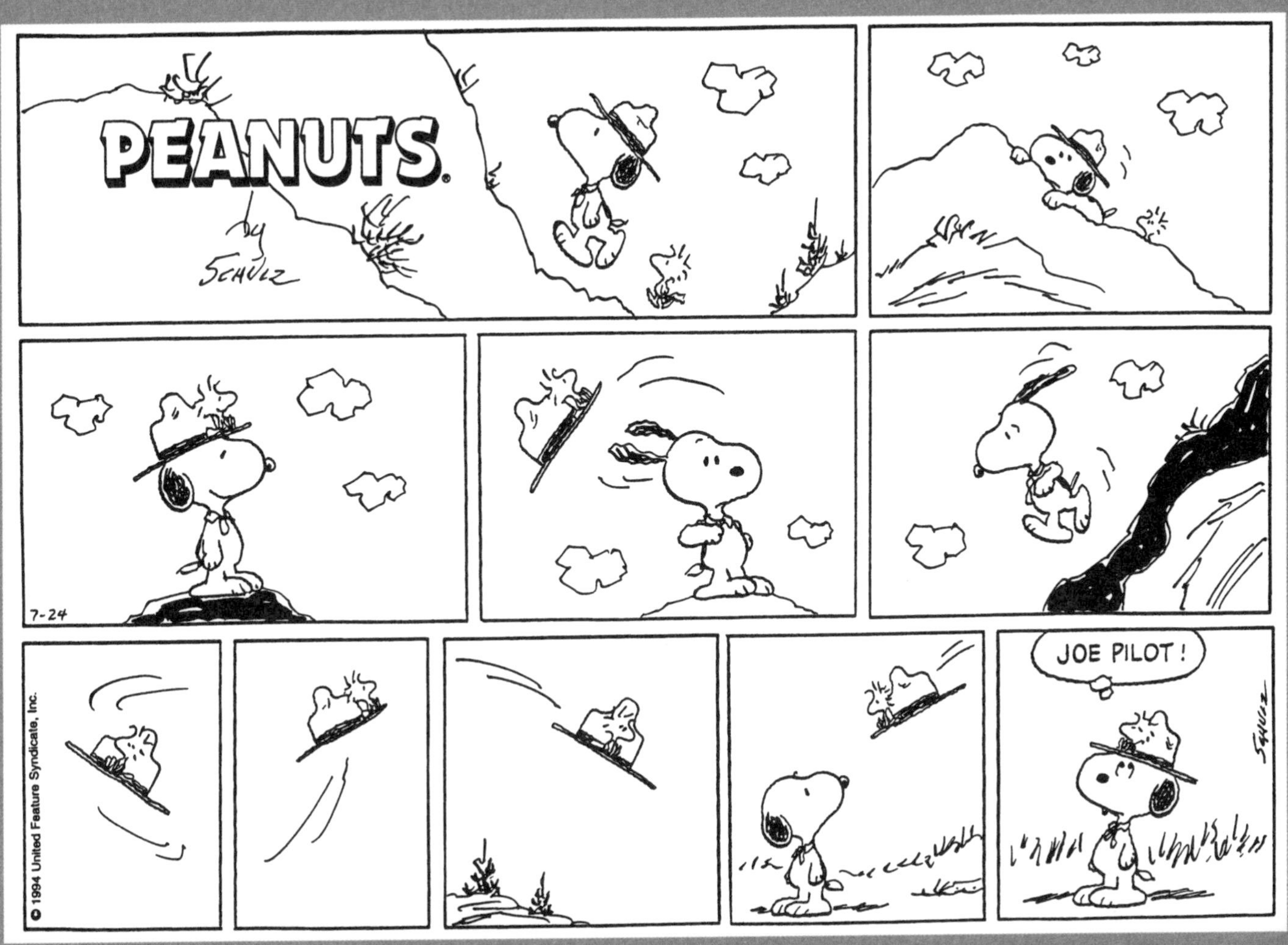
PEANUTS
by Schulz
7-24
© 1994 United Feature Syndicate, Inc.
JOE PILOT!
Schulz

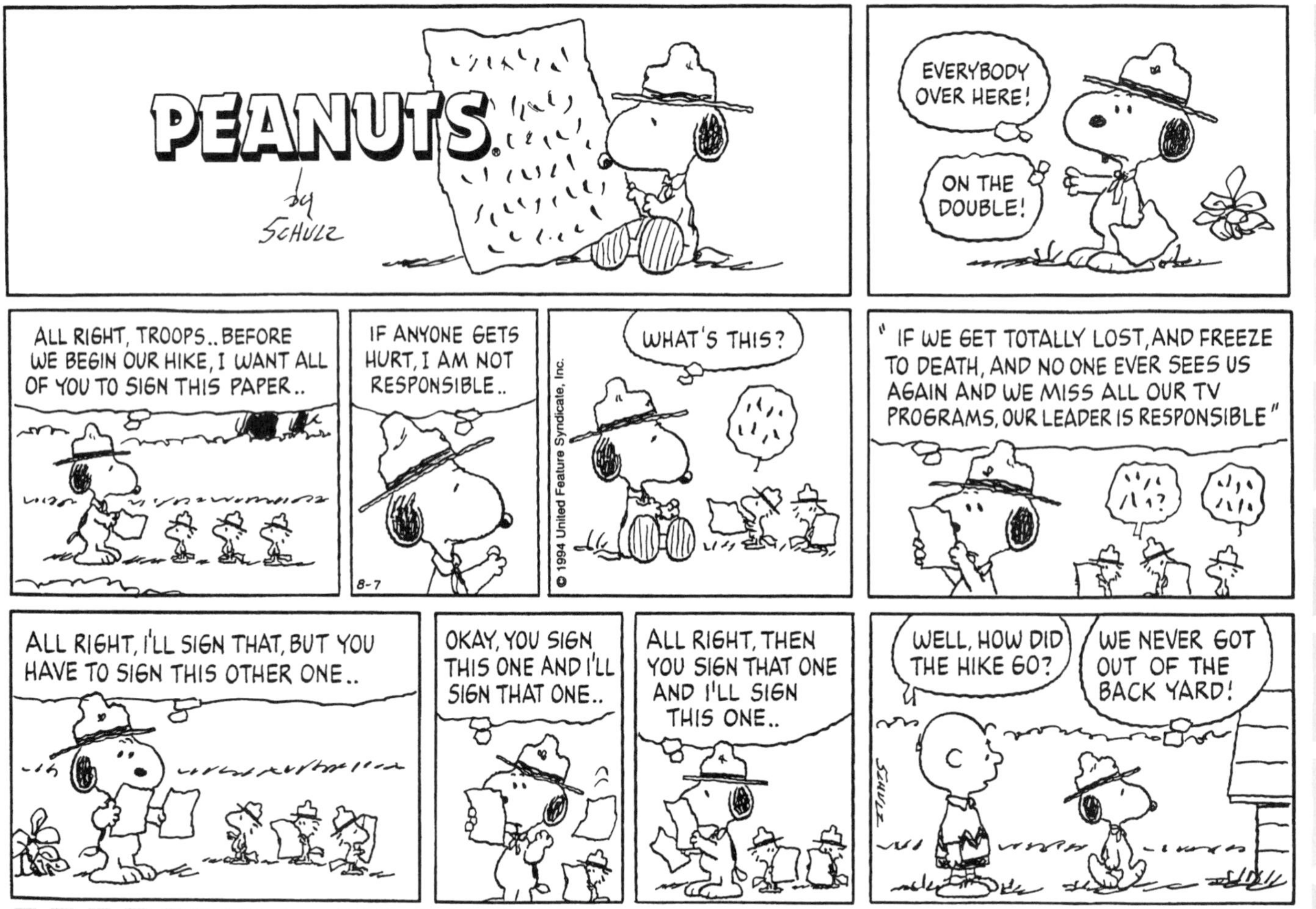
PEANUTS
by SCHULZ
EVERYBODY OVER HERE!
ON THE DOUBLE!
ALL RIGHT, TROOPS.. BEFORE WE BEGIN OUR HIKE, I WANT ALL OF YOU TO SIGN THIS PAPER..
IF ANYONE GETS HURT, I AM NOT RESPONSIBLE..
8-7
© 1994 United Feature Syndicate, Inc.
WHAT'S THIS?
" IF WE GET TOTALLY LOST, AND FREEZE TO DEATH, AND NO ONE EVER SEES US AGAIN AND WE MISS ALL OUR TV PROGRAMS, OUR LEADER IS RESPONSIBLE "
ALL RIGHT, I'LL SIGN THAT, BUT YOU HAVE TO SIGN THIS OTHER ONE..
OKAY, YOU SIGN THIS ONE AND I'LL SIGN THAT ONE..
ALL RIGHT, THEN YOU SIGN THAT ONE AND I'LL SIGN THIS ONE..
WELL, HOW DID THE HIKE GO?
WE NEVER GOT OUT OF THE BACK YARD!
SCHULZ

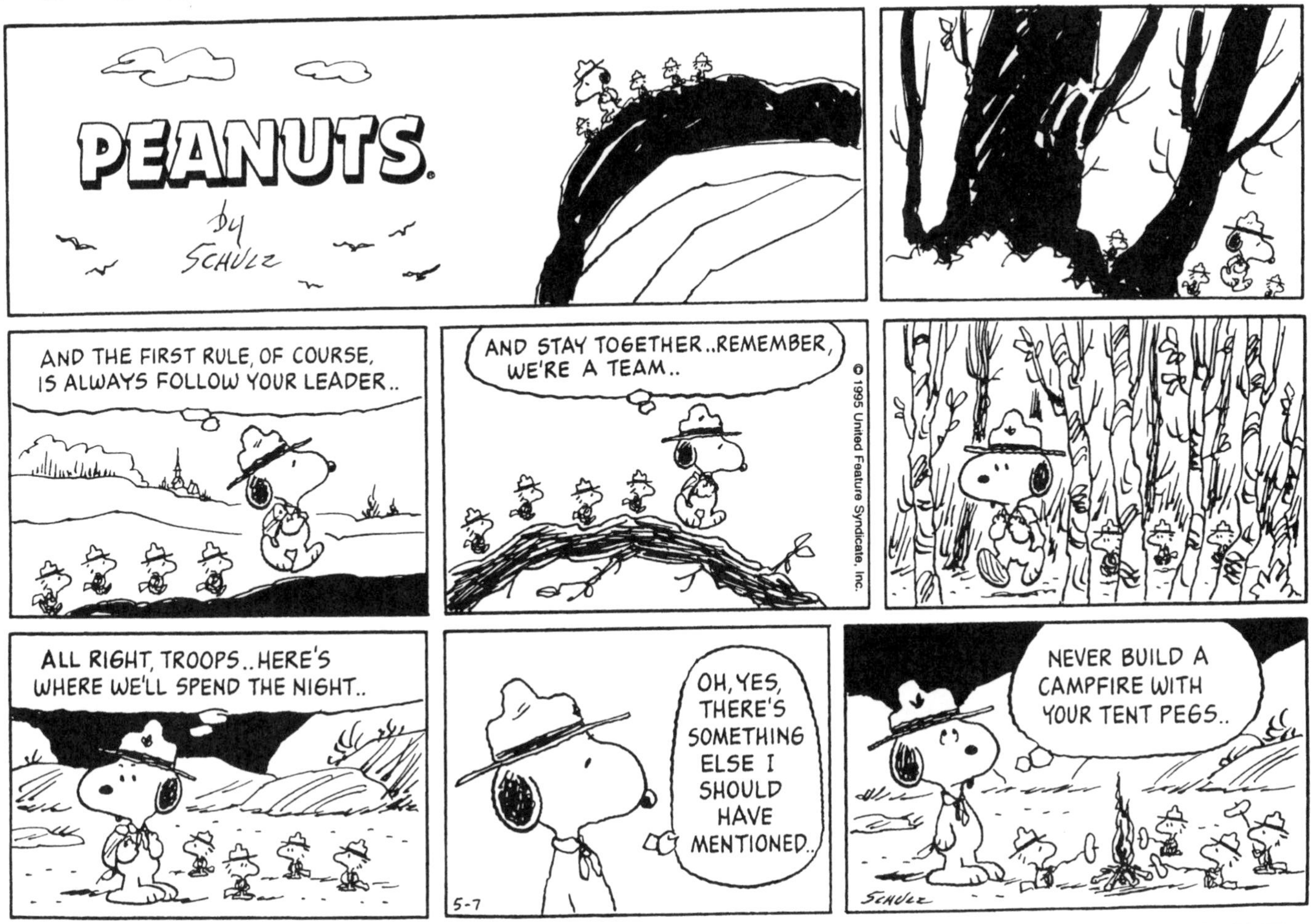
PEANUTS
by SCHULZ
AND THE FIRST RULE, OF COURSE, IS ALWAYS FOLLOW YOUR LEADER..
AND STAY TOGETHER..REMEMBER, WE'RE A TEAM..
© 1995 United Feature Syndicate, Inc.
ALL RIGHT, TROOPS..HERE'S WHERE WE'LL SPEND THE NIGHT..
OH, YES, THERE'S SOMETHING ELSE I SHOULD HAVE MENTIONED..
5-7
NEVER BUILD A CAMPFIRE WITH YOUR TENT PEGS..
SCHULZ

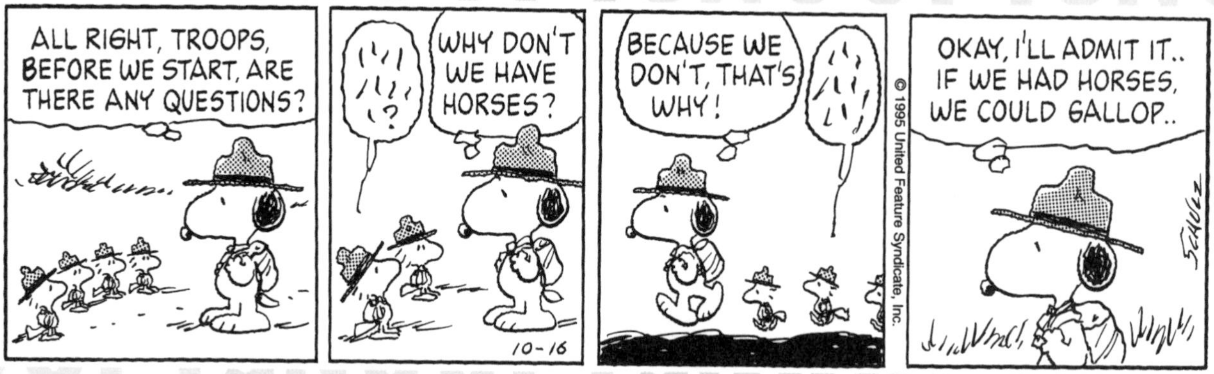
ALL RIGHT, TROOPS, BEFORE WE START, ARE THERE ANY QUESTIONS?
WHY DON'T WE HAVE HORSES?
10-16
BECAUSE WE DON'T, THAT'S WHY!
© 1995 United Feature Syndicate, Inc.
OKAY, I'LL ADMIT IT.. IF WE HAD HORSES, WE COULD GALLOP..
SCHULZ

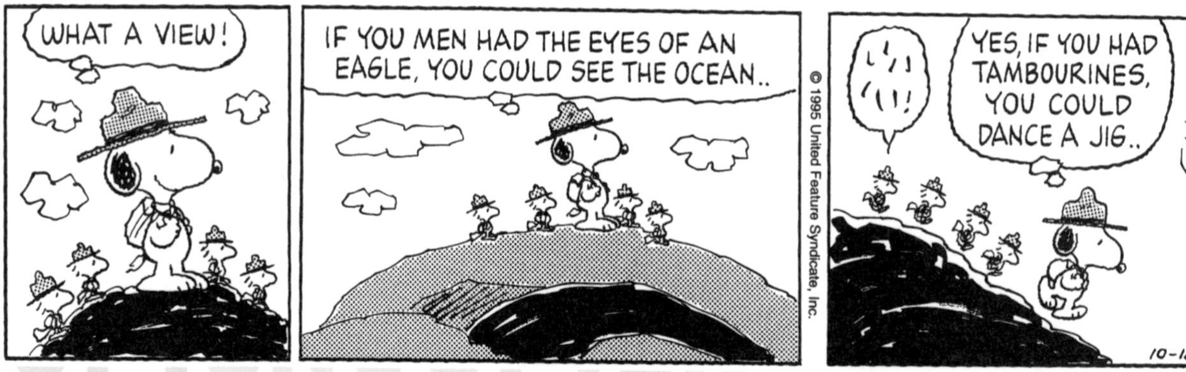
WHAT A VIEW!
IF YOU MEN HAD THE EYES OF AN EAGLE, YOU COULD SEE THE OCEAN..
© 1995 United Feature Syndicate, Inc.
YES, IF YOU HAD TAMBOURINES, YOU COULD DANCE A JIG..
SCHULZ
10-18

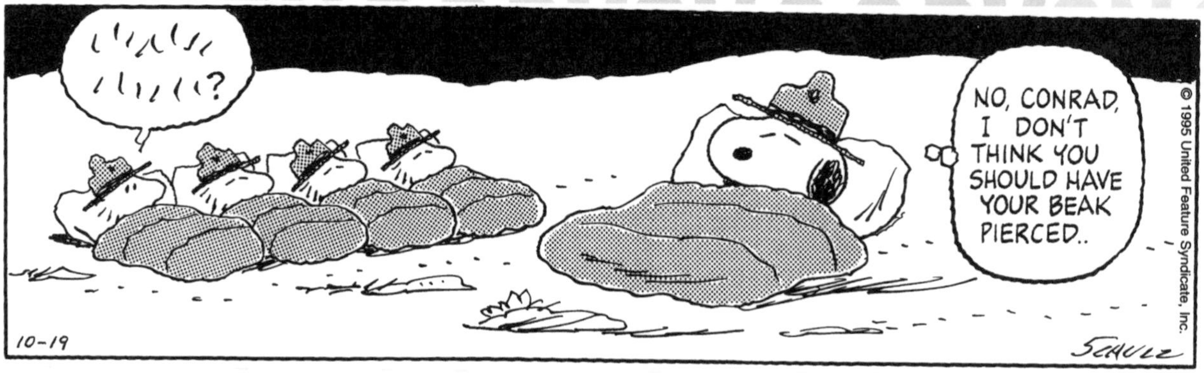
NO, CONRAD, I DON'T THINK YOU SHOULD HAVE YOUR BEAK PIERCED..
© 1995 United Feature Syndicate, Inc.
10-19
SCHULZ

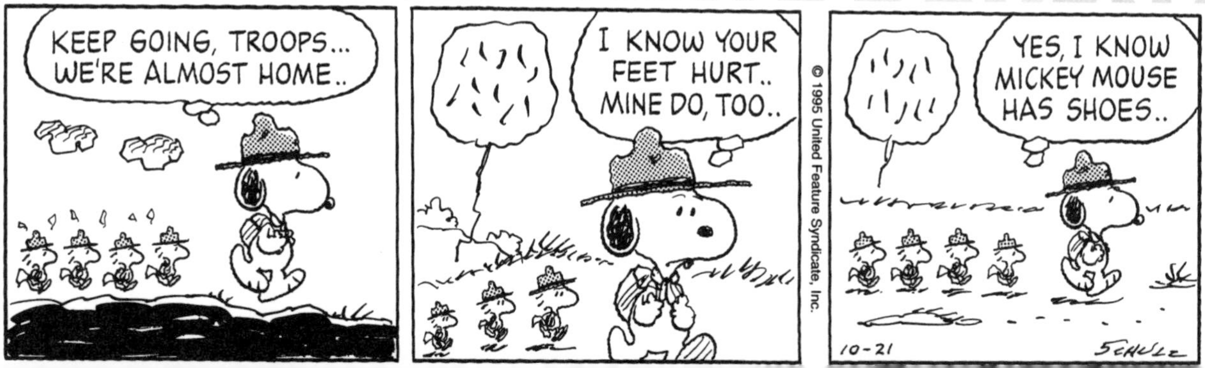
KEEP GOING, TROOPS... WE'RE ALMOST HOME..
I KNOW YOUR FEET HURT.. MINE DO, TOO..
© 1995 United Feature Syndicate, Inc.
YES, I KNOW MICKEY MOUSE HAS SHOES..
10-21
SCHULZ

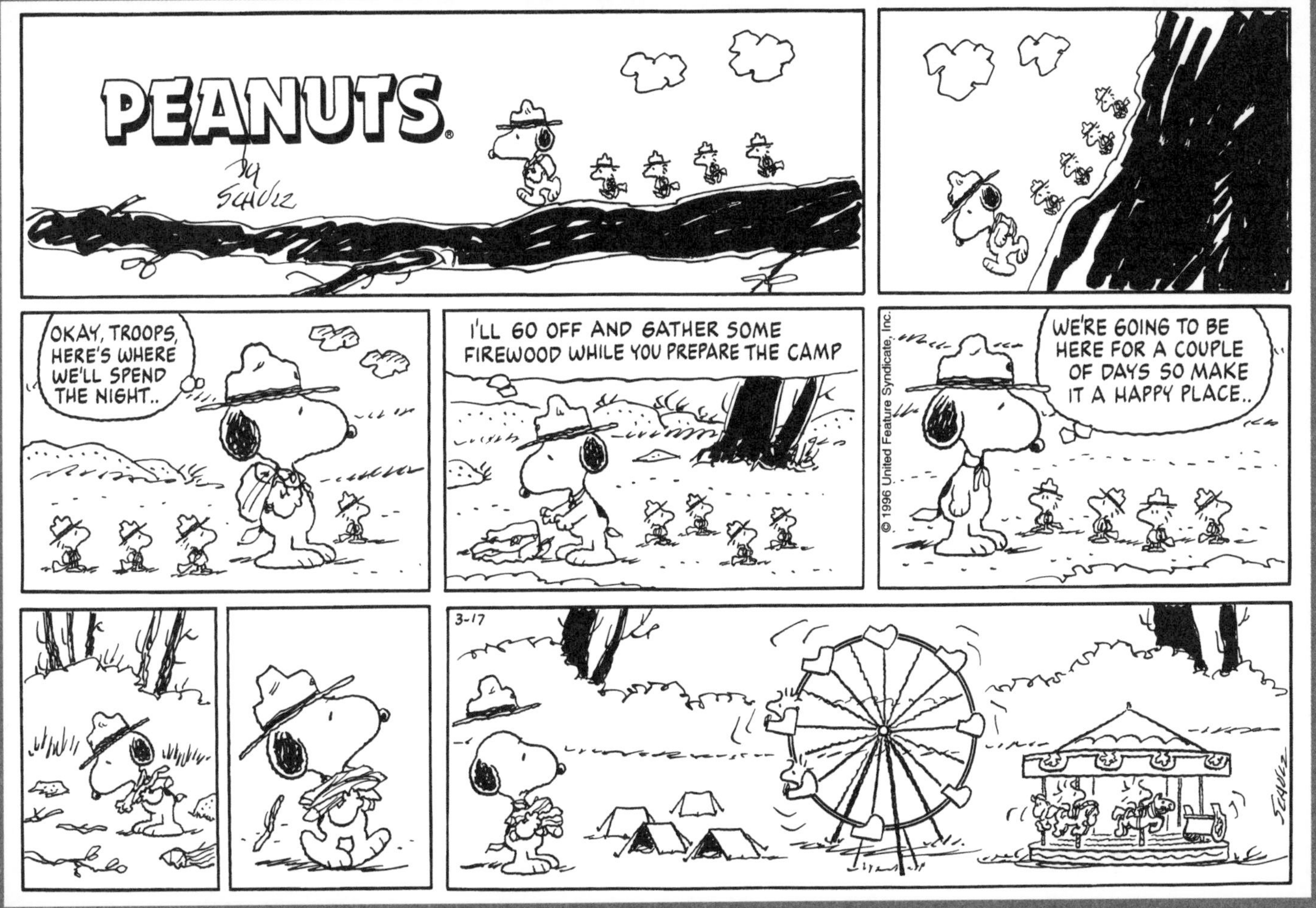
PEANUTS
by SCHULZ
OKAY, TROOPS, HERE'S WHERE WE'LL SPEND THE NIGHT..
I'LL GO OFF AND GATHER SOME FIREWOOD WHILE YOU PREPARE THE CAMP
© 1996 United Feature Syndicate, Inc.
WE'RE GOING TO BE HERE FOR A COUPLE OF DAYS SO MAKE IT A HAPPY PLACE..
3-17
SCHULZ

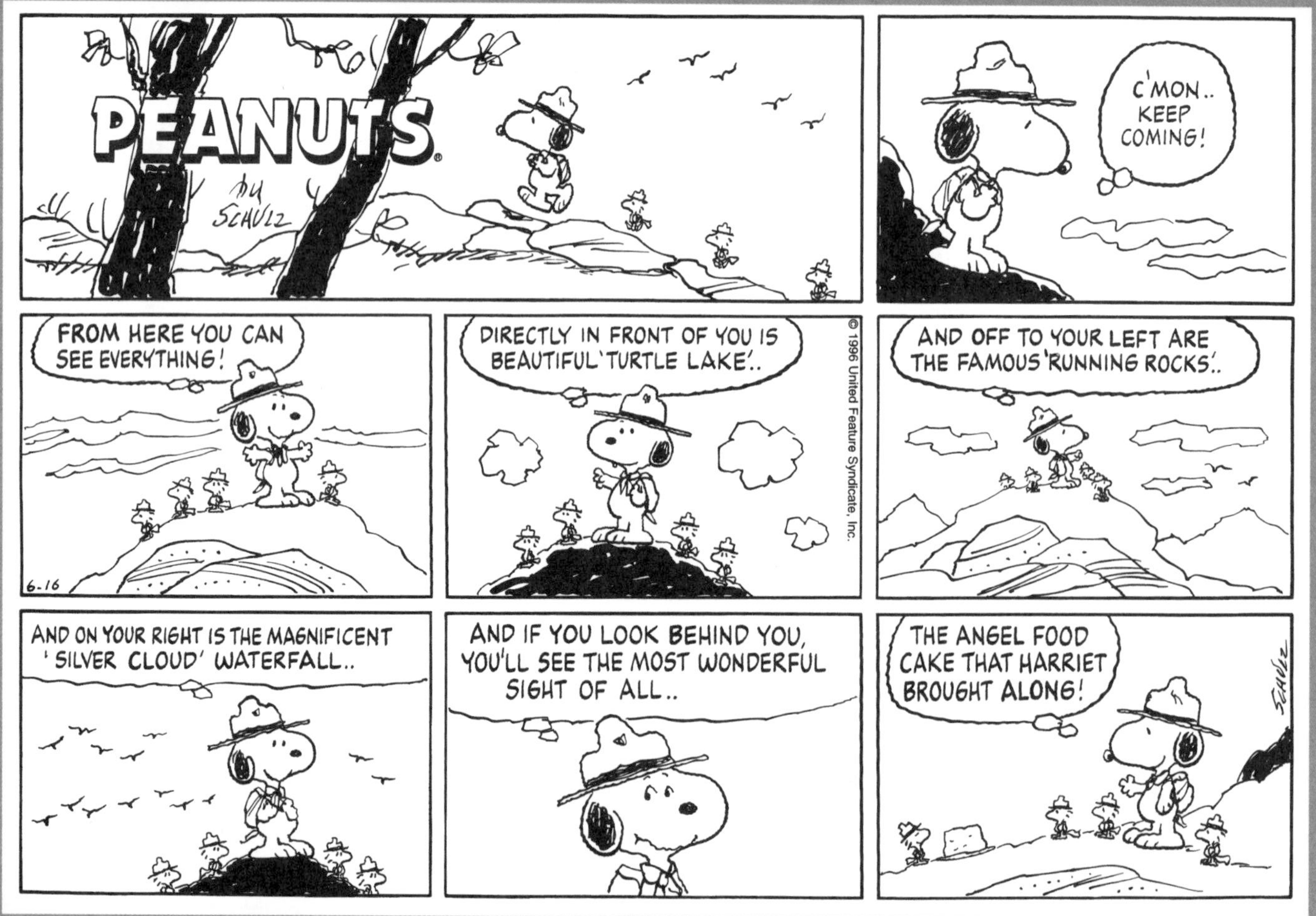
PEANUTS
by SCHULZ
C'MON.. KEEP COMING!
FROM HERE YOU CAN SEE EVERYTHING!
6-16
DIRECTLY IN FRONT OF YOU IS BEAUTIFUL 'TURTLE LAKE'..
© 1996 United Feature Syndicate, Inc.
AND OFF TO YOUR LEFT ARE THE FAMOUS 'RUNNING ROCKS'..
AND ON YOUR RIGHT IS THE MAGNIFICENT 'SILVER CLOUD' WATERFALL..
AND IF YOU LOOK BEHIND YOU, YOU'LL SEE THE MOST WONDERFUL SIGHT OF ALL..
THE ANGEL FOOD CAKE THAT HARRIET BROUGHT ALONG!
SCHULZ

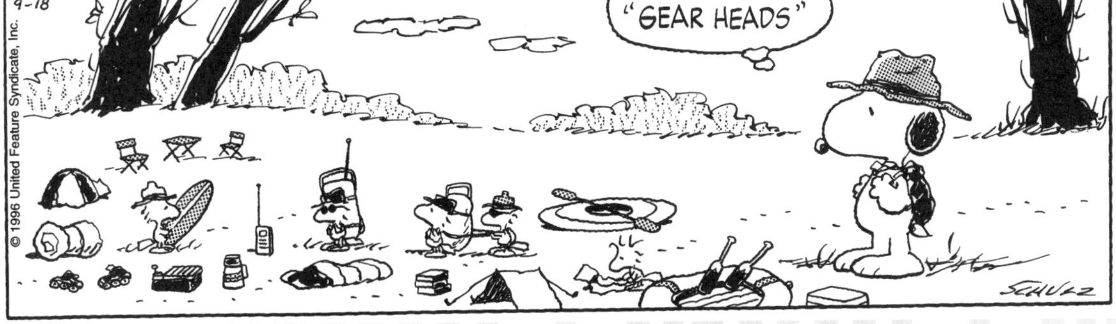
9-18
© 1996 United Feature Syndicate, Inc.
"GEAR HEADS"
SCHULZ

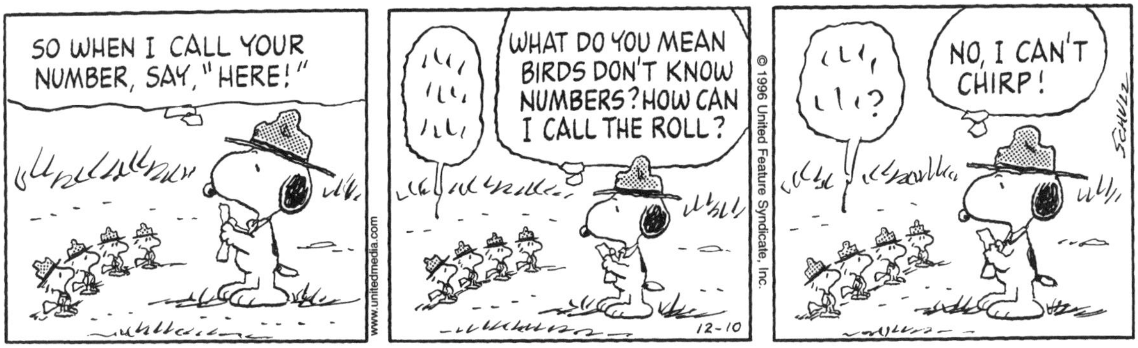
SO WHEN I CALL YOUR NUMBER, SAY, "HERE!"
www.unitedmedia.com
WHAT DO YOU MEAN BIRDS DON'T KNOW NUMBERS? HOW CAN I CALL THE ROLL?
12-10
© 1996 United Feature Syndicate, Inc.
NO, I CAN'T CHIRP!
SCHULZ

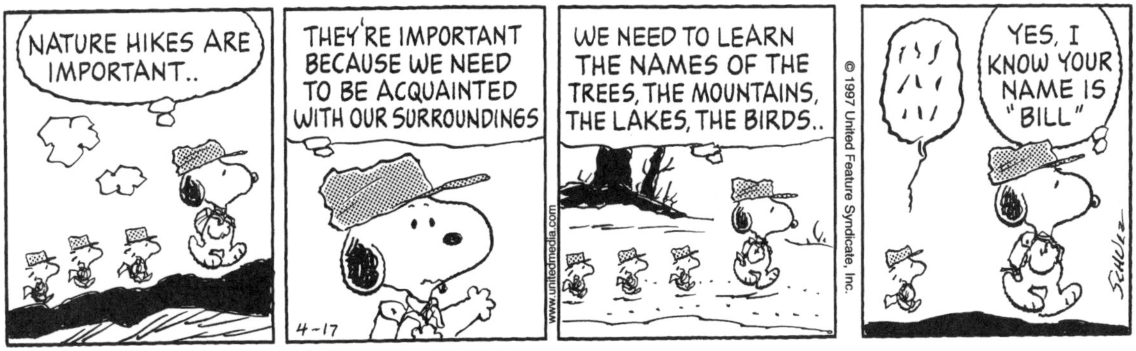
NATURE HIKES ARE IMPORTANT..
THEY'RE IMPORTANT BECAUSE WE NEED TO BE ACQUAINTED WITH OUR SURROUNDINGS
4-17
www.unitedmedia.com
WE NEED TO LEARN THE NAMES OF THE TREES, THE MOUNTAINS, THE LAKES, THE BIRDS..
© 1997 United Feature Syndicate, Inc.
YES, I KNOW YOUR NAME IS "BILL"
SCHULZ

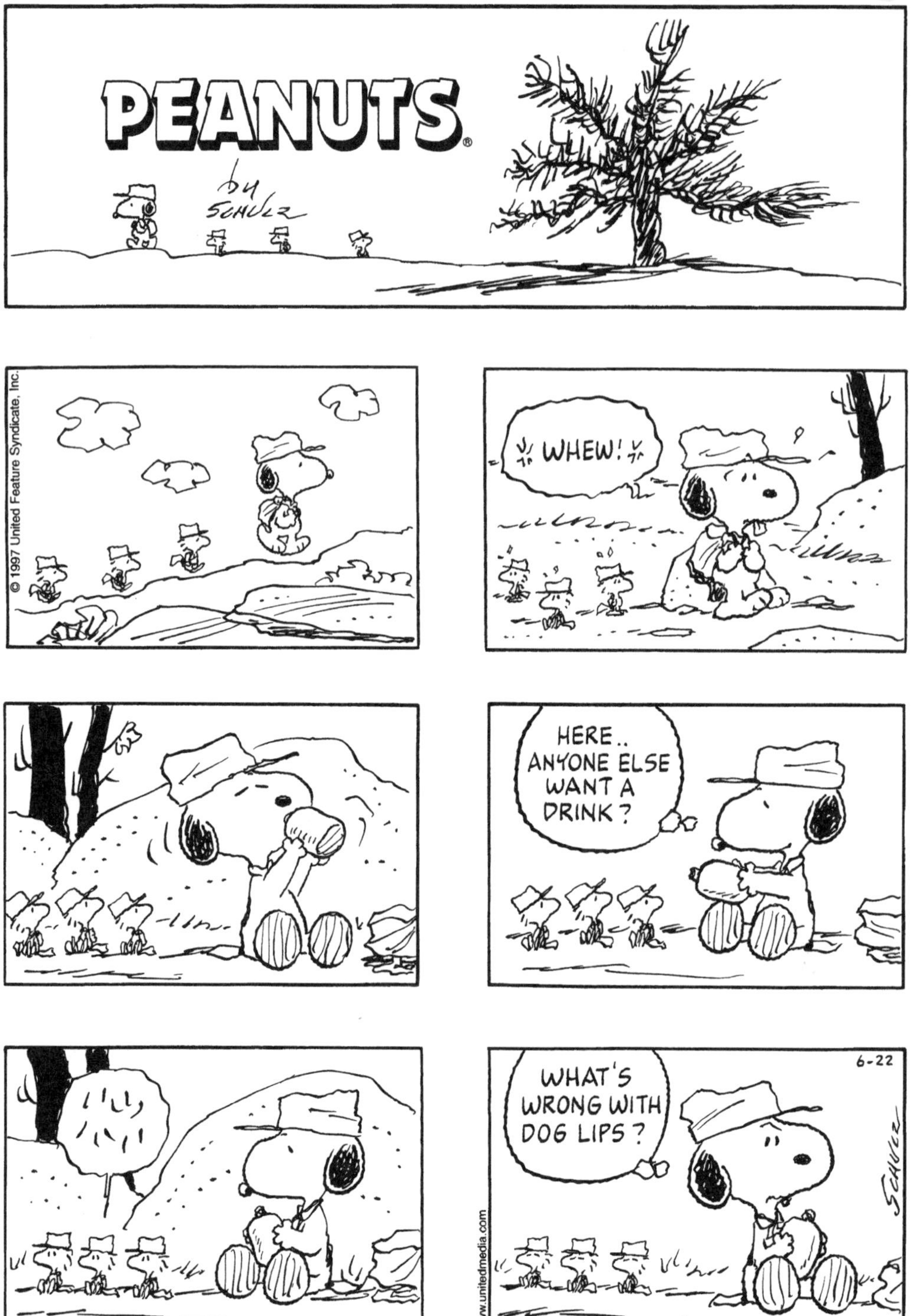
PEANUTS
by SCHULZ
© 1997 United Feature Syndicate, Inc.
WHEW!
HERE.. ANYONE ELSE WANT A DRINK?
WHAT'S WRONG WITH DOG LIPS?
6-22
SCHULZ
www.unitedmedia.com

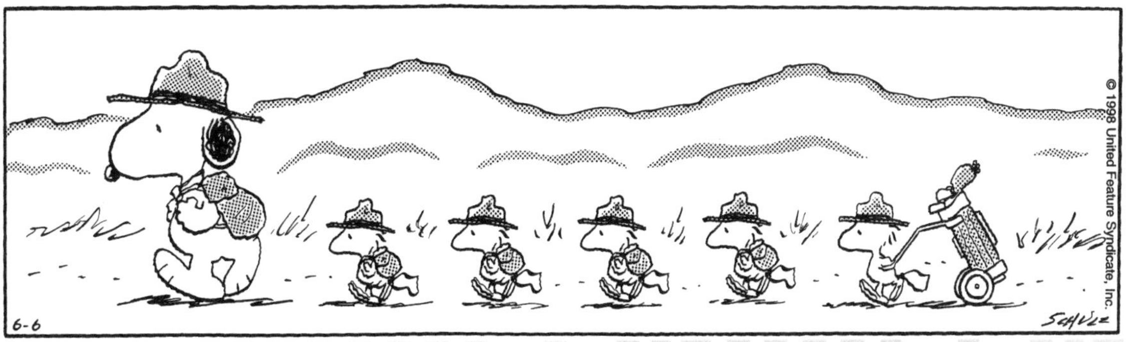
© 1998 United Feature Syndicate, Inc.
6-6
SCHULZ

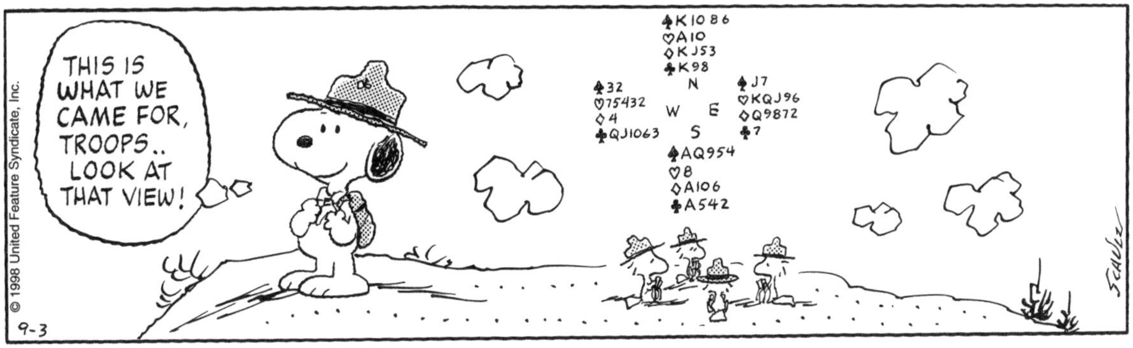
THIS IS WHAT WE CAME FOR, TROOPS.. LOOK AT THAT VIEW!
♠K 10 8 6
♡A 10
◇K J 5 3
♣K 9 8
♠3 2
♡7 5 4 3 2
◇4
♣Q J 10 6 3
N
W E
S
♠J 7
♡K Q J 9 6
◇Q 9 8 7 2
♣7
♠A Q 9 5 4
♡8
◇A 10 6
♣A 5 4 2
© 1998 United Feature Syndicate, Inc.
9-3
SCHULZ

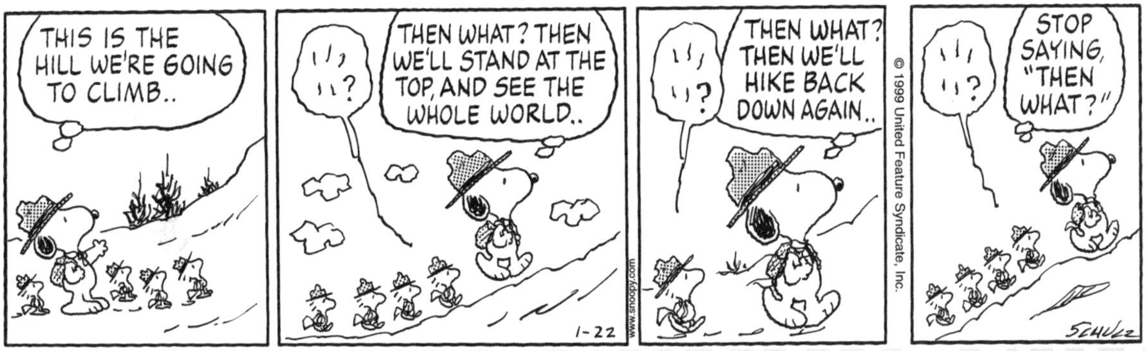
THIS IS THE HILL WE'RE GOING TO CLIMB..
" ?
THEN WHAT? THEN WE'LL STAND AT THE TOP, AND SEE THE WHOLE WORLD..
" ?
THEN WHAT? THEN WE'LL HIKE BACK DOWN AGAIN..
" ?
STOP SAYING, "THEN WHAT?"
1-22
www.snoopy.com
© 1999 United Feature Syndicate, Inc.
SCHULZ

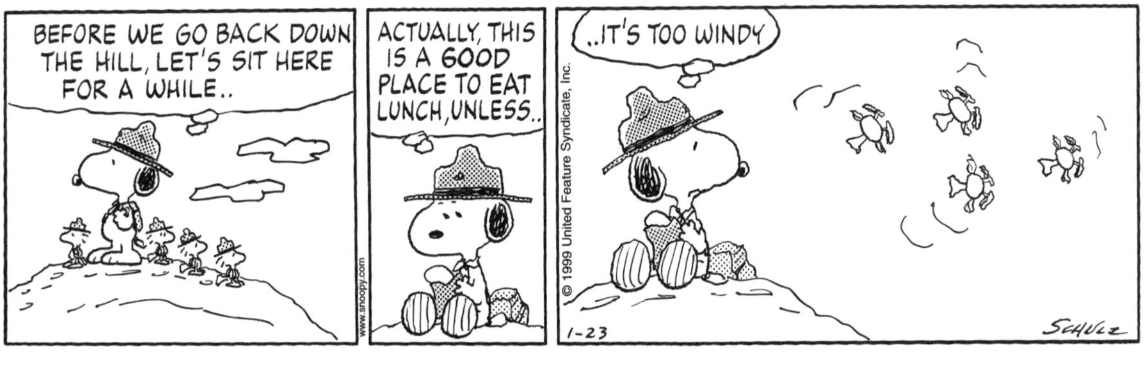
BEFORE WE GO BACK DOWN THE HILL, LET'S SIT HERE FOR A WHILE..
ACTUALLY, THIS IS A GOOD PLACE TO EAT LUNCH, UNLESS..
..IT'S TOO WINDY
www.snoopy.com
© 1999 United Feature Syndicate, Inc.
1-23
SCHULZ

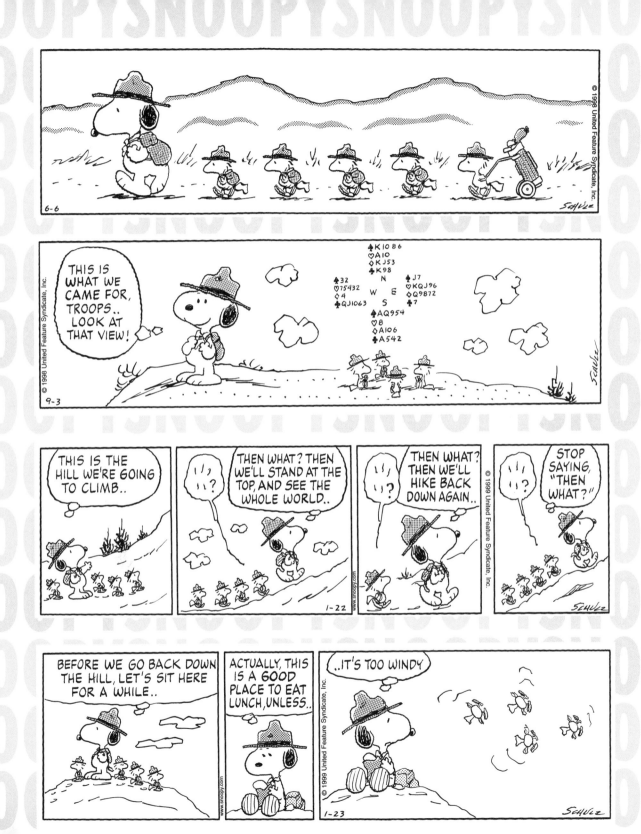

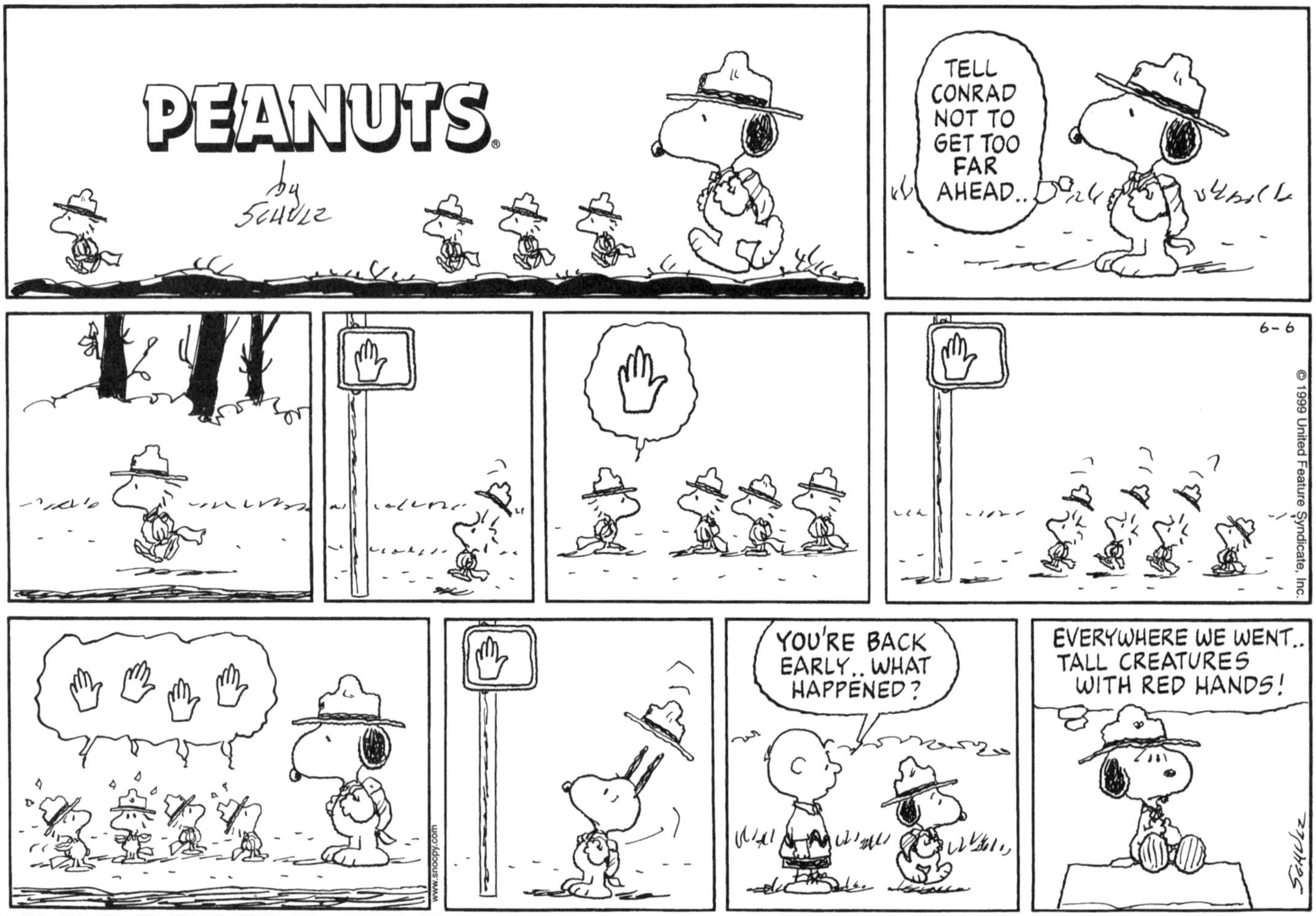
PEANUTS
by SCHULZ
TELL CONRAD NOT TO GET TOO FAR AHEAD..
6-6
© 1999 United Feature Syndicate, Inc.
www.snoopy.com
YOU'RE BACK EARLY.. WHAT HAPPENED?
EVERYWHERE WE WENT.. TALL CREATURES WITH RED HANDS!
SCHULZ

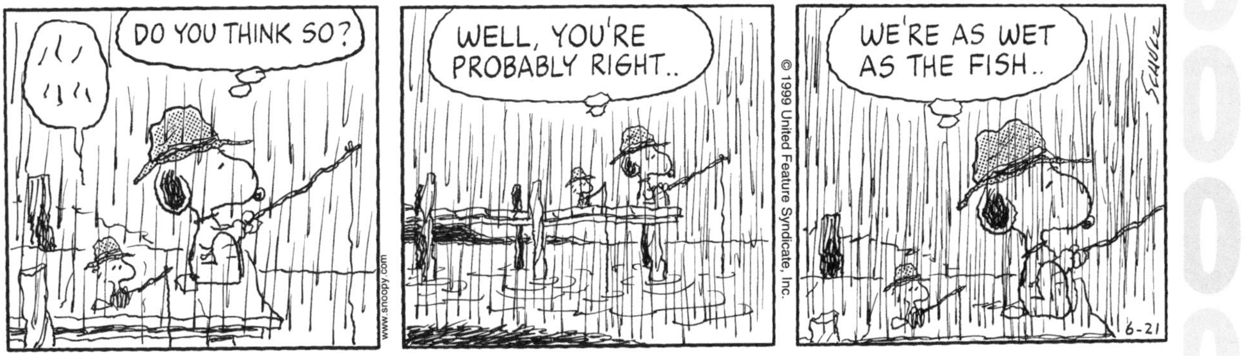
DO YOU THINK SO?
www.snoopy.com
WELL, YOU'RE PROBABLY RIGHT..
© 1999 United Feature Syndicate, Inc.
WE'RE AS WET AS THE FISH..
SCHULZ
6-21

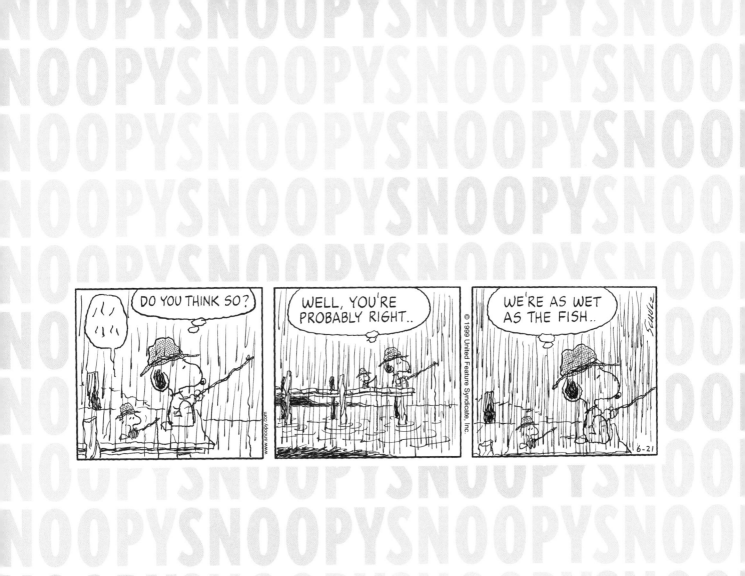

NOOPYSNOOPYSNOOPYSNOO
NOOPYSNOOPYSNOOPYSNOO
NOOPYSNOOPYSNOOPYSNOO
NOOPYSNOOPYSNOOPYSNOO
NOOPYSNOOPYSNOOPYSNOO
NOOPYSNOOPYSNOOPYSNOO
NOOPYSNOOPYSNOOPYSNOO
NOOPYSNOOPYSNOOPYSNOO
NOOPYSNOOPYSNOOPYSNOO
NOOPYSNOOPYSNOOPYSNOO
NOOPYSNOOPYSNOOPYSNOO
NOOPYSNOOPYSNOOPYSNOO
NOOPYSNOOPYSNOOPYSNOO

Literary Ace

SNOOPY

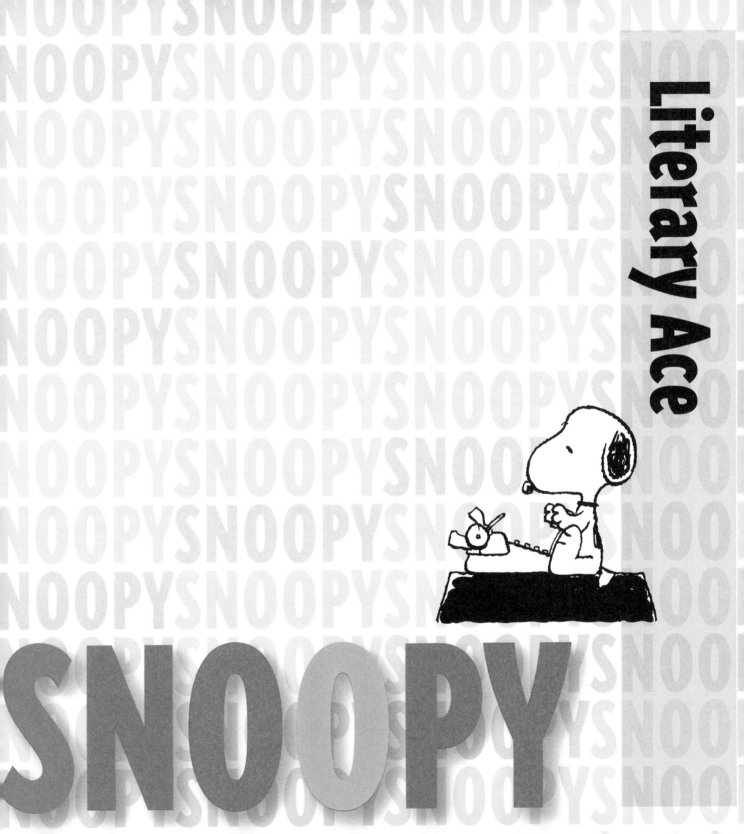

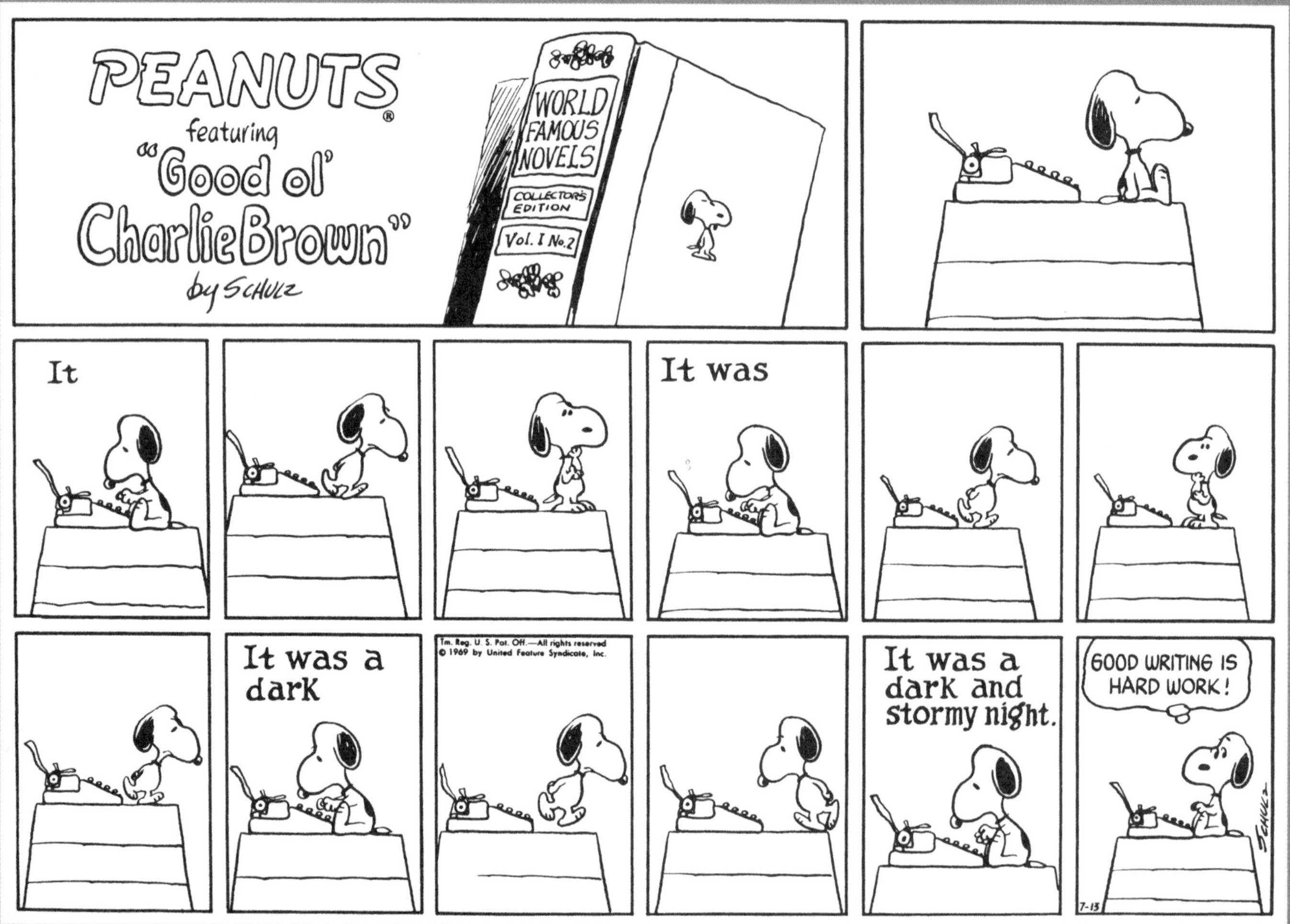
PEANUTS®
featuring
"Good ol' CharlieBrown"
by SCHULZ
WORLD FAMOUS NOVELS
COLLECTOR'S EDITION
Vol. I No. 2
It
It was
It was a dark
Tm. Reg. U. S. Pat. Off.—All rights reserved © 1969 by United Feature Syndicate, Inc.
It was a dark and stormy night.
GOOD WRITING IS HARD WORK!
SCHULZ
7-13

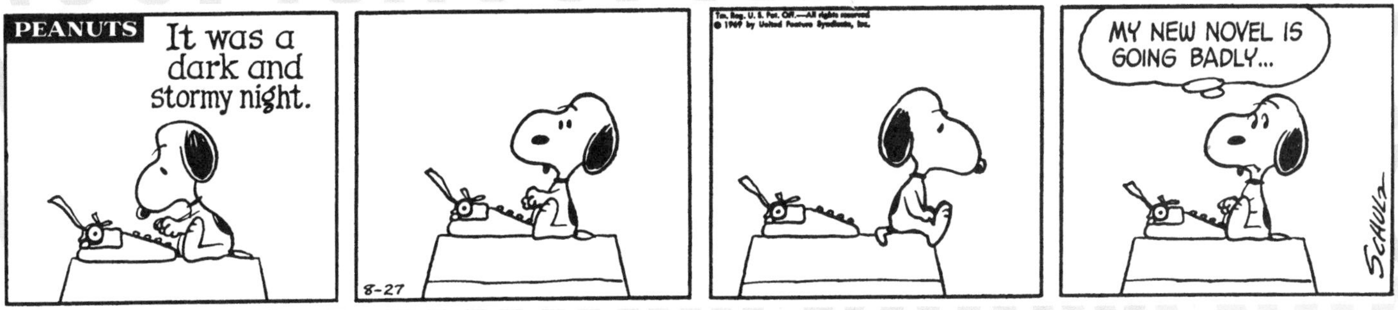
PEANUTS
It was a dark and stormy night.
8-27
Tm. Reg. U. S. Pat. Off.—All rights reserved © 1969 by United Feature Syndicate, Inc.
MY NEW NOVEL IS GOING BADLY...
SCHULZ

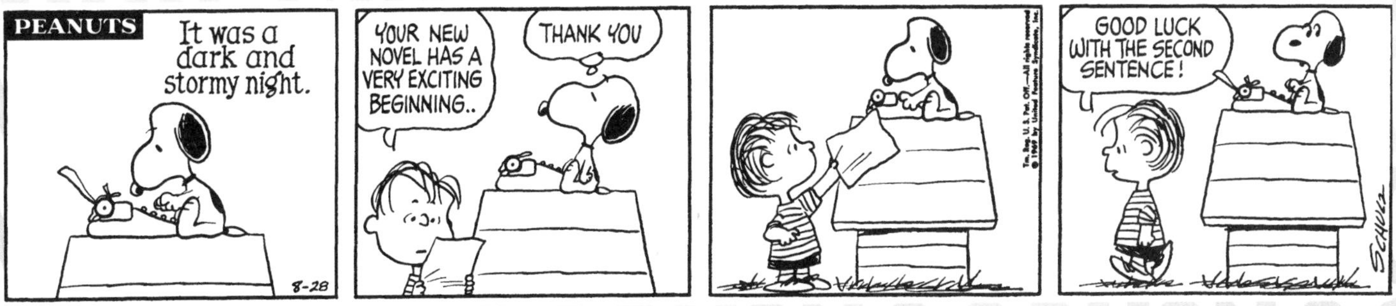
PEANUTS
It was a dark and stormy night.
8-28
YOUR NEW NOVEL HAS A VERY EXCITING BEGINNING..
THANK YOU
Tm. Reg. U. S. Pat. Off.—All rights reserved © 1969 by United Feature Syndicate, Inc.
GOOD LUCK WITH THE SECOND SENTENCE!
SCHULZ

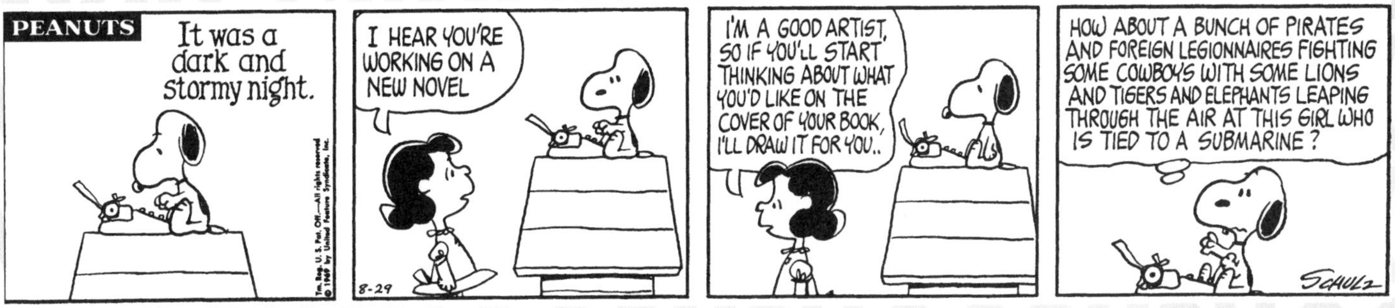
PEANUTS
It was a dark and stormy night.
Tm. Reg. U. S. Pat. Off.—All rights reserved © 1969 by United Feature Syndicate, Inc.
I HEAR YOU'RE WORKING ON A NEW NOVEL
8-29
I'M A GOOD ARTIST, SO IF YOU'LL START THINKING ABOUT WHAT YOU'D LIKE ON THE COVER OF YOUR BOOK, I'LL DRAW IT FOR YOU..
HOW ABOUT A BUNCH OF PIRATES AND FOREIGN LEGIONNAIRES FIGHTING SOME COWBOYS WITH SOME LIONS AND TIGERS AND ELEPHANTS LEAPING THROUGH THE AIR AT THIS GIRL WHO IS TIED TO A SUBMARINE?
SCHULZ

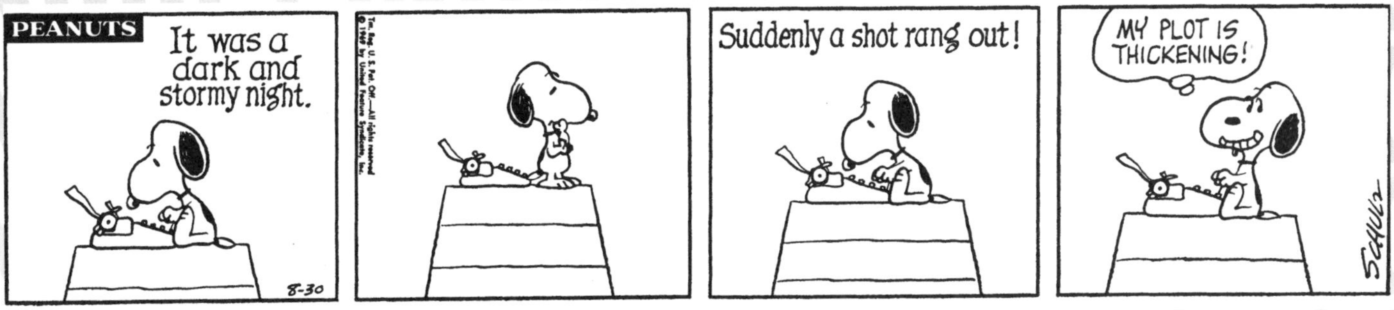
PEANUTS
It was a dark and stormy night.
8-30
Tm. Reg. U. S. Pat. Off.—All rights reserved © 1969 by United Feature Syndicate, Inc.
Suddenly a shot rang out!
MY PLOT IS THICKENING!
SCHULZ

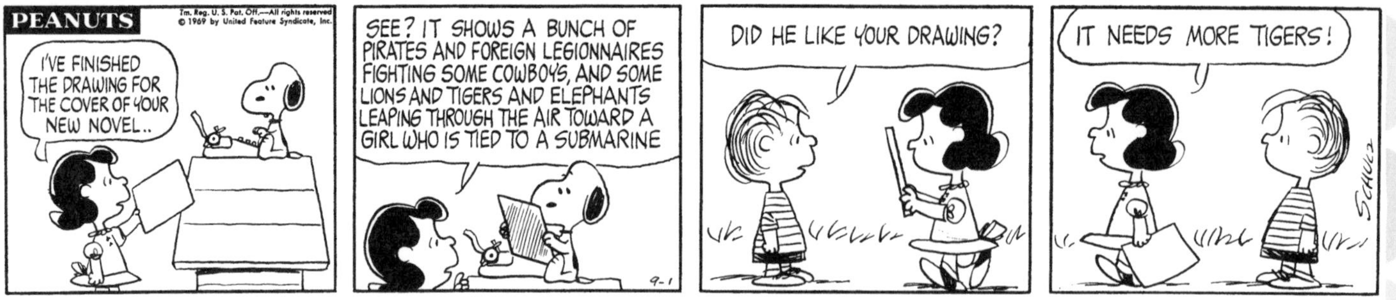
PEANUTS
Tm. Reg. U. S. Pat. Off.—All rights reserved © 1969 by United Feature Syndicate, Inc.
I'VE FINISHED THE DRAWING FOR THE COVER OF YOUR NEW NOVEL..
SEE? IT SHOWS A BUNCH OF PIRATES AND FOREIGN LEGIONNAIRES FIGHTING SOME COWBOYS, AND SOME LIONS AND TIGERS AND ELEPHANTS LEAPING THROUGH THE AIR TOWARD A GIRL WHO IS TIED TO A SUBMARINE
DID HE LIKE YOUR DRAWING?
IT NEEDS MORE TIGERS!
SCHULZ

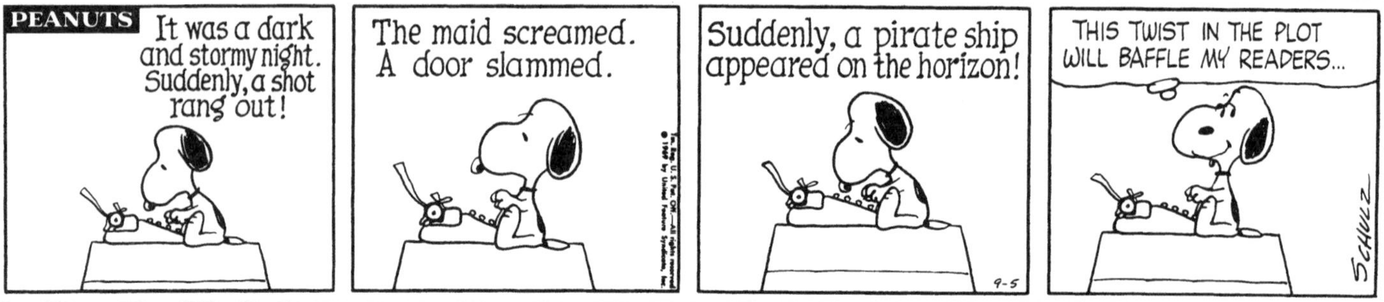
PEANUTS
It was a dark and stormy night. Suddenly, a shot rang out!
The maid screamed. A door slammed.
Tm. Reg. U. S. Pat. Off.—All rights reserved © 1969 by United Feature Syndicate, Inc.
Suddenly, a pirate ship appeared on the horizon!
THIS TWIST IN THE PLOT WILL BAFFLE MY READERS...
SCHULZ

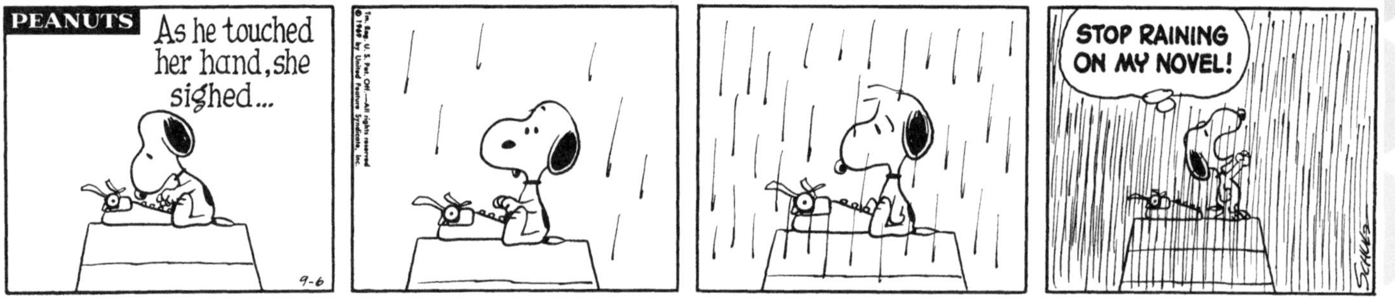
PEANUTS
As he touched her hand, she sighed...
Tm. Reg. U. S. Pat. Off.—All rights reserved © 1969 by United Feature Syndicate, Inc.
STOP RAINING ON MY NOVEL!
SCHULZ

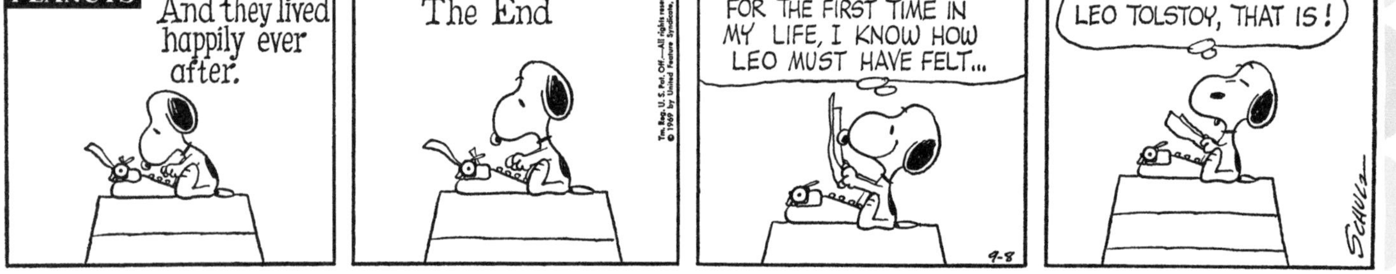
PEANUTS
And they lived happily ever after.
The End
Tm. Reg. U. S. Pat. Off.—All rights reserved © 1969 by United Feature Syndicate, Inc.
FOR THE FIRST TIME IN MY LIFE, I KNOW HOW LEO MUST HAVE FELT...
LEO TOLSTOY, THAT IS!
SCHULZ

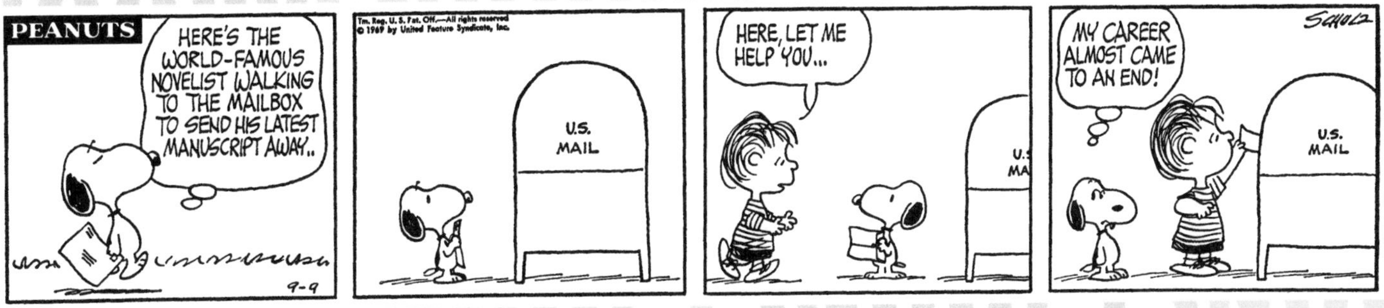
PEANUTS
HERE'S THE WORLD-FAMOUS NOVELIST WALKING TO THE MAILBOX TO SEND HIS LATEST MANUSCRIPT AWAY..
9-9
Tm. Reg. U.S. Pat. Off.—All rights reserved
© 1969 by United Feature Syndicate, Inc.
U.S. MAIL
HERE, LET ME HELP YOU...
MY CAREER ALMOST CAME TO AN END!
SCHULZ
U.S. MAIL

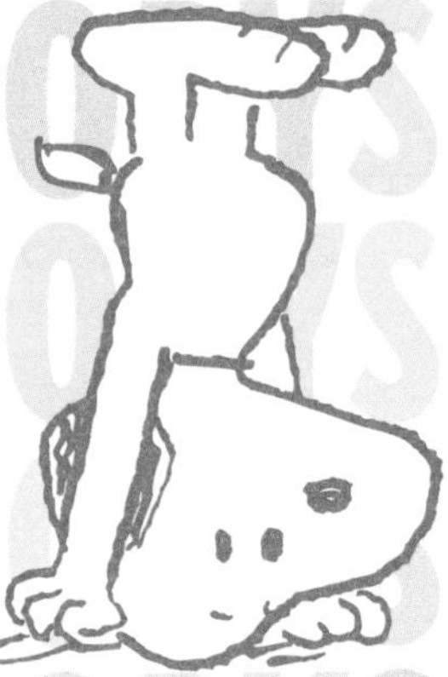

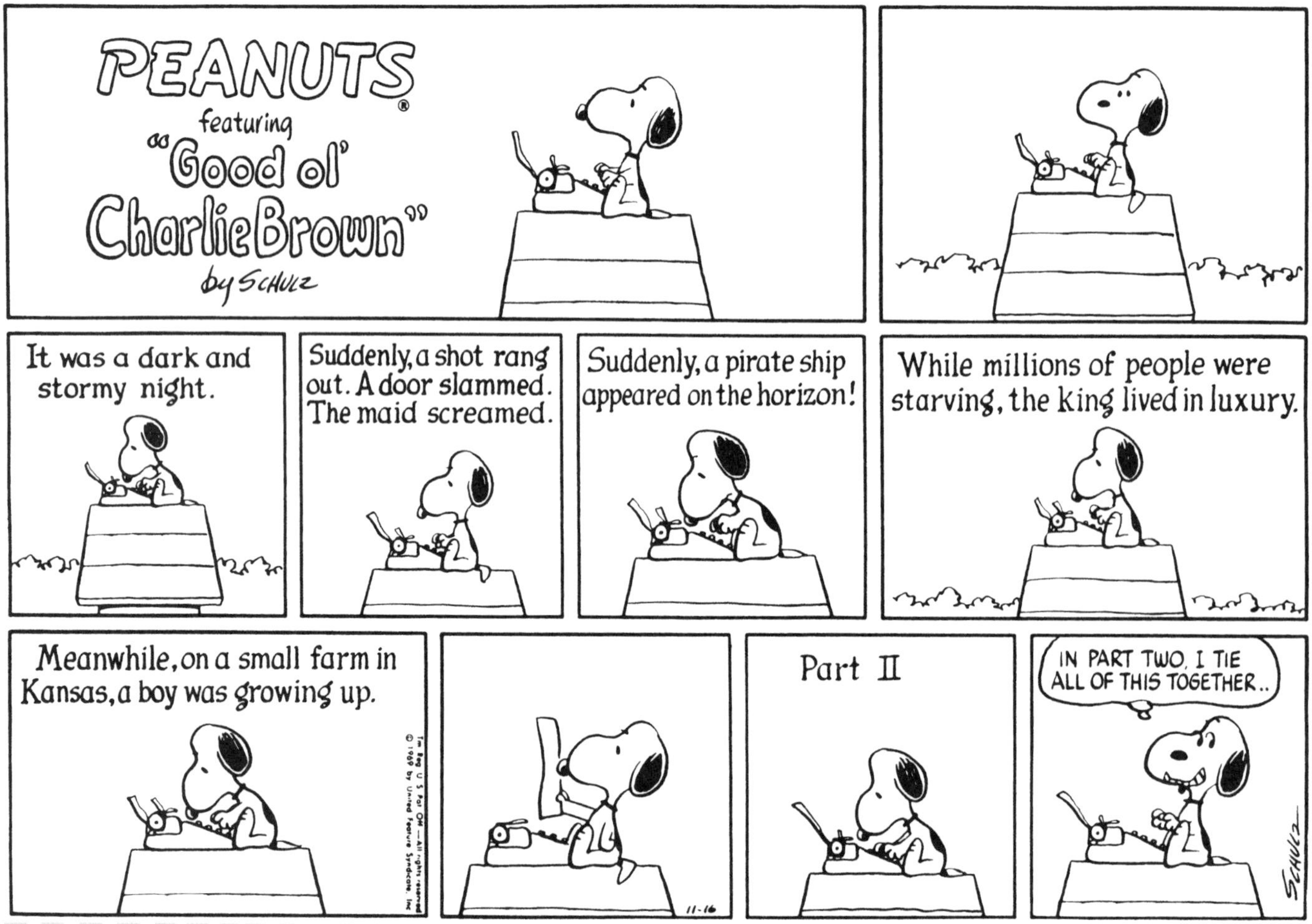
PEANUTS®
featuring
"Good ol' Charlie Brown"
by SCHULZ
It was a dark and stormy night.
Suddenly, a shot rang out. A door slammed. The maid screamed.
Suddenly, a pirate ship appeared on the horizon!
While millions of people were starving, the king lived in luxury.
Meanwhile, on a small farm in Kansas, a boy was growing up.
Tm Reg U S Pat Off—All rights reserved
© 1969 by United Feature Syndicate, Inc
11-16
Part II
IN PART TWO, I TIE ALL OF THIS TOGETHER..
SCHULZ

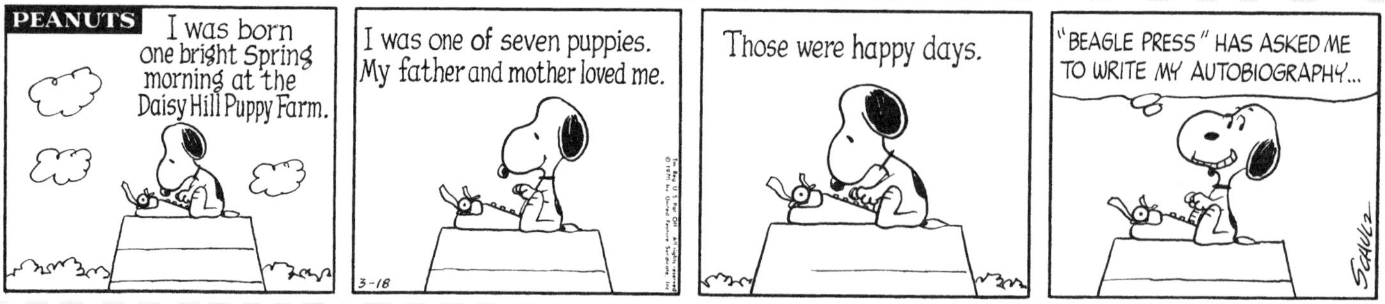
PEANUTS
I was born one bright Spring morning at the Daisy Hill Puppy Farm.
I was one of seven puppies. My father and mother loved me.
3-18
Those were happy days.
"BEAGLE PRESS" HAS ASKED ME TO WRITE MY AUTOBIOGRAPHY...
SCHULZ

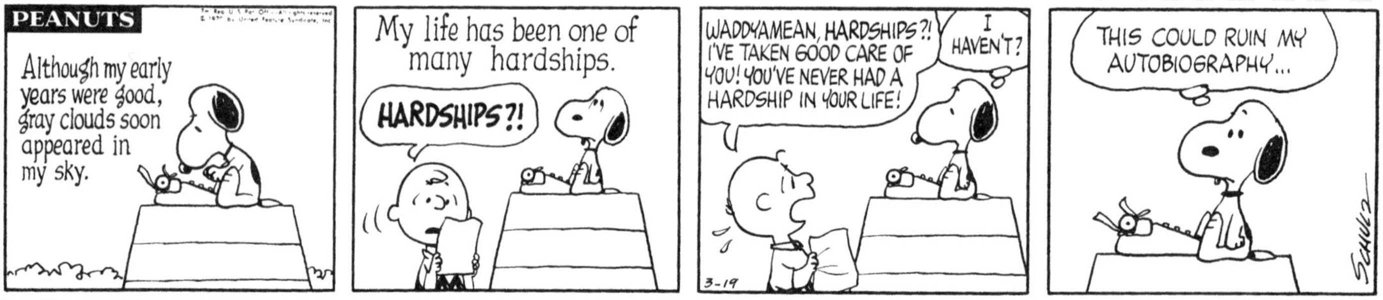
PEANUTS
Although my early years were good, gray clouds soon appeared in my sky.
My life has been one of many hardships.
HARDSHIPS?!
WADDYAMEAN, HARDSHIPS?! I'VE TAKEN GOOD CARE OF YOU! YOU'VE NEVER HAD A HARDSHIP IN YOUR LIFE!
I HAVEN'T?
3-19
THIS COULD RUIN MY AUTOBIOGRAPHY...
SCHULZ

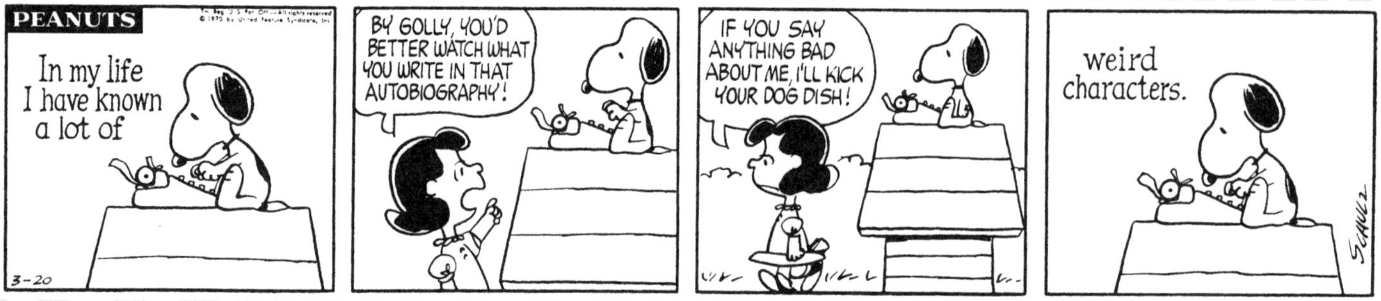
PEANUTS
In my life I have known a lot of
3-20
BY GOLLY, YOU'D BETTER WATCH WHAT YOU WRITE IN THAT AUTOBIOGRAPHY!
IF YOU SAY ANYTHING BAD ABOUT ME, I'LL KICK YOUR DOG DISH!
weird characters.
SCHULZ

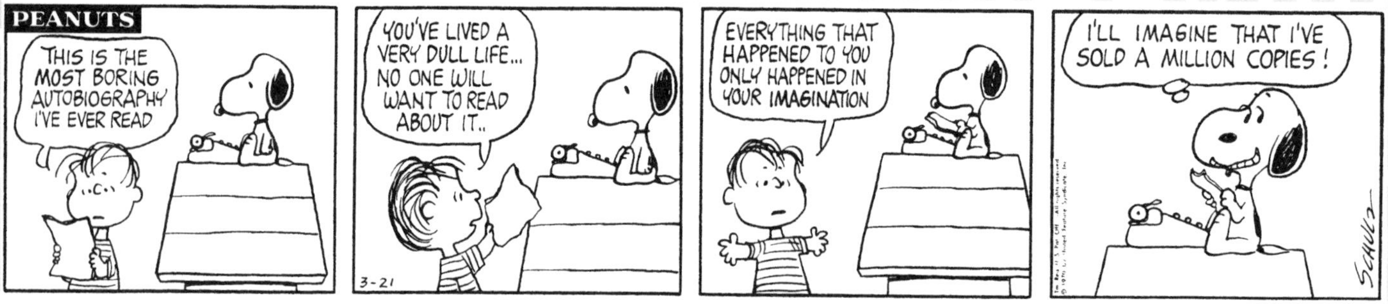
PEANUTS
THIS IS THE MOST BORING AUTOBIOGRAPHY I'VE EVER READ
YOU'VE LIVED A VERY DULL LIFE... NO ONE WILL WANT TO READ ABOUT IT..
3-21
EVERYTHING THAT HAPPENED TO YOU ONLY HAPPENED IN YOUR IMAGINATION
I'LL IMAGINE THAT I'VE SOLD A MILLION COPIES!
SCHULZ

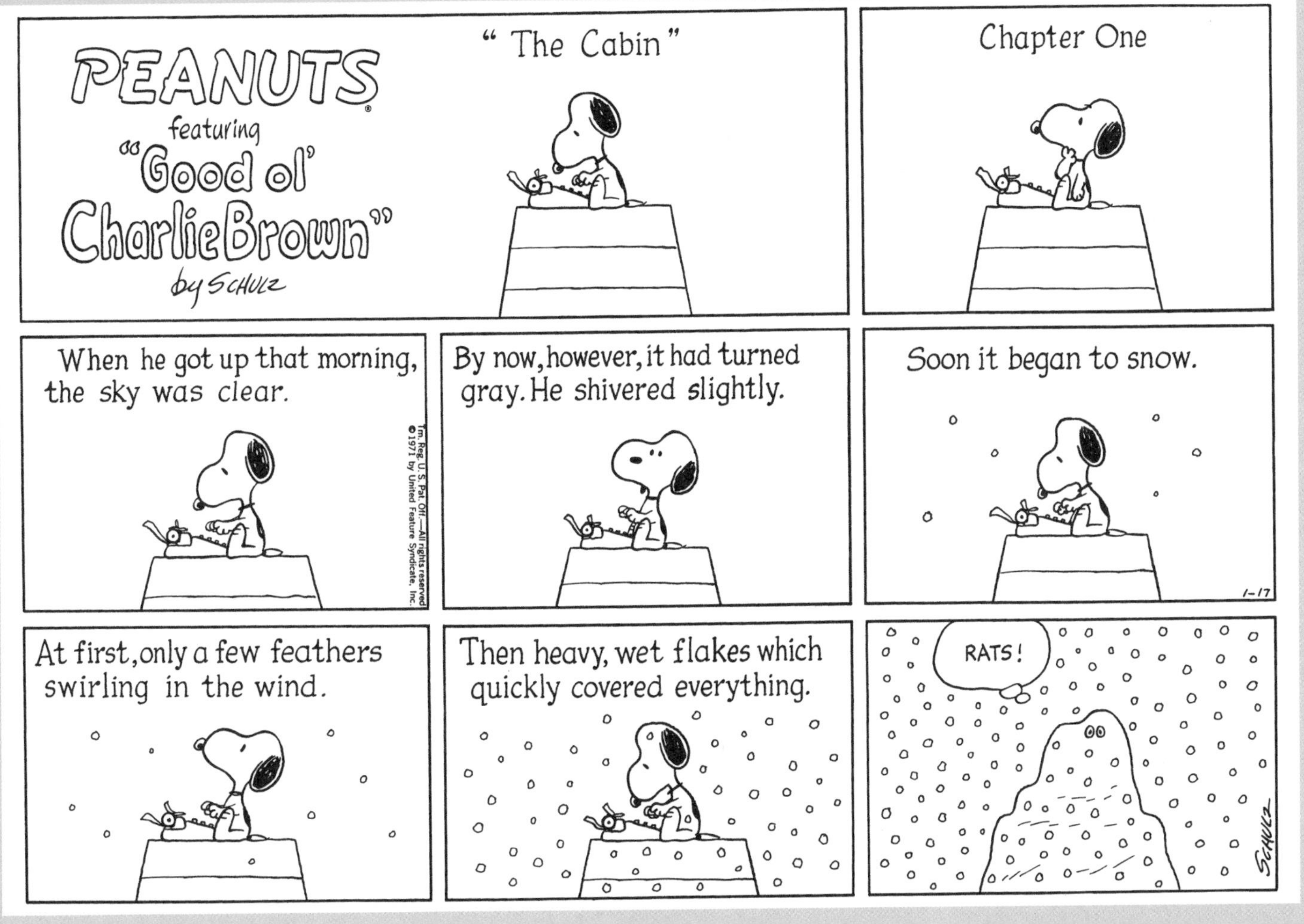
PEANUTS
featuring "Good ol' Charlie Brown"
by SCHULZ
" The Cabin"
Chapter One
When he got up that morning, the sky was clear.
Tm. Reg. U.S. Pat. Off.—All rights reserved © 1971 by United Feature Syndicate, Inc.
By now, however, it had turned gray. He shivered slightly.
Soon it began to snow.
1-17
At first, only a few feathers swirling in the wind.
Then heavy, wet flakes which quickly covered everything.
RATS!
SCHULZ

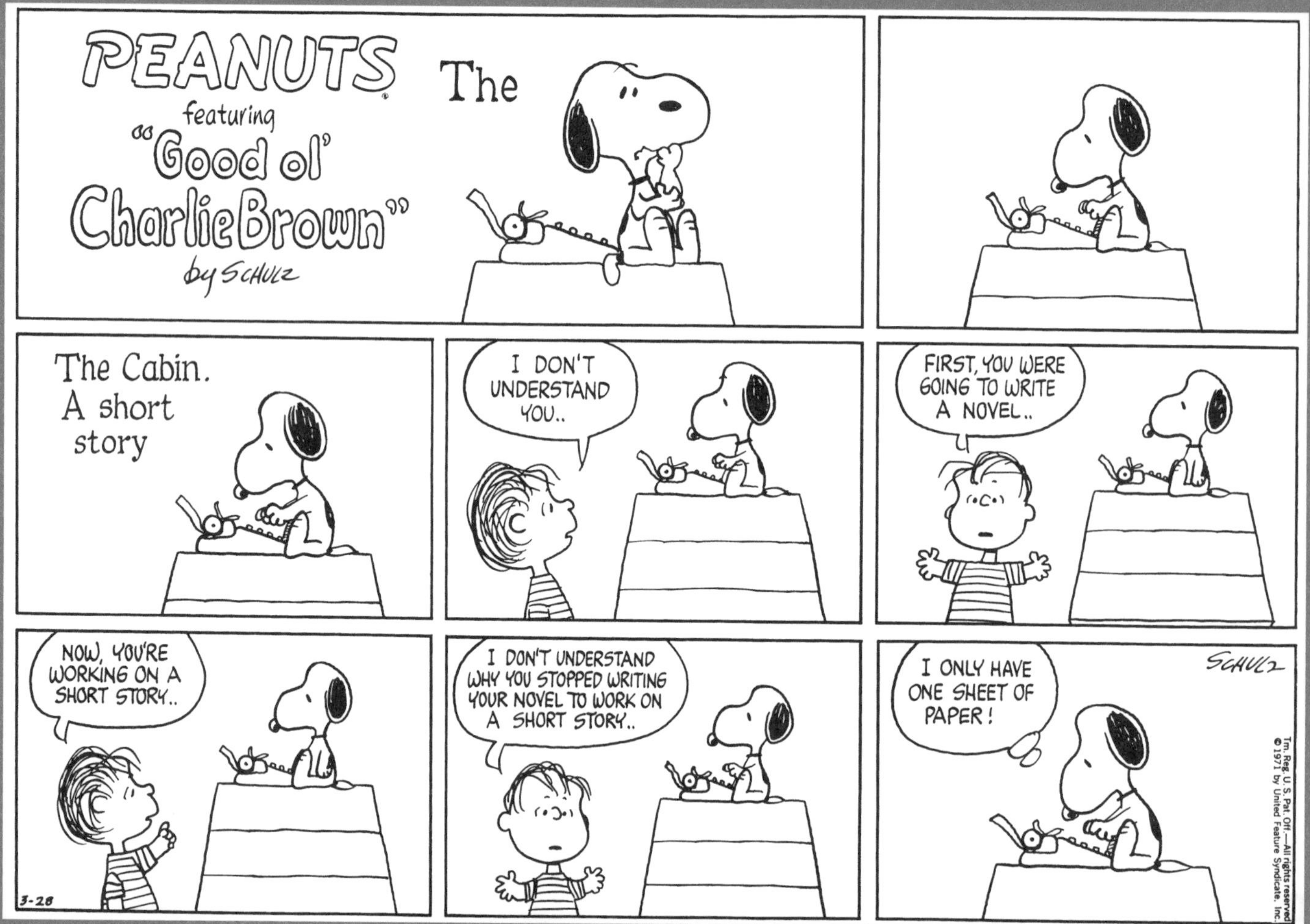
PEANUTS
featuring "Good ol' CharlieBrown"
by SCHULZ
The
The Cabin. A short story
I DON'T UNDERSTAND YOU..
FIRST, YOU WERE GOING TO WRITE A NOVEL..
NOW, YOU'RE WORKING ON A SHORT STORY..
I DON'T UNDERSTAND WHY YOU STOPPED WRITING YOUR NOVEL TO WORK ON A SHORT STORY..
I ONLY HAVE ONE SHEET OF PAPER!
SCHULZ
3-28
Tm. Reg. U. S. Pat. Off.—All rights reserved
© 1971 by United Feature Syndicate, Inc.

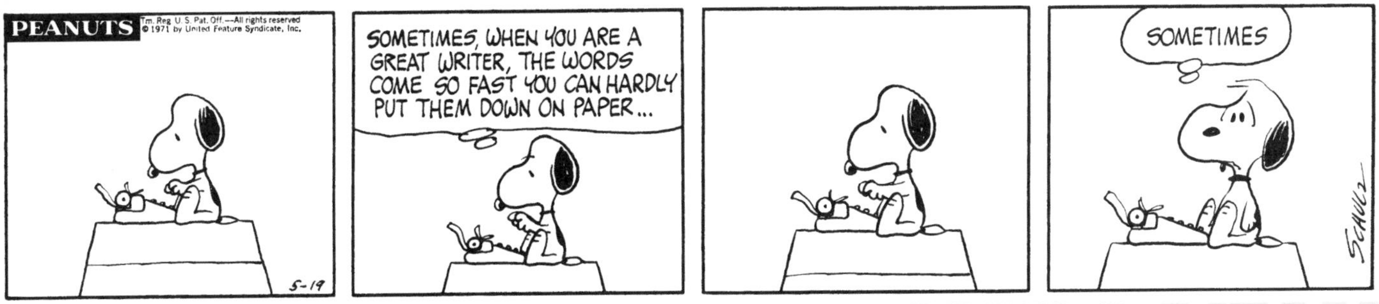
PEANUTS
Tm. Reg. U.S. Pat. Off.—All rights reserved © 1971 by United Feature Syndicate, Inc.
5-19
SOMETIMES, WHEN YOU ARE A GREAT WRITER, THE WORDS COME SO FAST YOU CAN HARDLY PUT THEM DOWN ON PAPER...
SOMETIMES
SCHULZ

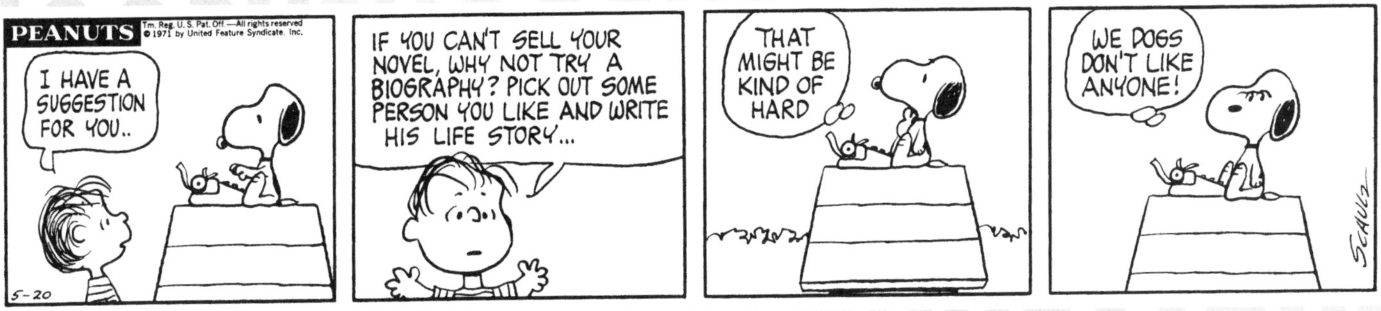
PEANUTS
Tm. Reg. U.S. Pat. Off.—All rights reserved © 1971 by United Feature Syndicate, Inc.
I HAVE A SUGGESTION FOR YOU..
5-20
IF YOU CAN'T SELL YOUR NOVEL, WHY NOT TRY A BIOGRAPHY? PICK OUT SOME PERSON YOU LIKE AND WRITE HIS LIFE STORY...
THAT MIGHT BE KIND OF HARD
WE DOGS DON'T LIKE ANYONE!
SCHULZ

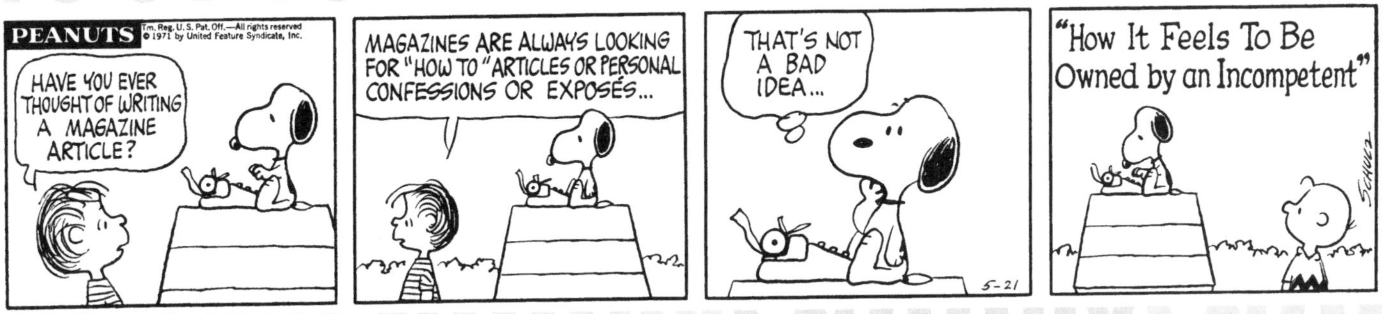
PEANUTS
Tm. Reg. U.S. Pat. Off.—All rights reserved © 1971 by United Feature Syndicate, Inc.
HAVE YOU EVER THOUGHT OF WRITING A MAGAZINE ARTICLE?
MAGAZINES ARE ALWAYS LOOKING FOR "HOW TO" ARTICLES OR PERSONAL CONFESSIONS OR EXPOSÉS...
THAT'S NOT A BAD IDEA...
5-21
"How It Feels To Be Owned by an Incompetent"
SCHULZ

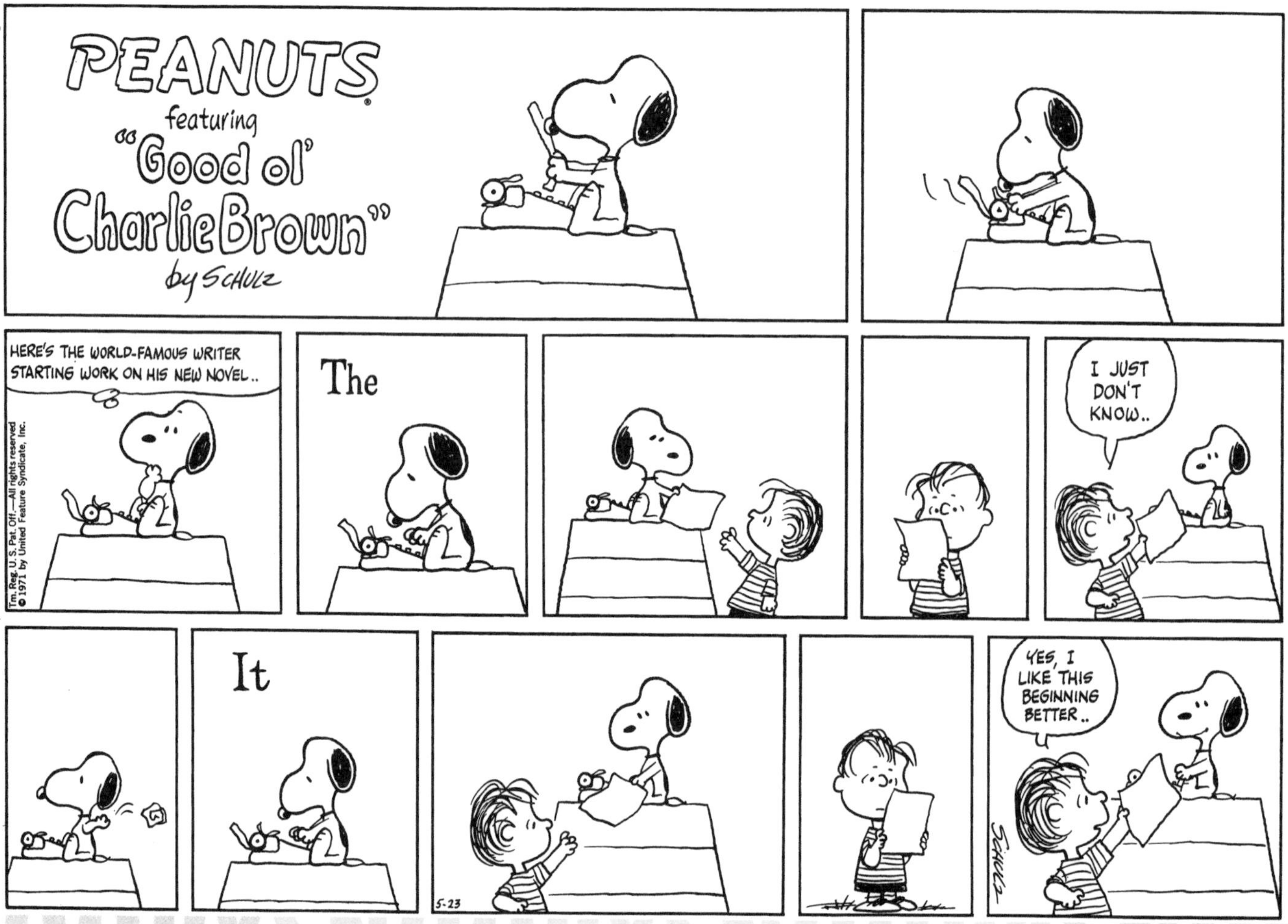
PEANUTS
featuring
"Good ol' Charlie Brown"
by SCHULZ
HERE'S THE WORLD-FAMOUS WRITER STARTING WORK ON HIS NEW NOVEL..
Tm. Reg. U.S. Pat. Off.—All rights reserved
© 1971 by United Feature Syndicate, Inc.
The
I JUST DON'T KNOW..
It
5-23
SCHULZ
YES, I LIKE THIS BEGINNING BETTER..

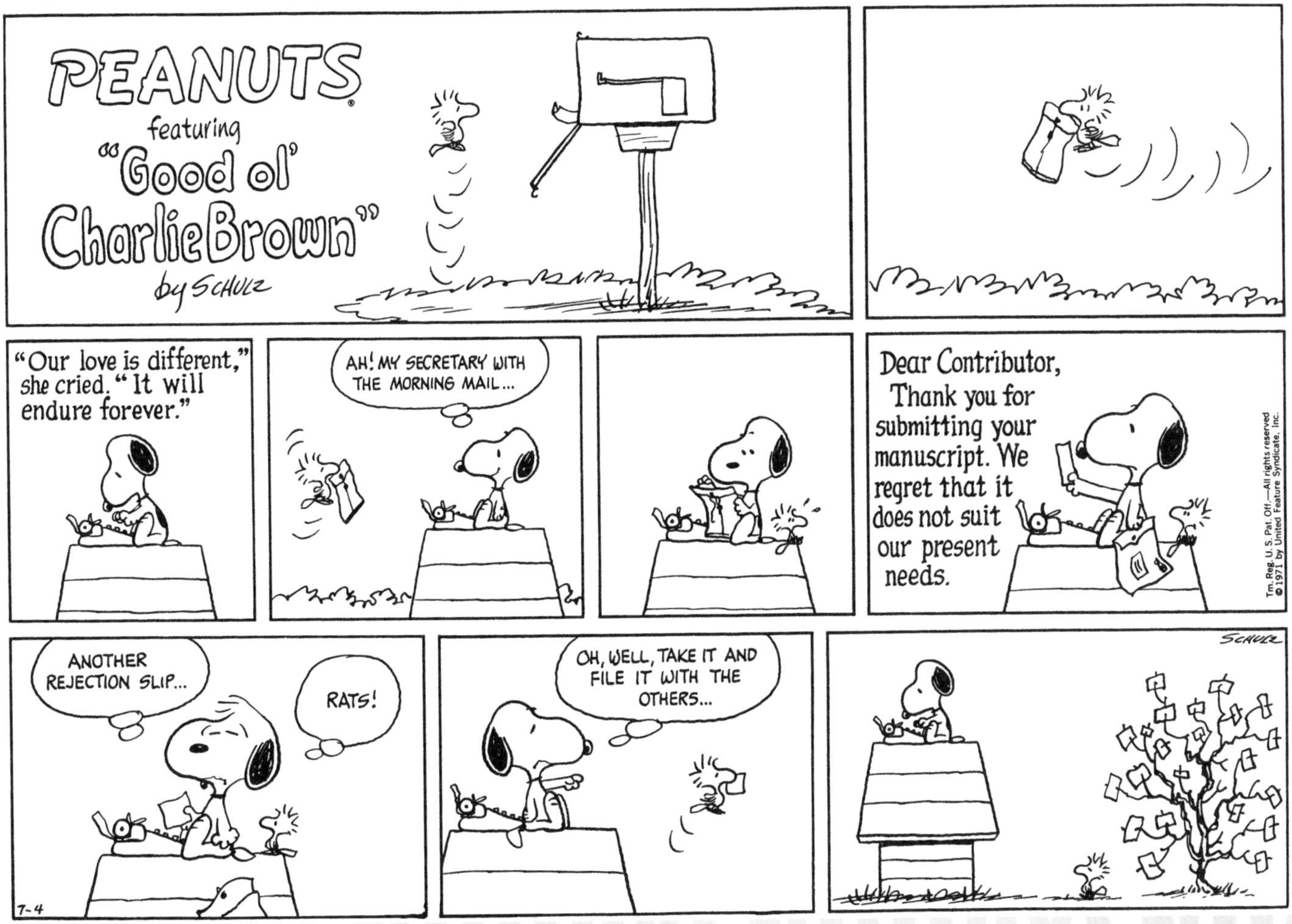
PEANUTS®
featuring
"Good ol' CharlieBrown"
by SCHULZ
"Our love is different," she cried. "It will endure forever."
AH! MY SECRETARY WITH THE MORNING MAIL...
Dear Contributor,
Thank you for submitting your manuscript. We regret that it does not suit our present needs.
Tm. Reg. U.S. Pat. Off.—All rights reserved ©1971 by United Feature Syndicate, Inc.
ANOTHER REJECTION SLIP...
RATS!
7-4
OH, WELL, TAKE IT AND FILE IT WITH THE OTHERS...
SCHULZ

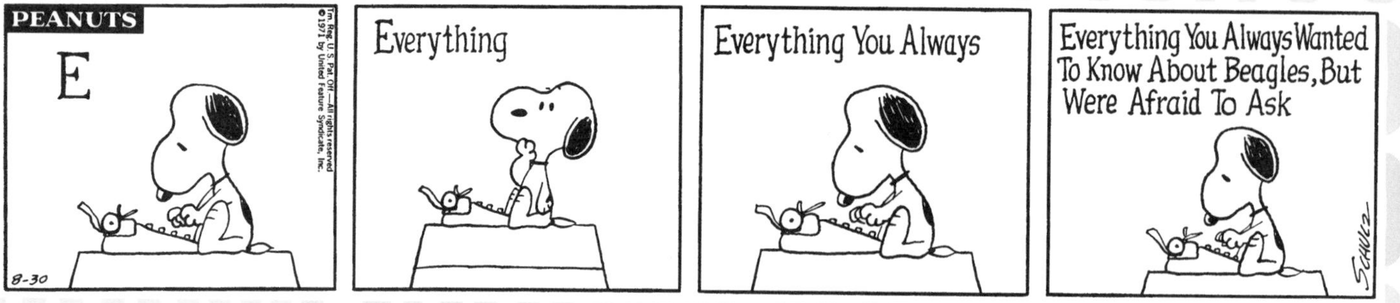
PEANUTS
Tm. Reg. U. S. Pat. Off.—All rights reserved © 1971 by United Feature Syndicate, Inc.
E
8-30
Everything
Everything You Always
Everything You Always Wanted To Know About Beagles, But Were Afraid To Ask
SCHULZ

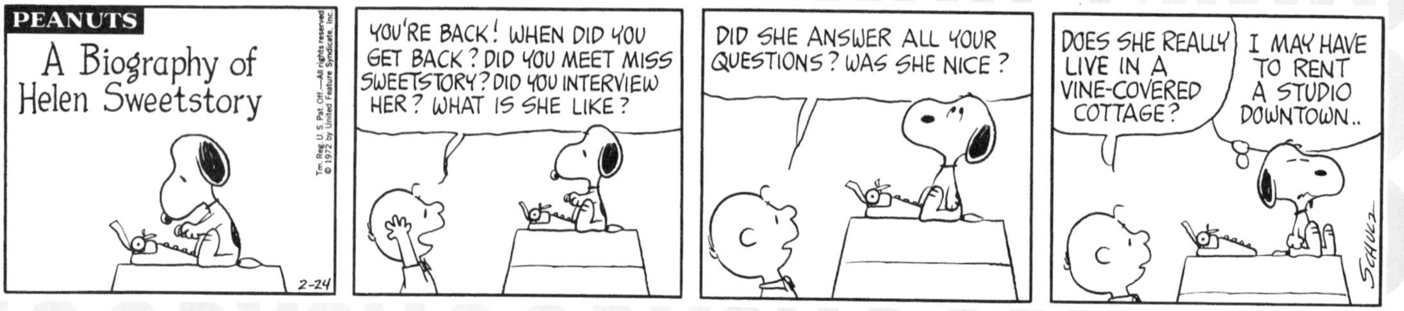
PEANUTS
A Biography of Helen Sweetstory
Tm. Reg. U. S. Pat. Off.—All rights reserved © 1972 by United Feature Syndicate, Inc.
2-24
YOU'RE BACK! WHEN DID YOU GET BACK? DID YOU MEET MISS SWEETSTORY? DID YOU INTERVIEW HER? WHAT IS SHE LIKE?
DID SHE ANSWER ALL YOUR QUESTIONS? WAS SHE NICE?
DOES SHE REALLY LIVE IN A VINE-COVERED COTTAGE?
I MAY HAVE TO RENT A STUDIO DOWNTOWN..
SCHULZ

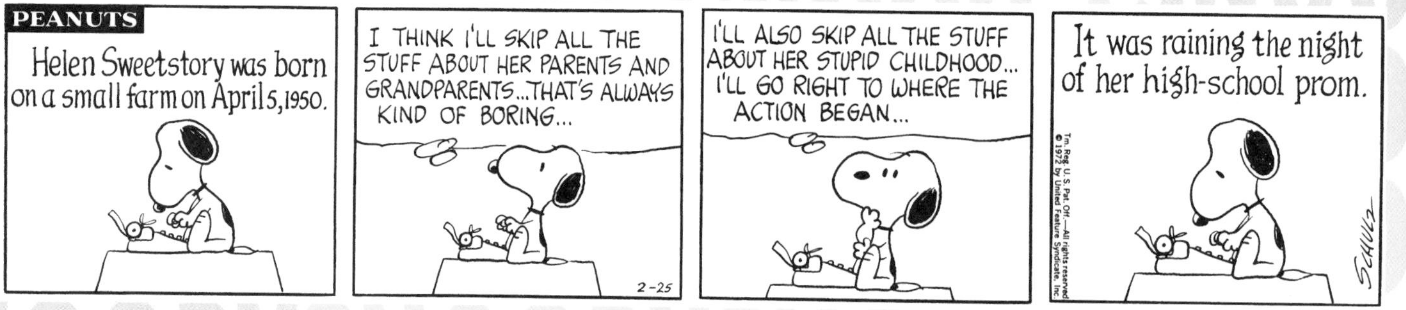
PEANUTS
Helen Sweetstory was born on a small farm on April 5, 1950.
I THINK I'LL SKIP ALL THE STUFF ABOUT HER PARENTS AND GRANDPARENTS...THAT'S ALWAYS KIND OF BORING...
2-25
I'LL ALSO SKIP ALL THE STUFF ABOUT HER STUPID CHILDHOOD... I'LL GO RIGHT TO WHERE THE ACTION BEGAN...
It was raining the night of her high-school prom.
Tm. Reg. U. S. Pat. Off.—All rights reserved © 1972 by United Feature Syndicate, Inc.
SCHULZ

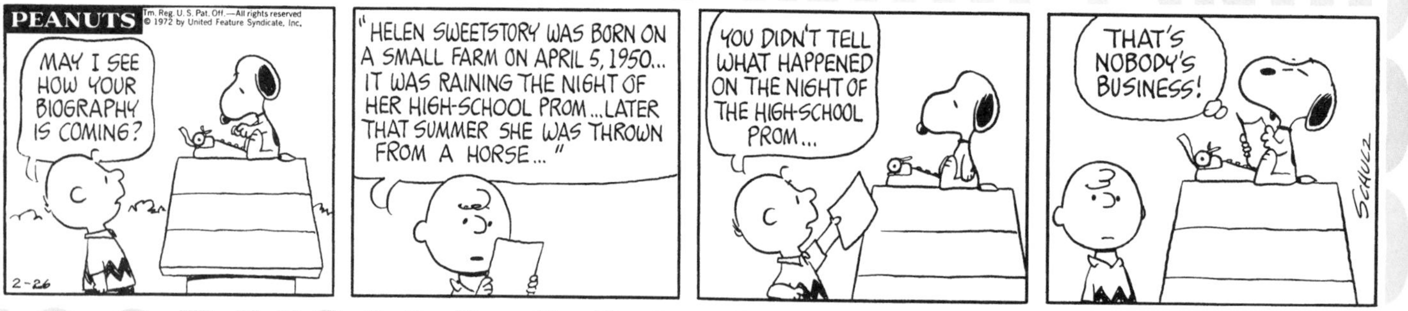
PEANUTS
Tm. Reg. U. S. Pat. Off.—All rights reserved © 1972 by United Feature Syndicate, Inc.
MAY I SEE HOW YOUR BIOGRAPHY IS COMING?
2-26
"HELEN SWEETSTORY WAS BORN ON A SMALL FARM ON APRIL 5, 1950... IT WAS RAINING THE NIGHT OF HER HIGH-SCHOOL PROM...LATER THAT SUMMER SHE WAS THROWN FROM A HORSE..."
YOU DIDN'T TELL WHAT HAPPENED ON THE NIGHT OF THE HIGH-SCHOOL PROM...
THAT'S NOBODY'S BUSINESS!
SCHULZ

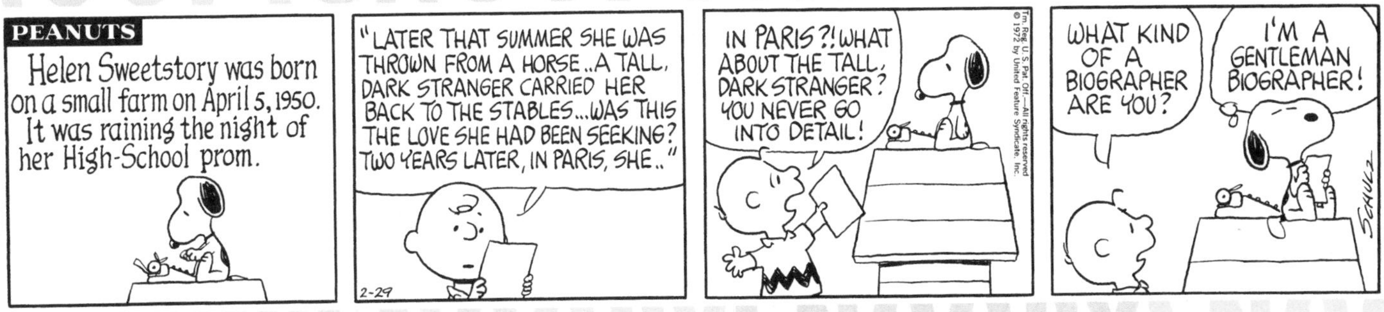
PEANUTS
Helen Sweetstory was born on a small farm on April 5, 1950. It was raining the night of her High-School prom.
"LATER THAT SUMMER SHE WAS THROWN FROM A HORSE..A TALL, DARK STRANGER CARRIED HER BACK TO THE STABLES...WAS THIS THE LOVE SHE HAD BEEN SEEKING? TWO YEARS LATER, IN PARIS, SHE.."
2-29
IN PARIS?! WHAT ABOUT THE TALL, DARK STRANGER? YOU NEVER GO INTO DETAIL!
Tm. Reg. U.S. Pat. Off.—All rights reserved © 1972 by United Feature Syndicate, Inc.
WHAT KIND OF A BIOGRAPHER ARE YOU?
I'M A GENTLEMAN BIOGRAPHER!
SCHULZ

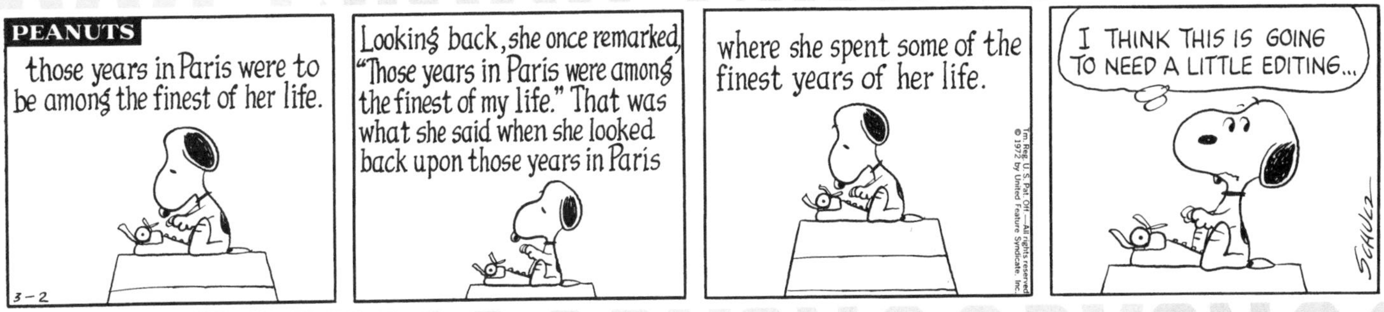
PEANUTS
those years in Paris were to be among the finest of her life.
3-2
Looking back, she once remarked, "Those years in Paris were among the finest of my life." That was what she said when she looked back upon those years in Paris
where she spent some of the finest years of her life.
Tm. Reg. U.S. Pat. Off.—All rights reserved © 1972 by United Feature Syndicate, Inc.
I THINK THIS IS GOING TO NEED A LITTLE EDITING...
SCHULZ

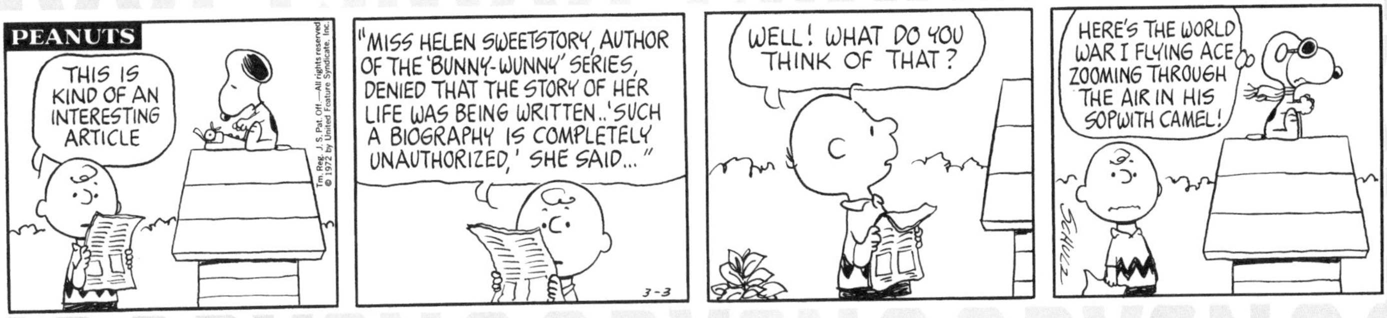
PEANUTS
THIS IS KIND OF AN INTERESTING ARTICLE
Tm. Reg. U.S. Pat. Off.—All rights reserved © 1972 by United Feature Syndicate, Inc.
"MISS HELEN SWEETSTORY, AUTHOR OF THE 'BUNNY-WUNNY' SERIES, DENIED THAT THE STORY OF HER LIFE WAS BEING WRITTEN..'SUCH A BIOGRAPHY IS COMPLETELY UNAUTHORIZED,' SHE SAID..."
3-3
WELL! WHAT DO YOU THINK OF THAT?
HERE'S THE WORLD WAR I FLYING ACE ZOOMING THROUGH THE AIR IN HIS SOPWITH CAMEL!
SCHULZ

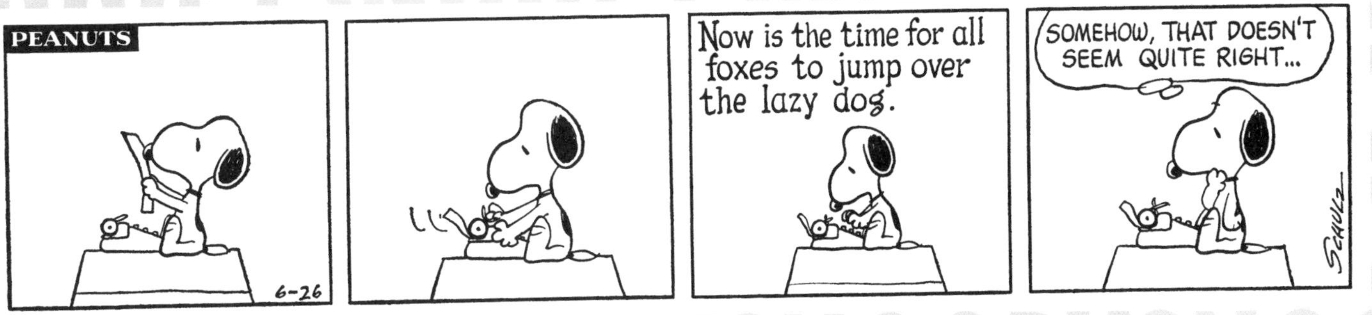
PEANUTS
6-26
Now is the time for all foxes to jump over the lazy dog.
SOMEHOW, THAT DOESN'T SEEM QUITE RIGHT...
SCHULZ

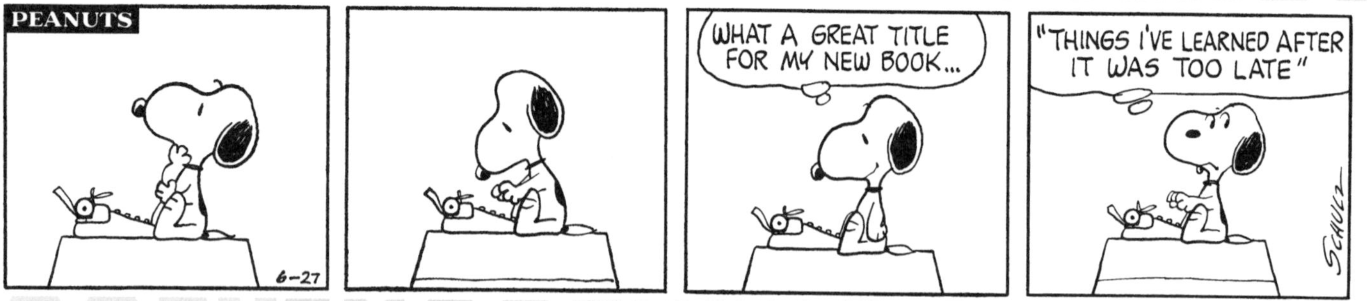
PEANUTS
WHAT A GREAT TITLE FOR MY NEW BOOK...
"THINGS I'VE LEARNED AFTER IT WAS TOO LATE"
6-27
SCHULZ

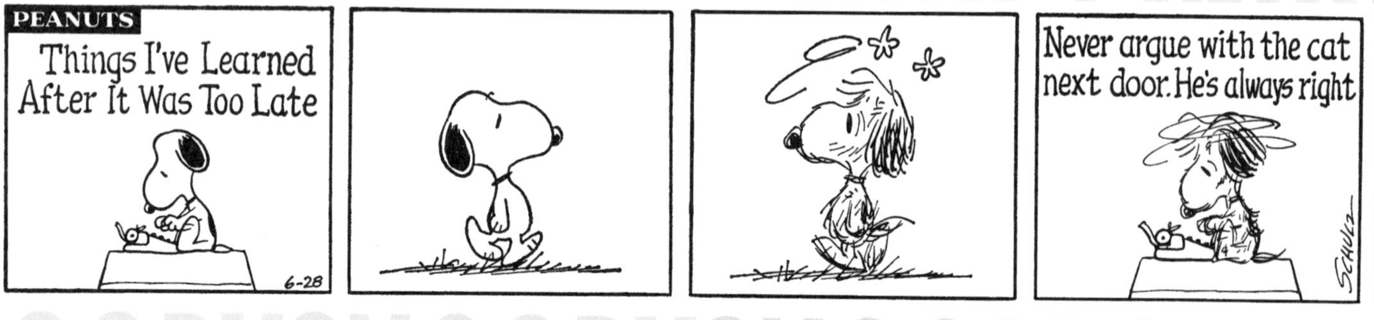
PEANUTS
Things I've Learned After It Was Too Late
6-28
Never argue with the cat next door. He's always right
SCHULZ

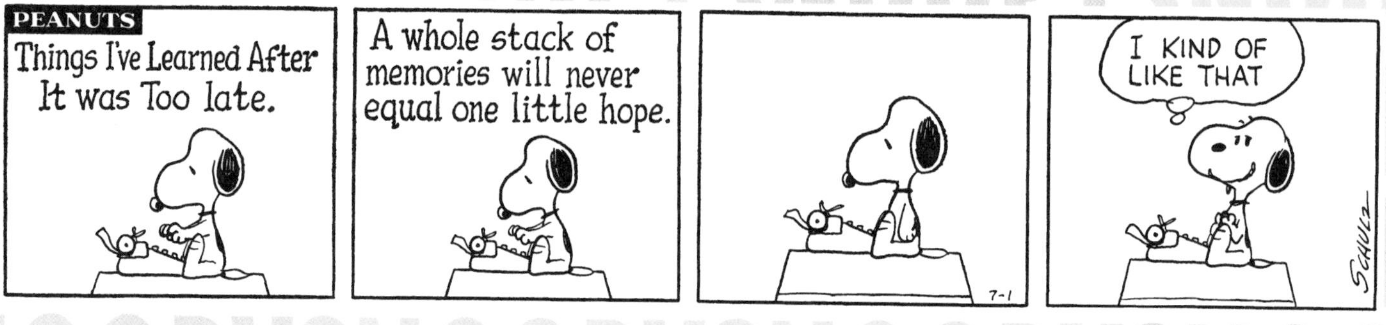
PEANUTS
Things I've Learned After It was Too late.
A whole stack of memories will never equal one little hope.
7-1
I KIND OF LIKE THAT
SCHULZ

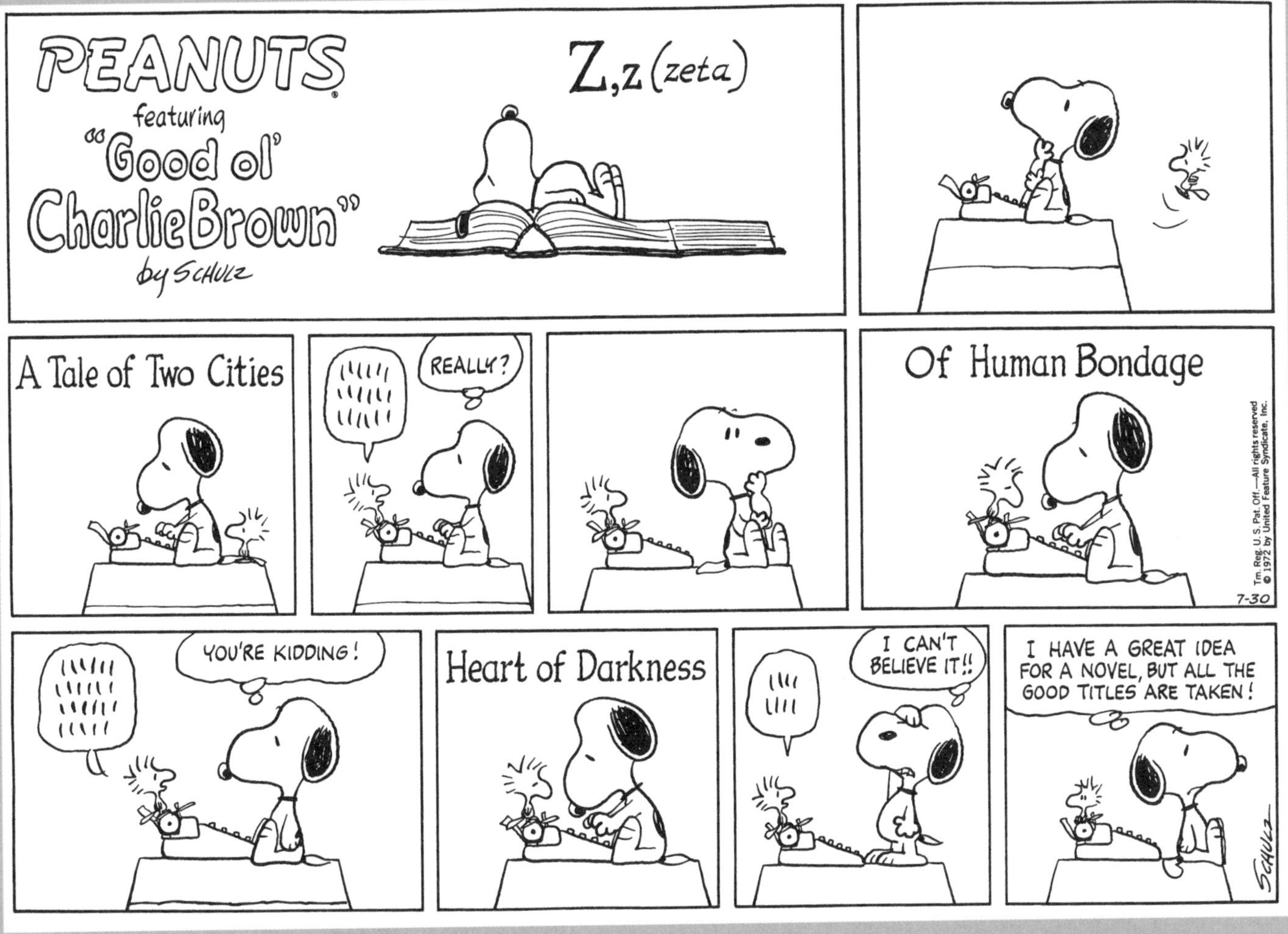
PEANUTS
featuring
"Good ol' Charlie Brown"
by SCHULZ
Z,z (zeta)
A Tale of Two Cities
REALLY?
Of Human Bondage
Tm. Reg. U. S. Pat. Off.—All rights reserved
© 1972 by United Feature Syndicate, Inc.
7-30
YOU'RE KIDDING!
Heart of Darkness
I CAN'T BELIEVE IT!!
I HAVE A GREAT IDEA FOR A NOVEL, BUT ALL THE GOOD TITLES ARE TAKEN!
SCHULZ

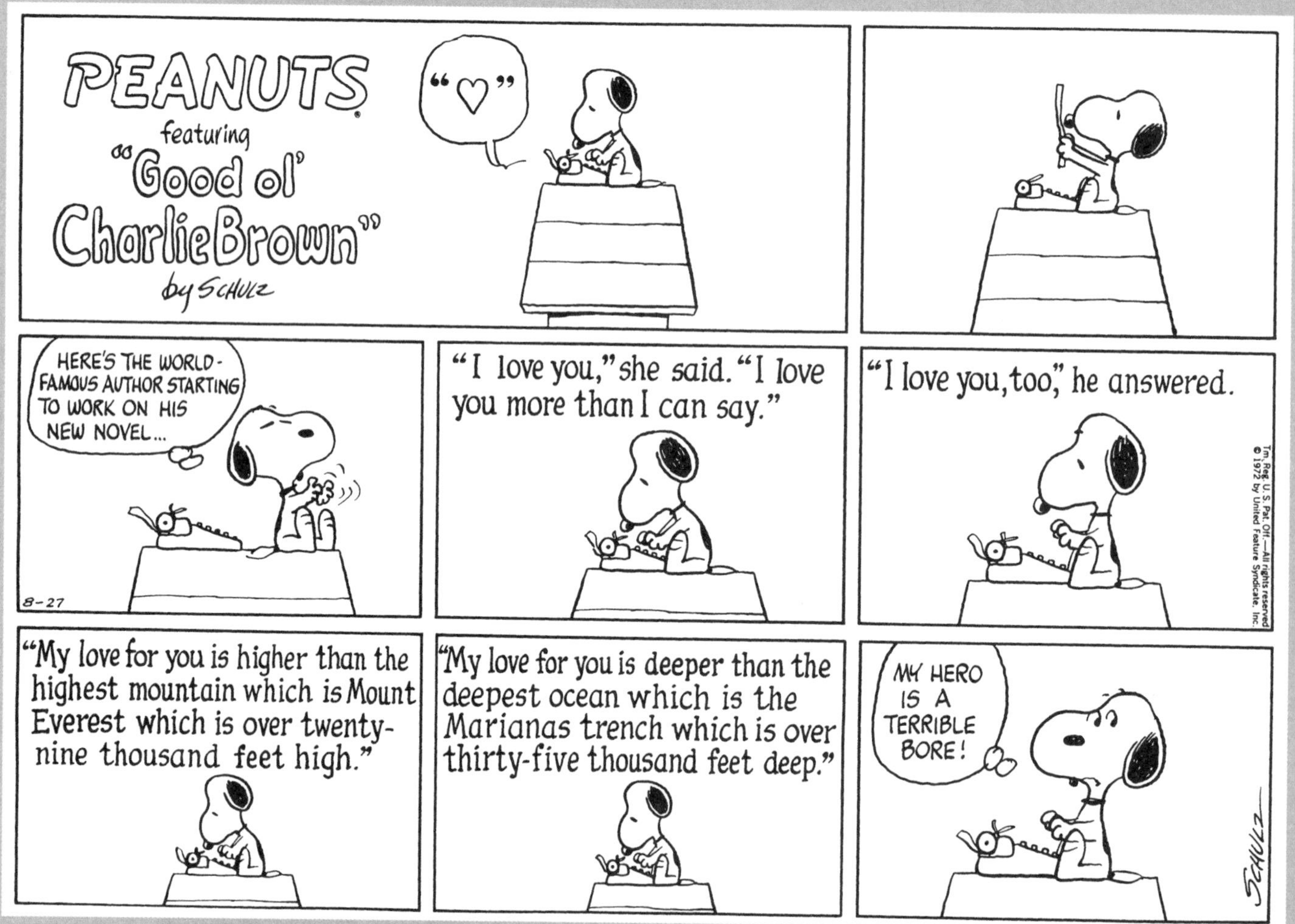
PEANUTS
featuring
"Good ol' Charlie Brown"
by SCHULZ
"♡"
HERE'S THE WORLD-FAMOUS AUTHOR STARTING TO WORK ON HIS NEW NOVEL...
8-27
"I love you," she said. "I love you more than I can say."
"I love you, too," he answered.
Tm. Reg. U.S. Pat. Off.—All rights reserved © 1972 by United Feature Syndicate, Inc.
"My love for you is higher than the highest mountain which is Mount Everest which is over twenty-nine thousand feet high."
"My love for you is deeper than the deepest ocean which is the Marianas trench which is over thirty-five thousand feet deep."
MY HERO IS A TERRIBLE BORE!
SCHULZ

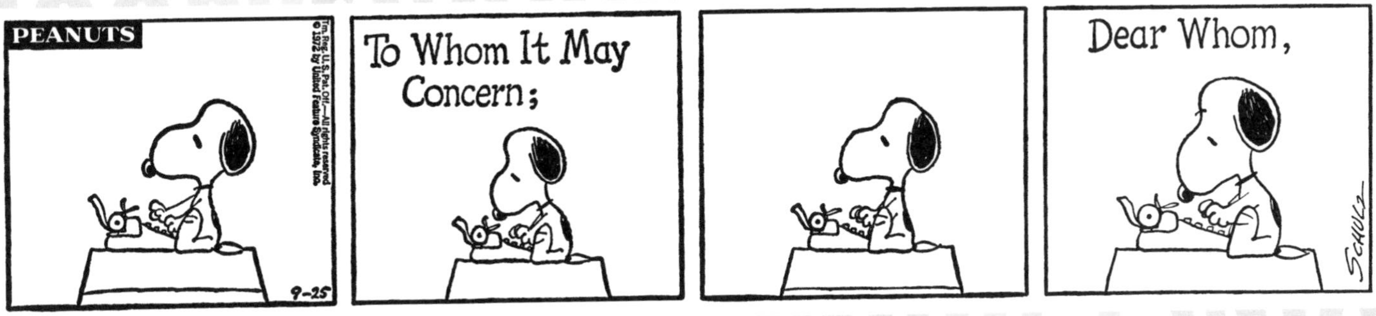
PEANUTS
Tm. Reg. U.S. Pat. Off.—All rights reserved
© 1972 by United Feature Syndicate, Inc.
9-25
To Whom It May Concern;
Dear Whom,
SCHULZ

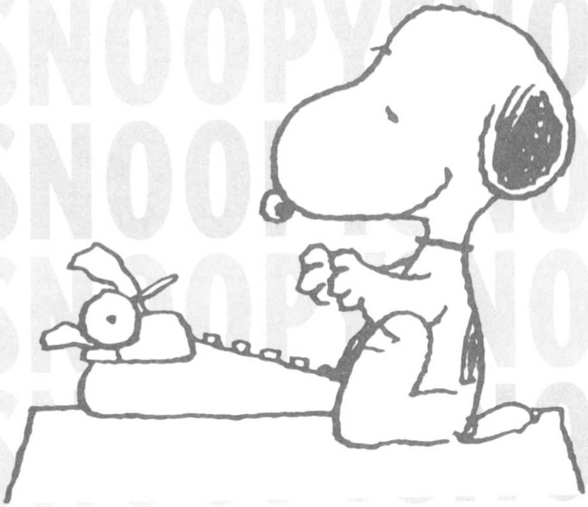

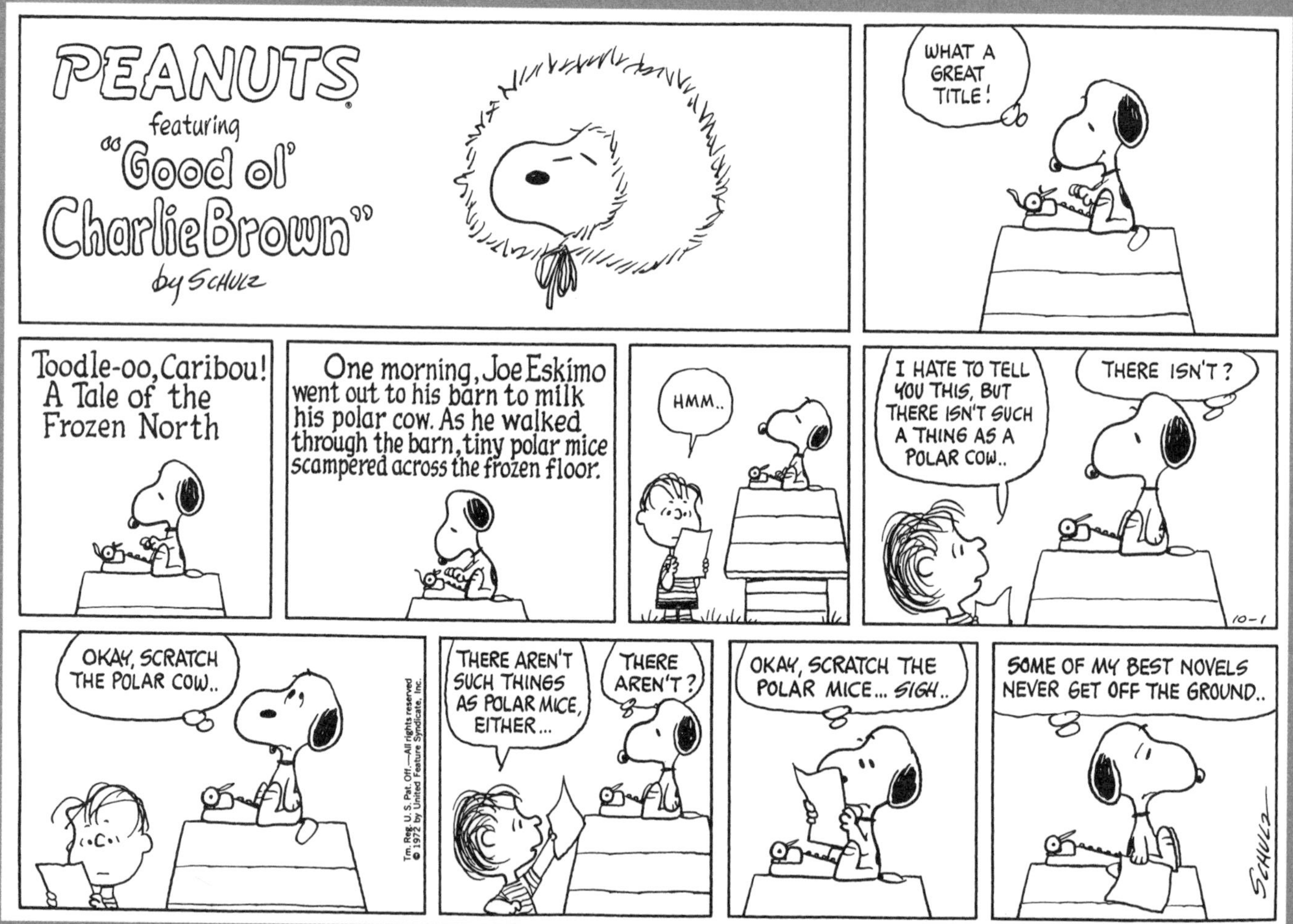

PEANUTS
featuring
"Good ol' Charlie Brown"
by SCHULZ
WHAT A GREAT TITLE!
Toodle-oo, Caribou! A Tale of the Frozen North
One morning, Joe Eskimo went out to his barn to milk his polar cow. As he walked through the barn, tiny polar mice scampered across the frozen floor.
HMM..
I HATE TO TELL YOU THIS, BUT THERE ISN'T SUCH A THING AS A POLAR COW..
THERE ISN'T?
10-1
OKAY, SCRATCH THE POLAR COW..
Tm. Reg. U. S. Pat. Off.—All rights reserved © 1972 by United Feature Syndicate, Inc.
THERE AREN'T SUCH THINGS AS POLAR MICE, EITHER...
THERE AREN'T?
OKAY, SCRATCH THE POLAR MICE... SIGH..
SOME OF MY BEST NOVELS NEVER GET OFF THE GROUND..
SCHULZ

PEANUTS

Report to the
Head Beagle

10-13

Subject: Our Beagle in
the field, Thompson.

Subject attempted to
subdue ten-thousand
rabbits by himself. End
came quickly.

Rabbit-tat-tat, and
it was all over!

Tm. Reg. U.S. Pat. Off.—All rights reserved
© 1972 by United Feature Syndicate, Inc.

SCHULZ

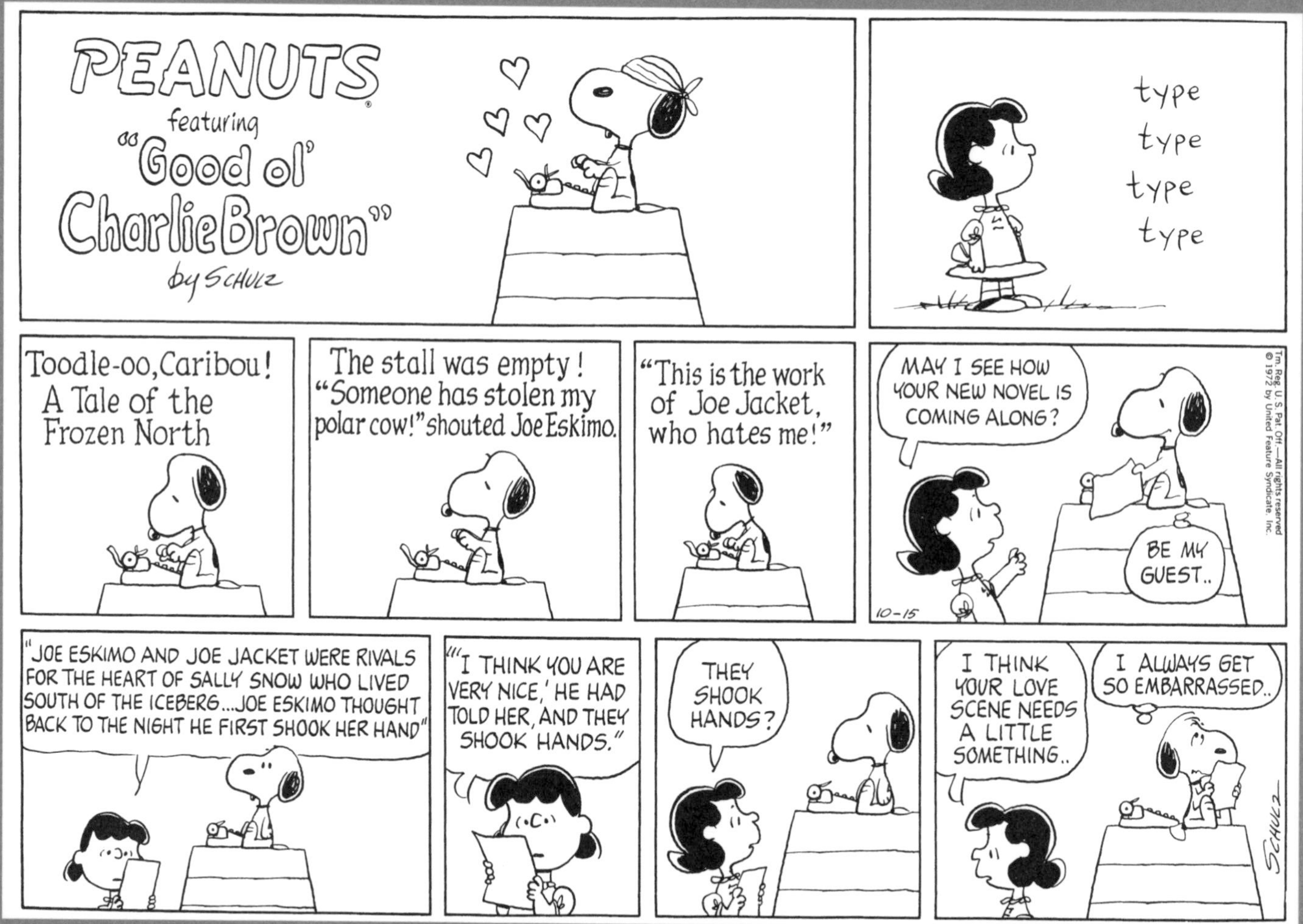
PEANUTS
featuring
"Good ol' CharlieBrown"
by SCHULZ
type
type
type
type
Toodle-oo, Caribou! A Tale of the Frozen North
The stall was empty! "Someone has stolen my polar cow!" shouted Joe Eskimo.
"This is the work of Joe Jacket, who hates me!"
MAY I SEE HOW YOUR NEW NOVEL IS COMING ALONG?
BE MY GUEST..
Tm. Reg. U.S. Pat. Off.—All rights reserved
© 1972 by United Feature Syndicate, Inc.
10-15
"JOE ESKIMO AND JOE JACKET WERE RIVALS FOR THE HEART OF SALLY SNOW WHO LIVED SOUTH OF THE ICEBERG....JOE ESKIMO THOUGHT BACK TO THE NIGHT HE FIRST SHOOK HER HAND"
"'I THINK YOU ARE VERY NICE,' HE HAD TOLD HER, AND THEY SHOOK HANDS."
THEY SHOOK HANDS?
I THINK YOUR LOVE SCENE NEEDS A LITTLE SOMETHING..
I ALWAYS GET SO EMBARRASSED..
SCHULZ

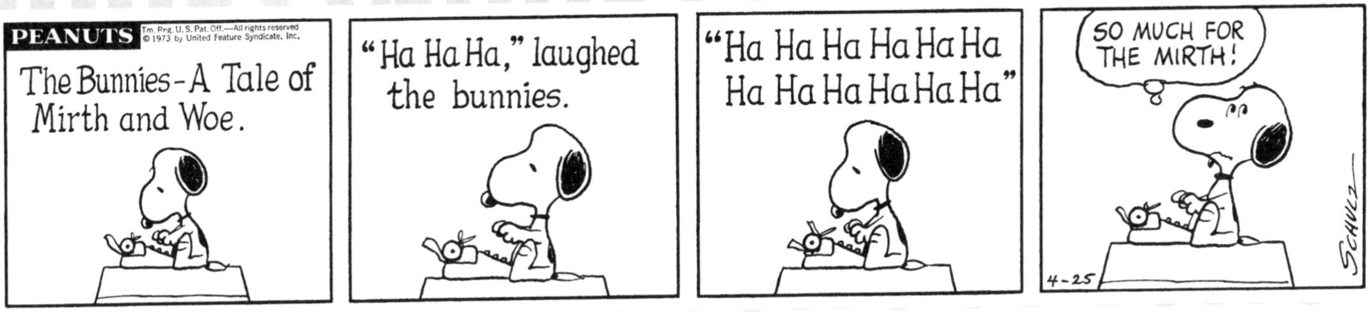
PEANUTS
Tm. Reg. U.S. Pat. Off.—All rights reserved © 1973 by United Feature Syndicate, Inc.
The Bunnies - A Tale of Mirth and Woe.
"Ha Ha Ha," laughed the bunnies.
"Ha Ha Ha Ha Ha Ha Ha Ha Ha Ha Ha Ha"
SO MUCH FOR THE MIRTH!
SCHULZ
4-25

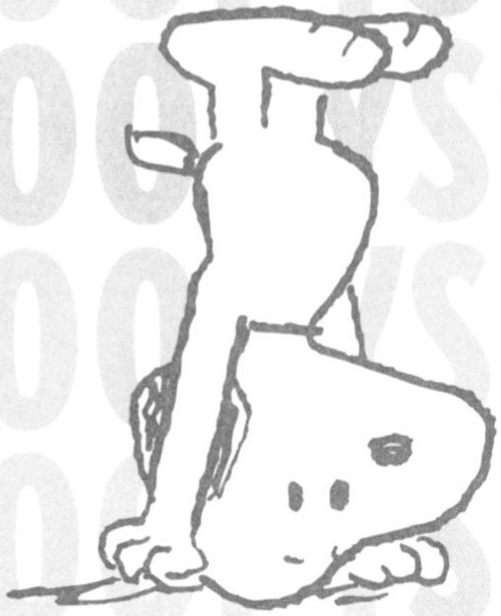

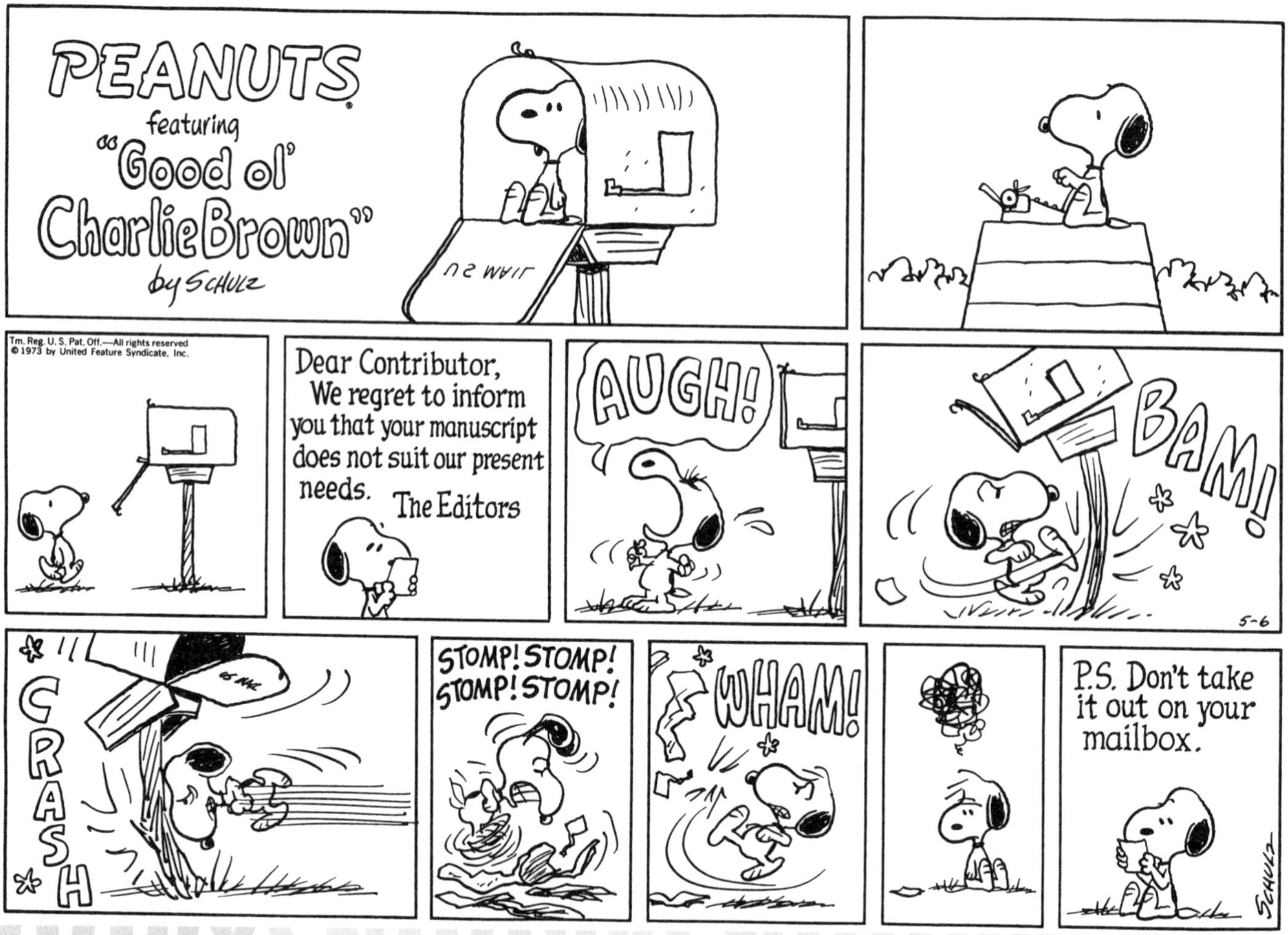
PEANUTS
featuring
"Good ol' Charlie Brown"
by SCHULZ
US MAIL
Tm. Reg. U. S. Pat. Off.—All rights reserved
© 1973 by United Feature Syndicate, Inc.
Dear Contributor,
We regret to inform you that your manuscript does not suit our present needs. The Editors
AUGH!
BAM!
5-6
CRASH
STOMP! STOMP! STOMP! STOMP!
WHAM!
P.S. Don't take it out on your mailbox.
SCHULZ

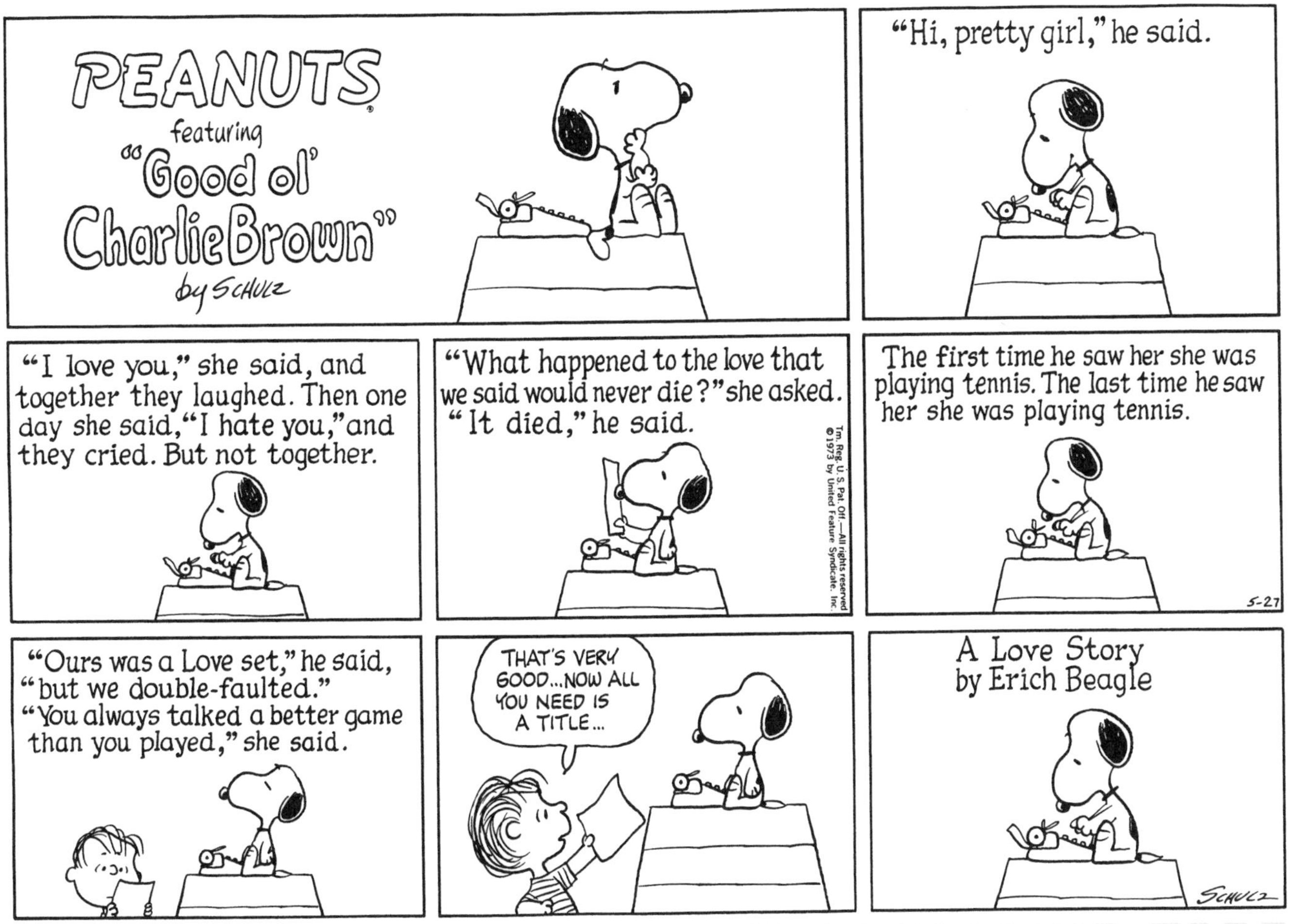
PEANUTS®
featuring
"Good ol' Charlie Brown"
by SCHULZ
"Hi, pretty girl," he said.
"I love you," she said, and together they laughed. Then one day she said, "I hate you," and they cried. But not together.
"What happened to the love that we said would never die?" she asked. "It died," he said.
Tm. Reg. U.S. Pat. Off.—All rights reserved
© 1973 by United Feature Syndicate, Inc.
The first time he saw her she was playing tennis. The last time he saw her she was playing tennis.
5-27
"Ours was a Love set," he said, "but we double-faulted." "You always talked a better game than you played," she said.
THAT'S VERY GOOD...NOW ALL YOU NEED IS A TITLE...
A Love Story
by Erich Beagle
SCHULZ

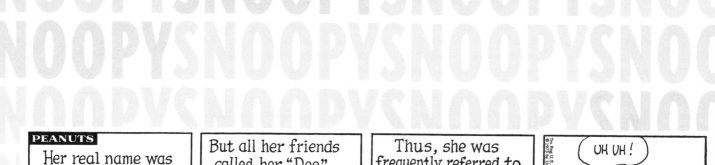

PEANUTS
Her real name was Dorothy Fledermaus.
7-12
But all her friends called her "Dee."
Thus, she was frequently referred to as "Dee Fledermaus."
Tm.Reg. U.S. Pat. Off.—All rights reserved
© 1973 by United Feature Syndicate, Inc.
UH UH!
SCHULZ

PEANUTS
Though her husband often went on business trips, she hated to be left alone.
8-6
"I've solved our problem," he said. "I've bought you a St. Bernard. It's name is Great Reluctance."
"Now, when I go away, you shall know that I am leaving you with Great Reluctance!"
Tm.Reg. U.S. Pat. Off.—All rights reserved
© 1973 by United Feature Syndicate, Inc.
She hit him with a waffle iron.
SCHULZ

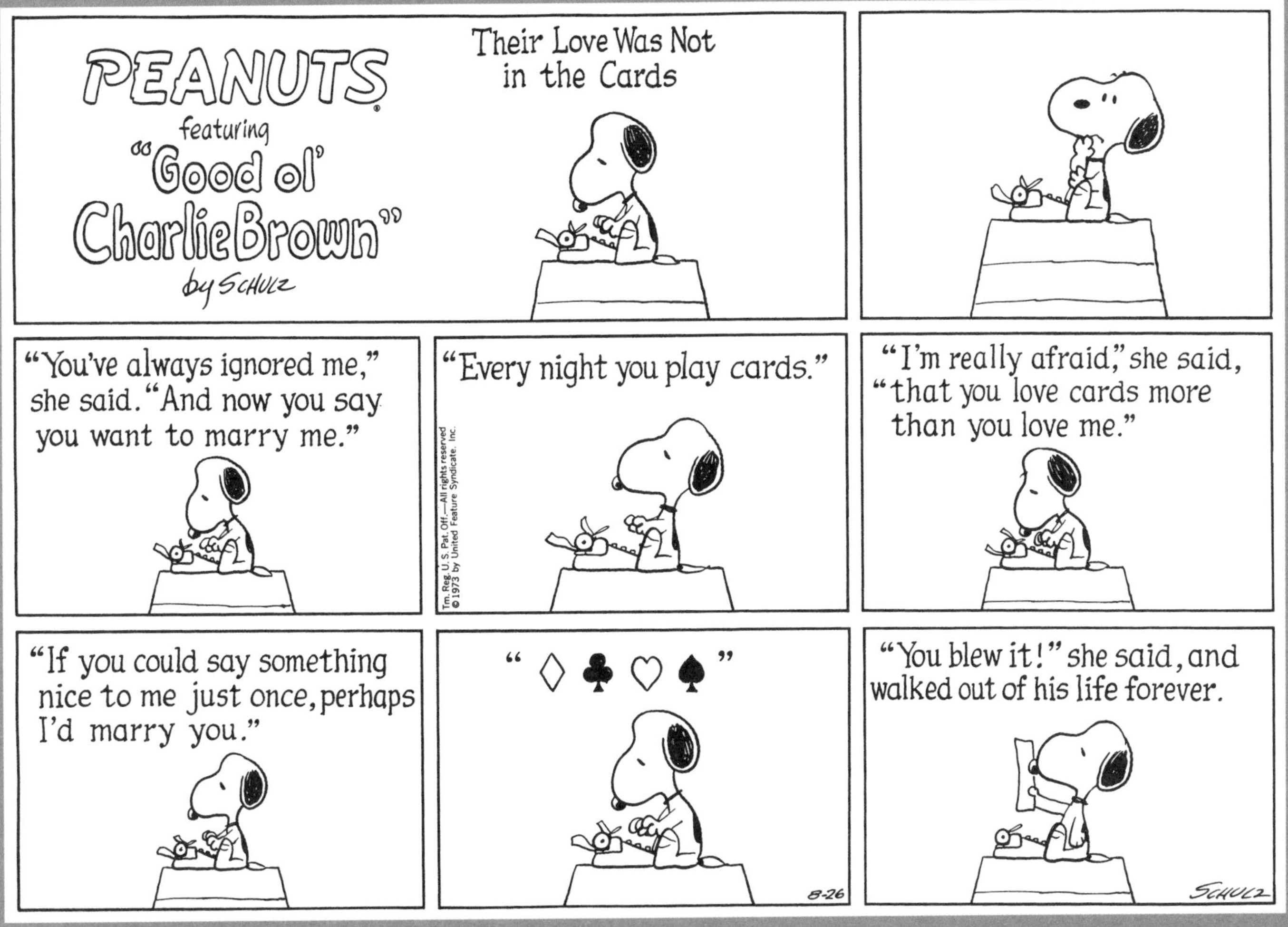
PEANUTS®
featuring
"Good ol' Charlie Brown"
by SCHULZ
Their Love Was Not in the Cards
"You've always ignored me," she said. "And now you say you want to marry me."
"Every night you play cards."
"I'm really afraid," she said, "that you love cards more than you love me."
"If you could say something nice to me just once, perhaps I'd marry you."
" ◇ ♣ ♡ ♠ "
8-26
"You blew it!" she said, and walked out of his life forever.
SCHULZ

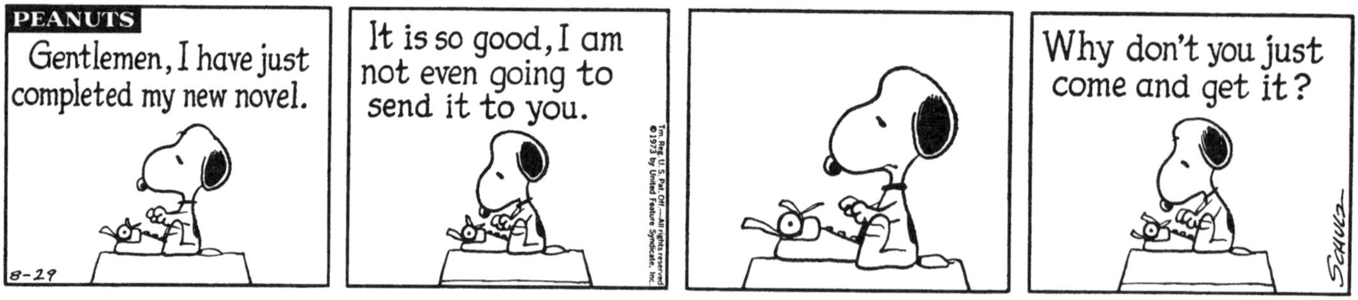
PEANUTS
Gentlemen, I have just completed my new novel.
It is so good, I am not even going to send it to you.
Tm. Reg. U.S. Pat. Off.—All rights reserved ©1973 by United Feature Syndicate, Inc.
Why don't you just come and get it?
8-29
SCHULZ

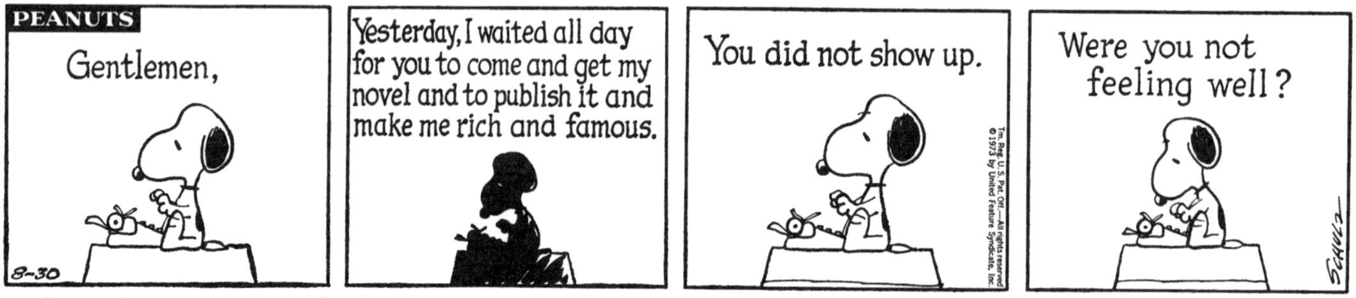
PEANUTS
Gentlemen,
Yesterday, I waited all day for you to come and get my novel and to publish it and make me rich and famous.
You did not show up.
Tm. Reg. U.S. Pat. Off.—All rights reserved ©1973 by United Feature Syndicate, Inc.
Were you not feeling well?
8-30
SCHULZ

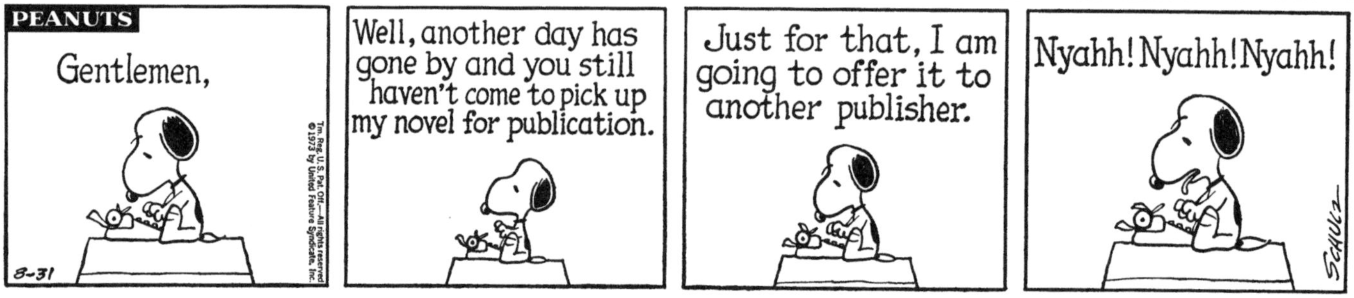
PEANUTS
Gentlemen,
Tm. Reg. U.S. Pat. Off.—All rights reserved ©1973 by United Feature Syndicate, Inc.
Well, another day has gone by and you still haven't come to pick up my novel for publication.
Just for that, I am going to offer it to another publisher.
Nyahh! Nyahh! Nyahh!
8-31
SCHULZ

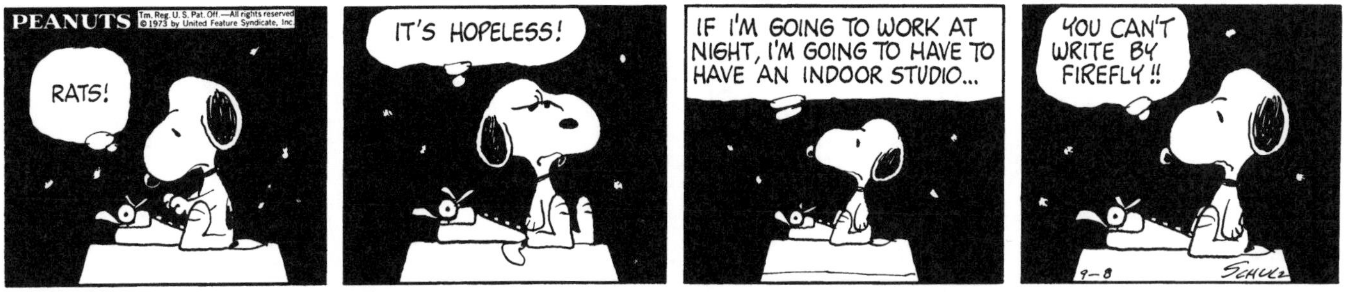
PEANUTS
Tm. Reg. U.S. Pat. Off.—All rights reserved
© 1973 by United Feature Syndicate, Inc.
RATS!
IT'S HOPELESS!
IF I'M GOING TO WORK AT NIGHT, I'M GOING TO HAVE TO HAVE AN INDOOR STUDIO...
YOU CAN'T WRITE BY FIREFLY!!
9-8
SCHULZ

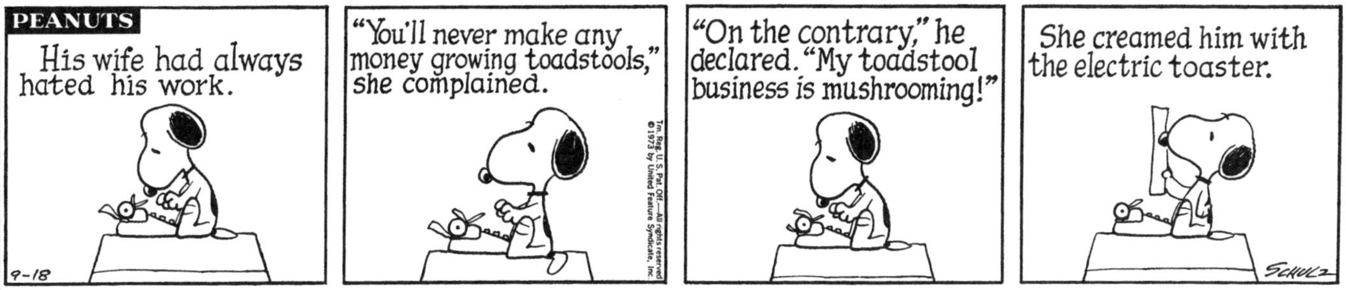
PEANUTS
His wife had always hated his work.
9-18
"You'll never make any money growing toadstools," she complained.
Tm. Reg. U.S. Pat. Off.—All rights reserved
© 1973 by United Feature Syndicate, Inc.
"On the contrary," he declared. "My toadstool business is mushrooming!"
She creamed him with the electric toaster.
SCHULZ

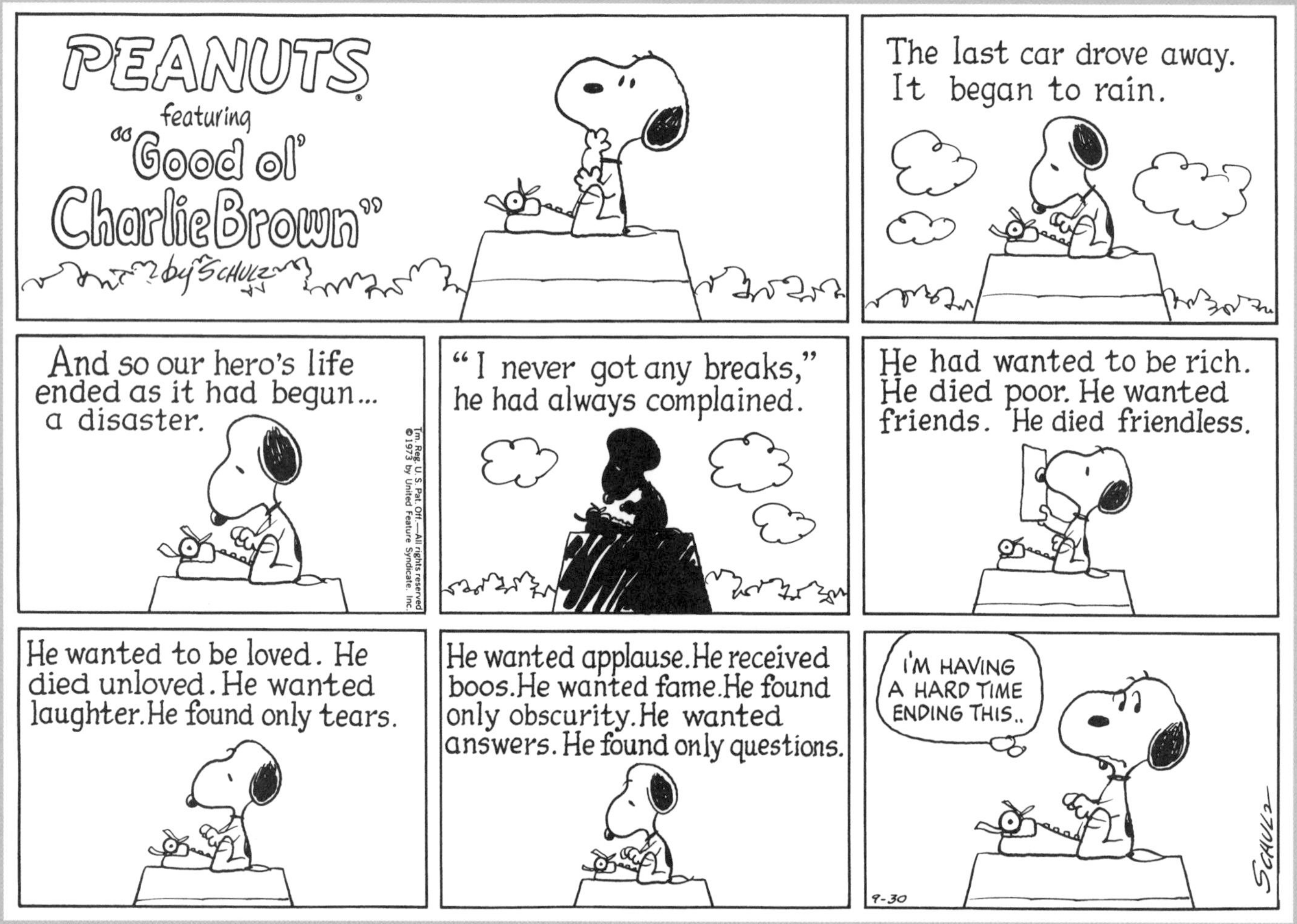
PEANUTS®
featuring "Good ol' Charlie Brown"
by SCHULZ
The last car drove away. It began to rain.
And so our hero's life ended as it had begun... a disaster.
Tm. Reg. U.S. Pat. Off.—All rights reserved © 1973 by United Feature Syndicate, Inc.
"I never got any breaks," he had always complained.
He had wanted to be rich. He died poor. He wanted friends. He died friendless.
He wanted to be loved. He died unloved. He wanted laughter. He found only tears.
He wanted applause. He received boos. He wanted fame. He found only obscurity. He wanted answers. He found only questions.
I'M HAVING A HARD TIME ENDING THIS..
9-30
SCHULZ

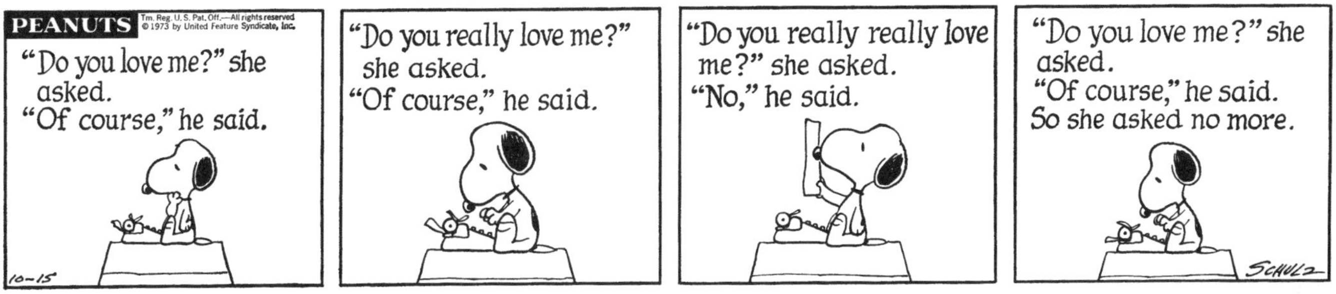
PEANUTS
Tm. Reg. U.S. Pat. Off.—All rights reserved © 1973 by United Feature Syndicate, Inc.
"Do you love me?" she asked.
"Of course," he said.
10-15
"Do you really love me?" she asked.
"Of course," he said.
"Do you really really love me?" she asked.
"No," he said.
"Do you love me?" she asked.
"Of course," he said.
So she asked no more.
SCHULZ

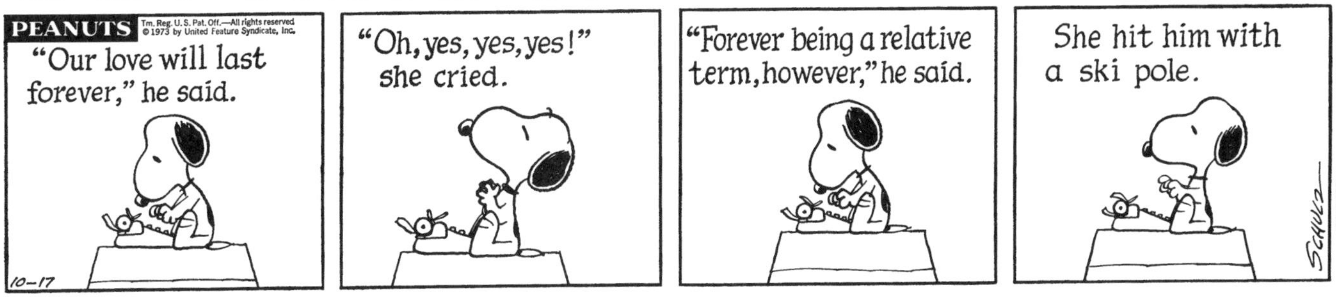
PEANUTS
Tm. Reg. U.S. Pat. Off.—All rights reserved © 1973 by United Feature Syndicate, Inc.
"Our love will last forever," he said.
10-17
"Oh, yes, yes, yes!" she cried.
"Forever being a relative term, however," he said.
She hit him with a ski pole.
SCHULZ

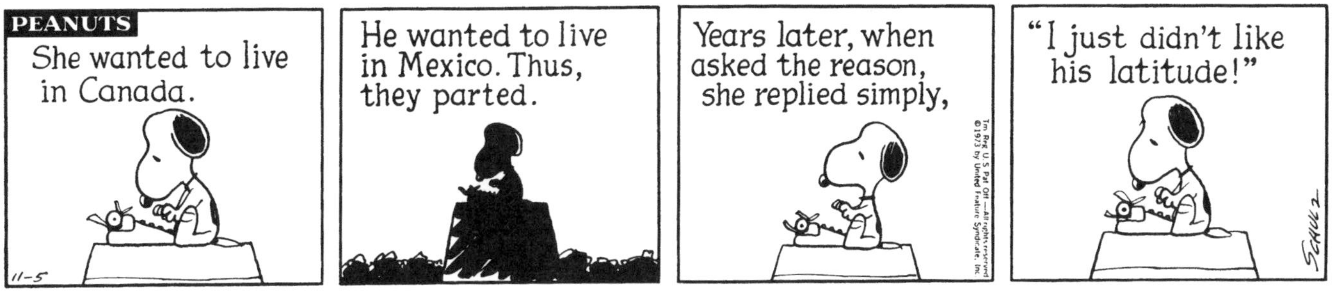
PEANUTS
She wanted to live in Canada.
11-5
He wanted to live in Mexico. Thus, they parted.
Years later, when asked the reason, she replied simply,
Tm. Reg. U.S. Pat. Off.—All rights reserved © 1973 by United Feature Syndicate, Inc.
"I just didn't like his latitude!"
SCHULZ

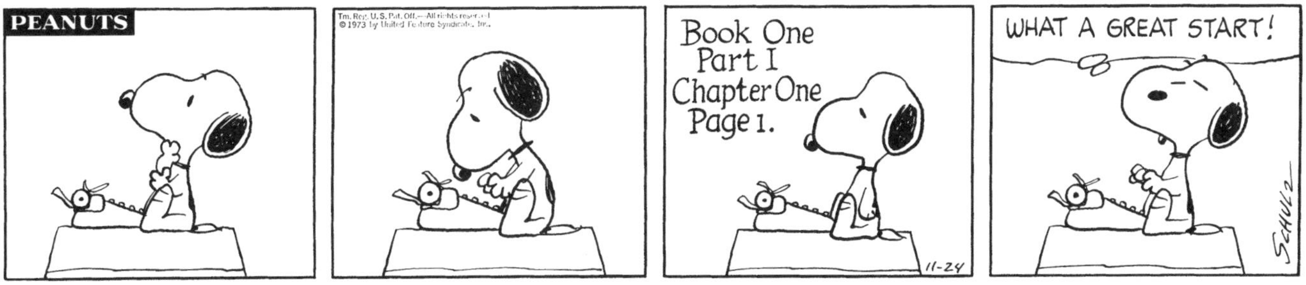
PEANUTS
Tm. Reg. U.S. Pat. Off.—All rights reserved © 1973 by United Feature Syndicate, Inc.
Book One
Part I
Chapter One
Page 1.
11-24
WHAT A GREAT START!
SCHULZ

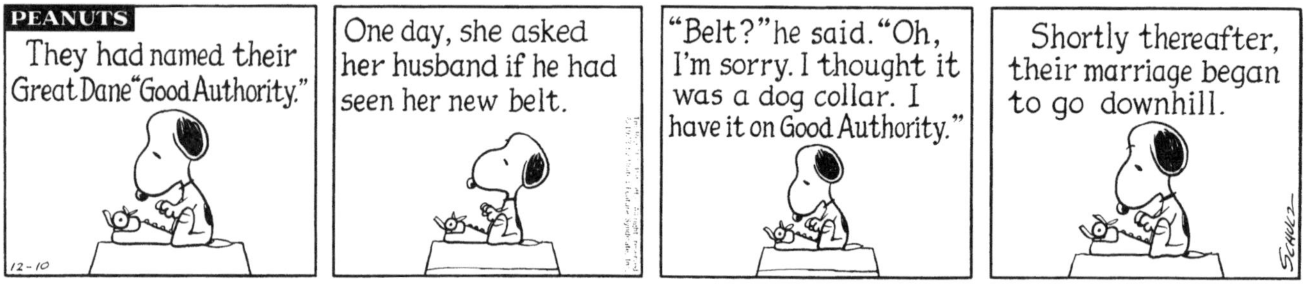
PEANUTS
They had named their Great Dane "Good Authority."
12-10
One day, she asked her husband if he had seen her new belt.
"Belt?" he said. "Oh, I'm sorry. I thought it was a dog collar. I have it on Good Authority."
Shortly thereafter, their marriage began to go downhill.
SCHULZ

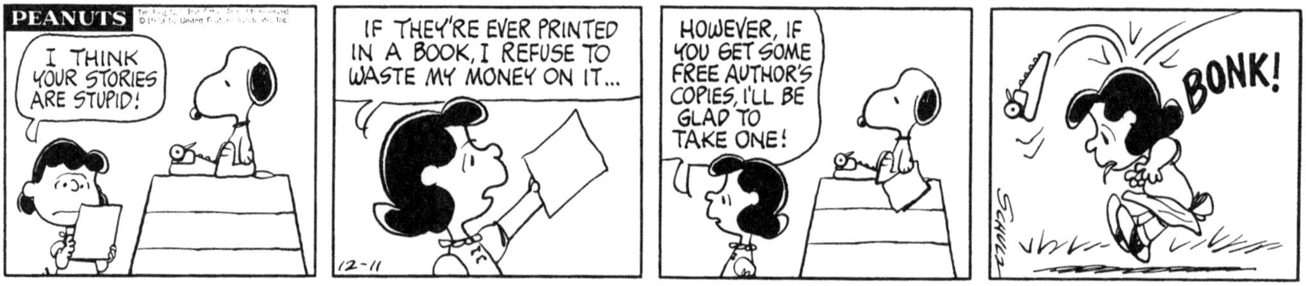
PEANUTS
I THINK YOUR STORIES ARE STUPID!
IF THEY'RE EVER PRINTED IN A BOOK, I REFUSE TO WASTE MY MONEY ON IT...
12-11
HOWEVER, IF YOU GET SOME FREE AUTHOR'S COPIES, I'LL BE GLAD TO TAKE ONE!
BONK!
SCHULZ

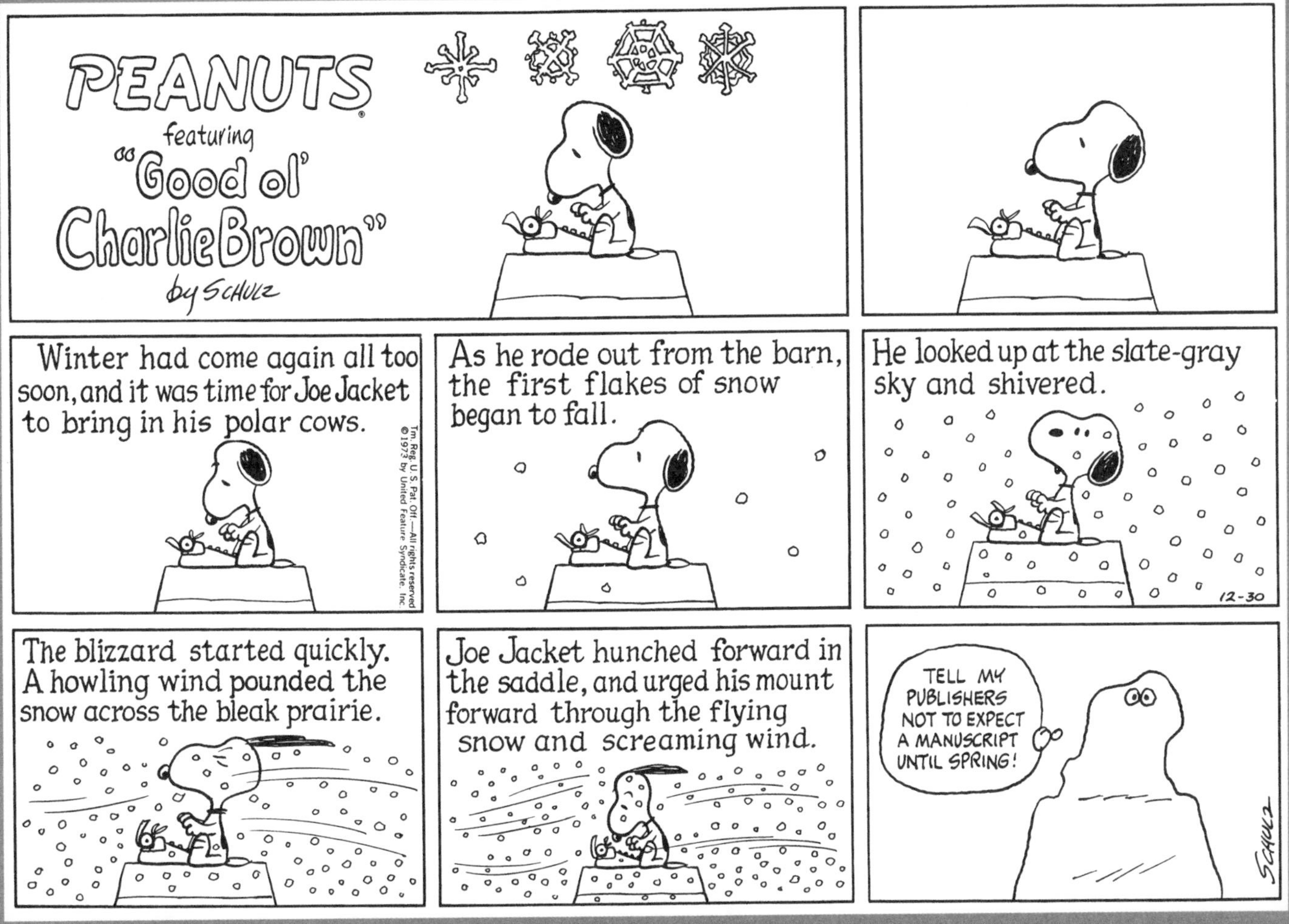
PEANUTS
featuring
"Good ol' Charlie Brown"
by SCHULZ
Winter had come again all too soon, and it was time for Joe Jacket to bring in his polar cows.
Tm Reg. U.S. Pat. Off.—All rights reserved © 1973 by United Feature Syndicate, Inc.
As he rode out from the barn, the first flakes of snow began to fall.
He looked up at the slate-gray sky and shivered.
12-30
The blizzard started quickly. A howling wind pounded the snow across the bleak prairie.
Joe Jacket hunched forward in the saddle, and urged his mount forward through the flying snow and screaming wind.
TELL MY PUBLISHERS NOT TO EXPECT A MANUSCRIPT UNTIL SPRING!
SCHULZ

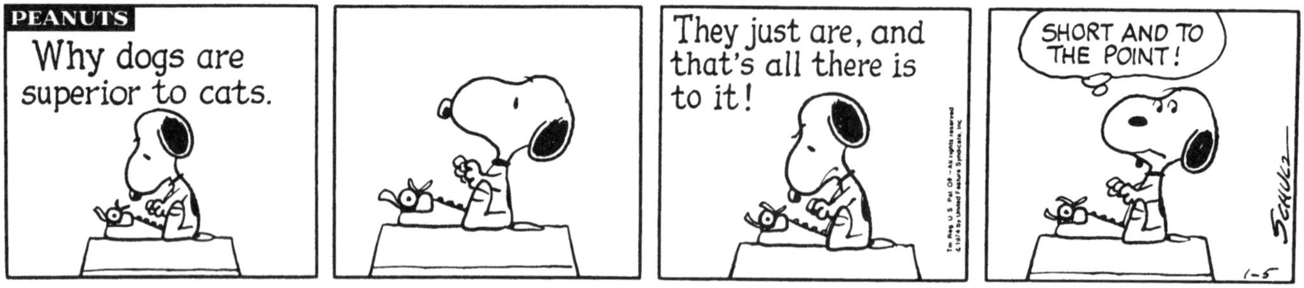
PEANUTS
Why dogs are superior to cats.
They just are, and that's all there is to it!
Tm Reg U S Pat Off — All rights reserved
© 1974 by United Feature Syndicate, Inc
SHORT AND TO THE POINT!
SCHULZ
1-5

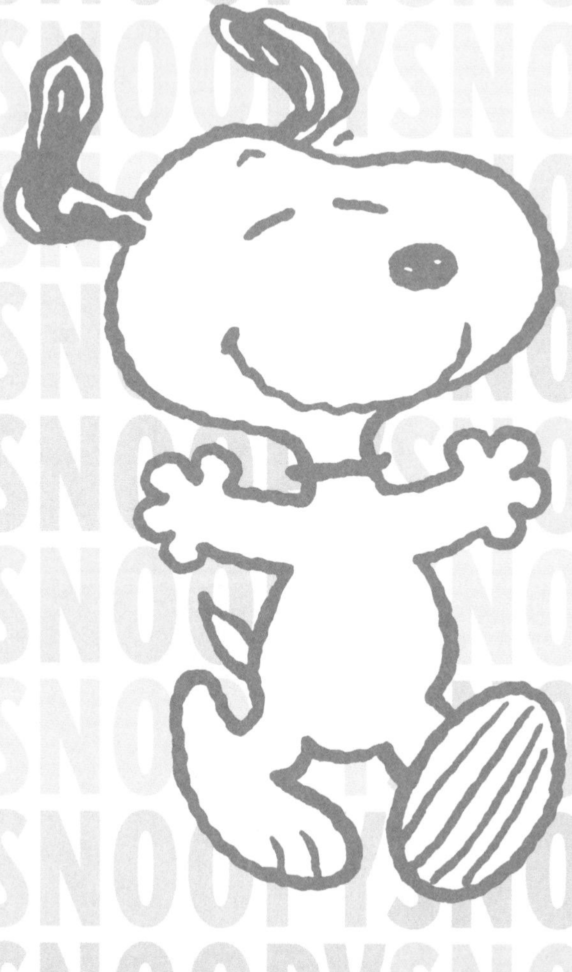

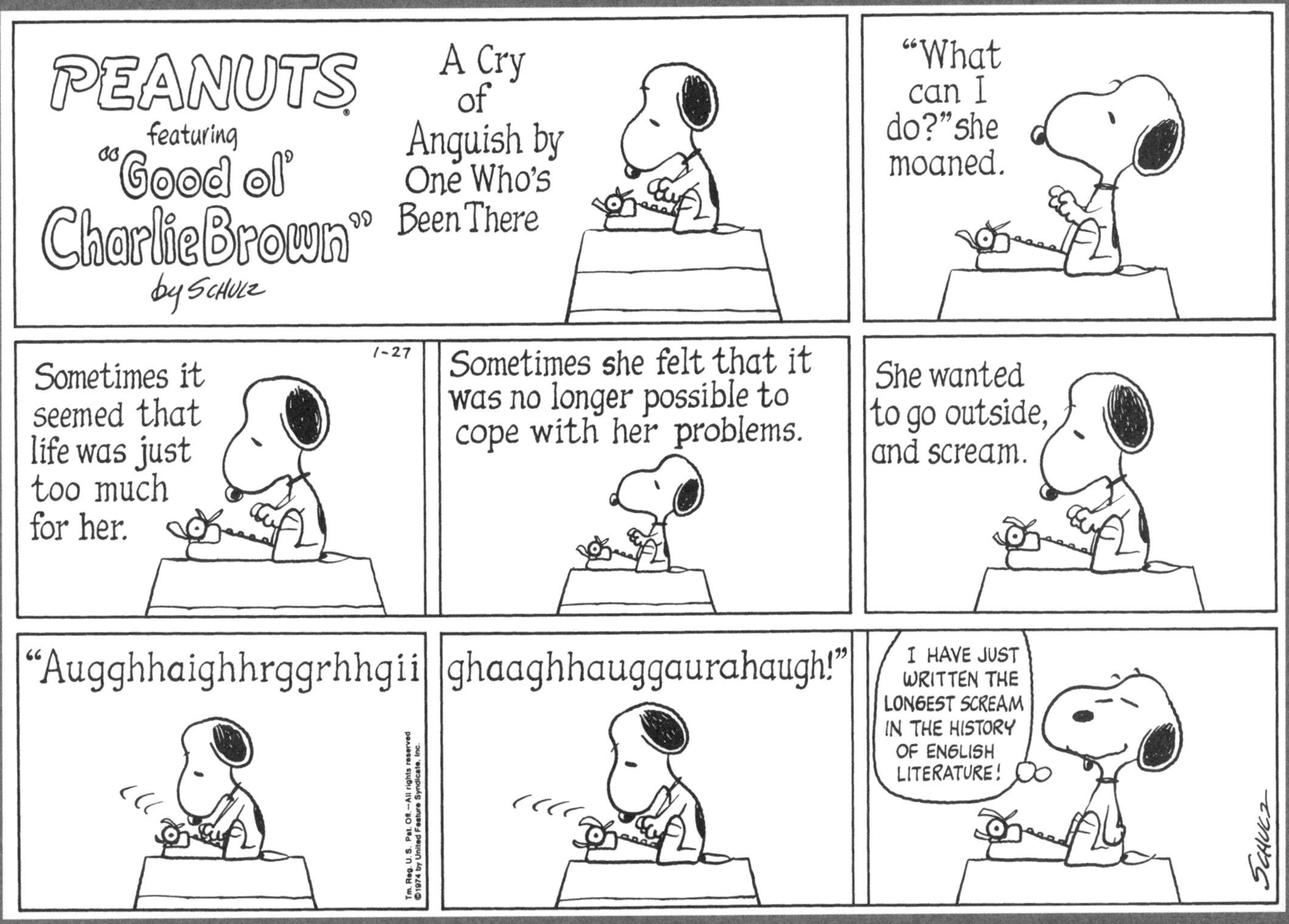
PEANUTS
featuring
"Good ol' CharlieBrown"
by SCHULZ
A Cry of Anguish by One Who's Been There
"What can I do?" she moaned.
1-27
Sometimes it seemed that life was just too much for her.
Sometimes she felt that it was no longer possible to cope with her problems.
She wanted to go outside, and scream.
"Augghhaighhrggrhhgii
Tm. Reg. U.S. Pat. Off.—All rights reserved
©1974 by United Feature Syndicate, Inc.
ghaaghhauggaurahaugh!"
I HAVE JUST WRITTEN THE LONGEST SCREAM IN THE HISTORY OF ENGLISH LITERATURE!
SCHULZ

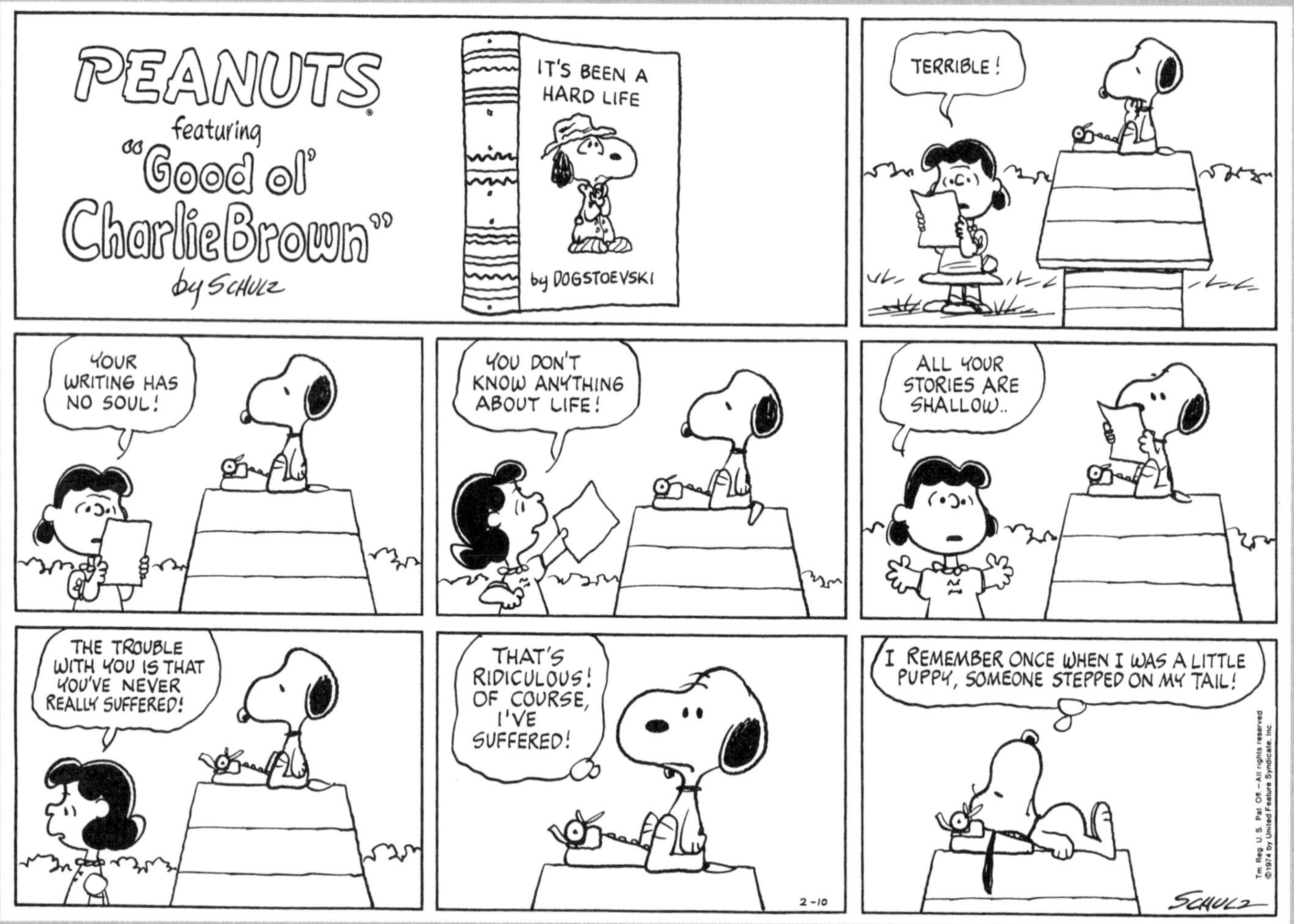
PEANUTS
featuring
"Good ol' Charlie Brown"
by SCHULZ
IT'S BEEN A HARD LIFE
by DOGSTOEVSKI
TERRIBLE!
YOUR WRITING HAS NO SOUL!
YOU DON'T KNOW ANYTHING ABOUT LIFE!
ALL YOUR STORIES ARE SHALLOW..
THE TROUBLE WITH YOU IS THAT YOU'VE NEVER REALLY SUFFERED!
THAT'S RIDICULOUS! OF COURSE, I'VE SUFFERED!
2-10
I REMEMBER ONCE WHEN I WAS A LITTLE PUPPY, SOMEONE STEPPED ON MY TAIL!
Tm. Reg. U.S. Pat. Off.—All rights reserved
©1974 by United Feature Syndicate, Inc.
SCHULZ

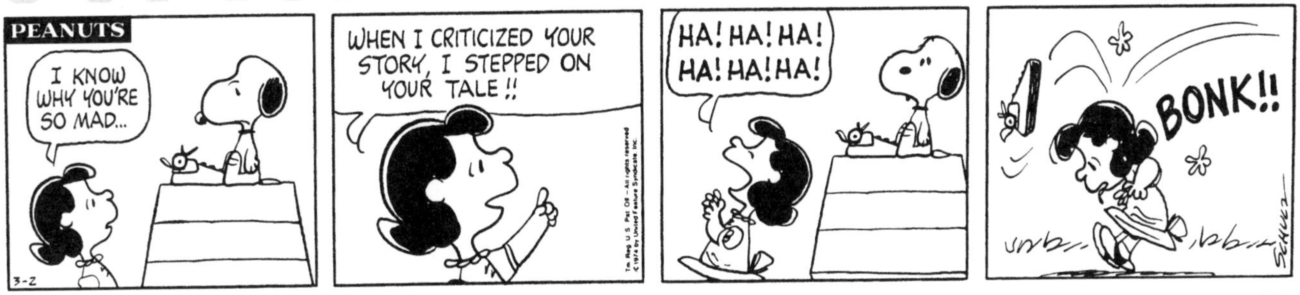
PEANUTS
I KNOW WHY YOU'RE SO MAD...
3-2
WHEN I CRITICIZED YOUR STORY, I STEPPED ON YOUR TALE !!
HA! HA! HA! HA! HA! HA!
BONK!!
SCHULZ

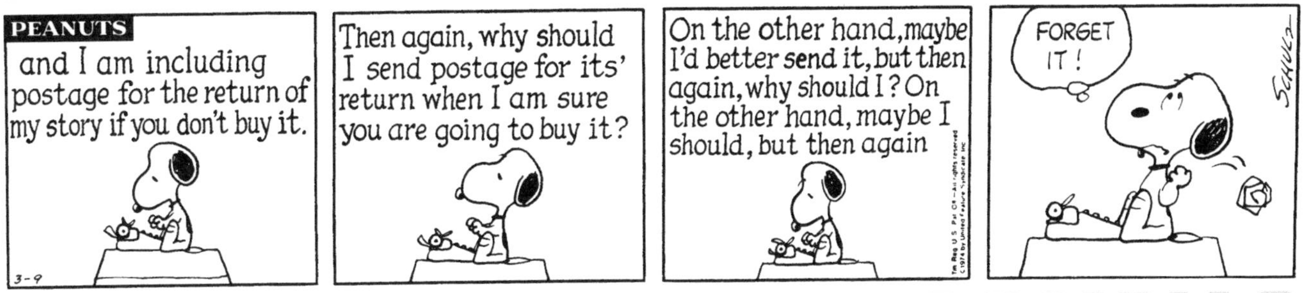
PEANUTS
and I am including postage for the return of my story if you don't buy it.
3-9
Then again, why should I send postage for its' return when I am sure you are going to buy it?
On the other hand, maybe I'd better send it, but then again, why should I? On the other hand, maybe I should, but then again
FORGET IT!
SCHULZ

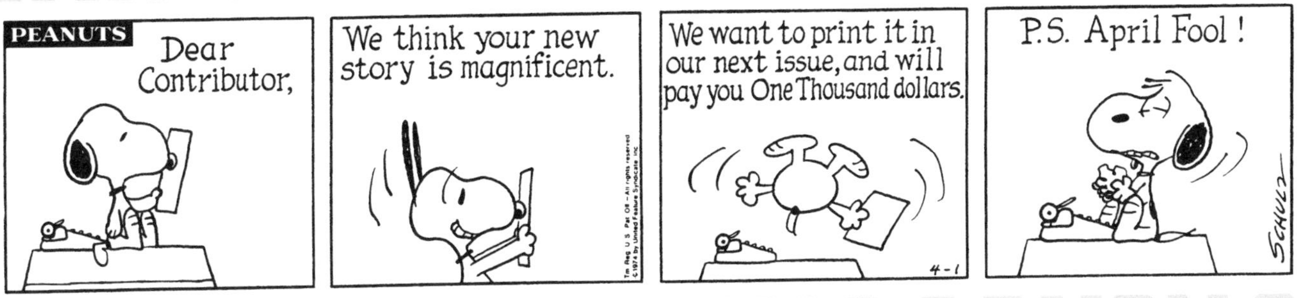
PEANUTS
Dear Contributor,
We think your new story is magnificent.
We want to print it in our next issue, and will pay you One Thousand dollars.
4-1
P.S. April Fool!
SCHULZ

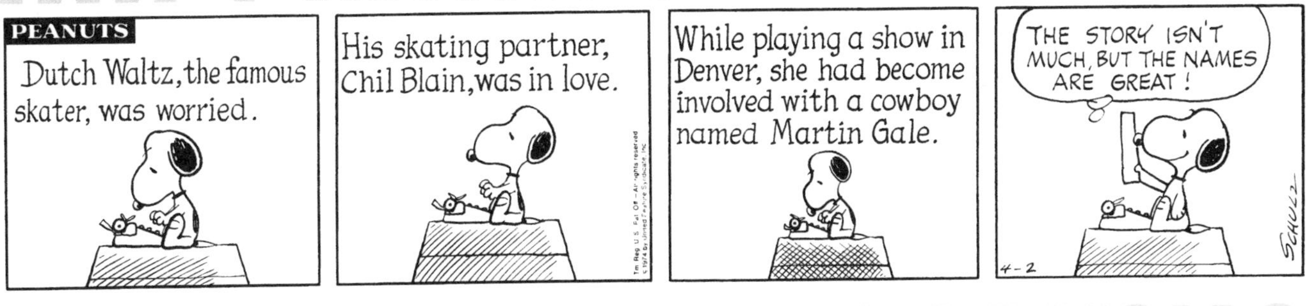
PEANUTS
Dutch Waltz, the famous skater, was worried.
His skating partner, Chil Blain, was in love.
While playing a show in Denver, she had become involved with a cowboy named Martin Gale.
THE STORY ISN'T MUCH, BUT THE NAMES ARE GREAT!
4-2
SCHULZ

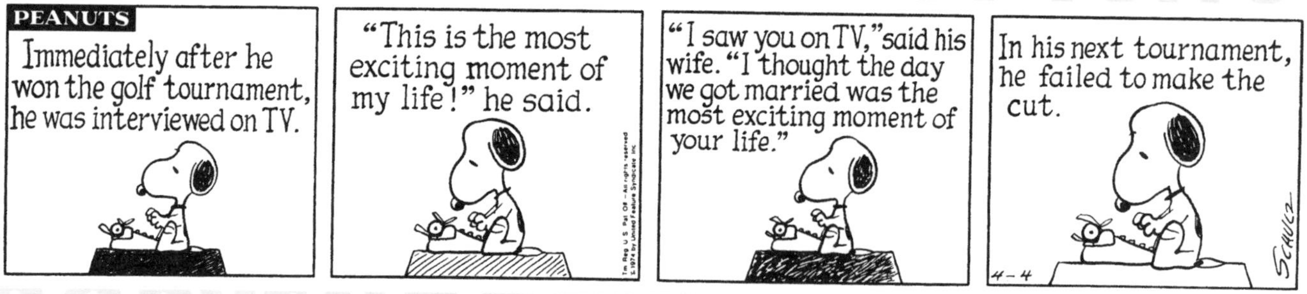
PEANUTS
Immediately after he won the golf tournament, he was interviewed on TV.
"This is the most exciting moment of my life!" he said.
"I saw you on TV," said his wife. "I thought the day we got married was the most exciting moment of your life."
In his next tournament, he failed to make the cut.
4-4
SCHULZ

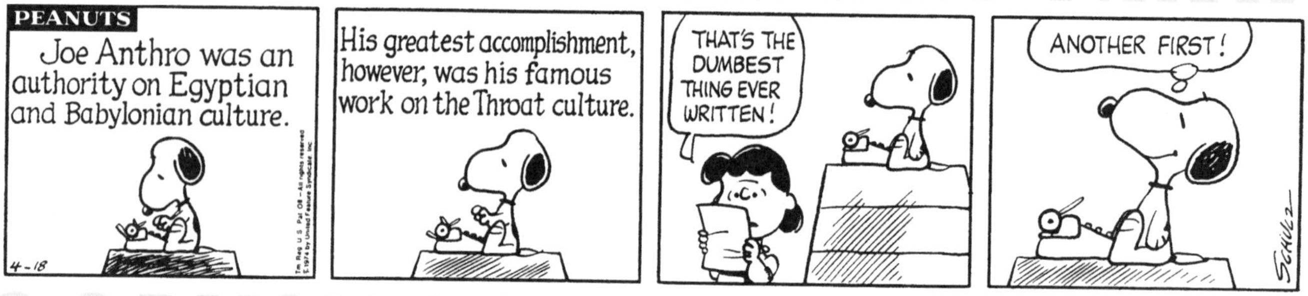
PEANUTS
Joe Anthro was an authority on Egyptian and Babylonian culture.
4-18
His greatest accomplishment, however, was his famous work on the Throat culture.
THAT'S THE DUMBEST THING EVER WRITTEN!
ANOTHER FIRST!
SCHULZ

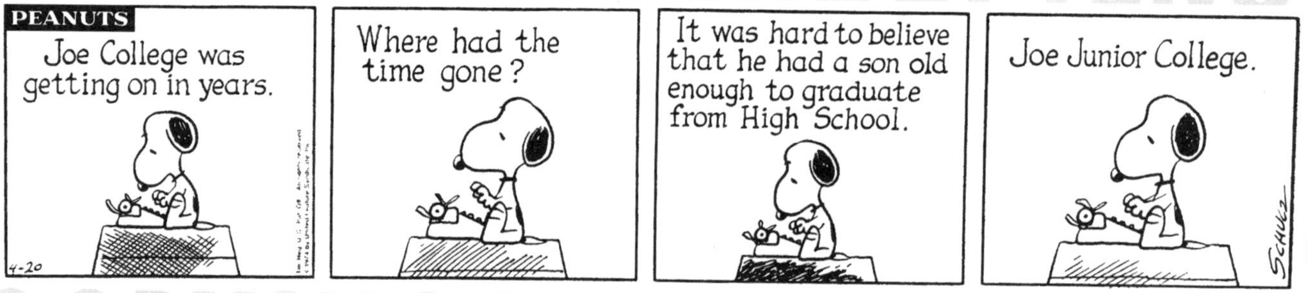
PEANUTS
Joe College was getting on in years.
4-20
Where had the time gone?
It was hard to believe that he had a son old enough to graduate from High School.
Joe Junior College.
SCHULZ

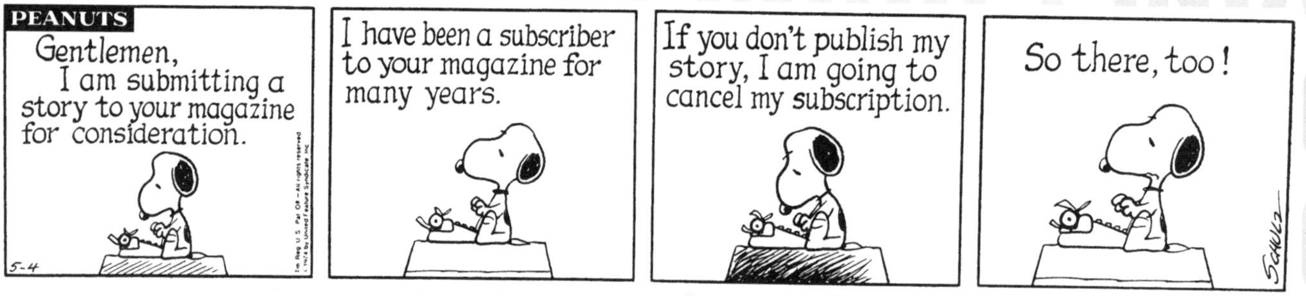
PEANUTS
Gentlemen,
I am submitting a story to your magazine for consideration.
5-4
I have been a subscriber to your magazine for many years.
If you don't publish my story, I am going to cancel my subscription.
So there, too!
SCHULZ

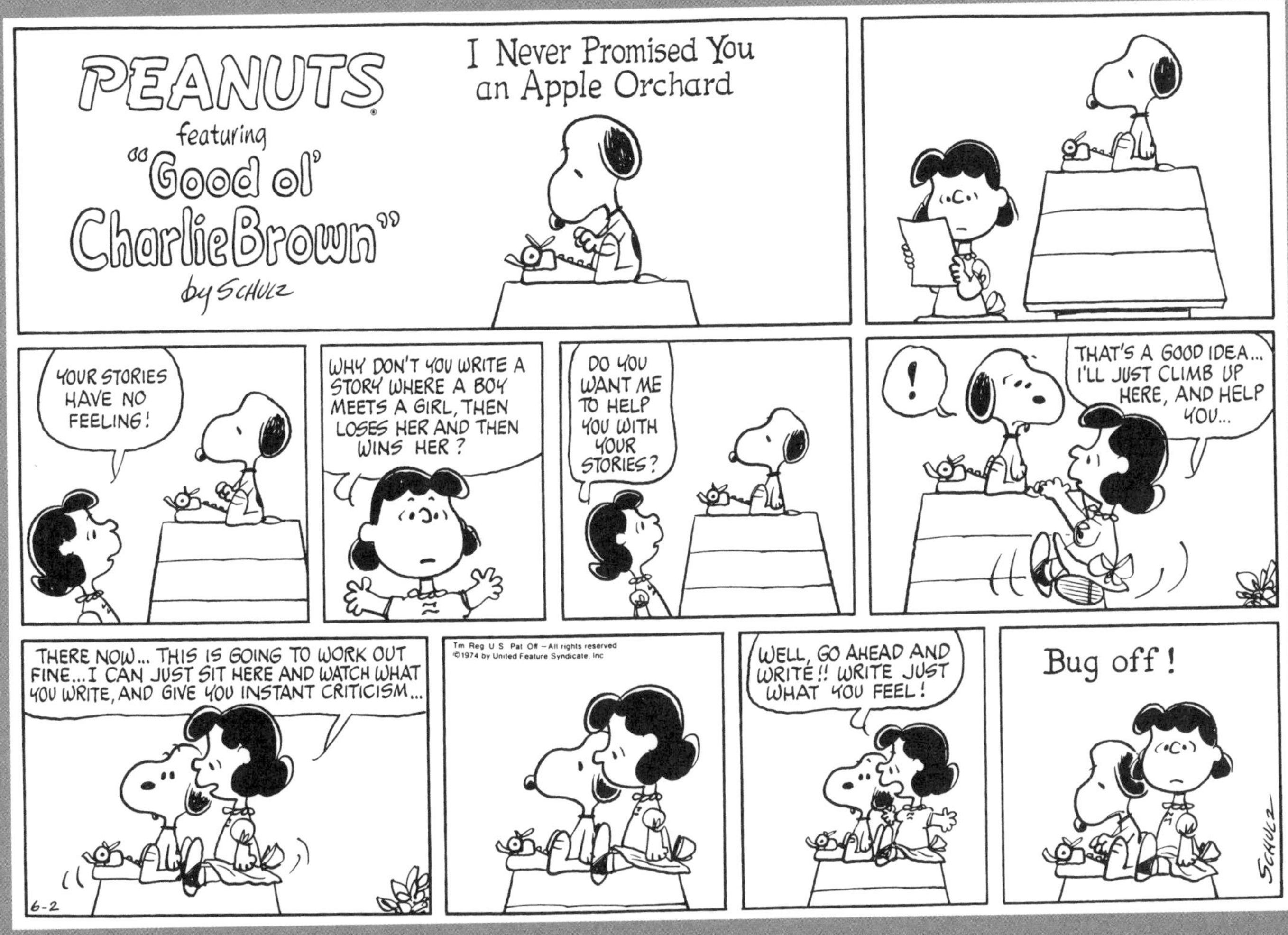
PEANUTS®
featuring "Good ol' Charlie Brown"
by SCHULZ
I Never Promised You an Apple Orchard
YOUR STORIES HAVE NO FEELING!
WHY DON'T YOU WRITE A STORY WHERE A BOY MEETS A GIRL, THEN LOSES HER AND THEN WINS HER?
DO YOU WANT ME TO HELP YOU WITH YOUR STORIES?
!
THAT'S A GOOD IDEA... I'LL JUST CLIMB UP HERE, AND HELP YOU...
THERE NOW... THIS IS GOING TO WORK OUT FINE... I CAN JUST SIT HERE AND WATCH WHAT YOU WRITE, AND GIVE YOU INSTANT CRITICISM...
6-2
Tm Reg U.S. Pat Off — All rights reserved
©1974 by United Feature Syndicate, Inc
WELL, GO AHEAD AND WRITE!! WRITE JUST WHAT YOU FEEL!
Bug off!
SCHULZ

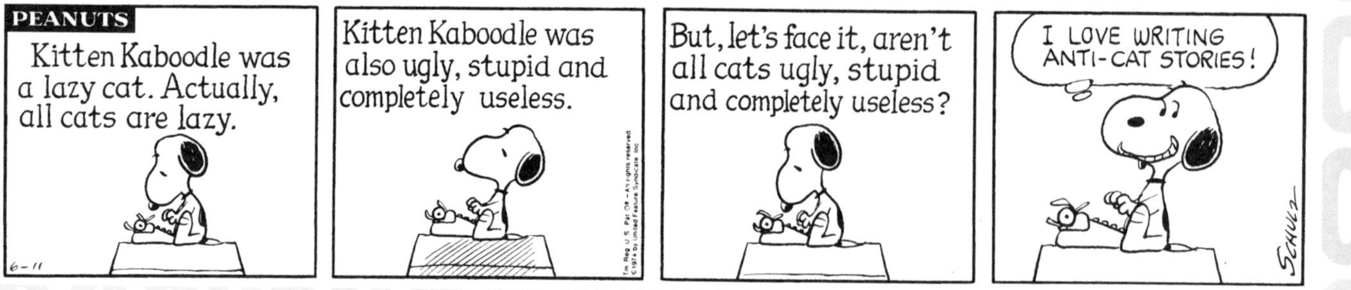
PEANUTS
Kitten Kaboodle was a lazy cat. Actually, all cats are lazy.
6-11
Kitten Kaboodle was also ugly, stupid and completely useless.
But, let's face it, aren't all cats ugly, stupid and completely useless?
I LOVE WRITING ANTI-CAT STORIES!
SCHULZ

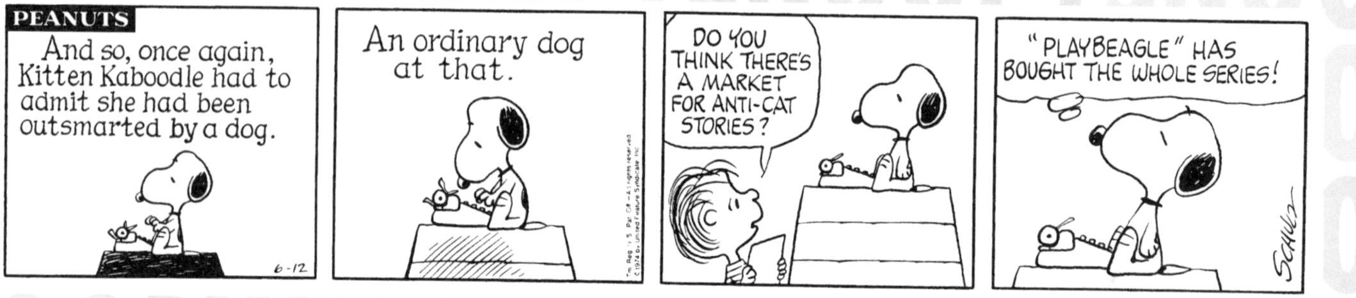
PEANUTS
And so, once again, Kitten Kaboodle had to admit she had been outsmarted by a dog.
6-12
An ordinary dog at that.
DO YOU THINK THERE'S A MARKET FOR ANTI-CAT STORIES?
"PLAYBEAGLE" HAS BOUGHT THE WHOLE SERIES!
SCHULZ

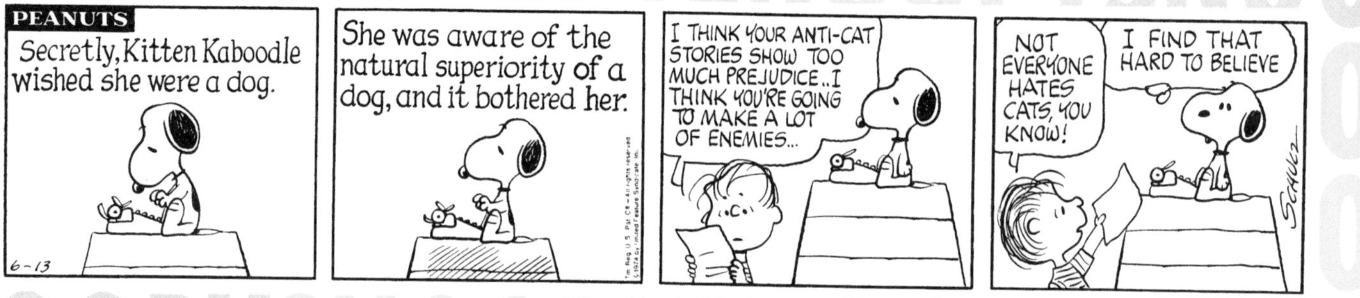
PEANUTS
Secretly, Kitten Kaboodle wished she were a dog.
6-13
She was aware of the natural superiority of a dog, and it bothered her.
I THINK YOUR ANTI-CAT STORIES SHOW TOO MUCH PREJUDICE..I THINK YOU'RE GOING TO MAKE A LOT OF ENEMIES...
NOT EVERYONE HATES CATS, YOU KNOW!
I FIND THAT HARD TO BELIEVE
SCHULZ

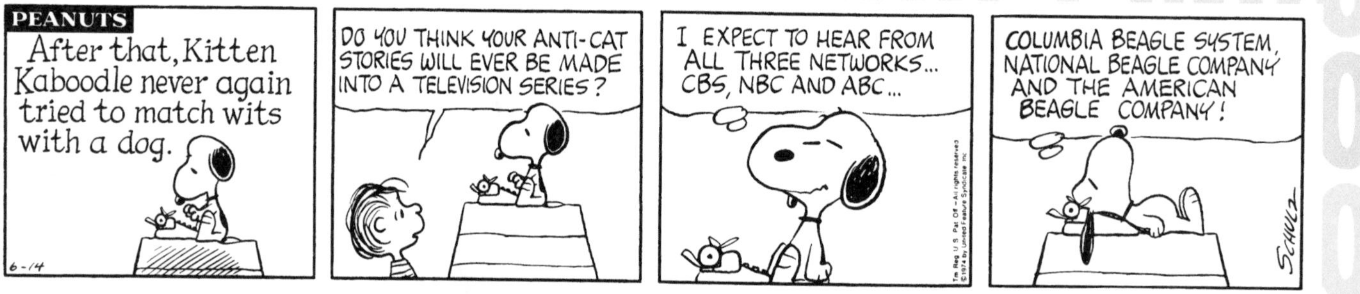
PEANUTS
After that, Kitten Kaboodle never again tried to match wits with a dog.
6-14
DO YOU THINK YOUR ANTI-CAT STORIES WILL EVER BE MADE INTO A TELEVISION SERIES?
I EXPECT TO HEAR FROM ALL THREE NETWORKS... CBS, NBC AND ABC...
COLUMBIA BEAGLE SYSTEM, NATIONAL BEAGLE COMPANY AND THE AMERICAN BEAGLE COMPANY!
SCHULZ

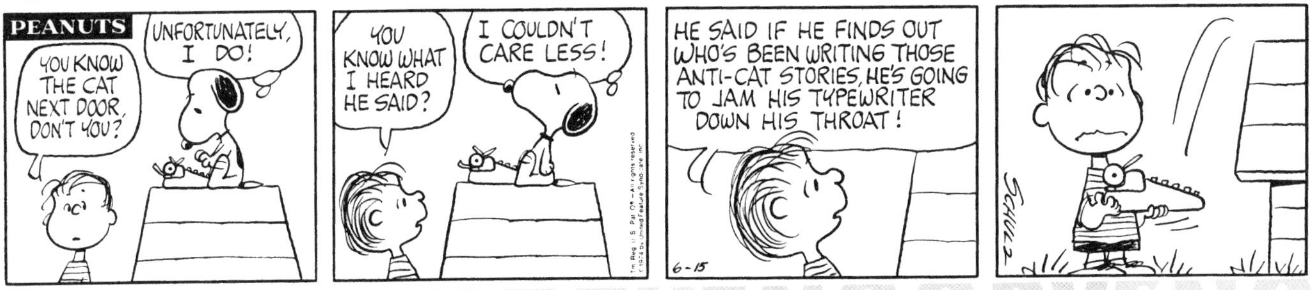
PEANUTS
YOU KNOW THE CAT NEXT DOOR, DON'T YOU?
UNFORTUNATELY, I DO!
YOU KNOW WHAT I HEARD HE SAID?
I COULDN'T CARE LESS!
HE SAID IF HE FINDS OUT WHO'S BEEN WRITING THOSE ANTI-CAT STORIES, HE'S GOING TO JAM HIS TYPEWRITER DOWN HIS THROAT!
6-15
SCHULZ

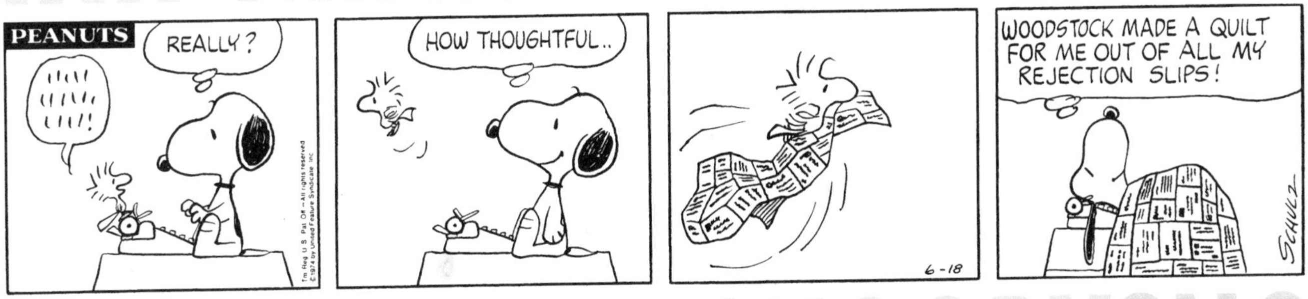
PEANUTS
REALLY?
HOW THOUGHTFUL..
6-18
WOODSTOCK MADE A QUILT FOR ME OUT OF ALL MY REJECTION SLIPS!
SCHULZ

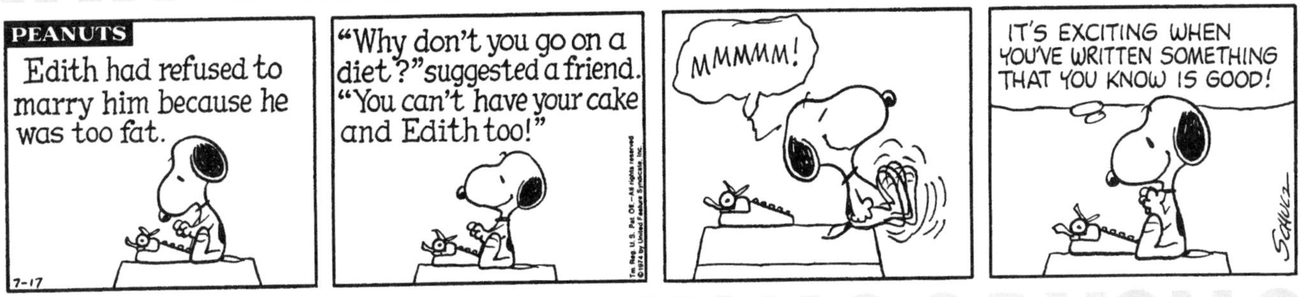
PEANUTS
Edith had refused to marry him because he was too fat.
7-17
"Why don't you go on a diet?" suggested a friend. "You can't have your cake and Edith too!"
MMMMM!
IT'S EXCITING WHEN YOU'VE WRITTEN SOMETHING THAT YOU KNOW IS GOOD!
SCHULZ

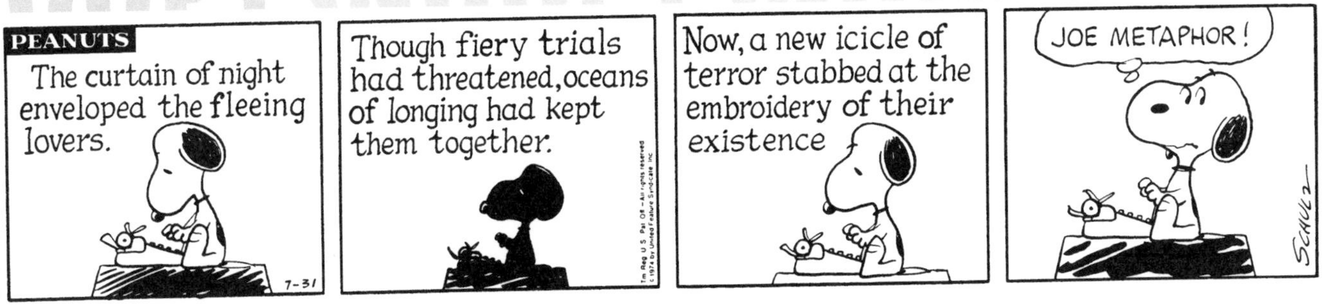
PEANUTS
The curtain of night enveloped the fleeing lovers.
7-31
Though fiery trials had threatened, oceans of longing had kept them together.
Now, a new icicle of terror stabbed at the embroidery of their existence
JOE METAPHOR!
SCHULZ

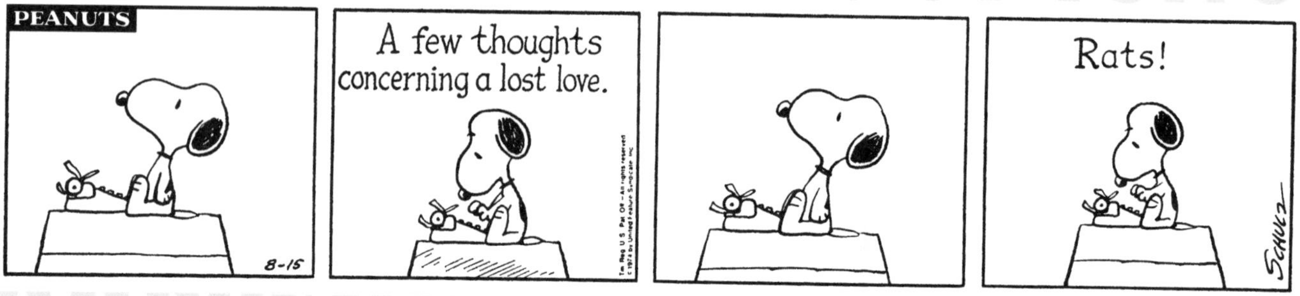
PEANUTS
A few thoughts concerning a lost love.
Rats!
8-15
SCHULZ

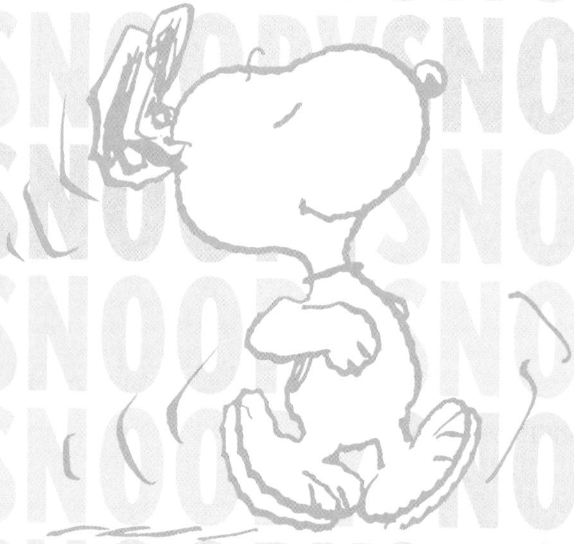

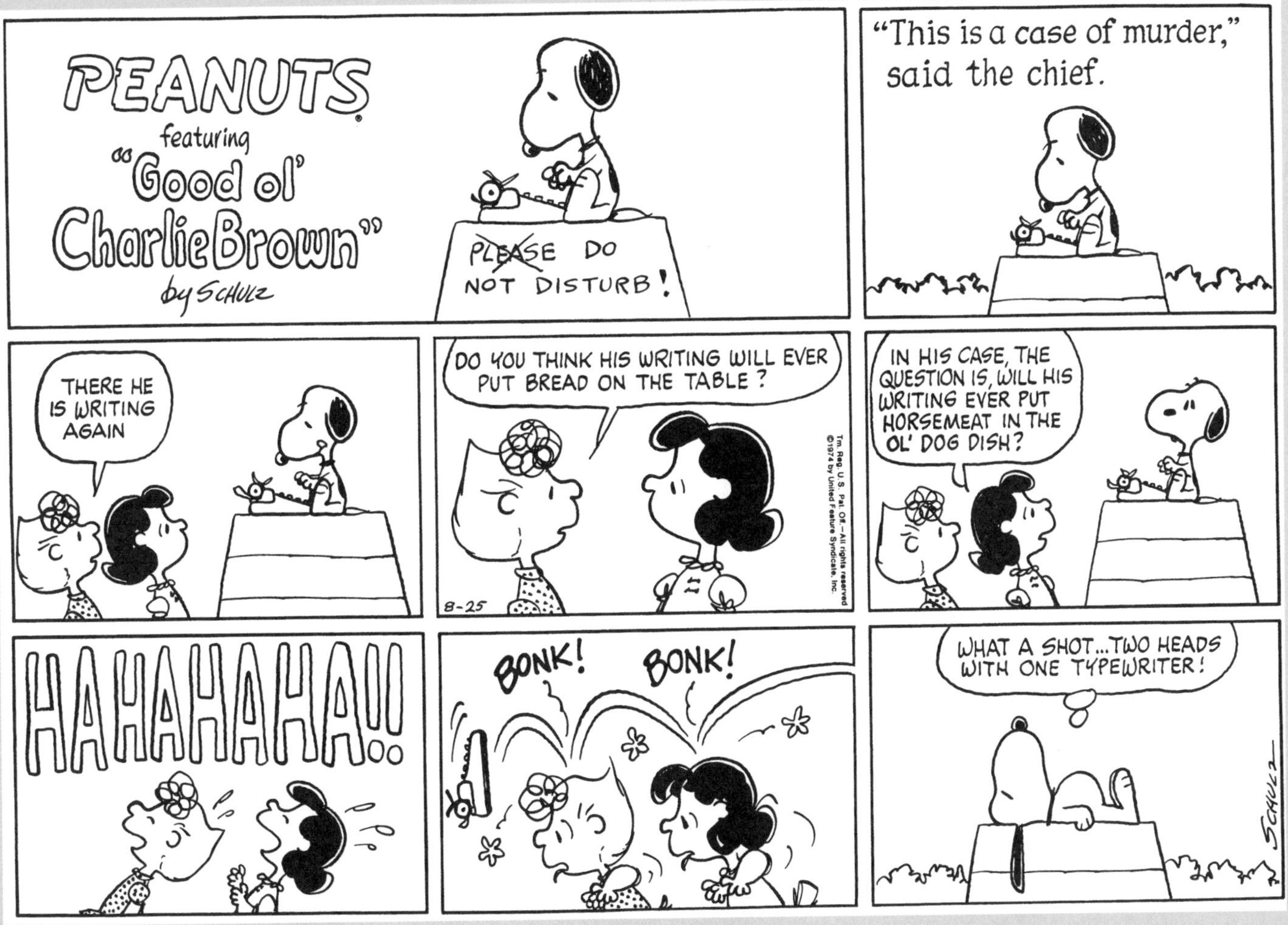
PEANUTS
featuring
"Good ol' CharlieBrown"
by SCHULZ
PLEASE DO NOT DISTURB!
"This is a case of murder," said the chief.
THERE HE IS WRITING AGAIN
DO YOU THINK HIS WRITING WILL EVER PUT BREAD ON THE TABLE?
8-25
Tm Reg. U.S. Pat. Off.—All rights reserved
©1974 by United Feature Syndicate, Inc.
IN HIS CASE, THE QUESTION IS, WILL HIS WRITING EVER PUT HORSEMEAT IN THE OL' DOG DISH?
HAHAHAHA!!
BONK!
BONK!
WHAT A SHOT...TWO HEADS WITH ONE TYPEWRITER!
SCHULZ

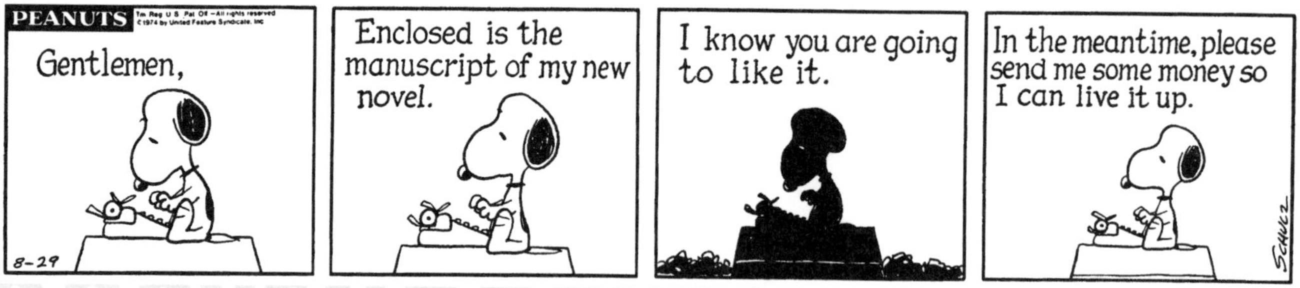
PEANUTS
Tm Reg U S Pat Off —All rights reserved © 1974 by United Feature Syndicate, Inc
Gentlemen,
8-29
Enclosed is the manuscript of my new novel.
I know you are going to like it.
In the meantime, please send me some money so I can live it up.
SCHULZ

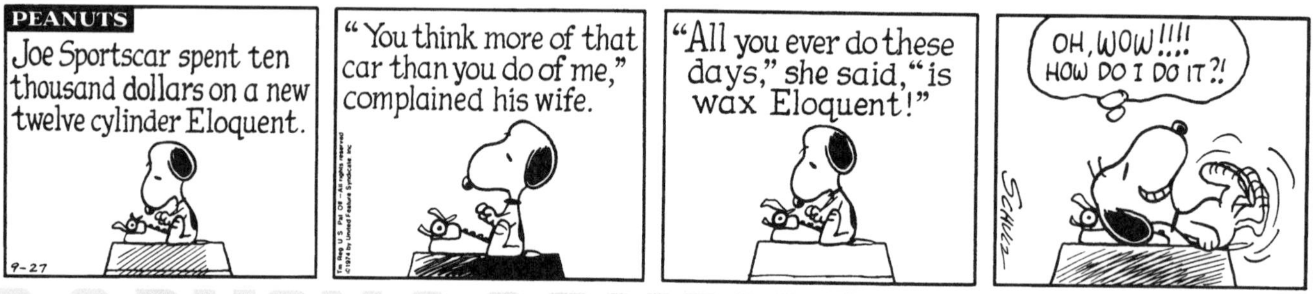
PEANUTS
Joe Sportscar spent ten thousand dollars on a new twelve cylinder Eloquent.
9-27
"You think more of that car than you do of me," complained his wife.
"All you ever do these days," she said, "is wax Eloquent!"
OH, WOW!!!! HOW DO I DO IT?!
SCHULZ

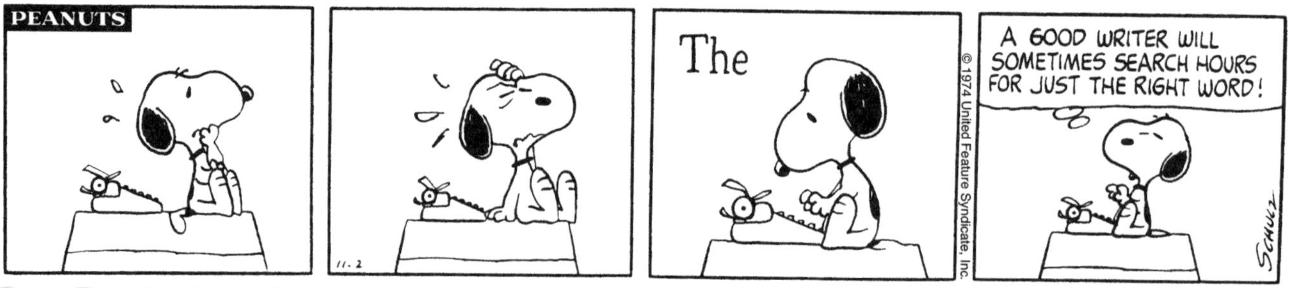
PEANUTS
11-2
The
© 1974 United Feature Syndicate, Inc.
A GOOD WRITER WILL SOMETIMES SEARCH HOURS FOR JUST THE RIGHT WORD!
SCHULZ

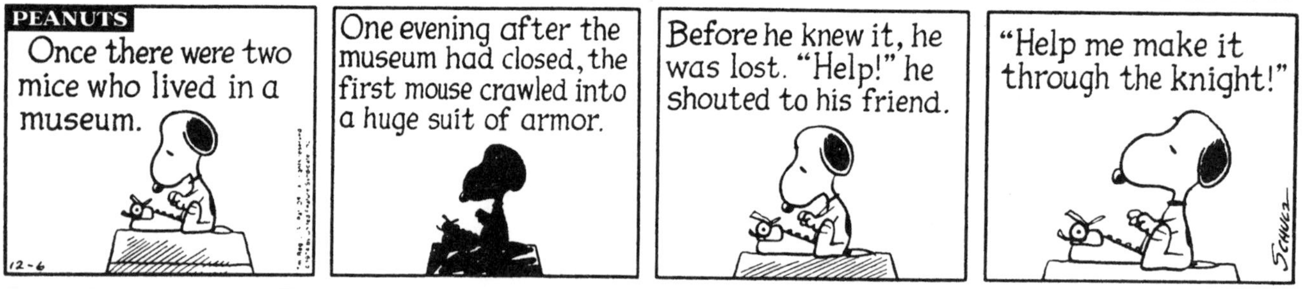
PEANUTS
Once there were two mice who lived in a museum.
12-6
One evening after the museum had closed, the first mouse crawled into a huge suit of armor.
Before he knew it, he was lost. "Help!" he shouted to his friend.
"Help me make it through the knight!"
SCHULZ

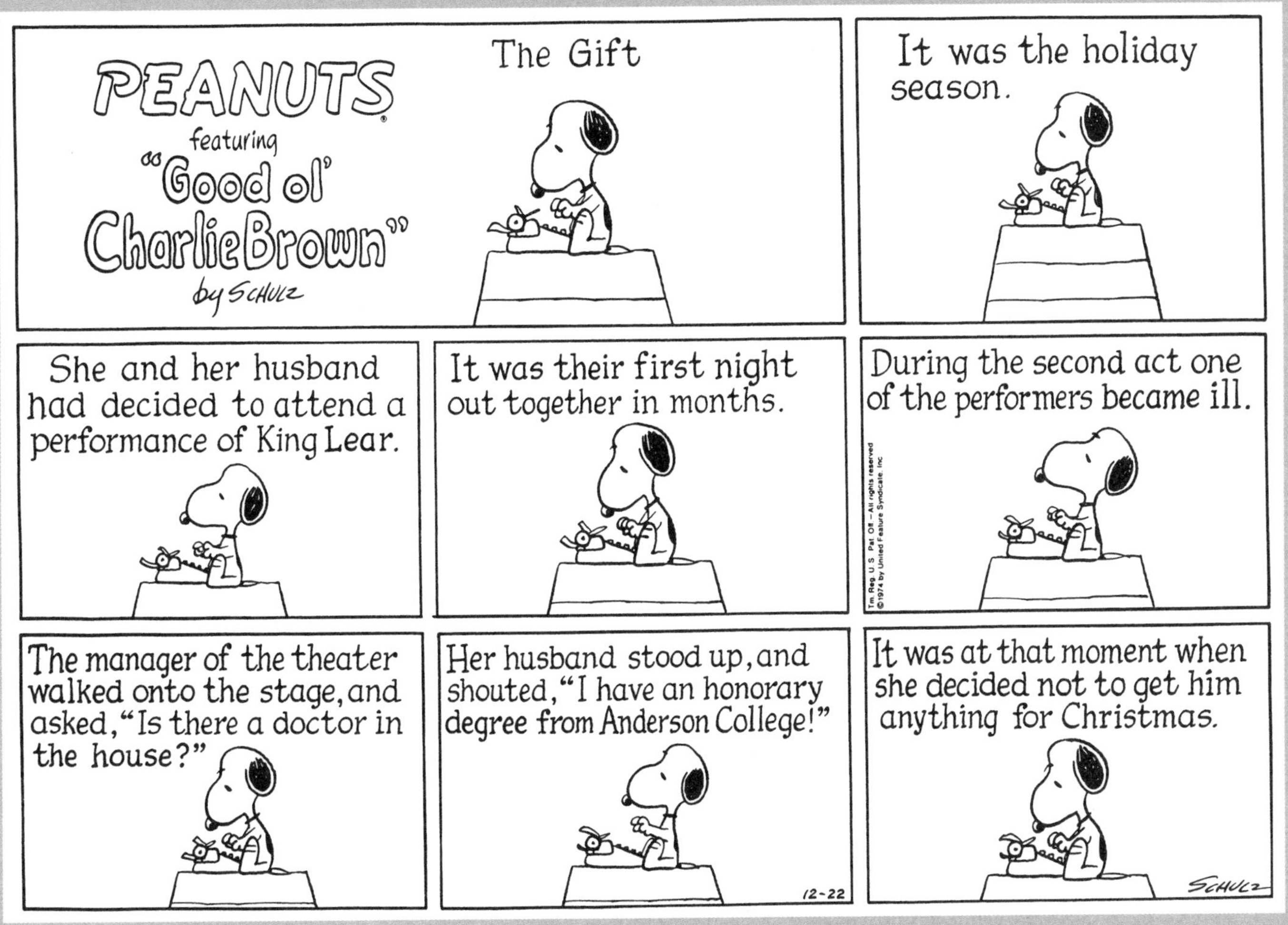
PEANUTS
featuring
"Good ol' Charlie Brown"
by SCHULZ
The Gift
It was the holiday season.
She and her husband had decided to attend a performance of King Lear.
It was their first night out together in months.
During the second act one of the performers became ill.
Tm. Reg. U.S. Pat. Off.—All rights reserved
©1974 by United Feature Syndicate, Inc.
The manager of the theater walked onto the stage, and asked, "Is there a doctor in the house?"
Her husband stood up, and shouted, "I have an honorary degree from Anderson College!"
12-22
It was at that moment when she decided not to get him anything for Christmas.
SCHULZ

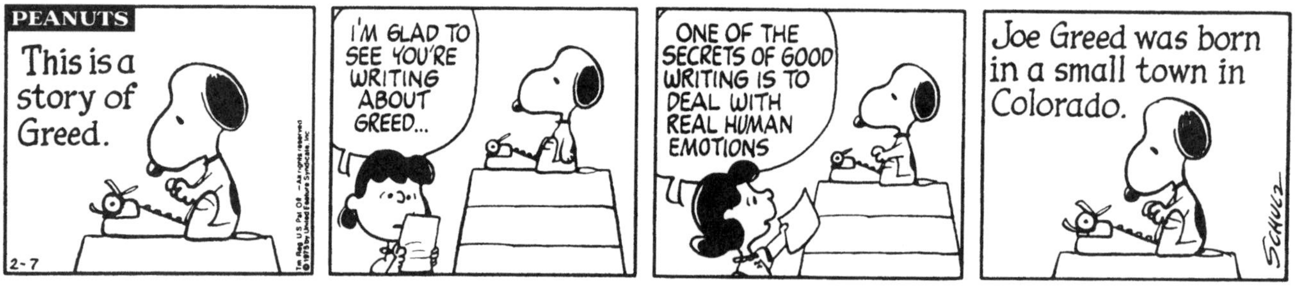
PEANUTS
This is a story of Greed.
2-7
I'M GLAD TO SEE YOU'RE WRITING ABOUT GREED...
ONE OF THE SECRETS OF GOOD WRITING IS TO DEAL WITH REAL HUMAN EMOTIONS
Joe Greed was born in a small town in Colorado.
SCHULZ

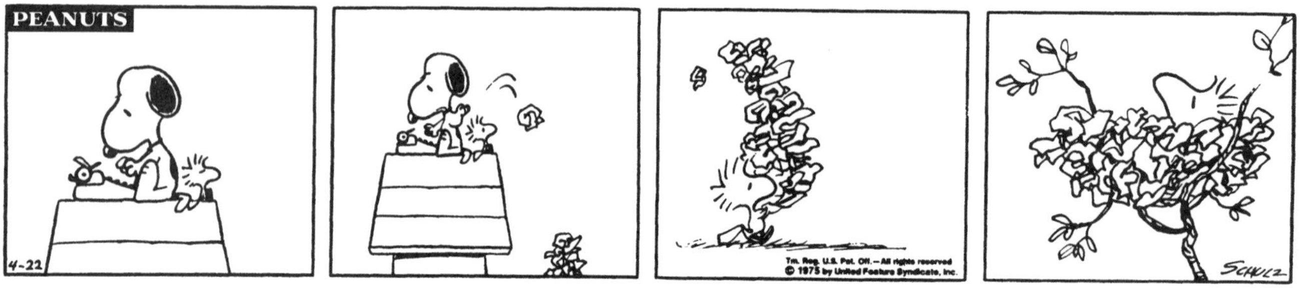
PEANUTS
4-22
Tm. Reg. U.S. Pat. Off.—All rights reserved
© 1975 by United Feature Syndicate, Inc.
SCHULZ

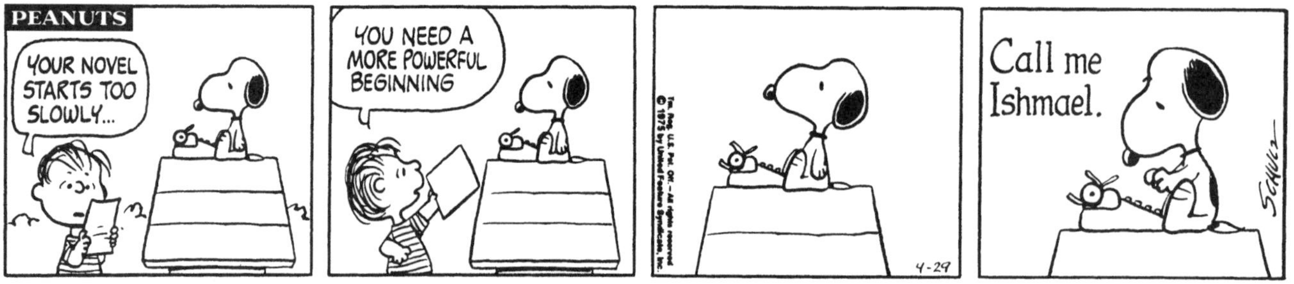
PEANUTS
YOUR NOVEL STARTS TOO SLOWLY...
YOU NEED A MORE POWERFUL BEGINNING
Tm. Reg. U.S. Pat. Off.—All rights reserved
© 1975 by United Feature Syndicate, Inc.
4-29
Call me Ishmael.
SCHULZ

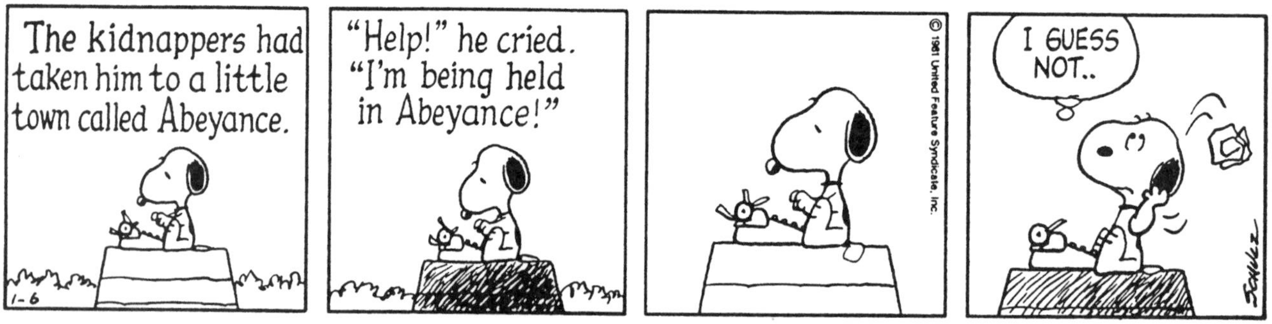
The kidnappers had taken him to a little town called Abeyance.
1-6
"Help!" he cried. "I'm being held in Abeyance!"
© 1981 United Feature Syndicate, Inc.
I GUESS NOT..
SCHULZ

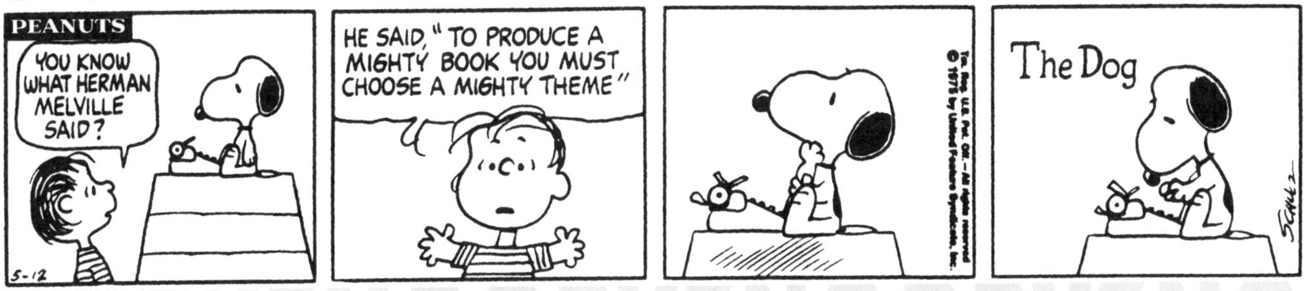
PEANUTS
YOU KNOW WHAT HERMAN MELVILLE SAID?
5-12
HE SAID, "TO PRODUCE A MIGHTY BOOK YOU MUST CHOOSE A MIGHTY THEME"
Tm. Reg. U.S. Pat. Off.—All rights reserved © 1975 by United Feature Syndicate, Inc.
The Dog
SCHULZ

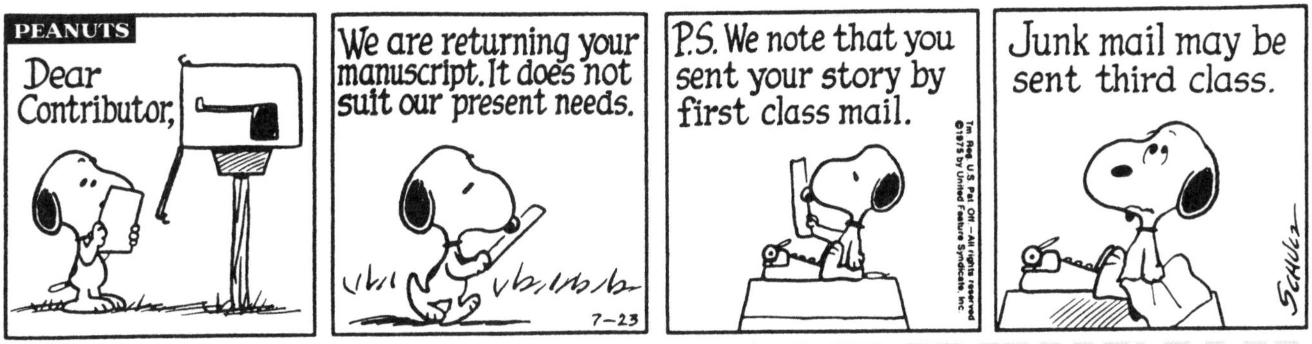
PEANUTS
Dear Contributor,
We are returning your manuscript. It does not suit our present needs.
7-23
P.S. We note that you sent your story by first class mail.
Tm. Reg. U.S. Pat. Off.—All rights reserved © 1975 by United Feature Syndicate, Inc.
Junk mail may be sent third class.
SCHULZ

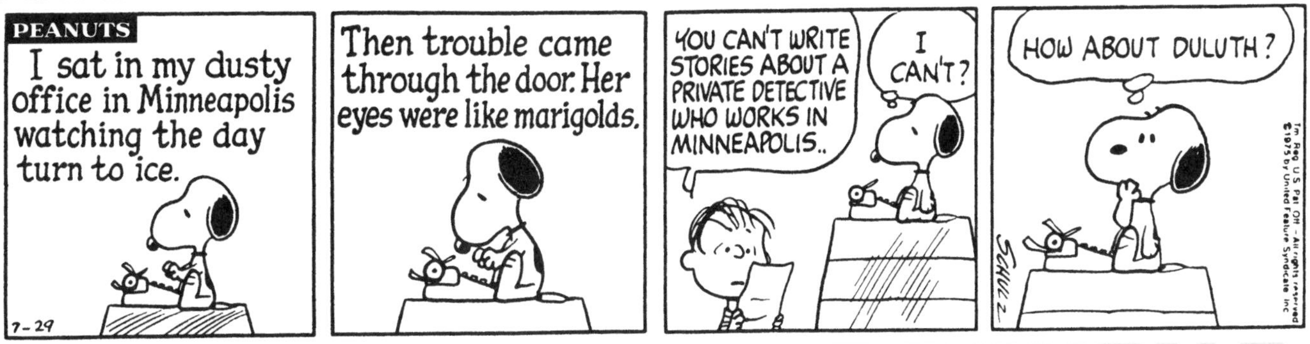
PEANUTS
I sat in my dusty office in Minneapolis watching the day turn to ice.
7-29
Then trouble came through the door. Her eyes were like marigolds.
YOU CAN'T WRITE STORIES ABOUT A PRIVATE DETECTIVE WHO WORKS IN MINNEAPOLIS..
I CAN'T?
SCHULZ
HOW ABOUT DULUTH?
Tm. Reg. U.S. Pat. Off.—All rights reserved © 1975 by United Feature Syndicate, Inc.

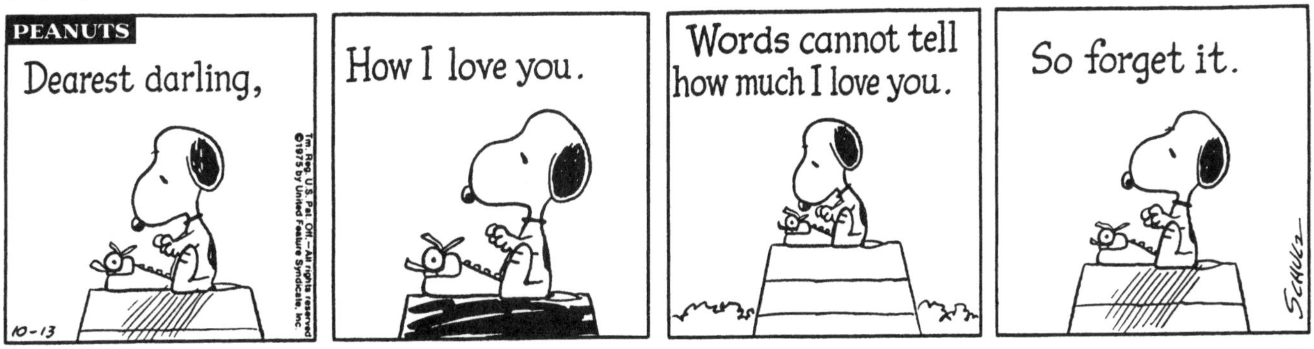
PEANUTS
Dearest darling,
10-13
Tm. Reg. U.S. Pat. Off.—All rights reserved © 1975 by United Feature Syndicate, Inc.
How I love you.
Words cannot tell how much I love you.
So forget it.
SCHULZ

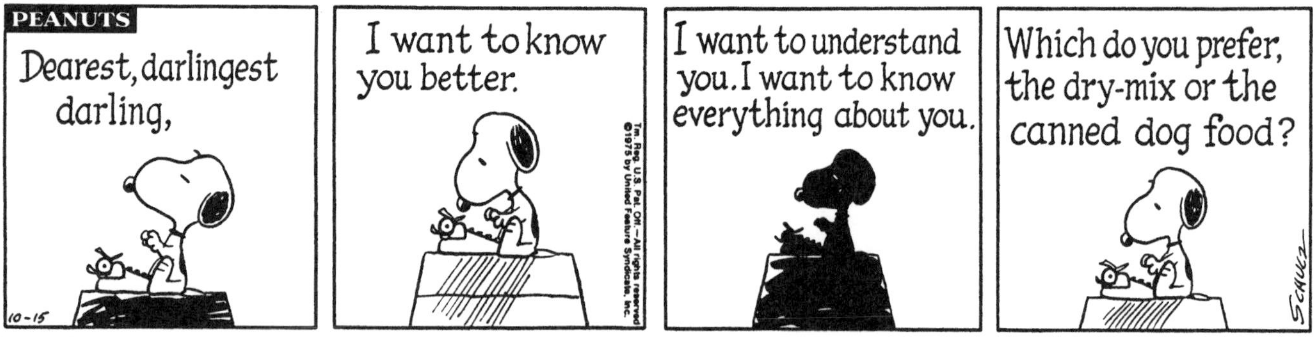
PEANUTS
Dearest, darlingest darling,
10-15
I want to know you better.
I want to understand you. I want to know everything about you.
Which do you prefer, the dry-mix or the canned dog food?
SCHULZ

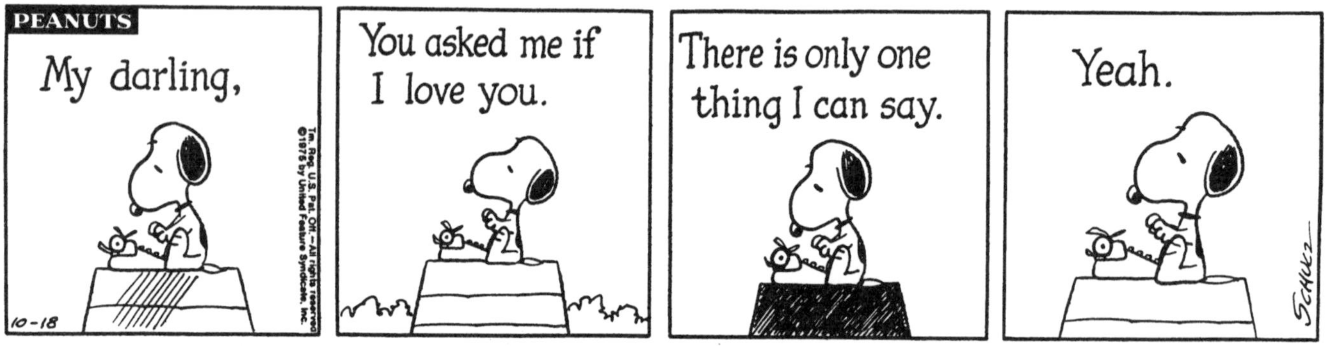
PEANUTS
My darling,
10-18
You asked me if I love you.
There is only one thing I can say.
Yeah.
SCHULZ

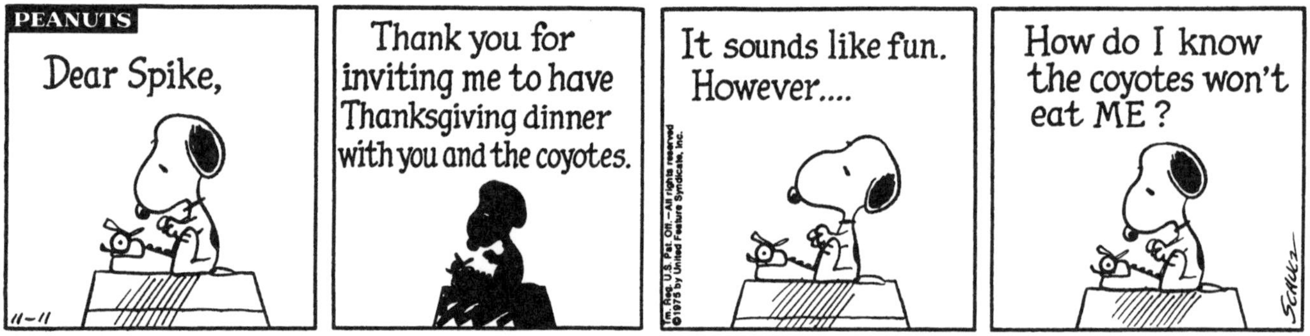
PEANUTS
Dear Spike,
11-11
Thank you for inviting me to have Thanksgiving dinner with you and the coyotes.
It sounds like fun. However....
How do I know the coyotes won't eat ME?
SCHULZ

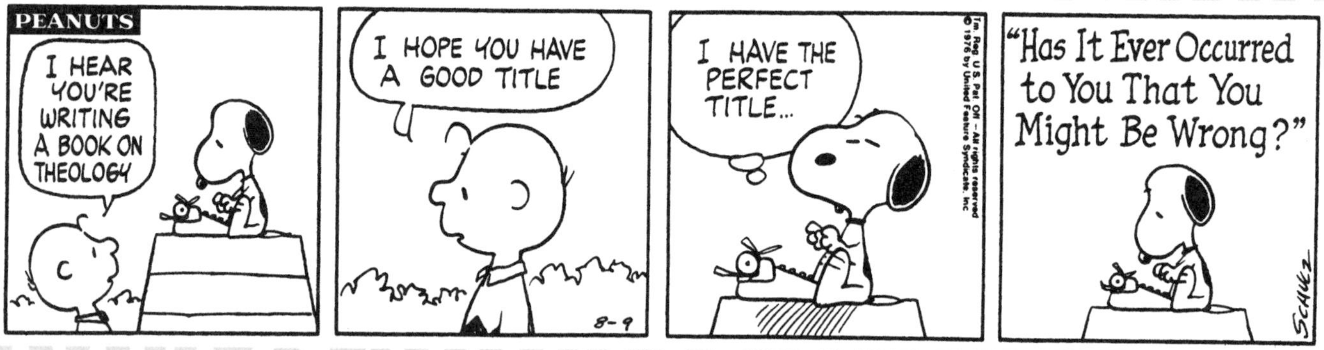
PEANUTS
I HEAR YOU'RE WRITING A BOOK ON THEOLOGY
I HOPE YOU HAVE A GOOD TITLE
8-9
I HAVE THE PERFECT TITLE...
"Has It Ever Occurred to You That You Might Be Wrong?"
SCHULZ

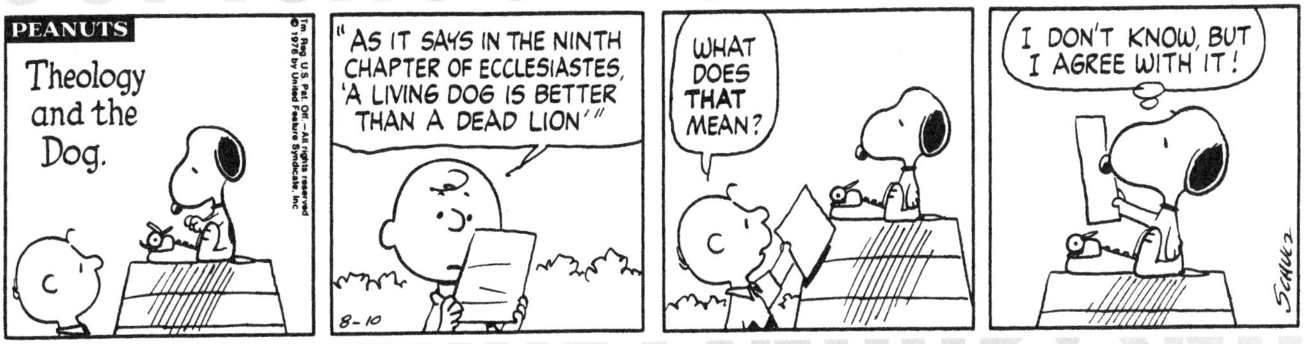
PEANUTS
Theology and the Dog.
Tm. Reg. U.S. Pat. Off.—All rights reserved © 1976 by United Feature Syndicate, Inc.
"AS IT SAYS IN THE NINTH CHAPTER OF ECCLESIASTES, 'A LIVING DOG IS BETTER THAN A DEAD LION'"
8-10
WHAT DOES THAT MEAN?
I DON'T KNOW, BUT I AGREE WITH IT!
SCHULZ

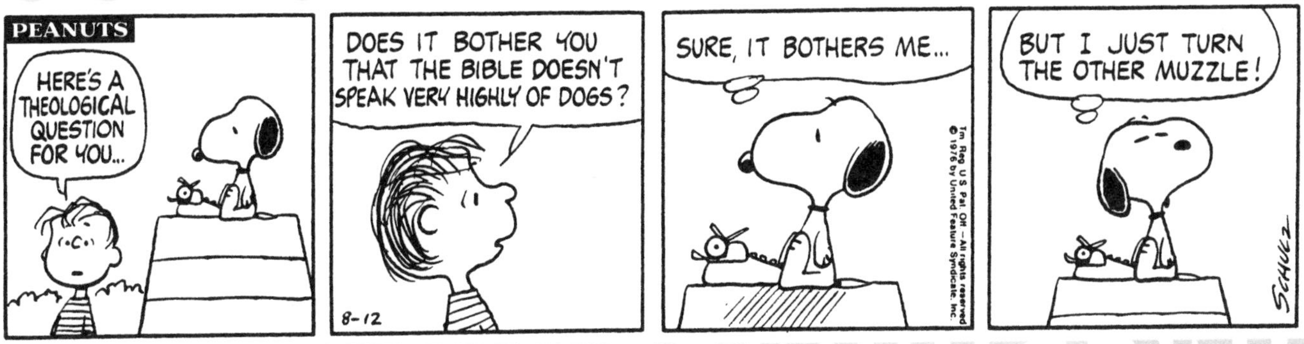
PEANUTS
HERE'S A THEOLOGICAL QUESTION FOR YOU...
DOES IT BOTHER YOU THAT THE BIBLE DOESN'T SPEAK VERY HIGHLY OF DOGS?
8-12
SURE, IT BOTHERS ME...
Tm. Reg. U.S. Pat. Off.—All rights reserved © 1976 by United Feature Syndicate, Inc.
BUT I JUST TURN THE OTHER MUZZLE!
SCHULZ

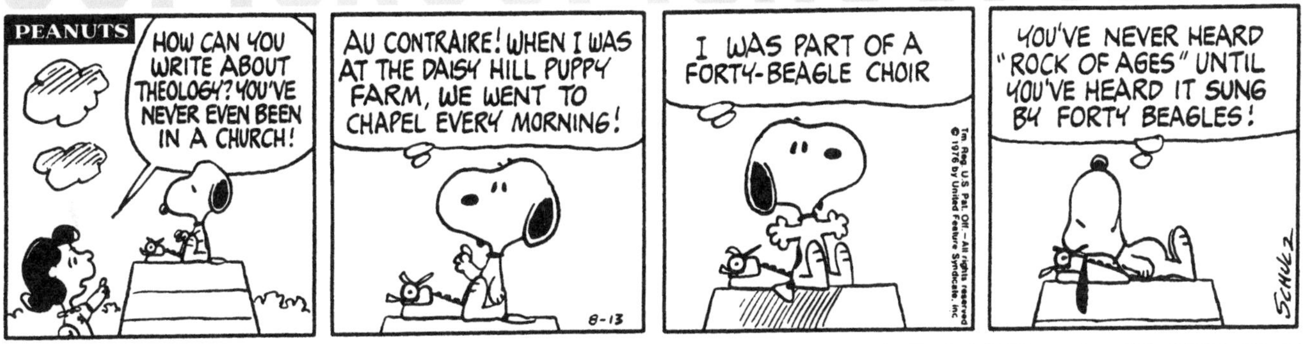
PEANUTS
HOW CAN YOU WRITE ABOUT THEOLOGY? YOU'VE NEVER EVEN BEEN IN A CHURCH!
AU CONTRAIRE! WHEN I WAS AT THE DAISY HILL PUPPY FARM, WE WENT TO CHAPEL EVERY MORNING!
8-13
I WAS PART OF A FORTY-BEAGLE CHOIR
Tm. Reg. U.S. Pat. Off.—All rights reserved © 1976 by United Feature Syndicate, Inc.
YOU'VE NEVER HEARD "ROCK OF AGES" UNTIL YOU'VE HEARD IT SUNG BY FORTY BEAGLES!
SCHULZ

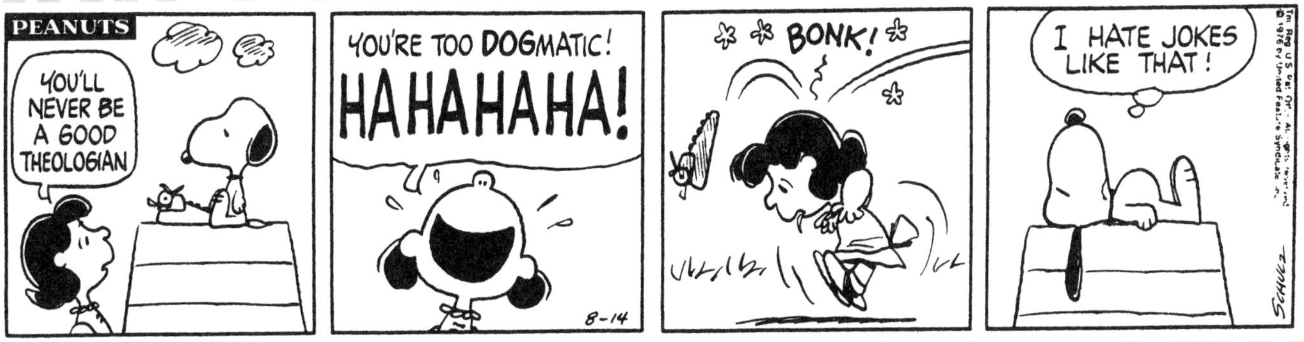
PEANUTS
YOU'LL NEVER BE A GOOD THEOLOGIAN
YOU'RE TOO DOGMATIC!
HAHAHAHA!
8-14
BONK!
I HATE JOKES LIKE THAT!
SCHULZ

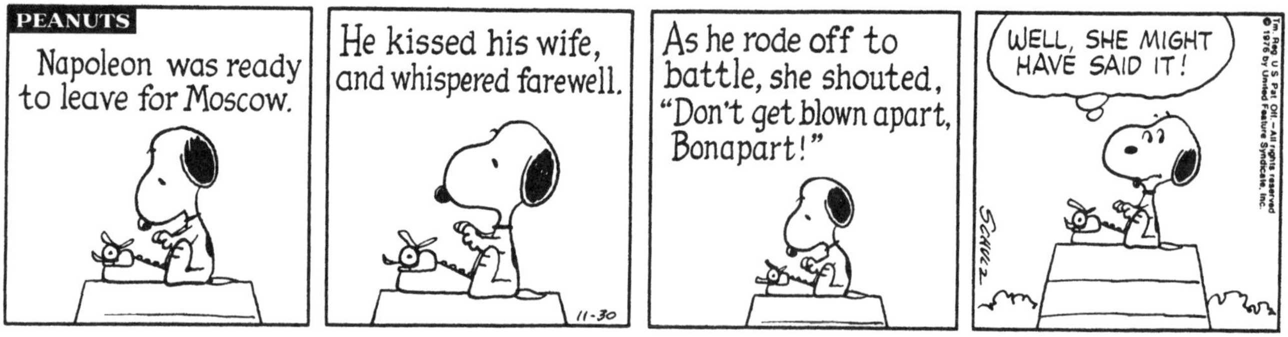
PEANUTS
Napoleon was ready to leave for Moscow.
He kissed his wife, and whispered farewell.
As he rode off to battle, she shouted, "Don't get blown apart, Bonapart!"
WELL, SHE MIGHT HAVE SAID IT!
SCHULZ
11-30
Tm. Reg U.S. Pat. Off.—All rights reserved © 1976 by United Feature Syndicate, Inc.

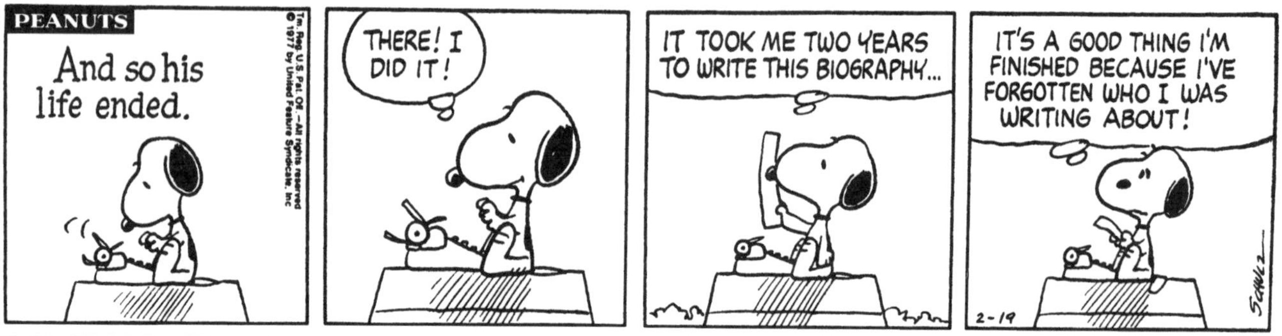
PEANUTS
And so his life ended.
Tm. Reg. U.S. Pat. Off.—All rights reserved © 1977 by United Feature Syndicate, Inc
THERE! I DID IT!
IT TOOK ME TWO YEARS TO WRITE THIS BIOGRAPHY...
IT'S A GOOD THING I'M FINISHED BECAUSE I'VE FORGOTTEN WHO I WAS WRITING ABOUT!
2-19
SCHULZ

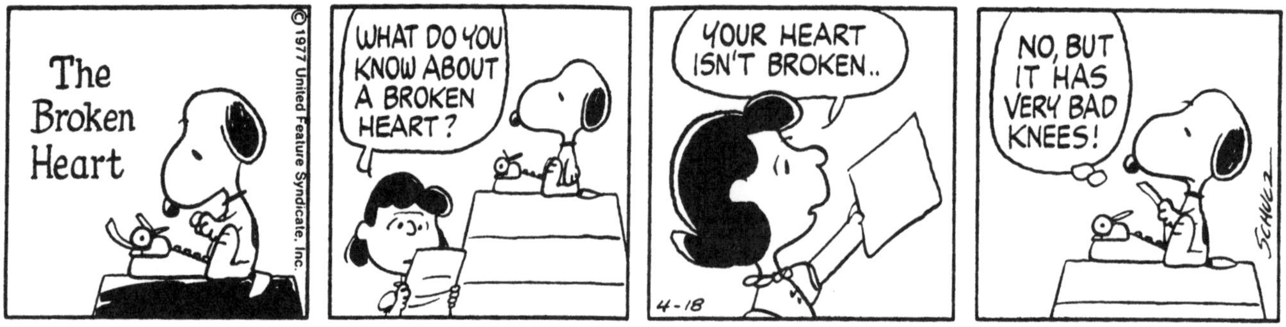
The Broken Heart
© 1977 United Feature Syndicate, Inc.
WHAT DO YOU KNOW ABOUT A BROKEN HEART?
YOUR HEART ISN'T BROKEN..
4-18
NO, BUT IT HAS VERY BAD KNEES!
SCHULZ

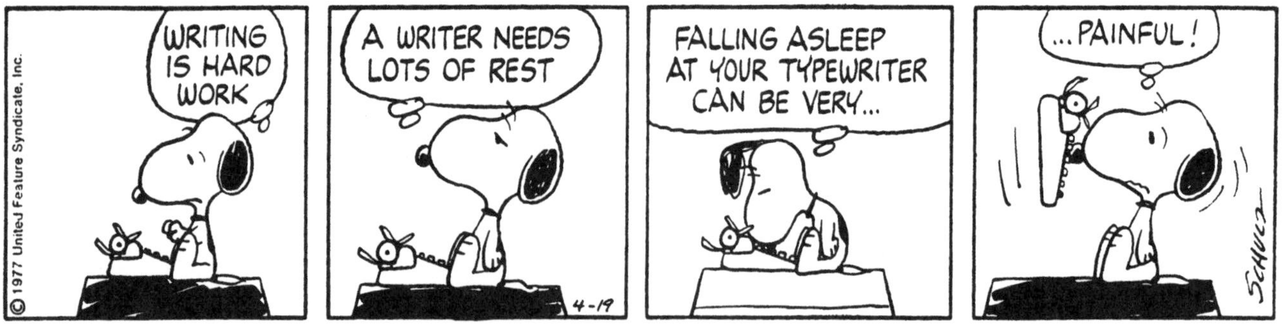
© 1977 United Feature Syndicate, Inc.
WRITING IS HARD WORK
A WRITER NEEDS LOTS OF REST
4-19
FALLING ASLEEP AT YOUR TYPEWRITER CAN BE VERY...
...PAINFUL!
SCHULZ

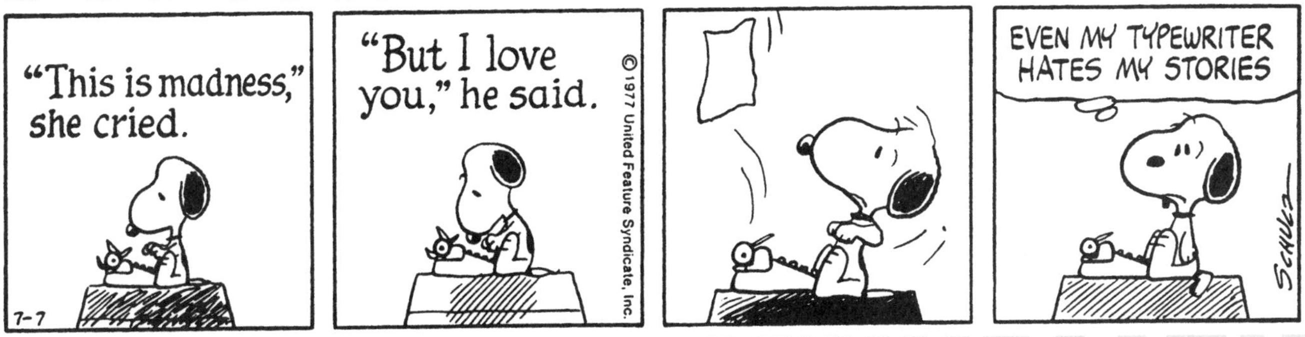
"This is madness," she cried.
7-7
"But I love you," he said.
© 1977 United Feature Syndicate, Inc.
EVEN MY TYPEWRITER HATES MY STORIES
SCHULZ

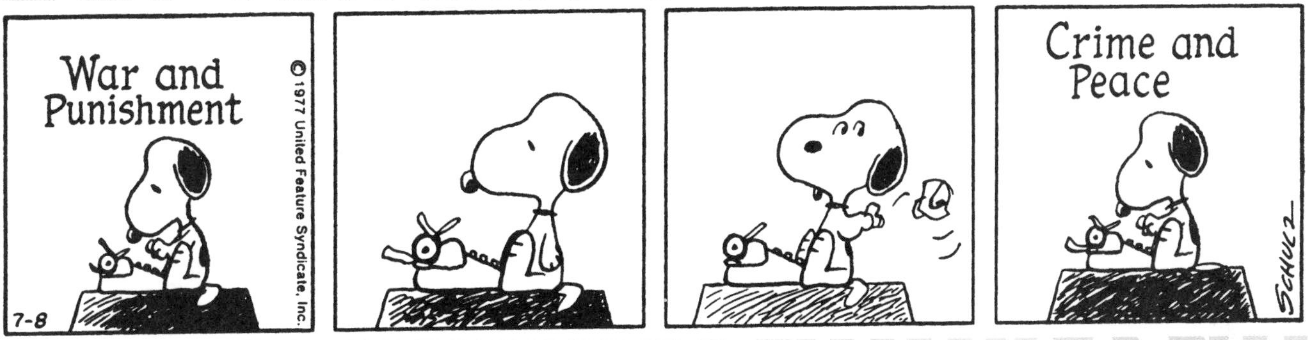
War and Punishment
7-8
© 1977 United Feature Syndicate, Inc.
Crime and Peace
SCHULZ

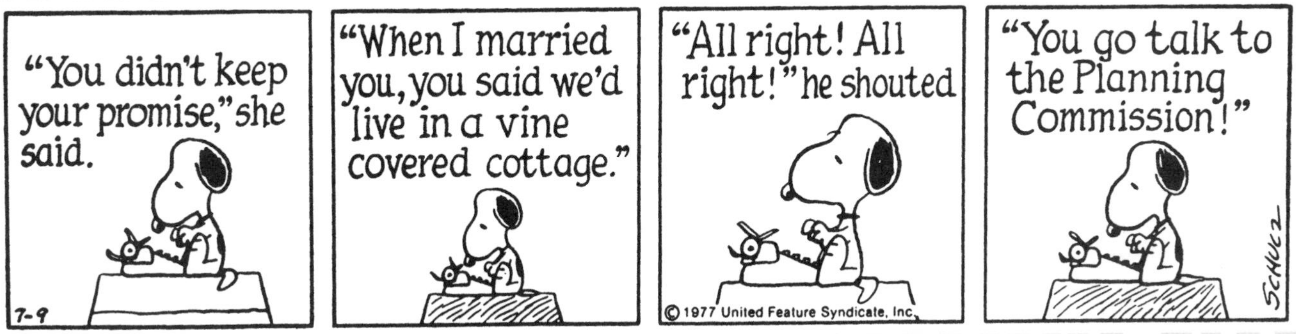
"You didn't keep your promise," she said.
7-9
"When I married you, you said we'd live in a vine covered cottage."
"All right! All right!" he shouted
© 1977 United Feature Syndicate, Inc.
"You go talk to the Planning Commission!"
SCHULZ

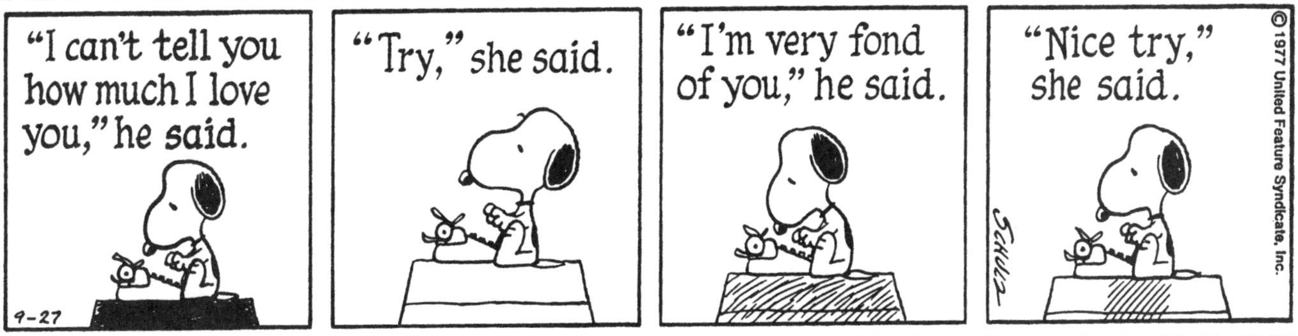
"I can't tell you how much I love you," he said.
9-27
"Try," she said.
"I'm very fond of you," he said.
SCHULZ
"Nice try," she said.
© 1977 United Feature Syndicate, Inc.

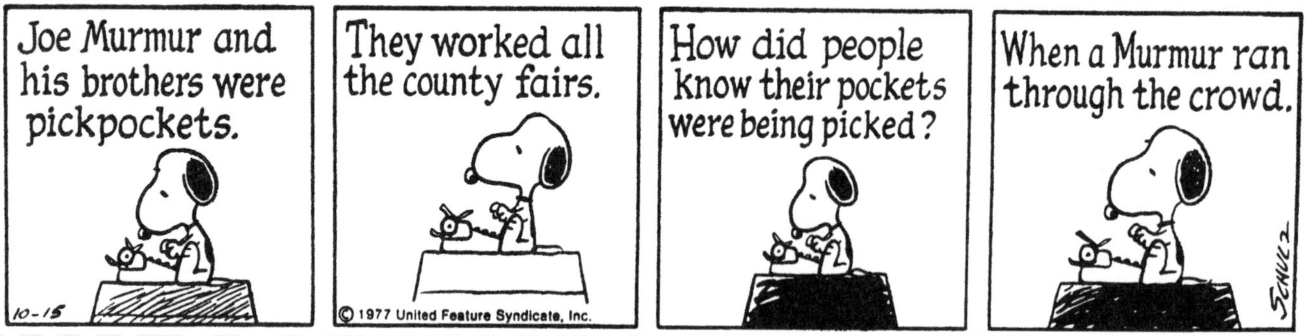
Joe Murmur and his brothers were pickpockets.
They worked all the county fairs.
How did people know their pockets were being picked?
When a Murmur ran through the crowd.
10-15
© 1977 United Feature Syndicate, Inc.
SCHULZ

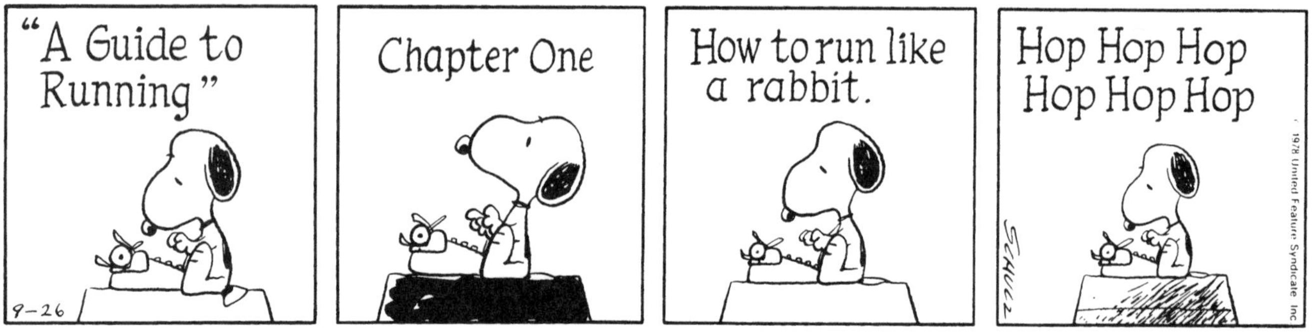
"A Guide to Running"
Chapter One
How to run like a rabbit.
Hop Hop Hop Hop Hop Hop
9-26
SCHULZ
© 1978 United Feature Syndicate, Inc.

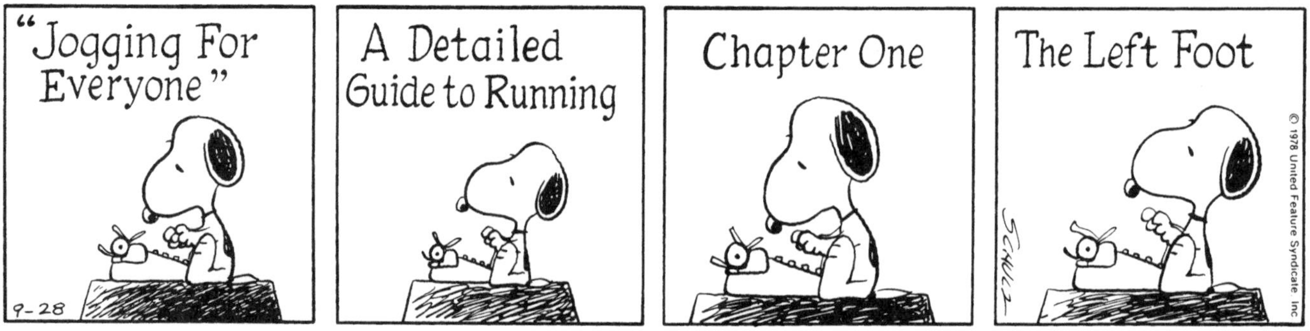
"Jogging For Everyone"
A Detailed Guide to Running
Chapter One
The Left Foot
9-28
SCHULZ
© 1978 United Feature Syndicate, Inc.

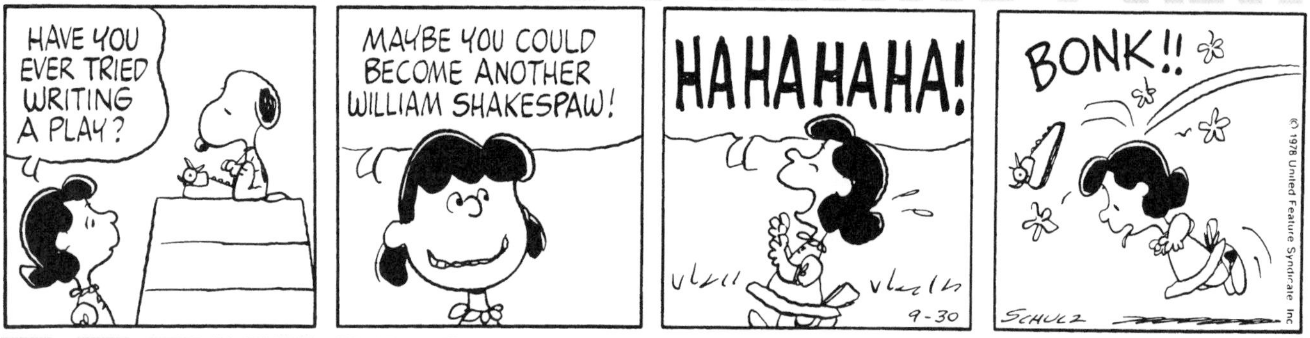
HAVE YOU EVER TRIED WRITING A PLAY?
MAYBE YOU COULD BECOME ANOTHER WILLIAM SHAKESPAW!
HAHAHAHA!
BONK!!
9-30
SCHULZ
© 1978 United Feature Syndicate, Inc.

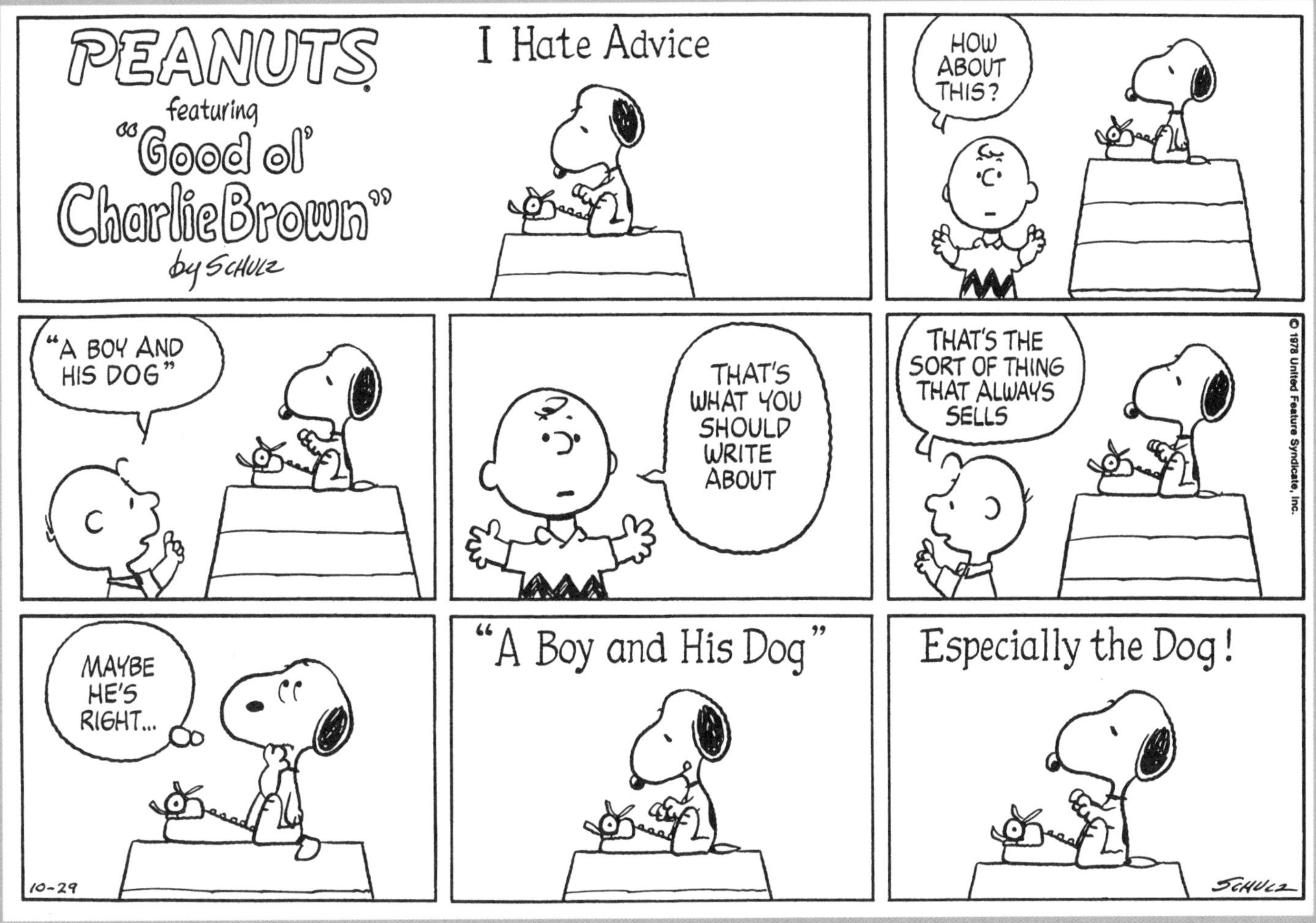
PEANUTS
featuring
"Good ol' CharlieBrown"
by SCHULZ
I Hate Advice
HOW ABOUT THIS?
"A BOY AND HIS DOG"
THAT'S WHAT YOU SHOULD WRITE ABOUT
THAT'S THE SORT OF THING THAT ALWAYS SELLS
© 1978 United Feature Syndicate, Inc.
MAYBE HE'S RIGHT...
10-29
"A Boy and His Dog"
Especially the Dog!
SCHULZ

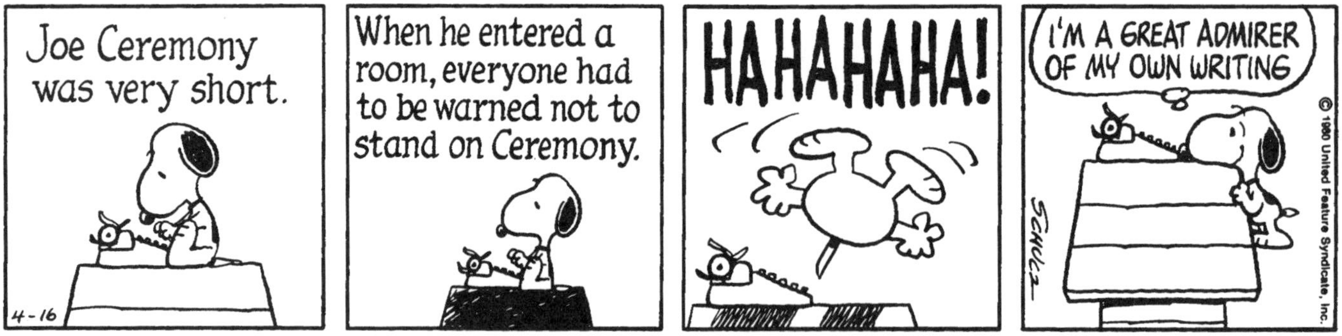
Joe Ceremony was very short.
4-16
When he entered a room, everyone had to be warned not to stand on Ceremony.
HAHAHAHA!
I'M A GREAT ADMIRER OF MY OWN WRITING
SCHULZ
© 1980 United Feature Syndicate, Inc.

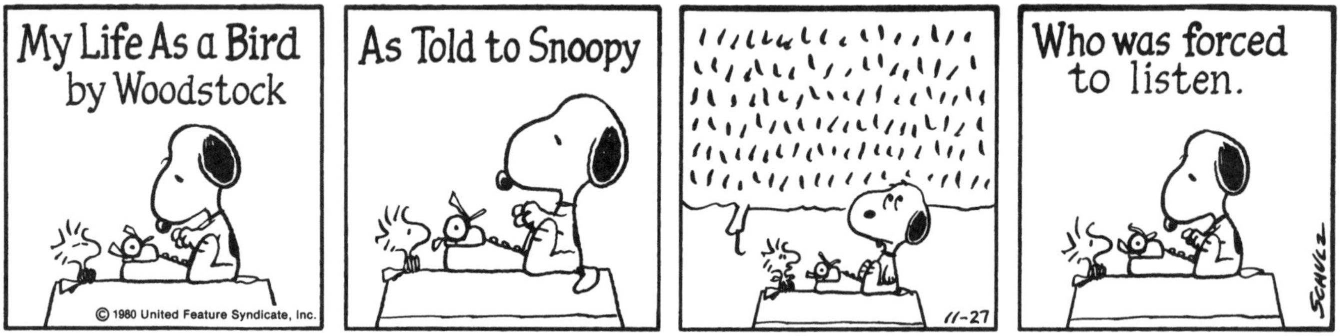
My Life As a Bird by Woodstock
© 1980 United Feature Syndicate, Inc.
As Told to Snoopy
11-27
Who was forced to listen.
SCHULZ

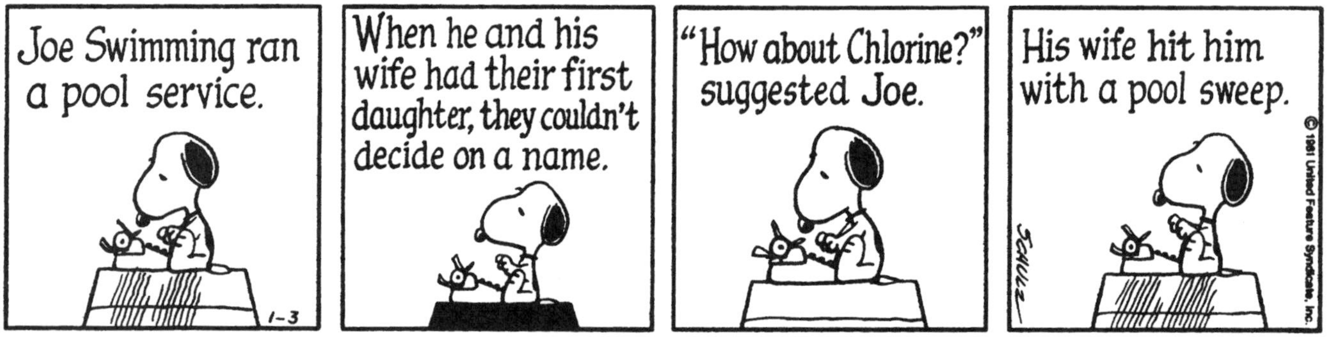
Joe Swimming ran a pool service.
1-3
When he and his wife had their first daughter, they couldn't decide on a name.
"How about Chlorine?" suggested Joe.
SCHULZ
His wife hit him with a pool sweep.
© 1981 United Feature Syndicate, Inc.

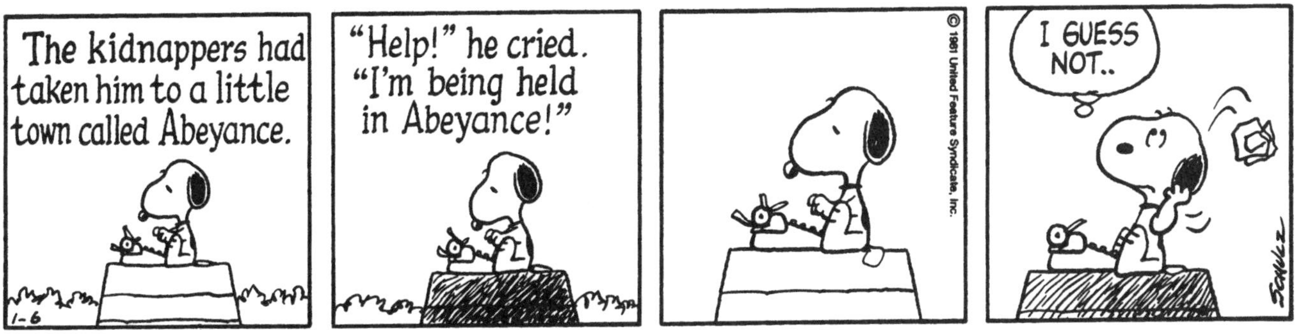
The kidnappers had taken him to a little town called Abeyance.
1-6
"Help!" he cried. "I'm being held in Abeyance!"
© 1981 United Feature Syndicate, Inc.
I GUESS NOT..
SCHULZ

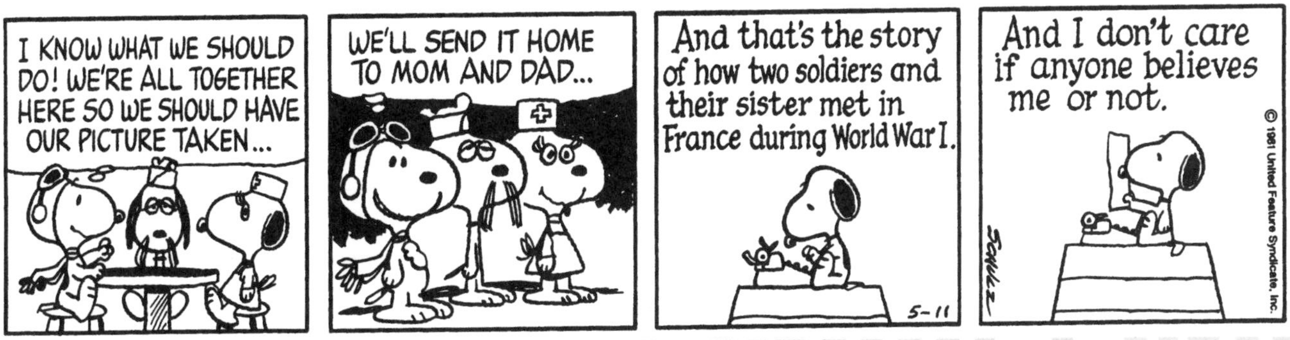
I KNOW WHAT WE SHOULD DO! WE'RE ALL TOGETHER HERE SO WE SHOULD HAVE OUR PICTURE TAKEN...
WE'LL SEND IT HOME TO MOM AND DAD...
And that's the story of how two soldiers and their sister met in France during World War I.
SCHULZ
5-11
And I don't care if anyone believes me or not.
© 1981 United Feature Syndicate, Inc.

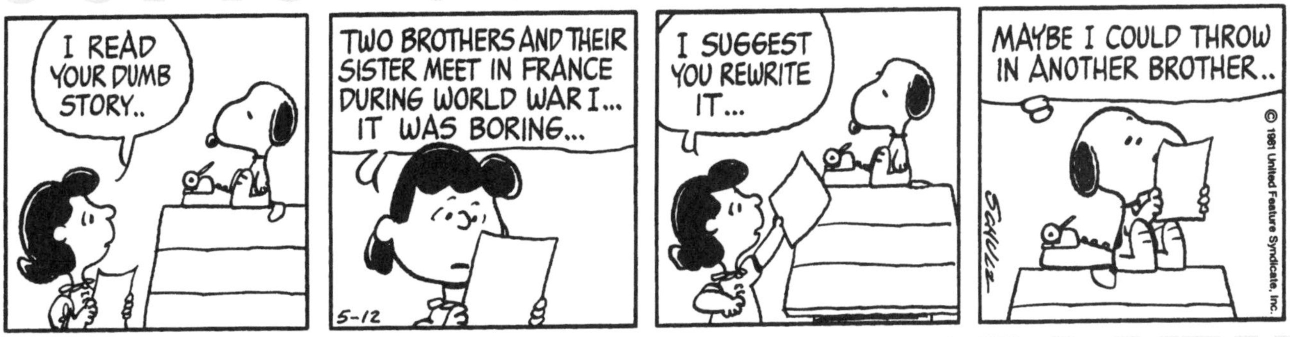
I READ YOUR DUMB STORY..
TWO BROTHERS AND THEIR SISTER MEET IN FRANCE DURING WORLD WAR I... IT WAS BORING...
5-12
I SUGGEST YOU REWRITE IT...
SCHULZ
MAYBE I COULD THROW IN ANOTHER BROTHER..
© 1981 United Feature Syndicate, Inc.

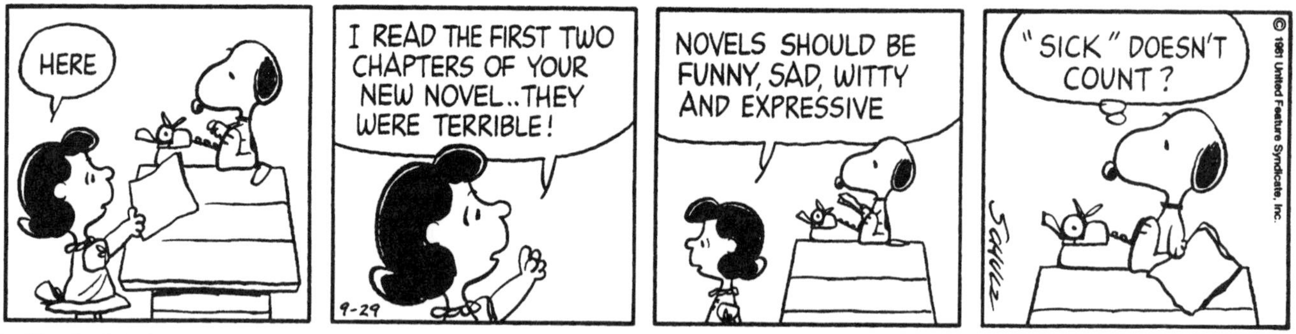
HERE
I READ THE FIRST TWO CHAPTERS OF YOUR NEW NOVEL..THEY WERE TERRIBLE!
NOVELS SHOULD BE FUNNY, SAD, WITTY AND EXPRESSIVE
"SICK" DOESN'T COUNT?
© 1981 United Feature Syndicate, Inc.

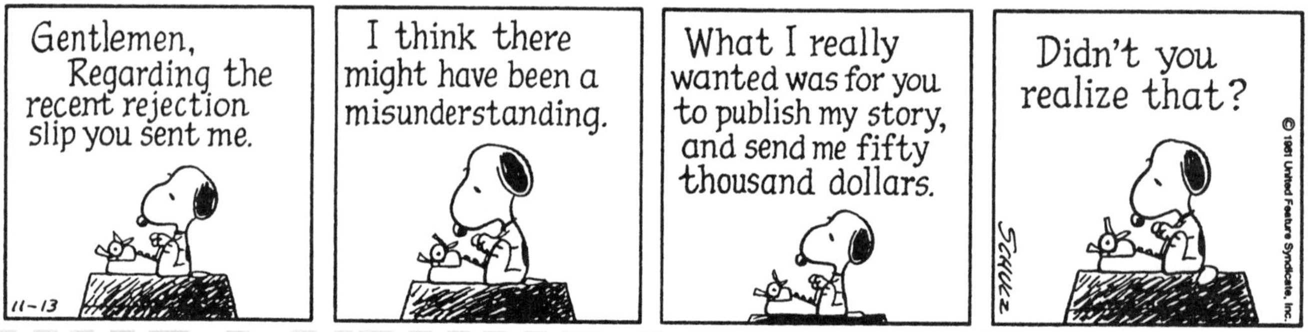
Gentlemen,
Regarding the recent rejection slip you sent me.
I think there might have been a misunderstanding.
What I really wanted was for you to publish my story, and send me fifty thousand dollars.
Didn't you realize that?
© 1981 United Feature Syndicate, Inc.

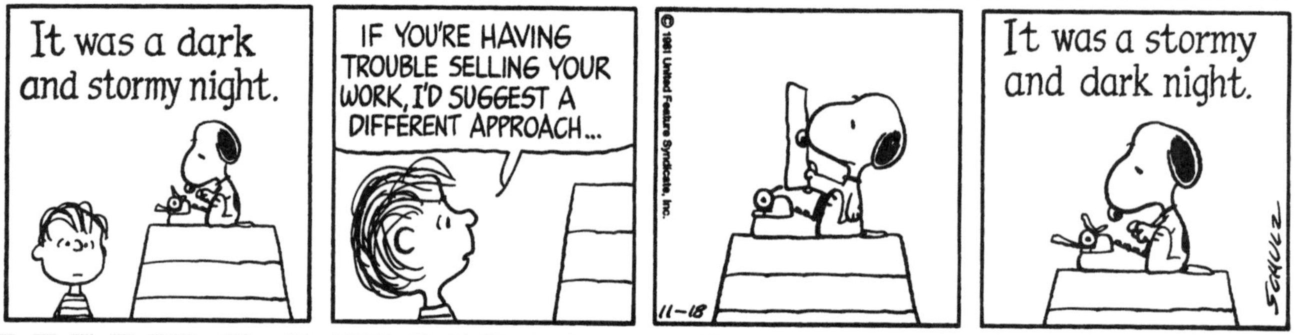
It was a dark and stormy night.
IF YOU'RE HAVING TROUBLE SELLING YOUR WORK, I'D SUGGEST A DIFFERENT APPROACH...
© 1981 United Feature Syndicate, Inc.
It was a stormy and dark night.

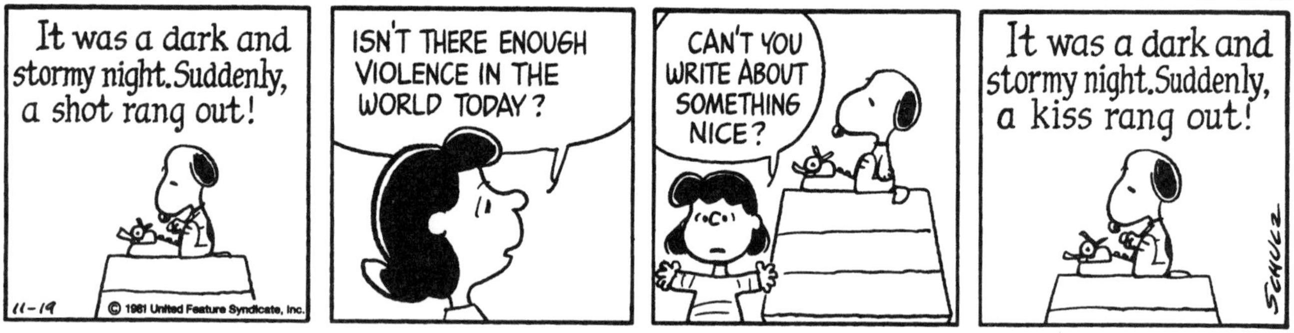
It was a dark and stormy night. Suddenly, a shot rang out!
© 1981 United Feature Syndicate, Inc.
ISN'T THERE ENOUGH VIOLENCE IN THE WORLD TODAY?
CAN'T YOU WRITE ABOUT SOMETHING NICE?
It was a dark and stormy night. Suddenly, a kiss rang out!

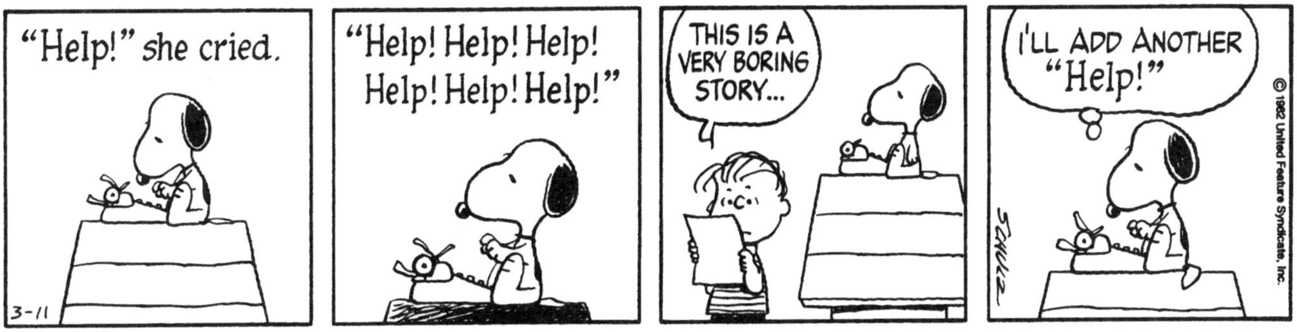
"Help!" she cried.
3-11
"Help! Help! Help! Help! Help! Help!"
THIS IS A VERY BORING STORY...
I'LL ADD ANOTHER "Help!"
© 1982 United Feature Syndicate, Inc.
SCHULZ

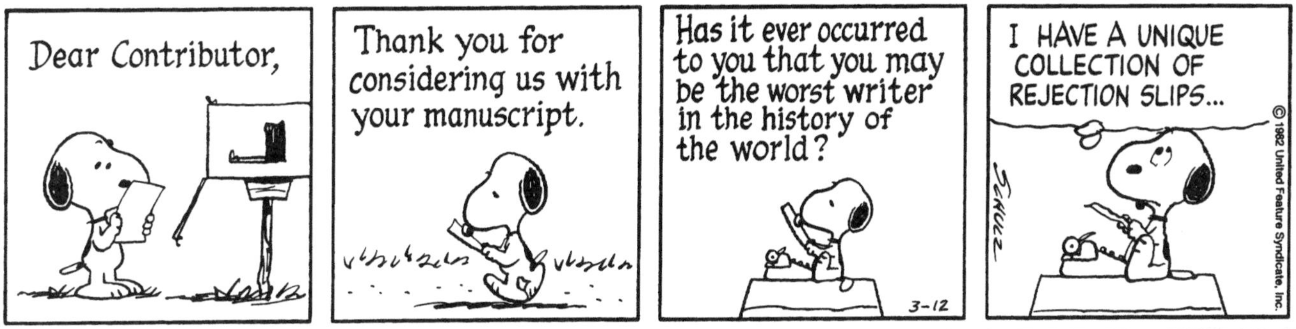
Dear Contributor,
Thank you for considering us with your manuscript.
Has it ever occurred to you that you may be the worst writer in the history of the world?
3-12
I HAVE A UNIQUE COLLECTION OF REJECTION SLIPS...
© 1982 United Feature Syndicate, Inc.
SCHULZ

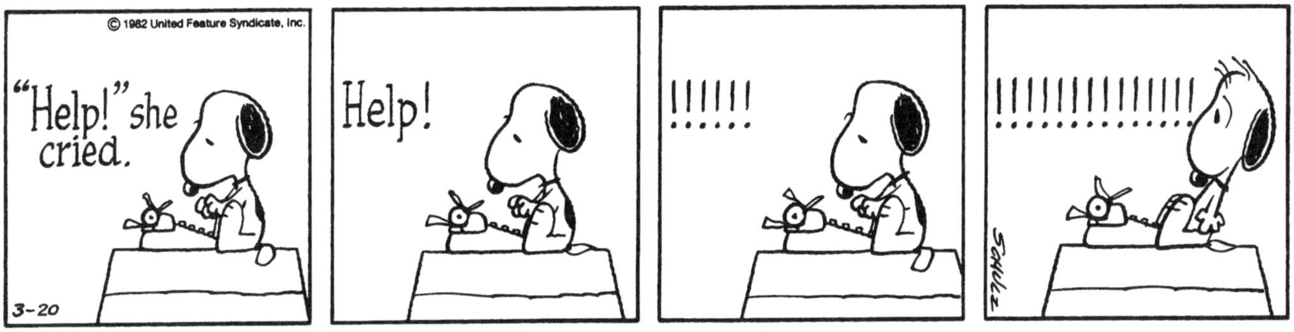
© 1982 United Feature Syndicate, Inc.
"Help!" she cried.
3-20
Help!
!!!!!!
!!!!!!!!!!!!!!
SCHULZ

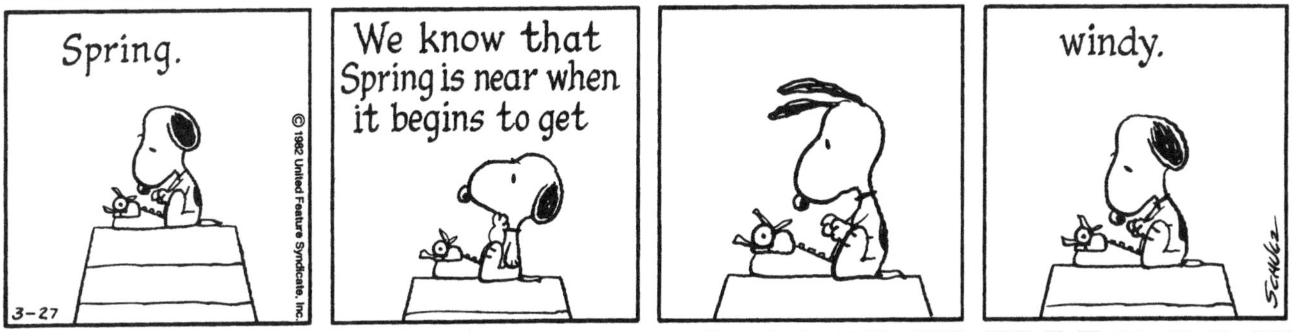
Spring.
3-27
© 1982 United Feature Syndicate, Inc.
We know that Spring is near when it begins to get
windy.
SCHULZ

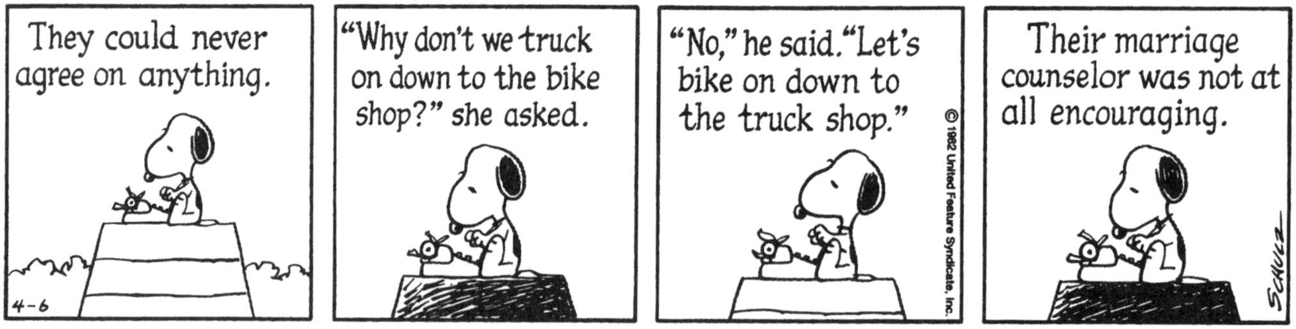
They could never agree on anything.
4-6
"Why don't we truck on down to the bike shop?" she asked.
"No," he said. "Let's bike on down to the truck shop."
© 1982 United Feature Syndicate, Inc.
Their marriage counselor was not at all encouraging.
SCHULZ

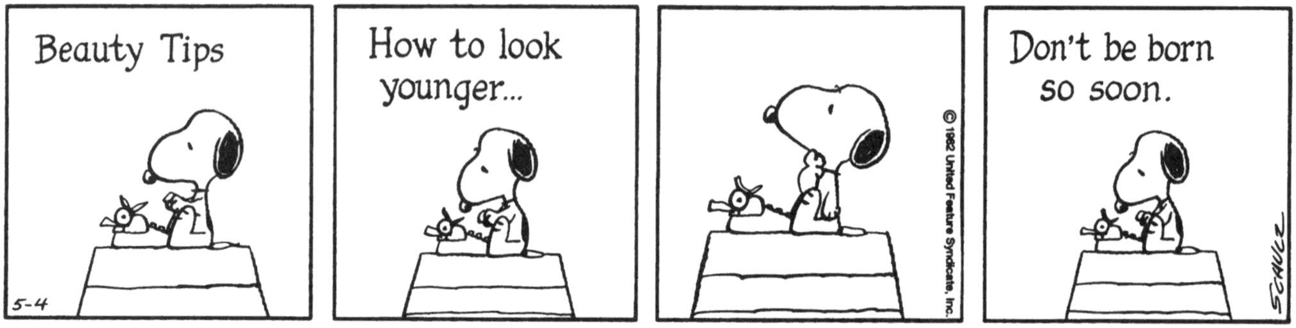
Beauty Tips
5-4
How to look younger...
© 1982 United Feature Syndicate, Inc.
Don't be born so soon.
SCHULZ

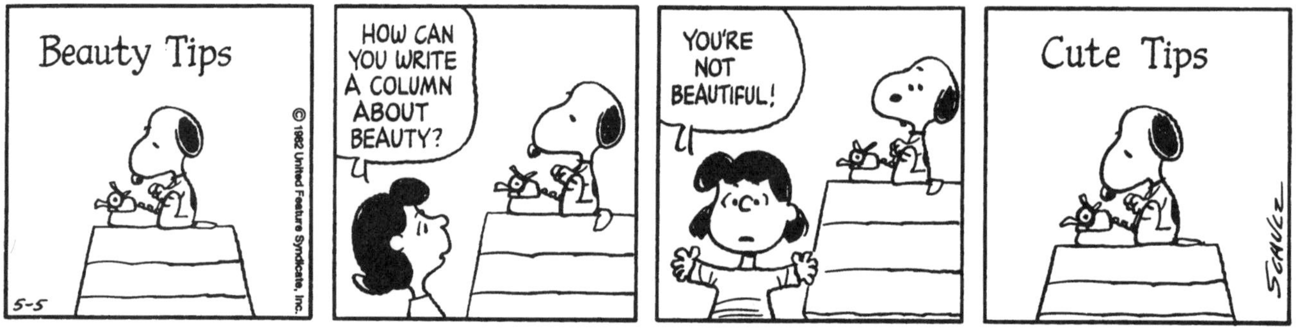
Beauty Tips
5-5
© 1982 United Feature Syndicate, Inc.
HOW CAN YOU WRITE A COLUMN ABOUT BEAUTY?
YOU'RE NOT BEAUTIFUL!
Cute Tips
SCHULZ

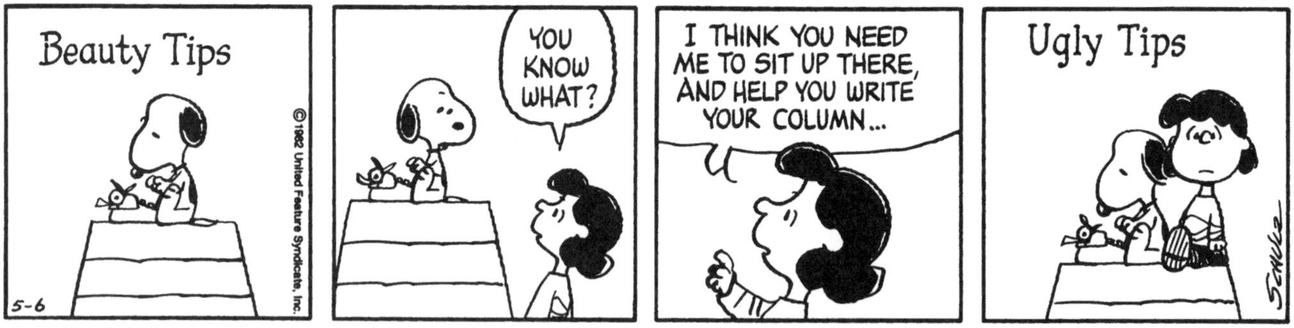
Beauty Tips
5-6
© 1982 United Feature Syndicate, Inc.
YOU KNOW WHAT?
I THINK YOU NEED ME TO SIT UP THERE, AND HELP YOU WRITE YOUR COLUMN...
Ugly Tips
SCHULZ

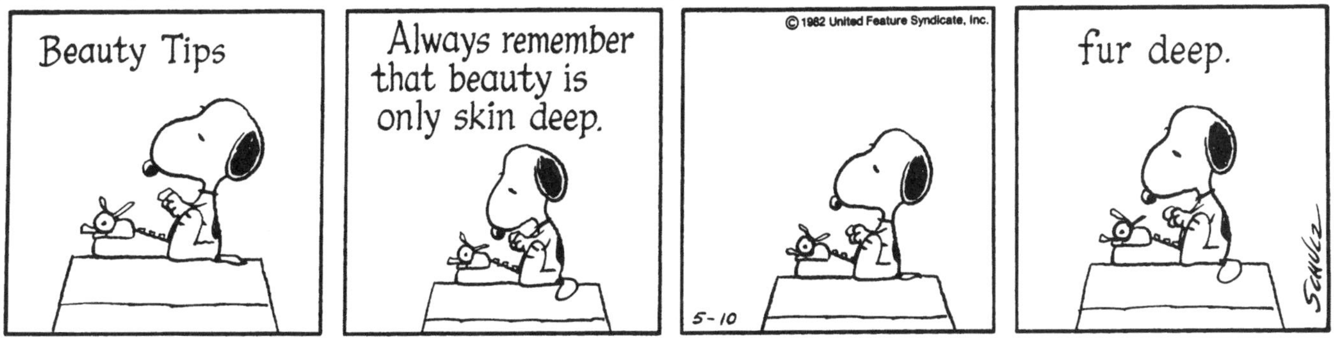
Beauty Tips
Always remember that beauty is only skin deep.
© 1982 United Feature Syndicate, Inc.
5-10
fur deep.
SCHULZ

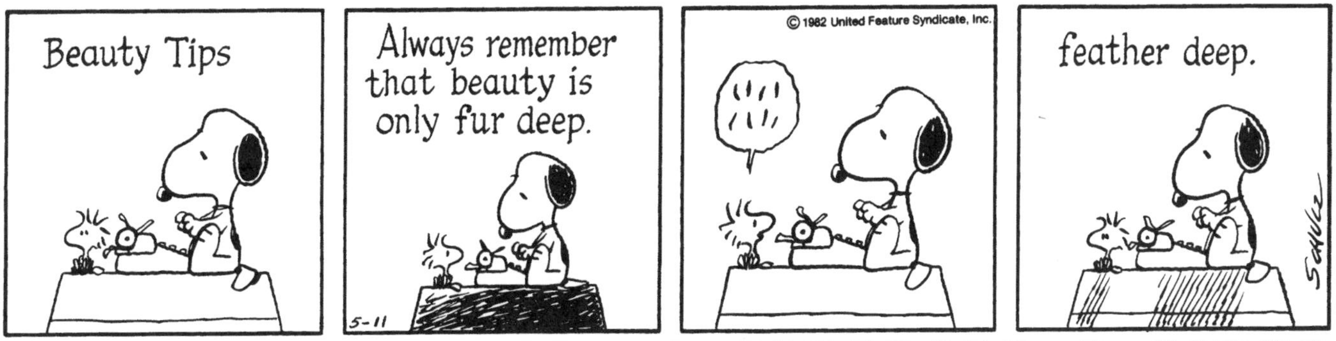
Beauty Tips
Always remember that beauty is only fur deep.
5-11
© 1982 United Feature Syndicate, Inc.
feather deep.
SCHULZ

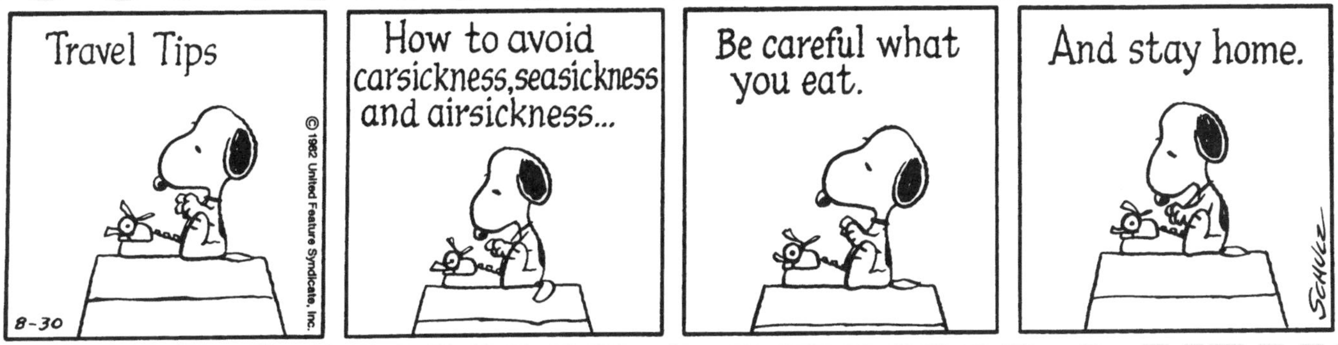
Travel Tips
8-30
© 1982 United Feature Syndicate, Inc.
How to avoid carsickness,seasickness and airsickness...
Be careful what you eat.
And stay home.
SCHULZ

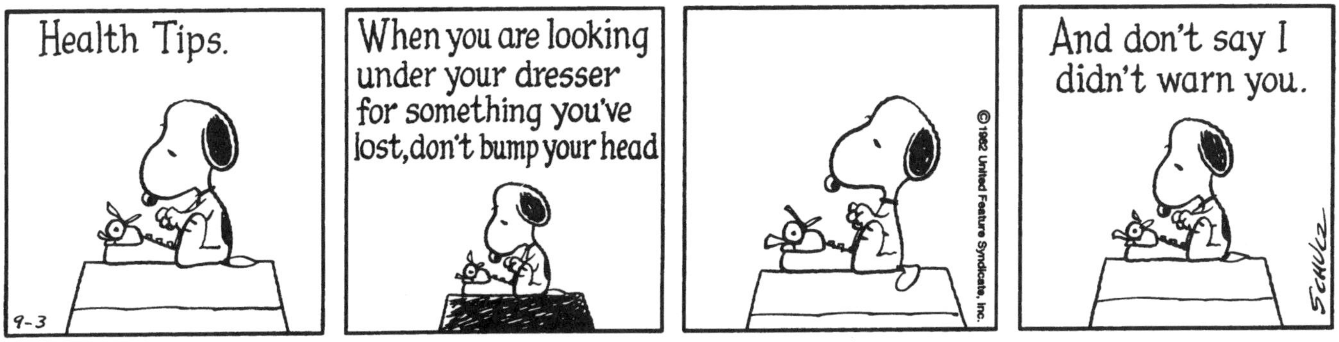
Health Tips.
9-3
When you are looking under your dresser for something you've lost,don't bump your head
© 1982 United Feature Syndicate, Inc.
And don't say I didn't warn you.
SCHULZ

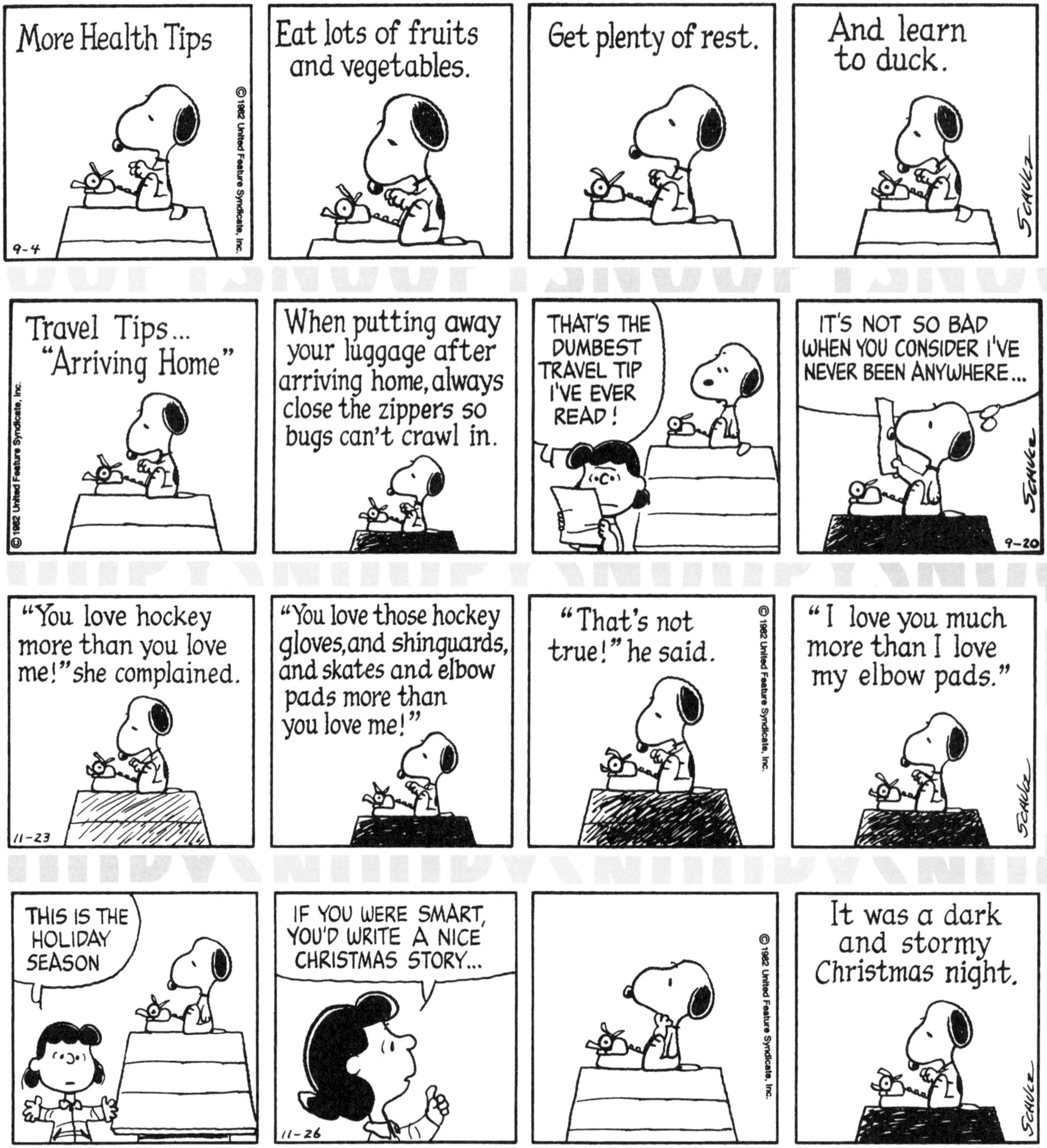
More Health Tips
© 1982 United Feature Syndicate, Inc.
9-4
Eat lots of fruits and vegetables.
Get plenty of rest.
And learn to duck.
SCHULZ
Travel Tips... "Arriving Home"
© 1982 United Feature Syndicate, Inc.
When putting away your luggage after arriving home, always close the zippers so bugs can't crawl in.
THAT'S THE DUMBEST TRAVEL TIP I'VE EVER READ!
IT'S NOT SO BAD WHEN YOU CONSIDER I'VE NEVER BEEN ANYWHERE...
SCHULZ
9-20
"You love hockey more than you love me!" she complained.
11-23
"You love those hockey gloves, and shinguards, and skates and elbow pads more than you love me!"
"That's not true!" he said.
© 1982 United Feature Syndicate, Inc.
"I love you much more than I love my elbow pads."
SCHULZ
THIS IS THE HOLIDAY SEASON
IF YOU WERE SMART, YOU'D WRITE A NICE CHRISTMAS STORY...
11-26
© 1982 United Feature Syndicate, Inc.
It was a dark and stormy Christmas night.
SCHULZ

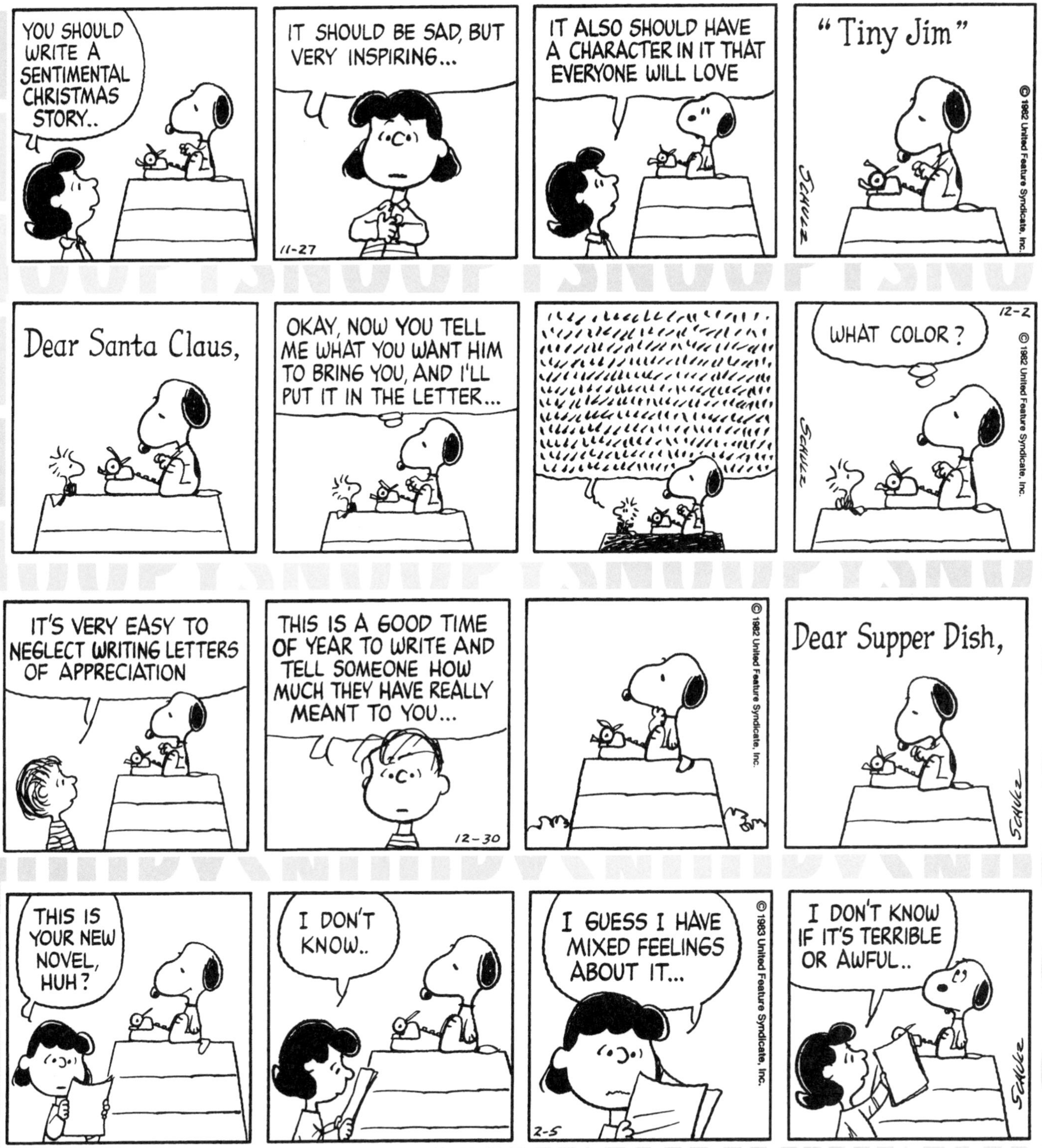

YOU SHOULD WRITE A SENTIMENTAL CHRISTMAS STORY..
IT SHOULD BE SAD, BUT VERY INSPIRING...
11-27
IT ALSO SHOULD HAVE A CHARACTER IN IT THAT EVERYONE WILL LOVE
"Tiny Jim"
SCHULZ
© 1982 United Feature Syndicate, Inc.
Dear Santa Claus,
OKAY, NOW YOU TELL ME WHAT YOU WANT HIM TO BRING YOU, AND I'LL PUT IT IN THE LETTER...
SCHULZ
WHAT COLOR?
12-2
© 1982 United Feature Syndicate, Inc.
IT'S VERY EASY TO NEGLECT WRITING LETTERS OF APPRECIATION
THIS IS A GOOD TIME OF YEAR TO WRITE AND TELL SOMEONE HOW MUCH THEY HAVE REALLY MEANT TO YOU...
12-30
© 1982 United Feature Syndicate, Inc.
Dear Supper Dish,
SCHULZ
THIS IS YOUR NEW NOVEL, HUH?
I DON'T KNOW..
I GUESS I HAVE MIXED FEELINGS ABOUT IT...
2-5
© 1983 United Feature Syndicate, Inc.
I DON'T KNOW IF IT'S TERRIBLE OR AWFUL..
SCHULZ

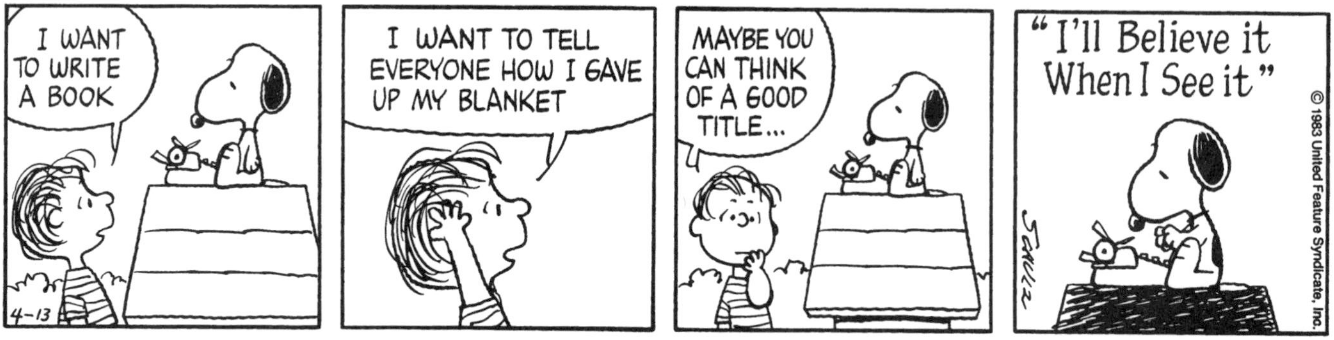
I WANT TO WRITE A BOOK
4-13
I WANT TO TELL EVERYONE HOW I GAVE UP MY BLANKET
MAYBE YOU CAN THINK OF A GOOD TITLE...
"I'll Believe it When I See it"
© 1983 United Feature Syndicate, Inc.
SCHULZ

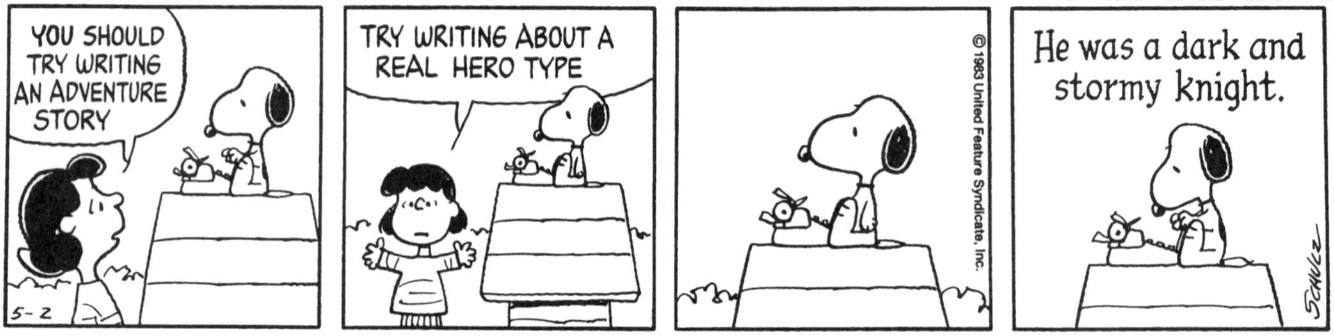
YOU SHOULD TRY WRITING AN ADVENTURE STORY
5-2
TRY WRITING ABOUT A REAL HERO TYPE
© 1983 United Feature Syndicate, Inc.
He was a dark and stormy knight.
SCHULZ

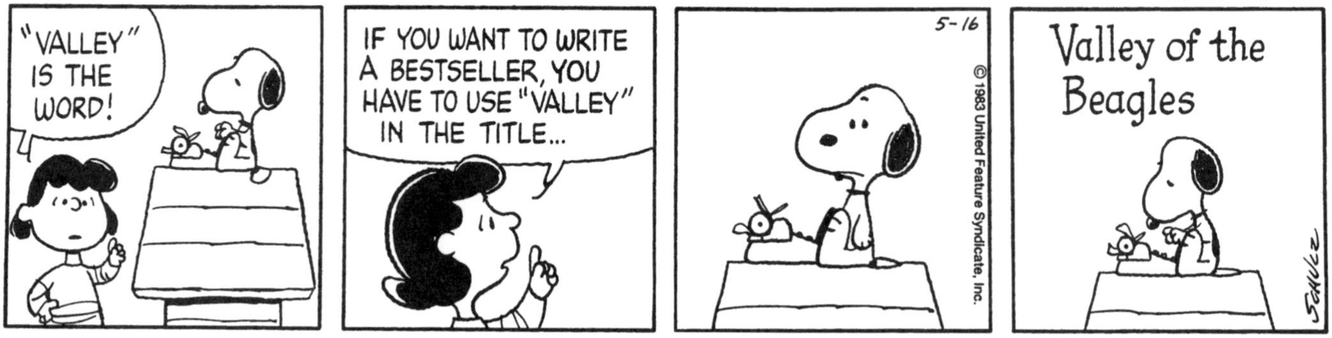
"VALLEY" IS THE WORD!
IF YOU WANT TO WRITE A BESTSELLER, YOU HAVE TO USE "VALLEY" IN THE TITLE...
5-16
© 1983 United Feature Syndicate, Inc.
Valley of the Beagles
SCHULZ

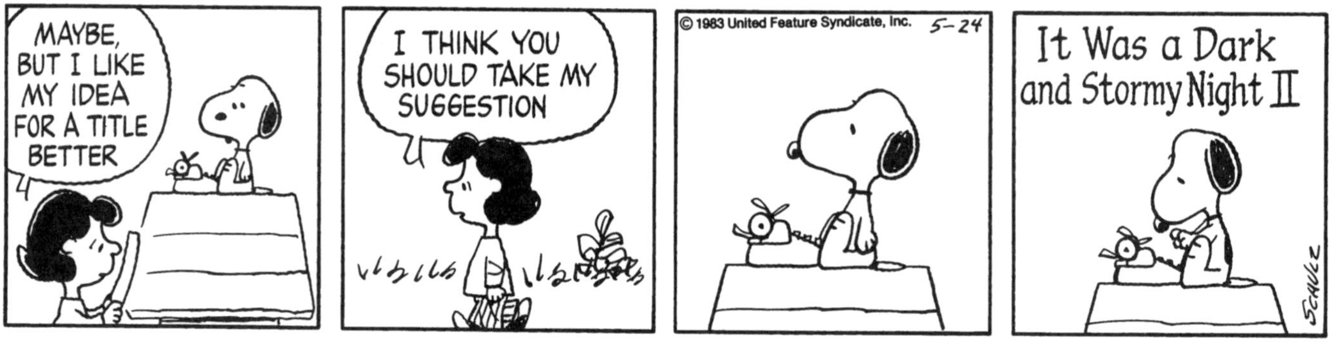
MAYBE, BUT I LIKE MY IDEA FOR A TITLE BETTER
I THINK YOU SHOULD TAKE MY SUGGESTION
© 1983 United Feature Syndicate, Inc.
5-24
It Was a Dark and Stormy Night II
SCHULZ

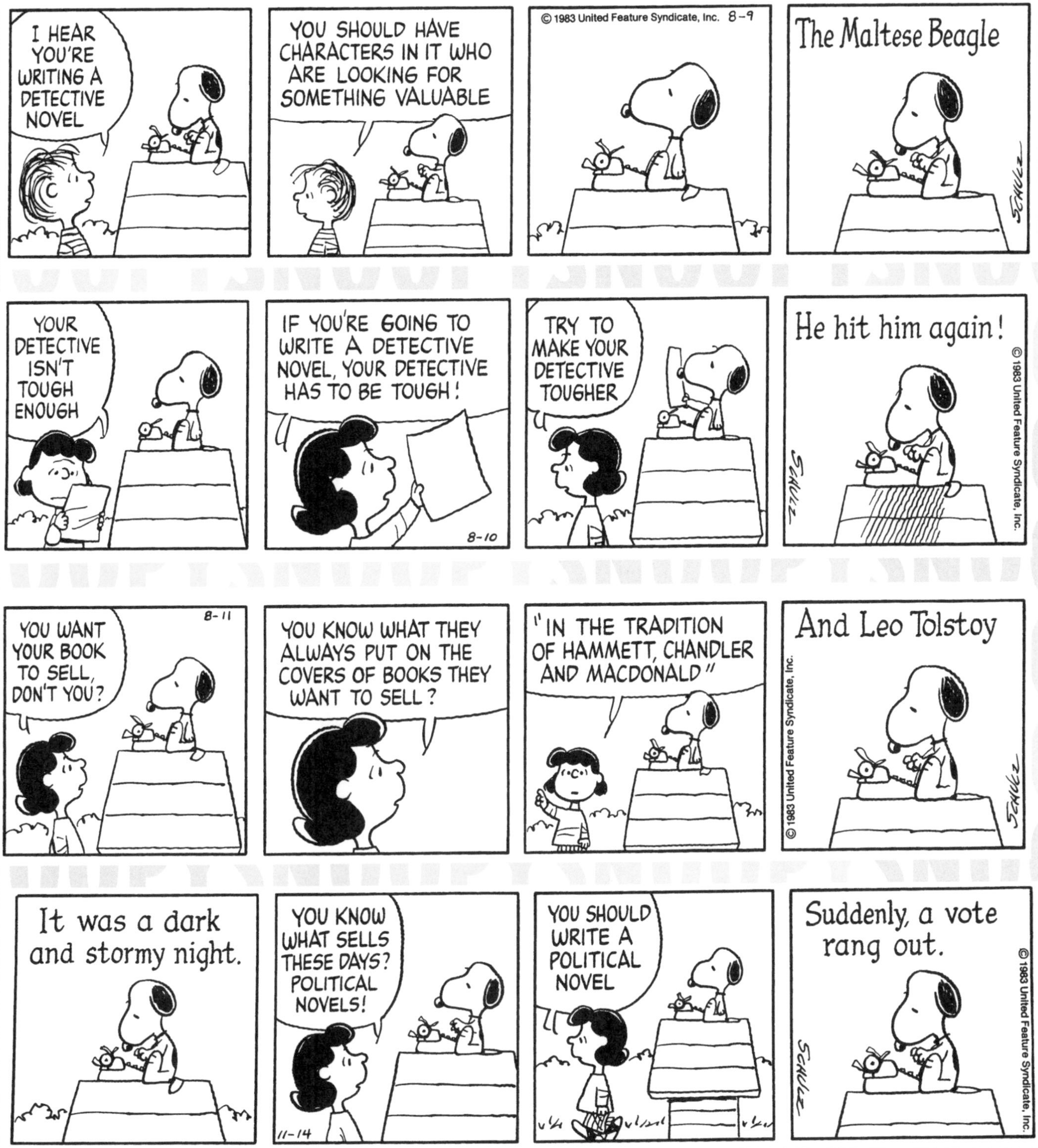
I HEAR YOU'RE WRITING A DETECTIVE NOVEL
YOU SHOULD HAVE CHARACTERS IN IT WHO ARE LOOKING FOR SOMETHING VALUABLE
© 1983 United Feature Syndicate, Inc. 8-9
The Maltese Beagle
SCHULZ
YOUR DETECTIVE ISN'T TOUGH ENOUGH
IF YOU'RE GOING TO WRITE A DETECTIVE NOVEL, YOUR DETECTIVE HAS TO BE TOUGH!
8-10
TRY TO MAKE YOUR DETECTIVE TOUGHER
SCHULZ
He hit him again!
© 1983 United Feature Syndicate, Inc.
8-11
YOU WANT YOUR BOOK TO SELL, DON'T YOU?
YOU KNOW WHAT THEY ALWAYS PUT ON THE COVERS OF BOOKS THEY WANT TO SELL?
"IN THE TRADITION OF HAMMETT, CHANDLER AND MACDONALD"
© 1983 United Feature Syndicate, Inc.
And Leo Tolstoy
SCHULZ
It was a dark and stormy night.
YOU KNOW WHAT SELLS THESE DAYS? POLITICAL NOVELS!
11-14
YOU SHOULD WRITE A POLITICAL NOVEL
SCHULZ
Suddenly, a vote rang out.
© 1983 United Feature Syndicate, Inc.

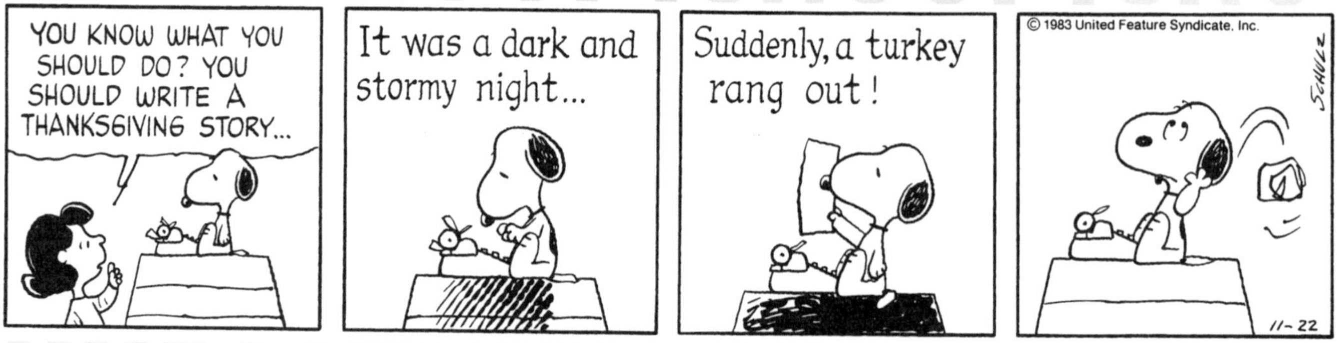
YOU KNOW WHAT YOU SHOULD DO? YOU SHOULD WRITE A THANKSGIVING STORY...
It was a dark and stormy night...
Suddenly, a turkey rang out!
© 1983 United Feature Syndicate, Inc.
SCHULZ
11-22

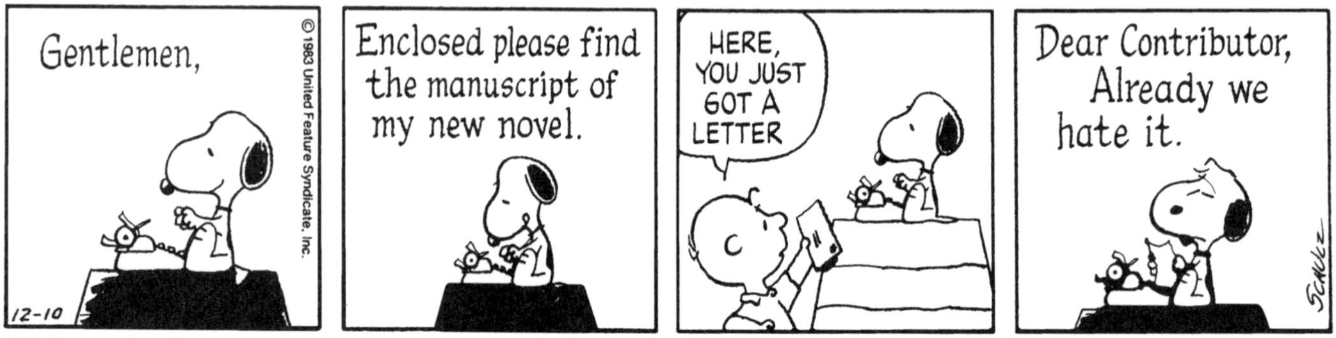
Gentlemen,
© 1983 United Feature Syndicate, Inc.
12-10
Enclosed please find the manuscript of my new novel.
HERE, YOU JUST GOT A LETTER
Dear Contributor, Already we hate it.
SCHULZ

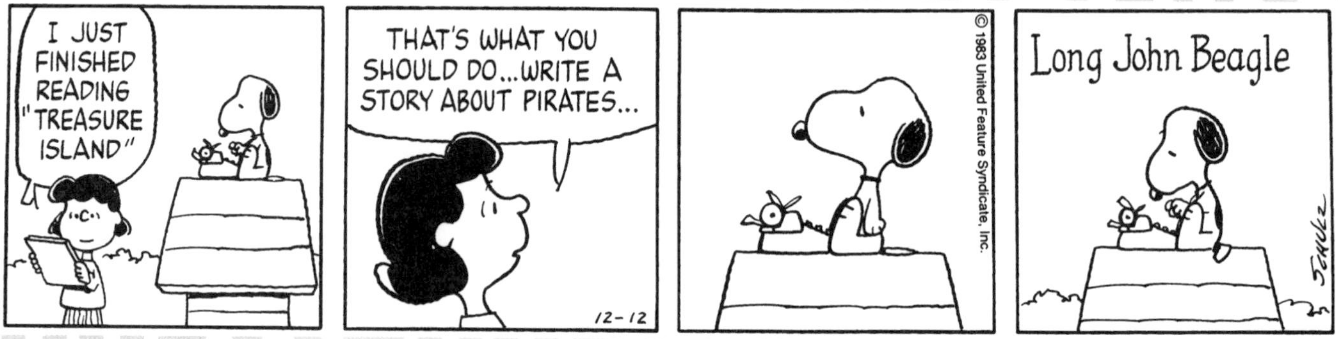
I JUST FINISHED READING "TREASURE ISLAND"
THAT'S WHAT YOU SHOULD DO...WRITE A STORY ABOUT PIRATES...
12-12
© 1983 United Feature Syndicate, Inc.
Long John Beagle
SCHULZ

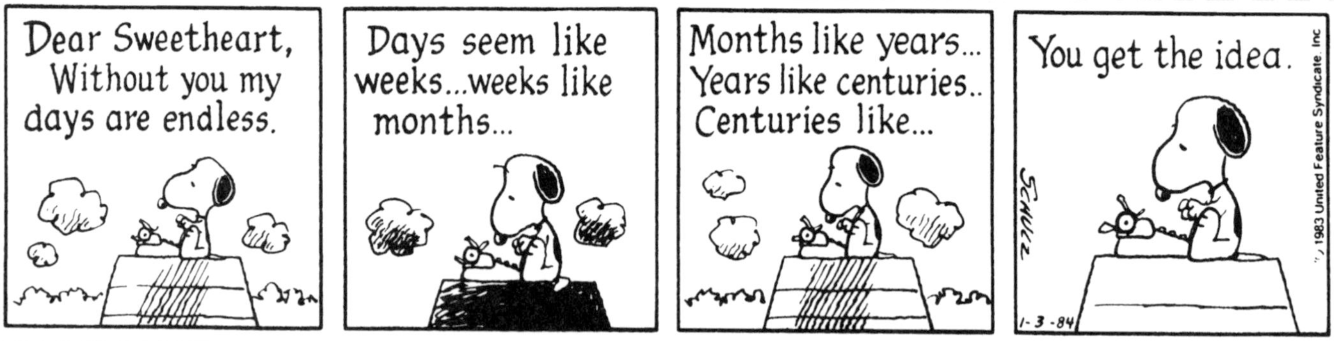
Dear Sweetheart, Without you my days are endless.
Days seem like weeks...weeks like months...
Months like years... Years like centuries.. Centuries like...
SCHULZ
1-3-84
You get the idea.
© 1983 United Feature Syndicate, Inc.

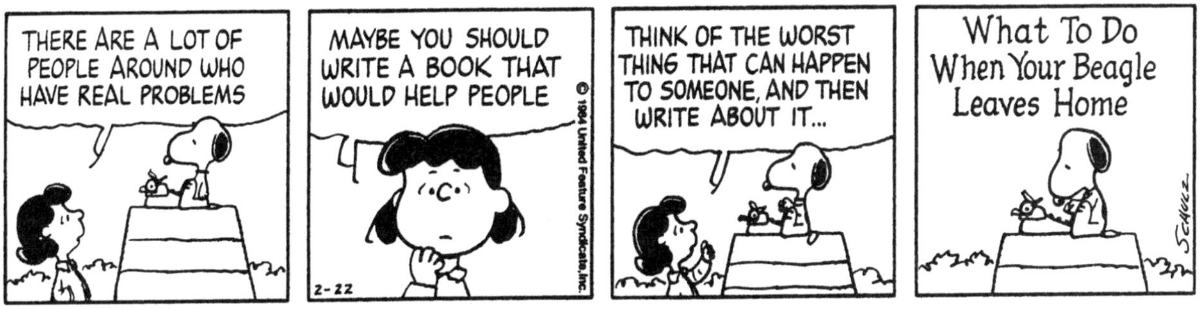
THERE ARE A LOT OF PEOPLE AROUND WHO HAVE REAL PROBLEMS
MAYBE YOU SHOULD WRITE A BOOK THAT WOULD HELP PEOPLE
2-22
© 1984 United Feature Syndicate,Inc.
THINK OF THE WORST THING THAT CAN HAPPEN TO SOMEONE, AND THEN WRITE ABOUT IT...
What To Do When Your Beagle Leaves Home
SCHULZ

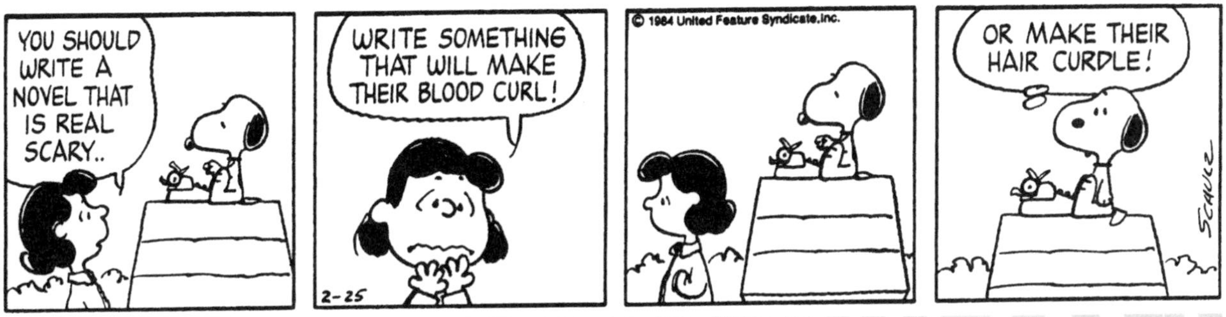
YOU SHOULD WRITE A NOVEL THAT IS REAL SCARY..
WRITE SOMETHING THAT WILL MAKE THEIR BLOOD CURL!
2-25
© 1984 United Feature Syndicate,Inc.
OR MAKE THEIR HAIR CURDLE!
SCHULZ

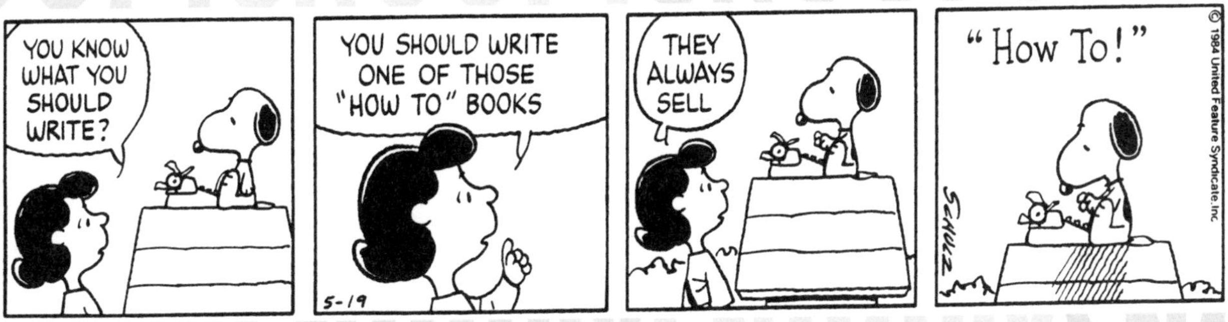
YOU KNOW WHAT YOU SHOULD WRITE?
YOU SHOULD WRITE ONE OF THOSE "HOW TO" BOOKS
5-19
THEY ALWAYS SELL
SCHULZ
"How To!"
© 1984 United Feature Syndicate,Inc.

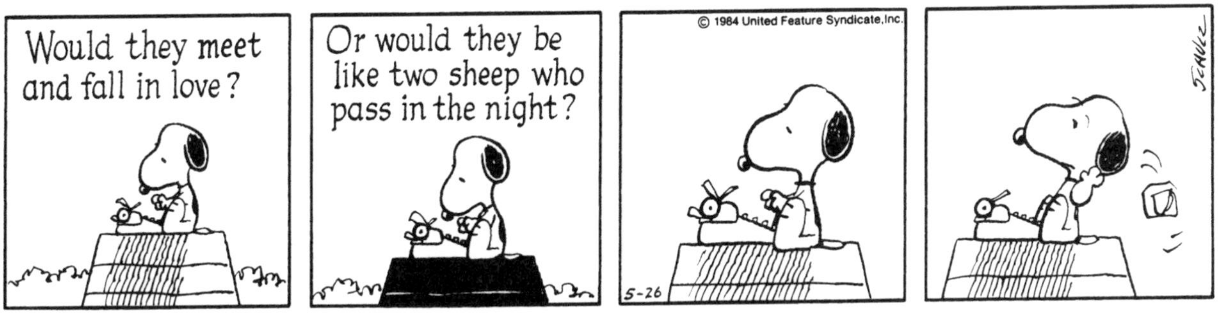
Would they meet and fall in love?
Or would they be like two sheep who pass in the night?
© 1984 United Feature Syndicate,Inc.
5-26
SCHULZ

LISTEN TO THIS..
IT'S A REVIEW OF YOUR LATEST NOVEL
YOUR WRITING HAS BEEN COMPARED TO FAULKNER AND HEMINGWAY...
8-28
UNFAVORABLY!
SCHULZ
© 1984 United Feature Syndicate, Inc.

As she climbed into the carriage, he waved goodbye.
"HE WAVED GOODBYE"?
© 1984 United Feature Syndicate, Inc.
YOU CALL THAT ROMANTIC?!
10-3
He also said, "Have a nice day!"
SCHULZ

It was a crowded room. He was lonely. Then he saw her...
11-20
Their eyes met... Five minutes later they were married.
THAT'S THE DUMBEST THING I'VE EVER READ
SCHULZ
I LIKE QUICK ROMANCES..
© 1984 United Feature Syndicate, Inc.

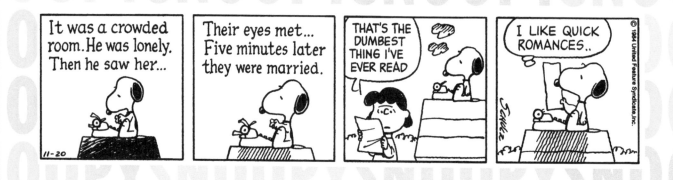

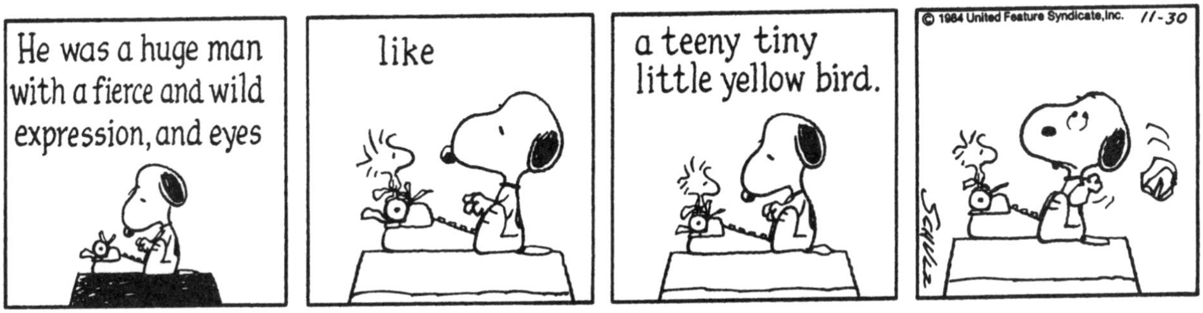
He was a huge man with a fierce and wild expression, and eyes
like
a teeny tiny little yellow bird.
© 1984 United Feature Syndicate,Inc. 11-30

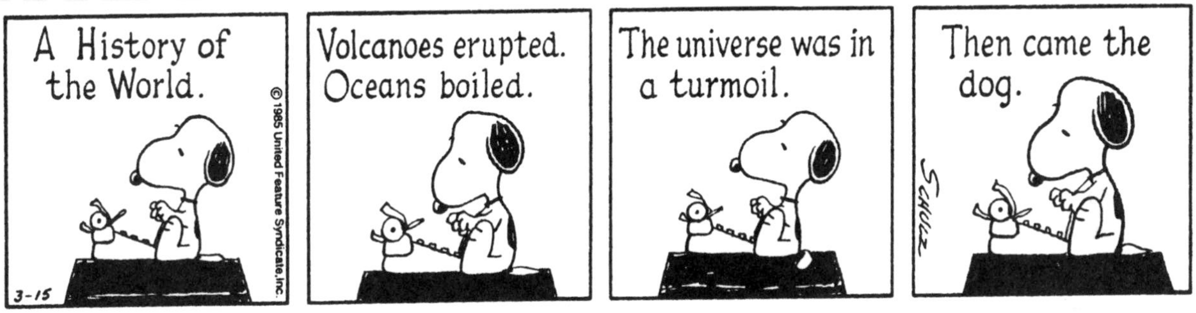
A History of the World.
3-15
© 1985 United Feature Syndicate,Inc.
Volcanoes erupted. Oceans boiled.
The universe was in a turmoil.
Then came the dog.

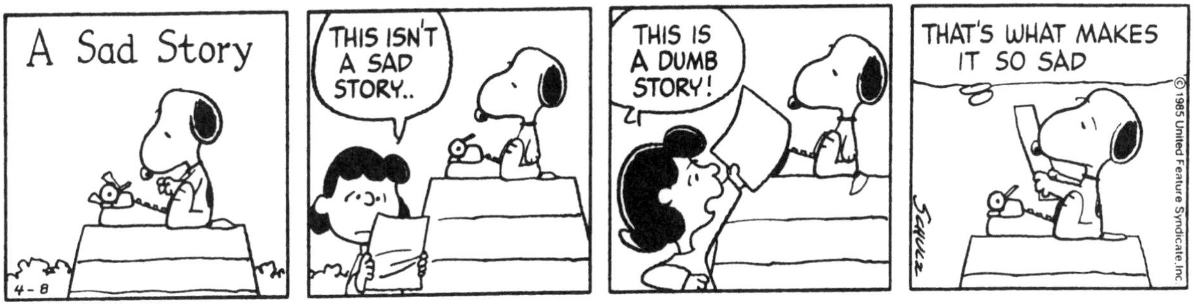
A Sad Story
4-8
THIS ISN'T A SAD STORY..
THIS IS A DUMB STORY!
THAT'S WHAT MAKES IT SO SAD
© 1985 United Feature Syndicate,Inc.

YOU KNOW WHAT YOU SHOULD WRITE?
YOU SHOULD WRITE A FAMILY STORY.. WRITE A STORY ABOUT FOUR SISTERS...
© 1985 United Feature Syndicate, Inc.
4-9
Small Women
SCHULZ

YOU SHOULD WRITE MORE ABOUT LOVE..
WRITE ABOUT ITS AGONY
WRITE SOMETHING THAT WILL EXPRESS THE PAIN OF A LOST LOVE...
5-20
Rats!
SCHULZ
© 1985 United Feature Syndicate, Inc.

"I used to think you were a great engineer," she said.
8-14
"Once, I even loved you..."
"But you've gotten too big for your bridges."
SCHULZ
© 1985 United Feature Syndicate, Inc.

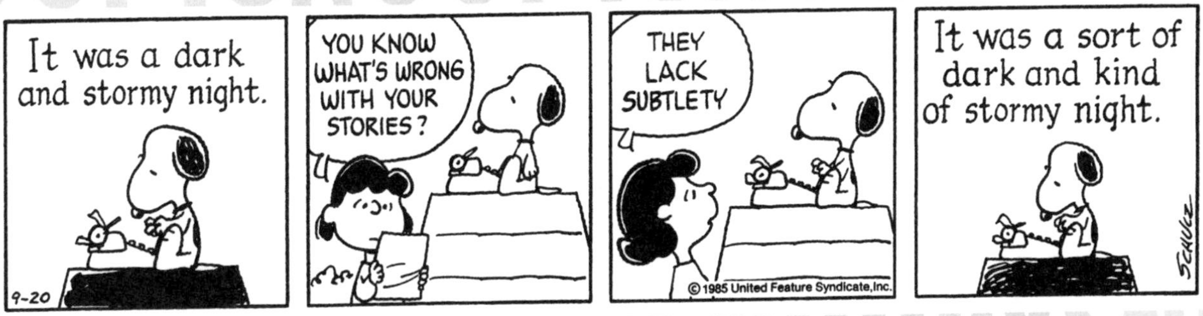
It was a dark and stormy night.
9-20
YOU KNOW WHAT'S WRONG WITH YOUR STORIES?
THEY LACK SUBTLETY
© 1985 United Feature Syndicate, Inc.
It was a sort of dark and kind of stormy night.
SCHULZ

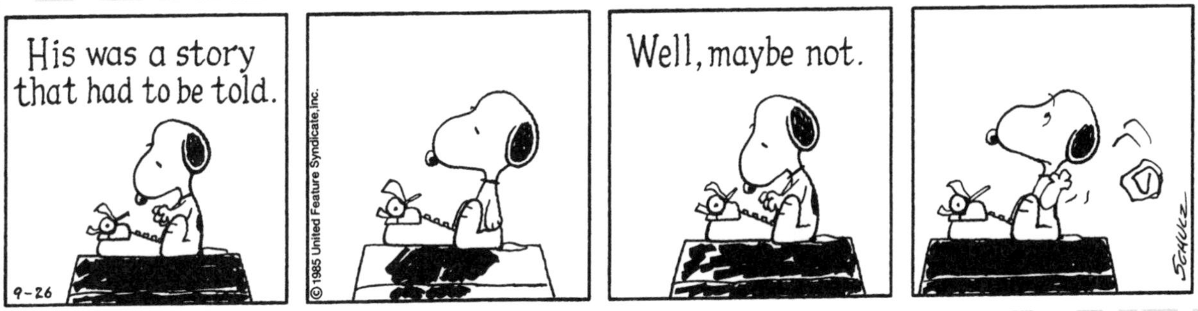
His was a story that had to be told.
9-26
© 1985 United Feature Syndicate, Inc.
Well, maybe not.
SCHULZ

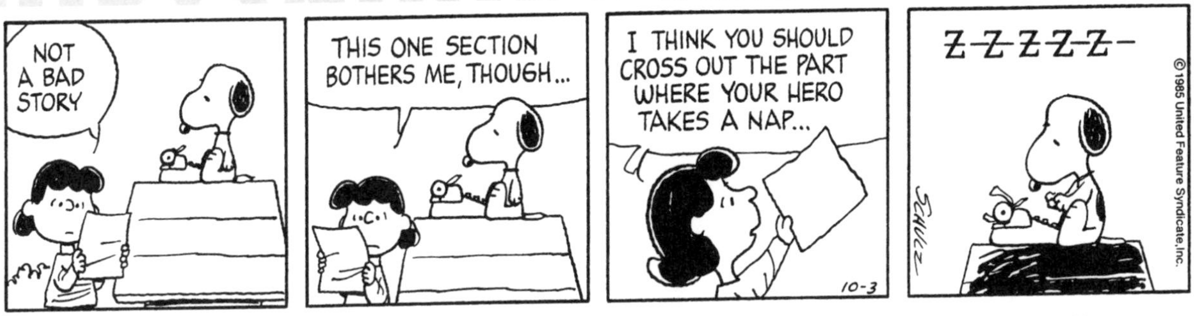
NOT A BAD STORY
THIS ONE SECTION BOTHERS ME, THOUGH...
I THINK YOU SHOULD CROSS OUT THE PART WHERE YOUR HERO TAKES A NAP...
10-3
SCHULZ
Z-Z-Z-Z-Z-
© 1985 United Feature Syndicate, Inc.

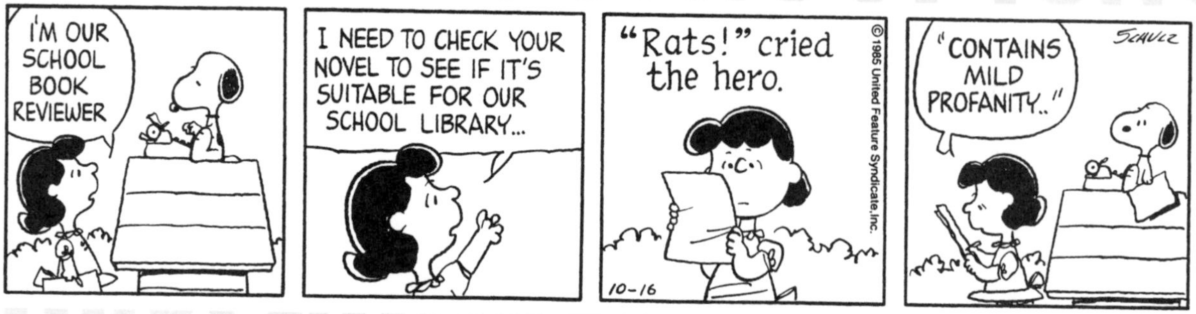
I'M OUR SCHOOL BOOK REVIEWER
I NEED TO CHECK YOUR NOVEL TO SEE IF IT'S SUITABLE FOR OUR SCHOOL LIBRARY...
"Rats!" cried the hero.
© 1985 United Feature Syndicate, Inc.
10-16
"CONTAINS MILD PROFANITY.."
SCHULZ

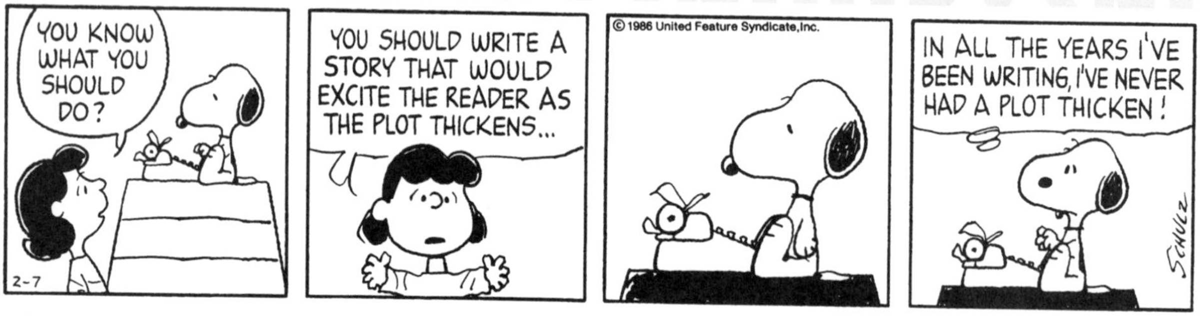
YOU KNOW WHAT YOU SHOULD DO?
2-7
YOU SHOULD WRITE A STORY THAT WOULD EXCITE THE READER AS THE PLOT THICKENS...
© 1986 United Feature Syndicate, Inc.
IN ALL THE YEARS I'VE BEEN WRITING, I'VE NEVER HAD A PLOT THICKEN!
SCHULZ

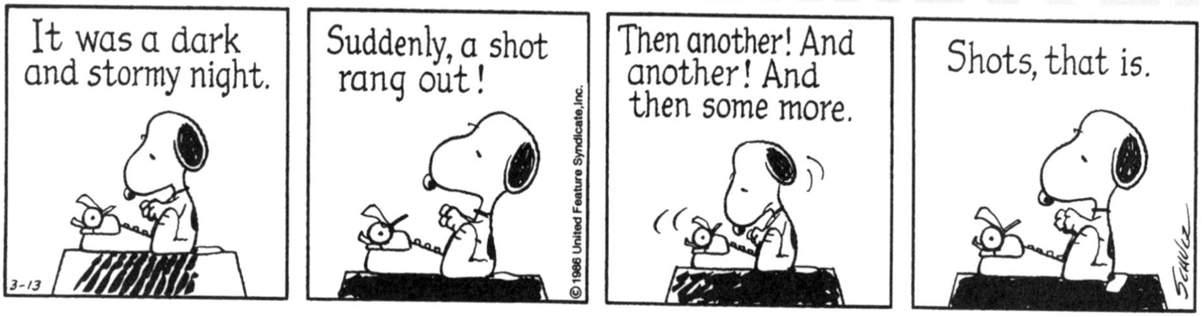
It was a dark and stormy night.
3-13
Suddenly, a shot rang out!
© 1986 United Feature Syndicate, Inc.
Then another! And another! And then some more.
Shots, that is.
SCHULZ

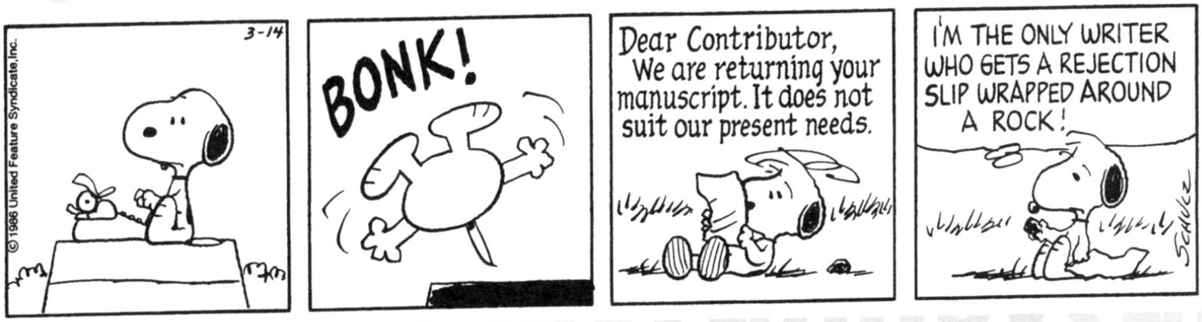

3-14
© 1986 United Feature Syndicate, Inc.
BONK!
Dear Contributor,
We are returning your manuscript. It does not suit our present needs.
I'M THE ONLY WRITER WHO GETS A REJECTION SLIP WRAPPED AROUND A ROCK!
SCHULZ

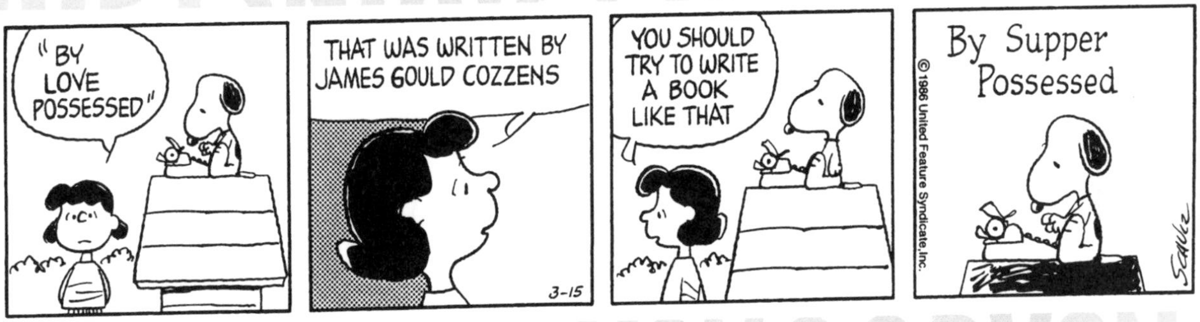

"BY LOVE POSSESSED"
THAT WAS WRITTEN BY JAMES GOULD COZZENS
3-15
YOU SHOULD TRY TO WRITE A BOOK LIKE THAT
© 1986 United Feature Syndicate, Inc.
By Supper Possessed
SCHULZ

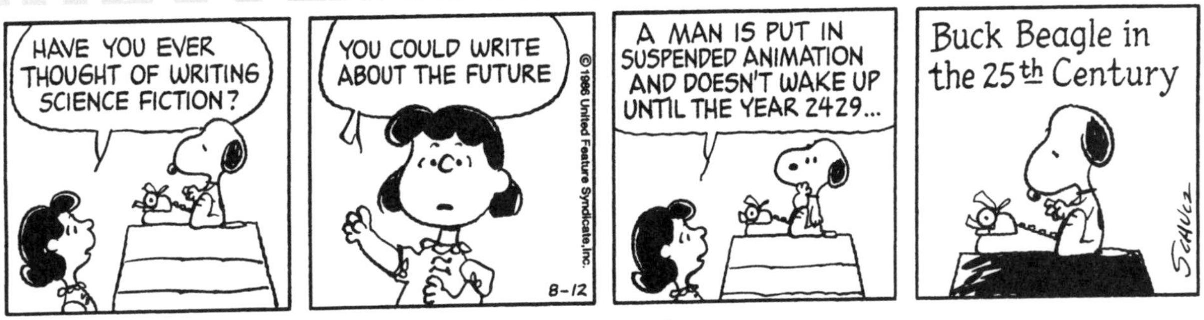

HAVE YOU EVER THOUGHT OF WRITING SCIENCE FICTION?
YOU COULD WRITE ABOUT THE FUTURE
© 1986 United Feature Syndicate, Inc.
8-12
A MAN IS PUT IN SUSPENDED ANIMATION AND DOESN'T WAKE UP UNTIL THE YEAR 2429...
Buck Beagle in the 25th Century
SCHULZ

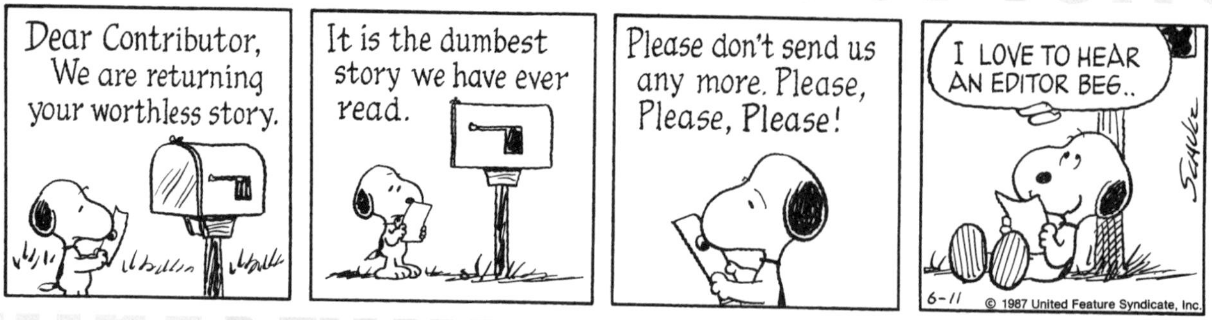
Dear Contributor, We are returning your worthless story.
It is the dumbest story we have ever read.
Please don't send us any more. Please, Please, Please!
I LOVE TO HEAR AN EDITOR BEG..
SCHULZ
6-11
© 1987 United Feature Syndicate, Inc.

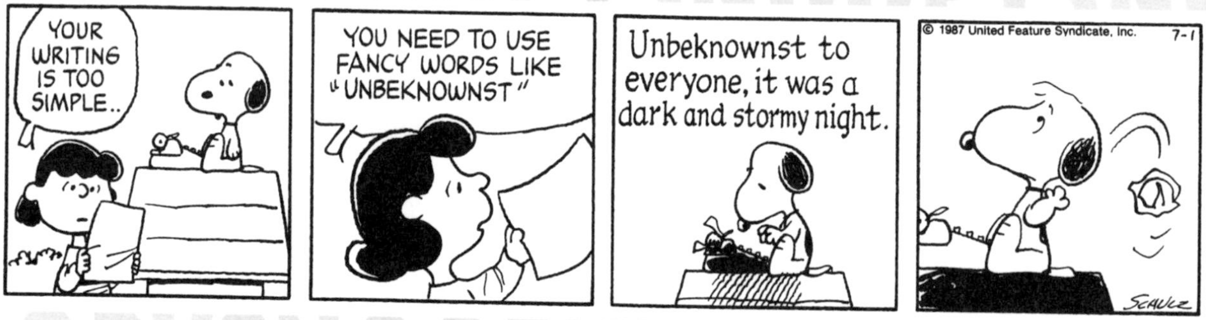
YOUR WRITING IS TOO SIMPLE..
YOU NEED TO USE FANCY WORDS LIKE "UNBEKNOWNST"
Unbeknownst to everyone, it was a dark and stormy night.
© 1987 United Feature Syndicate, Inc.
7-1
SCHULZ

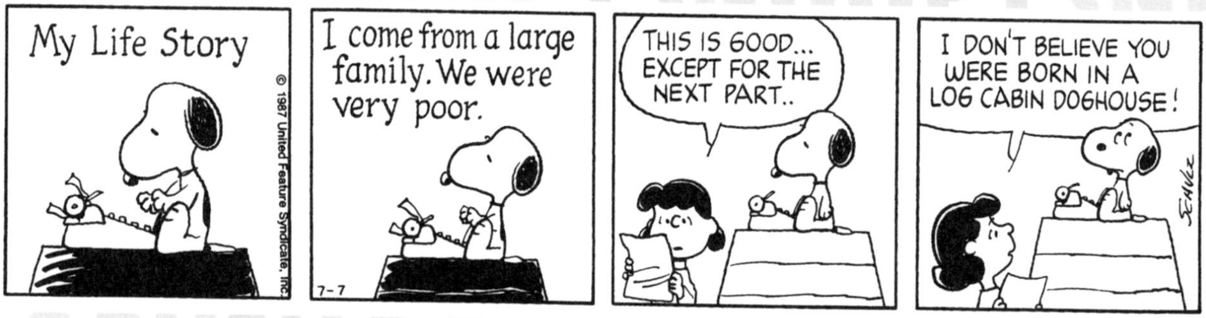
My Life Story
© 1987 United Feature Syndicate, Inc.
I come from a large family. We were very poor.
7-7
THIS IS GOOD... EXCEPT FOR THE NEXT PART..
I DON'T BELIEVE YOU WERE BORN IN A LOG CABIN DOGHOUSE!
SCHULZ

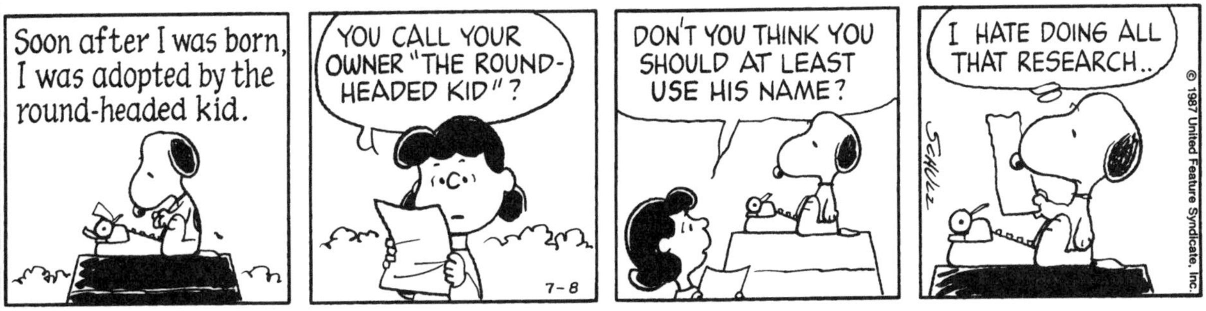
Soon after I was born, I was adopted by the round-headed kid.
YOU CALL YOUR OWNER "THE ROUND-HEADED KID"?
7-8
DON'T YOU THINK YOU SHOULD AT LEAST USE HIS NAME?
I HATE DOING ALL THAT RESEARCH..
© 1987 United Feature Syndicate, Inc.

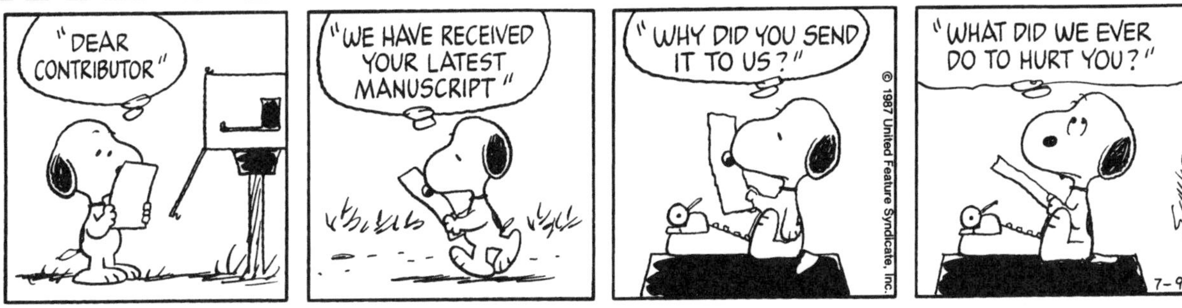
"DEAR CONTRIBUTOR"
"WE HAVE RECEIVED YOUR LATEST MANUSCRIPT"
"WHY DID YOU SEND IT TO US?"
© 1987 United Feature Syndicate, Inc.
"WHAT DID WE EVER DO TO HURT YOU?"
7-9

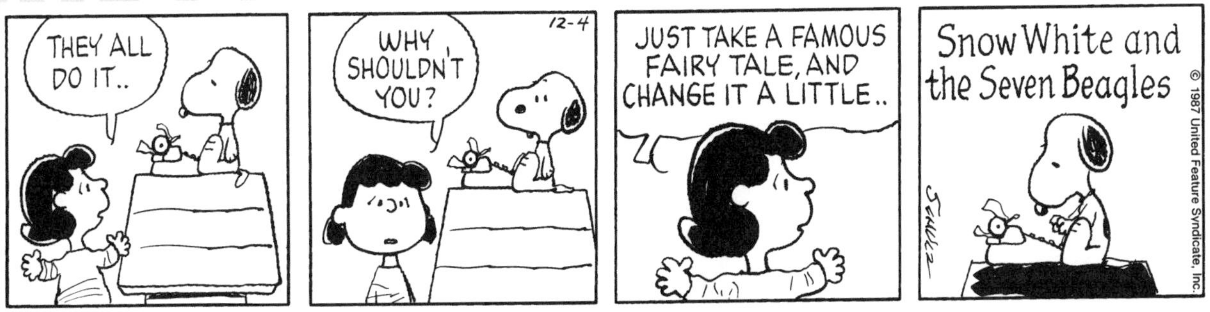
THEY ALL DO IT..
12-4
WHY SHOULDN'T YOU?
JUST TAKE A FAMOUS FAIRY TALE, AND CHANGE IT A LITTLE..
Snow White and the Seven Beagles
© 1987 United Feature Syndicate, Inc.

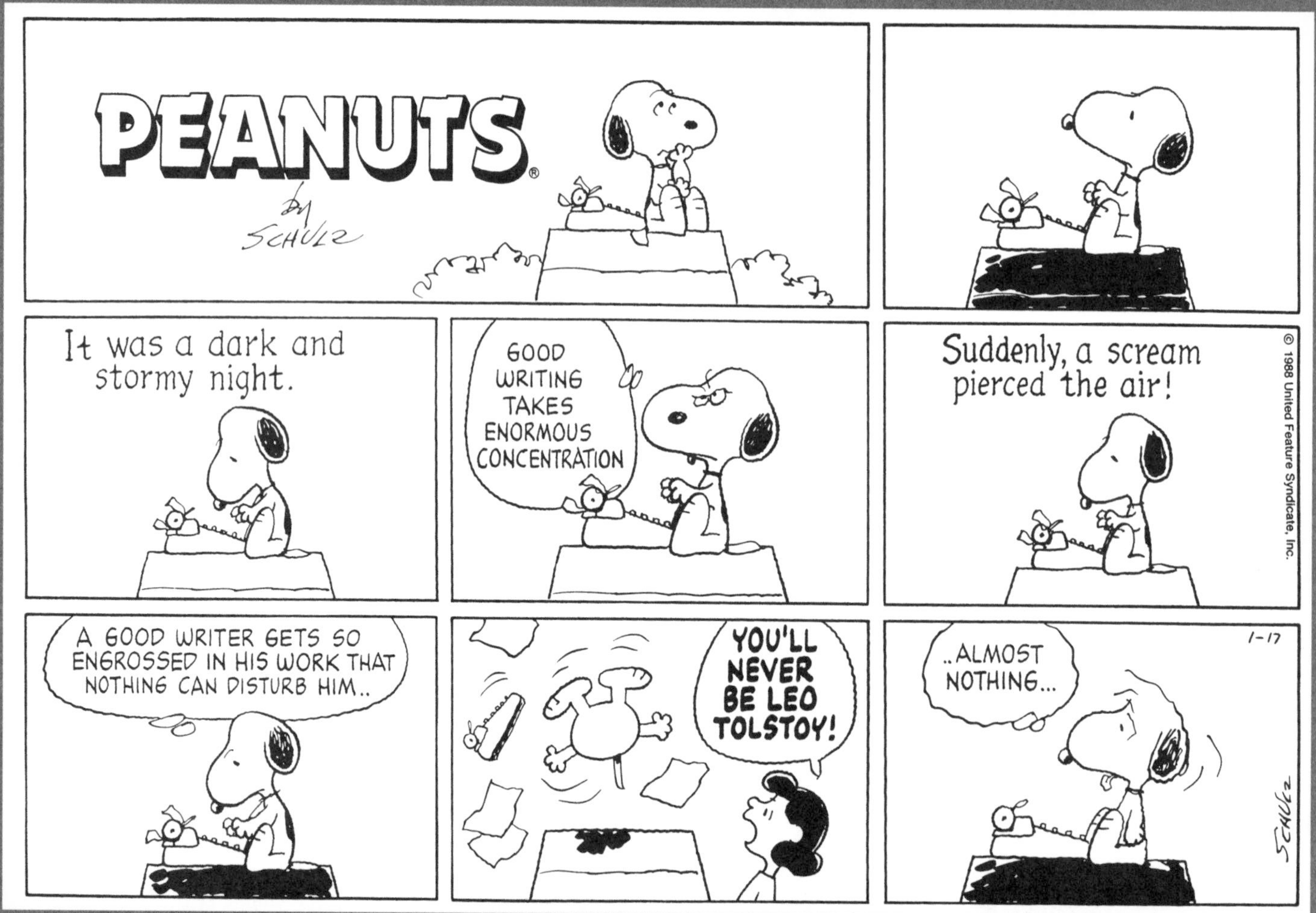
PEANUTS
by SCHULZ
It was a dark and stormy night.
GOOD WRITING TAKES ENORMOUS CONCENTRATION
Suddenly, a scream pierced the air!
© 1988 United Feature Syndicate, Inc.
A GOOD WRITER GETS SO ENGROSSED IN HIS WORK THAT NOTHING CAN DISTURB HIM..
YOU'LL NEVER BE LEO TOLSTOY!
1-17
..ALMOST NOTHING...
SCHULZ

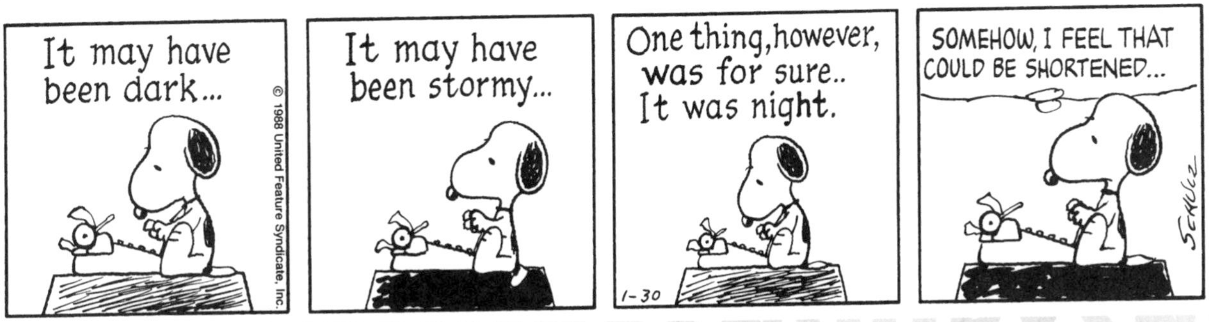
It may have been dark...
© 1988 United Feature Syndicate, Inc.
It may have been stormy...
One thing, however, was for sure.. It was night.
1-30
SOMEHOW, I FEEL THAT COULD BE SHORTENED...

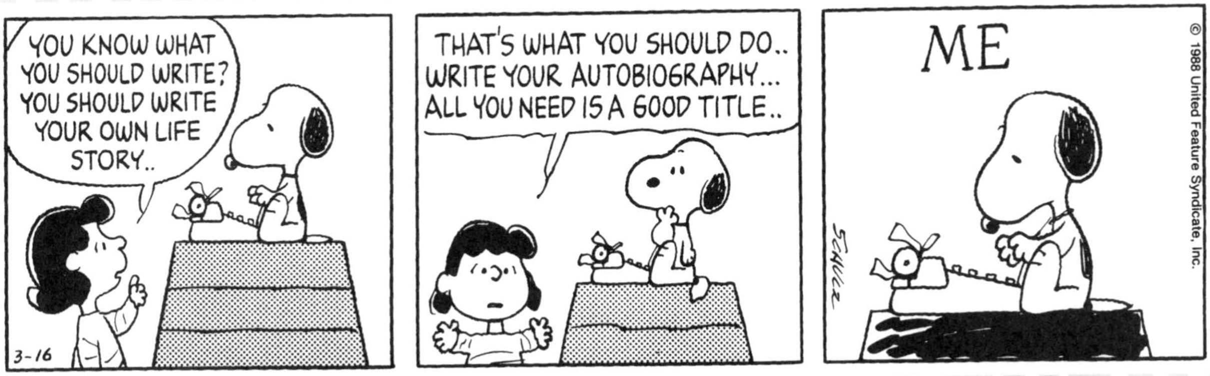
YOU KNOW WHAT YOU SHOULD WRITE? YOU SHOULD WRITE YOUR OWN LIFE STORY..
3-16
THAT'S WHAT YOU SHOULD DO.. WRITE YOUR AUTOBIOGRAPHY... ALL YOU NEED IS A GOOD TITLE..
ME
© 1988 United Feature Syndicate, Inc.

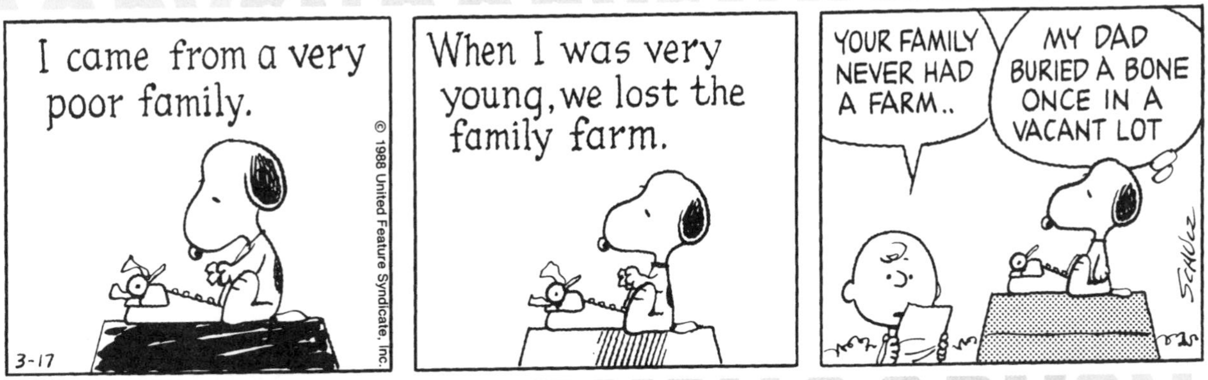
I came from a very poor family.
© 1988 United Feature Syndicate, Inc.
3-17
When I was very young, we lost the family farm.
YOUR FAMILY NEVER HAD A FARM..
MY DAD BURIED A BONE ONCE IN A VACANT LOT

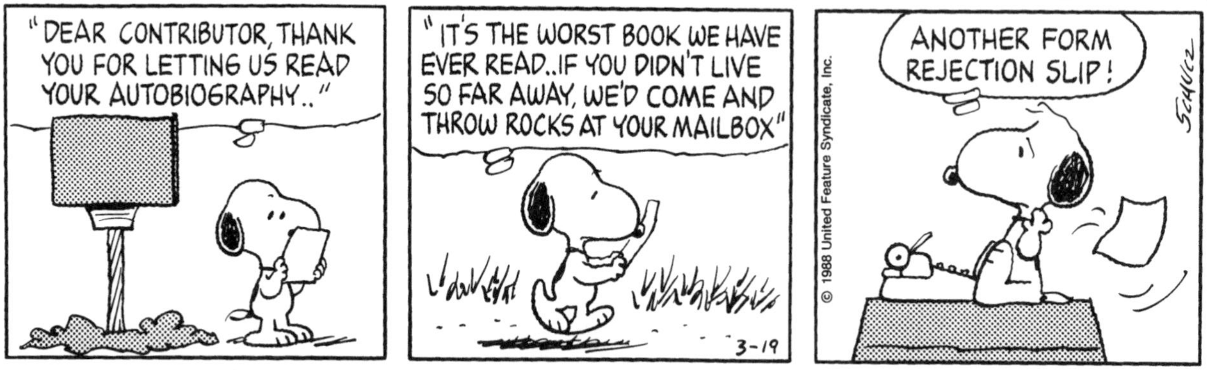
"DEAR CONTRIBUTOR, THANK YOU FOR LETTING US READ YOUR AUTOBIOGRAPHY.."
"IT'S THE WORST BOOK WE HAVE EVER READ..IF YOU DIDN'T LIVE SO FAR AWAY, WE'D COME AND THROW ROCKS AT YOUR MAILBOX"
3-19
© 1988 United Feature Syndicate, Inc.
ANOTHER FORM REJECTION SLIP!
SCHULZ

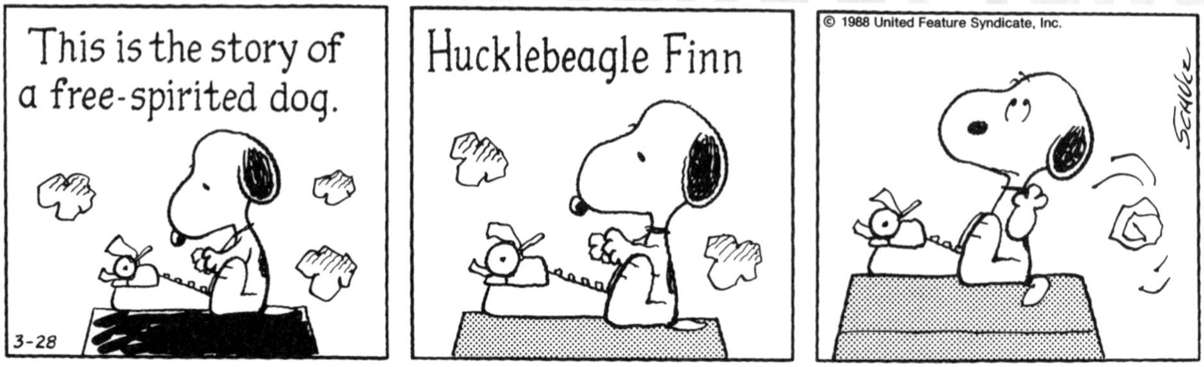
This is the story of a free-spirited dog.
3-28
Hucklebeagle Finn
© 1988 United Feature Syndicate, Inc.
SCHULZ

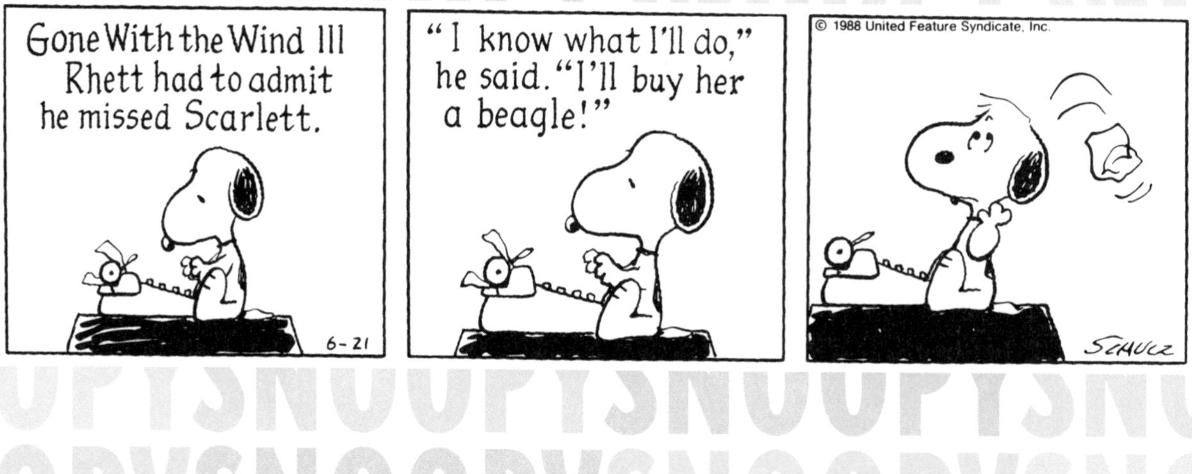
Gone With the Wind III
Rhett had to admit he missed Scarlett.
6-21
"I know what I'll do," he said. "I'll buy her a beagle!"
© 1988 United Feature Syndicate, Inc.
SCHULZ

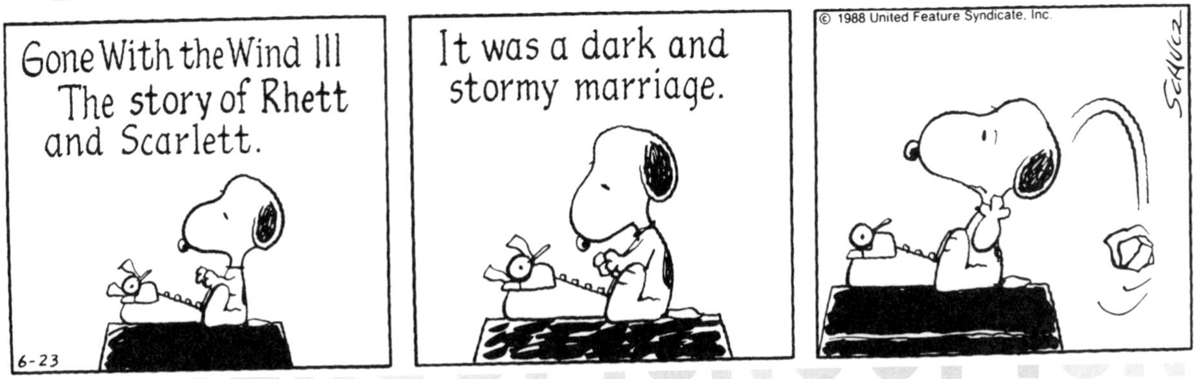
Gone With the Wind III
The story of Rhett and Scarlett.
6-23
It was a dark and stormy marriage.
© 1988 United Feature Syndicate, Inc.
SCHULZ

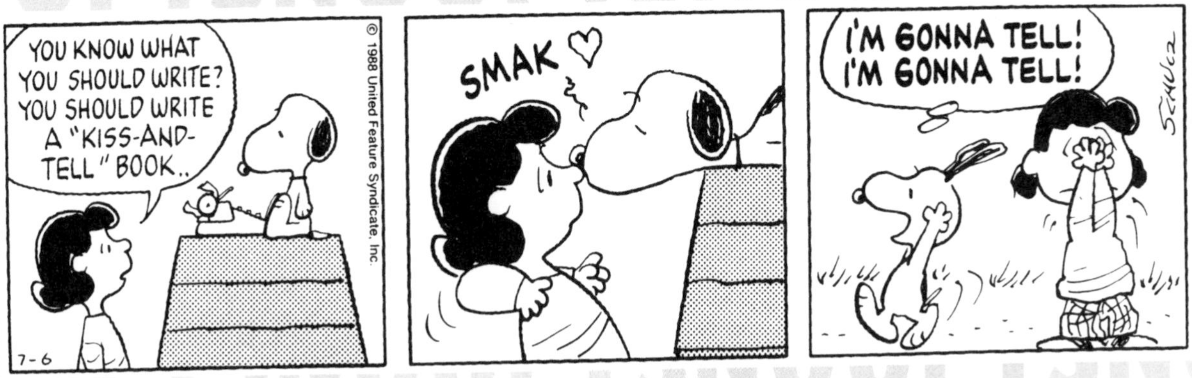
YOU KNOW WHAT YOU SHOULD WRITE? YOU SHOULD WRITE A "KISS-AND-TELL" BOOK..
7-6
© 1988 United Feature Syndicate, Inc.
SMAK
I'M GONNA TELL! I'M GONNA TELL!
SCHULZ

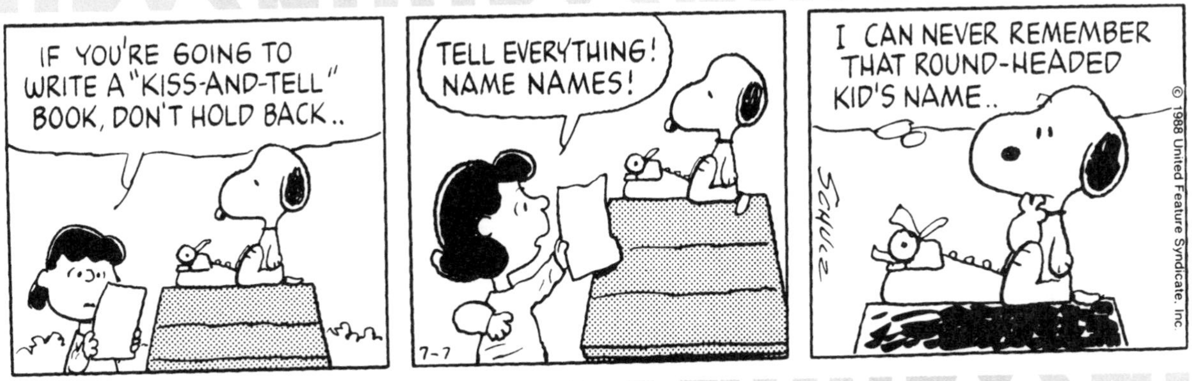
IF YOU'RE GOING TO WRITE A "KISS-AND-TELL" BOOK, DON'T HOLD BACK..
TELL EVERYTHING! NAME NAMES!
7-7
I CAN NEVER REMEMBER THAT ROUND-HEADED KID'S NAME..
SCHULZ
© 1988 United Feature Syndicate, Inc.

YOU STUPID BEAGLE! IF YOU PUT ME IN YOUR "KISS-AND-TELL" BOOK, I'LL TEAR YOU LIMB FROM LIMB!
7-8
© 1988 United Feature Syndicate, Inc.
OF COURSE, I DON'T WANT TO BE LEFT OUT, EITHER..
SCHULZ

I HEAR YOUR "KISS-AND-TELL" BOOK HAS MADE A LOT OF PEOPLE MAD..
7-9
I'VE BEEN WONDERING IF THE THREATENING LETTERS WORRY YOU...
JUST THE ONE WHERE THEY SAID THEY'D BLOW UP MY SUPPER DISH..
SCHULZ
© 1988 United Feature Syndicate, Inc.

Why Dogs Are Superior To Cats
7-27
Who says we're not?
SCHULZ
© 1988 United Feature Syndicate, Inc.

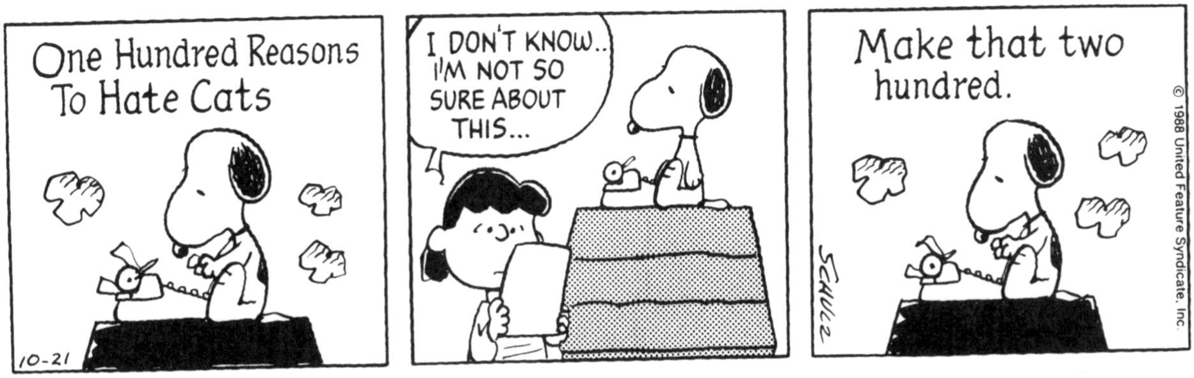
One Hundred Reasons To Hate Cats
10-21
I DON'T KNOW.. I'M NOT SO SURE ABOUT THIS...
Make that two hundred.
SCHULZ
© 1988 United Feature Syndicate, Inc.

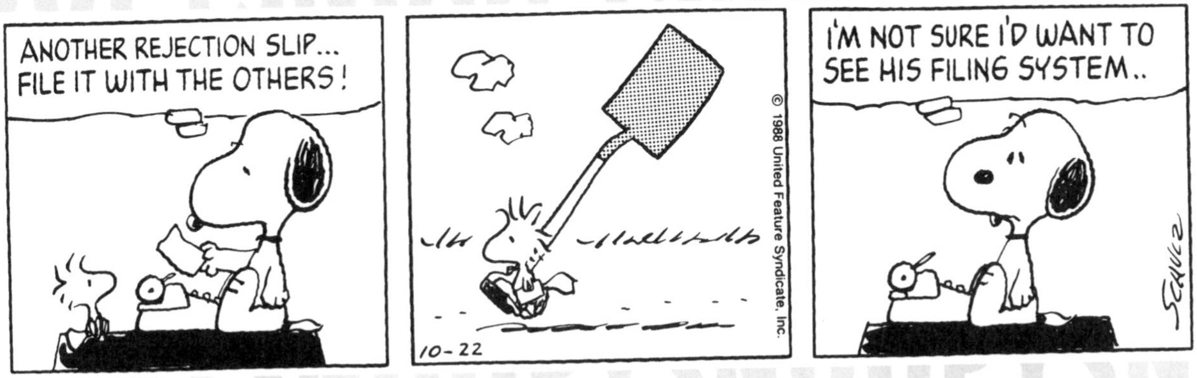
ANOTHER REJECTION SLIP... FILE IT WITH THE OTHERS!
10-22
© 1988 United Feature Syndicate, Inc.
I'M NOT SURE I'D WANT TO SEE HIS FILING SYSTEM..
SCHULZ

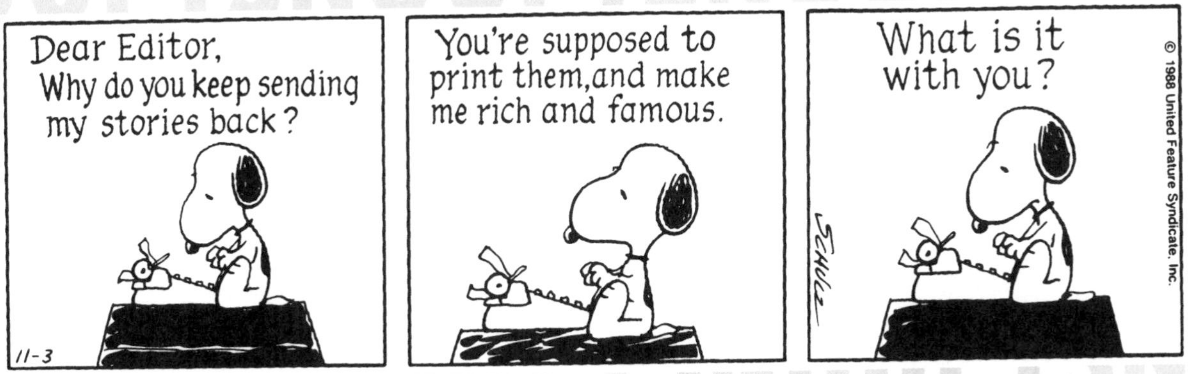
Dear Editor, Why do you keep sending my stories back?
11-3
You're supposed to print them, and make me rich and famous.
What is it with you?
SCHULZ
© 1988 United Feature Syndicate, Inc.

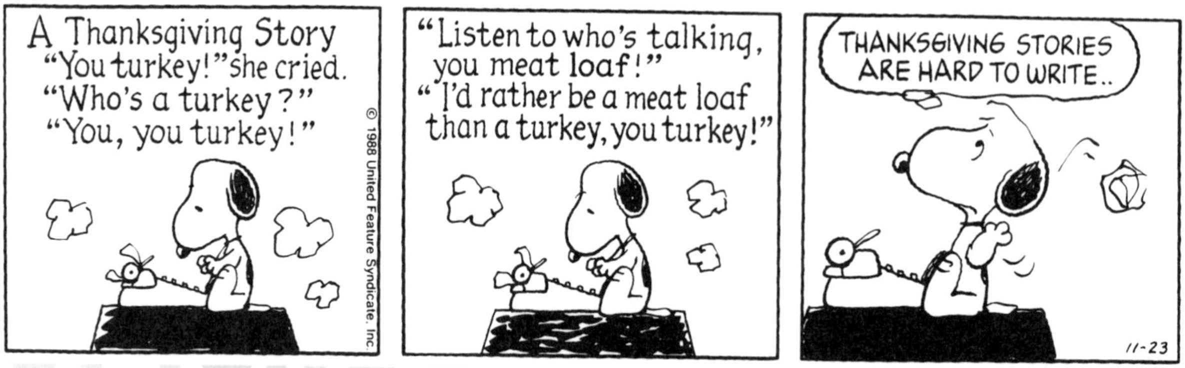
A Thanksgiving Story
"You turkey!" she cried.
"Who's a turkey?"
"You, you turkey!"
© 1988 United Feature Syndicate, Inc.
"Listen to who's talking, you meat loaf!"
"I'd rather be a meat loaf than a turkey, you turkey!"
THANKSGIVING STORIES ARE HARD TO WRITE..
11-23

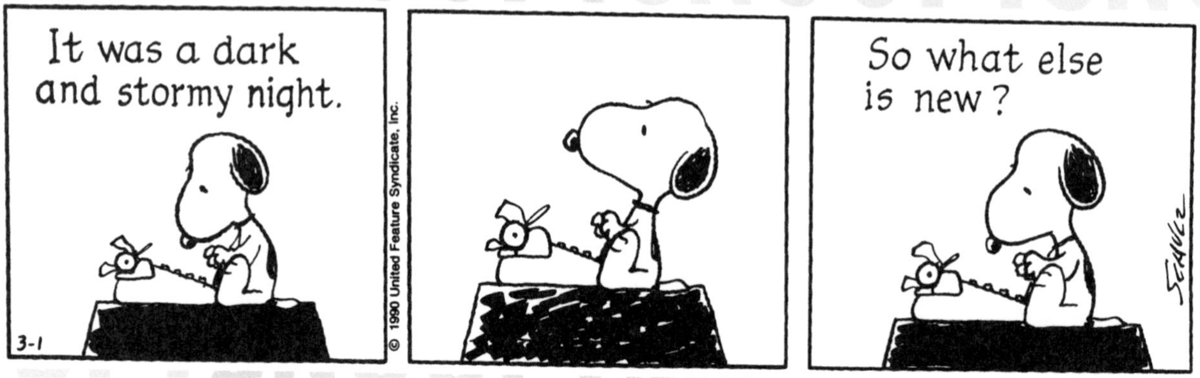
It was a dark and stormy night.
3-1
© 1990 United Feature Syndicate, Inc.
So what else is new?
SCHULZ

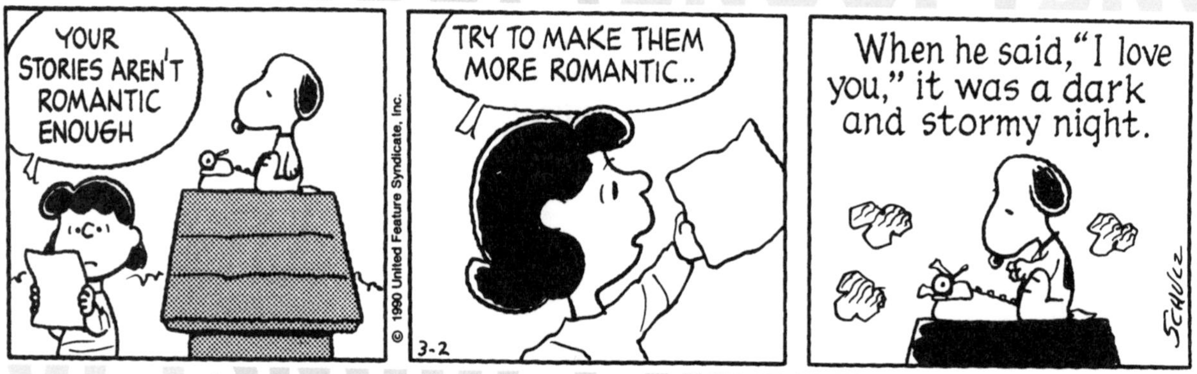
YOUR STORIES AREN'T ROMANTIC ENOUGH
© 1990 United Feature Syndicate, Inc.
TRY TO MAKE THEM MORE ROMANTIC..
3-2
When he said, "I love you," it was a dark and stormy night.
SCHULZ

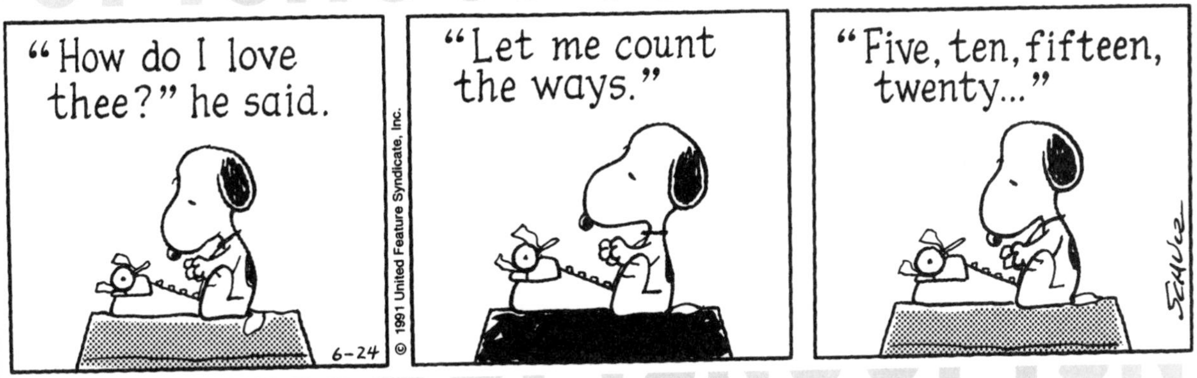
"How do I love thee?" he said.
6-24
© 1991 United Feature Syndicate, Inc.
"Let me count the ways."
"Five, ten, fifteen, twenty..."
SCHULZ

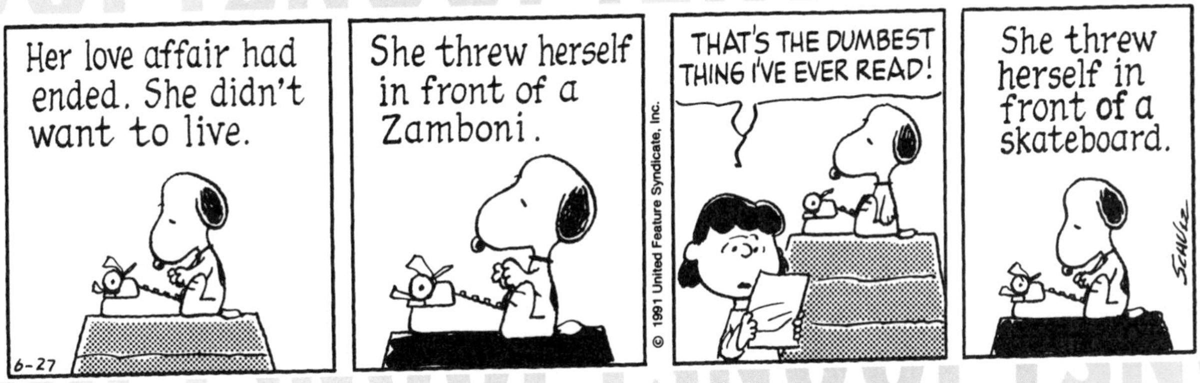
Her love affair had ended. She didn't want to live.
6-27
She threw herself in front of a Zamboni.
© 1991 United Feature Syndicate, Inc.
THAT'S THE DUMBEST THING I'VE EVER READ!
She threw herself in front of a skateboard.
SCHULZ

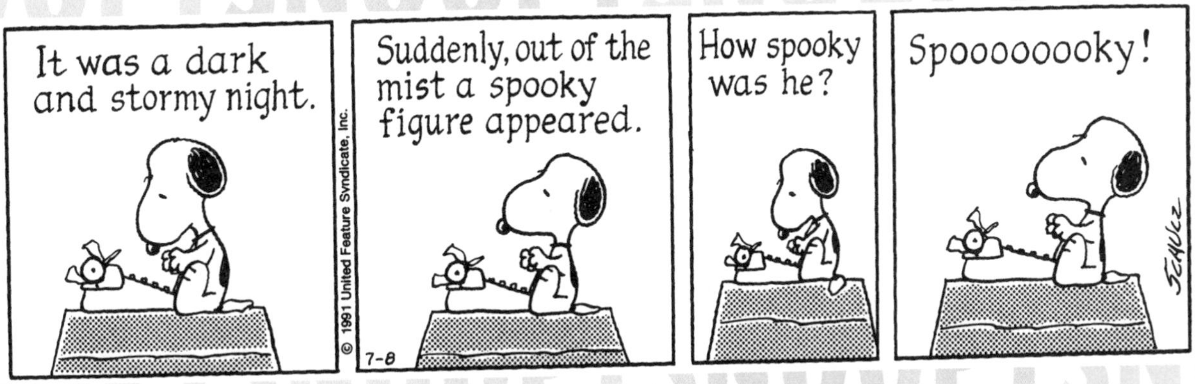
It was a dark and stormy night.
© 1991 United Feature Syndicate, Inc.
Suddenly, out of the mist a spooky figure appeared.
7-8
How spooky was he?
Spoooooooky!
SCHULZ

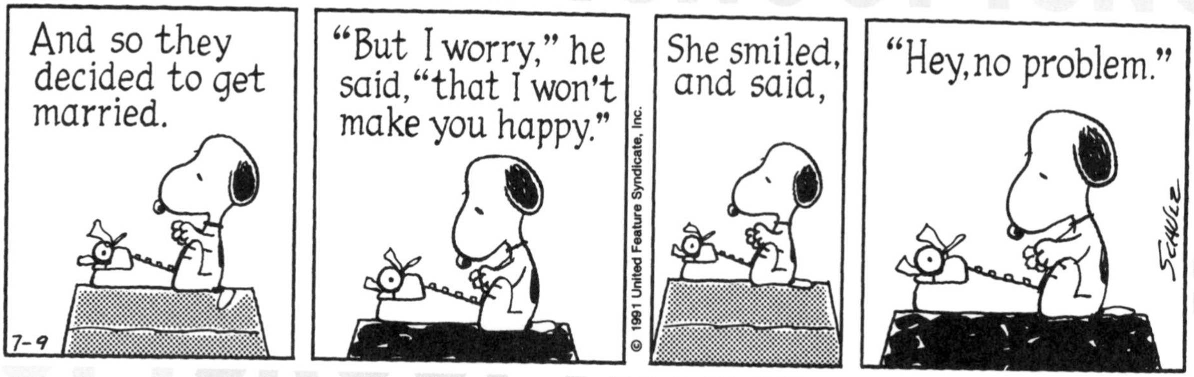
And so they decided to get married.
"But I worry," he said, "that I won't make you happy."
She smiled, and said,
"Hey, no problem."
© 1991 United Feature Syndicate, Inc.
7-9
SCHULZ

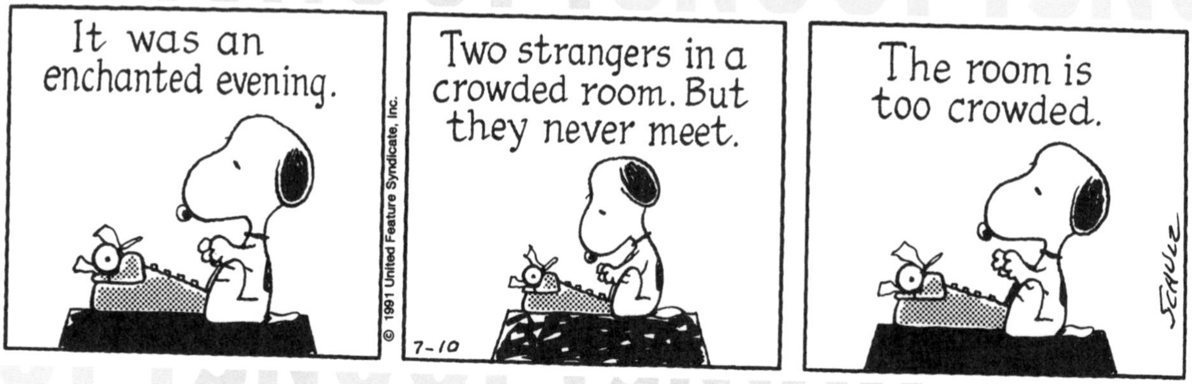
It was an enchanted evening.
Two strangers in a crowded room. But they never meet.
The room is too crowded.
© 1991 United Feature Syndicate, Inc.
7-10
SCHULZ

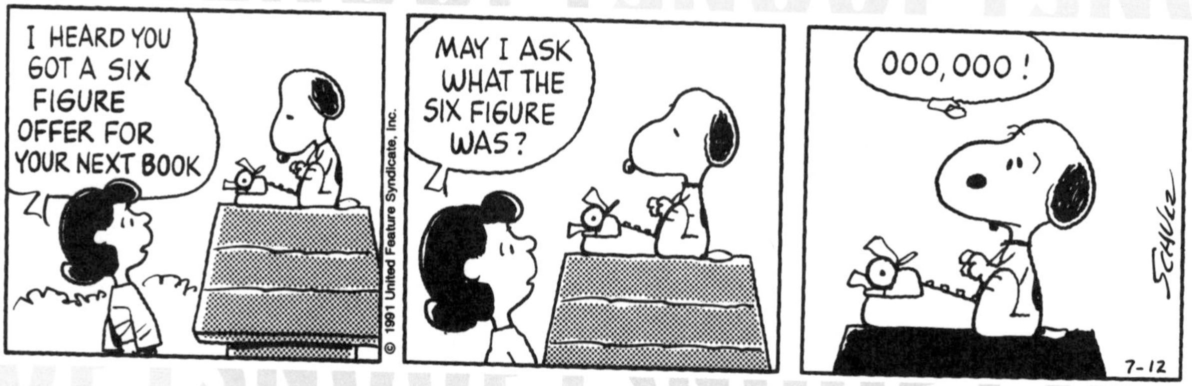
I HEARD YOU GOT A SIX FIGURE OFFER FOR YOUR NEXT BOOK
MAY I ASK WHAT THE SIX FIGURE WAS?
000,000!
© 1991 United Feature Syndicate, Inc.
7-12
SCHULZ

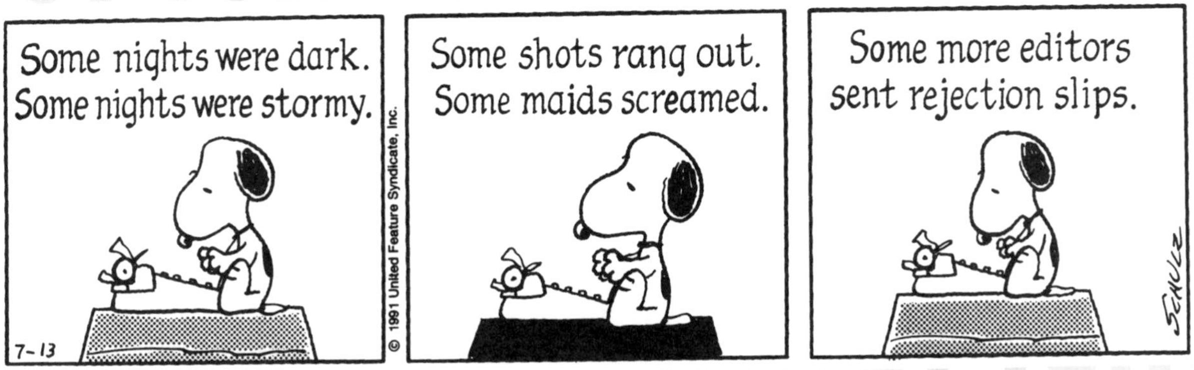
Some nights were dark. Some nights were stormy.
© 1991 United Feature Syndicate, Inc.
7-13
Some shots rang out. Some maids screamed.
Some more editors sent rejection slips.
SCHULZ

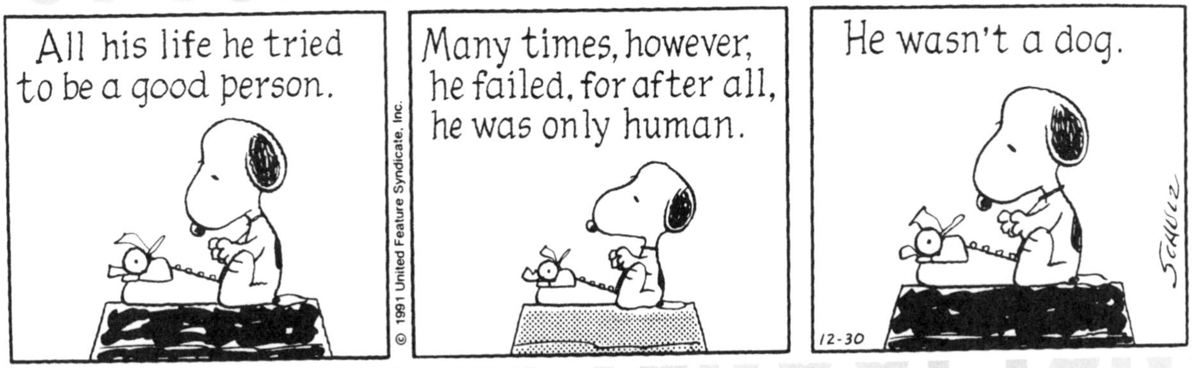
All his life he tried to be a good person.
© 1991 United Feature Syndicate, Inc.
Many times, however, he failed, for after all, he was only human.
He wasn't a dog.
SCHULZ
12-30

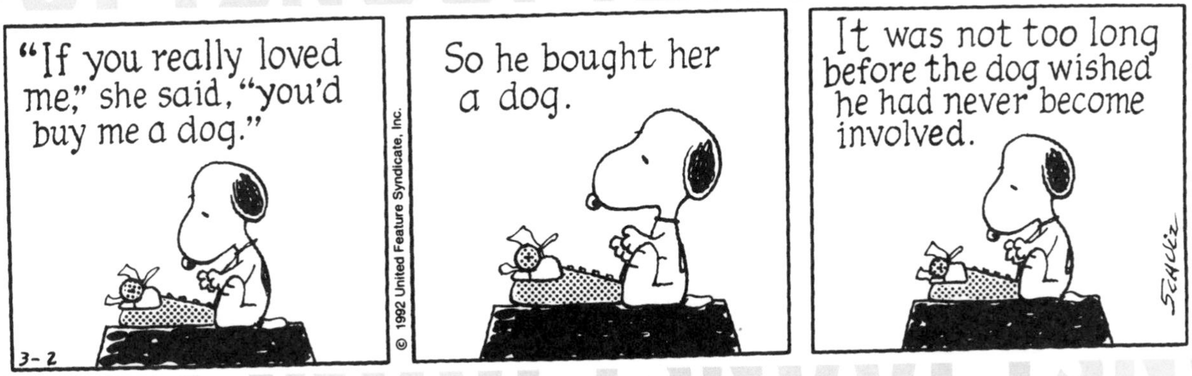
"If you really loved me," she said, "you'd buy me a dog."
3-2
© 1992 United Feature Syndicate, Inc.
So he bought her a dog.
It was not too long before the dog wished he had never become involved.
SCHULZ

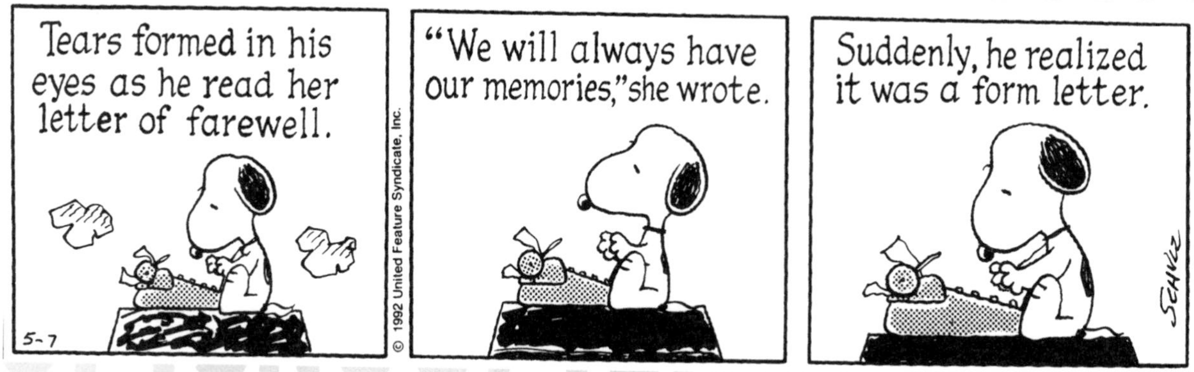
Tears formed in his eyes as he read her letter of farewell.
5-7
© 1992 United Feature Syndicate, Inc.
"We will always have our memories," she wrote.
Suddenly, he realized it was a form letter.
SCHULZ

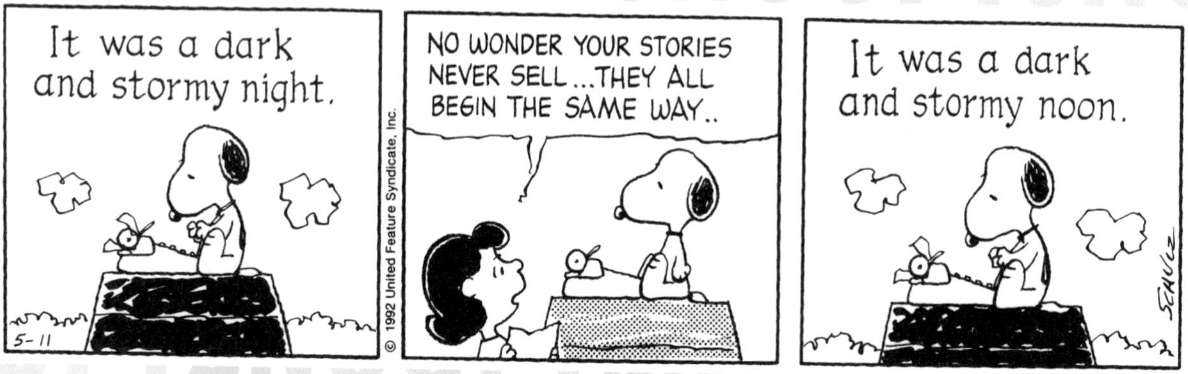
It was a dark and stormy night.
5-11
© 1992 United Feature Syndicate, Inc.
NO WONDER YOUR STORIES NEVER SELL ... THEY ALL BEGIN THE SAME WAY..
It was a dark and stormy noon.
SCHULZ

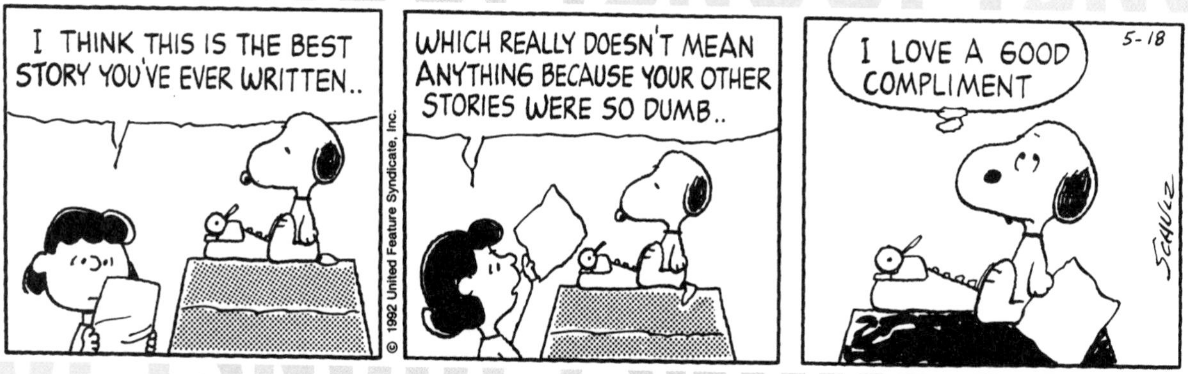
I THINK THIS IS THE BEST STORY YOU'VE EVER WRITTEN..
© 1992 United Feature Syndicate, Inc.
WHICH REALLY DOESN'T MEAN ANYTHING BECAUSE YOUR OTHER STORIES WERE SO DUMB..
5-18
I LOVE A GOOD COMPLIMENT
SCHULZ

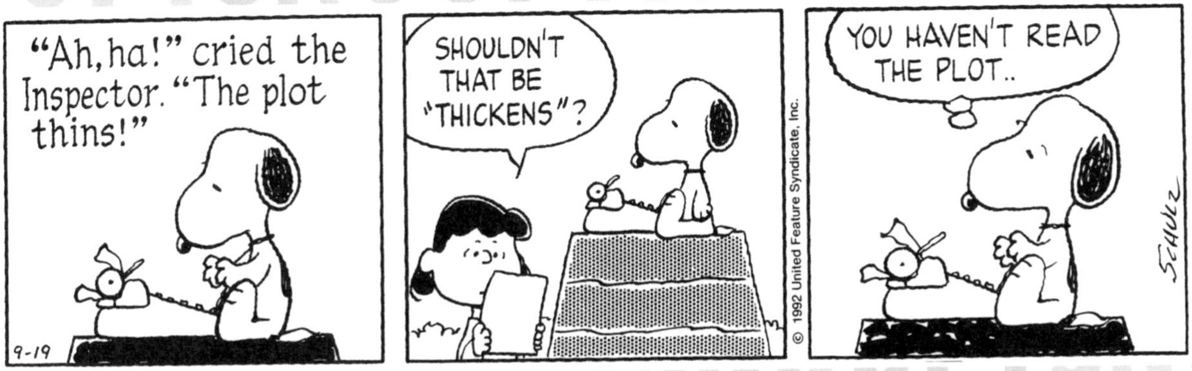
"Ah, ha!" cried the Inspector. "The plot thins!"
9-19
SHOULDN'T THAT BE "THICKENS"?
© 1992 United Feature Syndicate, Inc.
YOU HAVEN'T READ THE PLOT..
SCHULZ

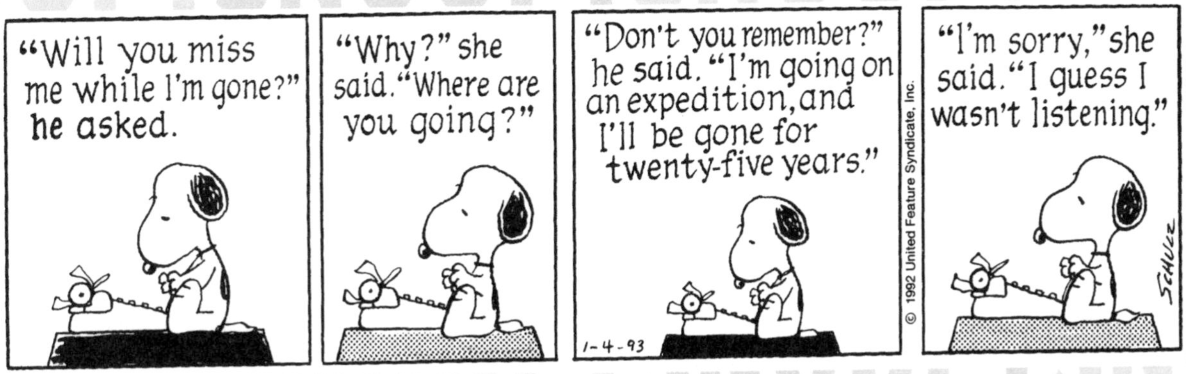
"Will you miss me while I'm gone?" he asked.
"Why?" she said. "Where are you going?"
"Don't you remember?" he said. "I'm going on an expedition, and I'll be gone for twenty-five years."
1-4-93
© 1992 United Feature Syndicate, Inc.
"I'm sorry," she said. "I guess I wasn't listening."
SCHULZ

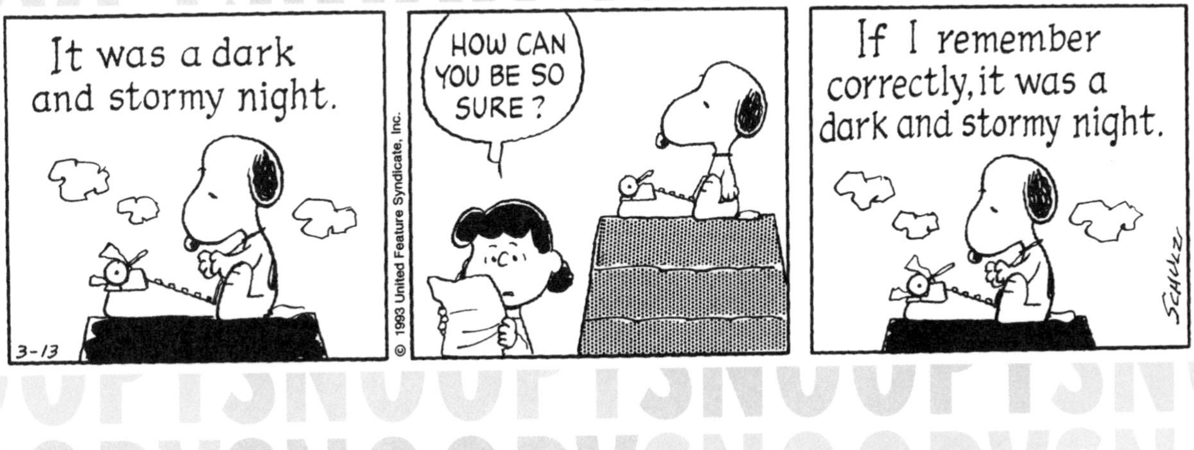
It was a dark and stormy night.
3-13
© 1993 United Feature Syndicate, Inc.
HOW CAN YOU BE SO SURE?
If I remember correctly, it was a dark and stormy night.
SCHULZ

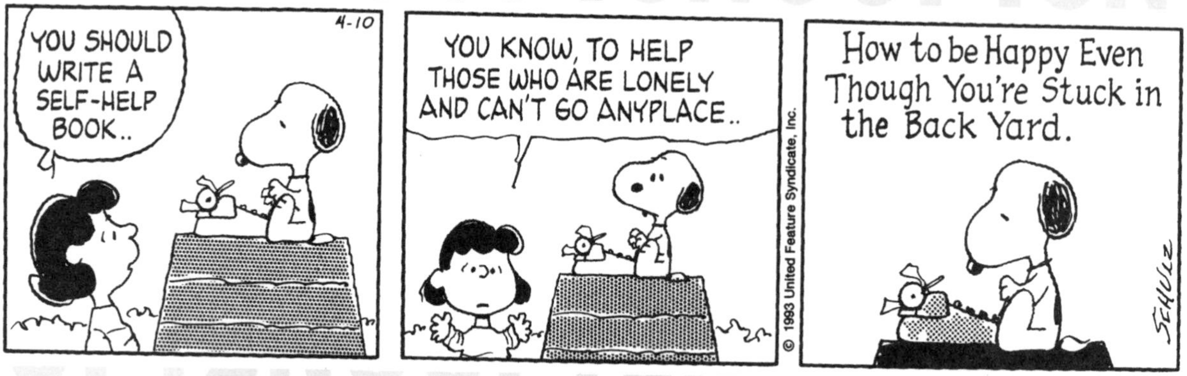
4-10
YOU SHOULD WRITE A SELF-HELP BOOK..
YOU KNOW, TO HELP THOSE WHO ARE LONELY AND CAN'T GO ANYPLACE..
© 1993 United Feature Syndicate, Inc.
How to be Happy Even Though You're Stuck in the Back Yard.
SCHULZ

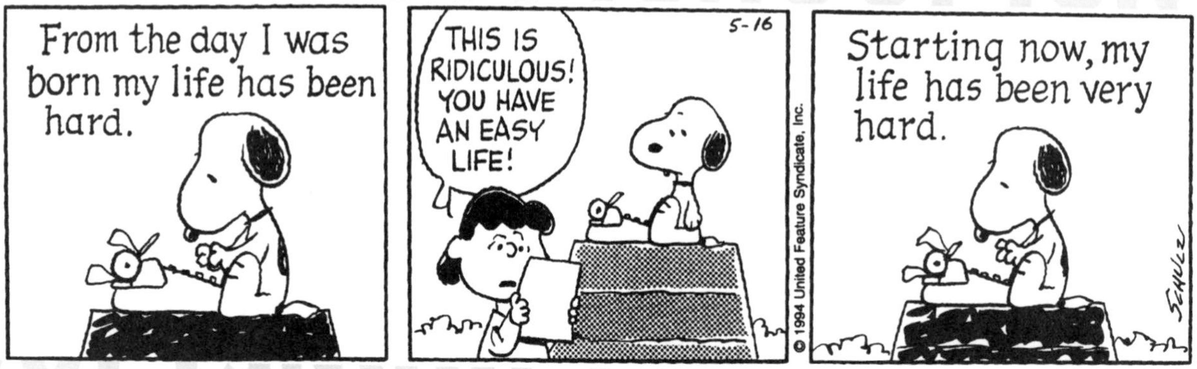
From the day I was born my life has been hard.
5-16
THIS IS RIDICULOUS! YOU HAVE AN EASY LIFE!
© 1994 United Feature Syndicate, Inc.
Starting now, my life has been very hard.
SCHULZ

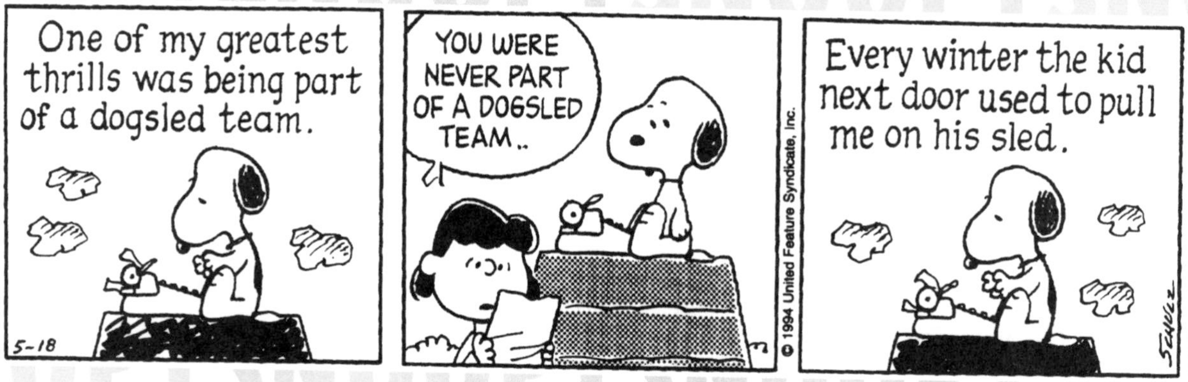
One of my greatest thrills was being part of a dogsled team.
5-18
YOU WERE NEVER PART OF A DOGSLED TEAM..
© 1994 United Feature Syndicate, Inc.
Every winter the kid next door used to pull me on his sled.
SCHULZ

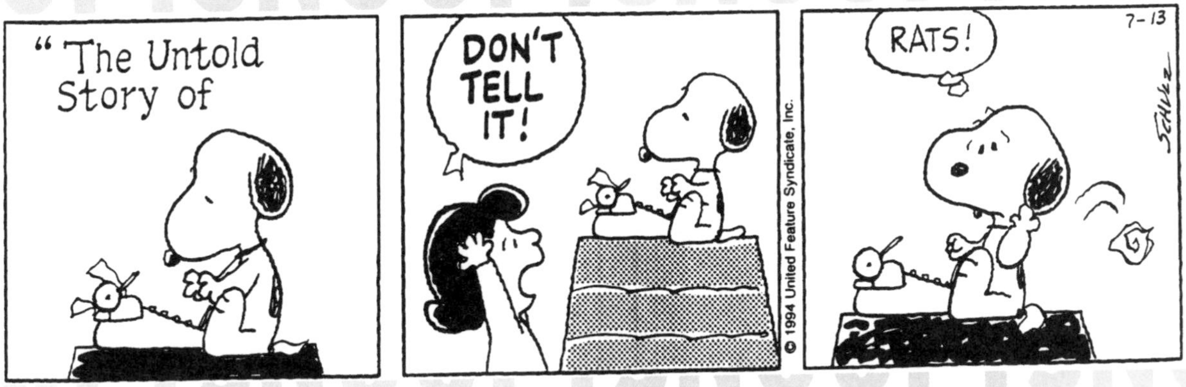
"The Untold Story of
DON'T TELL IT!
RATS!
7-13
SCHULZ
© 1994 United Feature Syndicate, Inc.

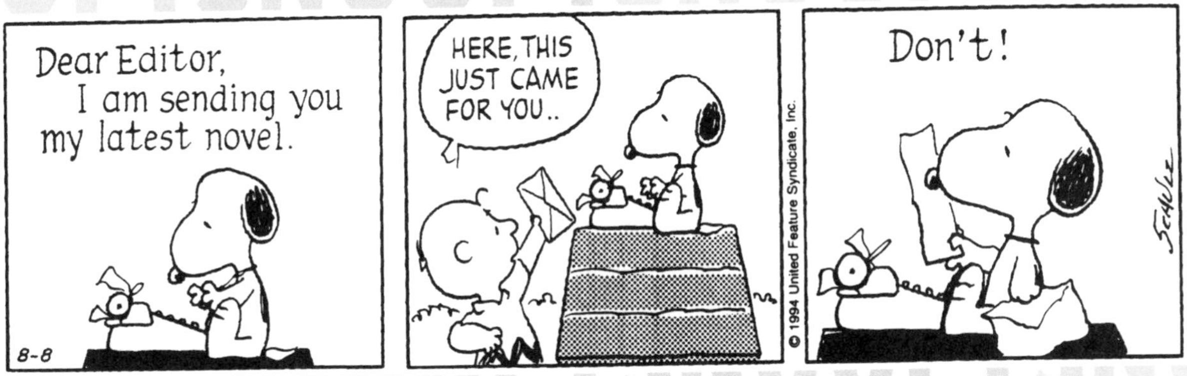
Dear Editor,
I am sending you my latest novel.
8-8
HERE, THIS JUST CAME FOR YOU..
Don't!
SCHULZ
© 1994 United Feature Syndicate, Inc.

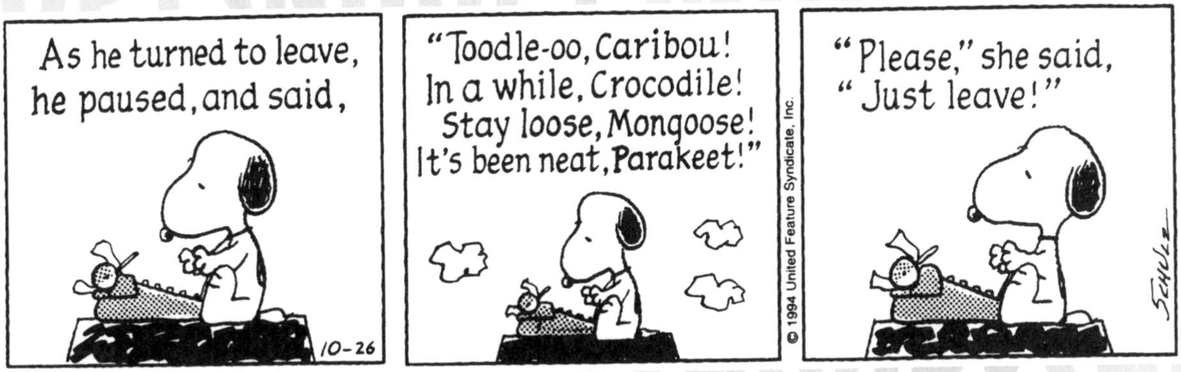
As he turned to leave, he paused, and said,
10-26
"Toodle-oo, Caribou! In a while, Crocodile! Stay loose, Mongoose! It's been neat, Parakeet!"
"Please," she said, "Just leave!"
SCHULZ
© 1994 United Feature Syndicate, Inc.

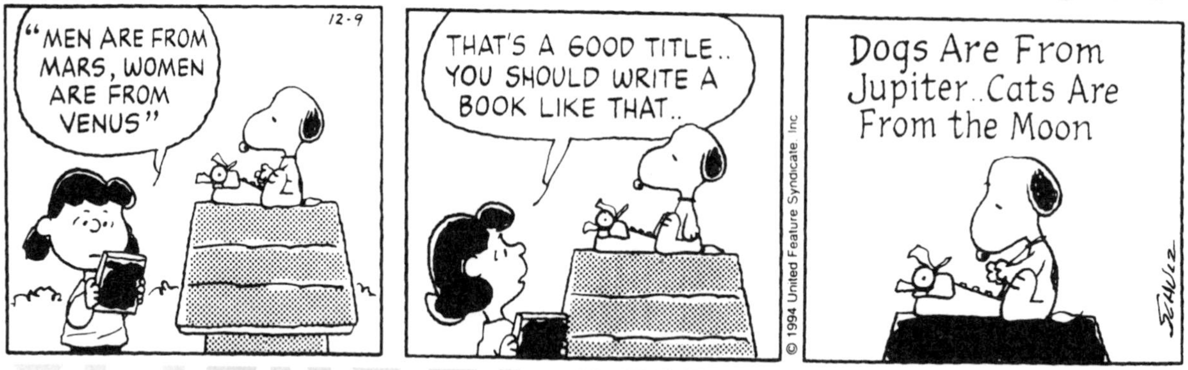
12-9
"MEN ARE FROM MARS, WOMEN ARE FROM VENUS"
THAT'S A GOOD TITLE.. YOU SHOULD WRITE A BOOK LIKE THAT..
© 1994 United Feature Syndicate, Inc.
Dogs Are From Jupiter..Cats Are From the Moon
SCHULZ

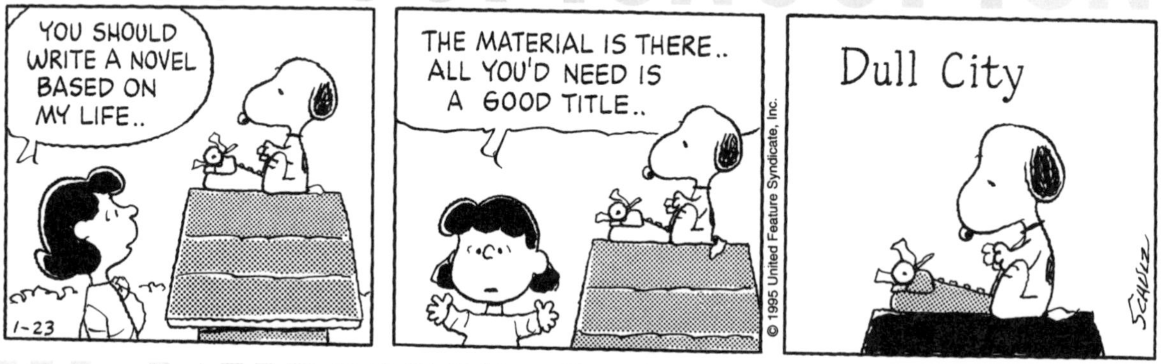
YOU SHOULD WRITE A NOVEL BASED ON MY LIFE..
1-23
THE MATERIAL IS THERE.. ALL YOU'D NEED IS A GOOD TITLE..
© 1995 United Feature Syndicate, Inc.
Dull City
SCHULZ

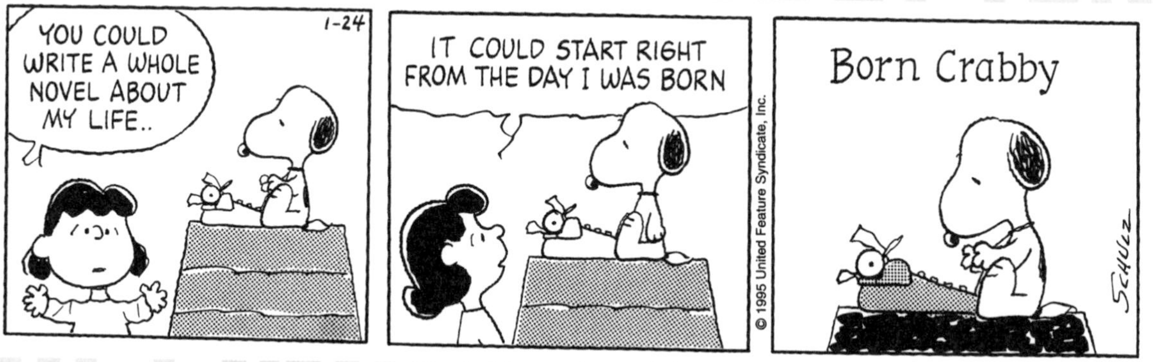
1-24
YOU COULD WRITE A WHOLE NOVEL ABOUT MY LIFE..
IT COULD START RIGHT FROM THE DAY I WAS BORN
© 1995 United Feature Syndicate, Inc.
Born Crabby
SCHULZ

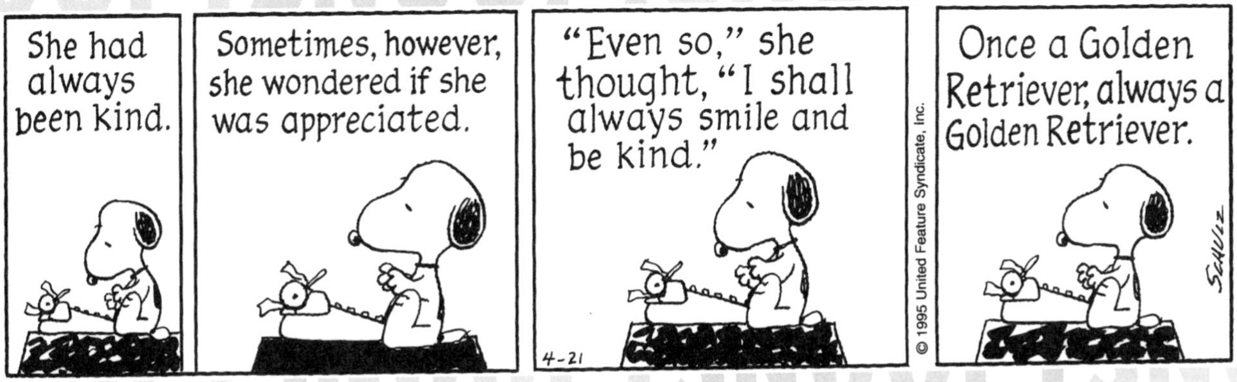
She had always been kind.
Sometimes, however, she wondered if she was appreciated.
"Even so," she thought, "I shall always smile and be kind."
4-21
© 1995 United Feature Syndicate, Inc.
Once a Golden Retriever, always a Golden Retriever.
SCHULZ

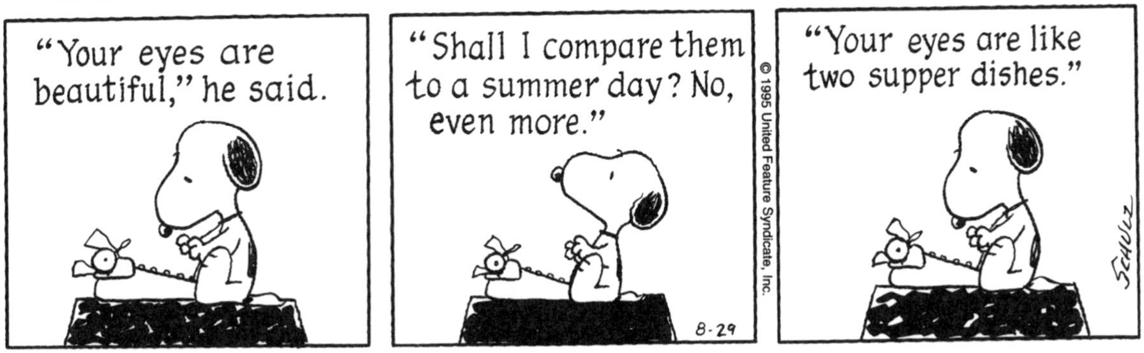
"Your eyes are beautiful," he said.
"Shall I compare them to a summer day? No, even more."
8-29
© 1995 United Feature Syndicate, Inc.
"Your eyes are like two supper dishes."
SCHULZ

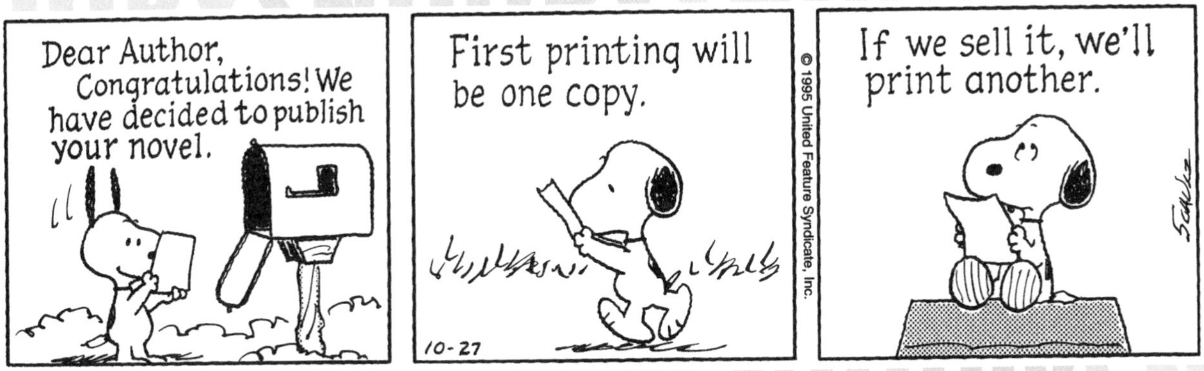
Dear Author,
Congratulations! We have decided to publish your novel.
First printing will be one copy.
10-27
© 1995 United Feature Syndicate, Inc.
If we sell it, we'll print another.
SCHULZ

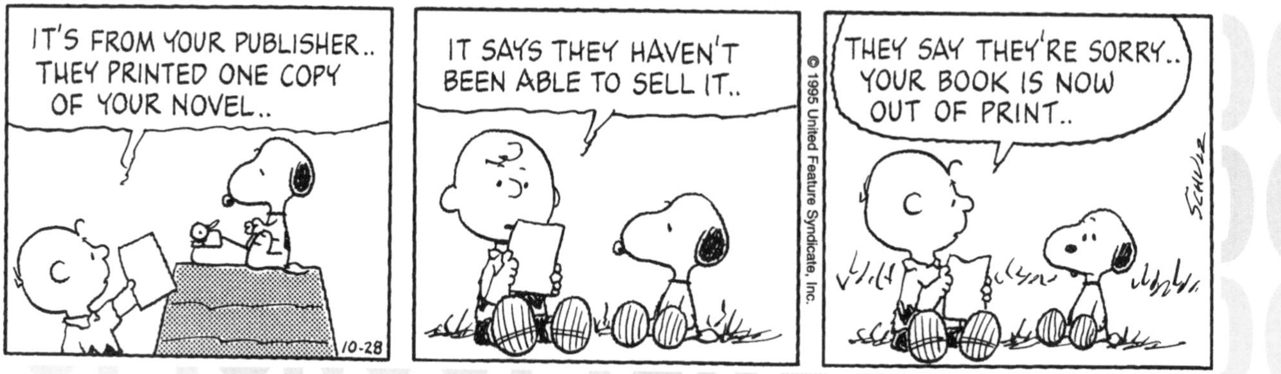
IT'S FROM YOUR PUBLISHER.. THEY PRINTED ONE COPY OF YOUR NOVEL..
10-28
IT SAYS THEY HAVEN'T BEEN ABLE TO SELL IT..
© 1995 United Feature Syndicate, Inc.
THEY SAY THEY'RE SORRY.. YOUR BOOK IS NOW OUT OF PRINT..
SCHULZ

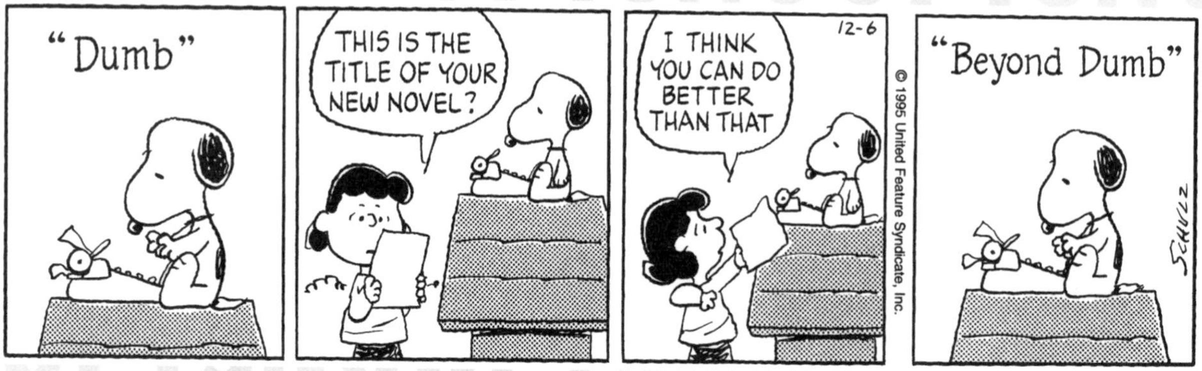
"Dumb"
THIS IS THE TITLE OF YOUR NEW NOVEL?
I THINK YOU CAN DO BETTER THAN THAT
12-6
© 1995 United Feature Syndicate, Inc.
"Beyond Dumb"
SCHULZ

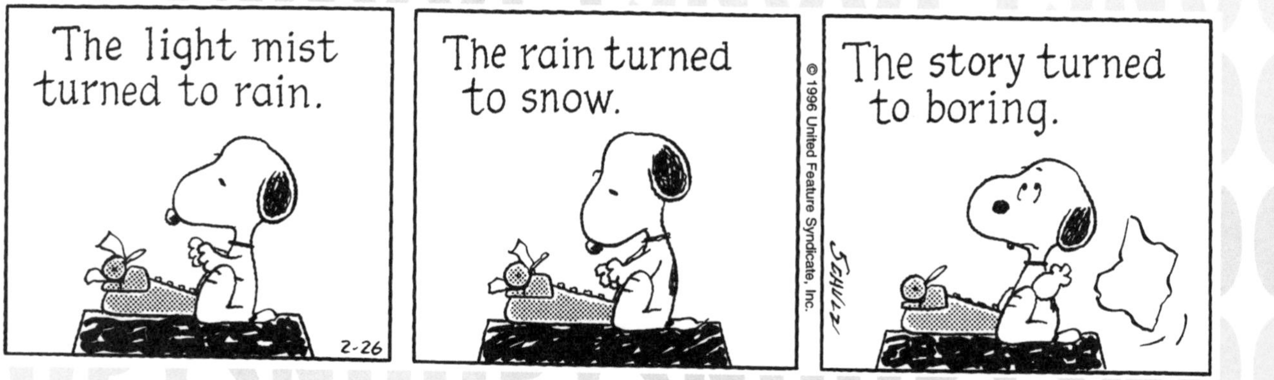
The light mist turned to rain.
2-26
The rain turned to snow.
© 1996 United Feature Syndicate, Inc.
The story turned to boring.
SCHULZ

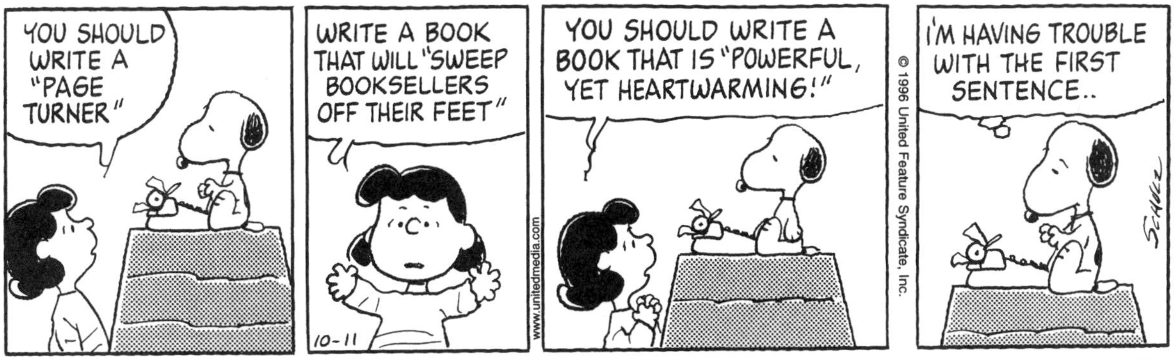
YOU SHOULD WRITE A "PAGE TURNER"
WRITE A BOOK THAT WILL "SWEEP BOOKSELLERS OFF THEIR FEET"
YOU SHOULD WRITE A BOOK THAT IS "POWERFUL, YET HEARTWARMING!"
I'M HAVING TROUBLE WITH THE FIRST SENTENCE..
10-11
www.unitedmedia.com
© 1996 United Feature Syndicate, Inc.
SCHULZ

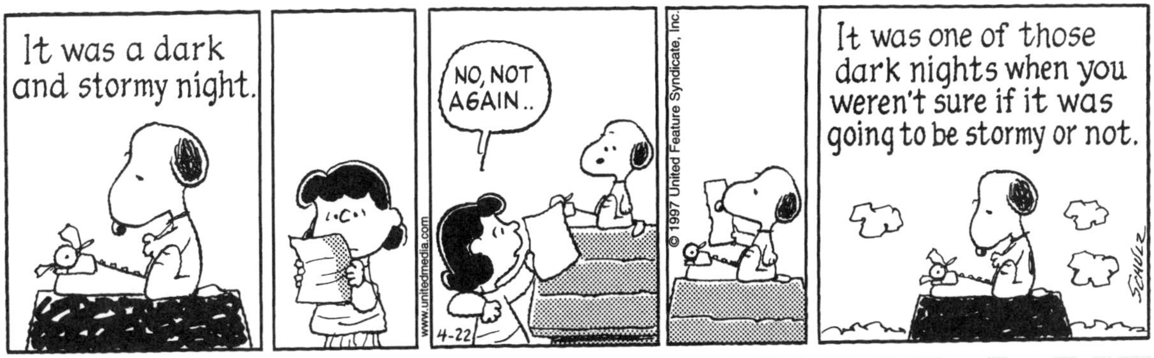
It was a dark and stormy night.
NO, NOT AGAIN..
It was one of those dark nights when you weren't sure if it was going to be stormy or not.
4-22
www.unitedmedia.com
© 1997 United Feature Syndicate, Inc.
SCHULZ

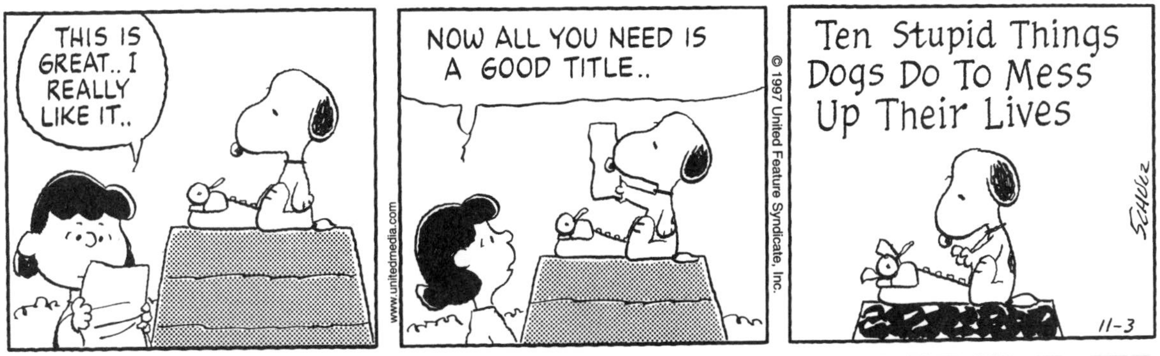
THIS IS GREAT.. I REALLY LIKE IT..
NOW ALL YOU NEED IS A GOOD TITLE..
Ten Stupid Things Dogs Do To Mess Up Their Lives
11-3
www.unitedmedia.com
© 1997 United Feature Syndicate, Inc.
SCHULZ

VIDEO GAME Available Fall 2006

SNOOPY VS THE RED BARON ™

BEAGLE OR BARON –
Who will rule the skies?

- JOIN SNOOPY AND AN INCREDIBLE CAST OF PEANUTS® CHARACTERS AS THEY TAKE ON THE NEFARIOUS BARON AND HIS COHORTS IN THIS ENCHANTING AERIAL ADVENTURE

- BECOME A VIRTUOSO FLYING ACE PILOTING SNOOPY'S FAMOUS SOPWITH CAMEL AND OTHER UNIQUE AIRCRAFT

- COLLECT CLUES TO REVEAL THE WHEREABOUTS OF THE RED BARON'S TOP SECRET HIDEOUT

FOR MORE INFORMATION, VISIT:
HTTP://WWW.NAMCO.COM/GAMES/SNOOPY/

 RATING PENDING RP CONTENT RATED BY ESRB — Visit www.esrb.org for updated rating information.

 PC DVD-ROM SOFTWARE

 United Media

Charles M. Schulz Creative Associates

 BANDAI NAMCO Games ™

PEANUTS © United Feature Syndicate, Inc. Game program © 2006 NAMCO BANDAI Games America Inc. "PSP" is a trademark and "PlayStation" and the "PS" Family logo are registered trademarks of Sony Computer Entertainment Inc. Memory Stick Duo™ may be required (sold separately). The ratings icon is a trademark of the Entertainment Software Association. All other trademarks belong to their respective owners.